FINANCIALACCOUNTING

A CRITICAL APPROACH

JOHN FRIEDLAN

YORK UNIVERSITY

Prentice
Hall

Toronto

National Library of Canada Cataloguing in Publication

Friedlan, John Michael
    Financial accounting: a critical approach/John Friedlan.
— 1st ed.

Includes index.
ISBN 0-13-019372-0

1. Accounting. I. Title.

HF5635.F75 2002   657   C2002-902216-9

0-13-019372-0

Vice President, Editorial Director: Michael J. Young
Senior Acquisitions Editor: Samantha Scully
Executive Marketing Manager: Cas Shields
Developmental Editor: Laurie Goebel
Production Editor: Mary Ann McCutcheon
Copy Editor: Lesley Mann
Production Coordinator: Janette Lush
Page Layout: Bill Renaud
Art Director: Julia Hall
Interior and Cover Design: Amy Harnden
Cover Image: Photonica/Ken Takewaki
Author Photograph: David West

1 2 3 4 5   07 06 05 04 03

Printed and bound in United States.

Brief Contents

Contents

Chapter 4

Income Measurement and the Objectives of Financial Reporting   189

Chapter 5

Generally Accepted Accounting Principles   257

Chapter 6

Cash Flow, Profitability, and the Cash Flow Statement   314

Chapter 7

Cash, Receivables, and the Time Value of Money   371

Chapter 8

Inventory   433

Chapter 9

Capital Assets   499

Chapter 10

Liabilities   567

Chapter 11

Owners' Equity   657

Preface

Objectives

My primary objective in writing *Financial Accounting: A Critical Approach* was to create an introductory financial accounting text that would be accessible to newcomers to accounting *and* provide solid insights into the real nature of accounting information. I expect (hope?) that a person who studies the book thoroughly will have a reasonably good understanding of financial statements.

The title of the book requires some explanation. The *Critical Approach* to financial accounting means that students are guided to look critically at accounting information. The book emphasizes the crucial importance of accounting information as a decision making tool, but also addresses the limitations, controversies, problems, and shortcomings with accounting and accounting information. Students learn not to simply accept the numbers in financial statements at face value. They learn that the people who prepare financial statements can often choose among reasonable, acceptable alternative ways of accounting for transactions and economic events and that different choices can affect the numbers that appear in the financial statements and have economic consequences for an entity's stakeholders and for the entity itself. Students also learn that accounting information provided by an entity cannot be all things to all people—the information provided by an entity might be useful to some decision-makers but not others. Students learn to critically evaluate whether the information is appropriate for the decisions *they* are making.

The importance of using a critical approach to the study of accounting is more evident today than ever. For decades accounting received little attention in the media beyond regular earnings announcements made by public companies. Then, around the time *Financial Accounting* was being written accounting became headline news. Almost on a daily basis the media reported new accounting "scandals" and controversies. The names of companies embroiled in controversies—names like Enron—became familiar even to people with very little interest in business. Increasingly, people began to question the numbers reported in financial statements and the motivations of managers for reporting accounting information as they do. *Financial Accounting: A Critical Approach* provides students with the tools to understand the issues behind these controversies and to make sense of accounting information.

While *Financial Accounting* is not primarily a book about how to do accounting, the "how to" part is fully covered. Chapter 3 is devoted to explaining how transactions and economic events are recorded and the data converted into financial statements. Chapter 3 serves to develop the building blocks that are necessary for students who choose to study accounting beyond the introductory level. In the context of this book an understanding of the procedural aspects of accounting are essential to understanding the relationship between transactions and economic events and the resulting financial statements.

One of the important features of this book is the use of short, decision-oriented "mini-cases." The cases and the process for solving them are first introduced in Chapter 4. Cases with solutions are provided in the Solved Problems of Chapters 4, 5, and 9. Cases for assignment and exam purposes appear in Appendix C of the book. The placement of the cases should not suggest that they are of secondary importance. I consider the cases and the problem solving process that is developed to solve them to be an integral part of the book. The cases are placed in an appendix because they often cover a range of accounting topics and as a result they do not fit well at the end of any particular chapter. The cases serve two purposes. First, they help develop critical thinking and problem solving skills; second, they help develop an appreciation of the context-specific nature of accounting. With these cases accounting comes to life as students grapple with the real nature of accounting and accounting information. The cases force students to think about alternative ways of accounting for transactions and economic events and to consider the impact the different alternatives can have on decisions and economic outcomes.

Pedagogical Features

Besides the cases mentioned above, this text is full of other useful pedagogical tools.

Chapter Outline—A chapter outline at the start of each chapter shows students where the chapter is going and how the chapter topics are related.

Chapter Outline

Introduction	Commitments
What Are Liabilities?	Subsequent Events
Current Liabilities	Financial Statement Analysis Issues
Bonds and Other Forms of Long-Term Debt	Solved Problem
Leases	Summary of Key Points
Pensions and Other Post-Retirement Benefits	Key Terms and Similar Terms

Learning Objectives and Summary—The Learning Objectives at the beginning of each chapter focus students' attention on the key points of that chapter. This is reinforced by the Chapter Summary that corresponds to the Learning Objectives.

Learning Objectives

After studying the material in this chapter you will be able to:

LO 1.   Describe the purpose and nature of accounting information systems and the accounting cycle.

LO 2.   Use an accounting equation spreadsheet to record transactions and economic events, and prepare balance sheets, income statements, and statements of retained earnings.

LO 3.   Record economic events and transactions using journal entries and debits and credits.

LO 4.   Discuss how financial statements are affected by how the accounting for transactions and economic events is done.

Summary of Key Points

LO 1. The key to producing accounting information is having an accounting system that captures raw data and organizes, summarizes, and classifies the data into a form that is useful for decision making. The information provided by an accounting system is limited by the data that are entered into it.

The accounting cycle is the process by which data about economic events are entered into an accounting system, processed, organized, and used to produce information, such as financial statements. An accounting system is very important because if data were not processed and organized it would be very difficult for anyone to understand

Key Terms and Glossary—Key Terms are printed in bold in the text. All the key terms are defined in the text and appear with their definitions and a page reference in the Glossary at the end of the book.

referenced to the key term definition.

absorption costing (page 462) A method of costing inventory that includes all prime and overhead costs in the cost of inventory.

accelerated amortization (page 510) Amortization methods that allocate more of the cost of an asset to expense in the early years of its life and less in the later years.

account (page 98) A category of asset, liability, or owners' equity. Each column in an

receivable.

accrual basis of accounting (page 50) A system of accounting that measures the economic impact of transactions and economic events rather than cash flows.

accrued asset (page 132) An asset that is recorded before cash is received.

accrued liability (page 130) A liability that is recognized and recorded in the financial statements but that is not triggered by an external event such as receipt of a bill or invoice.

Mark's Work Wearhouse—The financial statements and annual report for Mark's Work Wearhouse Limited are used as a focal point for discussion throughout the book. Most of the topics discussed in the book are related to the accounting and presentation used by Mark's Work Wearhouse. Each chapter's Assignment Materials contains a set of questions entitled *Analyzing Mark's Work Wearhouse* that give students the opportunity to apply the material from the chapter to Mark's Work Wearhouse's financial statements.

■ Analyzing Mark's Work Wearhouse

M5-1.   Examine MWW's financial statements and give examples of how basic assumptions is reflected in the statements.

M5-2.   Examine MWW's financial statements, including the notes, and how each of GAAP's qualitative characteristics of accounting is reflected ments and notes.

M5-3.   Examine MWW's financial statements, including the notes, and how each of GAAP's measurement conventions is reflected in the

Questions for Consideration—Each chapter contains a number of Questions for Consideration that provide opportunities for students to stop and think about what they have read so far in the chapter. The nature of the Questions for Consideration range from testing knowledge of information presented to practising calculations to critical thinking questions that require application of the material in the chapter.

Question for Consideration

Your aunt recently won $100,000 in a lottery. She has approached you for advice on which of two investments she should place her money. Your aunt wants to invest for ten years, at which time she plans to retire. Your aunt is only interested in investments that she considers safe, so she has narrowed her choice to two investments with large banks. The first investment is a ten-year investment certificate that bears an interest rate of 8%, with interest calculated annually. The second investment is also a ten-year certificate, but interest on that investment is calculated and compounded at the rate of 4% every six months (this means that there are 20 six-month investment periods at 4% rather than 10-one year investment periods at 8%). Which investment would you recommend to your aunt? Explain your answer. Make sure

Comment Boxes—Throughout the text, commentary on key points in the text is provided in Comment Boxes. The Comment Boxes provide insights into the nature and interpretation of accounting information.

> It is assumed that only Mr. Irving will receive the letter, whereas the report itself may be made available to Mr. Floor and the arbitrator. It is not appropriate to discuss the objectives of reporting in a document that will be shared with other parties. Neutrality assumes that financial statements are not prepared in a way that attempts to influence or manipulate the decisions of the users. However, when faced with acceptable and reasonable alternatives, a preparer will likely choose the ones that are in his or her self-interests. This is not to imply that the preparers will intentionally misstate the financial statements. Rather, when there are legitimate alternatives, the ones that are more favourable will be selected. It is reasonable to assume that the other parties will take a similar position—that Jim Floor will argue for accounting treatments that will tend to lower the selling price of Savoy.

Use of extracts from actual entities' financial statements—Many of the issues, concepts, and points raised in the book are demonstrated through extracts from the financial statements of actual entities, presented as they appeared in the entity's annual report. Students are able to see first hand the presentation of the topic in a real world setting.

Panel A: Dylex Limited / **Panel B: Newfoundland Power Inc.**

Solved Problems—Each chapter provides a detailed problem with a solution that addresses the key concepts in the chapter.

■ Solved Problem

In November 2005 Chedder Inc. (Chedder) set up operations as the exclusive western Canada distributor of Pligs, the newest children's toy sensation. Pligs first became popular in Europe and then the fad came to North America. Chedder's lone shareholder contributed $37,000 of her own money to purchase shares in Chedder and borrowed $50,000 from the bank. The terms of the loan required that Chedder have a current ratio of greater than 1.4 on December 31, 2006 or the loan is fully repayable immediately. Chedder began selling Pligs in early 2006. For its December 31, 2005 year end Chedder did not select an inventory cost flow assumption because it had not yet sold anything.

Chedder's December 31, 2005 balance sheet is shown in Table 8-8 and informa-

Similar Terms List—This feature provides a list of accounting terms used in the text compared to other terms that mean essentially the same thing that students may encounter in the media, in financial documents, and in accounting practice.

Similar Terms

The left column gives alternative terms that are sometimes used for the accounting terms introduced in this chapter, which are listed in the right column.

lender	**creditor, p. 24**
non-profit organization	**not-for-profit organization, p. 12**
stockholder	**shareholder, p. 10**
stock market	**stock exchange, p. 11**

Using Financial Statements—Each chapter's Assignment Material provides extensive extracts from an entity's financial statements and asks a series of questions that provide students with the opportunity to work with actual financial statement material and apply the coverage of the chapter in a real world setting.

■ Using Financial Statements

BCE Emergis Inc.

BCE Emergis Inc. (BCE Emergis) is a premier business-to-business e-commerce infrastructure provider, strategically focusing on market leadership in the transaction-intensive eHealth and financial services sectors. BCE Emergis' services are fully integrated, offering a comprehensive e-commerce solution that electronically transforms business processes, such as buying, selling, invoicing, payment, logistics, and customer services and that enables success in the web-centric, cost-driven, and highly competitive global Internet economy.[4]

Assignment Material—Each chapter contains a large number of questions, exercises, and problems that provide students with the opportunity to apply the knowledge and skills from the chapter. Much of this material is keyed to the Learning Objectives in the text.

Assignment Materials

Questions

Q6-1. Explain the difference between cash accounting and accrual accounting.

Q6-2. Why is the cash flow statement included in the general purpose financial statement package? Explain your answer fully.

Q6-3. What are some of the possible components that can be included in the definition of "cash" in the cash flow statement? Explain the usefulness and limitations of including each of the components in the definition.

Organization and Content

Financial Accounting: A Critical Approach provides considerable depth on a number of topics not normally covered in introductory accounting texts or courses. Chapter 4 provides extensive coverage of revenue recognition. This coverage is intended to introduce the concept of accounting choice and demonstrate the impact of different ways of reporting economic events on the financial statements. The purpose is to show early on that accounting for economic events is often not easy or straightforward and that preparers often have to choose among alternative ways of accounting.

Chapter 10 covers leases, pensions, and future income taxes. Chapter 11 examines employee stock options. Chapter 12 is devoted entirely to investments in other companies. This coverage is intended to ensure that readers are familiar with elements that are commonly seen in financial statements. Most of the financial statements students will be exposed to, both as students and in their careers, will be consolidated and will have leases, pensions, and/or future income taxes in them, and often these accounts will have large dollar amounts associated with them. If students are to be able to make sense of the entire set of statements they must be reasonably familiar and comfortable with these topics, even if they tend to be complex. Some instructors may prefer not to cover some of leases, pensions, future income taxes, and investments in other companies. These topics can be easily skipped without causing any problems with the use of the book.

The material on liquidity and the cash flow statement appears early in the book, in Chapter 5. This is done so that coverage of the complete set of the financial statements is provided together and so that students think about cash flow as well as accrual accounting throughout the book.

Names of Entities

One final note: Some readers may wonder about the origins of the names given to the entities used in the examples and end-of-chapter material in each chapter. *Financial Accounting* provides names for more than 500 entities throughout the book. It was a challenge to find names for all of these entities. I met this challenge by using an atlas of Canada. Virtually all the names used in the book are the actual names of places in Canada.

Quisibis Inc.
Account Balances
On December 31, 2005 and 2006

	2006	2005
Cash	$ 15,000	$ 10,000
Accounts receivable	22,000	18,000
Inventory	35,000	37,000
Capital assets	119,000	100,000
Accumulated amortization	(17,000)	(12,000)

Balzac Ltd.
Cash Flow Statement For the Year Ended May 31, 2004

Net income	$150,000	
Add: Amortization expense	30,000	
Loss on sale of land	20,000	
		$200,000
Changes in current operating accounts:		
Accounts receivable	(25,000)	
Inventory	20,000	

Rivulet Inc.
Current Operating Assets and Liabilities as of December 31, 2004 and 2005

	2005	2004		2005	2004
Accounts receivable	$124,000	$101,000	Accounts payable	$192,000	$217,000
Inventory	275,000	315,000	Accrued liabilities	49,000	32,000

Rivulet Inc.
Income Statement
For the Year Ended December 31, 2005

Revenue	$1,075,000

Supplements

The following supplements are available to assist instructors using this text:

Instructor's Solutions Manual
The Instructor's Solutions Manual, prepared by Dan Armishaw, contains full solutions to all Questions, Exercises, Problems, Using Financial Statement questions, and Mark's Work Wearhouse cases. In addition, solutions to the cases in Appendix C are provided here.

Instructor's Manual with Video Guide
The Instructor's Manual, written by John Friedlan, contains teaching tips, chapter outlines, suggested readings, extra Using Financial Statement questions and solutions and CBC Video Cases that can be used on their own or in conjunction with the CBC Videos listed below.

CBC/Pearson Education Canada Video Library
This 60 minute VHS cassette contains segments from the CBC series *Venture* that can be shown to a class and used in conjunction with the CBC Video Cases in the Instructor's Manual.

Test Item File
The Test Item File, created by Jeff Power, contains approximately 1000 multiple choice questions, 200 calculation exercises, and 100 short essay questions from which instructors can create their own tests and exams. Answers are provided along with page references and difficulty ratings.

TestGen
Pearson Education Canada's TestGen is a special computerized version of the Test Item File that enables instructors to view and edit the existing questions, add questions, generate tests, and print the tests in a variety of formats. Powerful search and sort functions make it easy to locate questions and arrange them in any order desired. TestGen also enables instructors to administer tests on a local area network, have the tests graded electronically, and have the results prepared in electronic or printed reports. Issued on a CD-ROM, the Pearson TestGen is compatible with IBM or Macintosh systems.

PowerPoint Presentations and Electronic Solutions
Available on CD-ROM, the PowerPoint Presentations provide slide shows for each chapter of the text focusing on the key points of the chapter. In addition, electronic copies of all the solutions are also provided as jpeg files. The PowerPoint Presentations were created by David McConomy.

Solutions Acetates
A hard copy of all the solutions is provided along with blank acetates so instructors can create overheads of the solutions they need.

Students will benefit from access to the following student supplements:

Study Guide
The Study Guide, written by John Friedlan, contains valuable study tools for students such as chapter reviews and study problems.

Student Solutions Manual
The Student Solutions Manual contains full solutions for all of the even-numbered Questions, Exercises, and Problems in the text.

Companion Website
The Companion Website contains chapter quizzes, weblinks, a glossary, internet exercises, and much more. Instructors will find useful material in the Instructor's Resources section of the site. Visit the site often at www.pearsoned.ca/friedlan.

Acknowledgements

Many people contributed to the development of this book and I take this opportunity to thank them.

Thanks to faculty reviewers who devoted significant time and effort reading the manuscript as it developed and who provided valuable comments, suggestions, and criticisms, all of which served to make the book better:

Hilary Becker, Carleton University
Peggy Coady, Memorial University
Roger Collins, University College of the Cariboo
Ian Feltmate, Acadia University
Leo Gallant, St. Francis Xavier University
Dennis Huber, University of New Brunswick, Saint John
Linda Lindsay, University of Saskatchewan
Don Lockwood, University of British Columbia
Cameron Morrill, University of Manitoba
Peter Norwood, Langara College
Jan Nyholt, Southern Alberta Institute of Technology
Jeff Pai, University of Manitoba
Fred Phillips, University of Saskatchewan
Jan Thatcher, Lakehead University

The students in accounting courses at the Schulich School of Business who used the manuscript in various stages of development and who offered feedback and identified errors also deserve mention. It is not possible to individually thank all the students in these classes, but special recognition goes to three students who seemed to take it upon themselves to provide ongoing feedback. These students are:

Elizabeth Allan
Ilya Soubbotin
Yueyin Zhang

Faculty colleagues and staff at the Schulich School of Business who provided support and encouragement throughout the development of the manuscript include:

Kate Bewley
Janne Chung
Teresa Colavecchia
Ashley Dafel
Gail Drory
Elizabeth Farrell
Rosa Fortura
Amin Mawani
Alan Mak
Filomena Petrilli
Paul Roy
Linda Thorne
Shanker Trivedi
Paul Wayne

Thanks to Lois Lieff and Ellin Bessner who provided valuable editorial feedback on the manuscript.

Various instructors assisted me by preparing selected supplements. Dan Armishaw worked on the Instructor's Solutions Manual, David McConomy prepared the PowerPoint Presentations that accompany the text, and Jeff Power authored the Test Item File for this book. My thanks to all of these individuals for providing these supplements, which are invaluable to instructors and students alike.

Thanks to John Gunn and Bruce Byford at Grant Thornton for providing financial statement information.

The staff at Pearson Education Canada provided outstanding support to help develop and market the book. Many thanks to

Laurie Goebel, Developmental Editor
Lesley Mann, Copyeditor
Mary Ann McCutcheon, Production Editor
Samantha Scully, Acquisitions Editor
Anita Smale, Technical Checker

Finally, a special acknowledgement to Professor Al Rosen who helped shape and develop the way I think about and teach accounting. His contribution to this book is significant.

Writing this book has been the greatest challenge of my professional life. It has also been one of the most exciting and fulfilling. I hope that all users of *Financial Accounting: A Critical Approach* find the book a valuable part of their study of accounting and business.

John Friedlan
Schulich School of Business, York University

About the Author

From a job counting peanuts to cracking the nuts and bolts of financial statements, John Friedlan has devoted more than twenty years to training future managers and accountants. An award-winning teacher at York University's Schulich School of Business, Friedlan strives to get students to think critically about balance sheets, net income, and how accounting numbers can be often managed to turn losses into profits, and vice versa. As a consultant to the Canadian Institute of Chartered Accountant's Board of Examiners, Friedlan has helped ensure that a generation of CA candidates meet the standards required to enter the Chartered Accountancy profession.

A Montreal native, Friedlan completed high school, wanting to be a scientist. But after trying to unravel the mysteries of genetics, with a Bachelor of Science (McGill 1976), he switched career paths to the business world, completing his MBA at York University in 1978. Friedlan entered the working world as an auditor with the Toronto office of Deloitte, Haskins and Sells, Chartered Accountants and qualified as a CA two years later (1980).

A two-year stint teaching accounting at York University followed, but the corporate world beckoned. It was Nabisco Brands, where Friedlan moved from bean counting to peanut counting as a manager with Planters nuts. Next came a staff position with the Board of Examiners at the Canadian Institute of Chartered Accountants. But Friedlan soon realized that his true passion was in the academic world and he moved to Seattle in 1985 to pursue his Ph.D. at the University of Washington. After graduating in 1990, Friedlan returned to York University's Schulich School of Business's Accounting area where he is now an associate professor. At York, Friedlan has inspired classrooms full of students with his energetic lectures, and his challenging questioning of the why's behind corporate financial reporting choices. He won the Educator of the Year Award for undergraduates in 1992 and a Seymour Schulich Award for Teaching Excellence in 2000.

Friedlan's articles have been published in top accounting journals including *Contemporary Accounting Research* (1994) and *Issues in Accounting Education* (1995), and in practitioner journals *CGA Magazine* (1994) and *CA Magazine* (1996). He has also presented papers at meetings of the American Accounting Association, Canadian Academic Accounting Association, and Canadian Finance Association.

In his private life, Friedlan is an avid runner, a fan of Peter, Paul and Mary, and Blue Rodeo, and believes "Star Trek" is real. Most of all, he is devoted to his family. He's married to a Toronto television news journalist, Ellin Bessner, and they have two children, Alex and Evan. Friedlan enjoys nothing better than chasing his boys around the house, playing hockey with them, doing car pool, and attending and participating in the boys' many programs. The Friedlan family lives in Richmond Hill, Ontario, just north of Toronto.

Chapter 1

The Accounting Environment: What Is Accounting and Why Is It Done?

Chapter Outline

Learning Objectives

Introduction

A Challenge to the Reader

About Mark's Work Wearhouse Ltd.

What Is Accounting?

Why Do People Need and Want Accounting Information?

The Two Fields of Accounting: Financial Accounting and Managerial Accounting

The Accounting Environment

Accounting Is for Measurement

The Rules of the Game

Solved Problem

Summary of Key Points

Key Terms and Similar Terms

Questions, Exercises, and Problems

Learning Objectives

After studying the material in this chapter you will be able to:

LO 1.   Explain accounting and its uses, and differentiate between financial and managerial accounting.

LO 2.   Describe the accounting environment.

LO 3.   Discuss how the interests of the people who prepare accounting information can conflict with the interests of the people who use the information.

LO 4.   Understand the importance of accounting information for measuring the attributes of an entity.

LO 5.   Describe generally accepted accounting principles in basic terms.

Introduction

Accounting is full of mystery and intrigue. The reader of an accounting report, like the reader of a good mystery, must sort through clues, interpret and analyze information, exercise judgment, decide which information is relevant and which should be ignored, and use the information to come to a conclusion. In an accounting mystery the question is not who is the murderer or thief. Instead, an accounting detective might have to decide whether to invest, lend, do business with a particular organization, or ask for an increase in wages.

Solving an accounting mystery requires detective work. The numbers tell a story, but it is usually necessary to read between the lines. You cannot just take the numbers at face value. Working with accounting information is not cold, calculating, and impersonal. The effective accounting detective must also understand human behaviour. *People* prepare accounting information—people who have their own interests regarding how the accounting information will be used. So just as a detective investigates a crime, an accounting detective must weigh the source of the accounting information.

Over the years accounting has endured a bad reputation. The stereotype is of dull people doing dreary work—it is not a field people think of as "sexy". Can you name any famous accountants? Have there ever been any television shows or movies about accounting? Probably the most famous accountants are the PricewaterhouseCoopers representatives who deliver the results for the Academy Awards.

But accounting's dreary reputation is not fair. There may be some dull accountants; there may even be a lot of dull accountants. But accounting definitely is not dull. In fact, using, preparing and understanding accounting information requires a set of high-level cognitive skills—skills that include judgment, analysis, synthesis, evaluation, problem solving, critical thinking, and creativity.

The goal of *Financial Accounting: A Critical Approach* is to help you become an effective accounting detective. You will examine accounting from the perspectives of people who prepare the information and those who use it. You will learn to interpret and understand financial statements and financial reporting, and master the tools to unravel their mysteries. And you will discover that accounting information raises questions, but does not usually provide answers.

Regardless of whether you plan to become a professional accountant, pursue a career in another business discipline, or just learn something about accounting, *Financial Accounting: A Critical Approach* will provide you with some tools to help you make sense of the information in accounting reports and understand the strengths and limitations of accounting information. For those of you who are considering careers in accounting, the book will provide the foundation for future accounting courses. If you want to understand accounting information to make informed investment decisions, gain insight into information produced by the company you work for, make important business decisions, or simply understand the many news items that draw on accounting information, *Financial Accounting: A Critical Approach* will start you on your way to being a sophisticated user of accounting information. However, this book is not about bookkeeping. You will learn some basic elements of how information is recorded in an accounting system, but these lessons in bookkeeping will not be ends in themselves. Instead, they will provide you with the tools to understand accounting information.

A Challenge to the Reader

Business and accounting are real-world subjects. They are easier to understand when you can connect them to real-world events. As we move through this book, links will be made with actual business problems and entities so that you can develop an understanding of accounting in context. These links will make more sense to you if you can relate them to your own understanding of business. However, many of you may have little or no experience with business. As a result it will be difficult to form links between what you read in the book, what you hear in the classroom, and your personal experience. Your challenge is to develop some context by exposing yourself to business situations and thinking about them.

Your first step will be to regularly read the business press to learn about Canadian and international business issues, problems, and companies. At first you may be confused and very unfamiliar with what you read. But the more you read, the more you will understand. You will begin to see links between your reading and what is happening in your accounting course (and other business courses). Canada has many fine business publications, such as *The Globe and Mail's Report on Business* and the *Financial Post* (published in *The National Post*). There are also many good business magazines that will help you learn about Canadian and global business issues, personalities, and entities. Most of these publications have online (Internet) editions on which current articles can be read.

Here are some well-known Canadian and international publications and their companion web sites. However, there are thousands of business-related web sites that can be explored for valuable and interesting information.

Publication	Web Site
The Globe and Mail	www.globeandmail.com
The National Post	www.nationalpost.com
Canadian Business	www.canadianbusiness.com
The Wall Street Journal (U.S.)	www.wsj.com
The Financial Times (U.K.)	www.ft.com
The Economist (U.K.)	www.economist.com
CGA Magazine	www.cga-canada.org
CA Magazine	www.camagazine.com
CMA Management	www.managementmag.com

In addition, the following web sites are particularly helpful if you are looking for financial information about Canadian and U.S. publicly traded companies:

Canadian companies	www.sedar.com
U.S. companies	www.sec.gov/edgar.shtml

Your next step to familiarize yourself with the real-world business environment will be to observe the business world and economic activity as you go through your day-to-day affairs. Business is everywhere. Think about the businesses you frequent (grocery stores, restaurants, clubs, gas stations, convenience stores, movie theatres, retail stores, pharmacies, and so on). Think about what makes them work. What are the keys to their success? How do they make money? What do they offer to customers? Talk to people about their businesses. You'll find that most business people enjoy discussing their companies.

By building an understanding of business through these methods, your experience with accounting will make more sense and you will find learning the subject more interesting and enjoyable.

About Mark's Work Wearhouse Ltd.

Throughout this book Mark's Work Wearhouse Ltd. (MWW) will serve as the real-world focus of our discussions of various accounting issues. Portions of MWW's 2001 annual report are reproduced in Appendix A on pages A-000 to A-000. The full annual report is available for downloading from www.sedar.com. Take some time to read the annual report and visit a MWW store so that the company will mean more to you than words on paper.

Mark's Work Wearhouse[1] describes itself as Canada's largest men's specialty apparel retailer. MWW sells outdoor gear, work clothes, and footwear. In the last decade MWW has also carved out a market niche in the field of "business casual" clothes that people wear to work. In fact, MWW aggressively targets customers who "do not wear a suit and tie to work."[2] MWW had sales of almost $500 million in 2001.

Mark Blumes launched the company that still bears his name with the opening of the first store in Calgary in 1977. MWW went public on the Toronto Stock Exchange in 1981. By 2001 MWW had over 300 stores in Canada, divided into three divisions: the flagship Mark's Work Wearhouse (L'Équipeur stores in Quebec); Work World; and the company's newest venture, DOCKERS®, which sells Levi's products. Most of the 157 Mark's Work Wearhouse stores are owned and operated by MWW, while 25 are franchises. On the Work World side, 90 of the 144 stores are franchised. The DOCKERS division opened its first five test stores in 2000 and opened three more in 2001. Since 1998 MWW has changed its strategy at Work World and begun converting the franchises to corporate-owned stores. The company is aiming to expand to 450 stores within a few years. About 3,000 people work for MWW in all divisions.

Generally, Mark's Work Wearhouse stores are located in urban areas and are destination locations situated in so-called "power centres". Mark's Work Wearhouse stores are generally 8,000 to 15,000 square feet in size. The Work World stores are typically located in smaller towns and cities across Canada and average 3,000 square feet. The DOCKERS stores are 3,000 to 4,000 square feet and are located in major malls in large- and mid-sized markets.

The Mark's Work Wearhouse and L'Équipeur stores stock apparel and footwear for customers' work needs, as well as for people who simply want casual and outdoor clothing and shoes. Seventy percent of the customers in the Mark's Work Wearhouse division are between 25 and 60 years old, divided equally among trades and blue-collar workers, sales and administration personnel, and professionals. Half the customers are women, and 25% of the purchases are by women who buy items for themselves. The Work World stores have very similar customers. DOCKERS stores are aiming to attract conservative dressers who prefer golf-inspired work wear and casual wear.

By 2001 MWW claimed to be the number one retailer in Canada of work, safety, winter, and hiking footwear, the number two retailer of men's outerwear, and the number one retailer of primary industry work wear apparel. MWW's Denver Hayes pant was the second largest brand of casual pants in the country, and MWW was the fourth largest retailer of denim in Canada. MWW does 70% of its business in its own private and captive label products. Mark's also calls itself "Canada's cold weather store". Indeed, the company's business remains very seasonal: 40% of annual sales—and most of its annual profits—occurs in the quarter leading up to the Christmas holiday season.

Through 2001 MWW invested about $25 million to renovate or build stores to make them more attractive places to shop. Mark's calls it their "On Concept" program. By 2001 the company had completed 86% of the makeover.

One significant attribute of MWW has been its extremely informative and open disclosure of financial information to the public. The company's annual reports have consistently won awards from the Canadian Institute of Chartered Accountants and other organizations for the straightforward way in which they describe the year's economic activities. MWW has also won the Best Investor Relations in Canada award for smaller companies.

In addition to its "bricks and mortar" stores, MWW also runs an e-commerce division at the www.marks.com web site, as well as selling customized uniforms to businesses and recreational clubs in Canada.

www.canadiantire.ca

In December 2001 Canadian Tire Corporation, Limited offered $116,000,000 to purchase MWW from its owners. The purchase was finalized on February 7, 2002. As a result of the purchase, MWW is no longer traded on the Toronto Stock Exchange and its shares cannot be purchased by individual investors. In future, information about MWW's activities will be incorporated into the accounting information prepared and presented by Canadian Tire Corporation, Limited.

What Is Accounting?

Accounting is a system for producing information about an **entity** (that is, an economic unit of some kind) and communicating that information to people who want or need the information for making decisions. Like any business activity, the purpose of accounting is to produce something: carmakers produce cars, movie studios produce entertainment, and accounting produces information.

Let's consider an analogy. A movie studio invests money to produce a film. The film is then distributed through theatres, television, and video stores for the entertainment of viewers. Some movies are more effective at entertaining than others. Of course, how entertaining a movie is depends on the taste of the viewer: a movie loved by some is hated by others, as a glance at different movie reviews will confirm. But if you buy a copy of a movie, what is of value is not the physical tape or the DVD. It is the images, the creative work of the actors, director, editors, and others, that are valuable.

The same applies to accounting. An organization invests money to produce information. This includes organizing an accounting department, setting up a computer system to accumulate data, hiring staff, and producing accounting reports. The information is distributed to users who need it to make decisions. Some information is more useful than other information, and what is useful depends on who you are and what decisions you are making. The value of an accounting report is not in the paper on which it is printed or the web site where it is posted, but the extent to which it aids and improves decision making.

The crucial purpose of accounting is communication of information about an entity, but as with any form of communication there are plenty of opportunities for misunderstanding, confusion, and misdirection. You probably know the game "telephone" in which several people sit in a row and the first person whispers a message into the ear of the second person, who whispers the message to the next person, and so on down the line. The fun comes from comparing the initial message to the one reported by the last person. Usually the two are very different! This analogy shows that communication down a line is not as straightforward as one might imagine. We can think of other examples of barriers to communication: consider the speaker whose words are inflammatory to some and innocuous to others, or the politician who is deliberately ambiguous so that what he or she says can be interpreted favourably by a wide range of people, many of whom would agree on very little.

Like other forms of communication, accounting is not always (or perhaps not even usually) straightforward. The people who prepare accounting information often have many choices and techniques available to them. These different ways of accounting mean that accounting reports could present the same situation in several different ways, depending on the choices made. If you cannot navigate through the choices that exist in accounting reports, you stand to be one of the people who misunderstands, becomes confused, or is misdirected. The consequences of not understanding accounting information are poor decisions that in turn can result in economic losses.

Many different people rely on information about entities for making important decisions. As with any kind of communication, the meaning and intent of accounting information are not always obvious. Sometimes you get confused. Sometimes you have to read between the lines. Sometimes ambiguity—deliberate or not—prevents you from understanding a situation. That is why accounting is full of mystery and intrigue.

Why Do People Need and Want Accounting Information?

The more and better information or knowledge a person has about a situation, the better the decisions he or she can make. Without information or knowledge, a "decision" is nothing more than a guess. For example, suppose you wanted to take a vacation over the winter break. You see an advertisement in the newspaper promoting Aruba as a fabulous winter vacation destination. Assuming you have never been to Aruba before and know little about it, would you simply accept the advertisement at face value? Most people wouldn't. You would probably want to find out what Aruba was like and whether it suited your requirements for a winter vacation. You would want to know what the weather will be like, whether the beaches are nice, what entertainment and activities are offered, and whether many people your age go there. You would also want to know whether the cost will fit your budget and if flight and hotel availability suit your schedule. To obtain information you might ask friends and relatives if they know anything about Aruba. You could do research in the library or on the Internet. You would gather information until you were comfortable making a decision. Some people might not do all this research on their own. They might consult with expert sources that specialize in gathering travel information. For example, a good travel agent or a travel guide published by an independent company might provide the needed information.

Not all information is equal. In making a decision, you will generally place more weight on the information that is the most reliable and most relevant to your needs. For example, travel brochures published by Aruba's government travel department will likely be very attractive, but would they be as credible as information provided by an independent travel company? Would you rely on the opinions of an acquaintance whose likes and dislikes are very different from yours, or trust the advice of a good friend with whom you share many similarities?

As a practical matter, it is usually not possible or worthwhile to collect all information available on a subject. First, gathering information is costly. It takes time and may cost money. At some point the benefit of obtaining more information is not worth the cost. This is known as the **cost/benefit trade-off**. The cost/benefit trade-off is the concept of comparing the benefits of an action with the costs of the action, and taking the action only if the benefits are greater than the costs. Information should be collected only if the benefit is greater than the cost. (For example, it is probably not worth the cost in time and money for most people to call a hotel to find out the colour of the carpeting.) Second, it is not possible for people to effectively manage large quantities of information. Too much information, or information overload, can impair a person's ability to make decisions.

Question for Consideration

Explain why a potential vacationer to Aruba would likely find travel information published by Aruba's government travel department less credible than information provided by an independent travel company.

Answer: The objective of Aruba's government travel department is to encourage people to visit the island. It is likely that its publications will emphasize the favourable qualities of the island and downplay or ignore negative ones. In contrast, an independent travel company's objective is likely to provide a useful service to its customers and encourage them to use the company's services again (the company will make more money if it can generate repeat business). As a result, the information from the independent travel agent is less likely to be biased in a way that is disadvantageous to a traveller. The vacationer is therefore likely to find the independent travel company's information more credible and useful.

What does a trip to Aruba have to do with studying accounting? Every day people make important decisions for themselves and on behalf of other entities. Individuals decide how to invest their retirement money. Bankers decide whether to lend money to struggling businesses. Labour union leaders assess how to approach negotiations with employers. Consumers decide whether to purchase products from a company. Taxation authorities assess whether a taxpayer has paid the appropriate amount of tax. We could add many more decision makers and decisions to this list, but in the final analysis, to make good decisions, whether they relate to a winter vacation or a business strategy, people must have good information available to them.

One important source of information for many business decisions is the accounting reports produced by entities. Accounting reports can be the standard financial statement package that many entities provide each year, which includes balance sheets, income statements, statements of retained earnings, cash flow statements, and notes to the financial statements. Alternatively, accounting reports can be information that is designed for the use of a particular decision maker. (We will explore the standard financial statement package in depth in Chapter 2.)

Let's consider an example of how accounting information can help improve a business decision. Suppose you were approached by a person who was referred to you by a distant cousin and this person wanted you to lend a significant amount of your own money to her corporation. What would you want to know before you would agree to make the loan? Your first key question would be, "Will the company be able to pay back the money it borrowed, plus interest?" A second question would be, "If the company were unable to pay me back, what resources does it have that I could take and sell to recover my money?" What information would help you answer these questions? You could simply size up the person by examining how she is dressed, what she looks like, and how she speaks. However, this assessment would probably not tell you much that would allow you to answer the two questions we posed.

This is where accounting comes in. Accounting information could be very helpful for answering the two questions. Accounting could tell you how well the corporation has performed in the past and it could show you the amount of cash the company is able to produce. Cash, of course, is important because that is what you hope to receive when the loan is supposed to be paid back. You might also want a list of the resources the corporation owns so that you could see what would be available to you if the loan were not repaid. You might also like a list of whom else the corporation owes money to. You can probably think of additional information that would help you make your decision. In addition, there is non-accounting information that would be helpful in your decision. For example, information about the people managing the corporation would be very useful. In short, there is a wealth of accounting information that could help you make an effective decision.

The Two Fields of Accounting: Financial Accounting and Managerial Accounting

The study of accounting is usually divided into two broad fields: financial accounting and managerial accounting. **Financial accounting** refers to the field of accounting that provides information to people who are external to an entity. These external users of accounting information include investors, lenders, taxation authorities (Canada Customs and Revenue Agency), competitors, and many more. Usually users of financial accounting information do not have inside access to information about the entity and must rely on the entity to provide information to them. This book focuses on financial accounting.

Managerial accounting refers to the field of accounting that provides information to the managers of the entity and other decision makers who work for the entity. This information assists them in making decisions related to operating the entity, including setting the price of products, deciding whether the company should expand, determining which products are successful and which are not, figuring out how much should be produced, and so on. Managerial accounting information is often much more detailed than financial accounting information, and its content and organization are more flexible. That is, financial accounting information is often prepared using known and accepted methods. Managerial accounting information is organized in whatever way the mangers want, usually to allow them to make the best decisions for the organization.

Readers should recognize that financial and managerial accounting are not independent. Entities usually collect and organize information in a single accounting system, so that even though it is presented differently for the two different classes of users, information for "financial" and "managerial" accounting comes from the same pool of data.

Question for Consideration

Explain the difference between financial and managerial accounting. Give an example of a decision that reflects each of these two fields of accounting.

Answer: Financial accounting refers to the field of accounting that provides information to people who are external to an entity—people who do not have direct access to an entity's information. Managerial accounting refers to the field of accounting that provides information to the managers of the entity and other decision makers who work for the entity to assist them in making decisions related to operating the entity. Examples that reflect financial accounting include whether to lend money to a company or whether to contribute money to a charitable organization. Decisions that reflect managerial accounting include determining the selling price of a product and whether a company should expand.

The Accounting Environment

Before we start our examination of accounting information (something we will do in earnest in Chapter 2), it is important to define and explain the environment in which accounting operates. It may come as a surprise that there cannot be a single accounting report that suits all possible interested parties. It may be helpful to consider an analogy to clarify this point.

Suppose your uncle approaches you to help him buy a car. He is very busy and does not really know much about cars, and he wants you to take care of the purchase for him. What car would you suggest he buy? Well, you might buy the car that appeals to you most, in the hope that he will let you borrow it. However, if you are going to buy a car that is suitable for your uncle, you will have to gather a lot of information before you can decide. You will need to know how much he wants to spend, how many people will be travelling in it, and how much importance he places on characteristics such as safety, style, colour, make, fuel economy, speed, leg and head room, resale value, reliability, trunk/storage space, number of doors, and so on. If you do not consider these factors you might be left with your uncle saying, "Nice car, but a two-seater sports car doesn't leave any room for the baby," or "I love the Rolls-Royce, but I make only $35,000 a year. How will I pay for it?"

This example illustrates that no one car will be suitable for all drivers: the choice will depend on the circumstances. Accounting is much the same. You cannot sensibly use or provide accounting information without considering the circumstances and addressing the many questions that must be asked before you can assess the accounting information. Who will be using the accounting information? Are there any constraints that limit how the accounting may be done? What industry does the entity belong to? Who owns the entity?

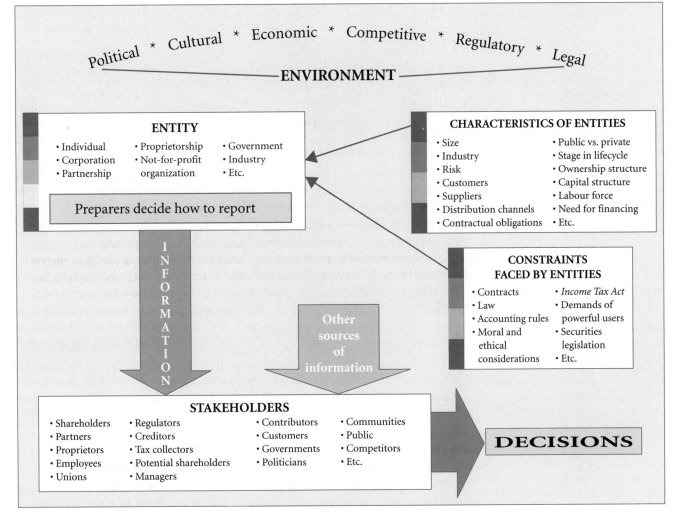

Figure 1-1

The Accounting Environment

There are four key elements of the accounting environment that form the framework for examining accounting information: entities, constraints, stakeholders, and overall environmental factors. These elements are displayed in Figure 1-1 (page 9) and discussed in detail below.

Environment

Every society has structures that guide the way people live their lives. Canada, for example, is a constitutional democracy with a mixed economy and a legal system based on British common law. The environmental "umbrella" at the top of Figure 1-1 identifies some of the important societal parameters that establish the structure of the society: that is, the political, cultural, economic, competitive, regulatory, and legal parameters. Accounting must be thought of as an activity that takes place within these environmental parameters.

Entities

As mentioned earlier, an entity is simply an economic unit of some kind. An entity can be an individual, a business, part of a business, a charity, a school, a government, a club, or an industry—almost anything you care to define. In an accounting context, an entity is an economic unit about which someone wants accounting information. Of course, it is not always possible to obtain information about an entity; perhaps no one collected it. But even if the information is collected the entity may not be obliged to provide it. As we will see, whether an entity will provide information to someone depends on the characteristics of the entity and the relationship the person has with the entity.

There are many different types of entities for which accounting can provide information, including the three different types of business entities—corporations, proprietorships, and partnerships—as well as not-for-profit organizations, governments, individuals, and others such as trade publications and interest groups. These entities are described in more detail below.

Corporations   A **corporation** is a separate legal entity created under the corporation laws of Canada or of a province, or of some other jurisdiction in the world. A corporation has many of the rights and responsibilities that an individual has. For example, a corporation must file a tax return (unlike a proprietorship or a partnership). A corporation can be sued. A corporation can enter into contracts (for example, to borrow money or to provide goods or services to a customer).

When a corporation is formed, shares in the corporation are issued to the owners. The **shares** represent ownership of the corporation. An entity that owns shares of a corporation and that is, therefore, an owner of the corporation is known as a **shareholder**. Shares can also be issued at any time through the life of a corporation, usually, but not always, in exchange for cash.

One of the most important features of a corporation is that it provides **limited liability** to its shareholders. Limited liability means that the shareholders of a corporation are not liable for the obligations of the corporation or the losses it suffers. For example, if a corporation borrows money and is unable to repay the loan, the lender cannot demand repayment from the shareholders. The lender can take action only against the corporation. Also, if the corporation is sued, the shareholders are not responsible for settling the suit—it is the corporation's responsibility. In effect, shareholders' liability is usually limited to the amount of money they invested in the corporation.

Another attractive feature of corporations is that it is relatively easy to transfer ownership from one shareholder to another without any effect on the corporation. The corporation simply carries on business with a new owner. (Of course, if the new owner has enough influence he or she could make changes to the corporation. However, the transfer of ownership itself does not imply any changes.) For other types of entities, a transfer of ownership can be more difficult.

The shares of some corporations are publicly traded, usually on a **stock exchange** such as the Toronto Stock Exchange (TSX) or TSX Venture Exchange (formerly CDNX). A stock exchange is a place (physical or virtual) where entities can buy and sell shares and other securities of publicly traded entities. The shares of a publicly traded entity can be purchased by anyone who is interested in owning a piece of the entity and has the money to buy the shares. Corporations such as Air Canada, Bombardier, and Nortel Networks are traded on the Toronto Stock Exchange and their shares can be purchased with a call to a stockbroker or on-line using a discount broker such as E*Trade or TD Waterhouse. These are known as **public corporations**.

www.tsx.ca
www.tdwaterhouse.com
www.etrade.com

Corporations can also be privately held. The ownership of the shares of a **private corporation** is limited. A private corporation is one whose shares and other securities are not available for purchase without agreement by the private corporation or its shareholders. For example, you might set up a corporation to run a small business. (The cost of setting up a corporation is relatively small, perhaps $1,500.) You could be the sole shareholder of the corporation and no one else could obtain shares of your corporation unless you wanted to sell them. Individuals, families, or other groups of people may hold shares of private corporations. Many small- and medium-sized businesses in Canada are operated as private corporations. There are also some well-known companies in Canada that are privately owned. For example, the shares of McCain Foods Limited, the world's largest producer of french fries, are owned by members of the McCain family of New Brunswick.

You can tell that an entity is incorporated if it has Inc., Corp., Ltd., Limited, Corporation, Incorporated, or plc (in the case of non-Canadian corporations) in its name. Shares can be owned by almost any entity, including individuals, other corporations, charities, governments, or mutual funds. But while public corporations are the most prominent business entities in Canada, there are far more businesses operating as private corporations, partnerships, and proprietorships.

www.mccain.com

Proprietorships A **proprietorship** is an unincorporated business that has one owner. Unlike a corporation, a proprietorship is not a separate legal entity. A proprietorship does not pay taxes. Instead, the **proprietor**, the person who owns the proprietorship, includes the money made by the proprietorship in his or her personal tax return, along with money made from other sources, such as employment. If the proprietorship does not meet its obligations, the entities that are owed money can attempt to recover what is owed to them by taking the proprietor's personal assets such as his or her house, car, or bank account. One of the attractive features of a proprietorship is that it is easy and inexpensive to set up.

Partnerships   A **partnership** is an unincorporated business owned by two or more individuals called **partners**. A partnership is like a proprietorship except that there is more than one owner. Partnerships do not pay taxes. Instead, the money earned by the partnership is included in the income of the partners. A partnership does not have limited legal liability. A lawsuit against a partnership places the assets of the partners at risk. Like a proprietorship, a partnership is relatively easy and inexpensive to set up. However, since a partnership involves more than one person, it is wise to have a partnership agreement laying out the rights and responsibilities of the partners. A partnership agreement adds cost and complexity to this form of business.

Not-for-profit Organizations   Business entities organized as corporations, partnerships, or proprietorships are formed with the intention of making money or profit. But not all economic activity in Canada is designed to make money. In fact, a large component of the Canadian economy is devoted to not-for-profit activities. **Not-for-profit organizations** provide services in Canadian communities or in other parts of the world. Not-for-profit organizations include hospitals, charities, religious organizations, unions, clubs, daycare centres, universities, and many others.

Governments   Government plays a large role in the lives of Canadians. The various levels of government in Canada raise hundreds of billions of dollars each year, mainly through different types of taxes. Given the large amount of money, financial reporting by governments is important if citizens are to evaluate how their tax dollars are being spent.

Questions for Consideration

Identify and describe the three types of business entities.

Answer: The three types of business entities are proprietorships, partnerships, and corporations. *Proprietorships* are unincorporated businesses owned by a single individual. A *partnership* is an unincorporated business owned by two or more entities. (Partners do not have to be people; they can be corporations.) *Corporations* are separate legal entities created under the corporation laws of Canada or of a province, or of some other jurisdiction in the world. Corporations have many of the rights and responsibilities that an individual has, including having to file a tax return. One of the main benefits of setting up a business as a corporation is that the corporation's shareholders have limited liability, a benefit not available to partnerships and proprietorships.

Explain the differences between public and private corporations.

Answer: The shares (or other securities) of a public corporation can be purchased by any entity with the money and desire to invest in them. The shares of a public corporation are usually purchased and sold on a stock exchange. In contrast, the shares and other securities of a private corporation are not available for purchase without agreement from the private corporation or its shareholders.

Individuals   Individual people are also accounting entities. Individuals often must produce information in a quantitative form to meet the demands of everyday life. Consider the following examples:

www.ccra-adrc.gc.ca

- Most individuals must file a tax return each year with the **Canada Customs and Revenue Agency** (CCRA), the Canadian government agency responsible for the administration and enforcement of the Canadian federal tax laws. This requires the accumulation and organization of information to complete the return.

- Most people insure their homes and belongings. To determine the appropriate amount of home-owner insurance that is needed, an individual must list his or her personal belongings and estimate a value for them.

- Most people keep a chequing account. The cheque register, where you record each cheque that you write, represents a simple accounting system that is needed so that you know how much money is in the bank.

- Many people prepare budgets. A student may want to estimate how much it will cost to attend university each year and plan monthly or weekly spending to ensure that enough money is available to meet all financial needs for the year.

Others   Though most common entities have been identified, accounting information can be compiled on an endless list of entities, depending on the users' needs. For example, some people may want data on a particular industry such as the automobile industry. One source of this kind of information would be **Statistics Canada,**

Canada's national statistical agency. Statistics Canada has a mandate to collect, compile, analyze, abstract, and publish statistical information on virtually every aspect of the nation's society and economy. Other sources of information include trade associations, industry publications, and public interest groups.

www.statcan.ca

Stakeholders: Different Users, Different Decisions, Different Information

There are many different groups and individuals that are interested in—or have a "stake" in—an entity. These groups and individuals are referred to as **stakeholders** and may include entities such as owners, lenders, taxation authorities, government, consumers, and regulators. (See Figure 1-1, page 9.) Of course not every possible stakeholder will be interested in every possible entity. Each stakeholder has his or her own perspective on an entity, and each stakeholder has specific decisions to make. An owner will be concerned about different things than a lender, who will be concerned about different things than the public, employees, or government. Therefore, the information that would be most useful to a particular stakeholder group would not be the same as the information that would be most useful to some other stakeholder.

Stakeholders are often people who do not have direct and unlimited access to an entity's databases and must rely on the entity to provide information for decision making. While information is usually available from other sources, the entity itself is an important source. Each stakeholder ideally would like to receive information that is tailored to his or her own needs. However, an entity will not likely provide information that is tailored to every user group. That is why it is important for stakeholders to assess the appropriateness of the available information for the decision being made.

For example, imagine you are deciding in which university's business program you should enrol and you contact a number of schools to send you information. One university sends you information about the overall university instead of detailed information about the business program. While the general university calendar might have some information about the business program, it would not be as useful as the business program calendar. To make the most informed decision about the business program you need its particular calendar.

Let's examine some of the stakeholders of an entity and look at how accounting information can be useful to them.

Owners   Often, the owners of a business do not manage it and are not involved in its day-to-day affairs. When the owners are separate from management, the owners need information from the company to evaluate how well their investment is doing, whether management is doing a good job, or whether they should sell their interest in the company or replace the managers. Remember that the owner of a business can be a proprietor, a partner or a shareholder.

Lenders   Many entities need to borrow money at times. Before lending money a prospective lender, such as a banker, would want to investigate whether the borrower would be able to pay back the loan. The prospective lender would assess the risk of the borrower being unable to pay back the loan and, in the event of the loan not being paid back, whether the borrower would have assets that the lender could take and sell to recover the money it lent. For this type of evaluation the banker would want to assess future cash flows and the market value of the entity's assets.

Taxation Authorities   The Canada Customs and Revenue Agency uses accounting information to assess the taxes owed by a business or individual. In Canada each individual and corporation must file a tax return each year. The Canada Customs and

Revenue Agency requires taxpayers to calculate their taxes using methods that are consistent with the *Income Tax Act*, Canada's federal tax legislation. Provinces also have tax rules that must be followed.

Governments   Other government departments also have an interest in accounting information. For example, governments may decide whether certain entities should receive government support or subsidies. Accounting information also has political impact. Companies may attract the attention of politicians by making what the public perceives as "too much money."

Consumers   When someone buys an expensive product such as a computer, he or she may be concerned about whether the company will be around in the future to support the product. While most people who buy computers do not consult the accounting reports of the manufacturers, there are many sources that convey the information reflected in the manufacturer's accounting reports. For example, the popular media will usually report when a well-known company is in financial trouble. As a result, a potential customer might decide not to buy from that company even though the product is attractive for other reasons.

Regulators   Some industries and businesses in Canada are subject to regulation, including cable television providers and local telephone companies, which are regulated by the Canadian Radio-television and Telecommunications Commission (CRTC), and pipeline companies that transport oil and natural gas, which are regulated by the National Energy Board (NEB). Accounting information is used to help the regulators set rates so that customers pay a reasonable price for the service and investors receive a reasonable return on their investment. Regulators sometimes may even define the accounting rules that a regulated company can use.

Question for Consideration

What are stakeholders? Give some examples of different stakeholders. Indicate a possible reason each stakeholder you identify might want information about an entity.

Answer: Stakeholders are entities that have an interest or a stake in an entity. The interest a stakeholder has depends on its relationship with the entity.

Stakeholder	Information is required to:
Shareholders	Evaluate management.
Partners	Determine the amount of money that should be paid for their interest in the partnership.
Taxation Authorities	Determine whether the provisions of the *Income Tax Act* have been followed and whether the appropriate amount of tax has been paid.
Regulators	Evaluate whether the entity should receive an increase in its rates and determine the amount of the increase.
Donors	Determine whether a charity should receive a donation based upon how efficiently the charity uses the money it receives.

Characteristics of Entities

Like people, no two entities are identical. Each has a set of characteristics that makes it unique. Some characteristics are obvious—for example, an entity's industry. Canada has businesses in a vast range of industries, including natural resources, agriculture, finance, manufacturing, high technology, hospitality, and services, to name a few. And even though several companies may be in the same industry, each may have different characteristics. Some may be public and others private, some may be large and others small, some may be unionized and others not, and each may do business in different markets. All of these characteristics are important for understanding an entity, what it does, and in the end how it does its accounting.

Figure 1-1 (page 9) identifies a number of characteristics of entities. We will explore many of these as we proceed through the book. At this point it is important to keep in mind that entities are not all the same and that an entity's characteristics may help determine the accounting choices it makes.

Constraints

How an entity does its accounting and what information it reports are not entirely up to the people who prepare the information. Often, the choices available are constrained by contracts, laws, accounting rules, and the information needs and demands of powerful users of accounting information. Consider the following examples:

- The *Income Tax Act* requires for certain situations that particular accounting methods be used for purposes of calculating the amount of income tax that must be paid.
- Companies that trade on Canadian stock exchanges must meet the requirements of the securities laws of their province.
- Companies that trade on the Toronto Stock Exchange (TSX), which includes many of Canada's largest and most well-known companies (including the Royal Bank of Canada, Bell Canada Enterprises and Alcan Inc.) must at a minimum meet the requirements stated in the *Ontario Securities Act* and the requirements of the TSX.

Stakeholders versus Preparers

Accounting information must be considered from two perspectives: the stakeholders' perspective and the preparers' perspective. **Preparers** are the people responsible for deciding what, how, and when information is going to be presented in an entity's financial statements and other accounting reports. Preparers are the people who make the decisions—senior managers such as controllers, chief financial officers, and even chief executive officers—and not the people who physically prepare the statements.

It is important to recognize that preparers are not neutral providers of accounting information. Their own personal interests may influence their preparation of accounting reports. Consider the following situations:

- Managers' bonuses are sometimes based on the numbers contained in accounting reports. (The preparer might want to enhance the accounting numbers to improve his or her bonus.)
- The amount of tax an entity pays is related to its accounting numbers. (The preparer might account in a way so as to pay as little tax as is legally possible.)
- When a business is sold, the selling price can be based on the accounting numbers. (The preparer might want to enhance the accounting numbers to increase the selling price of the business.)

It should be clear that there is potential for conflict. Stakeholders want information that will be useful for their decision making. Preparers will have an interest in supplying useful information to stakeholders, but they will also be inclined to pursue their own interests. Making matters more complicated are the rules under which most Canadian entities report—generally accepted accounting principles or GAAP. As we will see later in this chapter and throughout the book, GAAP provide preparers a great deal of latitude in deciding what, how, and when information is presented in an entity's accounting statements.

At this point sirens might be going off in your head. "This doesn't sound very honest." "They cook the books!" "You can't trust accounting numbers." "Are accountants unethical?" Sometimes these reactions are valid. However, the reliability of accounting information is a very tricky question. Even though GAAP allow preparers considerable leeway in choosing how to account, in most situations preparers stay within the rules. The fact that there is choice does allow the preparers to serve their self-interest. However, choice also provides preparers with flexibility so that they can supply accounting information in a way that best suits the varied information needs of different stakeholders and allows accounting to adapt to new situations.

Unfortunately for stakeholders, it is often difficult to figure out whether preparers' choices are motivated by their concern about providing useful information to stakeholders or by their own self-interest. We can discuss at length the merits of allowing preparers a lot of choice when they prepare their accounting information. However, the reality is that preparers and stakeholders both operate in this confusing and conflicting environment. If you are going to be a successful user or preparer of accounting information, it is essential that you understand this environment.

The apparent conflict between stakeholders and preparers creates the need for people who can examine the information provided by the preparers and offer assurance to the stakeholders that the information meets certain stated principles. The people who examine entities' financial information on behalf of external stakeholders are called **external auditors.** Their examination of an entity's information is known as an **external audit**. An external audit involves examining an entity's financial statements and the data supporting the information in the financial statements. In most circumstances in Canada, auditors audit to ensure that the financial statements are fair representations of the underlying economic activity of the entity and that the accounting is done in accordance with GAAP.

However, an external auditor can also audit to other principles besides GAAP. In fact, more than financial information can be audited. What is necessary is a person who has expertise in a field and a willingness to offer his or her expert opinion on the information. For example, a food company might make claims about the nutritional value of its products—perhaps that the products have certain levels of fat, protein, vitamins, and minerals. An independent testing lab could test the products and offer a statement that the products do meet the nutritional claims of the company. The opinion of the independent lab would provide some assurance to consumers that the company's claims were legitimate.

For external auditors to add credibility to the information provided by an entity, it is important that the auditors be independent of the entity they are auditing. That means an auditor cannot be involved in managing the entity, have an ownership interest, or participate in any type of relationship that will bring the independence of the auditor into question. For example, if you were buying a used car and wanted to be sure that the car you were interested in buying was in excellent condition, would you have more confidence in the opinion of the used car dealer or that of an independent mechanic? Clearly, the car dealer has an interest in making you believe that the car is of high quality since he or she will benefit from the sale.

There are other types of auditors in addition to the external auditors described above:

- Internal auditors are employed by an entity and conduct audits on behalf of the entity's management. Internal audits help ensure the credibility of the information produced by the entity for management decision making.

- The Canada Customs and Revenue Agency has auditors whose job is to verify that taxpayers adhere to the *Income Tax Act* and pay the appropriate amount of tax.

To place this discussion in context, consider this statement by Paul Beeston, former president of the Toronto Blue Jays Baseball Club, former president and chief operating officer of Major League Baseball, and an accountant:

> "Anyone who quotes profits of a baseball club is missing the point. Under generally accepted accounting principles, I can turn a $4 million profit into a $2 million loss, and I can get every national accounting firm to agree with me."[3]

We will examine the role of audits and auditors further in Chapter 5.

Question for Consideration

Our discussion of auditing noted that Paul Beeston, former president of the Toronto Blue Jays Baseball Club, former president and chief operating officer of Major League Baseball, and an accountant, once said, "Anyone who quotes profits of a baseball club is missing the point. Under generally accepted accounting principles, I can turn a $4 million profit into a $2 million loss, and I can get every national accounting firm to agree with me."[3] What do you think Mr. Beeston meant by his statement?

Answer: Mr. Beeston was making the point that accounting rules, even under GAAP, are flexible and allow preparers considerable latitude in choosing how, what, and when accounting information is presented. The implication of this flexibility is that the numbers reported in financial statements can vary depending on the choices that the preparers make and that a range of numbers can be considered as being "within the rules."

It must be emphasized that while choice exists in accounting for good reason, it is possible to go too far. Choice is available because it is often difficult and counterproductive to try to set rules that apply to all situations. The diversity of entities, stakeholders, and entity characteristics requires enough flexibility to allow information to be presented in an appropriate way for the situation. However, such flexibility allows some preparers to play fast and loose with the rules. Sometimes preparers become overly concerned about their personal interests and the interests of their organizations, forgetting that stakeholders rely on the information to make good decisions. If stakeholders cannot rely on the accounting information, there can be significant economic implications. Preparers of accounting information have an ethical and moral responsibility to provide information that is a reasonable economic representation of the organization.

Let's conclude this section with an accounting example. On December 15, 2004 Mark's Work Wearhouse (MWW) receives a large order from a customer to ship 2,000 pairs of work gloves to a work site in Québec. MWW does not have the gloves in stock at this time but assures the customer that it will be able to ship them by the middle of February. The customer has agreed to pay for the gloves 60 days after they are received. When would be an appropriate time for MWW to report that it has sold the gloves? Sound arguments could be made for reporting the sale when the order was received from the customer, when the gloves were shipped to the customer, or when the customer pays. Which do you think makes sense? The fact that reasonable cases exist for three different points in time highlights the fact that accounting is not clear-cut and precise.

It is crucial to understand that while the accountants are scratching their heads about when to report this sale, the economic activity proceeds unaffected by their pondering. In other words, when the accountants decide to record this sale does not change when the order was received, when MWW received the goods from its supplier, when the gloves were shipped to the customer, or when the customer paid MWW.

Let's consider the implications of the different possible times for reporting the sale of the gloves. When MWW records this transaction can have an impact on both preparers and stakeholders. The choice can affect the amount of tax MWW pays, the amount of bonus the president and other senior executives receive, approval of an increase in the company's loan from the bank, and even the shareholders' perception of how well MWW is doing and therefore its share price. As remarkable as it may seem, accounting information can have significant economic consequences for the preparers and the various stakeholders of an entity. It is the economic consequences of accounting information that make it so important to understand the nature of accounting.

As we move through the book you will see the choices that are available and how they can be used and abused. At this point the purpose for introducing this unexpected side of accounting is to make you aware of its true nature. Accounting is not certainty, it is not truth, and there are few right answers.

Accounting Is for Measurement

Accounting systems are designed to accumulate data that are then organized, processed, and converted into information that is useful to stakeholders. This is valuable because the information produced by accounting systems allows stakeholders to measure different attributes of an entity. Some of the attributes that accounting can be used to measure include:

- the performance of an entity
- the efficiency of an entity
- the performance of the entity's managers and how much bonus they should receive
- how much an entity owes to lenders
- the worth of a business for determining its selling price
- the amount of tax an entity should pay

Two characteristics of accounting information make it especially useful for measuring the attributes of an entity. First, accounting information is quantitative. That is, data entered into an accounting system always have numeric values assigned to them. For example, when MWW purchases goods that it will sell to its customers, say 1,000 pairs of size large work gloves, the quantity purchased and the amount paid are recorded in the accounting system. Second, the accounting information that is produced by an accounting system is presented in terms of a single unit of measure, usually money. For example, in its financial statements MWW will report the number of dollars customers spent purchasing clothing from MWW stores and the number of dollars MWW spent for the clothing that the customers purchased. Imagine how difficult it would be to make sense of the activities of an entity if accounting reports did not summarize data in terms of dollars or some other unit of measure—for example, if MWW provided only a detailed list of the items it sold.

Consider a simple example. A large bowl of fruit contains six apples, five oranges, four pears, four bananas, three kiwis, three peaches, and a pineapple. Without having a single unit of measure, all we can do is list the types of fruit in the bowl. It would be difficult to do any type of analysis of the contents of the fruit bowl. If we use fruit as the unit of measure we can come up with the total amount of fruit in the bowl: 26 pieces. With this number we can compare our fruit bowl with others. If we use the number of pieces of fruit in a bowl as a measure of the size of the fruit bowl, we could then easily compare our fruit bowl with others by simply counting the number of pieces of fruit in each bowl. A comparison of the sizes of different fruit bowls would be very difficult without a single unit of measure. There are other units that we could use to summarize the contents of the fruit bowl. We could also use the cost of the fruit, the price we could sell the fruit for, the weight of the fruit, and perhaps others as the basis of measurement.

While this example may strike you as trivial, remember that a company like MWW has hundreds of different products, many of which come in different sizes, colours, and styles. Think about how difficult it would be to analyze MWW if you received only a detailed list of each separate type of clothing item MWW sold, without a dollar value.

However, there are drawbacks to using a single unit of measure. Measuring on a single dimension can result in the loss of useful information. To go back to our fruit bowl example, note that by measuring the contents of the fruit bowl on the basis of the number of pieces of fruit we lose information that might be useful for some decisions. For example, data about the type and quality of fruit in the basket is not available if quantity of fruit is used as the basis of measurement. And it would be easy to argue that the number of pieces of fruit is not the best measure of the size of a bowl of fruit. Indeed, the "best" measure of the basket of fruit would depend on the decision that was being made. Similarly, if MWW aggregated the sales of different clothing, a user would be unable to tell what sales were of specific items.

Question for Consideration

Identify and explain the two characteristics that make accounting information especially useful for measurement.

Answer: The two characteristics are (1) accounting information is always quantified, and (2) accounting reports are stated in terms of a single unit of measure. These characteristics allow the data that is accumulated by the accounting system to be organized, processed, and converted into information that is useful to stakeholders. For example, without quantification and a single unit of measure, it would not be possible to come up with "totals" of often-dissimilar pieces of information.

Let's look at some examples of how accounting can be used for measuring. Suppose that over the summer you had a job in a mining town in northern Canada. At the end of the summer you wanted to know how much money you made and what you spent your money on. If you looked at your pay stubs you would find out how much the company paid you, but the pay stubs would not tell you how much money you spent over the summer. If you looked at your bank account you could figure out how much was deposited and how much you withdrew. With that information plus your pay stubs you could figure out what you spent. However, the bank account might also have deposits and withdrawals unrelated to your summer job, and it would not tell you what you spent your money on.

Fortunately, you decided to keep track of the money you spent during the summer by recording the information in a notebook. You kept a list of the hours you worked and the amount you were paid. An excerpt from the "book" is shown in Table 1-1. Your book represents a very basic accounting system.

Table 1-1	Your Summer Expenses: An Example of a Basic Accounting System

Listing of Money Spent During the Summer

Date	Purpose	Amount
•	•	•
•	•	•
•	•	•
June 13	Rent	$225.00
June 13	Magazines	5.75
June 13	Entertainment	22.50
•	•	•
•	•	•
•	•	•
July 17	Groceries	45.25
July 18	Entertainment	12.75
July 19	Miscellaneous	4.50
•	•	•
•	•	•
•	•	•
August 12	Groceries	22.98
August 12	Airfare home	475.68
•	•	•
•	•	•
•	•	•

The book itself is just raw data. To be useful, the data have to be organized, processed, and converted into information. You could go through your book and classify expenditures into categories such as food, entertainment, and rent. Table 1-2 shows an example of how you could present the information in your book.

With the information organized as in Table 1-2 it is easy to see how much money you made, how much you spent and what you spent it on, and how much you have left over. However, there are many things you cannot tell from this statement, including how much rent you paid each month, the type of entertainment you enjoyed, or what groceries you bought.

A crucial point to keep in mind is that how you organize the data depends on what you or some other stakeholder wants to know. If you didn't care how you spent your money, a statement like the one in Table 1-3 might suffice. On the other hand, you might want more detail about the type of entertainment you spent your money on.

Another important point to remember is that your ability to extract information from the accounting system is limited to the data that were entered in the system. For example, it would be possible to find out how much money you spent on different kinds of groceries only if you initially broke down your grocery spending into the appropriate categories. That is, you could not find out how much money you spent on soft drinks during the summer if you recorded soft drink spending with your spending on groceries.

Table 1-2	Classifying Your Summer Earnings and Spending: An Example of a Basic Accounting Report

Summary of Summer Earnings and Spending

Amount earned (gross pay)	$8,990.87	
Amount withheld*	1,712.98	
Deposited in the bank (net pay)		$7,277.89
Amounts spent		
Airfare	955.68	
Books, magazines, etc.	75.33	
Clothes	121.01	
Entertainment	375.25	
Groceries	448.65	
Local transportation	45.56	
Miscellaneous	99.98	
Rent	900.00	
Amount spent		3,021.46
Amount saved over the summer		$4,256.43

*Employers are required to withhold money from employees' pay for taxes, employment insurance, and Canada Pension Plan contributions. The amount earned before withholding is called gross pay. The amount after deductions is called net pay.

Table 1-3	Summarizing Your Summer Earnings and Spending: An Example of a Basic Accounting Report

Summary of Summer Earnings and Spending

Amount earned (gross pay)	$8,990.87	
Amount withheld	1,712.98	
Deposited in the bank (net pay)		$7,277.89
Amount spent		3,021.46
Amount saved over the summer		$4,256.43

This example demonstrates how accounting can summarize information in an informative way. It also shows how, by using a single unit of measure, totals can be obtained that provide useful information. Let's consider another example.

Imagine you are a first-year student who has just moved into a new apartment near your university or college. You need to get insurance for the apartment. You have furnished it with personal belongings, and it also has appliances supplied by the building's owner. How much insurance do you need? You want to have enough insurance to protect the things you own and the things you are responsible for, such as the building owner's appliances. The insurance company needs to know how much insurance you require so that it can write a policy and set a premium for you, based on the amount and type of insurance you want.

Table 1-4   Items in a Student's Apartment

Inventory of Apartment Contents

Column 1 Item	Column 2 What it cost	Column 3 What it would cost to replace	Column 4 What it could be sold for
Television	$ 500	$ 650	$ 225
Computer	1,900	1,500	700
Furniture	1,200	1,350	900
Books	750	875	300
Clothes	1,600	1,950	1,000
Stereo	900	1,100	700
Jewellery	500	625	300
Appliances	2,000	2,600	1,400
Art	300	300	200
Other	1,000	1,200	750
Total	$10,650	$12,150	$6,475

To estimate the amount of insurance you need, you will have to go through the apartment and take an "inventory" of the things you want to insure. (An inventory is a list of the items in your apartment, as provided in Table 1-4.)

Column 1 of Table 1-4 lists the contents of the apartment, but the list alone is not very helpful for deciding the amount of insurance you need. It indicates what you need to insure, but it does not say anything about how much insurance coverage you need. You have to assign a measure of value to each item so that you can "sum up" to a total that will help you decide how much insurance coverage you need. The total is important because if you do not know the worth of what you want to insure you may buy too little insurance, leaving you ill-prepared in the event of a fire or robbery. If you get too much insurance you are wasting money on premiums, since the insurance company will not pay out more than the amount of the loss. (For example, if you have $50,000 of insurance coverage and everything you own is destroyed in a fire but is worth $10,000, the insurance company will pay you only $10,000.)

Now things get more complicated. What is the appropriate "value" to assign to each item? In Table 1-4 three different measurements of value have been used for each item, as follows:

- Column 2 provides the amount paid for each item.

- Column 3 shows the amount that would have to be paid for a similar item. (For example, the TV might be a ten-year-old model that is no longer made. The TV could not be replaced by an identical item, so you would have to get something comparable that is available today.)

- Column 4 is the amount each item could be sold for. Insurance companies might refer to this amount as the "depreciated" value, or the value after the item has been used.

Notice that the total of each column is quite different from the others.

Any one of these three approaches might be a reasonable measure of the amount of insurance coverage required. The one you choose depends on the type of insurance coverage you want, and the type of insurance that companies will sell. Using Column 3 would allow replacement of the items lost (this is called replacement cost insurance). Using Column 4 would allow recovery of the amount you invested in the items, less an amount that reflects how much the items were used. (The insurance company would not get estimates of the worth of the specific items, but would use a formula to estimate the extent to which they were used, based, for example, on their age.)

There are two important points to note from our insurance example. The first is the importance of measurement. To decide on the amount of insurance needed, it was necessary to come up with a measure of the total worth of the items in the apartment. The second point is that there is often more than one way to measure the same thing. We have easily come up with three ways to measure the "value" in terms of dollars of the items in your apartment. Which one is best? That question cannot be answered in absolute terms. The "best" one depends on the situation.

> **Comment:** It is important to keep in mind that while most accounting reports use money as the unit of measure, it is not the only possible measure. Accounting and accountants can provide information in many different ways. In many situations where users want and require quantitative information, accounting can help. For example, accountants could be involved in providing information on the amount of pollution that a company produces. They could be involved in measuring the effectiveness of a medical care system (mortality rates, utilization of beds and equipment, etc.). Accountants could help develop measures of customer satisfaction or evaluate whether a government is getting value for the money it spends. These examples require measurements that are not measured in terms of money.

The Rules of the Game

Accounting is a tool that has been developed by people as a means of providing information for decision making. Unlike gravity, accounting has no natural laws that define how it should be done. As a result, it is necessary to establish rules of the game. If there were no rules it would be much more costly and difficult to make sense of the information contained in accounting reports because it would be necessary to learn and understand the rules that each entity was using.

The rules in accounting are known as **generally accepted accounting principles or GAAP**. GAAP are the principles, conventions, practices, procedures, and rules that define acceptable accounting practices and guide the preparation of financial statements in certain situations. In other words, GAAP represent a structure for preparing financial statements.

The importance of a set of rules can be demonstrated with an analogy. When we drive, there are certain conventions and rules that people follow that contribute to safe driving. In every community in Canada a red light means stop and a green light means go. A yellow light is a bit more ambiguous and different drivers respond differently to yellow lights. (This is actually just like GAAP, where some of the "rules" can be interpreted differently by different preparers of accounting information.) On traffic lights the red light is always on top and the green on the bottom. Everywhere in Canada we drive on the right side of the road. However, in the United Kingdom, Jamaica, and Zimbabwe, people drive on the left side of the road. This is an example of how traffic rules and GAAP can vary from jurisdiction to jurisdiction.

Now imagine the difficulty a driver would have if every community had different rules of the road—if there were different coloured lights in different positions. The result would be chaos. Traffic would move more slowly as visiting drivers tried to figure out the rules in each community. Getting around the community would be more costly in terms of time, fuel expense, insurance (since there would probably be more accidents), and fines (since people would likely violate the rules more often and there would be more tickets issued). The potential for damage to vehicles because of traffic mishaps would likely increase significantly. In sum, the existence of standardized rules of the road reduces the cost of getting around. However, even within Canada the rules are not completely uniform. For example, some provinces allow vehicles to make right-hand turns on red lights. Others do not. Similarly, some jurisdictions have delays when the lights change colours so that the lights are red in all directions for a brief time. Some jurisdictions do not have a delay. As we will see, the world of GAAP is very similar.

There are a few limitations worth noting about GAAP:

- GAAP are not universal. GAAP in each country differ. Canadian GAAP are quite similar but not identical to GAAP in the United States. Canadian GAAP differ dramatically from GAAP in some other countries in the world. For example, GAAP used by some European countries are very dissimilar to Canadian GAAP.

- Not every entity follows GAAP or has to follow GAAP. GAAP will be followed carefully by public corporations because public corporations are regulated by provincial securities commissions and by the stock exchanges on which the securities are traded. However, GAAP do not have to be followed by private corporations, partnerships, or proprietorships unless there is some specific reason for doing so. For example, shareholders of a private corporation or bankers may prefer GAAP accounting information because the information is prepared according to the prevailing set of "rules."

- GAAP are flexible. They offer preparers many choices that can affect the information contained in financial statements. The flexibility of GAAP require that users be very careful when examining and interpreting financial statements.

www.cica.ca

We will explore GAAP in depth in Chapter 5, but at this point we can take a look at some of the basic principles. The conceptual groundwork for Canadian GAAP is laid out in the *CICA Handbook,* published by the Canadian Institute of Chartered Accountants. The *CICA Handbook* is also the source of some specific GAAP, but there are in fact many sources of GAAP, including the accounting methods actually being used by entities. The *CICA Handbook* has the force of law behind it because the provincial securities commissions in Canada and the federal and provincial laws that regulate corporations specifically recognize the *CICA Handbook* as the source of GAAP in Canada. The *CICA Handbook* recognizes that an entity can have many stakeholders who are interested in receiving information about the entity. However, it also recognizes the practical limitations of providing information that is tailored to the needs of all stakeholders, and focuses on investors who own and lend money to entities, along with other creditors of an entity. (A **creditor** is an entity to which the reporting entity has an obligation to provide cash or other assets in the future.) As a result, Canadian GAAP are not intended to address the information needs of many stakeholders.

The *CICA Handbook* describes four qualitative characteristics that financial statement information must have if it is to be useful to users. The four characteristics are:

1. **Understandability**. Users must be able to understand information if it is to be useful to them. This characteristic does not mean that the information must be made simple enough for the most unsophisticated user to understand. Rather, the characteristic assumes that users will have a reasonable understanding of business and accounting, and a willingness to study the information provided.

2. **Relevance**. The information provided to users must be relevant or useful for the decisions they have to make. The *CICA Handbook* goes on to explain that relevant information is information that helps users make predictions about the future performance of the entity, provides feedback on decisions that were made in the past, and is provided to users in a timely manner so that it will be useful for decision making.

3. **Reliability**. The information provided to users must be a reasonable measure of what it is intended to measure. In other words, the information must be precise and unbiased.[4] For example, in many jurisdictions companies must limit the amount of pollution that they allow into the air and water. Independent agencies, often government agencies, are responsible for measuring the amount of pollution an entity produces. An independent agency that has the proper equipment can provide a precise and probably unbiased measure of the amount of pollution. Without the proper equipment, the measurement of the pollution would probably not be very precise. The polluter itself could not be relied on to provide reliable information about its polluting activities, even if it had the proper equipment, because the company is not unbiased—it might benefit from or be harmed by its pollution report.

4. **Comparability**. Users should be able to compare the accounting information provided by different entities and the information of a particular entity from period to period. For example, the ability to make predictions about the future performance of an entity can be aided by looking at historical performance trends of the entity. If the entity changes its accounting in each period, the ability to interpret the trends would be impaired.

If all of these characteristics could be met in all situations, there would be few critical comments that could be made about accounting information. The reality is, however, that in most cases it is not possible to achieve all the characteristics in every situation. In many cases trade-offs must be made among the characteristics. A particular user of the accounting information may find that the trade-offs that are made under GAAP may not suit his or her decision needs.

It is essential for any user or preparer of accounting information to know and understand GAAP. No user or preparer of accounting information can afford not to have an understanding of the concepts, principles, and rules that underlie GAAP. However, every user, preparer, and accountant must also understand that GAAP have significant problems and limitations. GAAP are not applicable to every user and every decision in every situation. Sophisticated users of financial statements will know when not to rely on GAAP-based statements, when to adjust the GAAP statements, and when to look elsewhere for information. Sophisticated users will also understand the flexibility that preparers of financial statements have even under GAAP and understand that this flexibility can have a significant effect on the appearance of the statements.

One of the main objectives of this book is to help readers understand and appreciate financial statements with all their blemishes. We will look at accounting practice and accounting information with a critical eye so that you will become sophisticated users and preparers of accounting information.

■ Solved Problem

Bayton Ltd.—Part 1

Bayton Ltd. (Bayton) is an operator of garbage dumps in western Canada. Bayton operates by purchasing land from private owners, having the land zoned for a garbage dump, and then developing and operating the dump. The planning and development of the dumps is done in close cooperation with the local communities that the dump will serve. Bayton does not provide garbage collection services; these are provided by local governments or by private companies that have contracts with local governments. The garbage collectors pay a fee to Bayton based on the weight of the garbage dumped.

Bayton is a privately owned corporation. The company has 15 investors who live all across Canada. A team of professional managers who have considerable experience in the waste management business runs Bayton. The managers are paid a salary plus a bonus based on the performance of the company, as measured by its accounting information. The company employs over 500 people, many of whom are unionized. In addition to money invested by the owners of the company, Bayton has borrowed heavily from several banks and other lenders.

Required:

Identify all of the stakeholders in Bayton and explain their "stake" in the company. Not all the stakeholders are explicitly referred to in the scenario. You will have think about the business situation carefully to identify some of the stakeholders. (You may be able to identify other stakeholders in addition to those in the Solution.)

Solution:

Stakeholders	Stake
1. Shareholders (owners)	The shareholders are Bayton's owners. Part of their wealth is invested in the company.
2. Lenders	Bayton owes the lenders money. The lenders will be concerned about Bayton's ability to repay amounts owed to them.
3. Managers	Managers are interested in maintaining their jobs and enhancing their reputations in the job market. In addition, part of the managers' compensation is based on the performance of Bayton.
4. Canada Customs and Revenue Agency (CCRA)	Bayton Ltd. is a taxpaying entity and the CCRA will be interested in ensuring that it pays its taxes and complies with the *Income Tax Act*.
5. People located in communities where dumps are or will be located	Garbage dumps are often unpopular neighbours. People who live near existing garbage dumps want to ensure that the dumps are being managed responsibly and that Bayton will be able to carry out its obligations in the future. People living near prospective garbage dumps may want to take steps to prevent a dump from being set up near their homes.
6. Government	Garbage dumps can be politically very sensitive issues. Governments will want to ensure that Bayton Inc.'s garbage dumps do not cause them political problems.
7. Employees/unions	Bayton Ltd.'s employees rely on the company for their incomes. Unions negotiate contracts with Bayton Ltd. on behalf of their employees.
8. Environmental regulatory agencies	Because of the potential environmental problems associated with Bayton's garbage dumps, many jurisdictions will have regulatory agencies whose responsibilities will include monitoring the company's waste management practices, ensuring compliance with government standards, and reporting to the government and public.
9. Communities	Communities require a means of disposing of their garbage. Ensuring a reliable method of disposal is crucial for many communities. Bayton provides the means for these communities to dispose of their garbage.
10. Garbage collection companies	Garbage collection companies require a place to dump the garbage they collect and must pay fees to do so.

11. Environmental groups Garbage dumps pose potentially serious environmental problems. Improper waste management practices can lead to contamination of land and ground water. Private environmental groups monitor the dumps and the companies operating them.

Bayton Ltd.—Part 2

In 1975 Bayton paid $250,000 ($500 per hectare) for a 500-hectare piece of land that it intended to develop into a garbage dump. For various reasons Bayton has not yet developed the land, but Bayton's president has stated that it will do so at the appropriate time. Over the last two years there have been two transactions involving the sale of land located near Bayton's property. In the first transaction, which occurred 20 months ago, the land was sold for $825 per hectare. In the second transaction, which occurred eight months ago, the land was sold for $730 per hectare.

Recently a business person made an offer for Bayton's land of $690 per hectare or $345,000. The president of Bayton hired an independent appraiser to estimate the value of the land so that he could assess the offer. The appraiser estimated that the land was worth between $340,000 and $390,000. For the purpose of calculating municipal property taxes, two years ago the municipality where the land is located placed a value on it of $290,000. The president himself thinks that Bayton could sell the land for $410,000 if Bayton chose to sell it.

Required:

Identify and explain the different measurements of the value of Bayton's land. Discuss the relevance and reliability of the different measurements. Make sure you refer to the decisions that have to be made by some of the stakeholders.

Solution:

There are a number of different measurements available for valuing Bayton's land, none of which represent the actual current value of the land. The measurements are: Note to formatter: see hard copy for set up.

Measurement	Explanation	Relevance and Reliability
Cost: $250,000	The amount Bayton paid for the land.	Cost is a very reliable measure of the value of the land because documentation exists indicating the price that Bayton paid for the land in 1975. This measure will be precise and unbiased. The cost is relevant for income tax purposes because the amount of tax paid when Bayton sells the land will be related to the price it paid for it. The cost may also be relevant to shareholders if they want to know how much profit Bayton made by holding the land since 1975 and then selling it. The cost of the land is not very relevant for most other decisions. Cost is not useful for determining whether or not the land should be sold, the amount of money that a lender would lend to Bayton based on the market value of land, or the amount that a buyer should pay for the land if Bayton decided to sell it. For these decisions the market value of the land is more relevant.
Property tax value: $290,000	The value assigned to the land by the municipality for determining property taxes.	This amount is relevant for determining the amount of property tax that Bayton must pay. Otherwise this value does not likely have any other useful purpose. The value was determined two years ago, which makes it somewhat out of date, and since it is not clear how the amount was determined, its relevance for non-property-tax purposes is difficult to determine.

Bayton's president's estimate: $410,000	The amount that Bayton's president thinks the company can sell the land for.	This amount may be relevant as a benchmark for management for determining whether the land should be sold or kept. The value is not very reliable for prospective buyers of the land because it is biased, as it is in the president's self-interest to make a high estimate.
Independent appraiser's estimate: $340,000–$390,000	The price range that an independent appraiser estimated the land is worth.	This estimate will be somewhat relevant and reliable to some stakeholders. The estimate is reliable because it comes from an unbiased source, but it is not very precise because the appraiser has given quite a broad estimate. It is also difficult to know what land will sell for before it is sold. The estimate would be relevant to lenders who are interested in lending money to Bayton because the lender would want to know how much money could be recovered if Bayton were unable to repay the loan. The estimate would also be relevant to Bayton itself and to prospective buyers of the land because it provides an unbiased estimate of the land's current market value.
Sale of nearby land: $412,500 based on the first sale and $365,000 based on the second sale.	These amounts are calculated by multiplying Bayton's 500 hectares by the price per hectare paid in the transactions for the nearby land.	The values for the land that was sold are reliable: they are supported by independent transactions and so there is no question about the amounts involved. However, these amounts are not necessarily reliable with respect to Bayton's land. There are three significant problems regarding the relevance of these amounts: (1) the transactions took place some time ago, so they may not reflect current market conditions, which would be an important concern to prospective lenders or buyers; (2) the land that was sold may not be similar to Bayton's land despite being nearby; and (3) the price does not inform us about the circumstances surrounding the sales (the seller in one of the transactions may have required cash urgently and therefore could not wait to get a higher price). These three factors limit the relevance of the selling price of the other pieces of land.

Summary of Key Points

LO 1. Accounting is a system for producing information about an entity and communicating that information to people who want or need the information for making decisions. Effective decision making requires information, and accounting is a crucial source of information. The numbers in an accounting report tell a story but the numbers cannot be taken at face value. Using, preparing, and understanding accounting information requires a set of high-level cognitive skills, including judgment, analysis, synthesis, evaluation, problem solving, critical thinking, and creativity.

Preparers of accounting information often have considerable leeway and choice in how they will do their accounting. The existence of choices makes it necessary for users to exercise a great deal of care to ensure they are aware of the choices that the preparer made and of how those choices affect their decisions.

Financial accounting is the field of accounting that provides information to people who are external to an entity—people who do not have direct access to an entity's information. Managerial accounting is the field of accounting that provides information to the managers of the entity and other decision makers who work for the entity to assist them in making decisions related to operating the entity.

LO 2. Accounting does not operate in a vacuum. You cannot sensibly use or provide accounting information without considering the accounting environment, which includes the social, political, legal, cultural, and economic environment of a society, the types of entities that are of interest to stakeholders and the characteristics of those entities, the different stakeholders that may have an interest in an entity, and the constraints that limit the accounting choices an entity can make. The diversity of the accounting environment makes it impossible for a single accounting report to be appropriate for all situations. Accounting reports must be tailored to suit the circumstances of an entity's accounting environment.

LO 3. The stakeholders in an entity who require accounting information for their decision making rely on the entity to provide the information. The preparers are not neutral. When preparing accounting reports preparers may be influenced by their own personal interests, and these interests may conflict with those of the stakeholders.

LO 4. The most valuable use of the information produced by accounting systems is that it allows stakeholders to measure different attributes of an entity. Two characteristics of accounting information make it especially useful for measuring the attributes of an entity. First, accounting information is quantitative; second, accounting information is presented in terms of a single unit of measure, usually money. These characteristics make it possible for the data entered into an accounting system to be organized, processed, and converted into information that is useful to stakeholders.

LO 5. GAAP are the principles, conventions, practices, procedures, and rules that define acceptable accounting practices and guide the preparation of financial statements in certain situations. A set of rules for preparing accounting information can help reduce the cost and difficulty of communication between entities and users. Canadian GAAP describe four qualitative characteristics that financial statement information must have to be useful to users: understandability, relevance, reliability and comparability. GAAP do not provide solutions to all accounting problems. GAAP are not universal, not every entity needs or is required to follow GAAP, and GAAP are flexible.

Key Terms

accounting, p. 5

Canada Customs and Revenue Agency (CCRA), p. 12

comparability, p. 25

corporation, p. 10

cost/benefit trade-off, p. 6

creditor, p. 24

entity, p. 5

external audit, p. 16

external auditors, p. 16

financial accounting, p. 8

generally accepted accounting principles (GAAP), p. 23

limited liability, p. 10

managerial accounting, p. 8

not-for-profit organization, p. 12

partner, p. 11

partnership, p. 11

preparers, p. 15

private corporation, p. 11

proprietor, p. 11

proprietorship, p. 11

public corporation, p. 11

relevance, p. 25

reliability, p. 25

share, p. 10

shareholder, p. 10

stakeholder, p. 13

Statistics Canada, p. 12

stock exchange, p. 11

understandability, p. 24

Similar Terms

The left column gives alternative terms that are sometimes used for the accounting terms introduced in this chapter, which are listed in the right column.

lender   **creditor, p. 24**

non-profit organization   **not-for-profit organization, p. 12**

stockholder   **shareholder, p. 10**

stock market   **stock exchange, p. 11**

Assignment Materials

Questions

Q1-1. Provide a definition of accounting that someone without a business background would understand.

Q1-2. Explain the difference between managerial and financial accounting.

Q1-3. Explain why it is important when studying business and accounting to make links between the classroom and the real world.

Q1-4. There are many different stakeholders in an entity. Explain why the same information may not be suitable or appropriate for all stakeholders.

Q1-5. Distinguish between preparers and users of accounting information.

Q1-6. Explain why the self-interests of accounting information preparers can affect what information is reported to stakeholders and how it is reported.

Q1-7. What is a corporation? What are the attractive features of organizing a business as a corporation?

Q1-8. What is a publicly owned corporation? How does it differ from a privately owned corporation?

Q1-9. What is a not-for-profit organization? Give an example of a not-for-profit organization. What is the purpose of the organization you identified?

Q1-10. What are some of the benefits of measuring things in terms of a single unit of measure such as money? What are the drawbacks?

Q1-11. Why is information important for good decisions?

Q1-12. Explain the cost/benefit trade-off. What are its implications for decision making?

Q1-13. When you make a decision, should you collect all possible related information? What limits would you set on the information you gather?

Q1-14. What are generally accepted accounting principles (GAAP)?

Q1-15. Why is it useful to have a set of rules such as GAAP to guide preparers of accounting information?

Q1-16. Why is it necessary for a user of accounting information to understand the rules (such as GAAP) that the preparer used when preparing the information?

Q1-17. According to the *CICA Handbook*, what are the four qualitative characteristics that financial statement information must have to be useful to users?

Q1-18. Describe and explain some of the limitations of GAAP that were described in this chapter.

Q1-19. What is an external audit of financial information and why can it be important for many stakeholders of an entity?

Exercises

E1-1. **(Consider the information relevant for making a decision, LO 2)** You meet a stranger on a street corner in Edmonton. She asks you for instructions on the best way to get from Edmonton to Ottawa. What would you tell her?

E1-2.   **(Understanding the qualitative characteristics of accounting, LO 5)** According to the *CICA Handbook* there are four qualitative characteristics that financial statement information must have if it is to be useful to users. Describe these characteristics in detail:
a. Understandability.
b. Relevance.
c. Reliability.
d. Comparability.

E1-3.   **(Considering the stakeholders in a university or college, LO 2)** Consider the university or college you attend. Who are the stakeholders in your university? Explain the interest or "stake" each stakeholder has in the university. What types of decisions would each of these stakeholders have to make regarding the university? What type of information would be useful to each of these stakeholders? Explain.

E1-4.   **(Assessing the credibility of information, LO 3)** You are looking to buy a new computer. You read an advertisement in a computer newspaper that describes Aylsham Computer Products Inc.'s (Aylsham) computer as the best value for the money for students. Based on this advertisement, would you purchase the computer? Why? What additional information would you require to decide whether to buy an Aylsham computer?

E1-5.   **(Assessing the credibility of information, LO 3)** A chain of donut shops claims to have the world's best coffee. Do you believe the claim? Explain. How would you go about determining whether the chain had the world's best coffee?

E1-6.   **(Consider the information relevant for making a decision, LO 2)** Your brother has just asked you to lend him $5,000 to help him buy a car. Would you lend him the money? How would you decide? What would you want to know before you made a final decision?

E1-7.   **(Consider the information relevant for making a decision, LO 2)** Your cousin is in her last year of high school and is in the process of deciding which university to attend. Since you went through the process just a few years ago, she has asked you for advice about the best university to attend. What would you tell your cousin? What questions would you ask her before you could provide an answer?

E1-8.   **(Considering different ways of measuring, LO 4)** For each of the following situations, explain which method of valuing the item in question would be most useful:

Measurement method	Explanation of the method
Cost	What you paid for the item.
Replacement cost	What it would cost to replace the item with an identical item in the same condition.
Replacement cost new	What it would cost to replace the item with an identical item that is new.
Net realizable value	What the item could be sold for now.

a. You lost your favourite CD and want to get another copy of it.
b. You need to get some money fast and you have nothing in your bank account, so you are thinking of selling your car.
c. You purchased a DVD player from a store that had a special sale offering to let you "use it for a year and if you don't like it you can get your money back." You decide you don't like the DVD player.
d. Your 1995 Ford Mustang was stolen and you are looking to get another one just like it.

E1-9.   **(Consider the different ways of measuring the attributes of a car, LO 4)** There are many attributes of an item that you can measure. For a car you could measure how fast it can go, its gas mileage, the number of doors it has, what you could sell it for, and many more. Notice that only one of these measures is stated in terms of money. Now consider your home. How many different attributes of your home could you measure? What would be the use for each measurement? Which measure of your home is best? Explain.

E1-10. **(Consider different ways of organizing information, LO 4)** Your 99-year-old grandfather died recently and he left you his beloved library of books. At the time of his death your grandfather's library contained over 5,000 books. The books had been packed away in boxes and the boxes have been delivered to you. After opening the boxes you realize that the books were not organized in any particular way. You decide to build a library in your basement and organize and catalogue the books. What are some of the ways you could organize the books in the library? What are the benefits and limitations of the different organizational principles? What are the benefits of organizing the books at all?

E1-11. **(Take a first look at an annual report, LO 1, 2, 3, 4, 5)** Read the Mark's Work Wearhouse annual report for 2001 provided in Appendix A. List seven questions that came to mind while reading the annual report. Your questions can relate to any part of the annual report, but some of them should pertain to the financial statements that are provided on pages A-000 to A-000. Your questions should cover topics such as why particular information is reported or what it means.

Problems

P1-1. **(Explain the reason stakeholders would want information about an entity, LO 2)** Consider the following stakeholders in an entity. Why would the stakeholder want information about the entity? Explain.
   a. A customer considering a major purchase (such as a computer or an appliance).
   b. A government minister evaluating whether to provide assistance to a business.
   c. The head of the CRTC (the regulatory agency responsible for the cable industry) determining whether a rate increase should be awarded to a cable company.
   d. A shareholder in a company.

P1-2. **(Explain the reason stakeholders would want information about an entity, LO 2)** Consider the following stakeholders in an entity. Why would the stakeholder want information about the entity? Explain.
   a. A person considering making a donation to a charity.
   b. Canada Customs and Revenue Agency (the federal government department responsible for tax collection).
   c. A banker considering whether to lend money to a small business.
   d. The head of a labour union preparing for negotiations with management of a company.

P1-3. **(Identify the stakeholders in an entity and the decisions they make, LO 2)** Consider the following entities. Identify the stakeholders in each of these entities. What types of decisions would each of these stakeholders want to make?
   a. Air Canada.
   b. Government of Canada.
   c. The Canadian Cancer Society.
   d. McCain Foods Limited.

P1-4. **(Identify the stakeholders in an entity and the decisions they make, LO 2)** Consider the following entities. Identify the stakeholders in each of these entities. What types of decisions would each of these stakeholders want to make?
   a. A local convenience store owned and operated by a family.
   b. A large, publicly owned company.
   c. A private, not-for-profit golf club.
   d. The government of a small Canadian city.

P1-5. **(Consider the decisions stakeholders make and the nature of the information they require, LO 1, 2)** Consider the following decisions that a stakeholder of an entity might have to make. For each decision, identify the stakeholder who would likely be making the decision and indicate whether the decision would be considered a financial or managerial accounting decision. Remember that the classification of financial or managerial accounting depends on who the decision maker is. Explain your answer.

a. The price a manufacturer's products should sell for.

b. Whether a loan should be made to a small business.

c. Whether a corporation has paid an appropriate amount of tax.

P1-6.   **(Consider the decisions stakeholders make and the nature of the information they require, LO 1, 2)** Consider the following decisions that a stakeholder of an entity might have to make. For each decision, identify the stakeholder who would likely be making the decision and indicate whether the decision would be considered a financial or managerial accounting decision. Remember that the classification of financial or managerial accounting depends on who the decision maker is. Explain your answer.

a. Whether a local clothing store should move to a larger location so that it could sell a wider range of clothes.

b. Whether to purchase the shares of a large oil company.

c. Whether unionized employees should receive a significant wage increase.

P1-7.   **(Considering the information needed to decide whether to invest in a business, LO 1, 2, 4)** A friend of yours has just called you up with "a great business opportunity." Your friend is starting up a new e-business and needs money to purchase computer equipment. Your friend says he is going to invest $10,000 in the business and wants to know whether you want to invest as well. Would you invest in the new e-business? Why or why not? What additional information would you want to have before making a decision?

P1-8.   **(Considering the information needed to decide whether to invest in a business, LO 1, 2, 4)** Two of your friends own and operate a business that rents bicycles and inline skates at a local lake. They have told you that they want to expand the business but said they are short of the money needed for the expansion and have asked you to become a partner by investing $8,000. Would you invest the $8,000? How would you decide? What additional information would you want to have before making a final decision?

P1-9.   **(Classify and organize information so that it is useful for decision making, LO 1, 4)** Mike is a university student who is often short of cash. A month may pass and he has no idea where his money went. After suffering with this problem for several months, Mike decides to monitor his spending for the next month. He buys a small pad to write down the amount spent and the purpose of the spending. The summary of Mike's spending for the month is below:

Date	Amount	Purpose
Feb 4	$ 8.75	Starting balance (cash in wallet)
Feb 4	50.00	Cash from ATM
Feb 4	−15.75	Movie and beer
Feb 6	−3.00	Photocopy of Steve's notes
Feb 6	−4.50	Lunch
Feb 10	−22.50	Book for course
Feb 11	−2.50	Snacks
Feb 12	50.00	Cash from ATM
Feb 12	−18.25	Date with Alex
Feb 15	−10.00	Long-distance phone card
Feb 17	−3.00	Contribution to charity drive
Feb 19	50.00	Cash from ATM
Feb 19	−22.50	Card and gift for Dad
Feb 20	−8.75	Overdue fees at library
Feb 20	−17.40	Share of phone bill for dorm room
Feb 21	10.00	Borrow from Lisa
Feb 21	−23.00	Food/drink for dorm room
Feb 24	50.00	Cash from ATM
Feb 24	−10.00	Pay Lisa back
Feb 27	−18.75	Partying after exam
Feb 28	$ 38.85	Amount remaining in wallet

Required:

Prepare a statement that organizes the information from the month's spending in a useful way. Explain why you organized the information the way that you did. How could you use the information if you were Mike?

P1-10. **(Classify and organize information so that it is useful for decision making, LO 1, 4)** Mei is a university student who has been unable, so far, to find a summer job. While she has enough money to pay for school next year, she is concerned that she is not managing her money as well as she could. She decides to monitor her spending for the next month so that she can get an idea of where her money is going. She buys a small pad and writes down the amount spent and the purpose of the spending. Mei's summary of her spending for July is shown below:

Date	Amount	Purpose
July 4	$ 0.00	Starting balance (cash in purse)
July 4	100.00	Cash from ATM
July 4	−15.75	Partying with friends
July 6	−45.00	Clothes
July 6	−4.50	Lunch
July 10	−22.50	Novel
July 11	−8.50	Movie
July 12	70.00	Cash from ATM
July 12	−38.25	Software
July 15	−22.45	Gift for Dad's birthday
July 17	−3.00	Coffee and donuts with friends
July 19	50.00	Cash from ATM
July 19	−15.50	Beverages for party
July 20	−8.75	Snacks
July 20	−12.50	Monthly Internet access fee
July 21	−23.00	Cosmetics
July 21	100.00	Borrowed from Mom
July 24	50.00	Cash from ATM
July 24	−20.00	Tennis lesson
July 27	−125.00	Deposit for university courses in fall
July 31	$5.30	Amount remaining in purse

Required:

Prepare a statement that organizes the information from the month's spending in a useful way. Explain why you organized the information the way that you did. How could you use the information if you were Mei?

P1-11. **(Evaluate different ways of measuring the value of a house, LO 4)** Rajiv owns a home in suburban Ottawa. You obtain the following information about the home:

a. Purchase price in 1978	$175,000
b. Selling price of a similar house on another street last year	$625,000
c. Price offered (and turned down) for Rajiv's house two months ago	$575,000
d. What it would cost to rebuild the house if it were destroyed	$235,000

Required:

Explain how each of the measures of the "value" of Rajiv's house could be used by a decision maker. What decision would the person be making? How would the information be useful?

P1-12. **(Evaluate different ways of measuring the value of a vintage automobile, LO 4)** Otto Collector owns a vintage 1925 Ford automobile. You obtain the following information about the car:

a. What Otto paid for the car in 1983	$29,000
b. Selling price of a similar car one year ago	$80,000
c. Price offered (and turned down) by Otto for his car last month	$95,000
d. What the car sold for new in 1925	$800

Required:

Explain how each of the measures of the "value" of Otto's car could be used by a decision maker. What decision would the person be making? How would the information be useful?

P1-13. **(Consider the usefulness of audited information, LO 1, 2, 3)** For each of the following situations explain whether and why having an independent review of the information provided—that is, an audit—would be useful. Suggest the type of person who might be appropriate for conducting the audit.

a. A donut shop advertises that it has the world's best coffee.

b. A used car dealer says that a car you are interested in is in excellent condition.

c. A store's rent to the mall owner is $1,200 per month plus 5% of the amount of sales the store makes. For the year just ended the store reports to the mall owner that its sales were $250,000.

d. A graduate university program requests a list of grades a student earned in her undergraduate program.

P1-14. **(Consider the usefulness of audited information, LO 1, 2, 3)** For each of the following situations explain whether and why having an independent review of the information provided—that is, an audit—would be useful. Suggest the type of person who might be appropriate for conducting the audit.

a. An individual files an income tax return with the Canada Customs and Revenue Agency in which she reports the amount of money her business earned during the previous year.

b. An electronics store states that it has "the lowest prices, guaranteed!"

c. A public corporation predicts that it will double its profit next year.

d. A job applicant submits a résumé to a prospective employer outlining his employment history and educational background.

P1-15. **(Identify the characteristics of different entities, LO 2, 3)** Identify two separate entities. These could be corporations, partnerships, proprietorships, not-for-profit organizations, or any other type of entity you are familiar with or can obtain information about. Identify the characteristics of each entity. (You can use the characteristics listed in Figure 1-1 on page 9.) Explain how the entities differ.

P1-16. **(Identify the characteristics of different entities, LO 2, 3)** Identify two different corporations that are in a similar business. Identify the characteristics of each corporation. (You can use the characteristics listed in Figure 1-1 on page 9 as a guide). Explain how the corporations are similar and how they differ.

Endnotes

1. This section is based on material from Mark's Work Wearhouse Ltd.'s web site, www.marks.com (accessed March 1, 2002); Mark's Work Wearhouse Ltd.'s 2001 annual report; and Zena Olijnyk, "All dressed up: Mark's Work Wearhouse may get bought—or go private," *Canadian Business*, November 26, 2001, p. 20.

2. Mark's Work Wearhouse Ltd. web site, www.marks.com (accessed March 1, 2002).

3. Andrew Zimbalist, *Baseball and Billions*, updated ed. (New York: Basic Books, 1994), p. 62.

4. William Scott, *Financial Accounting Theory*, 2nd ed. (Scarborough, ON: Prentice Hall Canada, 2000), p. 16.

Chapter 2

Financial Statements:
A Window on an Entity

Chapter Outline

Learning Objectives

After studying the material in this chapter you will be able to:

LO 1.   Recognize the components of a set of general purpose financial statements.

LO 2.   Describe the accounting equation and be able to record transactions by adjusting the accounting equation.

LO 3.   Explain the nature of assets, liabilities, owners' equity, revenues and expenses.

LO 4.   Characterize the accounts that are reported on entities' financial statements.

LO 5.   Prepare simple financial statements.

LO 6.   Differentiate between accrual-basis and cash-basis accounting.

LO 7.   Use financial statement information to assess the liquidity, risk and profitability of an entity.

Introduction

The most familiar products of accounting and accountants are financial statements. The financial statements most people see are published by public companies whose shares trade on stock exchanges. These companies have an obligation to make this information available to shareholders, and as a result of this wide publication anyone who is interested can get a copy of this information. While the financial statements of public companies are readily available to the public, virtually all businesses, governments, and not-for-profit organizations in Canada produce a set of financial statements at least once a year. But while financial statements are the most common products of accounting and accountants, they are by no means the only ones. Accounting systems can provide a wide range of information presented in an array of different forms.

In this chapter we will explore the five elements of the financial statement package, which are:

- the balance sheet
- the income statement
- the statement of retained earnings
- the cash flow statement
- the notes to the financial statements

The financial statements of Mark's Work Wearhouse Ltd. (MWW) in Appendix A will be used to illustrate our discussion. We will examine how the information in financial statements can be used for decision making.

General Purpose Financial Statements

MWW's financial statements are known as **general purpose financial statements**. Such statements are intended for use by many different stakeholders and for many different purposes, and are not necessarily tailored to the needs of any or all stakeholders or purposes. In other words, general purpose financial statements are intended for no one in particular and for everyone in general. (The alternative to general purpose financial statements is special purpose reports, which provide information designed for a specific user and/or a specific use. We'll discuss special purpose reports in more detail later in the chapter.)

A general purpose statement is like the jack of all trades but master of none—someone who can do many things, but none of them expertly. Sometimes the jack of all trades may not be able to do a job at all. You may be willing to trust a jack of all trades to change the oil in your car, but for a major problem you would probably prefer to use an expert mechanic, or bear the consequences later. The same is true for general purpose financial statements. A set of general purpose financial statements might provide a particular user with some of the information required for that user's decisions, but because the statements are not prepared with that particular user's needs in mind, they are not likely to be exactly what the user needs. In fact, general purpose statements may provide some users with little or none of the information they need.

Clearly, statements that are prepared for a wide range of stakeholders and decisions cannot be well suited for the specific needs of every stakeholder and every decision. For example, general purpose financial statements prepared according to GAAP, which show assets at the amount that the entity paid for them, would be of limited use to a lender who is interested in knowing the market value of the assets offered as collateral for a loan. It is important for users of financial information to understand that the information in general purpose financial statements may not be suitable for their particular needs and may even be misleading.

The financial statements of public companies like MWW are always general purpose. The preparers might tailor the general purpose financial statements to suit their own needs, but because the financial statements are available to anyone who wants them, they can be considered general purpose. Every entity will prepare a set of general purpose financial statements at least once a year, if for no other reason that they must be included with the entity's tax return. After that, the entity can produce any number of special purpose reports as required. Public companies are required to prepare their general purpose financial statements in accordance with GAAP. Entities that are not publicly traded companies do not face the same requirement.

An obvious question is, "If these statements are not especially useful for many of the decisions that users have to make, why devote an entire chapter, indeed a good chunk of a book, to examining them?" This is a good question. The answer is that users of accounting information can usually count on receiving GAAP-based general purpose financial statements. As a result, if you are going to use these statements intelligently, you have to know their strengths and limitations. You have to know what questions to ask. And you have to know when to look elsewhere for information.

MWW's Financial Statements: An Overview

Examining financial statements can be an intimidating task. What do the numbers mean? Where do they come from? The discussion below weaves a general discussion of each financial statement with an examination of MWW's statements. Before we examine the financial statement package in detail, let's take a broad look at MWW's financial statements. Four important points are worth noting:

1. All of MWW's financial statements are **consolidated**. Consolidated means that the financial information of more than one corporation is combined into a single set of statements. MWW statements contain the information of Mark's Work Wearhouse, Work World Enterprises, and DOCKERS®. Consolidated statements are prepared when a corporation controls another corporation (usually meaning it owns 50% or more of the other corporation). (We will discuss consolidated financial statements later in more detail in Chapter 12.)

2. Financial statements are presented for three years. This provides the users of the financial statements with some context. It is very difficult to make sense of accounting information without some perspective on other companies, the industry, performance in other years, and the economy in general. As we will discuss in more detail as we go through the book, making comparisons using accounting information can be very difficult and misleading. However, not making comparisons makes it very difficult to interpret the accounting information we have.

3. MWW prepares its financial statements for a fiscal year. A **fiscal year** is the 12-month or 52-week period for which performance of an entity is measured and at the end of which a balance sheet is prepared. While many companies prepare their financial statements as of the same date each year, such as December 31 or June 30, MWW's fiscal year is a period of 52 weeks that ends on the last Saturday in January of each year. The most recent fiscal year reported on in MWW's consolidated financial statements is the 52-week period ended January 27, 2001. Comparison information is provided for the 52-week periods ended January 29, 2000 and January 30, 1999.

4. Everything in MWW's financial statements is measured in terms of money, specifically in Canadian dollars. All amounts included in the statements must be

reasonably measurable in dollars. (We will discuss what accountants consider reasonable as we go through the book.) Numbers in the financial statements are rounded to the nearest thousand dollar. MWW's balance sheet reports cash and cash equivalents on January 27, 2001 of $6,993,000, but because the thousands are dropped, the amount of cash held by MWW could be anywhere between $6,992,499.99 and $6,993,500.00. The thousands are dropped to make the statements less cluttered in appearance. This rounding can be done only because dropping the thousands is not expected to affect the decisions of the users of the information. In this case, ignoring the thousands is not likely to affect, for example, whether an investor will buy more MWW shares or sell what he or she already owns.

The Balance Sheet

Let's begin our tour of financial statements by examining the balance sheet. The **balance sheet** provides information about the financial position of an entity at a specific point in time. It is also known as the statement of financial position. (One of the confusing aspects of accounting is that different names are often given to the same thing. The confusion will pass with time, but be prepared to scratch your head sometimes when a new term is used to describe a familiar concept. The list of Similar Terms at the end of each chapter will help you sort out any confusion.)

In a balance sheet, financial position means information about assets, liabilities, and owners' equity. These terms are defined as follows:

- **Assets** are economic resources that provide future benefits to an entity for carrying out its business activities.
- **Liabilities** are the obligations of an entity, such as to pay debts or provide goods or services to customers.
- **Owners' equity** is the investment the owners have made in the entity.

If you look at MWW's balance sheet you will see these three headings—but note that owners' equity is called shareholders' equity on MWW's balance sheet because MWW is a corporation and the owners of a corporation are called shareholders.

MWW's balance sheet conforms to the **accounting equation,** which is the conceptual foundation of accounting. The accounting equation is:

$$\text{Assets} = \text{Liabilities} + \text{Owners' Equity}$$

The left side of the equation represents the assets, the entity's valuable economic resources. The right side of the equation represents how those assets were financed; that is, where the entity's assets come from. Assets can be financed by **creditors** (entities to which money is owed) or owners. Financing by creditors results in liabilities. Financing by owners is represented by owners' equity. Any event that is entered into the accounting system must affect the accounting equation so that the equality between the left side and right side of the equation is maintained.

We can tie MWW's balance sheet amounts into the accounting equation as follows:

Assets	=	Liabilities	+	Owners' (Shareholders') Equity
$157,060,000	=	$92,339,000	+	$64,721,000

Examine MWW's balance sheet in Appendix A and find these amounts on the balance sheet.

All economic events that are entered into an accounting system are summarized in terms of the accounting equation; that is, each event is recorded based on its effect on assets, liabilities, and owners' equity. In this book we will use the accounting equation as the basis for a spreadsheet in which we will record transactions and economic events. The columns of the spreadsheet will represent assets, liabilities, and owners' equity, and each economic event that affects the entity will be recorded based on its effect on each of the columns. Ultimately, the spreadsheet will provide us with the information needed to prepare the financial statements. The spreadsheet will also provide us with a method for seeing how different accounting choices affect the financial statements. We will develop the spreadsheet method further in Chapter 3. For now, we will look at a simple example to learn about the balance sheet.

Suppose an entrepreneur named Tamara decides to start a house-painting business to earn money over the summer. In starting the business she has the following transactions. (See Table 2-1 for the spreadsheet summarizing the events.)

1. Tamara contributes $1,000 of her savings to the business. She sets up her business as a proprietorship (that is, a business that is not incorporated and is owned by one person) and opens a bank account under the name Tamara's Painting Business (TPB). As a result of this transaction the business now has $1,000 in cash. The cash is an asset because it is a resource that can be used to purchase the materials and equipment necessary to paint houses. Owner's equity increases by $1,000 because Tamara, the proprietor, has invested $1,000 in the business.

2. Tamara then borrows $500 from her mother. Tamara promises to pay back the money at the end of the summer. The assets increase by $500, reflecting the money that has come into the company. This time, however, liabilities increase by $500 because a creditor, a person who has lent money to the business, has supplied the money.

3. With $1,200 of TPB's cash Tamara purchases equipment for her business, including ladders, brushes, and trays. In this case there has been an asset exchange. One asset, cash, has been exchanged for other assets, equipment.

4. Tamara opens an account with a paint store. She plans to buy most of her paint from the store and the store grants her 60 days to pay her bills. She purchases $400 worth of supplies from the store. Assets increase because now Tamara's Painting Business has supplies that are necessary for painting. Because the supplies were purchased on credit, TPB has a liability. It has to pay the paint store within the next 60 days for the supplies purchased.

5. After canvassing several houses in her neighbourhood, Tamara gets her first job. An elderly man wants the outside of his house painted and pays a $200 deposit. Tamara expects to begin work in about 10 days when the weather improves. Assets have increased by $200 because Tamara received cash. But Tamara also has a liability, which is to paint the elderly man's house. In this case the liability is to provide a service, not to pay back cash, as was the case in event 4.

For each entry made the accounting equation is maintained. We could expand the spreadsheet so that instead of a single column for each of assets, liabilities, and owner's equity, a separate column could be created for each type of asset, liability, and owner's equity. In this case we could have asset columns for Cash, Supplies, and Equipment, and liability columns for Accounts Payable, Loans, and Services to be provided.

We can summarize the information in the spreadsheet into a balance sheet as shown in Table 2-2. The total assets, total liabilities, and total owner's equity correspond with the balances at the bottom of each column in Table 2-1. The total amounts have been separated on the balance sheet into the different types of assets and liabilities.

Table 2-1   Spreadsheet for TPB

Tamara's Painting Business
Spreadsheet

	Assets	=	Liabilities	+	Owner's Equity
1.	+ $1,000 cash				+$1,000 investment by owner
Balance	$1,000	=	$0	+	$1,000
2.	+$500 cash		+$500 loan from mother		
Balance	$1,500	=	$500	+	$1,000
3.	+$1,200 equipment −$1,200 cash				
Balance	$1,500	=	$500	+	$1,000
4.	+$400 supplies		+$400 account payable to paint store		
Balance	$1,900	=	$900	+	$1,000
5.	+$200 cash		+$200 service to be provided		
Balance	$2,100	=	$1,100	+	$1,000

Table 2-2   Balance Sheet for TPB

Tamara's Painting Business
Balance Sheet

Assets		Liabilities and Owner's Equity	
Cash	$ 500	Loans	$ 500
Supplies	400	Accounts payable	400
Equipment	1,200	Services to be provided	200
		Total liabilities	1,100
		Owner's equity	1,000
Total assets	$2,100	Total liabilities and owner's equity	$2,100

From Table 2-2 we see at a glance that when the balance sheet was prepared TPB had $500 in cash, supplies that cost TPB $400, and equipment that cost $1,200. Notice that the supplies and equipment are reported at their cost. This is important. According to Canadian GAAP, the basis for valuing an entity's assets is the transaction value—in the case of supplies and equipment, the amount that was paid or the cost. The liabilities side of the balance sheet shows the $500 loan from the proprietor's mother, the $400 owed to the paint store, and the $200 advance from the customer. The liability to the customer is the amount of the deposit, not the value of the entire job. This again is the rule of GAAP. The balance sheet also shows the amount invested by the proprietor—$1,000.

> Comment: It is important to recognize that the accounting equation is a tool for recording information in an accounting system. It is not unique to Canada or to GAAP. Recall the example in Chapter 1 where we valued the contents of an apartment in three ways—what the items cost, what they could be sold for, and what it would cost to replace them. All of these ways of valuing the items in the apartment are legitimate, although GAAP use cost as their basis of valuation. The accounting equation can accommodate all of these ways of measuring assets. In general, regardless of how assets, liabilities, and equities are defined, the accounting equation model can be used to record them. The idea that accounting can measure assets, liabilities, and equities in different ways will become clearer as we proceed through the book.

A balance sheet is like a photograph—it captures the scene at the moment the photo is taken. The scene could be dramatically different the moment before or after the picture is taken. When my first son was born, we had a baby photographer come to our house to take pictures. The pictures were amazing. Almost as amazing were the scenes just before and after the photographer snapped the pictures. The baby was moving, making strange expressions, and falling over, but the pictures showed a perfectly posed smiling baby. The same discrepancy between one moment and the next is true for a balance sheet. MWW reports cash and cash equivalents of $6,993,000 on January 27, 2001. But it is possible that on January 28, 2001 MWW could have spent that money. The balance sheet would not show that the money was spent the very next day.

Question for Consideration

Explain how the following events would affect the accounting equation for Tamara's Painting Business:
1. TPB pays $50 for some new paintbrushes.
2. TPB purchases $40 worth of new paintbrushes and promises to pay the store in 30 days.
3. Tamara contributes an additional $500 of her own money to ensure that TPB has enough cash to operate.

Answer:
1. No effect. This transaction simply transforms one asset, Cash (decreases by $50), into another asset, Equipment or paint brushes (increases by $50). There is no change in total assets or in liabilities or owner's equity.
2. Assets increase by $40 (the asset Equipment or paint brushes increases by $40) and liabilities increase by $40 (Accounts Payable, or amount owed to suppliers, increases by $40).
3. Assets increase by $500 (Cash) and owner's equity increases by $500 (Tamara, the owner, has contributed $500 to TPB).

Now we will take a closer look at assets, liabilities and owners' equity.

Assets

Assets are economic resources available to an entity that provide potential future benefits to the entity. Let's look at some of the assets on MWW's balance sheet and consider why they are assets (see the box on page 43).

An entity does not have to own an economic resource for it to be considered an asset. For example, according to GAAP, assets that are leased are sometimes included as assets if the lease meets certain criteria. (We will discuss these criteria in Chapter 10.) Over two-thirds of MWW's capital assets are leased rather than owned. When an asset is leased, the entity obtains some of the rights associated with owning the asset, but not all—for example, MWW can use the furniture that it leases, but it cannot sell

Type of Asset	What is it?	Why is it an asset?
Cash	Money.	The whole purpose of being in business is to generate more cash than the business started out with. Cash is used to buy needed goods and services, pay bills, pay debts, and pay dividends to shareholders.
Accounts receivable	Money owed by customers who bought on credit. MWW also includes amounts owed by other entities such as franchise stores and landlords (see Note 4 to MWW's financial statements).	Accounts receivables are assets because they represent the right to receive cash from customers and other entities.
Merchandise inventory	The clothing MWW has available to sell to customers. Generally, inventory is goods available for sale to customers or materials that that will be used to produce goods that will be sold.	Inventory is an asset because MWW can sell it to customers for cash or accounts receivable.
Capital assets	The furniture, display cases, mannequins, signs, computers, and so on that are part of MWW's offices and stores. These are the economic resources that are used on an ongoing basis to earn revenue, but that are not sold in the ordinary course of business.	These items are assets because they provide the resources necessary to operate a store and thereby provide the conditions to sell the inventory.

it. (Information on MWW's leased assets can be found in Note 7 to the financial statements on page A-53.)

MWW's balance sheet identifies certain assets as **current assets**. Current assets are assets that will be used up, sold, or converted to cash within one year or one operating cycle. An **operating cycle** is the time it takes from the initial investment an entity makes in goods and services to when cash is received from customers. A retail business such as MWW will expect to sell its inventory within one year, so its Inventory is classified as current. Since MWW's credit terms likely require customers to pay for their goods in less than one year, its Accounts Receivable are classified as current. Wine production is a business that would have operating cycles of longer than one year because wine can be aged for many years before it is sold.

Assets that are not classified as current are **non-current assets**. These are assets that will not be used up, sold, or converted to cash within one year or one operating cycle. Capital assets are classified as non-current because they will usually provide benefits to the entity for more than one year. For example, MWW would expect its display cases to provide useful service for several years. Similarly, a building can house a store for many years (although MWW does not own any of the buildings that house its stores). If MWW sold goods to a customer and agreed that the customer could pay in two years, the account receivable from that customer would be classified as non-current because the cash would be received more than one year after the sale. Notice that on MWW's balance sheet there is no indication of which assets are non-current. This presentation is common in financial statements. If an asset is not specified as a current asset, then it is understood to be non-current.

Believe it or not, accountants sometimes have a great deal of difficulty deciding what is an asset. Often our intuition about what is an asset may differ from what an accountant defines as an asset. For example, MWW spends a great deal of money on advertising. The advertising attracts people to the stores and helps build a brand name. By building its brand name, people will think of MWW when they want to buy clothes. Therefore, we could argue that the money spent on advertising has future benefit and should be classified as an asset. Yet the money companies spend on advertising rarely appears on the balance sheet as an asset.

The reason that every economic resource with potential future benefits does not appear on the balance sheet has to do with how accountants define and measure assets. Because the financial statements of MWW and many other Canadian companies are prepared according to GAAP, GAAP's criteria must be followed. The criteria require that:

- an asset must be the result of a transaction with another entity

- the cost of an asset can be determined (GAAP requires that an asset be valued at the amount paid for it—that is, its cost—whether the payment was in cash or some other form)

- an asset must provide a future benefit to the entity and the benefit must be reasonably measurable (if you are not sure what the benefit is, the amount of the benefit, or that there will be a benefit, you cannot call an item an asset)

According to these criteria, advertising is not classified as an asset because its future benefit is very uncertain and difficult to measure. Other examples show how application of the criteria leads to accounting treatments that are not always consistent with our intuition. One of the most valuable resources any company has, its employees, does not appear as an asset. Even research and development, the lifeblood of many companies, is explicitly prohibited by GAAP from being called an asset, except in very limited situations.

Another example of how GAAP's rules define an asset is the value at which assets are reported on the balance sheet. For example, a piece of land purchased for $1,000,000 many years ago, but which has a market value today of $5,000,000, appears on the balance sheet at $1,000,000. This is because there was a transaction with another entity to support the $1,000,000; however, there is no transaction supporting the $5,000,000 value. Because GAAP require that assets be recorded at their cost, the market value of an asset does not appear in the financial statements.

It is important to understand that the assets and amounts reported on MWW's balance sheet are the result of GAAP. If a different set of rules were used, you would get a different balance sheet. Accounting information is merely a representation of the economic activities of an entity. There are many different ways that assets and other financial statement components can be defined and measured. Canadian GAAP represent just one way of defining and measuring what is reported in financial statements.

Liabilities

Liabilities are an entity's obligations to pay money or provide goods or services to suppliers, lenders, and customers. If an entity borrows money from a bank, the entity reports a liability because the amount borrowed is owed to the bank. The amount of the liability is the amount borrowed from the bank. If a customer pays an entity in advance for goods or services, such as paying in advance for tickets to a concert, the entity reports a liability. In that case the liability is to provide a concert to the ticket holder. The amount of the liability is the amount the customer paid for the ticket.

A liability does not have to be a legal obligation. For example, many companies

Question for Consideration

Explain why under GAAP an "asset" such as money spent on research does not appear as an asset on an entity's balance sheet, whereas insurance purchased in advance would be reported as an asset.

Answer: Under GAAP three criteria must be met for an item to be considered an asset: an asset must be the result of a transaction with another entity; the cost of an asset can be determined; and an asset must provide a future benefit to the entity, a benefit that must be reasonably measurable. For research, the first two criteria are met (there are transactions with other entities—payment to researchers, purchase of supplies, etc.—and it would be possible to determine the amount of money spent), but the third criterion is not met. The future benefit of money spent on research is considered, under GAAP, to be too uncertain to classify the amount spent as an asset, since it is hard to know whether the research will result in the entity making any money. In contrast, insurance paid for in advance meets all three criteria. The insurance is purchased from another entity (an insurance company), the cost of the insurance in known, and the future benefit is the insurance coverage provided by the insurance. In the case of insurance the benefit is clear since the entity is protected from losses that are covered by the insurance policy.

provide warranties with their products. The warranty provides a customer with assurance that the company will repair certain problems with a product. Companies will usually set up a liability for the estimated cost of repairing warrantied items when the item is sold. This is not a legal liability since at the time the balance sheet is prepared the company does not owe anything to the customer. Only if and when a customer has a problem is there an obligation.

MWW's balance sheet reports several different liabilities:

Type of Liability	What is it?	Why is it a liability?
Accounts payable and accrued liabilities	Amounts owed to suppliers for goods and services that MWW purchased on credit.	MWW buys the clothing it sells from manufacturers. The manufacturers give MWW time to pay its bills, which is why so much is owing on January 27, 2001.
Income taxes payable	Money that is owed to the government for income taxes.	MWW owes money to the government.
Current portion of long-term debt	Money borrowed for more than one year that is due to be repaid within the next year.	MWW owes money to lenders.
Long-term debt	Money borrowed that has to be repaid in more than one year.	MWW owes money to lenders.

Most of MWW's liabilities consist of money owed to suppliers, lenders, and the government. An entity could also have obligations to provide goods or services to customers. For example, when Air Canada sells tickets and collects travellers' money in advance of a flight, the amount paid by the traveller appears on Air Canada's balance sheet as a liability called "advance ticket sales." Air Canada fulfills its obligation when the passenger takes the flight. In this case the liability is to provide transportation to a passenger.

Like assets, liabilities are classified on MWW's balance sheet as current and non-current. **Current liabilities** will be paid or satisfied within one year or one operating cycle. **Non-current liabilities** will be paid or satisfied in more than one year or one operating cycle. As was the case with assets, MWW does not specifically identify non-current liabilities on its balance sheet. If a liability is not identified as a current liability, then it is understood to be non-current. MWW has over $27,000,000 of long-term debt reported on its January 27, 2001 balance sheet. This means that these debts will not have to be paid until after January 2002.

The classification of assets and liabilities into current and non-current components is important because many users of financial statements want to assess an entity's liquidity. **Liquidity** is the entity's ability to pay its obligations as they come due; it refers to the availability of cash or near-cash resources to meet obligations. Liquidity is important to creditors who are expecting to be paid and to potential creditors who are considering extending credit. Liquidity is also important to shareholders because a company that is unable to meet its obligations is at significant risk of going out of business.

Current assets represent the resources that are or will soon be available to meet obligations that are coming due. Current liabilities represent the obligations that must be fulfilled. Taken together, current assets and current liabilities provide important information about the liquidity of an entity. Current assets minus current liabilities is called **working capital**. MWW's working capital on January 27, 2001 was:

$$\text{Working Capital} \quad = \quad \text{Current Assets} \quad - \quad \text{Current Liabilities}$$
$$\$47,165,000 \quad = \quad \$110,387,000 \quad - \quad \$63,222,000$$

Positive working capital suggests that an entity has the resources to meet its upcoming obligations. MWW's working capital a year earlier, on January 29, 2000, was $44,179,000. MWW's working capital has increased over the previous year.

Another way of examining working capital is with a ratio. The ratio of current assets to current liabilities is called the **current ratio,** or **working capital ratio**, and is defined as:

$$\text{Current ratio} \quad = \quad \frac{\text{Current assets}}{\text{Current liabilities}}$$

MWW's current ratio on January 27, 2001 was:

$$\text{Current ratio} \quad = \quad \frac{\text{Current assets}}{\text{Current liabilities}}$$
$$= \quad \frac{\$110,387,000}{\$63,222,000}$$
$$= \quad 1.75$$

The current ratio gives the relative amounts of current assets to current liabilities. The larger the ratio, the more current assets that are available to meet current liabilities. Therefore, on the surface at least, the more likely the entity is to meet its obligations. On January 29, 2000, the current ratio was 1.77.

Ratios are attractive tools for analyzing a company's financial information because they eliminate the effect of size. Instead of having to evaluate the meaningfulness of $47,165,000 of working capital on January 27, 2001 versus $44,179,000 on January 29, 2000, we can evaluate the ratio of 1.75 versus 1.77. This makes comparisons with other years and other entities simpler.

Making sense of financial information is not usually straightforward; it can require a lot of detective work. The numbers in the financial statements can raise questions in the mind of a user, but they will rarely provide answers. Users must analyze, assess, evaluate, and compare the information in financial statements to make sense of it. Calculating ratios is a part of the analysis and assessment of financial data, but is often just a first step. After some preliminary investigation it may be necessary to gather more information. For example, is a current ratio of 1.75 good news? It is not possible to tell. The fact that the ratio has remained fairly stable over the last two years may be a positive sign since it indicates that the company has been able to operate at that level. Comparisons with similar companies would also be helpful, although care must be taken because other companies differ from MWW in the way they account for certain types of transactions.

> Comment: Often people learn that a "good" current ratio is 2:1. This is entirely false. Different industries have different norms. For example, industries that have very predictable cash flows, such as regulated utilities, can operate successfully with a lower current ratio than industries with more uncertain cash flows.

MWW has over $84,000,000 in merchandise inventory, which is over 75% of its current assets. When we calculate working capital and the current ratio we assume that the inventory is liquid and that MWW will receive at least $84,000,000 for it. But the fashion industry is notoriously fickle. What happens if MWW bought too much inventory and cannot sell all of it, or if some of the styles are not very popular? Inventory may prove to be not very liquid and our interpretation of MWW's current ratio may change.

Owners' Equity

Owners' equity is the investment that the owners of an entity have made in the entity. Equivalent terms you may see in a financial statement include:

- *shareholders' equity,* which refers to the owners' equity of a corporation
- *partners' equity,* which refers to the owners' equity of a partnership
- *owner's* or *proprietor's equity,* which refers to the owner's equity of a proprietorship

Owners' investments in entities can be direct or indirect. Owners can make direct investments by purchasing shares of a corporation or units in a partnership, or by contributing money to a proprietorship. Direct investment is usually cash, but in some cases other assets can be invested in exchange for an ownership interest. The investment is direct because the investors contribute their own assets directly to the entity.

Indirect investment occurs when the net income of an entity is not distributed to the owners and is thus "reinvested" in the entity. (MWW uses the similar term net earnings instead of net income.) The net income of a company is a measure of how the owners' wealth has changed over a period of time. As we will discuss when we examine the income statement (page 49), net income is an entity's revenue less all the expenses incurred to earn that revenue. If the net income is not paid to the owners, then it is kept in the company. It can, therefore, be considered an investment in the entity by the owners.

In the owners' equity section of the financial statements of partnerships and proprietorships, the direct and indirect investments are usually combined. Partnerships can have separate lines for each partner, with each line combining the partner's direct and indirect investments, or the equity of the partners can be combined into a single line. (Partnerships will be discussed in more detail in Chapter 11.)

In a corporation's financial statements the shareholders' equity section separates direct investments and the reinvestment of net income, as follows:

- Direct investments by shareholders are reported in the Capital Stock account. **Capital stock** represents the amount of money (or other assets) that shareholders have contributed to the corporation in exchange for shares in the corporation.

- Reinvested net incomes are accumulated in the Retained Earnings account. **Retained earnings** is the sum of all the net incomes a corporation has earned since it began operations, less the dividends paid to shareholders. (**Dividends** are payments of a corporation's assets, usually cash, to its shareholders.) Dividends represent distributions of the corporation's net income to the shareholders. The term retained earnings is descriptive because the account represents the accumulated net incomes of a corporation that have not been distributed to the shareholders—the net income or earnings that have been retained by the corporation.

The separation of investments by shareholders into capital stock and retained earnings is actually quite important, especially if the shareholders and managers are not the same people. Shareholders need to know whether the money being distributed to them is due to the profits earned by the corporation, or if it is just a return of the money that they invested. When a dividend is paid because the corporation has been profitable, it represents a sharing of the success of the corporation with the shareholders. When a dividend is paid from amounts directly invested, it is simply a return of the money that the shareholders invested.

> Comment: A pyramid scheme is an example of how failure to know the source of payments can create problems. Consider the classic case of Ivar Kreuger, known as the Swedish Match King. In the early 1900s Kreuger raised money from new investors and used some of that money to pay dividends to existing investors. Investors found Kreuger's companies very attractive because of the high dividends they were paying. The high dividends attracted new investors, who in turn expected to be paid high dividends. This type of scheme requires a continual inflow of new capital, which, of course, becomes impossible once the number of investors gets too large. Kreuger's companies did not produce very much with the money they raised; they simply redistributed it among investors, with some finding its way into Kreuger's pocket. Investors were unable to detect what was going on because Kreuger's companies did not provide much financial information to them. Eventually the whole scheme collapsed and Kreuger committed suicide in disgrace.[1]

www.qikrux.com/Kreuger

MWW, which is a corporation, reports capital stock of $31,228,000 in its January 27, 2001 balance sheet. This means that since the company's inception investors have paid MWW $31,228,000 in exchange for MWW shares. (Actually, MWW has received more than $31,228,000 from investors, but the amount in the capital stock account has decreased in recent years because MWW has been buying back some of its shares from investors. We will discuss this further in Chapter 11.) MWW reports retained earnings on January 27, 2001 of $33,493,000. This means that since MWW began in 1977 it has generated net income of over $33 million that has not been paid to shareholders. You can see the relationship between retained earnings and net income by examining the following calculation for MWW:

Retained earnings on January 29, 2000	$26,856,000
+ Net income for the 52 weeks ended January 27, 2001	8,180,000
– Amount paid in dividends during the year ended January 27, 2001	0
– Purchase of capital stock during the year ended January 27, 2001	(1,543,000)
Retained earnings on January 27, 2001	$33,493,000

Dividends reduce the amount of retained earnings because they represent distributions of a corporation's profits. Each year retained earnings increases by the net income for the year less dividends paid to shareholders. MWW did not pay dividends in fiscal 2001, and has not paid dividends since at least 1987. The retained earnings account was also reduced by $1,543,000 in 2001 to reflect the repurchase of capital stock from investors. (Be sure you can find these numbers in the calculation in MWW's income statement and balance sheet. MWW calls its income statement a statement of earnings; see page 48 in Appendix A.).

Another common balance sheet analytical tool is the **debt-to-equity ratio**. The ratio provides a measure of how an entity is financed. The higher the ratio, the more debt an entity is using relative to equity. MWW's debt-to-equity ratio is

$$\text{Debt-to-equity ratio} \quad = \quad \frac{\text{Liabilities}}{\text{Shareholder's equity}} \quad = \quad \frac{\$92,339,000}{\$64,721,000} \quad = \quad 1.43$$

The debt-to-equity ratio is a measure of risk. The more debt an entity has, the greater the risk because debt has a fixed cost associated with it called interest. **Interest** is the cost of borrowing money and is usually calculated as a percentage of the amount borrowed. For example, if an entity borrows $10,000 at a 10% interest rate, interest for the year would be $1,000 ($10,000 × 0.10). The amount borrowed is called the **principal**. Regardless of whether an entity is doing well or poorly, it must pay its interest and principal on time. An entity is legally required to make its interest and principal payments when they are due. If an entity does not pay on time, the lenders can take action against it by compelling the borrower to sell assets, forcing it into bankruptcy, or requiring it to renegotiate the terms of the loan. In contrast, dividends are voluntary. An entity does not have to pay dividends at any time and shareholders cannot take any action if dividends are not paid.

A debt-to-equity ratio of 1.43 tells us that MWW has about 40% more liabilities than equity. The ratio has increased from 1.40 on January 29, 2000, meaning that the amount of liabilities held by MWW has increased slightly relative to the amount of equity. Is a ratio of 1.43 too much? Is the increase over 2000 good news or bad news? Well, it depends. There is nothing wrong with financing with debt—in fact, in some ways it is attractive to do so. Careful analysis is necessary to decide when enough is too much, and even then it is a judgment call. How an entity is financed is an important responsibility of management.

Question for Consideration

On December 31, 2002 Didzbury Inc. had retained earnings of $275,000. During 2003 Didzbury had net income of $95,000 and paid dividends to shareholders of $30,000. Calculate Didzbury's retained earnings on December 31, 2003.

Answer:

Ending retained earnings	=	Beginning retained earnings	+	Net income	−	Dividends
	=	$275,000	+	$95,000	−	$30,000
	=	$340,000				

The Income Statement

If a balance sheet is like a photograph, then an income statement is like a movie: it shows events over a period of time. The **income statement** is a "how did we do?" statement, reporting the economic performance of the entity over a period of time such as a year. **Net income**, the bottom line of the income statement, is a measure of how an entity performed and how the owners' wealth changed over a period of time. Performance measurement is considered one of the most important uses of accounting information. In particular, net income receives considerable attention from users trying to evaluate how an entity performed. Stock prices often change when a company announces its net income. Managers' bonuses are often based on net income. Income taxes are related to net income, and the selling price of a small business can be based on net income.

The income statement and net income are often referred to by many different names. The income statement is also known as the statement of operations, statement of earnings, and the statement of profit and loss. Net income is also called income, earnings, net earnings, profit, net profit, and the bottom line. If a company "loses money" (that is, net income is negative), the bottom line might be called a loss or net loss. Once again, do not be put off by the lack of consistent terminology.

Measuring the economic performance of an entity is more challenging than you might think. After all, what does economic performance mean? There are different ways performance can be measured. The two most commonly used methods in accounting are the cash basis of accounting and the accrual basis of accounting. They are distinguished as follows:

- The **cash basis of accounting** is relatively straightforward. It simply reports the cash flowing into and out of the entity. Under this method, economic performance is the change in cash over the period.

- The **accrual basis of accounting** measures the economic impact of transactions and economic events rather than cash flows. Accrual accounting, as we will refer to it throughout the book, attempts to measure economic changes rather than simply changes in cash.

Let's go back to our painting entrepreneur Tamara and see how the cash basis of accounting reports the performance for Tamara's Painting Business (TPB). TPB got off to a slow start in April and May, but by mid-June TPB was extremely busy. During July the following events occurred:

1. TPB started and completed seven painting jobs. TPB collected $3,500 for these jobs and was still owed $800 by one of its customers. The customer told Tamara that she would give her the money on August 15. TPB also collected $500 during July for jobs completed during June.

2. TPB paid $1,450 to people Tamara hired to help with the work. At the end of July TPB owed its employees $350. TPB would pay the amount owed in early August.

3. TPB purchased and used $1,250 of paint for the seven jobs undertaken in July. Since TPB had credit terms from the paint store, it did not pay for any of the paint used in July, but it did pay $900 for paint purchased previously.

An income statement for the month of July prepared on the cash basis is shown in Table 2-3.

This income statement shows that TPB had $1,650 more in cash at the end of July than at the beginning. This measure of performance is useful because it lets a user know the amount of cash that TBP generated during July, and that information can give an indication of TPB's ability to generate cash to meet its obligations. By generating $1,650 in cash during July, Tamara would know that enough money came in to pay her employees and to pay for the paint she bought. It would not be necessary for TPB's cash reserves to be used up.

For general purpose reporting in Canada accountants find the cash basis of accounting too limiting and an incomplete measure of performance. (This is not to understate how extremely important cash flow information is. Cash flow information

Table 2-3	Income Statement Prepared for TPB Using the Cash Basis

Tamara's Painting Business
Income Statement
For the Month Ended July 31

Revenue (cash collected)	$4,000
($3,500 for the seven July jobs plus $500 for jobs completed in June)	
Less: Expenses (cash spent)	
For employees	(1,450)
($1,450 paid to employees in July)	
For paint	(900)
($900 paid for paint purchased in previous months)	
Net income (cash flow)	$1,650

is reported in depth in the cash flow statement, which is discussed on page 58.) Accountants generally prefer to use accrual accounting because it gives a broader measure of performance than is reflected by cash flows. Accrual accounting attempts to reflect economic or wealth changes rather than cash changes. For a complex entity, trying to reflect economic changes makes sense because cash flows do not always take place at the same time as economic changes. However, reflecting economic changes is a lot more complicated than simply reporting cash flows. For general purpose reporting in Canada accountants usually use accrual accounting.

The format of the income statement can be stated as:

$$\begin{array}{r} \text{Revenue} \\ - \text{ Expenses} \\ \hline \text{Net income} \end{array}$$

An entity can have many different types of revenues and expenses, but the structure of the income statement always comes down to this simple arrangement. This equation is an expansion of the owners' equity section of the balance sheet. Even though the income statement is always presented separately, it is really just a part of the owners' equity section of the balance sheet. We could rewrite the accounting equation to reflect the current year's income statement as:

$$\text{Assets} = \text{Liabilities} + \begin{array}{c}\text{Owners' Equity at the} \\ \text{beginning of the period}\end{array} + \text{Revenue} - \text{Expenses}$$

or

$$\text{Assets} = \text{Liabilities} + \begin{array}{c}\text{Owners' Equity at the} \\ \text{beginning of the period}\end{array} + \text{Net income}$$

Owners' equity at the end of a period equals owners' equity at the beginning of the period plus revenues earned during the period less expenses incurred during the period (assuming no dividends). The reason for this is that with accrual accounting, net income is intended to reflect the change in the owners' wealth over a period of time. Net income represents an increase in the owners' investment in the entity.

Revenue (or sales or sales revenue) refers to economic benefits earned by providing goods or services to customers. Revenue results in an increase in owners' equity or the wealth of the owners of the entity. Revenue represents an increase in owners' equity because the revenue is associated with an increase in assets or a decrease in liabilities. When MWW makes a sale to a customer, there must be an increase in assets or decrease in liabilities in exchange for the clothes sold. MWW might receive cash, a promise of payment, or even some other asset such as equipment or store space. The customer could also forgive a liability. For example, if MWW owed a customer money, the customer could reduce the amount that MWW owed by the amount of the purchase.

Regardless of whether assets increase or liabilities decrease, for the accounting equation to remain in balance after a sale owners' equity must increase. Consider the following arrangements MWW could have for selling $500 of clothes:

	Assets	=	Liabilities	+	Owners' (Shareholders') Equity
The clothes are sold for cash	+$500 (Cash)	=		+	+$500 (Sales Revenue)
The clothes are sold for a promise of payment	+$500 (Accounts Receivable)	=		+	+$500 (Sales Revenue)
The clothes are sold for some other asset such as furniture	+$500 (Furniture)	=		+	+$500 (Sales Revenue)
The clothes are sold in exchange for the reduction in a liability		=	−$500 (Accounts Payable)	+	+$500 (Sales Revenue)

Expenses are economic sacrifices or costs made or costs incurred to earn revenue. Sacrifices can be the result of using up an asset or incurring a liability. Expenses decrease owners' equity because they represent what an entity must give up to earn the revenue. To make a sale MWW must exchange clothing for a customer's money. Thus owner's equity decreases because something of value—clothes—is being given up to make the sale. When an expense is incurred, assets must decrease or liabilities must increase to reflect the economic cost. Like revenue, an expense does not have to correspond with a cash flow. MWW's clothing, for example, might be paid for before or after it is expensed. Below are some examples of how the accounting equation can be affected by the different ways MWW might pay employees for work that they did worth $500:

	Assets	=	Liabilities	+	Owners' (Shareholders') Equity
Employees are paid in cash for work they have done	−$500 (Cash)	=		+	−$500 (Wages Expense)
Employees will be paid $500 cash for work they have done	−$500 (Inventory)	=		+	−$500 (Wages Expense)
Employees work but are promised payment later		=	+$500 (Wages Payable)	+	−$500 (Wages Expense)

Table 2-4	Income Statement Prepared for TPB Using the Accrual Basis

Tamara's Painting Business
Income Statement
For the Month Ended July 31

Revenue	$4,300
($3,500 for the six July jobs that were paid for	
plus $800 for the July job that was not paid for by the end of July)	
Less: Expenses	
Employees	(1,800)
($1,450 paid for work done by employees in July	
plus $350 owed for work done in July)	
Paint	(1,250)
($1,250 for paint purchased and used in July.	
This paint will not be paid for until later.)	
Equipment	(50)
(Tamara estimates that she will be able to use the equipment	
for 24 painting months, after which time she will have to replace	
the equipment. The charge for the month is $1,200 ÷ 24 = $50.)	
Net income	$1,200

An income statement for Tamara's Painting Business for the month of July using the accrual method is shown in Table 2-4.

This statement is very different from the income statement prepared using the cash basis. Different amounts are reported for each line in the statement, including net income. In this statement, revenue reflects work done in July. Even though not all of the money was collected by the end of July, revenue includes all the money TPB earned on the seven jobs done in the month. The money collected for the June job is not included in July's revenue because it has nothing to do with the work done in July. The revenue for that job would have been included in June's income statement. The expenses include the cost of paint used in July and the cost of the work done by employees in July even though these items were not fully paid for. Remember, these are costs that were incurred to earn the revenue in July—when cash changed hands doesn't matter.

One additional expense is included in TPB's income statement: the cost of the equipment. The equipment was bought and paid for when Tamara began her business, but it contributes to earning revenue in every month in which it is used. As a result, under accrual accounting a portion of the cost of the equipment is expensed each month. Expensing an asset over its life is called amortization. **Amortization** is the allocation of the cost of a capital asset to expense over the asset's useful life. Amortization reflects the "using up" of the asset in helping the entity to earn revenue. ("Depreciation" is a term often used to describe the using up of assets instead of amortization.)

What does net income mean in this statement? It is certainly more difficult to interpret than the cash flow statement, where the $1,650 bottom line just represented the increase in cash. Here the $1,200 of net income means that Tamara's wealth increased by $1,200 during July when the benefits (revenue) and the costs of earning those benefits (expenses) are considered. The $1,200 does not, however, represent cash.

The nature of accrual accounting will be examined in more detail in Chapter 3.

For TPB the difference in the amount of revenue between the two methods is the $500 that was collected in July for the job done in June and the $800 owed at the end of July for the work done in July. Revenue on the cash basis includes the $500 from June and excludes the $800 owing at the end of July. Revenue on the accrual basis excludes the $500 from June and includes the $800 owing at the end of July. Both methods include as revenue the amounts for jobs completed and paid for in July.

MWW's Statement of Earnings (Income Statement)

Let's take a look at MWW's statement of earnings (see page A-000). MWW reported net earnings of $8,180,000 for the year ended January 27, 2001. Remember that this does not mean that MWW had $8,180,000 more in cash. In terms of the accounting equation, when a company reports net income, the shareholders' equity (shareholders' equity is used here because MWW is a corporation) increases and **net assets** (assets – liabilities) must increase by the same amount. That is,

$$
\underbrace{\begin{array}{c} \text{Assets} - \text{Liabilities} \\ +\$8{,}180{,}000 \end{array}}_{\text{Net assets}} \quad \begin{array}{c} = \\ = \end{array} \quad \begin{array}{c} \text{Shareholders' Equity} \\ +\$8{,}180{,}000 \end{array}
$$

What does a net income of $8,180,000 mean? Standing alone, net income is very difficult to interpret. In an accrual accounting context it means that the wealth of the shareholders of the entity has increased by $8,180,000 or that the economic benefits enjoyed by MWW exceeded the economic costs it incurred by $8,180,000. But is that good or bad? That question must be evaluated in the context of how MWW was expected to perform, how similar firms performed, and how MWW performed compared with previous years. For example, if investors were expecting MWW's net earnings to be $9,500,000, then the actual amount could be considered disappointing. As we proceed through the book we will examine tools that will allow you to evaluate and interpret what net income means.

But there is more to MWW's statement of earnings than net income; it also includes important information about how it earned the net income. Consider the following:

- During fiscal 2001 MWW sold $363,870,000 of merchandise in the stores it owns.

- The cost of those sales was $214,361,000. **Cost of sales** is the cost of the inventory that is sold to customers. For MWW, cost of sales represents the cost of the clothes sold.

- When cost of sales is deducted from sales, gross margin is obtained. **Gross margin** is the amount by which an entity can sell its goods for more than their cost. The amount of gross margin is then available for covering the other costs of operating the business and for providing profit to the owners. MWW's gross margin was $149,509,000 (sales − cost of sales = $363,870,000 − $214,361,000).

This calculation shows that MWW sold its clothes for $149,509,000 more than what they cost. That amount is available to cover other costs.

A convenient way of analyzing gross margin is as a percentage of sales. The **gross margin percentage** is the ratio of gross margin to sales. It indicates the percentage of each dollar of sales that is available to cover other costs and return a profit to the entity's owners. Using the gross margin percentage makes it easier to compare the performance of different entities and the same entity year to year. MWW's gross margin percentage is:

$$\text{Gross Margin Percentage} = \frac{\text{Gross margin}}{\text{Sales}} = \frac{\text{Sales} - \text{Cost of sales}}{\text{Sales}}$$

$$= \frac{\$149,509,000}{\$363,870,000} = \frac{\$363,870,000 - \$214,361,000}{\$363,870,000}$$

$$= 0.41, \text{ or } 41\%$$

MWW's gross margin percentage in fiscal 2001 was 41%, which means that for every dollar of sales, it has $0.41 to apply to costs other than the cost of clothing and for profit. This percentage has been consistent over the last three years at around 40%. Higher gross margins are better than lower ones. In some businesses very small declines in the gross margin percentage can lead to a loss instead of a profit. For a more thorough analysis it would be valuable to examine competitors' gross margin percentages. However, as we will see through the book, it can be difficult to compare gross margins of different entities if the entities do not account for revenues and cost of sales the same way.

Many companies are very secretive about their gross margin percentages. They will combine cost of sales with other expenses to obscure the actual amount and thereby hide valuable information from competitors. For example, the statement of earnings of the Loblaw Companies Limited combines almost all of its expenses into a single line. The Loblaw statement of earnings is shown in Exhibit 2-1.[2]

www.loblaw.com

Exhibit 2-1

Loblaw Companies Limited Consolidated Statement of Earnings for Fiscal 2000 and 1999

Consolidated Statements of Earnings				
52 Weeks Ended December 30, 2000 ($ millions)			2000	1999
Sales			$ 20,121	$ 18,783
Operating Expenses	Cost of sales, selling and administrative expenses		18,862	17,706
	Depreciation		283	266
			19,145	17,972
Operating Income			976	811
Interest Expense (Income)	Long term		172	139
	Other		(29)	(27)
			143	112
Earnings Before Income Taxes			833	699
Income Taxes (note 4)	Provision		321	280
	Other		(4)	
			317	280
Earnings Before Goodwill Charges			516	419
Goodwill Charges, net of tax of $1 (1999 − $1)			43	43
Net Earnings for the Period			$ 473	$ 376
Per Common Share ($)	Earnings before goodwill charges		$ 1.87	$ 1.52
	Net earnings		$ 1.71	$ 1.37

Below the gross margin, MWW's statement of earnings reports the other expenses it incurred during the year. MWW breaks its expenses into front-line and back-line expenses. Front-line expenses are expenses incurred dealing directly with customers—essentially the costs of operating the stores—such as personnel, advertising, rent, amortization of furniture and fixtures, and some interest. Back-line expenses reflect the costs that are not related to operating the stores (see page 000).

MWW incurred a total of $111,248,000 in front-line expenses during 2001, representing about 30% of sales. The line "Front-line contribution" tells us how much MWW's store operations made during the year—the amount that is available to cover non-store costs and for profit. We can express the front-line contribution in terms of a percentage of sales, the front-line contribution margin percentage or ratio. In fiscal 2001 MWW made $38,261,000 from store operations, so its front-line contribution margin percentage was 10.5%. The calculation of front-line contribution margin percentage is:

$$\begin{aligned}\text{Front-line Contribution} \atop \text{Margin Percentage} &= \frac{\text{Sales} - \text{Cost of Sales} - \text{Front-line expenses}}{\text{Sales}} \\ &= \frac{\$363,870,000 - \$214,361,000 - \$111,248,000}{\$363,870,000} \\ &= 10.5\%\end{aligned}$$

The front-line contribution margin percentages in 2000 and 1999 respectively were 10.1% and 10.3%. Further investigation is needed to explain why this margin is higher than in the previous years. We will explore this type of analysis in more depth in a later chapter.

Remember that MWW owns some of its stores and some stores are operated as franchises. Sales for all stores in the MWW chain during fiscal 2001 were $487,979,000, as shown on the very top line of the statement of earnings. The sales made by the franchise stores are not included in the calculation of MWW's net earnings, but MWW earns a royalty on each sale a franchise store makes. That means that MWW receives a percentage of each sale as part of the franchise agreement. These revenues are included in the line "Franchise royalties and other."

Back-line expenses are the costs of behind-the-scenes activities such as office space, the accounting department, computer equipment, and so on. These costs are necessary to operate the business but are not store operating costs.

The line "Earnings before provision for closure of U.S. pilot stores, income taxes and goodwill amortization" is very important. It is a measure of earnings before events that are not an ordinary part of operations are considered. All revenues and expenses to this point can be considered regular costs of MWW's business. This amount is a good starting point if one wanted to estimate future years' earnings.

In fiscal 1999 MWW reported an expense of $2,961,000 for "Provision for closure of U.S. pilot stores." MWW tried to expand into the U.S. in the 1990s but was unsuccessful and decided to end the experiment in fiscal 1999. MWW reported the cost of closing the U.S. pilot stores on a separate line on its statement of earnings in fiscal 1999. By doing so MWW provided useful information to users of the financial statements. The cost of closing these stores will not be repeated year after year, so by showing the information separately the statements give users an idea of which expenses will occur in future years and which are non-recurring. Stakeholders trying to predict future earnings will find this information very valuable.

Because MWW is a corporation, it must pay taxes. For fiscal 2001 MWW recorded an income tax expense of $8,346,000, which is deducted in the calculation of net earnings. (As we will see in Chapter 10, the income tax expense does not mean

MWW has to pay $8,346,000 to the government that year.) In contrast, the income statement of a partnership or proprietorship would not show an income tax expense because with these types of entities income taxes are the responsibility of the partners or the proprietor. Not-for-profit organizations would not have an income tax expense because they do not pay taxes.

MWW does not pay dividends. However, when dividends are paid they are not treated as an expense when net income is calculated. This is because net income is a measure of the change in the owners' wealth from an entity's business activities, while payment of dividends does not reduce the wealth of the owners, it just distributes the wealth to them. In contrast, payments to stakeholders other than owners are treated as expenses because they reduce the wealth of the owners. For example, interest payments to creditors, taxes to governments, and wages to employees are all treated as expenses when net income is calculated.

Question for Consideration

During the summer Hank operated a cart that sold hot dogs and cold drinks. At the end of the summer Hank had collected $6,500 from customers and paid $3,300 to suppliers. At the end of the summer Hank owed suppliers $500 and he was owed $200 from customers. The amortization on his cart for the summer was $800. What was Hank's net income on the cash basis for the summer? What was his accrual net income?

Answer: Hank's income on the cash basis is simply cash in – cash out. Since Hank collected $6,500 from customers and paid suppliers $3,300, his income on the cash basis is $6,500 – $3,300 = $3,200.

On the accrual basis, revenues and expenses incurred to earn the revenue are considered regardless of whether cash was involved, so the amounts owed and owing as well as amortization must be included in the calculation. Therefore, Hank's accrual income is $6,500 (cash collected) + $200 (amounts owed by customers) – $3,300 (paid to suppliers) – $500 (owed to suppliers) – $800 (amortization of cart) = $2,100.

The Statement of Retained Earnings

The **statement of retained earnings** summarizes the changes to retained earnings during a period and serves as the bridge between the balance sheet and the income statement. (You can find MWW's statement of retained earnings at the bottom of its statement of earnings and retained earnings on page A-000.) Remember, earlier in the chapter it was pointed out that retained earnings represents the accumulation of an entity's net incomes over its life. The statement of retained earnings is where net income is added to retained earnings at the beginning of the period to obtain retained earnings at the end of the period. The statement of retained earnings shows all transactions and economic events that affected retained earnings during a period. In equation form the statement of retained earnings can be expressed as:

$$\begin{array}{l}\text{Retained earnings} \\ \text{at the end} \\ \text{of the year}\end{array} = \begin{array}{l}\text{Retained earnings} \\ \text{at the beginning} \\ \text{of the year}\end{array} + \begin{array}{l}\text{Net income} \\ \text{for the year}\end{array} - \begin{array}{l}\text{Dividends declared} \\ \text{during the year}\end{array}$$

To highlight the link between the income statement and the balance sheet this equation can be expanded to:

$$\begin{array}{l}\text{Retained earnings} \\ \text{at the end} \\ \text{of the year}\end{array} = \begin{array}{l}\text{Retained earnings} \\ \text{at the beginning} \\ \text{of the year}\end{array} + \text{Revenue} - \text{Expenses} - \begin{array}{l}\text{Dividends declared} \\ \text{during the year}\end{array}$$

There are a number of other transactions and economic events that can have an effect on retained earnings but that are not reflected in these equations. These include the effect of repurchases by an entity of its own capital stock from investors. During fiscal 2001 MWW paid $3,102,000 to repurchase 1,379,348 of its shares from investors. Of the $3,102,000 paid, $1,543,000 reduced retained earnings and the remainder reduced the capital stock account. (See Note 12, page A-57.)

An expression commonly used to describe the payment of dividends is that "dividends are paid out of retained earnings." The expression means that when dividends are paid, retained earnings decrease. However, paying a dividend requires cash. If a company does not have enough cash it cannot pay a dividend, no matter how large its retained earnings. Notice that MWW had over $33,000,000 in retained earnings on January 27, 2001 but only $6,993,000 in cash. It could not pay out all its retained earnings in dividends even if it wanted to (unless it borrowed money or sold some of its other assets).

The Cash Flow Statement

Readers of the business press might get the impression that the most important information about the performance of an entity comes from its income statement. This impression is far from accurate. While net income is an important indicator of performance, it is vital not to forget cash. As has been said and sung, money makes the world go round. Cash is necessary to pay bills and meet obligations as they come due. No matter how large a company's net income, if it does not have the cash to meet its obligations, it is in serious trouble.

Because of the importance of cash, the general purpose financial statement package usually includes a cash flow statement. The **cash flow statement** shows how cash was obtained and used during a period. The cash flow statement is another "how did we do?" statement. However, it measures "how we did" differently than the income statement. The cash flow statement shows users how the entity managed its cash during the reporting period. It is another source of information about an entity's liquidity.

The cash flow statement is usually broken down into three parts: cash from (1) operations, (2) investing activities, and (3) financing activities. Let's look at each part in more detail.

1. **Cash from operations** (CFO) is the cash an entity generates from or uses in its regular business activities. For MWW, CFO is the cash it generated or used selling clothes. CFO would include cash collected from sales of clothing and money spent on buying the clothes, renting stores, paying employees—anything spent on the day-to-day operation of the business.

   For fiscal 2001 MWW had CFO of $21,140,000. (On page A-47 the number appears about half way down the statement on an unnamed line; do not confuse it with the line called "Funds provided by operations," which is a little different). CFO means that during fiscal 2001 MWW's ordinary business operations generated $21,140,000 in cash. This is internally generated cash that could be used for expansion, purchasing capital assets, retiring debt, paying dividends, and so on. Notice that CFO is much different from net earnings. Remember that under accrual accounting net income measures economic flows, not cash flows. That means that net income includes amounts that are not cash flows, whereas cash from operations simply reflects the movement of cash.

2. The **cash from investing activities** section of the cash flow statement provides information about cash spent buying capital and other long-term assets and the

cash received from selling those types of assets. This reflects the fact that it is necessary for most entities to invest in assets that contribute indirectly to the success of the entity over more than one period. For a company like MWW these investments could include store items such as furniture, display cases, mannequins, in-store computer terminals, carpeting, and signs. In addition, the administrative offices could include furniture, computers, communications equipment, and so on. These assets contribute indirectly because they are not bought and sold in the ordinary course of business, but provide support for the ordinary business activities. It would be difficult to operate MWW stores without display cases, racks, signs, and so on.

During fiscal 2001 MWW spent $5,807,000 in cash on investing activities, including $2,485,000 on the purchase of various capital assets such as furniture, fixtures, and equipment and $3,054,000 on purchasing stores from franchisees. MWW also received $36,000 from selling capital assets.

3. **Cash from financing activities** is the cash an entity raises and pays to equity investors and lenders. Cash from financing activities includes cash raised from borrowing and from issuing shares, and cash paid for repaying loans, repurchasing shares, and paying dividends. (Interestingly, interest payments are usually included in CFO even though they are a cost of financing.)

During fiscal 2001 MWW had a net cash outflow of $10,114,000 from financing activities. The amount included retirement of $3,278,000 in long-term debt, $6,506,000 in payments on capital lease liabilities, and the issuing of $2,700,000 in new long-term debt.

Overall, what does the MWW's cash flow statement tell us? Internal generation of cash provided $21,140,000 (CFO), which was plenty to cover the $5,807,000 required for its investing activities and to allow it to pay out $10,114,000 for financing purposes. MWW also increased its cash on hand by $5,219,000.

Notes to the Financial Statements

Some users of financial statements say that the notes to the financial statements provide more useful information than the statements themselves. Certainly, it is not possible to understand the financial statements without a careful reading of the notes. The notes expand and explain the information in the statements and provide additional information that may help users assess an entity. If you look again at MWW's financial statements you will find that many of the lines on each statement refer to specific notes.

Let's look at two examples of financial statement notes.

- The balance sheet line for capital assets refers to Note 7. Note 7 (page A-53) lists the types of capital assets that MWW has and provides information about how certain transactions affected the capital assets. By examining Note 7 a user has an idea of the types of capital assets the entity has, how much each type cost, and how much has been amortized. In Note 7 we learn that a significant portion of MWW's assets are leased, not owned.

- Note 10 provides information about MWW's long-term debt (see page A-000). While the balance sheet tells users that the company has $37,921,000 in long-term debt ($10,905,000 due currently and the rest due in more than one year), the note lists the individual loans that MWW has, when each is due, the interest rate, and other relevant terms. If you were interested in predicting the future cash flows of an entity, this information would be crucial.

One of the most important notes is the one that explains the accounting policies used by the entity. **Accounting policies** are the methods, principles, and practices used by an entity to report its financial results. MWW describes its significant accounting policies in Note 1 (see pages A-000 to A-000). Preparers of accounting information can often choose from more than one way to account for economic events and transactions. Without a description of the entity's accounting choices it would be virtually impossible to make any sense of the numbers in the financial statements. We will explore many of the accounting choices available to preparers as we move through this book.

Question for Consideration

You are a loan officer for a major bank and an executive from MWW has come to ask for a $5,000,000 loan. What information on the balance sheet and cash flow statement would be of interest to you?

Answer: As a banker, your main concern is MWW's ability to repay the loan. You would be interested in whether MWW has the cash flow to support the interest on the loan. If the interest rate on the loan were 8%, MWW would have to pay the bank $400,000 per year in interest. In 2001, MWW had cash from operations of $21,140,000, which is ample to cover the additional interest cost. If you were confident that MWW could continue to generate that much cash from operations each year, you could assume that it would have little trouble paying the interest on the loan.

You would also be interested in knowing what other debts MWW has. The liability section of the balance sheet identifies amounts owed to other creditors. The liability section of the balance sheet also refers you to the notes to the financial statements, which provide you with more details on the terms of MWW's outstanding loans, and importantly, when they have to be repaid.

Users of MWW's Financial Statements

MWW's financial statements give us some insights into the identity of some of the stakeholders of the company. From the information in the financial statements we can surmise that potential stakeholders include:

- **Shareholders.** Since MWW is a public company that is traded on the Toronto Stock Exchange, shareholders are an important stakeholder group. Some of MWW's shareholders are small investors who may not have access to information other than what is publicly available.

- **Creditors.** The balance sheet shows that MWW has almost $38 million in long-term debt. That means that there are creditors, such as bankers, who have lent MWW money and will want to use the financial statements to evaluate the company to determine the status of their loans.

- **Franchise owners.** Many of MWW's stores are franchises. People owning franchises may want to use the financial statements to assess MWW's financial position to obtain some assurance that their investment in a franchise is safe—that the franchisor, MWW, will not go out of business.

- **Potential investors.** One of MWW's corporate strategies is to buy stores operated as franchises. This strategy may require MWW to raise money from debt or equity investors, which suggests that potential investors are another stakeholder.

Comment: The identification of the users of MWW's financial statement presumes it is a public company. As explained in Chapter 1, MWW was purchased by Canadian Tire Corporation, Limited in early 2002, at which time it stopped being a public company. As a private company MWW will have different prospective users. They will be fewer in number and have far less access to MWW's financial statements. The *shareholder* will still be interested in MWW, but now Canadian Tire Corporation, Limited is the only shareholder. *Creditors* will continue to be interested in MWW financial statements and they will regularly receive financial statements because the lending agreements will require that they do so. *Franchise owners* may still be interested in MWW's financial position but they are not likely to be able to obtain information because disclosure is at the discretion of the owners and managers. There will no longer be *potential purchasers* of MWW's stock, since it is a private company, but prospective lenders will likely receive the financial statements if MWW approaches them for a loan.

Format of General Purpose Financial Statements

There is no one right way to organize a set of financial statements. Even under GAAP there are no requirements for how financial statements should be presented. The *CICA Handbook* requires that certain information be included in the financial statements, but the preparer decides how that information is presented. Preparers' decisions about how to organize the financial statements can be influenced by what the preparers are trying to emphasize in their statements and what is common practice in the entity's industry.

Two examples of companies' balance sheets that have formats that are quite different from MWW's are shown in Exhibit 2-2.[3]

Panel A of Exhibit 2-2 shows Dylex Ltd.'s balance sheet for fiscal 2000. Dylex was a Canadian clothing retailer that operated the Tip Top, Fairweather, and BiWay chains. Dylex did not use the Assets = Liabilities + Owner's Equity format of the financial equation for its balance sheet. Instead, Dylex rearranged the accounting equation so that one side showed "assets employed" (working capital [current assets less current liabilities] plus capital assets) and the other side showed "capital employed" (non-current liabilities plus owners' equity). This arrangement emphasized the working capital position of the company, which was important because the company had ongoing liquidity problems beginning in the 1990s. The balance sheet included current liabilities as "negative" operating assets, so that the capital employed side of the balance sheet reflects the company's long-term financing. The balance sheet, of course, still balances, but what is on each side is different. Ultimately, Dylex did not survive and all its retail chains were sold or ceased operations by late 2001.

Panel B of Exhibit 2-2 shows the balance sheet of Newfoundland Power Inc. (Newfoundland Power), a producer and supplier of electricity. Newfoundland Power arranges its balance sheet in a way opposite to what we normally see. The fixed (capital) assets and other non-current assets are at the top of the asset side of the balance sheet, while current assets are at the bottom. One explanation for this arrangement is that non-current assets represent over 93% of the company's total assets, so management may want to give more prominence to the more significant asset classes. On the liabilities and equities side, shareholder equity is on the top of the statement, not on the bottom as is usually seen. This format is quite common for electrical utilities.

www.nfpower.nf.ca

Financial statements are a method of communication between an entity and its stakeholders. As in any type of communication the preparer will tailor the message to suit the situation. These examples highlight the variation that can exist in the financial

Exhibit 2-2

Examples of General Purpose Financial Statements

Panel A: Dylex Limited

consolidated statements of financial position

(thousands of dollars)	January 29 2000	January 30 1999
Current assets		
Cash and short-term investments	$ –	$ 29,498
Accounts receivable	7,138	9,605
Inventories	162,861	166,347
Prepaid expenses	2,225	3,126
Income taxes recoverable	318	499
Notes and other investments due within one year	399	411
	172,941	209,486
Current liabilities		
Bank indebtedness (note 9)	35,187	–
Accounts payable and accrued liabilities	102,570	108,062
Other taxes payable	3,564	4,459
Long-term debt due within one year (note 5)	116	116
Obligations under capital leases due within one year (note 6)	1,856	803
	143,293	113,440
Working capital	29,648	96,046
Other assets		
Notes and other investments	41	154
Fixed assets (note 2)	124,374	98,366
Assets under capital leases (note 3)	6,298	4,793
Deferred charges and goodwill (note 4)	9,730	5,463
	140,443	108,776
Assets employed	$ 170,091	$ 204,822
Financed by		
Other liabilities		
Long-term debt (note 5)	$ 206	$ 313
Obligations under capital leases (note 6)	4,484	3,888
Deferred revenue	20,248	15,661
	24,938	19,862
Shareholders' equity		
Share capital (note 7)	113,636	115,730
Retained earnings	31,517	69,230
	145,153	184,960
Capital employed	$ 170,091	$ 204,822

Panel B: Newfoundland Power Inc.

Balance Sheets

As at December 31

	2000	1999
	(in thousands)	
Assets		
Fixed Assets (Note 4)		
Property, plant and equipment	$ 865,406	$ 844,598
Less: accumulated depreciation	353,078	344,506
	512,328	500,092
Corporate Income Tax Deposit (Note 9)	13,636	15,595
Deferred Charges (Note 5)	58,969	49,015
Current Assets		
Accounts receivable	35,033	33,108
Materials and supplies at average cost	3,910	5,492
Rate stabilization account	4,376	4,828
	43,319	43,428
	$ 628,252	$ 608,130
Shareholders' Equity and Liabilities		
Shareholders' Equity		
Common shares (Note 6)	$ 70,321	$ 70,321
Retained earnings	180,010	172,527
Common shareholder's equity	250,331	242,848
Preference shares (Note 6)	9,890	9,890
	260,221	252,738
Long-term Debt (Note 7)	277,108	280,158
Current Liabilities		
Bank indebtedness	–	3,600
Short-term borrowings	19,224	16,026
Accounts payable and accrued charges (Note 1)	68,649	52,558
Current installments of long-term debt	3,050	3,050
	90,923	75,234
	$ 628,252	$ 608,130

statements of entities. How financial statements are organized does not affect the information itself, only the appearance of the information.

Other Accounting Information

The general purpose financial statement package described above is the most common format for financial reporting purposes. However, accountants may prepare any type of report to satisfy the needs of users. The only limitations are the willingness of the entity to provide the information and the availability of the information in the accounting system (an accounting system can provide only information that is entered into it).

Accounting reports that are prepared to meet the needs of specific users and/or a specific use are called **special purpose reports**. Special purpose reports normally would not be made publicly available even by public companies. For example, a creditor might want a statement of cash inflows and outflows, along with budgeted cash flows for the next year, to assess the borrower's ability to pay its debts. A property manager might want a statement of revenues so that the appropriate amount of rent could be charged, if rent is based in part on a store's sales. The list of special purposes is endless.

■ Solved Problem

Snowflake's Snow Removal Company (SSRC)—Part 1

Stan Snowflake recently decided to start a new business clearing snow from residential driveways. Stan is a construction worker, and while he tends to have a lot of work during the spring, summer, and fall, he does not usually work during the winter months. Stan finds being idle quite frustrating, so after some thought he decided that a snow removal business would be a good way to make some money and keep busy during the winter. As a result he organized Snowflake's Snow Removal Company (SSRC), an unincorporated business. In October, before the first snowfall, SSRC entered into the following transactions:

1. Stan opened a bank account in the name of SSRC and deposited $10,000 of his savings into the account.
2. SSRC borrowed $5,000 from the bank.
3. SSRC purchased a used pickup truck and a snowplough attachment for $17,500. SSRC paid $11,000 in cash and promised to pay the remainder in four months.
4. SSRC purchased shovels and an axe for $200 cash.
5. Stan went door-to-door in his neighbourhood signing up people for SSRC. SSRC offered snow removal for $250 for the entire winter or $50 per month for the five months SSRC would be operating. Ten people paid for the entire winter. Other people will begin paying in November.

Required:

Record SSRC's transactions into a spreadsheet like the one in Table 2-1 on page 41. Use the spreadsheet to prepare a balance sheet as of October 31 (before the first snowfall).

Solution:

Snowflake's Snow Removal Company Spreadsheet					
	Assets	=	Liabilities	+	Owner's Equity
1.	+$10,000 cash				+$10,000 investment by owner
Balance	$10,000	=	$0	+	$10,000
2.	+$5,000 cash		+$5,000 bank loan		
Balance	$15,000	=	$5,000	+	$10,000
3.	+$17,500 equipment −$11,000 cash		+$6,500 payable to vendor of truck		
Balance	$21,500	=	$11,500	+	$10,000
4.	+$200 equipment −$200 cash				
Balance	$21,500	=	$11,500	+	$10,000
5.	+$2,500 cash		+$2,500 obligation to provide snow removal services		
Balance	$24,000	=	$14,000	+	$10,000

Snowflake's Snow Removal Company
Balance Sheet
As at October 31

Assets		Liabilities and Owner's Equity	
Cash	$ 6,300	Bank loan	$ 5,000
Equipment	17,700	Accounts payable	6,500
		Services to be provided	2,500
			14,000
		Owner's equity	10,000
Total assets	$24,000	Total liabilities and owner's equity	$24,000

Notice that the liabilities are broken down into three different types. This format allows Stan to see the different types of obligations that SSRC has.

Snowflake's Snow Removal Company (SSRC)—Part 2

November and December were very busy for Stan and SSRC. There were a number of snowfalls, two of them quite heavy.

1. SSRC had 75 regular customers (remember that 10 of the customers paid in full in October). By the end of December Stan had collected $5,600 from the customers who agreed to pay each month and was owed $900 by these customers. In addition, SSRC received $800 from people who stopped Stan on the street and asked him to clean their driveways during heavy snowfalls.

2. SSRC was so busy that Stan sometimes had to hire a person to help him do shovelling. He paid the person $450 for work done and owed her $100 at the end of December.

3. SSRC spent $700 on gas, oil, and service on the truck.

4. Stan estimates that the monthly amortization of the truck and other equipment should be $700.

Required:

Prepare income statements on the cash basis and on the accrual basis for the two months ended December 31.

Solution:

Snowflake's Snow Removal Company
Income Statement
For the Two Months Ended December 31
(Prepared using the cash basis)

Revenue (cash collected)	$6,400
($5,600 from customers who pay monthly plus $800 from people who stopped Stan on the street)	
Less: Expenses (cash spent)	
For employee	(450)
($450 paid to the person for work done)	
For oil, gas, and service	(700)
($700 for gas, oil, and service)	
Net income (cash flow)	$5,250

Snowflake's Snow Removal Company
Income Statement
For the Two Months Ended December 31
(Prepared using the accrual basis)

Revenue	$8,300
($5,600 from customers who pay monthly + $900 owed by customers who pay monthly + $1,000 for the people who paid in advance [10 customers × $50 per month × 2 months]* + $800 from people who stopped Stan on the street)	
Less: Expenses	
For employee	(550)
($450 paid to the person for work done + $100 owed)	
For oil, gas, and service	(700)
($700 for gas, oil, and service)	
Equipment	($1,400)
(Stan estimates that monthly amortization should be $700)	
Net income	$5,650

*Even though customers paid in advance, SSRC earns the money on a monthly basis. Therefore, one-fifth of advance payment should be recognized each month.

Snowflake's Snow Removal Company (SSRC)—Part 3

Required:
Use the information from SSRC's balance sheet on October 31 to calculate the following amounts. Discuss the information provided by these amounts.

a. Working capital.

b. Current ratio.

c. Debt to equity ratio.

Solution:

a. Working capital = Current assets − Current liabilities

($7,700) = $6,300 − $14,000

b. Current ratio $= \dfrac{\text{Current assets}}{\text{Current liabilities}} = \dfrac{\$6,300}{\$14,000} = 0.45$

c. Debt-to-equity ratio $= \dfrac{\text{Liabilities}}{\text{Owner's equity}} = \dfrac{\$14,000}{\$10,000} = 1.4$

The working capital calculation and current ratio show that SSRC has more current liabilities than current assets. This is potentially a cause of concern because if cash were not forthcoming in the near future, SSRC would not be able to pay the bank or the vendor of the truck. On October 31 this would not have been much of a concern because customers were expected to begin paying in November. The main concern on October 31 might have been signing up enough customers and ensuring that they paid the amounts they owed. The debt-to-equity ratio indicates that SSRC has more liabilities than equity. It is not possible to tell whether this is a problem because there is no benchmark for comparison. However, the more debt an entity has, the more risk it faces. In this case, if SSRC were not successful (if it didn't have enough paying customers), Stan would still be obliged to pay the bank and the vendor of the truck.

Summary of Key Points

LO 1. There are five components of a set of general purpose financial statements: the balance sheet, the income statement, the statement of retained earnings, the cash flow statement, and the notes to the financial statements. The balance sheet summarizes the financial position of the entity—its assets, liabilities, and owners' equity—at a specific point in time. The income statement provides a measure of the economic performance of an entity over a period. The income statement summarizes an entity's revenues and expenses for a period. The statement of retained earnings summarizes the changes to retained earnings during a period. The cash flow statement shows how cash during a period was obtained from and used for operating, investing, and financing activities. The notes to the financial statements expand and explain the information in the statements and provide additional information that may be helpful in assessing an entity.

General purpose financial statements are designed to suit a broad set of users and uses. General purpose financial statements are usually prepared according to GAAP.

LO 2. The accounting equation is the conceptual foundation of accounting and is defined as:

$$\text{Assets} = \text{Liabilities} + \text{Owners' Equity}$$

LO 3. All economic events that are entered into an accounting system must be summarized in terms of the accounting equation. The equality between assets, and liabilities and equities must always be maintained.

LO 4. There are five basic elements in the financial statements: assets, liabilities, owners' equity, revenues, and expenses. Assets are economic resources that provide future benefits to an entity for carrying out its business activities. Liabilities are an entity's obligations to pay debts or provide goods or services. Owners' equity represents the owners' investment in an entity. Owners' investments can be made directly by contributing assets to the entity or indirectly by reinvesting profits back into the entity instead of distributing them to the owners. Revenues represent economic benefits earned by providing goods and services to customers. Expenses are economic sacrifices made to earn revenue.

LO 5. While there are only five basic elements reported in financial statements (assets, liabilities, owners' equity, revenues, and expenses), entities report a large number of different types of these elements. For example, MWW reports eight different asset accounts, five liability accounts, and two equity accounts on its balance sheet. The accounts reported on the financial statements represent a much larger number of accounts in MWW's actual records. One of the main purposes of accounting is to record economic events and transactions in an accounting system so that the raw data can be converted into useful information for stakeholders in the form of financial statements and special purpose reports.

LO 6. Two of the most common methods of accounting are the cash basis of accounting and the accrual basis of accounting. The cash basis of accounting records only economic events and transactions that involve cash. Under the cash basis of accounting, revenues are recorded when cash is received and expenses are recorded when cash is paid. The accrual basis of accounting attempts to measure the economic impact of transactions and economic events rather than cash flows. Under the accrual basis revenue is recorded when it is earned and expenses are recorded when costs are incurred to earn the revenue, regardless of when the cash is received or spent.

LO 7. Obtaining and examining financial statements are often only the first steps in evaluating an entity. Financial statement numbers can be analyzed to obtain additional insights. One of the analytical tools available to financial statement users is ratios. The current ratio (current assets ÷ current liabilities) provides information about an entity's liquidity. The debt-to-equity ratio (debt ÷ equity) gives an indication of an entity's risk, and the gross margin percentage (gross margin ÷ sales) gives an indication of an entity's profitability.

Key Terms

accounting equation, p. 39

accounting policies, p. 60

accounts payable, p. 45

accounts receivable, p. 43

accrual basis of accounting, p. 50

amortization, p. 53

asset, p. 39

balance sheet, p. 39

capital assets, p. 43

capital stock, p. 48

cash basis of accounting, p. 50

cash flow statement, p. 58

cash from financing activities, p. 59

cash from investing activities, p. 58

cash from operations, p. 58

consolidated financial statements, p. 38

cost of sales, p. 54

creditor, p. 39

current asset, p. 43

current liability, p. 46

current portion of long-term debt, p. 45

current ratio, p. 46

debt-to-equity, p. 49

dividend, p. 48

expense, p. 52

fiscal year, p. 38

general purpose financial statements, p. 37

gross margin, p. 54

gross margin percentage, p. 55

income statement, p. 49

interest, p. 49

inventory, p. 43

liability, p. 39

liquidity, p. 46

long-term debt, p. 45

net assets, p. 54

net income, p. 49

non-current assets, p. 43

non-current liability, p. 46

operating cycle, p. 43

owners' equity, p. 47

principal, p. 49

retained earnings, p. 48

revenue, p. 51

special purpose report, p. 62

statement of retained earnings, p. 57

working capital, p. 46

working capital ratio, p. 46

Similar Terms

The left column gives alternative terms that are sometimes used for the accounting terms introduced in this chapter, which are listed in the right column.

accrual accounting	**accrual basis of accounting, p. 50**
cash accounting	**cash basis of accounting, p. 50**
cash from operating activities	**cash from operations, p. 58**
common stock	**capital stock, p. 48**
cost of goods sold	**cost of sales, p. 54**
depletion	**amortization, p. 53**
depreciation	**amortization, p. 53**
earnings, net earnings	**net income, p. 49**
fixed assets	**non-current assets, p. 43**
gross profit	**gross margin, p. 54**
long-term assets, long-lived assets	**non-current assets, p. 43**
partners' equity (for a partnership)	**owners' equity, p. 47**
profit, net profit	**net income, p. 49**
sales, sales revenue	**revenue, p. 51**
share capital	**capital stock, p. 48**
shareholders' equity (for a corporation)	**owners' equity, p. 47**
statement of cash flow	**cash flow statement, p. 58**
statement of earnings, statement of profit and loss, statement of operations	**income statement, p. 49**
statement of financial position	**balance sheet, p. 39**
stockholders' equity (for a corporation)	**owners' equity, p. 47**

Assignment Materials

Questions

Q2-1.   What are the components of a complete financial statement package?

Q2-2.   Explain the difference between cash and accrual accounting.

Q2-3.   Why is it important for direct and indirect investments by a corporation's shareholders to be reported separately on the balance sheet?

Q2-4.   What are general purpose financial statements? What problems does any individual stakeholder have with using general purpose statements?

Q2-5.   Why are the financial statements produced by public companies in Canada considered general purpose financial statements?

Q2-6.   The balance sheet has been compared to a photograph. Explain.

Q2-7.   Explain each of the following terms in your own words and give an example of each:
   a. asset
   b. liability
   c. owners' equity
   d. dividend
   e. revenue
   f. expense

Q2-8.   Explain the following accounting measurements and explain how and why they would be used when evaluating an entity:
   a. working capital
   b. current ratio
   c. debt-to-equity ratio
   d. gross margin
   e. gross margin percentage

Q2-9.   Explain why each of the following would be classified as assets on an entity's balance sheet:
   a. cash
   b. rent paid for in advance
   c. land
   d. shares of other corporations owned by the entity

Q2-10. Explain why each of the following would be considered liabilities on an entity's balance sheet:
   a. amounts owing to suppliers of inventory
   b. advances received from customers for services to be provided in the future
   c. long-term debt

Q2-11. Under GAAP, money spent on research by companies in the biotechnology, pharmaceutical, high technology, and other industries is not reported on the balance sheet as an asset. In your opinion, is the money companies spend on research an asset? Explain your thinking. Based on what you read in this chapter, why do you think money spent on research is not considered an asset under GAAP? What do you think the implications of this treatment of research costs are for users of the financial statements?

Q2-12. Explain the difference between capital stock and retained earnings in the shareholders' equity section of a corporation's balance sheet.

Q2-13. Explain the concept of liquidity. Why is evaluating liquidity important?

Q2-14. By law, distillers of Irish whiskey must age the whiskey for a minimum of three years, although the whiskey is often aged for a much longer time. If you were evaluating the liquidity of a distiller of Irish whiskey, how would you deal with the whiskey inventory?

Q2-15. Explain why net income results in an increase in owners' equity.

Q2-16. Explain why paying dividends results in a decrease in retained earnings of a corporation.

Q2-17. Readers of financial statements are always encouraged to read the notes to the statements. Why do you think the notes are considered so important? What impact would *not* reading the notes have on a user's ability to evaluate an entity? Use MWW's financial statements as a reference when answering this question.

Q2-18. Why is knowing the ability of an entity to generate cash flow so important to assessing the survival of the entity?

Q2-19. Virtually all entities prepare financial statements on an annual basis. For example, MWW prepares its statements for the 52 or 53 weeks ending on the last Saturday in January. Other entities prepare financial statements for years ending on a specific date such as December 31 or June 30. Provide three reasons why entities report on an annual basis. In answering, consider the question from the point of view of the users of the information.

Q2-20. It is normal for entities to present financial statements for more than one year rather than for just the most recent year. Provide three reasons why it is useful to users of financial statements to receive more than one year's financial statements.

Q2-21. Explain why different entities will organize the presentation of their financial statements in different ways (use different formats). For example, why would some companies present a lot of detail in their statements, whereas others might present as little as possible? In answering, consider different users and uses of the statements.

Q2-22. Do you think all entities should be required to use the same format for financial statements? Explain.

Exercises

E2-1.   (**Accounting equation, LO 2**) For each of the following independent situations, fill in the shaded area with the appropriate dollar amount.

	Assets	=	Liabilities	+	Owners' Equity
Situation 1	$135,000		$		$ 75,000
Situation 2			300,000		750,000
Situation 3	900,000		400,000		
Situation 4	175,000				95,000

E2-2.   (**Classification of balance sheet accounts, LO 1, 4**) Classify each of the following balance sheet accounts as a current asset, non-current asset, current liability, or non-current liability. Briefly explain your classification:
a. inventory
b. accounts payable that are usually paid within 60 days of receiving an invoice from a supplier
c. accounts receivable from customers that are expected to be paid within 30 days
d. land
e. furniture in the company's head office
f. bank loan that the bank can ask the company to repay at any time
g. account receivable that will be paid by the customer in two years
h. bank loan that must be repaid in full in three years

E2-3.   (**Prepare a statement of retained earnings, LO 1, 5**) On December 31, 2004, Canmore Inc. (Canmore) reported retained earnings of $120,000. For the year ended December 31, 2005, Canmore had net income of $30,000 and paid dividends of $10,000.

Required:

Prepare a statement of retained earnings for Canmore for the year ended December 31, 2005.

E2-4. **(Prepare a statement of retained earnings, LO 1, 5)** Minden Corporation was incorporated on August 1, 2005 by five shareholders who each invested $50,000 in cash in exchange for common shares. Minden's year end is July 31. In its first year of business Minden had net income of $97,500. For its years ended July 31, 2007 and 2008, its second and third years of operation, Minden reported net income of $189,000 and $224,000 respectively. In its first year Minden did not pay any dividends, but in fiscal 2007 it paid $25,000 in dividends and in 2008 it paid $40,000 in dividends.

Required:

Prepare a statement of retained earnings for the year ended July 31, 2008.

E2-5. **(Classification of cash flows, LO 1)** Classify each of the following cash flows as operating, financing, or investing activities:
   a. cash paid for inventory
   b. cash collected from customers
   c. cash paid to suppliers
   d. repayment of a long-term loan
   e. purchase of computer equipment
   f. sale of a building for cash
   g. sale of common stock to investors
   h. cash spent to purchase advertising on radio
   i. payment of a dividend to shareholders

E2-6. **(Prepare a balance sheet, LO 1, 4, 5)** You have received the following alphabetical list of balance sheet accounts for Picton Corporation (Picton). Organize the accounts into Picton's balance sheet.

Accounts receivable	35,000	Insurance paid for in advance	10,000
Advances paid by customers		Inventory	85,000
for goods to be provided in		Land	125,000
the future	20,000	Loans made to the corporation	
Amounts owed to suppliers	75,000	by shareholders	50,000
Bank loan	100,000	Long-term debt	30,000
Capital stock	150,000	Retained earnings	80,000
Cash	12,000	Wages payable to employees	12,000
Furniture and fixtures	250,000		

E2-7. **(Complete statements of income and retained earnings, LO 1, 2, 3)** Selkirk Corporation began operation in 2005. Its summarized financial statements are presented below. Fill in the shaded areas to complete the financial statements. Begin your work in 2005 and move forward from there.

	2007	2006	2005
Revenues	$	$275,000	$250,000
Expenses	235,000	215,000	
Net income	65,000		52,000
Retained earnings at the beginning of the year			0
Dividends declared during the year		18,000	
Retained earnings at the end of the year	125,000		40,000
Capital stock at the end of the year		75,000	75,000
Liabilities at the end of the year	200,000	190,000	
Assets at the end of the year	415,000		265,000

E2-8. **(Record the effect of transactions on the accounting equation, LO 2, 3, 4)** Show the effect that each transaction described below has on the elements of the accounting equation. Also, specify the type of asset, liability, or owners' equity account that would be affected.

Transaction	Assets	=	Liabilities	+	Shareholders' Equity
Example: Shareholders purchase shares for $10,000	$10,000 + Cash +				$10,000 + Capital stock +
a. Equipment is purchased for $2,000 cash.					
b. $3,000 cash is borrowed from a bank.					
c. Goods are sold to customers for $4,000. The customer will pay in 45 days.					
d. $4,500 cash is paid to employees for work done in the current year.					
e. A cash dividend of $5,000 is paid to the shareholders.					

E2-9.   **(Record the effect of transactions on the accounting equation, LO 2, 3, 4)** Show the effect that each transaction described below has on the elements of the accounting equation. Also, specify the type of asset, liability or owners' equity account that would be affected.

Transaction	Assets	=	Liabilities	+	Partners' Equity
Example: Partners purchase partnership units for $10,000.	$10,000 + Cash +				$10,000 + Partners' equity +
a. The partnership purchases new office furniture for $10,000. The furniture will be paid for in 90 days.					
b. Partners take out a $1,000,000 mortgage on a building that was purchased several years ago.					
c. Services are sold for $15,000. The customer paid in cash.					
d. $6,000 cash is paid to employees for work done last year.					
e. A client makes a $10,000 deposit for work that will be done next year.					
f. Last year, the partnership purchased liability insurance. The policy cost $12,000 and covered three years beginning at the start of the current year. The policy was paid for in cash.					

E2-10.   **(Classification of cash flows, LO 1)** During 2004 Argentia Ltd. entered into the following cash transactions. Classify each transaction as operating, financing or investing cash flows. Explain your thinking in each case.

    a.   Inventory is purchased for $100,000.

    b.   Dividends of $75,000 are paid to shareholders.

c. A $500,000 loan is received from the bank.

d. Office furniture is purchased for $20,000 to furnish the president's office.

e. Four delivery trucks are sold for $22,500.

f. Common shares are sold to investors for $500,000.

E2-11. **(Classification of cash flows, LO 1)** During 2005 Argyle & Chester, a partnership, entered into the following cash transactions. Classify each transaction as an operating, financing, or investing cash flow. Explain your thinking in each case.

a. Payments of $30,000 are received from clients.

b. The two partners take drawings of $10,000 each for personal expenses.

c. Land is purchased for $250,000 as the site of Argyle & Chester's new office building.

d. The $3,000 phone bill is paid.

e. Insurance for the next two years costing $8,000 is purchased.

f. Old computer equipment is sold for $7,500.

E2-12. **(Calculation of ratios, LO 4, 7)** Below is a simplified balance sheet for Summerside Inc. (Summerside):

Summerside Inc.
Balance Sheet
As at December 31, 2005

Assets		Liabilities and shareholders' equity	
Current assets	$1,250,000	Current liabilities	$ 750,000
Non-current assets	8,250,000	Non-current liabilities	4,500,000
		Shareholders' equity	4,250,000
Total assets	$9,500,000		$9,500,000

Required:

Calculate the following on December 31, 2005, using Summerside's balance sheet. Provide an explanation for each:

a. working capital

b. current ratio

c. debt-to-equity ratio

E2-13. **(Calculation of ratios, LO 4, 7)** Consider the following alphabetic list of income statement accounts for Sussex Ltd. (Sussex) for the year ended September 30, 2006:

Cost of sales	$212,000
General and administrative expenses	82,000
Income tax expense	54,000
Interest expense	45,000
Revenue	760,000
Selling expenses	70,000
Wage expense	195,000

Required:

a. Prepare an income statement for Sussex for the year ended September 30, 2006.

b. What is net income for the year?

c. What is Sussex' gross margin for 2006?

d. What is Sussex' gross margin percentage for 2006?

E2-14. **(Prepare income statements using cash and accrual accounting, LO 1, 6)** You have been provided the following information about Kedgwick Company, a small proprietorship, as of the end of its first year of operations. Assume that all supplies were used up at year end.

Cash collected from customers	$8,000
Amounts owing from customers	1,200
Amounts paid to suppliers	4,700
Amounts owing to suppliers	1,100

Required:

Calculate income on the cash basis and on the accrual basis for Kedgwick Company. Explain why the cash basis and the accrual basis result in different amounts of income.

E2-15. **(Prepare income statements using cash and accrual accounting, LO 1, 6)** You have been provided the following information about Lunenberg Ltd. (Lunenberg) as of the end of its first year of operations. Lunenberg began business just over a year ago.

Cash collected from customers	$118,000
Amounts owing from customers	11,200
Amounts paid to suppliers for business supplies	34,700
Amounts owing to suppliers for business supplies	8,100
Business supplies on hand at the end of the year	2,800
Amounts paid to employees for work done	17,500
Amounts owing to employees for work done	2,200
Advances paid to employees for work that will be done in the future	1,000
Amortization of assets	4,000
Income taxes	7,500

Required:

Calculate income on the cash basis and on the accrual basis of accounting for Lunenberg. Explain why the cash basis and the accrual basis result in different amounts of income.

E2-16. **(Prepare a personal balance sheet, LO 1, 3, 4, 5)** Make a list of your personal assets and liabilities and try to organize them into an accounting balance sheet format. Assign values to the assets and the liabilities. Answer the following questions about your balance sheet:
a. How did you determine your equity in your assets?
b. How did you decide what amount to assign to each asset and liability?
c. Did you include your education among your assets? Why or why not? If your personal balance sheet was being prepared according to GAAP, would your education be included as an asset? Explain.

Problems

P2-1. **(Complete a set of financial statements, LO 1, 2, 4)** Below are three years of balance sheets, income statements, and statements of retained earnings for Auburndale Ltd.

Required:
a. Replace the missing information in the shaded areas with the appropriate amount. Begin your analysis in 2004 and work forward.
b. If you were a banker, would you lend Auburndale Ltd. $5,000,000? Explain your answer. What additional information would you require to make your decision whether to lend? Explain.

Auburndale Ltd.
Statements of Retained Earnings
For the Year Ended December 31
(in thousands of dollars)

	2006	2005	2004
Retained Earnings, Beginning of Year	$	$	$11,900
Net income			
Dividends	262	262	
Retained Earnings, End of year	$	$	**$14,694**

Auburndale Ltd.
Balance Sheets
As at December 31
(in thousands of dollars)

	2006	2005	2004
Current Assets			
Cash	$	$	$ 952
Accounts Receivable	7,378	6,664	5,950
Inventory	13,090	10,472	9,520
Prepaid Assets	714	238	476
Total Current Assets		21,278	
Land	2,975	2,975	2,975
Plant and Equipment	17,850	16,422	14,518
Accumulated Amortization	(8,806)	(7,378)	(6,426)
Other Assets	1,095	1,950	2,437
Total Non-Current Assets		13,969	
Total Assets	$	$35,247	$
Current Liabilities			
Accounts Payable	$ 7,140	$ 6,901	$ 5,474
Bank Loan Payable	795	2,056	952
Total Current Liabilities	7,935		6,426
Mortgage Payable	4,046	4,760	5,236
Total Liabilities		13,717	11,662
Shareholders' Equity			
Common Shares			4,046
Retained Earnings			14,694
Total Shareholders' Equity	24,695		18,740
Total Liabilities and Shareholders' Equity	$	$	$

Auburndale Ltd.
Income Statements
For the Year Ended December 31
(in thousands of dollars)

	2006	2005	2004
Sales Revenue	$	$53,550	$48,790
Cost of Goods Sold	41,650	36,890	
Gross Margin	17,850		15,470
Expenses			
Selling	7,378	6,545	
Administrative	3,570	3,332	3,213
Amortization	1,547	1,190	952
Interest	595	904	952
Total Expenses			11,067
Income Before Income Taxes		4,689	4,403
Income Taxes	1,809	1,637	
Net Income	$	$	$3,032

P2-2. **(Complete a set of financial statements, LO 1, 2, 4)** Following are three years of balance sheets, income statements, and statements of retained earnings for Alymer Ltd.

Required:

a. Replace the missing information in the shaded areas with the appropriate amount. Begin your analysis in 2004 and work forward.

b. If you were a banker, would you lend Alymer Ltd. $5,000,000? Explain your answer. What additional information would you require to make your decision whether to lend? Explain.

Alymer Ltd.
Balance Sheets
As at December 31
(in thousands of dollars)

	2006	2005	2004
Current Assets			
Cash	$ 1,000	$ 800	$ 400
Accounts Receivable	3,100	2,800	
Inventory		4,400	4,000
Prepaid Assets	300	100	200
			7,100
Long-Lived Assets			
Land	1,250	1,250	1,250
Plant and Equipment	7,500	6,900	
Accumulated Amortization	(3,700)	(3,100)	(2,700)
Goodwill	800	900	1,000
		5,950	6,050
Total Assets	$	$14,050	$13,150
Current Liabilities			
Accounts Payable	$ 3,000	$	$ 2,300
Bank Loan Payable	334	864	
		3,664	3,486
Long-Term Liabilities			
Bonds		2,000	2,200
Shareholders' Equity			
Capital Stock	1,900	1,700	1,700
Retained Earnings	7,716	6,686	
		8,386	7,464
Total Liabilities and Shareholders' Equity	$14,750	$14,050	$

Alymer Ltd.
Income Statements
For the Year Ended December 31
(in thousands of dollars)

	2006	2005	2004
Sales Revenue	$25,000	$22,500	$
Cost of Goods Sold	17,500		14,000
Gross Margin		6,750	6,000
Expenses			
Selling	3,100	2,750	2,500
Administrative	1,500	1,400	
Amortization	650	500	400
Interest		380	400
	5,600		4,560
Income Before Income Taxes		1,720	1,440
Income Taxes	760	688	576
Net Income	$ 1,140	$	$ 864

Alymer Ltd.
Statement of Retained Earnings
For the Year Ended December 31
(in thousands of dollars)

	2006	2005	2004
Retained Earnings, Beginning of Year	$6,686	$	$5,000
Net income		1,032	
Dividends		110	100
Retained Earnings, End of year	$7,716	$ 6,686	$5,764

P2-3.   **(Record information on a spreadsheet, prepare a balance sheet, LO 1, 2, 5)** Andrea Reed is in her fourth year at a business school in Nova Scotia. Recently Andrea was asked by her brother Dennis to help him prepare a personal balance sheet. Dennis needed the balance sheet because he was applying for a scholarship at a prestigious art school and the school required the information to help it assess Dennis' financial need. Andrea sat down with Dennis to go over his situation and she obtained the following information:

i.   Dennis's bankbooks show that he has $844 in his bank accounts.

ii.   Dennis purchased a used car from his uncle three years ago. He paid $4,500 for the car and he thinks he should be able to continue to use it for another two years.

iii.   Dennis is owed $750 for some decorating he did for a local social group's recent fund-raising party.

iv.   Dennis owes $2,000 to a local bank for a job training program he took a couple of years ago. He must begin to pay back the money once he accepts a full-time job or in five years, whichever comes first.

v.   About six months ago Dennis bought a computer from a local store. The computer cost $1,200 and he paid the seller $700 at the time he purchased it and he must pay $50 a month until the computer is paid for.

vi.   Dennis's personal property such as clothes, books, jewellery, etc., cost him about $6,000.

Required:

a.   Set up a spreadsheet like the one in Table 2-1 on page 41 and record each of the above events into the worksheet. For each entry make sure to state the type of asset, liability, or equity that is affected (cash, accounts receivable, accounts payable, etc.).

b.   Use the information in the spreadsheet to prepare a balance sheet for Dennis.

c.   How do you think the balance sheet would help the art school assess whether Dennis should receive financial assistance?

d.   What additional information do you think the school would want to have before making a decision to offer financial assistance?

P2-4.   **(Record information on a spreadsheet, prepare a balance sheet, LO 1, 2, 5)** In addition to the information provided in Problem 2-3, you also learn the following about Dennis's assets:

i.   Dennis thinks the car could be sold for about $2,200.

ii.   A friend of Dennis recently offered him $1,000 for the computer.

iii.   Dennis is unlikely to receive more than $1,000 for his personal property.

Required:

a.   Revise the spreadsheet that you prepared in Problem 2-3 so that you use the additional information that Dennis provided you about his assets.

b.   Use the revised spreadsheet to prepare a personal balance sheet for Dennis.

c.   Compare your balance sheet with the one you prepared in Problem 2-3. Which do you think would be more useful to the art school in assessing Dennis's need for financial assistance? Explain.

d.   What problems arise when using market values of Dennis's assets instead of the cost? What are some of the benefits of using the cost of the assets? Is the balance sheet prepared using market value information more or less useful than the balance sheet prepared using the cost information?

P2-5. **(Record information on a spreadsheet, prepare a balance sheet, LO 1, 2, 5)** Louis Langer is a dentist with a practice in a small town in Manitoba. Recently, he separated from his wife and they are currently negotiating how they will divide their assets when their divorce proceedings conclude. As part of the process, Louis's lawyer has asked for a balance sheet for his practice. The balance sheet will be used to help value Louis' practice. Louis has asked you to prepare the balance sheet. You gather the following information from Louis:

i.   Louis purchased all his equipment eight years ago when he started his practice. The total cost of all the equipment was $100,000. He expects to replace all the equipment in four years.

ii. He purchased furniture and decorations for his office four years ago for $22,000. He expects the furniture and decorations to last for about ten years.

iii. Patients owe Louis $19,000.

iv. Louis owes various suppliers $12,000 for various goods and services that he used in his practice.

v.   The practice has $4,750 in its bank account.

vi. Louis owes his staff $2,500. This amount will be paid on the next payday in two weeks.

vii. Louis has a bank loan outstanding for $10,000.

viii. Louis keeps various supplies that he needs in his practice. The cost of the supplies he currently has on hand is $750.

Required:

a. Set up a spreadsheet like the one in Table 2-1 on page 41 and record each of the above events into the worksheet. For each entry make sure to state the type of asset, liability, or equity that is affected (cash, accounts receivable, accounts payable, etc.).

b. Use the information in the spreadsheet to prepare a balance sheet for Louis' dental practice.

c. As a judge in this case, how would you use the balance sheet in deciding how to value Louis' practice?

d. What additional information do you think that you as judge might want to have before deciding how to value Louis' practice?

P2-6. **(Record information on a spreadsheet, prepare a balance sheet, LO 1, 2, 5)** In addition to the information provided in Problem 2-5, you also learn the following about Louis's assets:

i.   Louis thinks that if he closed his practice he could sell his list of patients to another dentist for $125,000.

ii. If Louis tried to sell his equipment he would receive about $25,000.

iii. Louis would be unlikely to receive any money if he tried to sell the furniture and decorations.

Required:

a. Revise the spreadsheet that you prepared in Problem P2-5 so that you use the additional information that Louis provided you about his assets.

b. Use the revised spreadsheet to prepare a balance sheet for Louis' dental practice.

c. Compare your balance sheet with the one you prepared in Problem 2-5. Which do you think would be more useful for valuing Louis' practice? Explain.

d. What problems arise when using market values of Louis' assets instead of the cost? What are some of the benefits of using the cost of the assets? Is the balance sheet prepared using market value information more or less useful than the balance sheet prepared using the cost information?

P2-7.   **(Analyze financial information, LO 4, 7)** Below are the income statements and balance sheets for Penticton Inc. (Penticton) for 2005 and 2006:

Penticton Inc.
Balance Sheets
As of December 31

	2006	2005		2006	2005
Assets			**Liabilities and shareholders' equity**		
Cash	$ 5,000	$ 10,000	Bank loan	$ 100,000	$ 75,000
Accounts			Accounts payable	200,000	150,000
receivable	205,000	175,000	Goods to be provided		
Inventory	264,200	225,000	to customers	42,000	35,000
Equipment,			Long-term debt	250,000	150,000
furniture and					
fixtures (net of					
accumulated			**Shareholders' equity**		
amortization)	720,000	680,000	Capital stock	260,000	250,000
Other non-			Retained earnings	417,200	380,000
current assets	75,000	100,000			
			Total liabilities and		
Total assets	$1,269,200	$1,190,000	shareholders' equity	$1,269,200	$1,190,000

Penticton Inc.
Income Statements
For the Years Ended December 31

	2006	2005
Revenue	$2,475,000	$1,925,000
Cost of goods sold	1,350,000	1,098,000
Selling, general, and administrative expenses	550,000	495,000
Amortization expense	120,000	100,000
Interest expense	125,000	120,000
Tax expense	132,000	44,800
Net income	$ 198,000	$ 67,200

Required:

a. Calculate the following for Penticton for 2005 and 2006:
   i.   working capital
   ii. current ratio
   iii. debt-to-equity ratio
   iv. gross margin
   v.   gross margin percentage
b. Explain why the amounts you calculated in (a) changed from 2005 to 2006.
c. Comment on Penticton's liquidity position on December 31, 2006. As a prospective lender of money to Penticton, what concerns would you have about its current liquidity position?
d. What could Penticton's management do to improve liquidity?

P2-8. (**Analyze financial information, LO 4, 7**) Below are the summarized income statements and balance sheets for Miramichi Inc. (Miramichi) for 2004 and 2005:

Miramichi Inc.
Balance Sheets
As at December 31

	2005	2004		2005	2004
Assets			**Liabilities and shareholders' equity**		
Cash	$ 15,000	$ 10,000	Bank loan	$ 50,000	$ 35,000
Accounts			Accounts payable	100,000	60,000
receivable	120,000	75,000	Current portion of		
Inventory	170,000	105,000	long-term debt	20,000	15,000
Plant and			Long-term debt	140,000	80,000
equipment (net					
of accumulated			**Shareholders' equity**		
amortization)	348,800	220,000	Capital stock	120,000	100,000
Other non-			Retained earnings	308,800	220,000
current assets	85,000	100,000			
			Total liabilities and		
Total assets	$738,800	$510,000	shareholders' equity	$738,800	$510,000

Miramichi Inc.
Income Statements
For the years ended December 31

	2005	2004
Revenue	$1,225,000	$1,015,000
Cost of goods sold	730,000	595,000
Selling, general and administrative expenses	210,000	175,000
Amortization expense	65,000	48,000
Interest expense	72,000	59,000
Tax expense	59,200	55,200
Net income	$ 88,800	$ 82,800

Required:
   a. Calculate the following for Miramichi for 2004 and 2005:
      i.   working capital
      ii. current ratio
      iii. debt-to-equity ratio
      iv. gross margin
      v.   gross margin percentage
   b. Explain why the amounts you calculated in (a) changed from 2004 to 2005.
   c. Comment on Miramichi's liquidity position on December 31, 2005. As a prospective lender of money to Miramichi, what concerns would you have about its current liquidity position?
   d. What could Miramichi's management do to improve liquidity?

P2-9. (**Understanding the impact of transactions on financial ratios, LO 4, 7**) Victoria Ltd. (Victoria) is a small tool and die manufacturer in British Columbia. Victoria recently obtained financing from a local bank for an expansion of the company's facilities. The agreement with the bank requires that Victoria's current ratio and debt-to-equity ratio be within ranges stated in the agreement. If the ratios fall outside of these ranges Victoria would have to repay the new loans immediately. At this time Victoria has a current ratio of 1.80 (based on current assets of $900,000 and current liabilities of $500,000) and a debt-to-equity ratio of 2 to 1 (based on total liabilities of $2 million and total equity of $1 million). The chief financial officer of Victoria is concerned about the effect a number of transactions scheduled for the last few days of the year will have on the company's current ratio and debt-to-equity ratio.

Required:

Determine the effect that each of the following transactions will have on the current ratio and the debt-to-equity ratio. Calculate what each ratio will be after each transaction takes place and indicate the effect each transaction has on each ratio (increase, decrease, or no effect). Treat each item independently.

	Transaction	Current ratio	Effect of the transaction on the current ratio	Debt-to-equity ratio	Effect of the transaction on the debt-to-equity ratio
	Example: $27,000 owing from customers is collected.	1.80	No effect	2 to 1	No effect
1.	Purchase of equipment for $150,000. The supplier of the equipment must be paid in two years.				
2.	Purchase of inventory for $40,000 cash. The inventory was unsold at the end of the year.				
3.	Sale of capital stock to investors for $300,000 cash.				
4.	Declaration and payment of $100,000 of dividends.				
5.	Repayment of $150,000 on a long-term loan.				
6.	Repayment of $75,000 on a short-term bank loan.				
7.	Dividends of $50,000 are declared and will be paid after the year end. (Once the dividends have been declared they become a liability called Dividends Payable.)				

P2-10. **(Understanding the impact of transactions on financial ratios, LO 4, 7)** Longueuil Ltd. (Longueuil) is a small shirt manufacturer in Québec. Longueuil recently obtained financing from a local bank for an expansion of the company's facilities. The agreement with the bank requires that Longueuil's current ratio and debt-to-equity ratio be within ranges stated in the agreement. If the ratios fall outside of these ranges Longueuil would have to repay the new loans immediately. At this time Longueuil has a current ratio of 2.0 (based on current assets of $700,000 and current liabilities of $350,000) and a debt-to-equity ratio of 1.5 to 1 (based on total liabilities of $900,000 and total equity of $600,000). The chief financial officer of Longueuil is concerned about the effect a number of transactions that will be occurring in the last few days of the year will have on the company's current ratio and debt-to-equity ratio.

Required:

Determine the effect that each of the following transactions will have on the current ratio and the debt-to-equity ratio. Calculate what each ratio will be after each transaction takes place and indicate the effect each transaction has on each ratio (increase, decrease, or no effect). Treat each item independently:

Transaction	Current ratio	Effect of the transaction on the current ratio	Debt-to-equity ratio	Effect of the transaction on the debt-to-equity ratio
Example: $27,000 owing from customers is collected.	2.00	No effect	1.5 to 1	No effect
1. Purchase of equipment for $250,000. The supplier of the equipment must be paid within six months.				
2. Bonuses of $75,000 cash are paid to senior managers.				
3. Sale of capital stock to investors for $100,000 cash.				
4. Declaration and payment of $100,000 of dividends.				
5. A loan of $100,000 from a bank is arranged and the cash received. The loan must be repaid in 18 months.				
6. A short-term bank loan for $50,000 is arranged and the cash received.				
7. Dividends of $50,000 are declared and will be paid after year end. (Once the dividends have been declared they become a liability called Dividends Payable.)				

P2-11. (Prepare an income statement and balance sheet from a list of accounts, LO 4, 5)

You have been provided with the following alphabetical list of accounts for Sudbury Ltd. for 2004. Use the information to prepare an income statement for the year ended December 31, 2004 and balance sheet as of December 31, 2004. You should be able to figure out how to treat accounts that have names that are unfamiliar to you by applying your understanding of the financial statements learned in this chapter. Amounts are in thousands of dollars.

Accounts payable	$ 525	Equipment, furniture and fixtures	$8,000
Accounts receivable	550	Income tax expense	1,500
Accrued liabilities	100	Income taxes payable	75
Accumulated amortization	7,500	Income taxes recoverable from government	45
Advances to employees	25	Interest expense	1,400
Advertising expenses	950	Interest revenue	10
Amortization expense	2,300	Inventory	850
Building	12,000	Investments in the shares of other corporations	1,200
Capital stock	10,000	Land	1,000
Cash	100	Long-term debt (non-current portion)	9,000
Cash revenue	2,250	Mortgage payable (non-current portion)	5,000
Charitable donations made	1,000	Other expense	200
Cost of assets lost in fire	900	Other non-current assets	500
Cost of sales	3,750	Patents	2,000
Credit revenue	14,500	Prepaid assets	20
Current portion of long-term debt	250	Retained earnings at the beginning of the year	7,520
Current portion of mortgage payable	300	Selling expenses	1,350
Deposits from customers	25	Wages expense	2,200
Dividends	250	Wages payable	35

P2-12. **(Prepare an income statement and balance sheet from a list of accounts, LO 4, 5)** You have been provided with the following alphabetical list of accounts for Thaxted Ltd. for 2005. Use the information to prepare an income statement for the year ended December 31, 2005 and balance sheet as of December 31, 2005. You should be able to figure out how to treat accounts that have names that are unfamiliar to you by applying your understanding of the financial statements learned in this chapter. Amounts are in thousands of dollars.

Accounts payable	$ 110	Interest expense	105
Accounts receivable	200	Interest revenue	22
Accrued liabilities	46	Inventory	300
Accumulated amortization	750	Loans to shareholders	25
Advertising expenses	75	Long-term debt (non-current portion)	1,250
Amortization expense	210	Marketable securities	250
Capital assets	2,000	Other current assets	10
Capital stock	1,500	Other expenses	50
Cash	25	Other non-current assets	75
Cost of closing west coast division	75	Research costs	950
Cost of sales	950	Retained earnings at the beginning of the year	7,520
Current portion of long-term debt	50	Revenue from sale of products	1,750
Deposits and prepaid assets	52	Revenue from sale of services	1,250
Deposits from customers	25	Selling, general, and administrative expenses	275
Dividends	25	Trademarks and intellectual property	1,200
Income taxes payable	20	Wages expense	420
Income taxes recoverable from government	31	Wages payable	15

P2-13. **(Evaluate the format of a balance sheet, LO 1, 5)** Look at the balance sheet of Dylex Ltd. in Panel A of Exhibit 2-2 (page 62). Redo Dylex Ltd.'s balance sheet in the more traditional format used by MWW. How does your statement differ from the one prepared by the company? Which statement is more informative, the one you prepared or the one the company prepared? Should it make any difference to users how the balance sheet is formatted? Explain.

P2-14. **(Evaluate the format of a balance sheet, LO 1, 5)** Look at the balance sheet of Newfoundland Power Inc. in the Panel B of Exhibit 2-2 (page 62). Redo Newfoundland Power Inc.'s balance sheet in the more traditional format used by MWW. How does your statement differ from the one prepared by the company? Which statement is more informative, the one you prepared or the one the company prepared? Should it make any difference to users how the balance sheet is formatted? Explain.

P2-15. **(Prepare a cash flow statement, LO 5)** The Pas Ltd. was organized on August 1, 2005 with a cash investment of $500,000 by its shareholders. The Pas arranged a mortgage with a local lender for $400,000 and purchased a warehouse for $600,000. During its fiscal year ended July 31, 2006 The Pas collected $325,000 in cash from customers, paid $200,000 in cash for operating expenses, and paid $20,000 in cash dividends to its shareholders.

Required:

a. Classify each of the cash flows described above as operating, investing, or financing.
b. Organize the cash flows into a cash flow statement.
c. Explain what your cash flow statement tells you that an income statement does not.

P2-16. **(Prepare a cash flow statement, LO 5)** Markham Ltd. was organized on September 1, 2004 with a cash investment of $700,000 by its shareholders. Markham arranged a long-term loan with a local bank for $500,000 and purchased a small office building for $800,000. During its fiscal year ended August 31, 2005 Markham collected $500,000 in cash from customers, paid $340,000 in cash for operating expenses, and paid $40,000 in cash dividends to its shareholders.

Required:

    a. Classify each of the cash flows described above as operating, investing, or financing.

    b. Organize the cash flows into a cash flow statement.

    c. Explain what your cash flow statement tells you that an income statement does not.

P2-17. **(Explain whether and why an expenditure is an asset, LO 3)** For each of the following, explain whether and why each would be considered:

    a. An asset by a non-accountant (use your intuition and judgment to decide whether the item in question should be considered an asset).

    b. An asset according to GAAP (use the GAAP criteria that were discussed in the chapter).

        i.   A large grocery store purchases land adjacent to the store for $300,000 so that it can expand its parking lot.

        ii. A student has paid university tuition totalling $15,000 to study business. The student plans to become a professional accountant in two years and hopes to open his own accounting practice within five years.

        iii. A trucking company regularly changes the oil in its trucks to ensure that they operate efficiently and that they last their full expected lives.

        iv. A fast food chain's brand name is known around the world. The chain has invested heavily over the years in making its restaurants popular for people by advertising its food and restaurants.

        v. A major retailer repeatedly is found to have the most satisfied customers in its industry in surveys conducted by independent market research companies.

P2-18. **(Explain whether and why an expenditure is an asset, LO 3)** For each of the following, explain whether and why each would be considered:

    a. An asset by a non-accountant (use your intuition and judgment to decide whether the item in question should be considered an asset).

    b. An asset according to GAAP (use the GAAP criteria that were discussed in the chapter).

        i.   An auto parts manufacturer spends $200,000 to clear land to prepare it for construction of a new factory.

        ii. A company that operates call centres spends over $1 million per year providing training for staff so that they can provide informed and courteous service to people contacted.

        iii. A metal fabricating shop is owed $25,000 by one of its customers. The customer recently filed for bankruptcy because it was unable to pay its debts.

        iv. A popular newsmagazine has a list of current and past subscribers.

        v. A major news organization has an internationally renowned team of journalists and broadcasters.

P2-19. (Classify the effect of economic events on income on the cash and accrual bases, LO 3, 6) Indicate whether each of the following events would be included in a calculation of net income on the cash basis, the accrual basis, or both:

Economic Event	Net income on the cash basis	Net income on the accrual basis
Example: An entity sells merchandise for cash.	Yes	Yes
a. An entity sells merchandise on credit.		
b. An entity collects cash for goods that were sold in a previous period.		
c. Inventory that was paid for in a previous period is sold in the current period.		
d. Inventory is paid for and sold in the current period.		
e. Inventory is purchased and paid for in the current period but is unsold as of the year end.		
f. A delivery vehicle is amortized.		

P2-20. (Classify the effect of economic events on income on the cash and accrual bases, LO 3, 6) Indicate whether each of the following events would be included in a calculation of net income on the cash basis, the accrual basis, or both:

Economic Event	Net income on the cash basis	Net income on the accrual basis
Example: An entity sells merchandise for cash.	Yes	Yes
a. An entity receives a deposit from a customer for services that will be provided in the future.		
b. An entity provides services to a customer in the current period who paid in a previous period.		
c. An advance is paid to an employee for work she will do in the future.		
d. Supplies that were paid for in a previous period are used in the current period to provide services to a customer.		
e. Supplies are bought, paid for, and used in the current period to provide services to a customer.		

P2-21. (Prepare balance sheets using different asset values, LO 5) In Chapter 1 we asked you to imagine you were a student needing insurance on your apartment and examined different ways of valuing the contents of the apartment. We identified three different ways of valuing the contents of the apartment. Table 1-4 from Chapter 1 is reproduced next. All the items on the list are owned by you, except for the appliances, which are owned by the building.

Inventory of Apartment Contents

Item	What it cost	What it would cost to replace	What it could be sold for
Television	$ 500	$ 650	$ 225
Computer	1,900	1,500	700
Furniture	1,200	1,350	900
Books	750	875	300
Clothes	1,600	1,950	1,000
Stereo	900	1,100	700
Jewellery	500	625	300
Appliances	2,000	2,600	1,400
Art	300	300	200
Other	1,000	1,200	750
Total	$10,650	$12,150	$6,475

In addition to the above, the following information is available:

Item	Amount
Student loans	$7,500
Loans from parents	3,000
Cash in bank	1,100
Owing from employer	800

Required:

a. Prepare three separate balance sheets using the information in each column above. Make sure to include the "other information" in each balance sheet.
b. Explain the benefits and limitations of each balance sheet to the people who might use them. Make sure to discuss specific entities that might use each balance sheet.
c. Which balance sheet do you think would be appropriate under GAAP?
d. Which balance sheet do you think is best? Explain.

Using Financial Statements

Anderson Exploration Ltd.

Anderson Exploration Ltd. (Anderson Exploration) is a senior Canadian oil and gas producer based in Calgary, Alberta. The company evolved from a program of oil and gas exploration, acquisition, and development commenced by Mr. J.C. Anderson in 1968. Anderson Exploration became a public company in 1988. The company operates exclusively in western and northern Canada and is heavily leveraged to natural gas, with 66% of its reserves and 72% of its production made up of natural gas. Until October 2001 the common shares of the Company were widely held and traded on The Toronto Stock Exchange. Effective October 15, 2001 Devon Energy Corporation acquired the outstanding shares of Anderson Exploration Ltd. for Cdn$40.00 per share in cash.[4]

Anderson Exploration's consolidated balance sheets, statements of earnings, retained earnings, and cash flows, along with some extracts from the notes to the financial statements, are provided in Exhibit 2-3. Use this information to respond to questions FS2-1 to FS2-9.

FS2-1. Examine Anderson Exploration's balance sheet and confirm that the accounting equation equality holds (Assets = Liabilities + Owners' Equity).

FS2-2. What is Anderson Exploration's year end?

FS2-3. Examine Anderson Exploration's statement of earnings. Does the statement give you information about the different ways the company makes its money? Explain.

FS2-4. Find the following information in Anderson Exploration's financial statements:
a. Earnings (net income) for the year ended September 30, 2000.
b. Revenue for the year ended September 30, 2000.
c. Operating expenses for the year ended September 30, 2000.
d. Total assets on September 30, 2000.
e. Bank indebtedness on September 30, 2000 (bank indebtedness is the amount of money that is owed to banks).
f. Long-term debt on September 30, 2000.
g. Retained earnings on September 30, 2000.
h. Dividends paid to shareholders during 2000.
i. Cash from operations for 2000. (This is a bit tricky. The line on the statement of cash flow called "cash from operations" is not really cash from operations. You have to look a little farther down on the statement to find it. You might find it helpful to use MWW's cash flow statement as a comparison.)
j. The amount Anderson spent on additions to property, plant, and equipment during 2000.
k. The amount of long-term debt that was retired (paid off) during 1999.
l. The amount of long-term debt that was issued during 2000.
m. The amount of cash raised by selling common shares during 2000.
n. The amount that was spent repurchasing common shares during 2000.
o. What number on the balance sheet does the line on the statement of cash flows called "cash position, end of year" correspond with?

FS2-5. Use Anderson Exploration's financial statement to calculate and answer the following:
a. Working capital for the years ended September 30, 1999 and 2000.
b. Current ratio on September 30, 1999 and 2000.
c. How much did working capital change between the end of fiscal 1999 and the end of fiscal 2000?
d. Debt-to-equity ratio on September 30, 1999 and 2000.
e. Explain why the debt-to-equity ratio changed from the end of fiscal 1999 to the end of fiscal 2000.

FS2-6. Examine the note to Anderson Exploration's financial statements that describes property, plant, and equipment. Describe the different types of property, plant, and equipment assets that the company has.

FS2-7. The note to the financial statement on property, plant, and equipment explains that amount reported on the balance sheet for oil and gas properties includes all the costs incurred exploring for and developing oil and gas properties. What does this information tell you about the value of the oil and gas that Anderson Exploration has available to it in the ground to extract and sell? How useful is this information to an investor who is considering buying shares in Anderson Exploration?

FS2-8. List five questions that you would ask Anderson Exploration's management if you were considering lending money to the company. Your question should pertain to information that you cannot obtain from the financial statements.

FS2-9. Compare Anderson Exploration's balance sheet with MWW's. Describe how the composition of assets differs between the two companies. Given the different industries that these two companies are in, does the difference make sense? Explain. In answering this question it may be helpful for you to calculate on a percentage basis what each asset represents as a portion of total assets.

Exhibit 2-3

Anderson Exploration Ltd. Consolidated Financial Statements

CONSOLIDATED BALANCE SHEETS

SEPTEMBER 30 (stated in millions of dollars)	2000	1999
ASSETS		
Current assets		
Accounts receivable	$ 227.7	$ 125.0
Inventories	17.8	11.2
	245.5	136.2
Property, plant and equipment (note 3)	3,728.1	2,470.0
	$ 3,973.6	$ 2,606.2
LIABILITIES AND SHAREHOLDERS' EQUITY		
Current liabilities		
Bank indebtedness	$ 32.4	$ 14.7
Accounts payable and accrued liabilities	272.9	136.2
Taxes payable	3.2	14.3
Current portion of long term debt	–	0.9
	308.5	166.1
Long term debt (note 4)	1,126.9	545.2
Other credits (note 5)	133.6	136.7
Deferred income taxes	841.1	622.4
	2,410.1	1,470.4
Shareholders' equity		
Share capital (note 6)	905.3	791.1
Retained earnings	658.2	344.7
	1,563.5	1,135.8
	$ 3,973.6	$ 2,606.2

See accompanying notes to consolidated financial statements.

Exhibit 2-3 (continued)

Anderson Exploration Ltd. Consolidated Financial Statements

CONSOLIDATED STATEMENTS OF EARNINGS

YEARS ENDED SEPTEMBER 30 (stated in millions of dollars, except per share amounts)	2000	1999
Revenues		
Oil and gas	$ 1,417.1	$ 770.9
Royalties, net of ARTC of $0.7 million (1999 – $1.5 million)	(291.8)	(125.9)
	1,125.3	645.0
Expenses		
Operating	209.4	153.6
Depletion and depreciation	312.0	260.7
General and administrative	52.9	40.7
Interest (including $58.3 million on long term debt; 1999 – $41.9 million)	58.3	42.5
Future site restoration	18.6	18.5
	651.2	516.0
Earnings from continuing operations before taxes	474.1	129.0
Taxes (note 8)		
Current	7.8	20.5
Deferred	218.1	42.1
	225.9	62.6
Earnings from continuing operations	248.2	66.4
Earnings from discontinued operations (note 2)	65.3	4.0
Earnings	$ 313.5	$ 70.4
Basic earnings per common share		
From continuing operations	$ 1.95	$ 0.54
From discontinued operations	0.51	0.03
	$ 2.46	$ 0.57
Diluted earnings per common share (note 7)		
From continuing operations	$ 1.92	$ 0.54
From discontinued operations	0.51	0.03
	$ 2.43	$ 0.57
Weighted average number of common shares outstanding (millions)	127.4	124.1

See accompanying notes to consolidated financial statements.

CONSOLIDATED STATEMENTS OF RETAINED EARNINGS

YEARS ENDED SEPTEMBER 30 (stated in millions of dollars)	2000	1999
Retained earnings, beginning of year	$ 344.7	$ 274.3
Earnings	313.5	70.4
Retained earnings, end of year	$ 658.2	$ 344.7

See accompanying notes to consolidated financial statements.

Exhibit 2-3 (continued)

Anderson Exploration Ltd. Consolidated Financial Statements

CONSOLIDATED STATEMENTS OF CASH FLOWS

YEARS ENDED SEPTEMBER 30 (stated in millions of dollars, except per share amounts)	2000	1999
Cash provided by (used in):		
Operations		
Earnings from continuing operations	$ 248.2	$ 66.4
Add (deduct) non-cash items:		
Depletion and depreciation	312.0	260.7
Future site restoration	18.6	18.5
Deferred taxes	218.1	42.1
Other	–	(0.1)
Cash flow from continuing operations	796.9	387.6
Cash flow from discontinued operations (note 2)	4.4	8.0
Cash flow from operations	801.3	395.6
Change in deferred revenue	(10.4)	(10.6)
Change in non-cash working capital related to:		
– continuing operations (note 9)	(17.6)	21.1
– discontinued operations (notes 2 and 9)	0.9	1.0
	774.2	407.1
Investments		
Additions to property, plant and equipment	(679.8)	(293.4)
Proceeds on disposition of property, plant and equipment	10.4	9.6
Acquisition of Ulster Petroleums Ltd. (note 2)	(550.1)	–
Proceeds on disposition of Federated Pipe Lines Ltd. (note 2)	103.3	–
Site restoration expenditures	(10.1)	(6.3)
Change in non-cash working capital related to investments (note 9)	(2.0)	4.8
Discontinued operations (notes 2 and 9)	(0.2)	(8.0)
	(1,128.5)	(293.3)
Financing		
Increase (decrease) in long term debt	331.7	(150.3)
Issue of common shares	49.4	42.7
Repurchase of common shares	(38.7)	–
Discontinued operations (note 2)	(5.8)	–
	336.6	(107.6)
Increase (decrease) in cash	(17.7)	6.2
Cash position, beginning of year	(14.7)	(20.9)
Cash position, end of year	$ (32.4)	$ (14.7)
Basic cash flow from operations per common share		
From continuing operations	$ 6.26	$ 3.13
From discontinued operations	0.03	0.06
	$ 6.29	$ 3.19
Diluted cash flow from operations per common share (note 7)		
From continuing operations	$ 6.17	$ 3.12
From discontinued operations	0.03	0.06
	$ 6.20	$ 3.18

See accompanying notes to consolidated financial statements.

Cash position includes cash net of current bank indebtedness. Current bank indebtedness includes outstanding cheques.

The Ulster acquisition amount represents the value assigned to property, plant and equipment of $1,000.7 million less share consideration of $103.5 million and debt and non-cash working capital deficiency of $347.1 million assumed from Ulster. The Federated disposition amount represents net proceeds of $102.5 million plus bank indebtedness of $0.8 million assumed by the purchaser.

Exhibit 2-3 (continued)

Anderson Exploration Ltd. Consolidated Financial Statements

3. PROPERTY, PLANT AND EQUIPMENT

	2000		1999	
	Cost	Accumulated depletion and depreciation	Cost	Accumulated depletion and depreciation
Oil and gas properties, including plant and production equipment	$ 6,440.0	$ (2,743.1)	$ 4,777.7	$ (2,436.1)
Buildings, land and other	83.9	(52.7)	73.4	(47.8)
Discontinued operations (note 2)	–	–	155.9	(53.1)
	$ 6,523.9	$ (2,795.8)	$ 5,007.0	$ (2,537.0)
Net book value		$ 3,728.1		$ 2,470.0

At September 30, 2000, oil and gas properties included $375.0 million (1999 – $179.0 million) relating to unproved properties which have been excluded from depletion and depreciation calculations. Future development costs of proven undeveloped reserves of $340.3 million (1999 – $301.7 million) are included in depletion and depreciation calculations.

At the balance sheet dates, the Company had substantial surpluses in its ceiling tests using balance sheet date prices.

(c) PROPERTY, PLANT AND EQUIPMENT

The Company follows the full cost method of accounting for oil and gas properties. Under this method, all costs relative to the exploration for and development of oil and gas reserves are capitalized into cost centres on a country by country basis. Capitalized costs include lease acquisitions, geological and geophysical costs, lease rentals on non-producing properties, costs of drilling productive and non-productive wells and plant and production equipment costs. General and administrative costs are not capitalized, except to the extent of the Company's working interest in operated capital expenditure programs to which overhead fees have been charged under standard industry operating agreements. Overhead fees are not charged on 100 percent owned projects. Proceeds received from disposals of oil and gas properties and equipment are credited against capitalized costs unless the disposal would alter the rate of depletion and depreciation by more than 20 percent, in which case a gain or loss on disposal is recorded.

■ Analyzing Mark's Work Wearhouse

Read the annual report provided in Appendix A (page A-000), including the financial statements, notes, and management discussion and analysis and discuss the following questions. (Instructors may supplement the MWW annual report with one they obtain themselves directly from an alternative company or download from the Internet at www.sedar.com.)

M2-1. What is the purpose of the annual report?

M2-2. How much credibility do you attach to the financial statements and related notes? Explain. What about the management discussion and analysis?

M2-3. What do the financial statements tell you? Explain. How would you use the information contained in the statements for decision making? What additional information would you want?

M2-4. Among the "Other assets" of $1,056,000 that MWW reports on its balance sheet is $583,000 for "Store opening expenses" (see Note 6 of the financial statements in Appendix A). The nature of the store opening expenses is explained in Note 1-I of the financial statements. Store opening expenses could include staff training, advertising and promotion of new stores, and similar costs. Store opening costs do not include the cost of inventory and capital assets.

Required:

Do you think that store opening expenses represents an asset? Explain. Consider the definition of an asset and GAAP's criteria for assets in your answer, and also express your opinion.

M2-5. Find the following amounts in MWW's financial statements:
  a. Accounts receivable on January 27, 2001.
  b. The amount of capital assets on January 27, 2001.
  c. Total assets on January 27, 2001.
  d. Income taxes payable on January 27, 2001.
  e. Deferred gains on January 27, 2001.
  f. Retained earnings on January 27, 2001.
  g. Sales during the year ended January 27, 2001.
  h. Total occupancy costs for the year ended January 27, 2001.
  i. Front-line personnel, advertising, and other expenses during the year ended January 27, 2001.
  j. Total interest expense for the year ended January 27, 2001.
  k. Net earnings for the year ended January 27, 2001.

Endnotes

1. Summarized from Dale L. Flesher and Tonya K. Flesher, "Ivar Kreuger's Contribution to U.S. Financial Reporting," *The Accounting Review*, Vol. 61 (July 1986), p. 421.

2. Extracted from Loblaw Companies Ltd.'s 2000 annual report.

3. Panel A extracted from Dylex Ltd.'s 2000 annual report. Panel B extracted from Newfoundland Power Inc.'s 2000 annual report.

4. Extracted from Anderson Exploration Ltd.'s 2000 annual report.

Chapter 3

The Accounting Cycle

Chapter Outline

Learning Objectives

After studying the material in this chapter you will be able to:

LO 1. Describe the purpose and nature of accounting information systems and the accounting cycle.

LO 2. Use an accounting equation spreadsheet to record transactions and economic events, and prepare balance sheets, income statements, and statements of retained earnings.

LO 3. Record economic events and transactions using journal entries and debits and credits.

LO 4. Discuss how financial statements are affected by how the accounting for transactions and economic events is done.

LO 5. Differentiate between the different types of adjusting journal entries and understand their purpose.

LO 6. Explain the purpose of closing journal entries and describe how to prepare them.

Introduction

In Chapter 1 we became familiar with financial statements and began exploring some of the steps for recording accounting data and preparing financial statements. In this chapter we will examine in more detail how transactions and other economic events are recorded in an accounting system, and how those raw data are organized, processed, and converted into information that is useful to stakeholders.

The recording and processing aspect of accounting is crucial for entities. It is the recording and processing that allows preparation of the information needed by managers and stakeholders. Consider all the activities that take place in an MWW store—merchandise is purchased by customers, wages are earned by salespeople, utilities are consumed, goods are returned and exchanged, and so on. MWW's accounting system must gather information from hundreds of stores across Canada and account for countless transactions each year. All of that information gets synthesized and summarized in the company's financial statements.

Procedures for recording and processing accounting data are the heart and soul of many accounting courses. However, this focus misses the forest for the trees. Learning accounting procedures is useful and, if you decide to pursue a career in accounting, essential. But to understand financial statements and other accounting information you must do more than simply learn the procedures. And that is important for accountants and non-accountants alike. As historian Diane Ravitch put it, "The person who knows HOW will always have a job. The person who knows WHY will always be his boss." A bookkeeper knows "how," but an accountant or sophisticated user of financial statements knows "why."

As you study the accounting cycle in this chapter, remember that you are learning tools that will help you become a sophisticated user of accounting information and, if it is your career goal, a capable accounting professional. It is easy to focus on the procedural side of accounting because, frankly, accounting procedures are the easy part—once you master the basic rules. (This is not to say that learning accounting procedures is easy. It is hard work and often challenging.) Focusing on accounting procedures is attractive because there is little judgment, analysis, and evaluation required. Once you know the rules, you follow the recipe and presto...you have the "one right answer." Unfortunately, just focussing on procedures ignores the judgment that is required to decide how *to apply* the rules. In other words, a bookkeeper will be told how to record any out of the ordinary transaction or economic event. The accountant must understand the circumstances to *decide* how.

In the main body of this chapter a "short-cut" approach is used to explain the accounting cycle. This approach will show you the "how" of accounting and provide you with the necessary tools to understand accounting and work through the material in the rest of the book. For the reader who requires a more in-depth discussion of the accounting cycle, the appendix to this chapter on pages 146–156 provides full coverage.

Double-Entry Bookkeeping

Accounting and record keeping have been with us for thousands of years. There has been a need for record keeping ever since people began accumulating large amounts of wealth and had to hire people to help look after it, ever since governments began collecting taxes, and ever since people began entering into transactions that were not initiated and completed at the same time. One of the earliest reasons for keeping records was for control—simply keeping track of what was going on. For example, when a person accumulated a large amount of wealth it was sometimes necessary to hire other people to help look after the wealth. However, the person doing the hiring needed to ensure that the people looking after the wealth were accountable for what happened to it. The result was the development of **stewardship accounting**. Stewardship accounting provides the owners of assets with information about how those responsible for looking after the assets have carried out their responsibilities.

Stewardship is still one of the important uses of accounting information today. Many corporations are managed by people who do not own all the shares of the corporation. For example, most of the shares of MWW are owned by public investors who do not have access to the financial records of the company. As a result there is a need for the managers (the stewards) to provide information to the shareholders (the owners) about how they have managed the company.

As business became more complex the demands on the record-keeping systems increased. A very important step in the evolution of modern accounting was the development of **double-entry bookkeeping**. In the double-entry system each transaction or economic event is recorded in two places in the accounts. Recall that this was what we did when we recorded transactions for Tamara's Painting Business in Chapter 2. The effect of each transaction had to be recorded in two places so that the accounting equation held.

Double-entry bookkeeping was first described by Luca Paciolo, a Franciscan monk in Venice, who published the first bookkeeping text, the *Summa*, in 1494. The double-entry system was in use before Paciolo published his work, but the *Summa* made the method known to the world. What is truly remarkable is that this system of recording and organizing accounts has remained essentially unchanged for over 500 years. Though accounting issues have grown more complex over the years, the nature of the double-entry system has remained much the same.

www.acaus.org/history
Accounting History

The double-entry system provides a safeguard against errors because an error would be detected if the accounting equation were out of balance. Historian A. C. Littleton argues that the true value of the double-entry system is that it allows separation of revenue and capital accounts. This makes it possible for users of the information to see the performance of an entity and for owners to see the amount of capital they have in the entity.[1] In other words, the double-entry system permits the calculation of profit.

Question for Consideration

Explain why a record-keeping or accounting system is necessary when people enter into transactions that are not initiated and completed at the same time. In other words, why is it important to keep records if you owe or are owed money, goods, or services?

Answer: Record keeping and accounting become important when transactions are not initiated and completed at the same time because it is necessary to know whom you owe or who owes you money, goods, or services. Without records it would be easy to lose track of what an entity owes and is owed.

The Accounting Cycle

The **accounting cycle** is the process by which data about economic events are entered into an accounting system, processed, organized, and used to produce information, such as financial statements. An accounting system is very important because without processing and organizing it would be very difficult for anyone to understand and use the data. If Tamara of Tamara's Painting Business simply placed receipts and invoices into a shoebox each time a transaction took place, she would find it difficult to assess the performance of her business or examine its financial position. The spreadsheet we used in Chapter 2 for Tamara's Painting Business (see Table 2-1 on page 41) is a simple accounting system.

Suppose you wanted to track the amount of money you spent in a month and how you spent it. Each time you spend money you get a receipt and put it in an envelope. At the end of the month you have an envelope stuffed with 64 receipts. You cannot determine the amount of money you spent or how you spent it until you classify the receipts by type of spending—entertainment, meals, clothing, transportation, etc.—and determine the amount that was spent in each category. The data do not become useful until processed and organized into a useful format. The process of organizing the information in your receipts represents a simple accounting system. Even a chequebook represents an accounting system because it allows you to keep track of whom you paid, what you paid, and how much money you have.

Figure 3-1 provides a schematic overview of the role of an accounting system in capturing raw data, processing it, and producing financial statements and other financial information. Let's look at each step of the process. Economic events occur around an entity continuously. Some economic events are transactions the entity enters into with others, such as buying and selling assets, incurring and settling liabilities, raising capital, and supplying its goods and services to clients and customers and incurring the costs of doing so. Many economic events affect an entity but are not the result of transactions involving the entity. For example, decisions by competitors and government, technological changes, and economic conditions all have economic effects on an entity.

An accounting system is designed to capture economic events that affect the entity. However, as shown in Figure 3-1, not all economic events are captured by the accounting system. An entity's managers decide which economic events and transactions will be captured by the accounting system, based on the information the managers want the system to produce.

In Canada financial reporting by most entities is based on transactions that have actually occurred. Amounts recorded in these accounting systems tend to be the transaction values. This means that if a piece of land is purchased for $2,000,000, the land is recorded in the accounting system at $2,000,000 and remains at that amount for as long as it is owned by the entity. Economic events that the accounting system is not designed to capture are ignored. For example, the accounting systems of most Canadian entities would not reflect an increase in the value of land. However, an accounting system does not have to be limited in this way. The designers of the accounting system can include and exclude any economic events that affect the entity. The key is for the accounting system to meet the decision-making needs of the users and the reporting requirements of the entity.

Figure 3-1

Overview of an Accounting System

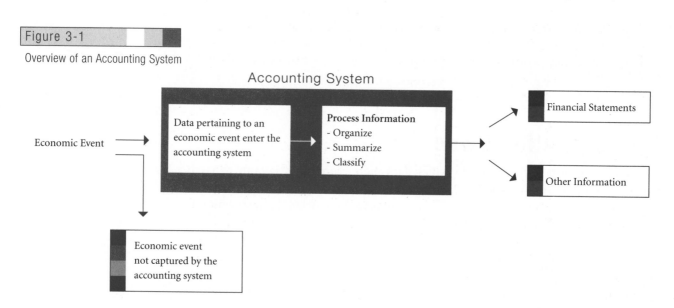

An economic event that is relevant to an entity must be physically entered into the accounting system in some way. An accounting system does not capture data automatically. Each sale or purchase, payment or collection, and change in the value of an asset must be recorded. Once entered into the accounting system, the data are processed so that useful information can be produced. Processing involves organizing, classifying, and summarizing the data into a useful form.

An accounting system operates in a way that is similar to the editorial process of a newspaper. (Figure 3-2 shows a schematic overview of the newspaper editorial process.) Each day the editors of the newspaper assign reporters to cover stories. Many newsworthy events take place in the world each day and it is not possible to cover all the stories or report all the stories in the newspaper. A newspaper will cover the stories that the editors think are most relevant to its readers. If a story is not covered, it cannot appear in the newspaper.

The newspaper's processing of the stories it collects involves editing them, placing them on a particular page, writing headlines, and so on. Readers expect a newspaper to be organized in a rational, predictable way. It would be much more difficult for a reader to use the newspaper efficiently and effectively if sports, business, and international news were spread randomly throughout the newspaper.

You can think of a newspaper as a general purpose report. All people who buy the newspaper get the same paper regardless of their interests or information needs. The newspaper is designed for a wide range of different readers. However, newspapers can also provide special purpose reports by using the Internet to allow readers to "build their own papers." Readers decide which topics are of particular interest to them and the newspaper sends them e-mail reports that are tailored to their needs.

The fact that accounting systems do not capture all economic events that affect the entity (and newspapers do not report all newsworthy stories) highlights a very important point. Financial statements cannot give a complete picture of the entity, just as newspapers cannot give a complete picture of the world. After all, a newspaper cannot report on a city council debate if no reporter covered it. Financial statements can report only information that is entered into the accounting system. Therefore, if the accounting system does not gather information on the current market value of land, that information cannot be presented in the financial statement. This reinforces the point made in Chapter 2 that financial statements are a window (but only *one* window) on an entity.

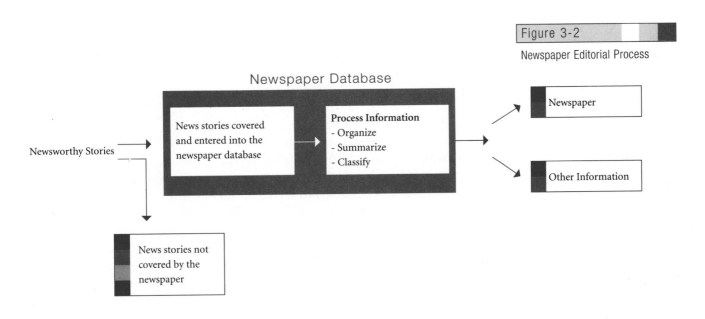

Figure 3-2

Newspaper Editorial Process

Devices for Doing Accounting

We will use two devices to show the effect of transactions and economic events on financial statements. Both devices will be used throughout the book to show the effect economic events have on the accounting information of an entity. (The appendix on page 146 presents an expanded description of how data are recorded and processed, and how financial statements are prepared.)

The first device is the *accounting equation spreadsheet* that was introduced in Chapter 2 (see page 39). The spreadsheet captures the full accounting cycle in an easy-to-use way, and preparation of financial statements is straightforward. A spreadsheet is not very practical for an entity that has hundreds or thousands or even millions of transactions in a year, and hundreds or thousands of different types of asset, liability, and equity accounts. Nonetheless, it is a convenient device for learning accounting.

The second device is **journal entries**. Journal entries are used *in practice* to enter information about economic events into the accounting system. Whenever an economic event or transaction occurs that is to be entered into the accounting system, a journal entry is made. We will use journal entries because they summarize the effect of an economic event in a compact and concise way that makes it easy to see and understand the effect of the event on the financial statements.

For any economic event that is to be entered into an accounting system, no matter what device is used, it is necessary to determine the following:

1. Which elements of the accounting equation are affected—assets, liabilities, and/or owners' equity, including revenues and expenses?

2. Which specific asset, liability, owners' equity, revenue, and expense accounts have been affected?

3. How are the accounts affected—that is, does the amount in each account increase or decrease?

4. By how much has each specific asset, liability, owners' equity, revenue, and expense account increased or decreased?

By answering these questions we will ensure that economic events are properly recorded in the accounting system. We answered these questions implicitly in Chapter 2 when we examined Tamara's Painting Business. Now we will consider them explicitly.

The Accounting Equation Spreadsheet

The accounting equation spreadsheet was introduced in Chapter 2 when we recorded events for Tamara's Painting Business. In that situation the spreadsheet was very simple: we classified economic events by their effect on the broad categories of assets, liabilities, and owners' equity. The format introduced in Chapter 2 was:

$$\text{Assets} \quad = \quad \text{Liabilities} \quad + \quad \text{Owners' Equity}$$

In practice, asset, liability, and owners' equity are divided into separate categories called accounts to reflect an entity's different types of assets, liabilities, and owners' equity. Instead of having a single column for assets, the assets column is divided into categories such as Cash, Accounts Receivable, Inventory, Furniture, Land, and any other assets that the managers would like identified specifically. The number and type of separate accounts that an entity has are determined by the information managers want to have in their accounting system. The division of assets, liabilities, and owners' equity into a larger number of accounts makes more detailed information available. The cost of having more accounts is that the accounting system may be more complicated and more costly to set up and run.

Let's use the accounting equation spreadsheet in a realistic business setting. In June 2004 two friends from business school, Filomena and Teresa, decide to open a small restaurant near their school campus. The friends think that the variety of food available to students and faculty on campus is limited and they believe their restaurant will be successful by offering large portions of good quality, fresh food at reasonable prices.

Filomena and Teresa develop a business plan and set to work opening their restaurant. They will use July and August to ready the restaurant and will open for business on September 1. Filomena and Teresa decide that their restaurant's accounting system will be designed to provide the information they need to prepare tax returns and to evaluate the performance of the restaurant. Thus the accounting system will process mainly transactional information and historical costs.

The accounting equation spreadsheet that will be used for this example is:

	Assets					=	Liabilities		+	Shareholders' Equity	
Transaction	Cash	Accounts Receivable	Food, Drinks, and Supplies Inventory	Prepaid Rent	Renovations, Equipment, and Furniture		Bank Loan	Accounts Payable		Capital Stock	Retained Earnings
Balance before transaction											
Transaction											
Balance after transaction											

The very top line of the spreadsheet states the accounting equation in the familiar format, with the difference that owners' equity has been replaced by shareholders' equity. This is because Filomena and Teresa are going to operate their restaurant as a corporation, and as you'll recall from Chapter 2 the owners of a corporation are called shareholders.

Under each of the accounting equation categories the different asset, liability, and shareholders' equity accounts are shown. These accounts are used because they are the ones relevant to Filomena and Teresa. When a transaction or economic event affects an account, the dollar amount will be placed in that account's column. (An **account** is a category of asset, liability, or owners' equity. Each column in an accounting equation spreadsheet represents an account.) This format will be used to discuss each transaction and economic event in the example.

At this stage of the discussion the income statement accounts are not shown. Revenue and expense transactions will be included in the retained earnings account at first. The income statement details will be shown later in the example.

To record transactions in the spreadsheet we'll follow these procedures:

- The row just under the account headings shows the balance in each account before the transaction being discussed is recorded in the spreadsheet.

- The transaction under discussion will be recorded in the next row and given a number for easy reference.

- The final row will give the balance in each account after the transaction is recorded. This row is the sum of the beginning balance and the current transaction.

- The amounts in the "balance after transaction" row are carried forward to the next transaction as the amounts in the "balance before transaction" row.

Now let's look at the specific transactions.

1. The first step Filomena and Teresa take is to set up a corporation as they have decided that the corporate form of organization is the most appropriate for both tax and legal liability purposes. Filomena and Teresa each contribute $20,000 to the corporation and each receives 1,000 shares of the corporation's shares in exchange. At this point Filomena and Teresa each own 50% of the corporation. They name their corporation Strawberries Inc. and their restaurant Strawberries. The entry to the spreadsheet would be:

Transaction	Assets					=	Liabilities		+	Shareholders' Equity	
	Cash	Accounts Receivable	Food, Drinks, and Supplies Inventory	Prepaid Rent	Renovations, Equipment, and Furniture		Bank Loan	Accounts Payable		Capital Stock	Retained Earnings
Balance before transaction											
1	$40,000									$40,000	
Balance after transaction	$40,000									$40,000	

Strawberries Inc.'s Cash (an asset) has increased by $40,000 because Filomena and Teresa contributed $40,000 in cash. In exchange for their $40,000 Filomena and Teresa received shares of Strawberries Inc. The shares represent an ownership interest in Strawberries, so the Capital Stock account increases by $40,000 because the investment was a purchase of company shares.

2. Filomena and Teresa realize that they probably do not have enough cash to start their business. They approach a banker for a loan to provide additional cash. The banker examines their business plan and is satisfied that it is reasonable. The banker offers a $20,000 loan. Interest of $150 must be paid to the bank at the end of each month, beginning in September. Strawberries Inc. must begin paying back the loan in one year.

Transaction	Assets					=	Liabilities		+	Shareholders' Equity	
	Cash	Accounts Receivable	Food, Drinks, and Supplies Inventory	Prepaid Rent	Renovations, Equipment, and Furniture		Bank Loan	Accounts Payable		Capital Stock	Retained Earnings
Balance before transaction	$40,000									$40,000	
2	$20,000						$20,000				
Balance after transaction	$60,000						$20,000			$40,000	

The money from the bank loan increases Strawberries Inc.'s cash by $20,000. Strawberries Inc. now has a liability—it owes the bank $20,000. As a result of the loan, Cash and Bank Loan each increase by $20,000. The cost of borrowing the money, the interest, is not recorded at this time because under accrual accounting the cost of using money occurs with the passage of time. Therefore, an interest expense will be recorded only after Strawberries Inc. has had the use of the money for some period of time. We will record the interest cost later.

3. Now Filomena and Teresa go to work setting up their business. They find a suitable space in a shopping centre near the campus and Filomena negotiates a two-year lease with the owner. The lease requires Strawberries Inc. to pay $1,250 per month in rent. Rent is due on the first day of each month, with the first three months' rent due on signing of the lease. Filomena writes a cheque for $3,750 when she signs the lease. The owner of the shopping centre has agreed that Strawberries Inc. will not have to pay rent until September, so no payment is required for the use of the space before then.

Transaction	Assets					=	Liabilities		+	Shareholders' Equity	
	Cash	Accounts Receivable	Food, Drinks, and Supplies Inventory	Prepaid Rent	Renovations, Equipment, and Furniture		Bank Loan	Accounts Payable		Capital Stock	Retained Earnings
Balance before transaction	$60,000						$20,000			$40,000	
3	($3,750)*			$3,750							
Balance after transaction	$56,250			$3,750			$20,000			$40,000	

*Brackets indicate a decrease in an account.

The payment to the owner of the shopping centre represents an asset to Strawberries. The $3,750 gives Strawberries Inc. the right to use the location for three months beginning in September, so when the payment is made in early July it represents a future benefit and, therefore, an asset. Strawberries Inc. has exchanged one asset, Cash, for another asset, the right to use the location for three months, which we call Prepaid Rent. As a result Cash decreases by $3,750 and Prepaid Rent increases by $3,750. (A decrease in an account is recorded in brackets on the spreadsheet.)

Only the amount paid to the property owner is recorded as an asset. Even though the lease is for two years, only the portion actually paid in cash is typically recorded under accrual accounting in Canada. The right to use the location for two years at an agreed-upon price is not recorded, even though having the lease is a benefit to Strawberries. This is an example of a type of future benefit that does not usually appear on the financial statements of Canadian entities.

4. To get the restaurant ready for business Filomena and Teresa undertake some renovations, including painting, refinishing the floors, and adding appropriate décor. In addition, some plumbing and electrical work is required. Filomena and Teresa do some of the work themselves and hire and pay tradespeople to do the rest. The total cost of renovations is $15,000. All payments for materials and tradespeople were made in cash.

Transaction	Assets					=	Liabilities		+	Shareholders' Equity	
	Cash	Accounts Receivable	Food, Drinks, and Supplies Inventory	Prepaid Rent	Renovations, Equipment, and Furniture		Bank Loan	Accounts Payable		Capital Stock	Retained Earnings
Balance before transaction	$56,250			$3,750			$20,000			$40,000	
4	($15,000)				$15,000						
Balance after transaction	$41,250			$3,750	$15,000		$20,000			$40,000	

The renovations are an asset because they will contribute to the environment of the restaurant while it is in business—after all, a restaurant's ambiance is part of the attraction of dining out. The cost of the renovations was paid in cash so Cash decreases by $15,000. The cost of the renovations was $15,000, so the asset Renovations, Equipment, and Furniture increases by $15,000. This is another example of one asset, Cash, being converted into another asset, Renovations, Equipment, and Furniture.

5. Teresa arranges for the purchase of equipment, furniture, dishes, and other necessary materials from a restaurant supply company. The total cost of the purchase is $25,000. Half of the purchase is paid in cash and the remainder is owed to the supplier and must be paid in 90 days.

Transaction	Assets					=	Liabilities		+	Shareholders' Equity	
	Cash	Accounts Receivable	Food, Drinks, and Supplies Inventory	Prepaid Rent	Renovations, Equipment, and Furniture		Bank Loan	Accounts Payable		Capital Stock	Retained Earnings
Balance before transaction	$41,250			$3,750	$15,000		$20,000			$40,000	
5	($12,500)				$25,000			$12,500			
Balance after transaction	$28,750			$3,750	$40,000		$20,000	$12,500		$40,000	

This is a slightly more complicated transaction because more than two accounts are affected, reflecting the fact that the purchase of the items was partly a cash transaction and partly a credit transaction. As a result, Cash decreases by $12,500, the amount that was paid to the supplier, and there is a liability, Accounts Payable, to pay the supplier $12,500 in 90 days. Accounts Payable are amounts owed to suppliers for goods or services purchased on credit. Accounts Payable are usually classified as current liabilities.

The items Teresa purchased are assets because they will help Strawberries Inc. earn revenue by providing the equipment to prepare meals, the dishes on which to serve meals, and so on, over several years. These assets are recorded under Renovations, Equipment, and Furniture at $25,000 because that is the amount being paid for them. Under accrual accounting it doesn't matter that the full amount was not paid in cash at the time of purchase. The $12,500 promised to the supplier at a later date is considered a part of the cost of the asset. In general, the cost of a capital asset represents what an entity sacrifices to acquire the asset. In the case of the purchases from the restaurant supply company, Strawberries Inc. has already paid $12,500 in cash and will pay an additional $12,500 in cash in 90 days, for a total a $25,000.

Comment: The sacrifice an entity makes need not be in cash. Strawberries Inc. could have even paid the restaurant supply company in meals at the restaurant. The trading of goods or services instead of paying cash is called a **non-monetary transaction**. The word barter is often used to describe trades of goods or services.

Under GAAP capital assets are always reported at their cost. If the market value of a capital asset increases after it is purchased, the cost recorded when the asset was purchased does not change. GAAP accounting is not intended to capture changes in the market values of capital assets.

The spreadsheet for Strawberries Inc. includes several different kinds of capital assets in a single account. The renovations, equipment, furniture, etc., are included in a single account called Renovations, Equipment, and Furniture. It would be possible to use separate accounts for each type of asset but Teresa and Filomena thought that a single account would be adequate for their needs. This demonstrates the flexibility that preparers have in organizing their records. In practice, though, the different types of capital assets would probably be placed in separate accounts if for no other reason than different types of capital assets receive different treatments for tax purposes and, therefore, separate classification would be useful.

6. As opening day approaches, Strawberries Inc. hires staff, including a server and kitchen help. The new employees will begin work when Strawberries Inc. opens. The restaurant also purchases non-perishable food items and supplies at a cost of $900.

Transaction	Cash	Accounts Receivable	Food, Drinks, and Supplies Inventory	Prepaid Rent	Renovations, Equipment, and Furniture	=	Bank Loan	Accounts Payable	+	Capital Stock	Retained Earnings
Balance before transaction	$28,750			$3,750	$40,000		$20,000	$12,500		$40,000	
6	($900)		$900								
Balance after transaction	$27,850		$900	$3,750	$40,000		$20,000	$12,500		$40,000	

The purchase of food items and supplies for cash reduces Strawberries Inc.'s Cash by $900 and increases another asset, Food, Drinks, and Supplies Inventory, by $900. The food items and supplies will contribute to making meals for customers, so they are assets. The food items and supplies will become expenses when they are used to prepare meals for customers. Under GAAP, the inventory is recorded in the accounting system at its cost.

The hiring of employees is not recorded in the accounting system because the employees have not yet provided any work or added any value to Strawberries Inc. and Strawberries Inc. has not paid the employees. If one or both of the parties had fulfilled its part of the contract—by working, in the case of the employees, or by making a payment, in the case of Strawberries Inc.—an entry would have been made in the accounting system. Under GAAP these executory contracts are not usually recorded in the accounting system. (An **executory contract** is an exchange of promises where one party promises to supply goods or services and the other party promises to pay for them, but neither side has fulfilled its side of the bargain.) We will see situations later in the book where this GAAP treatment does not provide the most useful information to the users.

7. Strawberries is ready to open for business! The restaurant becomes popular with students, staff, and faculty almost immediately, attracting large crowds especially at lunch and on weekends. During September Strawberries Inc. purchases $12,000 of food and drinks to serve to customers. The food and drinks are paid for in cash.

Transaction	Cash	Accounts Receivable	Food, Drinks, and Supplies Inventory	Prepaid Rent	Renovations, Equipment, and Furniture	=	Bank Loan	Accounts Payable	+	Capital Stock	Retained Earnings
			Assets			=	Liabilities		+	Shareholders' Equity	
Balance before transaction	$27,850		$900	$3,750	$40,000		$20,000	$12,500		$40,000	
7	($12,000)		$12,000								
Balance after transaction	$15,850		$12,900	$3,750	$40,000		$20,000	$12,500		$40,000	

The food and drinks are recorded as inventory when they are purchased because they are available for sale to customers. Cash decreases by $12,000 and Food, Drinks, and Supplies Inventory increases by $12,000, the amount paid for the food and drinks. Under accrual accounting inventory is an asset until it is sold. The food and drinks that Strawberries Inc. has in inventory will be expensed when they are sold to people who eat at the restaurant. In contrast, if Strawberries Inc. were using a cash accounting system, the purchase of food and drinks would be treated as a cost when they are paid for.

8. During September Strawberries had sales of $17,200 to people who visited the restaurant. All of these sales were for cash. Strawberries also catered a faculty party, for which it charged $700. Payment from the faculty is due in the middle of October.

Transaction	Assets					=	Liabilities		+	Shareholders' Equity	
	Cash	Accounts Receivable	Food, Drinks, and Supplies Inventory	Prepaid Rent	Renovations, Equipment, and Furniture		Bank Loan	Accounts Payable		Capital Stock	Retained Earnings
Balance before transaction	$15,850		$12,900	$3,750	$40,000		$20,000	$12,500		$40,000	
8	$17,200	$700									$17,900
Balance after transaction	$33,050	$700	$12,900	$3,750	$40,000		$20,000	$12,500		$40,000	$17,900

In total, Strawberries had sales of $17,900 during September. Sales represent an economic benefit or gain to the entity and an increase in the wealth of the owners, so Retained Earnings increases by $17,900. Sales of $700 for the faculty party were unpaid at the end of September, so Strawberries Inc. is owed money by the customer. The amount owed is an asset because it represents the right to receive $700 in cash, so $700 has been entered in Accounts Receivable, the usual account name for amounts owed by customers. Sales of $17,200 were for cash, so Cash increased by $17,200.

The recording of sales or revenue in the accounting system is a very important accounting decision made by preparers. The recording of revenue reflects an economic gain by the entity and when it is recorded it can have significant implications for many of the users and uses of accounting information. However, it is not always obvious or clear when the actual economic gain occurs. For example, Strawberries Inc. recorded the sale from the faculty party when the food was provided for the party. But that was not the only possible time to record the revenue. Strawberries Inc. might have considered recording the revenue for the faculty party when the order to cater the party was received, or it could have decided to wait until the cash was collected. When did the economic benefit occur? As you can see, the answer is not at all clear. Arguments can be made in support of each of the three times described.

Under GAAP and accrual accounting it is not necessary to wait until cash is received to record a sale unless there is unmeasurable uncertainty about whether the cash will actually be collected. On the other hand, GAAP encourage caution in deciding when to record a sale. As we discussed in Chapter 1, one of the important qualitative characteristics of GAAP is reliability. According to GAAP, if revenue is recorded too soon many outcomes could arise that render the information unreliable. For example, if Strawberries Inc. recorded the revenue from the faculty party when the order was received, it is possible that the party could have been cancelled at the last minute. In that case Strawberries Inc. would have reported revenue that never actually happened. It might also be difficult for Strawberries Inc. to know what it would cost to cater the party. In that situation the amount of profit that Strawberries Inc. could expect to make from the party would be uncertain. Under GAAP these uncertainties would suggest that Strawberries Inc. should delay recording the revenue.

In contrast, there is little choice about when to record revenue from the sales to people who visit the restaurant. It is not possible to anticipate that a person will have a meal at Strawberries until he or she actually comes to the restaurant. But once the customer has paid the bill and left the restaurant, both Strawberries and the customer have fulfilled their part of the bargain. There is no reason to wait to record the sale. As a result, in the case of Strawberries Inc.'s cash transactions, recording revenue at the time the meal is ordered, eaten, and paid for is the only possibility. (We will explore the recording of sales and revenue in depth in Chapter 4.)

Although the $17,900 of sales was recorded on a single line on the accounting equation spreadsheet on page 105, in fact a separate line would be added for each individual sale or each day's sales. Since the sales represent hundreds of separate transactions with customers, it is not practical to include each one in the example. However, you should recognize that each individual sale or each day's sales would likely be recorded separately.

9, 10. At the end of September, Strawberries Inc. pays $525 for utilities and $925 in wages to its employees. These payments were made by cheque. Cheques are recorded as Cash in the accounting system because an entity can exchange the cheque for cash by presenting it at the bank. In other words, a cheque is as good as cash. Once a cheque is cashed the amount of the cheque is removed from the bank account of the entity that wrote the cheque.

Transaction	Assets					=	Liabilities		+	Shareholders' Equity	
	Cash	Accounts Receivable	Food, Drinks, and Supplies Inventory	Prepaid Rent	Renovations, Equipment, and Furniture		Bank Loan	Accounts Payable		Capital Stock	Retained Earnings
Balance before transaction	$33,050	$700	$12,900	$3,750	$40,000		$20,000	$12,500		$40,000	$17,900
9	($525)										($525)
10	($925)										($925)
Balance after transaction	$31,600	$700	$12,900	$3,750	$40,000		$20,000	$12,500		$40,000	$16,450

The utilities and wages payments are costs of operating the restaurant in September and represent expenses for the month. Expenses reduce retained earnings because they represent economic sacrifices or costs to the entity and reduce the wealth of the owners. Therefore, Retained Earnings decreases by $1,450 ($525 + $925). Since these expenses were paid in cash, Cash decreases by $1,450.

11. At the end of September, Strawberries Inc. pays the bank $150 interest for the loan.

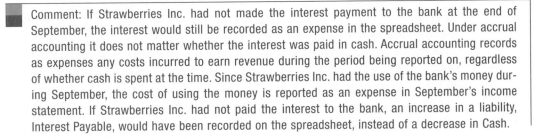

Transaction	Assets					=	Liabilities		+	Shareholders' Equity	
	Cash	Accounts Receivable	Food, Drinks, and Supplies Inventory	Prepaid Rent	Renovations, Equipment, and Furniture		Bank Loan	Accounts Payable		Capital Stock	Retained Earnings
Balance before transaction	$31,600	$700	$12,900	$3,750	$40,000		$20,000	$12,500		$40,000	$16,450
11	($150)										($150)
Balance after transaction	$31,450	$700	$12,900	$3,750	$40,000		$20,000	$12,500		$40,000	$16,300

Interest is the cost incurred to use the bank's money. The $150 is a cost of doing business during September and so is treated as an expense in September. Therefore, Retained Earnings decreases by $150, as does Cash, since the interest was paid to the bank in cash.

Comment: If Strawberries Inc. had not made the interest payment to the bank at the end of September, the interest would still be recorded as an expense in the spreadsheet. Under accrual accounting it does not matter whether the interest was paid in cash. Accrual accounting records as expenses any costs incurred to earn revenue during the period being reported on, regardless of whether cash is spent at the time. Since Strawberries Inc. had the use of the bank's money during September, the cost of using the money is reported as an expense in September's income statement. If Strawberries Inc. had not paid the interest to the bank, an increase in a liability, Interest Payable, would have been recorded on the spreadsheet, instead of a decrease in Cash.

12. One of Strawberries' major operating costs is the cost of the food, drinks, and supplies used in preparing meals for customers. One way of determining the amount of food, drinks, and supplies used is to subtract the amount of food, drinks, and supplies inventory on hand at the end of the month from the Food, Drink, and Supplies Inventory available for sale during the month. At the end of September Teresa counted the Food, Drinks, and Supplies Inventory and found that there was food, drink, and supplies left that cost $1,000. Since Strawberries Inc. had $12,900 of Food, Drinks, and Supplies Inventory available during September and there was $1,000 left at the end of September, this means that $11,900 was used (Food, Drinks, and Supplies Inventory on hand during the month – Food, Drinks, and Supplies Inventory remaining at the end of the month = $12,900 – $1,000).

Transaction	Assets					=	Liabilities		+	Shareholders' Equity	
	Cash	Accounts Receivable	Food, Drinks, and Supplies Inventory	Prepaid Rent	Renovations, Equipment, and Furniture		Bank Loan	Accounts Payable		Capital Stock	Retained Earnings
Balance before transaction	$31,450	$700	$12,900	$3,750	$40,000		$20,000	$12,500		$40,000	$16,300
12			($11,900)								($11,900)
Balance after transaction	$31,450	$700	$ 1,000	$3,750	$40,000		$20,000	$12,500		$40,000	$4,400

To reflect the use of food, drinks, and supplies, Food, Drinks, and Supplies Inventory must be decreased by $11,900. The food, drinks, and supplies were used to prepare meals that were sold to customers, so they are an expense incurred to earn the revenue that we recorded in Transaction 8. Therefore, the use of food, drinks, and supplies to provide meals to customers results in a decrease in Retained Earnings of $11,900.

The term **matching** is used for the process of recording and reporting expenses in the same period as when the revenue those expenses help earn is recorded and reported. Matching is a fundamental concept of accrual accounting. The association between benefits (revenues) and costs (expenses) is necessary if profit is to measure the change in wealth, which is a primary objective of accrual accounting.

Although matching expenses to revenues is a sensible way to account for many uses of accounting information, it may not be suitable for all users. For example, for entities whose main purpose is minimizing taxes, preparers would be willing to sacrifice matching in favour of recording expenses as soon as possible so that tax payments could be minimized. As we proceed through the book, we will find that while matching is often conceptually a good idea, it can be hard to accomplish because it is difficult to know the association between some costs and revenues.

13. Strawberries Inc. must account for the use of the space leased in the shopping centre. When Filomena paid $3,750 to the shopping centre owner, the amount was recorded as an asset because it represented a future benefit—the right to use the space from September through November. Now, at the end of September, Strawberries Inc. has used up part of the right to occupy the space. When an asset is used up or consumed, it becomes an expense. (This is another example of matching.)

In this case, the use of the leased space in September helped earn the revenue recorded in September by providing Strawberries Inc. a place to operate the business. Therefore, it makes sense to match the $1,250 cost of leasing the space in September to revenues recorded in September. The remaining $2,500 balance in Prepaid Rent represents the right to use the space in the shopping centre in October and November, so it is therefore classified as an asset.

Transaction	Assets					=	Liabilities		+	Shareholders' Equity	
	Cash	Accounts Receivable	Food, Drinks, and Supplies Inventory	Prepaid Rent	Renovations, Equipment, and Furniture		Bank Loan	Accounts Payable		Capital Stock	Retained Earnings
Balance before transaction	$31,450	$700	$1,000	$3,750	$40,000		$20,000	$12,500		$40,000	$4,400
13				($1,250)							($1,250)
Balance after transaction	$31,450	$700	$1,000	$2,500	$40,000		$20,000	$12,500		$40,000	$3,150

Since the beginning balance of Prepaid Rent is $3,750, Prepaid Rent must be reduced by $1,250, or one month's rent, so that the balance at the end of September reflects the cost of the future benefit that is available to Strawberries Inc.—that is $2,500, the rent for October and November. To look at it another way, one month of prepaid rent, or $1,250, has been used up, so the balance must decrease by $1,250. Under either interpretation, Prepaid Rent must decrease by $1,250. Retained Earnings must also decrease by $1,250 because the rent is a cost of doing business in September.

14. During September Strawberries Inc. will have consumed some of its capital assets—renovations, equipment, and furniture—in the process of operating its business. The renovations to the restaurant space have future benefit to Strawberries Inc. as long as the restaurant occupies that particular location. As the lease period expires, so do the benefits associated with the renovations. The equipment and furniture will eventually wear out, break down, or otherwise become obsolete. As a result an amortization expense should be recorded to reflect consumption of these assets.

Transaction	Assets					=	Liabilities		+	Shareholders' Equity	
	Cash	Accounts Receivable	Food, Drinks, and Supplies Inventory	Prepaid Rent	Renovations, Equipment, and Furniture		Bank Loan	Accounts Payable		Capital Stock	Retained Earnings
Balance before transaction	$31,450	$700	$1,000	$2,500	$40,000		$20,000	$12,500		$40,000	$3,150
14					($1,042)						($1,042)
Balance after transaction	$31,450	$700	$1,000	$2,500	$38,958		$20,000	$12,500		$40,000	$2,180

Amortization is the allocation of the cost of a capital asset to expense over the capital asset's useful life. (The term depreciation is often used in place of amortization and is usually applied to the amortization of **tangible capital assets,** which are capital assets that have physical form or substance, such as buildings, equipment, computers, and vehicles.) Amortization is another example of matching. Since capital assets contribute to an entity's earning of revenue, it is necessary under accrual accounting and GAAP to match the cost of a capital asset to the revenue it helped earn. To calculate the amount of amortization that should be expensed in a period it is necessary to estimate the useful life of the capital asset and to choose an acceptable method for amortizing the asset. However, it is often very difficult to come up with the "right" useful life and the "right" amortization method. As we will see in Chapter 9, there are several acceptable ways to amortize capital assets.

The first capital asset that we will consider is the renovations. The renovations will be amortized over two years, which is the period of the lease Strawberries Inc. signed with the property owner. Other amortization periods are possible. For example, if the lease had an option that allowed Strawberries Inc. to renew its lease, it would be reasonable to amortize the renovations over the initial period of the lease plus the renewal period. Since there is no indication that Strawberries can or will remain in its present location beyond the two-year lease period, we will amortize the renovation costs over two years.

This decision represents a conservative approach to reporting. **Conservatism** is a fundamental GAAP accounting concept that serves to ensure that assets, revenue, and net income are not overstated and that liabilities and expenses are not understated. The implication is that when preparers are faced with reasonable alternative accounting treatments, they should choose the one that is more conservative. In the case of renovations, a two-year amortization is more conservative because it is not clear that Strawberries will be in its present location for more than two years. Amortizing the renovations over two years rather than, say, three or four years is more conservative because the renovations are expensed more quickly. (We will discuss conservatism in more detail in Chapter 5.)

Since it is not reasonably possible to determine the contribution that the renovations will make to earning revenue each month, we will simply allocate an equal amount of amortization to each month of the lease. Therefore, the amount of amortization that should be expensed in September for the renovations is $625 ($15,000 ÷ 24 months).

The process is similar for the equipment and furniture. However, the useful lives of equipment and furniture are not limited to the life of the lease. The equipment and furniture could be moved to another location if the restaurant changed premises. Therefore, to calculate an amortization expense we must make an assumption about how long the furniture and equipment will provide future benefit. We will assume that the useful life of the equipment and furniture is five years. This assumption is a simplification since it is likely that the individual assets have a variety of useful lives. For purposes of this example, though, we will assume that all these assets have the same useful life.

A more important point to recognize is the flexibility that is available to preparers when making estimates of this kind. While there are limits on the estimates that can be made—for example, it would not be reasonable to estimate the useful life of the furniture at 50 years—how could one argue with estimates of four years versus six years versus eight years? The accounting choices and estimates made by the preparers can have a significant effect on the net income of the entity in a period. The amount of amortization that should be expensed in September for the equipment and furniture is $417 ($25,000 ÷ 60 months). Therefore, the amortization expense for September is $1,042 ($625 + $417).

Three final comments on amortization. First, Renovations, Equipment, and Furniture was reduced by $1,042, the amount of the amortization expense. In practice, the amortization is usually accumulated in a separate account called Accumulated Amortization. Second, amortization is the allocation of the cost of a capital asset to expense. Amortization provides no information whatsoever about the market value of an asset. Third, amortization has no effect on cash flow.

These points will be discussed further as we proceed through the book

15. At the end of September Filomena and Teresa decide to declare and pay a dividend of $0.50 per share, or $1,000 ($0.50 × 2,000 shares). The two friends need some money to meet personal expenses and are satisfied that the restaurant can afford to pay out the cash. A dividend is a distribution of the assets of the corporation to its shareholders.

Transaction	Assets					=	Liabilities		+	Shareholders' Equity	
	Cash	Accounts Receivable	Food, Drinks, and Supplies Inventory	Prepaid Rent	Renovations, Equipment, and Furniture		Bank Loan	Accounts Payable		Capital Stock	Retained Earnings
Balance before transaction	$31,450	$700	$1,000	$2,500	$38,958		$20,000	$12,500		$40,000	$2,180
15	($1,000)										($1,000)
Balance after transaction	$30,450	$700	$1,000	$2,500	$38,958		$20,000	$12,500		$40,000	$1,108

By paying a cash dividend Strawberries Inc.'s Cash decreases by $1,000 and Retained Earnings decreases by $1,000 because part of Strawberries Inc.'s earnings have been paid to the shareholders. (Remember from our discussion in Chapter 2 that retained earnings is the accumulated earnings of a business over its life, less dividends paid to shareholders over its life.)

While dividends reduce Retained Earnings, they are not included in the calculation of net income. Under GAAP in Canada net income is designed to measure the change in wealth from the perspective of the owners. From this perspective, net income represents the residual amount that is available to the owners after all other stakeholders (such as employees, lenders, and suppliers) have been considered. Because net income is a residual amount that belongs to the owners, payments of dividends to owners are not included in the calculation of net income.

We have now considered all the transactions and other economic events that affected Strawberries Inc. in September and recorded them in its accounting system. Using the accounting equation spreadsheet it is very simple to prepare the balance sheet for the end of September. The bottom line of the spreadsheet provides the total in each balance sheet account on September 30, 2004. To create the balance sheet we reorganize the information into a more traditional format. For example:

Strawberries Inc.
Balance Sheet
As of September 30, 2004

Assets		Liabilities and Shareholders' Equity	
Cash	$30,450	Bank loan	$20,000
Accounts receivable	700	Accounts payable	12,500
Food, drinks, and supplies inventory	1,000	Total liabilities	32,500
Prepaid rent	2,500		
Renovations, equipment,		**Shareholders' Equity**	
and furniture	38,958	Capital stock	40,000
		Retained earnings	1,108
		Total shareholders' equity	41,108
		Total liabilities	
Total assets	$73,608	and shareholders' equity	$73,608

Note how the account titles and balances on the balance sheet correspond with the column names and ending balances on the accounting equation spreadsheet. In practice, an accounting system contains many more accounts than are reported in the financial statements. For example, the accounting system might have separate accounts for renovations, equipment, and furniture but the balance sheet might show a single line that aggregates them. Similarly, the accounting system might have separate accounts for different types of inventory, but the balance sheet might report all those accounts in a single line. However, for the accounting equation to hold, the amount in each balance sheet account must be reflected in the balance sheet.

Preparing an income statement from the spreadsheet is slightly more difficult. On our accounting equation spreadsheet we have recorded all revenue, expense, and dividend transactions directly to the Retained Earnings account. This approach allowed us to easily prepare the balance sheet, but does not provide the information to easily prepare the income statement.

We can solve this problem by breaking down the Retained Earnings account into its component accounts. Remember that revenue and expense accounts are sub-accounts of the retained earnings account. Table 3-1 (pages 114–115) shows the accounting equation spreadsheet for Strawberries Inc. with the revenue and expense accounts shown. Now the amounts in each of the revenue and expense accounts can be easily identified from the bottom line of the spreadsheet and placed in the income statement.

Strawberries Inc.
Income Statement
For the Month Ended September 30, 2004

Sales		$17,900
Expenses		
Cost of sales	$11,900	
Rent	1,250	
Amortization	1,042	
Wages	925	
Utilities	525	
Interest	150	
Total expenses		15,792
Net income		$ 2,108

You might notice that the ending balance in the retained earnings account in Table 3-1 is not the same as the amount on the balance sheet. The reason is because the income statement balances are kept separate from Retained Earnings in Table 3-1.

They are not included in Retained Earnings. To get the correct Retained Earnings ending balance, the balances in the income statement accounts must be included in the retained earnings account. (This process will be discussed later in this chapter in the section on closing entries on page 134.)

Now that we have prepared Strawberries Inc.'s balance sheet and income statement, what do we do with them? What do they tell us? In general, financial statements raise questions rather than provide definite answers. Strawberries Inc.'s financial statements must be used with special care because they provide information for only the first month of operations. Nonetheless, a number of questions can be asked and observations made.

1. How well has Strawberries Inc. done? It is difficult to say. We have only one month's performance, the first month, and nothing to compare it with. Perhaps if we had information about how restaurants do when they first begin operations we would have a better idea. After Strawberries Inc. has been operating for a few years, we will be better able to compare its performance with other years or other restaurants. It is important to recognize a user must be very cautious when making comparisons using the accounting information of different entities. As we will discover, preparers of accounting information have many ways to account for similar situations. Nonetheless, it is not possible to make sense of accounting information without some benchmarks or bases of comparison.

2. Some analysis we can do suggests that Strawberries Inc. has done reasonably well in its first month:

    *   It has "turned a profit" of $2,108 for the month, which is positive news because it is very difficult to succeed in the restaurant business.

    *   The net income of $2,108 represents a return on equity of about 5% on Filomena and Teresa's $41,108 equity in Strawberries Inc. (return on equity = net income ÷ shareholders' equity = $2,108 ÷ $41,108). **Return on equity (ROE)** is a measure of the profitability of an entity and its effectiveness in using the assets provided by the owners of the entity to generate net income.

    *   Strawberries Inc.'s profit margin ratio (net income ÷ sales) is almost 12%, meaning that for every dollar of sales it makes it earns $0.12. The **profit margin ratio** is a measure of how effective the entity is at controlling expenses and reflects the amount of income earned for each dollar of sales.

        However, as we have already pointed out, it is very difficult to draw conclusions from this analysis without benchmarks or bases for comparison.

3. Why does Strawberries Inc. have so much cash? The new restaurant borrowed $20,000 from the bank, yet has more than that amount in cash on September 30. Strawberries Inc. owes $12,500 to the restaurant supply company that it must repay in two months, so at this point it has the cash to meet that obligation. Should Strawberries Inc. reduce its bank loan? Or do Teresa and Filomena have plans for the money? Perhaps major purchases are still required. Certainly some of the cash will be needed to buy more food inventory. How is the cash being managed? Is the cash being held in a business bank account earning no interest, or has it been invested so that it can earn a return until it is needed? Since the income statement does not report any interest or investment income, we can assume that it is being held in a non-interest-bearing bank account.

4. While Strawberries Inc. seems to have a large cash balance, starting up the business and operating it for a month consumed a significant amount of cash. Strawberries Inc.'s cash flow since it was incorporated is shown in Table 3-2.

Table 3-1   Complete Accounting Equation Spreadsheet for Strawberries Inc.

| | Assets | | | | | = | Liabilities | |
Transaction	Cash	Accounts Receivable	Inventory	Prepaid Rent	Renovations, Equipment, and Furniture		Bank Loan	Accounts Payable
1	$40,000							
2	$20,000						$20,000	
3	($3,750)			$3,750				
4	($15,000)				$15,000			
5	($12,500)				$25,000			$12,500
6	($900)		$900					
7	($12,000)		$12,000					
8	$17,200	$700						
9	($525)							
10	($925)							
11	($150)							
12			($11,900)					
13				($1,250)				
14					($1,042)			
15	($1,000)							
Balance	$30,450	$700	$1,000	$2,500	$38,958		$20,000	$12,500

Table 3-2   Strawberries Inc.'s Cash Flow

Strawberries Inc.
Calculation of Net Cash Flow
For the Period Ended September 30, 2004

Cash inflows:		
Shareholders	$40,000	
Bank	20,000	
Sales	17,200	
Total cash inflows		$77,200
Cash outflows		
Capital assets	27,500	
Inventory	12,900	
Rent	3,750	
Utilities	525	
Wages	925	
Interest	150	
Dividends	1,000	
Total cash outflows		46,750
Net cash flow		$30,450

If we ignore the money obtained from shareholders and the bank, net cash flow is actually negative (cash inflows from sales − cash outflows = $17,200 − $46,750 = $29,550). Note that this statement was prepared by organizing the transactions that are included in the Cash column of the accounting equation spreadsheet.

Also, cash from operations (cash from or used by an entity's regular business activities) is also negative, which shows that actual business operating costs are using more cash than they are generating. Cash from operations for Strawberries Inc. is shown in Table 3-3.

+

		Shareholders' Equity						
Capital Stock	Retained Earnings	Sales	Cost of Sales	Rent Expense	Wages Expense	Utilities Expense	Amortization Expense	Interest Expense
$40,000								
		$17,900						
						($525)		
					($925)			
								($150)
			($11,900)					
				($1,250)				
							($1,042)	
	($1,000)							
$40,000	($1,000)	$17,900	($11,900)	($1,250)	($925)	($525)	($1,042)	($150)

Table 3-3   Strawberries Inc.'s Cash from Operations

Strawberries Inc.
Calculation of Net Cash Flow
For the Period Ended September 30, 2004

Cash inflows from sales		$17,200
Cash outflows		
Inventory	12,900	
Rent	3,750	
Utilities	525	
Wages	925	
Interest	150	18,250
Net cash flow		$(1,050)

5. The large amount of cash Strawberries Inc. has means it can easily pay the accounts payable as well as purchase needed inventory. Therefore, Strawberries Inc.'s liquidity position appears to be solid because it will be able to pay its debts as they come due. Strawberries Inc.'s current ratio (current assets ÷ current liabilities = $34,650 ÷ $32,500) is 1.07 to 1, which usually is not considered to be very high. But the bank loan does not have to be paid for almost a year, which suggests that the low current ratio is not a significant problem yet.

6. The income statement does not tell us much about how Strawberries Inc. will perform in the next month or the next year. September was the first month of operations and Strawberries' encouraging performance may have been due to curiosity by local people who may not come back. Alternatively, next month may be even better as more people learn about the new restaurant. It is not possible to predict what will happen based on the first month's performance of a restaurant.

In general, one of the limitations of general purpose financial statements is that they are prepared mainly on the basis of transactional information and historical costs. They do not tell us explicitly very much about the future. Historical cost, transactional-based statements can sometimes be used as a starting point to predict the future. However, in the case of new entities such as Strawberries Inc., or even for established entities that are facing significant change, the statements may not be very helpful for predicting what will happen in the future.

Journal Entries

The accounting equation spreadsheet is one device for recording the effects of economic events and for showing the effects of accounting choices on financial statements. The second device that will be used extensively in this book is the journal entry. Journal entries are used in practice as the method of initially entering a transaction or economic event into the accounting system. For learning purposes in this book, journal entries will be used to summarize transactions or other economic events so that the effects on the financial statements can be seen easily. The appendix to this chapter on pages 146–156 shows how journal entries fit into the complete accounting cycle.

A journal entry accomplishes exactly the same thing as an entry to an accounting equation spreadsheet, but in a different format. The format of a journal entry is:

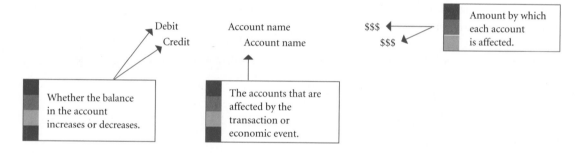

A journal entry provides the following information:

- the accounts that are affected by the transaction or economic event
- whether the balance in each account increases or decreases
- the amount by which each account is affected

The account name identifies the account that is affected by the transaction or economic event and $$$ is the amount by which each account is affected. The account names correspond to the column headings on the spreadsheet. The terms **debit** and **credit** tell whether the balance in the account has increased or decreased. These terms have very precise meanings in accounting. The precise meanings of debit and credit are described in the following list:

Debit (Dr.)	Credit (Cr.)
Increase assets	Decrease assets
Decrease liabilities	Increase liabilities
Decrease owners' equity	Increase owners' equity
Decrease revenues	Increase revenues
Increase expenses	Decrease expenses

We can see the effect of debits and credits on assets, liabilities, and owners' equity in the accounting equation in the diagram below:

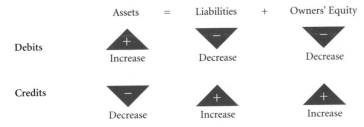

The diagram below shows the effect of debits and credits on revenues and expenses:

At first these terms may be confusing and cumbersome to work with. It is probably worthwhile to memorize the debit and credit lists (page 116) so that you know what debits and credits mean right from the start. Rest assured that as you work with journal entries the terms will become second nature to you.

> Comment: It is easy to fall into the trap of assigning qualities to debits and credits: credits are good, debits are bad. While the term "credit" does have positive connotations in ordinary language, it does not share that positive meaning in an accounting context. The terms simply refer to whether the balance in an account increases or decreases. Sometimes debit and credit or their abbreviations Dr. and Cr. are omitted completely from a journal entry. In those cases debits can be distinguished from credits because credits are indented. In a journal entry the debits must equal the credits. Since journal entries are manipulations of the accounting equation, if the debits do not equal the credits the accounting equation will not balance.

Questions for Consideration

Describe the effect (increase or decrease) that debits and credits have on asset, liability, owners' equity, revenue, and expense accounts.

Answer: Debits increase asset and expense accounts, and decrease liability, owners' equity, and revenue accounts. Credits decrease asset and expense accounts, and increase liability, owners' equity, and revenue accounts.

Explain why an expense is a debit.

Answer: Expenses represent economic sacrifices made by an entity to earn revenue. Economic sacrifices result in a decrease in owners' equity or the wealth of the owners. A debit increases owners' equity. Since an expense results in a decrease in owners' equity, it must be a debit.

Let's return to Strawberries Inc. to show how journal entries work. Journal entries will be recorded for each of the transactions that were recorded in the spreadsheet. The number of each journal entry corresponds to the number assigned to each transaction in the spreadsheet. In the first transaction Filomena and Teresa each contributed $20,000 cash in exchange for shares of Strawberries Inc. The journal entry to record this transaction is:

1.   Dr. Cash (asset +)   40,000
      Cr. Capital stock (shareholders' equity +)   40,000
   To record the sale of shares for cash.

Cash is debited because the amount of cash has increased and an increase in an asset is a debit.

Teresa and Filomena purchased shares of Strawberries Inc., which means that Capital Stock, a shareholders' equity account, increases, requiring a credit entry. Note that the debits equal the credits. At this point you might find it helpful to keep track of the type of account (asset, liability, shareholders' equity) that is being affected in the journal entry and the direction of the change on that account.

The journal entry corresponds to the entry made to the accounting equation spread sheet:

Transaction	Cash	Accounts Receivable	Inventory	Prepaid Rent	Renovations, Equipment, and Furniture	=	Bank Loan	Accounts Payable	+	Capital Stock	Retained Earnings
			Assets				Liabilities			Shareholders' Equity	
Balance											
1	$40,000									$40,000	
Balance	$40,000									$40,000	

The $40,000 debit to Cash corresponds to the $40,000 added to the Cash column. The $40,000 credit to Capital Stock corresponds to the $40,000 added to the Capital Stock column.

The second transaction was the loan Strawberries Inc. obtained from the bank. Cash is debited because Strawberries Inc.'s cash has increased by $20,000. Strawberries Inc. also has a liability to repay the bank $20,000. As a result, the Bank Loan account is credited for $20,000 because liabilities have increased and an increase in a liability is a credit.

2.   Dr. Cash (asset +)   20,000
      Cr. Bank loan (liability +)   20,000
   To record the acquisition of a $20,000 bank loan.

The journal entries for the remainder of Strawberries Inc.'s transactions are shown below. Make sure you can explain the debits and credits in each entry.

3.   Dr. Prepaid rent (asset +)   3,750
      Cr. Cash (asset −)   3,750
   To record the prepayment of three months' rent.

4.   Dr. Renovations, equipment, and furniture (asset +)   15,000
      Cr. Cash (asset −)   15,000
   To record the cost of renovating the restaurant.

5.   Dr. Renovations, equipment, and furniture (asset +)   25,000
      Cr. Cash (asset −)   12,500
      Cr. Accounts payable (liability +)   12,500
   To record the purchase of equipment and furniture.

6. Dr. Food, drinks, and supplies inventory (asset +)   900
        Cr. Cash (asset −)   900
    To record the purchase of inventory.

7. Dr. Food, drinks, and supplies inventory (asset +) 12,000
        Cr. Cash (asset −)   12,000
    To record the purchase of food during September. (In practice,
    each purchase of food inventory would require a separate
    journal entry, but for the purpose of the example all purchases
    are recorded in a single entry.)

Journal entries 8 through 15 affect income statement accounts. Recall that income statement accounts are actually sub-accounts of the shareholders' equity section of the balance sheet. For clarity, the type of account (asset, liability, shareholders' equity, revenue, or expense) and the direction of the change are shown. For income statement accounts, the effect on the income statement account (revenue or expense) and the effect on shareholders' equity (retained earnings) are shown. However, you should recognize that these are two ways of describing the same thing.

8. Dr. Cash (asset +)   17,200
    Dr. Accounts receivable (asset +)   700
        Cr. Sales (shareholders' equity +, revenue +)   17,900
    To record sales for the month of September.

9., 10. Dr. Utilities expense (shareholders' equity −, expense +)   525
         Dr. Wage expense (shareholders' equity −, expense +)   925
             Cr. Cash (asset −)   1,450
         To record the payment of utilities and wages expenses for the
         month of September.

11. Dr. Interest expense (shareholders' equity −, expense +)   150
         Cr. Cash (asset −)   150
     To record the payment of interest expense for the month of
     September.

12. Dr. Cost of sales (shareholders' equity −, expense +)   11,900
         Cr. Food, drinks, and supplies inventory (asset −)   11,900
     To record the cost of food, drinks, and supplies used to
     provide meals to customers.

13. Dr. Rent expense (shareholders' equity −, expense +)   1,250
         Cr. Prepaid rent (asset −)   1,250
     To record the rent expense for September.

14. Dr. Amortization expense (shareholders' equity −, expense +)   1,042
         Cr. Renovations, equipment, and furniture (asset −)   1,042
     To record the amortization of renovations, equipment,
     and furniture.

15. Dr. Retained earnings (shareholders' equity −)   1,000
         Cr. Cash (asset −)   1,000
     To record the payment of a dividend of $0.50 per share.

One final point: for both journal entries and the accounting equation spreadsheet, making sure that the debits equal the credits or that the accounting equation equality is maintained does not guarantee that your accounting decisions make sense. You could incorrectly classify an asset as an expense or a liability as a revenue, and your entries would balance but not necessarily make sense.

Accrual Accounting

In Chapter 2 accrual accounting was introduced as one of the ways of measuring performance. Now we are going to explore accrual accounting in more detail.

Accrual accounting is the basis of GAAP. Even entities that do not follow GAAP will usually (not always) use accrual accounting. Accrual accounting is necessary for control purposes—keeping track of receivables and payables, for example—and it can provide a more useful measure of economic performance than cash accounting. The concept behind accrual accounting is the measurement of economic activity and economic changes, rather than the measurement of cash and cash flows that is the basis of the cash accounting system. Accountants believe that by measuring economic activity and economic changes, they will provide more relevant information to users in the financial statements. Because of its widespread use, it is important to have a good understanding of accrual accounting so that you can understand the strengths and limitations of financial reporting.

A good way to explain accrual accounting is to contrast it with cash accounting. Under cash accounting the economic event that triggers recording in the accounting system is the exchange of cash. A sale is recorded when the customer pays cash; an expense is recorded when cash is paid to a supplier. With accrual accounting the exchange of cash is not necessarily the economic event that triggers recording (although it may). If inventory were purchased on credit, the inventory would be recorded as an asset and the obligation to pay the supplier would be recorded as a liability. The economic event is reflected in the financial statements even though no cash is involved in the transaction. Revenues and expenses can be recorded before cash changes hands, when cash changes hands, or after cash changes hands.

If you think about it, a cash system is very inadequate for providing information about what is going on in an entity. Consider the following events that have economic implications on an entity but do not involve cash:

* Exchanges between entities are often done on credit. Knowing that an entity owes or is owed money is very useful information.

* Entities usually have assets that contribute to their success over many years.

* Customers sometimes pay for goods or services in advance. It is useful to know that the entity has an obligation to the customer.

* Assets sometimes change in value. It is sometimes useful to know about these changes in value.

An accrual accounting system can capture these effects because accrual accounting reflects economic changes, not just cash changes. In general an accrual accounting system (or any accounting system) is not designed to capture all economic changes. For example, under GAAP in Canada, the decrease in the value of investments is sometimes recorded. However, the increase in the value of investments is almost never recorded.

Let's use Mark's Work Wearhouse (MWW) to demonstrate how the recording of revenue differs under cash and accrual accounting. It is common practice for businesses using accrual accounting to record revenue when goods are shipped or delivered to customers. In January 2004 MWW receives a large order for work gloves from a corporate customer. The order is delivered in November 2004. Figure 3-3 shows how the cash flows could differ under different business arrangements. Each of the three situations has payment from the customer coming at a different time.

* Situation 1: cash is received when the order is placed (in January 2004, which is in fiscal 2004).

* Situation 2: cash is received on delivery of the goods to the customer (in November 2004, which is in fiscal 2005).

Panel A: Three Possible Cash Flow Situations

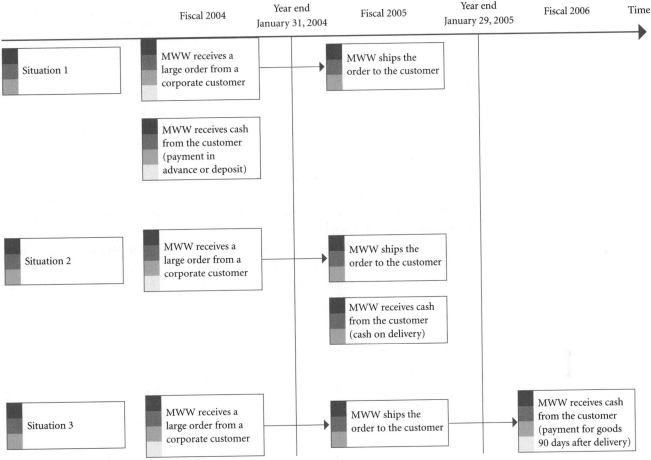

Panel B: Journal Entries for Each of the Three Cash Flow Situations

	Situation 1 Cash paid in advance when order placed		Situation 2 Cash paid on delivery		Situation 3 Cash paid 90 days after delivery	
Year	Accrual Accounting	Cash Accounting	Accrual Accounting	Cash Accounting	Accrual Accounting	Cash Accounting
2004	Dr. Cash (assets +) Cr. Advance payment (Liabilities +)	Dr. Cash (assets +) Cr. Sales (revenue +, shareholders' equity +)	No entry	No entry	No entry	No entry
2005	Dr. Advance payment (Liabilities −) Cr. Sales (revenue +, shareholders' equity +)	No entry	Dr. Cash (assets +) Cr. Sales (revenue +, shareholders' equity +)	Dr. Cash (assets +) Cr. Sales (revenue +, shareholders' equity +)	Dr. Accounts receivable (assets +) Cr. Sales (revenue +, shareholders' equity +)	No entry
2006	No entry	No entry	No entry	No entry	Dr. Cash (assets +) Cr. Accounts receivable (assets −)	Dr. Cash (assets +) Cr. Sales revenue +, shareholders' equity +)

Figure 3-3

Cash versus Accrual Accounting

- Situation 3: the customer agrees to pay for the goods 90 days after delivery (in February 2005, which is in fiscal 2006) (remember that MWW's year end is the last Saturday in January).

With accrual accounting the revenue would be reported in fiscal 2005 regardless of when the cash was received. The reason is that the key economic event is shipment or delivery of goods. Panel B of Figure 3-3 shows the journal entries that would be made in each situation using accrual accounting and cash accounting. Note that the credit to sales occurs in fiscal 2005 in all three situations with accrual accounting. With cash accounting, the credit to sales depends on when the cash was received. However, the accounting is not entirely rigid. If MWW believed that there was a significant risk that the customer would not pay, then under accrual accounting it would be appropriate to recognize the revenue when the cash was collected. More on this later.

A similar story exists for expenses. Under accrual accounting, accountants try to find the costs that were incurred to earn the revenue, and expense those costs in the same period that the revenue was recorded. For MWW's sale to its corporate customer it makes no difference when MWW paid for the work gloves it sold. What matters is when the gloves were considered sold for accounting purposes. Regardless of when MWW paid for the gloves, the cost would be expensed at the same time that MWW recorded the revenue from the sale of the gloves.

While accrual accounting may provide more relevant information to users in many situations, it also introduces some complexities. Unlike cash accounting, where it is fairly easy to decide when to record an economic event or transaction (recording occurs when cash changes hands), accrual accounting often requires the careful exercise of judgment. Since revenue is reported when the entity enjoys an economic benefit, someone has to decide when the benefit occurred. This is the revenue recognition question.

Revenue recognition refers to the point in time when revenue is recorded in the accounting system and is reported in the income statement. When revenue should be recognized is not always straightforward. Sometimes there are choices. It is easy for a hotdog vendor with a cart on a street corner to recognize revenue. When the customer turns over her money and the vendor provides the hotdog, the vendor is better off—revenue has happened. But consider a more complicated example. An engineering consulting firm signs a contract to build a new gas pipeline from western Canada to Chicago. The pipeline will take five years to build. The consulting firm will receive 18% of its fee each year and the remaining 10% one year after the project is completed. When should the revenue be recognized? How much should be recognized each year?

We will explore the criteria for recognizing revenue in Chapter 4. For now, it is important to realize that *when* revenue should be recognized is not always an easy question to answer and can require the exercise of judgment.

Under accrual accounting, once revenue has "happened" you look for the costs that were incurred to earn those revenues and expense those costs. This is the matching concept we discussed earlier. By matching expenses to revenues, the income statement provides a measure of the net change in the wealth of the owners: economic benefits minus economic costs. But matching expenses to revenues is not necessarily easy either, even for our hotdog vendor. While matching the cost of the hotdog to the sale is easy, what about the condiments? How can the vendor determine how much mustard or how many pickles each person puts on his or her hotdog? This question is more easily answered if the vendor looks at condiment costs for a month or a year. A more difficult question arises when we consider the hotdog vendor's cart. How can the cost of the cart, which will probably be used to sell hotdogs for many years, be matched to the sale of a single hotdog, or to the hotdogs sold in a month or a year? The answer has significant implications for the income statement.

Figure 3-4 summarizes the relationship between revenue and expense recognition and cash flow.

In describing accrual accounting and revenue and expense recognition, we raised a number of questions without finding clear-cut answers. Unfortunately, these questions do not have clear-cut answers. Accounting is easy if you are told exactly when

Accrual Accounting

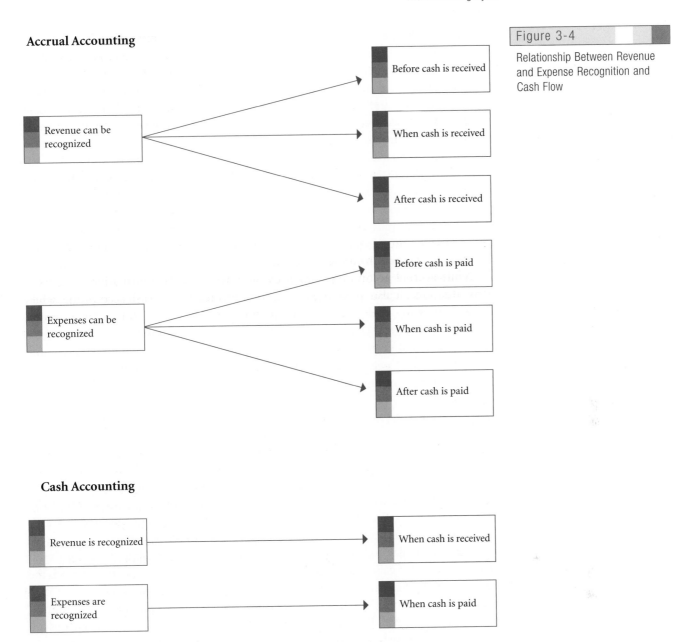

Figure 3-4

Relationship Between Revenue
and Expense Recognition and
Cash Flow

Cash Accounting

revenue is supposed to be recognized and how expenses should be matched to revenues. But doing as you are told hides the choices that are available, the judgment that must be exercised, and the thought that goes along with making these choices. Accrual accounting makes accounting less clear-cut. To understand financial statements you have to realize that revenue and expenses can often be recognized at different times, and that alternative choices can have significant effects on the financial statements.

A Question of Timing

We saw in the last section that revenues and expenses do not have to appear in the income statement at the same time as the cash transaction takes place. But if revenues and expenses are not recognized when cash is exchanged, when are they recognized? This is a question that gets a lot of attention from accountants. The answer is important because of the effect it has on the financial statements—and because of the economic effects that the financial statements can have on the stakeholders of an entity.

The reason accountants have to deal with sticky questions about when things happen is because financial statements must be prepared from time to time over the life of the entity. If an entity had to prepare financial statements only at the end of its life, the job of an accountant would be much simpler because over the life of an entity accrual accounting and cash accounting provide the same results—there would be no need to decide when to recognize revenue and expenses. In other words, the cause of most accounting problems is the fact that financial statements are prepared periodically—monthly, quarterly, or annually.

In the 15th and 16th centuries the need to measure income periodically during the life of a business was not particularly important. At that time many business opportunities were operated as short-term ventures. Investors would put money in a venture such as a trade voyage to the New World. The organizers would purchase all they needed for the venture, including a ship. At the end of the venture everything would be sold off and the proceeds would be distributed among the investors. Income measurement during the trade voyage was not necessary.

As business became more complex and business itself became continuous, it was no longer possible or appropriate to sell all of a company's resources from time to time. But stakeholders wanted to know how the entity was doing, so the need for a periodic statement of performance arose. You will see as we go through the book that the need to report periodically during the life of an entity is at the heart of most accounting problems and controversies.

Adjusting Entries

An entry into an accrual accounting system is usually triggered by a transaction—an exchange between the entity and a party external to the entity. In the Strawberries Inc. example all the entries that were made to the spreadsheet involved interactions with outside parties (bankers, shareholders, suppliers, and customers), except for entries 12, 13, and 14. But sometimes economic changes occur that are not triggered by transactions, and these changes must be recorded in the accounting system.

Entries to an accrual accounting system that are not triggered by exchanges with outside entities are called **adjusting entries**. At the end of each reporting period, the preparers of the financial statements must identify any economic changes that may have occurred during the period but that have not been reflected in the accounting system and make any adjustments that are necessary. In contrast, adjusting entries are not required in a cash accounting system because recording is triggered only by the exchange of cash, which must involve an outside entity.

Adjusting entries are necessary in accrual accounting because recognition of revenues and expenses—measures of economic changes—does not always correspond with cash flows. Once again, recall Strawberries Inc. In July Filomena signed a two-year lease and paid rent for September, October, and November. We recorded that transaction as an asset that we called Prepaid Rent. There was an exchange between Strawberries Inc. and the property owner. At the end of September we took a look at the accounts and realized that we had used up one month of the three months' rent. To adjust the accounts we reduced the amount in the asset account because at the end of September only two months' rent was prepaid (October and November), and we expensed one month's rent because it had been consumed in September. Note that the entry at the end of September did not involve another entity. The owner of the shopping centre did not phone us and tell us to adjust the accounting records. However, there was clearly a change. An asset had been consumed and the account balances had to be adjusted to reflect the change. To reiterate: The cash transaction occurred before the asset was used. When the asset was eventually used, there was no transaction with another entity.

Comment: Adjusting entries are not intended to capture all economic changes that are not the result of transactions. The adjusting entries only reflect the changes that the method of accounting is designed to capture. For example, according to GAAP adjusting entries are not recorded to recognize increases in the market value of property that has not been sold as of the end of the period.

There are four types of adjusting entries. (See the summary in Table 3-4.) Before discussing adjusting entries in detail, you should note the following general points:

1. The situations that give rise to adjusting entries revolve around the timing of the cash flow versus the timing of revenue or expense recognition—revenue and expense recognition can happen at a different time than the cash flows.

2. Each adjusting entry involves a balance sheet account and an income statement account.

3. Each adjusting entry is associated with a transaction that is recorded before or after the adjusting entry. A **transactional entry** is a journal entry that is triggered by an exchange with another entity.

Table 3-4   Four Types of Adjusting Entries

Type	Situation	Example	Entry made in the current or previous period (Transactional Entry)	Entry made at the end of the current period (Adjusting Entry)	Entry made in the next period (Transactional Entry)
Deferred expense/ prepaid expense	Cash is paid before the expense is recognized	Prepaid insurance Prepaid rent Capital assets	Dr. Asset Cr. Cash	Dr. Expense Cr. Asset	No entry
Deferred revenue	Cash is received before revenue is recognized	Deposits Subscriptions Advances Gift certificates	Dr. Cash Cr. Liability	Dr. Liability Cr. Revenue	No entry
Accrued liability	Expense is recognized before cash is paid	Wages Utilities Interest expense	No entry	Dr. Expense Cr. Liability	Dr. Liability Cr. Cash
Accrued asset	Revenue is recognized before cash is received	Interest earned	No entry	Dr. Asset Cr. Revenue	Dr. Cash Cr. Asset

Here are three tips to keep in mind as you study adjusting entries:

1. Adjusting entries are required only when financial statements are prepared.

2. Adjusting entries never involve cash. If cash is part of the entry, it is not an adjusting entry.

3. Adjusting entries always include at least one balance sheet account and one income statement account.

Question for Consideration

Why are adjusting entries required when using accrual accounting? Why are they not necessary when using cash accounting?

Answer: Accrual accounting attempts to measure economic changes. Not all economic changes are triggered by an interaction with an outside entity. As a result it is necessary to "adjust" the accounts for economic changes that occur during a period but are not triggered by interactions with outside entities. Adjusting entries are not required in a cash accounting system because recording in the accounting system is triggered only by an exchange of cash, which always involves an outside entity.

Let's examine the four types of adjusting entries in detail. Assume the year end in each case is December 31.

1. Deferred Expense/Prepaid Expense

Entities often purchase assets that provide benefits for more than one period, including insurance policies, equipment, buildings, and patents, to name a few. Usually, as time passes or as an asset is used by the entity, the future benefits are consumed. As a result, the portion consumed in a period must be expensed. Expensing an asset as it is consumed serves to match the cost of the asset with the revenue the asset helped earn.

The terms **deferred expense** and **prepaid expense** refer to assets that are acquired in one period but not expensed, at least in part, until a later period or periods. Deferred expense and prepaid expense adjusting entries record the consumption of assets that provide benefits to an entity for more than one period. These entries reduce the amount of the asset that is reported on the balance sheet and recognize an expense for the portion of the asset that has been consumed. They are adjusting entries because they are not triggered by an interaction or exchange with another entity.

On January 5, 2005 Dahlia Ltd. (Dahlia) purchases three years of insurance coverage for $9,000 cash. The insurance covers the period January 1, 2005 to December 31, 2007.

When Dahlia purchases the insurance it makes the following journal entry:

Dr. Prepaid insurance (asset +)	9,000	
Cr. Cash (asset −)		9,000

To record the purchase of insurance for the period
January 1, 2005 to December 31, 2007.

This is a transactional entry because an exchange has taken place between Dahlia and the insurance company. The insurance is set up as an asset because the policy will provide Dahlia with three years of coverage, a future benefit.

On December 31, 2005 an adjusting entry is required because one year of the insurance coverage has been used up. If no adjusting entry were made Dahlia's balance sheet would report $9,000 of insurance coverage, implying that there are three years of coverage available when there are really only two. What the balance sheet should report on December 31, 2005 is $6,000 of prepaid insurance, representing two years of coverage. As a result, Prepaid Insurance must be decreased by $3,000. Dahlia must also report an expense of $3,000 in its income statement to reflect the cost of insurance consumed in 2005. The adjusting entry that Dahlia would make on December 31, 2005 is:

Dr. Insurance expense (expense +, shareholders' equity −)	3,000	
Cr. Prepaid insurance (asset −)		3,000

To record the cost of insurance used in the year ended
December 31, 2005. ($9,000 ÷ 3 years of coverage = $3,000).

This is an adjusting entry because Dahlia makes it without the involvement of another entity. The adjusting entry assumes that the cost of the insurance in each year of the policy is the same, which is a reasonable assumption based on the information given.

One year later on December 31, 2006 another adjusting entry would be required to reflect the use of the second year of insurance. The adjusting entry would be the same as the one recorded in 2005. The entry on December 31, 2006 is:

Dr. Insurance expense (expense +, shareholders' equity −)	3,000	
Cr. Prepaid insurance (asset −)		3,000

To record the cost of insurance used in the year ended
December 31, 2006 ($9,000 ÷ 3 years of coverage = $3,000).

The December 31, 2006 balance sheet would now show prepaid insurance of $3,000 ($9,000 − $3,000 − $3,000). A similar adjusting entry would be required on December 31, 2007. The financial statement effects are shown using the spreadsheet in Table 3-5. (This is a summarized spreadsheet showing entries and balances only in the accounts that are relevant to the situation.)

Table 3-5   Dahlia Ltd. Summary Spreadsheet

	Assets			= Liabilities +	Shareholders' Equity				
Date	Cash	Prepaid Insurance	All other assets	All liabilities	Capital Stock	Retained Earnings	Insurance Expense	All other income statement accounts	
Jan. 5, 2005	($9,000)	$9,000							Trans-actional entry
Dec. 31, 2005		($3,000)					($3,000)		
Balance on Dec. 31, 2005		**$6,000**					**($3,000)**		Adjusting entry
Dec. 31, 2006		($3,000)					($3,000)		
Balance on Dec. 31, 2006		**$3,000**					**($3,000)**		
Dec. 31, 2007		($3,000)					($3,000)		
Balance on Dec. 31, 2007		**$0**					**($3,000)**		

You may notice that the balance in the insurance expense column does not add up over the three years (that is, the insurance expense on December 31, 2007 is $3,000, not $9,000). The reason is because income statement accounts reflect only the expenses that occurred during a period. (We will discuss this in more detail later.) The expenses from one year are not carried forward in an expense (or revenue) account to the next year. As a result, the balance in expense (and revenue) accounts at the beginning of each year is zero.

If Dahlia's insurance policy came into effect on July 1, 2005 and ran until June 30, 2008, the adjusting entry would be a bit different. In that case on December 31, 2005, only half of a year's insurance would have been used up. The amount expensed would be $1,500 because one year's coverage costs $3,000, so half a year's coverage is $3,000 ÷ 2 or $1,500. Therefore, the adjusting entry would be:

Dr. Insurance expense (expense +, shareholders' equity −)   1,500
    Cr. Prepaid insurance (asset −)   1,500
To record the cost of insurance used from
July 1, 2005 to December 31, 2005
([$9,000 ÷ 3 years of coverage] × 1/2 year = $1,500).

The transactional entry would be the same in this situation.

Another example of this type of adjusting entry is the amortization of capital assets. Capital assets are the assets an entity uses to produce or supply the goods or services it offers to its customers. These assets contribute indirectly to the earning of revenue—indirectly because selling them is not part of the ordinary activities of the entity. Examples include buildings, vehicles, machinery, patents, copyrights, and so on. Capital assets contribute to earning revenue over more than one period and the cost of these assets must be expensed over the asset's life. Conceptually, amortizing the cost of a capital asset is the same as expensing prepaid insurance over the life of a policy. But amortization deserves special notice because it is such a common part of financial statements.

There are many different ways that an asset can be amortized. We will discuss some of these methods in Chapter 9. For now, here is an example of one way the cost of a capital asset can be amortized over its life.

On January 2, 2004, Kaslo Ltd. (Kaslo) purchased a new delivery truck for $50,000 cash. Kaslo's management estimates that the truck will be useful to the company for five years. The truck will be amortized using the straight-line amortization method. **Straight-line amortization** allocates an equal amount of the cost of a capital asset to expense in each year of the asset's life. The adjusting entry that would be recorded at the end of each year would be:

Dr. Amortization expense (expense +, shareholders' equity −)   10,000
    Cr. Accumulated amortization (asset −)   10,000
Adjusting entry to record amortization of the truck
(Cost of the asset ÷ estimated useful life = $50,000 ÷ 5 years =
$10,000 per year).

The accumulated amortization account is referred to as a contra-asset account. A **contra-asset account** is an account that is used to accumulate subtractions from a related asset account. Thus, the **accumulated amortization** account accumulates subtractions from capital asset and other amortizable asset accounts. Instead of crediting the asset account directly for the amortization expense, the credit is made to a separate account. This treatment makes information about the cost of an asset readily available from the accounting system. Knowing the original cost of an asset can be important for various reasons, including for tax purposes. The balance in the accumulated amortization account is not meaningful by itself. Taken together, the cost of a capital asset less the accumulated amortization gives the asset's **net book value (NBV)**.

The spreadsheet for Kaslo is shown in Table 3-6. Notice that the balance in the capital asset account itself remains at $50,000 all the time. The accumulated amortization increases by $10,000 each year, the amount of the annual amortization expense. Combining the amount in the capital asset account with the amount in the accumulated amortization account at any time gives the NBV. On December 31, 2004 the NBV of the truck is $40,000 ($50,000 − $10,000) and on December 31, 2007 the NBV is $10,000 ($50,000 − $40,000).

If you look at the consolidated balance sheet of MWW on page A-45 you will see that $28,148,000 in capital assets is reported. Check Note 7 to the financial statements, page A-53) and you will see that the cost of those capital assets was $45,847,000. The difference between the cost and the amount reported on the balance sheet, $17,699,000, is the accumulated amortization. (The actual amount of accumulated amortization is not stated but can be calculated as the difference between cost and net book value.)

2. Deferred Revenue

Sometimes an entity will receive payment for goods or services before it recognizes the revenue. For example, a fan might purchase tickets to a concert months before the performance, or a customer might pay a deposit to ensure delivery of goods some time later. In these examples, the entity might recognize revenue when the concert is performed or the goods are delivered. When the payment is received, the entity records a liability. The liability represents the obligation to provide the good or service that the customer has paid for. An adjusting entry is necessary when the revenue is recognized and the obligation is fulfilled.

On May 20, 2003 Fatfish Magazine Ltd. (Fatfish) received $52 for a new two-year subscription to its popular monthly magazine. The subscription begins in the first week of July. When Fatfish received the cheque from the new subscriber, it made the following journal entry:

Table 3-6   Spreadsheet for Kaslo Ltd.: Amortization of its Truck

| | Assets | | | | = Liabilities + | Shareholders' Equity | | | | |
Date	Cash	Capital Assets (Vehicles)	Accumulated Amortization	All other assets	All liabilities	Capital Stock	Retained Earnings	Amortization Expense	All other income statement accounts	
Jan. 2, 2004	($50,000)	$50,000								Transactional entry
Dec. 31, 2004			($10,000)					($10,000)		
Balance on Dec. 31, 2004		**$50,000**	**($10,000)**					**($10,000)**		
Dec. 31, 2005			($10,000)					($10,000)		
Balance on Dec. 31, 2005		**$50,000**	**($20,000)**					**($10,000)**		
Dec. 31, 2006			($10,000)					($10,000)		Adjusting entry
Balance on Dec. 31, 2006		**$50,000**	**($30,000)**					**($10,000)**		
Dec. 31, 2007			($10,000)					($10,000)		
Balance on Dec. 31, 2007		**$50,000**	**($40,000)**					**($10,000)**		
Dec. 31, 2008			($10,000)					($10,000)		
Balance on Dec. 31, 2008		**$50,000**	**($50,000)**					**($10,000)**		

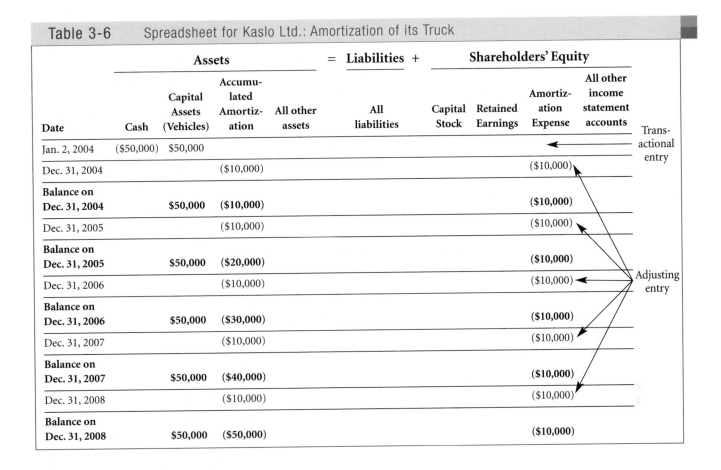

Dr. Cash (asset +)   52
    Cr. Unearned revenue (liability +)   52
To record cash received for a two-year subscription.

This is a transactional entry because it involves interaction with an outside entity, namely the new subscriber. When Fatfish received the new subscriber's cheque, revenue was not recognized because the company had not yet provided magazines to the subscriber. The unearned revenue liability means that Fatfish has an obligation to deliver the magazine to the subscriber over the next two years. **Unearned revenue** is a liability that is recorded when cash is received before revenue is recognized.

In this situation revenue is recognized when the magazine is delivered. At the end of the year Fatfish would make an adjusting entry to recognize revenue. Since 25% of the subscription will have been delivered as of December 31, 2003, 25% of the revenue can be recognized. The journal entry would be:

Dr. Unearned revenue (liability −)   13
    Cr. Revenue (revenue +, shareholders' equity +)   13
To record revenue earned from subscriptions. (Percentage of subscription delivered × price of subscription
= 6 months ÷ 24 months × $52 = $13.)

This is an adjusting entry because it does not involve an outside entity. Fatfish makes this entry in its accounting records to reflect the fact that revenue has been earned. The entry recognizes revenue for six months—from the delivery of the first magazine in July until December 2003. But this entry assumes that financial statements are prepared only at the end of the year. If financial statements were prepared monthly, an adjusting entry would be required at the end of each month to recognize the revenue earned in that month. In that case, the adjusting entry each month would record $2.17 of revenue and reduce the liability by the same amount, representing the sale of the magazine delivered in each month ($52 ÷ 24 months = $2.17 per month). Remember that it is necessary to make adjusting entries only if financial statements are being prepared.

Adjusting entries would be required on December 31, 2004 and December 31, 2005 to recognize the revenue earned in 2004 and 2005 respectively. The effects on the balance sheet and income statement for each year of the subscription are summarized in the condensed spreadsheet in Table 3-7.

When Fatfish recognizes the revenue, it would recognize the costs of earning the revenue at the same time. (This is matching costs to revenues.) Examples of the journal entries that might be made to recognize the cost of the subscription include:

Dr. Cost of subscriptions (expense +, shareholders' equity –)   xx
    Cr. Paper inventory (assets –)   xx
To record the cost of paper used in the production of the magazine.

Dr. Wage expense (expense +, shareholders' equity –)   xx
    Cr. Cash (assets –)   xx
To record the wages of magazine production employees.

Dr. Amortization expense (expense +, shareholders' equity –)   xx
    Cr. Accumulated amortization (contra assets +)   xx
To record amortization of equipment used in the production of the magazine.

3. Accrued Liability An **accrued liability** is a liability that is recognized and recorded in the financial statements but is not triggered by an external event such as receipt of a bill or invoice. The accrued liability type of adjusting entry is recorded when an entity has incurred an expense, but the recording of the expense and related liability have not been triggered by an external event. Recognition of the expense gives rise to a liability to pay for the resource that was consumed. The entry is necessary to ensure that all resources consumed in a period are expensed in that period—in other words, to ensure that expenses are matched to revenues. Without an external trigger, such as an invoice, to initiate the recording process, an adjusting entry is required so that the expense is recorded. It is important to recognize that an adjusting entry to accrue a liability is required only if the entity has not received an invoice or has not

Table 3-7   Fatfish Magazine Ltd. Spreadsheet Summary

Date	Assets Cash	All other assets	= Liabilities Unearned revenues	All liabilities	+ Shareholders' Equity Capital Stock	Retained Earnings	Revenue	All other income statement accounts	
May 20, 2003	$52		$52						Trans-actional
Dec. 31, 2003			($13)				$13		entry
Balance on Dec. 31, 2003			**$39**				**$13**		
Dec. 31, 2004			($26)				$26		
Balance on Dec. 31, 2004			**$13**				**$26**		Adjusting entry
Dec. 31, 2005			($13)				$13		
Balance on Dec. 31, 2005			**$0**				**$13**		

paid for the resource by the end of the period. If the entity receives an invoice from the supplier before the end of the period, an adjusting entry is not required because an external trigger, the invoice, triggers the recording process.

Babbit Inc. (Babbit) is billed every two months by Richmond Hill Hydro for the power Babbit consumes. In late December 2004, Babbit received an invoice for $8,250 for power consumed in October and November 2004. The invoice for power used in December 2004 and January 2005 will not be received until late February 2005.

This situation is a bit tricky because the adjusting entry is made before the transactional entry and so the amount of the expense and the amount of the liability must be estimated. At the end of December Babbit knows that it has not been invoiced for the electricity it used in December. If Babbit's income statement is to include all costs incurred in the year ended December 31, 2004, then the cost of electricity used in December must be recorded. Because no invoice will have been received by the time the financial statements are prepared, it is necessary to estimate the cost of electricity used in December and accrue the amount in the 2004 financial statements. Let's assume that Babbit estimates that the cost of electricity in December will be half of its cost for October and November combined. (There are other ways that Babbit could estimate the expense, such as using the December 2003 amount.) Babbit would make the following adjusting entry on December 31, 2004:

Dr. Utilities expense—electricity		
(expense +, shareholders' equity −)	4,125	
Cr. Accrued liabilities (liabilities +)		4,125
To accrue electricity expense for December. (Cost of		
electricity for [October and November] ÷ 2		
= $8,250 ÷ 2 = $4,125.)		

The entry records an estimated expense for electricity used in December and creates an accrued liability that recognizes the obligation to pay for the electricity even though Babbit has not yet been billed for it. The transactional entry is recorded when Babbit receives the invoice from Richmond Hill Hydro in February 2005. Assume that Babbit's invoice from Richmond Hill Hydro for electricity usage in December 2004 and January 2005 is for $8,250 and that Babbit's estimate of the cost for December was correct. Assuming that Babbit pays the invoice in February, the transactional entry would be:

Dr. Accrued liabilities (liabilities −)	4,125	
Dr. Utilities expense—electricity		
(expense +, shareholders' equity −)	4,125	
Cr. Cash (assets −)		8,250
To record payment of December 2004 and January 2005		
electricity bill from Richmond Hill Hydro. The December		
portion of $4,125 had been accrued at December 31, 2004.		

There are two things happening in this entry:

1. The payment of the amount that was accrued for December. This part of the entry removes the liability that was accrued for the estimated cost of December's electricity.

2. The recording of the expense and payment of January's electricity cost. The January cost is invoiced, expensed, and paid in 2005, so it is not related to the adjusting entry. (If financial statements were prepared monthly, perhaps because a banker wants monthly statements, an adjusting entry would be needed at the end of January for January's electricity use.)

The February 2005 entry is a transactional entry because the invoice sent by Richmond Hill Hydro triggers it. The effects of the accrued liability on the balance sheet and income statement are summarized in the condensed spreadsheet in Table 3-8.

An important aspect of this adjusting entry is that the amount of the liability had to be estimated. It is unlikely that Babbit would know the exact cost of the electricity it used in December. If the financial statements were prepared before the invoice was received from Richmond Hill Hydro, the amount of the liability and the corresponding expense would be an estimate—an "educated guess." Financial statements are filled with estimates like these. Other examples of estimates used in accounting are the useful lives of capital assets (what is the life of a delivery truck?) and the amount of accounts receivable that will be collected in cash (not everyone pays their debts).

Because estimates represent uncertain future amounts, you cannot assume that numbers in financial statements are exact. Keep in mind too the fact that estimates are made by managers, and managers may have reporting objectives such as maximizing their own bonuses, satisfying lenders so they keep lending money, and maximizing profits to keep investors happy. Hence the need for careful detective work when you examine a company's financial statements.

4. Accrued Asset An **accrued asset** is an asset that is recorded before cash is received. This type of adjusting entry is required when an entity has earned revenue but no transaction with another entity has triggered the recording of the revenue. Recognizing the revenue gives rise to a receivable that reflects that payment is forthcoming. As was the case for accrued liabilities, the adjusting entry recording an accrued asset is made before the transactional entry is made. The debit side of the entry is a receivable because cash will be received in the future.

On October 1, 2005 Jalobert Ltd. (Jalobert) invested $1,000,000 of surplus cash in Government of Canada bonds that have an interest rate of 5%. Interest on the bonds is paid semi-annually on September 30 and March 31 of each year. Interest revenue is earned simply by the passage of time. Jalobert earns interest for each minute it holds the bonds. On December 31, 2005, Jalobert Ltd. should recognize the interest it earned by holding the bonds from October 1 to December 31. The adjusting entry is:

Dr. Interest receivable (asset +)	12,603	
Cr. Interest revenue (revenue +, shareholders' equity +)		12,603

To record accrual of revenue earned from October 1 to December 31 from investment in Government of Canada bonds ($92 \div 365 \times \$1,000,000 \times 5\%$).

The entry recognizes interest revenue earned over the 92 days from October 1 to December 31 ($92 \times \$1,000,000 \times 5\%$) and the interest receivable. While the government does not have an obligation to pay the interest until March 31, 2006, in an

| Table 3-8 | Babbit Inc. Summary Spreadsheet |

	Assets		=	Liabilities		+	Shareholders' Equity			
Date	Cash	All other assets		Accrued Liabilities	All other liabilities		Capital Stock	Retained Earnings	Utilities Expense	All other income statement accounts
Dec. 31, 2004				$4,125					($4,125)	← Adjusting entry
Balance on Dec. 31, 2004				**$4,125**					**(4,125)**	Trans- actional entry
Feb. 22, 2005	($8,250)			($4,125)					($4,125)	

Notice that the balance in the accrued liability account is zero after the payment has been made to Richmond Hill Hydro.

The expense recorded on February 25, 2005 is for electricity used in January 2005.

accounting and economic sense the money is owed to Jalobert. When a cheque is received from the government on or about March 31, 2006, Jalobert would record the following transactional entry:

Dr. Cash (asset +)	24,932	
Cr. Interest revenue (revenue +, shareholders' equity +)		12,329
Cr. Interest receivable (asset −)		12,603

To record cash received for interest earned from investment in Government of Canada bonds between October 1, 2005 and March 31, 2006 [(182 ÷ 365) × $1,000,000 × 5%]. The October 1, 2005 to December 31, 2005 portion of the payment had been accrued on December 31, 2005.

The transactional entry reflects two events:

1. Collection of the interest revenue that was earned in the last three months of 2005 and recorded as a receivable for the December 31, 2005 year end.

2. Recognition of the interest revenue earned during the first three months of 2006. (The amount of interest earned in the last three months of 2005 is greater than the amount earned in the first three months of 2006 because the number of days in the two periods is different.)

The effects on the balance sheet and income statement of the accrued asset are summarized in the condensed spreadsheet in Table 3-9.

Question for Consideration

A sports fan buys tickets for a game. The game will be played in six months, which is in the team's next fiscal accounting year. When the fan purchases the ticket the team records the following journal entry:

Dr. Cash	xxx	
Cr. Unearned revenue		xxx

The team recognizes revenue from its games when the games are actually played. Explain why an adjusting entry is necessary to recognize revenue when the game is played.

Answer: The exchange between the fan and the team occurs when the fan pays money for the tickets. There is no exchange or interaction between the fan and the team when the game is actually played. However, the team recognizes the revenue from tickets sold for the game when the game is played. Therefore, an adjusting entry is required so that the revenue can be reported in the income statement for the period in which the game is played.

Table 3-9   Jalobert Ltd. Summary Spreadsheet

	Assets			= Liabilities +	Shareholders' Equity				
Date	Cash	Interest Receivable	All other assets	All liabilities	Capital Stock	Retained Earnings	Interest Revenue	All other income statement accounts	
Dec. 31, 2005		$12,603					$12,603 ◄		Adjusting entry
Balance on Dec. 31, 2005		**$12,603**					**$12,603**		Trans-actional entry
Mar. 31, 2006	$24,932	($12,603)					$12,329 ◄		

Notice that the balance in the interest receivable account is zero after the payment has been received from the government.

The revenue recorded on March 31, 2006 is for interest earned between January 1 and March 31, 2006.

Closing Journal Entries

All accounts that are reported on the income statement are referred to as **temporary accounts**. They are temporary because at the end of each period they are reset to zero so that accumulation of revenues and expenses can begin anew in the next period. The balances in temporary accounts are not carried forward from one period to the next. This is important because an income statement reports results for a period of time. For example, a year-end income statement reports revenues and expenses "For the Year Ended December 31, 2005." If the income statement accounts are not reset to zero, then the revenues and expenses for the year ended December 31, 2006 would be combined with those of 2005, making it almost impossible to understand what belonged to which year.

Consider the analogy of the trip odometer in a car. You want to find out how many kilometres you are able to travel per litre of gas. When you fill up your car you set the trip odometer to zero. The next time you fill up you note the distance travelled and the amount of gas that you used so that you can do the calculation. If you wanted to repeat the test, you would have to reset the trip odometer to zero when you fill up the car. Otherwise you would not know how far you travelled on the second tank of gas because the trip odometer would reflect the distance travelled on two fill-ups.

Setting each of the income statement accounts to zero simply involves making an entry to the accounting equation spreadsheet that is opposite in amount to the ending balance in each account. So if the ending balance in sales is $1,000,000, an entry of −$1,000,000 is made. But how do we make the accounting equation's equality hold? Remember that the income statement accounts are part of the shareholders' or owners' equity section of the balance sheet. When the income statement accounts are set to zero, or *closed*, the amounts in those accounts are moved to owners' or shareholders' equity. For a corporation, the income statement accounts are closed to Retained Earnings. For a partnership or proprietorship, the amounts are closed to the owners' capital accounts.

We maintain the integrity of the accounting equation when we reset the sales account to zero by entering −$1,000,000 to the spreadsheet (or debit sales for $1,000,000) and also make an entry to Retained Earnings (if the entity is a corporation) for $1,000,000 (or credit Retained Earnings for $1,000,000). In effect, the economic benefit reflected by the $1,000,000 in sales is transferred from the sales account to the retained earnings account. The process of resetting temporary account balances to zero and transferring the balances in the temporary accounts to Retained Earnings or Owners' Equity is accomplished using **closing journal entries**.

Let's return to the Strawberries Inc. example. Shown in Table 3-10 is the bottom line of the Shareholders' Equity section of the spreadsheet from Table 3-1. For each of the temporary accounts (that is, the income statement accounts), an entry is made that is equal and opposite in amount to the ending balance for the month (that is, the amounts on the last line of the spreadsheet). The "other side" of each entry is made to Retained Earnings. The final balance in Retained Earnings now corresponds to the amount we included in the balance sheet. The income statement accounts are now at zero so the accounting records are ready to accumulate amounts for the next period. The end result is that we have "transferred" the balances in each income statement account to Retained Earnings.

Table 3-10 Strawberries Inc. Spreadsheet: Shareholders' Equity Section

	Capital Stock	Retained Earnings	Sales	Cost of Sales	Rent Expense	Wages Expense	Utilities Expense	Amortization Expense	Interest Expense
Shareholders' Equity									
Balance before closing entry on Sept. 30, 2004	$40,000	($1,000)	$17,900	($11,900)	($1,250)	($925)	($525)	($1,042)	($150)
Closing entry		$17,900	($17,900)						
Closing entry		($11,900)		$11,900					
Closing entry		($1,250)			$1,250				
Closing entry		($925)				$925			
Closing entry		($525)					$525		
Closing entry		($1,042)						$1,042	
Closing entry		($150)							$150
Ending balance on Sept. 30, 2004	$40,000	$1,108	$0	$0	$0	$0	$0	$0	$0

The corresponding journal entry would be:

Dr. Sales	17,900	
Cr. Cost of sales		11,900
Cr. Rent expense		1,250
Cr. Wages expense		925
Cr. Utilities expense		525
Cr. Amortization expense		1,042
Cr. Interest expense		150
Cr. Retained earnings		2,108

To record the closing entry at September 30, 2004.

Question for Consideration

What are closing journal entries and why are they necessary?

Answer: Closing journal entries are made at the end of a reporting period when the financial statements are prepared. Closing entries reset the temporary (income statement) account balances to zero and transfer the balances in the temporary accounts to Retained Earnings or Owners' Equity. Closing journal entries are necessary so that the temporary accounts have zero balances at the beginning of the next period so that they will include revenue and expense information for only that period. Closing journal entries are also necessary so that Retained Earnings/Owners' Equity at the end of the period includes the activities recorded in the temporary accounts during the period.

When Are Adjusting and Closing Entries Made?

You might think that at the stroke of midnight on December 31 a team of accountants races to get the adjusting and closing entries done as quickly as possible. In fact, the year-end process can go on for weeks after the end of the year. For example, MWW's year end in 2001 was January 27, but Management's Responsibility for Financial Statements (a statement by management included in the annual report explaining its responsibility for preparing the financial statements) is dated March 9, 2001, more than a month after the year end. (See page A-44.) This means that MWW's management agreed that the financial statements were final on March 9.

There is a trade-off in this delay. On the positive side, with the passage of time there will be less and less uncertainty surrounding some of the estimates that must be made at year end. For example, if the financial statements of Babbit Inc. were not finalized until late February, it would not be necessary to estimate the cost of the electricity used in December because Babbit would have received the invoice for December before the financial statements were finalized. On the negative side, the more time that passes from the end of the period to the issuing of financial statements, the less timely and relevant is the information.

Comprehensive Example

Child First Safety Ltd. (CFS) is a small business that provides safety advice and equipment to parents and daycare centres that want to have a safe, childproofed environment for infants and toddlers. The company has been in business for approximately two years. CFS is owned and operated by Yehuda Bigalli, who owns 100% of the shares of the company. Yehuda has never been much of a bookkeeper and his accounting system has tended to be a bag where he puts all information pertaining to CFS, including receipts, invoices, cancelled cheques (a cheque that has been cashed and returned by the bank to the writer of the cheque), and so on. At the end of the year he brings the bag to an accountant friend, who organizes the information and prepares financial statements that Yehuda uses for calculating his taxes and to show his bank because he has a bank loan.

In answering the question we will play the role of Yehuda's accountant friend.

We begin by examining the October 31, 2005 (last year's) balance sheet, which is shown in Table 3-11.

We organize and summarize the data in the bag and determine the following:

1. On November 1, 2005 CFS purchased a two-year insurance policy for $3,000 cash.

2. During the year CFS sold safety equipment and advising services to customers for $199,000; $140,000 of the sales were for cash, with the remainder on credit.

3. CFS purchased $65,000 of inventory during the year. All purchases were on credit.

4. CFS paid $62,000 during the year to suppliers for inventory purchases.

5. On November 15, 2005 CFS purchased a used car for $12,000 in cash. Yehuda uses the car for service calls and deliveries instead of using his personal vehicle. He estimates that the car will last for four years.

6. During the year CFS paid Yehuda and a part-time sales person $70,000 in salary and commission.

7. During the year CFS collected $45,000 from customers for purchases they had made on credit.

Table 3-11   Child First Safety Ltd. Balance Sheet

Child First Safety Ltd.
Balance Sheet
As of October 31, 2005

Assets			Liabilities and Shareholders' Equity		
Current assets			**Current liabilities**		
Cash		$ 12,800	Bank loan		$ 15,000
Accounts receivable		22,000	Accounts payable		49,000
Inventory		52,000	Taxes payable		5,000
		86,800	Unearned revenue		3,000
					72,000
Non-current assets			**Shareholder's equity**		
Capital assets		24,000	Capital stock		15,000
Accumulated amortization		(8,000)	Retained earnings		15,800
		16,000			30,800
			Total liabilities and		
Total assets		$102,800	shareholder's equity		$102,800

8. On October 31, 2006 CFS paid interest of $900 for the year on its bank loan.

9. On October 31, 2006 CFS repaid $2,000 of its bank loan.

10. During the year, CFS incurred other expenses of $20,000, all paid in cash.

11. CFS paid a dividend of $15,000 on September 15, 2006.

12. During the year CFS paid the $5,000 in taxes payable that was owing to the federal and provincial governments on October 31, 2005.

13. In November 2005 CFS supplied $3,000 of equipment to a large daycare centre. The daycare centre had paid in advance for the equipment in October 2005. The payment was reported as unearned revenue on the October 31, 2005 balance sheet.

14. At the end of the year CFS owed the part-time sales person $1,500 in salary and commissions. The amount owing will be paid in mid-November 2006.

15. Amortization of capital assets is $6,000, including the used car that was purchased on November 15, 2005.

16. The cost of the safety equipment sold during the year was $72,000.

17. CFS will have to pay $6,700 in income taxes for the 2006 fiscal year. No payments had been made with respect to the 2006 fiscal year as of October 31, 2006.

To prepare the balance sheet as of October 31, 2006 and the income statement and statement of retained earnings for the year ended October 31, 2006, we will use an accounting equation spreadsheet to record all of the above transactions and events. Table 3-12 provides the completed spreadsheet for the year ended October 31, 2006. Most of the entries should be clear, but note the following points:

- The first line of the spreadsheet, which is called "beginning balance", contains the values on the balance sheet on October 31, 2005. Remember that balance sheet accounts are permanent, so the ending balances in last year's balance sheet are always the beginning balances in this year's balance sheet. The income statement accounts all have beginning balances of zero. This is because the income statement accounts are closed each year to retained earnings, as we saw in the previous section.

Table 3-12 Child First Safety Completed Spreadsheet

| | | Assets | | | | | | = | Liabilities | | |
Transaction	Type of entry	Cash	Accounts Receivable	Inventory	Prepaid Insurance	Capital Assets	Accumulated Amortization		Bank Loan	Accounts Payable	Salaries Payable
Beginning Balance		12,800	22,000	52,000	0	24,000	(8,000)		15,000	49,000	0
1	Transactional	(3,000)			3,000						
2	Transactional	140,000	59,000								
3	Transactional			65,000						65,000	
4	Transactional	(62,000)								(62,000)	
5	Transactional	(12,000)				12,000					
6	Transactional	(70,000)									
7	Transactional	45,000	(45,000)								
8	Transactional	(900)									
9	Transactional	(2,000)							(2,000)		
10	Transactional	(20,000)									
11	Transactional	(15,000)									
12	Transactional	(5,000)									
13	Adjusting										
14	Adjusting										1,500
15	Adjusting						(6,000)				
16	Adjusting			(72,000)							
17	Adjusting										
18	Adjusting				(1,500)						
		7,900	36,000	45,000	1,500	36,000	(14,000)		13,000	52,000	1,500
19	Closing										
Ending Balance		7,900	36,000	45,000	1,500	36,000	(14,000)		13,000	52,000	1,500

- The amortization expense in item 14 is the portion of the cost of capital assets that is matched to sales in the current period. As shown above, the amortization of the capital assets is usually made to a separate contra-asset account and not directly to the capital asset account itself.

- Item 18 is tricky because the question does not specifically state that part of the prepaid insurance has to be expensed at year end. This is typical of adjusting entries. Because adjusting entries are generated within the entity, the accountant or bookkeeper has to examine the accounts and decide when an adjusting entry is necessary.

The balance sheet, income statement, and statement of retained earnings are shown in Table 3-13 (page 140).

How Did Child First Safety Ltd. (CFS) Do?

Since we have put these financial statements together on behalf of Yehuda, who does not seem too concerned about the accounting information, we should probably give him some insights into what these statements say. We should warn Yehuda that the financial statements do not provide clear-cut answers to questions about an entity's situation. The statements raise flags for further investigation.

1. As was the case with Strawberries Inc., our ability to analyze the performance of CFS is hampered by the absence of comparable income statement data. We do have the October 31, 2005 balance sheet for making comparisons between balance sheet accounts.

2. It can be difficult to evaluate the financial statements of an entity when the owner

Liabilities (cont'd)		+	Shareholders' Equity									
Taxes Payable	Unearned Revenue		Capital Stock	Retained Earnings	Sales	Cost of sales	Insurance Expense	Salaries Expense	Amort. Expense	Other Expenses	Tax Expense	Interest Expense
5,000	3,000		15,000	15,800								
					199,000							
						(70,000)						
												(900)
										(20,000)		
				(15,000)								
(5,000)												
	(3,000)				3,000							
								(1,500)				
									(6,000)			
						(72,000)						
6,700											(6,700)	
							(1,500)					
6,700	0		15,000	800	202,000	(72,000)	(1,500)	(71,500)	(6,000)	(20,000)	(6,700)	(900)
				23,400	(202,000)	72,000	1,500	71,500	6,000	20,000	6,700	900
6,700	0		15,000	24,200	0	0	0	0	0	0	0	0

also manages the entity. One reason is that the salary the owner receives may not bear any relationship to market value of the work he or she provides to the entity. That is because owner-managers are free to pay themselves any amount they choose and the payments can take different forms, including salary, dividends, and loans. Remember that only salary reduces net income so different combinations of payments made to owner-managers will have different effects on net income. Often, an important objective of owner-managers of private corporations is to minimize the overall tax burden on themselves and their corporation.

3. Without knowing his share of the salaries expense, we cannot make a conclusive statement about how well-paid Yehuda was this year, but it appears that he had a reasonably good year. If we assume that Yehuda's share of the Salaries Expense was $45,000 (which is probably a reasonable assumption given that the sales person was a part-time employee), Yehuda took home $60,000 in salary and dividends ($45,000 in salary + $15,000 in dividends). In addition, his business made money so that also added to his wealth.

4. At first glance CFS's liquidity position seems adequate. Its current ratio has been stable for the two years available (1.23 in 2006, 1.21 in 2005). We would need to compare these current ratios with other businesses of this type to get some perspective of the adequacy of this current ratio. Of some concern is the low amount of cash and receivables (current assets that are cash or will be cash very soon) relative to the liabilities that will require cash very soon (accounts, wages, and taxes payable). If sales slow down, there may be a cash problem if the conversion of inventory to cash is delayed. In other words, CFS faces the possibility that it might run out of cash. However, CFS's liquidity position was similar a year ago and it seems to have managed through it.

5. CFS generated a return on equity of about 67% (Net income ÷ Average shareholders' equity), a very good return on investment. The profit margin for the year is 11.6%. This ratio is difficult to assess without some comparative data from similar businesses.

6. Compared with October 31, 2005, the amount of inventory on hand on October 31, 2006 has decreased, while the amount of accounts receivable has increased. Without comparable income statements to tell us how sales changed from fiscal 2005, it is difficult to interpret these changes. For example, the increase in accounts receivable could be due to much higher sales, more generous credit terms being offered by CFS to attract more business, customers paying less frequently than last year, or other reasons.

Table 3-13   Child First Safety Ltd. Balance Sheet, and Income Statement and Statement of Retained Earnings

Child First Safety Ltd.
Balance Sheet
As of October 31, 2006

Assets		Liabilities and Shareholders' Equity	
Current assets		**Current liabilities**	
Cash	$ 7,900	Bank loan	$ 13,000
Accounts receivable	36,000	Accounts payable	52,000
Inventory	45,000	Salaries payable	1,500
Prepaid insurance	1,500	Taxes payable	6,700
	90,400		73,200
Non-current assets		**Shareholder's equity**	
Capital assets	36,000	Capital stock	15,000
Accumulated amortization	(14,000)	Retained earnings	24,200
	22,000		39,200
		Total liabilities and	
Total assets	$112,400	shareholder's equity	$112,400

Child First Safety Ltd.
Income Statement and Statement of Retained Earnings
For the Year Ended October 31, 2006

Sales		$202,000
Cost of sales		72,000
Gross margin		130,000
Expenses		
Insurance expense	$ 1,500	
Salaries expense	71,500	
Amortization expense	6,000	
Other expenses	20,000	
Interest expense	900	
Total expenses		99,900
Income before taxes		30,100
Income tax expense		6,700
Net income		23,400
Retained earnings at the beginning of the year		15,800
Dividends		(15,000)
Retained earnings at the end of the year		$ 24,200

Analyzing accounting information can be difficult. There are rarely answers and usually many questions. You should already see that the numbers reported in financial statements cannot simply be taken at face value. When managers have choices for how to account for transactions and other economic events, the choices they make will affect the accounting numbers that are reported, which in turn may affect how the numbers are interpreted and what decisions stakeholders make. That is why it is always necessary to look behind the numbers.

■ Solved Problem

Gary's Computer Maintenance Ltd. (GCML) is a small computer repair shop owned and operated by Gary Armstrong. Gary's wife Susan is a 50% shareholder in GCML but she is not involved in the operations of the company. GCML has been in business for three years since being incorporated in 2002. Because he has been so busy recently and lacks expertise in financial matters, Gary has asked you to prepare the financial statements for GCML for 2005. Gary provides you with the company's balance sheet for the year ended December 31, 2004 (Table 3-14) and the following information about GCML's activities in the year.

Information about GCML's activities during 2005:

1. In August 2005 GCML signed a lease for a new shop on the main street in town. Monthly rent is $1,200. GCML paid six months' rent in advance when it signed the lease. The lease came into effect when GCML occupied the new shop on November 1, 2005. GCML paid rent of $10,000 in cash from January though October 2005 for its previous location.

2. During 2005 GCML earned revenues of $188,000. Credit sales accounted for $56,000 of the revenues earned.

3. GCML purchased capital assets for $12,000 cash during 2005.

4. During 2005 GCML purchased inventory of parts and supplies for $52,000. All inventory purchases were on credit.

5. During 2005 GCML collected $65,000 in amounts due from customers.

6. GCML paid suppliers $24,000 for inventory it purchased during 2005. It also paid $26,000 to suppliers for amounts owing on December 31, 2004.

Table 3-14   Gary's Computer Maintenance Ltd. Balance Sheet

Gary's Computer Maintenance Ltd.
Balance Sheet
As of December 31, 2004

Assets			Liabilities and Shareholders' Equity	
Current assets			**Current liabilities**	
Cash	$ 12,000		Bank loan	$ 15,000
Accounts receivable	47,000		Accounts payable	26,000
Inventory	38,000		Taxes payable	3,000
	97,000		Interest payable	400
				44,400
Non-current assets			**Shareholders' equity**	
Capital assets	22,000		Capital stock	30,000
Accumulated amortization	(10,000)		Retained earnings	34,600
	12,000			64,600
			Total liabilities and	
Total assets	$109,000		shareholders' equity	$109,000

7. On March 2, 2005 GCML borrowed an additional $8,000 from the bank.

8. During 2005 GCML paid cash dividends of $30,000 to its shareholders.

9. GMCL paid employees salaries of $45,000. In addition, Gary was paid a salary of $25,000. All salaries paid pertained to work done in 2005. At the end of 2005 GMCL owed employees $1,000.

10. During 2005 GMCL incurred other expenses of $27,000, all paid in cash.

11. During the year GCML paid the $3,000 in taxes payable that was owing to the federal and provincial governments on December 31, 2004.

12. In December 2005 GCML signed a number of one-year contracts to provide ongoing 24-hour service to customers' computers at their places of business. All of the contracts take effect in January 2006. The customers paid $10,000 in cash to GCML in December 2005 as deposits against future services to be provided.

13. During 2005 GCML paid the bank $2,000 in interest. Of that amount, $1,600 pertained to 2005 and the remainder was owed to the bank from fiscal 2004. On December 31, 2005 GCML owed the bank $600 in interest, which will be paid in March 2006.

14. On December 31, 2005 Gary counted the inventory of parts and supplies on hand. His count showed that there was $41,000 of inventory on hand. (Use this information to figure out how much inventory was used during 2005.)

15. Amortization of capital assets was $5,000.

Table 3-15   GCML Completed Spreadsheet for the Year Ended December 31, 2005

		Assets						=	Liabilities			
Transaction	Type of entry	Cash	Accounts Receivable	Parts and Supplies Inventory	Prepaid-Rent	Capital Assets	Accumulated Amortization		Bank Loan	Accounts Payable	Salaries Payable	Taxes Payable
Beginning Balance		12,000	47,000	38,000	0	22,000	(10,000)		15,000	26,000	0	3,000
1	Transactional	(7,200)			7,200							
1	Transactional	(10,000)										
2	Transactional	132,000	56,000									
3	Transactional	(12,000)				12,000						
4	Transactional			52,000						52,000		
5	Transactional	65,000	(65,000)									
6	Transactional	(50,000)								(50,000)		
7	Transactional	8,000							8,000			
8	Transactional	(30,000)										
9	Transactional	(70,000)										
10	Transactional	(27,000)										
11	Transactional	(3,000)										(3,000)
12	Transactional	10,000										
13	Transactional	(2,000)										
13	Adjusting											
14	Adjusting			(49,000)								
15	Adjusting						(5,000)					
16	Adjusting											3,200
17	Adjusting				(2,400)							
18	Adjusting										1,000	
		15,800	38,000	41,000	4,800	34,000	(15,000)		23,000	28,000	1,000	3,200
19	Closing											
Ending Balance		15,800	38,000	41,000	4,800	34,000	(15,000)		23,000	28,000	1,000	3,200

16. GCML will have to pay $3,200 in income taxes for the year. No payments had been made with respect to the fiscal 2005 year as of December 31, 2005.

Required:

Use an accounting equation spreadsheet to record all of the above events and transactions for GCML during 2005. Make sure to include the adjusting and closing entries. Prepare the balance sheet as of December 31, 2005 and the income statement and the statement of retained earnings for the year ended December 31, 2005.

Solution:

Table 3-15 gives the completed spreadsheet for the year ended December 31, 2005. The balance sheet, income statement, and statement of retained earnings are shown in Table 3-16. Most of the entries should be clear, but note the following points:

- The spreadsheet shows two entries for transaction 1. This was necessary to show the prepayment of rent for the new location ($7,200) and the rent expense for the previous location ($10,000).

- Item 14 provides the ending inventory balance for GCML on December 31, 2005. This information can be used along with the inventory on hand at the beginning of the year and the inventory purchased during 2005 to calculate Cost of Sales.

$$
\begin{aligned}
\text{Cost of Sales} &= \text{Beginning Inventory} + \text{Purchases} - \text{Ending Inventory} \\
&= \$38,000 + \$52,000 - \$41,000 \\
&= \$49,000
\end{aligned}
$$

Liabilities (cont'd)		+				Shareholders' Equity							
Unearned Revenue	Interest Payable		Capital Stock	Retained Earnings	Sales	Cost of Sales	Rent Expense	Salaries Expense	Amort. Expense	Other Expenses	Tax Expense	Interest Expense
0	400		30,000	34,600								
							(10,000)					
					188,000							
				(30,000)								
								(70,000)				
										(27,000)		
10,000												
	(400)											(1,600)
	600											(600)
						(49,000)						
									(5,000)			
											(3,200)	
							(2,400)					
								(1,000)				
10,000	600		30,000	4,600	188,000	(49,000)	(12,400)	(71,000)	(5,000)	(27,000)	(3,200)	(2,200)
				18,200	(188,000)	49,000	12,400	71,000	5,000	27,000	3,200	2,200
10,000	600		30,000	22,800	0	0	0	0	0	0	0	0

Table 3-16   Gary's Computer Maintenance Ltd. Balance Sheet, and Income Statement and Statement of Retained Earnings

Gary's Computer Maintenance Ltd.
Balance Sheet
As of December 31, 2005

Assets		Liabilities and Shareholders' Equity	
Current assets		**Current liabilities**	
Cash	$ 15,800	Bank loan	$ 23,000
Accounts receivable	38,000	Accounts payable	28,000
Inventory	41,000	Salaries payable	1,000
Prepaid rent	4,800	Taxes payable	3,200
	99,600	Unearned revenue	10,000
		Interest payable	600
			65,800
Non-current assets		**Shareholder's equity**	
Capital assets	34,000	Capital stock	30,000
Accumulated amortization	(15,000)	Retained earnings	22,800
	19,000		52,800
		Total liabilities and	
Total assets	$118,600	shareholders' equity	$118,600

Gary's Computer Maintenance Ltd.
Income Statement and Statement of Retained Earnings
For the Year Ended December 31, 2005

Sales		$188,000
Cost of sales		49,000
Gross margin		139,000
Expenses		
Rent expense	$ 12,400	
Salaries expense	71,000	
Amortization expense	5,000	
Other expense	27,000	
Interest expense	2,200	
Total expenses		117,600
Income before taxes		21,400
Income tax expense		3,200
Net income		18,200
Retained earnings, January 1, 2005		34,600
Dividends		(30,000)
Retained earnings, December 31, 2005		$ 22,800

- Entry 17 is an adjusting entry that expenses two months' rent for the new location (November and December). Prepaid Rent decreases by $2,400 ($1,200 per month × 2 months) because two of the prepaid months' rent have been consumed.

- Entry 18 is an adjusting entry that records salaries earned by employees but not paid as of December 31, 2005. This information is from item 9 in the question.

Summary of Key Points

LO 1. The key to producing accounting information is having an accounting system that captures raw data and organizes, summarizes, and classifies the data into a form that is useful for decision making. The information provided by an accounting system is limited by the data that are entered into it.

The accounting cycle is the process by which data about economic events are entered into an accounting system, processed, organized, and used to produce information, such as financial statements. An accounting system is very important because if data were not processed and organized it would be very difficult for anyone to understand and use it.

LO 2. The accounting equation spreadsheet is a device that is used to record transactions and economic events in a way that allows the information to be conveniently collected and organized, and then presented in financial statements. The accounting equation spreadsheet has columns for each account in the entity's records. Each transaction or economic event is recorded on a separate line in the spreadsheet. Each entry to the spreadsheet must maintain the accounting equation of Assets = Liabilities + Owners' (Shareholders') Equity. The ending balance in each column of the spreadsheet represents the ending balance in that account at a point in time and can be used to prepare balance sheets, income statements, and statements of retained earnings.

LO 3. The journal entry is the method used in practice to enter information about economic events into the accounting system. Whenever an economic event or transaction occurs that is to be entered into the accounting system, a journal entry is made. Journal entries provide compact and concise summaries of economic events in a way that makes it easy to see and understand the effect the event has on the financial statements. Debits and credits are the notations used to record the effects of an economic event on the accounts. Debits represent increases in assets and expenses, and decreases in liabilities, owners' (shareholders') equity, and revenue. Credits represent decreases in assets and expenses, and increases in liabilities, owners' (shareholders') equity, and revenue.

LO 4. Devices such as accounting equation spreadsheets and journal entries are only means to an end. These devices give us the ability to record and organize, summarize, and classify data into information that is useful for decision making. Accounting methods such as accrual accounting and GAAP often provide preparers of accounting information with choices for how to record and report transactions and economic events. When managers have choices for how to account for transactions and other economic events, their decisions will affect the accounting numbers that are reported, which in turn may affect how the numbers are interpreted and the decisions stakeholders make. That is why it is always necessary to look behind the numbers.

LO 5. Accrual accounting attempts to measure the economic activity and economic changes of an entity. An entry into an accrual accounting system is usually triggered by a transaction—an exchange between the entity and a party external to the entity. Sometimes, however, economic changes occur that affect the wealth of the entity but that are not triggered by transactions. These changes must be recorded in the accounting system. Entries to the accounting system that are not triggered by exchanges with outside entities are called adjusting entries.

There are four types of adjusting entries:

1. Deferred expense/prepaid expense where cash is paid before the expense is recognized;

2. Deferred revenue where cash is received before revenue is recognized;

3. Accrued liability where the expense is recognized before cash is paid; and

4. Accrued asset where revenue is recognized before cash is received.

LO 6. Income statement accounts are sub-accounts of an entity's owners' equity account (retained earnings account in the case of a corporation). Separate income statement accounts are maintained so that information about revenues and expenses can be collected. At the end of each period the balances in the income statement, or temporary accounts, must be set to zero and the balances in those accounts transferred to their permanent place in the owners' equity section of the balance sheet. The balances in the income statement accounts are set to zero so that they can accumulate information about transactions and economic events that pertain only to the next period. The setting of temporary accounts to zero and the transferring of the balances in those accounts to owners' equity is achieved by a closing journal entry.

Appendix: The Accounting Cycle

Introduction

The accounting equation spreadsheet approach discussed in the main part of Chapter 3 is a straightforward method to show how transactions and economic events affect the financial statements. The spreadsheet approach provides a technique for preparing financial statements without getting into many of the details of bookkeeping. This appendix will go though the steps that are followed in keeping formal accounting records so those students who wish to learn the complete accounting cycle may do so. The steps in the accounting cycle are shown in Figure 3-A1.

Prepare Journal Entries

As described in the main part of Chapter 3, the initial recognition of a transaction or other economic event is made by a journal entry. The journal entry is recorded in the **general journal**, a chronological record of the journal entries that have been entered into the accounting system. The general journal is referred to as the book of original entry because an event is first recorded in the accounting system in the general journal. The general journal can be an actual book where entries are physically written down or a computerized accounting package.

An example of a general journal is shown in Figure 3-A2. Figure 3-A2 shows that the general journal is a dated list of the journal entries that are made by the entity. The reference number is useful because it allows for easy tracing of entries as they proceed through the accounting system. Regardless of whether data are recorded in the accounting system manually or by computer, the process of the accounting cycle is the same. Review the section on journal entries on pages 116–119 to ensure you understand them.

Post Journal Entries to the General Ledger

The next step in the accounting cycle is posting the journal entry to the general ledger. The **general ledger** is a record of all the accounts of an entity. **Posting** a journal entry to the general ledger is the process of transferring each line of a journal entry to the corresponding account in the general ledger. You can picture the general ledger as a book where each page represents a different account, although again computerized general ledgers are common. There will be a page for Cash, a page for Inventory, a page for Sales, and so on. The general ledger organizes information on an account-by-account basis, rather than on a transaction-by-transaction basis as is the case with the general journal. In the spreadsheet method, each column represents a general ledger account.

Figure 3-A1

The Accounting Cycle

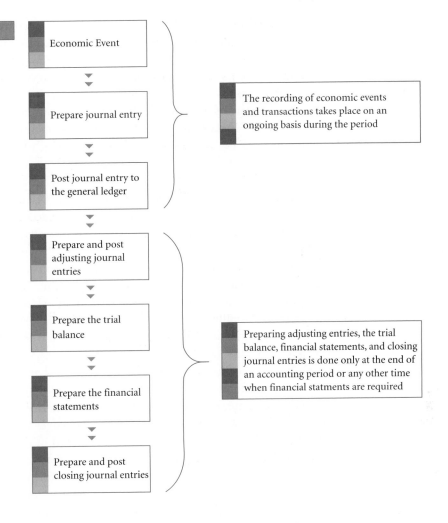

Economic Event

↓

Prepare journal entry

↓

Post journal entry to the general ledger

The recording of economic events and transactions takes place on an ongoing basis during the period

↓

Prepare and post adjusting journal entries

↓

Prepare the trial balance

↓

Prepare the financial statements

↓

Prepare and post closing journal entries

Preparing adjusting entries, the trial balance, financial statements, and closing journal entries is done only at the end of an accounting period or any other time when financial statments are required

---

Figure 3-A2

The General Journal

The reference number provides easy tracing through the accounting system

Accounts affected by the tranaction or economic event and a description of the entry

		General Journal		
Reference Number	**Date**	**Transaction**	**Debit**	**Credit**
1	Aug 15	Cash	10,000	
		Accounts receivable		10,000
		Collection from customer.		
2	Aug 16	Inventory	20,000	
		Accounts payable		20,000
		Purchase of inventory on credit.		

The general journal is a chronological record of transactions and other economic events that are entered into the accounting system

Amount by which each account is affected

In accounting textbooks a device called the **T-account** is used to represent general ledger accounts. (The name "T-account" is used because the device has the shape of the letter T.) Each T-account corresponds with an account in the accounting system and represents a page in the general ledger or a column on the accounting equation spreadsheet.

The structure of the T-account is shown in Figure 3-A3. The name of the account is written on the horizontal line at the top. The vertical line separates the debits and credits made to the account. The beginning balance—the balance in the account at the beginning of the period—is shown between the horizontal lines at the top of the T-account. The ending balance is shown between the horizontal lines at the bottom. If an account has a debit balance at the beginning or end of the period, the balance is recorded on the left side of the vertical line. If an account has a credit balance at the beginning or end of the period, the balance is recorded on the right side of the vertical line.

When a journal entry is posted to the T-accounts, debits are recorded on the left side of the vertical line and credits on the right side. The difference between the debits and credits in an account plus the beginning balance gives the ending balance in the account. Usually, asset accounts have debit balances and liability and owners' equity accounts have credit balances, although there are exceptions. The posting process is shown in Figure 3-A4.

Whereas a journal entry allows you to see which accounts a transaction or economic event affects, a general ledger account allows you to see the activity in the account over time. If you wanted to examine the activity in inventory over the last year, you would look at the inventory general ledger account. If you then wanted to examine the individual events that were recorded in the general ledger account, you would go back to the journal entry, which describes the specific event.

In practice, an entity will have many more accounts in its general ledger than are shown on the financial statements because many account balances are combined and shown as one total. For example, MWW would maintain separate accounts for different types of inventory. There could be hundreds of separate inventory accounts, one for each type of inventory that MWW sells. However on the balance sheet only a single amount for inventory is shown. The many separate inventory accounts provide detail that is useful for management decision making and control.

This detail is excluded from the financial statements so that the statements are easier to use. It also prevents too much information from being disclosed to competitors.

Prepare and Post Adjusting Journal Entries

Preparation of journal entries and posting them to the general ledger occurs on an ongoing basis during a reporting period. The remaining steps in the accounting cycle occur at the end of a period when the entity wants to prepare financial statements.

Adjusting journal entries were discussed in detail on pages 124–134. At the end of the period the managers examine the general ledger accounts and determine the adjusting entries that must be made. Many adjusting entries are automatic, as man-

Figure 3-A3

The T-Account

	Account Name	
Beginnning Balance		
Debits		Credits
Ending Balance		

Figure 3-A4

The Posting Process

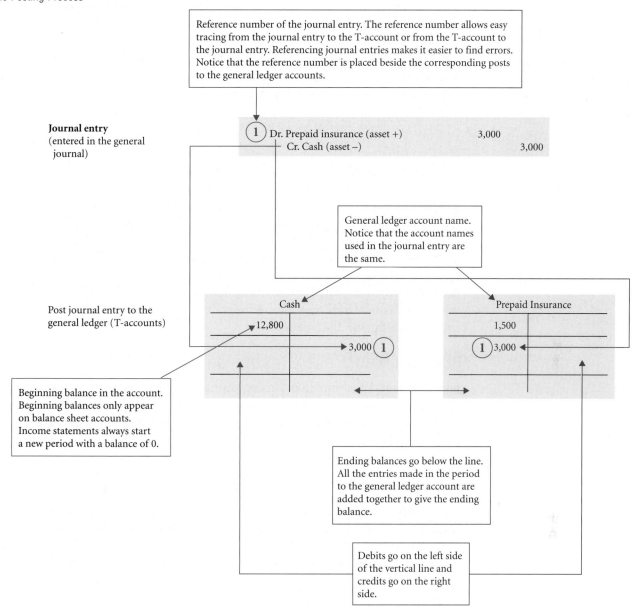

Reference number of the journal entry. The reference number allows easy tracing from the journal entry to the T-account or from the T-account to the journal entry. Referencing journal entries makes it easier to find errors. Notice that the reference number is placed beside the corresponding posts to the general ledger accounts.

Journal entry
(entered in the general journal)

① Dr. Prepaid insurance (asset +)   3,000
    Cr. Cash (asset −)   3,000

General ledger account name. Notice that the account names used in the journal entry are the same.

Post journal entry to the general ledger (T-accounts)

Cash
12,800
3,000 ①

Prepaid Insurance
1,500
① 3,000

Beginning balance in the account. Beginning balances only appear on balance sheet accounts. Income statements always start a new period with a balance of 0.

Ending balances go below the line. All the entries made in the period to the general ledger account are added together to give the ending balance.

Debits go on the left side of the vertical line and credits go on the right side.

agers know that certain adjustments have to be made each period. Other adjustments do not occur regularly and managers must be careful to make sure that these are also recorded.

Prepare the Trial Balance

The **trial balance** is a listing of all the accounts in the general ledger with their balances. The main purpose of the trial balance is to ensure that the debits equal the credits and to provide a summary of the balances in each account. If debits and credits are unequal there is an error somewhere in the accounts that must be corrected.

However, having equal debits and credits does not mean that the accounting has been done properly. It simply means that all journal entries and postings to the general ledger accounts were balanced. For example, if an entity purchases land and promises to pay for the land in one year, the correct entry would be to debit Land (asset) and credit Payables (liability). But if the accountant incorrectly debited the Cash account instead of the Land account, the debits and credits would still balance but the account balances would not be correct.

Sometimes several trial balances are prepared at the end of a period. Trial balances are sometimes prepared before and after preparation of the adjusting entries, as well as after the closing entry has been prepared. Each trial balance helps ensure that the posting of the journal entries balances at each step.

Prepare the Financial Statements

The list of the accounts and balances in the trial balance is a useful source of information for preparing the financial statements. All the information required to prepare the balance sheet and income statement is in the trial balance. The accounts in the trial balance have to be aggregated and organized into the format desired by the managers. However, at this stage there is one piece of information missing from the trial balance that prevents complete preparation of the financial statements. The missing information is the ending balance in Retained Earnings that will be reported on the year-end balance sheet. The ending balance in Retained Earnings is not known because the income statement accounts have not yet been closed. Once the income statement accounts have been closed, the ending balance in Retained Earnings is available for inclusion on the balance sheet.

Prepare and Post Closing Journal Entries

Preparation and posting of the closing journal entry is the last step in the accounting cycle. The closing entry sets the income statement accounts to zero and updates the balance in retained earnings to its year-end balance. (Closing entries are discussed on pages 134–136).

Comprehensive Example

The description of the accounting cycle has so far been rather abstract. We will now work through the full accounting cycle using the Child First Safety Ltd. (CFS) example developed in the main body of Chapter 3. The mechanics of the accounting cycle are relatively straightforward. Learning them is just a matter of practice.

Prepare Journal Entries

1.	Dr. Prepaid insurance (asset +)	3,000	
	Cr. Cash (asset −)		3,000
	To record the purchase of insurance for two years.		
2.	Dr. Cash (asset +)	140,000	
	Dr. Accounts receivable (asset +)	59,000	
	Cr. Sales (revenue +, shareholders' equity +)		199,000
	To record sales for the year.		
3.	Dr. Inventory (asset +)	65,000	
	Cr. Accounts payable (liability +)		65,000
	To record the purchase of inventory on credit.		
4.	Dr. Accounts payable (liability −)	62,000	
	Cr. Cash (asset −)		62,000
	To record the payment to suppliers for inventory purchased.		

5. Dr. Capital assets (asset +)   12,000
        Cr. Cash (asset −)   12,000
    To record the purchase of a car.

6. Dr. Salaries expense (expenses +, shareholders' equity −)   70,000
        Cr. Cash (asset −)   70,000
    To record salaries paid.

7. Dr. Cash (asset +)   45,000
        Cr. Accounts receivable (asset −)   45,000
    To record collection of accounts receivable.

8. Dr. Interest expense (expense +, shareholders' equity −)   900
        Cr. Cash (asset −)   900
    To record the payment of interest on the bank loan.

9. Dr. Bank loan (liability −)   2,000
        Cr. Cash (asset −)   2,000
    To record payment of principal on the bank loan.

10. Dr. Other expenses (expense +, shareholders' equity −)   20,000
        Cr. Cash (asset −)   20,000
    To record the payment of other expenses

11. Dr. Retained earnings (shareholders' equity −)   15,000
        Cr. Cash (asset −)   15,000
    To record the payment of a dividend.

12. Dr. Taxes payable (liability −)   5,000
        Cr. Cash (asset −)   5,000
    To record the payment of taxes payable.

Post Journal Entries to the General Ledger

Next, the elements of each journal entry are posted to the appropriate general ledger accounts. T-accounts will be used to represent the general ledger accounts. The T-accounts are shown in Figure 3-A5. On the left side of each line in each T-account there is a number that corresponds to the number of the journal entry. This cross-referencing is important because it makes it easy to trace back from the general ledger account to the journal entry. For students this is important because it is common to make posting errors. The cross-referencing makes it easy to find the journal entry associated with each ledger entry when you are trying to find errors.

In addition, for each balance sheet T-account a beginning balance is shown. This is the amount that was in the account on October 31, 2005. Remember that income statement accounts do not have beginning balances because they were set to zero on October 31, 2005 when the temporary accounts were closed.

Prepare and Post Adjusting Journal Entries

At the end of the period the accounts are examined and any necessary adjusting entries are made. The adjusting entries are then posted to the corresponding general ledger accounts. Posting of the adjusting entries to the T-accounts is shown in Figure 3-A6, while the journal entries are shown below. The adjusting entries in Figure 3A-6 are posted to the T-accounts in bold.

13. Dr. Unearned revenue (liability −)   3,000
        Cr. Sales (revenue +, shareholders' equity +)   3,000
    Adjusting entry to record recognition of revenue on
    merchandise paid for in advance.

14. Dr. Salaries expense (expense +, shareholders' equity −)   1,500
    Cr. Salaries payable (liability +)   1,500
    Adjusting entry to accrue salaries owed but not paid.

15. Dr. Amortization expense (expense +, shareholders' equity −)   6,000
    Cr. Accumulated amortization (contra-asset +)   6,000
    Adjusting entry to record the amortization of capital assets.

16. Dr. Cost of sales (expense +, shareholders' equity −)   72,000
    Cr. Inventory (asset −)   72,000
    Adjusting entry to record cost of sales.

17. Dr. Tax expense (expense +, shareholders' equity −)   6,700
    Cr. Taxes payable (liability +)   6,700
    Adjusting entry to record income tax expense and accrue the liability for income taxes.

18. Dr. Insurance expense (expense +, shareholders' equity −)   1,500
    Cr. Prepaid insurance (asset −)   1,500
    Adjusting entry to record insurance used during the year.

Figure 3-A5

T-Accounts for Child First Safety Ltd. before Adjusting Entries are Posted

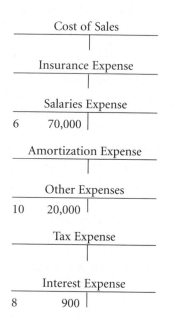

Cash

Bal	12,800	
1		3,000
2	140,000	
4		62,000
5		12,000
6		70,000
7	45,000	
8		900
9		2,000
10		20,000
11		15,000
12		5,000

Accounts Receivable

Bal	22,000	
2	59,000	
7		45,000

Inventory

Bal	52,000	
3	65,000	
16		72,000

Prepaid Insurance

Bal	0	
1	3,000	

Capital Assets

Bal	24,000	
5	12,000	

Accumulated Amortization

Bal		8,000

Bank Loan

Bal		15,000
9	2,000	

Accounts Payable

Bal		49,000
3		65,000
4	62,000	

Salaries Payable

Bal		0

Taxes Payable

Bal		5,000
12	5,000	

Unearned Revenue

Bal		3,000

Capital Stock

Bal		15,000

Retained Earnings

Bal		15,800
11	15,000	

Sales

2		199,000

Cost of Sales

Insurance Expense

Salaries Expense

6	70,000	

Amortization Expense

Other Expenses

10	20,000	

Tax Expense

Interest Expense

8	900	

Prepare the Trial Balance

The ending balance in each general ledger account (T-account) is organized into a trial balance. The ending balance in each T-account with a debit balance is placed in the left column of the trial balance and the ending balance in each T-account with a credit balance is placed in the right column. The trial balance is shown in Table 3-A1. The trial balance in Table 3-A1 was prepared after the adjusting journal entries had been made and posted to the appropriate ledger accounts. It would also be possible to prepare a trial balance before the adjusting entries were made.

Figure 3-A6

T-Accounts for Child First Safety Ltd. After Adjusting Entries Are Posted

Cash

Bal	12,800		
1		3,000	
2	140,000		
4		62,000	
5		12,000	
6		70,000	
7	45,000		
8		900	
9		2,000	
10		20,000	
11		15,000	
12		5,000	
Bal	7,900		

Accounts Receivable

Bal	22,000		
2	59,000		
7		45,000	
Bal	36,000		

Inventory

Bal	52,000		
3	65,000		
16		**72,000**	
Bal	45,000		

Prepaid Insurance

Bal	0		
1	3,000		
18		**1,500**	
Bal	1,500		

Capital Assets

Bal	24,000		
5	12,000		
Bal	36,000		

Accumulated Amortization

Bal		8,000	
15		**6,000**	
Bal		14,000	

Bank Loan

Bal		15,000	
9	2,000		
Bal		13,000	

Accounts Payable

Bal		49,000	
3		65,000	
4	62,000		
Bal		52,000	

Salaries Payable

Bal		0	
14		**1,500**	
Bal		1,500	

Taxes Payable

Bal		5,000	
12	5,000		
17		**6,700**	
Bal		6,700	

Unearned Revenue

Bal		3,000	
13	**3,000**		
Bal		0	

Capital Stock

Bal		15,000	
Bal		15,000	

Retained Earnings

Bal		15,800	
11	15,000		
Bal		800	

Sales

2		199,000	
13		**3,000**	
Bal		202,000	

Cost of Sales

16	**72,000**		
Bal	72,000		

Insurance Expense

18	**1,500**		
Bal	1,500		

Salaries Expense

6	70,000		
14	**1,500**		
Bal	71,500		

Amortization Expense

15	**6,000**		
Bal	6,000		

Other Expenses

10	20,000		
Bal	20,000		

Tax Expense

17	**6,700**		
Bal	6,700		

Interest Expense

8	900		
Bal	900		

Table 3-A1   Child First Safety Ltd. Trial Balance

Child First Safety Ltd.
Trial Balance
October 31, 2006

	Debits	Credits	
Cash	$ 7,900		
Accounts receivable	36,000		
Inventory	45,000		
Prepaid insurance	1,500		
Capital assets	36,000		
Accumulated amortization		$ 14,000	Balance sheet accounts
Bank loan		13,000	
Accounts payable		52,000	
Salaries payable		1,500	
Taxes payable		6,700	
Unearned revenue		0	
Capital stock		15,000	
Retained earnings		800	
Sales		202,000	
Cost of sales	72,000		
Insurance expense	1,500		
Salaries expense	71,500		Income statement accounts
Amortization expense	6,000		
Other expenses	20,000		
Tax expense	6,700		
Interest expense	900		
	$305,000	$305,000	→ Debits = Credits

Prepare the Financial Statements

The balances listed in the trial balance can then be used to prepare the financial statements. (The financial statements are the same as the ones in Table 3-13 on page 140.) The financial statements are prepared before the closing entry because at this stage the balances in the income statement accounts are still present. Once the closing entry is made, the balances in the income statement accounts become zero. However, preparing the statements before the closing entry is made means that the ending balance in retained earnings is not known from the trial balance. (Ending retained earnings can be calculated by using the following formula: Ending retained earnings = beginning retained earnings + total revenues − total expenses − dividends.)

Prepare and Post Closing Journal Entries

The last step in the accounting cycle is the closing entry that sets all the income statement accounts to zero and transfers those amounts to retained earnings. The closing journal entry is shown on page 156 and the T-accounts after the closing entry has been posted are shown in Figure 3-A7. The after-closing trial balance (the trial balance prepared after the closing entry has been posted) is shown in Table 3-A2. Notice that the income statement accounts all have zero balances and the balance in the Retained Earnings corresponds with the amount on the October 31, 2006 balance sheet. The closing entries in Figure 3A-7 are posted to the T-accounts in bold.

Figure 3-A7

Post-closing T-Accounts for Child First Safety Ltd.

Cash		
Bal	12,800	
1		3,000
2	140,000	
4		62,000
5		12,000
6		70,000
7	45,000	
8		900
9		2,000
10		20,000
11		15,000
12		5,000
Bal	7,900	

Accounts Receivable		
Bal	22,000	
2	59,000	
7		45,000
Bal	36,000	

Inventory		
Bal	52,000	
3	65,000	
16		72,000
Bal	45,000	

Prepaid Insurance		
Bal	0	
1	3,000	
18		1,500
Bal	1,500	

Capital Assets		
Bal	24,000	
5	12,000	
Bal	36,000	

Accumulated Amortization		
Bal		8,000
15		6,000
Bal		14,000

Bank Loan		
Bal		15,000
9	2,000	
Bal		13,000

Accounts Payable		
Bal		49,000
3		65,000
4	62,000	
Bal		52,000

Salaries Payable		
Bal		0
14		1,500
Bal		1,500

Taxes Payable		
Bal		5,000
12	5,000	
17		6,700
Bal		6,700

Unearned Revenue		
Bal		3,000
13	3,000	
Bal		0

Capital Stock		
Bal		15,000
Bal		15,000

Retained Earnings		
Bal		15,800
11	15,000	
19		**23,400**
Bal		24,200

Sales		
2		199,000
13		3,000
Bal		202,000
19	**202,000**	
Bal		0

Cost of Sales		
16	72,000	
Bal	72,000	
19		**72,000**
Bal	0	

Insurance Expense		
18	1,500	
Bal	1,500	
19		**1,500**
Bal	0	

Salaries Expense		
6	70,000	
14	1,500	
Bal	71,500	
19		**71,500**
Bal	0	

Amortization Expense		
15	6,000	
Bal	6,000	
19		**6,000**
Bal	0	

Other Expenses		
10	20,000	
Bal	20,000	
19		**20,000**
Bal	0	

Tax Expense		
17	6,700	
Bal	6,700	
19		**6,700**
Bal	0	

Interest Expense		
8	900	
Bal	900	
19		**900**
Bal	0	

Table 3-A2   Post-Closing Trial Balance

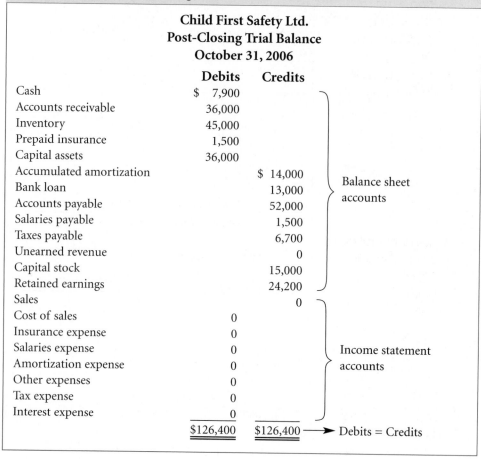

Child First Safety Ltd.
Post-Closing Trial Balance
October 31, 2006

	Debits	Credits	
Cash	$ 7,900		⎫
Accounts receivable	36,000		
Inventory	45,000		
Prepaid insurance	1,500		
Capital assets	36,000		
Accumulated amortization		$ 14,000	Balance sheet
Bank loan		13,000	accounts
Accounts payable		52,000	
Salaries payable		1,500	
Taxes payable		6,700	
Unearned revenue		0	
Capital stock		15,000	
Retained earnings		24,200	⎭
Sales		0	⎫
Cost of sales	0		
Insurance expense	0		
Salaries expense	0		Income statement
Amortization expense	0		accounts
Other expenses	0		
Tax expense	0		
Interest expense	0		⎭
	$126,400	$126,400	→ Debits = Credits

19.	Dr. Sales	202,000	
	Cr. Cost of sales		72,000
	Cr. Insurance expense		1,500
	Cr. Salaries expense		71,500
	Cr. Amortization expense		6,000
	Cr. Other expense		20,000
	Cr. Tax expense		6,700
	Cr. Interest expense		900
	Cr. Retained earnings		23,400

To close income statement accounts to retained earnings.

Key Terms

account, p. 99

accounting cycle, p. 95

accrued asset, p. 132

accrued liability, p. 130

accumulated amortization, p. 128

adjusting entry, p. 124

closing journal entry, p. 134

conservatism, p. 110

contra-asset account, p. 128

credit, p. 116

debit, p. 116

deferred expense, p. 126

double-entry bookkeeping, p. 95

executory contract, p. 104

general journal, p. 146

general ledger, p. 146

journal entry, p. 98

matching (matching concept), p. 108

net book value (NBV), p. 128

non-monetary transaction, p. 103

Similar Terms

The left column gives alternative terms that are sometimes used for the accounting terms introduced in this chapter, which are listed in the right column.

carrying value

barter transaction

deferred expense, deferred charge,
   deferred cost, deferred debit

nominal account

deferred revenue

depreciation

net book value (NBV), p. 128

non-monetary transaction, p. 103

prepaid expense, p. 126

temporary accounts, p. 134

unearned revenue, p. 129

amortization, p. 128

Assignment Materials

Questions

Q3-1. Explain why much more judgment is required with accrual accounting than with cash accounting.

Q3-2. What are closing journal entries and why are they necessary? When do closing entries have to be prepared?

Q3-3. In 2002 Taymouth Inc. reported net income of $100,000. What would be the effect on retained earnings on Taymouth's 2002 balance sheet and on its 2003 income statement if it did not record a closing journal entry?

Q3-4. Explain why adjusting entries are necessary in accrual accounting, but not required when the cash basis of accounting is used.

Q3-5. What is stewardship accounting? Why is stewardship accounting important for public corporations? Why would stewardship accounting not be very important for an owner-managed corporation?

Q3-6. Why do you think that accounting and record keeping have always been so important for taxation purposes?

Q3-7. Explain the difference between transactional journal entries and adjusting journal entries.

Q3-8. Identify the four types of adjusting entries and explain why each type is necessary.

Q3-9. For each type of adjusting entry, explain the impact on assets, liabilities, owners' equity, revenue, expenses and net income if the required adjusting entry were not made.

Q3-10. When do adjusting entries have to be made? Explain.

Q3-11. What do the terms *debit* and *credit* mean?

Q3-12. What is a contra-asset account? Why are contra-asset accounts used?

Q3-13. When a dividend is declared and paid by a corporation, a debit is made to retained earnings. Explain.

Q3-14. Describe the two devices used in Chapter 3 for recording accounting information.

Q3-15. If cash increases when a debit is made to the cash account, why does the bank credit your account when you make a deposit?

Q3-16. What is an executory contract? How do GAAP usually account for executory contracts?

Q3-17. Identify and explain the four things that must be known if data are to be entered into an accounting system.

Q3-18. Why do entities divide assets, liabilities, and owners' equity into sub-accounts rather than accumulating data simply as assets, liabilities, and owners' equity?

Q3-19. How should an entity determine the number of accounts it should keep in its general ledger?

Q3-20. Why can preparers sometimes choose among alternative ways of accounting for transactions and economic events when accrual accounting is used? What are the implications of these choices on the financial statements and to the users of financial statements?

Q3-21. Figure 3-1 (page 96) shows that not every economic event that has an effect on an entity is entered into the entity's accounting system. What do you think are the implications for financial statements and financial statement users of not having every economic event recorded in the accounting system?

Q3-22. Figure 3-1 (page 96) shows that not every economic event that has an effect on an entity is entered into the entity's accounting system. Give three examples of economic events that might have an effect on an entity but are not recorded in the entity's accounting system.

Q3-23. Explain the matching concept. Give some examples of matching. Why is matching important for financial accounting? Why is matching sometimes difficult to do in practice?

Q3-24. Explain the accounting concept of conservatism.

Appendix Questions

Q3-25. Identify and explain the steps of the accounting cycle.

Q3-26. What is a T-account? Why are T-accounts used?

Q3-27. What does "posting" journal entries to the general ledger mean? Why are journal entries posted to the general ledger?

Q3-28. What is a trial balance and what is its purpose? Why doesn't a trial balance guarantee that your accounting is "correct"?

Q3-29. Why is it useful to cross-reference journal entries to the posting to the general ledger account (T-account)?

Q3-30. Explain how information that is recorded in the general journal (using journal entries) is organized differently from the information in the general ledger (posted from the general journal).

Exercises

E3-1. **(Types of events, LO 5)** For each of the events listed below, indicate whether the event will give rise to a transactional entry, an adjusting entry, or not result in any entry in the accounting system. Assume that the accounting system is designed to collect information on an accrual and a GAAP basis.
a. Amortization of equipment.
b. Collection of accounts receivable from a customer.
c. Increase in the market value of a building while it continues to be owned.
d. Recognition of revenue for work done in the current period but paid for in the previous period.
e. Hiring of a new vice-president of finance.
f. Purchase of inventory on credit from a supplier.

g. Earning of interest on an investment. The interest will not be paid until next year.

h. Customer pays in advance for work to be done next year.

i. Sale of land to a buyer in exchange for a promise to pay $1,000,000 in cash in two years.

j. Payment of a dividend to shareholders.

k. Company agrees to supply cleaning services to a customer. The customer agrees to pay each time the work is done.

E3-2. **(Preparing closing entries using spreadsheets and journal entries, LO 2, 3, 6)**
Below is a summarized income statement for St. Bruno Inc. (St. Bruno).

St. Bruno Inc.
Income Statement for the Year Ended December 31, 2004

Revenue	$10,250,000
Expenses	6,450,000
Net income	$ 3,800,000

a. Prepare a spreadsheet and make the entry that is necessary to close the temporary accounts.

b. Prepare the journal entry necessary to close the temporary accounts.

c. Explain why closing entries are necessary and when they should be recorded.

d. What would be the effect on net income in 2005 if St. Bruno Inc. forgot to prepare a closing entry?

E3-3. **(Preparing closing entries using spreadsheets and journal entries, LO 2, 3, 6)**
Below is Niagara Falls Ltd.'s (Niagara Falls) summarized income statement for the year ended August 31, 2005.

Niagara Falls Ltd.
Income Statement for the Year Ended August 31, 2005
(in thousands of dollars)

Sales		$75,240
Cost of sales		25,400
Gross margin		49,840
Expenses		
Selling and marketing	$7,580	
General and administrative	5,150	
Research and development	3,225	
Amortization	3,140	
Interest	1,500	
Other	1,105	21,700
Income before taxes		28,140
Income taxes		10,130
Net income		$18,010

a. Prepare a spreadsheet and make the entries that are necessary to close the temporary accounts.

b. Prepare the journal entry necessary to close the temporary accounts.

c. Explain why closing entries are necessary and when they should be recorded.

d. What would be the effect on net income in 2006 if Niagara Falls Ltd. forgot to prepare a closing entry?

E3-4. **(Recognizing the effects of debits and credits, LO 3)** Indicate whether each of the following would be treated as a debit or a credit in a journal entry.

a. Increase in cash.

b. Decrease in unearned revenue.

c. Decrease in prepaid rent.

d. Increase in interest revenue.

e. Increase in interest expense.

f. Increase in capital stock.

   g. Decrease in amortization expense.

   h. Decrease in mortgage payable.

E3-5.   **(Identifying different types of adjusting entries, LO 5)** Refer to Table 3-4 in this chapter (page 125). For each of the situations described below, identify the type of adjusting entry that would ultimately be required as a result of the event. Explain the reason for your choice.

	Type	Situation
Example	Deferred expense/ prepaid expense	Two year's rent is paid in advance
a.	_____	Water used by the company has not yet been billed or paid for.
b.	_____	Rent is owed by a tenant but not yet paid.
c.	_____	A customer pays in advance for services to be rendered.
d.	_____	Salaries earned by employees are not yet paid.
e.	_____	Computers are purchased.
f.	_____	Interest earned on an investment is not due to be received until next year.
g.	_____	Membership to a golf club is paid in advance.
h.	_____	A golf club receives membership fees in advance.

E3-6.   **(Recording transactions using an accounting equation spreadsheet, LO 2)** Set up an accounting equation spreadsheet and enter each of the following independent economic events into the spreadsheet.

   a. A car is purchased for $25,000 cash.

   b. A car is purchased for $15,000 cash and $10,000 financed through the dealer.

   c. A corporation sells shares to investors for $100,000.

   d. A corporation pays dividends to shareholders of $1,000,000.

   e. A corporation declares dividends of $1,000,000. The dividends will be paid in 30 days.

   f. A corporation pays $1,000,000 of dividends that were previously declared.

   g. A company sells goods to a customer for $300 cash. The goods cost $200. (Hint: the company records the reduction in inventory and cost of sales at the time the sale is recorded.)

   h. A company sells goods to a customer for $300 cash. The goods cost $200. The customer promises to pay in 30 days. (Hint: the company records the reduction in inventory and cost of sales at the time the sale is recorded.)

   i. A company collects $1,000 that is due from a customer.

E3-7.   **(Recording transactions using journal entries, LO 3)** For each of the events described in Exercise E3-6, make the journal entry necessary to record the event.

E3-8.   **(Recording transactions using an accounting equation spreadsheet, LO 2)** Set up an accounting equation spreadsheet and enter each of the following independent economic events into the spreadsheet:

   a. A company pays $25,000 in wages to its employees.

   b. A company buys a building and the vendor takes back a mortgage for the full price of $5,000,000.

   c. A company uses services costing $10,000. The company will pay in 30 days.

   d. A partnership borrows $25,000 from the bank.

   e. A proprietorship repays a $10,000 bank loan plus $1,000 interest on the loan.

   f. A company borrows $10,000,000 from a bank and uses the money to buy a piece of land.

   g. A company pays a $5,000 deposit to a supplier who will provide maintenance on its equipment next year.

   h. A company receives a $3,000 deposit from a customer for services that will be provided next year.

E3-9. **(Recording transactions using journal entries, LO 3)** For each of the events described in Exercise E3-8, make the journal entry necessary to record the event.

E3-10. **(Calculate inventory related amounts, LO 4)** In each of the following situations, calculate the missing information.

a.	Beginning inventory	=	$125,000
	Purchases	=	525,000
	Ending inventory	=	135,000
	Cost of goods sold	=	▓▓▓▓
b.	Beginning inventory	=	$425,000
	Purchases	=	▓▓▓▓
	Ending inventory	=	85,000
	Cost of goods sold	=	975,000
c.	Beginning inventory	=	$125,000
	Purchases	=	525,000
	Ending inventory	=	▓▓▓▓
	Cost of goods sold	=	595,000

E3-11. **(Explaining journal entries, LO 3, 4, 5)** Provide a description of the event represented by each of the following journal entries.

a.	Dr. Cash	1,000,000	
	Cr. Land		1,000,000
b.	Dr. Accounts receivable	20,000	
	Cr. Revenue		20,000
c.	Dr. Cash	7,500,000	
	Cr. Capital stock		7,500,000
d.	Dr. Capital assets—equipment	350,000	
	Cr. Notes payable		350,000
e.	Dr. Rent expense	5,000	
	Cr. Prepaid rent		5,000
f.	Dr. Unearned revenue	10,000	
	Cr. Revenue		10,000
g.	Dr. Accounts payable	15,000	
	Cr. Cash		15,000
h.	Dr. Supplies expense	2,000	
	Cr. Supplies inventory		2,000

E3-12. **(Explaining journal entries, LO 3, 4, 5)** Provide a description of the event represented by each of the following journal entries.

a.	Dr. Equipment	1,100,000	
	Cr. Cash		350,000
	Cr. Notes payable		750,000
b.	Dr. Interest receivable	25,000	
	Cr. Interest revenue		25,000
c.	Dr. Cash	1,500,000	
	Dr. Long-term receivable	3,500,000	
	Cr. Land		5,000,000
d.	Dr. Wages expense	8,500	
	Cr. Wages payable		8,500
e.	Dr. Sales commissions	21,000	
	Cr. Commissions payable		21,000
f.	Dr. Bond payable	250,000	
	Cr. Capital stock		250,000
g.	Dr. Cash	35,000	
	Cr. Revenue		25,000
	Cr. Unearned revenue		10,000
h.	Dr. Rent expense	2,500	
	Cr. Prepaid rent		2,500

E3-13. **(Recording economic events in an accounting equation spreadsheet and preparing financial statements, LO 2, 4, 5, 6)** Fitness For All Ltd. is a new health club operating in a suburb of Winnipeg. The following transactions take place in September and October 2005:

   i.   September 1: Fitness For All Ltd. is incorporated. The owner pays $125,000 for 5,000 shares of company stock.

   ii. September 3: Fitness For All Ltd. signs a three-year lease for space for the club in a strip mall. The owner pays $3,000 cash in rent for October and November.

   iii. September 3–20: Renovations on the location are carried out at a cost of $20,000 cash.

   iv. September 21: Equipment worth $125,000 is purchased from a supplier. Fitness For All Ltd. pays $75,000 in cash and promises to pay the remainder in six months. The estimated life of the equipment is five years.

   v. September 25: Supplies are purchased on credit for $5,000.

   vi. During September and October: Memberships to the club are sold to 300 people at $350 per person. Members pay 50% immediately and promise to pay the remainder in 30 days.

   vii. During September and October: Employees are paid wages of $10,000. At the end of October Fitness For All Ltd. owes employees $1,200.

   viii. During September and October: Utilities costing $2,000 are paid.

   ix. During September and October: Fitness For All Ltd. pays $2,700 toward the supplies purchased on credit on September 25.

   x. During September and October: Fitness For All Ltd. collects $30,000 owed by members.

   xi. During September and October: $3,900 of supplies was used.

Required:

   a. Use an accounting equation spreadsheet to record the transactions that occurred during September and October.

   b. Make adjusting entries for amortization of equipment, expensing of rent, use of supplies, and wages owing to employees.

   c. Make the closing entry.

   d. Prepare the balance sheet as of October 31, 2005 and an income statement and statement of retained earnings for the period ending October 31, 2005.

E3-14. **(Making adjusting entries, LO 2, 3, 5)** For each of the following situations prepare the required adjusting entries. Also show the related transactional entries and the date the entries would be made. Assume a December 31 year end. This question can be done using an accounting equation spreadsheet or journal entries.

   a. On June 30 a company purchases a building for $10,000,000. The estimated life of the building is 25 years.

   b. A company pays its salaried employees monthly, on the 15th of the month. On December 31 the company owes its employees $4,500.

   c. On July 10 a company received a $10,000 deposit for services that were to be provided over the next 10 months, beginning on August 1. The services provided are worth the same amount each month.

   d. On October 1 a company invested $100,000 in an investment account that pays interest of 6% per year, payable on March 31 and September 31.

   e. On January 1 the office supplies account had a balance of $4,300. During the year office supplies costing $7,000 were purchased. A count of office supplies on December 31 found supplies worth $2,100 on hand.

E3-15. **(Making adjusting entries, LO 3, 5)** The account balances before and after the adjusting entries have been made are presented below for a number of accounts. For each account, prepare the adjusting entry that gave rise to the change in the account balance and provide an explanation for each entry.

Account	Balance before adjusting entry	Balance after adjusting entry
Unearned revenue	$ 10,000	$ 7,500
Interest receivable	0	2,000
Accumulated amortization	125,000	160,000
Prepaid rent	8,000	5,000
Supplies inventory	15,000	8,000
Wages payable	0	4,500
Interest payable	0	2,500

E3-16. **(Understanding the relationship between closing entries and the income statement, LO 6)** Below is the closing journal entry prepared by Bellburn Ltd. on December 31, 2004. Use the closing journal entry to prepare Bellburn Ltd.'s income statement for the year ended December 31, 2004.

Dr. Sales	650,000
Dr. Interest revenue	3,000
Cr. Retained earnings	112,000
Cr. Wage expense	125,000
Cr. Advertising expense	35,000
Cr. Amortization expense	25,000
Cr. Cost of goods sold	225,000
Cr. Selling and administrative expense	32,000
Cr. Interest expense	12,500
Cr. Rent expense	18,000
Cr. Income tax expense	59,000
Cr. Miscellaneous expense	9,500

E3-17. **(Evaluating the effect that not recording adjusting entries has on net income, LO 4, 5)** For each of the following situations, indicate whether not recording the necessary adjusting entry will result in (i) an overstatement of net income (net income is higher than it would otherwise be), (ii) an understatement of net income (net income is lower than it would otherwise be), or (iii) no effect on net income. Provide an explanation for your conclusion.

		Effect on Net Income	Explanation
	Wages earned by employees in the last week of the year but not paid until next year are ignored.	Overstatement	The adjusting entry would record a wage expense and a wages payable liability. Therefore, by not making the necessary entry, expenses will be understated and liabilities understated.
a.	Amortization expense is not recorded.		
b.	Interest earned on an investment but not receivable until next year is not recorded.		
c.	A property owner records four months' rent received in advance as unearned revenue. The property owner does not make an adjustment at the end of the year for the two months that the tenant has used the space.		

d.	A company purchases a two-year insurance policy on the first day of the year and records the purchase as prepaid insurance. At the end of the year no adjustment is made to reflect the portion of the policy that was consumed.		
e.	Interest on a loan that is incurred but is not payable until next month is not recorded.		

E3-18. **(Using an accounting equation spreadsheet to determine the opening balance in an account, LO 2)** The chief financial officer of Afton Ltd. (Afton) is trying to determine the amount of cash the company had on hand one month ago on March 1, 2005. A problem with the company's computer system resulted in the loss of the information. Use an accounting equation spreadsheet and the following information to determine the information the chief financial officer requires. Afton Ltd. had a cash balance of $75,000 on March 31, 2005.

     a. On March 15 Afton purchased equipment costing $100,000 by paying $20,000 in cash and promising to pay the remainder in 90 days.

     b. On March 20 Afton made payments of $10,000 on its bank loan.

     c. During March Afton collected $110,000 from customers and paid suppliers $90,000.

     d. During March Afton paid employees $22,000.

     e. During March Afton had other cash receipts of $2,500 and other cash payments of $8,000.

E3-19. **(Using an accounting equation spreadsheet to determine missing information, LO 2)** Use an accounting equation spreadsheet and the following information to determine the amount of cash that was collected from customers during November 2004:

     a. On November 1, 2004 the balance in the accounts receivable account was $175,000.

     b. During November 1, 2004 sales of $220,000 were made on credit.

     c. The balance in the accounts receivable account on November 30, 2004 was $190,000.

E3-20. **(Effect of adjustments on financial ratios, LO 4, 5)** For each of the following adjusting entries, complete the table by indicating the effect that the adjustment has on each financial ratio. Indicate the effect as increasing, decreasing, or having no effect on each ratio.

a.	Dr. Amortization expense	10,000	
	Cr. Accumulated amortization		10,000
b.	Dr. Unearned revenue	5,000	
	Cr. Revenue		5,000
c.	Dr. Interest receivable	2,000	
	Cr. Interest revenue		2,000
d.	Dr. Utilities expense	500	
	Cr. Accrued utility expense payable		500
e.	Dr. Rent expense	1,000	
	Cr. Prepaid rent		1,000

	Current ratio $\left(\dfrac{\text{Current assets}}{\text{Current liabilities}}\right)$	Debt-to-equity ratio $\left(\dfrac{\text{Liabilities}}{\text{Owners' equity}}\right)$	Profit margin ratio $\left(\dfrac{\text{Net income}}{\text{Sales}}\right)$	Return on equity $\left(\dfrac{\text{Net income}}{\text{Owners' equity}}\right)$
a.				
b.				
c.				
d.				
e.				

E3-21. **(Correcting errors, LO 2, 3, 4)** Zhoda Ltd. has been having problems with its bookkeeper. The bookkeeper is a cousin of the president of the company and is very nice, but does not understand accounting very well. Recently errors have been observed in the bookkeeper's work. Examine each of the items below and make any journal entry that is necessary to correct the entries originally made. This question can also be answered using an accounting equation spreadsheet.

a. Zhoda Ltd. received an advance from a customer for work that was going to be done in the next fiscal year. The bookkeeper debited Cash and credited Revenue for $10,000

b. Zhoda Ltd. sold shares to investors for $200,000. The bookkeeper debited Cash and credited Revenue for $200,000.

c. Zhoda Ltd. purchased four computers for $10,000. The bookkeeper debited Computer Expense and credited Cash for $10,000.

d. Zhoda Ltd. paid a dividend to shareholders of $50,000. The bookkeeper debited Dividend Expense and credited Cash for $50,000.

E3-22. **(Correcting errors, LO 2, 3, 4)** Examine the accounting errors described in Exercise E3-21. For each error explain the impact the error (and failure to correct the error) would have on the financial statements.

E3-23. **(Preparing a balance sheet and income statement using a trial balance, LO 3, 4, 6)** Below is Kuskonook Inc.'s (Kuskonook) December 31, 2005 trial balance that was prepared before the closing journal entry was recorded. Use the trial balance to prepare Kuskonook's balance sheet as of December 31, 2005 and the income statement for the year ended December 31, 2005. The accounts in the trial balance are listed alphabetically.

Kuskonook Inc.
Trial Balance
December 31, 2005

Account	Debit	Credit
Accounts payable	$	$ 200,000
Accounts receivable	125,000	
Accrued liabilities		18,000
Amortization expense	250,000	
Bank loan payable		150,000
Buildings	2,500,000	
Capital stock		1,250,000
Cash	25,000	
Cost of sales	2,445,000	
Current portion of long-term debt		300,000
Furniture and equipment	1,750,000	
Income tax expense	350,000	
Income taxes payable		15,000
Interest expense	180,000	
Interest payable		12,000
Inventory	224,000	
Land	750,000	
Loan receivable	48,000	

Long-term debt		2,100,000
Long-term loan receivable	110,000	
Other expenses	182,000	
Prepaid assets	18,000	
Retained earnings		808,000
Revenue		5,750,000
Selling, general, and administrative expense	725,000	
Wages and salaries expense	950,000	
Wages and salaries payable		29,000
	$10,632,000	$10,632,000

Problems

P3-1. **(Prepare adjusting entries, LO 3, 5)** For each of the following situations provide the necessary adjusting entries for Truax Ltd. for the year ended June 30, 2004. (These situations are tricky. When preparing each adjusting entry, compare what is recorded in the accounting system before you make your entry with what you think should be in the accounting system. Your adjusting entry should take the accounting system from "what is" recorded to "what should be" recorded.)

a. On January 2, 2004 Truax Ltd. purchased a two-year insurance policy for $20,000 cash. The transactional journal entry debited Insurance Expense for $20,000 and credited Cash for $20,000.

b. On June 1, 2004 Truax Ltd. received $5,000 for goods that it would produce and deliver to a customer in November 2004. Truax Ltd. recorded the transaction by debiting Cash for $5,000 and crediting Revenue for $5,000.

c. On March 1, 2004, Truax Ltd. invested $200,000 of surplus cash in a one-year investment certificate that paid 0.5% per month. The $200,000 initial investment plus the interest of $12,000 were to be paid on February 28, 2005. On March 1, 2004 Truax Ltd. recorded the investment by debiting Investments for $200,000 and crediting Cash for $200,000. It also debited Accounts Receivable for $12,000 and credited Interest Revenue for $12,000.

P3-2. **(Prepare adjusting entries, LO 3, 5)** For each of the following situations provide the necessary adjusting entries for Carberry Inc. for the year ended December 31, 2005. (These situations are tricky. When preparing each adjusting entry, compare what is recorded in the accounting system before you make your entry with what you think should be in the accounting system. Your adjusting entry should take the accounting system from "what is" recorded to "what should be" recorded.)

a. On January 2, 2005, Carberry Inc. paid $10,000 cash for the right to use a vacant lot to store some of its equipment for the next two years. The transactional journal entry debited Prepaid Rent for $10,000 and credited Cash for $10,000.

b. On November 1, 2005, Carberry Inc. received $25,000 as an advance for services to be rendered in 2006. Carberry Inc. recorded the transaction by debiting Cash for $25,000 and crediting Revenue for $25,000.

c. On April 1, 2005, Carberry Inc. invested $100,000 of surplus cash in a one-year investment certificate that paid 0.6% per month. The $100,000 initial investment plus the interest of $7,200 were to be paid on March 31, 2006. On April 1, 2005 Carberry Inc. recorded the investment by debiting Investments for $100,000 and crediting Cash for $100,000. It also debited Accounts Receivable for $7,200 and credited Interest Revenue for $7,200.

P3-3. **(The effect of different lease arrangements on the financial statements, LO 3, 4, 5)** Liscomb Consulting is a partnership of business consultants located in Halifax. The company has been successful since it began business five years ago and the partners have decided to move into new offices. On August 20, 2004, the partners came to terms with a property owner and signed a three-year lease for space at a prestigious address. Liscomb Consulting occupied its new offices on September 1, 2004. Monthly rent is $1,000. For each situation below show what would appear on Liscomb Consulting's balance sheet and income statement if these statements were prepared on September 1, 2004 and on September 30, 2004. For each situation show all journal entries prepared in August and September 2004. Indicate whether each journal entry is a transactional or adjusting journal entry. Consider each situation separately

a. On August 20, 2004 Liscomb Consulting pays the property owner rent for September and agrees to pay each month's rent on the first day of the month (so October's rent is due on October 1).

b. The property owner agrees to allow Liscomb Consulting to pay its rent in arrears so that the rent is due on the first day of the next month (so September's payment is due October 1, and so on).

c. The property owner agrees to allow Liscomb Consulting to pay its rent on the 15th of each month. The first month's rent is paid August 20 (so the payment on September 15 is for October).

d. The property owner agrees to allow Liscomb Consulting to pay its rent on the 15th of each month. The first month's rent is paid on September 15 (so the payment on September 15 is for September).

P3-4. **(The effect of different lease arrangements on the financial statements, LO 3, 4, 5)** Kashabowie Properties Ltd. (Kashabowie) owns and operates several commercial real estate properties in Halifax. On August 20, 2004 Kashabowie signed a three-year lease with a consulting firm for space in one of its buildings. Monthly rent is $1,000. For each situation below show what would appear on Kashabowie's balance sheet and income statement if these statements were prepared on September 1, 2004 and on September 30, 2004. For each situation show all journal entries prepared in August and September 2004. Indicate whether each journal entry is a transactional or adjusting journal entry.

a. On August 20, 2004 Kashabowie receives the $1,000 rent payment for September. The lease agreement requires the consulting firm to pay each month's rent on the first day of the month (so October's rent is due on October 1).

b. Kashabowie agrees to allow the consulting firm to pay its rent in arrears so that its rent is due on the first day of the next month (so September's payment is due October 1 and so on).

c. Kashabowie agrees to allow the consulting firm to pay its rent on the 15th of each month. The first month's rent is paid on August 20 (so the payment on September 15 is for October).

d. Kashabowie agrees to allow the consulting firm to pay its rent on the 15th of each month. The first month's rent is paid on September 15 (so the payment on September 15 is for September).

P3-5. **(Understanding the effect of errors on the elements of the accounting equation, LO 4, 5)** For each of the following situations, indicate how the recording errors affect the amount of assets, liabilities, owners' equity, revenues, and expenses reported in the 2004 financial statements. Indicate whether each category is overstated (too high), understated (too low), or unaffected by the error. Assume that the year end is June 30. Briefly explain why the effects occur and state any assumptions that you make.

Example:

On January 3, 2004 a three-year insurance policy was purchased for $9,000 cash. The bookkeeper debited insurance expense for $9,000 when the policy was purchased. No adjusting entry was made at year end.

Situation	Assets	Liabilities	Owners' Equity	Revenue	Expense	Explanation
Example	Understated	No effect	Understated	No effect	Overstated	By expensing 100% of the insurance cost in the current year, three years of insurance is expensed in a single year, thereby overstating expenses. Since expenses are closed to owners' equity, the equity section of the balance sheet would be understated. Assets would be understated because the two years of insurance that should be reported on the balance sheet would not be. After three years the financial statements would be correct if the error were not corrected.

a. On January 3, 2004 a company purchased a new delivery truck for $35,000. The company estimates the truck will be used for five years. No adjusting entry was made at year end.

b. On June 15, 2004 a sports fan purchased seasons tickets for her city's hockey team's games for $6,000 cash. The hockey season begins in October and the team recognizes its revenue when the hockey games are played. The bookkeeper credited revenue for $6,000 when the cash was received.

c. On June 30, 2004 no entry was made to reflect the use of water during June. The water bill will not be received until late August. In June 2003, the company used $5,000 of water and the managers estimate that about the same amount of water was used this year.

d. On September 1, 2004 a company borrowed $1,000,000 from a private lender. The interest rate on the loan is 6% per year. Interest must be paid on August 31 and February 28 of each year. The loan principal must be paid in full on August 31, 2008. No adjusting entry was made by the borrower with respect to the loan and interest on June 30, 2004.

e. On April 17, 2004 a $9,570 cash expenditure for capital assets was recorded as $7,570.

P3-6. **(Understanding the effect of errors on the elements of the accounting equation, LO 4, 5)** For each of the following situations, indicate how the recording errors affect the amount of assets, liabilities, owners' equity, revenues, and expenses reported in the 2005 financial statements. Indicate whether each category is overstated (too high), understated (too low), or unaffected by the error. Assume that the year end is December 31. Briefly explain why the effects occur and state any assumptions that you make.

Example:

On January 3, 2005, a three-year insurance policy was purchased for $9,000 cash. The bookkeeper debited insurance expense for $9,000 when the policy was purchased. No adjusting entry was made at year end.

Situation	Assets	Liabilities	Owners' equity	Revenue	Expense	Explanation
Example	Understated	No effect	Understated	No effect	Overstated	By expensing 100% of the insurance cost in the current year, three years of insurance is expensed in a single year, thereby overstating expenses. Since expenses are closed to owners' equity, the equity section of the balance sheet would be understated. Assets would be understated because the two years of insurance that should be reported on the balance sheet would not be. After three years the financial statements would be correct if the error were not corrected.

a. On January 3, 2005 a three-year insurance policy was purchased for $9,000 cash. The bookkeeper debited Prepaid Insurance for $9,000 when the policy was purchased. No adjusting entry was made at year end.

b. On December 15, 2005 $400 was received from a customer paying in advance for lawn care services that were going to be provided in 2006. The bookkeeper credited Revenue for $400 when the cash was received.

c. On December 31, 2005 no entry was made to reflect the use of electricity during the month of December. The bill for electricity will not be received until late February. In December 2004 the company used $2,000 of electricity and management estimates that about the same amount was used this year.

d. On September 1, 2005 the company invested $1,000,000 in government bonds that pay interest on September 1 and March 1 of each year. The interest rate is 6% per year. No adjusting entry was made.

e. On July 17, 2005 a $5,750 cash expenditure for some required items was recorded as $7,570.

P3-7. **(Using the accounting equation spreadsheet to record transactions and prepare financial statements, LO 1, 2, 5, 6)** Paul Byrne is a first-year student in a business program in Toronto. Toward the end of the academic year he was approached by a friend who offered to sell him his hot dog vending cart. The friend was finishing his university studies and was going to be starting a permanent job in the summer, so he no longer needed the cart. Paul thought about the offer for a few days and decided to buy the cart. He thought that it would be a way to make money to finance his education and learn how to manage a business at the same time.

Paul operated his business from late April, when the weather started to warm up, to early September, when it was time to get back to school. Paul was so busy running the business, he had no time to keep any accounting records. So on September 10, after he had put away the cart until the next year, he sat down with all the data he had carefully collected throughout the summer about his business and placed in a shoebox. From the information in the shoebox he obtained the following:

a. On April 1, Paul opened a bank account in the name of his company Paul's Dogs. He deposited $2,000 from his bank account into the account. Paul decided he would operate the business as a proprietorship. (Remember, in a proprietorship the owners' equity section of the balance sheet includes only a single account called Owner's Equity or Owner's Capital. This is different from a corporation where there will be a Capital Stock account and a Retained Earnings account.)

b. Paul purchased the cart from his friend on April 8 for $1,500. He gave his friend $1,000 in cash and promised to pay him the rest at the end of the summer. The cart is already four years old and Paul's friend says it should be good for another three or four years, after which time it will probably be junk.

c. Paul took the cart to a repair shop. He had the cart painted, serviced, and repaired. Paul paid the shop $300 in cash.

d. Paul went to city hall and obtained a license to operate his cart in the city. The license cost $250 and Paul wrote a cheque for that amount. The license is valid for two years and expires at the end of the next calendar year.

e. During the summer Paul sold hot dogs and drinks for $15,750.

f. In late August Paul was asked to bring his cart to a softball tournament where he would be the official supplier of hot dogs to participants. The agreement was that Paul would keep track of the hot dogs and drinks he handed out to the players and send a bill to the tournament organizers. At the end of the tournament Paul sent a bill to the organizers for $1,115. The organizers said they would pay on September 20.

g. During the summer Paul bought hot dogs, buns, drinks, condiments, napkins, plastic cutlery, paper plates, and other supplies for $8,525. All of these items were paid for in cash.

h. At the end of the summer Paul had about $750 in non-perishable items stored in his basement at home (he had used $7,775 of the supplies he had bought).

i. On several days during the summer Paul was unable to operate the cart himself. On those days he hired his brother to do it. For the entire summer Paul paid his brother $375. As of today Paul still owes him $75.

j. During the summer Paul incurred $1,000 in other expenses. All of these were paid in cash.

k. On August 15 Paul withdrew $1,500 from the business to pay for tuition and other school-related items.

l. On September 5 Paul paid his friend the $500 he owed him.

Required:

a. Enter each of the transactions onto an accounting equation spreadsheet. You can use a computer spreadsheet program or create a spreadsheet manually, although the computer spreadsheet will probably be easier because you will be able to correct mistakes more easily. Create a separate column on the spreadsheet for each account.

b. Provide explanations for each of your entries. You should explain why you have treated the economic events as you have (that is, why you have recorded an asset, liability, etc.)

c. Prepare a balance sheet as of September 10 and an income statement for the period ended September 10 from your spreadsheet. Make sure to make a closing entry.

d. Explain why the financial statements you have prepared would be useful to Paul.

e. If Paul asked you for some feedback on his business from examining the financial statements, what would you be able to tell him from your examination?

P3-8. **(Using the accounting equation spreadsheet to record transactions and prepare financial statements, LO 1, 2, 5, 6)** We've Got Wheels, Inc. (Wheels) was formed on May 1, 2004 by two university friends who thought they could make money renting bikes and inline skates to visitors at a busy lake-front area near their homes. The friends thought the business would be a good way to spend their summer near the beach while making enough money to finance next year's university costs. If the business is successful the friends hope to operate it for as long as they attend university.

The two owners closed down Wheels for the year after the Labour Day weekend. It was a very hectic summer and they didn't have nearly as much time to have fun as they thought they would. They were also so busy that they didn't pay much attention to keeping any accounting records. They did, however, keep all the receipts, invoices, and deposit slips that accumulated over the summer.

It is now September 10. The owners have asked you to compile useful information about Wheels for them. After summarizing the data they provided, you have the following information for the summer of 2004:

i. May 1: Each friend contributed $10,000 in cash to Wheels in exchange for stock in the company.

ii. May 5: Purchased 15 new and used bicycles for a total of $7,000. Wheels agreed to pay $4,000 immediately and the remainder on September 30, 2004. The owners think the bikes will last for at least three summers, after which time they will no longer be useful for the business.

iii. May 9: Obtained a permit to operate a business at the lake. The cost of the permit was $100 for the summer.

iv. May 10: Purchased 25 sets of inline skates and 25 sets of protective equipment for $4,500 in cash. The owners think that the most they will get out of this equipment is about two summers of use.

v. During the summer: Wheels rented bicycles and skates to customers for $27,750 cash.

vi. During the summer: Purchased packaged snacks for $1,200. At the end of the summer there were $275 of snacks left over. The snacks were sold to customers through the summer for $1,800.

vii. During the summer: Purchased advertising on a local radio station. Advertising was paid for by cheque once an ad was played. Total amount spent during the summer was $900. Nothing was owing at the end of the Labour Day weekend.

viii. During the summer: Wheels provided inline skating lessons to children on behalf of the local Parks and Recreation Department. Wheels billed the department $4,500 for the lessons. As of September 10, $1,500 was still owed to Wheels. The amount owed is due on October 15.

ix. During the summer: Wheels incurred other expenses amounting to $12,700. All were paid in cash.

x. During the summer: The owners took $5,000 each to meet their personal needs.

Required:

a. Enter each of the transactions onto an accounting equation spreadsheet. You can use a computer spreadsheet program or create a spreadsheet manually, although the computer spreadsheet will probably be easier because you will be able to correct mistakes more easily. Create a separate column on the spreadsheet for each account.

b. Provide explanations for each of your entries. You should explain why you have treated the economic events as you have (that is, why you have recorded an asset, liability, etc.).

c. Prepare a balance sheet as of September 10, 2004 and an income statement for the period ended September 10, 2004 from your spreadsheet. Make sure to make a closing entry.

d. Explain why the financial statements you have prepared would be useful to the owners of Wheels.

e. Compare Wheels' net income with the amount of cash that was generated by the business. Which is a better indicator of how Wheels did? Why are they different? (When looking at the cash flow, consider the cash flows after the owners made their initial $20,000 investment.)

f. If Wheels' owners asked you to evaluate the financial statements for them, what would you be able to tell them based on your evaluation?

P3-9. **(Using the accounting equation spreadsheet to record transactions and prepare financial statements, LO 1, 2, 5, 6)** Harry Neighbourly is the owner and operator of Harry's Appliance Emporium Ltd. (HAEL), Yarksis' largest independent household appliance store. Harry supplies appliances to retail customers as well as to builders of the many new homes and apartments that are going up in the community. Sales to builders have grown substantially in the last year. HAEL has been in business for five years and Harry has been happy with its performance.

HAEL's balance sheet for August 31, 2004, the company's year end, is shown below. Harry uses the financial statements mainly for tax purposes and to show the holders of the long-term notes.

Harry's Appliances Emporium Ltd.
Balance Sheet
As of August 31, 2004

Assets		Liabilities and shareholders' equity	
Cash	$ 30,000	Accounts payable	$265,000
Accounts receivable	123,000	Taxes payable	20,000
Inventory	446,500	Interest payable	8,500
Prepaids	14,000	Long-term notes payable	100,000
Furniture and fixtures	190,000		
Accumulated		Capital stock	110,000
amortization	(40,000)	Retained earnings	260,000
	$763,500		$763,500

It is now mid-September 2005. HAEL needs to prepare its financial statements for the year ended August 31, 2005. The following information has been obtained about the fiscal year just ended:

i. HAEL purchased appliances from suppliers for $850,000. All purchases were made on credit.

ii. Sales during the year were $1,350,000. Cash sales were $775,000. The remainder was on credit, mainly to builders.

iii. The cost of the appliances sold during fiscal 2005 was $745,000.

iv. HAEL paid salaries and commissions to employees of $200,000. On August 31, 2005, employees were owed $7,500 by HAEL.

v. HAEL collected $375,000 during the year from customers who purchased on credit.

vi. HAEL paid suppliers $600,000 for appliances it purchased on credit.

vii. During the year HAEL paid the taxes it owed at the end of fiscal 2004. During fiscal 2005 HAEL paid $15,000 in instalments on its taxes. At year end the accountant estimates that HAEL owes an additional $12,000 in taxes.

viii. HAEL accepted $10,000 in deposits from customers who wanted a guarantee that their appliances would be delivered when they needed them. The deposits pertained to a particularly hard-to-get appliance. HAEL expects that the appliances will be delivered in early November 2005.

ix. Beginning July 1, 2005 HAEL pays $4,000 a month for the rent of its store. The terms of the lease require that rent be paid six months in advance on January 1 and July 1 of each year. Before July 1, 2005 HAEL paid $3,500 a month in rent. In addition, HAEL must pay 2% of annual sales to the property owner 60 days after the year end.

x. Harry recently redecorated his kitchen at home. He took a refrigerator, stove, and microwave that cost $4,500 from the store and installed them in his new kitchen.

xi. During 2005 HAEL purchased new capital assets (furniture and fixtures) for $25,000 cash.

xii. Amortization expense for 2005 is $22,000.

xiii. During the year HAEL paid $8,500 in interest to the holders of the long-term notes. Interest is paid annually on September 1. In addition to the interest payment, HAEL paid $20,000 on September 1, 2004 to reduce the balance owed on the long-term notes. The interest rate on the notes is 8.5%.

xiv. HAEL paid $225,000 in cash for other expenses related to operating the business in fiscal 2005.

Required:

a. Enter each transaction onto an accounting equation spreadsheet. Create a separate column on the spreadsheet for each account. Make sure to prepare all adjusting entries and the closing entry to the spreadsheet. Indicate whether each entry to the spreadsheet is a transactional entry, an adjusting entry or a closing entry.

b. Provide explanations for each of your entries. You should explain why you have treated the economic events as you have (that is, why you have recorded an asset, liability, etc.)

c. Prepare a balance sheet, an income statement, and a statement of retained earnings from your spreadsheet.

d. Harry is considering expanding HAEL to include a wider range of products. Harry has approached you about purchasing common shares of HAEL to help finance the expansion. Based on your examination of the statements, what can you tell about HAEL that would be useful to your decision to invest? Also, list five questions you might ask Harry that would help you use the financial statements more effectively.

P3-10. **(Using the accounting equation spreadsheet to record transactions and prepare financial statements, LO 1, 2, 5, 6)** Majestic Trucking Inc. (Majestic) is a small trucking company that carries freight between centres in central Canada and the northeastern United States. The Mozart family of Cobourg owns Majestic, but professional managers manage it. One member of the Mozart family serves as the chair of the board of directors. No other family members are actively involved with Majestic.

Majestic's balance sheet for December 31, 2004, the company's year end, is shown below. Majestic uses its financial statements for tax purposes, to show to the holders of the long-term notes that the company issued to finance the purchase of some of its trucks, and to provide information to the shareholders.

Majestic Trucking Inc.
Balance Sheet
As of December 31, 2004

Assets		Liabilities and shareholders' equity	
Cash	$ 77,340	Accounts payable	$42,220
Accounts receivable	81,500	Taxes payable	15,000
Prepaid insurance	18,000	Wages payable	10,000
Capital assets	465,000	Customer deposits	27,000
Accumulated		Interest payable	11,900
amortization	(201,700)	Long-term notes payable	140,000
		Capital stock	80,000
		Retained earnings	114,020
	$440,140		$440,140

It is now January 2006. Majestic needs to prepare its financial statements for the year ended December 31, 2005. The following information has been obtained about the fiscal year just ended:

i.   Shipping revenue for the year was $1,065,225. Majestic gives credit to all its customers and there were no cash sales during the year.

ii. Majestic purchased $275,000 worth of fuel during the year. All purchases were on credit. At the end of 2005 Majestic had not been billed for an additional $10,000 of fuel that it purchased.

iii. Majestic incurred maintenance costs of $125,000 during 2005. At the end of 2005 Majestic owed mechanics $8,000.

iv. Majestic paid salaries and bonuses of $475,000 to employees. At December 31, 2005 Majestic owed employees $27,500.

v.   During the year Majestic collected $1,075,000 from customers.

vi. Majestic paid its fuel suppliers $250,000 during 2005.

vii. During the year Majestic paid the taxes it owed at the end of 2004. It also paid $11,000 in instalments on its 2005 income taxes. It is estimated that Majestic owes an additional $12,000 in income taxes for 2005.

viii. The deposits reported on the 2004 balance sheet pertained to customers who were perceived to be high risk and to whom Majestic was not prepared to offer credit. These customers were required to give deposits against shipping to be done during 2005. These customers used shipping services during 2005 in excess of the amount of the deposits. Majestic decided in 2005 to offer credit to these customers.

ix. Members of the Mozart family sometimes used Majestic employees for personal work at their homes and cottages. Usually the work was done on weekends and the employees were paid at overtime rates. Majestic pays the employees' wages for the work done for the family members and accounts for the cost as a wage expense. The wages paid for work done on behalf of Mozart family members was $11,000.

x. During 2005 Majestic purchased a new truck for $98,000 in cash.

xi. Amortization expense for 2005 was $48,000.

xii. Prepaid insurance pertains to insurance on its truck fleet and premises. During 2005 it used $15,000 of insurance that was recorded as prepaid on December 31, 2004. In late 2005 Majestic purchased and paid for insurance for 2006. The insurance cost $21,000.

xiii. During the year Majestic paid $11,900 in interest to the holders of the long-term notes. Interest is paid annually on January 2. In addition to the interest payment, Majestic paid $20,000 on January 2, 2005 to reduce the balance owed on the long-term notes. The interest rate on the notes is 8.5%.

xiv. Majestic paid $75,000 in cash for other expenses related to operating the business in fiscal 2005.

xv. Majestic paid dividends of $55,000 to shareholders.

Required:

a. Enter each of the transactions onto an accounting equation spreadsheet. You can use a computer spreadsheet program or create a spreadsheet manually, although the computer spreadsheet will probably be easier because you will be able to correct mistakes more easily. Create a separate column on the spreadsheet for each account. Make sure to prepare all adjusting entries and the closing entry to the spreadsheet. Indicate whether each entry to the spreadsheet is a transactional entry, an adjusting entry or a closing entry.

b. Provide explanations for each of your entries. You should explain why you have

P3-11.

Transaction	Assets					=	Liabilities		
	Cash	Supplies Inventory	Prepaid Rent	Capital Assets	Accumulated Amortization		Accounts Payable	Unearned Revenue	Wages Payable
Balance before adjusting entries	$30,000	$22,000	$3,000	$40,000	($14,000)		$8,000	$14,000	
Balance after adjusting entries	$30,000	$10,000	$1,000	$40,000	($22,000)		$8,000	$6,000	$4,000

P3-12.

Transaction	Assets					=	Liabilities		
	Cash	Inventory	Prepaid Insurance	Capital Assets	Accumulated Amortization		Bank Loan	Accounts Payable	Salaries Payable
Balance before adjusting entries	$50,000	$325,000	$25,000	$120,000	($44,000)		$58,000	$78,000	
Balance after adjusting entries	$50,000	$145,000	$15,000	$120,000	($69,000)		$58,000	$78,000	$12,000

treated the economic events as you have (that is, why you have recorded an asset, liability, etc.).

c. Prepare a balance sheet as of December 31, 2005 and an income statement for the year ended December 31, 2005 from your spreadsheet.

d. The North American economy is booming and there is a lot of work for shipping companies like Majestic. However, the competition is fierce and success and failure are defined by how efficient a company is and how well it services its customers. Majestic's managers would like to upgrade its fleet by adding two new trucks and making significant improvements to its existing vehicles. Based on your examination of the statements, what can you tell about Majestic that would be useful to your decision to lend it $125,000? Also, list five questions you might ask Majestic's management that would help you use the financial statements more effectively.

P3-11. **(Reconstructing adjusting entries, LO 2, 4, 5)** The spreadsheet below provides the balances in Takhini Inc.'s accounts on December 31, 2004, before and after the adjusting entries have been made.

Required:

Reconstruct the adjusting entries that were made to Takhini Inc.'s spreadsheet on December 31, 2004.

P3-12. **(Reconstructing adjusting entries, LO 2, 4, 5)** The spreadsheet below provides the balances in Smithers Inc.'s accounts on May 31, 2006, before and after the adjusting entries have been made.

Required:

Reconstruct the adjusting entries that were made to Smithers Inc.'s spreadsheet on May 31, 2006.

P3-13. **(Evaluating the effect that not recording adjusting entries has on net income, LO 4, 5)** For each of the following economic events, indicate the effect that *not* recording the necessary adjusting entry at year end would have on the financial statements. Indicate whether not recording the adjusting entry would result in (i) an overstatement of assets, liabilities, owners' equity, or net income (they are higher than they would be otherwise), (ii) an understatement of assets, liabilities, owners'

+		Shareholders' Equity					
Capital Stock	Retained Earnings	Services Revenue	Supplies expense	Rent Expense	Wage Expense	Amortization expense
$10,000	$12,000	$58,000		$5,000	$16,000	
$10,000	$12,000	$66,000	$12,000	$7,000	$20,000	$8,000

Liabilities (cont'd)		+			Shareholders' Equity					
Unearned Revenue	Interest Payable		Capital Stock	Retained Earnings	Revenue	Cost of Goods Sold	Insurance Expense	Salaries Expense	Interest Expense	Amortization Expense
$55,000			$50,000	$55,000	$258,000			$78,000		
$55,000	$6,000		$50,000	$55,000	$258,000	$180,000	$10,000	$90,000	$6,000	$25,000

equity, or net income (they are lower than they would be otherwise), or (iii) no effect on assets, liabilities, owners' equity, or net income. Provide an explanation for your conclusion and state any assumptions you make. Assume a December 31 year end. For this question it is necessary for you to determine what is the adjusting entry required.

		Effect on Assets	Effect on Liabilities	Effect on Owners' Equity	Effect on Net Income	Explanation
	Wages earned by employees in the last week of the year are not paid until next year.	No effect	Understatement	Overstatement	Overstatement	The adjusting entry would record a wage expense and a wages payable liability. Therefore, by not making the necessary entry, expenses will be understated and liabilities understated.
a.	Equipment costing $100,000 is purchased.					
b.	Work is performed for a customer who paid for the work in a previous period.					
c.	An investment in a long-term government bond pays interest on March 31 and September 30 of each year. (Consider this from the perspective of the entity investing in the bond.)					
d.	The issuer of a long-term bond pays interest to investors on April 30 and October 31 of each year.					

P3-14. **(Evaluating the effect that not recording adjusting entries has on net income, LO 4, 5)** For each of the following economic events, indicate the effect on the financial statements of not recording at year end the necessary adjusting entries. Indicate whether not recording the adjusting entry would result in (i) an overstatement of assets, liabilities, owners' equity, or net income (they are higher than they would be otherwise), (ii) an understatement of assets, liabilities, owners' equity, or net income (they are lower than they would be otherwise), or (iii) no effect on assets, liabilities, owners' equity, or net income. Provide an explanation for your conclusion and state any assumptions you make. Assume a December 31 year end. For this question it is necessary for you to determine what is the adjusting entry required.

		Effect on Assets	Effect on Liabilities	Effect on Owners' Equity	Effect on Net Income	Explanation
	Wages earned by employees in the last week of the year are not paid until next year.	No effect	Understatement	Overstatement	Overstatement	The adjusting entry would record a wage expense and a wages payable liability. Therefore, by not making the necessary entry, expenses will be understated and liabilities understated.
a.	A bus company sells tickets to customers in advance and recognizes revenue when travel takes place.					
b.	A property owner receives part of the rent on his property three months after the year end.					
c.	On October 1 a tenant pays $12,000 to cover six months' rent. The tenant records the payment as prepaid rent.					
d.	A retail store pays a percentage of its sales as rent to the property owner. The payment is made three months after its year end, when the financial statements are released.					

P3-15. **(Use the information in the accounting equation spreadsheet to make journal entries, LO 2, 3, 5)** For each transaction recorded in the accounting equation spreadsheet below, prepare the corresponding journal entry.

Transaction	Cash	Accounts Receivable	Inventory	Prepaid Rent	Capital Assets	Accumulated Amortization	Accounts Payable	Salaries Payable	Capital Stock
1	100,000								100,000
2	(10,000)				30,000		20,000		
3	(3,000)			3,000					
4			15,000				15,000		
5		25,000							
7			(10,000)						
8	(25,000)						(25,000)		
9	18,000	(18,000)							
10	(7,000)								
11	(9,000)								
12						(5,000)			
13				(1,000)					
14								500	

P3-16. **(Use the information in the accounting equation spreadsheet to make journal entries, LO 2, 3, 5)** For each transaction recorded in the accounting equation spreadsheet below, prepare the corresponding journal entry.

Transaction	Cash	Accounts Receivable	Inventory	Prepaid Rent	Capital Assets	Accumulated Amortization	Bank Loan	Accounts Payable	Unearned Revenue
1	20,000								
2	10,000						10,000		
3	(12,000)				25,000			13,000	
4			10,000					10,000	
5	10,000	11,000							
7	(12,000)							(12,000)	
8	8,000	(8,000)							
9	(1,000)						(900)		
10	2,000								2,000
11	(5,000)								
12	(2,000)								
13			(8,000)						
14						(2,500)			
15									

P3-17. **(Understanding the effect of different estimates on net income, LO 4)** In 2005 Otis Knight opened a small business that he called The Corner Coffee Cart. The Corner Coffee Cart sells a variety of coffee-based beverages from a portable cart that Otis can move from place to place. Otis purchased the cart for $12,000 cash when he began the business. All of The Corner Coffee Cart's transactions are for cash. Otis pays cash for all supplies and all sales to customers are for cash. At the end of 2005 Otis decided he wanted to get an idea about how well The Corner Coffee Cart performed in its first year. He assembled the following information:

i. Sales to customers $22,000 (all in cash)

ii. Cost of providing coffee to customers $13,000 (all in cash, includes coffee, milk, cups, stir sticks, etc.)

From this information Otis concluded that he had made $9,000, which he was satisfied with. A friend who had recently taken an accounting course told Otis that his

Retained Earnings	Sales	Cost of Sales	Rent Expense	Salaries Expense	Amortization Expense	Other Expenses
	25,000					
		(10,000)				
				(7,000)		
						(9,000)
					(5,000)	
			(1,000)			
				(500)		

Interest Payable	Capital Stock	Retained Earnings	Sales	Cost of Sales	Interest Expense	Salaries Expense	Amortization Expense	Other Expenses
	20,000							
			21,000					
					(100)			
						(5,000)		
								(2,000)
			(8,000)					
							(2,500)	
800					(800)			

profit of $9,000 was not correct because he did not amortize the cost of the coffee cart. Otis asked his friend to help him calculate the "correct" amount of profit based on the friend's knowledge of accounting.

Required:

    a. Why did Otis's friend tell Otis that his measure of profit was not correct without an amortization expense for the cart? Do you agree with the friend's position?

    b. If Otis assumes that the useful life of the cart is six years and he amortizes the cost of the cart using the straight-line method (an equal amount is expensed each year), what would The Corner Coffee Cart's net income for 2005 be? Assume that the cart would not have any value at the end of its life.

    c. Calculate The Corner Coffee Cart's net income assuming that the cost of the cart is amortized over three years. Calculate net income assuming the cost of the cart is amortized over ten years.

d. What is the difference in The Corner Coffee Cart's net income using the three different periods for amortizing the cart in (b) and (c)?

e. How is your evaluation of how The Corner Coffee Cart performed during 2005 affected by using different periods for amortizing the cart?

f. Assume that the different periods used for amortizing the cart simply represent different reasonable estimates of the cart's useful life. Is the actual performance of The Corner Coffee Cart really different even though the net income under each estimate is different? Explain.

g. What is the "correct" number of years over which to amortize the cart?

Appendix Problems

P3-18. **(Following the steps of the accounting cycle, LO 1, 3, 5, 6)** Use the information provided in Problem P3-7 about Paul's Dogs to do the following:

a. Prepare all necessary journal entries until September 10.

b. Prepare T-accounts and post each journal entry to the appropriate T-account.

c. Prepare and post adjusting journal entries to their appropriate T-accounts. Adjusting entries are needed for the cart and the license.

d. Prepare a trial balance as of September 10.

e. Prepare a balance sheet for Paul's Dogs as of September 10 and an income statement covering the period until September 10.

f. Prepare the closing journal entry and post the closing entry to the appropriate T-accounts.

g. Prepare a trial balance as of September 10 that includes the closing entry.

h. If Paul asked you for some feedback on his business from examining the financial statements, what would you be able to tell him from your examination?

P3-19. **(Following the steps of the accounting cycle, LO 1, 3, 5, 6)** Use the information provided in Problem P3-8 about We've Got Wheels, Inc. (Wheels) to do the following:

a. Prepare all necessary journal entries until September 10.

b. Prepare T-accounts and post each journal entry to the appropriate T-account.

c. Prepare and post adjusting journal entries to their appropriate T-accounts. Adjusting entries are needed for the bikes, inline skates and equipment, and the permit.

d. Prepare a trial balance as of September 10.

e. Prepare a balance sheet as of September 10, 2004 and an income statement for the period ended September 10, 2004 from your spreadsheet. Prepare the closing journal entry and post the closing entry to the appropriate T-accounts.

f. Prepare a trial balance as of September 10, 2004 that includes the closing entry.

g. Compare Wheels' net income with the amount of cash that was generated by the business. Which is a better indicator of how Wheels did? Why are they different? (When looking at the cash flow, consider the cash flows after the owners made their initial $20,000 investment.)

h. If Wheels' owners asked you evaluate the financial statements for them, what would you be able to tell them based on your evaluation?

P3-20. **(Following the steps of the accounting cycle, LO 1, 3, 5, 6)** Use the information about Harry's Appliance Emporium Ltd. (HAEL) provided in Problem P3-9 to do the following:

a. Prepare all necessary transactional journal entries for the year ended August 31, 2005.

b. Prepare T-accounts and post each journal entry to the appropriate T-account.

c. Prepare and post adjusting journal entries to their appropriate T-accounts.

d. Prepare a trial balance as of August 31, 2005.

e. Prepare a balance sheet for HAEL as of August 31, 2005 and an income statement and statement of retained earnings for the year ended August 31, 2005.

f. Prepare the closing journal entry and post the closing entry to the appropriate T-accounts.

g. Prepare a trial balance as of August 31, 2005 that includes the closing entry.

h. Harry is considering expanding HAEL to include a wider range of products. Harry has approached you about purchasing common shares of HAEL to help finance the expansion. Based on your examination of the statements, what can you tell about HAEL that would be useful to your decision to invest? Also, list five questions you might ask Harry that would help you use the financial statements more effectively.

P3-21. **(Following the steps of the accounting cycle, LO 1, 3, 5, 6)** Use the information about Majestic Trucking Inc. (Majestic) provided in Problem P3-10 to do the following:

a. Prepare all necessary transactional journal entries for the year ended December 31, 2005.

b. Prepare T-accounts and post each journal entry to the appropriate T-account.

c. Prepare and post adjusting journal entries to their appropriate T-accounts.

d. Prepare a trial balance as of December 31, 2005.

e. Prepare a balance sheet for Majestic as of December 31, 2005 and an income statement and statement of retained earnings for the year ended December 31, 2005.

f. Prepare the closing journal entry and post the closing entry to the appropriate T-accounts.

g. Prepare a trial balance as of December 31, 2005 that includes the closing entry.

h. The North American economy is booming and there is a lot of work for shipping companies like Majestic. However, the competition is fierce and success and failure are defined by how efficient a company is and how well it services its customers. Majestic's managers would like to upgrade its fleet by adding two new trucks and making significant improvements to its existing vehicles. Based on your examination of the statements, what can you tell about Majestic that would be useful to your decision to lend it $125,000? Also, list five questions you might ask Majestic's management that would help you use the financial statements more effectively.

■ Using Financial Statements

WestJet Airlines Ltd.

WestJet Airlines Ltd. (WestJet), based in Calgary, Alberta, is Canada's leading low-fare air carrier. In 2000, WestJet carried 3.4 million guests to the fifteen destinations of Victoria, Vancouver, Abbotsford/Fraser Valley, Prince George, Kelowna, Calgary, Edmonton, Grande Prairie, Saskatoon, Regina, Winnipeg, Thunder Bay, Hamilton, Ottawa and Moncton. As of December 31, 2000, WestJet operated 22 Boeing 737-200 aircraft and employed over 1500 people. WestJet is a publicly traded company on the Toronto Stock Exchange.[2]

www.westjet.com

WestJet's consolidated balance sheets, statements of earnings, retained earnings, and cash flows along with some extracts from the notes to the financial statements, are provided in Exhibit 3-1.

Use this information to respond to questions FS3-1 to FS3-11.

FS3-1. Examine WestJet's balance sheets. Which accounts do you think would require adjustments at the year end? Explain.

FS3-2. WestJet includes among its current liabilities $18,764,000 for "Advance Ticket Sales." Note 1(b) provides some additional information about this account.

a. When does WestJet recognize its revenue?

b. What does Advance Ticket Sales represent?

c. Why is Advance Ticket Sales reported as a liability? Describe the circumstances that would give rise to an increase in this account.

d. What journal entry would be made to record an increase in Advance Ticket Sales?

Exhibit 3-1

WestJet Airlines Ltd. Financial
Statements

WESTJET AIRLINES LTD.
CONSOLIDATED
BALANCE SHEETS

December 31, 2000 and 1999
(Stated in Thousands of Dollars)

Assets	2000	1999
Current assets:		
Cash and short-term investments	$ 79,025	$ 50,740
Accounts receivable	6,447	5,168
Prepaid expenses and deposits	6,099	4,123
Inventory	604	462
	92,175	60,493
Capital assets (note 2)	239,320	121,974
Other long-term assets (note 3)	5,677	4,131
	$ 337,172	$ 186,598

Liabilities and Shareholders' Equity		
Current liabilities:		
Accounts payable and accrued liabilities	$ 43,616	$ 21,059
Income taxes payable	10,471	7,410
Advance ticket sales	18,764	10,907
Non-refundable passenger credits	6,996	3,863
Current portion of long-term debt (note 4)	9,336	6,550
Current portion of obligations under capital lease (note 5)	1,597	137
	90,780	49,926
Long-term debt (note 4)	40,953	29,341
Obligations under capital lease (note 5)	8,519	335
Future income tax (note 7)	15,828	12,509
	156,080	92,111
Shareholders' equity:		
Share capital (note 6)	125,390	69,039
Retained earnings	55,702	25,448
	181,092	94,487
Commitments (notes 5 and 8)		
	$ 337,172	$ 186,598

Exhibit 3-1 (continued)

WestJet Airlines Ltd. Financial Statements

WESTJET AIRLINES LTD.
CONSOLIDATED STATEMENTS OF EARNINGS AND RETAINED EARNINGS

Years ended December 31, 2000 and 1999
(Stated in Thousands of Dollars, Except Per Share Data)

	2000	1999
Revenues:		
Passenger revenues	$ 315,931	$ 193,715
Charter and other	16,588	9,859
	332,519	203,574
Expenses:		
Passenger services	64,090	43,955
Aircraft fuel	55,875	30,480
Maintenance	49,512	31,854
Sales and marketing	21,763	13,907
Amortization	17,959	8,272
Employee profit share provision	13,549	6,633
Flight operations	13,923	8,826
Reservations	12,497	9,550
General and administration	12,147	9,410
Inflight	10,972	7,531
Aircraft leasing	6,770	2,687
	279,057	173,105
Earnings from operations	53,462	30,469
Non-operating income (expense):		
Interest income	2,463	1,657
Interest expense	(2,937)	(2,871)
Gain (loss) on disposal of assets	(282)	93
	(756)	(1,121)
Earnings before income taxes	52,706	29,348
Income taxes (note 7):		
Current	18,102	7,696
Future	4,350	5,820
	22,452	13,516
Net earnings	30,254	15,832
Retained earnings, beginning of year	25,448	9,616
Retained earnings, end of year	$ 55,702	$ 25,448
Earnings per share:		
Basic	$ 0.72	$ 0.42
Fully diluted	$ 0.69	$ 0.39

Exhibit 3-1 (continued)

WestJet Airlines Ltd. Financial
Statements

WESTJET AIRLINES LTD.
CONSOLIDATED STATEMENTS
OF CASH FLOWS

Years ended December 31, 2000 and 1999
(Stated in Thousands of Dollars)

	2000	1999
Cash provided by (used in):		
Operations:		
Net earnings	$ 30,254	$ 15,832
Items not involving cash:		
Amortization	17,959	8,272
Gain on disposal of capital assets	(633)	(93)
Future income tax	4,350	5,820
Cash flow from operations	51,930	29,831
Increase in non-cash working capital	35,483	17,948
	87,413	47,779
Financing:		
Increase in long-term debt	22,417	15,314
Repayment of long-term debt	(8,019)	(5,335)
Issuance of common shares	57,689	30,591
Share issuance costs	(2,369)	(2,356)
Increase in other long-term assets	(3,818)	(4,195)
Decrease in obligations under capital lease	(137)	(96)
	65,763	33,923
Investments:		
Aircraft additions	(97,269)	(39,318)
Aircraft disposals	12,239	—
Other capital asset additions	(40,043)	(5,350)
Other capital asset disposals	182	206
	(124,891)	(44,462)
Increase in cash	28,285	37,240
Cash, beginning of year	50,740	13,500
Cash, end of year	$ 79,025	$ 50,740

Exhibit 3-1 (continued)

WestJet Airlines Ltd. Financial
Statements

WESTJET AIRLINES LTD.
NOTES TO CONSOLIDATED
FINANCIAL STATEMENTS

Years ended December 31, 2000 and 1999
(Tabular Amounts are Stated in Thousands of Dollars)

1. Significant accounting policies:

(a) Principles of consolidation:
These consolidated financial statements include the accounts of the Corporation and its wholly-owned subsidiaries.

(b) Revenue recognition:
Passenger revenue is recognized when air transportation is provided. The value of unused tickets is included in the balance sheet as advance ticket sales under current liabilities.

(c) Non-refundable passenger credits:
The Corporation, under certain circumstances, may issue future travel credits which are non-refundable and which expire one year from the date of issue. The utilization of passenger credits are recorded as revenue when the passenger has flown.

(d) Foreign currency:
Monetary assets and liabilities, denominated in foreign currencies, are translated into Canadian dollars at rates of exchange in effect at the balance sheet date. Other assets and revenue and expense items are translated at rates prevailing when they were acquired or incurred.

Exchange gains and losses arising on the translation of long-term monetary items that are denominated in foreign currencies are deferred and amortized on a straight-line basis over the remaining term of the related monetary item.

(e) Inventory:
Materials and supplies are valued at the lower of cost and replacement value. Aircraft expendables and consumables are expensed as incurred.

(f) Deferred costs:
Sales and marketing and reservation expenses attributed to the advance ticket sales are deferred and expensed in the period the related revenue is recognized. Included in prepaid expenses are $2,435,000 (1999 - $1,169,000) of deferred costs.

(g) Capital assets:
Capital assets are depreciated over their estimated useful lives at the following rates and methods.

Asset	Basis	Rate
Aircraft net of estimated residual value	Flight hours	Hours flown
Spare engines and parts	Flight hours	Hours flown
Aircraft under capital lease	Straight-line	Over the term of the lease
Flight simulators	Straight-line	10 and 25 years
Computer hardware and software	Straight-line	5 years
Equipment	Straight-line	5 years
Leasehold improvements	Straight-line	Over the term of the lease
Buildings	Straight-line	40 years

h) Maintenance costs:
Maintenance costs related to the cost of acquiring the aircraft and preparation for service are capitalized and included in aircraft costs.

Heavy maintenance ("D" check) costs incurred on aircraft are deferred and amortized over the remaining useful service life of the aircraft.

All other maintenance costs are expensed as incurred.

e. What circumstances would give rise to a decrease in Advance Ticket Sales?

f. What journal entry would be made to record a decrease in Advance Ticket Sales?

FS3-3. WestJet includes among its current liabilities $6,996,000 for "Non-refundable traveller credits." Note 1(c) provides some additional information about this account. When a traveller books a WestJet flight he or she has 24 hours to cancel the reservation and get a refund. If the traveller cancels after the 24-hour period, the amount paid is not refunded but the traveller receives a credit that can be used against the price of a WestJet flight in the next 12 months.

a. What journal entry would WestJet record when a traveller makes the initial reservation? Remember that when a traveller pays for a ticket in advance of a flight the amount is credited to "Advance Ticket Sales" (see Note 1(b)).

b. What adjusting entry is required if a traveller cancels his or her flight after the 24-hour grace period for getting a refund?

c. What journal entry would WestJet make if a traveller who has a travel credit calls to book another flight?

FS3-4. Read note 1(f) to WestJet's financial statements. The note explains how WestJet accounts for "Deferred Costs."

a. Where on WestJet's balance sheet are the deferred costs reported?

b. What amount of deferred costs is reported on WestJet's December 31, 2000 balance sheet?

c. What are the deferred costs?

d. WestJet's treatment of the deferred costs can be considered an application of the matching principal. Explain.

e. What journal entry would WestJet make to record the deferred costs?

f. What journal entry would WestJet make when it was time to expense the deferred costs?

FS3-5. Note 1(h) explains that WestJet capitalizes some of the maintenance costs that it incurs and expenses others. How do you think an accountant might explain why maintenance costs done for different purposes are accounted for differently?

FS3-6. Suppose that WestJet expensed all of the maintenance costs described in Note 1(h) in the year in which they were incurred rather than capitalizing some of them. What would be the effect on the financial statements of this different treatment? Would a different accounting treatment change the actual economic activity and performance of WestJet? How might the perceptions of users of the financial statements be affected by different accounting treatments?

FS3-7. Calculate the following ratios for WestJet for 1999 and 2000:

a. Profit margin.

b. Return on equity.

c. Current ratio.

FS3-8. Prepare the closing journal entry that WestJet would make on December 31, 2000.

FS3-9. During 2000 WestJet generated a significant amount of cash, as reflected by the significant increase in the amount of cash on hand and in the amount of money invested in capital assets (remember that on a GAAP balance sheet capital assets are recorded at the amount paid for them, less the total amount of amortization expensed). Examine WestJet's balance sheets and statements of cash flow. How did WestJet obtain the cash used to increase its cash balance and for its investment in capital assets? You should be able to find information in both statements to help you answer this question.

FS3-10. How much inventory does WestJet report on its December 31, 2000 balance sheet? Why do you think WestJet has so little inventory?

FS3-11. Compare WestJet's balance sheet and income statement with MWW's. Describe how the statements differ. Explain. In responding, consider the different types and relative amounts of assets, liabilities, revenues, and expenses that are reported on the statements. In answering this question consider assets as a percentage of total assets, liabilities as a percentage of total liabilities and shareholders' equity, and expenses as a percentage of revenues.

Analyzing Mark's Work Wearhouse

M3-1. See Appendix A for the Mark's Work Wearhouse Annual Report. Examine MWW's balance sheet and income statement for the year ended January 27, 2001 (pages A-45 to A-46). What adjusting journal entries do you think MWW had to make when preparing the statements? Explain. (Reading the notes associated with some of the balance sheet and income statement items might help in answering this question.)

M3-2. How much would MWW "close" to retained earnings at the end of its 2001 fiscal year? Explain.

M3-3. Prepare the closing journal entry that MWW would make on January 27, 2001.

M3-4. What accounts on MWW's income statement and balance sheet indicate that it is using accrual accounting? Explain.

M3-5. How much depreciation and amortization did MWW expense in the year ended January 27, 2001? (Look carefully at the income statement, as this expense appears more than once.) What journal entry would MWW make to record the depreciation and amortization expense? What amount would be in the accumulated amortization account for MWW's capital assets on January 27, 2001?

M3-6. MWW reports $6,993,000 of cash and cash equivalents on its January 27, 2001 balance sheet. This amount does not mean that all this cash is kept in a single bank account. Speculate as to possible different locations where MWW might hold its cash. Explain. If cash is held in many locations, why is it reported as a single amount on the balance sheet?

Endnotes

1. A.C. Littleton, *Accounting Evolution to 1900*, 2d ed. (New York: Russell & Russell, 1966).

2. Extracted from WestJet Airlines Ltd.'s 2000 annual report.

Chapter 4

Income Measurement and the Objectives of Financial Reporting

Chapter Outline

Learning Objectives

Introduction

Revenue Recognition

Gains and Losses

Expense Recognition

The Objectives of Financial Reporting

Can Preparers Do Whatever They Want?

Solving Accounting Choice Problems

Solved Problem

Summary of Key Points

Key Terms

Questions, Exercises, and Problems

Using Financial Statements

Analyzing Mark's Work Wearhouse

Learning Objectives

After studying the material in this chapter you will be able to:

LO 1.   Explain and apply the GAAP criteria for revenue recognition.

LO 2.   Describe the critical-event and gradual approaches of recognizing revenue.

LO 3.   Explain the effects that different approaches to recognizing revenue have on the income statement and on financial ratios.

LO 4.   Apply the percentage-of-completion and completed-contract methods of recognizing revenue.

LO 5.   Describe expense recognition and the matching principle.

LO 6.   Explain the reasons for, the implications of, and limitations to flexible accounting rules that give the preparers of accounting information the opportunity to choose how they account.

LO 7.   Apply an approach to solving accounting choice problems.

Introduction

We have now covered the fundamentals of accounting principles. In Chapters 1 to 3 you have explored the accounting environment, become familiar with financial statements, and learned the basics of the accounting cycle. We can now begin our exploration of accounting information in depth. In the remainder of the book we will examine how economic events are reported (and not reported) in financial statements. It is now time to don our detective gear and learn how to sleuth through accounting information.

In this chapter we will explore revenue and expense recognition. The term *recognition* refers to when revenues and expenses appear on the income statement. There are different ways and times that revenues and expenses can be recognized, and the methods chosen can affect the amount of revenues, expenses, and income that an entity reports in a period. Different revenue and expense recognition methods also affect many accounting and financial ratios—tools that stakeholders often use to analyze an entity. Even though the appearance of an income statement will vary depending on the revenue and expense recognition methods used, the underlying economic activity of the entity is the same regardless of the methods chosen. That is, the same entity can be represented in different ways by its accounting information.

We will learn in this chapter that preparers of accounting information have considerable latitude selecting when and how revenues and expenses are recognized. Through the remainder of this book we will also see that most accounting issues provide preparers with choices as to how to account. But before going on, it is important to explain why preparers have choices to make. In other words, why are there different ways to account for particular economic events?

One of the reasons that preparers of accounting information are given choice is the nature of accounting itself. Accounting has been created by people and is not subject to any natural laws. Unlike gravity, which is a law of nature, accounting rules are created and defined to suit needs. These may be the needs of individual users or of a society as a whole. Different needs and different users often require different information. As a result, there is rarely one right or best way to account for an economic event that serves everyone's needs or interests. Another reason for giving preparers choice is that sometimes it is very difficult to say definitively that there is one best way of accounting for a particular economic event or transaction. Accounting "translates" complex economic events into numbers in the financial statements. That translation can be difficult and the interpretation of economic events can be subject to judgment. It is the preparers of the financial statements who make these judgments.

The availability of accounting choice raises important ethical questions. How do preparers choose among legitimate alternatives? Which user group's interests should be considered most important if it is necessary to choose among competing interests? In the end, the preparers must often make difficult choices about what information to present in the general purpose financial statements and how to present that information. These choices may make the financial statements more useful and informative to some users, and less useful and informative to others. The choices may have different economic implications for different users and user groups. Sometimes the preparers may make accounting choices that serve their own interests rather than the interests of the users of the financial statements. The sheer number of possible accounting choices, and the variety of possible users and uses of accounting information, make it difficult to determine whether preparers have made their choices to produce more informative statements or to serve their own interests. Users of financial statements must read and interpret them very carefully to avoid being misled or confused.

Revenue Recognition

In Chapter 3, when the topic of revenue recognition was introduced, we saw that under accrual accounting it is necessary to decide when revenue "happens." In other words, with accrual accounting the economic event that should trigger revenue recognition is not always obvious. Someone has to decide what the economic event is that triggers revenue recognition. *When* revenue is recognized and *how* expenses are matched to revenue can have a significant impact on the income statement and the balance sheet, on financial ratios, and, more generally, on a person's perception of how a business is performing. Once you determine *when* revenue should be recognized, the journal entry to record revenue is straightforward. The journal entry is:

Dr. Cash (asset +) or Accounts Receivables (asset +)   xxx
   or Unearned Revenue (liabilities −)
     Cr. Revenue (revenue +, owners' equity +)   xxx
  To record revenue.

When revenue is recognized, an income statement account for a revenue (or sales or sales revenue) account is credited and a balance sheet account is debited. The entry to the balance sheet account either increases assets or decreases liabilities. The balance sheet effect is an increase in net assets (assets − liabilities). This reflects the concept that revenue represents economic benefits gained by the entity (increase in assets or decrease in liabilities) or an increase in the wealth of the owners of the entity.

Conceptually, earning revenue is a continuous process. Each activity an entity undertakes that increases the economic value of a good or service represents revenue, since by adding value an entity makes its goods or services more valuable to consumers and ultimately, revenue is the amount consumers will pay for that good or service. Therefore, by adding value to its goods or services an entity is earning revenue.

For Mark's Work Wearhouse (MWW) the actual sale of goods to a customer is the culmination of a series of actions. Before a customer buys an item, MWW must:

- invest in stores to provide a place where the customer can shop
- purchase inventory from suppliers
- distribute the inventory to stores and display it
- advertise its products
- provide heat, light, and a suitable shopping environment
- provide staff, etc.

Each of these steps adds value to MWW's products by bringing them closer and making them more conveniently available to customers, by making customers aware of the goods' existence, availability, and attractiveness, and by creating an environment that makes shopping a positive experience. Each step along the way represents revenue to MWW, at least in a conceptual sense.

As a practical matter, it is very difficult for accountants to determine *when* and *how much* revenue should be recognized along the series of actions that culminates in an actual sale to a customer. For example, how much revenue does a particular television advertisement broadcast at 8:13 PM on Thursday create? It is impossible to know. In reality, there are practical limitations in recognizing this economic or conceptual revenue. Despite the difficulties, though, revenue must somehow be reflected in the income statement in a logical and rational way. Broadly, accountants have devised two approaches for recognizing revenue.

The first approach for recognizing revenue we can call the **critical-event approach**. Under the critical-event approach, an entity chooses an instant in the earnings process that it considers an appropriate time to recognize revenue. That instant is called the critical event. When the critical event occurs, 100% of the revenue is recognized. The critical-event approach is "all or nothing." Before the critical event occurs no revenue is recognized. Once the critical event has occurred, all the revenue is recognized. With the critical-event approach, the continuous nature of the revenue-earning process is ignored.

The second approach recognizes revenue gradually over a period of time. We can call this approach to recognizing revenue the **gradual approach.** The gradual approach is often used when an entity has long-term contracts, such as construction projects, that last for more than one accounting period. With the gradual approach, revenue is recognized little by little as a project progresses. The entity must identify a basis for determining how much revenue should be recognized each period.

Both revenue recognition approaches will be discussed in more detail later in the chapter. Before we come to that discussion, we will define some criteria that can be used for determining when to recognize revenue. These criteria will form the basis for our discussion of the two revenue recognition approaches. This section on revenue recognition will also explain why it matters when and how an entity recognizes its revenue and will discuss why preparers can often choose when to recognize revenue (and make other accounting choices).

Criteria for Recognizing Revenue

To recognize revenue in a logical and rational manner we need some criteria to guide the choice. Without some guidance financial reporting could become a free-for-all that could impair the usefulness of financial statements. (Some critics argue that financial reporting is already a free-for-all!) The criteria that we will use to evaluate when revenue should be recognized are listed below. The criteria are reflective of the conditions necessary to recognize revenue under GAAP. We use GAAP as our benchmark for examining financial reporting because GAAP-based financial statements are the type of statements that we most commonly encounter. Remember, however, we are examining financial reporting with a critical eye, so it is important not to think of these criteria as the best or only criteria for recognizing revenue. The criteria are:

1. The revenue has been earned.
2. The amount of revenue can be reasonably measured.
3. The costs required to earn the revenue can be reasonably measured.
4. Collection of payment is reasonably assured.

The first criterion requires that the revenue has been earned. The notion of "earned" can be explained in different ways. One way is that the entity has completed a significant portion of the effort required to provide the goods or services to customers. In other words, the entity has done most of what it is supposed to do to be entitled to the benefits associated with the effort being provided. Another explanation comes from the *CICA Handbook*, which characterizes the notion of "earned" as the transfer of the significant rights and risks of ownership from the seller to the buyer.

Criteria 2 and 3 deal with measurability. For revenue to be recognized it must be measurable—the entity must be able to make a reasonable estimate of the amount of revenue. In addition, the costs associated with earning the revenue must be measurable so that they can be matched to the revenue—the entity must be able to make a reasonable estimate of the costs. Remember that matching is a key accrual accounting concept.

The fourth criterion is collectability. The entity must have a reasonable expectation that it will be paid.

These criteria provide guidance to preparers, but they are open to interpretation and judgment. After all, at what point has revenue been "earned"? When has a "significant portion of effort" been completed? When have the "significant rights and risks of ownership" been transferred? For criteria 2 through 4, what does "reasonably" mean? These fairly vague terms provide flexibility for choosing when to recognize revenue. These criteria are, however, fairly *conservative* in that they tend to delay the recognition of revenue until fairly late in the revenue-generating process.

The intent of this more conservative approach is to limit the uncertainty surrounding the numbers in the financial statements so that the information reported can be meaningful. If there is too much uncertainty about revenues and/or expenses, the amounts reported can be virtually meaningless. Financial statement numbers that are too uncertain are not much better than random numbers. They do not provide financial statement users with much information that is useful for decision making. On the other hand, waiting until there is no uncertainty may not be useful either because the users will not receive information in time to influence their decisions. While the criteria listed above tend to limit uncertainty, they do not eliminate it. For uncertainty to be eliminated, revenue would have to be recognized very late—in most cases long after cash is collected.

Here is one more criterion that we can add: the revenue-recognition point selected should provide a reasonable and fair representation of the entity's activities, given the needs of the people who will be using the accounting information. This means that after deciding that a revenue recognition point satisfies the criteria on page 192, a preparer should step back and assess whether the choice is a reasonable and fair representation of the entity's activities, given the needs of the users. If the preparer believes that the choice of revenue recognition point may be misleading or confusing, an alternative should be considered. We can think of this criterion as pervasive and overriding. Remember that above all, accounting information must provide useful information about an entity to stakeholders so that they can make

---

Question for Consideration

What are the four criteria for recognizing revenue under GAAP? Explain each criterion.

Answer: The four criteria are:

Criterion	Explanation
1. The revenue has been earned.	To recognize revenue, the entity must have fulfilled most of what it had to do to receive the benefits associated with the effort being provided. In the words of the *CICA Handbook*, revenue is earned when the significant rights and risks of ownership have been transferred from the seller to the buyer.
2. The amount of revenue can be reasonably measured.	It is necessary to know the amount of revenue that will be earned. That is, the amount that the customer has agreed to pay must be known.
3. The costs required to earn the revenue can be reasonably measured.	It is necessary to know the costs that will be incurred to earn the revenue. This criterion is necessary if expenses are going to be matched to revenue. Costs include not only those incurred to the time the revenue is recognized, but also costs related to the revenue that will be incurred in the future.
4. Collection of payment is reasonably assured.	For revenue to be recognized there must be a reasonable expectation that payment will be received. If the revenue is not collected, there is no economic gain.

informed decisions. As our discussion proceeds we will refer mainly to the first four criteria. However, this fifth criterion should always be kept in mind.

One final remark on these revenue-recognition criteria: they are not universal. One could devise a different set of criteria that would be equally appropriate for particular stakeholders in particular situations. For example, stakeholders in a real estate company might benefit from having the increases in the value of the property owned by the company reported as revenue. Recognizing increases in value before property is sold is, in most cases, contrary to GAAP and would not meet our revenue-recognition criteria. However, alternative criteria could be set up that would allow for recognition of these increases in value. The reason other sets of criteria are possible is that there is no natural set of accounting rules. People create accounting rules to suit their needs and the environments in which they function.

The Critical-Event Approach to Recognizing Revenue

Under the critical-event approach to recognizing revenue, the occurrence of the critical event triggers the recording of revenue and the matching of the related expenses. Revenue is recognized in full when the critical event occurs. Until the critical event occurs revenue is not recorded.

Entities have some flexibility in choosing what the critical event for recognizing their revenue should be. The critical events for similar transactions could be different, depending on the circumstances of the transactions. In many situations, there is not one and only one possible critical event. In situations where there is more than one possible critical event, the one an entity chooses will be influenced by its accounting environment—factors such as the characteristics of the entity (industry, type of transactions, risk, and so on), constraints, stakeholder needs, and the interests of the preparers of the accounting information. (See Figure 1-1 on page 9.)

If the entity is following GAAP, the critical event must meet the revenue-recognition criteria and must occur at a reasonable and fair point in the earnings process. One of the most common critical events chosen by companies is when the goods or services offered by the companies are delivered to the customer. However, different critical events are commonly seen in practice and these critical events can be before or after the goods or services are delivered. Let's take a look at some of the critical events that trigger the recognition of revenue.

Delivery   Delivery occurs when the buyer takes possession of the goods being sold or receives the service being purchased. For retail businesses like MWW the revenue-recognition criteria are met when a customer buys an item, such as a shirt, at a store. When a customer buys a shirt at MWW most of the effort required to sell the shirt has occurred. The customer has been attracted to the store, the salesperson has assisted the customer, and the customer has chosen the shirt and made the purchase. The amount of revenue is known since the customer has paid for the shirt. The cost of the shirt is also known. Collection is reasonably assured (actually, it is certain) since people usually pay at retail stores with cash, a debit card, or a credit card. (Collection will be less certain for retail stores that have their own credit cards, such as Canadian Tire and The Bay.) In the MWW case, there are still uncertainties at the time of delivery, since the customer may return the shirt or, if credit is offered, some customers may not pay. However, these uncertainties are identifiable and can usually be estimated. Note that using delivery as the critical event means that revenue can be recognized before cash is received, after cash is received, or at the same time cash is received.

Most retail, manufacturing, and service businesses use delivery as their critical event because for these businesses the revenue-recognition criteria are not met until delivery occurs. In contrast, there is too much uncertainty before delivery occurs, and recognizing revenue after delivery would delay recognition beyond a reasonable time. That said, there are always exceptions. For example, a retail business that sells to high-risk customers (customers who have a high likelihood of not paying on time) could reasonably delay recognizing revenue until cash is collected.

Using delivery as the critical event for revenue recognition is so common that many companies that use it do not disclose this fact in their financial statements. They assume that users realize that revenue is recognized at the point of delivery, unless another critical event is disclosed. If you look at MWW's financial statements, you will find no explanation of how MWW recognizes revenue from its sale of clothing. Note 1C (page A-49) explains the revenue-recognition method for MWW's franchise operations, but there is no reference to how revenue is recognized for its main line of business.

Completion of Production

In some situations the four revenue-recognition criteria can be considered met as soon as the product is produced, even if it has not been sold or delivered to the customer. If the sale of the product is assured and the costs of selling and distributing it are minor, revenue can be reasonably recognized when production is complete. Commodities, such as gold, are a good example. Once a gold mining company has found gold, extracted it from the ground, and refined it into the pure precious metal, the revenue can be considered earned. The gold mining company will have completed a significant amount of the effort required to provide the gold to the final customer and there are few costs left to incur. Actually selling the gold is easy. There is an active market for gold that can purchase any amount of gold a producer has to sell. The price of gold is set by the market and can easily be determined at any time. (Gold prices are reported every day in most media business reports. Prices for other commodities are also readily available, but are not as widely reported as the price of gold. Look for commodity prices in the business section of *The Globe and Mail* or *The National Post*.) There may be uncertainty about the final selling price because market prices fluctuate. As a result, the price of gold when the gold mining company produces the gold could be different from the price when the gold is actually sold.

www.globeandmail.com
www.nationalpost.com

Exhibit 4-1 shows the revenue recognition note from the financial statements of Richmont Mines Inc. (Richmont), which operates mines in Quebec and Newfoundland.[1] Richmont recognizes revenue as soon as the gold bullion is produced. The fact that there is no customer, no sale transaction, and no delivery of the gold does not prevent revenue from being recognized.

www.richmont-mines.com

Cash Collection

Sometimes it is very difficult for an entity to reasonably estimate

---

Exhibit 4-1

Revenue Recognition Method
Used by Richmont Mines Inc.

NOTES TO CONSOLIDATED FINANCIAL STATEMENTS

Years ended December 31, 2000, 1999 and 1998
(Amounts are presented in Canadian dollars)

1. SIGNIFICANT ACCOUNTING POLICIES

b) Precious metals recognition

Precious metals revenue, based upon spot metal prices or forward sales contracts, is recorded when gold bullion is produced. Revenue may be subject to adjustment on final settlement to reflect changes in metal market prices.

the amount that will be collected from customers. In these situations collection becomes the critical event because the fourth criterion for revenue recognition requires that collection of payment be reasonably assured. For example, a retail store that sells to high-risk customers may delay recognizing revenue until the cash is received. The key is that it is difficult to estimate the amount that will be collected.

With most credit sales there is some risk of non-collection. However, just because there is some chance that money owed will not be collected, this does not mean that revenue recognition should be delayed until the money is collected. *If* the amount that *will be* collected can be reasonably estimated, then revenue can be recognized before cash is collected. For example, companies that sell goods on credit would usually recognize their revenue on delivery, even though it is likely that some customers will not pay for the goods they received.

Remember that receiving cash does not automatically mean that revenue can be recognized. Collection is only one of the revenue-recognition criteria, and all of the criteria must be met before revenue can be recognized. If the other criteria are not satisfied when the cash (or other compensation) is received, then revenue recognition should be deferred.

Consider the following example. Many travellers pay for their plane tickets well in advance of their flights, but airlines such as Air Canada usually recognize revenue only when the flight occurs. As shown in Exhibit 4-2, which reproduces the note from Air Canada's fiscal 2000 financial statements explaining how air transportation revenue is recognized, Air Canada does not recognize revenue just because it has received cash from its passengers.[2] It faces many uncertainties before a flight occurs that might prevent the earning of revenue, including the possible cancellation of a flight or cancellations by travellers. The flight itself represents a significant portion of the effort required to earn the revenue, and until a traveller takes the flight Air Canada has not earned the revenue.

Sometimes a customer does not make full payment all at once. For example, it is common to see advertisements for a range of products that allow customers to make their purchases in "five easy payments." If the entity cannot reasonably determine the collectability of the amounts owed by customers, then a method known as the **instalment method** can be used. The instalment method recognizes revenue when each payment is received. The expenses incurred to earn the revenue are matched on a proportional basis. For example, if an instalment payment is received that represents 20% of the expected revenue, then 20% of the expenses are matched to the revenue. The instalment method is not, strictly speaking, a critical-event approach because 100% of the revenue is not recognized when the critical event occurs. Instead, the amount of the cash that is collected is recognized. However, because revenue is recognized on the occurrence of a critical event (the collection of cash), the instalment method is a critical-event approach.

Exhibit 4-2

Revenue Recognition Method
Used by Air Canada

Notes to Consolidated Financial Statements

(currencies in millions, except per share figures)

1. Significant Accounting Policies

f) Air Transportation Revenue

Airline passenger and cargo sales are recognized as operating revenues when the transportation is provided. The value of unused transportation is included in current liabilities.

Completion of Warranty Period or Right-of-Return Period   When there are uncertainties about significant costs that may be incurred after delivery, it may be appropriate to recognize revenue only when those uncertainties have been resolved. For example, a company develops a sophisticated product that relies on a new technology and sells the product with an unconditional warranty. (A **warranty** is a promise by a seller or producer of a product to correct specified problems with the product.) Because the product relies on a new technology, it may be impossible to estimate the cost of repairing any problems that may arise. It would be appropriate to defer revenue recognition until the warranty period ends because of the uncertainty about the warranty costs. In this case, criterion 3 (that costs required to earn the revenue can be reasonable measured) is not fulfilled and revenue should not be recognized.

However, the existence of a warranty does not always justify delaying revenue recognition. Revenue can be recognized earlier if the warranty costs associated with a product can be reasonably estimated. That would occur for a product that has been produced for some time. To satisfy the matching principle it is necessary to accrue the estimated warranty costs when the revenue is recognized, even though the warranty costs will not be actually incurred until a later period.

Right-of-return periods are similar to warranties when assessing the revenue-recognition criteria. Revenue recognition could be delayed when customers have the right to return goods purchased. If the amount to be returned is unpredictable, it would be appropriate to delay revenue recognition until after the right-of-return period has expired.

Other Critical Events   There are other points in time that can be used as the critical event for recognizing revenue, including when an order is received from a customer or when an order from a customer is accepted and the terms of the sale are finalized. When working in a GAAP environment, one should always assess the appropriateness of a critical event in light of the revenue-recognition criteria.

Unrealized Gains—A Non-GAAP Critical Event   The revenue-recognition criteria used under GAAP do not capture all of an entity's economic gains and losses. Sometimes the market value of an entity's assets can change while the entity continues to own them. That is, the market value of inventory, capital assets, investments, and other assets can increase and decrease over time. Increases or decreases in the market value of assets that are not supported by a transaction with an outside party are called **unrealized gains and losses**. A gain or loss is *realized* when there is a transaction—that is, when the asset is sold. Under GAAP gains are recognized only when they are realized. (Because of conservatism, unrealized losses are sometimes recognized before they are realized.) When a gain is unrealized, most or all of the four revenue-recognition criteria are not met. This accounting treatment for unrealized gains represents a limitation of GAAP. The change in market value of an entity's assets could be useful information for some stakeholders, but it is not provided in GAAP financial statements.

Now let's consider a real example. Companies in the real estate industry can hold land and other property for a long time before it is sold. Exhibit 4-3 (page 198) shows the notes to the financial statements of Genesis Land Development Corp. (Genesis) that explain its revenue recognition policies and valuation policy for real estate held for development and sale.[3] When Genesis purchases land it is recorded at cost. All costs incurred over the years prior to the land being developed are added to the cost of the land. Even if the land is held for many years, there is no income statement effect reported until the land is sold.

www.genesisland.com

As you can imagine, the market value of land can change dramatically over the years. However, GAAP-based financial statements provide very little information about the changing value of land, even though these changes can be economically significant to the entity and the information could be very valuable to some stakeholders. Again, the reason Genesis and similar companies do not report these unrealized gains is conservatism. Another way of explaining conservatism is that gains should not be anticipated—they should be recorded only when they are realized.

Canadian accounting standard setters have been reluctant to include information about unrealized changes in the value of land and other assets in financial statements because it can be very difficult to estimate the market value of land before it is sold. The people responsible for setting accounting standards in Canada believe that estimates of the market value of certain assets are so uncertain and unreliable that including such estimates could be misleading to users. This perspective demonstrates the trade-off that exists in accounting between reliable information and relevant information.

This discussion about the critical-event approach may lead some people to conclude that it is easy and straightforward to choose the critical event for recognizing revenue. In most cases, it is. However, every now and then situations arise where the facts allow for more than one reasonable choice for recognizing revenue. Those situations make working with accounting information challenging.

Why Does It Matter When a Company Recognizes Revenue?

Let's look at an example to show the effects on the income statement of using different critical events for recognizing revenue. Escuminac Copper Mines Ltd. (Escuminac) is a Canadian company that operates a copper mine in South America. The mine began producing copper in 2005. Escuminac has contracted to sell all the copper it produces between 2005 and 2007 to customers at a fixed price. After 2007 Escuminac will have to arrange new fixed price contracts or sell its copper on the open market. Under the contracts, Escuminac receives $3,000 per tonne of copper. Copper is delivered to customers about 60 days after it is produced and customers pay, on

Exhibit 4-3	
Revenue Recognition Policies at Genesis Land Development Corp.	

Genesis Land Development Corp.

Notes to Consolidated Financial Statements

December 31, 2000

1. Significant accounting policies

   (3) Revenue recognition

       (1) Residential lot sales

           Revenue is recognized when a contract for sale is signed, 15% of the sale proceeds has been received and the sale is unconditional.

       (2) Housing and construction sales

           The sale is recognized when the completed unit is conveyed to the purchaser.

   (4) Real estate held for development and sale

       Land held for future development, land under development, and housing and construction projects under development are recorded at lower of cost and estimated net realizable value.

       Capitalized costs include all direct costs related to development and construction, carrying costs including interest on debt used to finance projects, property taxes and land acquisition costs. Land acquisition costs are prorated to a phase of a project on an acreage basis when the first sale occurs in the phase. During the year, interest of $2,516,948 (1999 - $6,474,112) was capitalized to real estate held for development and sale.

       No general and administration costs are capitalized.

average, 90 days after receiving the copper. The table below shows how much copper was produced, delivered, and paid for in each year of the contracts. The amounts of copper produced, delivered, and paid for are not equal because some of the production will be delivered and paid for in 2008.

Tonnes of copper	2005	2006	2007
Produced by Escuminac	1,100	1,300	1,700
Delivered to customers	917	1,266	1,634
Paid for by customers	688	1,225	1,550

Now let's look at Escuminac's financial results in the years 2005 to 2007. Three sets of income statements have been prepared and are shown in Table 4-1. Each set is prepared using a different critical event to recognize revenue. The three critical events used are:

1. When the copper is produced.

2. When the copper is delivered to customers.

3. When cash is received from customers.

All three statements assume that the direct costs of producing the refined copper, called *production expenses* in Table 4-1, are 60% of the selling price of the copper. These costs are expensed when the revenue is recognized, as required by the matching principle. This means that it costs $1,800 ($3,000 × 60%) to produce each tonne of copper. In addition, there are $950,000 of other costs, such as executive salaries, cost

Table 4-1   Income Statements for Escuminac Copper Mines Ltd.

Escuminac Copper Mines Ltd.
Income Statements
(in thousands of dollars)

	1. Revenue recognized when the copper is produced			2. Revenue recognized when the copper is delivered			3. Revenue recognized when cash is received from customers		
	2005**	2006	2007	2005	2006	2007	2005	2006	2007
Revenue*	$3,300.0	$3,900.0	$5,100.0	$2,751.0	$3,798.0	$4,902.0	$2,064.0	$3,675.0	$4,650.0
Production Expenses	1,980.0	2,340.0	3,060.0	1,650.6	2,278.8	2,941.2	1,238.4	2,205.0	2,790.0
Gross Margin	$1,320.0	$1,560.0	$2,040.0	$1,100.4	$1,519.2	$1,960.8	$ 825.6	$1,470.0	$1,860.0
Other Expenses (assumed)	$ 950.0	$ 950.0	$ 950.0	$ 950.0	$ 950.0	$ 950.0	$ 950.0	$ 950.0	$ 950.0
Net Income	$ 370.0	$ 610.0	$1,090.0	$ 150.4	$ 569.2	$1,010.8	($ 124.4)	$ 520.0	$ 910.0
Financial Ratios:									
Gross Margin Percentage	0.400	0.400	0.400	0.400	0.400	0.400	0.400	0.400	0.400
Profit Margin	0.112	0.156	0.214	0.055	0.150	0.206	–0.060	0.141	0.196

* The total amount of revenue, expenses and net income over the three years is different for each critical event because some of the copper will not be delivered until 2008 and so recognition of some of the revenue at the delivery and cash collection points will not be recognized until 2008. If results for 2008 were also shown for these contracts, the total of revenue, expenses and net income over 2005 through 2008 would be the same. Over the term of the contracts the amount of revenue earned is not affected by the critical event chosen. Only the timing of when the revenue is recognized is affected.

**Below are sample calculations for the amounts shown in the exhibit. Calculations are shown for 2005 when revenue is recognized when the copper is produced.

Revenue = Quantity produced × Selling price per tonne = 1,100 tonnes × $3,000 per tonne = $3,300,000
Production Expenses = 60% × Selling price per tonne = 60% × $3,000 × 1,100 tonnes = $1,980,000
Gross Margin = Revenue − Production Expenses = $3,300,000 − $1,980,000 = $1,320,000
Other Expenses = $950,000 (fixed amount)
Net Income = Gross Margin − Other Expenses = $1,320,000 − $950,000 = $370,000
Gross Margin Percentage = Gross Margin/Revenue = $1,320,000 ÷ $3,300,000 = 0.40 = 40%
Profit Margin = Net Income ÷ Revenue = $370,000 ÷ $3,300,000= 0.112 = 11.2%

of support staff, and so on, that are expensed in the period the work is done. The example ignores income taxes.

The numbers in each set of income statements are very different. In 2005 net income ranges from $370,000, using production of copper as the critical event, to a loss of $124,400, using cash collection as the critical event. Net income in 2006 and 2007 is also different with each of the critical events. The gross margin percentage is the same across years and critical events because it was assumed that Production Expenses were a constant percentage (60%) of the selling price of the copper. The profit margin percentage differs across years and critical events because Other Expenses is a constant $950,000 per year. A key point to recognize is that using different critical events for recognizing revenue yields very different financial statements. However, the underlying economic activity of Escuminac is the same regardless of which statement is prepared.

Many of Escuminac's other financial ratios will also be affected, depending on which of these different critical events is used to recognize revenue. For example, the current ratio (current assets ÷ current liabilities) will be different because the amount of accounts receivable, inventory, and liabilities will be different with each critical event. The debt-to-equity ratio (debt ÷ equity) will also be affected by the different critical events. Escuminac's shareholders' equity will be different because net income is different in each year and, therefore, retained earnings is different under each method. Again, it is important to remember that these different financial ratios are representations of the same entity under the same economic circumstances.

Now we can consider some important questions. Which critical event for recognizing revenue is best? Which one reports the "right" amount of revenue? How do these different critical events affect users of Escuminac's financial statements? The following conclusions are suggested:

- Recognizing revenue on production or on delivery are both reasonable alternatives in the case of Escuminac. In fact, both are used in practice. Given that contracts are in place fixing the price for all copper produced and the costs of production are known when the copper is produced, recognizing revenue on production is clearly supportable. There will be some uncertainties, including shipping costs, collection, and other after-production costs but these could be interpreted as being relatively minor and measurable.

- Recognizing revenue on delivery is also supportable if you contend that delivery represents a significant portion of the effort required to provide the copper to customers. It is clear that both critical events could be justified under the revenue-recognition criteria.

- Recognizing revenue when cash is collected is probably too conservative and therefore inappropriate in most cases.

Unless there is significant uncertainty about whether the customers will pay (perhaps the copper is being sold to a poor and unstable government) or there is some other significant and immeasurable uncertainty, the four revenue-recognition criteria seem to be met before collection. Which critical event is *best* is a question that cannot be answered. The best or most appropriate choice of critical event depends on the situation—the stakeholders, the preparers, and the facts underlying the entity's economic transactions.

Which critical event reports the "right" amount of revenue and income? This question too does not have a single correct answer. Each critical event represents a legitimate point at which to recognize revenue. Even recognizing revenue when cash is collected, which we dismissed as inappropriate according to the revenue-recognition criteria, could be appropriate under a different set of criteria or a different set of facts.

The three critical events are different ways of measuring the same underlying economic events. Because revenue is earned continuously, using a critical event is a convenient way to overcome the difficulty of measuring revenue as it is earned in an economic sense. However, it is important to recognize that using a critical event to recognize revenue is convenient but arbitrary. And most importantly, regardless of which critical event is selected, Escuminac Copper Mines Ltd. is the same. The accounting choices an entity makes do not change the underlying economic activities that an entity is reporting. Different accounting choices simply change how the underlying economic activities are reported. This is not to say, however, that different accounting choices do not have economic implications for the entity and for stakeholders. They certainly do.

This leads us to the final question: How are users affected by these alternative critical events, the alternative points for recognizing revenue? If there are contracts or agreements that are based on accounting numbers such as revenue or net income, the accounting choices an entity makes can have an effect on the stakeholders. If the president of Escuminac receives a bonus of 1% of net income, her bonus is directly affected by the critical event that is chosen for recognizing revenue. The amount of tax that Escuminac pays may be related to the critical event chosen. Unionized employees might feel more confident about seeking wage increases if Escuminac reported net income determined using production as the critical event because the higher net income suggests a more successful company and a greater ability to pay higher wages. In fact, there are many different contracts and agreements that rely on accounting numbers, which makes accountants' measurement of things like revenue very important.

Even more subtle is the effect that different choices have on the perceptions of users. Does a more "rosy" income statement make a company more attractive to investors and lenders? Do higher revenues and higher net incomes make users think that managers have done a better job, even if the difference in the numbers was due to an entity's accounting choices, rather than real economic differences? While it is hard to give definite answers, it seems likely that if a user cannot determine what the numbers would be under alternative accounting methods, or if a user is not aware of the effect of different accounting approaches, perceptions about the entity will be affected. There is certainly evidence that the managers who prepare the financial statements are concerned about the numbers that are reported and will use accounting flexibility to report numbers more to their liking.

In summary, here are some of the important issues to keep in mind while you think about the Escuminac Copper Mines Ltd. example:

1. When you receive an income statement, you are not shown what revenue or income would have been under alternative choices of critical events. That means the income statement you receive shapes your perceptions of the entity. You do not get the benefit of an alternative view, although financial statements *do* disclose the revenue-recognition and other significant accounting policies of an entity in the notes to the financial statements. A sophisticated user might be able to develop an alternative view, but the analysis required can be difficult and time consuming.

2. The preparer chooses the critical event for recognizing revenue. That means that the self-interest of Escuminac's management's can affect its choice. (Self-interest in an accounting choice situation means that the managers might choose accounting methods that, for example, give them higher bonuses rather than providing more useful information to stakeholders.) When faced with reasonable and acceptable alternatives, the preparers' self-interest may sway their final decision. However, it is not possible for a user to determine the extent to which self-interest plays a role in accounting choice.

3. The economic activity of Escuminac is not affected by how or when it recognizes revenue. Regardless of which critical event is chosen, the same amount of copper was produced each year, the same amount of copper was delivered each year, and the same amount of cash was collected each year. What is affected is how the activities are accounted for and reported. This is the essential point. While it is true that in some situations an entity will make economic decisions based on the accounting effects, in this situation we are focussing on reporting a single set of economic facts in different ways.

Question for Consideration

Suppose you are an investor and you were evaluating the liquidity of Escuminac Copper Mines Ltd. Assume that Escuminac's current ratio in 2005 is 2.11 when revenue is recognized as when copper is produced and 1.62 when revenue is recognized as when the copper is delivered to customers. Does the actual liquidity of Escuminac Copper Mines Ltd. differ depending on the method of revenue recognition used? Explain. Assume that income taxes are not affected by the choice of revenue-recognition method.

Answer: The actual liquidity of Escuminac Copper Mines Ltd. is the same regardless of the revenue-recognition method that is used. The current ratio and all other accounting measures are representations of an entity's underlying economic activity. The underlying economic activity of an entity is not affected by how accounting measures the activity. Thus, regardless of how revenue is recognized, the same amount of copper was produced each year, the same amount of copper was delivered each year, and the same amount of cash was collected each year. This discussion assumes that the accounting numbers do not affect cash flow, which is not always the case. Bonuses, taxes, and other payments can be affected by accounting choices.

Why Do Preparers Have So Much Choice?

The discussion of Escuminac Copper Mines Ltd. might make you wonder why preparers are given so much power to affect the information in financial statements. Can't rules be established to limit choices and effectively capture economic reality? Wouldn't it be easier if there were just one way to recognize revenue? These are questions with which accounting has been dealing for a long time. Some countries have addressed these questions by developing much more stringent accounting rules than the ones in Canada, rules that specify how certain types of transactions are accounted for. However, while eliminating choice may make all financial statements consistent in when they recognize revenue, the same policy may not make the statements comparable. For example, consider two furniture distributors. One sells to high-risk customers, where collecting money owed is a significant part of the earnings process and there is significant uncertainty about the amount that will be collected. The other sells to reliable customers like governments and large corporations, which tend to pay. Does it make sense for both companies to recognize revenue at the same time? The circumstances are different and the financial statements would probably be more informative if different critical events for recognizing revenue were used.

In theory, allowing choice for recognizing revenue and for other accounting issues is sensible because the economic activities of the Canadian and world economies are too complex to precisely define accounting rules to suit every situation. The challenge with accounting choice is ensuring that the people who prepare accounting information focus on providing the most useful information to users instead of focussing on their own interests. This is the ethical challenge faced by accountants and other financial professionals.

A simple analogy shows that being able to present information in different ways can be useful and sensible. When most people look for a job they create a résumé to show to prospective employers. A résumé is usually a short, concise document describing a person's experience, education, skills and abilities, interests, activities, and any other information considered appropriate by the job hunter. When preparing a résumé, you would presumably try to highlight your strengths and downplay your weaknesses. You would not add false university degrees or work experience, but you would certainly organize the information and describe your accomplishments in ways that would put you in the best light. Further, if you were applying for several quite different jobs (perhaps in accounting, marketing, and finance), it is possible that you might even prepare a different résumé for each job, with each résumé highlighting the attributes that are best suited for each job.

Is it dishonest to give different résumés to different prospective employers, provided that the information in each résumé is truthful? Given that there are many ways that a résumé can be written and organized, how would you describe the "right" way to prepare one? In many ways, someone preparing financial statements is like someone writing a résumé. Most will have an honest desire to provide useful and relevant information to the users. At the same time, preparers of the financial statements, like preparers of a résumé, will want to put themselves in a good light. Without strict rules for the right way to prepare financial statements or résumés, a lot of power and judgment is given to the people preparing the information. Even under GAAP the rules are not strict. GAAP provide considerable room for judgment and flexibility. In the absence of GAAP, flexibility is even greater. However, with GAAP or in the absence of GAAP, there can be many acceptable or "right" ways to prepare financial statements, *but* there are also many unacceptable or "wrong" ways.

The Gradual Approach to Recognizing Revenue

The gradual approach recognizes revenue bit by bit over the entire earnings process rather than when a particular critical event occurs. The gradual approach is consistent with the conceptual nature of the revenue-earning process because it reflects earnings as a continuous rather than a discrete process. As we discussed earlier, in most situations recording revenue gradually is not practical. However, there are a number of situations where the gradual method is practical and necessary to provide useful information to users of the financial statements. In these situations, the gradual approach is not an *alternative* to the critical-event approach; it is used in situations where the critical-event approach is not appropriate.

We have already considered one example of the gradual approach to revenue recognition. In Chapter 3 we examined how adjusting journal entries are made to accrue interest earned on investments such as bonds and bank accounts. These adjusting entries, referred to as the accrued-asset type, are made so that the income statement will reflect interest earned to date even though cash has not been received and is not owed as of the date on which the financial statements are being prepared. In effect, the revenue is recognized continuously for accounting purposes with the passage of time. Notice that with this type of revenue there is no critical event triggering revenue recognition and there is no all-or-nothing situation. Instead the revenue is earned and recorded gradually over time.

The gradual approach to revenue recognition is appropriate for providing useful and timely information to stakeholders regarding long-term projects, such as long-term service contracts and construction projects such as dams and large buildings. With a long-term contract an entity is earning revenue in more than one reporting period. If a critical-event approach were used to recognize revenue, one of the reporting periods would have all the revenue associated with the long-term contract, while the others would have none. Since the revenue-recognition criteria usually lead to later rather than earlier revenue recognition, the early years of long-term contracts would have no revenue or income and a later or the final year would have it all. The critical-event approach to revenue recognition would lead to erratic revenues and earnings, and potentially would be misleading about the economic activity of the entity. In addition, if an entity waited to recognize revenue until a long-term contract were almost finished, the delay would prevent stakeholders from receiving timely and relevant information for their decision making.

The Percentage-of-Completion Method   A gradual-approach method that has become generally accepted for recognizing revenue on long-term contracts is known as the percentage-of-completion method. With the **percentage-of-completion method**, revenues and expenses associated with a long-term contract are spread over the life of the contract, based on a measure of the effort completed in each period. The approach reduces the erratic reporting of revenues and earnings, and provides useful economic information to users on a more timely basis. The percentage-of-completion method can be considered a compromise because the four revenue-recognition criteria are usually not met when revenue is recognized early on in the contract. For a long-term project such as the construction of a dam, the entity will not have earned the revenue (criterion 1) in the early periods of the contract. Also, in most cases, there will be uncertainties about future costs to be incurred and possibly uncertainty about the amount of revenue that will be received. Notice that the description of the percentage-of-completion method requires allocation of both revenues and expenses. Remember that under accrual accounting and the matching concept, expenses must be recognized in the period when the revenues they helped earn are recognized.

To use the percentage-of-completion method, it is necessary to have a way of determining how much revenue to recognize in each period. One of the common ways is to base the estimate on the proportion of total costs incurred to date on the contract. This can be done by using the ratio of the actual costs incurred on the project during the period to the project's total estimated costs. Thus, the revenue recognized in a period is:

$$\text{Revenue for the period} \quad = \quad \frac{\text{Cost incurred during the period}}{\text{Total estimated costs for the project}} \quad \times \quad \begin{array}{c} \text{Estimated revenue} \\ \text{for the project} \end{array}$$

Note that it is necessary to estimate total revenues as well as total costs for the project to calculate the revenue that should be recognized in a period. These estimates would be made before a company bids on a project and would be revised as the project progresses.

The Completed-Contract Method   Sometimes it is not possible to use the percentage-of-completion method for a long-term contract. If the revenues or expenses cannot be reasonably estimated, or if it is difficult to estimate the portion of the project that has been completed, then the **completed-contract method** is used instead. The completed-contract method is a critical-event approach to revenue recognition that recognizes revenue in full when a contract is completed. There are no effects on the income statement until the contract is complete. All the costs incurred are accumulated in balance sheet asset accounts until the revenue is recognized. When the revenue is recognized the balances in these asset accounts are expensed and matched to the revenue.

Comparing the Completed-Contract and Percentage-of-Completion Methods   As long as a project is profitable, the percentage-of-completion method is used as described above. However, if a project is found to be unprofitable—that is, the expenses are expected to be greater than the revenue—then 100% of the loss is recognized immediately. The loss is not spread over the entire contract. The reason this treatment is used is conservatism. As we have discussed, conservatism requires a cautious approach to reporting, so whenever a loss becomes known it is accounted for in full immediately, even though reporting 100% of the loss is not consistent with the percentage-of-completion method. Under the completed-contract method a loss is also reported as soon as it is known. That means that the loss would be reported before the contract is completed.

Let's compare the effects on the income statement and the balance sheet of the completed-contract and percentage-of-completion methods. On December 15, 2004 Judique Construction Corporation (Judique) entered into a three-year contract to build a factory for Hallam Corp. (Hallam). Hallam agreed to pay $75,000,000 for the factory, from which Judique would cover all costs of construction. Hallam paid $5,000,000 when it signed the contract and agreed to pay $20,000,000 on July 2 of each of the next three years. The final $10,000,000 is to be paid six months after the factory is completed. The expected completion date is August 1, 2007. Table 4-2 shows Judique's estimated annual costs and the amount of revenue that would be recognized each year using the percentage-of-completion method. Judique's year end is December 31.

It is important to recognize that cash flows and revenue and expense flows do not have to correspond. Revenue is recognized based on the portion of the job that has been completed. When cash is received is not relevant because we are not using the receipt of cash as the basis for recognizing revenue. Hallam could have paid in full when the contract was signed or could have paid when the factory was completed. The amount of revenue recognized each year would be the same in each case.

For the completed-contract method all the revenue would be recognized in 2007 when the factory is completed. Net income under the percentage-of-completion method and the completed-contract method for each year of the contract is shown in Table 4-3 (page 206). The total amount of revenue and expense under the two methods is the same. What differs is the amount that is reported in each period. With the completed-contract method, all the revenue and expenses are recognized in 2007, the year construction of the factory is finished.

The problem with the completed-contract method is clear. In years when no contracts are completed, no revenue and no expenses are reported on the income state-

Table 4-2   Judique Construction Corporation: Amount of Revenue Recognized Using Percentage-of-Completion Method

Year	Column A Cash payments by Hallam to Judique	Column B Judique's estimated annual cost of building the factory	Column C Percentage of project completed each year based on estimated costs	Column D Amount of revenue recognized each year Calculated as: $\frac{\text{Year's cost}}{\text{Total estimated cost}} \times$ Total revenue	
2004	$ 5,000,000				
2005	$20,000,000	$ 9,000,000	18.8%*	$14,063,000	$\frac{\$9,000,000}{\$48,000,000} \times \$75,000,000$
2006	$20,000,000	$18,000,000	37.5%*	$28,125,000	$\frac{\$18,000,000}{\$48,000,000} \times \$75,000,000$
2007	$20,000,000	$21,000,000	43.7%*	$32,812,000	$\frac{\$21,000,000}{\$48,000,000} \times \$75,000,000$
2008	$10,000,000				
Total	$75,000,000	$48,000,000	100%	$75,000,000	

*The percentage of the project completed each year = $\dfrac{\text{Year's cost (Column B)}}{\text{Total estimated cost (total of Column B)}}$

Table 4-3   Judique Construction Corporation: Percentage-of-Completion versus Completed-Contract Methods for Accounting for Long-Term Contracts

	Judique Construction Corporation Income Statements (thousands of dollars)									
	Percentage-of-Completion Method					Completed-Contract Method				
	2004	2005	2006	2007	Total	2004	2005	2006	2007	Total
Income Statements										
Revenue	$0	$14,063	$28,125	$32,812	$75,000	$0	$0	$0	$75,000	$75,000
Expenses	0	9,000	18,000	21,000	48,000	0	0	0	48,000	48,000
Net income	$0	$ 5,063	$10,125	$11,812	$27,000	$0	$0	$0	$27,000	$27,000

ment, and Judique appears to be an inactive company. This could be very misleading to users who are unaware of how Judique conducts its business. At a minimum the financial statements are not very informative. If a company is involved in a small number of long-term contracts at any one time, the use of the completed-contract method can produce wild fluctuations in earnings, depending upon when the contracts are completed.

The percentage-of-completion method gives a more realistic indication of Judique's economic activity. Over the term of the contract Judique is earning revenue by building the factory. The percentage-of-completion method reflects this economic activity in the financial statements. The disadvantage of the percentage-of-completion method is that it allows management some latitude in deciding how much revenue and income to report in each period. This latitude exists because estimates are required to determine the amount of revenue to be reported in a period. The completed-contract method reduces the subjectivity because revenues and expenses are known when the contract is completed.

In practice, the accounting for long-term contracts can get much more complicated than the example indicates. For instance, the example assumes that actual costs equal estimated costs. In most cases actual costs will differ from estimated costs, sometimes dramatically. Many other problems can arise over the course of a long-term contract that can affect the accounting for the project. For the purpose of this book, the example was kept simple to compare the financial statement implications of the percentage-of-completion and completed-contract methods.

The journal entries for the two methods are shown in Table 4-4. The transactional entries in Column A of Table 4-4 are recorded regardless of which approach is used. These entries record the day-to-day transactions, such as invoicing and receipt of payments from Hallam and costs incurred during construction. Note that all of the accounts used to record the transactional entries are balance sheet accounts; none of the transactional entries affect the income statement. The income statement effects occur when revenue and expenses are recognized. The entries affecting revenue and expenses are shown in Column B of Table 4-4 for the percentage-of-completion method and in Column C of Table 4-4 for the completed-contact method.

Each year Judique sends an invoice to Hallam for $20,000,000 as specified in the contract. Journal entry 2 in Table 4-4 is an example of the journal entry prepared in 2005 to record the invoicing of Hallam. When the invoice is sent, Judique records an account receivable for the amount due. The offsetting credit is to unearned revenue because the billing is done independent of how and when revenue is recognized. Adjustments to the unearned revenue account will be done later, when Judique

Table 4-4 Judique Construction Corporation: Percentage-of-Completion versus Completed-Contract Methods for Accounting for Long-Term Contracts

Column A	Column B	Column C
Transactional Entries	**Percentage-of-Completion Method**	**Completed-Contract Method**

2004

1. Dr. Cash (B/S)*   5,000,000
    Cr. Unearned revenue (B/S)   5,000,000
To record the initial payment of $5,000,000.

(Column B) No entry

(Column C) No entry

2005

2. Dr. Accounts receivable (B/S)   20,000,000
    Cr. Unearned revenue (B/S)   20,000,000
To record invoicing Hallam Corp. for the amount due on July 2, 2005.

3. Dr. Cash (B/S)   20,000,000
    Cr. Accounts receivable (B/S)   20,000,000
To record receipt of payment from Hallam Corp. on July 2, 2005.

4. Dr. Construction-in-progress (B/S)   9,000,000
    Cr. Cash, payables, etc. (B/S)   9,000,000
To record the costs incurred to build the factory during 2005.

(Column B)

12. Dr. Unearned revenue (B/S)   14,063,000
    Cr. Revenue (I/S)   14,063,000
To record revenue for 2005.

13. Dr. Cost of construction (I/S)   9,000,000
    Cr. Construction-in-progress (B/S)   9,000,000
To expense costs incurred earning the revenue recognized in 2005.

(Column C) No entry

2006

5. Dr. Accounts receivable (B/S)   20,000,000
    Cr. Unearned revenue (B/S)   20,000,000
To record invoicing Hallam Corp. for the amount due on July 2, 2006.

6. Dr. Cash (B/S)   20,000,000
    Cr. Accounts receivable (B/S)   20,000,000
To record receipt of payment from Hallam Corp. on July 2, 2006.

7. Dr. Construction-in-progress (B/S)   18,000,000
    Cr. Cash, payables, etc. (B/S)   18,000,000
To record the costs incurred to build the factory during 2006.

(Column B)

14. Dr. Unearned revenue (B/S)   28,125,000
    Cr. Revenue (I/S)   28,125,000
To record revenue for 2006.

15. Dr. Cost of construction (I/S)   18,000,000
    Cr. Construction-in-progress (B/S)   18,000,000
To expense costs incurred earning the revenue recognized in 2006.

(Column C) No entry

2007

8. Dr. Accounts receivable (B/S)   20,000,000
    Cr. Unearned revenue (B/S)   20,000,000
To record invoicing Hallam Corp. for the amount due on July 2, 2007.

9. Dr. Cash (B/S)   20,000,000
    Cr. Accounts receivable (B/S)   20,000,000
To record receipt of payment from Hallam Corp. on July 2, 2007.

10. Dr. Construction-in-progress (B/S)   21,000,000
    Cr. Cash, payables, etc. (B/S)   21,000,000
To record the costs incurred to build the factory during 2007.

(Column B)

16. Dr. Unearned revenue (B/S)   22,812,000
   Dr. Accounts receivable (B/S)   10,000,000
    Cr. Revenue (I/S)   32,812,000
To record revenue for 2007 and record the receivable for the $10 million that will be paid in 2008 by Hallam Corp.

17. Dr. Cost of construction (I/S)   21,000,000
    Cr. Construction-in-progress (B/S)   21,000,000
To expense costs incurred earning the revenue recognized in 2007.

(Column C)

18. Dr. Unearned revenue (B/S)   65,000,000
   Dr. Accounts receivable (B/S)   10,000,000
    Cr. Revenue (I/S)   75,000,000
To record revenue for the entire Hallam Corp. project.

19. Dr. Cost of construction (I/S)   48,000,000
    Cr. Construction-in-progress (B/S)   48,000,000
To expense costs incurred in building the factory for Hallam Corp.

2008

11. Dr. Cash (B/S)   10,000,000
    Cr. Accounts receivable (B/S)   10,000,000
To record receipt of the final payment from Hallam Corp.

*In this exhibit "B/S" signifies a balance sheet account and "I/S" an income statement account.

recognizes the revenue on the contract. When Judique receives its money from Hallam, Accounts Receivable is credited and Cash is debited. Journal entry 3 in Table 4-4 shows the journal entry recorded in 2005 when cash is received.

During construction Judique incurs costs for work done by employees, materials and services purchased, use of capital assets such as construction equipment, and so on. These costs are debited to the Construction-in-Progress account on the balance sheet (see journal entries 4, 7, and 10 in Table 4-4). The Construction-in-Progress account is like an inventory account. Costs are accumulated in this account until the revenue associated with the costs—in the example, the revenue from the contract with Hallam—is recognized. The credits could be cash, payables to workers, and payables to suppliers, or the credits could reflect the use of capital equipment.

The entries made under each revenue-recognition method are shown in Column B (percentage-of-completion) and Column C (completed-contract) of Table 4-4. Under the percentage-of-completion method a portion of the revenue is recognized each year, based on the proportion of total costs that was incurred in the period. Since invoices sent to Hallam are recorded as unearned revenue, unearned revenue is reduced when the revenue is recognized. Journal entry 12 in Table 4-4 shows the entry to recognize revenue in 2005. Costs incurred to earn the revenue are expensed by crediting Construction-in-Progress on the balance sheet and debiting an expense account that we can call Cost of Construction. Cost of Construction is conceptually equivalent to cost of sales or cost of goods sold. Judique incurred $9,000,000 in costs to build the factory in 2005. Column B of Table 4-4 shows that when revenue was recognized in 2005, the $9,000,000 of construction costs was expensed to Cost of Construction (journal entry 13). In the example, all the costs incurred during a year are expensed in the year, leaving a zero balance in Construction-in-Progress at the end of each year. This does not have to be the case, however. It is possible to have a non-zero balance in Construction-in-Progress at year end.

When the completed-contract method is used, no revenue is recognized until the factory is completed. As a result, no entry to record revenue is made until 2007 (see Column C of Table 4-4). Costs incurred are accumulated in the construction-in-progress account over the life of the project and all of these costs are expensed when the revenue is recognized. As shown in Column C of Table 4-4, the entire $75,000,000 of revenue is recognized and the $48,000,000 in costs is expensed in 2007 (see journal entry 18 in Table 4-4). At the end of each of 2005 and 2006 there will be a balance in the construction-in-progress account. At the end of 2005 the balance in Construction-in-Progress would be $9,000,000, the costs incurred to build the factory during 2005. The balance in Construction-in-Progress at the end of 2006 would be $27,000,000 ($9,000,000 + $18,000,000). Balances in selected balance sheet accounts under the percentage-of-completion and the completed-contract methods are shown for each year of the contract in Table 4-5.

Table 4-5 Percentage-of-Completion versus Completed-Contract Methods for Accounting for Long-Term Contracts: Selected Balance Sheet Accounts

	Judique Construction Corporation Selected Balance Sheet Accounts							
	Percentage-of-Completion Method				Completed-Contract Method			
	2004	2005	2006	2007	2004	2005	2006	2007
Selected Balance Sheet Accounts								
Accounts Receivable (Asset)	0	0	0	10,000,000	0	0	0	10,000,000
Construction-in-Progress (Asset)	0	0	0	0	0	9,000,000	27,000,000	0
Unearned Revenue (Liability)	5,000,000	10,937,000	2,812,000	0	5,000,000	25,000,000	45,000,000	0

Question for Consideration

Identify and explain the two broad approaches used to recognize revenue.

Answer: The two broad approaches for recognizing revenue are the critical-event approach and the gradual approach.

Under the *critical-event approach*, an entity chooses an instant in the earnings process that it considers an appropriate time to recognize revenue. That instant is called the critical event. When the critical event occurs, 100% of the revenue is recognized. The critical-event approach is "all or nothing." Before the critical event occurs, no revenue is recognized. Once the critical event has occurred, all the revenue is recognized.

The *gradual approach* recognizes revenue bit-by-bit over the entire earnings process rather than when a particular critical event occurs. The gradual approach is used for long-term projects and continuous earnings processes such as the earning of interest revenue.

For both the percentage-of-completion and completed-contract methods, an account receivable arises in 2007 because all the revenue has been recognized but Hallam still owes Judique $10,000,000. The $10,000,000 is to be paid in 2008.

One of the reasons an entity would choose to use the completed-contract method rather than the percentage-of-completion method is that the Canada Customs and Revenue Agency allows the use of completed-contract accounting for contracts that are less than two years long. The benefit of the completed-contract method for tax purposes is that it delays payment of taxes. The *Income Tax Act* requires that the percentage-of-completion method be used for contracts that are longer than two years in length. The following example shows the tax benefit of using the completed-contract method.

Joynt Corp. (Joynt) signs a contract to do major renovations to an office building. The work will be completed over two years. Joynt estimates that half the work will be done in 2005 and half in 2006. Joynt's year end is December 31. Joynt will be paid $300,000 for the job and will incur tax-deductible costs of $120,000. If Joynt uses the percentage-of-completion method it will report $90,000 of income that can be taxed in each year. At a tax rate of 25% Joynt will pay tax of $22,500 each year. If Joynt uses the completed-contract method, it will pay no tax in 2005 since it will not report any income in that year, but will pay $45,000 in tax in 2006. The income statements for Joynt showing these results are given in Table 4-6. While Joynt pays the same amount of tax over the two years, it defers the payment of $22,500 in tax for a year without any penalty by using the completed-contract method. This deferral means that Joynt has an extra $22,500 to use or invest for a year. If cash were tight, the $22,500 would be useful. It could reduce the amount of borrowing that is required or be invested to earn additional money.

Table 4-6   Tax Benefits of Using the Completed-Contract Method

	Joynt Corp. Income Statements			
	Percentage-of-Completion Method		Completed-Contract Method	
	Years Ended		Years Ended	
	2005	2006	2005	2006
Revenue	$150,000	$150,000	$0	$300,000
Expenses	60,000	60,000	0	120,000
Taxes	22,500	22,500	0	45,000
Net income	67,500	67,500	$0	$135,000

Question for Consideration

Ryley Inc. (Ryley) recently entered into a three-year contract to build a small office building for a growing law firm. The law firm will pay Ryley $7,000,000 for the building. Ryley is required to pay all costs itself. Ryley estimates that its total cost to build the building will be $5,200,000. It estimates the cost to be $1,700,000 in the first year, $2,500,000 in the second year, and $1,000,000 in the third year. Assuming that Ryley's cost estimates prove to be correct, how much revenue will it recognize in each year of the contract using (1) the percentage-of-completion method and (2) the completed-contract method?

Answer:

1. Percentage-of-completion method:

$$\text{Revenue for the period} = \frac{\text{Cost incurred during the period}}{\text{Total estimated costs for the project}} \times \text{Estimated revenue for the project}$$

Year 1:

$$\text{Revenue} = \frac{\$1,700,000}{\$5,200,000} \times \$7,000,000 = \$2,288,461$$

Year 2:

$$\text{Revenue} = \frac{\$2,500,000}{\$5,200,000} \times \$7,000,000 = \$3,365,385$$

Year 3:

$$\text{Revenue} = \frac{\$1,000,000}{\$5,200,000} \times \$7,000,000 = \$1,346,154$$

2. Completed-contract method

Under the completed-contract method, all revenue is recognized when the contract is completed, in this case, in year 3.

Year 1:
Revenue = $0

Year 2:
Revenue = $0

Year 3:
Revenue = $7,000,000

Revenue Recognition at Microsoft Corporation

The way most companies recognize their revenue is not very controversial. However, every now and then one comes across a revenue recognition policy that seems unusual.

When Microsoft Corporation (Microsoft) sells its Windows® operating system or software such as Excel® or PowerPoint®, it does not recognize 100% of the selling price as revenue in the year that the software is sold. Instead, it defers a portion of the revenue because it provides additional services and products, such as technical support and browser technologies, to customers over the life of the product. The most common accounting treatment in this type of situation would be to recognize the full selling price as revenue when the product was shipped, despite the additional products and services. However, when Microsoft ships certain products, it makes a journal entry similar to this:

www.microsoft.com/msft

Dr. Accounts receivable	100	
Cr. Revenue		80
Cr. Unearned revenue		20

The effect of this entry is that some of Microsoft's revenue is deferred to later periods. As a result of this treatment, Microsoft reported unearned revenue of $5.6 billion on June 30, 2001 and $4.8 billion on June 30, 2000. The $5.6 billion of unearned revenue represents over 22% of the revenue that Microsoft reported in its 2001 income statement. The notes to Microsoft's financial statements explaining its revenue recognition policies are shown in Exhibit 4-4.[4]

Exhibit 4-4

Microsoft Corporation's Revenue
Recognition Policies

Revenue recognition

Revenue from products licensed to original equipment manufacturers is recorded when OEMs ship licensed products while revenue from certain license programs is recorded when the software has been delivered and the customer is invoiced. Revenue from packaged product sales to and through distributors and resellers is recorded when related products are shipped. Maintenance and subscription revenue is recognized ratably over the contract period. Revenue attributable to undelivered elements, including technical support and Internet browser technologies, is based on the average sales price of those elements and is recognized ratably on a straight-line basis over the product's life cycle. When the revenue recognition criteria required for distributor and reseller arrangements are not met, revenue is recognized as payments are received. Costs related to insignificant obligations, which include telephone support for certain products, are accrued. Provisions are recorded for returns, concessions, and bad debts.

Unearned revenue

A portion of Microsoft's revenue is earned ratably over the product life cycle or, in the case of subscriptions, over the period of the license agreement. End users receive certain elements of the Company's products over a period of time. These elements include items such as browser technologies and technical support. Consequently, Microsoft's earned revenue reflects the recognition of the fair value of these elements over the product's life cycle. Upon adoption of American Institute of Certified Public Accountants (AICPA) Statement of Position (SOP) 98-9, Modification of SOP 97-2, With Respect to Certain Transactions, during the fourth quarter of fiscal 1999, the Company was required to change the methodology of attributing the fair value to undelivered elements. The percentages of undelivered elements in relation to the total arrangement decreased, reducing the amount of Windows and Office revenue treated as unearned, and increasing the amount of revenue recognized upon shipment. The percentage of revenue recognized ratably decreased from a range of 20% to 35% to a range of approximately 15% to 25% of Windows desktop operating systems. For desktop applications, the percentage decreased from approximately 20% to a range of approximately 10% to 20%. The ranges depend on the terms and conditions of the license and prices of the elements. In addition, in the fourth quarter of fiscal 1999, the Company extended the life cycle of Windows from two to three years based upon management's review of product shipment cycles. Product life cycles are currently estimated at 18 months for desktop applications. At June 30, 2000 and 2001, Desktop Applications unearned revenue was $1.84 billion and $2.19 billion. Desktop Platforms unearned revenue was $2.34 billion and $2.59 billion. Enterprise Software and Services unearned revenue was $433 million and $413 million. Unearned revenue associated with Consumer Software, Services, and Devices, and Other was $200 million and $427 million at June 30, 2000 and 2001.

Is Microsoft's treatment justifiable? The answer is yes, and that is the problem. In effect, Microsoft is arguing that when it sells some of its products it is really selling a series of products and services that are provided over more than one period. Microsoft contends that when it ships the initial product it has not earned the revenue on the product and services that will be delivered later. It is hard to argue with Microsoft's position. The approach is more conservative than recognizing 100% of the selling price as revenue when a product is shipped to a customer, which is usually very appealing to accountants.

However, some critics argue that Microsoft's accounting treatment is really designed to allow it to "smooth" its earnings, report steadily increasing profits, and meet the earnings targets set by financial analysts. ("Smoothing income" refers to managing revenues and expenses to smooth out the "peaks" and "valleys" that can appear in reported earnings from period to period.) When Microsoft releases a new version of some of its products, there is a sales spike as people rush to purchase the latest software. The spike adds significantly to revenue and earnings when the product is released, but revenue and earnings will be lower in the next period once that initial burst of demand has been satisfied. By deferring revenue, Microsoft takes some of that sales spike and moves it and the related profits into later periods, thereby "smoothing" its earnings.

Smoothing income and meeting analysts' targets are important aspects of financial reports because of how the capital markets work (or are believed to work). Financial analysts play an important role in the functioning of the markets by predicting the earnings of public companies. These predictions become the market's expectations—the benchmarks for assessing how well an entity has performed. If the market's expectations are not met because a company reports lower-than-expected earnings, the stock price of the company will usually fall, sometimes significantly. As a result, managers will sometimes use the accounting choices available to them to try to ensure that the company's earnings meet the market's expectations.

Is Microsoft's accounting bad or wrong? No, it is just new and different. The approach does make it more difficult to use financial statements because similar companies may be using different accounting principles. On the other hand, the software business is relatively new and it is not surprising that new accounting approaches arise to meet different circumstances. This is one of the ways new accounting approaches become generally accepted. GAAP in particular, and accounting principles in general, are evolving. As changes take place in the world that affect how entities operate and transact, and as the needs of stakeholders change, accounting must respond to keep up with the changes.

Gains and Losses

A gain or loss arises when an entity sells an asset that it does not usually sell in the ordinary course of its business for an amount that is different from the net book value of the asset. For example, if MWW sells furniture and fixtures from stores or old computers, a gain or a loss arises rather than revenue and expenses because the sale of these assets is not part of MWW's normal business activities. The sale of these assets is a necessary part of the business, but an incidental one.

Let's consider some examples. An entity owns land that has a net book value of $500,000. If the land is sold for more than $500,000 a gain results; if it is sold for less than $500,000 a loss results. For example:

1. If the land were sold for $600,000, a gain of $100,000 would be reported on the income statement (selling price − net book value = $600,000 − $500,000 = $100,000).

2. If the land were sold for $425,000, a loss of $75,000 would be reported (selling price − net book value = $425,000 − $500,000 = −$75,000). The journal entries to record the gain and loss would be:

1.	Dr. Cash	600,000	
	Cr. Gain on sale of land (income statement)		100,000
	Cr. Land		500,000
	To record the gain on the sale of land.		
2.	Dr. Cash	425,000	
	Dr. Loss on sale of land (income statement)	75,000	
	Cr. Land		500,000
	To record the loss on the sale of land.		

In both cases the land account must be credited for $500,000. According to GAAP, land is recorded at its cost. When the land is sold the full cost must be removed from the accounting system, regardless of the amount received. The difference between the amount received and the amount recorded in the accounting system is the gain or loss.

The difference between the income statement presentation of the sale of an asset that results in a gain or loss and the sale of inventory is one of detail. When inventory is sold, the revenue and the cost of the inventory are shown separately (revenue – cost of sales). When the sale of an incidental asset occurs, the proceeds from the sale and the cost of the asset sold are shown net—only the net amount, the gain or loss, is shown. The examples here are limited to the sale of land—an asset that is not amortized. Gains and losses also arise when assets that are amortized are sold. We will look at the accounting for the sale of amortizable assets in Chapter 9. For now, recognize that the net book value of an asset that is amortized equals the cost of the asset less the amount of the asset that has been amortized up to the date the asset is sold.

A couple of points are worth mentioning:

1. The amount of a gain or loss is related to the accounting choices that were made regarding the asset. The costs that were capitalized, the amortization method selected, and the estimates of residual value and useful life will all affect the net book value of the asset and, therefore, the gain or loss.

2. Proceeds from the sale of a capital asset should not be affected by the book value. The price a buyer will pay for an asset will be based the economic value of an asset to the buyer. The net book value of the asset will make no difference to the buyer. Sellers may be affected by the accounting effect of a potential sale because they may be concerned about the effect of the gain or loss on the financial statements. This behaviour by sellers (managers) is not especially prudent because they should focus on the economic effects of a transaction, not its accounting effects.

Generally, gains and losses should be reported separately from revenues and expenses on the income statement. Disclosing gains and losses separately is important because if they are included in normal operating revenues and expenses, it can be much more difficult for financial statement users to interpret the performance of the entity. Gains and losses are different from ordinary revenue and expenses, and users such as investors should interpret them differently. For example, if a gain is included in revenue, the amount of operating revenue reported by the entity is overstated, which would make it difficult for an investor to predict future earnings.

Exhibit 4-5 (page 214) provides an example of how a gain is reported on the income statement.[5] In 2000 Printera Corporation, a producer of consumer labels, packaging, and promotional printing, reported a gain on the sale of equipment of $128,547. A loss could be shown in similar fashion.

www.printera.com

Expense Recognition

As we have discussed, a key concept in accrual accounting for determining income is the matching concept, which was introduced in Chapter 3. According to the matching concept, expenses are reported on the income statement in the same period as the revenue that those expenses helped earn. The order of the accounting is important: *expenses* are matched to *revenues*. First revenue is recognized and then the costs incurred to earn that revenue are expensed. This process is generally the reverse of actual economic activity. Usually an entity first incurs the costs that will help generate revenues and then later earns the revenue. For example, MWW must invest in furniture and fixtures to create the appropriate buying environment for its stores, then purchase inventory, advertise, and so on, before sales can be made.

The matching principle makes sense, at least for some uses and users of accounting information. If an income statement is to give information about the economic

Exhibit 4-5

Printera Corporation Reports a
Gain on the Sale of Equipment

CONSOLIDATED STATEMENTS OF OPERATIONS

Year ended September 30	note	2000	1999
			note 15
Sales		$ 61,876,693	$ 57,146,422
Cost of Sales		45,980,851	42,426,625
Gross Profit		15,895,842	14,719,797
Dividend and interest income		1,231,322	1,179,090
Gain on sale of equipment		128,547	—
Selling, general and administrative expenses		(10,443,677)	(7,620,467)
Earnings before amortization, interest expense, taxes and discontinued operations		6,812,034	8,278,420
Amortization expense		3,933,739	3,992,199
Earnings before interest expense, taxes and discontinued operations		2,878,295	4,286,221
Interest expense	6	2,755,923	2,269,719
Earnings before income taxes and discontinued operations		122,372	2,016,502
Recovery of income taxes	9	2,267,286	2,110,635
Earnings from continuing operations		2,389,658	4,127,137
Loss from discontinued operations, net of income taxes	12	(214,814)	(1,401,344)
Provision for discontinued operations, net of income taxes	12	—	(1,198,627)
		(214,814)	(2,599,971)
Net earnings		$ 2,174,844	$ 1,527,166

(as opposed to cash flow) activity and performance of an entity, it makes sense to associate costs and benefits. If you sell a pair of pants and want to know how much better off you are as a result of the sale, it makes sense to subtract the cost of the pants, along with any other costs incurred to sell them, from the revenue that you earned. That way you know how much better off you are. Accrual accounting requires that all costs be matched to the revenue—regardless of whether cash was paid before, at the same time as, or after the revenue is recognized. As the revenue-recognition criteria state, the costs required to earn the revenue must be reasonably measurable if revenue is to be recognized.

In a perfect accrual accounting world, all costs could be matched to the related revenues. Practically that cannot be done. The problem is that often there are many costs that are difficult to match. Consider the costs that MWW incurs to sell a pair of pants. First there is the cost of the pants. This cost is easy to match to the revenue earned from selling the pants. Then there are wages to salespeople and rent for the stores. But how do you match a salesperson's wage or the store rent to the sale of a particular pair of pants? It is even more difficult to match the cost of the capital assets used in the store. For example, how can the cost of display cases be matched to the sale of a particular item? As you can see, many costs do not lend themselves well to matching.

The result is that the income statement does not perfectly match costs and benefits. That is, when it is difficult or impossible to reasonably match costs and benefits, accountants do not try to force a match. Instead, costs that cannot be reasonably matched to revenue are expensed in the period in which they are incurred. The wages MWW pays to its store employees and the rent it pays for its stores are expensed when the employees do their work or when the space being rented is used. Costs that are expensed in the period that they are incurred are called **period costs**. Costs that can be matched to specific revenues, such as the cost of pants that are sold, are called **product costs**. Product costs are expensed when the revenue they help generate is recognized. Product costs are usually accumulated in inventory on the balance sheet (or in some other balance sheet account) until the revenue is recognized.

Like so many things in accounting, the distinction between product costs and period costs is not always clear. One cannot say that a certain type of cost will always be a product cost or a period cost. For example, wages paid to sales people in a MWW store would likely be treated as a period cost. However, wages paid to the people who make the clothing that MWW sells would probably be treated as a product cost. The cost of the work done to make the clothes can be associated with the revenue earned from the sale of the clothes. The wages paid to the people making the clothing is included as part of the cost of inventory and is expensed when the clothes are sold. The classification of a cost as a product or period cost is not always obvious. Similar entities can classify certain costs in different ways, making it even more challenging to compare and interpret the financial statements of the entities.

It is also necessary to estimate costs that have not yet been incurred so that they can be matched to revenues. For example, bad debts, returns, and warranty costs are all incurred after revenue is recognized. Let's look at these situations in more detail.

- The bad debt expense is an estimate of the amount that will not be collected from customers who purchased on credit. Of course, it is not possible to identify the customers who are not going to pay at the time of the transaction because if you could, you wouldn't sell to those customers. However, bad debts are a cost of selling on credit and should, under accrual accounting, be matched to the related revenue.

- When merchandise is returned it represents revenue that never happened. As a result, returns should be accrued in the period the related revenue is recognized.

- Many businesses offer to repair, adjust, or service their goods or services after a customer buys them—sometimes for a long time after the sale. For example, many new cars come with a 36-month or 60,000-kilometre warranty covering the complete vehicle against defects in factory-supplied materials or workmanship. Warranties often represent an important feature of a product for a customer and potentially a costly one to the seller. Warranty costs should also be accrued when the revenue from the product or service under warranty is sold.

It is worth pointing out that when a customer buys something, he or she buys more than a physical good or service. Warranties, the right to return goods, and customer service are all part of the package that a customer buys. All of these components of the package can be considered product costs because they can easily be matched to the sale of product. The difficult part of accounting for these costs is estimating how much they will be. Preparers rely on historical information and their knowledge of the business and products to come up with estimates. Of course, if it is not possible to reasonably estimate these costs, and if they are significant, then the recognition of revenue should be deferred because not all of the revenue-recognition criteria are met.

It is important to remember that not all users or uses of accounting information benefit from matching. For example, for tax purposes recognizing expenses as early as possible, regardless of matching, reduces the amount of income tax that has to be paid. Lenders might be interested in cash flow information so that they can assess the liquidity of the entity, again, regardless of matching. One must always keep in mind that the usefulness of information has to be assessed in the context of the needs of the user. As a result, it cannot be said that GAAP financial statements are the best way to present accounting information to all users or in all situations. However, in the context of accrual accounting and GAAP, matching is a central concept.

The Objectives of Financial Reporting

Preparers of accounting information can often choose from a number of reasonable accounting treatments for transactions and other economic events, even under GAAP. The discussion of revenue recognition in this chapter highlights this idea. But how do the preparers decide which accounting methods to choose?

Broadly, the choices of preparers are influenced by two factors: the information needs of stakeholders and the self-interest of preparers. Providing relevant information to stakeholders is the reason for financial accounting, but as we have seen preparers may take their own needs into consideration when making accounting choices, including such needs as maximizing their compensation, keeping their jobs, increasing the price of shares or the apparent value of the business, and so on. Information needs and self-interest will often conflict. The accounting choice that provides the "best" information to stakeholders (or at least to particular stakeholders) will not always be the one that best satisfies the interests of preparers. Ideally, self-interest should not play a role in the accounting choices an entity makes, but given human nature self-interest is often a factor. In fact, there is considerable evidence that preparers' accounting choices are influenced by self-interest. Given the reality of self-interested behaviour by managers, it is crucial for users of accounting information to understand the nature of this behaviour and the impact it can have on their ability to analyze and interpret financial statements. The factors that affect accounting choice are shown in Figure 4-1.

Figure 4-1 shows the two factors influencing preparers' accounting choices and provides a list of some of the factors that drive preparers' interests. Stakeholder information needs are also shown (these were first shown in Figure 1-1 on page 9). While preparers often have choice in how to account, they usually cannot account in whatever way they like. There are mechanisms in place to restrict the self-interest of preparers. These mechanisms include the following:

- GAAP
- the involvement of independent accountants and auditors who assess, on behalf of stakeholders, the accounting choices made by the preparers
- contracts
- the information demands of powerful stakeholders who may dictate accounting treatments and disclosures
- the facts surrounding an economic event or transaction that is being accounted for

Of course, there would be no need to limit the choices of preparers who are not influenced by self-interest since they would be motivated only to provide useful information. However, it is human nature for people to consider their own interests when making decisions.

Determining the extent to which self-interest influences accounting choices is a challenge. But even if preparers considered only the information needs of stakeholders when making accounting choices, they would still have choices to make and stakeholders would not be assured of receiving information that was useful for their decisions. The reason for this is that, as we saw in Chapter 1, there are many stakeholders who can use accounting information, and the information appropriate for each stakeholder group is not necessarily the same. However, an entity can prepare only one set of general purpose financial statements. That means that some stakeholders' information needs are not going to be satisfied by an entity's general purpose report. (An entity can produce any number of special purpose reports that are

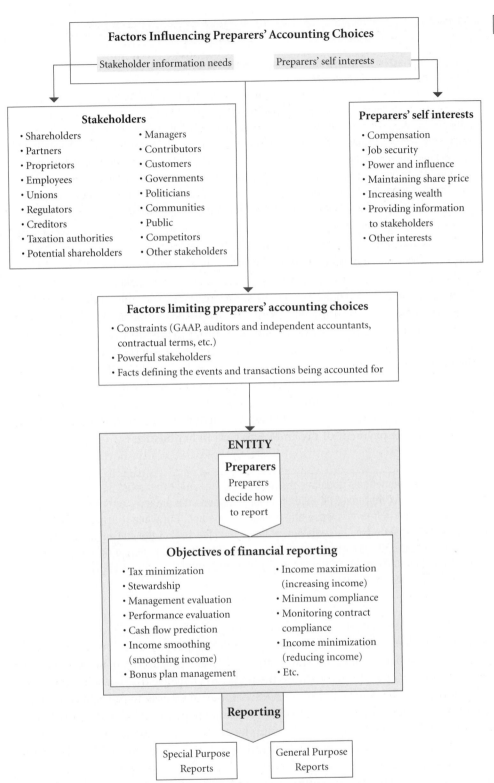

Figure 4-1

Factors That Affect Accounting Choices and Objectives of Financial Reporting

designed for a specific purpose, but special purpose reports will be prepared only for powerful stakeholders who have the ability to demand information that is tailored to their needs.)

For example, consider a small business owned and managed by Ellin Bamboo. Ms. Bamboo's company's financial statements are used primarily for tax purposes. When a Canadian business files a tax return, it must include its general purpose income statement and balance sheet. In some instances tax rules require that businesses use the same accounting treatments for tax purposes that are used in their general purpose statements. If choosing one accounting treatment over another reduces the amount of tax that has to be paid, it makes sense for the tax-lowering treatment to be used. This is not illegal, dishonest, or unethical. If Canada Customs and Revenue Agency allows you to choose among alternatives, you are well within your rights to do so. If Ms. Bamboo uses the completed-contract method of revenue recognition for her business's long-term contracts that are less than two years in duration, she legitimately delays the payment of tax and keeps cash in her business.

Comment: Tax law sometimes specifies the accounting treatment that must be used for calculating the amount of tax that must be paid. In those situations the preparer of the general purpose financial statements is free to choose any accounting method. But when it comes time to calculate the tax that must be paid, an adjustment must be made so that the calculation of tax is consistent with tax law. Tax law does not impose accounting rules for preparing general purpose financial statements. The rules of the tax laws of Canada and the provinces apply only to the calculation of the amount of tax that must be paid.

Now suppose that Ms. Bamboo decides to sell her business. Prospective buyers would want to examine the financial statements as part of their assessment of the business. Would the financial statements that were prepared for tax purposes be appropriate for a person evaluating a business? No, because the financial statements prepared using the completed-contract method could misstate the economic activity of Ms. Bamboo's business. This is because recognition of activity in the statements is delayed until a contract is completed. The financial statements prepared for tax purposes may not give a fair and reasonable reflection of Ms. Bamboo's business even though they are perfectly acceptable for tax purposes. If these financial statements were used to set the price for Ms. Bamboo's business without taking into consideration that the statements were prepared to minimize taxes, it is possible that Ms. Bamboo would not receive and the buyer would not pay a fair price for the business.

This example highlights the problem that one set of financial statements will not satisfy all users and uses. But because only one set of general purpose financial statements can be prepared, some stakeholders may have to be satisfied with statements that have not been tailored to their specific needs. A preparer's accounting choices will affect the usefulness of the financial statements to stakeholders and may have economic implications for them.

Figure 4-1 (page 217) lists some of the objectives of reporting that an entity can have. Let's look at these in detail.

Tax Minimization

When a taxpayer pursues the objective of *tax minimization,* the taxpayer will follow the tax laws to pay as little tax as possible. The accounting choices an entity makes can have a bearing on the amount of tax it pays because the policies used in general purpose financial statements are sometimes also used for tax purposes. A business's general purpose financial statements must be filed with its tax return. (In the case of partnerships or proprietorships, the general purpose financial statements must be filed along with the tax return of the partners or proprietor.) To minimize its taxes, an entity will make accounting choices that lower taxable income. In principle, this objective makes good economic sense because it keeps cash in the hands of the entity for as long as possible. However, many entities do not pursue this objective because they believe that the lower income that results from minimizing taxes may jeopardize the company's other objectives.

Stewardship

When the people who provide money or other resources to an entity are different from the people who manage the resources, a stewardship relationship exists. People want to know how the resources they have invested in an organization have been handled. Has the money been used efficiently and effectively and in a way that is satisfactory to the investors? A stewardship relationship can exist for businesses, governments, and not-for-profit organizations. Information provided for this purpose should allow the stakeholders to understand easily what has taken place during the reporting period. Stewardship is one of the explicit objectives of Canadian GAAP as stated in the CICA Handbook.

Management Evaluation

Stakeholders will often want to evaluate the performance of the people managing an entity. The financial statements should provide information that reflects the decisions of an entity's managers and the effects of those decisions on the performance of the entity. Information should be provided to allow stakeholders to separate the effects of management's decisions from the effects of luck and factors beyond management's control.

Performance Evaluation

Performance evaluation is similar to management evaluation but broader in scope, in that the stakeholders want to evaluate the overall performance of the entity. People will always be interested in evaluating the performance of the corporations in which they have invested so that they can decide whether they should continue to invest, invest more, or invest less in these corporations. MWW provides supplementary information in its annual report that allows stakeholders to evaluate performance. For example, MWW provides corporate goals for the next fiscal year, strategic targets for the next three fiscal years and forecasted financial statements for the next year under conservative and optimistic assumptions. (See the Corporate Goals, Strategic Plan update and Forecast Range sections of MWW's Annual Report on pages A-10 to A-22). Many of these forecasts and targets are accounting measures that are useful for evaluating company and management performance. For example, it would be easy to compare MWW's forecast net income for 2002 with the actual amount it reports. Unfortunately, most entities do not provide nearly as much useful information for evaluating performance as MWW does.

Cash Flow Prediction

Many decisions that stakeholders make are future oriented. The cash flows an entity will generate are especially important. Knowledge of future cash flows can help a lender evaluate whether a borrower will be able to pay back the interest and principal on a loan, whether the price of a stock will go up or down, or whether the purchase price of a business is reasonable. Prediction of future cash flows is explicitly stated in the *CICA Handbook* as one of the objectives of accounting information. However, information that is presented in accordance with GAAP in general purpose financial statements is historical in nature—it reflects what *happened*, not what *will happen*. Stakeholders who want to predict future cash flows can use the information in historical cost, GAAP financial statements as a basis for predicting the future, but they would need additional information to do so. This is because GAAP financial statements are not designed to be predictions of the future.

Monitoring Contract Compliance

In the course of business, entities often enter into contracts that require them to meet certain terms and conditions. These terms and conditions are intended to limit the actions that management can take and they are often stated in terms of financial statement numbers. For example, a lending agreement may require that a borrower maintain its current ratio above a specified amount or its debt-to-equity ratio below a specified amount. Failure to meet these requirements could mean that the loan would have to be repaid or renegotiated. Another condition often seen in contracts restricts the payment of dividends if retained earnings are not above a specified amount. Covenants are included in contracts to restrict the behaviour of an entity so that, for example, a lender is not exposed to unforeseen risks when making a loan, such as the entity taking on additional debt. When contract terms and conditions are based on financial statement numbers, the financial statements serve as tools for monitoring compliance with the terms of the contract by the entity.

Earnings Management

Managing earnings means that the preparers use accounting choices to report financial statement numbers that satisfy the objectives or self-interests of the entity or its managers. Earnings management can serve the purpose of providing more useful information to stakeholders, as well as allowing the managers to satisfy their personal objectives. Earnings management can also be used to benefit some stakeholders at the expense of others.

While the term *earnings management* suggests that the focus is exclusively on earnings, the objective should be interpreted to apply to accounting choices made by preparers to affect *any* financial statement numbers with the intent of satisfying the self-interests of the preparers. For example, accounting choices might be made that prevent an entity from violating a current ratio or debt-to-equity requirement that is specified in a contract. There are many different reasons why preparers would want to manage their earnings, such as reducing income, increasing income, and smoothing income. When you read and think about earnings management, it is crucial to remember that earnings management means using accounting choices to change the reported information about an entity. Earnings management has no impact on the underlying economic activity of the entity.

Remember that in almost all cases earnings management takes places within the parameters of GAAP or whatever basis of accounting that is being used. In other words, when managers manage their accounting information, they are playing by the rules. The managers are choosing among legitimate reasonable alternatives. It cannot even be said that the alternative selected by the managers is inferior to some other alternative. The choice is simply more beneficial to the objectives of the managers than the alternatives.

Managing Earnings to Reduce Income

It may come as a surprise, but there are many situations in which preparers will want to manage earnings downward. Companies in politically sensitive businesses may find themselves under pressure if they make "too much money." (Canadian banks were in that position in the 1990s. Because of the huge profits banks were reporting, some citizens and politicians proposed regulation and extra taxes for banks.) One way that managers can address this pressure is by making accounting choices that reduce what might be seen as excessive profits. Another situation when reducing income might be a good strategy for an entity is when the entity is looking for government support or subsidies. By making the entity's performance appear poor through accounting choices that reduce net income, the entity might be more likely to convince governments to provide support. Lower reported earnings could also be used to influence the outcome of labour negotiations by convincing workers and unions to accept lower wage settlements.

On an ongoing basis, reducing income can be achieved by recognizing revenue late in the earnings cycle and recognizing expenses early. Preparers can significantly lower earnings in a particular period by taking a "big bath." A **big bath** is the expensing of a significant amount of assets that normally would have been amortized or otherwise expensed in future periods. The benefit of a big bath is that while net income is lowered in the current period, income will be higher in future periods compared with what it would have been had there not been a big bath. The reason income will be higher after the big bath is that the assets that were expensed as part of the big bath do not affect income in later periods—in other words, there are fewer expenses in later periods.

A company must be able to justify a big bath—assets cannot be written off on the whim of management. That said, it is usually very easy for management to provide a "reasonable" justification. Because of the emphasis in GAAP accounting on conservatism, an argument by management that certain assets are overvalued is usually acceptable. Big baths are sometimes seen when a company replaces its management. The new management takes a big bath, blames the poor performance and the big bath on the previous management, and then takes the credit when earnings improve subsequently.

Even not-for-profit organizations can benefit from this strategy, even though they do not report earnings. (Remember that not-for-profit organizations do not operate to make a profit and, therefore, do not report earnings. However, they do report surpluses or deficits, which reflect the extent to which their "revenues" are greater than or less than their "expenses.") If the revenues of a not-for-profit organization exceed its expenses by a large amount, contributors might doubt the organization is in need and take their money elsewhere. Managers of not-for-profit organizations might use accounting choices to make their organizations look less successful and more in need of contributions.

Managing Earnings to Increase Income

At the other end of the spectrum are preparers who want to make accounting choices that increase an entity's reported income. By managing earnings upwards preparers may influence some stakeholders' perceptions about how well the entity and its managers are performing. Situations in which preparers might make such choices include the following:

- Preparers may try to influence the stock price of publicly traded companies. There is a well-established relationship between accounting earnings and stock prices, and preparers might believe that by increasing reported earnings they can increase the stock price.

- Before a private company is to be sold, preparers might make accounting choices that increase income in order to increase the selling price. Accounting information is crucial information for determining the market value of a private company, and managing earnings may increase the amount of money received by the sellers.

- Preparers might manage accounting information to maximize income to increase the likelihood of receiving a loan.

- Managers who have bonus plans that are based on net income or other accounting numbers might use accounting choice to maximize income and increase their bonuses.

- Preparers might manage earnings to avoid violation of the terms of debt agreements or other kinds of contractual agreements.

Managing Earnings to Smooth Income   As we have seen earlier, "smoothing" income refers to managing revenues and expenses to smooth out the "peaks" and "valleys" that can appear in reported earnings from period to period. Fluctuating net income can be an indicator of risk, and many managers would prefer to avoid having stakeholders believe that their companies are risky. Some have suggested that Microsoft's revenue recognition policy for new operating systems and software that we discussed earlier in this chapter was chosen to smooth income. By deferring some of its revenue from a year with a high level of sales into later periods, Microsoft smoothes its revenues and earnings.

The list of circumstances where the preparers of financial statements would have incentives to manage earnings and other financial statement numbers is endless and well documented. However, it should be clear that this behaviour could have a payoff for the preparers. An Internet search will provide many real world examples of this behaviour.

Minimum Compliance

Preparers of accounting information sometimes provide the minimum amount of information necessary to comply with reporting requirements. Minimum reporting requirements are defined in various pieces of federal and provincial legislation. For example, public corporations must meet the requirements defined in the *Canada Business Corporations Act* or the equivalent provincial corporations act. Further, public companies must meet the requirements of the appropriate provincial securities act and of the stock exchange, if any, on which the company's shares trade. The *Canada Business Corporations Act* requires that companies prepare financial statements according to GAAP as defined in the *CICA Handbook*. As a result, the accounting standards presented in the *Handbook* have the force of law. Private companies have fewer legal constraints to follow, but they *may* still have to meet the reporting requirements defined in the appropriate corporations act. (We will explore the legal requirements of GAAP further in Chapter 5.)

Some public companies will pursue minimum compliance if they are concerned about providing information to competitors or if they are not concerned about negative reactions by the stock markets to supplying limited information. Private companies may prepare minimum compliance statements if the shareholders are active in the entity and, therefore, have other sources of information, or if other stakeholders are able to receive the information they require in special purpose reports. Also, by providing as little information as they can, preparers make it even more difficult for users to figure out how the preparers' accounting choices affect the financial statements and make it difficult for users to make good decisions. Exhibit 4-6 shows the December 31, 2000 income statement of Stelco Inc. (Stelco), Canada's largest steel

Exhibit 4-6

Stelco Inc.'s Income Statement

Stelco Inc.

Consolidated Statement of Income

Years ended December 31, (in millions, except per share amounts)

	2000	1999
Net sales	$ 2,837	$ 3,101
Costs	2,638	2,765
EBITDA*	199	336
Depreciation and amortization	149	142
OPERATING INCOME	50	194
FINANCIAL EXPENSE		
Interest on long-term debt	(55)	(57)
Other interest – net	7	13
INCOME BEFORE INCOME TAXES	2	150
Income taxes (Note 4) – current	10	18
– future	(12)	
– deferred		25
NET INCOME	$ 4	$ 107

producer.[6] Stelco's income statement provides the minimum amount of information that is required. Compare Stelco's income statement with the MWW's income statement, which provides much more information.

When you begin the study of accounting it is easy to get the impression that all the accounting choices preparers can make are transparent to users of the information. You might believe that a user who carefully examines the financial statements and the notes can find any skulduggery that the preparers have chosen to pursue. This is far from true. Accounting policies *do* have to be disclosed in the notes to the financial statements, so a user will know, for example, how an entity recognizes revenue. However, it is not always clear what effect these choices have on the reported numbers.

Accounting estimates pose even more problems. **Accounting estimates** (in contrast with accounting policies) are amounts reflected in the financial statements that are the result of uncertainties in the outcomes of economic events and transactions that have been recorded in the accounting system. Examples of accounting estimates include the amount of accounts receivable that will not be collected, the useful lives of capital assets, and the cost of warranty services that have not yet been provided. Many (if not most) financial statement numbers are estimates and it is not always required that preparers disclose their estimates. This provides the preparers with powerful tools for managing financial statement numbers in ways that cannot be observed by the users.

After reading this discussion of the different objectives of financial reporting, especially earnings management, one might come to the conclusion that accounting information cannot be relied on or used for decision making. This is not true. Accounting information is an absolutely essential source of information for most decisions regarding an entity. To ignore accounting information would be a mistake. The message that readers should take from this discussion is that accounting information must be analyzed and interpreted carefully before decisions are made. Understanding the nature of accounting information and the motivations of the preparers of the information will serve to make you a more sophisticated user whose decisions are less likely to be affected by preparers' accounting choices.

It is also important to recognize that accounting is not different from any other business discipline or, for that matter, any other form of communication. Take advertising for example. When a company advertises a product, it tries to project an image of the product that makes it attractive to consumers. Advertisers do not go out of their way to highlight the shortcomings of their products. They highlight the positive aspects, and minimize or even ignore the negative. It is the responsibility of consumers to do their research to assure themselves they are getting what they bargained for. Accounting is no different.

Question for Consideration

Which objective of financial reporting is most important?

    Answer: There is no "most important" objective of financial reporting. The question must be assessed in the context of the entity's accounting environment. For a small, private company with little demand for information by external stakeholders, income tax minimization would probably be the most important objective. For a company that urgently requires a loan, the most important objective would be providing information that would increase the likelihood that a loan could be obtained—perhaps by reporting higher net income or by providing detailed cash flow forecasts. For senior managers who have a net income-based bonus plan, the most important objective might be receiving a large bonus. From a stakeholder's perspective, the most important objective would be to receive information or have the information organized and presented in a way that best served that particular stakeholder's needs.

Can Preparers Do Whatever They Want?

One could get the impression from our discussion that preparers of accounting information are completely unconstrained when they prepare their financial statements and that they can do whatever they want to accomplish their accounting objectives. This is not true. As was mentioned earlier in the chapter, constraints, powerful stakeholders, and the economic circumstances surrounding transactions and economic events limit the choices that preparers have.

The constraints preparers face include GAAP, securities laws, tax laws, corporations laws, the terms of contracts, and others. Constraints may reduce or eliminate choice in some circumstances. For example, Canadian GAAP require that money spent on research be expensed—there is no choice. However, it is rarely possible to limit completely by law or by contract the accounting choices preparers have. The economy is far too complex and dynamic to design rules that can apply to every possible situation.

Even companies that are not constrained by GAAP are really not free to do whatever they want. It is unlikely that an entity would invent a radically new set of accounting rules on which to base its financial statements because it would be very difficult for the users to understand them. Remember that accounting is a mode of communication. If the people receiving the accounting information cannot understand it, then it serves no purpose. Imagine receiving a set of financial statements prepared in a language that you didn't understand. Those statements would be of little use to you.

Sometimes powerful stakeholders can make reporting demands on an entity. For example, if an entity needs a loan, a banker can demand information and special reports that meet the specific information needs of the bank. The entity is not required to meet the information demands of the bank, but if it does not, the bank may decide not to make the loan. Another example of a powerful stakeholder is a shareholder of a corporation who owns a large proportion of the shares the company. Since shareholders ultimately control a company, a large shareholder will often be able to specify the accounting policies and other accounting choices that the entity uses in its general purpose financial statements. A large shareholder may also be able to demand special purpose reports that provide information that is not available in the general purpose report. In contrast, a small shareholder in a public company—for example, a person who owned 100 shares of MWW—would not be able to obtain information beyond what was in the general purpose financial statements and what MWW was otherwise prepared to provide.

The economic circumstances surrounding transactions can also impose some limits on the choices preparers have. Consider a vendor selling hotdogs for cash from a mobile cart on the street. No matter what objectives of reporting that hotdog vendor might have, it is hard to imagine recognizing revenue at a time other than when a hotdog is exchanged for cash. On the other hand, in the case of Escuminac Copper Mines Ltd. (pages 198 to 202) three viable alternatives for recognizing revenue were presented. Though there are other alternatives that could be identified for Escuminac, these would be far less viable. For example, it is difficult to see how revenue could be recognized before the copper was produced. There would be too little information about costs and the amount of copper that could actually be mined. (This is not to say that information about the amount of copper available for extraction would not be valuable—it is potentially very valuable to some stakeholders. It would just be very difficult to justify recognizing revenue in accordance with the GAAP criteria before the copper was produced.)

Accounting choices must reflect the economic circumstances that surround the entity. That is why it is necessary, for example, to evaluate revenue recognition alternatives in the context of the revenue-recognition criteria. Those criteria provide a framework for making a choice. While the framework does not always limit the choice to a single alternative, it does link the choice to the entity's economic circumstances.

Solving Accounting Choice Problems

This chapter has examined two important accounting topics: revenue and expense recognition, and the objectives of financial reporting. The link between these two topics is that when and how an entity chooses to recognize revenue can be significantly influenced by the entity's objectives of financial reporting. This section develops a problem-solving technique that will help you understand how preparers make accounting choices and how users of accounting information can use and are limited by the information provided to them by entities.

Constraints, Facts, and Objectives

Before looking at the problem-solving approach, let's examine the factors that guide the accounting choices made by entities and that will form the central analytical tool for making accounting choices. The accounting choices made by preparers are affected by three factors:

1. The *constraints* that formally limit the choices that are available to preparers.

2. The *facts* surrounding the transaction or economic event that is being accounted for.

3. The *objectives* of financial reporting.

The application of the constraints, facts, and objectives is shown schematically in Figure 4-2.

Constraints are specific external limitations on the accounting choices that preparers can make, including legal requirements, GAAP, or the terms of contracts. Constraints can eliminate choice by requiring that a particular economic event or transaction be treated in one and only one way, or limit choice by reducing the set of available alternatives. For example, GAAP limit the choices available for recognizing revenue. Under GAAP, as we discussed earlier, changes in the market value of assets cannot be recognized as revenue. If the constraints limit or eliminate choice, there is

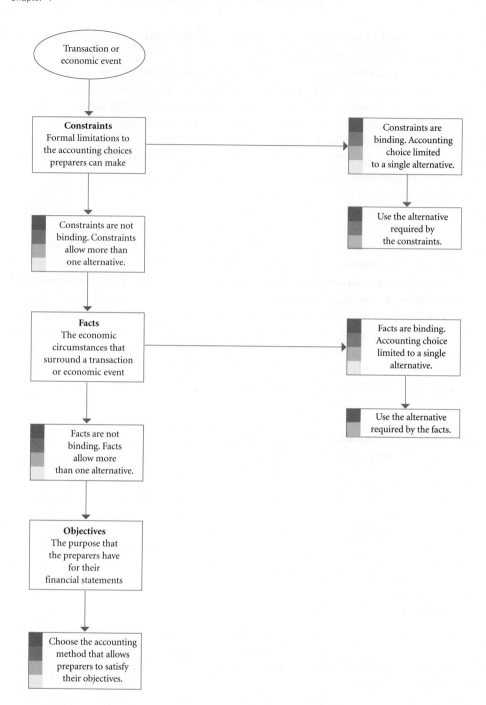

Figure 4-2

The Impact of Constraints, Facts, and Objectives on Accounting Choices

not much purpose to considering alternatives that violate the constraints because those alternatives cannot be used. If the constraints require the preparer to use one and only one method, then that method must be used—no further evaluation is necessary. If there are no constraints, or if the constraints allow more than one alternative, then the facts can be examined.

The *facts* are the economic circumstances that surround a transaction or economic event. The facts must be interpreted to determine an appropriate accounting method. A key question to address is: What do accounting principles, fair reporting and ethics, and common sense tell us about how the accounting should be done? The facts can be ambiguous. Ambiguity allows for different interpretations of the facts, which leads to more than one possible, reasonable accounting method. For example, in the Escuminac Copper Mines Ltd. example (pages 198 to 202), more than one reasonable point for recognizing revenue could be justified. On the other hand, it would be difficult for MWW to justify recognizing revenue at a time other than at the time of sale to a customer who buys merchandise using a MasterCard®. When the facts are binding (that is, when the facts point to one and only one accounting treatment), then that treatment must be used. If the facts allow for more than one possible accounting treatment for a transaction or economic event, then the objectives can be considered.

If there is more than one acceptable accounting alternative remaining after assessing the constraints and the facts, then the final choice depends on the preparers' *objectives* of financial reporting. From the remaining alternatives, the preparers choose the one that best suits the objectives. It is crucial to remember that the remaining alternatives have survived scrutiny in light of the constraints and the facts. That means that each is justifiable in terms of the constraints and the facts. To be acceptable, a recommendation that satisfies the objectives *must* satisfy the constraints and the facts. For example, if we have a GAAP constraint, the choice of revenue-recognition method must be justifiable in terms of the revenue-recognition criteria.

From a preparer's standpoint, it would be ideal if only the objectives of financial reporting had to be considered when making accounting choices. In that case, the preparer would make the choice that best satisfied the objective. However, that approach is not acceptable. Before the objectives of financial reporting play a role, the constraints and the facts surrounding the transaction or economic event must be considered. That is why preparers sometimes have to choose accounting methods that do not satisfy their objectives. The constraints and facts may prevent the preparers from selecting the best alternative for purposes of satisfying the objectives. Being able to justify an accounting choice in terms of the constraints and facts is important for another reason: an accounting choice will rarely be justified in terms of the objectives of financial reporting. Managers would not say that they made an accounting choice to maximize their income. Instead, the choice would be couched in terms of accounting concepts—in terms of the facts.

Analyzing Accounting Problems

The constraints, facts, and objectives model can be used in a decision-making approach to understand how accounting choices are made. The steps described below attempt to formalize the problem-solving process so that all important constraints, facts, and objectives are identified and integrated into the analysis. Note that this approach to problem solving is not unique to accounting—it can be used for any type of problem.

Also note that the steps in the approach take the perspective of the preparers of the financial statements: they follow a process that preparers might follow in making their accounting choices. However, this does not mean that looking at accounting choices from the perspective of different users is not important. As we proceed through the book we will modify the steps of the process to fit the perspective of users. For now, we will focus on the preparers' perspective. Be aware that looking at accounting choices from the perspective of a user can be very different from looking at them from the perspective of a preparer.

The steps are:

1. Assess the entity and its environment. What are the entity's key characteristics (industry, size, ownership, management, and so on)? What problems is it facing? What are the entity's crucial success factors (what are the keys to the entity's success)? How does the business make money (if it is a for-profit organization)? The purpose is to understand the entity from an operational perspective (rather than an accounting perspective) so that you can make accounting choices that suit the needs of the organization. Remember that accounting serves the needs of an entity and its stakeholders. It is not an end in itself.

2. Create a framework for analyzing the accounting issues. The framework provides the parameters by which the accounting problems will be analyzed. The framework includes:

    a. Identifying the users and uses of accounting information.

    b. Identifying the objectives of financial reporting, based on the users and uses of the accounting information.

    c. Ranking the objectives of financial reporting in order of importance and explaining the ranking made. (The ranking is necessary so that the analysis can be oriented toward accomplishing the most important objectives.)

    d. Considering the accounting implications of the objectives. That is, you must understand how the objectives will affect *accounting* choices.

    e. Identifying constraints that can limit or eliminate accounting choices.

    When the preparers rank the objectives, the ranking is done from their perspective. The preparers determine what they believe is most important for the entity (and perhaps themselves) and proceed accordingly. As a result, the needs of some stakeholders may not be served since the decisions (accounting and otherwise) that the managers make may not be the ones that are in the best interests of a particular stakeholder. This point highlights the difference between a preparer perspective and a user perspective.

3. Identify the accounting problems. Sometimes the accounting problems an entity faces are clearly laid out. Other times problems may be hidden and need to be detected through analysis and inference.

4. Rank the problems in order of importance and emphasize the more important problems in the analysis. More time and effort should be spent on the accounting problems that have the greatest impact on the entity. There is not much point to devoting resources to solving problems that do not matter.

5. Analyze the accounting problems. For each accounting problem:

    a. Identify possible alternative accounting treatments.

    b. Determine which alternatives, if any, violate the constraints. Alternatives that do not satisfy the constraints must be discarded. If the constraints allow only a single alternative, then the analysis of the problem is complete because the accounting treatment is determined by the constraints.

    c. Analyze each alternative to determine whether it is consistent with and can be supported by the facts. That means that the circumstances surrounding an economic event or transaction must be examined in light of the appropriate accounting principles. For example, analyzing a revenue recognition problem for an entity that is constrained by GAAP requires applying the revenue-recognition criteria discussed in this chapter to the revenue being earned.

        The existence of an alternative does not make it acceptable. Also, an alternative is not acceptable simply because it satisfies the objectives of financial reporting. For an alternative to be acceptable, it must be supportable and justifiable by the facts. If the facts do not support an alternative, it must be discarded. If the facts support only one alternative, then that alternative must be used regardless of whether it is useful for meeting the objectives. When the facts support only a single alternative, the analysis of the problem is complete because the accounting treatment is determined by the facts. If the facts support an alternative that is not allowed by the constraints, then that alternative cannot be used because constraints take precedence over the facts.

    d. Assess the appropriateness of the remaining alternatives in relation to the objectives. Determine which alternative best suits the objective or objectives of financial reporting that were identified and ranked in step 2.

6. Make a recommendation and explain why the recommendation is consistent with the framework for analysis that you initially set up.

The above approach can be applied to real-world problems as well as to textbook problems designed to develop problem-solving and critical-thinking skills. When you work on textbook problems there are some additional points to remember:

- First, you must be aware of your role. Normally when you face a real-life problem you will implicitly understand the perspective from which you are supposed to tackle the problem. However, in a textbook problem you are placed in a role and you must try to understand the perspective. There are many different roles one can be asked to play. Roles include advisors to management, the board of directors, and various user groups. Other roles include arbitrators (a person who helps resolves disputes between parties), external auditors, and auditors for the Canada Customs and Revenue Agency.

  Broadly, there are two perspectives a role can have: user and preparer. A preparer perspective requires an assessment of the landscape of users and users' needs, and identification and ranking of possible objectives. This approach is necessary because preparers must decide how to orient their financial reporting in relation to the environment the entity faces. The preparer must decide what is important and determine how to achieve those goals. A user perspective is much narrower. Users assess accounting information from their own perspectives. Typically, a user will receive accounting information from an entity and will have to assess its appropriateness for the intended purpose. The objectives of the preparers or other users are not important because users are concerned about their own needs. Understanding the broader reporting environment will be helpful to users because it may provide insights into the accounting information that was provided by the entity. (Examples of preparer-perspective cases are provided as the solved problems in this chapter and in Chapter 5. A user-perspective case is the solved problem in Chapter 9.)

- Second, in any problem situation, real or textbook, it is never possible to have all the information that exists or that you might like to have. Time, cost, and limitations to a person's ability to process information prevent this. As a result, it is necessary to make assumptions—to fill in the blanks—when information is missing. It is very important to recognize when you make assumptions and to state them explicitly. Failure to state assumptions can make it difficult to understand the recommendations made. Note that knowing when assumptions are being made and what those assumptions are is not always easy—it takes skill and practice to do it well. Also, textbook problems usually have less information than what is available in real-world problems, and there are usually greater constraints on obtaining additional information. However, the differences between textbook and real world problems do not make textbook problems less valuable for learning how to analyze accounting choice situations.

- Third, many accounting problems do not have a single, correct answer. The appropriateness of a response depends on the weightings given to various factors, the assumptions made, and the interpretation of events. There can be and are, however, many wrong answers. It is also possible to come up with a reasonable recommendation that is poorly supported. The quality and usefulness of a recommendation lies in the support provided for it, not in the recommendation itself.

The solved problem following shows an application of this decision-making approach.

■ Solved Problem

Pizzazz Pizza Parlours Ltd. (PPPL) is a small chain of take-out/delivery pizza shops located in Atlantic Canada. The Pizzazz family owns the chain. Until recently several of the Pizzazzes managed the company. Many other family members are passive shareholders who are not involved in managing PPPL, including some who rely on the company for their incomes.

In early fiscal 2005 PPPL underwent a number of organizational and strategic changes. First, the family decided that instead of opening just pizza parlours that they owned themselves, PPPL would also sell franchises to people interested in owning their own businesses. (In a franchise arrangement, entities obtain the right to operate a business—in this case a Pizzazz Pizza Parlour— from the owner.)

Next, the members of the family who were running the business realized that they were not fully qualified to manage the business they envisioned. As a result, PPPL's board of directors, which is made up mostly of members of the Pizzazz family, hired as president a person who had many years of experience in the pizza industry. The new president signed an employment contract that entitled him to a salary plus a bonus based on net income. Some of the Pizzazzes remained as part of the management team. One of the first actions taken by the new president was to arrange a large bank loan to finance the expansion of the company.

As of PPPL's year end on August 31, 2005, PPPL's new strategy was developing nicely. Fourteen Pizzazz Pizza Parlour franchises had been sold, of which eight were already operating. The remaining six are expected to open by the end of December 2005. Franchises are sold for $70,000. A franchise owner pays PPPL $5,000 when the franchise agreement is signed, $15,000 when the restaurant opens, and $10,000 per year for five years on the anniversary of the opening of the pizza parlour. In addition, franchises pay PPPL a royalty of 5% of sales and are required to purchase pizza dough, sauce, cheese, and some other items either from PPPL or from designated suppliers.

Franchises receive help from PPPL in selecting a location, advice on operating the business, training, policy manuals, and the benefits of centralized purchasing, advertising, and centralized order taking from customers.

PPPL's 2005 fiscal year has just ended and it has not yet determined how to recognize revenue on the franchises it sells. You have been asked by PPPL's board of directors to prepare a report that responds to the following questions:

Required:

1. What business is PPPL in? How does it make its money? What do you think are some crucial success factors for PPPL's franchise business?

2. Who are the likely users of PPPL's financial statements? For what purposes will these users want the financial statements?

3. From the perspective of the board of directors of PPPL (which we will assume is responsible for approving major accounting policies used by PPPL), what are the possible objectives of financial reporting? The discussion in part (2) should help answer this question. Which objective of financial reporting do you think is most important? Explain. How would you rank the remaining objectives? Are there any conflicts among the objectives?

4. Are there any constraints that limit the accounting choices that PPPL can make?

5. What are some possible alternatives for when PPPL could recognize the revenue from the sale of franchises? (You should be able to identify at least three different revenue-recognition points.)

6. Do any of the revenue-recognition points you identified in (5) violate the constraints? Which of the alternatives can be justified and supported by the facts?

7. For each revenue-recognition alternative you identify, calculate the amount of franchise fee revenue that would be recognized in the years ended August 31, 2005 and 2006, for franchise agreements signed during fiscal 2005 and assuming that all payments are received on time.

8. Which revenue-recognition method would you recommend PPPL use to recognize franchise fee revenue? Explain.

9. What information about the franchise revenue would it be important to disclose in the financial statements for the users? Explain.

Solution:

1. PPPL is in three businesses:

   a. It owns and operates pizzerias, making money by selling pizzas to customers.

   b. It sells franchise rights to people who are interested in operating their own Pizzazz Pizza Parlour, making money from the franchise fees and royalties paid by the Pizzazz Pizza Parlour franchises.

   c. PPPL is also a supplier of ingredients to the franchised pizzerias, possibly making money by selling the ingredients at a profit.

   For the franchise business, the crucial success factors include:

   - Having strong management to run the company, especially during this period of strategic change. Strong management is crucial because the Pizzazz family did not feel it had the ability to manage the expansion of the business on its own through franchises.

   - Availability of financing for the franchising program. The franchise business requires cash because the pizzerias open before most of the cash is received from the franchises. For the expansion to continue successfully, credit must be available as required.

   - Capable people with adequate resources to buy and operate the franchises. The franchises must be successful so that money will be available to pay debts and royalties to PPPL and to help attract new franchises in the future.

   - PPPL must successfully promote its name so that people will have a preference for eating at a Pizzazz Pizza Parlour.

2. There are a number of possible users and uses of PPPL's financial statements:

Possible users	Decisions that will be assisted by the financial statements and how the information will help users make the decisions
Pizzazz family members	Pizzazz family members will have a number of uses that could be helped by financial statements: • They will want to evaluate the performance of the new president to decide whether he is managing the company well. Since the president's bonus is based on net income, they will want the income statement to reflect the president's accomplishments. • Pizzazz family members, especially those who depend on PPPL for their incomes, will want information that will allow them to assess the performance of PPPL and evaluate the amount of cash that will be available to pay dividends. • Family members who are not involved in management will want information for stewardship purposes. • From PPPL's perspective, the board of directors may want to show the Pizzazz family members that PPPL is performing well.

Lenders and potential lenders	• Existing lenders will want to assess whether their loan is safe and check whether any restrictions (such as current-ratio or debt-to-equity ratio restrictions), if any, have been violated.
	• Additional loans might be required if the franchising program continues. Potential lenders will want to assess PPPL's ability to generate the cash flows necessary to make interest and principal payments. They will also be interested in the market value of available collateral, which would have to be sold in the event that PPPL were unable to pay back the loan. Potential lenders would want to know the terms of existing loans such as amounts already borrowed, the interest rate, repayment schedule, and collateral pledged to other lenders.
	• From PPPL's perspective, the company will want the financial statements to indicate to lenders that existing loans are and future loans would be secure, and that any restrictions have not been violated.
Canada Customs and Revenue Agency (CCRA)	• The CCRA will want to ensure PPPL complies with the *Income Tax Act.*
	• From PPPL's perspective, the company will want to pay as little tax as possible and still comply with the *Income Tax Act.*
New president of PPPL	• The president receives a bonus based on net income so he will want to see high net income.
	• From PPPL's perspective, the company would want the president to receive a bonus that reflects his contribution to the performance of the company.
Prospective franchise owners	• Prospective franchise owners may want to assess the financial position of PPPL to obtain some confidence that the company is financially solid. If a franchise is purchased, but PPPL is unable to support it, the franchise owner does not benefit from owning a PPPL pizzeria. Depending on the level of sophistication, prospective franchise owners may want information about cash flows, the number of franchises sold and being negotiated, expansion plans, and information on the performance of operating franchises. PPPL is under no obligation to provide its financial statements to prospective franchisees unless it chooses to do so as part of its effort to sell franchises.
	• From PPPL's perspective, the company will want to give prospective franchise owners confidence that PPPL will be able to support its franchises and that a PPPL franchise is a good investment.
Suppliers	• If they are major suppliers, they may want assurances that PPPL will be able to pay for goods and services purchased. They will be interested in cash flows and liquidity.
	• From PPPL's perspective, the company will want to give confidence to the suppliers that it is able to meet its obligations to pay for supplies. PPPL is under no obligation to provide its financial statements to suppliers, unless it chooses to do so.

3. From the analysis of the users and uses of accounting information, a number of possible objectives emerge. Based on our analysis of the crucial success factors in part (1), the important users from PPPL's perspective are:

    •   prospective lenders, because additional loans will be required if PPPL continues to sell franchises

    •   new franchise owners, who are key to PPPL's expansion strategy

    •   the president of PPPL, who has been hired to implement the new business strategy

Of these three groups, the president is most important because PPPL's board chose him to lead the company in this phase of its development. To lose him at this stage would probably be a serious blow to PPPL's new strategy. A good president will probably be able to effectively manage the relationship with the bank and help attract good franchise owners. Without good management, borrowing from the bank would likely be much more difficult.

Therefore, the objective of financial reporting should be to ensure that the financial statements reflect the performance of management and adequately compensate the president for his accomplishments—that is, the objective of management evaluation. The board would probably want to make sure that the net income of PPPL was a reasonable reflection of the president's actions so that he would receive a bonus that he felt was fair. The needs of lenders would probably be satisfied by the statements used for management evaluation along with supplementary information on cash flows. While people who buy franchises are important users, PPPL would probably not be making financial statement information available to them.

Members of the Pizzazz family are also important and powerful users, but their needs must be considered secondary to the users who are important to expanding PPPL. In addition, the board could provide special purpose reports to members of the family to satisfy their information needs.

Everything else being equal, all businesses want to pay as little tax as possible, and PPPL's need for cash makes the objective of tax minimization even more important. However, the need for strong management also makes tax minimization a secondary objective.

Suppliers are a minor user and will not likely be granted access to the financial statements.

Note that there are conflicts among the objectives. In particular, the tax minimization objective, which suggests lower net income, conflicts with the management evaluation objective, which suggests "fair" or net income that is representative of the entity's underlying economic activity.

It is interesting to note that had we examined the objectives from the perspective of the president of PPPL rather than from that of the board of directors, the primary objective might have been bonus maximization rather than management evaluation. The president's self-interest might have had a stronger influence since he would have been making accounting choices that directly affected his personal wealth.

Finally, remember that this ranking is not the only one or the best one. Many other rankings are possible, reasonable, and supportable. However, any proposed ranking must be supported.

4. There do not appear to be any statutory constraints stated in the question. PPPL is a private company and therefore it does not have to provide audited financial statements. Some users may prefer audited, GAAP-based financial statements, such as the bank, the shareholders that are not involved in management, and prospective franchise owners. For purposes of preparing tax returns, PPPL will have to comply with the *Income Tax Act*. The lending agreement with the bank may have minimum requirements for accounting ratios, such as the current ratio or the debt-to-equity ratio, but without any information about these ratios it is not possible to make a reasonable assumption regarding specific amounts. Given the number of external users of the financial statements, it will be assumed that GAAP financial statements will be prepared.

5. Possible points for recognizing revenue from the sale of franchises include:
   - when a franchise agreement is signed with a new owner of a franchise
   - when a franchised Pizzazz Pizza Parlour opens
   - when cash is collected from a franchise (instalment method)

    • when full payment is received from a franchise

6.   Since it was assumed that GAAP will be followed, each revenue-recognition point must be evaluated in relation to the four revenue-recognition criteria:

- *When a franchise agreement is signed with a new owner of a franchise.* It may be difficult to argue that the revenue has been earned at this point. Perhaps the case could be made that most of the effort is the actual recruitment of franchise owners and that the actual start-up is minor. This is not an especially credible argument. More likely, getting a new franchise operating is a major part of fulfilling PPPL's obligation to new franchises. The amount of revenue earned is known when the contract is signed because the amount is specified in the contract. Costs are uncertain because PPPL still has work to do providing assistance to the franchisee. These costs may be fairly predictable, although at this stage PPPL has no history on which to base its estimates. Collection is a potential problem because payment depends on the success of the franchises and PPPL has no track record for evaluating how successful the franchised pizzerias will be, so it is not clear that the franchises will be able to pay the $65,000 each owes after the contracts are signed. This alternative is very aggressive and likely is not supportable using the four revenue-recognition criteria.

- *When a franchised Pizzazz Pizza Parlour opens.* The revenue can probably be considered earned at this point, since once a pizza parlour is open most of the effort required by PPPL has been completed. In addition, the franchise owner has an operating business at this point so one could argue that the rights and risks of ownership are with the owners of the franchise restaurant. While PPPL will still have work to do on an ongoing basis, especially in the first while after the franchise has opened, the amount of effort is likely relatively small compared with the start-up itself. The amount of revenue is known at this point because the amount is specified in the contract. Most costs are probably known at this time, although some cost uncertainty likely exists regarding the cost of the support that must be provided to the franchisee (especially given that PPPL is new to the franchising business), which may make estimating future costs difficult. Of course, at some point the support provided by PPPL can be considered paid for by the royalties paid by the franchises rather than from the initial franchise fee. Collection from the franchises is still an open question. At the time the pizza parlour opens, the franchise will have paid $20,000 of the $70,000 of the franchise fee. The fact that PPPL is new to the business makes it difficult to estimate the amount that will not be collected. This alternative meets the four criteria, provided that a reasonable estimate of the amounts that will not be collected from the franchises can be made.

- *When cash is collected from a franchise.* Restaurants are a notoriously risky business and franchises can fail. As a result, collection is not a foregone conclusion. Waiting until cash is in hand is conservative but not unreasonable because collection may prove to be costly and unpredictable. Except for the payment received when the franchise agreement is signed, the instalment method meets the four revenue-recognition criteria. The $5,000 received when the contract is signed would probably have to be deferred until the pizza parlour opened because if the opening does not go as planned PPPL might have to return the initial payment.

- *When full payment is received from a franchise.* This method is very conservative. It would require that there be significant and unpredictable costs occurring in the later years of the contract, or that PPPL had not earned the revenue once a restaurant opened or once it had been opened for a few months. The most likely reason for delaying revenue recognition for this long would be for tax purposes. However, this method would not be allowed under the *Income Tax Act.*

7. Amount of revenue that would be recognized in the years ended August 31, 2005 and 2006, using each revenue recognition point:

   - When a franchise agreement is signed with a new owner of a franchise
     Revenue in 2005: $980,000 (14 stores × $70,000 per store)
     Revenue in 2006: $0

   - When a franchised Pizzazz Pizza Parlour opens
     Revenue in 2005: $560,000 (8 × $70,000)
     Revenue in 2006: $420,000 (6 × $70,000)

   - When cash is collected from a franchise (except for the payment on signing of the franchise agreement, which must be recognized when the franchise restaurant opens—see the discussion above)
     Revenue in 2005: $160,000 (8 × $20,000)
     Revenue in 2006: $200,000 (6 × $20,000 + 8 × $10,000)

   - When full payment is received from a franchise
     Revenue in 2005: $0
     Revenue in 2006: $0

8. The analysis above supports using either the opening of a Pizzazz Pizza Parlour or collection of cash as acceptable points to recognize revenue. Because more than one alternative is available after the constraints and the facts are addressed, the objectives of financial reporting can be considered. To satisfy the objective of management evaluation, our first objective, revenue should be recognized when a franchised Pizzazz Pizza Parlour opens. While cash collection is a significant uncertainty in PPPL's earnings process, using cash collection as the basis for evaluating and rewarding the president would likely undermine the incentive value of the bonus plan because the bonus would be significantly delayed. While recognizing revenue when the store opens might make the president less selective in choosing franchise owners (he may focus more on making sure the franchises open rather than making sure that the franchises are able to pay their debts), the disincentive overrides this problem. When a restaurant opens, the president has done his job of expanding the chain. At this point, the franchise owners have made a significant financial investment and would likely work hard to make sure that their restaurants succeed.

9. Information that would be important to users includes, but is not limited to, the following:

   - The revenue-recognition method used.
   - When cash will be received from franchisees.
   - Collectability of receivables.
   - Costs to PPPL of selling franchises.
   - Whether PPPL can generate the cash flow to support the expansion.
   - Whether PPPL has enough credit/cash available to meet the needs of the franchise business.
   - How many franchises have been sold and how many have been opened.

   (Note: The usefulness of any piece of information would depend on who the user is.)

Summary of Key Points

LO 1. To recognize revenue in a logical and rational matter we need some criteria to guide the choice. Under GAAP the following four criteria are used:

1.   The revenue has been earned.

2.   The amount of revenue can be reasonably measured.

3.   The costs required to earn the revenue can be reasonably measured.

4.   Collection of payment is reasonably assured.

These criteria provide guidance to preparers, but they are open to interpretation and judgment. An additional, overriding criterion requires that the revenue recognition point selected provide a reasonable and fair representation of the entity's activities, given the needs of the people who are using the accounting information.

LO 2. Conceptually, earning revenue is a continuous process. Each activity an entity undertakes that increases the value of a good or service represents an economic gain or benefit to the entity. As a practical matter it can be very difficult for accountants to determine when and how much revenue should be recognized along the series of actions leading to a sale to a customer. Accountants have devised two approaches for recognizing revenue: the critical-event approach and the gradual approach.

Under the critical-event approach, an entity chooses an instant in the earnings process that it considers an appropriate time to recognize revenue. That instant is called the critical event. When the critical event occurs, 100% of the revenue is recognized.

Under the gradual approach, revenue is recognized gradually over a period of time. The gradual approach, which is often used when an entity has long-term contracts, provides useful and timely information to stakeholders about long-term contracts.

LO 3. There are different ways and times that revenues and expenses can be recognized, and the methods chosen can affect the amount of revenue, expense, and income that an entity reports. Different revenue and expense recognition methods also affect many accounting and financial ratios. Even though the income statement will be affected by different revenue and expense recognition methods used, the underlying economic activity of the entity is the same regardless of the methods chosen.

LO 4. The percentage-of-completion method is a gradual approach method that allocates revenues and related expenses over more than one reporting period, based on a measure of the effort completed in each period.

If the revenues or expenses of a long-term project cannot be reasonably estimated, or if it is difficult to estimate the portion of the project that has been completed, then the completed-contract method is used. The completed-contract method is a critical-event approach to revenue recognition that recognizes revenue in full when a contract is completed.

LO 5. Accrual accounting requires that all costs be matched to revenue in the same period as that in which the revenue that those expenses helped earn is recognized—whether the costs are incurred before, at the same time as, or after the revenue is recognized. Not all costs are easy to match to revenue. Costs that are expensed in the period that they are incurred are called period costs. Costs that can be matched to specific revenues (for example, the cost of MWW pants that are sold) are called product costs. Product costs are expensed when the revenue they help generate is recognized.

LO 6. Preparers of accounting information can often choose from a number of reasonable accounting treatments for transactions and other economic events, even under GAAP. Some of the reasons for, implications of, and limitations to flexible accounting rules are:

- The economic circumstances surrounding a transaction or economic event can sometimes make it difficult to identify one best way to account. As a result there is often more than one reasonable way to account for a transaction or economic event. The people who prepare the financial statements must exercise judgment.

- The choices made by the people preparing the financial statements can be influenced by two broad factors: the information needs of stakeholders and the self-interest of preparers.

- Entities are allowed to prepare only one set of general purpose financial statements (but many additional special purpose reports).

- There is often a variety of stakeholders with different decisions to make and different information needs. A single general purpose report may not be useful or appropriate for all stakeholders.

- There are many different objectives of financial reporting. Different objectives of financial reporting can result in very different financial statements. It is the preparer who gets to choose which objective or objectives the financial statements will serve.

- It can be very difficult for a user to determine what the preparer's objectives are.

- There are limitations to the choices that preparers can make. The constraints include GAAP, securities laws, tax laws, corporations laws, the terms of contracts, and others. Constraints may reduce or eliminate choice in some circumstances. However, it is rarely possible to eliminate by law or by contract all accounting choices.

LO 7. The existence of alternative accounting treatments makes it necessary to decide which accounting alternative to choose. Choosing among accounting alternatives requires consideration of the relevant constraints, facts, and objectives, and application of a problem-solving approach that incorporates the following steps:

1. Assess the entity and its environment.

2. Create a framework for analyzing the accounting issues.

3. Identify the accounting problems.

4. Rank the problems in order of importance and emphasize the more important problems in the analysis.

5. Analyze the accounting problems.

6. Make a recommendation and explain why the recommendation is consistent with the framework for analysis that you initially set up.

Key Terms

accounting estimate, p. 223
big bath, p. 221
completed-contract method, p. 204
critical-event approach, p. 191
gradual approach, p. 192
instalment method, p. 196

percentage-of-completion method, p. 204
period costs, p. 214
product costs, p. 214
unrealized gain (loss), p. 197
warranty, p. 197

Assignment Materials

Questions

Q4-1. Explain why it is not possible to have a single set of financial statements that will satisfy all the stakeholders of an entity.

Q4-2. Explain the difference between period and product costs. How is each type of cost accounted for?

Q4-3. Explain what is meant by the accounting term "revenue recognition."

Q4-4. How is the balance sheet affected when revenue is recognized? Explain your answer and give examples.

Q4-5. The revenue-recognition criteria introduced in this chapter require that revenue should be recognized when it is "earned." Explain when revenue is "earned."

Q4-6. Do you think it is good or bad that entities have flexibility in choosing when to recognize revenue? Explain.

Q4-7. Costs can be classified as period costs or product costs. How are the income statement and balance sheet affected by the classification? How might the objectives of accounting be affected by the classification?

Q4-8. Does the percentage-of-completion method of recognizing revenue meet the revenue-recognition criteria discussed in the chapter? Explain. How do accountants justify using the percentage-of-completion method for recognizing revenue on long-term contracts?

Q4-9. What effects do the objectives of financial reporting have on when an entity recognizes revenue? Explain.

Q4-10. What are constraints, facts, and objectives? How does each affect the accounting methods an entity uses? Why does each have to be considered when making an accounting choice?

Q4-11. What is the matching concept? Why is it relevant to revenue recognition?

Q4-12. Can a single set of financial statements satisfy all objectives of financial reporting? Explain.

Q4-13. Explain why recognizing revenue and expenses in different ways has no effect on the underlying economic activity of an entity.

Q4-14. Why can it be difficult for accountants to determine when revenue should be recognized?

Q4-15. What is the instalment method of recognizing revenue? Under what circumstances should it be used?

Q4-16. Why is determining when to recognize revenue more difficult under accrual accounting than under cash accounting?

Q4-17. Distinguish between the percentage-of-completion method and the completed-contract method of revenue recognition. Which method requires the exercise of more judgment by the preparers of the financial statements? Explain.

Q4-18. Do you think that the managers of entities should be responsible for selecting the accounting methods and estimates that they use, or should that responsibility be given to an independent third party? Explain your view. Make sure to consider both sides of the argument.

Q4-19. Do you think accounting would be more useful and reliable if only a single method of revenue recognition were allowed, such as when cash is collected or when the goods or services are provided to the customer? Explain.

Q4-20. Identify and explain the four revenue-recognition criteria.

Q4-21. What difference does it make when the revenue is recognized? How and why does it matter? Explain.

Q4-22. Under what circumstances should the completed-contract method of revenue recognition be used instead of the percentage-of-completion method?

Q4-23. What are gains and losses? How do they arise? How are gains and losses reported in the financial statements?

Q4-24. Why are gains and losses usually shown separately from revenues and expenses from ordinary business activities? What are the implications to the users of the financial statements if gains and losses are included in revenues and/or expenses?

Q4-25. Identify and explain the two factors that influence the accounting choices that are made by preparers of financial statements.

Q4-26. Why does self-interest play a role in accounting choice? In an ideal world, should it?

Q4-27. Why do preparers have the opportunity to choose some of the accounting methods they use? Should preparers have a choice? Explain.

Q4-28. Conceptually, why can the earning of revenue be considered to be a continuous process? In spite of the continuous conceptual nature of revenue, why is revenue usually recognized at a single instant in time?

Q4-29. Why is it not possible to use the gradual approach to revenue recognition for sales of clothing by a retailer such as Mark's Work Wearhouse?

Q4-30. Explain what each of the following objectives of financial reporting means:
   a. Tax minimization.
   b. Management evaluation.
   c. Minimum compliance.
   d. Cash flow prediction.
   e. Stewardship.
   f. Earnings management.

Q4-31. What is an unrealized gain? Why are unrealized gains not usually recorded under GAAP?

Q4-32. What does it mean when accountants refer to recognizing revenue when a "critical event" occurs?

Exercises

E4-1. **(Classifying period and product costs, LO 5)** Oxbow Toy Ltd. (Oxbow) develops, manufactures, markets, and distributes a broad range of toys and games for children from newborns to teenagers. The principal markets for Oxbow's products are Canada, the United States, and Australia, where Oxbow markets and distributes both company-developed and licensed products. In addition to sales in these countries, Oxbow's products are marketed in more than 50 countries worldwide. For each of the costs described below, state whether you would treat the cost as a product cost or a period cost. Explain your choices.
   a. Plastic, wood, metal and other materials that are used to produce toys.
   b. Commissions paid to salespeople who sell toys to distributors and retailers.
   c. Salaries paid to head office staff and senior executives.
   d. Electricity and other utilities used in the manufacturing plant.
   e. Amortization of equipment used to manufacture toys.
   f. Amounts paid to trucking companies for delivering toys to customers.
   g. Amounts paid to research and develop new toys.
   h. Television and print advertising to promote one of Oxbow Toy Ltd.'s toys.
   i. Television and print advertising to promote the entire line of Oxbow Toy Ltd.'s toys.

E4-2. **(Recording journal entries for recording revenue at different critical events, LO 1, 2, 5)** Risteen Telephone Services Ltd. (Risteen) designs and installs telephone systems for commercial customers. For example, in December 2004, Risteen signed a contract with Yarm Telemarketing Systems Ltd. (Yarm) to design and install a phone system for Yarm's new call centre in New Brunswick. The following events pertain to the contract with Yarm:
   i. December 13, 2004: The contract between Risteen and Yarm is signed. Yarm will pay $500,000 for the system and the system will cost Risteen $300,000 to design, produce, and install. The contract provides an 18-month warranty to make any repairs or adjustments required. Yarm will pay within 90 days of completion of the installation of the system.
   ii. October 15, 2005: Installation of the system is completed.
   iii. December 12, 2005: Warranty work costing $15,000 is performed.
   iv. January 8, 2006: Risteen receives payment in full from Yarm.
   v. April 15, 2006: Warranty expires.

Required:
   Prepare the journal entries required for the above events assuming that:
   a. Revenue is recognized when the contract is signed.
   b. Revenue is recognized when installation of the system is complete.

c. Revenue is recognized when cash is collected.

d. Revenue is recognized when the warranty period expires.

E4-3.   **(Identifying the objectives of financial reporting, LO 6, 7)** For each of the following entities, identify the objectives of financial reporting that the preparers of the financial statements might have. In answering, consider who the users of the financial statements might be and which user(s) would be most important to the preparers. Explain how the objectives of financial reporting would influence the accounting choices made by the preparers.

a. A family-owned corporation that is planning to sell shares to the public and become a public company that is traded on a stock exchange.

b. A charity that raises money to buy and distribute food to hungry children around the world.

c. A private corporation that provides consulting services to restaurants. The company has one shareholder who is also president of the company. The company has a small bank loan and no other major creditors.

d. A private company with a large labour union that is preparing for negotiations with the union.

e. An accounting firm partnership that uses accounting income to determine the amount of tax the partners pay and the compensation the partners receive.

f. A public company that has been adversely affected by international competition and that is trying to receive subsidies from government.

g. A private corporation that repairs commercial vehicles. The company has one shareholder who is also president of the company. The company urgently needs cash.

E4-4.   **(Determining when to recognize revenue, LO 1, 2)** For each of the following situations, use the four GAAP revenue-recognition criteria to determine when revenue should be recognized. Explain your reasoning.

a. An ice cream vendor sells an ice cream sandwich to a child at a local park for $1.50 cash.

b. A parents' magazine sells a three-year subscription to a new subscriber for $33. The subscriber makes the payment when she subscribes.

c. A furniture store has a "don't pay for a year" event. Customers take delivery of their furniture immediately but do not have to pay until twelve months later.

d. A software manufacturer sells a computer game. The company promises to provide the next two upgrades to the program free of charge.

E4-5.   **(Determining when to recognize revenue, LO 1, 2)** For each of the following situations, use the four GAAP revenue-recognition criteria to determine when revenue should be recognized. Explain your reasoning.

a. A jewellery store offers a lay-away plan whereby a customer pays 10% of the purchase price of an item and the store holds the item until the customer has paid 60% of the selling price.

b. A professional hockey team sells season tickets to its fans. Fans pay the full price of the tickets before the season begins and receive tickets for the all of the team's home games.

c. An auto parts manufacturer sells wheel assembly parts to a major car manufacturer. The car manufacturer pays for the parts within 60 days of delivery. The manufacturer is entitled to return all parts that it decides are defective.

d. An electronics store sells customers extended warranties on the products that it sells. The extended warranty provides "free" parts and labour for three years beyond the one-year warranty that is provided by the manufacturer.

E4-6.   **(Calculating revenue using the percentage-of-completion and completed-contract methods, LO 2, 4)** Whipporwill Ltd. (Whipporwill) is a small construction company in northern Ontario. Whipporwill recently signed a contract to build a new town hall in one of the region's larger cities. Whipporwill will receive $12,500,000 from the city for building the town hall and will have to pay the costs of construction from that amount. Construction will begin in September 2005 and is expected to be completed in March 2007. Whipporwill's year end is December 31. Whipporwill estimates that construction costs in each year will be:

	2005	2006	2007	Total
Estimated costs	$1,750,000	$4,500,000	$2,200,000	$8,450,000

Required:

Calculate the amount of revenue and expense that Whipporwill would recognize in each year of the contract using the percentage-of-completion method and the completed-contract method. Prepare the journal entries required for each method.

E4-7. **(The effect of using different ways of estimating the proportion of a long-term contract that has been completed on the amount of revenue recognized, LO 2, 3, 4)** Hectanooga Ltd. (Hectanooga) is a large construction engineering company. In 2004, Hectanooga was awarded a contract to build a small hydroelectric generating plant adjacent to an aluminum smelting plant. The aluminum company decided that it would be cheaper to generate its own power than to buy power from a supplier, so it is having a generating plant built. Hectanooga will receive $62,000,000 to build the dam, from which it must pay the costs of construction. Information regarding the yearly progress of the contract measured in different ways is provided below:

	2004	2005	2006	2007	Total
Costs	$8,000,000	$13,000,000	$16,000,000	$5,000,000	$42,000,000
Percentage completed in each year as estimated by an independent engineering expert	15%	35%	42%	8%	100%
Labour hours worked	66,000	185,000	310,000	99,000	660,000

Required:

Hectanooga's new vice-president of finance understands that there are different ways to calculate the percentage-of-completion of a project. The vice-president has asked you to calculate the amount of revenue that would be recognized in each year of the contract using three different methods of estimating the percentage completed:

a. Costs incurred.
b. Percentage completed in each year as estimated by an independent engineering expert.
c. Labour hours worked.

The vice-president would also like you to explain how he should choose among the three methods.

E4-8. **(Preparing journal entries for percentage-of-completion and completed-contract methods, LO 3, 4)** Hazelbrook Corp. (Hazelbrook) is a custom builder of luxury homes. On November 27, 2005 Hazelbrook signed a contract to build a mansion just outside of Charlottetown for an entrepreneur who made a fortune selling her stake in an e-business to a large US company. The entrepreneur agreed to pay $1,750,000 for the mansion. At the time the contract was signed, the entrepreneur paid Hazelbrook $200,000. Construction is scheduled to begin in March 2006 and end in late 2007. The contract stipulates that the final $150,000 must be paid six months after the entrepreneur takes possession of the mansion.

	2005	2006	2007	2008	Total
Costs incurred during the year	$0	$525,000	$610,000	$0	$1,135,000
Billings	$200,000*	$700,000	$700,000	$150,000	$1,750,000
Cash collected	$200,000	$700,000	$700,000	$150,000	$1,750,000

*The $200,000 was paid when the contract was signed, so this $200,000 was not actually billed to the entrepreneur. However, it is included for completeness.

Required:

a. Prepare the transactional journal entries that would be prepared each year by Hazelbrook.

b. Prepare the journal entries that Hazelbrook would make if it recognized revenue using the completed-contract method.

c. Prepare the journal entries that Hazelbrook would make if it recognized revenue using the percentage-of-completion method. Use the costs incurred during each year divided by total costs to estimate the percentage completed.

E4-9. **(Using the instalment method, LO 2)** Red Pheasant Inc. (Red Pheasant) sells a range of consumer products. The company buys half-hour blocks of time on local television stations to promote the products to potential buyers. For example, recently Red Pheasant has been promoting a sophisticated home gym. Customers can purchase the home gym for 36 monthly payments of $75. The cost of a home gym to Red Pheasant is $1,400. Red Pheasant used the instalment method for recognizing revenue.

Required:

a. Why do you think that Red Pheasant uses the instalment method to recognize revenue on the sale of its home gym?

b. What journal entries would Red Pheasant record when it receives a payment from a customer?

E4-10. **(Accounting for gains and losses, LO 5)** For each of the following land sales, prepare the journal entry that would be recorded and indicate the amount of the gain or loss that would be reported. Assume that in each case, the sale of land is not a main business activity of the entity.

a. Land costing $350,000 is sold for $200,000.

b. Land costing $700,000 is sold for $1,000,000.

c. Land costing $1,800,000 is sold for $1,800,000.

E4-11. **(Explaining and understanding different roles that accounting problems can be viewed from, LO 6, 7)** Listed below are some of the roles that a person addressing accounting problems can have. The role can affect how the role-player approaches and analyzes an accounting problem. For each role listed below, explain the perspective that the role brings to the analysis. (Example: an auditor for the Canada Customs and Revenue Agency examines accounting information to ensure that an entity complies with the *Income Tax Act* and, as a result, pays an appropriate amount of tax.) In answering, consider the entity the person in the role is working for and the objectives of that entity, and apply these factors to explain how the role-player would approach providing advice on accounting problems.

a. Arbitrator. (An arbitrator is a person who helps resolve disputes between parties. In an accounting setting, an arbitrator might be asked to resolve disagreements over the accounting choices an entity made when, for example, the selling price of the entity is based on net income.)

b. Advisor to management of the entity.

c. Advisor to the board of directors of the company.

d. External auditor.

e. Advisor to a prospective lender.

f. Advisor to a major shareholder who is not involved in the day-to-day management of the entity.

E4-12. **(Choosing when to recognize revenue according to the objectives of financial reporting, LO 1, 2, 7)** Pisquid Ltd. (Pisquid) is a manufacturer of kitchen furniture. In November 2004, Pisquid received an order for 15,000 sets of specially designed furniture from a large retail chain. The contract with the retail chain guaranteed the price that the retailer would pay and the quantity it would buy from Pisquid. The furniture is to be delivered monthly, in equal quantities each month, beginning in March 2005 and continuing through August 2006. The retail chain is to pay Pisquid within 45 days of receiving each shipment. Because Pisquid had excess capacity in its plant when the contact was signed, it decided to manufacture the full order as soon as it could. Pisquid began producing the furniture in January 2005 and completed making the 15,000 sets in November 2005.

Required:

a. Identify the different possible critical events that could be used to recognize revenue.

b. For the purposes of satisfying each of the following objectives, which critical event would you recommend for recognizing revenue? Explain. For purposes of answering, do not consider the constraints and the facts.

   i.   Tax minimization.
   ii. Evaluation of management by outside shareholders.
   iii. Income smoothing.
   iv. Managing earnings to increase income.
   v.   Cash flow prediction.

c. Which of the revenue-recognition methods that you identified in (a) satisfy the four revenue recognition criteria? Explain.

E4-13. **(Assessing different ways of recognizing revenue, LO 1, 2, 6)** Valhalla Furniture Emporium Ltd. (Valhalla) sells poor-quality furniture at low prices. Customers take delivery of their furniture after making a down payment of 10% of the selling price. The customers agree to pay the balance owing in 36 equal monthly payments. Valhalla repossesses between 40% and 60% of the furniture sold because customers default on their payments. Repossessed furniture can be resold if it requires only minor repairs and cleaning. Some repossessed furniture is unsaleable and must be disposed of.

Required:

a. What are the possible points at which Valhalla could recognize revenue?

b. Explain what objectives of reporting each revenue-recognition point would satisfy?

c. Which revenue-recognition points can you support with the four GAAP criteria?

Problems

P4-1. **(Choosing a revenue-recognition point to achieve an objective of financial reporting, LO 1, 2, 3, 6, 7)** For each of the following independent situations, recommend how you would want to recognize revenue if your objective of financial reporting were to minimize taxes. Support your answer. (To respond you should identify alternative points for recognizing revenue and choose the one that best satisfies the objective of minimizing taxes *and* can be reasonably supported.)

a. A construction company signs a contract to build a warehouse for a food distribution company. The project is to take 18 months from the signing of the contract and the construction company will receive $10,000,000. At the construction company's fiscal year end 60% of the project has been completed.

b. An investment company purchases shares of publicly traded companies for its portfolio. During the year, the market value of the portfolio increases from $2,300,000 to $3,745,000. None of the shares were sold during the year.

c. A national bus company sells passes that allow the passenger unlimited travel on the company's buses for 60 days from the day the pass is first used. Passes must be purchased at least 90 days before they are first used. Once purchased, the passes are not refundable.

d. A computer software company sells a software package that entitles the owners to receive the next two upgrades of the package at no additional charge, plus technical support for 18 months from the date of purchase.

e. A law firm charges clients who wish to have legal advice available to them 24 hours a day, seven days a week, a fee of $10,000 per year for the service. (The $10,000 fee is simply for the privilege of having a lawyer available all the time. These clients then have to pay the lawyer's hourly rate for the advice given.)

P4-2. **(Evaluating when to recognize revenue to try to achieve an objective of financial reporting, LO 1, 2, 3, 6, 7)** For each of the following independent situations, recommend how you would want to recognize revenue if you were the president of the company, you received a significant bonus based on net income, and your objective of financial reporting was to receive as high a bonus as is reasonably possible. Support your answer. (To respond you should identify alternative points for recognizing revenue and choose the one that best satisfies the objective of achieving a high bonus *and* can be reasonably supported.)

a. A construction company signs a contract to build a warehouse for a food distribution company. The project is to take 18 months from the signing of the contract and the construction company will receive $10,000,000. At the construction company's fiscal year end 60% of the project has been completed.

b. An investment company purchases shares of publicly traded companies for its portfolio. During the year, the market value of the portfolio increases from $2,300,000 to $3,745,000. None of the shares were sold during the year.

c. A national bus company sells passes that allows the passenger unlimited travel on the company's buses for 60 days from the day the pass is first used. Passes must be purchased at least 90 days before they are first used. Once purchased, the passes are not refundable.

d. A computer software company sells a software package that entitles the owners to receive the next two upgrades of the package at no additional charges plus technical support for 18 months from the date of purchase.

e. A law firm charges clients who wish to have legal advice available to them 24 hours a day, seven days a week, a fee of $10,000 per year for the service. (The $10,000 fee is simply for the privilege of having a lawyer available all the time. These clients then have to pay the lawyer's hourly rate for the advice given.)

P4-3. **(Observing the effects of different revenue-recognition methods on financial ratios, LO 1, 2, 3, 4, 5, 6)** On November 15, 2004 Desert Renovations Ltd. (Desert) signed a contract to renovate a 75-year-old building so that it would be suitable to house the head office of a real estate company. Desert has provided you with the following information about the contract:

i. Desert expects the renovations to take three years.

ii. Desert will receive $10,000,000 for the renovations. Desert will receive payments on the following schedule:
  - $2,500,000 when the contract is signed.
  - $3,000,000 on September 1, 2005.
  - $3,000,000 on June 1, 2006, the expected completion date of the project.
  - $1,500,000 on January 15, 2007.

iii. The total cost of the renovations is expected to be $6,500,000:
  - 2004: $0
  - 2005: $2,400,000
  - 2006: $4,100,000
  - 2007: $0

iv. Other costs associated with the contract are $700,000 in each of 2005 and 2006. These costs are treated as period costs in the calculation of income.

v. Desert's year end is December 31.

Required:

a. Calculate revenue, expenses, gross margin, and net income for each year using the following revenue-recognition methods:

     i.   Percentage-of-completion.

     ii. Completed-contract.

     iii. Cash collection. (Hint: match expenses based on the proportion of cash collected in each year)

  b. Calculate the gross margin percentage and the profit margin percentage for each year.

  c. Does it matter how Desert accounts for its revenue from the renovation contract? To whom does it matter and why?

  d. Is the actual economic performance of Desert affected by how it accounts for the revenue from the renovation contract? Explain.

P4-4. **(Observing the effects of different revenue-recognition methods on financial ratios, LO 1, 2, 3, 4, 5, 6)** On, July 15, 2005 Tidnish Vessel Refitters Ltd. (Tidnish) signed a contract to refit a 25-year-old supertanker to meet new environmental standards and operate more efficiently. Tidnish has provided you with the following information about the contract:

i. Tidnish expects the refitting to take three years.

ii. Tidnish will receive $25,000,000 for the refitting. Tidnish will receive payments on the following schedule:

- $5,000,000 when the contract is signed.
- $6,000,000 on June 1, 2006.
- $10,000,000 on February 1, 2007, the expected completion date of the project.
- $4,000,000 on August 15, 2008.

iii. The total cost of the renovations is expected to be $16,000,000:

- 2005: $0
- 2006: $10,000,000
- 2007: $6,000,000
- 2008: $0

iv. Other costs associated with the contract are $2,000,000 in each of 2006 and 2007. These costs are treated as period costs in the calculation of income.

v. Tidnish's year end is July 31.

Required:

  a. Calculate revenue, expenses, gross margin, and net income for each year using the following revenue-recognition methods:

     i.   Percentage-of-completion.

     ii   Completed-contract

     iii. Cash collection. (Hint: match expenses based on the proportion of cash collected in each year).

     iv. Calculate the gross margin percentage and the profit margin percentage for each year.

  b. Does it matter how Tidnish accounts for its revenue from the refitting contract? To whom does it matter and why?

  c. Is the actual economic performance of Tidnish affected by how it accounts for the revenue from the refitting contract? Explain.

P4-5. **(Observing the effects of different revenue-recognition methods on financial ratios, LO 2, 3, 5, 6)** Antler Manufacturing Ltd. (Antler) is a newly formed company specializing in the production of high-quality machine parts. Paul Wayne incorporated Antler on the understanding that it would receive a large contract from his previous employer, Pocologan Inc. (Pocologan), to manufacture parts. Antler has rented the space and equipment it needs to operate its business. During Antler's first year of operations, the following transactions and economic events take place:

     i.   January 3, 2005: Paul Wayne contributes $500,000 cash in exchange for 100,000 common shares in Antler.

     ii. January 5, 2005: Antler borrows $250,000 from Pocologan. The loan carries an interest rate of 10% per year. No interest or principal needs to be paid until 2008.

iii. January 8, 2005: Antler rents space and equipment to operate the business. Rent of $200,000 for two years is paid.

iv. January 10, 2005: Antler signs the contract with Pocologan. The contract requires that Antler manufacture and deliver $4,000,000 in parts over the period July 1, 2005 to December 31, 2007. The contract requires payment by Pocologan within 90 days of each delivery by Antler. The selling price of all parts is specified in the contract. Antler begins production of the parts immediately.

v. During 2005 Antler produced and delivered parts, and collected cash in the following amounts:

Selling price of parts *produced* during 2005	$1,400,000
Cost of parts *produced* during 2005	840,000
Selling price of parts *delivered* to Pocologan during 2005	900,000
Cost of parts *delivered* to Pocologan during 2005	540,000
Cash collected from Pocologan during 2005	525,000
Cost of parts that were paid for by Pocologan during 2005	315,000

vi. All costs incurred to produce the parts were purchased on credit. Of the $840,000 incurred to produce parts in 2005, $760,000 had been paid by December 31, 2005.

vii. During 2005 Antler incurred additional costs of $210,000, all on credit. As of December 31, 2005, $175,000 of these costs had been paid. Because these costs were not directly related to the production of parts, Antler plans to expense them in full in 2005. This amount does not include the amount paid for rent and the interest expense.

viii. Antler has a December 31 year end.

Required:

a. Use an accounting equation spreadsheet to record the transactions and economic events that occurred in 2005 for Antler. Prepare a separate spreadsheet using the following critical events for recognizing revenue:
i. Production.
ii. Delivery.
iii. Collection of cash.

b. Prepare Antler's income statement for 2005 and its balance sheet as of December 31, 2005, using each of the three critical events (production, delivery, and collection of cash). Your income statements should show revenue, cost of goods sold, gross margin, other expenses, and net income.

c. Calculate the gross margin percentage, profit margin percentage, current ratio, and the debt-to-equity ratio for 2005 for each critical event.

d. Which method of calculating the ratios in (c) gives the best indication of Antler's performance and liquidity? Explain.

e. Does it matter how Antler recognizes revenue? To whom does it matter and why?

f. Is the actual economic performance of Antler affected by how it recognizes revenue? Explain.

P4-6. **(Observing the effects of different revenue-recognition methods on financial ratios, LO 2, 3, 5, 6)** Kinkora Manufacturing Ltd. (Kinkora) is a newly formed company specializing in the production of a new type of pizza oven. Lisa Volente organized Kinkora on the understanding that it would receive a large contract for pizza ovens from her previous employer, Cascumpec Inc. (Cascumpec), which was planning to renovate its chain of pizza restaurants. Cascumpec is one of the largest pizza restaurant chains in central Canada. Kinkora has rented the space and equipment it needs to operate its business. During Kinkora's first year of operations, the following transactions and economic events took place:

i. July 3, 2006: Lisa Volente contributes $100,000 cash in exchange for 100,000 common shares in Kinkora.

ii.   July 5, 2006: Kinkora borrows $200,000 from Cascumpec. The loan carries an interest rate of 10% per year. No interest or principal must be paid until 2009.

iii.   July 8, 2006: Kinkora rents space and equipment to operate the business. Rent of $100,000 for two years is paid.

iv.   July 10, 2006: Kinkora signs the contract with Cascumpec. The contract requires that Kinkora manufacture and deliver $2,000,000 in pizza ovens over the period August 1, 2006 to June 30, 2008. The contract requires that Cascumpec pay within 90 days of delivery by Kinkora. The selling price of the pizza ovens is specified in the contract. Kinkora begins production of the pizza ovens immediately.

v.   During fiscal 2007 Kinkora produced and delivered pizza ovens, and collected cash in the following amounts:

Selling price of ovens *produced* during 2007	$650,000
Cost of ovens *produced* during 2007	325,000
Selling price of ovens *delivered* to Cascumpec during 2007	400,000
Cost of ovens *delivered* to Cascumpec during 2007	200,000
Cash collected from Cascumpec during 2007	230,000
Cost of ovens that were paid for by Cascumpec during 2007	115,000

vi.   All costs incurred to produce the ovens were purchased on credit. Of the $325,000 incurred to produce ovens in fiscal 2007, $290,000 had been paid by June 30, 2007.

vii.   During fiscal 2007 Kinkora incurred additional costs of $95,000, all on credit. As of June 30, 2007, $80,000 of these costs had been paid. Because these costs were not directly used in the production of ovens, Kinkora plans to expense them in full in fiscal 2007. This amount excludes the amount paid for rent and the interest expense.

viii.   Kinkora has a June 30 year end.

Required:

a.   Use an accounting equation spreadsheet to record the transactions and economic events that occurred in fiscal 2007 for Kinkora. Prepare a separate spreadsheet using the following critical events for recognizing revenue:

    i.   Production.

    ii.   Delivery.

    iii.   Collection of cash.

b.   Prepare Kinkora's income statement for the year ended June 30, 2007 and its balance sheet as of June 30, 2007, using each of the three critical events (production, delivery, and collection of cash). Your income statements should show revenue, cost of goods sold, gross margin, other expenses, and net income.

c.   Calculate the gross margin percentage, profit margin percentage, current ratio, and the debt-to-equity ratio for fiscal 2007 for each critical event.

d.   Which method of calculating the ratios in (c) gives the best indication of Kinkora's performance and liquidity? Explain.

e.   Does it matter how Kinkora recognizes revenue? To whom does it matter and why?

f.   Is the actual economic performance of Kinkora affected by how it recognizes revenue? Explain.

P4-7.   **(Evaluating objectives of financial reporting and recommending how to recognize revenue, LO 1, 2, 6)** Notigi Mines Ltd. (Notigi) is a mining venture that recently began operations in northern Manitoba. The mine has been under development for the last two years and will produce its first shipments of refined metal before the end of the current fiscal year. Two senior executives who have extensive mining experience manage the mine. The mine is owned by a syndicate of 20 investors—mainly professionals such as accountants, doctors, lawyers, and dentists—who live in various locations in western Canada.

Notigi extracts ore from the ground and ships it to another company for processing into refined metal. The processing company then returns the refined metal to Notigi for sale and shipment to buyers. Notigi has already entered into long-term contracts with several buyers to purchase virtually all of the mine's production at prices specified in the contract. Any production not covered by the long-term contracts can easily be sold at prevailing prices in the open market.

Required:

    a. What do you think could be Notigi's objectives of accounting? Explain.

    b. How would you rank the objectives? Explain.

    c. When would you recommend that revenue be recognized on the sale of the refined metal? Explain your recommendation. Make sure that you consider the constraints, facts, and objectives in your answer.

P4-8.   **(Evaluating objectives of financial reporting and recommending how to recognize revenue, LO 1, 2, 6)** Opeongo Construction Ltd. (Opeongo) is a recently formed company that builds commercial and industrial buildings in the Ottawa area. All of Opeongo's common stock is owned by five people: Adam and Nikki, a brother and sister who operate the company; two cousins of Adam and Nikki who live and work in Vancouver; and a wealthy aunt who is retired and lives in Europe. Opeongo borrowed money from the bank to cover the costs of starting the business. All the money that was initially borrowed from the bank has been spent.

Recently, Opeongo won a contact to build a warehouse in suburban Ottawa. This will be its first large job. The warehouse will take about 18 months to build. Opeongo will receive $1.96 million to build the warehouse. The contract specifies the following payment schedule:

• On commencement of construction	$ 100,000
• On the first day of each month beginning with the month after construction begins ($70,000 per month for 18 months)	1,260,000
• On completion of construction	400,000
• 90 days after the purchaser takes possession of the warehouse	200,000
• Total	$1,960,000

From this amount Opeongo will have to pay the costs of construction, which it estimates to be about $1,500,000.

Required:

    a. What do you think Opeongo's objectives of accounting could be? Explain.

    b. How would you rank the objectives? Explain.

    c. When would you recommend that revenue be recognized on the warehouse construction project? Explain your recommendation. Make sure that you consider the constraints, facts, and objectives in your answer.

P4-9.   **(Considering when to recognize revenue, LO 1, 2, 6, 7)** Teslin Inc. (Teslin) is a medium-sized manufacturer of plastic storage containers. Teslin is a private corporation that is owned entirely by a single shareholder, Kim Chung. Ms. Chung is not involved in the day-to-day management of Teslin, but she does speak regularly with Teslin's president, Mr. Krajden. Mr. Krajden is compensated with a salary plus a bonus based on Teslin's net income.

On October 1, 2005 Teslin signed a $1,000,000 contract with the Government of Canada to design and manufacture storage containers for all the tax dollars they collect from Canadians. The storage containers must be delivered by April 1, 2007. The government will pay $250,000 on April 1, 2006, $250,000 on January 15, 2007, and the balance 30 days after all the containers have been delivered. Teslin plans to begin production of the containers in early 2006. Teslin plans to ship 10% of the contracted number of containers per month beginning in September 2006. The contract stipulates that Teslin pay a penalty of $20,000 per week if the containers are not completely delivered by April 1, 2007. Teslin had to borrow $300,000 from the bank to provide cash to finance the project. Teslin expects to earn $225,000 from this contract.

You have been hired by Mr. Krajden to provide advice to him on how to recognize revenue on the contract with the government. Teslin's year end is December 31.

Required:

a. Who are the possible users of Teslin's financial statements and what use do they have for the statements?

b. What objectives of financial reporting would you suggest that Mr. Krajden consider when preparing Teslin's financial statements? Explain.

c. How would you advise Mr. Krajden to rank the objectives? Explain.

d. What possible critical events for recognizing the revenue on the container contract can you identify for Mr. Krajden? Explain.

e. When would you recommend that Teslin recognize the revenue on the contract? Make sure that you consider the constraints, facts, and objectives when responding.

P4-10. **(Evaluating when a partnership of lawyers should recognize revenue, LO 1, 2, 3, 6, 7)** Elnora and Partners is a recently formed partnership of lawyers. The partnership has ten partners (all of whom are practising lawyers) and 15 associate lawyers (lawyers who work for the partnership but who are not partners), along with 12 other employees. The partnership's financial statements will be used to determine:

- the amount of income tax that each partner pays (remember, partners, not the partnership, pay income tax).
- the amount of money that is paid to each partner, based on the net income of the partnership.
- the amount that a new partner pays to join the partnership and the amount a departing partner is paid for his or her partnership interest. In addition, the financial statements are provided to the bank because the partnership has a large line of credit available to it.

The partnership's September 30 year end has just passed and the managing partner of the firm has asked for your advice on how to recognize revenue. The managing partner provides you with the following information on how the partnership generates revenue:

i.   Some clients are billed at the completion of a case, based on the number of hours lawyers worked on the case. (Each lawyer has an hourly billing rate.) Lawyers keep track of the time they spend on each case and report the number of hours each month to the accounting department, which keeps track of the hours spent on each case by each lawyer. The amount actually billed to a client may differ from the actual charges generated by the lawyers who worked on the case. (That is, the amount billed may differ from number of hours worked multiplied by the hourly billing rate.) The final amount billed is based on the judgment of the partner in charge of the case. Clients have 60 days from receipt of their bill to pay.

ii. Some clients pay only if their cases are successful. The partnership receives a percentage of the settlement if the client wins the case. It can be difficult to determine whether a client will win a case and the amount that will be received if the client does win.

iii. Some clients pay amounts called retainers, which is an amount paid to the partnership before services are provided. The retainer is used to pay for legal services as they are provided. If the amount of retainer is not used by the end of the year, the remaining amount is applied against future years' legal services.

iv. Clients who wish to have legal advice available to them 24 hours a day, seven days a week, pay a fee of $10,000 per year for the service. (The $10,000 fee is simply for the privilege of having a lawyer available all the time. These clients then have to pay the lawyer's hourly rate for the advice given.)

Required:

a. What are the possible objectives of financial reporting? Explain each objective that you identify. Are there any conflicts among the objectives? Explain.

b. Rank the objectives in order of importance. Explain your ranking.

c. When should the partnership recognize its revenue? Explain your recommendations fully. Make sure to discuss constraints, facts, and objectives in your answer.

P4-11. (**Preparing income statements under different revenue-recognition methods, LO 1, 2, 3, 6**) Igloolik Mines Inc. (Igloolik) operates three nickel mines in the Yukon. In 2002 gold was discovered on one of its mining properties and Igloolik developed the gold mine. The gold mine went into production in 2004. The ore is extracted from the ground and refined into pure gold at a refinery that Igloolik built on the mine property. The gold is stored until it is shipped to customers. The following information on the contracts and the operation of the mine is obtained from the mine manager:

i.   In the first three years the mine was in production, 30,000 ounces of gold were produced in each year.

ii. Just before the mine began production, Igloolik had signed contracts with several buyers to purchase 30,000 ounces of gold per year for the next three years.

iii. The contracts set the purchase price that the customers must pay for the gold each year at $420 per ounce for each ounce of gold delivered.

iv. The cost of mining, refining, and delivering an ounce of gold to customers in the first three years was $275 per ounce in the first year, $290 per ounce in the second year, and $300 per ounce in the third year. These costs are accounted for as product costs.

v.   Amortization expense in each of the first three years was $1,600,000.

vi. Other non-production costs were $1,000,000 in the first year, $1,050,000 in the second year, and $900,000 in the third year.

vii. The mine pays 30% of income before taxes in income taxes.

viii. Other information:

	2004	2005	2006
Gold produced	30,000 ounces	30,000 ounces	30,000 ounces
Gold shipped and delivered to customers	27,000 ounces	32,000 ounces	31,000 ounces
Payments received from customers	24,000 ounces	28,000 ounces	38,000 ounces

Required:

a. Prepare an income statement for each of the three years assuming that:
   i.   Revenue is recognized when a contract is signed.
   ii. Revenue is recognized when the gold is produced.
   iii. Revenue is recognized when the gold is shipped and delivered to customers.
   iv. Revenue is recognized when payment is received from customers.
   When preparing the statements, assume that the cost of mining, refining, and delivery of the gold is accounted for as a product cost, and the amortization expense and the non-production costs are accounted for as period costs.

b. Which objective of financial reporting would be served by each method of recognizing revenue?

c. Under GAAP, which revenue-recognition methods could be justified? Try to think of circumstances that would allow you to justify using each of the four revenue-recognition points.

P4-12. (**Selecting and justifying revenue-recognition alternatives to suit the objectives of financial reporting, LO 2, 3, 6, 7**) Eyebrow Technologies Ltd. (Eyebrow) is a Canadian-owned developer of computer hardware and software. Eyebrow is owned by 20 private investors, most of whom are not involved in the day-to-day management of the company. Eyebrow has borrowed extensively from banks, and management believes that additional loans will be required in the near future. Senior executives own a small number of Eyebrow's shares and are compensated with a salary plus a bonus based on the performance of the company.

Eyebrow is completing development of a new product. The product combines a modification of Eyebrow's existing computer hardware with a newly developed proprietary software program. The new product is targeted at firms in the financial services industry (firms such as Canadian banks, mid- to large-sized trust companies, and insurance companies). The design of the product requires that customers purchase both Eyebrow's hardware and software (a customer cannot purchase only the software, and the hardware is not useful without the software).

The new product (hardware and software) sells for $325,000. Eyebrow has 12 firm orders for the new product. In January 2005 Eyebrow shipped the computer hardware component to the 12 customers. The software will be provided to customers when it is completed in May 2005. The software was originally expected to be ready in February 2005, but unexpected programming problems delayed its completion. Eyebrow now expects to complete testing and debugging of the software in time to meet the May shipping date. Costs of the product include the hardware, software development, and marketing, sales and administrative costs.

Customers have already paid 25% of the cost of their orders. They will pay an additional 60% 30 days after the product is delivered and operating, and the balance six months after that.

Eyebrow's year end is February 28.

Required:

a. Identify the stakeholders who would have an interest in the financial information of Eyebrow. Explain each stakeholder's interest in the information (i.e., why would they want it?).

b. Identify possible objectives of financial reporting that Eyebrow's management might have. Explain why each objective might be relevant.

c. Identify possible critical events that Eyebrow could use to recognize the revenue on the new product. (In answering this question, consider whether the new product is really two products instead of one.)

d. Select two of the stakeholders and recommend a revenue and expense recognition policy to Eyebrow's management that could be used to satisfy the information needs of each of the two stakeholders. (Note: You should come up with two *different* policies, one for each stakeholder.) Fully explain your choices by justifying them in terms of the constraints, facts, and objectives.

■ Using Financial Statements

travelbyus.com ltd.

travelbyus.com ltd. (travelbyus) is an integrated travel company providing consumers, primarily located in the United States, with various travel products including travel packages, cruises, discounted airfares, and other services. These travel products are provided through various travel agencies, some of which are owned by the company, and a substantial number of which are considered member agencies under various programs offered by the company, and the company's 800-i-travel call centre and Internet booking engines. The majority of these travel products are provided on an agency basis for the various travel providers. The company also provides products, marketing services, and support to non-owned travel agencies, travel providers and other corporate customers. The company is in the process of developing a new travel magazine and television show.[7]

travelbyus' statements of operations and deficit and consolidated balance sheets, along with some extracts from the notes to the financial statements, are provided in Exhibit 4-7. Use this information to answer to questions FS4-1 to FS4-11.

FS4-1. Why does travelbyus not report any income for the period ended September 30, 1999? Why is the period ended September 30, 1999 less than one year? What are some of the problems with using these financial statements? Explain.

FS4-2. Identify and explain the different ways that travelbyus makes money.

FS4-3. What are travel product sales and travel commissions? How much of each of these types of revenue did travelbyus earn in fiscal 2000? How is each of these types of

Exhibit 4-7

travelbyus.com ltd. Financial Statements

travelbyus.com ltd.
Consolidated Statements of Operations and Deficit

(expressed in 000's of Canadian dollars except for per share amounts)

	Year ended September 30, 2000 $	Period from January 1, 1999 to September 30, 1999 $
Revenues		
Travel product sales	4,574	-
Travel commissions	10,582	-
Associate marketing program	605	-
Advertising	887	-
Technology sales	1,561	-
	18,209	-
Expenses		
Cost of travel product sales	4,469	-
Cost of services	723	-
Cost of technology product sales	1,592	-
Advertising	4,231	-
Amortization of software and other assets	6,555	40
Amortization of property, plant and equipment	607	4
Foreign exchange loss (gain)	62	(2)
Gain on marketable securities	-	(53)
General and administration	26,267	927
Interest	1,560	92
Interest and other income	(380)	(7)
Web site costs	1,457	363
Write-down of contract rights (note 12(b))	10,347	-
Capital taxes	283	186
Write-down of programming library, investment, barter credits, and advances	16,090	14
	73,863	1,564
Loss before income tax and write-off and amortization of goodwill	(55,654)	(1,564)
Income tax recovery	11,754	-
Loss before write-off and amortization of goodwill	(43,900)	(1,564)
Write-off and amortization of goodwill - net of tax of $nil (1999 - $nil)	(76,099)	-
Loss for the year	(119,999)	(1,564)
Deficit - Beginning of year	(12,850)	(11,286)
Deficit - End of year	(132,849)	(12,850)
Basic and diluted loss per common share	(1.71)	(0.05)
Weighted average number of common shares outstanding	70,086,465	31,781,090

revenues recognized? Explain what distinguishes the two types of revenue and why what is recognized as revenue differs. Do you agree with the difference in the accounting for these two types of revenue?

FS4-4. What is marketing program revenues? How much did travelbyus earn in marketing program revenues in fiscal 2000? How is marketing program revenue recognized? Do you agree with the method used? Explain.

FS4-5. What is advertising revenues? How much did travelbyus earn in advertising revenues in fiscal 2000? How is advertising revenue recognized? Do you agree with the method used? Explain. What are the costs associated with advertising revenues and how are they accounted for? Does the accounting for these costs make sense? Explain.

FS4-6. What is television programming revenues? How much did travelbyus earn in television programming revenues in fiscal 2000? How is television programming revenue recognized? Do you agree with the method used? Explain. Given the amount of television programming revenue recognized during fiscal 2000, why do you think there is an accounting policy stated?

FS4-7. What is technology sales revenues? How much did travelbyus earn in technology sales revenues in fiscal 2000? How is technology sales revenue recognized? Do you agree with the method used? Explain.

Exhibit 4-7 (continued)

travelbyus.com ltd. Financial Statements

travelbyus.com ltd.
Consolidated Balance Sheets
As at September 30, 2000 and 1999

(expressed in 000's of Canadian dollars)

	2000 $	1999 $
Assets		
Current assets		
Cash and cash equivalents	3,016	3,256
Accounts receivable and prepaid expenses (note 5)	3,865	51
Inventory and barter credits (note 5)	755	-
Marketable securities (note 4)	231	231
	7,867	3,538
Investment (note 5)	1,091	-
Advances and other receivables (note 7)	4,330	436
Cash deposits for acquisitions (note 8)	-	7,200
Security deposits (note 9)	1,534	-
Deferred financing costs - net of accumulated amortization of $812 (1999 - $40) (note 13(a))	482	1,255
Deferred acquisition costs	-	194
Programming library (note 11)	2,700	-
Property, plant and equipment - net of accumulated amortization of $622 (1999 - $4) (note 10)	4,112	79
Software and other assets - net of accumulated amortization of $5,783 (1999 - $nil) (note 12)	31,438	-
	53,554	12,702
Liabilities		
Current liabilities		
Bank indebtedness (note 3)	419	-
Accounts payable and accrued liabilities (note 5)	6,758	301
Due to related parties (note 17(c), (d) and (e))	886	219
Customer deposits	445	-
Debentures (note 13)	13,136	-
	21,644	520
Debentures (note 13(a))	-	11,950
	21,644	12,470
Shareholders' Equity		
Capital stock (note 14)		
Authorized		
Unlimited number of common shares without par value		
Issued		
96,804,569 common shares (1999 - 41,539,178)	137,723	12,846
Share capital to be issued (note 14(e))	4,096	-
Convertible debenture (note 13(b))	938	-
Warrants and special warrants (notes 13(a) and (b) and 14(c) and (d))	21,614	236
Deficit	(132,849)	(12,850)
Cumulative translation adjustment	388	-
	31,910	232
	53,554	12,702

FS4-8. How are advertising costs accounted for? How would you justify this accounting treatment? How are costs incurred for television and radio advertisements accounted for *before* the advertising is used for the first time? Where would these costs appear in the financial statements before the advertising is used for the first time?

travelbyus.com ltd.
Notes to Consolidated Financial Statements
For the year ended September 30, 2000 and for the period from January 1, 1999 to September 30, 1999

2. Summary of significant accounting policies

Revenue recognition

a)   Travel product sales and commissions

Travel sales consist of revenues derived from the sale of travel products including airline tickets, hotel and vacation property accommodations, car rentals, vacation packages including cruises and tours, and volume bonuses and overrides from suppliers of these products.

Where the company sells airline tickets or provides travel bookings as an agent, at prices determined by the supplier, commission revenue is recognized at the time the ticket is issued to the customer, which generally corresponds to the time the payment is processed, less an allowance for returns and cancellations based on the companyís historical experience.

Where the company acquires an inventory of travel services from airlines, hotels, vacation properties, car rental companies and vacation package providers and the company determines the selling price of these products, revenue for these services is recognized upon the customer's scheduled departure date, provided that collection is reasonably assured. Travel product sales are recorded at the gross amount collected from the customer only where the company has acquired an inventory which is non-returnable and non-refundable and bears general inventory risk, has latitude in establishing pricing, bears credit risk and is the merchant of record. Where these conditions do not exist, sales are recorded at the amount paid by the customer net of the travel product costs.

The company also earns commissions for booking accommodations and vehicle rentals, and receives certain volume bonuses and overrides from the travel product suppliers (overrides represent commissions earned on the basis of volumes). Revenues related to accommodations and vehicle rentals are recognized on the customersí scheduled departure dates. Volume bonus and override commission revenues are recognized as specified in the contractual arrangement when the specified targets have been achieved.

b)   Marketing program revenues

The company provides retail travel agencies with access to certain travel product suppliers under preferred supplier agreements, as well as administrative, Web site and marketing services. Under these associate marketing programs, the member agencies are charged an annual or monthly license fee. The license fees are recognized on a straight-line basis over the license period, when collectibility is reasonably assured.

c)   Advertising revenues

Advertising revenues are derived from travel product suppliers' advertising included in printed marketing and promotional materials prepared by the company and delivered to travel agents and customers. Advertising revenues are recognized at the time the marketing and promotional materials are distributed to the travel agents and customers, when collectibility is reasonably assured. Costs of sales comprise the direct costs of developing and producing the marketing and promotional materials.

d)   Technology sales

Revenue from the sales of computer data storage equipment is recognized upon delivery of the equipment, provided collectibility is reasonably assured.

e)   Television programming revenues

Revenues from the license of television program material are recognized when the license period begins and all of the following conditions have been met: a) the license fee is known, b) the cost of the episodes provided under the license agreement is known or reasonably determinable, c) collectibility of the license fee is reasonably assured, d) the episodes have been accepted by the licensee in accordance with the license agreement and e) the episodes are available for the first telecast.

f)   Management fees

Fees earned in connection with services provided to related parties (note 17(d)) are recognized when received following the provision of the related services.

Other intangibles

Proprietary software, trademarks, airline contracts, sales channels, workforce, and the agency network are being amortized on a straight-line basis over three years. The costs of acquiring the right to the 800-i-TRAVEL number are being amortized on a straight-line basis over five years.

Programming library

The costs to acquire television programming are capitalized and amortized in the same ratio that current gross revenues bear to anticipated total gross revenues. Estimates of anticipated total gross revenues are reviewed periodically and revised when necessary to reflect more current information. Where the carrying value of the unamortized costs exceeds the estimated fair value, the carrying value is written down to the fair value.

Advertising costs

Advertising costs are expensed as incurred except for television and radio advertisements, which are expensed, the first time the advertising takes place.

FS4-9.   travelbyus paid $1,372,000 for the rights to its 1-800-i-travel phone number. How is the phone number being accounted for? What justification is there for accounting for the phone number in this way? Do you agree with this accounting treatment? What would be the implications for the financial statements if the phone number was amortized over a shorter period of time or expensed when purchased?

FS4-10. How are costs incurred to acquire television programming accounted for? What are the problems with this method of expensing these costs? Does the method provide management with the opportunity to manage its earnings? Explain. Do you agree, conceptually at least, with the method used to account for the television programming acquisition costs? Explain.

FS4-11. Examine travelbyus' income statement for the year ended September 30, 2000 and the balance sheet as of September 30, 2000. Do you think travelbyus is in good financial shape? Explain.

■ Analyzing Mark's Work Wearhouse

M4-1.   What do you think are MWW's objectives of financial reporting? Explain.

M4-2.   How does MWW recognize revenue from initial franchise fees paid by purchasers of Mark's Work Wearhouse or Work World franchises? How does MWW recognize revenue from royalties on sales made by franchisees?

M4-3.   Examine MWW's income statement and Note 14 (pages A-46 and A-61) to the financial statements and respond to the following:
   a. What were total combined corporate and franchise sales during fiscal 2001? Where does this amount appear on the year ended January 27, 2001 income statement?
   b. What were sales by MWW's company-owned stores during fiscal 2001?
   c. What were sales by Mark's Work Wearhouse and Work World franchise stores during fiscal 2001?
   d. Why does MWW not include sales by its franchise stores in the calculation of net income?
   e. Why does MWW disclose sales by franchise stores on its income statement and in the notes to the financial statements?

M4-4.   Examine MWW's income statement and Note 15 to the financial statements (pages A-46 and A-61) and respond to the following:
   a. How much revenue from royalties did MWW report in its income statement for the year ended January 27, 2001? How much of that revenue was earned from Mark's Work Wearhouse stores and how much was earned from Work World stores?
   b. What is royalty revenue?
   c. On a per store basis, did royalty revenue earned by MWW from Work World stores increase or decrease from fiscal 2000 to fiscal 2001? (To answer calculate the average amount of royalty revenue earned from Work World stores in fiscal 2000 and compare that amount with the royalty revenue earned from Work World stores in fiscal 2001.)
   d. Where in the income statement is royalty revenue reported? Why do you think it is reported there instead of including it in sales?

M4-5.   Examine MWW's income statement. Which costs that are shown on the income statement could be reasonably matched to the sale of merchandise? Which costs would be difficult to match? Explain.

M4-6.   Examine Table 5 and the related discussion in the "Management's Discussion and Analysis" section of MWW's 2001 annual report (page A-27).
   a. What are MWW's major product categories?
   b. Which product category makes up the largest percentage of MWW's sales?
   c. Which product category grew fastest between fiscal 2000 and fiscal 2001?
   d. What objectives of financial reporting might be served by analyzing sales by major product category information?

M4-7. Examine MWW's financial goals as reported in its annual report (page A-12).

    a. What are MWW's conservative and optimistic forecasts for combined corporate and franchise store sales for fiscal 2002?

    b. Is it useful for stakeholders to receive forecasts of revenues? Explain. What are some of the concerns you might have about receiving forecasts from MWW's management? Can you think of alternatives for who should prepare forecasts of future years' sales?

Endnotes

1. Extracted from Richmont Mines Inc.'s 2000 annual report.

2. Extracted from Air Canada's 2000 annual report.

3. Extracted from Genesis Land Development Corp.'s 2000 annual report.

4. Extracted from Microsoft Corporation's 2000 annual report.

5. Extracted from Printera Corporation's 2000 annual report.

6. Extracted from Stelco Inc.'s 2000 annual report.

7. Extracted from travelbyus ltd.'s 2000 annual report.

Chapter 5

Generally Accepted Accounting Principles

Chapter Outline

Learning Objectives

Introduction

What Are Generally Accepted Accounting Principles (GAAP)?

The World According to GAAP

The Auditors' Report

Solved Problem

Summary of Key Points

Key Terms and Similar Terms

Questions, Exercises, and Problems

Using Financial Statements

Analyzing Mark's Work Wearhouse

Learning Objectives

After studying the material in this chapter you will be able to:

LO 1.   Explain the need for, sources of, and applicability of GAAP.

LO 2.   Describe the four basic assumptions that underlie GAAP.

LO 3.   Recognize the strengths and limitations of the four qualitative characteristics of GAAP.

LO 4.   Explain the measurement conventions that determine the amounts that are reported in the financial statements.

LO 5.   Identify the four different opinions auditors can provide on financial statements and interpret the meaning of an unqualified audit report.

Introduction

Financial reporting in Canada and in most places around the world is played by a set of rules. These rules are known as generally accepted accounting principles or GAAP. We have mentioned GAAP several times in the book so far. In this chapter we will take a more comprehensive look at GAAP.

As we discussed in Chapter 1, GAAP represent the rules of the accounting game. In most games, rules are subject to interpretation. For example, hockey has a detailed and lengthy set of rules of how the game is to be played. Some rules are straightforward and not subject to judgment: if an offensive player precedes the puck over the offensive zone blue line, the linesman must blow the whistle and stop play because the play is offside. Other hockey rules are subject to the referee's interpretation: a player who holds an opponent with hands, stick, or in any other way will receive a minor penalty for holding. Hockey fans know that a holding penalty is not given every time holding occurs. The referees exercise judgment in applying the holding rule. They take into consideration the extent of the holding, the impact a particular holding infraction has on the play, and when during a game the infraction occurs.

Judgment is not uniform among referees. Different referees are known to have different styles—some may be more lax in calling holding penalties, while others are stricter. Yet despite these inconsistencies rules are necessary in hockey, other games, and more generally in a civilized society. Without rules a hockey game would be chaos. Some players might choose to pick the puck up in their hands and skate with it until an opposing player tackled them. Other players might think that the best way to stop opponents is to club them over the head with a stick. A clever coach might decide to use two or three goaltenders simultaneously to reduce the likelihood of a goal being scored. The rules of hockey add order to the play and make the game understandable to the people who watch it.

The rules of hockey are not universal. Hockey organizations modify the rules to meet their own needs. For example, younger children's leagues and some recreational leagues do not allow physical contact. Many leagues below the professional level require players to wear full facial protection. In Europe the game is played on a larger ice surface, players who fight are thrown out of the game, and ties are resolved by a "shootout."

And so it is with GAAP. GAAP are not universal. Different countries have different GAAP. Canadian GAAP require the application of judgment. Canadian accounting standards are written in a way that requires the interpretation of the circumstances in applying the standard. GAAP are not a clear-cut, rigid set of rules. GAAP are easy to criticize. Various stakeholders could examine a set of GAAP financial statements and come up with suggestions to "improve" financial reporting.

In this chapter we will look at the assumptions, characteristics, and conventions that form the foundation of GAAP in Canada and that define Canadian financial reporting. GAAP are crucial to Canadian financial reporting. Having a common basis of communication that all stakeholders can know and understand makes it easier and more straightforward for an entity to communicate with its stakeholders. Like hockey, without a set of "rules" financial reporting would be chaos. Stakeholders would have to invest heavily to learn and understand the accounting of each entity they are interested in. To understand the financial information of a number of institutions would be a huge task and the benefit of doing so would often be dwarfed by the cost.

Despite the importance and value of a somewhat standardized set of rules, it is important to look at GAAP critically. This book offers a critical examination of accounting, with the objective of making readers sophisticated users of accounting information. This means recognizing that GAAP have significant limitations as well as benefits. What will become clear is that when GAAP are used, the information needs of some users of financial statements will not be met.

Explain why it is necessary to have rules for accounting and for games like hockey. Explain why it is very difficult to establish a set of rules that can be uniformly applied without judgment or interpretation.

Answer: Rules are necessary for games and for accounting to ensure that, in broad terms at least, all participants and observers can know and understand how the game is played. Without rules hockey and accounting would be wild free-for-alls. For accounting, without some commonly known and accepted set of rules, communication by entities to stakeholders would be costly and inefficient because stakeholders would have to learn and understand the accounting principles used by each entity they want to examine.

It is very difficult to establish a set of rules that can be uniformly applied without judgment or interpretation because the circumstances that give rise to the application of the rules can vary greatly. In hockey, some holding penalties may be inconsequential to the game. Calling these penalties would disrupt the flow of the game and reduce the fans' enjoyment of the game for no real reason. That is why the judgment of the referees is so important.

In accounting, the circumstances surrounding economic events and transactions are so varied that if rigid rules were created there would be uniformity in financial reporting, but the accounting itself would not necessarily provide a reasonable representation of the economic activity. For example, the revenue recognition rules discussed in Chapter 4 are flexible so as to allow the financial statements to reflect the economic substance of transactions and economic events, rather than simply requiring that revenue be recognized at a specific point in time, such as collection of cash or delivery of the goods or services.

What Are Generally Accepted Accounting Principles (GAAP)?

Chapter 1 explained that accounting is a tool that has been developed by people as a means of providing information for decision making. There are no natural laws that define how accounting should be done. As a result, it is necessary to establish rules for accounting. If there were no rules it would be much more costly and difficult to make sense of the information contained in accounting reports because it would be necessary to learn and understand the rules that each entity was using. GAAP are the characteristics, assumptions, principles, conventions, practices, procedures, and rules that define acceptable accounting practices and guide the preparation of financial statements in certain situations. In other words, GAAP represent a structure for preparing financial statements.

While not all entities are required to follow GAAP, most of the financial statements we will examine in this book, and most of the financial statements we come across day-to-day, are prepared in accordance with GAAP. The reason for this is that the financial statements that are available to the public are the statements of publicly traded companies, and these companies are compelled to follow GAAP.

Despite how pervasive GAAP-based financial statements are, GAAP are surprisingly difficult to define. It is not possible to point to a single source that documents all GAAP. In fact, much of GAAP are not recorded at all. The most prominent source of GAAP is the *CICA Handbook*. When Canadian accounting standard setters establish an accounting practice, the practice is recorded in the *CICA Handbook*. The *CICA Handbook* is a rather thick document containing a wide range of pronouncements that state how entities should account for certain types of transactions and economic events. The *CICA Handbook* also identifies the broad concepts that provide guidance to accountants and preparers of accounting information for making accounting choices. Some of these broad concepts were discussed in Chapter 1, including the four qualitative characteristics of accounting information:

- understandability
- relevance
- reliability
- comparability

www.cica.ca
www.cga-canada.org
www.cma-canada.org

The *CICA Handbook* is published by the Canadian Institute of Chartered Accountants (CICA), the organization that has responsibility for setting accounting standards in Canada. The Accounting Standards Board (ASB) of the CICA is specifically responsible for setting the accounting standards that are included in the *CICA Handbook*. The ASB is made up mainly of Chartered Accountants, but it also attempts to give representation to the groups that have an interest in accounting standards, such as financial executives, financial analysts, accounting academics, and the other two major accounting groups in Canada, the Certified General Accountants (CGA) and Certified Management Accountants (CMA). The process of setting standards is fairly elaborate and provides opportunities for interested parties to respond to proposed accounting standards before they are approved and included in the *CICA Handbook*.

However, despite the prominence of the *CICA Handbook*, most of GAAP are not set out in it. Much of GAAP are simply what entities actually do in practice. If an accounting practice is used successfully by an entity, that practice becomes generally accepted. An accounting practice does not have to be widely used to be considered a GAAP, and there can be more than one way of accounting for a particular type of economic event or transaction, all of which can be considered GAAP. (Think back to our discussion of revenue recognition in Chapter 4 and recall the number of acceptable ways that revenue could be recognized.) Some accounting methods are GAAP only in specific industries—a certain accounting treatment might be acceptable in one industry, but not used or generally acceptable in others. And because the world is always changing, accountants and preparers are often faced with new and different transactions and economic events to account for. Accountants and preparers must develop ways of accounting for these. As a result, GAAP are always evolving and changing to meet the changing environment.

Federal and provincial corporations acts and the provincial securities acts require that the financial statements of corporations be filed with the appropriate government and/or regulator, and that the financial statements comply with GAAP. This suggests that all corporations in Canada must comply with GAAP. However, this is not exactly the case. Public companies must follow GAAP. If a public company does not follow GAAP, the securities regulators have the authority to stop the trading of the company's stock. This is a very severe sanction, and as a result public companies follow GAAP.

For private entities the situation is more complicated. While the corporations acts apply to private corporations and require them to provide audited financial statements to their shareholders, the shareholders are entitled to waive this requirement if they agree unanimously to do so. Of course, private corporations can choose to have an audit and to follow GAAP. For example, a private corporation might have an audit and follow GAAP as part of a borrowing agreement with a bank. Partnerships and proprietorships are not covered by any constraints that require them to follow GAAP. Following GAAP is voluntary by these types of entities and the decision to do so will be motivated by the needs of the stakeholders.

However, even when entities do not follow GAAP, they will generally not abandon them entirely. (That would mean inventing an entirely new and different method of accounting.) Rather, these entities are likely to follow some GAAP, but not all. For example, most entities will use historical cost and accrual accounting. Most will do some matching of expenses to revenues. But private companies may choose not to follow GAAP because some of the standards may be too complex and may not help the entity achieve its reporting objectives, or because alternative accounting methods are more appropriate for the information needs of the stakeholders. (For example, if an entity has tax minimization as its primary objective, the entity might use accounting policies that are allowed by the *Income Tax Act*, even if the policies are not consistent with GAAP.) It is worth remembering that most entities in Canada are private. Therefore, most entities in Canada do not *have* to follow GAAP.

Canadian GAAP are not the same as GAAP in other countries. Accounting principles in countries evolve as they do for many reasons, including the economic, political, and social conditions that exist. Because of the close relationship between Canada and the United States, Canadian GAAP have many similarities to U.S. GAAP but are not identical to U.S. GAAP. One of the major differences between accounting in Canada and the U.S. is that Canadian accounting standards place a heavy emphasis on professional judgment, whereas U.S. standards tend to be much more rule-oriented.

www.transcanada.com

Recognizing that there are differences in the GAAP used in different countries helps one understand there is no one right or best way to account. Exhibit 5-1 (page 262) shows a reconciliation between net income from continuing operations as reported in accordance with Canadian GAAP and net income from continuing operations in accordance with U.S. GAAP for TransCanada Pipelines Limited (TCPL).[1] This type of reconciliation is common for companies whose shares are traded on Canadian and U.S. stock exchanges. Continuing operations is a measure of performance of an entity, exclusive of the parts of the business that the entity does not plan to operate in the future. Net income from continuing operations is different in each of the three years under U.S. and Canadian GAAP, sometimes by a fairly large amount. Which measure is right? Probably the best way to answer that question is to say that the amounts shown for Canadian GAAP are acceptable under Canadian GAAP and the amounts shown under U.S. GAAP are acceptable under U.S. GAAP. You cannot say that one is better than the other. They are just different.

www.iasc.org.uk

While accounting principles used in a jurisdiction evolve from conditions in that jurisdiction, the globalization of business makes the development of a single global set of GAAP logical. Having different accounting rules in different countries when many companies are doing business and raising capital in many countries can be inefficient, expensive, and confusing. International Accounting Standards (IAS) are an attempt to redress this problem. IAS are a harmonized set of accounting standards that could be used around the world and are being increasingly accepted worldwide, particularly by securities regulators. IAS are also being used in many countries as the basis for reporting domestically. Because of the increasing importance of IAS, users of accounting information should be aware of them.

The purpose of this chapter is to introduce the underpinnings of GAAP. However, it is crucial that you not look at GAAP as the one, the only, or the best way to account. Despite the usefulness of having a set of guidelines and rules for preparing financial statements, GAAP are not without flaws. To be a sophisticated user of financial information it is necessary to know and understand what GAAP-based information tells you, how it can help you, and what its limitations are.

The World According to GAAP

In this section we will examine three groups of accounting principles that form the essence of GAAP. The three groups of principles are:

1. The basic assumptions.

2. The qualitative characteristics.

3. The measurement conventions.

Exhibit 5-1

TransCanada Pipelines Limited: Net Income Reconciliation Due to Differences Between Canadian and U.S. GAAP

CANADA PIPELINES LIMITED

NOTE 21

Significant Differences Between Canadian and U.S. GAAP

NET INCOME RECONCILIATION

Year ended December 31 (millions of dollars except per share amounts)	2000	1999	1998
Net income from continuing operations as reported in accordance with Canadian GAAP	590	542	463
U.S. GAAP adjustments			
Preferred securities charges[1]	(78)	(82)	(40)
Tax impact of preferred securities charges	34	36	19
Income taxes[2]	–	(15)	–
Tax recoveries from substantively enacted tax rates[3]	(28)	–	–
Gain on early retirement of long-term debt[4]	(15)	–	–
Tax impact on gain on early retirement of long-term debt	2	–	–
Transaction costs of business combination[5]	–	–	(182)
Income from continuing operations in accordance with U.S. GAAP	505	481	260
Net income/(loss) from discontinued operations in accordance with U.S. GAAP[6]	200	(476)	(143)
Income before extraordinary item in accordance with U.S. GAAP	705	5	117
Extraordinary item:			
Gain on early retirement of long-term debt, net of tax	13	–	–
Net income in accordance with U.S. GAAP	718	5	117
Basic and diluted net income/(loss) per share in accordance with U.S. GAAP			
Continuing operations	$ 0.99	$ 0.91	$ 0.45
Discontinued operations	0.42	(1.01)	(0.31)
Extraordinary item	0.03	–	–
	$ 1.44	$ (0.10)	$ 0.14

[1] Under U.S. GAAP, the financial charges related to Preferred Securities are recognized as an expense, rather than dividends.

[2] Under U.S. GAAP, the liability method is used to calculate deferred income taxes and deferred income tax expense is calculated as the net change in the deferred tax asset or liability in the year. Prior to 2000, the deferral method was used under Canadian GAAP.

[3] Under U.S. GAAP, only enacted rates can be used in measuring deferred tax assets and liabilities; use of substantively enacted rates is not permitted. The February 2000 and October 2000 Federal budgets would not be considered enacted until the proposals were completely enacted into law and accordingly the related tax recoveries are not recognized.

[4] Under U.S. GAAP, gain on early retirement of long-term debt is recognized as an extraordinary item, rather than ordinary income from operations.

[5] Under U.S. GAAP, the transaction costs related to the business combination with NOVA are recognized as an expense, rather than a charge to retained earnings.

[6] Net income/(loss) from discontinued operations reconciliation

As you read about these principles, keep in mind the fact that they do not always work in harmony. The principles often conflict, which makes it difficult to develop consistent, coherent solutions to accounting problems. These conflicts help explain how it is possible to have more than one solution to an accounting problem while still being consistent with the accounting principles. One could argue these principles are flawed because they do not provide a consistent basis for resolving accounting issues and problems.

Basic Assumptions of GAAP

There are four basic assumptions that underlie financial reporting under GAAP. We have discussed three of the four assumptions—the unit-of-measure, entity, and periodic-reporting assumptions—in the first four chapters of the book. The fourth basic assumption is the going-concern assumption.

Unit of Measure   The **unit-of-measure assumption** states that the economic activity of an entity can be effectively stated in terms of a single unit of measure. The unit of measure that is almost always used is money, and in Canada the monetary unit used is usually the Canadian dollar. However, some Canadian companies use the U.S. dollar as the unit of measure in their financial statements: Nortel Networks Corporation, Alcan Inc., and Hummingbird Ltd. all report in U.S. dollars. Interestingly, Alcan prepares its financial statements in accordance with Canadian GAAP, and Nortel and Hummingbird prepare one set of financial statements in accordance with U.S. GAAP and another set in accordance with Canadian GAAP.

www.nortelnetworks.com
www.alcan.com
www.hummingbird.com

As we discussed in Chapter 1, there are benefits and drawbacks to using a single unit of measure. The major benefit of using a single unit of measure is that it allows diverse information to be aggregated and summarized. If a single unit of measure were not used, MWW could not calculate total assets because it would not be possible to add together different types of assets such as cash, inventory, and capital assets into a single amount. Similarly, it would not be possible to calculate income.

There are also drawbacks to using a single unit of measure:

- First, the major benefit of using a single unit of measure—the ability to summarize and aggregate information—creates one of the major drawbacks, which is that by stating everything in currency units, considerable information is lost about the individual items being measured. For example, when cost of goods sold is reported as a single dollar amount on the income statement, it is not possible to tell the quantity or type of inventory that was sold.

- Second, by measuring in terms of Canadian dollars, characteristics of an entity that are not easily measured in terms of dollars are not accounted for. For example, intellectual and human capital and social costs are typically not reported in GAAP financial statements.

As a result of these drawbacks, financial accounting measures for an entity prepared in accordance with GAAP cannot be comprehensive.

Another drawback to using a single unit of measure is the fact that the unit of measure required under Canadian GAAP is not simply the Canadian dollar, it is the *nominal* Canadian dollar. The term nominal dollar means that no consideration is given to the fact that the purchasing power of a dollar changes over time. If you went grocery shopping with $100 in 1980 you came home with a lot more groceries than if you went shopping with $100 in 2002. A 1980 dollar bought a lot more groceries than a 2002 dollar because the prices of goods in the economy generally increased between 1980 and 2002. This does not mean that the price of everything increased between 1980 and 2002, just that the average price of goods and services increased. However, Canadian GAAP ignore the changing purchasing power of the dollar over time.

A related problem exists with the Canadian dollar in relation to other currencies. For example, the amount of U.S. dollars that a Canadian dollar can buy at any moment in time is always changing with the exchange rate. We will examine these issues in more depth in Chapter 7.

Entity   Accounting systems are designed to provide information about some defined entity. When providing information about an entity, it is necessary to exclude transactions and economic events that do not pertain to that entity from the accounting records and the financial statements. This assumption is not as straightforward as it may seem. It is very common, especially in proprietorships and private corporations, for personal transactions of the owners to be intermingled with the entity's business activities. In some cases it is very difficult to determine whether an expense is a personal expense or a business expense, and in those circumstances the shareholder or proprietor might make choices that serve his or her self-interests rather than the "right" accounting choice.

Consider the following situation. If a business is run from the home of the shareholder or proprietor, how are the operating expenses of the home allocated between business and personal? For tax purposes it might be desirable to expense as much as is legitimately possible to minimize the amount of tax that must be paid. For a prospective investor in such a business, the financial statements may not provide information that is representative of the economic activity of the entity itself. To have valid measurements of the entity's activities, it is appropriate to exclude the transactions of other entities from the financial statements. Users of financial statements need to be very wary of the possibility that transactions that do not belong to the entity are included in the statements.

An accounting entity does not have to be a separate legal entity. Partnerships and proprietorships are legitimate economic entities for accounting purposes, but they are not separate legal entities. Partnerships and proprietorships are simply extensions of the partners or proprietor. In general, an entity is any economic unit that is of interest to a stakeholder. What is crucial is that the economic activities that do not belong to the entity are excluded or adjusted for in the financial statements.

Going Concern   In popular language, a going concern is a person or business that is active and thriving. In accounting, a **going concern** is an entity that will be continuing its operations for the foreseeable future. GAAP accounting assumes that, absent information to the contrary, an entity operates as a going concern. This means that under GAAP an entity is expected to complete its current plans, use its existing assets, and meet its obligations in the normal course of business. For MWW operating as a going concern means that it will sell its inventory, collect its receivables, use up its capital assets for the purpose they were acquired, and settle its liabilities as they come due.

If the going-concern assumption does not apply—for example, because an entity is going out of business or because an entity was formed as a short-term venture, such as a summer business set up by a student—then it is not appropriate to use historical cost as the basis for valuing assets and liabilities. In other words, if an entity cannot be considered a going concern, then the primary valuation method used in GAAP accounting—historical cost—is invalid and should not be used. If an entity cannot be considered a going concern, then assets and liabilities should be valued on a liquidation basis: assets at the amount that will be received from their immediate sale and liabilities at the amount that will be required to settle them immediately. The reason for this treatment is that if an entity is closing down, it can be assumed that its assets will be disposed of and liabilities will be settled in a relatively short period of time, rather than used in the operation of the entity.

Similarly, the classification of assets and liabilities as current and non-current is not meaningful if an entity is not a going concern because the entity will not exist beyond the short term. The going-concern assumption is also the reason that capital assets are amortized over their useful lives. If an entity is not a going concern, amortization does not make sense because assets are amortized to match the cost of the assets to the revenue they generate. More likely, these assets will be sold and not used for the purpose for which they were originally purchased.

An interesting problem that accountants sometimes face is deciding when the going-concern assumption no longer applies. There is always some probability that an entity will go out of business. The question is, when should the basis of valuation used in the financial statements be changed to a liquidation basis to reflect that an entity is no longer a going concern? It is not easy to decide when the going-concern assumption is no longer valid. Waiting until the entity is actually out of business is too late in the process to provide useful information to stakeholders. Making the decision too early can even push a struggling entity "over the brink" and out of business if stakeholders such as creditors see the financial statements prepared on a liquidation basis and in response take steps to protect their own interests.

Periodic Reporting   The **periodic-reporting assumption** states that meaningful financial information about an entity can be provided for periods of time that are shorter than the life of an entity. In Chapter 3 we saw that one of the major reasons why working with accounting information can be tricky is that financial statements have to be prepared periodically through the life of an entity. Accounting would be much easier if it was only necessary for an entity to prepare financial information once—at the end of its life.

At the end of an entity's life everything about the entity's activities is known with certainty and there are no decisions or estimates to make about when to record and how much to record of assets, liabilities, revenues, and expenses. The problem with waiting until the end of an entity's life is that stakeholders need information for making decisions more frequently and more regularly. Waiting until the end of some entities' lives can be a long time. Molson's Breweries, now a subsidiary of The Molson Companies Limited, was founded in 1786; The Hudson's Bay Company was founded in 1670. While these are extreme examples, they highlight the fact that an entity's life can be very long. It is unlikely that governments would be willing to wait for centuries to collect income taxes from these entities!

To provide necessary information to stakeholders frequently and regularly, financial statements are prepared more often than at the end of an entity's life. At a minimum, financial statements are prepared annually, although it is common for entities to produce financial statements more often than that. Some stakeholders, such as banks, may require statements monthly or quarterly as part of a loan agreement, and some stock exchanges and securities commissions require quarterly reports from public companies.

Providing information to stakeholders frequently and regularly is crucial for the efficient operation of the economy. Stakeholders need and want up-to-date information to allow them to make the best possible decisions. However, reporting periodically instead of at the end of an entity's life has many problems. Once the life of an entity is broken down into small pieces, there can be difficulty determining in which periods revenues and expenses should be reported. We saw in Chapter 4 that there are many different legitimate ways to recognize revenue. Using alternative revenue recognition methods and points results in different measurements of revenues, expenses, assets, and liabilities in a given period. The underlying economic activity is not affected by the different choices, but the representation of that economic activity in financial statements can differ significantly. In addition, the shorter the time period that an entity reports on, the more difficult are the problems of allocating expenses and revenues among periods. As we pointed out in Chapter 3, the requirement to report periodically over the life of an entity is at the heart of most accounting problems and controversies.

> ## Question for Consideration
>
> Identify and briefly explain the four basic assumptions that underlie GAAP.
>   Answer:
> 1. *Unit-of-measure:* The economic activity of an entity can be effectively stated in terms of a single unit of measure. The unit of measure that is almost always used is money, and in Canada the monetary unit used is usually the Canadian dollar.
> 2. *Entity:* An economic unit being reported on. Information about an entity should exclude transactions and economic events that do not pertain to the entity, such as personal transactions by the owners of the entity.
> 3. *Going concern:* An entity is expected to continue its operations for the foreseeable future such that it will be able to complete its current plans, use its existing assets, and meet its obligations in the normal course of business.
> 4. *Periodic reporting:* Meaningful financial information about an entity can be provided for periods of time that are shorter than the life of an entity.

Qualitative Characteristics

Chapter 1 of the book introduced the four qualitative characteristics that the *CICA Handbook* states financial information should have if it is to be useful to users. The four characteristics are understandability, comparability, relevance, and reliability. Let's review these characteristics in more detail.

Understandability   Imagine having to study from a textbook written in a language you do not understand very well or at all. It would be virtually impossible for you to learn anything from the book. The same difficulties apply to working with accounting, the language of business. Users must be able to understand the information presented to them in financial statements if it is to be useful to them for making decisions. Understandability does not mean that information must be presented simply enough for the most unsophisticated user to understand. The *CICA Handbook* states that accounting information should be understandable to users who have a reasonable understanding of business and accounting, and a willingness to study the information provided, and if they do not, it is assumed that they will obtain advice.

Targeting accounting information at moderately sophisticated users is a choice made by standard setters. There is no compelling reason that moderately sophisticated users represent the appropriate audience for accounting information. It is simply the choice the standard setters made when formalizing their framework. What is important about the choice is that it has implications for the nature and sophistication of the information that is presented in accordance with GAAP. If information were targeted at the least sophisticated users, financial statements would have to be much simpler than they are now, but they would have a wider audience. If accounting information were targeted at the most sophisticated users (financial analysts, mutual fund and pension fund managers, accountants, and other experts) the financial statements could be much more detailed and sophisticated, but many people who might have an interest in examining financial statements would be excluded and forced to rely more on experts for their information.

Comparability   Accounting information is very difficult to evaluate in absolute terms. An entity's revenue, net income, current ratio or debt-to-equity ratio, assets, or any other accounting measurement for a single period are very difficult to interpret without a benchmark or basis of comparison. Broadly, there are two types of comparisons that users can make:

1. An entity's accounting numbers can be compared with the accounting numbers of other similar entities.

2. The entity's numbers can be compared with its own accounting numbers from previous years.

Comparisons are easier to make if the similar entities being compared use the same accounting methods and if the entity itself uses the same accounting methods every year. If different accounting methods are used, it is difficult to know whether differences in the numbers are due to real economic differences or to the different accounting methods. If preparers change the accounting practices each year, it is impossible to draw sensible inferences from any patterns that are observed. Accountants often use the term **consistency** to describe the use by an entity of the same accounting policies from period to period.

Ensuring that financial statements are consistent and comparable is a worthwhile goal in principle. In practice, however, there are many problems and concerns with achieving comparability. As we have discussed, GAAP frequently provide legitimate alternative accounting treatments for certain types of transactions. Preparers can choose among the acceptable alternatives without constraint. In a way, GAAP undermine comparability by allowing alternatives. As a result, one must use a great deal of caution when comparing the financial information of different entities. If entities do not have the same set of constraints, facts, and objectives, then it is not reasonable to expect that the entities will use the same accounting methods.

GAAP provide some protection for users by requiring entities to disclose the accounting policies they choose. This disclosure allows users to assess whether comparable accounting policies are being used. However, the disclosure of the accounting policies being used does not tell users what the accounting numbers would be using different accounting policies. And while GAAP require that entities disclose the accounting policies that they use, GAAP do not require entities to disclose much information about the estimates they make. (For example, an entity does not have to disclose the amount of its accounts receivable it does not expect to collect.) Differences between entities in the estimates they make can have a significant effect on accounting numbers the entities report and can make comparisons difficult, especially since it can be very difficult for users to determine the existence and extent of the differences.

A dramatic example of the difficulty in comparing financial statements can be seen in the way Canada's major banks accounted for the costs of their proposed mergers. In 1998 mergers were proposed between the Bank of Montreal and the Royal Bank, and between CIBC and TD Bank. Paul Martin, then Canada's minister of finance, rejected the mergers in December 1998. The banks incurred significant costs in trying to bring about these mergers. The merging banks were very similar, and since the costs related to the same transaction, one would expect the facts to be the same for each bank. Yet the banks accounted for the merger costs differently:

- The Bank of Montreal did not reflect its merger costs in the income statement at all. Instead, it reduced retained earnings in fiscal 1999 by the amount of the costs incurred for the merger, after the proposed mergers were rejected.

- The Royal Bank expensed all its merger costs when the merger was rejected in December 1998. The full effect of the merger costs was reflected in its income statement for the year ended October 31, 1999.

- CIBC and TD Bank expensed their merger costs when they were incurred. Some of the costs were reflected in these banks' income statements for the year ended October 31, 1998 and some of the costs were reflected in the income statements for the year ended October 31, 1999.

Figure 5-1

Accounting for Proposed
Canadian Bank Mergers Costs:
Effects on Income Statements

	Effect on the Income Statement	
	Fiscal 1998*	**Fiscal 1999***
Bank of Montreal	No effect	No effect
Royal Bank	No effect	Expense all costs associated with the proposed merger
TD Bank/CIBC	Expense costs incurred during the year	Expense costs incurred during the year

*Note that all the banks have October 31 year ends.

As a result of the different methods used by the banks for accounting for the merger costs, the financial statements of the banks cannot be compared straight up. The effects of the different accounting methods are summarized in Figure 5-1.

Consistency is easier to achieve than comparability between entities, and GAAP provide some protection to users from arbitrary changes in accounting policies. GAAP do not allow entities to change accounting policies without good reason. According to the *CICA Handbook*, a change in accounting policy must result in a more appropriate presentation of events or transactions in the financial statements. However, it is usually not very difficult for the preparers to come up with a good reason for an accounting change.

When a change in policy is made, the change must be disclosed, the effect of the change on the current period must be disclosed, and the effects of the change must be made *retroactively*. Making the change retroactively means that the entity has to present its financial statements for previous years as if it had been using the new accounting policy all along. For example, if MWW changed the way it accounted for its inventory in its 2001 financial statements, the financial statements for 2000 and 1999 that are included in the 2001 annual report for comparative purposes would have been restated to reflect the new accounting policy for inventory. In that situation, if you compared relevant 2000 financial statement numbers, as reported in the 2001 annual report, with the 2000 numbers, as reported in the 2000 annual report, the numbers would be different.

Retroactive restatement of financial statements is only done when an accounting policy is changed. Use of a different accounting policy for transactions that arise from different circumstances does not represent a change in an accounting policy. It is simply the selection of an accounting policy that is appropriate, given the facts surrounding the transaction. For example, consider an entity that has historically recognized its revenue when merchandise is delivered to customers. If the entity changes its business practices such that it is now taking on customers that are higher credit risks, the entity could legitimately recognize revenue from the new customers when cash is collected. This would not be considered a change in accounting policy.

Unlike a change in an accounting policy, a change in an accounting estimate is done *prospectively*. A prospective change means that the change is applied to the current year's financial statement and then in future years. Previous years' statements are not restated. Remember that a change in an accounting estimate does not have to be disclosed. If an entity changes an estimate, the financial statements may not be consistent and users may not be aware of the fact.

Relevance   It should be self-evident that accounting information must be relevant to the people who use it. If accounting information is not relevant, then what is the point of producing it? Relevant information is defined as information that is useful for the decisions a stakeholder has to make—information that will influence the stakeholder's decisions. This is a general definition. As a practical matter, the objectives of financial statements that are stated in the *CICA Handbook* (and, therefore, a part of GAAP) make the qualitative characteristic of relevance somewhat self-limiting.

The *CICA Handbook* narrows the focus of financial reporting of for-profit organizations to primarily present and potential debt and equity investors. The *CICA Handbook* goes on to state that debt and equity investors are interested in predicting an entity's ability to earn income and generate cash flows. Indeed, the *CICA Handbook* is explicit that it is not practical for financial statements to satisfy all the information needs of all users. The limitations imposed on financial reporting under GAAP may be realistic, reasonable, and practical. However, the limitations highlight the importance of recognizing that the relevance of financial reporting is not universal: GAAP financial statements are not designed to be relevant for all uses and to all users.

The *CICA Handbook* adds three characteristics that contribute to the relevance of information: predictive value, feedback value, and timeliness. These characteristics are distinguished as follows:

- *Predictive value:* As mentioned above, prediction of future earnings and future cash flows is an important use for financial statements. Many decisions that stakeholders make involve predicting the future. For example, lenders want to estimate future cash flows to determine whether an entity will be able to meet the repayment schedule required by a loan. Equity investors often want to predict future earnings as a basis for predicting the future stock price of public companies.

  Curiously, despite the stated importance of prediction, GAAP are decidedly backward-looking. GAAP financial statements focus on reporting transactions and economic events that have happened, not those that will happen. GAAP financial statements are useful for prediction because they can be used as a benchmark for predicting the future. Users are expected to begin with previous periods' financial statement information. By incorporating future-oriented information from other sources and by making assumptions, they can then make the predictions they require.

  This approach can be difficult and can require a great deal of sophistication by the users. For entities that are relatively stable and established the approach can probably be used effectively. However, for new entities and for entities that are subject to significant change, such as high-technology companies, Internet companies, and high-growth companies, the task can be exceedingly difficult because historical financial statements may not be a reasonable basis upon which to predict the future. Also, it is important to remember that the preparers of the financial statement information often have incentives to pursue their self-interests, which may make it more difficult to make predictions.

- *Feedback value:* When users make predictions, they require information that allows them to evaluate their predictions and to revise, update, correct, and adjust them. GAAP-based accounting is reasonably well suited for providing feedback because it presents the results of what happened. Financial analysts spend a lot of their time making estimates of what entities' future earnings will be. When an entity's actual earnings are released, comparisons are made between the actual earnings reported and the forecasts. If an entity's actual earnings are less than what is forecast, the stock price will often fall in response. This example shows how GAAP financial statements can be used to provide feedback on predictions made by analysts, and how the market responds to this feedback. (Remember, financial analysts only pay attention to publicly traded companies. The earnings of private companies are not made public and there is not the wide public interest in private companies that there is in public companies.)

- *Timeliness:* For information to be useful for decision making it must be available to stakeholders in time to influence their decisions. Information that does not arrive on a timely basis will have little impact on decision making. Some people argue that financial statements provided by entities are not timely. For example, MWW's 2001 fiscal year end was January 27, but its financial statements were not made available to the public until May 2001. (This long time lag is not unique to MWW. Most public companies have a similar lag.) One can question the timeliness and usefulness of information that arrives in the hands of stakeholders more than three months after the year end. This is especially true for businesses of the new economy—that is, knowledge-based industries—where change takes place very quickly.

Reliability   For information to be useful to users, it must provide a reasonable representation of what it is intended to measure. The *CICA Handbook* identifies the components of reliability as verifiability, representational faithfulness, and neutrality (freedom from bias). Let's examine these components more closely.

- *Verifiability:* Information is verifiable if independent and knowledgeable observers can come up with the same results for the measurement of an attribute. If a group of people were asked to measure the physical dimensions of a room, it is likely that each person would come up with approximately the same result. There might be some variation among the people, but it is reasonable to expect that the measurements would be very similar. Measurement of the dimensions of the room would be considered verifiable and therefore reliable. Now suppose the same group of people were asked to rate the attractiveness of the room. It is likely that the individuals in the group would have fairly diverse ratings of the room's attractiveness. The measurements of attractiveness are not as easily verified and therefore less reliable than the measurements of the dimensions of the room.

  In an accounting context, historical cost, transaction-based information is quite verifiable. Because financial statement amounts can be traced back to documents that underlie a transaction, the amounts are relatively easy to verify. For example, the amount paid for inventory can be traced to the invoice sent by the supplier. While there can be some variation in the amount that different people would come up with, the variation would normally fall within a narrow range. In contrast, measures of financial statement elements that are not supported by transactions would have much more variation, since the amounts would be based on individual judgments rather than observations of what actually took place. Verifiability is one of the main reasons why historical cost is the primary method of valuation used under GAAP.

- *Representational faithfulness:* If you examine a map of Canada, you expect the provincial boundaries and the locations of cities and towns on the map to be an accurate reflection of where the boundaries and the cities and towns are in fact. Representational faithfulness refers to the association between underlying information being represented (the actual locations of boundaries and communities) and the representation of that information (the map). Financial statements are a representation of the underlying economic activity of an entity. If the statements are to be representationally faithful, then they must capture the economic activity of an entity. This means that all the assets, liabilities, revenues, and expenses must be reflected in the statements.

  As we discussed in Chapter 2, all of an entity's assets are not reflected on a GAAP balance sheet. For example, the brand name that MWW has developed over the years is not reflected on its balance sheet. For some entities the brand name is its most valuable asset, yet traditional GAAP accounting does not reflect this asset. In our map analogy this would be equivalent to not showing the capital city of each province on the map. The difficulty of verifying the amount that should be reported for the MWW brand makes accounting for the brand inappropriate under GAAP. Curiously, problems with one dimension of reliability (verifiability) make it difficult to achieve another dimension of reliability (representational faithfulness)

- *Neutrality or freedom from bias:* Information is neutral or free from bias if it is not presented in a way that is designed to influence or manipulate users' decisions. This characteristic seems to be inconsistent with the objectives of financial reporting that we discussed in Chapter 4. The discussion in Chapter 4 stated that preparers of accounting information can often select accounting methods that allow them to achieve their objectives of accounting—objectives that can be in the self-interests of the preparers rather than in the interests of stakeholders. In contrast, neutrality suggests that accounting information should be presented in a way that does not serve any of the preparers' objectives. While neutrality is a worthwhile characteristic to have, evidence from research and casual observation of events reported in the popular press strongly suggest that preparers do use the accounting choices available to them to pursue their objectives.

  Neutrality is sometimes misinterpreted to mean that accounting information should have no effect on the decisions that users make. If this were the case, there would be no point in preparing accounting information because it would not serve a useful purpose: it would not have an impact on users' decisions. For information to be useful to a decision maker, it must have the possibility of influencing decisions.

Relevance versus Reliability: A Conflict   Both relevance and reliability are necessary if information is truly going to be useful to users. Information that is relevant but not reliable—meaning that users cannot be confident that the measurement being provided is a reasonable representation of the underlying economic activity—is not going to be useful to users. Similarly, information that is reliable but not

---

Question for Consideration

Identify and briefly explain the four qualitative characteristics that, according to the *CICA Handbook* and GAAP, accounting information should have if it is to be useful to users.

Answer:

1. *Understandability:* Users must be able to understand accounting information if it is to be useful to them. The *CICA Handbook* states that financial information should be understandable to users who have a reasonable understanding of business and accounting, and a willingness to study the information provided, and if they do not, it is assumed that they will obtain advice.

2. *Comparability:* Users should be able to compare the accounting information provided by different entities and the information of a particular entity from period to period. Comparability requires that the entities being compared use the same accounting methods for the same transactions and economic events, and that an entity use the same accounting methods from period to period.

3. *Relevance:* Accounting information is relevant if it is useful to users for making decisions. According to the *CICA Handbook* and GAAP, relevant information must help users—debt and equity investors in particular—predict the future performance of an entity (predictive value), allow users to evaluate their predictions and to revise, update, correct, and adjust them (feedback value), and arrive in time to be useful for making decisions (timeliness).

4. *Reliability:* Accounting information is reliable if it can be verified by independent and knowledgeable observers (verifiability), if it provides a reasonable representation of the underlying economic activity (representational faithfulness), and if it is not presented in a way that is intended to influence or manipulate users' decisions (neutrality/freedom from bias).

relevant—meaning that users can have confidence in the measurement, but the measurement is not appropriate for the decision being made—is not going to be useful to users. Ideally, all information that is provided to stakeholders should be both relevant and reliable. Unfortunately, in many situations this is not possible and as a result a trade-off occurs between these crucial characteristics. The information that is most relevant for a decision may be less reliable than other information or may even be unreliable. The most reliable information may not be relevant.

If users were free to choose the information they receive from entities, they could deal with this trade-off in a way they deemed appropriate. However, most users are not able to specify the information they want from an entity. Most users have to rely on the general purpose financial statements for their information. That is why GAAP are so important. GAAP help define the information that is provided in general purpose financial statements and therefore define how the trade-off between relevance and reliability is resolved. GAAP accounting tends to favour reliability over relevance. For example, GAAP use historical costs as the primary measurement method, even though it is widely acknowledged that for many decisions historical cost information is not very relevant.

Consider a lender who has been asked to make a large loan to a new borrower. Lenders are generally very cautious and they will often ask for insurance in the event that the borrower cannot repay the loan. The insurance takes the form of **collateral**. Collateral is assets that are pledged by a borrower and that are turned over to the lender if the borrower is unable to repay the loan. One of the concerns a lender will have is the value of the collateral that the borrower can offer. When we talk of "value of the collateral", we are interested in the market value of the collateral if and when the bank has to sell it. Of course, it is very difficult to project if and when it will be necessary to sell the collateral, and very difficult to determine what the collateral could be sold for at that time. So what information would satisfy the needs of the lender on the date the loan is made?

Figure 5-2 shows how different pieces of information reflect the relevance-reliability trade-off in the context of a lender's evaluation of collateral. Figure 5-2 shows that information can be considered to have low or high relevance and low or high reliability. Information that is in the top-right quadrant is best because it is both highly relevant and highly reliable. The market value of publicly traded shares fits into this quadrant for a lender because the current value of the shares provides the most current information about the market value of the collateral (the amount of cash that would be received in the event the loan is not paid). The information is reliable because the current market value of a share of a public company as set by a stock market is representationally faithful, verifiable, and neutral.

The most interesting quadrants are the lower-right and the upper-left quadrants because this is where we see the trade-offs. The information in the lower-right quadrant is relevant because the market value of real estate gives the lender an idea of what the real estate could raise in cash if sold today. The problem with determining the market value of real estate without actually selling it is that the information can be very unreliable. After all, how sure can you be about the selling price of a building, unless it is sold? In contrast, the information in the upper-left quadrant is highly reliable because the cost of the real estate is fairly easy to check by examining the documents supporting the original purchase of the real estate. But it is unlikely that the historical cost of real estate is relevant to the lender, especially if the real estate was purchased a long time ago. Historical cost tells the lender very little about the amount the real estate could be sold for today or in the future.

Information that is in the lower-left quadrant is of little interest because it is not relevant or reliable. A stakeholder would not be interested in the information at all. For example, the current market value of real estate that is secured to another creditor

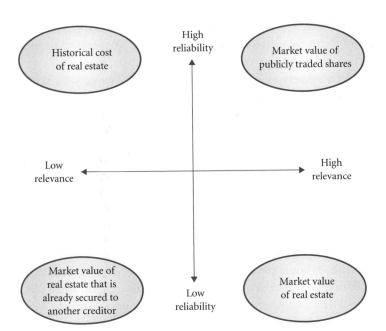

Figure 5-2

The Relevance-Reliability Trade-Off

could be placed in this quadrant. Real estate that is secured to another creditor has little relevance to our lender because the proceeds of sale would go to the other creditor. The market value of real estate has low reliability because it is difficult to estimate what it could be sold for.

Measurement Conventions

With the assumptions and qualitative characteristics underlying GAAP described, we can now examine the conventions that define the measurements that are recorded in an accounting system and the amounts that are reported in the financial statements. Ultimately, accounting is about measurement. GAAP have a number of conventions that help determine the amounts that are reported in the financial statements.

Valuation   There are many different ways that assets and liabilities can be valued. These methods include historical cost, replacement cost, net realizable value, and present value of future cash flows. While historical cost is the primary valuation method used in GAAP financial statements, the other methods are also used and are generally

Question for Consideration

Which characteristic is more valuable in financial statements: relevance or reliability?

Answer: This question does not have an answer. Both characteristics are important for information in financial statements and ideally all financial statement information should be both relevant and reliable. Unfortunately, there is often a trade-off between these two characteristics. If a user must use GAAP-based general purpose financial statements, then the trade-off is resolved by the preparers' choices and by the GAAP constraint. However, if a user had the ability to obtain the information he or she desired, the decision would be a personal one. To the extent that a user had to choose between relevance and reliability, some users and uses would find more relevance at the expense of less reliability more valuable (perhaps an estimate of the market value of real estate rather than the real estate's historical cost). Other users and uses might find reliability more valuable (for example, reliable information might be considered more appropriate by some users for purposes of evaluating how well the managers have done managing the entity).

accepted in some situations. We will first look at the secondary valuation methods of GAAP—replacement cost, net realizable value, and present value of future cash flows—and then discuss historical cost.

The **replacement cost** of an asset is the current price that would have to be paid to purchase an identical or equivalent asset. Replacement cost is a market-value measure, not a historical measure. Under certain circumstances replacement cost can be used under GAAP for reporting inventory on the balance sheet. Normally, inventory is reported at its cost—the price paid to purchase the inventory. However, if the market value of inventory is less than its cost, then the inventory is reported on the balance sheet at its replacement cost instead of its historical cost. (In fact, preparers can choose from a number of methods of estimating the market value of inventory, of which replacement cost is one.) This approach to valuing inventory is known as the lower of cost and market rule, and it is an application of the conservatism principle. The lower of cost and market rule (LCM) will be discussed in detail in Chapter 8.

Net realizable value is the amount of cash that is expected to be received from the sale or realization of an asset, after taking into consideration any additional costs. Accounts receivable are normally valued at their net realizable value on an entity's balance sheet. Under GAAP an entity reduces the actual amount that customers have promised to pay by an estimate of the amount of those receivables that are not expected to be collected. Thus the amount that appears on the balance sheet will be an estimate of the amount of cash that will actually be collected or realized. Net realizable value is also one of the methods used to estimate the market value of inventory when using the lower of cost and market rule. Net realizable value is also used to value assets and liabilities when the going-concern assumption is deemed not to apply.

The present value of future cash flows represents the amount of cash that would be paid today for cash flows that will be received in the future. We will discuss the present value method in detail in Chapter 7, but for now what you need to understand is that money today is worth more than money that will be received in the future. One situation that uses present valuing under GAAP is when an entity has an account receivable that will be collected in more than a year. If the receivable does not require that interest be paid or if the interest rate is not the market rate, the present value method is used to determine the amount that will be reported on the balance sheet for the receivable. Similarly, liabilities issued at interest rates that are different from the prevailing market rate on the date the debt is issued are adjusted using the present value method.

Historical cost or the transaction cost is the primary method used to measure financial statement elements under GAAP. **Historical cost** requires that transactions and economic events be valued in the financial statements at the actual dollar amounts involved when the transaction or economic event took place. For example, if MWW purchases new display cases for its stores for $100,000, the display cases will be reported on MWW's balance sheet at $100,000. The $100,000 becomes the permanent valuation amount for the display cases, and under ordinary circumstance it does not change. The display cases will be amortized over their useful lives so that costs can be matched to revenues. However, amortization under GAAP is simply the allocation of the cost of an asset to expense over time. The amount that is amortized under GAAP is only affected by the cost of the asset, its useful life, and the method used to amortize. Market value of an asset has no bearing on amortization.

The dominance of historical cost emerges from the assumptions and qualitative characteristics described earlier in this chapter. Historical cost is consistent with *reliability*. In almost all situations, the historical cost of an asset, liability, revenue, or expense is at least as reliable as any of the other possible alternatives. The terms of most transactions and economic events are usually easily determined at the time they occur and these terms can usually be readily verified. Other possible measures can be difficult to determine and verify. For example, determining the replacement cost or net realizable value of an old building can be difficult and is certainly less reliable than determining what the building cost. The use of historical cost in GAAP accounting indicates that the frequently occurring trade-off between reliability and relevance is often resolved in favour of reliability. Historical cost is the primary measurement method used under GAAP despite the limited usefulness of the measure for many users and uses of accounting information.

Historical cost is also consistent with the going-concern assumption. Recall that under the going-concern assumption it is assumed that an entity will continue its operations for the foreseeable future—long enough to carry out its current plans, use its assets, and meet its obligations. Therefore, according to GAAP, market value estimates of financial statement elements are not necessary because assets will be used up in the ordinary course of business and liabilities will be settled. This means that the cost of assets can be expensed as they are used up so that income can be determined.

Tax requirements also provide a practical reason for using historical cost for financial reporting in Canada. In most cases income for tax purposes requires a transaction (something has to be sold) and the amount of income is the amount received, less the costs incurred. For example, if a taxpayer purchases shares in a company for $10 per share, no income is reported for tax purposes until the shares are sold, regardless of any changes in the market value of the shares year to year. If the taxpayer sells the shares several years later for $25 per share, the amount of income reported is $15 per share ($25 − $10). If the shares pay dividends, the taxpayer would have to declare the dividends as income in the year received. Since the tax system is based on transactions and historical costs, an accounting system based on that approach makes sense.

Determining cost can sometimes be surprisingly difficult. Consider the example of MWW, where the cost of inventory at first glance seems quite straightforward. Suppose MWW orders a shipment of winter coats for $75,000 from an Asian manufacturer. The cost of the coats is "obviously" $75,000. Or is it so obvious? There are other costs that are required to make the coats available for sale. The coats must be shipped from Asia to MWW's distribution centre in Canada. There may be import duties. The coats must then be sent to MWW's stores across Canada. Since the goods are produced in a foreign country, there are potential costs involved in paying the producer in a currency other than Canadian dollars. There are also the costs of handling the goods when they are delivered to the individual stores. Store employees must unpack, check, and display the merchandise.

All of these costs can be considered costs of the MWW inventory. But will all of the costs be included in the cost of inventory? Not necessarily. Recall our discussion of period and product costs in Chapter 4. It can be difficult to attach some costs to the inventory and it is common to simply treat difficult-to-attach costs as period costs. What makes the situation most difficult from a user's standpoint is that different entities may treat similar types of costs differently. This makes comparability difficult to achieve.

We could give many more examples of the difficulty that exists in determining cost. The issue in each example would be essentially the same: Which costs, in the case of assets, are treated as period costs and which are treated as product costs?

Full Disclosure   For financial statements to fulfil their objective of providing relevant information to users, the statements must include all relevant information about the economic activities of the entity. The principle that financial statements should provide this information is known as **full disclosure**. In reality, financial statements do not provide all the information users require. Some of the information that users might want would represent deviations from GAAP. For example, some users might find cash flow forecasts useful. Some information might be inappropriate to disclose outside the entity for competitive reasons. Other information might be too voluminous to include in a traditional set of financial statements and would thereby violate the understandability criterion.

Thus once again GAAP come with a practical constraint. In principle it is certainly desirable for users to receive all relevant information, but in practice there are limits. However, the information in the financial statements should be adequate so as not to mislead users. Under GAAP certain disclosures are explicitly required, while in other cases the preparers must use their judgment when deciding if there should be disclosure of certain information and how that information should be disclosed.

Information can be disclosed in financial statements in a number of ways:

1. Quantified information can be incorporated into the financial statements without further explanation. For example, MWW shows its accounts payable and accrued liabilities on the balance sheet, with no additional explanation. What you see on the balance sheet is all you get.

2. Quantified information can be incorporated into the financial statements but the information can be segregated in a way that provides additional information about the particular item. For example, MWW provides a separate line in its 1999 income statement for the provision for closing its U.S. pilot stores. This separate disclosure gives users useful information for predicting future earnings (because the provision would not be necessary in future years) and for evaluating the performance of MWW.

3. Quantified information can be incorporated into the financial statements and supplementary information can be provided in the notes. Many of the items in MWW's financial statements reference specific notes. For example, long-term debt on the balance sheet refers the reader to Note 10, which provides information about the type, maturity, interest rate, and other information about MWW's long-term debt. (See pages A-45 and A-55).

4. Information may be provided only in the notes to the financial statements without being included in the financial statements themselves. Note 19 (page A-64) provides information to users about events that took place after MWW's year end—information that is not included in the financial statements themselves, but is considered relevant to stakeholders.

It can matter whether information is disclosed only in the notes to the financial statements or reflected in the statements themselves. Measurement is important if financial statement numbers are used to determine an outcome—for example, managers' bonuses, the selling price of a business, whether a borrower has met the terms of a loan agreement (such as a minimum current ratio), or the amount of tax that should be paid. Whether an economic event is disclosed in the notes or measured and incorporated in the financial statements will affect the financial statement numbers and may thereby have an economic impact on the entity and its stakeholders.

For highly sophisticated users of accounting information and for the capital markets, how the information is incorporated into the financial statement package is less important than whether it is incorporated. Sophisticated users can readily take information from various sources, including the financial statements and the notes, and organize it in ways that are appropriate for their decisions. How securities are priced on the capital markets, such as the Toronto Stock Exchange, is captured by a theory known as the Efficient Market Hypothesis.

The **Efficient Market Hypothesis** (EMH) states that all publicly available information is reflected quickly in the price of publicly traded securities such as stocks and bonds. According to the EMH, it does not make any difference how information is made available to the public. The information can be included in the financial statements, in the notes to the financial statements, or in some other way, such as a press release (an official statement the entity releases to the news media). It is important to emphasize that the EMH only applies to the prices set for publicly traded securities in the capital markets. The EMH is not relevant for purposes of setting the prices of the securities of private companies, or for outcomes that are dependent on actual financial statement numbers.

Recognition We explored revenue recognition in depth in Chapter 4. Revenue recognition represents the point when a sale transaction is recorded and is the first step in the process of determining income. The term **recognition** alone has a more general meaning in accounting. It refers to when any financial statement element—asset, liability, equity, expense or revenue—is entered into the accounting system and reported in the financial statements. Disclosing information in the notes to the financial statements is not recognition. Recognition only occurs when an item is included in the financial statements.

Matching Matching was also explored in Chapter 4. Recall that income is a measure of how the wealth of the owners of an entity has changed over a period of time. Under GAAP, matching is the process of associating costs (based on the historical costs) with the revenue the costs help generate so that income can be determined. Like many other of the principles discussed in this chapter, matching makes sense, at least for some objectives of accounting, and it is certainly consistent with the objectives of GAAP accounting as stated in the *CICA Handbook*. However, there are many practical problems with matching that are important to understand if GAAP financial statements are to be understood.

The process of matching means that expenditures are not reported as expenses until the expenditures have contributed to the generation of revenue. For some costs it is straightforward to determine when an expense should be recorded. For example, when MWW sells articles of clothing and the revenue is recognized, the cost of the clothing sold is expensed and matched to the revenue in the period in which the revenue is recognized. As long as the inventory is unsold, it is accounted for as an asset and is not expensed. As long as there is a clear link between the revenue and the costs, there is no problem with matching.

Matching the cost of capital assets to revenues is more problematic. Clearly, capital assets contribute to the generation of revenue, and they do so over a number of periods, so it makes sense that the cost of capital assets should be expensed over the life of the assets. This gives rise to amortization. The problem is, how should the cost of a capital asset be expensed? It is not possible to definitively show that one way of amortization results in better matching than another way. As a result, the amount that is amortized in a given period can be thought of as being somewhat arbitrary. However, how the cost of a capital asset is amortized will affect the amount of amortization and income that is reported in a period.

Another difficulty with matching is the problem of costs that are difficult to clearly associate with revenue. An entity incurs many costs that are difficult to associate with particular revenues, although the costs are likely to contribute to the generation of revenue. These are the period costs we discussed in Chapter 4. Period costs can include head office administration costs, compensation to senior executives, advertising, salaries to salespeople, and so on. Treating costs as period costs is a recognition that it is not possible to match all costs directly to the revenues they help generate, so instead these costs are "matched" to a period of time—usually the period in which the costs are incurred.

Matching also gives rise to the need to estimate expenses. Some expenditures are not made until after the revenue is recognized. For example, warranty costs on consumer goods and technical support costs for computer hardware and software are not usually incurred until after the revenue is recognized. Since these types of future costs are part of the cost of earning the revenue, good matching requires that they be matched against the revenue when it is recognized. This means that the expense must be estimated at the time that the revenue is recognized.

Conservatism   We initially discussed the accounting concept of conservatism in Chapters 3 and 4. Conservatism requires that measurements in financial statements should be made to ensure that assets, revenues, and net income are not overstated and that liabilities and expenses are not understated. Conservatism does not mean that there should be a deliberate understatement of assets, revenues, and net income, or a deliberate overstatement of liabilities and expenses. In principle there is no problem with using a conservative approach to accounting (although one should recognize that a conservative approach is only one of a number of approaches to accounting that could be legitimately used). One reason a conservative approach to accounting might make sense is because the managers who are usually responsible for an entity's financial statements tend to be optimistic about the prospects for the entities they manage. The managers also have incentives to act in their self-interests when making accounting choices. Conservatism can serve to dampen the effects of managerial optimism and self-interest.

Conservatism manifests itself in different ways in financial statements. When an entity purchases inventory or capital assets, the assets are initially recorded at their acquisition cost. This, of course, is the application of the historical cost convention. Under normal circumstances historical cost is the basis of valuation of inventory and capital assets. However, if the market value of these assets falls below cost, then the book value of the assets is reduced to market value. If the book value of assets were not reduced, the value of the assets on the balance sheet would be overstated. In contrast, if the market value of these assets increased, there would be no recognition of the increases until the assets were sold and the increases in value realized. Under GAAP gains are only recognized when they are realized (when the gain is supported by a transaction). It would not be conservative to recognize a gain until it was realized.

An example of conservative accounting can be seen in MWW's financial statements. In its January 30, 1999 income statement MWW reports a $2,961,000 expense called "Provision for closure of U.S. pilot stores." (See page A-46.) This expense represents the estimated cost of closing its pilot (test) stores in the United States. The cost of closing the stores had to be estimated because the costs would not be known until the stores were actually closed in fiscal 2000. This is an example of conservatism because the cost or loss from closing the U.S. pilot stores was expensed in fiscal 1999 when the decision was made, even though the actual closing of the stores and the costs incurred to close the stores would not occur until fiscal 2000. Conservatism requires that losses be recognized in the financial statements as soon as they are known, even if the transactions that ultimately give rise to the loss do not occur until later.

Conservatism also influences the estimates preparers make in their financial statements. Even though GAAP accounting presents information on past transactions and economic events, there are often uncertainties regarding the outcomes of these transactions and economic events that must be accounted for. For example, when revenue is recognized before cash is collected, there is uncertainty about the exact amount of cash that will be received. When an item is sold with a warranty, the exact cost of the warranty is not known until after the warranty expires. When an amortizable capital asset is purchased, it is necessary to estimate the useful life of the asset so its cost can be amortized. Thus, estimates of the amount of cash from credit sales that will not be collected, the cost of providing warranty service, and the lives of amortizable assets should be "conservative." Conservatism means that preparers should make cautious estimates.

One of the problems with conservatism is that today's conservative choices can lead to the opposite effects in later periods. For example, in 2004 Carcajou Ltd. (Carcajou) purchased computer equipment for $210,000. Carcajou's management decides to amortize the equipment over two years, a period of time that it believed was a reasonable but conservative estimate of the equipment's useful life. Carcajou's income statements for the years ended December 31, 2004, 2005, and 2006 are shown in Panel A of Table 5-1. The income statements are summarized so that all expenses, except for the amortization of the computer equipment, are shown on a single line.

Now, let's assume that Carcajou's management had decided instead to amortize the computer equipment over three years rather than two, a less conservative estimate of the equipment's useful life. Carcajou's income statements under this assumption are shown in Panel B of Table 5-1. When we use the more conservative two-year estimate of the useful life, net income in the first two years is lower than when the three-year estimate is used. However, in the third year, net income is much higher than when the three-year estimate is used. The reason for this is that the computer equipment is fully amortized after two years in the first case, so there is no amortization expense needed in the third year. As a result net income gets a boost in the third year when the more conservative estimate of the useful life of the equipment is used. This is why conservatism today can lead to the opposite effect in later periods. It is important to notice that over the three years total revenue, expenses, amortization, and net income are the same.

Another example of conservative accounting is write-downs and write-offs. Sometimes situations arise that impair the value of an asset. For accounting purposes, an asset is impaired when the future benefits that the asset will provide over its remaining life are less than its net book value (NBV of a capital asset: cost less the accumulated amortization). For example, a building could be destroyed by fire, market demand could reduce the production of a plant, declines in commodity prices

Table 5-1   Carcajou Ltd. Income Statements

Panel A

Carcajou Ltd.
Income Statements
For the Years Ended December 31

	2004	2005	2006	Total
Revenue	$750,000	$800,000	$825,000	$2,375,000
Expenses	620,000	660,000	680,000	1,960,000
Amortization of computer equipment*	105,000	105,000	0	210,000
Net income	$ 25,000	$ 35,000	$145,000	$ 205,000

*Computer equipment cost $210,000 and is amortized over two years.

Panel B

Carcajou Ltd.
Income Statements
For the Years Ended December 31

	2004	2005	2006	Total
Revenue	$750,000	$800,000	$825,000	$2,375,000
Expenses	620,000	660,000	680,000	1,960,000
Amortization of computer equipment*	70,000	70,000	70,000	210,000
Net income	$ 60,000	$ 70,000	$ 75,000	$ 205,000

*Computer equipment cost $210,000 and is amortized over three years.

could reduce the revenues to be earned from a mine, oil well, or forest, or the market value of inventory could fall. When assets become impaired, a write-down of the assets is required. A **write-down** is a reduction in the net book value of an asset to some measure of the market value of the asset. A write-down is achieved by debiting an expense and crediting the asset. When an asset is written down to zero the event is referred to as a **write-off**. A write-down reduces the book value of the asset (credit assets) and reduces income (debit to the income statement). A write-down does not affect cash. It is merely a bookkeeping entry that reduces assets and net income.

Let's look at an example. In its year ended December 31, 2000 Samuel Manu-Tech Inc. (Samuel) reported restructuring costs of $18,586,000. Samuel's income statements for those years and the related note to the financial statements are shown in Exhibit 5-2.[2] The note explains that the restructuring costs relate to major changes that Samuel made in its packaging segment. Included in the restructuring charge is a $6,994,000 write-down of assets affected by the restructuring. The write-down is considered conservative accounting because it reduces the book value of an asset on the balance sheet. Presumably the write-down is in response to information that led Samuel's management to conclude that these assets were overvalued on the balance sheet.

Write-downs are very subjective. Management decides when a write-down occurs. (Why was Samuel's write-down made in 2000 rather than 1999 or 2001? What changed between 1999 and 2000 that made 2000 the appropriate year for the write-down?) Management decides the amount of the write-down. (Why did Samuel's management write down the assets by $6,994,000 rather than $5,000,000 or $8,000,000?) Samuel's restructuring costs raises the question of whether the company was taking a *big bath* (big baths were explained in Chapter 4). It can be very difficult to determine whether an entity is taking a big bath or whether the write-downs represent reasonable adjustments to the book values of assets.

Conservatism tends to be one of the dominant accounting conventions. It can be used to justify deviating from the historical cost convention (assets such as inventory and capital assets are recorded at their market values in certain circumstances) and reliability (market values are used for assets such as inventory and capital assets even though there is no supporting transaction). One of the problems with conservatism is that it requires judgment by the preparers and these judgments can be highly subjective and open to abuse.

Non-Arm's Length Transactions   Financial reporting under GAAP assumes that the transactions that give rise to assets, liabilities, revenues, and expenses occur at arm's length. An **arm's length transaction** is a transaction that takes place between unrelated parties, each of whom is acting in his or her own self interests and therefore is trying to get the best deal for him- or herself. When a transaction takes place at arm's length, the exchange amount is considered to be the fair market value. The exchange or transaction amount is the basis of most valuation issues in GAAP accounting.

A non-arm's length transaction occurs between **related parties**. Related parties exist when one entity has the ability to influence the decision making of another. Examples of related parties include close family members, corporations owned or controlled by a single shareholder, and senior management. As we will see, non-arm's length transactions can cause serious problems for interpreting financial statements.

Suppose you decide that you are going to buy a used car and you find one that appears to meet your needs. When you negotiate with the person selling the car you try to get the best deal for yourself, while the person selling the car tries to get the best deal for him- or herself. Since each of you is trying to get the best deal, if you come to an agreement it is assumed that the agreed price is a reasonable representation of the fair market value of the car. For accounting purposes, the car would be reported at its cost—which is assumed to be a reasonable estimate of its fair market value.

Exhibit 5-2

Samuel Manu-Tech Inc. Income
Statements

Consolidated Statements of Earnings

(in thousands of dollars except per share amounts)
Years ended December 31, 2000 and 1999

	2000	1999
NET SALES	$806,482	$793,354
COSTS (INCOME) AND EXPENSES:		
Cost of sales, selling and administration	724,654	704,140
Depreciation and amortization	26,992	24,107
Interest on long-term debt	11,908	11,763
Interest on short-term debt	1,476	1,146
Interest income	(342)	(179)
	764,688	740,977
EARNINGS BEFORE RESTRUCTURING CHARGE, INCOME TAXES AND GOODWILL AMORTIZATION	41,794	52,377
RESTRUCTURING CHARGE (note 2)	18,586	—
EARNINGS BEFORE INCOME TAXES AND GOODWILL AMORTIZATION	23,208	52,377
INCOME TAXES:		
Current	10,822	15,533
Future	(7,672)	1,167
	3,150	16,700
EARNINGS BEFORE GOODWILL AMORTIZATION	20,058	35,677
GOODWILL AMORTIZATION, net of income taxes	1,883	1,909
NET EARNINGS	$18,175	$33,768
NET EARNINGS PER SHARE BEFORE GOODWILL AMORTIZATION	$ 0.59	$ 1.03
NET EARNINGS PER SHARE	$ 0.53	$ 0.98

See accompanying notes to consolidated financial statements.

2. RESTRUCTURING CHARGE:

The 2000 financial results of the Company include a pre-tax charge of $18,586 ($11,186 after tax) associated with restructuring actions within the Packaging segment comprising $3,797 for severance and other expenses associated with eliminating redundant or duplicated costs, a writedown of $6,994 relating to assets which were affected by the restructuring and $7,795 relating to goodwill which was determined to be permanently impaired. At December 31, 2000, the liability for restructuring charges included in accounts payable was $1,954.

Now, suppose instead that you were not buying the used car from a stranger but from your parents. In this case it is not possible to assume that the price paid for the car is its fair market value. There are factors other than getting the best deal for yourself that could have come into play in determining the selling price. For example, your parents may have been interested in helping you out by giving you a deal on the car (a stranger would not do that). Or you may have been helping out your parents by paying more than the fair market value. The point is that it is not possible to be sure whether the transaction took place at fair market value.

It is crucial for financial statement users to be aware of the existence and the terms of non-arm's length transactions because they can have serious implications for interpreting the financial statements. Consider the owner-manager of a small manufacturing business. As the owner, she can choose to pay herself as much or as little as she thinks appropriate. She can choose to pay herself a salary, which is an expense on the income statement, or pay herself a dividend, which has no effect on net income. Table 5-2 (page 282) shows the income statement for such a small business under three scenarios:

- In Scenario A the owner-manager does not pay herself a salary. The wage and salary expense pertains to employees.

- In Scenario B the owner-manager pays herself a large, above-market-value salary of $200,000 (the wage and salary expense is $200,000 higher in Scenario

Table 5-2	Non-Arm's Length Transactions: The Effect on Net Income of Different Methods of Compensating an Owner-Manager		
	Scenario A Owner-manager receives no salary	**Scenario B** Owner-manager receives a salary that is greater than the market value for the work done	**Scenario C** Owner-manager receives a reasonable salary
Revenue	$1,750,000	$1,750,000	$1,750,000
Cost of goods sold	675,000	675,000	675,000
Gross margin	1,075,000	1,075,000	1,075,000
Expenses:			
Wage and salary	370,000	570,000	470,000
Selling and marketing	275,000	275,000	275,000
Amortization	110,000	110,000	110,000
Interest	45,000	45,000	45,000
Taxes	105,000	105,000	105,000
Net income	$ 170,000	$ (30,000)	$ 70,000

B than in Scenario A). This means that the owner-manager is receiving a larger salary than she would receive if she were an employee in a similar capacity for a similar business.

- In Scenario C the owner-manager is receiving a fair market salary for the work she does.

For purposes of evaluating the performance of this entity, the net income under each of the scenarios tells a different story. Net income ranges from −$30,000 to $170,000 and the profit margin ranges from −1.7% to 9.7%. If you were interested in buying this business and hiring a manager to operate it, the most useful measure of performance would be Scenario C because it indicates what the entity would earn if a manager were paid the fair market value for his or her services.

The *CICA Handbook* requires that information about non-arm's length or **related party transactions** be disclosed in the financial statements. Related party transactions are transactions between related parties. These disclosures include information about existence of these transactions, descriptions of the relationship between the parties, and the amount of the transactions. Importantly, it is not necessary to disclose whether exchanges between related parties took place at fair market value or whether special arrangements were made between the parties. In other words, entities record transactions in the ordinary course of business at the actual exchange amount, regardless of whether the transaction took place at fair market value. As a result it is difficult for a user to determine the effect that the non-arm's length transactions have on the financial statements.

Examples of the information provided in the financial statements about related party transactions are shown in Exhibit 5-3. Notice that for Magna International Inc. and BCE Emergis (Panels A and C) it is difficult to determine whether the terms of the non-arm's length transactions were at fair market value. Quebecor Inc. states that its purchases of raw materials from Donohue Inc., a company that Quebecor Inc. controlled for part of 2000, occurred at open market terms, which leads one to believe that there were no preferential terms in the transactions (Panel B).[3]

Non-arm's length transactions are not illegal or unethical. However, their existence can have significant implications for the financial statements and users should be very aware of that fact.

www.quebecor.com
www.magnaint.com
www.emergis.com

Panel A: Magna International

17. TRANSACTIONS WITH RELATED PARTIES

The Company has agreements with an affiliate of the Chairman of the Board for the provision of business development and consulting services. In addition, the Company has an agreement with the Chairman of the Board for the provision of business development and other services. The aggregate amount expensed under these agreements with respect to the year ended December 31, 2000 was $28 million [for the year ended December 31, 1999 – $23 million; for the five month period ended December 31, 1998 – $9 million; for the year ended July 31, 1998 – $18 million].

During the year ended December 31, 2000, trusts, which exist to make orderly purchases of the Company's shares for employees either for transfer to the EPSP or to recipients of either bonuses or rights to purchase such shares from the trusts, borrowed up to $41 million [for the year ended December 31, 1999 – $18 million; for the five month period ended December 31, 1998 – $23 million; for the year ended July 31, 1998 – $31 million] from the Company to facilitate the purchase of Class A Subordinate Voting Shares of the Company. At December 31, 2000, the trusts' indebtedness to the Company, which is included in accounts payable, was $26 million [December 31, 1999 – $15 million].

Investments include $2 million [December 31, 1999 – $2 million], at cost, in respect of an investment in a company that was established to acquire shares of the Company for sale to employees.

During the year ended December 31, 2000, a subsidiary of the Company purchased from a company associated with members of the family of Mr. F. Stronach, Ms. B. Stronach and Mr. A. Stronach, the Chairman of the Board, Vice-Chairman and Chief Executive Officer, and Vice-President, Business Development, respectively of the Company, approximately 200 acres of land and improvements in Aurora, Ontario to the same company associated with members of the family of Mr. F. Stronach, Ms. B. Stronach and Mr. A. Stronach for approximately $0.2 million.

Panel B: Quebecor Inc.

19. RELATED PARTY TRANSACTIONS

During the year, the Company purchased raw materials from Donohue, Inc. The purchases amounted to $29.5 million ($89.3 million and $44.1 million for the years ended December 31, 1999 and 1998) in 2000 up to the date that the control over Donohue, Inc. ceased. These transactions were concluded at prices and conditions similar to those prevailing on the open market.

Panel C: BCE Emergis

15. Related party transactions

The following transactions occurred in the normal course of operations with BCE, the parent company, and other companies in the BCE group subject to commons control during the periods and were measured at the exchange value:

	Year ended December 31	
	2000	**1999**
Revenue (a)	122,578	50,505
Direct costs and expenses	117,169	74,276
Interest expense on convertible debenture due to parent	7,927	—

(a) Includes services for resale to third parties and for internal use.

The balance sheet includes the following balances with BCE, the parent company, and other companies in the BCE group subject to common control.

	Year ended December 31	
	2000	**1999**
Cash and temporary cash investments	15,000	35,000
Accounts receivable	16,534	17,038
Accounts payable and accrued liabilities	4,192	18,591
Convertible debenture due to parent	129,000	—
Option on convertible debenture due to parent	21,000	—
Long-term debt	2,083	3,083

Question for Consideration

Why does the existence of non-arm's length or related party transactions make it possible that the reporting entity's financial statements will be difficult to interpret?

Answer: Non-arm's length transactions cannot be assumed to take place at fair market value. However, for many types of transactions GAAP require that entities record non-arm's length transactions at their transaction value, not their fair market value. If transactions are not reported at fair market value on the date of the transaction, then all the elements of the financial statements and any ratios that might be calculated are potentially misstated. This misstatement makes comparing the statements with those of other entities more difficult.

Materiality   If you look at MWW's financial statements you will notice that all the numbers in the statements are rounded to the nearest thousand. Amounts in the financial statements of some very large entities, such as BCE Inc. or the Bank of Montreal, are rounded to the nearest million. Why are amounts in financial statements rounded at all? Why not show amounts right to the dollar, or even the cent? The reason is **materiality**. Materiality describes the significance of financial information to users. Information is material if its omission or misstatement would affect the judgment of a user of the information. All material information should be disclosed in financial statements because its absence may affect the decisions made by users. For entities like MWW, BCE Inc., and the Bank of Montreal, rounding the thousands or the millions is not expected to affect any of the decisions that users want to make. In fiscal 2001 MWW reported net income of $8,180,000. The fact that this amount is rounded to the nearest thousand means that the preparers do not think that the decisions of any users will change if the actual amount of income was $8,179,501 or $8,180,499.

Materiality can be thought of from a personal standpoint. If you lost a dollar, would it have any impact on your life? Probably not. Your behaviour, your plans, and your activities would probably stay the same. Suppose instead, you lost $1,000. Would there be any impact on your life? For many people there would be. You might have to forgo a vacation, computer equipment, some entertainment, or even education. The loss of one dollar would not be considered material, whereas the loss of $1,000 would be.

If materiality was not taken into consideration, financial statements would have to disclose every penny that was expended by the entity. MWW's financial statements would provide information on the cost of paper clips, hangers, and glass cleaner used during a period and held as assets at the end of a period. Would that much detailed information in financial statements be helpful to users? More likely, the extra detail would make the financial statements more cumbersome and difficult to work with. We can link materiality back to *full disclosure*. The need to disclose all relevant information to users is constrained by materiality. If certain information is not considered material, then it does not have to be disclosed because it will not have an effect on users' decisions.

Matters that are not material do not have to be treated in accordance with GAAP. For example, MWW may expense the cost of inexpensive capital assets that, strictly speaking, should be capitalized. Clothes hangers should be capitalized and amortized over their useful lives. However, because of their relatively small cost, the hangers might be expensed when they are purchased. The question then is, does this "incorrect" GAAP accounting mislead or confuse users in any way, or have an impact on their decisions? If the answer is no, then the accounting used is appropriate. In contrast, suppose MWW decided to expense the $1,000,000 cost of new furniture and fixtures when they were acquired. Would this accounting treatment potentially mislead or confuse users in any way, or have an impact on their decisions? In this case the answer is probably yes, so the accounting treatment would not be appropriate.

What then should be considered material? Materiality is a matter of judgment and it is difficult to establish firm rules. Materiality will depend on the size of the entity ($1,000,000 may not be material for a large multi-national corporation, whereas $500 might be material for the corner convenience store), the risks it faces, and the identity and needs of the users of the financial statements. In addition, as is typically the case with general purpose financial statements, it is not really possible to define a level of materiality that is appropriate for all decisions and users. Some information considered immaterial for purposes of preparing an entity's financial statements might be regarded as material by some users.

The Auditors' Report

One part of MWW's annual report that we did not examine in Chapter 2 was the auditors' report. The auditors' report gives the *external auditors' opinion* on the entity's financial statements. Remember from Chapter 1 that the external auditor is an independent person who adds credibility to an entity's financial information by assessing the information in relation to some standard, such as GAAP, and expressing an opinion on the information.

Audits are essential in an economy like Canada's, where the management of an entity is often separate from the owners and the other stakeholders. The owners and other stakeholders need information about the entity for decision making, and this information will almost always be produced by the entity itself. An audit adds credibility to information that could be biased by the managers, who may be inclined to pursue their own interests rather than the interests of the stakeholders. Without an external audit, information would be less reliable and users would have less confidence in it. However, despite the importance of audited information, the work of the auditor is heavily constrained by the rules that auditors report under. As we will see, a satisfactory opinion does not provide a guarantee.

Auditors examine an entity's financial statements and the accounting records that were used to prepare the financial statements to evaluate whether the financial statements are properly prepared in accordance with the relevant accounting rules. Based on the audit, an auditor issues an opinion on the financial statements. There are four opinions that auditors can give on financial statements: an unqualified opinion, which says the financial statements satisfy the standards the auditor is using, and three opinions that indicate problems with the financial statements or the audit. The audit opinions that indicate problems are qualified opinions, adverse opinions, and a denial of opinion.

Our discussion will focus on the unqualified opinion because that is the one most commonly seen. (MWW's financial statements received an unqualified opinion.) For entities that follow GAAP, an **unqualified opinion** means that the auditors are satisfied that the financial statements present the financial situation of the entity fairly and that the statements follow GAAP.

MWW's auditors' report, prepared by the accounting firm PricewaterhouseCoopers, is on page A-44 in the appendix. Refer to it as we proceed through the discussion.

MWW's auditors' report is addressed to MWW's shareholders. The auditors' report is always addressed to the entity that appointed the auditor. In the case of a public company, it is always the shareholders that appoint the auditors. Management nominates the auditor but it is up to the shareholders to vote for the auditor, which they do at the entity's annual general meeting. A possible conflict of interest for auditors exists because while the auditors' report is usually addressed to some entity other than the management of the entity being audited, the auditors' fee is authorized by management and paid by the entity being audited.

The auditors' report usually follows a standard format, making it easy for users to see at a glance whether the entity has received an unqualified opinion. An unqualified auditors' report always consists of three paragraphs. The other opinions always have more than three paragraphs, which is why it is easy to tell whether an entity received an unqualified opinion or not.

The first paragraph of an unqualified auditors' report is known as the introductory paragraph. The introductory paragraph tells the reader what the auditor did. The paragraph explains that an audit was conducted, identifies the financial statements that were audited, and describes the periods that were audited. MWW's auditors' report states that MWW's consolidated balance sheets as of January 30, 1999, January 29, 2000, and January 27, 2001 and its consolidated statements of earnings and retained earnings and cash flows for each of those years were audited. The auditor also audits the notes to the financial statements, although this is not explicitly stated.

The introductory paragraph also tells readers that preparation of the financial statements is the responsibility of the management of the entity. The auditor does not prepare the financial statements—the auditor only audits and expresses an opinion on them. The entity's management makes all the accounting choices that go into preparing the financial statements. The significance of these responsibilities of management and the auditors is that the auditors do not have the power or authority to change the financial statements that have been prepared by management. The auditors will discuss any concerns they have with the management of the entity, but it is up to management to make any changes. Ultimately, if the auditors are not satisfied that the financial statements meet the appropriate standards, they can only express their dissatisfaction in the auditors' report.

The second paragraph of an unqualified auditors' report is called the scope paragraph. The scope paragraph describes what an audit involves. The paragraph states that the auditors "conducted our audits in accordance with Canadian generally accepted auditing standards." **Generally accepted auditing standards (GAAS)** is a set of general guidelines that are stated in the *CICA Handbook* and that provide guidance to auditors in the conduct of their audits. GAAS do not provide specific details as to how to do an audit, but offer a broad overview of how auditors should approach audits to ensure that they are done properly and that enough evidence is obtained to give on opinion on the financial statements. The *CICA Handbook* also provides more specific guidance to auditors, but ultimately how an audit is done is left to the professional judgment of the auditor.

The scope paragraph includes a number of terms that give valuable insights into the nature of an audit and the meaning of an audit opinion. The scope paragraph says that GAAS require that an audit be planned and performed to obtain "reasonable assurance" that the financial statements are free of "material misstatement." The use of the term "material" means that the auditor is only looking for errors and misstatements that will have an effect on the decisions of users, not minor mistakes that have no effect on users' decisions. This has two implications:

1. The financial statements cannot be considered precise or exact because the auditors' report acknowledges that there may be errors in the statements that are not material.

2. The notion of materiality assumes that the same level of materiality applies to all users. This is not necessarily the case. An error that is not material for one user of the financial statements may be material to another.

The term "reasonable assurance" means that an audit does not eliminate the possibility that there is a material error or misstatement in the financial statements. An audit means that there is a very good chance that the financial statements are free of material errors, but an audit is not a guarantee.

The scope paragraph also states that "an audit includes examining, on a test basis, evidence supporting the amounts and disclosures in the financial statements." This statement means that auditors do not examine every transaction and economic event in which an entity was involved. Instead, it means that a sampling of transactions and economic events is examined to reach an opinion on the financial statements. Auditors use their professional judgment to decide how many and which transactions and economic events should be audited. The last sentence of the scope paragraph explains that auditors assess the accounting principles used, estimates made by management, and the overall financial statement presentation.

In the third paragraph of an unqualified auditors' report the auditors' opinion on the financial statements is expressed. The opinion paragraph states that the financial statements present fairly, in all material respects, the financial situation of the entity, in accordance with GAAP. Once again it is important to emphasize that the auditor is offering an opinion, not a guarantee. There *appear* to be two elements to the opinion—that the financial statements present the financial situation of the entity fairly and that the financial statements comply with GAAP. In fact, there is only one element. The fairness of the financial statements is evaluated in relation to GAAP. In other words, to be fair, financial statements must comply with GAAP. If they do not comply with GAAP, they are not fair.

Within GAAP auditors must evaluate whether the choices made among alternative available accounting methods result in a fair representation of the entity's economic activities. In other words, simply because an entity chooses an alternative that is in accordance with GAAP or the choice can be justified in terms of GAAP does not automatically mean that the financial statements present the entity's financial situation fairly. Also, there can be situations where, in the professional judgment of the auditors, a non-GAAP accounting treatment can be used and an unqualified audit opinion given. However, such circumstances are rare. The opinion paragraph also states that the financial statements present fairly "in all material respects the financial position of the company." The phrase "in all material respects" reiterates the point that the financial statements are not precise or exact. Recently the auditing profession has been subject to substantial criticism as the result of management fraud (WorldCom), financial failures of major corporations (Enron) and other irregularities. The focus on the auditors in these situations highlights their importance in the operation of capital markets.

Other Auditors' Reports

The three other opinions that auditors can give on financial statements, in addition to an unqualified opinion, are described briefly as follows:

Qualified Opinion   A **qualified opinion** is used when, overall, the financial statements present the entity's situation fairly, but the statements do deviate from GAAP (or from whatever set of accounting standards the auditor is auditing to). A qualified audit opinion always contains the term "except for", which prefaces the explanation as to why the qualified audit report was given.

Adverse Opinion   An **adverse opinion** is given when the financial statements are so materially misstated or misleading that they do not present fairly the financial position, results of operations, and/or cash flows of the entity. Adverse opinions are rare and would never be given to a public company because an adverse opinion would be unacceptable to the securities regulators. If a public company received an adverse opinion, trading of the company's shares would not be allowed until the circumstances giving rise to the adverse opinion were rectified. If an adverse opinion were expressed on the financial statements of a private entity, the statements would likely be seen as having limited usefulness to the entities that received them.

Denial of Opinion   When auditors cannot obtain enough evidence to support an opinion on the financial statements, then the auditors do not give one. This is a **denial of opinion**. Instead the auditors state in their report that they are unable to express an opinion as to whether the financial statements are fair and in accordance with GAAP.

When the opinion given on financial statements is something other than an unqualified opinion, the format of the auditors' report is different than the three-paragraph format used with an unqualified auditors' report. In these cases, there will always be more than three paragraphs. Extra paragraphs are necessary to explain why an unqualified opinion was not given, and the different format highlights that the opinion is not the standard, unqualified opinion.

Other Assurance Accountants Can Provide

Audits are only one of the forms of assurance that accountants can provide. A **review engagement** provides less assurance to users about whether an entity's financial statements are in accordance with GAAP than an audit does. The benefit of a review engagement is that it is much less expensive than an audit and it therefore saves the entity money. When an accountant performs a review, the report that the accountant prepares is called a review engagement report. Review engagements are never performed on public companies because securities laws require audits. A review will be done for private companies when external stakeholders require some assurance, but these stakeholders are satisfied with less assurance than is provided by an audit.

Accountants can also provide reports on financial information other than financial statements (for example, a shopping mall may want a report on the amount of sales a store made because the rent the mall receives is based on sales) or in compliance with an agreement or regulations (for example, to see whether an entity has met the current-ratio requirement of a lending agreement).

Question for Consideration

You are the property manager for a large mall. Most of the tenants in the mall pay a fixed amount of rent each month based on the number of square metres rented plus a percentage of sales made in the store each year. Would you require the stores in the mall to have their sales audited by an independent auditor? Explain.

Answer: An audit would be essential. Since the people managing and owning the stores in the mall prepare the accounting information that you rely on to determine the amount of rent, there is a possibility that some of these people might understate the amount of sales. The benefit to stores' understating their sales is a smaller rent payment. An audit would add reliability to the accounting information that the store presented. Audited sales figures would provide you with greater assurance that the amount of sales a store was reporting in its statement to you represented the actual sales the store earned during the year.

■ Solved Problem

The solved problem in this chapter will build on the problem-solving skills that were developed in Chapter 4. Some of the issues raised in this and similar types of questions may have actual rules that GAAP prescribe. However, at this stage of the book it is not necessary for you to be aware of the rules. It is more important that you develop the ability to use the knowledge you have acquired to come up with sensible responses to accounting issues. For example, if you are faced with a situation where an entity chooses to conform with GAAP, proposed accounting treatments should be assessed in relation to the GAAP discussed in this chapter. When reviewing the problem, keep in mind that the objective is to provide a well-reasoned and well-supported set of recommendations that address and attempt to resolve the accounting issues faced by the entity.

Savoy Health Club Ltd.

Fred Irving, the founder, owner and operator of the Savoy Health Club Ltd. (Savoy or the club) recently agreed in principle to sell Savoy to Jim Floor. The parties have agreed in principle to make the purchase price equal to five times net income for the year ended June 30, 2005. However, the deal cannot be finalized until Jim Floor receives the June 30, 2005 financial statements and agrees to them. In the event that Jim Floor does not agree to the financial statements, outstanding accounting issues can be submitted to an independent arbitrator for resolution. Until the agreement in principle was signed, Savoy's financial statements were prepared exclusively for tax purposes. Fred Irving is in the process of finalizing the June 30, 2005 financial statements, but he is unsure about how to account for a number of issues.

Fred Irving has hired you to prepare a report explaining appropriate accounting treatments for the issues he is concerned about. Fred wants full explanations and justifications for the recommendations you make so that he can explain them to Jim Floor and to the arbitrator, if necessary. Your discussions with Fred Irving provide the following information:

1. People join the club by paying an initiation fee of $600. The initiation fee is paid only once when the member joins. Provincial legislation requires that health clubs allow members to pay their initiation fees in equal instalments over 12 months. Most new members pay their initiation fees monthly. In the past between 10% and 20% of people who join the club stop paying their initiation fees sometime during the year.

    In addition, each member must pay a monthly fee of $80. Members can pay their continuing monthly fees on the first day of each month or they can pay the full annual amount on the renewal date of their contract, in which case they receive a $160 reduction in their annual fee. (Members sign a one-year contract each year.) Approximately 40% of members pay in a lump sum at the start of the year. Some members who pay their monthly fees each month stop paying sometime during the year.

2. During fiscal 2005 the club began selling passes that allow non-members to participate in aerobics classes put on by the club. Passes for individual classes can be purchased for $8 each, or monthly passes can be purchased for one month ($70), three months ($200), or six months ($375). A monthly pass allows the holder to attend 15 classes per month, but the pass can only be used in the month for which it was issued. Aerobics instructors receive $1.50 for each participant in their classes.

3. Normal maintenance work on some of the athletic equipment has been delayed for the last two months. The work will cost about $4,000. The delay is apparently due to scheduling problems with the contractor and the work is now scheduled for July 2005.

4. During the year three pieces of equipment were damaged by vandals and cannot be repaired for a reasonable price. The equipment cost $5,000 and has a net book value of $2,200. The cost to replace the equipment is $6,500.

5. The club pays monthly rent of $3,000. Rent is paid six months in advance on October 1 and April 1.

6. Fred Irving has never taken a salary.

Required:
    Prepare the report requested by Fred Irving.

Solution:
When you examine this solution it is important to remember that there is not a single right answer to this question. There are many wrong answers, but more than one good answer. The important quality for responding to this type of question is the thinking that goes into supporting the recommendations that are made, not the recommendations themselves. A recommendation that is not well supported is not part of a good answer. In supporting your recommendations, you should try to use the accounting assumptions, qualitative characteristics, and measurement conventions discussed in this chapter, as well as the concepts raised in earlier chapters.

The answer below is prepared as a report to Fred Irving. It is useful to respond to these types of questions in the role you are asked to play. Throughout the report are comments on the answer, which are not part of the report itself, but provide some additional explanation.

Mr. Fred Irving
2334 Piché St.
Bordeaux, Québec

Dear Mr. Irving:

Attached is the report you requested recommending accounting treatments for unresolved items in the financial statements of Savoy Health Club Ltd. In preparing this report I have attempted to provide reasonable, justified alternatives for the outstanding accounting issues that were identified. There is often more than one reasonable choice for treating accounting problems. In situations where there is more than one acceptable alternative, I have attempted to choose the one that serves the objective of increasing net income and thereby increasing the selling price of Savoy.

In previous years Savoy's financial statements have been prepared primarily for income tax purposes. Presumably the accounting choices made for those statements served to legitimately reduce Savoy's tax burden. Financial statements prepared for tax purposes meet the requirements of the *Income Tax Act* but are often not appropriate for determining the selling price of a business. Financial statements prepared for tax purposes will tend to understate income because they are designed to reduce taxes. Using such statements for determining the selling price of a business will unfairly reduce the proceeds you receive from the sale of Savoy.

Financial statements prepared for determining the selling price of a business should provide a reasonable representation of the ongoing and continuing earning ability of the business. Because these financial statements will be used by Mr. Jim Floor, the prospective buyer of Savoy, and potentially by an arbitrator, it is important to use a recognized standard as the basis for preparing the statements. Accordingly, I recommend using GAAP. While GAAP are not necessarily the best criteria for setting the selling price of a business, GAAP are widely known and recognized. It is possible that the buyer will reject some of the accounting choices that you incorporate into the financial statements. You may have to concede some issues to come to an agreement. However, all recommendations made in this report are supportable in terms of GAAP, fairness, and accrual accounting.

If you have any questions, please contact me.

Yours truly,

Accountant

Comment: The letter to Fred Irving, the person who engaged the accountant, lays out the perspective that the accountant will take in pursuing the engagement. The letter is an important part of effective role-playing and serves the purpose of providing a vehicle for discussing the constraints, facts, and objectives that are relevant to the case. In this case, the objective of preparing financial statements for determining the selling price of Savoy is clearly most important. The perspective that the accountant brings to the report is to work within the constraints and the facts, but when possible to attempt to serve the objectives of the client to get a good price for Savoy.

It is assumed that only Mr. Irving will receive the letter, whereas the report itself may be made available to Mr. Floor and the arbitrator. It is not appropriate to discuss the objectives of reporting in a document that will be shared with other parties. Neutrality assumes that financial statements are not prepared in a way that attempts to influence or manipulate the decisions of the users. However, when faced with acceptable and reasonable alternatives, a preparer will likely choose the ones that are in his or her self-interests. This is not to imply that the preparers will intentionally misstate the financial statements. Rather, when there are legitimate alternatives, the ones that are more favourable will be selected. It is reasonable to assume that the other parties will take a similar position—that Jim Floor will argue for accounting treatments that will tend to lower the selling price of Savoy.

Report to Fred Irving

Terms of Reference

You have asked me to prepare a report recommending appropriate accounting treatments for a number of issues that must be resolved before presenting the financial statements of Savoy Health Club Ltd. (Savoy) to Mr. Jim Floor, who has agreed in principle to purchase Savoy from you. The financial statements, net income specifically, will be used to determine the final selling price of Savoy. I understand that if Mr. Floor does not accept the financial statements as presented to him, you and Mr. Floor will attempt to resolve any differences through negotiations. If outstanding issues cannot be resolved through negotiations, the remaining issues will be presented to an arbitrator for resolution

My objective in preparing this report is to come up with reasonable and justified treatments for the accounting problems that will result in an income measure that reflects normalized earnings (earnings that can reasonably be expected to repeat in future years). Generally accepted accounting principles will be used as the basis for my evaluation of the accounting issues.

> Comment: Materiality will be low in this situation. Each dollar change in net income has a five-dollar effect of the price of Savoy. That is, if an accounting choice results in a $1,000 increase in net income, the selling price of Savoy increases by $5,000. Also, disclosure cannot be used to resolve any accounting issues. Because the selling price of Savoy depends on net income, measurement of all accounting events is necessary for them to be relevant.

Issues

The issues I deal with in this report are revenue recognition, maintenance costs, vandalized equipment, rent costs, and owner's salary.

Revenue Recognition

There are three revenue recognition issues that must be addressed: initiation fees, monthly membership fees, and aerobics fees, as follows.

1. *Initiation fees:* Under GAAP there are four criteria that must be met if revenue is to be recognized. The first criterion is that the revenue must be earned. Initiation fees allow an individual to be a member of the club for however long the person wishes, provided that he or she pays the monthly fee. In my opinion, the initiation fee is earned when a new member agrees to join the club. The initiation fee simply represents the right to join the club. To continue as a member a person must pay the monthly fee. Savoy is entitled to the initiation fee once the member signs the contract—no refunds are possible once the contract is signed. One of the key success factors of operating a health club is enlisting new members. Considerable effort and expense go into recruiting new members. Once a new

member signs a contract agreeing to become a member and pay the initiation fee, the recruiting process is complete. The initiation fee is the reward for successful recruitment.

The second criterion requires that the amount of revenue be known. Since new members must sign contracts in which they agree to pay the $600 initiation fee, the amount of revenue is known when the member joins.

The third criterion is that the costs of earning the revenue must be known when revenue is recognized. The costs of recruiting new members include advertising, salespeople, promotions, office space for meeting with prospective members, and so on. These costs are treated as period costs and are expensed when incurred. No portion of the costs incurred in recruitment are carried forward to future periods.

The fourth criterion for recognizing revenue is collectability of amounts owing. Collectability is an issue because a significant number of people do not pay their initiation fees. However, the key issue is measurability of the amount that will be collected. Based on its history, Savoy is able to estimate the amount that will not be collected. The amount of the allowance should be based only on members who pay over an entire year. There is no uncertainty about amounts that will be received when a new member pays in full when the contract is signed.

> Comment: The most difficult revenue recognition issue is initiation fees because other alternatives for recognizing the revenue can be defended. For example, a case could be made for spreading the initiation fee revenue over the average time a member belongs to the club. Since the role in this case is to support Fred Irving's position, an alternative that is favourable to Mr. Irving was selected. The key point to recognize is that there are reasonable alternatives available for recognizing revenue. The solution provided is not an obviously inferior alternative chosen simply because it is consistent with Mr. Irving's position. The accountant did not twist and bend the rules to come up with a recommendation that met Mr. Irving's needs. Notice that in analyzing the problem the GAAP constraint was adhered to (because GAAP were established as a constraint, adhering to GAAP is very important), and that the recommendation was justified in terms of the facts. It is not adequate to recommend a solution only because it meets the objectives. The constraints and facts must be satisfied for a recommendation to be acceptable. Mr. Floor would not accept an accounting method simply because it made Mr. Irving richer (and Mr. Floor poorer).

> Comment: There is an implied assumption in the discussion of this and several other issues in the question. If we use the recommended revenue recognition method, consistency requires that the same method be used in other years. If membership in the club is growing, then recognizing revenue early increases income. If membership in the club is decreasing and there are fewer members paying the initiation fee in the current year than in previous years, then it may be preferable for purposes of satisfying the objectives to use a different revenue recognition method. If membership is stable, then it does not matter when revenue is recognized. The analysis of this question assumes that membership is growing.

2. *Monthly membership fees*: Monthly fees should be recognized as time passes and members have access to the club. The monthly fee entitles members to use the club for a period of time. This means that revenue is earned as time passes. Therefore, revenue should be accrued to reflect portions of monthly membership fees earned as of the date the financial statements are prepared. This accounting approach should be used regardless of whether a member pays monthly or at the start of the year. If the member pays in full on the renewal date of the contract, the amount paid should be treated as unearned revenue and an adjusting entry should be prepared to recognize the appropriate amount of revenue when the financial statements are prepared.

There are no legitimate alternatives for recognizing revenue for the monthly fees. Revenue is earned as members have access to the club. The revenue is known since the monthly fee is set in the contract signed by the member. Costs of earning the revenue are known because these are the costs of operating the club. Collection may be an issue for some members, although it should be possible to make an estimate of the amounts that will not be collected.

> Comment: Accounting for the monthly membership fees is an example of a situation where the facts dictate the accounting method. It would be desirable from Mr. Irving's point of view to recognize revenue earlier, say when a member signs a contract, because this would place more revenue in the current period. However, these choices would not be appropriate under GAAP (our constraint) because the revenue has not been earned before the members can use the club (the facts).

3. *Aerobics fees*: Non-members can attend aerobics classes at the club by purchasing passes for individual classes, or monthly passes that entitle a person to attend 15 aerobics classes per month. Payment is made when the pass is purchased. Clearly, revenue is earned when a person attends a class. The service being provided is an aerobics class, and it is difficult to argue that revenue is earned at any time other than when a person attends a class. The fee earned by the instructor should be matched to the revenue when it is recognized.

The difficult problem is how to handle classes not attended. Some people will not attend all 15 classes they are entitled to attend by the end of a month. The revenue from the unattended classes should be recognized in the month that the person was entitled to attend the classes because classes cannot be carried forward to another month. Unattended classes do not incur an instructor fee because instructors only get paid for classes attended by the client. The four revenue recognition criteria are clearly met at the time the class is given (or at the end of the month for unattended classes) because: (a) the revenue is earned when the class is given (or the month ends for unattended classes); (b) the amount of revenue is known because the price of the passes is specified; (c) costs are known (most costs are club operating costs that must be treated as period costs plus the fee paid to the instructor, which is known once a class is given); and (d) collection is not an issue because people pay in advance.

> Comment: The timing of aerobics fee revenue is also dictated by the facts. An alternative might be to recognize revenue when passes are purchased, but under the GAAP criteria point of purchase is too early because the service being purchased has not been provided when a pass is purchased. Considerable effort is still required to put on the aerobics class. An aggressive accountant might try to use point of purchase as the revenue recognition point, which would increase club revenue and net income, but Mr. Floor would likely challenge it.

Maintenance Costs Maintenance costs are incurred to ensure that the equipment lives up to its operating potential. Without proper maintenance the useful lives of the equipment will be shorter than expected. While regularly scheduled maintenance is necessary for proper operation of the equipment and for customer satisfaction, the judgment of management is the ultimate determinant for whether maintenance is required at a point in time. It is senseless from a business perspective to do maintenance unless it is required.

In this case we must rely on management's judgment that maintenance was not required at the time and therefore should not be included as an expense in the income statement in the current period. This is not a situation where an expense should be accrued, such as a good or service consumed but not billed (such as electricity costs) or an expense that should be matched to revenue recognized in the current period but that will not be incurred until a future period (such as a warranty expense). This is an independent transaction that has not taken place. GAAP are a transactions-based accounting system. Since there has been no transaction, it is inappropriate under GAAP to accrue the maintenance costs.

> Comment: Strictly speaking, the maintenance expense should be recorded when it is incurred. There are many uncertainties surrounding this cost, including the amount and whether it will be incurred (perhaps Mr. Floor will decide, should he buy Savoy, that this particular service call is not necessary). Since GAAP record transactions and economic events that have happened, it is easy to make a case that these maintenance costs should not be accounted for in 2005.
>
> However, as the accountant explained in the letter to Mr. Irving, the financial statements should be a reasonable representation of the ongoing and continuing earning ability of the business. After all, future earnings and future cash flow is what Mr. Floor is buying. An ongoing and regular cost of operating a health club is maintenance. By excluding this particular maintenance cost in fiscal 2005, net income is overstated in relation to ongoing and continuing earnings (although the accounting is consistent with GAAP). So while the treatment proposed by the accountant is consistent with GAAP, we can question whether it is fair. The accountant's choice is consistent with Mr. Irving's objectives and with the constraints and the facts, and therefore is a reasonable recommendation. Mr. Floor and the arbitrator may see things differently. This demonstrates some of the practical limitations of using GAAP accounting for setting the price of a business. Similar problems are seen with the vandalized equipment and Mr. Irving's compensation.

Vandalized Equipment   The vandalized equipment appears to be of no value to Savoy because it cannot be repaired at a reasonable cost. Therefore, the equipment does not meet the definition of an asset because it does not provide any future benefit. According to conservatism, the equipment should be written down to its net realizable value—the amount that it could be sold for. The problem is that while recognizing a loss in the June 30, 2005 financial statements is consistent with GAAP, it does not result in a net income that is representative of ongoing and continuing earnings. Any loss suffered by writing down the vandalized equipment is a cost that is not likely to recur on an ongoing basis. By recognizing the loss in the June 30, 2005 financial statements, the price that will be received for Savoy will be lower than is appropriate. This is an undesirable and unfair outcome for Mr. Irving.

One alternative would be to contend that the equipment is serviceable and should not be written off. However, given my understanding of the situation, this treatment would be a misrepresentation of the facts and is therefore unethical. Also, Mr. Floor would certainly discover that the equipment could not be used once he took over the club. A reasonable approach to take would be to argue that because the loss on the vandalized equipment is unusual, it should not be included in the amount that is used to calculate the selling price. Since the loss is a one-time event, the loss should be subtracted from the selling price but not subject to the five-times multiplier.

> Comment: The costs associated with the vandalized equipment are a non-recurring item that reduces net income. This item shows the problems with using net income in a single year to set the selling price of a business. There will sometimes be non-recurring items that can distort the representativeness of net income of ongoing and continuing earnings. The proposed solution addresses this problem, but strictly speaking it is not consistent with the agreement in principle since the agreement bases the price on net income, which should include this loss.

Rent Costs   Clearly, rent should be accrued on a monthly basis. Rent expense should reflect the cost of the space used during the period in question because it is only that cost that contributed to earning revenue. Savoy paid $18,000 to the property owner on April 1, 2005 to cover rent for April 1 to September 30, 2005. A rent expense of $9,000 should be accrued in the June 30, 2005 financial statements.

> Comment: This is a clear application of accrual accounting. The rent should be expensed in the period when the space was used, regardless of when the cash is expended.

Owner's Salary   The owner's salary is a non-existent expense. Over the life of the business Mr. Irving never took a salary so it is inappropriate to include it in the calculation of net income. Historical cost financial statements are intended to be representations of what happened. Including a salary for Mr. Irving means that the statements would include something that did not happen.

> Comment: The issue here is whether the selling price should include a cost of management. An owner manager has the option of removing money from the company as salary or dividend (a question that has significant tax implications), or not at all. From an entity standpoint, the financial statements do not reflect all the costs of operating Savoy because the cost of management is a part of the cost. The method and amount of compensation received by an owner-manager is a non-arm's length transaction and can distort net income for purposes of setting the price of Savoy. There is no simple solution to this issue. The treatment recommended by the accountant is consistent with GAAP and is the best choice to achieve Mr. Irving's objectives. Ultimately, this issue, along with the accounting for the maintenance cost and the vandalized equipment, may be better resolved through negotiations.

Summary of Key Points

LO 1. The rules of accounting are known as generally accepted accounting principles or GAAP. GAAP are the characteristics, assumptions, principles, conventions, practices, procedures and rules that define acceptable accounting practices and guide the preparation of financial statements in certain situations. It is not possible to point to a single source that documents all GAAP. In fact, much of GAAP are not recorded at all, but are simply what is done in practice. GAAP often allow more than one way of accounting for a particular type of economic event or transaction.

All public companies must adhere to GAAP. However, private companies can waive compliance with unanimous consent of all shareholders. Partnerships and proprietorships are not required to use GAAP unless they choose to.

LO 2. There are four basic assumptions that underlie GAAP. The assumptions are:

- Unit of measure: The economic activity of an entity can be effectively stated in terms of a single unit of measure.
- Entity: Accounting systems are designed to provide information about some defined entity.
- Going concern: The entity will continue its operations for the foreseeable future.
- Periodic reporting: Meaningful financial information can be provided for periods of time that are shorter than the life of the entity.

LO 3. The *CICA Handbook* defines four qualitative characteristics that financial information should have if it is to be useful to users. The four qualitative characteristics are:

- Understandability.
- Comparability.
- Relevance: According to the *CICA Handbook* and GAAP, relevant information must have predictive value, feedback value, and timeliness.

- Reliability: According to the *CICA Handbook* and GAAP, reliable information must be representationally faithful, verifiable, and neutral/free from bias.

LO 4. Accounting is about measurement. GAAP have a number of conventions that help determine the amount at which financial statement elements will be recorded. The conventions are:

- Valuation: The primary valuation method used in GAAP financial statements is historical cost, although replacement cost, net realizable value, and the present value of future cash flows are also used in certain circumstances.
- Full disclosure.
- Recognition.
- Matching.
- Conservatism.
- Non-arm's length transactions: Non-arm's length or related party transactions can distort financial statements because they may not occur at fair market value. Generally, it is assumed that transactions occur at fair market value; non-arm's length transactions may undermine that assumption.
- Materiality.

LO 5. An audit adds credibility to information that could be biased by the managers who may be inclined to pursue their own interests, rather than the interests of the users. Without an external audit, information would be less reliable and users would have less confidence in the information. However, audits are not guarantees that the financial statements are true, exact, precise, or correct.

There are four opinions that auditors can give on financial statements. The most common opinion is an unqualified opinion, which says the financial statements satisfy the standards the auditor is using (GAAP, for example). The three other opinions indicate that there are problems with the financial statements or the audit. These opinions are a qualified opinion, an adverse opinion, and a denial of opinion.

Key Terms

adverse opinion, p. 287

arm's length transaction, p. 280

collateral, p. 272

consistency, p. 267

contingent liability, p. 312

denial of opinion, p. 287

Efficient Market Hypothesis (EMH), p. 276

full disclosure, p. 275

generally accepted auditing standards
  (GAAS), p. 286

going-concern assumption, p. 264

historical cost, p. 274

materiality, p. 284

net realizable value, p. 274

periodic-reporting assumption, p. 265

qualified opinion, p. 287

recognition, p. 277

related parties, p. 280

related party transactions, p. 282

replacement cost, p. 274

review engagement, p. 288

unit-of-measure assumption, p. 263

unqualified opinion, p. 285

write-down, p. 280

write-off, p. 280

Similar Terms

The left column gives alternative terms that are sometimes used for the accounting terms introduced in this chapter, which are listed in the right column.

clean audit opinion   **unqualified audit opinion, p. 285**

non-arm's length transactions   **related party transactions, p. 282**

Assignment Materials

Questions

Q5-1. Which entities are required to follow GAAP? Which entities do not have to follow GAAP? Why would entities that do not have to follow GAAP choose to follow GAAP? Explain your answers.

Q5-2. What are the benefits of having a set of rules like GAAP to guide financial reporting in Canada? What are some of the drawbacks? Explain.

Q5-3. Where do GAAP come from? Who decides what are GAAP?

Q5-4. You are a fairly sophisticated Canadian investor who has experience investing in Canadian companies. You have been asked in a phone solicitation to invest in a small distributing company. You receive the financial statements and discover they are not prepared according to Canadian GAAP. What problems do the fact the statements are not prepared in accordance with GAAP create for you? Explain.

Q5-5. How is it possible that GAAP are different in different countries? Should GAAP not be the same in all countries? Do you think it is a problem that GAAP are different in different countries? Explain your response.

Q5-6. Explain the historical cost convention. Why is historical cost the primary valuation method used under GAAP?

Q5-7. Explain conservatism. Which accounting concepts are sometimes violated when conservative accounting is used?

Q5-8. Why does making accounting choices conservative today sometimes result in non-conservative effects in later periods?

Q5-9. Explain the conflict that sometimes exists between relevance and reliability. Provide examples of the conflict.

Q5-10. Identify and explain the four assumptions that underlie GAAP accounting.

Q5-11. Explain why the periodic reporting assumption is the cause of many of the problems and controversies that face the accounting professions today.

Q5-12. Explain what accountants mean when they speak of a going concern. What are the implications for financial reporting of an entity not being a going concern? Do you think these implications make sense? Explain.

Q5-13. Explain how the going-concern assumption is used as a justification for using historical cost for valuing capital assets.

Q5-14. What is the unit of measure that is typically used in the financial statements of Canadian companies? What are the some of the benefits and drawbacks of using the Canadian dollar as the unit of measure?

Q5-15. Identify and explain the characteristics that make information (i) relevant and (ii) reliable.

Q5-16. What do accountants mean when they say that an accounting change is made retroactively? What kinds of accounting changes are made retroactively?

Q5-17. What do accountants mean when they say that an accounting change is made prospectively? What kinds of accounting changes are made prospectively?

Q5-18. What is the Efficient Market Hypothesis (EMH)? Explain why the EMH does not apply to situations where the numbers in the financial statements are used to determine an outcome such as a manager's bonus or the selling price of a business.

Q5-19. According to the Efficient Market Hypothesis (EMH), does it matter whether an entity provides information to the capital markets in the financial statements or the notes to the financial statements? Explain.

Q5-20. Identify and explain each of the audit opinions that an auditor can express on an entity's financial statements.

Q5-21. As a prospective investor in a company, would you be concerned if the company did not receive an unqualified audit opinion? Explain.

Q5-22. What is comparability? Why is it important to users that financial statements be comparable?

Q5-23. One of the qualitative characteristics of GAAP accounting is that financial information must be understandable. Should financial information be tailored such that it is understandable to the most unsophisticated possible users? Explain.

Q5-24. Accounting by Canada's big banks for the costs of their aborted mergers was discussed in this chapter. As a user of financial statements, do you think that it makes sense that the different banks would treat the merger costs in such different ways? Suppose you learned that the same auditor audited more than one of these banks, and the banks that this firm audited used different accounting treatments for the merger costs. Do you think that the auditor should have accepted the different treatments for these costs? Explain. (See pages 267–268.)

Q5-25. Despite what some people think, an audit does not provide a guarantee that the financial statements are perfect, correct, or exact. Explain.

Q5-26. Neutral information is sometimes interpreted to mean that the information does not influence the decisions made by the users of the information. Why is this not a sensible definition to use for neutral accounting information? Explain.

Q5-27. Based on what we have discussed thus far in the book, do you think that accounting information is likely to be neutral? Explain.

Q5-28. What is a non-arm's length transaction? Why do non-arm's length transactions present serious problems for users of financial statements?

Exercises

E5-1. **(Examining relevance and reliability, LO 3)** You are trying to decide which business school to attend. You receive a package of information from one of the schools that contains the following:
a. A list of some graduates and their current jobs.
b. An article from a major Canadian newsmagazine with a ranking of all business schools in Canada.
c. Letters from existing students and recent graduates praising various aspects of the school's academic and non-academic programs.
d. A catalogue of courses offered by the Physical Education department.
e. A letter from the dean of the school stating that the school is the best in Canada.
f. A list of faculty and some background information on them.
g. A brief history of the school.
h. An article from the university newspaper that claims the university is the "best party university in the province."

Required:

Evaluate the relevance (including predictive value, feedback value, and timeliness) and reliability (including representational faithfulness, verifiability, and neutrality/freedom from bias) of each piece of information for purposes of choosing a business school.

E5-2. **(Examining relevance, LO 3)** For each of the following situations, indicate the information that the specific user would require. Explain. Do you think the information required would be available in general purpose GAAP financial statements? Explain.
a. A banker is asked to lend money and accept a building as collateral for the loan. The banker can lend only 90% of the fair market value of the collateral.
b. A tenant in a mall must pay 5% of its gross sales in a year as rent to the mall owner. The rent must be paid within 60 days of the end of the year.
c. An investor wants to predict the amount of cash a company will have to spend on replacing old equipment.

d. An investor wants to know the current market value of the Loblaw Companies Limited shares that she owns.

E5-3. **(Examining the entity assumption, LO 2)** Mazeppa Ltd. (Mazeppa) is a producer of electronic parts that it sells to manufacturers of electronic equipment. Mazeppa has organized itself by setting up a number of separate corporations to operate different parts of its business. The corporate organization chart is shown below. Each box represents a separate corporation and the percentage shown represents the percentage of that corporation that is owned the corporation above it in the chart. For example, Mazeppa Ltd. owns 100% of Mazeppa US Ltd. and Mazeppa Distributing Ltd. owns 60% of Mazeppa Retail Ltd. (The other 40% of Mazeppa Retail Ltd. is owned by other investors).

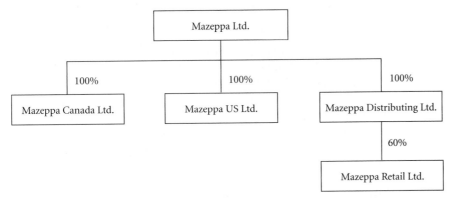

Required

For each of the following situations, indicate which entity the party described would want information about. Explain your answer:

a. An investor purchases shares in Mazeppa Ltd. and wishes to evaluate the performance of the company.

b. A bank is evaluating a loan application from Mazeppa US Ltd. The loan will not be guaranteed by any other entity.

c. The 40% shareholders in Mazeppa Retail Ltd. wish to evaluate their investment in that company.

d. The Canada Customs and Revenue Agency is assessing the tax return filed by Mazeppa Distributing Ltd.

E5-4. **(Examining neutrality, LO 3)** In each of the following situations, indicate whether the information being provided is neutral. Explain your reasoning.

a. A newspaper publishes an editorial recommending that readers vote for a particular political party.

b. Environment Canada reports that 15 centimetres of snow fell overnight.

c. An advertisement for a donut shop states that it has the "world's best coffee."

d. An arbitrator issues a report based on her meetings with disputing parties that makes recommendations designed to help the parties come to an agreement.

e. A candidate for employment prepares a résumé for a prospective employer.

f. A manager prepares the financial statements that will be presented to the board of directors and the shareholders of the company.

E5-5. **(Examining historical cost, LO 4)** For each of the following situations, determine what amount Sangudo Ltd. (Sangudo) should record as the cost of the asset. Explain your reasoning and indicate any practical problems that may be influencing your decisions.

a. Sangudo purchased new computer equipment for its head office. The equipment itself cost $250,000. Delivery, installation, and necessary renovations to the office cost an additional $175,000. Staff training cost $10,000. Taxes were $20,000.

b. Sangudo purchased inventory at a list price of $25,000. Sangudo paid for the inventory early so it received a 5% discount from the list price.

c. Sangudo purchased inventory for $30,000. Delivery charges were $2,000. The inventory was stored in a warehouse on shelving that cost $10,000. Utilities for the warehouse for the year this inventory was stored were $25,000. The manager of the warehouse earns $40,000 per year and wages for warehouse workers are $145,000 per year.

E5-6.   **(Identifying accounting assumptions, qualitative characteristics, and measurement conventions, LO 2, 3, 4)** For each of the following situations, identify the accounting assumptions, qualitative characteristics, and/or measurement conventions that Exmoor Corp. (Exmoor) would be violating by the accounting choices that it made. Explain your answer.

a. The president of Exmoor decided to increase the value of land the company was holding for resale because the amount originally recorded significantly understated the value.

b. Exmoor's sole shareholder used Exmoor personnel, material, and equipment to build his mansion. All costs incurred were reported on Exmoor's income statement as other expenses.

c. A foreign government has threatened to expropriate some of Exmoor's production facilities in that country without compensation. The country has a history of expropriating the assets of foreign corporations. Exmoor has not provided any information about this possibility in its financial statements because the company is still having discussions with the government and is hopeful that "things will work out."

d. Exmoor recently signed a contract to sell specially designed equipment to a poor Third World country for use in agriculture. Exmoor's engineering staff just began working on the design and it is hoped that the equipment will be delivered in four years. Exmoor recognized the revenue when the contract was signed with the country.

e. Exmoor expenses the cost of inventory when the inventory is received from the supplier.

f. Exmoor decided to change the method for recognizing revenue on some of its long-term contracts from the completed-contract method to the percentage-of-completion method to be consistent with its competitors. Due to certain complexities, Exmoor is not changing the revenue reported in previous years.

g. Exmoor purchased new computer equipment for its head office. The equipment itself cost $250,000. Delivery, installation, and renovations to the office to allow the computer equipment to be installed and operated cost an additional $175,000, which were expensed when incurred.

h. Some of Exmoor's inventory was seriously damaged in a fire. The company is currently looking for a buyer and is hoping to receive about 25% of the original cost of the inventory. Exmoor's controller is not writing down the inventory because "it has not been sold yet."

E5-7.   **(Identifying accounting assumptions, qualitative characteristics, and measurement conventions, LO 2, 3, 4)** Identify the accounting assumption, characteristic, or convention that best suits each of the situations below. Explain your choice.

a. Financial statements should include all relevant information about the economic activity of an entity.

b. The financial statements of a proprietorship should exclude the personal assets, liabilities, revenues, and expenses of the proprietor.

c. Capital assets are reported at their historical cost.

d. Shareholders receive an annual report from the corporation each year.

e. A company uses the percentage-of-completion method for recognizing revenue on long-term projects. The company determines that one of the projects is generating a loss and so recognizes the full amount of the loss immediately, rather than spreading the loss over the life of the contract.

f. Financial statement analysis is easier if similar entities use similar accounting methods.

g. The financial statements of most Canadian companies are presented in Canadian dollars.

h. The financial statements of many entities round amounts to the nearest thousand or even the nearest million.

i. A business that is ceasing operations values its assets and liabilities on a liquidation basis.

j. The cost of inventory sold is reported in the income statement in the same period in which the revenue that the inventory helped earn is recognized.

k. The cost of some low-cost assets is expensed when they are purchased, even though they have useful lives of more than one year.

E5-8. **(Examining verifiability, LO 3)** For each of the following transactions and economic events involving Hybla Ltd. (Hybla), indicate whether you think the amounts involved are easy to verify, moderately easy/moderately difficult to verify, or difficult to verify. Explain your reasoning.

a. Hybla purchases land from a developer for $5,000,000.

b. Land that Hybla has owned for 25 years has an estimated market value of $1,200,000.

c. Hybla trades a piece of land that it has owned for many years for shares in a privately held company. Hybla records the shares on its books at $5,000,000.

d. Hybla purchases a delivery vehicle and estimates that it will have a useful life of six years for purposes of calculating amortization.

e. Hybla sells merchandise to a customer for $100,000 and recognizes the revenue when the goods are delivered. The customer promises to pay in 90 days.

f. Hybla reports that it has $124,000 cash.

g. Hybla recognizes revenue on a percentage-of-completion basis on some of its long-term projects.

E5-9. **(Examining the periodic reporting assumption, LO 3)** For each of the following situations, explain the accounting problems and difficulties created because of the requirement for periodic reporting. Include other accounting assumptions, qualitative characteristics, and measurement conventions in your discussion if they are relevant.

a. An airline purchases a new Boeing 767 aircraft.

b. An engineering company decides to recognize revenue on a large dam project in a Third World country using the percentage-of-completion method.

c. A button manufacturer sells to clothing manufacturers around the world. Customers are required to pay within 60 days of delivery. The button manufacturer recognizes revenue when buttons are shipped to customers.

d. An oil refiner produces gasoline from crude oil and sells it to independent gas stations across Ontario. The crude oil is purchased at market prices and stored in large containers until it is refined. A single container mixes together different batches of crude oil that cost significantly different amounts because the price of crude can vary greatly.

E5-10. **(Examining materiality, LO 4)** For each of the following situations, explain whether you think the amount involved is material.

a. Students in an accounting course receive a grade of A if they get 80% or more on the final exam. A student receives 79% on the final exam, but the instructor made an adding error and the actual grade is 80%. Is the one-mark adding error material?

b. Students in an accounting course receive a grade of A if they get 80% or more on the final exam and a grade of B if they get between 65% and 79%. A student receives a 69% on the final exam, but the instructor made an adding error and the actual grade is 70%. Is the one-mark adding error material?

c. A company with annual sales of $1,000,000, net income of $150,000, and total assets of $500,000 accidentally did not include a $100,000 sale made near the end of the year in its current year's income statement. All costs associated with the sale were expensed in the current year's income statement. Is the $100,000 omission material?

d. A company with annual sales of $1,000,000, net income of $150,000, and total assets of $500,000 accidentally did not include a $1,000 sale made near the end of the year in its current year's income statement. All costs associated with the sale were expensed in the current year's income statement. Is the $1,000 omission material?

e. An agreement to sell a business sets the selling price at five times average net income. A $10,000 expenditure that is normally expensed when incurred was capitalized. Net income, without considering the capitalized $10,000 item, was $200,000.

f. In 2003 a company spent $200,000 on advertising and promotion. In 2004, because the company was short of cash, it spent $30,000 on advertising and promotion. Since the amount spent in 2004 was relatively small, management decided to include advertising and promotion in the general and administrative account on the income statement instead of reporting it separately as it did in its 2003 financial statements. In the 2004 financial statements, the 2003 amount was restated for consistency purposes so that it was also included in general and administrative expenses.

g. A company paid $500 for inventory it purchased from another company owned by the same shareholder.

E5-11. **(Examining non-arm's length transactions, LO 4)** For each of the following transactions entered into by Nootka Ltd. (Nootka), indicate whether it should be considered a non-arm's length transaction. In each case indicate whether information about the transaction should be disclosed separately according to GAAP. Explain your thinking. Assume you are a small shareholder in Nootka.

a. The CEO of Nootka purchases land owned by Nootka so that she can build a home.

b. Forty percent of Nootka's sales are to a single customer.

c. Nootka obtains consulting services from a firm operated by the majority shareholder's brother. All transactions occur at standard terms for the industry.

d. A number of Nootka's employees are close relatives of the majority shareholder. These people receive compensation that is the same as other employees carrying out similar duties.

e. The husband of Nootka's CEO is the "special consultant to the CEO." The special consultant receives a fee of $100,000 annually. The special consultant does not have special training or experience in the field and is rarely seen in Nootka's offices.

f. A friend of the CEO is Nootka's main supplier of office equipment.

g. Nootka sells goods to the Government of Canada and several of the provinces.

E5-12. **(Applying accounting assumptions, characteristics, and measurement conventions, LO 2, 3, 4)** What accounting assumption, characteristic, or measurement convention would Pilger Ltd. (Pilger) use to justify the following accounting treatments for the year ended June 30, 2004?

a. Pilger writes down capital assets to their net realizable value if the net realizable value is less than the cost of the asset.

b. Pilger discloses in the notes to the financial statements the fact that a fire destroyed a major production facility in July 2004. The effect of the fire is not recorded in Pilger's financial statements for the year ended June 30, 2004.

c. Pilger records the purchase of inventory at the amount of money it paid.

d. Pilger expenses the cost of inventory when the inventory is sold to a customer and the revenue is recognized.

e. Pilger allocates the cost of its amortizable assets over the estimated life that Pilger expects the asset to contribute to earning revenue.

E5-13. **(Examining conservatism, LO 4)** Anvil Ltd. (Anvil) adheres to GAAP in its financial statements. For each of the following independent situations, explain how Anvil should account for the transaction or economic event. Explain your reasoning. In each case, provide the journal entry that Anvil should prepare.

a. A piece of equipment that was purchased for $25,000 was destroyed during initial installation in an accident. The equipment had not yet been amortized.

b. Inventory with a cost of $100,000 has gone out of style and it will have to be sold at a discount. Management estimates that Anvil will be able to sell the inventory for $60,000.

c. Several years ago Anvil invested $200,000 in the shares of a new technology company. Last year the technology company went public and its shares are now traded on the Toronto Stock Exchange (TSX). Based on the most recent price on the TSX, the market value of Anvil's shares in the technology company is $7,000,000. None of the shares have been sold.

d. Several years ago Anvil invested $300,000 in the shares of a biotechnology company. Last week the biotechnology company announced that it was bankrupt and would be liquidating all of its assets and going out of business. Anvil will receive nothing for its shares in the biotechnology company and cannot sell the shares.

E5-14. **(Audit opinions, LO 5)** For each of the following situations, indicate the type of audit opinion that you think would be appropriate. The possible audit opinions are unqualified, qualified, adverse, and denial of an opinion.

a. Instead of using historical cost to value its inventory and capital assets on its balance sheet, Chocolate Cove Corp. used net realizable value, which was significantly higher than the cost of these assets.

b. Kitchimanitou Ltd. complied with GAAP in all material respects except that it expensed $330 worth of office supplies (staplers, hole punches, etc.) rather than capitalizing and amortizing them over their useful lives.

c. The auditor of Salt Harbour Inc. was prevented from determining the amount of inventory the company had at year end and as a result was unable to verify the amount of cost of goods sold, net income, and total assets.

d. Heart's Desire Inc. refused to write off inventory that in the auditor's opinion could not be sold. The amount is material and, as a result, the amount of inventory on the balance sheet is overstated and net income is understated. In the auditor's opinion, except for this item, the financial statements are fair and are in accordance with GAAP.

Problems

P5-1. **(Examining relevance and reliability, LO 3)** You are a corporate loan officer at a major bank. Itivia Inc. (Itivia) has applied to your bank for a $1,000,000 line of credit to finance operations. You have been given Itivia's file and find the following information:

a. Audited financial statements for the last three years.

b. Forecasted financial statements for the next two years prepared by management.

c. A letter from management providing assurances that Itivia is a solid company in good financial position.

d. A letter from the major shareholder offering a portfolio of securities as collateral against the loan.

e. Job descriptions and biographies of Itivia's senior executives.

f. A credit history (including a listing of loans obtained during the last 10 years) prepared by Itivia's management.

Required:

Evaluate the relevance (including predictive value, feedback value, and timeliness) and reliability (including representational faithfulness, verifiability, and neutrality/freedom from bias) of each piece of information in Itivia's file for the purpose of making the lending decision.

P5-2. **(Examining relevance and reliability, LO 3)** You are a prospective investor contemplating purchasing shares in Whyac Ltd. (Whyac), a publicly traded Canadian corporation. In the course of your research you obtain the following information:

a. Whyac's audited financial statements for the last three years.

b. The remainder of Whyac's annual report, including the president's letter and management's discussion and analysis.

c. A tip from a broker friend of yours indicating that "some big things are about to happen at Whyac."

d. A research report prepared by an independent financial research company that does in-depth analyses of companies and their prospects.

e. A research report prepared by a brokerage firm. The brokerage firm is in the process of finalizing a deal with Whyac that will have the brokerage firm selling Whyac's new issue of shares to the public.

f. An anonymous tip from an Internet investment chat room.

g. A newspaper item assessing the future prospects of Whyac's industry.

h. An economic outlook written by the chief economist of one of Canada's major banks.

Required:

Evaluate the relevance (including predictive value, feedback value, and timeliness) and reliability (including representational faithfulness, verifiability, and neutrality/ freedom from bias) of each piece of information for the purpose of deciding whether to invest in Whyac.

P5-3. **(Considering comparability, LO 3)** Thoburn Ltd. (Thoburn) and Nitro Inc. (Nitro) are two companies in the same industry. The net incomes for the year ended October 31, 2005 for the companies are shown below:

	Net income for the year ended October 31, 2005
Thoburn Ltd.	$125,000
Nitro Inc.	$ 75,000

Upon reviewing the financial statements you discover that the two companies use identical accounting policies except for inventory and amortization of capital assets. Thoburn uses a method for accounting for inventory called FIFO, while Nitro uses a method called average cost (these methods will be discussed in Chapter 8). Also, Thoburn uses a method called straight-line amortization for amortizing its capital assets while Nitro uses a method called accelerated amortization (these methods of accounting for amortization will be discussed in Chapter 9).

Had Thoburn used average cost for accounting for inventory, its net income would have been $30,000 lower than it reported in its financial statements. Had Nitro used FIFO instead of average cost for accounting for inventory, its net income would have been $30,000 higher than it reported in its financial statements. Had Thoburn used accelerated amortization instead of straight-line amortization, its net income would have been $20,000 lower than it reported in its financial statements. Had Nitro used straight-line amortization instead of accelerated amortization, its net income would have been $20,000 higher than it reported in its financial statements.

Required:

a. Compute net income for Thoburn and Nitro under the following circumstances:

Inventory Method	Amortization Method	Net Income for Thoburn Ltd.	Net Income for Nitro Inc.
FIFO	Straight line		
FIFO	Accelerated		
Average cost	Straight line		
Average cost	Accelerated		

b. Which company performed better during the year ended October 31, 2005? Explain.

c. Why do you think the managers of Thoburn and Nitro selected the accounting policies they did? Explain.

d. What are the implications of having more than one acceptable accounting method under GAAP on a user's ability to use the financial statements?

P5-4. **(Considering comparability, LO 3)** Donjek Ltd. (Donjek) and Quigley Inc. (Quigley) are two companies in the same industry. The net incomes for the companies for the year ended May 31, 2006 are shown below:

	Net income for the year ended May 31, 2006
Donjek Ltd.	$425,000
Quigley Inc.	$350,000

Upon reviewing the financial statements you discover that the two companies use identical accounting policies except for inventory and amortization of capital assets. Donjek uses a method for accounting inventory called FIFO, while Quigley uses a method called average cost (these methods of accounting for inventory will be discussed in Chapter 8). Also, Donjek uses a method called straight-line amortization for amortizing its capital assets while Quigley uses a method called accelerated amortization (these methods of accounting for amortization will be discussed in Chapter 9).

Had Donjek used average cost for accounting for inventory, its net income would have been $50,000 lower than it reported in its financial statements. Had Quigley used FIFO instead of average cost for accounting for inventory, its net income would have been $50,000 higher than it reported in its financial statements. Had Donjek used accelerated amortization instead of straight-line amortization, its net income would have been $25,000 lower than it reported in its financial statements. Had Quigley used straight-line amortization instead of accelerated amortization, its net income would have been $25,000 higher than it reported in its financial statements.

Required:

a. Compute net income for Donjek and Quigley under the following circumstances:

Inventory Method	Amortization Method	Net Income for Donjek Ltd.	Net Income for Quigley Inc.
FIFO	Straight line		
FIFO	Accelerated		
Average cost	Straight line		
Average cost	Accelerated		

b. Which company performed better during the year ended May 31, 2006? Explain.

c. Why do you think the managers of Donjek and Quigley selected the accounting policies they did? Explain.

d. What are the implications of having more than one acceptable accounting method under GAAP on a user's ability to use the financial statements?

P5-5. **(Applying accounting assumptions, qualitative characteristics, and measurement conventions, LO 2, 3, 4)** For each of the following items pertaining to Dollarton Ltd. (Dollarton), indicate which accounting assumptions, qualitative characteristics, and measurement conventions are influencing the accounting treatment used. Explain your reasoning.

a. A corporation that is owned by Dollarton is going out of business and values its assets and liabilities at their net realizable value. Dollarton and the other companies owned by it do not value their assets and liabilities at their net realizable value.

b. Dollarton records the purchase of new heavy equipment at $22,000,000, the price paid. The $20,000 cost of inspecting the equipment is expensed when the equipment was purchased as a maintenance expense.

c. Dollarton holds a portfolio of shares of publicly traded companies. The shares are recorded on the balance sheet at their cost, which is significantly lower than their market value. Dollarton reports the market value of the portfolio in the notes to the financial statements.

d. Dollarton prepares financial statements for its December 31 year end and amounts in the statements are stated in U.S. dollars.

e. Because of zoning problems with a piece of land, Dollarton writes down the cost of the land to $500,000 from its cost of $1,200,000.

f. A person who claims to have been injured using one of Dollarton's products launches a lawsuit against the company. Dollarton includes a note describing the lawsuit in its financial statements but does not accrue any amount in the financial statements themselves.

P5-6. **(Applying accounting assumptions, qualitative characteristics, and measurement conventions, LO 2, 3, 4)** For each of the following items pertaining to Magpie Ltd. (Magpie), indicate which accounting assumptions, qualitative characteristics, and measurement conventions are influencing the accounting treatment used. Explain your reasoning.

a. During the year just ended Magpie changed the method it uses to account for inventory. Magpie restated previous years' financial statements so that all years in the financial statements would reflect the same accounting method. As a result of the change Magpie now uses the same accounting policy as its major competitors.

b. Magpie, which has assets of $3,000,000 and revenues of $4,000,000, includes the $20,000 cost of renting storage space in general and administrative expenses rather than providing a separate line on the income statement for the amount.

c. Magpie receives an advance payment from a customer for goods that will be delivered in four months. The payment is credited to the unearned revenue account.

d. The cost of capital assets is amortized over their useful lives.

e. For the year just ended Magpie recorded a bad debt expense of $20,000, which is its estimate of the amount of accounts receivable that will not be collected. The $20,000 was credited to the allowance for doubtful accounts account, which is a contra-asset account to accounts receivable.

f. Some land owned by Magpie has more than doubled in value since it was purchased two years ago. Magpie plans to sell the land in the next year, but to date the increase in the value of the land has not been reflected in the financial statements.

P5-7. **(Examining conservatism, LO 4)** Kitscoty Inc. (Kitscoty) is a chain of retail sporting goods stores located across western Canada. Kitscoty has a policy of capitalizing the cost of opening new stores and amortizing the cost over five years. In the last year and a half Kitscoty has not been performing well and in late 2005 the shareholders of the company, none of whom are involved in the management, decided to replace the existing management with a new team of managers. Kitscoty is in the process of preparing its December 31, 2005 financial statements. In light of the company's recent poor performance, the new management has decided to write off the entire $5,200,000 of store opening costs that were recorded as an asset on the balance sheet.

a. If a new store incurred $400,000 in opening costs, what journal entity would Kitscoty make to capitalize the cost of the store opening cost as an asset? Assume that $250,000 of the opening costs was in cash and the remainder are liabilities.

b. What journal entry would Kitscoty record when it writes off the $5,200,000 in store opening costs? What is the effect on income in 2005 of writing off the store opening costs?

c. What accounting concepts justify the write-off of the store opening costs?

d. What possible motivations could Kitscoty's new management have for writing off the store opening costs in 2005?

e. If Kitscoty had not written off the store opening costs, it would have incurred about $1,300,000 in amortization expense for the store opening costs in each of fiscal 2005, 2006, and 2007. Assuming that income including all revenues and expenses except for the store opening costs in 2005 was $4,600,000, and was estimated to be the same for 2006 and 2007, calculate net income in 2005, 2006, and 2007:

    i.   Assuming that Kitscoty wrote off the store opening costs in 2005.

    ii. Assuming that Kitscoty did not write off the store opening costs in 2005 and amortized $1,300,000 in each year.

f. Using your results in (e), explain the effect of the write off in 2005 on future years' earnings, and the problems that users might have interpreting financial statements as a result of the write-off.

P5-8. **(Applying accounting assumptions, qualitative characteristics, and measurement conventions, LO 2, 3, 4)** Internet Access Ltd. (IAL) is a large Canadian Internet service provider (ISP). A key to success for IAL is enlisting new customers and the company aggressively markets its service by sending out free IAL Internet Access Software in newspapers, magazines, and direct mailings. The software allows potential customers to gain access to the Internet at no charge and IAL hopes that after the trial period expires the potential customers will become paying customers by signing up with IAL as their ISP. The costs of attracting new customers in this way include printing, production, and distributing the Internet Access Software. IAL capitalizes theses costs of attracting new customers and amortizes them over 24 months. The 24-month amortization period is used because IAL estimates that the customers will generate revenue for IAL for an average of 24 months.

IAL is the only company in the industry that accounts for attracting customers in this way; in general, most companies expense these types of costs when they are incurred. IAL's costs of attracting new customers have increased significantly in each of the last five years.

Required:

a. Explain the effect on IAL's earnings of capitalizing the costs of attracting new customers and amortizing them over 24 months.

b. Use the accounting assumptions, qualitative characteristics, and measurement conventions identified in this chapter to make a case for:

    i.   Capitalizing the costs of attracting new customers and amortizing them over a reasonable period.

    ii. Expensing the costs of attracting new customers as they are incurred.

P5-9. **(Applying accounting assumptions, qualitative characteristics, and measurement conventions, LO 2, 3, 4)** Live Theatre Productions Ltd. (LTPL) produces major theatrical productions in major centres across Canada. Usually LTPL selects shows that have had or are having successful runs in the United States or in Europe, and then mounts Canadian productions of the show. Most productions that are successful outside of Canada do well in Canada, but this is not always the case.

It can take well over a year from the time LTPL decides to put on a show to the first performance. Many costs must be incurred before the show is ever performed, including purchasing the rights to the show, paying performers and other personnel, creating costumes and sets, holding rehearsals, and so on. LTPL capitalizes all costs incurred before a show begins its run and classifies them as an asset on the company's balance sheet. LTPL then amortizes these costs over the estimated life of the show.

Required:

Use the accounting assumptions, qualitative characteristics, and measurement conventions identified in this chapter to make a case for:

a. Capitalizing the costs incurred before a show begins and amortizing them over the estimated life of the show.

b. Expensing the costs as they are incurred, before a show begins.

P5-10. **(Applying accounting assumptions, qualitative characteristics, and measurement conventions, LO 2, 3, 4)** Companies in the oil and gas exploration industry can choose the method they use to account for the cost of finding oil or gas. The cost of finding these resources is very expensive and significant amounts of money must be spent before a single drop of oil or gas finds its way to market.

The first method available to oil and gas exploration companies is the successful efforts method. When oil and gas companies explore, they often look in a number of places and find the resource only in some of the places. Thus a company may drill a dozen wells and find oil or gas in five of them. Under the successful efforts method of accounting, only the costs incurred to find wells that actually contain oil or gas are capitalized. The costs incurred to find wells that are empty are expensed once it is known that a well is empty. The capitalized costs are then amortized over the estimated amount of oil or gas that will be extracted from the well. (If a well is estimated to have 1,000,000 barrels of oil and the well cost $5,000,000 to find and develop, then $5 is expensed for each barrel of oil that is removed from the well. If at the same time another $5,000,000 were spent on a well that proved to be empty, the $5,000,000 would be expensed immediately.)

The second method of accounting for the costs of exploring for oil and gas is called the full cost method. Under the full cost method all costs incurred to find oil or gas are capitalized regardless of whether the wells explored for are full or empty. All of the costs incurred would be amortized over the estimated amount of oil or gas that will be extracted from the well successful wells. (Thus, if a well is estimated to have 1,000,000 barrels of oil in it and that well and an unsuccessful well cost $10,000,000 to find and develop, then $10 is expensed for each barrel of oil that is removed from the successful well.)

Required:

a. Explain the effect on earnings that using the successful efforts method would have versus the full costing method. Which method do you think entities would prefer to use? Explain.

b. You have been asked to prepare a brief for the accounting standard setters that argues in favour of using successful efforts accounting for oil and gas exploration costs and against the full cost method. Use the accounting assumptions, qualitative characteristics, and measurement conventions identified in this chapter as appropriate to develop your arguments.

c. You have been asked to prepare a brief for the accounting standard setters that argues in favour of using full cost accounting for oil and gas exploration costs and against the successful efforts method. Use the accounting assumptions, qualitative characteristics, and measurement conventions identified in this chapter as appropriate to develop your arguments.

P5-11. **(Case analysis, LO 2, 3, 4)** Re-read the Savoy Health Club Ltd. case that was given as the Solved Problem in this chapter (see pages 288–289).

Required:

Jim Floor has approached you to advise him regarding his pending acquisition of Savoy Health Club Ltd. Mr. Floor has become familiar with the accounting concerns being addressed by Fred Irving and he would like you to prepare a report explaining appropriate accounting treatments for the accounting issues. Mr. Floor wants full explanations and justifications for the recommendations you make so that he can explain them to Fred Irving and to the arbitrator, if necessary.

P5-12. **(Case analysis, LO 2, 3, 4)** Re-read the Savoy Health Club Ltd. case that was given as the solved problem in this chapter (see pages 288–295).

Required:

You are an arbitrator who has been engaged by Fred Irving and Jim Floor to help resolve the outstanding accounting issues that are delaying the completion of the deal that will sell Savoy Health Club Ltd. to Mr. Floor. Prepare a report recommending appropriate accounting treatments for the accounting issues. Mr. Irving and Mr. Floor would like full explanations and justifications for the recommendations you make.

P5-13. **(The impact of non-arm's length transactions and entity assumption, LO 2, 4)** Norboro Software Development Inc. (Norboro) is a small software development company that specializes in customizing computer software for small- to medium-sized professional practices. Norboro has developed a number of proprietary software packages that it modifies for clients. Norboro also modifies existing commercial packages to suit the needs of clients. Norboro is owned by James and Anita Norboro; each owns 50% of the shares of the company. Recently the Norboros were approached about selling their business to a competitor that is looking to expand. The Norboros are thinking seriously about selling and they have provided the following income statement for the year ended September 30, 2004:

Norboro Software Development Inc.
Income Statement
For the Year Ended September 30, 2004

Revenue		$825,000
Expenses:		
Salaries and wages	$325,000	
Amortization	75,000	
Advertising and promotion	60,000	
Other	35,000	
Interest	4,500	
Utilities	12,000	
Administration	10,000	
Consulting fees	80,000	601,500
Income before income taxes		$223,500

In discussions with the Norboros the prospective buyer has obtained some important information about the business. Norboro was originally financed five years ago by a $200,000 interest free loan from Anita Norboro's parents. An equivalent loan from the bank would have an interest rate of about 10%. The loan has not yet been repaid. The salaries and wages expense includes $60,000 per year that is paid to James and $60,000 per year that is paid to Anita. Anita does not work in the business, except to help out from time to time with some of the administration. If Norboro had to hire an employee to do the work done by Anita, the cost would be about $15,000. Hiring a person to do the work James does would cost about $75,000. Norboro's offices are located in a building owned by Anita. The company pays no rent for the space. Equivalent space in the building rents for about $100,000 per year. The consulting fees pertain to service provided by another company owned by James Norboro. These services are provided to Norboro Software Development Inc. at about 10% below the usual market rate.

Required:
a. Are the financial statements as shown above an appropriate basis for the prospective buyer to assess Norboro? Explain.
b. You have been asked by the prospective buyer of Norboro to recast the financial statements for the year ended September 30, 2004 as if the buyer had operated the company.

P5-14. **(Case analysis, LO 2, 3, 4)** Wanda's Fashions is a small tailor shop located in the centre of a medium-sized community. The shop is owned and operated by Wanda. Wanda makes alterations to clothing, tailors clothing to the specification of customers, and carries a line of ready-made clothing that she designs and makes herself. Wanda also makes all the uniforms worn by employees of her brother Wendel's businesses. Wanda has been in business for over 20 years and has many loyal customers. Wanda has a list of over 200 people who use her services regularly, both for tailoring new clothes and for repairing and altering clothes.

The store owns several sewing machines, pressing equipment, mannequins, and furniture and fixtures in the showroom portion of the store. There is also a large sign in front of the store. All capital assets are amortized using the rates required by the *Income Tax Act*.

Wanda has a large quantity of fabrics in stock so she can provide selection to customers who wish to have clothes made for them.

Wanda operates the store on her own. She has two tailors who work for her part-time, based on how busy she is. Her children, Wendy and Webster, sometimes work in the store when it is busy. Webster also helps his mother do alterations and some of the tailoring. The children are not paid for their work but Wanda pays for their university tuition fees and last year bought them a car.

The shop is located in a three-storey building owned by Wanda and her husband Willie. In addition to Wanda's shop, the building houses three other storefront businesses (a fruit store, a butcher shop, and a video store) and has two businesses and three apartments on the second floor. Each of the tenants (except Wanda's Fashions) pays a monthly rent.

Wanda, Willie, and family live on the third floor of the building.

Wanda and Willie prepare a single set of financial statements that are used for tax purposes. The statements encompass all income and expenses generated by Wanda and Willie's business activities (all of which are unincorporated), including Wanda's Fashions, building operations, and some of Willie's unincorporated business ventures.

Wolfgang Wondergarment has expressed interest in purchasing Wanda's shop. Wolfgang is an experienced tailor who arrived in Canada three years ago from an eastern European company. He has been working as a tailor for a major chain but he feels he is ready to have his own business. He will be meeting with Wanda next week to discuss the sale. Wanda has indicated that she will provide any information that is required.

Required:

Wolfgang Wondergarment has asked you for help in preparing for the meeting. Wolfgang would like a report outlining the information that should be requested from Wanda, including questions and concerns he should have about the financial statements that Wanda will show him. Wolfgang believes that Wanda's accountant (actually her cousin Wesley) will be present, so Wolfgang wants full explanations of what is needed and why it is required.

■ Using Financial Statements

Canada Bread Company, Limited

Canada Bread Company, Limited (Canada Bread) is a leading Canadian manufacturer and marketer of value-added flour-based products. The Company's products include fresh bread, rolls and bagels; frozen bagels and dough products; par-baked bread products; and specialty pasta and sauces. Canada Bread maintains a national presence with three principal brand names: Dempster's, Olivieri, and Tenderflake. Canada Bread Company, Limited is 68% owned by Maple Leaf Foods Inc.[4]

Canada Bread's consolidated balance sheets and statements of earnings, along with some extracts from the notes to the financial statements, are provided in Exhibit 5-4. Use this information to respond to questions FS5-1 to FS5-9. Incorporate the relevant GAAP assumptions, qualitative characteristics, and measurement conventions discussed in this chapter, when appropriate, in your answers.

FS5-1. What is the unit of measure used by Canada Bread in its financial statements? How do you know? Why is it important that this information be provided?

FS5-2. Why does Canada Bread round the dollar numbers in its financial statements to the nearest thousand? Does this rounding result in users of Canada Bread's financial statement losing important information? Could it? Explain.

FS5-3. What is the entity that Canada Bread's financial statements report on? Is this entity a single legal entity? Explain.

Exhibit 5-4

Canada Bread Company, Limited
Financial Statements

(in thousands of Canadian dollars) As at	December 31, 2000	December 31, 1999
Assets		
Current Assets:		
Accounts receivable (note 4)	$ 25,094	$ 25,324
Due from related company (note 14)	5,281	4,290
Inventories	16,065	17,898
Income and other taxes receivable	1,673	—
Future tax asset (note 12)	2,655	—
Prepaid expenses	1,740	1,945
	52,508	49,457
Investment in associated company	46,971	46,128
Property and equipment (note 5)	156,676	166,290
Goodwill	74,225	77,490
	$ 330,380	$ 339,365
Liabilities and Shareholders' Equity		
Current Liabilities:		
Bank indebtedness	$ 3,280	$ 1,436
Accounts payable and accrued charges	55,958	64,394
Dividends payable	1,285	1,285
Income and other taxes payable	—	2,707
Current portion of long term debt (note 6)	102	106
	60,625	69,928
Long term debt (note 6)	175	14,772
Future tax liability (note 12)	34,139	—
Deferred income taxes	—	23,505
Shareholders' equity (note 8)	235,441	231,160
	$ 330,380	$ 339,365

See accompanying notes to consolidated financial statements.
Contingencies and commitments (note 15)
Subsequent events (note 16).

(in thousands of Canadian dollars, except per share amount) Years ended	December 31, 2000	December 31, 1999
Sales	$ 553,660	$ 567,251
Earnings from operations, before unusual items	24,652	20,111
Unusual items (note 3)	—	(8,350)
Earnings from operations	24,652	11,761
Other income (note 10)	1,876	1,469
Earnings before interest and taxes	26,528	13,230
Interest expense (note 11)	2,323	2,174
Earnings before income taxes	24,205	11,056
Income taxes (note 2g and 12)	6,965	4,754
Net earnings	$ 17,240	$ 6,302
Earnings per share (note 8)	$ 0.80	$ 0.29

See accompanying notes to consolidatged financial statements.

FS5-4. How is the periodic reporting assumption reflected in Canada Bread's financial statements? Explain. How is accounting for capital assets such as property and equipment affected by the periodic reporting assumption? (When answering the latter question, consider how the cost of property and equipment is expensed over its life and the difficulty that might exist in estimating the amount to expense.)

FS5-5. Examine Canada Bread's statement of earnings. Do you think this statement satisfies the four qualitative characteristics discussed in this chapter? Explain.

2. SIGNIFICANT ACCOUNTING POLICIES

a) Principles of consolidation

The accompanying consolidated financial statements include the accounts of the Company and its subsidiaries. The Company owns a 25% interest in Multi-Marques Inc., a Quebec based bakery business, which is accounted for using the equity method.

e) Property and equipment

Property and equipment are recorded at cost including, where applicable, interest capitalized during the construction or development period. Depreciation is calculated using the straight-line basis at the following rates which are based on the expected useful life of the asset:

Buildings	2½% – 5%
Machinery and equipment	7½% – 33⅓%

5. PROPERTY AND EQUIPMENT

	2000	1999
Land	$ 13,219	$ 13,198
Building	52,039	50,272
Machinery and equipment	210,331	197,384
Construction in progress	4,388	13,511
	279,977	274,365
Less accumulated depreciation	123,301	108,075
Net book value	$ 156,676	$ 166,290

14. RELATED PARTY TRANSACTIONS

a) A significant portion of the Company's sales to the U.S. and other export markets are through related companies during the normal course of operations and have been recorded at market amounts.

b) Maple Leaf provides the Company with certain management services including treasury, taxation, internal audit, accounting and access to bulk purchasing programs. Pursuant to a Management and Affiliation Agreement entered into in August 1995, the Company paid a management and affiliation fee of $3.4 million (1999 – $3.2 million) to Maple Leaf which approximates the cost of providing these services.

15. CONTINGENCIES AND COMMITMENTS

a) The Company has been named as defendant in several legal actions and is subject to various risks and contingencies arising in the normal course of business. Management is of the opinion that the outcome of these uncertainties will not have a material adverse effect on the Company's financial position.

b) In the normal course of business, the Company enters into sales commitments with various customers, and purchase commitments with various suppliers. These commitments are for varying terms, and can provide for fixed or variable prices. The Company believes these contracts serve to reduce risk, and it is not anticipated that losses will be incurred on these contracts.

16. SUBSEQUENT EVENT

On January 22, 2001, the Company reached an agreement to increase its ownership in Multi-Marques Inc. from 25% to 100% by acquiring the remaining outstanding shares from all of the other shareholders. The purchase will represent a net investment of approximately $125 million and will be financed with new long term bank debt. Finalization of the transaction is dependant on clearance of the transaction under the Competition Act.

FS5-6. Examine Notes 2e and 5 to Canada Bread's financial statements. How are Canada Bread's property and equipment valued on the financial statements? Do you think the information provided about property and equipment is relevant, reliable, or both? Explain.

FS5-7. Examine Note 14 to Canada Bread's financial statements. What are related party transactions? Why are they reported in the financial statements? Describe the related party transactions that Canada Bread reports. Explain why this particular information is useful to users of the financial statements.

FS5-8. Examine Note 15 to Canada Bread's financial statements, which describes contingent liabilities. A **contingent liability** is a liability that may arise in the future if certain future events occur and a commitment is an executory contract.
   a. What is the nature of the economic events described in Note 15?
   b. Why do you think this information is included in the notes to the financial statements even though it is not incorporated in the financial statements themselves?

FS5-9. Examine Note 16 to Canada Bread's financial statements. As the title of the note, "Subsequent events" suggests, this note provides information about events that took place after Canada Bread's December 31, 2000 year end. Describe the subsequent event that Canada Bread reports in the notes to its financial statements. Since the events described in Note 16 occurred after Canada Bread's year end, why are they included in the financial statements? Tie your answer to the accounting assumptions, qualitative characteristics, and measurement conventions described in the chapter.

■ Analyzing Mark's Work Wearhouse

M5-1. Examine MWW's financial statements and give examples of how each of GAAP's basic assumptions is reflected in the statements.

M5-2. Examine MWW's financial statements, including the notes, and give examples of how each of GAAP's qualitative characteristics of accounting is reflected in the statements and notes.

M5-3. Examine MWW's financial statements, including the notes, and give examples of how each of GAAP's measurement conventions is reflected in the statements and notes.

M5-4. Examine Note 1I of MWW's financial statements (page A-50). Present arguments using the GAAP assumptions, characteristics, and conventions that are discussed in this chapter in support of the treatment used by MWW for its store opening costs and in opposition to the treatment used by MWW for its store opening costs.

M5-5. Examine Note 1P of MWW's financial statements (page A-51). Explain why this note is included in the statements. In your answer make reference to the relevant GAAP assumptions, qualitative characteristics, and measurement conventions that were discussed in the chapter.

M5-6. MWW does not report its brand name as an asset on its balance sheet. Explain why this is the case using the relevant GAAP assumptions, qualitative characteristics, and measurement conventions that were discussed in the chapter.

M5-7. Read the introductory paragraph to Note 1 and Note 1B to MWW's financial statements (page A-49). What is the entity that MWW's financial statements are reporting on?

M5-8. Note 11 to MWW's financial statements (page A-56) provides information on MWW's commitments and contingent liabilities. A contingent liability is a liability that may arise in the future if certain future events occur and a commitment is an executory contract.
   a. Describe the commitments and contingent liabilities that MWW has.
   b. Why is the information supplied in this note useful to users? Include in your answer a discussion of the relevant accounting assumptions, qualitative characteristics, and measurement conventions that were raised in this chapter.

Endnotes

1. Extracted from TransCanada Pipelines Limited's 2000 annual report.

2. Extracted from Samuel Manu-Tech Inc.'s 2000 annual report.

3. Panel A extracted from Magna International Inc.'s 2000 annual report. Panel B extracted from Quebecor Inc.'s 2000 annual report. Panel C extracted from BCE Emergis' 2000 annual report.

4. Extracted from Canada Bread Company, Limited 2000 annual report.

Chapter 6

Cash Flow, Profitability, and the Cash Flow Statement

Learning Objectives

After studying the material in this chapter you will be able to:

LO 1. Distinguish between cash and accrual accounting, and between cash from operations and net income.

LO 2. Describe the cash cycle.

LO 3. Read and interpret the information in the cash flow statement.

LO 4. Prepare a cash flow statement.

LO 5. Explain how cash flow information can be manipulated and how accrual accounting policy choices affect the cash flow statement.

Introduction

Money—cash money, that is—makes the world go round. A company like Mark's Work Wearhouse (MWW) must have cash to pay for operating costs such as inventory, employees, rent, and utilities. MWW also needs cash to repay amounts borrowed, purchase capital assets, and re-purchase franchise stores. Without cash, business will quickly grind to a halt.

When it comes to assessing an entity, however, it seems that net income and accrual information are the main criteria. Unfortunately, focusing on accrual information can be a very narrow and naïve way to view an entity for many of the decisions and assessments that stakeholders have to make. It is important to remember that earnings is a very abstract concept. Earnings reflects changes in wealth; *earnings do not pay the bills*. Paying bills and operating a business requires cash. A business can survive quite nicely without showing a profit, provided that it has adequate cash inflows or reserves. Conversely, as we will discover in this chapter, it is very possible for an entity to have good earnings and poor cash flow. An entity that cannot generate enough cash will eventually find itself in trouble because it will be unable to meet its obligations. Clearly, focusing only on earnings can give a misleading picture of how an entity is doing.

In this chapter we will explore the importance of cash flow and liquidity to an entity. Managing the liquidity of an entity is crucial to its success and survival. If an entity is too liquid (in other words, if it has too much cash), it stands to be unprofitable or less profitable than it could be. If it is not liquid enough, it can suffer financial distress. A useful source of information about the cash flow and liquidity of an entity is the cash flow statement. In this chapter you will learn how to read, interpret, and prepare a cash flow statement.

Cash Versus Accrual Accounting and the Cash Cycle

Accrual accounting is the primary accounting method used in Canada. While there are some exceptions—primarily small, simple businesses—accrual accounting is used by the vast majority of entities. Once the economic environment an entity faces becomes the least bit complex, there is a need for at least some elements of accrual accounting. For example, if an entity buys or sells on credit, there is a need for payables or receivables, both of which are accrual concepts. With accrual accounting, revenue is recognized when it is earned and expenses are matched to the revenue. Cash flows can occur before, after, or at the same time that revenues and expenses are recognized. Receivables arise in accrual accounting when an entity has a right to receive cash; payables arise when the entity has an obligation to pay cash. Capital assets are amortized over their useful lives, regardless of when or how they are paid for.

Cash accounting is much simpler than accrual accounting and requires far less judgment. The concepts of revenue and expense are replaced by receipt and disbursement, which simply reflect cash received and cash expended. Receivables and payables do not exist at all under cash accounting. Accrual accounting requires judgment as to when revenue is earned and how and what costs should be matched to revenues. Cash receipts are recorded when cash is received and disbursements are recorded when cash is paid—there is little room for judgment in either case. The standard measure of performance under accrual accounting, earnings, is a slippery, abstract economic concept that is intended to measure the change in wealth of the owners of a profit-oriented entity. Earnings are not designed to reflect flows of cash, but rather flows of wealth. Cash flow is a much more concrete concept than earnings. This is not to say that cash flow is a better or worse measure than earnings. Cash flow is just different from earnings, and each has its role to play.

In sum, cash accounting and accrual accounting tell us different things. Cash accounting provides information about the movement of cash in and out of an entity. This information is crucial for assessing liquidity. Accrual accounting provides information that can be viewed as giving a bigger economic picture. Both cash information and accrual information can be useful to stakeholders and it can be unwise for stakeholders to ignore either.

Question for Consideration

Provide five examples of why earnings differ from cash flow.

    Answer: There are many examples of why earnings and cash flow are different. Some include:

- Inventory is purchased and paid for before it is sold.
- Inventory is sold before it is paid for.
- Revenue is recognized before cash is received (sale on credit).
- Revenue is recognized after cash is received (payment received before revenue is earned).
- Capital assets are amortized over their useful lives.
- Insurance or rent is paid in advance but expensed when used.
- Wages are earned by employees but not paid until a later period.
- Wages are paid in advance.
- Store opening costs are deferred and amortized.
- Warranty expense/liability is set up when the related goods are sold but the cash flow occurs later when the warranty work is done.

The Cash Cycle

Being in business costs money. And entities usually must spend money before that spending generates cash from customers. There is almost always a lag between the expenditure of cash and the receipt of cash. For example, before a single sale is made in a new store MWW has to locate, rent, design, decorate, and equip the store, stock it with inventory, hire and train employees, and so on. Once the store is operating, inventory must be continually replaced and updated. Much of the inventory will be bought and paid for before a customer purchases it. It is not only the investment in capital assets that happens before cash comes in from customers. MWW must buy inventory before it is sold to customers. Even a relatively simple business such as a street-side hot dog vendor requires up-front investment for the cart and a supply of hot dogs, drinks, and condiments to do business.

We can get a better understanding of the lag between expenditure and receipt of cash by looking at some numbers. The effect of the lag is shown in Figure 6-1. Yellowknife Corp. (Yellowknife) is a distributor of outdoor clothing and equipment. On average Yellowknife has inventory in stock for 180 days before it is sold (inventory conversion period). In other words, the average length of time between Yellowknife receiving inventory from its suppliers and selling it to customers is 180 days. Yellowknife pays for its inventory, on average, 90 days after it receives goods from a supplier (payables deferral period). The average length of time between delivery of goods to customers and receipt of cash by Yellowknife is 40 days (receivables conversion period).

Figure 6-1 shows that 220 days pass from the time Yellowknife receives inventory from a supplier to when it receives cash from a customer. For 90 days Yellowknife does not have to pay for its inventory—suppliers finance the purchases. For the remaining

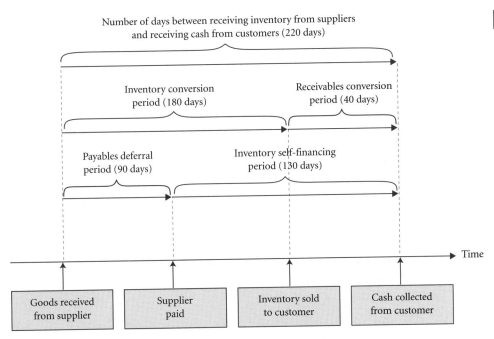

Figure 6-1

The Cash Lag for Yellowknife Corp.

130 days, Yellowknife has cash invested in inventory (inventory self-financing period). Even though Yellowknife will not have sold most of its inventory once it is paid for, the company must have cash available to pay for the inventory as well as other costs of operating the business, such as wages, rent, utilities, and so on. If Yellowknife does not have the cash to meet these obligations, suppliers may stop shipping inventory, employees may refuse to work, utilities may cut off their services, and property owners may evict the occupant. These outcomes would be disastrous for Yellowknife's business.

Ensuring that an entity has enough cash resources on hand or available to it is a crucial task for management. If cash inflows from customers do not occur as expected, the ability of an entity to meet its obligations can be impaired. In an economic slowdown cash inflows may be reduced because customers are slow in paying their debts (perhaps they themselves have cash flow problems or buy less than expected). If cash inflows are reduced, there might not be enough cash to pay suppliers, employees, and other creditors.

The cycle by which an entity begins with cash, invests in resources, provides goods or services to customers using those resources, and then collects cash from customers is called the **cash cycle**. The cash cycle is shown in Figure 6-2 (page 318). When you examine Figure 6-2 it is crucial to recognize that the cash expended purchasing resources usually occurs before the entity receives cash from customers. The length of the lag will vary depending on the industry, customers, terms and conditions of transactions, and so on. For example, in the mining industry huge amounts of money must be spent to find the resource and develop the mine before any cash is generated from sales.

If the future were perfectly predictable there would be few entities facing liquidity problems. Liquidity problems occur because what actually happens is not always the same as what managers expect to happen. For example, MWW's managers must buy merchandise for their stores many months before it will be made available for sale. When making their buying decisions MWW's managers must predict customers' tastes, weather conditions, economic conditions, and so on, in order to stock appropriate merchandise in the right quantities for sale at the right price. But many things can go wrong. If there is a downturn in the economy, there will be less demand for work clothes and people will have less money to spend on MWW merchandise. If the winter is warmer than expected, MWW will sell less cold weather clothing than

Figure 6-2

The Cash Cycle

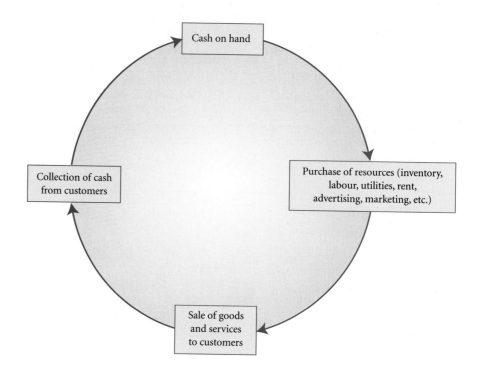

anticipated. If MWW purchases lines of merchandise that are not popular with customers, that merchandise will not sell very well. The upshot is that if any of these circumstances arise, MWW will have less cash coming in than expected. However, the suppliers of the merchandise still have to be paid.

Growing businesses also can face serious liquidity problems. Expansion and growth are positive times for businesses, but poor planning and excessive optimism can lead to serious cash shortages. Consider a successful restaurant that expands to accommodate the people whom the owners think are clamouring to eat at the restaurant. Expansion requires upfront capital costs to renovate the new space, purchase furniture and fixtures, perhaps buy additional kitchen equipment, and so on. Ongoing operating costs will increase with expansion as well. The owners may have to pay additional rent and increased utilities costs, hire additional staff, and purchase additional inventory. What happens if the customers do not come to the expanded location? Many of the higher operating costs still have to be paid. If loans were obtained to finance the upfront costs, interest must be paid on the loans. If cash inflows are not adequate to meet the cash requirements of the business, financial distress may occur.

Example: Cash Flow Scenarios at Peabody Corp.

Let's look at an example that demonstrates the cash flow problems an entity can face and the differences that can exist between earnings and cash flow. Peabody Ltd. (Peabody) began operations on January 1, 2005. Peabody purchases various types of candy in bulk from producers, packages the candy, and sells it to corporate customers. The corporate customers use the packaged candy as gifts for customers, suppliers, and employees. Peabody must maintain an inventory of candy and packaging so that it can meet the orders of customers quickly. The following information is available about Peabody's operation:

- All of Peabody's inventory purchases are for cash because suppliers are not ready to extend credit to the new company.

- Peabody allows customers up to 90 days to pay for their purchases. For the pur-

Question for Consideration

Ushta Ltd. is a manufacturer of auto parts. The company purchases materials from suppliers and stores them in a warehouse. Materials are held for 30 days, until they are used in the manufacturing process, and then the manufactured auto parts are held for 15 days until they are sold and shipped to customers. Ushta pays its suppliers 40 days after receiving the goods, and receives payments from customers 30 days after delivering auto parts. Calculate the following for Ushta and explain the cash implications of the inventory self-financing period:

a. Payables deferral period.
b. Inventory self-financing period.
c. Inventory conversion period.
d. Receivables conversion period.
e. Number of days between receiving inventory from suppliers and receiving cash from customers.

   Answer:

a. Payables deferral period = 40 days.
b. Inventory self-financing period = 35 days.
c. Inventory conversion period = 45 days (30 days holding materials from suppliers and 15 days holding manufactured auto parts).
d. Receivables conversion period = 30 days.
e. Number of days between receiving inventory from suppliers and receiving cash from customers = 75 days.

The inventory self-financing period is the length of time that Ushta has its own cash invested in the inventory. That means that Ushta must have enough cash available to maintain its inventory at the level necessary to operate efficiently. If Ushta does not have enough cash to pay suppliers on a timely basis, suppliers may not be willing to sell Ushta materials on credit, which will make it much more difficult for Ushta to operate.

---

pose of the example, assume that customers always pay in the quarter after they make their purchases.

- The amount of inventory Peabody has on hand at the start of a quarter is based on management's forecast of the amount of sales that will be made in the next quarter. All purchases of inventory are made on the first day of each quarter.

- Peabody has a mark-up on its product of 100%. (If a customer purchases candy that costs Peabody $100, the customer pays $200.)

- Operating costs, other than the cost of product sold, are $12,000 per quarter. These costs are paid in cash during the quarter.

- Peabody began operations with $40,000 in cash contributed by its shareholders.

- Peabody purchased $16,000 worth of inventory when it started operations.

- Sales by quarter for 2005 were:

1st Quarter	2nd Quarter	3rd Quarter	4th Quarter	Total sales in 2005
$20,000	$24,000	$27,500	$31,500	$103,000

Peabody's quarterly income statements for 2005 are shown in Table 6-1. Information about Peabody's inventory purchases are shown in Table 6-2 (page 320).

The income statements show that Peabody suffered a loss of $2,000 in the first quarter, broke even in the second quarter, and made profits in the third and fourth quarters. For the entire year Peabody made a profit of $3,500. The inventory information shows that the amount of inventory that Peabody has on hand increases over the year. This makes sense because Peabody's sales are growing. As sales increase it is

Table 6-1   Peabody Ltd. Quarterly Income Statements

Peabody Ltd.
Quarterly Income Statements for 2005

	1st Quarter	2nd Quarter	3rd Quarter	4th Quarter	Total 2005
Sales	$20,000	$24,000	$27,500	$31,500	$103,000
Cost of sales	10,000	12,000	13,750	15,750	51,500
Other costs	12,000	12,000	12,000	12,000	48,000
Net income	$ (2,000)	$ 0	$ 1,750	$ 3,750	$ 3,500

Table 6-2   Peabody Ltd. Inventory Information

Peabody Ltd.
Inventory Information for 2005

	1st Quarter	2nd Quarter	3rd Quarter	4th Quarter	Total 2005
Beginning inventory	$ 0	$ 6,000	$ 7,200	$ 8,250	$ 0
+ Purchases	16,000	13,200	14,800	16,950	60,950
− Cost of sales	10,000	12,000	13,750	15,750	51,500
= Ending inventory	$ 6,000	$ 7,200	$ 8,250	$ 9,450	$ 9,450

necessary to maintain more inventory to meet the needs of customers. The increasing amount of inventory means that more and more cash must be invested in inventory. Let's now compare these income statements with the cash flow statements for the same periods. Peabody's quarterly cash flow statements and beginning and ending cash balances for each quarter are shown in Table 6-3.

Peabody's cash flow statements tell a different story than the income statements. During 2005, Peabody expended considerably more cash than it collected, and at the end of 2005 most of the $40,000 it began operations with was gone. In every quarter during 2005 cash flow was negative. Over the entire year Peabody had a negative cash flow of $37,450 but a net income of $3,500. Why? Because Peabody is a new business, it was necessary to make a large initial purchase of inventory and then allow the inventory to increase as sales increased so that customer orders could be met. The build-up in inventory is not reflected in the income statement because only goods sold are expensed in an accrual income statement. However, the build-up of inventory did use cash.

If a user focused only on the income statement and ignored Peabody's cash flow statement, Peabody's performance would look positive, despite the fact that Peabody had just about run out of cash. If in late 2005 Peabody had to make a $5,000 cash payment, it would be unable to do so. The company would have to come up with additional cash to make the payment. This example highlights how earnings and cash flow can differ dramatically, and how important it is to examine both cash and accrual information.

Now let's look at 2006, Peabody's second year of operation. We will look at Peabody under two scenarios. The first scenario assumes that Peabody reached its maximum level of sales in the fourth quarter of 2005 and that level of sales ($31,500 per quarter) will continue in each quarter for the foreseeable future. Peabody's income statements, inventory information, cash flow statements, and cash balances by quarter for 2006 under this scenario are shown in Table 6-4.

Table 6-4 shows that when Peabody's sales stabilized at $31,500 per quarter, net income and cash flow were the same in each quarter. The reason is that Peabody

Table 6-3	Peabody Ltd. Comparison of Quarterly Cash Flow Statements and Cash Flow Balances

Peabody Ltd.
Quarterly Cash Flow Statements for 2005 and Quarterly Cash Balances

	1st Quarter	2nd Quarter	3rd Quarter	4th Quarter	Total 2005
Collections*	$ 0	$20,000	$24,000	$27,500	$ 71,500
Disbursements**	28,000	25,200	26,800	28,950	108,950
Cash flow	$(28,000)	$(5,200)	$(2,800)	$(1,450)	$(37,450)
Beginning cash balance	$ 40,000	$12,000	$ 6,800	$ 4,000	$ 40,000
Ending cash balance	$ 12,000	$ 6,800	$ 4,000	$ 2,550	$ 2,550

*Collections equal the amount of sales in the previous quarter.
**Disbursements equal the amount spent purchasing inventory plus $12,000 per month in other costs.

Table 6-4	Peabody Ltd. Financial Information: Scenario 1 (Sales Stable)

Peabody Ltd.
Quarterly Income Statements for 2006

	1st Quarter	2nd Quarter	3rd Quarter	4th Quarter	Total 2006
Sales	$31,500	$31,500	$31,500	$31,500	$126,000
Cost of sales	15,750	15,750	15,750	15,750	63,000
Other costs	12,000	12,000	12,000	12,000	48,000
Net income	$ 3,750	$ 3,750	$ 3,750	$ 3,750	$ 15,000

Peabody Ltd.
Inventory Information for 2006

	1st Quarter	2nd Quarter	3rd Quarter	4th Quarter	Total 2006
Beginning inventory	$ 9,450	$ 9,450	$ 9,450	$ 9,450	$ 9,450
+ Purchases	15,750	15,750	15,750	15,750	63,000
− Cost of sales	15,750	15,750	15,750	15,750	63,000
= Ending inventory	$ 9,450	$ 9,450	$ 9,450	$ 9,450	$ 9,450

Peabody Ltd.
Quarterly Cash Flow Statements for 2006 and Quarterly Cash Balances

	1st Quarter	2nd Quarter	3rd Quarter	4th Quarter	Total 2006
Collections*	$31,500	$31,500	$31,500	$31,500	$126,000
Disbursements**	27,750	27,750	27,750	27,750	111,000
Cash flow	$ 3,750	$ 3,750	$ 3,750	$ 3,750	$ 15,000
Beginning cash balance	$ 2,550	$ 6,300	$10,050	$13,800	$ 2,550
Ending cash balance	$ 6,300	$10,050	$13,800	$17,550	$ 17,550

*Collections equal the amount of sales in the previous quarter.
**Disbursements equal the amount spent purchasing inventory plus $12,000 per month in other costs.

simply has to replace the inventory it sells so that the amount of inventory sold is the same as the amount of inventory purchased. With a stable level of sales, Peabody no longer has to spend money building up inventory. An important point to note: the balance in the cash account in this situation builds up during the year such that at the end of 2006 there is an ending cash balance of $17,550. Cash builds up at this point because Peabody is selling the inventory for more than it costs, so cash levels increase.

The second 2006 scenario assumes that sales decline. After reaching a peak in the fourth quarter of 2005, interest in Peabody's products declines. Perhaps the attraction of offering candy as a gift has lost its appeal and is being replaced by something else, or competitors have moved into the market. Whatever the case, sales decline in 2006. However, management does not see that demand for its product is declining—perhaps management believes that the decline is to be short-lived or there is not enough information to identify the problem. Consequently, management targets its inventory levels to the level of sales in the fourth quarter of 2005. As a result, inventory builds up during 2006.

Peabody's income statements, inventory information, cash flow statements, and cash balances by quarter for 2006 under the sales decline scenario are shown in Table 6-5.

In this scenario we can see the effect of the sales decline and management's planning error. Peabody's management expected sales to level off at $31,500 per quarter, but instead they declined throughout the year. As a result, inventory increased significantly over the year. Despite the decrease in sales during 2006, Peabody was profitable in every quarter. However, cash flow declined through the year and in the last two quarters cash flow was negative. At the end of 2006 Peabody has a significant amount of money tied up in inventory.

Table 6-5 Peabody Ltd. Financial Information: Scenario 2 (Sales Decrease)

Peabody Ltd.
Quarterly Income Statements for 2006

	1st Quarter	2nd Quarter	3rd Quarter	4th Quarter	Total 2006
Sales	$28,500	$27,500	$26,500	$26,000	$108,500
Cost of sales	14,250	13,750	13,250	13,000	54,250
Other costs	12,000	12,000	12,000	12,000	48,000
Net income	$ 2,250	$ 1,750	$ 1,250	$ 1,000	$ 6,250

Peabody Ltd.
Inventory Information for 2006

	1st Quarter	2nd Quarter	3rd Quarter	4th Quarter	Total 2006
Beginning inventory	$ 9,450	$10,950	$12,950	$15,450	$ 9,450
+ Purchases	15,750	15,750	15,750	15,750	63,000
− Cost of sales	14,250	13,750	13,250	13,000	54,250
= Ending inventory	$10,950	$12,950	$15,450	$18,200	$18,200

Peabody Ltd.
Quarterly Cash Flow Statements for 2006 and Quarterly Cash Balances

	1st Quarter	2nd Quarter	3rd Quarter	4th Quarter	Total 2006
Collections*	$31,500	$28,500	$27,500	$26,500	$114,000
Disbursements**	27,750	27,750	27,750	27,750	111,000
Cash flow	$ 3,750	$ 750	$ (250)	$(1,250)	$ 3,000
Beginning cash balance	$ 2,550	$ 6,300	$ 7,050	$ 6,800	$ 2,550
Ending cash balance	$ 6,300	$ 7,050	$ 6,800	$ 5,550	$ 5,550

*Collections equal the amount of sales in the previous quarter.
**Disbursements equal the amount spent purchasing inventory plus $12,000 per month in other costs.

What happens if Peabody is unable to meet some of its obligations? Perhaps as a result of the build-up in inventory it does not have enough cash to pay its rent or employees. Then the company must take steps to come up with cash. There are a number of possible sources of cash. The owners could contribute additional cash in exchange for shares or as a loan. Peabody could approach a bank for a loan. (Of course, bankers may be reluctant to lend money to a company that is in financial difficulty, so a bank loan may not be a viable option.) Another alternative would be for Peabody to have a sale by lowering the prices of its products. A sale would lower or eliminate profits, but it would generate cash.

Understanding the Cash Flow Statement: An Overview

Our discussion of the differences between cash and accrual accounting and the cash cycle leads to an important conclusion: it is necessary for financial statement users to pay attention to cash and liquidity. The source of cash flow information in a set of general purpose financial statements is the **cash flow statement**. (The cash flow statement is also known by other names, including the statement of cash flows and the statement of changes in financial position.) The cash flow statement is intended to provide users with information about the historical changes in an entity's cash position.

While a document like the cash flow statement has long been part of the financial statement package, the emphasis on cash flow is actually relatively recent. Previous forms of the cash flow statement focussed on broader definitions of liquidity than cash, such as working capital. However, a number of high-profile business failures, where the entity in question was profitable and working capital indicated that the entity was liquid, led standard setters to conclude that cash flow information should be the basis for preparing the cash flow statement.

It is interesting to note that the *CICA Handbook* does not require private companies to include a cash flow statement in their financial statement packages, provided that the required cash flow information is available from the other financial statements and the notes to the statements. This means that while cash flow statements will always be available in the annual reports of public companies, they may not be included in the financial statements of private companies. This is one of the reasons why you will be shown how to prepare a cash flow statement later in the chapter.

The cash flow statement was introduced in Chapter 2. Before reading on, take another look at MWW's cash flow statement (which it calls the statement of cash flows) on page A-47 in Appendix A.

The cash flow statement provides information on an entity's historical cash flows. Cash flows are grouped into three categories: cash from operations, cash flows from investing activities, and cash flows from financing activities. Let's look at these categories in more detail:

1. **Cash from operations (CFO)** is the cash an entity generates from or uses in its regular business activities. Cash inflows from operations include cash collected from customers, along with other receipts of cash that are related to operations. Cash outflows from operations include cash payments made to generate operating cash inflows; for example, payments to suppliers and employees.

2. **Cash flows from investing activities** is the cash an entity spends on buying capital and other long-term assets and the cash it receives from selling those assets.

3. **Cash flows from financing activities** is the cash an entity raises and pays to equity investors and lenders.

Figure 6-3

Examples of Cash Flows

Examples of Cash Flows by Category	
Cash Flows From Operations	
Cash inflows	**Cash outflows**
Amounts received from customers Tax refunds Interest collected	Payments for inventory Payments to other suppliers Payments to employees Taxes paid Interest paid
Cash Flows From Investing Activities	
Cash inflows	**Cash outflows**

Sale of capital assets
Collection of principal on loans made by
    the entity
Proceeds from the sale of securities held
    for investment by the entity
    (i.e., stocks and bonds)
	Purchase of capital assets
	Loans made to other entities
	Purchase of securities of other entities
	    made for investment purposes
	Cash expended and capitalized as
	    intangible assets (e.g., pre-opening costs,
	    oil and gas exploration costs)

Cash Flows From Financing Activities	
Cash inflows	**Cash outflows**

Proceeds from the sale of shares to
    investors
Proceeds from the issuance of debt to
    investors
Amounts received from bank loans
	Dividends paid to shareholders
	Repurchase of the entity's shares from
	    investors
	Repayment of debt principal
	Repayment of bank loans

Examples of the different categories of cash flows are shown in Figure 6-3.

> Comment: The classification of the payment and collection of interest as cash flows from operations is debatable for most entities. According to the *CICA Handbook* these cash flows should be classified as cash from operations. However, interest collected often relates to activities that would be classified as investing activities, such as investments in bonds. Interest payments clearly pertain to borrowed amounts and borrowings are classified as cash flows from financing activities. An exception would be banks, where interest received and paid is a part of their regular business activities.

A question that might not seem interesting is, what does the *cash* in the cash flow statement include? Naturally, the answer is not as straightforward as one might think. A term that is often seen in the cash flow statement is "cash and cash equivalents." Look at MWW's cash flow statement and Note 1D to see the use of this term and the definition that MWW uses (pages A-47 and A-49). The term suggests that there is more to cash than the loose change in the owner's pocket. Some possible items that could be included in a definition of cash in the cash flow statement include:

- Cash on hand and petty cash (**petty cash** is cash kept on hand to make cash payments that are required on an immediate basis).

- Cash in bank accounts.

- Short-term liquid investments. (The *CICA Handbook* defines these types of investments as ones that can be easily converted to a known amount of cash and where there is little risk that the amount of cash that will be received will change. For example, a short-term guaranteed investment certificate would qualify but a bond would not because the market value of a bond changes with interest rates. Therefore, the amount of cash that would be received by selling a bond would change with interest rate changes.)

- Certain types of bank loans such as bank overdrafts and lines of credit where the loans are used as part of the day-to-day cash management of the entity. (A **bank overdraft** occurs when an entity removes more money from its bank account than there is in the bank account, effectively creating an amount owing to the bank. The amount of the overdraft is treated as a liability. For example, if an entity has $20,000 in its bank account and it writes cheques for $30,000 on the account, the account will be overdrawn by $10,000. The $10,000 would be treated as a liability. A **line of credit** is a prearranged loan that can be drawn on as required by an entity.)

GAAP, as stated in the *CICA Handbook*, are not specific as to what definition of cash should be used. The notion behind the *CICA Handbook* section is that the cash flow statement should show the movement of readily available cash resources, even if some of the cash is not on hand. Cash on hand and cash in bank accounts are obviously included in the definition of cash. Short-term liquid investments can be included because most entities will try not to keep a lot of cash in bank accounts that do not pay interest. If an entity has a surplus of cash it will invest it so that it can earn a return. Investments as short as overnight are often used by entities to "put their cash to work." To be considered short-term liquid assets these investments must be convertible into cash relatively quickly, perhaps in no more than a few months. Bank overdrafts and lines of credit can also be included in the definition of cash because these bank loans are sometimes used as pools of cash that can be used as needed by

Question for Consideration

Classify the following cash flows of Quick Motors Ltd. (Quick), a new car dealership, as operating, investing, or financing. Quick sells new cars and provides service to cars. Explain your reasoning.

a. Quick purchases a number of cars and vans for resale to customers for $375,000 cash.

b. Quick purchases a van for $40,000 cash that it will use to carry customers who leave their cars at the dealership for servicing to and from their homes.

c. Quick sells a car to a customer for $32,000 cash.

d. Quick repays a $500,000 loan from a bank that was used to renovate the showroom.

e. Quick sells old furniture and computers that were used by its salespeople for $25,000 cash.

f. Quick sells infrequently sold inventory from its auto parts department to a parts dealer who specializes in parts for older cars.

g. Quick sells a number of cars that were used by its salespeople to a charitable organization. The organization is given 12 months to pay for the cars.

Answer:

a. Operating: Cars and vans are Quick's inventory. Sale of these is its business. Clearly, this is an operating cash flow.

b. Investing: This van will not be resold, but rather is a capital asset that will be used to help generate revenue by providing convenience to customers.

c. Operating: Quick's line of business is selling cars. Cash received from a sale is an operating item.

d. Financing: Repayment of a loan is a financing activity.

e. Investing: Quick is in the car business, not the furniture and computer business. Selling furniture and computers is not part of Quick's regular business activities. When these assets were purchased they would have been considered capital assets and the cash spent on them classified as an investing activity.

f. Operating: Sale of auto parts is part of the regular business activities of a car dealership.

g. None: No cash is involved in this transaction so it does not appear on the cash flow statement.

an entity. For example, seasonal businesses will use their lines of credit to finance operations during the busy period; as cash is collected from sales in the busy period, the cash is used to pay back the bank. When bank overdrafts and the amount borrowed on a line of credit are included in the definition of cash and cash equivalents, the amount of the overdraft or amount borrowed on the line of credit is subtracted from the amount of other cash and cash equivalents when the amount of cash an entity has is determined.

The GAAP guidelines are reasonable ones. However, preparers who are constrained by GAAP are allowed to exercise some judgment in the exact definition of cash that they use. Therefore, there may be some variation in the definition of cash that is used in entities' cash flow statements. For example, MWW defines cash and cash equivalents as cash on hand, balances with banks, and investments in money market instruments. If you examine the financial statements of other entities, you will see that this definition may vary.

Understanding the Cash Flow Statement: Specific Activities

This section will focus on understanding the cash flow statement. The main emphasis of the section will be on the CFO section because it is more difficult to understand the calculation of CFO than the calculation of cash flows from investing and financing activities.

Cash Flows from Investing and Financing Activities

Cash flows from investing and financing activities are actually quite straightforward. In large measure, the items in the financing activities section simply show changes in the financing accounts on the balance sheet—accounts such as long-term debt, bank loans, mortgages, and capital stock. Similarly, the items in the investing activities section show changes in the investment accounts on the balance sheet—accounts such as capital assets and investments. In essence, these two sections reorganize the information that is presented in the balance sheet to reflect the cash flows related to investing and financing activities. However, if all the cash flow statement provided was a reorganization of the balance sheet accounts, there would be little benefit to having it at all. Users could simply reorganize the information themselves in a way that suited their needs.

One of the ways that the financing and investing activities sections provide additional information over and above what is in the balance sheet is by not combining positive and negative changes in balance sheet accounts. For example, MWW reports separate lines in its cash flow statement for "purchases of capital assets" and "dispositions of capital assets," and for "proceeds of long-term debt" and "retirement of long-term debt." It can sometimes be very difficult, if not impossible, to determine these more detailed changes from the information in the balance sheet and notes to the financial statements.

Another way that the cash flow statement provides information that cannot be determined from changes in balance sheet accounts is by including only transactions affecting cash. For example, if an entity purchases an asset and pays for it by issuing shares of the entity, that transaction is not reflected in the cash flow statement because cash is not involved. Or if a capital asset is sold and the entity takes a mortgage back from the buyer instead of cash, that too is a transaction that would not be reflected in the cash flow statement. However, while these transactions are not included in the cash flow statement, their existence is disclosed. For example, MWW provides

"Supplementary Schedules to Consolidated Statements of Cash Flows" (page A-48) that show non-cash investing and financing activities.

A look at MWW's cash flow statement during the year ended January 27, 2001 shows that it expended $5,807,000 in cash on investing activities, including $2,485,000 on capital assets. MWW also had a net cash outflow of $10,114,000 in respect to financing activities, mainly to retire long-term debt and repay capital leases. (A **lease** is a contractual agreement that calls for one entity to pay another entity for use of an asset that the latter entity owns. A **capital lease** is an accounting classification for a lease whereby the entity leasing the asset includes the leased asset on its balance sheet if the lease transfers the rights and risks of ownership to the leasing entity. We will discuss leases in Chapter 10.)

Cash from Operations

Cash from operations (CFO) is the cash that an entity generates from and consumes in its ordinary, day-to-day operations. For example, CFO for MWW is the cash from selling clothing and from earning royalties from franchised stores, less the cash spent generating those cash flows.

There are two ways that CFO can be calculated and reported in a cash flow statement:

1. The **indirect method** reconciles from net income to CFO by adjusting net income for non-cash amounts that are included in the calculation of net income and for operating cash flows that are not included in the calculation of net income.

2. The **direct method** reports CFO by showing cash collections and cash disbursements related to operations during the period.

MWW uses the indirect method. If you look at MWW's cash flow statement you will see that the starting point for calculating CFO is net earnings followed by a series of

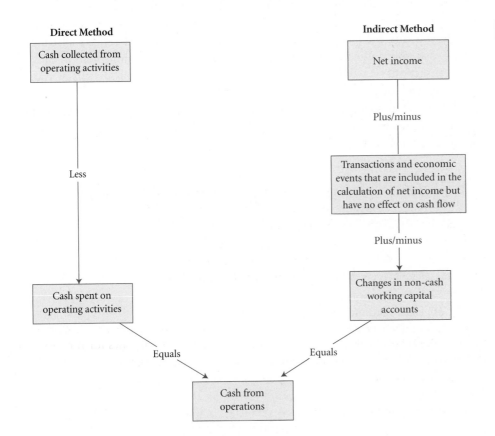

Figure 6-4

Comparison of the Direct and Indirect Methods of Calculating Cash from Operations adjustments. These adjustments reconcile net income to a cash number. In fiscal 2001 MWW had CFO of $21,140,000. (CFO is not the line called "funds provided by operations", which is actually something called working capital from operations. CFO is an untitled line about mid-way down the cash flow statement, just before the "Investing" section.) If MWW used the direct method, it would show cash collected from customers and for royalties, and show cash expended on inventory, employees, and so on.

While the direct method has more intuitive appeal, it is rarely used in practice. *Financial Reporting in Canada* reports that of 200 Canadian public companies surveyed in 2000, only one used the direct method.[1] A possible reason for the popularity of the indirect method is that it links the cash flow statement to the income statement. By starting with net income a user can see a relationship between income and cash flow. The *CICA Handbook* permits the use of both the direct and indirect methods, although the *Handbook* encourages the use of the direct method. The direct and indirect methods are compared schematically in Figure 6-4 (page 327).

Because the direct method of calculating CFO is rare in Canada, it is not possible to show an actual company's CFO calculated in this way, but an example of the direct method is shown in Table 6-6. In contrast with the indirect method, CFO calculated using the direct method is simply a listing of operating cash inflows and outflows from various sources. Magnolia Ltd. collected $1,854,000 from customers during 2005 and paid out $1,332,000 in cash to suppliers, employees, and for other operating expenses, income taxes, and interest.

The focus of the rest of this section will be on understanding the calculation of CFO using the indirect method. (We will look at the direct method again when we discuss how to prepare a cash flow statement.)

Broadly, there are two types of adjustments that must be made when reconciling from net income to CFO using the indirect method. The first type of adjustment removes transactions and economic events that are included in the calculation of net income but have no effect on cash flow. A simple way to conceptualize this adjustment is to imagine two sets of balls—a red set and a blue set. The red balls represent transactions that involve cash and the blue balls represent transactions that do not affect cash. If you mix the balls together, you have a set of balls that reflects all transactions—cash and non-cash. If you were then asked to provide information only on cash transactions, it would be necessary to remove the blue balls. In effect, you are removing the blue balls that you previously added in.

The most obvious example of this type of adjustment is the amortization expense. Amortization does not involve cash—it is the allocation of the cost of a capital asset to expense over the life of the asset. Since net income includes the non-cash

---

Table 6-6   Example of the Direct Method of Calculating Cash Flows from Operations

Magnolia Ltd.
Cash Flow Statement
for the Year Ended July 31, 2005

Cash flows from operations:		
Cash collected from customers		$1,854,000
Cash paid to suppliers	$525,000	
Cash paid to employees	372,000	
Cash paid for other operating expenses	295,000	
Cash paid for interest	75,000	
Cash paid for income taxes	65,000	1,332,000
Cash flows from operations		$ 522,000

amortization expense, it is necessary to remove the expense when reconciling from net income to CFO. The same is true for any transaction or economic event that does not affect cash. The amortization expense is eliminated from net income by adding it back because the amortization expense was subtracted in the calculation of net income. (Think of net income as the combined set of red and blue balls, and amortization as the blue balls.)

Let's consider an example. The income statement of Moose Jaw Company (Moose Jaw) is presented as follows:

Moose Jaw Company
Income Statement
For the Year Ended December 31, 2004

Revenue	$35,000
Expenses	18,000
Amortization expense	8,000
Net income	$ 9,000

All of Moose Jaw's revenues and expenses are in cash except for amortization. All of its cash flows are operating cash flows. It should be clear that Moose Jaw's CFO for 2004 is $17,000 ($35,000 − $18,000). However, we can see this directly by using a spreadsheet:

	Cash	Capital assets	Accum. amort.	Owners' equity	Revenue	Expenses	Amort. expense
Balance on December 31, 2003	5,000	80,000	(16,000)	69,000			
Revenue during 2004	35,000				35,000		
Expenses during 2004	(18,000)					(18,000)	
Amortization expense for 2004			(8,000)				(8,000)
Pre-closing balance on December 31, 2004	22,000	80,000	(24,000)	69,000	35,000	(18,000)	(8,000)
Closing entry for 2004				9,000	(35,000)	18,000	8,000
Balance on December 31, 2004	22,000	80,000	(24,000)	78,000	0	0	0

The Cash column of the worksheet gives us the information we need about cash flow. Since cash increased from $5,000 to $22,000, the CFO for the year is $17,000. (Remember, there were no cash flows from financing or investing activities.)

The difference between net income and CFO is simply the amount of the amortization expense. If we are trying to calculate CFO starting with net income, we adjust net income by adding back the amortization that was expensed in calculating net income in the first place. For Moose Jaw,

Net income	$ 9,000
Add: Amortization expense	8,000
Cash from operations	$17,000

The thinking is straightforward. If a non-cash item is subtracted in the calculation of net income (such as amortization), then it must be added back when reconciling from net income to CFO. Similarly, if a non-cash item is added in the calculation of net income, then it must be subtracted when reconciling from net income to CFO. If we were calculating CFO using the direct approach, we would not consider these non-cash items at all. We would simply prepare a statement that reflected operating cash inflows and outflows:

Revenue (all cash)	$35,000
Expenses (all cash)	18,000
Cash from operations	$17,000

Note that we get the same CFO by ignoring the non-cash items in the first place.

Question for Consideration

A friend suggests to you that a good way for an entity to maximize its CFO is to take as large an amortization expense possible. The friend reasons that because non-cash expenses such as amortization are added back to net income when calculating CFO using the indirect method, taking the maximum possible amortization expense will result in the maximum amount of cash from operations. Evaluate your friend's suggestion.

Answer: While amortization is added back to net income when calculating CFO using the indirect method, the amount of amortization that is expensed in a year has no effect on cash from operations. The reason amortization is added back to net income is that it is deducted as an expense in the calculation of net income. But amortization does not use any cash. Therefore, whether the amortization expense is large or small has no effect on cash from operations because you would just be adding back the same amount that was subtracted when calculating net income.

A list of non-cash items that are included in net income and that must be adjusted for when calculating CFO using the indirect method is given in Figure 6-5. (Some of the items on the list will not be discussed in detail until later in the book).

Figure 6-5

Non-Cash Items and Their Treatment in CFO Calculation Using the Indirect Method

Expense	**Description**	**Treatment (Add to or subtract from net income when reconciling net income to CFO)**
Amortization	Allocation of the cost of a capital asset to expense over the asset's life.	Add
Gains	The amount by which the selling price of an asset is greater than its net book value.	Subtract
Losses	The amount by which the selling price of an asset is less than its net book value.	Add
Future (deferred) taxes	Difference between how taxes are calculated for accounting purposes versus how they are calculated for the taxation authorities. Future taxes will be discussed later in the book.	Add or subtract
Write-offs and write-downs of assets	Occurs when an asset's book value is decreased to reflect a decline in market value that is not supported by a transaction.	Add

Comment: The treatment of gains and losses can be a bit confusing. When an asset is sold and gives rise to a gain or loss, there is often cash involved in the transaction. The cash component of the sale is classified as an investing activity. The gain or loss is just the difference between the book value of the asset and the proceeds from the sale; it does not actually represent cash. Net income, however, includes the gain or loss. If the cash proceeds from the sale are classified as an investing activity and if the reconciliation from net income to CFO does not remove the gain or the loss, there will be double counting. Double counting occurs because CFO will reflect the gain or loss *and* the full amount of the proceeds will be reported as an investing activity—the total will be different from the actual amount of cash actually received.

For example, Rife Inc. (Rife) sells land that cost $10,000 for $25,000 cash. This is the only transaction Rife has for the year. The gain on the sale of the land is $15,000 ($25,000 – $10,000) and that would be its net income, since there are no other transactions. CFO would be

Net income	$15,000
Less: Gain on sale of land	15,000
Cash from operations	$ 0

| Cash from investing activities: | |
| Sale of land | $25,000 |

If the gain were not subtracted from net income when reconciling to CFO, CFO would be $15,000 and cash from investing activities would be $25,000, for total inflow of $40,000. This is clearly wrong, since Rife only received $25,000. This is why it is necessary to adjust for gains and losses.

Question for Consideration

In 2005 Baltic Ltd. (Baltic) reported net income of $16,000, based on revenues of $100,000, expenses other than amortization of $70,000, amortization of $6,000, and a loss on the sale of a piece of land of $8,000. All of these revenues and expenses (other than amortization) were for cash. Assuming that there are no other transactions or economic events, calculate Baltic's CFO for 2005 using the indirect method.

Answer:

Net income	$16,000
Add: Amortization	6,000
Loss on sale of land*	8,000
Cash from operations	$30,000

*Note that the loss on the land is added back in the calculation of cash from operations because it is a non-cash item that was subtracted in the calculation of net income.

The second type of adjustment for the calculation of CFO using the indirect method adjusts accrual revenues and expenses so that the non-cash components are removed and so that operating cash flows that are not reflected in revenues and expenses are included. These adjustments are necessary because revenues and expenses are recognized on an accrual basis, which means that the cash flows associated with the revenues and expenses may occur before, after, or at the same time as recognition on the income statement. However, CFO should include cash spent on inventory regardless of whether it was sold. As we will see below, changes in the non-cash current operating accounts (non-cash working capital accounts such as accounts receivable, inventory, prepaids, accounts payable, wages payable, and accrued liabilities) over a period provide the information needed to make these adjustments. You can see this type of adjustment on MWW's cash flow statement in the bottom half of the CFO reconciliation titled "Changes in non-cash working capital" (see page A-47).

One might think that the simplest way to obtain this information is to identify operating cash inflows and outflows directly from the accounting system. However, accounting systems designed for accrual accounting purposes are usually unable to easily provide this information. As a result, it is necessary to make these adjustments by using changes in an entity's non-cash current operating accounts. Even when the direct approach is used, it is necessary to determine cash inflows and outflows in this roundabout way.

Converting accrual income statement amounts to cash flow amounts is actually quite straightforward. Understanding why the adjustments are made is less obvious. First, let's look at the process. Figure 6-6 (page 332) shows the adjustments that must be made when reconciling from net income to CFO. The box in Figure 6-6 entitled "Adjustments for non-cash transactions" represents the first type of adjustment that we discussed above. The remaining adjustments are the changes in the non-cash current operating accounts on the balance sheet. When calculating CFO using the indirect method, increases in current operating asset accounts such as accounts receivable,

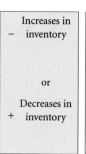
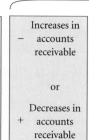
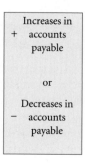
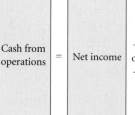
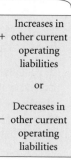
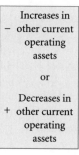
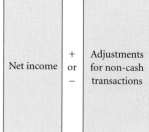

Second type of adjustment: adjusts accrual revenues and expenses so that the non-cash components are removed and so that operating cash flows not reflected in revenues and expenses are included

| Cash from operations | = | Net income | + or − | Adjustments for non-cash transactions | Increases in − accounts receivable / or / Decreases in + accounts receivable | Increases in − inventory / or / Decreases in + inventory | Increases in − other current operating assets / or / Decreases in + other current operating assets | Increases in + accounts payable / or / Decreases in − accounts payable | Increases in + other current operating liabilities / or / Decreases in − other current operating liabilities |

First type of adjustment: removes transactions and economic events that are included in the calculation of net income but have no effect on cash flow

inventory, and prepaids are subtracted from net income and decreases in these accounts are added. Increases in current operating liability accounts such as accounts payable, wages payable, and accrued liabilities are added to net income and decreases are subtracted.

At this point, take another look at MWW's cash flow statement to see this type of adjustment. Note that if you try to compare the changes in the current operating accounts as reported in MWW's cash flow statement with the changes in the same balance sheet accounts, you will find that the two are not the same. This is the case with the financial statements of many entities. For MWW part of the reason for this difference is due to how the acquisition of subsidiaries and franchise stores is accounted for in the cash flow statement.

Next we can ask, why do these adjustments remove the non-cash components in revenues and expenses, and result in the inclusion of operating cash flows that are not reflected in revenues and expenses? The reason is that differences between the accrual income statement numbers and the cash flow numbers are represented in the changes in these accounts. These effects can best be shown with examples. We will examine two examples. The first looks at cash collections and revenue; the second looks at cash disbursements for inventory and cost of goods sold. (While the discussion of disbursements is limited to inventory, the approach can be applied to any operating expense and related balance sheet accounts, such as wages expense and wages payable.)

Example 1: Kamloops Inc.   Consider the following information for Kamloops Inc. in Table 6-7 and the partial accounting equation spreadsheet in Table 6-8. The spreadsheet summarizes the entries that would have been made in 2005 regarding revenue, cash, and accounts receivable. Examine the spreadsheet to see how these entries affected the Revenue account in comparison with the Cash account.

Table 6-7	Kamloops Inc. Financial Information

Kamloops Inc.
Information About the Year 2005

Cash on December 31, 2004	$ 70,000	Cash on December 31, 2005	$566,000
Accounts receivable on December 31, 2004	60,000	Accounts receivable on December 31, 2005	89,000
Sales during 2005	525,000	Collections from customers in 2005	496,000

Table 6-8	Kamloops Inc. Partial Accounting Equation Spreadsheet

Kamloops Inc.
Partial Spreadsheet for 2005

	Cash	Accounts receivable	Revenue
Balance on December 31, 2004	70,000	60,000	
During 2005—revenue		525,000	525,000
During 2005—collection of receivables	496,000	(496,000)	
Balance on December 31, 2005	566,000	89,000	525,000

The difference between revenue recognized during 2005 and cash collected from customers during 2005 ($525,000 − $496,000 = $29,000) is the same amount as the increase in Accounts Receivable over 2005 ($89,000 − $60,000 = $29,000). This is not a coincidence. An increase in accounts receivable means that credit sales in the current year that are uncollected as of the year end are greater than the amount of cash collected in the current year from credit sales that were recognized in a previous year. When accounts receivable decrease, the opposite is true. The difference between these two amounts is the difference between the beginning and ending balances of accounts receivable and the difference between cash collections and revenue during the period. This effect can be expressed as follows:

$$\text{Cash collected from customers during the period} = \text{Revenue in the period} + \substack{\text{Cash collections during the period} \\ \text{that were recognized as revenue} \\ \text{in a previous period (beginning} \\ \text{accounts receivable)}} - \substack{\text{Credit sales during the year} \\ \text{that were not collected at} \\ \text{year end (ending accounts} \\ \text{receivable)}}$$

The difference between these two amounts is the difference between beginning and ending Accounts Receivable

Applying this equation to Kamloops Inc., cash collected from customers during 2005 is:

Cash collected from customers = $525,000 + 60,000 − 89,000
= $496,000

This is the same amount that was calculated in the spreadsheet. Therefore, by subtracting an increase in accounts receivable from net income or by adding a decrease in accounts receivable, we have adjusted revenues (which are included in net income) so that cash collections rather than accrual revenue is reflected.

Example 2: Rollingdam Ltd. For the second example we will examine cash disbursed for inventory and cost of goods sold. Consider the following information about Rollingdam Ltd. in Table 6-9 and the partial accounting equation spreadsheet in Table 6-10. The spreadsheet summarizes the entries that would have been made in 2006 regarding cost of goods sold, cash, inventory, and accounts payable. Examine the spreadsheet to see how these entries affected the cost of goods sold account in comparison with the cash account. This example is a bit more complicated than the Kamloops example because cash disbursed for inventory requires that we look at two balance sheet accounts—inventory and accounts payable—instead of one. The example assumes that accounts payable pertains only to inventory purchases.

Notice that the difference between cost of goods sold in 2006 and cash expended on inventory during 2006 ($325,000 − $270,000 = $55,000) is the same as the amount of the decrease in inventory in 2006 ($125,000 − $100,000 = $25,000) plus the amount of the increase in accounts payable in 2006 ($90,000 − $60,000 = $30,000) ($25,000 + $30,000 = $55,000). Once again, this is not a coincidence. A decrease in the amount of inventory means that the entity sold inventory acquired in previous periods. If inventory were paid for in cash when purchased, a decrease in inventory would mean that less cash was spent on inventory in the current year than the amount that was expensed as cost of goods sold. An increase in the amount of inventory means that the entity was building up its inventory. Again, if inventory were paid for in cash when purchased, an increase in inventory would mean that more cash was spent on inventory in the current year than was expensed as cost of goods sold.

Of course, most inventory is not paid for in cash when it is purchased, but is purchased on credit. As a result, accounts payable has an effect on the amount of cash that is expended in a period for inventory. Credit terms delay the payment of cash to suppliers. When accounts payable increases during a period, the amount of financing provided by suppliers has increased. The additional financing means that less cash is needed to buy inventory (or other goods and services). When accounts payable

---

Table 6-9   Rollingdam Ltd. Financial Information

Rollingdam Ltd.
Information About the Year 2006

Cash on December 31, 2005	$340,000	Cash on December 31, 2006	$ 70,000
Inventory on December 31, 2005	125,000	Inventory on December 31, 2006	100,000
Accounts payable on December 31, 2005	60,000	Accounts payable on December 31, 2006	90,000
Payments made to inventory suppliers during 2006	270,000	Inventory purchased during 2006 (All inventory is purchased	
Cost of goods sold during 2006	325,000	on credit)	300,000

Table 6-10   Rollingdam Ltd. Partial Accounting Equation Spreadsheet

Rollingdam Ltd.
Partial Spreadsheet for 2006

	Cash	Inventory	Accounts payable	Cost of goods sold
Balance on December 31, 2005	$340,000	$125,000	$ 60,000	
During 2006—inventory purchases		300,000	300,000	
During 2006—payments made for inventory	(270,000)		(270,000)	
During 2006—cost of goods sold		(325,000)		$(325,000)
Balance on December 31, 2006	70,000	100,000	90,000	(325,000)

decreases, the amount of financing provided by suppliers has declined so, in effect, the entity must use cash to reduce the amount of money owing.

Therefore, to determine the amount of cash spent on inventory during a period, we adjust cost of goods sold for the change in the inventory and accounts payable accounts on the balance sheet. The adjustment is achieved by subtracting from net income increases in inventory and decreases in accounts payable, and by adding to net income decreases in inventory and increases in accounts payable.

Question for Consideration

You are provided the following information about Ituna Inc. (Ituna) for 2005. Use this information to calculate the amount of cash that Ituna paid to suppliers for inventory during 2005.

Ituna Inc.
Information About the Year 2005

Inventory on December 31, 2004	$8,500	Inventory on December 31, 2005	$5,600
Accounts payable on	6,200	Accounts payable on	
December 31, 2004		December 31, 2005	4,900
Cost of goods sold during 2005	47,250		

Answer:

$$\text{Cash paid to suppliers} = \text{Cost of goods sold} - \text{Decrease in inventory} + \text{Decrease in accounts payable}$$

$$= \$47,250 - \$2,900 + \$1,300$$

$$= \$45,650$$

Some readers may be confused about the mathematical signs here. It appears that the decrease in inventory is being subtracted and the decrease in accounts payable added, rather than the opposite, as we discussed. This is not a mistake. The reason for the sign reversal is that cash paid to suppliers and cost of goods sold represent outflows. In other words, cash paid to suppliers is a cash outflow and cost of goods sold is a deduction in the calculation of net income (it is subtracted from revenue). As a result, when we examine cash flow and the related component of net income that is negative, but they are included in the calculation as positive numbers, as is done above, the signs reverse. We could make the signing consistent with our discussion simply by entering cost of goods sold as a negative number:

$$\text{Cash paid to suppliers} = \text{Cost of goods sold} + \text{Decrease in inventory} - \text{Decrease in accounts payable}$$

$$= -\$47,250 + \$2,900 - \$1,300$$

$$= -\$45,650$$

Now the signs associated with the decreases in inventory and accounts payable are consistent with what we discussed earlier.

Preparing a Cash Flow Statement

In this section we will examine how to prepare a cash flow statement. The method uses the spreadsheet approach that was used to explain the accounting cycle in Chapter 3. The preparation of a cash flow statement is essentially a reorganization of the information on the balance sheet and income statement. Usually the cash flow statement is constructed this way because, as was explained earlier, accounting information systems often do not organize data in a way that makes direct preparation of a cash flow statement straightforward.

There are six steps involved in preparing the cash flow statement:

Step 1. Obtain balance sheets as of the beginning and end of the period, the income statement for the period, and any other information that is available about the cash flows of the entity.

Step 2.   Prepare a spreadsheet with a column for each balance sheet and income statement account. On the first row of the spreadsheet enter the amounts from the beginning balance sheet. On the last row enter the amounts from the ending balance sheet and the period's income statement. Also, include a column to number each entry to the spreadsheet and a column to classify each entry as cash from operations, financing activities, or investing activities.

Step 3.   Make entries to the spreadsheet that explain the changes in each account. Explaining the changes means making entries that reconstruct the transactions and economic events occurring during the period that resulted in the ending balance sheet and income statement. You are not trying to recreate every transaction that the entity entered into during the period. You are trying to summarize the events of the period. Use the information provided to you to make appropriate entries to the spreadsheet.

Step 4.   For each entry that affects the cash account, classify it as an operating, financing, or investing cash flow.

Step 5.   Prepare the cash flow statement by organizing the amounts in entries that affected the cash account into CFO, investing activities, and financing activities. For CFO, cash inflows and outflows should be separately shown. Additional detail on inflows and outflows can be provided if considered useful. (Using this approach will result in the calculation of CFO using the direct method.)

Step 6.   Calculate totals for each of operating, financing, and investing cash flows and calculate total cash flow for the period by totalling operating, financing, and investing cash flows. Total cash flow for the period should be added to the beginning balance in the cash account to give the ending cash balance on the balance sheet.

We will use information for Flin Flon Inc. (Flin Flon) to prepare a cash flow statement. Flin Flon's balance sheets as of December 31, 2006 and 2007 and its 2007 income statement are shown in Table 6-11. The spreadsheet is shown in Table 6-12, pages 338–339).

Additional information regarding Flin Flon includes the following:

- All the company's sales are on credit.
- All inventory is purchased on credit. Cost of Goods Sold reflects the cost of inventory sold during the year.
- During the year the company sold land (which is included in capital assets) for $120,000 cash. The land originally cost $100,000, so a gain of $20,000 was recorded on the income statement.
- Selling, general, and administrative costs are all in cash except for the expensing of prepaid insurance. During the year, Flin Flon expensed $12,000 of insurance that was recorded as prepaid.
- All interest expenses are paid in cash.
- The tax expense for a year is recorded in full for that year and paid to the government in the following year.
- The company paid $10,000 in dividends to shareholders.

Let's look closely at Flin Flon's accounting equation spreadsheet (Table 6-12). Entry 1 shows Flin Flon's beginning balance sheet and entry 20 shows its ending balance sheet and the income statement for 2007.

Entries 2 and 3 reconstruct the change in accounts receivable during 2007. During 2007 accounts receivable increased by $80,000, from $242,000 to $322,000. We

Table 6-11   Flin Flon Inc. Balance Sheets and Income Statement

Flin Flon Inc.
Balance Sheets
As at December 31, 2006 and 2007
(in thousands of dollars)

	2007	2006
Current assets		
Cash	$ 9	$ 259
Accounts receivable	322	242
Inventory	453	312
Prepaid insurance	13	16
Total current assets	797	829
Capital assets	4,272	3,065
Accumulated amortization	(1,272)	(1,111)
	$3,797	$2,783
Current liabilities		
Accounts payable	$ 312	$ 199
Taxes payable	52	42
Total current liabilities	364	241
Notes payable	123	168
Bonds payable	1,591	1,102
Capital stock	1,363	974
Retained earnings	356	298
	$3,797	$2,783

Flin Flon Inc.
Income Statement
For the Year Ended December 31, 2007
(in thousands of dollars)

		2007
Revenue		$2,348
Cost of goods sold		1,815
Gross profit		533
Expenses:		
Selling, general and administrative expense	$149	
Interest expense	123	
Amortization expense	161	433
Gain on sale of land		20
Income before taxes		120
Tax expense		52
Net income		$ 68

can reconstruct this change by recording sales on credit (increase Accounts Receivable, increase Revenue) and collections from customers (decrease Accounts Receivable, increase Cash) to the spreadsheet. The additional information tells us that all sales were made on credit, so entry 2 records Flin Flon's revenue transactions by increasing Revenue and Accounts Receivable by $2,348,000, the amount of revenue reported in the income statement. We are not told how much cash was collected from customers, but we can figure it out because we know the beginning and ending balances of Accounts Receivable as well as the amount by which receivables increased as a result of new credit sales. The amount collected is:

Table 6-12   Flin Flon Inc. Accounting Equation Spreadsheet

	Entry number	Type	Cash	Accounts receivable	Inven-tory	Prepaid insurance	Capital assets	Accum. amort.	Accounts payable	Taxes payable
Balance Dec. 31, 2006	1		259	242	312	16	3,065	(1,111)	199	42
	2			2,348						
	3	O	2,268	(2,268)						
	4				(1,815)					
	5				1,956				1,956	
	6	O	(1,843)						(1,843)	
	7	F	(45)							
	8	F	489							
	9	F	389							
	10							(161)		
	11	I	120				(100)			
	12	I	(1,307)				1,307			
	13					(12)				
	14	O	(9)			9				
	15	O	(137)							
	16	O	(123)							
	17	O	(42)							(42)
	18									52
	19	F	(10)							
Pre-closing balance Dec. 31, 2007	20		9	322	453	13	4,272	(1,272)	312	52
	21									
Balance Dec. 31, 2007	22		9	322	453	13	4,272	(1,272)	312	52
Change in the non-cash current operating accounts from the beginning to the end of the year				80	141	(3)			113	10

Cash collections from customers	=	Beginning balance in Accounts Receivable	+ Credit sales during the period − Ending balance in Accounts Receivable
	=	$242,000	+ $2,348,000 − $322,000
	=	$2,268,000	

For Entry 3 we record the increase in cash and decrease in receivables of $2,268,000. This entry affects the Cash column and will therefore be included in the cash flow statement as an operating cash flow. The amount is an operating cash flow because the cash collected pertains to Flin Flon's sales.

The equation used above is simply a way of determining missing information from information that is available. For any account, we can use the following equation:

1		2		3		4
Ending balance in the account	=	Beginning balance in the account	+	Transactions and economic events that increase the balance in the account	−	Transactions and economic events that decrease the balance in the account

Elements 1 and 2 in the equation are the beginning and ending balances from the balance sheet. Elements 3 and 4 are the transactions and economic events that cause increases and decreases in the account. The nature of the adjustments that cause elements 3 and 4 will vary from account to account. Some examples:

- For Accounts Receivable, element 3 is credit sales and element 4 is collections from customers.

Notes payable	Bonds payable	Capital stock	Retained earnings	Revenue	Cost of goods sold	Selling, general, and admin. exp.	Interest expense	Amort. expense	Gain on sale of land	Tax expense
168	1,102	974	298							
				2,348						
					(1,815)					
(45)										
	489									
		389								
								(161)		
									(20)	
						(12)				
						(137)				
							(123)			
										(52)
			(10)							
123	1,591	1,363	288	2,348	(1,815)	(149)	(123)	(161)	(20)	(52)
			68	(2,348)	1,815	149	123	161	20	52
123	1,591	1,363	356	0	0	0	0	0	0	0

- For Accounts Payable, element 3 is credit purchases and element 4 is payments to suppliers.
- For Inventory, element 3 is inventory purchases and element 4 is sales of inventory or cost of goods sold.

The "trick" in working with these equations is to determine which elements you know and solve the missing one. In the case of Flin Flon's accounts receivable, elements 1, 2, and 3 are known (the beginning and ending balance sheet amounts and credit sales). Collections from customers had to be calculated.

Continuing with the Flin Flon example, entries 4, 5 and 6 in the spreadsheet reconstruct changes to the Cost of Goods Sold, Inventory, and Accounts Payable accounts. These three entries will record the following: the amount of inventory that was sold (cost of goods sold), the amount of inventory that was purchased, and the amount of inventory that was paid for. The income statement reports cost of goods sold of $1,815,000, so entry 4 reflects Cost of Goods Sold and a decrease in Inventory of $1,815,000.

Entry 5 shows the amount of inventory that was purchased during 2007. The amount is not given explicitly, but it can be figured out using the equation approach:

Inventory purchased	=	Ending balance in the inventory account	+	Cost of goods sold	–	Beginning balance in the inventory account
	=	$453,000	+	$1,815,000	–	$312,000
	=	$1,956,000				

The additional information tells us that all inventory was purchased on credit, so entry 5 records that during 2007 Inventory and Accounts Payable increased by

$1,956,000. (Note that entries 4 and 5 fully explain the change in the inventory account.)

Entry 6 records the amount that was actually paid to suppliers. Again we are not told this amount but we can figure it out:

Payments to suppliers	=	Beginning balance in the Accounts Payable account	+	Credit purchases during the period	−	Ending balance in the Accounts Payable account
	=	$199,000	+	$1,956,000	−	$312,000
	=	$1,843,000				

Therefore, $1,843,000 was paid to suppliers of inventory. Entry 6 is an operating cash flow because it involves the purchase of inventory.

Entries 7, 8 and 9 are all financing activities. Entry 7 records the repayment of $45,000 of a note payable. The balance in the Notes Payable account decreased by $45,000 during the year, suggesting that Flin Flon paid $45,000 in cash to the holder of the note. Entry 8 records Flin Flon's raising of $489,000 in cash by selling bonds to investors. We are assuming that the increase in bonds payable was due strictly to the issue of new bonds. Without any additional information it is not possible to tell whether some bonds were paid off and more than $489,000 worth was issued. However, given the available information our assumption is reasonable. Without additional information it is best to make the simplest assumption. Entry 9 records the issue of capital stock to investors in exchange for $389,000 in cash.

Entry 10 records the Amortization Expense and the corresponding increase in the Accumulated Amortization account. This entry does not affect cash flow.

Entries 11 and 12 are investing activities because they involve the purchase and sale of capital assets. Entry 11 records the sale for $120,000 cash, land that was recorded on Flin Flon's books at $100,000. Because the land was sold for more than its book value, a gain on the sale is reported on the income statement. The capital asset account is reduced by $100,000, the book value of the land—not by $120,000, the amount the land was sold for. When a capital asset is disposed of, the full book value is removed from the accounts, with the difference between the proceeds from the sale and the book value being the gain or loss.

Entry 12 records the purchase of capital assets for $1,307,000. This amount is determined by using the equation approach:

Purchase of capital assets	=	Ending balance in the Capital Assets account	+	Cost of capital assets sold	−	Beginning balance in the Capital Assets account
	=	$4,272,000	+	$100,000	−	$3,065,000
	=	$1,307,000				

Entries 13 and 14 explain the change in the prepaid insurance account. The additional information we have about Flin Flon says that during 2007 the company expensed $12,000 of insurance as a selling, general, and administrative expense. Entry 13 records the reduction in the Prepaid Insurance account, and the related Selling, General and Administrative expense. We also have to determine the amount of insurance that was purchased during 2007, but not used as of the end of 2007. From the equation we conclude that the amount added to the Prepaid Insurance account during 2007 is $9,000, which is recorded in entry 14. Insurance is classified as an operating cash flow.

Paid for prepaid insurance	=	Ending balance in the Prepaid Insurance account	+	Amount of prepaid insurance expensed	−	Beginning balance in the Prepaid Insurance account
	=	$13,000	+	$12,000	−	$16,000
	=	$9,000				

Entry 15 records the cash paid for selling, general, and administrative expenses during 2007. From the income statement we know that Flin Flon incurred $149,000 of selling, general, and administrative expenses. We also know from the additional information that all selling, general, and administrative expenses are paid in cash, except for $12,000 of insurance expense, which was recorded in entry 13. Since we have already accounted for $12,000 of the selling, general, and administrative expense in entry 13, the amount paid in cash for these expenses is $137,000 ($149,000 − $12,000). Entry 15 records a decrease in Cash and Selling, General, and Administrative expenses of $137,000. Cash flows for selling, general, and administrative purposes are classified as operating cash flows.

Flin Flon's income statement for 2007 reports an interest expense of $123,000. The additional information says that all interest expenses are paid in cash, so entry 16 records Interest Expense and a decrease in Cash of $123,000. Interest expense is classified as an operating cash flow.

Entries 17 and 18 record the recognition and payment of taxes. The additional information tells us that Flin Flon pays its taxes the year after they are expensed in the income statement. The beginning balance in the taxes payable account is $42,000, which means that during 2007 Flin Flon paid $42,000 in cash to the appropriate governments. Accordingly, entry 17 records a $42,000 reduction in the Cash and Taxes Payable accounts. Taxes are an operating cash flow. In 2007 Flin Flon has a tax expense of $52,000, which will be paid in 2008. Entry 18 records the tax expense and the increase in taxes payable of $52,000. Entry 18 does not affect cash.

Entry 19 records the payment of a $10,000 dividend to shareholders. Dividends are classified as a financing cash flow.

Entry 21 is the entry that closes the income statement accounts to retained earnings.

The accounting equation spreadsheet is now complete. All the changes in the accounts have been explained. The information from the spreadsheet can now be used to prepare the cash flow statement. The key is the Cash column. Since we want our statement to reflect just cash flows, only entries that affect the Cash column are relevant. All we have to do is organize the information so that operating, investing, and financing cash flows are grouped together.

The completed cash flow statement is shown in Table 6-13 (page 342). Note how the entries that are designated as operating cash flows are grouped together to give CFO using the direct method. Similarly, the entries designated as financing cash flows are grouped in the financing activities section, and entries designated as investing are grouped in the investing activities section.

Flin Flon's cash flow statement tells us that the company invested a lot of cash in capital assets. The investment may be due to expansion or the replacement of existing assets. The cash for the capital asset purchases was obtained mainly by issuing capital stock and bonds. Operations contributed $114,000 to the investment in capital assets. Most of the cash on hand at the beginning of the year was used during the year.

The cash flow statement tells more than do the income statement and balance sheets alone. The fact that Flin Flon sold land and purchased $1,307,000 in capital assets could not be determined from just the balance sheets and income statement.

CFO in Flin Flon's cash flow statement is calculated using the direct method. The spreadsheet approach lends itself well to the direct approach because all cash flows can be found in the cash column. The spreadsheet can also be used to calculate CFO using the indirect approach, but it is admittedly more cumbersome. Using the indirect approach requires identification of the two types of adjustments described earlier. For the first type of adjustment it is necessary to identify transactions and economic events that do not affect cash. (Figure 6-4 on page 327 lists the non-cash transactions and economic events that must be adjusted for.)

When we examine Flin Flon's spreadsheet we see there are two items that must be

Table 6-13   Flin Flon Cash Flow Statement

Flin Flon Inc.
Cash Flow Statement
For the Year Ended December 31, 2007

Cash from operations:		
Cash inflows (entry 3)		$2,268,000
Cash outflows:		
Cash spent on inventory (entry 6)	$1,843,000	
Cash spent on selling, general, and administrative		
activities (entries 14 and 15)	146,000	
Cash spent on interest (entry 16)	123,000	
Cash spent on taxes (entry 17)	42,000	2,154,000
Cash from operations		114,000
Investing activities:		
Sale of land (entry 11)	120,000	
Purchase of capital assets (entry 12)	(1,307,000)	(1,187,000)
Financing activities:		
Repayment of note payable (entry 7)	(45,000)	
Issuance of bonds (entry 8)	489,000	
Issuance of capital stock (entry 9)	389,000	
Payment of dividends (entry 19)	(10,000)	823,000
Cash flow for the year		(250,000)
Cash at the beginning of the year		259,000
Cash at the end of the year		$ 9,000

adjusted for: the amortization expense and the gain on the sale of the land. For the second type of adjustment it is necessary to adjust net income for changes in the non-cash current operating accounts. The changes to these accounts are shown on the bottom row of Table 6-12. Calculation of CFO using the indirect method is shown in Table 6-14. This calculation can be used in place of the CFO calculation in Table 6-13.

Interpreting the Cash Flow Statement

The cash flow statement provides important information to many users of an entity's financial statements. Prediction of future cash flows is key for estimating the value of an entity and its shares. Bankers and other lenders and creditors are interested in cash flow so that they can evaluate whether the entity will be able to meet its obligations. Of course, the cash flow statement in a set of GAAP-based general purpose financial statements is a *historical* statement—it provides information about cash flows that have already occurred, not cash flows that will occur. However, as was the case with earnings and the income statement, it is expected that users can use historical cash flow information as a starting point for predicting future cash flows. The usefulness of historical cash flows to predict future cash flows depends on the entity and its circumstances. A new or rapidly growing entity's historical cash flows may not be a good indication of its future cash flows. The cash flow statement would probably be a good starting point for an established, stable entity.

MWW's cash flow statement (see page A-47) shows that during fiscal 2001 it had CFO of $21,140,000. This means that MWW's ordinary business activities produced enough cash to pay the operating cash flows and have over $21,000,000 left to apply to other purposes. MWW used the CFO to purchase capital assets and other assets, purchase franchise stores, retire long-term debt, repay capital lease liabilities, and repurchase capital stock. MWW shows that CFO is crucial for assessing whether an

Table 6-14 Flin Flon Inc. Calculation of CFO (Indirect Method)

Flin Flon Inc. Calculation of Cash from Operations using the Indirect Method For the Year Ended December 31, 2007		
Cash from operations:		
Net income		$ 68,000
Adjustments for non-cash items:		
Add: Amortization	$161,000	
Less: Gain on sale of land	(20,000)	141,000
Changes in non-cash current operating accounts		
Add: Decrease in prepaid insurance	3,000	
Increase in accounts payable	113,000	
Increase in taxes payable	10,000	
Less: Increase in accounts receivable	(80,000)	
Increase in inventory	(141,000)	(95,000)
Cash from operations		$114,000

entity will be able to generate enough cash to achieve its objectives. Without generating adequate CFO it would be much more difficult for MWW to achieve its objectives of purchasing back franchised stores and opening new stores.

CFO provides cash that can be used for paying dividends, acquiring capital assets, paying off liabilities, financing expansion, and so on. CFO is crucial because an entity's ability to raise cash through financing and investing activities is limited. Lenders and equity investors will not provide an endless supply of cash. As the amount of debt increases, an entity becomes more risky because the amount of interest the entity must pay increases. Remember that interest must be paid in good times and bad, so increasing the amount of debt increases the likelihood that the entity will be unable to pay its interest and make principal payments as they come due. At some point the risk becomes too high and loans are so costly (the result of very high interest rates) that borrowing is no longer viable. Similarly, equity investors purchase the shares of an entity because they want to earn a return on their investments. Investors will not purchase shares of an entity (or will not pay very much for them) that is in financial difficulty.

Entities can also raise cash by selling capital assets and investments. (This is a common strategy for entities that are in financial difficulty and urgently require cash.) However, if an entity must sell a significant amount of its assets, the nature of the entity will change dramatically. Because the amount of cash that can be generated from financing and investing activities is limited, CFO is crucial for an entity to achieve its business objectives.

Negative CFO can therefore be a cause for concern. Negative CFO means that simply operating the business uses cash. If an entity has negative CFO, it must have sources of cash to make up the shortfall. In the short run, negative cash from operations can be taken care of by drawing on cash reserves, using available lines of credit, borrowing or raising equity capital, or selling capital assets. However, as noted above, there can be limits to an entity's ability to raise cash continually to compensate for negative CFO. Lenders and investors will certainly be wary about "throwing good money after bad." Thus when you evaluate an entity it is important to assess how long the entity can survive with negative CFO.

Unfortunately, as with so many situations we have seen already in the book, interpreting negative CFO is not black and white. Negative CFO is not necessarily bad news. Entities that are just starting up or are in a growth phase would be expected to have negative CFO because growth or expansion requires investment in current assets such as inventory and accounts receivable. And a new or expanded business does not reach its maximum sales capacity immediately. This takes time. However, many of the operating costs may still have to be incurred regardless of the amount of sales. As a result, the business may be operating at a loss (in accrual accounting terms) and have negative CFO. Still, debt and equity investors are often very willing to provide cash to new businesses with good ideas.

Like most accounting information, the cash flow statement does not provide many answers—only questions that require further investigation. An inventory build-up that is using up cash can indicate that a business is expanding (which is likely good news) or that the inventory cannot be sold (which is bad news).

While operating cash flows are crucial to an entity's main business activities, it is important to recognize that entities must regularly spend on capital assets to maintain their ability to operate. Even if an entity is not growing, equipment, buildings, furniture and fixtures, computers, and other capital assets must be replaced as they become old or out of date. When evaluating the cash flow of an entity, it is necessary to consider cash requirements to replace capital assets. What makes the evaluation of investing cash flow requirements difficult is that the cash outlays required for capital assets need not be the same each year. There can be great variation in investment spending. Therefore, when you try to evaluate the cash requirements of an entity it is important to examine the cash flow statement for a number of periods. It is also important to have an understanding of the business of the entity you are examining.

There are many combinations of cash flows from operations, investing activities, and financing activities that an entity can have, and each combination tells a different story. For example, one would expect that an expanding company would have negative CFO, cash inflows from financing activities, and cash outflows for investing activities. An expanding company would be spending cash from operations on establishing the expanded operations, raising financing, and investing in the required capital assets. A stable, mature entity might have positive CFO, negative cash from investing activities (meaning that the entity is investing in capital assets, presumably replacing assets as required), and positive cash from financing activities (meaning that the entity is raising debt and equity capital to help finance its capital assets).

Figure 6-7 shows the patterns of the components of cash flow for several Canadian firms. Innova LifeSciences Corporation, a company that develops, manufactures, and markets medical devices, shows the pattern of a growing company, with negative CFO and cash from investing activities, and positive cash from financing activities. The example of SMK Speedy International Inc. (Speedy) shows how net income can differ from CFO and net cash flow. Speedy, the auto service company, reported net income of $107,229,000 and negative CFO of $15,213,000 for the year ended January 1, 2000. The net income was due entirely to a gain on the sale of Speedy's European subsidiaries ($141,425,000). The proceeds from the sale of the subsidiaries were treated as an investing activity since the transaction was the sale of a capital asset. While the gain added nicely to Speedy's net income, the transaction did not affect CFO. By selling its European subsidiaries, Speedy was able to use the proceeds from the sale to eliminate most of its long-term debt, which makes it a financially stronger but much smaller company. If a user ignored CFO and instead focussed on net income to evaluate the financial strength of Speedy, the user could be misled about Speedy's liquidity and its ability to generate CFO. It is situations like this that the cash flow statement is designed to help financial statement users understand. Speedy's cash flow statement is shown in Exhibit 6-1 (page 346).[2]

Before moving on to the next section, let's take a look at the cash flow statements of a well-known Canadian company. The T. Eaton Company Ltd. (Eaton's) was a Canadian institution for 130 years until 1999, when it was forced to close because of serious financial problems that made it impossible for the company to meet its

www.innovatechcorp.com
www.speedy.com

Company and year end	Net income (000)	Cash from operations (000)	Investing activities (000)	Financing activities (000)	Net change in cash (000)
Mark's Work Wearhouse (January 27, 2001)	$8,180	$21,140 +	($5,807) −	($10,114) −	$5,219
Innova LifeSciences Corporation (December 31, 2000)	(73)	(1,052) −	(639) −	2,036 +	(388)[1]
The Second Cup Ltd. (June 24, 2000)	(972)	5,024 +	26,543 +	(30,934) −	6,241
Shaw Communications Inc. (August 31, 2000)	254,440	253,079 +	(970,711) −	698,622 +	(19,010)
QLT Inc. (December 31, 2000)	9,453	(47,145) −	124,424 +	65,062 +	143,341
Clearly Canadian Beverage Corporation (December 31, 2000)	(1,486)	(1,486) −	(427) −	(243) −	(2,319)
SMK Speedy International Inc. (January 1, 2000)	107,229	(15,213) −	223,865 +	(193,937) −	14,655

Figure 6-7

Cash Flow Patterns of Selected Canadian Corporations

+ Indicates a net cash inflow.
− Indicates a net cash outflow.
[1] Figures do not add up because the company also included a loss on cash held in foreign currency.

obligations to its creditors. Eaton's cash flow statements for 1996 through 1999 are shown in Exhibit 6-2 (page 347).[3]

Eaton's cash problem can be seen clearly in the cash flow statements. Over the four-year period shown in Exhibit 6-2, operations consumed over $630,000,000 in cash. That means that Eaton's used $630,000,000 just to keep its operations going! Eaton's covered that cash shortfall largely by selling off parts of its business. Over the four years Eaton's raised over $385,000,000 by selling real estate and by selling its credit card business. (See the line called "cash provided by discontinued operations." **Discontinued operations** represent the parts of an entity's operations that the entity has sold or plans to sell in the near future.) Eaton's also raised cash of $207,693,000 by selling shares to public investors in 1999 and by selling shares privately in fiscal 1998 to raise $60,000,000. Eaton's also issued over $126,000,000 in debt over the four years and retired over $215,000,000 in debt over the same period. But Eaton's was not able to sell enough merchandise at high enough margins to generate enough cash to get itself out of trouble. In the end, Eaton's was unable to obtain the cash it needed to stay in business and suppliers were unwilling to sell it merchandise on credit.

Manipulating Cash Flow Information and the Effect of Accrual Accounting Choices on the Cash Flow Statement

We have already spent a good deal of space in this book discussing how the preparers of accounting information can use the availability of alternative accounting methods and the judgment that is required by accrual accounting to manage earnings and

Exhibit 6-1

SMK Speedy International Inc.'s
Cash Flow Statements

SMK SPEEDY INTERNATIONAL INC.
CONSOLIDATED STATEMENTS OF CASH FLOWS
(in thousands of Canadian dollars)

	Year ended	
	January 1 2000	January 2 1999
Operating activities		
Net income (loss) for the year	$ 107,229	$ (2,559)
Add (deduct) items not involving cash		
Depreciation and amortization	4,366	23,333
Restructuring costs (recoveries)	209	(3,875)
Amortization of deferred charges	413	3,306
Gain on sale of European subsidiaries	(141,425)	–
Loss on extinguishment of debt (Note 11)	18,983	1,053
Deferred income taxes	8,200	(8,600)
Loss (gain) on disposal of fixed assets	284	(32)
	(1,741)	12,626
Changes in non-cash working capital balances (Note 13)	(13,472)	(30,703)
Cash used in operating activities	(15,213)	(18,077)
Investing activities		
Fixed asset additions	(4,846)	(15,781)
Proceeds on disposal of fixed assets	955	5,677
Proceeds on sale of European subsidiaries (Note 3)	243,472	–
Proceeds on sale of Speedy U.S.A. (Note 4)	–	76,800
Sale and leasebacks (Note 6)	(15,316)	14,675
Other	(400)	542
Cash provided by investing activities	223,865	81,913
Financing activities		
Issue of capital stock	1,185	–
Repayment of long-term debt	(193,586)	(35,736)
Decrease in bank indebtedness	(1,276)	(20,673)
Repayment of capital lease obligations	(260)	(7,693)
Cross currency swaps	–	(1,704)
Decrease in other liabilities	–	(152)
Cash used in financing activities	(193,937)	(65,958)
Foreign exchange (loss) gain on cash held in foreign currencies	(60)	2,036
Increase (decrease) in cash and cash equivalents for the year	14,655	(86)
Cash and cash equivalents, beginning of year (Note 13)	14,515	14,601
Cash and cash equivalents, end of year (Note 13)	$ 29,170	$ 14,515

other financial statement numbers. One of the attractions, it is said, of cash accounting and the information in a cash flow statement is that it cannot be managed or manipulated the way accrual information can be.

This conclusion is not true. Cash information can be manipulated. It is certainly true that cash information cannot be manipulated in the same way as accrual information, where preparers must decide the timing of revenue and expense recognition. Cash information is "cleaner" in the sense that a transaction has an impact on cash flow only if cash is involved in the transaction. As a result, the preparer cannot exercise any judgment on the accounting for cash *once a transaction involving cash has occurred*. However, preparers can manipulate cash by influencing the timing of cash flows.

One way an entity can affect the timing of cash flows is by reducing "discretionary" spending on research and development, advertising and promotion, marketing, or maintenance. These spending reductions increase CFO, but such decisions by management to reduce the spending might not be in the interests of the entity. For example:

- The reduction of maintenance spending by a company that relies on its production facilities would increase CFO in the short term, but could contribute to higher costs in the future. Equipment would eventually require more costly maintenance or need replacing sooner than would have been necessary had the equipment been properly maintained. Poorly maintained equipment could also reduce

	Fiscal years ended			
	January 31, 1999	**January 31, 1998**	**January 25, 1997**	**January 27, 1996**
			(thousands)	
			(restated – note 1)	
OPERATING ACTIVITIES				
Loss before earnings from discontinued operations	$(102,893)	$(167,295)	$(170,162)	$ (56,822)
Adjustments for non-cash items (*note 12*)	3,946	(109,972)	80,055	(12,741)
	(98,947)	(277,267)	(90,107)	(69,563)
Net change in non-cash working capital balances (*note 12*)	(27,798)	30,358	65,416	11,644
Settlement of liabilities under CCA A plan (*note 2*)		(174,081)	–	–
Cash used in operating activities	(126,745)	(420,990)	(24,691)	(57,919)
INVESTING ACTIVITIES				
Proceeds from pension surplus (*note 5*)	4,677	201,534	–	–
Additions to fixed assets	(111,028)	(22,008)	(43,376)	(39,596)
Proceeds on sale of fixed and other assets	11,020	7,995	1,447	33,077
Other		–	592	2,994
Cash provided by (used in) investing activities	(95,331)	187,521	(41,337)	(3,525)
FINANCING ACTIVITIES				
Debt				
– issued, net of expenses	2,389	107,916	6,186	10,304
– repaid	(137,538)	(47,576)	(14,796)	(15,574)
Additions to capital stock and contributed surplus	207,693	60,000	–	1,596
Shareholder advances		(41)	1,820	(8,679)
Dividends paid.		–	(10,000)	–
Cash provided by (used in) financing activities	72,544	120,299	(16,790)	(12,353)
Net decrease in cash before discontinued operations	(149,532)	(113,170)	(82,818)	(73,797)
Cash provided by discontinued operations (*note 13*)	122,790	102,494	118,065	41,718
Cash position, beginning of fiscal year	(82,403)	(71,727)	(106,974)	(74,895)
Cash position, end of fiscal year	$(109,145)	$ (82,403)	$ (71,727)	$(106,974)
Cash position represented by				
Cash and short-term investments	7,319	$ 7,514	$ 91,167	$ 31,305
Revolving operating line	(116,464)	(89,917)	(162,894)	(138,279)
	$(109,145)	$ (82,403)	$ (71,727)	$(106,974)

Exhibit 6-2

The T. Eaton Company Ltd. Cash Flow Statements

the efficiency of operations or the quality of the goods produced, which would increase costs and reduce revenues.

- An entity could also increase CFO by delaying payments to suppliers. The payments to suppliers would have to be made eventually, which would have consequences on cash flows in future periods, but by deferring the payment CFO increases in the period when the payment is not made.

- Management decisions could also influence cash flow if an entity decides to sell some of its capital or other long-term assets. Such sales would increase cash from investing activities, but may result in the disposal of assets that would be in the interests of the entity to have.

Of course, in all these examples it is difficult to be sure what is motivating management to make its decisions, which makes understanding the financial statement numbers more difficult.

One way for a cash flow statement user to overcome the difficulties caused by preparers who manage the timing of their cash flows is to examine cash flow statements for a number of periods. Many of these manipulations are simply moving cash flows among periods, which an alert user can observe by carefully examining a number of cash flow statements.

Another question about the cash flow statement is whether accrual accounting policy choices have an effect on cash flow. The answer to the question is no. Accrual accounting policy choices do not affect total cash flows for a period, but the choices may affect how the cash flows are classified in the cash flow statement. Note that this conclusion refers to the actual cash flows of a transaction, not the cash flow *implications* of an accounting choice. In other words, an accounting policy choice could affect the amount of tax an entity pays or the amount of bonus its managers receive.

For example, if an entity can choose between capitalizing a cash expenditure and amortizing it over a period of time, and expensing the expenditure when it is incurred, there will be an effect on CFO and cash from investing activities in the period that the expenditure is made. The reason is that if an expenditure is capitalized it is treated as an investing activity, whereas if it is expensed it is treated as CFO. Total cash flow is not affected, but the classification of cash flows is. (We will examine a detailed example of this effect in Chapter 9.)

■ Solved Problem

Use the information about Kabina Ltd. (Kabina) in Table 6-15 to prepare a cash flow statement for the year ended October 31, 2004. Use the direct method of calculating CFO.

Additional information:

- Income taxes are paid in full by the end of the year.

- During fiscal 2004 Kabina paid dividends to shareholders of $50,000.

- All inventory purchases are made on credit.

- All sales to customers are made on credit.

- Interest, selling, general, and administrative, and other expenses are all paid in cash in the year they are incurred.

- Wages are paid two weeks after the work is done.

- During fiscal 2004 Kabina sold land that had cost $50,000 for $10,000 cash.

Solution:

The accounting equation spreadsheet for Kabina Ltd. is provided in Table 6-16 and the cash flow statement is shown in Table 6-17 (pages 350–351).

Table 6-15 Kabina Ltd. Financial Statements

Kabina Ltd.
Balance Sheets
As of October 31, 2003 and 2004

Assets	2004	2003	Liabilities	2004	2003
Current assets			*Current liabilities*		
Cash	$ 58,600	$ 10,000	Bank loan	$ 32,000	$ 25,000
Accounts receivable	52,000	56,000	Accounts payable	65,000	70,000
Inventory	135,000	110,000	Wages payable	30,000	20,000
Total current assets	245,600	176,000	Total current liabilities	127,000	115,000
Capital assets	475,000	375,000	Long-term note payable	90,000	110,000
Accumulated amortization	(175,000)	(120,000)	**Shareholders' equity**		
			Capital stock	100,000	80,000
			Retained earnings	228,600	126,000
			Total liabilities and		
Total assets	$545,600	$431,000	shareholders' equity	$545,600	$431,000

Kabina Ltd.
Income Statement
For the Year Ended October 31, 2004

Revenue	$950,000
Cost of goods sold	310,000
Gross margin	640,000
Selling, general and administrative expense	137,000
Wages expense	156,000
Amortization expense	55,000
Loss on sale of land	40,000
Other expenses	20,000
Interest expense	14,000
Income before taxes	218,000
Income tax expense	65,400
Net income	$152,600

Table 6-16   Kabina Ltd. Accounting Equation Spreadsheet

	Entry number	Type	Cash	Accounts receivable	Inven-tory	Capital assets	Accum. amort.	Bank loan	Accounts payable	Wages payable	Long-term note payable
Bal. Oct. 31, 2003	1		10,000	56,000	110,000	375,000	(120,000)	25,000	70,000	20,000	110,000
	2			950,000							
	3	O	954,000	(954,000)							
	4				(310,000)						
	5				335,000				335,000		
	6	O	(340,000)						(340,000)		
	7	O	(137,000)								
	8									156,000	
	9	O	(146,000)							(146,000)	
	10	O	(14,000)								
	11	O	(65,400)								
	12	O	(20,000)								
	13						(55,000)				
	14	I	10,000			(50,000)					
	15	I	(150,000)			150,000					
	16	F	7,000					7,000			
	17	F	(20,000)								(20,000)
	18	F	20,000								
	19	F	(50,000)								
Pre-closing balance Oct. 31, 2004	20		58,600	52,000	135,000	475,000	(175,000)	32,000	65,000	30,000	90,000
	21										
Bal. Oct. 31, 2004	22		58,600	52,000	135,000	475,000	(175,000)	32,000	65,000	30,000	90,000

Table 6-17   Kabina Ltd. Cash Flow Statement

Kabina Ltd.
Cash Flow Statement
For the Year Ended October 31, 2004

		Notes		
Cash from operations:				
Cash inflows (entry 3)		1		$954,000
Cash outflows:				
Cash spent on inventory (entry 6)		2	$340,000	
Cash spent on selling, general and administrative activities (entry 7)		3	137,000	
Cash spent on wages (entry 9)		4	146,000	
Cash spent on interest (entry 10)		3	14,000	
Cash spent on income taxes (entry 11)		3	65,400	
Cash spent on other expenses (entry 12)		3	20,000	722,400
Cash from operations				231,600
Cash from investing activities:				
Sale of land (entry 14)		5	10,000	
Purchase of capital assets (entry 15)		6	(150,000)	(140,000)
Cash from financing activities:				
Increase in bank loan (entry 16)		7	7,000	
Repayment of long-term note payable (entry 17)		7	(20,000)	
Issuance of capital stock (entry 18)		7	20,000	
Payment of dividends (entry 19)		8	(50,000)	(43,000)
Cash flow for the year				48,600
Cash at the beginning of the year				10,000
Cash at the end of the year				$ 58,600

Notes:

1.	Cash collections from customers	=	Beginning balance in the Accounts Receivable account	+	Credit sales during the period	−	Ending balance in the Accounts Receivable account
	$954,000	=	$56,000	+	$950,000	−	$52,000

Capital stock	Retained earnings	Revenue	Cost of goods sold	Selling, general, and admin. exp.	Wages expense	Interest expense	Amort. expense	Other expenses	Loss on sale of land	Income tax expense
80,000	126,000									
		950,000								
			(310,000)							
				(137,000)						
					(156,000)					
						(14,000)				
										(65,400)
								(20,000)		
							(55,000)			
									(40,000)	
20,000										
	(50,000)									
100,000	76,000	950,000	(310,000)	(137,000)	(156,000)	(14,000)	(55,000)	(20,000)	(40,000)	(65,400)
	152,600	(950,000)	310,000	137,000	156,000	14,000	55,000	20,000	40,000	65,400
100,000	228,600	0	0	0	0	0	0	0	0	0

Table 6-17 (continued)

2.	Inventory purchased	=	Ending balance in the Inventory account	+	Cost of Goods Sold	−	Beginning balance in the Inventory account
	$335,000	=	$135,000	+	$310,000	−	$110,000
	Payments to suppliers	=	Beginning balance in the Accounts Payable account	+	Credit purchases during the period	−	Ending balance in the Accounts Payables account
	$340,000	=	$70,000	+	$335,000	−	$65,000

3. Expense was paid in cash during the year so the amount of cash paid is the same as the expense for the period.

4.	Amount paid in wages	=	Beginning balance in the Wages Payable account	+	Wage expense	−	Ending balance in the Wages Payable account
	$146,000	=	$20,000	+	$156,000	−	$30,000

5. Land was sold for $10,000 cash as stated in the additional information.

6.	Purchase of capital assets	=	Ending balance in the Capital Assets account	+	Cost of capital assets sold	−	Beginning balance in the Capital Assets account
	$150,000	=	$475,000	+	$50,000	−	$375,000

7. Financing can be determined by comparing the beginning and ending balances in the bank loan, long-term note payable, and capital stock accounts. Given that there was no detail about activity in each of these accounts, it is reasonable to assume that a single event gave rise to the change in each account.

8. Dividends of $50,000 are stated in the question. If the dividend payment was not stated, it could be calculated using the following equation:

	Dividends	=	Ending balance in the Retained Earnings account	+	Net income	−	Ending balance in the Retained Earnings account
	$50,000	=	$126,000	+	$152,600	−	$228,600

Summary of Key Points

LO 1. Accrual accounting is the primary method of accounting in Canada. Accrual accounting requires judgments as to when revenue is earned, and how and what costs should be matched to revenues. Cash accounting simply records cash inflows and outflows as they occur—there is little room for judgment. The standard measure of performance under accrual accounting, earnings, is not designed to reflect flows of cash, but rather flows of wealth. Cash flow is a much more concrete concept than is earnings. This is not to say that cash flow is a better or worse measure than earnings. Cash flow is just different from earnings, and each has its role to play. In sum, cash accounting and accrual accounting tell users different things. Cash flow information is crucial for assessing liquidity. Accrual accounting provides information that can be viewed as giving a bigger economic picture.

LO 2. The cycle of how an entity begins with cash, invests in resources, provides goods or services to customers using those resources, and then collects cash from customers is called the cash cycle. Entities usually have to invest cash in resources before cash is received from customers—there is almost always a lag between the expenditure of cash and the receipt of cash.

LO 3. The cash flow statement provides information on an entity's historical cash flows. Cash flows in the cash flow statement are grouped into three categories: cash from operations (CFO), cash flows from investing activities, and cash flows from financing activities. CFO can be calculated and reported in two ways on the cash flow statement. The indirect method reconciles net income to CFO by adjusting net income for non-cash amounts that are included in the calculation of net income and for operating cash flows that are not included in the calculation of net income. The direct method reports CFO by showing cash collections and cash disbursements related to operations during the period.

LO 4. The six steps for preparing a cash flow statement are:

Step 1: Obtain balance sheets as of the beginning and end of the period and the income statement for the period, along with any other information that is available about the cash flows of the entity.

Step 2: Prepare an accounting equation spreadsheet with a column for each balance sheet and income statement account, plus columns to number and classify entries. Enter the amounts from the beginning and ending balance sheet accounts and from the income statement accounts on the spreadsheet.

Step 3: Make entries to the spreadsheet that explain the changes in each account.

Step 4: For each entry that affects the cash account, classify it as an operating, financing, or investing cash flow.

Step 5: Prepare the cash flow statement by organizing the amounts in entries that affected the cash account into CFO, investing activities, and financing activities.

Step 6: Calculate totals for each of operating, financing, and investing cash flows and calculate total cash flow for the period.

LO 5. Some argue that one of the attractions of cash accounting information over accrual accounting information is that cash accounting information cannot be managed or manipulated. Cash accounting information cannot be manipulated the same way as accrual information, where preparers must decide the timing of revenue and expense recognition. Cash information is "cleaner" in the sense that a transaction has an impact on cash flow only if cash is involved in the transaction. However, preparers can manipulate cash information by influencing the timing of cash flows. Also, some accrual accounting choices made by preparers affect the classification of cash flows, but not the actual amount of the cash flow.

Key Terms

bank overdraft, p. 325

capital lease, p. 327

cash cycle, p. 317

cash flow statement, p. 323

cash flows from financing activities, p. 323

cash flows from investing activities, p. 323

cash from operations (CFO), p. 323

direct method (of calculating cash from
   operations), p. 327

discontinued operations, p. 345

indirect method (of calculating cash from
   operations), p. 327

lease, p. 327

line of credit, p. 325

petty cash, p. 324

Similar Terms

The left column gives alternative terms that are sometimes used for the accounting
terms introduced in this chapter, which are listed in the right column.

statement of cash flows, statement of changes in financial position   **cash flow statement, p. 323**

cash flow from operating activities   **cash from operations, p. 323**

Assignment Materials

Questions

Q6-1. Explain the difference between cash accounting and accrual accounting.

Q6-2. Why is the cash flow statement included in the general purpose financial statement
package? Explain your answer fully.

Q6-3. What are some of the possible components that can be included in the definition of
"cash" in the cash flow statement? Explain the usefulness and limitations of including each of the components in the definition.

Q6-4. Explain each of the following:
a. Payables deferral period.
b. Inventory self-financing period.
c. Inventory conversion period.
d. Receivables conversion period.
e. Number of days between receiving inventory from suppliers and receiving cash
    from customers.

Q6-5. What is cash from operations?

Q6-6. Which should be more important to a shareholder of a company: cash flow or
income? Explain your answer.

Q6-7. Why is amortization added back to net income when cash from operations is calculated using the indirect method?

Q6-8. Why are losses added back to and gains subtracted from net income when cash from
operations is calculated using the indirect method?

Q6-9. What does it mean when an entity has negative cash from operations? What are the
reasons for negative cash from operations? Why is negative cash from operations
cause for concern? Is negative cash from operations necessarily bad news for an
entity? Explain.

Q6-10. Which should be more important to the management of an entity: cash flow or
income? Explain your answer.

Q6-11. Explain the three types of activities that are reported in a cash flow statement. Give
examples of each and explain the classification for each example.

Q6-12. New businesses frequently fail because of poor cash flow. Explain why you think new
businesses have this problem.

Q6-13. What are the two methods for calculating and reporting cash from operations? Explain how each arrives at cash from operations. As a user of financial statements, which method of calculating cash from operations would you prefer to see in a cash flow statement? Explain.

Q6-14. How is interest paid classified in a cash flow statement prepared according to GAAP? Does this treatment make sense? Explain.

Q6-15. How are dividends paid classified in a cash flow statement prepared according to GAAP? Does this treatment make sense? Explain.

Q6-16. What information does the cash flow statement provide to users that is not in the income statement?

Q6-17. What is the cash cycle? Describe the cash cycle for a wine maker.

Q6-18. An entity has a very profitable year, yet its cash flow and cash from operations are negative. Explain how this can happen.

Q6-19. An entity reports a loss for the year. Explain how the entity could have positive cash flow and positive cash from operations in that year.

Q6-20. What does the term "cash" in the cash flow statement refer to? Explain.

Q6-21. Why does an increase in accounts receivable imply a decrease in cash from operations? Explain.

Q6-22. Why does a decrease in inventory imply an increase in cash from operations? Explain.

Q6-23. How is it possible for managers to manipulate the information in the cash flow statement?

Q6-24. What type of manipulation of accounting information do you think is more likely to cause operational problems for an entity: the manipulations that are done with accrual accounting, or the manipulations that are done with cash accounting? Explain your answer.

Q6-25. Managers often receive bonuses based on the net income of the entities they manage. Do you think that it would be better to use cash from operations as a basis to award bonuses rather than net income? Explain your answer.

Q6-26. What objectives of financial reporting does the cash flow statement serve? Explain.

Q6-27. One way for a biotechnology, software, or other high-technology company to increase cash from operations would be to reduce spending on research. Explain why reducing spending on research (which is expensed when incurred according to GAAP) would increase cash from operations. Explain why reducing spending on research is potentially a serious problem for these types of entities. Respond by discussing the business implications of reducing spending on research.

Q6-28. According to the *CICA Handbook*, non-cash transactions such as the acquisition of an asset in exchange for shares or a liability are not included in the cash flow statement. Explain how you think the cash flow statement would differ in appearance if $1,000,000 of equipment were acquired in exchange for $1,000,000 of the acquiring company's shares. Do you think it makes better sense to include or not include these non-cash transactions in the cash flow statement? Explain.

Q6-29. In a recent negotiation between labour and management of a major corporation, management argued that the company's low earnings made it imprudent to grant the requested wage increase. The labour union disagreed and argued that the company had ample resources to meet the wage demands of the union. What do you think might have been the basis of the union's argument? Do you think that it is adequate to base the ability of a company to grant a wage increase only on net income? Explain.

Q6-30. Give examples of the circumstances that could cause cash flow problems for an airline.

Q6-31. Explain why growing companies sometimes face cash flow problems.

Exercises

E6-1. **(Calculating the cash lag, LO 2)** Dickens Tailor Shop (Dickens) makes tailored-to-measure suits, jackets, and pants for men and women. Customers who are interested in purchasing tailored-to-measure clothing make an appointment with one of Dickens' tailors, at which time the customer decides on the style of clothing he or she wishes to buy, selects an appropriate fabric, and is measured by the tailor. Dickens keeps a large selection of fabrics so customers can see the actual fabric their clothing will be made from. A bolt of fabric is, on average, held in inventory for nine months before it is used to make a garment. Dickens pays for its fabric 60 days from the time it is received from the supplier. The time from a customer's first appointment to the completion and delivery of the garment is, on average, one month. Customers receive an invoice when the garment is delivered and payment is received from the customer, on average, 30 days from the time of delivery.

Required:

Calculate the following for Dickens Tailor Shop:
a. Payables deferral period.
b. Inventory self-financing period.
c. Inventory conversion period.
d. Receivables conversion period.
e. Number of days between receiving inventory from suppliers and receiving cash from customers.

E6-2. **(The effect of amortization on cash from operations, LO 1, 3)** In 2003 Anyox Ltd. (Anyox) reported net income of $100,000. All revenues and expenses were in cash, except for a $15,000 amortization expense.

Required
a. Calculate cash from operations for Anyox in 2003.
b. Suppose that instead of a $15,000 amortization expense in 2003, Anyox expensed $22,000 for amortization. Assume that all other revenues and expenses remained the same. What would Anyox's net income be in 2003? What would its cash from operations be in 2003? Explain the reasons for any differences or similarities in your answer for when the amortization expense was $15,000 and when it was $22,000.

E6-3. **(The effect of asset write-offs on cash from operations, LO 1, 3)** Hexham Inc. (Hexham) wrote off $1,000,000 in assets from its books in its December 31, 2004 income statement. Hexham's net income for the year, after taking into consideration the write-off, was $3,700,000. During 2004 accounts receivable increased by $100,000, inventory increased by $175,000, and accounts payable decreased by $15,000. Amortization expense in 2004 was $278,000.

Required:
a. What journal entry did Hexham make to record the write-off of the assets?
b. Calculate cash from operations using the indirect method.
c. Suppose that at the last minute, Hexham's management decided to delay writing off the assets from its books:
   i. What would Hexham's net income be in 2004?
   ii. What would Hexham's cash from operations be in 2004?
d. Explain the differences you found between the net incomes you calculated under c(i) and c(ii).
e. Explain the differences you found between the cash from operations numbers you calculated under c(i) and c(ii).

E6-4. **(Classifying transactions for a cash flow statement, LO 3)** For each of the following transactions and economic events, classify each as an operating, investing, or financing cash flow, or whether the item has no effect on cash flow. Also, indicate whether each item increases or decreases cash.
a. Equipment is purchased for cash.

b. Capital assets are amortized.

c. Cash dividends are paid to shareholders.

d. Interest is paid on a bond.

e. Accounts receivable are collected from customers.

f. Land is purchased in exchange for shares in the company.

g. Cash is obtained from a lender in exchange for a long-term note payable.

h. A bank loan is repaid.

i. Suppliers of inventory are paid in cash.

i. Inventory is purchased on credit.

E6-5. **(Classifying transactions for a cash flow statement, LO 3)** Mamalilaculla Ltd. (Mamalilaculla) is a small retail jewellery store. For each of the following, specify whether the item should be classified as an operating, financing, or investing cash flow, whether the item represents a cash inflow or outflow, and the amount of the transaction. Explain your reasoning.

a. Mamalilaculla paid $20,000 cash for a shipment of cut diamonds for engagement rings.

b. Mamalilaculla's amortization expense for the year was $8,000.

c. Mamalilaculla purchased new display cases for the store for $13,500 cash.

d. Mamalilaculla sold a number of old display cases for $3,500. The loss on the sale of the display cases was $2,000.

e. Mamalilaculla sold a pendant to a customer for $2,000. The customer paid with a Visa credit card.

f. Mamalilaculla's shareholder purchased additional shares of the corporation for $100,000. The cash will be used to purchase additional inventory.

g. Mamalilaculla repaid a $50,000 loan from the bank.

E6-6. **(Determining missing information, LO 3)** Calculate the missing information (indicated by shaded areas) from the following cash flow statements:

Cash from (used by)	Company 1	Company 2	Company 3	Company 4	Company 5
Operations	$10,000	($12,000)		$16,000	
Investing activities	(4,500)		500	(10,000)	(5,000)
Financing activities		15,000	(10,000)	(6,000)	2,000
Net increase (decrease) in cash	1,000	(5,000)	6,000		(8,000)

E6-7. **(Calculating cash from operations, LO 3)** You are provided the following information about Joggins Inc. (Joggins) for 2005:

Net income	=	$175,000
Accounts receivable on January 1, 2005	=	550,000
Accounts receivable on December 31, 2005	=	625,000
Inventory on January 1, 2005	=	700,000
Inventory on December 31, 2005	=	610,000
Accounts payable on January 1, 2005	=	475,000
Accounts payable on December 31, 2005	=	575,000
Amortization expense	=	105,000

Required:

Calculate cash from operations for Joggins for 2005.

E6-8. **(Adjustments to net income when using the indirect method of calculating cash from operations, LO 3)** Tracadie Inc. (Tracadie) uses the indirect method to calculate and report cash from operations in its cash flow statement. For each of the following items, indicate whether the item would be added to net income, deducted from net income, or not be relevant when calculating cash from operations.

a. Gain on the sale of equipment that was used by Tracadie to provide its services.

b. Amortization expense.

c. Decrease in accounts payable.

d. Purchase of equipment.

e. Decrease in inventory.

f. Increase in accounts receivables.

g. Increase in accrued liabilities.

h. Loss on the sale of office furniture used in Tracadie's executive offices.

i. Increase in long-term debt.

i. Dividends paid.

E6-9. **(Calculate cash from operations using the indirect method, LO 1, 3, 4)** Consider the following non-cash current operating account information of Yahk Ltd. (Yahk):

	2005	2004		2005	2004
Accounts receivable	$ 24,000	$ 19,000	Accounts payable	$52,000	$47,000
Inventory	75,000	87,000	Wages payable	9,000	12,000
Prepaids	10,000	8,000	Taxes payable	16,000	10,000
			Interest payable	9,500	13,000
Total current operating assets	$109,000	$114,000	Total current operating liabilities	$86,500	$82,000

Yahk's net income for 2005 was $72,000. In addition, Yahk reported an amortization expense of $20,000 and a loss on the sale of capital assets of $10,000.

Required:

a. Calculate cash from operations for Yahk using the indirect method and prepare the cash from operations section of Yahk's cash flow statement.

b. Explain why cash from operations is different from net income in 2005.

E6-10. **(Calculate cash collections using the direct method, LO 4)** In its April 30, 2005 annual report, Ebbsfleet Inc. (Ebbsfleet) reported a beginning Accounts Receivable balance of $121,000 and an ending Accounts Receivable balance of $152,000. Ebbsfleet reported Sales for the year ended April 30, 2005 of $1,542,000.

Required:

Calculate the amount of cash Ebbsfleet collected from customers during fiscal 2005.

E6-11. **(Calculate cash payments using the direct method, LO 4)** In its May 31, 2004 annual report, Maloneck Ltd. (Maloneck) reported that it had Inventory of $87,500 and Accounts Payable of $52,000 on May 31, 2003, and Inventory of $98,000 and Accounts Payable of $61,000 on May 31, 2004. Maloneck's income statement for the year ended May 31, 2004 reported Cost of Goods Sold of $610,000.

Required:

Calculate the amount of cash that Maloneck paid to suppliers for purchases of inventory during fiscal 2004. Assume that accounts payable pertain only to the purchase of inventory on credit.

E6-12. **(Calculate cash payments made to employees using direct method, LO 4)** In its August 31, 2005 annual report, Pitquah Corp. (Pitquah) reported Wages Payable on August 31, 2004 of $175,000, and Wages Payable on August 31, 2005 of $225,000. Pitquah's income statement reports Wages Expense of $2,346,000.

Required:

Calculate the amount of cash that Pitquah paid in wages to employees in fiscal 2005.

E6-13. **(Preparing a cash flow statement, LO 3, 4)** Use the following information to prepare a cash flow statement for Quisibis Inc. (Quisibis) for the year ended December 31, 2006. Assume that income statement amounts have already been closed to retained earnings. Also assume that dividends of $10,000 were paid during 2006.

Quisibis Inc.
Account Balances
On December 31, 2005 and 2006

	2006	2005
Cash	$ 15,000	$ 10,000
Accounts receivable	22,000	18,000
Inventory	35,000	37,000
Capital assets	119,000	100,000
Accumulated amortization	(17,000)	(12,000)
Accounts payable	15,000	14,000
Long-term debt	62,000	70,000
Capital stock	75,000	70,000
Retained earnings	22,000	(1,000)
Revenue	250,000	
Cost of goods sold	130,000	
Other expenses (all cash)	82,000	
Amortization	5,000	

E6-14. **(Preparing a cash flow statement, LO 3, 4)** Use the following information to prepare a cash flow statement for Maynooth Inc. for the year ended December 31, 2005. Assume that income statement amounts have already been closed to retained earnings. Also assume that dividends of $100,000 were paid during 2006.

Maynooth Inc.
Account Balances
On December 31, 2004 and 2005

	2005	2004
Cash	$ 47,000	$ 62,000
Accounts receivable	59,000	69,000
Inventory	98,000	87,000
Capital assets	248,000	210,000
Accumulated amortization	(112,000)	(77,000)
Accounts payable	63,000	70,000
Long-term debt	158,000	110,000
Capital stock	75,000	70,000
Retained earnings	44,000	101,000
Revenue	498,000	
Cost of goods sold	241,000	
Other expenses (all cash)	179,000	
Amortization	35,000	

Problems

P6-1. **(Calculating missing information about balance sheet accounts, LO 4)** The following general equation can be used to determine missing information about balance sheet accounts:

Ending balance in the account	=	Beginning balance in the account	+	Transactions and economic events that increase the balance in the account	−	Transactions and economic events that decrease the balance in the account

Use the equation to determine the missing information in each of the following independent situations. For each case assume that the year end is December 31:

a. On January 1, 2004 Ewart Ltd. (Ewart) had $175,000 of Inventory on hand. During 2004 Ewart sold $520,000 of inventory and purchased $615,000 of inventory. How much inventory did Ewart have on December 31, 2004?

b. On January 1, 2005 Peno Inc. (Peno) had $500,000 of Accounts Receivable and on December 31, 2005 it had $450,000 of Accounts Receivable. During 2005 Peno collected $2,450,000 from customers. What amount of credit sales did Peno make during 2005? Assume all of Peno's sales were on credit.

c. Noir Inc. (Noir) capitalizes its store opening costs and amortizes them over five years. On January 1, 2004 the balance in Noir's unamortized Store Opening Costs account on the balance sheet was $75,000. On December 31, 2004 the balance in the account was $85,000. During 2004 the amortization expense for store opening costs was $20,000. What amount of store opening costs did Noir capitalize to the Store Opening Cost account on the balance sheet during 2004? Assume that Noir does not have a separate contra-asset account for accumulating amortization for this account.

d. On December 31, 2005 Hythe Ltd. (Hythe) owed its employees $22,000. During 2005 Hythe's employees earned $200,000 and were paid $210,000. How much did Hythe owe its employees on December 31, 2004?

e. Cadzow Inc. (Cadzow) purchases all of its inventory on credit. On January 1, 2004 Cadzow had $1,250,000 of Inventory on hand and on December 31, 2004 it had $1,500,000 of Inventory. Cost of Goods Sold during 2004 was $5,350,000. The beginning and ending balances in Cadzow's Accounts Payable account on January 1, 2004 and December 31, 2004 were $950,000 and $1,100,000 respectively. How much did Cadzow pay its suppliers during 2004?

P6-2. **(Calculating missing information about balance sheet accounts, LO 4)** The following general equation can be used to determine missing information about balance sheet accounts:

Ending balance in the account	=	Beginning balance in the account	+	Transactions and economic events that increase the balance in the account	−	Transactions and economic events that decrease the balance in the account

Use the equation to determine the missing information in each of the following independent situations. For each case assume that the year end is June 30.

a. On July 1, 2004 Zincton Ltd. (Zincton) had $325,000 of Inventory on hand. During fiscal 2005 Zincton sold $980,000 of Inventory and purchased $815,000 of inventory. How much inventory did Zincton have on June 30, 2005?

b. On July 1, 2003 Winsloe Inc. (Winsloe) had $370,000 of Accounts Receivable and on June 30, 2004 it had $420,000 of accounts receivable. During fiscal 2004 Winsloe collected $2,150,000 from customers. What amount of credit sales did Winsloe make during fiscal 2004? Assume all of Winsloe's sales were on credit.

c. Union Inc. (Union) capitalizes its store opening costs and amortizes them over five years. On July 1, 2004 the balance in Union's unamortized Store Opening Costs account on the balance sheet was $115,000. On June 30, 2005 the balance in the account was $95,000. During fiscal 2005 the amortization expense for store opening costs was $30,000. What amount of store opening costs did Union capitalize to the Store Opening Costs account on the balance sheet during fiscal 2005? Assume that Union does not have a separate contra-asset account for accumulating amortization for this account.

d. On June 30, 2004 Sawbill Ltd. (Sawbill) owed its employees $152,000. During fiscal 2004, Sawbill's employees earned $1,250,000 and were paid $1,120,000. How much did Sawbill owe its employees on July 1, 2003?

e. Otter Inc. (Otter) purchases all of its inventory on credit. On July 1, 2004 Otter had $250,000 of Inventory on hand and on June 30, 2005 it had $200,000 of Inventory. Cost of Goods Sold during fiscal 2005 was $950,000. The beginning and ending balances in Otter's Accounts Payable account on July 1, 2004 and June 30, 2005 were $135,000 and $103,000 respectively. How much did Otter pay its suppliers during fiscal 2005?

P6-3. **(Reconstructing the beginning balance sheet using the ending balance sheet and the cash flow statement, LO 3, 4)** Use the balance sheet as of October 31, 2006 and the cash flow statement for the year ended October 31, 2006 that are shown below to prepare Factory Corp.'s balance sheet as of November 1, 2005.

Factory Corp.
Balance Sheet as of October 31, 2006

Assets		Liabilities and shareholders' equity	
Current assets		*Current liabilities*	
Cash	$ 100,000	Accounts payable	$ 375,000
Accounts receivable	210,000	Wages payable	45,000
Inventory	510,000	Total current liabilities	420,000
Total current assets	820,000	Long-term loan	912,500
Land	500,000	Capital stock	462,500
Furniture and fixtures	1,750,000	Retained earnings	800,000
Accumulated amortization	(475,000)	Total liabilities and	
Total assets	$2,595,000	shareholders' equity	$2,595,000

Factory Corp.
Cash Flow Statement for the Year Ended October 31, 2006

Net income		$375,000
Add: Amortization expense		105,000
Less: Gain on sale of land		(50,000)
		$430,000
Changes in current operating accounts:		
Accounts receivable	35,000	
Inventory	(45,000)	
Accounts payable	20,000	
Wages payable	(15,000)	(5,000)
Cash from operations		425,000
Investing activities:		
Sale of land	150,000	
Purchase of furniture and fixtures	(250,000)	
Cash from investing activities		(100,000)
Financing activities:		
Sale of stock	82,500	
Dividends paid	(95,000)	
Repayment of long-term loan	(287,500)	
Cash from financing activities		(300,000)
Increase in cash for the year		25,000
Cash balance on November 1, 2005		75,000
Cash balance on October 31, 2006		$100,000

P6-4. **(Reconstructing the ending balance sheet using the beginning balance sheet and the cash flow statement, LO 3, 4)** Use the balance sheet as of May 31, 2003 and the cash flow statement for the year ended May 31, 2004 that are shown below for Balzac Ltd. to prepare Balzac Ltd.'s balance sheet as of May 31, 2004.

Balzac Ltd.
Balance Sheet as of May 31, 2003

Assets		Liabilities and shareholders' equity	
Current assets		*Current liabilities*	
Cash	$ 22,000	Accounts payable	$ 75,000
Accounts receivable	60,000	Accrued liabilities	10,000
Inventory	110,000	Interest payable	5,000
Prepaids	10,000	Taxes payable	11,000
Total current assets	202,000	Total current liabilities	101,000
Land	100,000	Long-term loan	99,000
Furniture and fixtures	300,000	Capital stock	200,000
Accumulated amortization	(80,000)	Retained earnings	122,000
		Total liabilities and	
Total assets	$522,000	shareholders' equity	$522,000

Balzac Ltd.
Cash Flow Statement For the Year Ended May 31, 2004

Net income	$150,000	
Add: Amortization expense	30,000	
Loss on sale of land	20,000	
		$200,000
Changes in current operating accounts:		
Accounts receivable	(25,000)	
Inventory	20,000	
Prepaids	4,000	
Accounts payable	12,000	
Accrued liabilities	(2,500)	
Interest payable	7,000	
Taxes payable	(1,500)	14,000
Cash from operations		214,000
Investing activities:		
Sale of land	5,000	
Purchase of furniture and fixtures	(179,500)	
Cash from investing activities		(174,500)
Financing activities		
Sale of stock	50,000	
Dividends paid	(122,000)	
Long-term loan	22,500	
Cash from financing activities		(49,500)
Increase/(decrease) in cash for the year		(10,000)
Cash balance on May 31, 2003		22,000
Cash balance on May 31, 2004		$ 12,000

P6-5. (**Preparing a cash flow statement using the direct method to determine cash from operations, LO 4**) Examine Agu Inc.'s (Agu) balance sheets and income statement below.

Agu Inc.
Balance Sheets
As of March 31, 2004 and 2005

Assets	2005	2004	Liabilities and shareholders' equity	2005	2004
Current assets			*Current liabilities*		
Cash	$ 125,000	$ 62,000	Accounts payable	$ 27,000	$ 20,000
Accounts receivable	271,000	197,000	Accrued liabilities	125,000	140,000
Supplies inventory	45,000	53,000	Interest payable	42,000	37,000
Prepaids	13,000	22,000	Taxes payable	92,000	59,000
Total current assets	454,000	334,000	Total current liabilities	286,000	256,000
Capital assets	2,250,000	1,346,000	Note payable	951,000	659,000
Accumulated amortization	(610,000)	(443,000)	Capital stock	400,000	200,000
			Retained earnings	457,000	122,000
			Total liabilities and		
Total assets	$2,094,000	$1,237,000	shareholders' equity	$2,094,000	$1,237,000

Agu Inc.
Income Statement
For the Year Ended March 31, 2005

Sales		$2,750,000
Expenses:		
Salaries and wages	$1,135,000	
Supplies	375,000	
Amortization	195,000	
Advertising and marketing	95,000	
Interest	87,000	
General and administrative	175,000	
Other	52,000	2,114,000
Income before gains and income taxes		636,000
Gain on sale of capital assets		25,000
Income before income taxes		661,000
Income taxes		204,910
Net Income		$ 456,090

Additional information:

i. During 2005, dividends of $91,000 were paid to the shareholders of Agu Inc.

ii. $750,000 of Agu's sales were for cash. The remaining sales were made on credit.

iii. All of Agu's purchases of supplies were made on credit. Purchases of supplies on credit are reflected in the Accounts Payable account.

iv. During 2005 Agu sold for $97,000 capital assets that cost $100,000 and had a net book value of $72,000. (Remember that when amortizable capital assets are sold, the cost of the asset and the accumulated amortization associated with the asset must be removed from the books. In this situation, the Capital Assets account would be reduced by $100,000 and the Accumulated Amortization account would be reduced by $28,000.)

v. Advertising and Marketing and Other Expenses were fully paid in cash during 2005. General and Administrative Expenses are expensed and paid in cash when incurred, except for Prepaid Rent and Prepaid Insurance. During 2005 Agu expensed $35,000 of prepaid items.

vi. Accrued Liabilities pertain to salaries and wages.

Required:

a. Use the information provided to prepare a cash flow statement for Agu for the year ended March 31, 2005. Use the direct method for calculating cash from operations.

b. Assume the role of a lender who is evaluating Agu's situation. Analyze and interpret the cash flow statement you prepared and prepare a report to your manager describing what you learned about Agu from the statement.

P6-6. **(Preparing a cash flow statement using the indirect method to determine cash from operations, LO 4)** Refer to the information provided in Problem P6-5 and respond to the following:

a. Use the information provided to prepare a cash flow statement for Agu for the year ended March 31, 2005. Use the indirect method for calculating cash from operations.

b. Assume the role of a lender who is evaluating Agu's situation. Analyze and interpret the cash flow statement you prepared and prepare a report to your manager describing what you learned about Agu from the statement.

P6-7. **(Preparing a cash flow statement, using the direct method to calculate cash from operations LO 4)** Examine Jubilee Ltd.'s (Jubilee) balance sheets and income statement below:

Jubilee Ltd.
Balance Sheets for the Years Ended July 31, 2004 and 2005

Assets	2005	2004	Liabilities and shareholders' equity	2005	2004
Current assets			*Current liabilities*		
Cash	$ 10,000	$ 27,000	Accounts payable	$ 27,000	$ 48,000
Accounts receivable	50,000	35,000	Wages and salaries payable	20,000	27,000
Inventory	79,000	62,000	Interest payable	5,000	3,200
Due from shareholders	40,000	25,000	Taxes payable	5,000	9,000
Total current assets	179,000	149,000	Total current liabilities	57,000	87,200
Capital assets	250,000	285,000	Bank loan	40,000	55,000
Accumulated amortization	(160,000)	(148,000)	Capital stock	60,000	50,000
			Retained earnings	112,000	93,800
			Total liabilities and		
Total assets	$269,000	$286,000	shareholders' equity	$269,000	$286,000

Jubilee Ltd.
Income Statement
For the Year Ended July 31, 2005

Sales		$725,000
Cost of goods sold		325,000
Gross margin		400,000
Expenses:		
Salaries and wages	$175,000	
Amortization	57,000	
Advertising and marketing	48,000	
Interest	22,000	
General and administrative	31,000	
Other	17,000	350,000
		50,000
Loss on sale of capital assets		25,000
Income before income taxes		25,000
Income taxes		6,800
Net income		$ 18,200

Additional Information:
i. During fiscal 2005 $125,000 of Jubilee's sales were for cash and the remainder were on credit.
ii. All of Jubilee's inventory purchases were on credit.
iii. During 2005 Jubilee sold for $20,000 capital assets that cost $100,000 and had a net book value of $45,000. (Remember that when amortizable capital assets are sold, the cost of the asset and the accumulated amortization associated with the asset must be removed from the books. In this situation, the Capital Assets account would be reduced by $100,000 and the Accumulated Amortization account would be reduced by $55,000.)
iv. Advertising and Marketing, General and Administrative, and Other Expenses were fully paid in cash during 2005.
v. The amounts Due From Shareholders are loans made to shareholders by Jubilee. These loans are not considered operating items.

Required:
a. Use the information provided to prepare a cash flow statement for Jubilee for the year ended July 31, 2005. Use the direct method for calculating cash from operations.
b. Assume the role of an analyst for a mutual fund company who is evaluating Jubilee's situation. Analyze and interpret the cash flow statement you prepared and prepare a report to your manager describing what you learned about Jubilee from the statement.

P6-8.   **(Preparing a cash flow statement using the indirect method to calculate cash from operations, LO 4)** Refer to the information provided in Problem P6-7 and respond to the following:

Required:

    a. Use the information provided to prepare a cash flow statement for Jubilee for the year ended July 31, 2005. Use the indirect method for calculating cash from operations.

    b. Assume the role of an analyst for a mutual fund company who is evaluating Jubilee's situation. Analyze and interpret the cash flow statement you prepared and prepare a report to your manager describing what you learned about Jubilee from the statement.

P6-9.   **(Calculating cash from operations using both the direct and indirect methods, LO 1, 3, 4)** You are provided the following balance sheet information and summarized income statement for Rivulet Inc.:

Rivulet Inc.
Current Operating Assets and Liabilities as of December 31, 2004 and 2005

	2005	2004		2005	2004
Accounts receivable	$124,000	$101,000	Accounts payable	$192,000	$217,000
Inventory	275,000	315,000	Accrued liabilities	49,000	32,000

Rivulet Inc.
Income Statement
For the Year Ended December 31, 2005

Revenue	$1,075,000
Cost of goods sold	532,000
Gross margin	543,000
Other expenses	392,000
Amortization expense	215,000
Loss on sale of capital assets	25,000
Net loss	$ 89,000

Accounts Payable pertains exclusively to the purchase of inventory and Accrued Liabilities pertains exclusively to Other Expenses.

Required:

    a. Prepare Rivulet's cash from operations section of the cash flow statement using the direct method.

    b. Prepare Rivulet's cash from operations section of the cash flow statement using the indirect method.

    c. Which method do you think is more informative to users of the cash flow statement? Explain. What information is available when the direct method is used that is not available when the indirect method is used?

    d. Explain the difference between net income and cash from operations. Why did Rivulet have a loss on its income statement but positive cash from operations?

    e. What are the implications of having a loss on the income statement but positive cash from operations?

P6-10. **(Calculating cash from operations using both the direct and indirect methods, LO 1, 3, 4)** You are provided the following balance sheet information and summarized income statement for Katrime Ltd.:

Katrime Ltd.
Current Operating Assets and Liabilities
as of May 31, 2004 and 2005

	2006	2005		2006	2005
Accounts receivable	$427,000	$278,000	Accounts payable	$392,000	$315,000
Inventory	818,000	566,000	Wages payable	72,000	85,000
Prepaid insurance	72,000	35,000			

Katrime Ltd.
Income Statement
For the Year Ended May 31, 2006

Revenue	$2,762,000
Cost of goods sold	1,471,000
Gross margin	1,291,000
Wages expense	(666,000)
Amortization expense	(85,000)
Insurance expense	(60,000)
Other expenses	(275,000)
Gain on sale of capital assets	55,000
Net income	$ 260,000

Accounts payable pertains exclusively to the purchase of inventory. Other Expenses were fully paid in cash during the year.

Required:

    a. Prepare Katrime's cash from operations section of the cash flow statement using the direct method.

    b. Prepare Katrime's cash from operations section of the cash flow statement using the indirect method.

    c. Which method do you think is more informative to users of the cash flow statement? Explain. What information is available when the direct method is used that is not available when the indirect method is used?

    d. Explain the difference between net income and cash from operations. Why did Katrime have a profit on its income statement but negative cash from operations?

    e. What are the implications of showing a profit on the income statement but negative cash from operations?

P6-11. **(Preparing financial statements, LO 1, 4)** Exstew Ltd. (Exstew) is a newly formed advertising agency. The agency was formed on May 1, 2004 by three friends from university who graduated several years ago and had been working in advertising until recently. Each of the friends contributed $35,000 to Exstew in exchange for shares in the company. In addition, they arranged a $75,000 line of credit from the bank. On August 1, 2004 Exstew arranged to rent office space in prestigious downtown offices at a cost of $4,000 per month. Rent had to be paid in advance on the first day of August, December, and April. Each payment was for $16,000. Exstew also purchased office furniture and equipment for $30,000. The furniture and equipment is being amortized over five years.

During fiscal 2005 Exstew earned $110,000 providing services to customers. As of April 30, 2005 Exstew was owed $65,000 from customers. During fiscal 2005 it paid salaries of $57,000, incurred advertising costs of $25,000, and incurred various other costs of $17,000. At the end of the year Exstew owed employees $2,700 and owed various other suppliers $9,200. As of April 30, 2005 Exstew had borrowed $42,000 against its line of credit. Interest on the borrowed money was $2,300.

Required:

    Exstew's April 30, 2005 year end has recently passed and you have been approached by the three friends to prepare financial statements for the year. Use the information above to prepare a balance sheet, an income statement, and a cash flow statement. Exstew does not believe it will have to pay taxes for 2005. Use the financial statements you prepared to assess the financial situation of Exstew. Your assessment should consider information from all of the financial statements.

P6-12. **(Preparing financial statements, LO 1, 4)** Souvenirs-On-The-Go Ltd. (Souvenirs-On-The-Go) is a mobile souvenir stand that moves around the city to be "where the action is." Souvenirs-On-The-Go was started this summer by Evan Shayne as a way to earn money in the summer months to help pay for his education. Evan registered his corporation and contributed $10,000 of his savings to Souvenirs-On-The-Go in exchange for shares in the company. Souvenirs-On-The-Go borrowed $5,000 from

Evan's parents to provide additional cash. Souvenirs-On-The-Go purchased a used cart for $7,500 cash. If it is successful, Evan hopes to operate Souvenirs-On-The-Go for four years until he graduates from university. Souvenirs-On-The-Go obtained a municipal vending license for $500 that allows the cart to operate in designated areas around the city. The license is valid for two years.

Over the summer Souvenirs-On-The-Go sold $12,700 in souvenirs, all for cash. Souvenirs-On-The-Go purchased $5,100 worth of souvenirs, including $900 in souvenirs that were not paid for by the end of the summer. Souvenirs-On-The-Go incurred $525 of maintenance and repairs on the cart and $2,100 of miscellaneous expenses during the summer. As of the end of the summer the maintenance and repairs had been fully paid for and $250 of the miscellaneous expenses was still owed to the suppliers. At the end of the summer unsold souvenirs costing $600 remained. However, Evan thinks he will be able to sell them next summer. Also, Souvenirs-On-The-Go owes Evan's parents $300 in interest.

Required:

The summer is now over and Evan is back at school. Evan has not yet had a chance to evaluate the performance of Souvenirs-On-The-Go. Evan has asked you to prepare an income statement, balance sheet, and cash flow statement for the summer just ended. Use the financial statements you prepared to assess the financial situation of Souvenirs-On-The-Go. Your assessment should consider information from all of the financial statements.

P6-13. (**The effect of accrual accounting policies on the cash flow statement, LO 5**) The chief accountant of Phidias Publications Ltd. (Phidias) is thinking about how accrual accounting policy choices affect the cash flow statement. Phidias publishes a number of newspapers in mid-sized Canadian communities. One of the key success factors of the newspaper business is circulation of the papers. Phidias spends a significant amount of money recruiting and maintaining subscribers. The accountant thinks that sound arguments could be made for both expensing the cost of recruiting and maintaining subscribers when they are incurred, and capitalizing the costs and amortizing them over a number of years.

The accountant has prepared the following cash flow statement, which is complete except for how to account for the cost of recruiting and maintaining subscribers. During 2004 Phidias spent $135,000 recruiting and maintaining subscribers.

Phidias Publications Ltd.
Cash Flow Statement
For the Year Ended December 31, 2004

Cash from operations:		
Cash collected from customers	$2,346,000	
Cash paid to employees	(1,124,000)	
Cash paid to suppliers	(905,000)	
Cash paid in interest	(52,000)	
Cash from operations		$264,000
Cash from investing activities:		
Proceeds from sale of capital assets	110,000	
Purchase of capital assets	(300,000)	
Cash from investing activities		(190,000)
Cash from financing activities:		
Dividends paid	(75,000)	
Repayment of bank loan	(175,000)	
Proceeds of long-term debt	325,000	
Cash from financing activities		75,000
Cash generated during the year		149,000
Cash on hand on December 31, 2003		37,000
Cash on hand on December 31, 2004		$186,000

Required:

    a. Present arguments for and against the two proposed accounting treatments for the cost of recruiting and maintaining subscribers.

    b. Explain the effect of the two accounting alternatives on Phidias' income statement.

    c. Complete Phidias' cash flow statement assuming that cash spent on recruiting and maintaining subscribers is expensed when incurred.

    d. Complete Phidias' cash flow statement assuming that cash spent on recruiting and maintaining subscribers is capitalized and amortized over three years.

    e. Discuss the difference between the statements you prepared in (b) and (c) above. What are the implications of the different treatments to the underlying cash flow and liquidity of Phidias?

    f. Which cash flow statement do you think the managers of Phidias would prefer? Explain.

P6-14. **(Accrual and cash flow information analysis, LO 1, 3, 4)** In December 2004 Alexander Bedlam organized Soldit Properties Ltd. (Soldit), a company that sells real estate on behalf of clients. Alexander exchanged $20,000 in cash for 1,000 common shares of Soldit. When business actually began in January 2005 Alexander was very busy—so busy that he did not bother keeping any records. At the end of the month Alexander noticed that he had less than the $20,000 in cash that he started business with. He did not understand how he could be so busy and still have lost money. Alexander has come to you for help understanding his situation. From your conversation with Alexander you obtain the following information:

    i. During the month, five properties were sold with a sales value of $600,000. Soldit earns a commission of 5% of the sales value of the property.

    ii. Sales assistants sold three of the five properties sold in January. These three properties had a total sales value of $400,000. Sales assistants receive a commission of 4% of the sales value of the properties they sell.

    iii. The commission on one of the properties has not yet been received. The client owes Soldit $8,000.

    iv. During January Soldit made the following payments in cash:

Salaries	$ 2,200
Commissions to sales assistants	16,000
Down payment on car	3,000
Rent	1,200
Purchase of computer, fax, and copier	2,000
Utilities	500

    v. Soldit has taken delivery of the car and the computer, fax, and copier. The price of the car was $20,000 and the price of the computer, fax, and copier was $5,000.

Required:

    a. Prepare an income statement for the month of January for Soldit.

    b. Prepare a cash flow statement for January for Soldit.

    c. How did Soldit perform in January? How should Alexander interpret these two statements? Did Soldit perform as badly as Alexander seems to think? Explain your answer.

■ Using Financial Statements

BCE Emergis Inc.

BCE Emergis Inc. (BCE Emergis) is a premier business-to-business e-commerce infrastructure provider, strategically focusing on market leadership in the transaction-intensive eHealth and financial services sectors. BCE Emergis' services are fully integrated, offering a comprehensive e-commerce solution that electronically transforms business processes, such as buying, selling, invoicing, payment, logistics, and customer services and that enables success in the web-centric, cost-driven, and highly competitive global Internet economy.[4]

www.emergis.com

Exhibit 6-3

BCE Emergis Inc.'s Financial Statements

(in thousands of Canadian dollars)	Consolidated statements of cash flows	
	Year ended December 31	
	2000	**1999**
Operating activities		
Net loss	(279,305)	(66,059)
Depreciation and amortization	345,738	82,266
Accretion of convertible debenture due to parent, related to the option	25,236	—
Future income taxes	(16,780)	—
Gains on sale of exited activities, net	(16,169)	(13,795)
Changes in working capital (note 10)	(11,754)	36,151
Cash flows from operating activities	46,966	41,563
Investing activities		
Additions to capital assets	(53,825)	(26,360)
Acquisitions (note 11)	(810,648)	(164,354)
Cash acquired on acquisition of UP&UP	46,301	—
Cash acquired on acquisition of InvoiceLink	1,067	—
Note receivable from former majority shareholder of UP&UP	(11,600)	—
Advances to company under common control	(2,152)	—
Proceeds on sale of exited activities	7,700	29,326
Cash flows used for investing activities	(823,157)	(161,388)
Financing activities		
Repayment of long-term debt	(16,309)	(19,262)
Bank advances	(5,651)	5,651
Issue of convertible debentures due to parent	300,000	—
Repayment of convertible debentures due to parent	(150,000)	—
Issue of common shares	657,868	180,230
Cash flows from financing activities	785,908	166,619
Foreign exchange gain on cash held in foreign currencies	789	—
Cash and cash equivalents		
Increase	10,506	46,794
Balance, beginning of year	81,709	34,915
Balance, end of year	92,215	81,709
Cash and cash equivalents		
Cash	39,060	14,800
Temporary investments	53,155	66,909
	92,215	81,709
Supplemental disclosure of cash flow information		
Interest paid	6,632	1,113
Income taxes paid	9,310	—

BCE Emergis' consolidated statements of cash flows and earnings, along with extracts from the notes to the financial statements, are provided in Exhibit 6-3. Use this information to respond to questions FS6-1 to FS6-9.

FS6-1. What amounts does BCE Emergis report in its statement of cash flow for each of the following?
   a. Cash flows from operating activities.
   b. Cash flows used for investing activities.
   c. Cash from financing activities.

FS6-2. What method does BCE Emergis use to calculate cash flows from operating activities? How can you tell?

FS6-3. BCE Emergis' statement of cash flows uses the term cash and cash equivalents.
   a. What does BCE Emergis include in its definition of cash equivalents?
   b. How much "just plain" cash did BCE Emergis have on hand at the beginning and at the end of 2000?
   c. How much did BCE Emergis have invested in cash equivalents?
   d. Does it make sense to include cash and cash equivalents in a statement of cash flow, or would using cash only make better sense? Explain your answer.

FS6-4. BCE Emergis reported a large net loss on its statement of earnings, but positive cash flows from operating activities. Explain why there was such a large difference between the accrual measure of performance and cash flows from operating activities.

FS6-5. What activities by BCE Emergis consumed a lot of cash in 2000? Where did BCE Emergis get the cash to pay for these activities?

Exhibit 6-3 (continued)

BCE Emergis Inc.'s Financial Statements

Consolidated statements of earnings

(in thousands of Canadian dollars except per share data)

	Year ended December 31	
	2000	1999
Revenue	467,972	186,731
Direct costs	111,970	61,457
Gross margin	356,002	125,274
Expenses		
Operations	148,116	59,680
Sales and marketing	53,694	18,965
Research and development	28,005	22,205
General and administrative	51,372	20,577
	281,187	121,427
Earnings before under-noted items	74,815	3,847
Depreciation	27,983	9,544
Amortization of intangibles	317,755	75,722
Interest income	(5,588)	(3,557)
Interest expense	605	667
Interest on long-term debt	10,209	446
Accretion on convertible debenture due to parent, related to the option (note 11b)	25,236	—
Gains on sale of exited activities, net (note 9)	(16,169)	(13,795)
Other expenses	—	879
Net loss before income taxes	(285,216)	(66,059)
Income taxes (note 13)		
Current	10,869	—
Future	(16,780)	—
	(5,911)	—
Net loss	(279,305)	(66,059)
Loss per share ($)	(3.04)	(0.82)
Weighted average number of shares outstanding used in computing basic loss per share	91,743,796	80,333,535

2. Accounting policies

Cash equivalents

Investments with original maturities of three months or less are classified as cash equivalents.

10. Cash flow information

	Year ended December 31	
	2000	1999
Changes in working capital:		
Accounts receivable	(5,730)	(5,651)
Other current assets	4,993	(9,481)
Accounts payable and accrued liabilities	(22,655)	47,445
Deferred revenue	11,638	3,838
Non-cash investing and financing activities		
Additions to capital assets financed	29,160	11,746
Equity issued with respect to acquisitions (see notes 8 and 11)		
Common shares issued	49,164	82,540
Common shares to be issued	56,346	—
Options issued	14,571	—

FS6-6. During 2000 BCE Emergis reported a gain on the sale of exited activities (assets associated with businesses the company had chosen to leave) of $16,169,000. Why is the gain added back in the calculation of cash flows from operating activities?

FS6-7. The bottom panel of Note 10 refers to "non-cash activities." These activities are not included in the statement of cash flows, but are reported in a separate schedule.

a. How much is identified as "additions to capital assets financed"? What do you think this amount represents? Why do you think the amount is not included among investing activities on the statement of cash flows? (When answering give thought to what the statement of cash flows is designed to report and different ways that capital assets can be purchased.)

b. What value of its common shares did BCE Emergis issue with respect to companies it acquired during the year? Why is this amount not included in the statement of cash flows?

FS6-8. Suppose that on December 31, 1999 BCE Emergis had $70,659,000 of accounts receivable and $122,569,000 of accounts payable and accrued liabilities. Use the information in Exhibit 6-3 to determine the amounts in accounts receivable and in accounts payable and accrued liabilities on December 31, 2000.

FS6-9. Examine the statement of cash flows and Note 10 to BCE Emergis' financial statements. Explain how BCE Emergis' non-cash working capital accounts affected cash flows from operating activities during 2000. Explain why changes in non-cash working capital accounts affect cash flows from operating activities.

■ Analyzing Mark's Work Wearhouse

M6-1. In its 2001 statements of cash flow MWW reported cash from operations of $21,140,000. How did MWW use this cash?

M6-2. Examine Note 1D to the financial statements. What does MWW include in its definition of cash and cash equivalents?

M6-3. What amounts does MWW report in its 2000 and 2001 statements of cash flows for each of the following?
   a. Cash from operations.
   b. Cash from investing activities.
   c. Cash from financing activities.

M6-4. In its January 27, 2001 financial statements MWW reported net earnings of $8,180,000 but cash flow from operations of $21,140,000. Explain why MWW's net earnings in 2001 were so different from its cash from operations.

M6-5. Examine the Supplementary Schedules to Consolidated Statements of Cash Flow that follows MWW's consolidated statements of cash flows (see page A-48).
   a. Why do you think the first schedule (schedule of non-cash investing and financing activities) is included in the financial statement package? What information does the schedule provide that is not included in the cash flow statement?
   b. Describe the activities that are reported in the schedule of non-cash investing and financing activities.

M6-6. Note 1I describes how MWW accounts for its store opening costs (see page A-50).
   a. Explain how capitalizing the store opening costs and amortizing them over three years affects the cash flow statement in comparison with simply expensing these costs as they occur.
   b. Would changing the method of accounting for store opening costs affect MWW's cash flow? Explain.
   c. How might a user's interpretation of MWW's cash flows be affected by the accounting treatment for store opening costs?
   d. Calculate MWW's cash from operations assuming that it capitalized $250,000 in store opening costs in fiscal 2001 and amortized $417,000.

Endnotes

1. Clarence Byrd, Ida Chen, and Heather Chapman, *Financial Reporting in Canada*, 26th Edition. The Virtual Professional Library. CD-ROM. 2002.

2. Extracted from SMK Speedy International Inc.'s 2000 annual report.

3. Extracted from The T. Eaton Company Ltd.'s 1998 annual report.

4. Extracted from BCE Emergis Inc.'s web site at www.emergis.com (accessed April 2, 2002).

Chapter 7

Cash, Receivables, and the Time Value of Money

Chapter Outline

Learning Objectives

After studying the material in this chapter you will be able to:

LO 1. Discuss how cash is accounted for in financial statements and recognize the importance of cash management and internal controls over cash.

LO 2. Explain the concept of the time value of money and its relevance to accounting, and be able to do some basic time value of money calculations.

LO 3. Describe accounting for receivables and uncollectable amounts.

LO 4. Explain how managers can use accounting estimates to create hidden reserves to move earnings from one period to another, and recognize the implications of hidden reserves for financial statement users.

LO 5. Analyze and interpret information for evaluating the liquidity of an entity.

Introduction

To this point in the book we have examined accounting and accounting information from a broad perspective. For the remaining chapters we will delve more deeply into the accounting used for the major components of the financial statements. Do not be misled by the apparent focus of these chapters on the balance sheet. Never forget that the financial statements are all closely linked and accounting choices that affect one of the statements will invariably have an impact on others. Therefore, our discussion will look at the effect of the accounting on the income statement and the cash flow statement as well as on the balance sheet.

In this chapter we will examine some of an entity's most liquid assets: cash and receivables. Cash, of course, is the most liquid of assets and is vital for the effective operation and survival of an entity. Yet understanding accounting for cash is not always as straightforward as counting the amount of money in your pocket. Receivables represent amounts owed to the entity, usually, but not always, by customers. Our examination of receivables will show the effect that estimates have in determining the values that are assigned to the assets on the balance sheet and to the amount of income an entity reports.

The chapter will also introduce a powerful tool used in accounting and for financial analysis that takes into consideration the "time value of money"—the fact that money received today is more valuable than the same amount of money received sometime in the future.

Cash

Cash is a crucial asset. If an entity does not have enough cash, or at least access to enough cash, the consequences could be dire. Without cash an entity cannot pay its bills or meet other obligations, and as a result operations may grind to a halt if suppliers refuse to do business with the cash-strapped entity. We discussed the importance of cash and cash flow at length in Chapter 6. This chapter will cover some of the accounting issues pertaining to cash. Accounting for cash is relatively straightforward and does not generate much controversy, although there are some twists and turns that you should be aware of.

In its January 27, 2001 balance sheet Mark's Work Wearhouse (MWW) reports "Cash and cash equivalents" of $6,993,000 as a current asset. The cash part of this amount represents all of the cash that MWW has in all its bank accounts, cash registers, and safes throughout the organization. As long as the cash is readily available for use, it can be classified as a current asset. MWW must have enough cash in its bank accounts to cover cheques to suppliers and employees, and enough cash in its registers to allow its stores to operate efficiently. The cash equivalents part of the amount represents short-term investments that can be converted into a known amount of cash easily and quickly. This includes securities such as treasury bills, guaranteed investment certificates (GICs), and money market funds, and excludes equity investments such as common and preferred shares. Equity investments are excluded, even the equity of public companies, because the price of equity investments fluctuates day to day, meaning that a known amount of cash is not available.

Cash cannot all be considered a liquid asset that is readily available for use by the entity. Sometimes the use of an entity's cash is restricted in some way, perhaps because there is a legal or contractual obligation to use it in a particular way. For example, Cadillac Fairview Corporation (Cadillac Fairview) reports $10,835,000 in cash that must be used for specified purposes. This means that this cash cannot be used for day-to-day purposes and cannot be considered a liquid asset. Exhibit 7-1 shows the asset side of Cadillac Fairview's balance sheet, the note to the financial statements that

www.cadillacfairview.com

As at October 31, 1999 and 1998 (In thousands of Canadian dollars)	Note	1999	1998
ASSETS			
Real estate assets	3	$ 4,646,664	$ 4,486,312
Amounts receivable		58,341	56,259
Other assets	4	245,620	120,641
		$ 4,950,625	$ 4,663,212

4. OTHER ASSETS

	1999	1998
Unrestricted cash and short-term investments	$ 131,885	$ 26,038
Restricted cash	10,835	18,320
Prepaid expenses	70,900	40,712
Deferred charges less accumulated amortization	32,000	35,571
	$ 245,620	$ 120,641

Other assets increased by $125.0 million during 1999 to $245.6 million. Cash and short-term investments amounted to $142.7 million, with $10.8 million of the total restricted as to use under a November 1996 loan agreement governing the refinancing of eight United States properties. The restricted cash is available to fund certain capital spending, tenant inducements and other costs relating to these properties. The remaining other assets of $102.9 million are represented by prepaid expenses of $70.9 million and deferred charges of $32.0 million.

shows the company's cash and restricted cash balances, and an explanation of the restricted cash taken from Cadillac Fairview's management discussion and analysis in the 1999 annual report.[1]

An entity's cash may also be netted against its bank borrowings. Exhibit 7-2 (page 374) shows the balance sheet of The Boyd Group Inc. (Boyd), an operator of automotive collision repair centres in Canada and the United States.[2] Boyd shows no cash on its December 31, 2000 balance sheet. This apparent absence of cash might suggest that Boyd was in serious trouble. It seems unfathomable that a retail business would have no cash in its shops. After all, how can a business that deals with retail customers operate with no cash in the till?

www.boydgroup.com

In fact, Boyd does have cash. What Boyd has done is combine its cash with its bank borrowing. In other words, in preparing its financial statements Boyd defines cash as cash less bank borrowing. If that difference is positive, meaning Boyd has more cash than bank borrowings, the amount is reported as cash on the asset side of the balance sheet. If the difference is negative, the amount is reported as bank indebtedness on the liabilities side of the balance sheet. Note 7 to Boyd's financial statements shows that on December 31, 2000 the company had $901,995 of cash on deposit and $4,139,719 of bank indebtedness, which nets to the amount shown on the liability side of the balance sheet ($3,237,724). Boyd's disclosure in Note 7 is actually quite informative since the actual amount of cash is disclosed, although it is necessary to examine the notes to the financial statements to find the amount. Many entities that use this approach do not disclose the actual amount of cash and bank indebtedness, so the reader cannot tell the amount that has been borrowed.

Cash Management and Controls Over Cash

It would be easy to conclude that the more cash an entity has on hand, the better. That is far from true. Having too little cash, of course, is a potential threat to the survival of the entity. But having too much cash can be a problem as well. While cash provides insurance for the unexpected, cash is an unproductive asset. Businesses do not make money by holding cash. Business chequing accounts typically pay no interest. At best, cash will earn a very small return in an interest bearing account, but those earnings

<table>
<tr><td>

Exhibit 7-2

The Boyd Group Inc.: Combining Cash and Bank Borrowing

</td></tr>
</table>

CONSOLIDATED BALANCE SHEETS

December 31

ASSETS	2000	1999
CURRENT		
Accounts receivable	$ 11,183,811	$ 6,418,818
Due from C.C. Collision Repair Management Limited Partnership	–	8,977
Income taxes recoverable	1,089,508	174,702
Inventory	2,961,238	1,692,799
Prepaid expenses	1,230,335	711,045
	16,464,892	9,006,341
CAPITAL ASSETS (Note 4)	16,094,189	12,608,190
DEFERRED COSTS (Note 5)	501,397	457,014
OTHER ASSETS (Note 6)	34,932,950	12,896,981
	$ 67,993,428	$ 34,968,526
LIABILITIES		
CURRENT		
Bank indebtedness (Note 7)	$ 3,237,724	$ 416,977
Accounts payable and accrued liabilities	8,744,748	5,742,342
Due to C.C. Collision Repair Management Limited Partnership	16,012	–
Current portion of long-term debt (Note 8)	2,981,135	812,724
Current portion of obligations under capital leases (Note 9)	825,450	576,735
	15,805,069	7,548,778
LONG-TERM DEBT (Note 8)	23,772,367	9,977,940
OBLIGATIONS UNDER CAPITAL LEASES (Note 9)	1,098,433	1,305,409
CONVERTIBLE DEBENTURES – DEBT COMPONENT (Note 10)	1,678,485	1,782,013
FUTURE TAXES (Note 14)	317,005	619,422
UNEARNED INCOME (Note 11)	5,457,792	1,519,231
OTHER LONG-TERM LIABILITIES	347,195	–
NON-CONTROLLING INTEREST	–	7,936
	48,476,346	22,760,729
CONTINGENCIES (Note 17)		
EQUITY		
SHARE CAPITAL (Note 12)	15,505,193	10,463,151
CONVERTIBLE DEBENTURES – EQUITY COMPONENT (Note 10)	288,232	297,704
RETAINED EARNINGS	3,586,267	1,468,417
CUMULATIVE TRANSLATION ADJUSTMENT	137,390	(21,475)
	19,517,082	12,207,797
	$ 67,993,428	$ 34,968,526

7. BANK INDEBTEDNESS

	2000	1999
Funds on deposit	$ (901,995)	$ (1,131,487)
Operating demand loan at prime rate secured by a General Security Agreement securing all company assets	4,139,719	1,548,464
	$ 3,237,724	$ 416,977

would be far less than what could be earned if it were invested in the business. If a business is unable to find productive ways to use its cash, it would probably be best if the surplus cash were returned to shareholders, who could find more productive investments for their money. Or the surplus cash could be used to retire outstanding liabilities. Effective cash management is a key function for an entity's management. A balance must exist between having too little cash and too much.

One of the important stewardship responsibilities of management is to protect the entity's assets. Protection of assets is part of the internal controls that an entity maintains. **Internal controls** are the policies and procedures that management implements to protect the entity's assets and ensure the integrity of the accounting information system. Strong internal controls provide assurance to stakeholders that the entity's assets cannot be stolen, used inappropriately, or used without proper authorization, and that the information produced by the accounting system can be relied on. (For example, many retail stores place devices on more expensive inventory items that set off an alarm if the item is removed from the store without being paid for. The use of these devices is an internal control that helps prevent theft.) In general, poor internal controls can lead to significant losses. Every entity should take steps to ensure the protection of its assets and information system.

It is especially important to control cash. Cash is attractive to thieves because it is easy to hide and it cannot be identified once it is stolen. Most entities do not leave cash lying around so that it is easy for a thief to take, although entities that handle a lot of cash, such as retail stores, casinos, arcades, and laundromats, need internal controls to protect their cash. There are many ways that cash can be stolen in addition to being physically taken. Money can be stolen if weak internal controls allow an employee to make payments by cheque to non-existent suppliers and then cash the cheques him- or herself. Weak internal controls might also allow an employee to alter a payment so that a supplier receives more than is actually owed, or to alter records to cover up a theft of cash.

There are many controls that can be put in place to limit the likelihood that cash will somehow be stolen. One of the most important and effective controls that can be implemented for cash (and other assets as well) is **segregation of duties**. Segregation of duties means that people who handle an asset should not also be responsible for record keeping for that asset. If duties are not segregated, an employee may be able to steal cash and cover up the theft by making fictitious entries to the accounting records. For example, consider a person who receives mailed-in cheques from customers and deposits the cheques in the bank, and who is also responsible for recording the deposit in the accounting system. That person might be able to deposit some of the cheques in his or her own bank account and cover up the theft by making a journal entry that writes off accounts receivable in the amount stolen.

Bank Reconciliation

A **bank reconciliation** is an internal control procedure that is used to explain differences between the accounting records and the bank records. The bank records are represented by the bank statement that is sent for each of an entity's bank accounts. The bank reconciliation should be done by a person who is not responsible for writing or authorizing cheques or for recording transactions pertaining to the cash account. This is necessary to maintain segregation of duties and thereby allow an independent person to review the bank statement. If a person who is handling cash also prepares the bank reconciliation, that person may be able to cover up cash he or she is stealing.

The bank reconciliation serves a number of purposes:

1. It helps determine the cash balance that should be reported on the balance sheet at the end of a period. Usually neither the accounting records nor the bank statement provides the entity's actual cash balance. The accounting records will not represent the actual cash balance because it does not reflect bank service charges, interest earned, cash collected by the bank on behalf of the entity, errors in entering information into the accounting system, and returned cheques. (A **returned cheque** is a cheque that has been cashed by the receiving entity but has not been honoured by the bank because the entity that wrote the cheque did not have enough money in its bank account to cover the cheque.) The bank statement will not represent the actual cash balance because it does not reflect **outstanding cheques** (cheques the entity has written and recorded in the accounting system but that have not yet been cashed), **outstanding deposits** (deposits the entity has made and recorded in the accounting system but that have not been recorded by the bank as of the bank statement date), and bank errors.

2. The bank reconciliation serves to identify accounting and bank errors.

3. The bank reconciliation may help detect theft of cash by employees.

A bank reconciliation should be prepared each month, for each bank account. Figure 7-1 summarizes the common adjustments that must be made to reconcile the accounting and bank records.

Let's consider an example of a bank reconciliation. On December 31, 2005 the accounting records of Zephyr Inc. (Zephyr) showed a cash balance of $10,450.07. The balance reported in Zephyr's December 31, 2005 bank statement was $11,504.24. Examination of the bank statement and the accounting records showed the following:

*   Three cheques that had been written and mailed by Zephyr, and recorded in Zephyr's accounting records, had not been cashed by the entities to which the cheques had been written. The outstanding cheques were numbers #811 for $1,250.25, #813 for $2,210.37, and #816 for $105.09.

*   Zephyr deposited $3,365.55 in cash and cheques to its bank account through a bank machine late on December 31, 2005. The deposits were not recorded by the bank until January 2006 and as a result did not appear in the December 31, 2005 bank statement.

*   The bank collected $1,200.89 on behalf of Zephyr from one of Zephyr's customers.

*   Bank service charges for December 2005 were $57. The amount was deducted from Zephyr's bank account but not recorded in the accounting records.

*   A cheque received from one of Zephyr's customers was not honoured by the bank because the customer did not have enough money in its bank account to cover the cheque. The amount of the cheque was $812.02. Zephyr had recorded the cheque as a debit to cash when it was deposited.

*   Zephyr was paid $12.10 in interest during December. The amount was deposited in Zephyr's bank account but not recorded in the accounting system.

*   The bank made an error by depositing $510.04 to Zephyr's bank account. The amount should have been deposited to another account.

The bank reconciliation is shown in Table 7-1. The adjusted cash balance of $10,794.04 is the amount that will appear on Zephyr's December 31, 2005 balance sheet. Zephyr will have to make entries to account for the bank service charges, the collection by the bank, the interest earned, and the returned cheque. The entries required are:

Dr. Cash (asset +)	1200.89	
Cr. Accounts receivable (asset −)		1200.89
To record collection by the bank.		
Dr. Cash (asset +)	12.10	
Cr. Interest revenue (revenue +, shareholders' equity +)		12.10
To record interest earned and received from the bank.		
Dr. Bank service charges (expense +, shareholders' equity −)	57.00	
Cr. Cash (asset −)		57.00
To record bank service charges for December.		
Dr. Accounts receivable (asset +)	812.02	
Cr. Cash (asset −)		812.02
To record return of cheque.		

No adjustments are made to the bank records. The bank will adjust its own records when it processes the outstanding items.

Balance in the Accounting Records		Balance in Bank Records	
Add:	Interest earned	Add:	Outstanding (unrecorded) deposits
	Collections by the bank		Bank errors
Subtract:	Bank service charges	Subtract:	Outstanding (uncashed) cheques
	Returned cheques		Bank errors
	→ Adjusted cash balance ←		

Figure 7-1

Bank Reconciliation: Common Adjustments to Accounting and Bank Records

Is a Dollar a Dollar?

One of the fundamental GAAP accounting concepts explained in Chapter 5 was the unit-of-measure assumption. The unit-of-measure assumption requires that financial statement information must be measurable and stated in monetary units such as Canadian dollars. A dollar of cash reported on a balance sheet means a dollar in hand. But is a dollar always really worth a dollar? In fact, the value of a dollar is not constant over time. While the face value of a dollar is always the same, the value of a dollar will vary relative to what it can buy and relative to other currencies.

The Effect of Changes in Purchasing Power   If you take $10,000 and hide it under your mattress, your GAAP financial statements for financial reporting in Canada will always show that you have $10,000 in cash. While you will always have the $10,000, as time passes you will be less and less well off. Why? With the passage of time the purchasing power of cash declines because of **inflation**. Inflation refers to a period when, on average, prices in the economy are rising. If the amount of goods and services you can buy with your money declines, the value of the money has declined even though the face value of the money stays the same. The reverse logic is true if there is **deflation**, but deflation is far less common than inflation. Deflation refers to a period when, on average, prices in the economy are falling.

Using Canada's inflation rate as the base, let's say you hid your $10,000 under your mattress at the beginning of 1992. At the end of 2000 your $10,000 would purchase what $8,678 would have purchased in 1992. In other words, while the absolute or nominal number of dollars you had in 1992 and 2000 is the same, the amount of goods and services those dollars can buy is different. You would be able to buy fewer pairs of pants at MWW in 2000 than you could in 1992.

GAAP reporting in Canada does not take into consideration the changing purchasing power of money over time. The unit of measure is the "nominal" dollar. That

Table 7-1   Bank Reconciliation for Zephyr Inc.

Zephyr Inc.
Bank Reconciliation for December 2005

Balance per the accounting records on December 31, 2005		$10,450.07	Balance per bank statement on December 31, 2005			$11,504.24
Add:	Interest earned	12.10	Add:	Outstanding (unrecorded) deposits		3,365.55
Add:	Collections by the bank	1,200.89	Add:	Bank errors		0
Subtract:	Bank service charges	57.00	Subtract:	Outstanding (uncashed) cheques		
Subtract:	Returned cheques	812.02			#811	1,250.25
					#813	2,210.37
					#816	105.09
			Subtract:	Bank errors		510.04
	Adjusted cash balance	$10,794.04		Adjusted cash balance		$10,794.04

means that no adjustment is made for changes in purchasing power. Yet losses in the purchasing power of money represent a real economic cost to an entity.

How could a change in purchasing be reflected in the financial statements? One way would be to record the decrease in purchasing power as a loss. If an entity held $10,000 over a period where the purchasing power decreased by 10%, a loss of $1,000 would be reported on the income statement. By doing this, the financial statements would reflect the cost of holding cash. This approach to accounting is not used in Canada. However, in some countries such as Israel, Mexico, and Brazil, where inflation is much more of a problem, adjustments are made to financial statements to account for losses in purchasing power.

The Effect of Changing Prices of Foreign Currencies   Canada is a trading nation. Much of its economic activity involves transactions with entities in foreign countries and in foreign currencies. Many Canadian companies have business operations in other countries. For example, in the 1990s MWW attempted to expand its business into the U.S. While MWW's venture failed, it demonstrates how cross-border activities have become the norm. Transactions involving foreign currencies and foreign operations can have an impact on an entity's financial statements, including the amount of cash it reports.

For example, Quarry Ltd. (Quarry) has a bank account in which it has U.S. dollars. Because of the unit-of-measure assumption, all amounts reported in the financial statements must be stated in a single currency. If Quarry's financial statements are presented in Canadian dollars, its U.S. cash must be stated in Canadian dollars. Since **exchange rates** of currencies fluctuate, the number of Canadian dollars that a U.S. amount represents will vary. (The exchange rate is the price to buy one currency, stated in terms of another currency.)

Suppose that on December 31, 2005 Quarry had U.S.$1,000,000 and the exchange rate was $1.40—that is, US$1 could be exchanged for Cdn$1.40. When Quarry prepares its financial statements it must convert its U.S.$1,000,000 into the equivalent amount in Canadian dollars. This means that on its December 31, 2005 balance sheet Quarry would report $1,400,000 of Canadian cash (exchange rate × amount of foreign currency = $1.40 × U.S.$1,000,000). This amount is reported even though the money is still actually in U.S. dollars. One year later, on December 31, 2006, Quarry's U.S. bank account still has U.S.$1,000,000, but the exchange rate is $1.35. On its December 31, 2006 balance sheet Quarry would report $1,350,000 of Canadian cash.

The effect is that when exchange rates change, the amount of Canadian dollars reported changes even though the quantity of the foreign currency stays the same. The change in the exchange rate from December 31, 2005 to December 31, 2006 has resulted in Quarry having $50,000 less in Canadian dollars, even though the amount of U.S. dollars has not changed.

The Time Value of Money

Would you rather receive $1,000 today or $1,000 a year from now? The answer to that question should be easy. It is better to have cash now rather than the same amount of cash later. There are a number of reasons for this:

1. Having the money sooner allows you to earn a return on the money sooner. By investing in a one-year investment certificate that offers 4% interest per year, your $1,000 would turn into $1,040 a year later. You would have an extra $40. By waiting a year to receive the $1,000 you would lose the opportunity to earn that $40.

2. By getting the money today you can spend and enjoy it now. A person is likely to prefer having a high-definition TV or taking a holiday sooner rather than later, or at least have the option of doing so.

3. As explained in the previous section, because of inflation the purchasing power of money declines over time. With inflation of 2%, $1,000 in a year will only buy what $980 would have bought today.

4. Getting the money sooner reduces the likelihood that you are not going to be paid.

However you care to look at it, it should be clear that you are ahead of the game if you get your money sooner. This does not mean that a person will never decide to receive his or her money later rather than sooner. However, the delay should come with a price. The concept that people would prefer to receive a given amount of money sooner rather than later is known as the **time value of money.**

While conceptually it should make sense that it is preferable to receive a given amount of money sooner rather than later, how do you choose among different amounts that can be received at different times? For example, suppose you won a contest that allowed you to choose among receiving $10,000 today, $4,000 at the end of each of the next three years, or $14,000 in three years. Which would you choose?

It is hard to make a decision by just looking at these three alternatives. However, there is a powerful tool that allows you to evaluate this choice and other business and accounting problems that involve cash flows that occur at different times. Valuing cash flows that occur at different times can be viewed from two perspectives: the future value and the present value. The **future value** of cash flows is the amount of money you will receive in the future by investing today at a given interest rate. The **present value** of cash flows is the value today of money that will be received in the future.

The coverage in this book will be limited to a brief introduction of these time-value-of-money tools. The objective is to give you enough background to be able to understand the accounting issues that are affected by the time value of money and to understand the usefulness of these tools.

Future Value

We will begin our discussion with future value because it is a concept that most people are familiar with. The way that money in a bank account grows with the passage of time is an application of the future value concept. If you put $1,000 in a bank account that pays interest of 5% per year, in one year your bank account will have $1,050. You will have earned $50 in interest during the year. The amount of interest earned is calculated by multiplying the amount in your bank account by the interest rate. In this case the calculation is $1,000 \times 0.05 = 50. The amount of money in the account at the end of the year is calculated by multiplying the amount in the account by one plus the interest rate $(1 + 0.05)$. For our example the balance in the account would be $1,000 \times 1.05 = $1,050$. In time value of money terms, the future value of $1,000 invested at 5% for one year is $1,050.

If you leave your $1,050 in the bank for another year and continue to receive interest at 5% per year, at the end of the second year you will have $1,102.50 ($1,050 \times 1.05$). During the second year you will have earned $52.50 of interest ($1,050 \times 0.05$). The reason that you earned more than $50 in interest in the second year is that you earned compound interest. **Compound interest** is interest that is calculated on the principal amount and on interest accumulated in previous periods. In the second year, interest was not only earned on the original $1,000, but also on the $50 in interest that you earned in the first year. (If the interest were only calculated using the initial investment of $1,000, the interest every year would be $50. This type of interest is called simple interest. **Simple interest** is interest paid or earned on the principal amount only.) In time value of money terms, the future value of $1,000 invested at 5% for two years is $1,102.50.

The formula for calculating the amount that you will receive at some future time with an investment today is:

$$FV_{n, r} = (1 + r)^n \times \text{Amount invested}$$

FV (future value) is the amount you will receive in the future (the future value) by investing an amount (amount invested) for n periods at an interest rate of r per period. The formula incorporates the compounding of interest.

Using the formula to calculate the future value of an investment of $1,000 at 5% for two years, we find

$$\begin{aligned} FV_{2, 0.05} &= (1 + 0.05)^2 \times \$1,000 \\ &= 1.1025 \times \$1,000 \\ &= \$1,102.50 \end{aligned}$$

This is the same amount that we calculated earlier.

If you wanted to find out how much you would have if you invested $1,000 at 8% for 25 years, the formula would give you:

$$\begin{aligned} FV_{25, 0.08} &= (1 + 0.08)^{25} \times \$1,000 \\ &= 6.84848 \times \$1,000 \\ &= \$6,848.48 \end{aligned}$$

Using Future Value Tables

Using the future value formula (and, as we will see, present value formula) with pencil and paper or a basic calculator can be cumbersome. The easiest way to calculate future (and present) values is with a financial calculator or a computer spreadsheet program. Both of these devices have the formulas integrated into their software. All that you need to know, once you understand the formulas, is how to input each of the variables in the formula into the calculator or spreadsheet—and presto! The future (or present) value is known. If you do not have the benefit of a financial calculator or spreadsheet program, the task is made easier if you use tables that do part of the calculations for you. Using tables is not the leading-edge way to do future or present value analyses. However, for purposes of this introduction to future and present values, the tables will serve nicely.

Table B-1 in Appendix B (page B-2) shows the future value of $1 invested today at different interest rates and for different periods of time. In Table B-1 the left-hand column gives the number of periods that money will be invested for and the top row gives the interest rates at which the money will be invested for those periods. The values in the table at the intersection of a particular number of periods and a particular interest rate is the future value of $1 invested at that interest rate and for that number of periods. In our examples the periods are years, but periods could be days, weeks, months, or anything else. Since the values in the table are the future values of $1 investments, determining the future value of an amount that is different from $1 simply requires multiplying the value in the table by the amount of money that will be invested. The key to finding the appropriate future value factor is to go to the point in the table where the number of periods in the future that the cash flow will be received intersects with the interest rate that will be earned. For example, if you wanted to find out the future value of $1,000 invested at 8% for 25 years, you would go across the top row to the 8% column and look down to the 25-period row.

Table 7-2 (page 382) provides an extract from Table B-1 to show how to find the appropriate future value factor. The appropriate future value factor of 6.84848 is found where the 8% column and the 25-year row intersect. Since the table applies to investments of $1, you must multiply the future value factor from the table by the amount that you invest to get the future value of your investment. Make sure you can find the future value factor in both Table B-1 (Appendix B) and Table 7-2.

$$FV_{n,r} = \text{Future value factor (from table)} \times \text{Amount}$$
$$FV_{25,0.08} = 6.84848 \times \$1,000$$
$$= \$6,848.48$$

The $6,848.48 is the same amount that we calculated using the formula.

The future value technique is very useful and powerful. There are many questions that can be answered by using it. Let's look at a couple of examples.

Example 1: The Mayos

In 2004 Mr. and Mrs. Mayo received $2,500 from Mr. Mayo's parents as gift in honour of the birth of their first daughter, Ellin. Mr. and Mrs. Mayo plan to invest the money to help pay for Ellin's university education. They would like to know how much Ellin will receive if they invest the $2,500 in a 20-year investment certificate that earns 6% interest per year.

Table B-1 shows that the future value factor for 20 years and 6% is 3.20714.

$$FV_{n,r} = \text{Future value factor} \times \text{Amount}$$
$$FV_{20,0.06} = 3.20714 \times \$2,500$$
$$= \$8,017.85$$

Therefore, Ellin will receive $8,017.85 when the investment certificate matures in 2024.

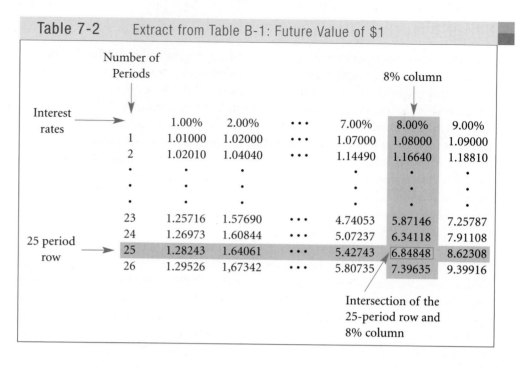

Table 7-2   Extract from Table B-1: Future Value of $1

Number of Periods	1.00%	2.00%	· · ·	7.00%	8.00%	9.00%
1	1.01000	1.02000	· · ·	1.07000	1.08000	1.09000
2	1.02010	1.04040	· · ·	1.14490	1.16640	1.18810
·	·	·		·	·	·
·	·	·		·	·	·
·	·	·		·	·	·
23	1.25716	1.57690	· · ·	4.74053	5.87146	7.25787
24	1.26973	1.60844	· · ·	5.07237	6.34118	7.91108
25	1.28243	1.64061	· · ·	5.42743	6.84848	8.62308
26	1.29526	1,67342	· · ·	5.80735	7.39635	9.39916

Interest rates

8% column

25 period row

Intersection of the 25-period row and 8% column

Example 2: Ms. Secretan   Ms. Secretan recently purchased a new car to replace her rusting 13-year-old vehicle. Ms. Secretan arranged a $35,000 three-year loan at 10% per year from the bank to pay for the car. Under the terms of the loan Ms. Secretan does not have to make any payments until the end of the three-year term, at which time she must pay the bank the principal and interest in full. Ms. Secretan would like to know how much she will have to pay the bank when the loan must be repaid.

Table B-1 shows that the future value factor for 3 years and 10% is 1.33100.

$$\begin{aligned}
\text{FV}_{n,r} &= \text{Future value factor} \times \text{Amount} \\
\text{FV}_{3,0.10} &= 1.33100 \times \$35,000 \\
&= \$46,585.00
\end{aligned}$$

Therefore, Ms. Secretan will have to pay the bank $46,585.00 in three years when the loan must be repaid.

Present Value

For accounting purposes, the present value technique is the more relevant tool. The present value technique looks at what cash received in the future is worth today. Consider the $1,102.50 that you had in your bank account after two years invested at 5% per year. The question asked in a present value analysis is, "At an interest rate of 5%, how much is the $1,102.50 that you will receive in two years equivalent to today?" Another way of posing the question is, "How much would you pay or invest today to receive $1,102.50 in two years, if the interest rate was 5%?" Based on the earlier example, you should guess that the present value of $1,102.50 to be received in two years at 5% is $1,000. This result can be shown by using the following formula:

$$\text{PV}_{n,r} = \frac{1}{(1+r)^n} \times \text{Amount to be received or paid}$$

PV (present value) is the equivalent to an amount of cash you will receive or pay in the future by investing an amount (amount to be received) for n periods at an interest rate of r per period. Note that the term discount rate is often used instead of interest rate in a present value analysis. The **discount rate** is the rate used to calculate the present value of future cash flows.

Your aunt recently won $100,000 in a lottery. She has approached you for advice on which of two investments she should place her money. Your aunt wants to invest for ten years, at which time she plans to retire. Your aunt is only interested in investments that she considers safe, so she has narrowed her choice to two investments with large banks. The first investment is a ten-year investment certificate that bears an interest rate of 8%, with interest calculated annually. The second investment is also a ten-year certificate, but interest on that investment is calculated and compounded at the rate of 4% every six months (this means that there are 20 six-month investment periods at 4% rather than 10-one year investment periods at 8%).

Which investment would you recommend to your aunt? Explain your answer. Make sure to explain why the quantitative result you obtain occurs.

Answer: Your aunt would be better off with the investment that has 4% interest calculated and compounded every six months. Quantitatively,

Investment 1: $FV_{n,r}$ = Future value factor × Amount
$FV_{10, 0.08}$ = 2.15892 × $100,000
= $215,892

Investment 2: $FV_{n,r}$ = Future value factor × Amount
$FV_{20, 0.04}$ = 2.19112 × $100,000
= $219,112

Investment 2 is more attractive because compounding occurs more often. Even though the interest rate appears to be the same for both investments, more interest is earned with Investment 2. For example, in the first year, your aunt earns 8% on $100,000 with Investment 1. But with Investment 2, she earns 4% on $100,000 in the first half of the first year ($4,000) and then 4% on $104,000 in the second half ($4,160) of year one, which gives a total of $8,160 of interest in the first year. The effect of the more frequent compounding builds over the life of the investment.

Present value is really nothing more than the amount that would be received in the future less the interest earned on the money over the investment period. Applying this formula to the example gives:

$$PV_{2, 0.05} = \frac{1}{(1 + 0.05)^2} \times \$1,102.50$$
$$= \$1,000$$

What this calculation tells us is that at a discount rate of 5%, having $1,000 now is equivalent to receiving $1,102.50 in two years. In other words, if you were offered a choice between $1,000 now and $1,102.50 in two years and your discount rate was 5%, you would be indifferent—the two amounts are equally valuable to you. However, instead if you were offered $1,100 in two years, you would prefer the $1,000 now. And if you were offered $1,110 in two years, you would prefer the $1,110 to $1,000. Remember that when the time value of money concept was first introduced, it was explained that people would accept money later rather than sooner, but at a price. That price is a larger amount of money.

Suppose that instead of using a discount rate of 5% to determine the present value of $1,102.50 to be received in two years, you decide that 7% is the appropriate discount rate. Then the present value of $1,102.50 to be received in two years is:

$$PV_{2, 0.07} = \frac{1}{(1 + 0.07)^2} \times \$1,102.50$$
$$= \$962.97$$

In other words, if your discount rate were 7%, the present value of the $1,102.50 would be $962.97. You would only be willing to pay up to $962.97 to receive $1,102.50 in two years. Having to pay anything more than $962.97 would not be satisfactory. To put it another way, you would prefer receiving any amount more than $962.97 today rather than $1,102.50 in two years. Anything less than $962.97 today would make $1,102.50 in two years preferable. At a discount rate of 7% you would be indifferent between $1,102.50 in two years and $962.97 today.

It is important to recognize the crucial role the discount rate plays in determining the present value. The higher the discount rate, the lower the present value of a future amount. This corresponds to the future value effect whereby the higher the interest rate paid on an investment, the more money that will be received in the future from that investment. The selection of the discount rate is somewhat subjective and there are many considerations that go into the choice, including risk and expected inflation. Further discussion about determining the discount rate is beyond the scope of this book.

Using Present Value Tables

As was the case with future value, present value tables are commonly used instead of the present value formula. Table B-2 in Appendix B (see page B-4) shows the present value of $1 to be received at various discount rates and at various periods in the future. The left-hand column of Table B-2 indicates how many periods in the future the cash will be received and the top row states the discount rate. As in the future value table, the values apply to cash flows of $1, so it is necessary to multiply the present value factor by the amount of cash that will be received. And also as in the future value table, the key to finding the appropriate present value factor is to find the value on the table where the row representing the number of periods in the future in which the cash flow will be received intersects with the discount rate column.

Continuing to use our example of finding the present value of $1,102.50 to be received in two years and at a discount rate of 7%, we find:

$$PV_{n,r} = \text{Present value factor (from table)} \times \text{Amount to be received}$$
$$PV_{2,0.07} = 0.87344 \times \$1,102.50$$
$$= \$962.97$$

This is the same as the result we calculated using the formula. As was the case with the future value tables, periods on the present value table can be years, months, weeks, or days.

Let's look at two applications of the present value technique. Table 7-3 provides an extract from Table B-2 to show how to find the appropriate discount factor from the table.

Example 1: Phil Maybutt   Phil Maybutt has decided to give his new nephew a gift of a university education. Phil estimates that it will cost $100,000 for a four-year education at a good school, including tuition and living expenses, when his nephew is ready for university in 18 years. Phil has an investment opportunity that will earn 12% per year. How much must Phil invest today to have the $100,000 required in 18 years? In other words, what is the present value of $100,000 to be received in 18 years using a discount rate of 12%?

At the intersection of 18 years and 12% in Table B-2, we find that the present value factor is 0.13004.

$$PV_{n,r} = \text{Present value factor} \times \text{Amount}$$
$$PV_{18,0.12} = 0.13004 \times \$100,000$$
$$= \$13,004$$

Therefore, Phil would have to invest $13,004 today at 12% so that his nephew would have $100,000 in 18 years to pay for his university education.

Table 7-3   Extract from Table B-2: Present Value of $1

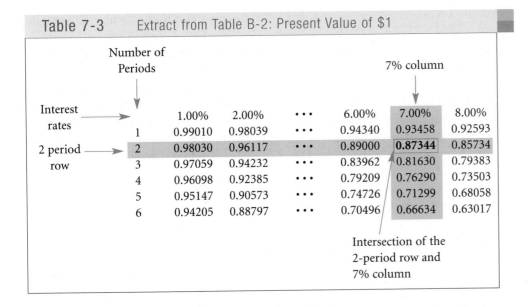

Number of Periods	1.00%	2.00%	...	6.00%	7.00%	8.00%
1	0.99010	0.98039	...	0.94340	0.93458	0.92593
2	0.98030	0.96117	...	0.89000	**0.87344**	0.85734
3	0.97059	0.94232	...	0.83962	0.81630	0.79383
4	0.96098	0.92385	...	0.79209	0.76290	0.73503
5	0.95147	0.90573	...	0.74726	0.71299	0.68058
6	0.94205	0.88797	...	0.70496	0.66634	0.63017

Interest rates →
2 period row →

7% column ↓

Intersection of the 2-period row and 7% column

Example 2: Quyon Ltd.   Quyon Ltd. (Quyon) recently purchased a machine for $500,000. The purchase agreement allows Quyon to pay for the machine in three years with no interest. What would be the equivalent price if Quyon had to pay for the machine in cash today, if the appropriate discount rate was 8%? In other words, what is the present value of $500,000 to be paid in three years using a discount rate of 8%?

At the intersection of three years and 8% in Table B-2 (page B-4), we find that the present value factor is 0.79383.

$$PV_{n,r} = \text{Present value factor} \times \text{Amount}$$
$$PV_{3,0.08} = 0.79383 \times \$500,000$$
$$= \$396,915$$

Therefore, the current cash amount that is equivalent to paying $500,000 in three years at a discount rate of 8% is $396,915.

Discounting, which is another term used for determining the present value of a future cash flow, is a very powerful tool because it allows for the comparisons of cash flows received at different times and in different amounts. So far we have looked at

Question for Consideration

You have the option of receiving $1,000 today, $1,500 in four years, or $1,700 in six years. Which would you choose? Assume a discount rate of 6%. Explain your answer.

Answer: To answer the question it is necessary to compare the present values of each of the cash flows and select the one with the highest present value. The cash flow with the highest present value is the most valuable. The present value of cash today is that amount of cash:

Option 1: $PV_{n,r}$ = Present value factor × Amount
$PV_{0,0.06}$ = 1.000 × $1,000
= $1,000

Option 2: $PV_{4,0.06}$ = 0.79209 × $1,500
= $1,188.14

Option 3: $PV_{6,0.06}$ = 0.70496 × $1,700
= $1,198.43

Option 3 is best because it has the largest present value. (Note that the present value factor applied to a cash flow to be received now is always 1.000, regardless of the discount rate.)

simple situations involving a single cash flow sometime in the future. The present value technique can be used in more complex situations. Let's add a fourth option to the three prizes offered in the previous Question for Consideration. Option 4 is that you could receive $250 per year for six years beginning in one year. How would option 4 stack up against receiving $1,700 in year six, the best option of the first three?

This calculation is a bit more complicated, but the concepts are the same. Option 4 requires that we determine the present value of a series of six cash flows occurring at different times. The approach is the same as with the simpler examples, but more calculations are involved. The calculation of the present value of this series of cash flows is shown in Table 7-4.

Since the present value of the cash flows in Option 4 is the largest of the four offered, it should be selected.

Present Value of an Annuity

For Option 4 in the example we've just discussed, you would receive a $250 payment at the end of each of the next six years. A series of equal cash flows (inflows or outflows), usually made at equally spaced time intervals, is known as an **annuity**. To calculate the present value of the series of six $250 payments requires the following steps:

1. Find the discount rate for each of the six years.
2. Multiply the cash flow in each year by the appropriate discount rate to determine the present value of the cash flow in each year.
3. Add up the present values from each year to get the present value of the entire series of cash flows.

However, there is an easier way to calculate this amount. It is common to have to evaluate a series of equal cash flows that are to be received over a period of time, so a third table is provided that allows you to easily calculate the present value of an annuity. Table B-3 in Appendix B (see page B-6) provides factors for determining the present value of an annuity. Table B-3 is used the same way as Tables B-1 and B-2. In the case of Option 4, you go to the intersection of the 6% column and the six-period row and find the present value factor of 4.91732. Multiplying this factor by the amount of cash to be received in each period gives the present value of the annuity. For Option 4 the present value is:

$$\text{PV of an annuity}_{n, r} = \text{Present value of an annuity factor} \times \text{Amount to be received}$$
$$\text{PV of an annuity}_{6, 0.06} = 4.91732 \times \$250$$
$$= \$1,229.33$$

Table 7-4   Option 4: Calculation of Present Value

Calculation of Present Value of Option 4
(Receive $250 per year for six years, beginning one year from now, at a discount rate of 6%)

Cash received	Amount of cash received	Discount factor (from Table B-2)	Present value of cash flow
Now	$ 0		
In one year	250	0.94340	$ 235.85
In two years	250	0.89000	222.50
In three years	250	0.83962	209.91
In four years	250	0.79209	198.02
In five years	250	0.74726	186.81
In six years	250	0.70496	176.24
Totals		4.91732	$1,229.33

This is the same amount that we calculated in Table 7-4. Note that the n in this formula refers to the number of periods for which the cash flow will be received. Also, note that the present value of an annuity factor is simply the sum of the present value factors for each of the years over the life of the annuity.

It is important to understand that Table B-3 can only be used in a limited set of circumstances. Table B-3 can only be used when:

- the cash flow is the same in each year;
- the same discount rate is applied to each year's cash flow; and
- the cash flow occurs in every year beginning one year from the present.

If *any* of these conditions is not met, then Table B-3 cannot be used and the individual cash flows must be evaluated using Table B-2. Let's consider an example that looks at the present value of an annuity.

Example 1: Tuttle Inc. Tuttle Inc. (Tuttle) can invest in a business opportunity that will pay it $5,000,000 at the end of each of the next five years. Assuming that the appropriate discount rate is 12%, what is the present value of the payments Tuttle would receive by investing in the opportunity? What is the maximum amount that Tuttle should pay to invest in the business opportunity?

The answer will be calculated by first using Table B-2 (page B-4) and then using Table B-3 (page B-6).

Using Table B-2
(Receive payments of $5,000,000 per year for five years using a discount rate of 12%)

Cash received	Amount of cash received	Discount factor	Present value
End of year 1	$5,000,000	0.89286	$ 4,464,300
End of year 2	5,000,000	0.79719	3,985,950
End of year 3	5,000,000	0.71178	3,558,900
End of year 4	5,000,000	0.63552	3,177,600
End of year 5	5,000,000	0.56743	2,837,150
			$18,023,900

Using Table B-3
(Receive an annuity of $5,000,000 for five years using a discount rate of 12%)

Cash received	Discount factor	Present value
End of each of the next five years $5,000,000	3.60478	$18,023,900

The present value of a series of $5,000,000 payments to be received at the end of each of the next five years, at a discount rate of 12%, is $18,023,900. The results using both approaches are the same, but you'll notice how much less time-consuming it is to use the annuity table (Table B-3). The present value calculation implies that $18,023,900 today is equivalent to a series of $5,000,000 payments to be received at the end of each of the next five years, at a discount rate of 12%. This means that Tuttle would pay no more than $18,023,900 to invest in this business opportunity. By paying $18,023,900 Tuttle is earning exactly 12% on its investment, which is what it requires (that is why the 12% discount rate is used). If Tuttle had to pay more than $18,023,900, it would earn less than 12%, which would not be acceptable.

There are a number of accounting issues for which discounting is relevant. For example, if a company makes sales on credit, where payment is not due for a long time and no interest is payable on the debt, discounting helps determine how much revenue should be recognized. Discounting is also relevant for many liabilities, such as

Question for Consideration

A famous professional athlete recently signed a one-year contract with his team for $15,000,000. Because the team was having financial problems, the athlete agreed to accept the $15,000,000 in equal payments of $750,000 over the next 20 years. The team stated at a press conference that the $15,000,000 justly rewarded the best player in the game with the highest one-year salary in the history of the sport, exceeding the previous high salary of $9,500,000.

Do you agree with the team's statement that the salary is the highest in the history of the sport? Explain your answer. Assume a discount rate of 10% and that payments are received at the end of each year.

Answer: If the previous high salary of $9,500,000 was paid in one year, the $15,000,000 salary is nowhere near the previous high. The present value of a series of $750,000 payments received over 20 years is:

$$\text{PV of an annuity}_{n,\,r} = \text{Present value of an annuity factor} \times \text{Amount to be received each year}$$
$$\text{PV of an annuity}_{20,\,0.10} = 8.51356 \times \$750,000$$
$$= \$6,385,170$$

Because the payments on the contract are spread over 20 years, the present value of the athlete's salary is $6,385,170. That means that receiving $750,000 over 20 years is equivalent to receiving $6,385,170 today. In nominal dollar terms, the athlete is receiving more money than any athlete before. However, comparing the present value of the payments made under different contracts is a more legitimate way of comparing the contracts.

leases, pensions, and other long-term obligations. Later in this chapter we will examine an accounting application of the time value of money.

Comment: This discussion of the time value of money is intended to briefly introduce the topic. For the purpose of this text it is necessary that you understand the fundamentals so that you can understand how the time value of money affects financial reporting. Any further discussion is beyond the scope of the text.

Receivables

Receivables represent amounts owing to an entity. Usually the amounts owing will be received in cash, but goods and services can also be receivable or owing. Most receivables result from selling goods and services to customers on credit. These are usually referred to as *accounts receivable.* Receivables can also represent amounts owing by shareholders and employees (shareholder/employee loans receivable), tax refunds (taxes receivable), amounts owing from investments (interest and dividends receivable), proceeds due from the sale of capital assets, and so on. Receivables are usually current assets, but if an amount owing is to be received in more than a year, it would be classified as non-current.

We will focus mainly on accounts receivable because these are the most common and most significant receivables seen on financial statements. For example, the retail chain Sears Canada Inc. (Sears) reports receivables of almost $1,000,000,000 on its January 1, 2001 balance sheet, which represents almost 24% of the company's total assets. Extracts from Sears' financial statements are shown in Exhibit 7-3.[3]

Sears reports two categories of receivables:

www.sears.ca

- *Charge account receivables* are amounts owed by customers for goods and services purchased on their Sears credit cards.

Exhibit 7-3

Sears Canada Inc. Receivables Information

Consolidated Statements of Financial Position

As at December 30, 2000 and January 1, 2000 (in millions)

	2000	1999 Restated (Note 2)
Assets		
Current Assets		
Cash and short-term investments	$ **135.5**	$ 148.1
Charge account receivables (Note 3)	**403.8**	403.9
Other receivables (Note 4)	**538.2**	666.0
Inventories	**1,015.2**	814.3
Prepaid expenses and other assets	**117.2**	98.8
Current portion of future income tax assets (Note 5)	**206.9**	184.8
	2,416.8	2,315.9
Investments and Other Assets (Note 6)	**71.3**	61.0
Net Capital Assets (Note 7)	**1,199.2**	983.6
Deferred Charges (Note 8)	**138.0**	133.4
Future Income Tax Assets (Note 5)	**129.7**	272.8
	$ **3,955.0**	$ 3,766.7

3. CHARGE ACCOUNT RECEIVABLES

Details of charge account receivables are as follows:

(in millions)	2000	1999
Charge account receivables	$ **1,949.3**	$ 1,822.6
Less: amounts securitized	**(1,545.5)**	(1,418.7)
Net charge account receivables	$ **403.8**	$ 403.9

4. OTHER RECEIVABLES

Other receivables consist of the following:

(in millions)	2000	1999
Deferred receivables	$ **737.9**	$ 668.0
Less: amounts securitized	**(268.2)**	(66.0)
Net deferred receivables	**469.7**	602.0
Miscellaneous receivables	**68.5**	64.0
Total	$ **538.2**	$ 666.0

Deferred Receivables

Deferred receivables are charge account receivables that have not yet been billed to the customers' accounts. Service charges are not accrued on these accounts over the deferral period which generally ranges from six to 13 months.

- *Other receivables* are mainly deferred receivables, which are amounts owed for purchases made on Sears' credit cards, but for which payment has been deferred for several months and customers have not yet been billed.

Interestingly, Exhibit 7-3 shows that Sears has actually generated charge account receivables of $1,949,300,000 and deferred receivables of $737,900,000, but the company has *securitized* over $1,545,500,000 of its charge account receivables and

$268,200,000 of its deferred receivables. This means that Sears has sold these receivables to investors as a way to raise cash to meet its needs. The receivables that have been sold are not reported on Sears' balance sheet.

Accounts receivable arise when revenue is recognized but payment is not received. As we discussed in Chapter 4, the journal entry to record revenue that is recognized before payment is received is:

Dr. Accounts receivable (asset +)	xxx	
Cr. Revenue (revenue +, owners' equity +)		xxx

When the customer pays the amount owed, the journal entry recorded is:

Dr. Cash (asset +)	xxx	
Cr. Accounts receivable (asset −)		xxx

Accounts receivable are essentially loans made by an entity to its customers. Most businesses would probably prefer to do business on a cash basis because selling on credit lengthens an entity's cash cycle and introduces the risk that amounts owed will not be collected. Selling on credit also incurs costs to administer the credit program—costs such as setting policies for determining whether customers are eligible for credit, doing credit checks on prospective credit customers, processing billings and collections, and pursuing customers that do not pay. However, if a company does not offer credit, some customers may take their business elsewhere. In many business situations, credit terms are an important part of the "package" that an entity offers its customers, especially for non-retail transactions.

For most retail businesses credit is offered through major credit cards such as MasterCard and Visa. However, credit can be an important and lucrative business in the retail industry. That is why companies such as Sears Canada Inc., Canadian Tire Corporation, Limited, and Hudson's Bay Company offer their own credit cards to their customers. These companies earn interest from customers who do not pay for their purchases within the allowed period of time.

GAAP financial statements report receivables at their net realizable value (NRV); that is, at the estimated amount that will be collected. When a company sells on credit, a number of events can reduce the amount that will actually be collected, including the following:

- Customers might not pay what they owe. Failure to pay may be due to financial problems, disputes over whether the goods or services were delivered or acceptable, or simply because some customers are dishonest.

- Some customers may demand refunds if they are not satisfied with the goods or services provided. Most people have purchased items or received gifts that they have returned for a refund or credit.

- Customers may receive a discount if they pay their bills early. For example, an entity may offer a customer a 2% discount if the amount owed is paid within 10 days. Thus if the customer owes $1,000, only $980 has to be paid if payment is made within 10 days. If the customer waits until the payment is actually due, perhaps 30 or 60 days from the date of purchase, then the full amount must be paid.

Under accrual accounting, bad debts, returns, and discounts are costs of doing business in the period when the revenue is recognized. The effect of accounting for bad debts, returns, and discounts is to reduce net income (by reducing sales or increasing expenses) and reduce accounts receivable. Each of these items is not usually known at the balance sheet date, so the amounts must be estimated.

Reporting receivables at their NRV makes sense for many users and uses of financial statements. For cash flow prediction and liquidity analysis, the NRV provides the most useful information because the amount represents the cash that will likely be received.

For the stewardship and management evaluation objectives, knowing the actual amount owed by customers and the estimated amount that will be collected are useful for assessing how well receivables, credit and collection, returns, and discounts are being managed. GAAP do not cooperate fully in providing this stewardship information. Under GAAP it is necessary to account for uncollectable receivables, sales returns, and discounts, but there is no requirement that information on these estimates be disclosed.

MWW provides information about its receivables in Note 4 to the financial statements (see page A-52). Note 4 lists the sources of amounts owed to MWW on January 27, 2001. (MWW groups different types of receivables in accounts receivable.) The gross amount owed is $15,305,000. This means that the entities listed in Note 4 have agreed to pay $15,305,000 to MWW. However, MWW only expects to collect $13,998,000, the amount at the bottom of the table in Note 4 and the amount that is reported on MWW's balance sheet. The $1,307,000 difference between the gross amount and the amount that MWW estimates that it will collect is MWW's estimate of uncollectables. In contrast, Sears does not provide information about uncollectable amounts (see Exhibit 7-3, page 389). Neither company provides information about sales returns or discounts.

For private companies, where adherence to GAAP may not be required, the amount reported for accounts receivable could represent gross receivables, net receivables, or receivables net of some estimates (such as bad debts), but not of others (such as returns). A user must be very careful to understand exactly what is represented by the numbers being reported. This is especially true for financial statements that are prepared primarily for tax purposes. Estimates such as returns and discounts cannot be deducted when calculating taxable income, so a preparer may not include these estimates when preparing the financial statements. For tax purposes an allowance for uncollectable accounts can be deducted.

When a MWW customer purchases merchandise using a credit card such as Visa or MasterCard, the amount does not appear as a receivable. The credit card receipt is equivalent to cash; MWW just has to take the receipt to the bank to receive cash. The account receivable belongs to the credit card company. MWW pays the credit card company a percentage of each sale as a fee for being able to accept the credit card. For example, a $100 purchase made using a MasterCard might cost MWW 1% of the charged amount, or $1. When MWW presents the credit card receipt at the bank, it would receive $99 instead of $100.

A credit card transaction could be recorded in two ways. The first way would be to simply record the sale in the amount of the cash received. For a $100 sale with a service charge of $1, the journal entry would be:

Dr. Cash (asset +)	99	
Cr. Revenue (revenue +, owners' equity +)		99
To record the sale of goods using a credit card at the net amount.		

The second way to record a credit card transaction would be to record the sale at the amount the customer agreed to pay and create a separate account for the service charge. In this case the journal entry would be:

Dr. Cash (asset +)	99	
Dr. Credit card service fee (expense +, owners' equity −)	1	
Cr. Revenue (revenue +, owners' equity +)		100
To record the sale of goods using a credit card at the gross amount.		

The second entry provides information about the cost of allowing customers to use credit cards. With the first entry this information is lost. The amount of revenue reported is not affected by how the customer paid. In other words, with the second entry $100 of revenue would be recorded regardless of whether the customer paid by cash, cheque, or credit card.

Accounting for Uncollectable Receivables

Amounts not collected from customers are a cost of selling on credit and these costs must be accounted for. Accounting for uncollectable receivables must address two effects. First, an expense must be recorded to reflect the costs incurred as a result of amounts that will not be collected. Second, accounts receivable must be decreased by the amount that will not be collected so that the amount on the balance sheet reflects the amount the entity will collect from customers.

The easiest way to account for uncollectable receivables, or bad debts, is to simply write off a receivable when it becomes clear that a customer will not be paying. This method is known as the direct write-off method. With the **direct write-off method**, a receivable is removed from the list of receivables and an expense recorded when management decides that the receivable will not be collected. The journal entry that would be recorded is:

Dr. Bad debt expense (expense +, owners' equity −)	xxx	
Cr. Receivables (assets −)		xxx

For example, in September 2004 the management of Killowen Inc. (Killowen) decided that $10,000 owed to it by Fredericton Ltd. would not be paid. The amount had been in dispute for 18 months and management decided that it was not worthwhile pursuing the matter any further. Killowen has a December 31 year end. If Killowen used the direct write-off method to account for bad debts, it would make the following journal entry in September 2004, when management decided that the amount owing would not be collected:

Dr. Bad debt expense (expense +, owners' equity −)	10,000	
Cr. Accounts receivable (assets −)		10,000
To write off an uncollectable account receivable.		

While the direct write-off method is simple and straightforward, it is not good matching. In the example, the expense for the bad debt would be recognized over 18 months after the transaction had taken place. However, matching requires that the cost of bad debts be expensed in the period when the related revenue is recognized. In other words, if Killowen were using accrual accounting, it should not wait until it is clear that a customer is not going to pay. Another problem with the direct write-off method is that it is easily manipulated because management can pick and choose exactly when it wants to write off accounts receivable.

If we are going to match and expense bad debts in the period in which the related revenue is recognized, an obvious question is, "How do we know which accounts to write-off?" We don't. If we knew at the time of the transaction that a customer was not going to pay, we would not have offered the customer credit. Under accrual accounting, an *estimate* of the amount that will not be collected is made without knowing which specific receivables will not be collected. We have to wait to find out which receivables will not be collected.

There are two methods used to estimate the cost of bad debts:

1. The percentage-of-receivables method.
2. The percentage-of-credit-sales method.

With either of these two methods, the following journal entry is made each period to account for bad debts:

Dr. Bad debt expense (expense +, owners' equity −)	xxx	
Cr. Allowance for uncollectable accounts (contra-asset +)		xxx

The bad debt expense is the cost of selling on credit during the period. The **allowance for uncollectable accounts** is a contra-asset account to accounts receivable or another receivables account that represents the amount of the receivables that management estimates will not be collected. A contra-asset account is used because it is not possible to identify the specific receivables that will not be collected when the estimate is made. The Accounts Receivable account represents a listing of the amount owed by each customer. For example, an extract from the detailed list for Killowen Inc. is presented in Table 7-5.

Because the accounts receivable account is a summary of individual amounts owed by customers and it is not known which receivables will not be collected, there is really no place to record the estimate for uncollectable receivables within the Accounts Receivable account. As a result, the allowance for uncollectable accounts is kept in a separate contra-asset account. The balance in the Allowance for Uncollectable Accounts account means, "We know that some of our receivables will not be collected: we just do not know which ones." Considered together, Accounts Receivable and Allowance for Uncollectable Accounts give an estimate of the NRV of accounts receivable.

The Percentage-of-Receivables Method The **percentage-of-receivables method** is a method of estimating uncollectable receivables that is based on management's estimate of the percentage of receivables at the end of the period that will not be collected. At the end of each reporting period, management estimates the amount of accounts receivable on hand at the end of the period that will not be collected. By doing this, management is estimating the NRV of the ending balance of receivables. To obtain the NRV of the Receivables account, the allowance account is debited or credited for whatever amount is needed to bring the balance in the Receivables account to the uncollectable amount estimated by management. This entry is an adjusting entry.

For example, Killowen Inc.'s management estimates that $71,500 of its ending accounts receivable of $1,194,000 on December 31, 2004 will not be collected. The balance in the allowance account before the end-of-period adjusting entry is recorded is a credit of $5,000. (The reason why there might be a balance in the allowance account before the adjusting entry is made will be made clear shortly.) To bring the balance in the allowance account to the desired credit balance of $71,500, a credit to the allowance account of $66,500 is required. The following journal entry is recorded:

Dr. Bad debt expense (expense +, owners' equity −)	66,500	
Cr. Allowance for uncollectable accounts (contra-asset +)		66,500
To record the bad debt expense for 2004.		

With the percentage-of-receivables method, the bad debt expense is not calculated directly. The bad debt expense is simply "the other side of the journal entry" that is required to bring the Allowance account to the desired level. If, as in the example, a

Table 7-5   Killowen Inc.: Selected Accounts Receivable

Killowen Inc.
Accounts Receivable Ledger
December 31, 2004

Customer	Account Balance
Charlottetown Inc.	$ 31,200.05
Dartmouth Ltd.	157,000.10
Fredericton Ltd.	25,000.92
Gander Inc.	38,500.68
Moncton Ltd.	22,250.25
Saint John Inc.	117,410.41
St. John's Ltd.	57,200.09
Total	$1,194,000.00

credit of $66,500 is required to bring the Allowance account to the desired level, the bad debt expense is debited for $66,500. This focus on the Allowance account is why the percentage-of-receivables method is called a *balance sheet approach*. The effect on the accounts can be seen in the partial spreadsheet in Table 7-6.

The NRV of Killowen's accounts receivable is $1,122,500 ($1,194,000 − $71,500). There is a balance in Allowance for Uncollectable Accounts before the adjusting entry is made on December 31, 2004 because management's estimate of the amount of receivables that would not be collected during 2004 was not exact. The estimate Killowen's management made on December 31, 2003 was $5,000 too high. This error is simply the result of having to predict the future. Errors that result from having to make estimates or predictions are commonplace in accrual accounting.

How does management estimate the amount of receivables that will not be collected? One way is to use an aging schedule. An **aging schedule** classifies accounts receivable by the length of time that they have been outstanding. In other words, the receivables are classified by how long it has been since the transaction with the customer took place. Current receivables are ones that are due within the period that the entity allows customers to pay. If the entity allows customers to pay within 30 days, receivables that have been outstanding for 30 days or less are current. The remaining receivables are then classified by how long overdue they are. For example, an entity might classify receivables as being between one and 30 days overdue, between 31 and 90 days overdue and over 90 days overdue.

Management uses its historical information about the proportion of each category of receivables that has been collected in the past, along with its knowledge of factors that might cause those historical percentages to change, to estimate the amount of end-of-period accounts receivable that will not be collected. Typically, the older a receivable, the less likely it is to be collected.

An aging schedule for Killowen is shown in Table 7-7.

Based on the aging schedule, Killowen would report gross accounts receivable of $1,194,000, less an allowance for uncollectable accounts of $71,500. How this information is disclosed in the financial statements varies. Killowen could disclose the allowance on the balance sheet, in the notes to the statements, or not at all. According to GAAP, entities are not required to disclose their bad debt expense in the income statement or the notes to the financial statements. In 2000, 158 of 200 firms surveyed in *Financial Reporting in Canada* did not disclose or refer to the allowance for uncollectable accounts in their financial statements.[4] As a result, it can be difficult for a user to assess the efficiency and effectiveness of an entity's credit and collection policies. Exhibit 7-4 shows how three different companies provide information about their accounts receivable in their financial statements and notes.[5]

It is important to remember that an estimate is a prediction of what will

---

Table 7-6   Partial Spreadsheet for Killowen Inc.

Killowen Inc.
Partial Spreadsheet
December 31, 2004

	Accounts Receivable	Allowance for Uncollectable Accounts	Bad Debt Expense
Balances on December 31, 2004, before adjusting entry	$1,194,000	$ (5,000)	
Adjusting entry		(66,500)	$(66,500)
Ending balances on December 31, 2004	$1,194,000	$(71,500)	

Table 7-7   Aging Schedule for Killowen Inc.

Killowen Inc.
Aging Schedule
December 31, 2004

	Current	1 to 30 days overdue	31 to 90 days overdue	Over 90 days overdue	Total
Amount	$950,000	$125,000	$72,000	$47,000	$1,194,000
Percentage estimated to be uncollectable	1%	4%	40%	60%	
Amount estimated to be uncollectable	$ 9,500	$ 5,000	$28,800	$28,200	$ 71,500

happen—in this case the amount of receivables that will not be collected. Historical information might be helpful for making a prediction, but that does not mean it will happen in the future. For example, circumstances such as a slowdown in the economy or a change in the credit terms an entity offers suggest that simply using the historical rate of bad debts is not always appropriate.

Users of financial statements are not likely to see the accounts receivable aging schedule unless they are powerful enough to successfully demand information from an entity. Banks will usually require a schedule of aged receivables if the receivables are used as collateral for a loan and the maximum amount that can be borrowed is a percentage of receivables. Banks will want an aging schedule because they will not

Consolidated statements of financial position

as at December 31   in millions of US dollars

	2000	1999
Assets		
Current Assets		
Cash and cash equivalents	$ 100.0	$ 44.0
Accounts receivable (Note 5)	326.6	269.3
Inventories (Note 6)	406.2	377.2
Prepaid expenses	38.9	35.7
	871.7	726.2
Property, plant and equipment (Note 7)	2,910.1	2,877.1
Goodwill (Note 8)	106.4	109.4
Other assets (Note 9)	257.5	204.1
	$4,145.7	$3,916.8

5. Accounts Receivable

	2000	1999
Trade accounts – Canpotex	$ 31.4	$ 37.6
– Other	268.8	215.0
Non-trade accounts	34.1	23.7
	334.3	276.3
Less allowance for doubtful accounts	7.7	7.0
	$ 326.6	$ 269.3

Exhibit 7-4

Four Examples of Accounts Receivable Information in Financial Statements

Panel A: Potash Corporation of Saskatchewan Inc.

www.potashcorp.com
www.rogers.com
www.ballard.com
www.huskyenergy.ca

Comment: Potash Corporation of Saskatchewan Inc. (PotashCorp.) reports the net amount of accounts receivable in its balance sheet and provides some detail on the receivables, including the amount of the allowance for doubtful accounts in a note to the financial statements. PotashCorp. does not disclose the bad debt expense.

Exhibit 7-4 (continued)

Four Examples of Accounts
Receivable Information in
Financial Statements

Panel B: Rogers Communications
Inc.

consolidated balance sheets

(In thousands of dollars) As at December 31	2000	(As restated — note 1D) 1999
Assets		
Fixed assets (note 3)	$ 4,047,329	$ 3,539,160
Goodwill and other intangible assets (note 4)	1,573,923	1,349,552
Investments (note 5)	972,648	554,241
Cash and short-term deposits	299,151	13,937
Accounts receivable, net of allowance for doubtful accounts of $66,296 (1999 — $48,628)	501,553	345,397
Deferred charges (note 6)	235,824	217,944
Other assets (note 7)	235,867	231,287
	$ 7,866,295	$ 6,251,518

Comment: Rogers Communications Inc. discloses its allowance for doubtful accounts parenthetically on the balance sheet. No information about the bad debt expense is provided.

Panel C: Ballard Power
Systems Inc.

CONSOLIDATED BALANCE SHEETS

December 31 (Expressed in thousands of Canadian dollars)	2000	1999
ASSETS		
Current assets		
Cash and cash equivalents	$ 288,729	$ 86,462
Short-term investments	480,944	272,089
Accounts receivable (notes 2 and 15)	23,054	26,518
Inventories (note 3)	17,643	8,649
Prepaid expenses	667	1,216
	811,037	394,934

	2000	1999
Long-term contracts	$ 11,899	$ 13,139
Short-term contracts	7,413	9,862
Other	3,742	3,517
	$ 23,054	$ 26,518

Comment: Ballard Power Systems Inc. provides additional detail about the nature of its accounts receivable, but no information about the allowance for doubtful accounts and the bad debt expense.

Panel D: Husky Energy Inc.

CONSOLIDATED BALANCE SHEETS

As at December 31 (millions of dollars)	2000	1999	1998
ASSETS			
Current assets			
Cash equivalents	$ -	$ -	$ 1
Accounts receivable	715	315	160
Inventories (note 4)	186	134	81
Prepaid expenses	27	14	16
	928	463	258

Comment: Husky Energy Inc. (Husky) provides an amount for accounts receivable on its balance sheet with no additional explanation. We can assume that the amount is net of the allowance for doubtful accounts since Husky follows accrual accounting. No information is provided about the bad debt expense for the year.

usually accept as security receivables that are more than 90 days old, since these receivables have a high risk of being uncollectable.

Question for Consideration

You have been given the following list of aged accounts receivable for Onward Inc. (Onward) on December 31, 2005:

Current	$175,000
1-30 days overdue	32,000
31-60 days overdue	12,500
61-90 days overdue	5,700
Over 90 days overdue	2,300

Onward's management estimates that it will collect 98% of the current accounts receivable, 94% of the receivables that are 1-30 days overdue, 80% of the receivables that are 31-60 days overdue, 65% of the receivables that are 61-90 days overdue, and 30% of the receivables that are more than 90 days overdue.

Onward uses the percentage-of-receivables method for estimating bad debts. Prepare the journal entry that Onward should make on December 31, 2005 to record the bad debt expense. There is a credit balance of $1,025 in Allowance for Uncollectable Accounts on December 31, 2005, before the adjusting entry is made.

Answer:

Calculation of the estimated amount of year-end receivables that will not be collected

Current	$175,000 × 0.02 =	$ 3,500
1-30 days overdue	32,000 × 0.06 =	1,920
31-60 days overdue	12,500 × 0.20 =	2,500
61-90 days overdue	5,700 × 0.35 =	1,995
Over 90 days overdue	2,300 × 0.70 =	1,610
		$11,525

The balance desired in the allowance account on December 31, 2005 is $11,525. There is a credit balance of $1,025 in the allowance account before making the adjusting entry, so a credit to the allowance account of $10,500 ($11,525 − $1,025) is required. The required journal entry is:

Dr. Bad debt expense (expense +, owners' equity −)	10,500	
Cr. Allowance for uncollectable accounts (contra-asset +)		10,500
To record the bad debt expense for 2005.		

Percentage-of-Credit-Sales Method   The second method for accounting for bad debts is the percentage-of-credit-sales method. The **percentage-of-credit-sales method** is a method of estimating uncollectable receivables that is based on management's estimate of the percentage of credit sales in a period that will not be collected. With this method the bad debt expense is estimated by taking a percentage of credit sales in the period. The logic is that in each period some portion of credit sales will not be collected. That percentage is the bad debt expense for the period. Only credit sales are considered because cash sales, of course, are 100% collected. Again, management bases its estimate on the historical collection rate of credit sales and knowledge of any changes that might cause the collection rate to change.

The form of the journal entry recorded using this method is the same as the one shown using the percentage-of-receivables approach, although the amounts recorded in the entry are usually different. The entry is:

Dr. Bad debt expense (expense +, owners' equity −)	xxx	
Cr. Allowance for uncollectable accounts (contra-asset +)		xxx

For example, if Killowen had credit sales of $9,375,000 during 2004 and management estimated that 0.8% of credit sales would not be collected, then the adjusting journal entry that Killowen would make on December 31, 2004 would be:

Dr. Bad debt expense (expense +, owners' equity −)   75,000
    Cr. Allowance for uncollectable accounts (contra-asset +)   75,000
To record the bad debt expense for 2004.

Unlike the percentage-of-receivables method, which takes a balance sheet approach, the percentage-of-credit-sales method takes an *income statement approach*. The focus of this method is the bad debt expense. By calculating the amount of credit sales that will not be collected, the "right" amount of bad debt expense is obtained. This method results in a better matching of the costs and benefits because the amount expensed is directly related to the amount of credit sales in the period. With the percentage-of-credit-sales method, the bad debt expense is calculated and the amount of the expense for the period is credited to the allowance account to complete the journal entry. Because the percentage-of-credit-sales method focuses on the income statement (and as a result does not focus on the balance sheet), the estimate of the NRV of accounts receivable may not be as accurate as with the percentage-of-receivables approach.

In some cases, the annual estimate that management makes to determine the bad debt expense is consistently too high or too low. The percentage of credit sales that management uses may be consistently above or below the actual amount of bad debts the entity incurs each year. The result is that there will be a build-up in the Allowance account. If the bad debt expense is consistently above the amount of receivables that are actually written off, then a credit balance builds up in the allowance account. If the bad debt expense is consistently below the actual amount written off, then a debit balance builds up. In either case an adjusting entry must eventually be made that puts the balance in the allowance account in line with the actual economic situation. If there is a credit balance build-up in the Allowance account, the adjusting entry is:

Dr. Allowance for uncollectable accounts (contra-asset −)   xxx
    Cr. Bad debt expense (expense −, owners' equity +)   xxx

The entry reduces the credit balance in the allowance account to a level that reflects the NRV of accounts receivable. The entry also reduces the bad debt expense, which increases net income for the period. In effect, in the previous years when the error was being made, net income was lower than it would have been had a better estimate of bad debts been made. If the Allowance account is not adjusted, the Allowance account combined with the Accounts Receivable account does not give a reasonable estimate of the NRV of accounts receivable. This adjustment corrects the error. The opposite is true of the effect for a debit build-up in the Allowance account.

The adjusting journal entry in the event of a debit balance build-up is:

Dr. Bad debt expense (expense +, owners' equity −)   xxx
    Cr. Allowance for uncollectable accounts (contra-asset +)   xxx

In principle, errors in estimates are not a major concern. Predicting the future is difficult and so there should be no expectation that management will get the estimate "right" each time. However, persistent errors (errors in the same direction each year) will introduce persistent errors into the financial statements.

From a user's perspective, financial statements usually do not provide enough information to allow effective analysis of credit and collection policies. It is rare for an entity to break down its sales into cash and credit components. Entities often do not disclose their bad debt expenses, and usually they do not disclose how uncollectables are estimated or the percentages used to make the estimates.

Writing Off a Receivable

The percentage-of-receivables and the percentage-of-credit-sales methods are used to estimate uncollectable accounts. But what happens when we finally know who is not going to pay? For both methods of estimating uncollectable accounts, when a specific account receivable is identified as not being collectable, that receivable is removed from the receivables listing, thereby reducing the balance in the Receivables account. The balance in the Allowance account is also reduced or debited. The Allowance account is reduced because when a specific uncollectable account is identified, that part of the estimate has become reality. Therefore, the amount of the estimate that has happened is transferred from the "estimate account" (Uncollectables) to the "actual account" (Receivables).

Once Killowen Inc.'s management decides that the $10,000 owing from Fredericton Ltd. was not going to be collected, it will make the following entry:

Dr. Allowance for uncollectable accounts (contra-asset −)   10,000
   Cr. Accounts receivable—Fredericton (asset −)   10,000
To write off a $10,000 account receivable from Fredericton Ltd.

Writing off an account receivable has no effect on the net balance of Accounts Receivable (Accounts Receivable − Allowance for Uncollectables). This can be seen by comparing Killowen's receivables before and after the write-off of the $10,000 owed by Fredericton. The comparison is shown in Table 7-8. Allowance for Uncollectable Accounts and Accounts Receivable both decrease by $10,000, but net Accounts Receivable remains the same.

If we examined the accounts receivable ledger shown in Table 7-5 (page 393) after the write-off, we would find that the amount owing by Fredericton would be $15,000.92 instead of $25,000.92.

Notice that the write-off of an account receivable has no effect on the income statement. The income statement effect occurs when the adjusting entry that records the bad debt expense and the adjustment to Allowance for Uncollectable Accounts is made.

Comparison of the Methods

Now let's compare how the three methods of accounting for uncollectables affect the financial statements. The amount that will be expensed each year with the three methods will usually be different, although over the life of the entity the amount expensed will be the same, regardless of the method. It is important to recognize that an entity's net income in a period may be affected by the method of accounting for uncollectables, even though the underlying economic circumstances of the entity are not affected by the method. However, outcomes that are based on net income and other accounting numbers that are affected by the accounting choice may be affected in turn—for example, management bonuses may differ with different net incomes.

The expense using the direct write-off method will be different from the other two methods because uncollectable receivables are expensed when they are determined to be uncollectable, not in the period the related revenue is recognized. This creates a difference in the timing of the expense between the direct write-off method and the other two methods.

The percentage-of-receivables and the percentage-of-credit-sales methods can also provide different bad debt expenses in a given period. One reason for the difference is that different methods are being used to estimate bad debts. Different methods will typically lead to different estimates. However, even if we assume that these two methods should, in principle, provide the same estimates, the amount expensed each year under each method will not be the same *unless* the estimated amount of bad debts proves to be accurate every year. In other words, if an entity records a bad debt

Table 7-8	Killowen Inc.: Accounts Receivable Before and After Write-Off	
	Before Write-Off	**After Write-Off**
Accounts receivable	$1,194,000	$1,184,000
Less: Allowance for uncollectable accounts	71,500	61,500
Accounts receivable, net	$1,122,500	$1,122,500

expense of $34,000, and ultimately $34,000 of receivables is written off, and this pattern occurs every year, then the two methods will provide the same bad debt expense and the same balance in the Allowance account each year.

Another way of making this point is that the bad debt expense with the two methods will be the same if the balance in the Allowance account before making the adjusting entry to account for bad debts each year is zero. However, since estimating bad debts is not an exact science, it is not likely that the estimate will be exactly right each year. As a result, the percentage-of-receivables and the percentage-of-credit-sales methods will often yield different bad debt expense estimates and different balances in the allowance account.

The differences can best be shown in an example. Information about Montreal Inc.'s (Montreal) receivables is provided in Panel A of Table 7-9. The entries to the worksheet under each method of accounting for uncollectable accounts are shown in Panel B of Table 7-9. As you work through the example, note that Cash, the gross

Table 7-9 Montreal Ltd.: Comparison of Different Methods of Accounting for Uncollectable Receivables

Panel A

	2006	2007	2008
Accounts receivable on December 31	$ 125,000	$ 175,000	$ 210,000
Credit sales (all sales are on credit)	1,168,953	1,418,329	1,701,995
Accounts receivable written off during the year	7,500	11,000	4,000
Percent of credit sales estimated to be uncollectable	0.802%	0.802%	0.802%
Percent of closing accounts receivable estimated to be uncollectable	7.5%	7.5%	7.5%

Panel B

	Cash	Accounts receivable (gross)	Revenue	Percentage-of-receivables approach — Allowance for uncollectable accounts	Percentage-of-receivables approach — Bad debt expense	Percentage-of-credit-sales approach — Allowance for uncollectable accounts	Percentage-of-credit-sales approach — Bad debt expense	Direct write-off approach[1] — Bad Debt expense
December 31, 2005 Balance Sheet		100,000		(7,500)		(7,500)		
During 2006—Revenue		1,168,953	1,168,953					
During 2006—Write-offs		(7,500)		7,500		7,500		(7,500)
During 2006—Collections	1,136,453	(1,136,453)						
31/12/2006 adjusting entries				(9,375)	(9,375)	(9,375)	(9,375)	
December 31, 2006 Balance Sheet	1,136,453	125,000		(9,375)		(9,375)		
During 2007—Revenue		1,418,329	1,418,329					
During 2007—Write-offs		(11,000)		11,000		11,000		(11,000)
During 2007—Collections	1,357,329	(1,357,329)						
31/12/2007 adjusting entries				(14,750)	(14,750)	(11,375)	(11,375)	
December 31, 2007 Balance Sheet	2,493,782	175,000		(13,125)		(9,750)		
During 2008—Revenue		1,701,995	1,701,995					
During 2008—Write-offs		(4,000)		4,000		4,000		(4,000)
During 2008—Collections	1,662,995	(1,662,995)						
31/12/2008 adjusting entries				(6,625)	(6,625)	(13,650)	(13,650)	
December 31, 2008 Balance Sheet	4,156,777	210,000		(15,750)		(19,400)		

[1]With the direct write-off approach there is no allowance for uncollectable accounts account.

amount of Accounts Receivable, and the amount of revenue recognized are the same under all three methods. How uncollectables are accounted for has no effect on these accounts. What differs under the three methods is the ending balance in the allowance account and the amount of bad debt expense each year.

On December 31, 2005 the balance in Montreal's allowance for uncollectable accounts account is $7,500 under both the percentage-of-receivables and percentage-of-credit-sales methods. During 2006 Montreal writes off $7,500 in receivables. Therefore, on December 31, 2006, the balance in the allowance account, before the adjusting entry is made, is zero. Because of the zero balance in the allowance account, the bad debt expense for 2006 is the same using both accrual methods. (The example is designed so that the two methods yield the same bad debt expense if the pre-adjusting entry balance in the allowance account is zero.) Since the balance in the allowance account is zero before the adjusting entries are made, the desired amount in the allowance account (the percentage-of-receivables method) and the desired bad debt expense (the percentage-of-credit-sales method) is $9,375. For the direct write-off method, the bad debt expense is $7,500, the amount of receivables written off during the year.

In 2007 things are different. During 2007, $11,000 of accounts receivable is written off even though we only have an allowance of $9,375. There is nothing unreasonable about the estimate not being exact. However, the estimate's inexactness affects the bad debt expense. Under the percentage-of-receivables method, the objective is to have the balance in the Allowance account be the amount of receivables that are estimated to be uncollectable. Whatever amount is required to obtain that ending balance is credited or debited to the allowance account.

In 2007 the desired ending balance in the Allowance account is a credit of $13,125 ($175,000 × 7.5%). The pre-adjusting entry balance in the Allowance account is a debit of $1,625, so to obtain the ending credit balance of $13,125 the allowance account must be increased by $14,750 (− $9,375 + $11,000 + $13,125). The bad debt expense is also $14,750 because with the percentage-of-receivables method, the bad debt expense is equal to the amount that must be credited to the Allowance account to bring it to the desired balance.

The focus is opposite using the percentage-of-credit-sales method. With the percentage-of-credit sales-method the bad debt expense is calculated directly—the objective is to get the bad debt expense "right." With this method the entry to the allowance account is that amount that is calculated as the bad debt expense for the period. In 2007 the desired bad debt expense is $11,375 ($1,418,329 × 0.802%). This amount is expensed and added to the Allowance account.

The effect of using the income statement approach is that the NRV of accounts receivable (Accounts Receivable less Allowance for Uncollectable Accounts) may not be the best possible estimate. If we assume that the best estimate of the NRV of accounts receivable is obtained using the percentage-of-receivables method, the NRV of accounts receivable is overstated when the percentage-of-credit-sales method is used ($161,875 with the percentage-of-receivables method versus $165,250 with the percentage-of-credit-sales method). The bad debt expense using the direct write-off method is $11,000, the amount of the receivables written off during the year.

In 2008 a smaller amount of receivables is written off than had been estimated. Once again, a difference between an estimate and the actual outcome is not surprising. You should examine and understand the entries for 2008 under each method in Table 7-9.

Which method is best? Under accrual accounting the direct write-off method is not acceptable because it does not match expenses and revenues. The estimation methods are different ways of achieving the same objective of accounting for uncollectable accounts. Neither is best and both are used in practice. The amount of the bad debt expense and the adjustments to the Allowance for Uncollectables account, as well as the decision to write off a specific account receivable, are all exercises of judgment by management. As a result of the need for judgment, estimating bad debts is a tool that managers can use to "manage the numbers" in the financial statements.

Long-Term Receivables

www.nortelnetworks.com

Receivables do not always have to be current assets. Even amounts owing from customers can be due in more than a year or an operating cycle. An entity can enter into any type of payment arrangement with customers that it chooses. If a receivable is due in more than a year or an operating cycle, it is classified as a long-term asset. Exhibit 7-5 shows an example of long-term receivables reported on the balance sheet of Nortel Networks Corporation.[6]

An interesting question surrounding the accounting for long-term receivables is the amount that should be reported on the balance sheet. When payment is not due for a long time, or if payment is spread out over a long period of time, then the time value of money becomes an issue. If a long-term receivable does not require the payment of interest or if the interest rate is less than the market rate, then the amount of revenue that is recognized and the receivable are too high if the time value of money is ignored.

Let's look at an example. On December 31, 2003 Winnipeg Inc. (Winnipeg) sold goods to Regina Ltd. (Regina) for $200,000. Because of Regina's financial difficulties, Winnipeg agreed to accept payment in full in three years, on January 2, 2007. The agreement does not require Regina to pay interest. Winnipeg was confident that it would receive its money because Regina's owners have personally guaranteed the debt, so Winnipeg recognized the revenue when the goods were shipped.

How much revenue should Winnipeg recognize when the goods are shipped and how should the receivable be accounted for in its accounting records? Clearly, Winnipeg has not earned $200,000 because the time value of money concept means the present value of the money Regina will pay in three years is less than $200,000.

For this example, assume that a discount rate of 8% is appropriate. The present value of $200,000 to be received in three years can be determined using the present value tables. Since the payment from Regina is a single payment to be received in the future, we use Table B-2 (see Appendix B, page B-4), the present value of $1 to be received at the end of period n. The factor at the intersection of the 8% column and the three-period row is 0.79383. Therefore, the present value of $200,000 to be received in three years is $200,000 \times 0.79383 = $158,766.

This means that if we consider the time value of money, Winnipeg should recognize $158,766 of revenue in 2003 for the sale to Regina. The journal entry that Winnipeg would make in 2003 to record the revenue is:

Dr. Long-term receivable (asset +)	158,766	
Cr. Revenue (revenue +, shareholders' equity +)		158,766
To record the sale of goods to Regina Ltd.		

Exhibit 7-5

Nortel Networks Corporation: Long-Term Receivables

NORTEL NETWORKS CORPORATION
Consolidated Balance Sheets
As at December 31
(millions of U.S. dollars)

	2000	1999
ASSETS		
Long-term receivables (less provisions of –$383 for 2000, $284 for 1999)	1,528	1,356

The spreadsheet entries for the sale to Regina are shown in Table 7-10. The difference between the $158,766 that Winnipeg recognizes as revenue in 2003 and the $200,000 in cash that it will receive in January 2007 is the interest implicit in the agreement between Winnipeg and Regina. Over the three-year period Winnipeg will recognize $41,234 in interest on this receivable. Each year Winnipeg will recognize interest revenue and increase the long-term receivable. The journal entry made each year would be:

Dr. Long-term receivable (asset +)   xxx
   Cr. Interest revenue (revenue +, shareholders' equity +)   xxx
To accrue interest revenue on the long-term receivable from Regina Ltd.

Note that revenue from the sale of goods is reduced and it is replaced with interest revenue. In other words, the sale to Regina is equivalent to selling the goods for $158,766 on the date of the transaction and then earning $41,234 in interest by financing the sale. Over the three years $200,000 of revenue is recognized, but taking the time value of money into consideration changes the timing and type of the revenue. Table 7-10 shows the amount of interest revenue that Winnipeg would recognize each year as a result of the contract with Regina. Notice that the amount of interest accrued each year is added to the long-term receivable column. On December 31, 2006 the amount of the receivable reported on the balance sheet is $200,000, the amount that Regina is expected to pay. On Winnipeg's December 31, 2006 balance sheet the long-term receivable would be classified as a current asset because as of the end of 2006 the payment from Regina is due within one year.

If Winnipeg's agreement with Regina required the payment of interest at the market rate it would be unnecessary to discount the cash flow. The revenue and receivable could be set up at $200,000 in 2003 and the interest revenue would be recorded each year.

Table 7-10   Partial Spreadsheet for Winnipeg Inc.

Winnipeg Inc. Partial Spreadsheet					
	Cash	Long-term receivable	Revenue	Interest revenue	
Ending balance sheet December 31, 2003		158,766	158,766		Recognition of revenue on sale of goods to Regina Ltd.
December 31, 2004 (adjusting entry)		12,701		12,701	Recognition of interest revenue earned in 2004. Interest is calculated based on the receivable on December 31, 2003. The interest is added to the long-term receivable account. Interest earned = $158,766 × 0.08. Note that amounts are rounded to the nearest dollar.
Ending balance sheet December 31, 2004		171,467			
December 31, 2005 (adjusting entry)		13,718		13,718	Recognition of interest revenue earned in 2005. Interest earned = $171,467 × 0.08.
Ending balance sheet December 31, 2005		185,185			
December 31, 2006 (adjusting entry)		14,815		14,815	Recognition of interest revenue earned in 2006. Interest earned = $185,184 × 0.08.
Ending balance sheet December 31, 2006		200,000			This amount would be classified as a current asset because it will be collected within one year.
January 2, 2007	200,000	(200,000)			Collection of the $200,000 from Regina Ltd.

Financial Statement Analysis Issues

Hidden Reserves

Hidden reserves are undisclosed accounting choices used to manage earnings and other financial information with the intention of satisfying the self-interests of the preparers. Using hidden reserves is an abuse of accounting information; they undermine the usefulness and credibility of financial statements. There are strong suspicions that hidden reserves are in wide use by many entities. Securities commissions in Canada and the U.S. have taken direct aim on this manipulation of financial statements. While hidden reserves are inappropriate, their apparent wide use makes them an interesting area of accounting and one users of accounting information need to understand.

A simple example will show how management can use accounting estimates to manage earnings. The example uses the allowance for uncollectable accounts and bad debt expense to show how profits can be moved from one period to another. Remember, under GAAP there are minimal disclosure requirements about the estimates that management makes when preparing the financial statements.

In 2004 Discovery Ltd. (Discovery), a public company, enjoyed its most successful year ever. Its performance exceeded the expectations of management as well as investors and stock market watchers. Sales in 2004 were $50,000,000 and net income should have been $3,000,000. However, in late 2004 management recognized that 2005 would be less successful and they feared that the poorer performance would have a negative effect on Discovery's stock price and management's bonuses. Historically, Discovery had set up an allowance for uncollectable accounts equal to 3% of its year-end accounts receivable. Over the years the 3% estimate had proven to be a reasonable estimate of amounts that would not be collected from customers.

For its December 31, 2004 financial statements, Discovery's management decided to increase the allowance for uncollectable accounts to 4.5% of the ending balance of accounts receivable. Management justified the change in estimate by arguing that it was concerned about the collectability of a number of receivables and as a result, a more conservative allowance for uncollectables was appropriate. Remember from Chapter 5 that conservatism is an easily abused accounting principle. Add to that the bias that exists in GAAP accounting towards conservative measurements and the fact that accounting estimates can be very difficult for auditors to verify, and you have a situation that managers can use to advantage.

By increasing the percentage-of-receivables that was expected to be uncollectable, Discovery's bad debt expense is higher and its net income lower than what would have been reported had Discovery continued to use the 3% estimate. The change in the estimate of uncollectables increased the bad debt expense from $405,000 to $607,500 and decreased net income by $202,500. Table 7-11 provides a partial worksheet for Discovery Ltd. that shows the entries it would have made if it were creating a hidden reserve.

In 2005, as expected, Discovery's performance was not as strong as in 2004. Sales declined to $47,000,000. During 2005, $405,000 of accounts receivable were written off (which turned out to be 3% of the December 31, 2004 accounts receivable). At the end of 2005 management decided that the receivables it was concerned about a year earlier were no longer problems and, accordingly, Discovery would return to the 3% estimate that it had used in previous years. Because only $405,000 of accounts receivable had to be written off during 2005, the balance in the Allowance account, before making the adjusting entry at the end of 2005, was a credit of $202,500. For the Allowance account to have the desired balance of $397,500 at the end of 2005 (representing 3% of the 2005 year-end accounts receivable—$13,250,000 × 3%), the

Table 7-11   Discovery Inc.: Partial Spreadsheet Showing How Hidden Reserves Can Be Used to Manipulate Earnings

The zero balance in the Allowance account means that during 2004 the exact amount of the estimate of bad debts made at December 31, 2003 was written off during 2004.

The pre-adjusting balance in the Bad Debt Expense account is zero because the account would have been closed at the end of 2003 and no entries would be made to the account until the adjusting entries were made.

The balance in Allowance for Doubtful Accounts is equal to 4.5% of closing Accounts Receivable.

	Cash (B/S)	Accounts Receivable (B/S)	Allowance for Doubtful Accounts (B/S)	Revenue (I/S)	Bad Debt Expense (I/S)
31/12/04 (pre-adjusting entries		13,500,000	0		0
31/12/04 adjusting entries			(607,500)		(607,500)
31/12/04 (final)		13,500,000	(607,500)		(607,500)[1]
During 2005					
Sales		47,000,000		47,000,000	
Collections	46,845,000	(46,845,000)			
Bad debts written off		(405,000)	405,000		
31/12/05 (pre-adjusting balances)		13,250,000	(202,500)		
31/12/05 adjusting entries			(195,000)		(195,000)
31/12/05 (final)		13,250,000	(397,500)		(195,000)[1]

During 2005 management writes off $405,000 in receivables that it decides are uncollectable.

[1] The balance in the Bad Debt Expense account would become zero when the closing entry is made. The closing entry is not shown in this example.

The amount that must be added to the allowance account for it to have the desired balance of 3% of year-end accounts receivable at the end of 2005. By making too large an estimate of uncollectables in 2004, the expense required in 2005 is lower than it would have been.

Allowance account would have to be increased by $195,000 and the Bad Debt Expense for 2005 would be $195,000. These entries can be seen in Table 7-11.

Table 7-12 (page 406) compares summarized income statements and accounts receivable information when Discovery creates a hidden reserve with the same information prepared using the 3% estimate for allowance for doubtful accounts in both years. By using a hidden reserve, Discovery Ltd. is able to report a profit increase of $207,500 from 2004 to 2005, an increase of over 7%, instead of a decline in profit of $197,500, a decline of almost 7%. By using a hidden reserve, Discovery is able to show a positive earnings trend rather than a negative trend. Note that total income over the two years is the same under both scenarios. But by altering the allowance for uncollectable accounts, Discovery is able to shift income from 2004 to 2005.

This example is set up to allow you to see how management can use the flexibility of accounting to satisfy its self-interests. The example makes the problem, the motivation, and effect transparent. In reality, users of financial statements cannot see these hidden choices that management makes and it is very difficult to know what

Table 7-12	Discovery Ltd. Extracts from Financial Statements

Discovery Limited
Extracts from the December 31, 2004 and 2005
Financial Statements (in thousands)

	No hidden reserves		Using hidden reserves	
	2004	**2005**	**2004**	**2005**
Revenue	$50,000	$47,000	$50,000	$47,000
Expenses (except bad debts)	46,595	43,800	46,595	43,800
Bad debt expense	405	397.5	607.5	195
Net income	$ 3,000	$ 2,802.5	$ 2,797.5	$ 3,005
Accounts receivable	$13,500	$13,250	$13,500	$13,250
Allowance for uncollectable accounts	405	397.5	607.5	397.5

management's motivation is. This is why these types of manipulations are called hidden reserves.

You might be wondering how preparers can get away with behaviour that is clearly inappropriate ethically, violates the spirit of fair presentation of the financial statements, and, as a result, is inconsistent with GAAP. One of the reasons is that it can be difficult to evaluate the reasonableness of estimates. As long as an estimate falls within a reasonable range and the managers can provide a reasonable explanation for it, a change can be difficult to quarrel with. After all, management knows the entity best, is best able to make estimates, and is responsible for the financial statements.

It is important to emphasize that the problem in the example is not that the estimate of uncollectables changed. The problem is the motivation for the change. For financial statement information to be useful, it must reflect the current economic circumstances. If management were legitimately concerned about the collectability of receivables, then increasing the allowance for uncollectables would be appropriate and would provide useful information to the stakeholders. The problem is that it can be difficult to tell whether management's intention is to provide information or to satisfy its self-interests.

The allowance for uncollectable accounts estimate is only one of many estimates available to management to create hidden reserves. Managers can use estimates like sales returns and warranty liabilities, among many others, to create hidden reserves. The procedure and effect for these other examples is similar to the treatment shown for the allowance for uncollectable accounts. The use of hidden reserves is not limited to public companies only. Many different scenarios could explain why preparers would want to have a "rainy day" fund.

Is this a real problem? Arthur Levitt, chairman of the Securities and Exchange Commission in the United States, commenting on the problems with financial reporting, said:

> Companies stash accruals in "cookie jar" reserves during the good economic times and reach into them when necessary in the bad times."[7]

Mr. Levitt's comments highlight the problem of entities using the flexibility available in GAAP to manage the information reported in their financial statements.

Current and Quick Ratios

In this chapter we examined two of an entity's most liquid assets—cash and receivables. One other liquid asset, temporary investments, will be discussed in Chapter 12. As we have discussed in a number of places in this book, liquidity is a crucial consideration when evaluating an entity. In Chapter 2 we examined the current ratio, an

Question for Consideration

Explain why managers would create hidden reserves and why securities commissions, in the case of public companies, would be so concerned about them.

Answer: Managers create hidden reserves because it gives them the ability to manage earnings and other financial statement numbers in a way that is very difficult for financial statement users to detect. If users are not able to detect management of earnings, then managers are better able to use accounting information to achieve their self-interests. For public companies, hidden reserves can be used to influence investors' perception of the company and possibly its stock price. Hidden reserves would be useful to management in any situation where earnings management would be beneficial—situations such as maximizing management bonuses, avoiding violation of covenants, and so on.

Securities commissions are concerned about the use of hidden reserves by entities because they undermine the integrity of the financial statements. If preparers are able to use hidden reserves to achieve their self-interests, then financial statements will be less useful for communicating with stakeholders and stakeholders will have less confidence in the information.

indicator of an entity's ability to meet its current obligations. The current ratio was defined as current assets divided by current liabilities. A potential problem with the current ratio is that the numerator includes all current assets and all current assets may not be liquid.

Let's look at Mark's Work Wearhouse as an example. Note 5 to MWW's financial statements (page A-53) describes the "Other current assets" that are reported on MWW's balance sheet. These other assets include prepaid expenses, representing items like insurance and rent paid in advance. Property owners are unlikely to return rent paid in advance, and while it might be possible to get a refund on an insurance policy, it would probably be unwise to operate MWW without insurance. The current portion of store opening costs represents costs incurred when new stores were opened. These costs were capitalized and are being amortized over three years; the current portion is the amount that will be expensed during the next year (see Note 1I of MWW's financial statements, page A-50). These store opening costs are not liquid at all. One could also question the liquidity of MWW's inventory. Over 76% of MWW's current assets are inventory and if faced with a cash crunch it may be difficult to convert the inventory to cash quickly. In a pinch MWW could probably sell off inventory to raise cash, but that would still take time.

To compensate for these problems with the current ratio, the **quick** or **acid test ratio** can be used to assess the liquidity of an entity. The quick ratio is a stricter test of an entity's ability to meet its obligations because it excludes less liquid assets such as inventory, prepaids and the current portion of store opening costs. The quick or acid test ratio is defined as

$$\text{Quick ratio} = \frac{\text{Quick assets}}{\text{Current liabilities}} = \frac{\text{Cash} + \text{Cash equivalents} + \text{Temporary investments} + \text{Receivables}}{\text{Current liabilities}}$$

Quick assets are assets that are cash or can or will be realized in cash fairly quickly. For MWW the quick ratio for 2001 is:

$$\text{Quick ratio} = \frac{\$6,993,000 + \$13,998,000}{\$63,222,000} = 0.332$$

MWW's quick ratio may seem quite low, but this is not surprising for a retail business. Retail businesses typically have a lot of money invested in inventory since they have to have enough stock to meet the needs of their customers. However, inventory is usually purchased on credit, so at any time there will usually be significant amounts owing to suppliers. The quick ratio excludes the inventory from the numerator, but includes the liabilities that were incurred to purchase the inventory in the denominator. This situation will result in a low quick ratio. If you examine the financial statements of other retail stores you will find very low quick ratios as well.

A low quick ratio is not necessarily a problem for retail stores, provided that they have reliable cash flows from the sale of the inventory to meet cash needs. Retail stores get into trouble when sales slow down and, as a result, the inflow of cash slows down. The implication is that evaluation of a quick ratio (or any other ratio) must be done in the broader context of the overall financial health of the entity and the economic environment it faces.

Figure 7-2 shows the current and quick ratios for a number of Canadian industries. These ratios are the averages for the firms in the industry over seven years, 1994 through 2000. Notice the wide variation in both ratios across the industries. If the table presented the ratios for each year, you would also see variation within each industry across time and across the companies in each industry.

Accounts Receivable Turnover Ratio

An important responsibility of management is to effectively manage the entity's credit program. The **accounts receivable turnover ratio** is one tool users have to assess how well credit is being managed. The ratio is defined as:

$$\text{Accounts receivable turnover ratio} = \frac{\text{Credit sales}}{\text{Average accounts receivable}}$$

The easiest way to calculate average accounts receivable is to add the balances in the accounts receivable account at the beginning and end of the year and divide by two. For MWW the average for fiscal 2001 would be calculated by taking accounts receivable on January 27, 2001 and January 29, 2000, adding them together, and dividing by two. Using this approach the average accounts receivable would be $14,504,000 ([$13,998,000 + $15,010,000] ÷ 2).

This ratio provides information on how quickly the entity is collecting its receivables. The higher the ratio, the more quickly the entity is collecting its receivables. The term *turnover* means how quickly receivables are collected and replaced by new receivables. An accounts receivable turnover ratio of eight means that the entity incurs, collects, and replaces its receivables eight times a year.

A more intuitive measure can be obtained by dividing the accounts receivable turnover ratio into 365 to give the **average collection period of accounts receivable**.

Figure 7-2

Seven-Year Averages for Current and Quick Ratios for Selected Canadian Industries

Seven-Year Averages (1994-2000) for Several Industries*		
Industry	**Current Ratio**	**Quick Ratio**
Auto, Parts & Transportation Equipment	1.88	0.98
Communications & Media	1.35	0.99
Food & Beverage	2.10	0.97
Gold & Precious Minerals	8.50	7.92
Hospitality	1.69	1.37
Oil & Gas	1.72	1.47
Paper & Forest Products	2.14	1.14
Steel	2.14	0.97
Technology	3.64	2.98
Telephone & Utility	1.11	0.93
Wholesale & Retail	1.76	0.66

*Data taken from the 2001 Industry Reports published by the *Financial Post*.

$$\text{Average collection period of accounts receivable} = \frac{365}{\text{Accounts receivable turnover ratio}}$$

The average collection period of accounts receivable gives the number of days, on average, it takes to collect receivables. Table 7-13 shows the accounts receivable turnover ratio and the average collection period of accounts receivable for MWW for 2001 and 2000.

Table 7-13 shows that from fiscal 2000 to fiscal 2001, the number of days MWW took to collect its receivables declined from 16.46 days to 14.55 days—a decrease of almost two days. On the surface, this is good news because a shorter collection period means that cash is realized more quickly, which shortens the cash cycle. However, a great deal of caution must be exercised when one uses and interprets this ratio. Let's look at some potential problems:

- First, correct application of the ratio requires credit sales. Table 7-13 uses total sales as reported in MWW's income statement because the financial statements of most companies do not provide separate credit and cash sales numbers. For retail businesses like MWW, this can be a problem because a large proportion of its sales are for cash. If the proportions of credit and non-credit sales change from year to year it can be very difficult to interpret the ratio. For many industries, cash sales are a relatively minor part of total sales, so using total sales is less of a problem.

  A quick example will demonstrate the problem. Castor Inc. (Castor) reported total sales in 2003 of $875,000 and in 2004 of $941,000. Average receivables were $132,500 and $150,000 in 2003 and 2004 respectively. Using this information, we find that the accounts receivable turnover ratio was 6.60 in 2003 and 6.27 in 2004. This result indicates that receivables management has deteriorated somewhat over the last two years. Now suppose that we learn that in 2003 credit sales made up $700,000 of the $875,000 total and in 2004 credit sales were $800,000 of the $941,000 total. (Average receivables, of course, would not be affected by this additional information.) Now if we calculate the accounts receivable turnover ratio we find that it was 5.28 in 2003 and 5.33 in 2004—a much more stable situation than was previously found. We would expect the level of the accounts receivable turnover ratio to be different using the two sets of data. However, the trends using the two sets suggest different situations. The reason for the difference is that in 2004 the proportion of credit sales increased to 85% of total sales from 80% in 2003. Without the credit sales information we could easily misinterpret Castor's credit management situation.

- Second, the ratio was calculated using the full amount of accounts receivable reported on the balance sheet and in Note 4. This was probably not appropriate. Note 4 indicates that a significant amount of accounts receivable are not related to sales, including landlord leasehold rebates receivable, co-op advertising receivable, and other accounts receivable. In addition, it is not clear whether

Table 7-13 Mark's Work Wearhouse: Accounts Receivable Turnover Ratio and Average Collection Period of Accounts Receivable

	Average accounts receivable (000)	Sales (000)	Accounts receivable turnover ratio	Average collection period of accounts receivable
For the year ended January 27, 2001	$14,504,000	$363,870,000	25.09	14.55 days
For the year ended January 29, 2000	14,187,000	314,547,000	22.17	16.46 days

amounts due from franchise stores pertain to franchise fees receivable or receivables for merchandise purchased. It would probably make more sense to use the receivables from franchise stores and from business accounts, which would give different accounts receivable turnover ratios.

- Third, using the year-end accounts receivables balances to calculate average receivables may not provide a good estimate of the average for the year. For seasonal businesses, accounts receivable will fluctuate, sometimes significantly, during the year. For example, in fiscal 2001 MWW made almost 38% of its sales during its fourth quarter, and its receivables, at the end of each quarter of the year, ranged from $11,394,000 to $21,458,000. This information is available from MWW's *quarterly financial statements*, which are public documents and available at www.sedar.com. In fact, MWW's average accounts receivable during fiscal 2001 were much higher than the average of the beginning and ending amounts.

- Fourth, the credit terms MWW (and other entities) offers its customers and franchisees are not found in the annual report. The credit terms are a benchmark for evaluating the effectiveness of the entity's collections. Compounding the problem is the fact that an entity may not offer all customers the same credit terms. The actual credit terms offered can serve as benchmarks for evaluating the ratios. For example, a major customer may receive a longer payment period than small customers. If users know that an entity normally gives 30 days to customers to pay, and the customers normally pay in 30 days, the accounts receivable turnover ratio should be about 12 because there would always be one month's credit sales in accounts receivable. The average collection period in this situation would be 30 days.

If a stakeholder is powerful, it will be able to get additional detail to carry out any analysis it deems necessary. For example, an entity's lenders could probably overcome many of the problems described above by requiring that certain information be provided as part of the loan agreement. Despite these limitations, the accounts receivable turnover ratio is a useful tool for assessing an entity's credit management. The limitations may make it difficult to compare different entities, but examining trends for an entity may be a reasonable way to apply this tool. Changes in the ratio will raise questions for further investigation but will likely not provide any definitive answers.

■ Solved Problem

You are provided with the following information about Nuwata Inc.'s (Nuwata) sales and accounts receivable:

1. On October 31, 2005 (Nuwata's year end), the balance sheet reported gross accounts receivable of $27,250 and an allowance for uncollectable accounts of $1,300.

2. During fiscal 2006 Nuwata wrote off $1,100 in bad debts.

3. During fiscal 2006 Nuwata had total sales of $347,000, including cash sales of $52,000.

4. Nuwata uses the percentage-of-credit-sales method for accounting for uncollectable receivables. For 2006 Nuwata's management will base the bad debt expense on 1.2% of credit sales for the year.

5. During fiscal 2006 Nuwata collected $285,000 from customers who purchased merchandise on credit.

6. Nuwata's credit terms require customers to pay outstanding amounts within 30 days of receiving merchandise. For 2005 Nuwata's average collection period of accounts receivable was 37.5 days.

Required:

a. Use an accounting equation spreadsheet to determine the balances in Accounts Receivable and Allowance for Uncollectable Accounts on October 31, 2006, and the bad debt expense for the year ended October 31, 2006.

b. Calculate Nuwata's accounts receivable turnover ratio and the average collection period of accounts receivable for fiscal 2006. Interpret the ratios you calculated.

Solution

a. Spreadsheet results:

	Cash	Accounts receivable	Allowance for uncollectable accounts	Revenue	Bad debt expense
Balances on October 31, 2005		$27,250	($1,300)		
Sales during 2006	$52,000	295,000		$347,000	
Cash collections during 2006	285,000	(285,000)			
Accounts written off during 2006		(1,100)	1,100		
Adjusting entry accruing bad debt expense for 2006			(3,540) [$295,000 × 1.2%]		($3,540)
Balances on October 31, 2006	$337,000	$36,150	($3,740)	$347,000	($3,540)

b. Accounts receivable turnover ratio and average collection of accounts receivable:

$$\text{Accounts receivable turnover ratio} = \frac{\text{Credit sales}}{\text{Average accounts receivable}}$$

$$= \frac{295,000}{(27,250 + 36,150) \div 2}$$

$$= \frac{295,000}{31,700}$$

$$= 9.31$$

$$\text{Average collection period of accounts receivable} = \frac{365}{\text{Accounts receivable turnover ratio}}$$

$$= \frac{365}{9.31}$$

$$= 39.2 \text{ days}$$

Nuwata's collection period has deteriorated from 2005. In 2005 Nuwata, on average, collected its receivables in 37.5 days. This year the collection period has increased by almost two days to 39.2 days. This increase is of concern because it delays the receipt of cash from customers and lengthens the cash cycle. This in turn may impair Nuwata's liquidity.

An increase in the average collection period may occur for a number of reasons:

1. Nuwata may have eased its credit terms, meaning that it grants credit to less credit-worthy customers. Easing credit terms can increase sales, but it comes at the potential cost of increasing the amount that is not collected from customers. This can be a reasonable business strategy for an entity to pursue, but the cost benefit of the strategy must be assessed.

2. Nuwata's internal controls over some aspect of the credit process may not be working effectively. For example, credit may have been given to inappropriate customers or the accounts receivable department may not be following up on unpaid accounts promptly or thoroughly.

3. Existing customers are having difficulty paying their bills, perhaps because of an

economic slowdown in general or because of problems faced by the particular customers.

From the information given, it is not possible to tell what is the cause of the increase in the average collection period. It is necessary to understand the cause before conclusions can be drawn about the implications for stakeholders.

In the case of explanation 1, the increase in the average collection period is reasonable and would be expected under the circumstances. In the case of explanation 2, steps could be taken to tighten the internal controls over credit and collections to ensure that company policies are being followed. Explanation 3 is most problematic. If customers are facing financial problems or if there is an economic downturn, the flow of cash through the whole economy is affected. Nuwata should aggressively pursue the amounts owed to it so that if customers are choosing which suppliers to pay, Nuwata will be one they choose first. Nuwata should also take steps to ensure that it will be able to meet its obligations even if the cash cycle is lengthened.

Summary of Key Points

LO 1. Cash reported on the balance sheet often includes cash equivalents, which includes short-term investments that can be converted into a known amount of cash easily and quickly. Good management requires that there be enough cash available to meet obligations, but not too much so as to result in the inefficient use of the entity's resources.

An important responsibility of management is to protect the entity's assets. Internal controls are the policies and procedures that management implements to protect the entity's assets and ensure the integrity of the accounting information system. Strong internal controls provide assurance to stakeholders that the entity's assets cannot be stolen, used inappropriately, or used without proper authorization, and that the information produced by the accounting system can be relied on. A bank reconciliation is an important internal control for cash.

The amount of cash reported on the balance sheet represents the face value of an entity's cash. GAAP in Canada do not consider changes in the purchasing power of cash. Also, because financial statements are stated in a single currency, cash held in foreign currencies must be translated into Canadian dollars so that they can be reported on the balance sheet.

LO 2. The time value of money is the concept that cash received in the future is not worth as much as the same amount of cash today. The future value of cash flows is the amount of money you will receive in the future by investing it today at a given interest rate. The present value of cash flows is the equivalent value today of money that will be received in the future, discounted to the present at a given discount rate. Present and future value analyses are valuable tools for comparing the values of cash flows that occur at different times and in different amounts.

LO 3. Receivables represent amounts owing to an entity. Under accrual accounting, receivables should be valued at their net realizable value (NRV). This means that uncollectables, discounts, and returns can reduce the amount of cash the entity will actually realize. There are three ways to account for uncollectable amounts:

- the direct write-off method
- the percentage-of-receivables method
- the percentage-of-credit-sales method

The percentage-of-receivables and percentage-of-credit-sales methods are accrual methods that attempt to match the cost of offering credit to customers to the revenue in the period. The direct write-off method does not result in the matching of costs and revenues. The three methods can lead to very different bad debt expenses in a given year, although over the life of an entity the amount expensed will be the same.

LO 4. Hidden reserves are undisclosed accounting choices used to manage earnings and other financial information with the intention of satisfying the self-interests of the preparers. Using hidden reserves is an abuse of accounting information and they undermine the usefulness and credibility of financial statements. Two factors contribute to the existence of hidden reserves: the need for estimates, which are subjective and require the judgment of management, and the fact that many of the estimates that managers make do not have to be disclosed in the financial statements.

LO 5. The current ratio has limitations because current assets often include assets that are not very liquid. The quick or acid test ratio, which is defined as quick assets ÷ current liabilities, is sometimes used to overcome this problem by including only liquid assets in the numerator of the ratio. Quick assets include cash, accounts receivable, and temporary investments.

The accounts receivable turnover ratio and the average collection period of accounts receivable are useful tools for assessing how well management is managing the entity's credit program. The accounts receivable turnover ratio is defined as credit sales ÷ average accounts receivable and the average collection period of accounts receivable is defined as 365 days ÷ accounts receivable turnover ratio.

Key Terms

accounts receivable turnover ratio, p. 408

acid test ratio, p. 407

aging schedule, p. 394

allowance for uncollectable accounts, p. 392

annuity, p. 386

average collection period of accounts receivable, p. 408

bank reconciliation, p. 375

compound interest, p. 380

deflation, p. 377

direct write-off method, p. 392

discount rate, p. 382

exchange rate, p. 379

future value, p. 380

hidden reserves, p. 404

inflation, p. 377

internal control, p. 374

outstanding cheque, p. 375

outstanding deposit, p. 375

percentage-of-credit-sales method, p. 397

percentage-of-receivables method, p. 393

present value, p. 380

quick or acid test ratio, p. 407

receivables, p. 388

returned cheque, p. 375

segregation of duties, p. 375

simple interest, p. 380

time value of money, p. 379

Similar Terms

The left column gives alternative terms that are sometimes used for the accounting terms introduced in this chapter, which are listed in the right column.

discounting	**determining present values, p. 380**
interest rate	**discount rate, p. 382**
allowance for doubtful accounts, allowance for bad debts	**allowance for uncollectable accounts, p. 392**

Assignment Materials

Questions

Q7-1. What is meant by the term "internal control"? Why are strong internal controls important to an entity?

Q7-2. What is a bank reconciliation? Why is it important to prepare a bank reconciliation every month when the bank statement is received from the bank? Why should the bank reconciliation be prepared by someone who is not responsible for writing or authorizing cheques or a person not responsible for recording transactions pertaining to the cash account?

Q7-3. What is meant by the term "segregation of duties"? Why is it important for internal control purposes for people who physically handle an asset to not also be responsible for accounting for the asset?

Q7-4. Why is cash considered an unproductive asset?

Q7-5. How is it possible that an entity can have too much cash?

Q7-6. You are examining the financial statements of a company in which you are interested in investing. The company reports a negative balance in the cash account (the cash account on the balance sheet is reported as a negative amount on the asset side of the balance sheet). How would you interpret the negative balance in the cash account?

Q7-7. In August 2005 you received a birthday gift of $500 in cash from a generous uncle. Your uncle wanted you to have the money so that you could enjoy yourself as you were beginning your studies at university. Unfortunately, you lose the $500 in your very messy room in your residence hall. In June 2009, when you graduate, you find the $500 when you clean out your room as you prepare to move out. With respect to the $500, are you as well off on the day you found the $500 as you were on the day you received the $500? Explain your answer.

Q7-8. According to GAAP in Canada, the unit of measure that is used is the *nominal* dollar. What is a nominal dollar? What real economic costs are ignored by using a nominal dollar as the unit of measure, rather than using a unit of measure that takes into consideration the changing purchasing power of a dollar?

Q7-9. What does it mean when cash on an entity's balance sheet is classified as restricted? What are the implications of restricted cash for users of the financial statements?

Q7-10. Why is a certain amount of cash today more valuable than the same amount of cash in the future?

Q7-11. What is the difference between compound interest and simple interest? Would you receive more interest from an investment that pays compound interest or from one that pays simple interest? Explain.

Q7-12. Which investment would be more attractive: 8% per year compounded annually or 8% per year compounded quarterly? Explain.

Q7-13. Explain the terms *present value* and *future value*. Give an example of when each measurement would be appropriate.

Q7-14. What is a "receivable"? How are receivables classified on a balance sheet? What are some of the different types of receivables that can be reported on a balance sheet?

Q7-15. How is the reported liquidity of an entity affected by how it recognizes revenue? Explain. Is the liquidity in an economic rather than an accounting sense affected by how revenue is recognized?

Q7-16. What is the relationship between an account receivable and the income statement? What is the relationship between an account receivable and the revenue recognition criteria discussed in Chapter 4?

Q7-17. What are some of the benefits and drawbacks to a business of offering credit terms to customers? Would a business prefer to do business in cash or on credit? Explain.

Q7-18. Why is the amount reported on a balance sheet for receivables usually not the same as the sum of the amount that customers and other people who owe the entity money have promised to pay?

Q7-19. When a customer makes a purchase from MWW using a credit card such as Visa or MasterCard, why does MWW not include the sale as an account receivable?

Q7-20. What are the three methods available for accounting for uncollectable amounts from customers? Explain each of the three methods.

Q7-21. Why is the direct write-off method of accounting for bad debts not appropriate in accrual accounting or GAAP?

Q7-22. Why is the percentage-of-credit-sales method of accounting for bad debts referred to as an income statement approach, whereas the percentage-of-receivables method is referred to as a balance sheet approach?

Q7-23. Explain why the percentage-of-credit-sales and the percentage-of-receivables methods to not usually give the same bad debt expense or the same balance in the allowance for uncollectable accounts.

Q7-24. If an entity uses the percentage-of-credit-sales method of accounting for uncollectable accounts, what are the effects on the financial statements if the entity consistently uses too low a percentage of credit sales for estimating bad debts? What are the effects on the financial statements if it consistently uses too high a percentage? Consider the effects on both the income statement and the balance sheet.

Q7-25. What is an aging schedule? How is the aging schedule used for calculating the bad debt expense?

Q7-26. How does management decide what percentage of receivables or what percentage of credit sales should be used to calculate the bad debt expense and the balance in the allowance for uncollectables account? Is this a subjective or objective decision? Explain.

Q7-27. How does management decide when to write off an account receivable or some other receivable? Is this an objective or subjective decision? Explain. How can management use the judgment required to decide when to write off a receivable to affect the numbers in the financial statements? Explain.

Q7-28. Canadian GAAP do not require companies to disclose the amount of the bad debt expense or the balance in the allowance for uncollectable accounts. Would this information be useful to users of financial statements? Why do you think some entities would not want to disclose this information?

Q7-29. Verlo Ltd. recently made a $100,000 sale to a customer. Terms of the sale agreement permit the customer to pay the $100,000 in two years. The customer will not have to pay any interest. If Verlo Ltd. recognizes the revenue in the current period, why should the amount of revenue recorded be less than $100,000? Explain.

Q7-30. What is a hidden reserve? Why would management create hidden reserves? Why is it possible for managers to create hidden reserves? Why is the existence of hidden reserves a problem for users of financial statements?

Q7-31. What is the quick or acid test ratio? How does the quick or acid test ratio differ from the current ratio? What would be a better measure of liquidity for a jewellery store, the quick ratio or the current ratio? Explain. What would be a better measure of liquidity for a mine holding a large inventory of gold bouillon, the quick ratio or the current ratio? Explain.

Exercises

E7-1. **(Classifying cash on the balance sheet, LO 1)** For each of the following items, explain whether the amount described should be included in "Cash and Cash Equivalents" on Jelly Inc.'s (Jelly) December 31, 2004 balance sheet:
   a. $22,300 in Jelly's chequing account at the bank.
   b. An investment certificate that will pay $10,000 plus accrued interest on the date it is cashed. The certificate can be cashed at any time by Jelly.
   c. A guaranteed investment certificate that matures on July 15, 2006. Jelly will receive $11,000 when the certificate matures.
   d. $250 kept in the office to pay for incidentals such as office supplies.
   e. $12,500 kept in a savings account at the bank.

f. $7,000 of cheques received from customers in mid-December, 2004, but not yet cashed.

g. $10,000 held by Jelly's lawyer for purposes of paying a particular supplier when equipment ordered is delivered. The supplier required that the lawyer hold the money so that it would be assured of payment. The equipment is due to be delivered in February 2005.

h. $4,200 that is owed by a senior executive. The amount is to be paid on January 5, 2004.

i. £3,000 (British pounds) held in an account at a major British bank.

E7-2.   **(Calculating future values, LO 2)** Calculate the future value in each of the following situations:

a. A senior citizen purchases a Canada Savings Bond for $1,000 that pays 5% interest per year for eight years, compounded annually. How much will the senior citizen receive when the Savings Bond matures in eight years?

b. An investor purchases a long-term investment for $50,000 that pays 8% interest per year for 15 years, compounded semi-annually. How much will the investor receive when the investment matures in 15 years?

c. An entity borrows $25,000 at 12% for three years. Interest and principal must be paid in full in three years, at the end of the term of the loan. How much will the entity have to pay the lender in three years?

d. A parent lends her child $20,000 to help finance his education. The loan bears no interest, but must be repaid in five years. How much will the parent receive from the child in five years?

E7-3.   **(Calculating present values, LO 2)** Answer the following questions:

a. A customer purchases $10,000 of goods. The goods will be paid for in cash in two years. How much revenue should be recorded on the date the goods are delivered, assuming a discount rate of 6%?

b. You are presented with an investment opportunity that will pay you $1,000 in one year, $2,000 in two years, and $3,000 in three years. At a discount rate of 10%, would you pay $5,000 for this investment?

c. A "zero coupon bond" is a type of long-term debt that pays no interest, but simply pays a single amount on the date the bond matures. Your broker offers you a zero coupon bond that will pay $10,000 in 20 years. How much would you pay for the bond today, if your discount rate were 12%?

d. You are presented with an investment opportunity that will pay you $3,000 in one year, $2,000 in two years, and $1,000 in three years. At a discount rate of 8%, what is the maximum amount you would pay for this investment?

E7-4.   **(Calculating the present value of annuities, LO 2)** Answer the following questions:

a. A contest promotes that the winner wins $1,000,000. The $1,000,000 prize is paid in equal installments over 20 years, with the first payment being made one year from the date the contest winner is announced. What is the "real" (present) value of the prize? Assume a discount rate of 8%.

b. You have the option of receiving $100,000 today or $12,000 a year for 15 years, beginning one year from now. If your discount rate is 10%, which would you choose?

c. A store allows you to purchase a new computer for $100 down and $25 a month for 50 months. If the appropriate discount rate is 1% per month, what would be the equivalent cash price today for the computer?

d. An investor can purchase an investment that pays interest of $100 per year for ten years as well as paying the investor $1,000 in the tenth year. If the appropriate discount rate for an investment of this type is 12%, what is the maximum amount that the investor should pay for the investment? (When answering, remember that calculating an annuity only applies to equal payments. In this question, the present value of the additional $1,000 received in the tenth year must be determined separately.)

E7-5. **(Preparing a bank reconciliation, LO 1)** On December 31, 2004 the accounting records of Ivujivik Inc. (Ivujivik) showed a cash balance of $21,550.15. The balance reported in Ivujivik's December 31, 2004 bank statement was $26,508.79. Examination of the bank statement and the accounting records showed the following:

i. Three cheques that had been written and mailed by Ivujivik, and recorded in Ivujivik's accounting records, had not been cashed by the entities to which the cheques had been written. The outstanding cheques were numbers #2117 for $10,505.10, #2118 for $4,375.26, and #2120 for $927.81.

ii. Ivujivik deposited $12,369.09 in cash and cheques to its bank account through a bank machine late on December 31, 2004. The deposits were not recorded by the bank until January 2005 and as a result did not appear in the December 31, 2004 bank statement.

iii. The bank collected $3,110.25 on behalf of Ivujivik from one of Ivujivik's customers. Ivujivik did not record this collection in its accounting records.

iv. Bank service charges for December 2004 were $92. The amount was deducted from Ivujivik's bank account but not recorded in the accounting records.

v. A cheque received from one of Ivujivik's customers was not honoured by the bank because the customer did not have enough money in its bank account to cover the cheque. The amount of the cheque was $1,125.58. Ivujivik had recorded the cheque as a debit to cash when it was deposited.

vi. Ivujivik was paid $19.99 in interest during December. The amount was deposited in Ivujivik's bank account but was not recorded in the accounting records.

vii. The bank made an error by removing $428.10 from Ivujivik's bank account that should have been taken from another entity's bank account.

Required:

a. Prepare a bank reconciliation for December 31, 2004.

b. What amount should Ivujivik report for cash on its December 31, 2004 balance sheet?

c. Prepare any journal entries required as a result of the bank reconciliation and the review of the bank statement.

E7-6. **(Preparing a bank reconciliation, LO 1)** On March 31, 2006 the accounting records of Nenagh Ltd. (Nenagh) showed a cash balance of $1,925.72. The balance reported in Nenagh's March 31, 2006 bank statement was $1,530.79. Examination of the bank statement and the accounting records showed the following:

i. Three cheques that had been written and mailed by Nenagh, and recorded in Nenagh's accounting records, had not been cashed by the entities to which the cheques had been written. The outstanding cheques were numbers #455 for $195.25, #459 for $88.88, and #461 for $12.55.

ii. Nenagh deposited $875.61 in cash and cheques to its bank account through a bank machine late on March 31, 2006. The deposits were not recorded by the bank until April 2006 and as a result did not appear in the March 31, 2006 bank statement.

iii. The bank collected $225.00 on behalf of Nenagh from one of Nenagh's customers. Nenagh did not record this collection in its accounting records.

iv. Bank service charges for March 2006 were $21. The amount was deducted from Nenagh's bank account but not recorded in the accounting records.

v. A cheque received from one of Nenagh's customers was not honoured by the bank because the customer did not have enough money in its bank account to cover the cheque. The amount of the cheque was $96.68. Nenagh had recorded the cheque as a debit to cash when it was deposited.

vi. The bank made an error by depositing $56.69 to Nenagh's bank account that should have been deposited to another account.

Required:

a. Prepare a bank reconciliation for March 31, 2006.

b. What amount should Nenagh report for cash on its March 31, 2006 balance sheet?

c. Prepare any journal entries required as a result of the bank reconciliation and the review of the bank statement.

E7-7.   **(Understanding the bank reconciliation, LO 1)** A new accounting clerk for Everell Ltd. (Everell) has been asked to prepare a preliminary bank reconciliation for the current month. The clerk is having some trouble with some of the items. Indicate whether each of the following items would be added to or subtracted from the entity's cash account, or added to or subtracted from the balance on the bank statement when preparing a bank reconciliation. Also indicate if any of the items should not be included in the bank reconciliation. Explain each of your choices.

a. Interest was withdrawn from Everell's account to cover the monthly interest cost of the company's bank loan. The amount was not accrued in the accounting records.

b. Several cheques that Everell had written and mailed had not yet been cashed.

c. The bank made an error by depositing money to Everell's bank account that should have been deposited to another company's account.

d. Late in the month, Everell deposited money to its bank account through a bank machine, but the amount was not recorded by the bank until the next month.

e. An automatic withdrawal was made from Everell's bank account to cover a monthly utility charge. The withdrawal was not recorded in the accounting records.

f. An automatic withdrawal was made from Everell's bank account to cover a monthly insurance charge. The withdrawal was recorded in the accounting records.

g. Cheques were returned by the bank because the entities that gave the cheques to Everell did not have enough money in their bank accounts to cover them.

h. The bank deducted its monthly service charge from the account.

i. Fifty cheques were written during the month and mailed and recorded in the accounting system. All of these cheques were cashed by the bank.

E7-8.   **(Basic journal entries, LO 3)** Prepare the journal entries necessary to record the following transactions and economic events for Sahali Ltd. (Sahali):

a. During 2005 Sahali had cash sales of $175,000 and credit sales of $625,000.

b. During 2005 $405,000 of accounts receivable were collected.

c. Management estimated that 5% of credit sales would not be collected.

d. During 2006 Sahali wrote off $34,000 of accounts receivables.

E7-9.   **(Writing off an account receivable, LO 3)** Malagash Ltd. (Malagash) recently learned that a major customer would be permanently shutting down its operations within 30 days. The reason for the shut-down was not clear, but Malagash's management assumed that there were probably financial problems underlying the decision. As of Malagash's year end it was not clear whether it would receive any of the $50,000 owed to it by the customer. Despite the uncertainty regarding collection, Malagash's management decided that it would write off the $50,000 receivable in the current fiscal year.

Required:

a. Prepare the journal entry that Malagash would prepare if it were using the direct write-off method of accounting for uncollectable amounts. What would be the effect on net income of the entry?

b. Prepare the journal entry that Malagash would prepare if it were using the percentage-of-credit-sales method of accounting for uncollectable amounts. What would be the effect on net income of the entry?

c. Prepare the journal entry that Malagash would prepare if it were using the percentage-of-receivables method of accounting for uncollectable amounts. What would be the effect on net income of the entry?

d. Why do you think that Malagash decided to write off the receivable in the current fiscal year, even though it did not know whether it would be paid or not?

In answering, consider accounting principles and the objectives of accounting.

E7-10. **(Accounting for long-term receivables, LO 2, 3)** On May 31, 2005 Namaka Ltd. (Namaka) sold an office building to Audy Inc. (Audy) for $15,000,000. The sale agreement required that Audy pay $3,000,000 to Namaka on May 31, 2005, and then $4,000,000 on each of May 31, 2006, 2007, and 2008. Namaka decided to recognize the sale of the building in the year ended May 31, 2005.

Required:

    a. How much revenue should Namaka recognize as a result of its sale of the office building to Audy? Prepare the journal entry that Namaka should prepare to record the sale. Assume a discount rate of 12%.

    b. How much interest revenue will be reported on Namaka's income statement for the years ended May 31, 2006, 2007, and 2008 as a result of the sale to Audy? Prepare the journal entry that should be prepared each year to record the interest revenue.

    c. How much would be reported as receivable from Audy on Namaka's balance sheets for the years ended May 31, 2005, 2006, 2007, and 2008? How would the receivable be classified on each year's balance sheet? Explain your answer.

    d. Suppose Namaka insisted on recognizing $15,000,000 as revenue in 2005. What would be the implications for users of its financial statements? Why might Namaka's management want to report the full $15,000,000 immediately?

E7-11. **(Calculating accounts receivable, LO 3)** Use an accounting equation spreadsheet and the following information to calculate accounts receivable on December 31, 2004:

	December 31,	
	2004	**2003**
Accounts receivable		$61,250
Allowance for uncollectable accounts	$ (3,960)	(3,210)
Unearned revenue	18,200	25,500
Revenue recognized during 2004*	431,500	
Payments of accounts receivable during 2004	385,000	
Bad debt expense for 2004	4,150	
Cash received from customers for services to be provided in the future during 2004	14,200	
Amount of accounts receivable written off during 2004	3,400	

*Includes recognition of revenue classified as unearned in previous periods. All other revenue is on credit.

E7-12. **(Calculating the bad debt expense and the allowance for uncollectable accounts, LO 3)** You are provided with the following information about Nyanza Corp.:

    i.   Accounts Receivable on December 31, 2005 = $575,000.

    ii. Sales during the year ended December 31, 2005 = $4,525,000 (all sales are on credit).

    iii. Accounts Receivable written off during 2005 = $79,200.

    iv. Balance in Allowance for Uncollectable Accounts on December 31, 2004 = $76,300.

    v. Historically, an average of 2% of credit sales has been uncollectable.

Required:

Calculate Nyanza's bad debt expense for the year ended December 31, 2005 and the allowance for uncollectable accounts on December 31, 2005, and prepare the journal entry that should be prepared to record the bad debt expense.

E7-13. **(The effect of errors on net income, LO 3)** Capstick Ltd. (Capstick) uses the percentage-of-credit-sales method of estimating the bad debt expense. Since 2000 Capstick has used too low a percentage in calculating the bad debt expense each year. In 2004 management realized the error and decided to make an adjusting entry to correct it. Credit sales every year from 2000 through 2004 were $500,000. Capstick determined the bad debt expense using 2% of net income as the basis of its estimate each year. Management decides it will use 2.3% beginning in 2005. Capstick has written off $11,500 of accounts receivable each year from 2000 through 2004. The balance in the allowance account on January 1, 2000 (the first day of Capstick's fiscal year) was $11,500.

a. What bad debt expense did Capstick record in each year from 2000 to 2004?
b. What was the effect on net income each year of using too low a bad debt expense estimate?
c. What was the balance in the allowance account at the end of each year?
d. What effect does correcting the error have on net income in 2004?
e. Prepare the journal entry that Capstick would make in 2004 to correct the error and leave an appropriate balance in the allowance account. Assume the adjusting entry to correct the error is made after the entry to record the 2004 bad debt expense.

E7-14. **(Comparing the percentage-of-receivables and percentage-of-credit-sales methods, LO 3)** The following information has been obtained about Elzevir Inc. (Elzevir) for 2004. The information was obtained before any year-end adjusting entries were made. Elzevir's year end is March 31:

Accounts receivable on March 31, 2004	$ 525,000
Credit sales for the year ended March 31, 2004	3,120,500
Allowance for uncollectable accounts on March 31, 2004 (credit balance)	3,750

Required:

a. Calculate the bad debt expense that Elzevir would record for the 2004 fiscal year, assuming that management expects that 6% of year-end accounts receivable will not be collected. What would be the balance in Allowance for Uncollectable Accounts on March 31, 2004? Prepare the journal entry to record the bad debt expense.
b. Calculate the bad debt expense that Elzevir would record for the 2004 fiscal year, assuming that management expects that 1.5% of credit sales during fiscal 2004 will not be collected. What would be the balance in Allowance for uncollectable accounts on March 31, 2004? Prepare the journal entry to record the bad debt expense.
c. What would your answers in (a) and (b) be if the balance in Allowance for Uncollectable Accounts on March 31, 2004 (before any year-end adjusting entries) was a debit of $3,750? Explain any differences you find.

E7-15. **(Using an aging schedule to calculate the bad debt expense, LO 3)** Pipestone Ltd. (Pipestone) uses an aging schedule to estimate the amount of receivables that will not be collected. Pipestone allows its customers up to 60 days to pay amounts owed. Any receivable outstanding for more than 60 days is considered overdue. Based on historical information, management estimates that it will collect 98% of current accounts receivable, 92% of receivables overdue by between 1 and 30 days, 80% of receivables overdue by between 31 and 90 days, and 50% of receivables overdue by more than 90 days. Management has provided you with the following aged receivable schedule:

Account age	**Balance on January 31, 2005**
Current	$175,000
1-30 days overdue	72,000
31-90 days overdue	32,100
More than 90 days overdue	14,700

The balance in Allowance for Uncollectable Accounts before the period-end adjusting entry is made is a debit of $2,700.

Required:

    a. What amount of closing accounts receivable is estimated to be uncollectable on January 31, 2005?

    b. Prepare the journal entry required to record the bad debt expense for Pipestone for the year ended January 31, 2005.

E7-16. **(Compute the accounts receivable turnover ratio and the average collection period for accounts receivable, LO 5)** The following information was obtained from Acamac Corp.'s (Acamac) 2004 financial statements:

Sales (all sales are on credit)	$3,234,000
Accounts receivable on December 31, 2004	410,000
Accounts receivable on December 31, 2003	375,000

Required:

    a. Calculate Acamac's accounts receivable turnover ratio for 2004.

    b. Calculate the average collection period for accounts receivable during 2004.

    c. Is Acamac's average collection period for 2004 reasonable? What information would you require to answer this question? Explain.

E7-17. **(Correcting the balance in Allowance for Uncollectable Accounts, LO 3)** Trilby Inc. (Trilby) uses the percentage-of-credit-sales method for estimating its bad debt expense. The percentage that Trilby uses is based on historical information. Trilby's management has not revised the percentage for several years, a period during which a number of environmental and business factors have changed. Trilby's management recently realized that over the last three years, the percentage of credit sales that the company used was too high. As a result, the balance in Allowance for Uncollectable Accounts is $53,000 higher than it would have been had a better estimate of bad debts been used each year.

Required:

    a. Prepare the adjusting journal entry that Trilby must make to have an appropriate balance in Allowance for Uncollectable Accounts.

    b. What is the effect of the error in estimating bad debts in each of the years the error is made? What is the effect of the adjusting entry on net income? Answer the question by comparing the reported net income with what net income would have been had the error not been made and the adjusting entry not required.

    c. What is the impact of this error and the adjusting entry on the users of the financial statements? Explain fully.

E7-18. **(Identifying quick assets, LO 5)** Which of the following assets would you classify as quick assets for purposes of calculating the quick ratio? Explain your reasoning.

    a. Accounts receivable

    b. Prepaid insurance

    c. Current portion of a long-term note receivable

    d. Interest receivable

    e. Inventory of gold bars

    f. An investment certificate that matures in 12 months

    g. Inventory of gravel

    h. Shares in Mark's Work Wearhouse

    i. A term deposit that matures in one month

E7-19. **(Compute current and quick ratios, LO 5)** Following are the balance sheets for the years ended June 30, 2005 and 2006 for Seahorse Inc.:

Seahorse Inc.
Balance Sheets
As of June 30, 2005 and 2006

Assets	2006	2005	Liabilities and Shareholders' Equity	2006	2005
Current assets			*Current liabilities*		
Cash and cash			Accounts payable	$ 70,000	$ 69,500
equivalents	$ 38,000	$ 42,000	Accrued liabilities	12,000	19,000
Accounts receivable	95,000	58,000	Unearned revenue	10,000	12,000
Inventory	110,000	98,000	Current portion of		
Prepaids	8,100	7,500	long-term debt	45,000	60,000
Current assets	251,100	205,500	Current liabilities	137,000	160,500
Capital assets (net)	372,900	410,000	Long-term debt	110,000	155,000
			Capital stock	165,000	125,000
			Retained earnings	212,000	175,000
			Total liabilities and		
Total assets	$624,000	$615,500	shareholders' equity	$624,000	$615,500

Required:

a. Calculate the current ratio and the quick ratio on June 30, 2005 and 2006.

b. Assess the change in the liquidity position of Seahorse Inc.

c. Can you think of any circumstances where a significant increase in the quick ratio could be an indicator of a deteriorating liquidity position?

E7-20. **(Working with the accounts receivable turnover ratio, LO 5)** During 2004 Oderin Inc. (Oderin) reported revenue of $2,356,000. Oderin's accounts receivable turnover ratio for 2004 was 5.18. What was Oderin's average amount of accounts receivable during 2004?

Problems

P7-1. **(Thinking about internal controls, LO 1)** For the following two scenarios, describe what you think are the weaknesses in the internal controls and explain the implications of the weaknesses:

a. The administrative assistant to the corporate controller keeps a cash box with up to $500 of company money in her desk so that she can pay for incidental expenses as they occur. These expenses include paying couriers, reimbursing other employees for expenditures that they made on behalf of the company, paying for food ordered for meetings and people who work late, and so on. The cash is kept in a locked box in a locked drawer in the administrative assistant's desk. The cash in the box is replaced when the administrative assistant tells the corporate controller that more is required. The administrative assistant has been with the company for over 20 years and is highly respected and trusted by all members of senior management.

b. A religious centre collects cash contributions from people who attend services. The cash is stored in the religious centre's office in an unlocked drawer until later in the week, when the volunteer treasurer takes the money and deposits it in the centre's bank account. The office is located near the entrance to the religious centre and visitors to the centre usually go to the office. Many of the members of the religious centre know where the money is stored because they have filled volunteer positions and so are familiar with the procedures the centre follows.

P7-2. **(Thinking about internal controls, LO 1)** For the following two scenarios, describe what you think are the weaknesses in the internal controls and explain the implications of the weaknesses:

a. A travelling amusement park hires people in the towns the park visits to operate the rides on the midway. A person hired is given full responsibility for the ride.

Responsibility includes collecting cash from the people who want to take the ride, making sure people get on and off the rides safely, and operating the ride. At the end of the day the person gives the cash collected from customers over to the park manager.

b. Because of its small size, Hochelaga Ltd. has only one person, Mathew Jordan, in its accounting department. For accounts payable, Mr. Jordan is responsible for ensuring that goods and services that had been ordered are received, authorizing payments to suppliers, preparing cheques, and entering transactions into the accounting system. He also prepares the bank reconciliation. The owner of the company signs all cheques and frequently reviews Mr. Jordan's work. The owner is often out of the country on business, sometimes for up to two weeks. Office staff are always aware of when the owner will be returning.

P7-3.   **(Time value of money calculations, LO 2)** For each of the following situations, do the calculations necessary to make a decision:

a. An entity purchases equipment for $50,000. The entity pays $10,000 on the delivery date, $15,000 one year from the delivery date, and $25,000 two years from the delivery date. How much should the entity record as the cost of the equipment? The purchase agreement does not require that the entity pay interest.

b. A woman saving for her retirement invests $10,000 in a long-term investment certificate. The certificate pays 7% interest per year compounded annually for 20 years. How much money will the woman receive when she retires in 20 years?

c. An investment promises to pay investors $10,000 per year for 10 years. The first payment will be received one year from the date the investment is made. If an investor has a discount rate of 10%, what is the maximum amount that the investor should pay for the investment?

d. A company borrows $1,000,000 for five years from a group of lenders. The company does not have to pay interest each year but must pay the principal and interest back at the end of the loan term. Assuming an interest rate of 8%, how much will the company have to give the lenders when the loan comes due in five years?

e. Would you prefer to receive $14,000 today, $25,000 in five years, or $4,000 at the end of each of the next five years? Assume a discount rate of 12%.

P7-4.   **(Analyzing changes to credit policy, LO 3, 5)** Magundy Inc. (Magundy) imports high-end merchandise from Europe and distributes it to retailers across eastern Canada. Magundy has tended to be very conservative in managing its operations. In late 2005 the shareholders of Magundy decided that they were not satisfied with the performance and growth of the company, and they decided to replace the president with a younger, more aggressive person whom they believed would be better able meet their performance and growth objectives.

In early 2006 the new president decided that Magundy had been too cautious in granting credit to customers and he implemented a new credit policy that significantly increased the number of retailers who would be able carry Magundy's merchandise. The new president thought that the new credit policy would increase sales significantly, which would meet the objectives of the owners. The new credit policy allowed businesses that were considered higher credit risks (customers that were more likely to not pay their debts) to obtain credit from Magundy. The new credit policy also allowed all customers more time to pay Magundy for purchases.

By the end of 2006, it appeared that the new president's strategy was working. Sales during the year had increased 20% over the previous year, to $2,395,000.

Required

You have been asked by the shareholders to prepare a report evaluating certain aspects of Magundy's performance during 2006. Your report should consider the following:

a. What should be Magundy's bad debt expense for 2006? In previous years

Magundy calculated its bad debt expense based on 2% of credit sales during the year. Explain your answer.

b. How would you expect Magundy's accounts receivable turnover ratio to change from 2005 to 2006? Explain.

c. How would the new credit strategy affect Magundy's liquidity?

d. Do you think the new president's credit strategy is a good one? What are the risks and benefits of the new strategy?

P7-5.   **(Comparing the effects of different methods of accounting for bad debts, LO 3)**
You have obtained the following information about Eskasoni Inc. (Eskasoni) from the company's 2005 annual report:

i.   Eskasoni's year end is November 30.

ii. Sales for the year ended November 30, 2005 were $4,235,000; 90% of sales are credit sales.

iii. The balance in Accounts Receivable on November 30, 2005 was $610,000.

iv. The balance in Allowance for Uncollectable Accounts on November 30, 2004 was $48,000.

v.   During fiscal 2005, Eskasoni wrote off $42,000 of accounts receivable.

vi. The bad debt expense can be estimated as 1.5% of credit sales or 9.5% of year-end accounts receivable.

vii. Net income for the year ended November 30, 2005, including all revenues and expenses except for the bad debt expense, was $250,000.

Required:

a. Determine the bad debt expense for the year ended 2005, assuming that Eskasoni used:
   i.   the direct-write-off method for accounting for uncollectable accounts.
   ii. the percentage-of-credit-sales method for accounting for uncollectable accounts.
   iii. the percentage-of-receivables method for accounting for uncollectable accounts.

b. What would be the balance in Allowance for Uncollectable Accounts on November 30, 2005 using the three methods identified in part (a)?

c. Prepare the journal entry required to record the bad debt expense under each of the three methods identified in part (a).

d. What would net income be for 2005 under each of the three methods identified in part (a)?

e. Explain why the three methods identified in part (a) provide different bad debt expenses.

f. Which method of determining the bad debt expense and the allowance for uncollectable accounts is best? Explain.

P7-6.   **(Comparing the effects of different methods of accounting for bad debts, LO 3)**
You have obtained the following information about Dogwood Inc. (Dogwood) from the company's 2005 annual report:

i.   Dogwood's year end is April 30.

ii. Sales for the year ended April 30, 2005 were $1,500,000; 80% of sales are credit sales.

iii. The balance in Accounts Receivable on April 30, 2005 was $290,000.

iv. The balance in Allowance for Uncollectable Accounts on April 30, 2004 was $27,000.

v.   During fiscal 2005 Dogwood wrote off $36,000 of accounts receivable.

vi. The bad debt expense can be estimated as 2.5% of credit sales or 10% of year-end accounts receivable.

vii. Net income for the year ended April 30, 2005, including all revenues and expenses except for the bad debt expense, was $90,000.

Required:

a. Determine the bad debt expense for the year ended 2005, assuming that Dogwood used:

    i. the direct-write-off method for accounting for uncollectable accounts.

    ii. the percentage-of-credit-sales method for accounting for uncollectable accounts.

    iii. the percentage-of-receivables method for accounting for uncollectable accounts.

b. What would be the balance in Allowance for Uncollectable Accounts on April 30, 2005 using the three methods identified in part (a)?

c. Prepare the journal entry required to record the bad debt expense under each of the three methods identified in part (a).

d. What would net income be for 2005 under each of the three methods identified in part (a)?

e. Explain why the three methods identified in part (a) provide different bad debt expenses.

f. Which method of determining the bad debt expense and the allowance for uncollectable accounts is best? Explain.

P7-7. **(Observing the effect of errors in estimating the bad debt expense and the allowance of uncollectable accounts on the financial statements, LO 3, 4)** Since 2002 Kyuquot Inc. (Kyuquot) has estimated that its bad debt expense would be approximately 3% of credit sales each year. In late 2003 Kyuquot made a number of changes to its internal control procedures that increased the effectiveness of its credit granting and receivables collection. As a result, in 2004 uncollectables decreased to about 2% of credit sales. However, the accounting department never bothered to lower the 3% rate that had been implemented in 2002.

The following information is also available about Kyuquot's receivables and bad debts:

i. Kyuquot's year end is December 31.

ii. The balance in Kyuquot's allowance account on January 1, 2002 was $19,600.

iii. Credit sales and write-offs by year and accounts receivable on December 31 of each year were:

Year	Credit sales made during the year	Accounts receivable written off during the year	Accounts receivable on December 31
2002	$ 750,000	$19,600	$275,000
2003	825,000	22,550	350,000
2004	930,000	21,000	475,000
2005	1,050,000	29,450	510,000
2006	1,195,000	29,070	625,000
2007	1,300,000	38,125	700,000

Required:

a. Calculate Kyuquot's bad debt expense in each year from 2002 through 2007.

b. Calculate the balance in Allowance for Uncollectable Accounts on December 31 of each year, after the adjusting entry recording the bad debt expense for the year was made.

c. Examine the balance in the allowance account over the period from 2002 through 2007. Explain what is happening to the allowance account as a result of using a percentage of credit sales that is consistently too high. (To answer, it may help to look at the balance in the allowance account as a percentage of Accounts Receivable.)

d. What is the effect on income each year of using a percentage of credit sales that is consistently too large? Explain.

e. What is the net amount of accounts receivable (accounts receivable – allowance for uncollectables) on Kyuquot's balance sheet on December 31, 2007? Does the balance on the balance sheet represent the net realizable value of the accounts receivable on December 31, 2007? Explain.

f. What would the balance in the allowance account be on December 31, 2007, after the adjusting entry for bad debts is made, if Kyuquot expensed 2% of credit sales as bad debts beginning in 2007?

g. Suppose that in 2007 management become aware of the error it was making estimating bad debts each year by using 3% of credit sales instead of 2%. What journal entry would Kyuquot have to make to reduce the balance in the allowance account to $35,000? What would be the effect of this journal entry on net income in 2007? What are some of the implications of these errors on users of the financial statements?

P7-8. **(The effect of transactions on ratios, LO 1, 3, 5)** Complete the following table by indicating whether each transaction results in an increase, a decrease, or has no effect on the financial ratios identified in the table. Assume that the current and quick ratios are greater than 1.0 before each of the items is considered.

	Transaction	Current ratio	Quick ratio	Accounts receivable turnover ratio	Average collection period of accounts receivable
1.	Collection of accounts receivable				
2.	Recording the bad debt expense				
3.	Writing off an uncollectable account				
4.	Credit sale				
5.	Cash sale				
6.	Purchase of inventory on credit				
7.	A new bank loan				
8.	Reclassification of a long-term receivable as current (because it will come due within 12 months)				

P7-9. **(Determine missing information, LO 5)** Use the information provided to determine the values for the missing information (indicated by screened boxes):

Current assets on December 31, 2004 = $925,000

Current ratio on December 31, 2004 = 1.32

Current liabilities on December 31, 2004 = $

Quick assets on December 31, 2004 = $210,000

Quick ratio on December 31, 2004 =

Accounts receivable on December 31, 2004 = $175,000

Accounts receivable on December 31, 2003 = $

Revenues (all on credit) during 2004 = $1,124,000

Average collection period of accounts receivable for 2004 = 47 days

Accounts receivable turnover ratio for 2004 =

P7-10. **(Determine missing information, LO 5)** Use the information provided to determine the values for the missing information (indicated by screened boxes):

Current assets on December 31, 2005 = $

Current ratio on December 31, 2005 = 1.25

Current liabilities on December 31, 2005 = $121,000

Quick assets on December 31, 2005 = $

Quick ratio on December 31, 2005 = 0.70

Accounts receivable on December 31, 2005 = $▨▨▨▨

Accounts receivable on December 31, 2004 = $45,000

Revenues (all on credit) during 2005 = $254,000

Average collection period of accounts receivable for 2005 = ▨▨▨▨

Accounts receivable turnover ratio for 2005 = 4.84

P7-11. **(The effect of transactions on ratios, LO 3, 5)** For the year ended December 31, 2004 Alpena Inc. (Alpena) had revenues (all on credit) of $2,456,000. Its average collection period of accounts receivable for 2004 was 62 days. Accounts receivable on December 31, 2004 was $420,000.

Calculate the effect on average collection period of accounts receivable and the accounts receivable turnover ratio if the following additional transactions occurred during 2004. Consider the effect of each transaction or economic event separately.
a. Alpena, which uses the percentage-of-credit-sales method of estimating the bad debt expense, wrote off an additional $7,000 of accounts receivable.
b. Alpena collected an additional $80,000 of accounts receivable from customers.
c. Alpena recognized additional cash revenue of $125,000.
d. Alpena recognized additional credit revenue of $125,000.

P7-12. **(Accounting for long-term receivables, LO 2, 3)** On July 31, 2005 Romanace Ltd. (Romanace) agreed to sell Youbou Inc. (Youbou) $1,500,000 of specialized equipment for use at its newly developed mine site in northern Manitoba. Because the mine had not yet begun to produce any metal, Youbou negotiated that it would pay for the equipment on August 6, 2007, at which time the mine would be generating the cash flow required to pay Romanace. Despite the fact that Romanace would not be receiving its cash for two years, it decided to recognize the revenue from the sale during the year ended July 31, 2005. The agreement between Romanace and Youbou states that Youbou does not have to pay any interest on the amount owed.

Required:

Use a spreadsheet similar to the one in Table 7-10 (page 403) to answer the following:
a. How much revenue should Romanace recognize in the year ended July 31, 2005 for the sale to Youbou? Prepare the journal entry that Romanace should prepare to record the sale. Assume a discount rate of 10%.
b. What amount would be reported on Romanace's July 31, 2005 balance sheet for accounts receivable as a result of the sale to Youbou? How would the receivable from Youbou be shown in the balance sheet? Explain your answer.
c. How much interest revenue would Romanace report on its July 31, 2006 income statement as a result of the sale to Youbou? Prepare the journal entry that Romanace would make to record the interest revenue. What amount would be shown as receivable from Youbou on Romanace's July 31, 2006 balance sheet? How would the receivable from Youbou be classified on the balance sheet?
d. How much interest revenue would Romanace report on its July 31, 2007 income statement as a result of the sale to Youbou? Prepare the journal entry that Romanace would make to record the interest revenue. What amount would be shown as receivable from Youbou on Romanace's July 31, 2007 balance sheet? How would the receivable from Youbou be classified on the balance sheet?
e. What journal entry would Romanace make when it received payment in full on August 6, 2007?

P7-13. **(Using an aging schedule to calculate the bad debt expense, LO 3)** Examine the following information about Weyakwin Inc. (Weyakwin):
i. Ending balance in Allowance for Uncollectable Accounts on April 30, 2005 = $16,950 (credit balance).

ii. Accounts receivable written off during the year ended April 30, 2006 = $14,500.

iii. Aging schedule for accounts receivable outstanding on April 30, 2006:

Account age	Balance on April 30, 2006	Percent estimated to be uncollectable
Current	$72,000	3%
1-30 days overdue	28,000	6%
31-60 days overdue	15,000	12%
61-120 days overdue	10,000	40%
More than 120 days overdue	15,000	80%

Required:

a. What amount of closing accounts receivable is estimated to be uncollectable on April 30, 2006?

b. Prepare the journal entry required to record the bad debt expense for Weyakwin for the year ended April 30, 2006.

c. What are some possible explanations for the change in the allowance account between April 30, 2005 and April 30, 2006?

P7-14. **(Correcting the balance in Allowance for Uncollectable Accounts, LO 3)** Trilby Inc. (Trilby) uses the percentage-of-credit-sales method for estimating its bad debt expense. The percentage that Trilby uses is based on historical information. Trilby's management has not revised the percentage for several years, a period during which a number of environmental and business factors have changed. Trilby's management recently realized that over the last three years the percentage of credit sales that the company used was too high. As a result, the balance in Allowance for Uncollectable Accounts is $53,000 higher than it would have been had a better estimate of bad debts been used each year.

Required:

a. Prepare the adjusting journal entry that Trilby must make to have an appropriate balance in allowance for uncollectable accounts.

b. What is the effect of the error in estimating bad debts in each of the years the error was made? What is the effect of the adjusting entry on net income? Answer the question by comparing the reported net income with what net income would have been had the error not been made and the adjusting entry not required.

c. What is the impact of this error and the adjusting entry on the users of the financial statements? Explain fully.

P7-15. **(Managing accounts receivable, LO 5)** A financial analyst is comparing the credit management of two companies, Zealand Inc. (Zealand) and Manotick Ltd. (Manotick). The two companies are in the same industry, but operate in different parts of the country. Through conversations with representatives of each of the companies, the analysts learned that Zealand gives its customers 45 days to pay for purchases, while Manotick gives its customers 60 days to pay. By examining the companies' financial statements, the analyst found that during 2004 Zealand had revenues of $2,475,000, of which 82% were on credit, while Manotick had revenues of $2,950,000, of which 74% were on credit. Average accounts receivable during 2004 were $286,000 for Zealand and $490,000 for Manotick.

Required:

a. Calculate the accounts receivable turnover ratio for Zealand and Manotick.

b. Calculate the average collection period of accounts receivable for Zealand and Manotick.

c. Which company does a better job managing its receivables? Explain.

P7-16. **(Creating hidden reserves, LO 4)** The president of Remo Ltd. (Remo) wants to use hidden reserves to "save" income for a year when the company is not performing very well. To accomplish this objective, the president instructed the accounting department to over-estimate the bad debt expense each year. Instead of using the historical norm of 1.5% of credit sales, the president suggested using 1.75% of credit sales. Remo commenced this "policy" in 2004 and it has continued through 2008, a period in which Remo has been very successful. The following information about Remo is available:

	2004	2005	2006	2007	2008
Credit sales	$2,527,000	$3,158,750	$3,632,563	$4,286,424	$4,929,387
Net income, excluding the bad debt expense	232,484	315,875	345,093	398,637	443,645
Accounts receivable write-offs	31,500	37,905	47,381	54,488	64,296

The balance in Remo's Allowance for Uncollectable Accounts on January 1, 2004 was $31,500.

Required:

a. Prepare a table that shows:
   i.   Remo's bad debt expense from 2004 through 2008 using the 1.5% rate.
   ii. Remo's bad debt expense from 2004 through 2008 using the 1.75% rate.
   iii. The Allowance for Uncollectable Accounts at the end of each year using each of the estimates.
   iv. Net income for each year using each of the two estimates.
b. How could the president of Remo justify using the 1.75% rate for estimating bad debts?
c. In 2009 Remo's net income fell slightly and the president was concerned about a negative response from shareholders and creditors. He was especially concerned that Remo was planning to approach new equity investors to invest in Remo. Credit sales during 2009 were $5,191,000 and net income, excluding the bad debt expense, for the year was $441,410. At this point the president "recognized" the error that had been made over the previous five years and decided it was time to correct it. The president instructed the accounting department to reduce the balance in the Allowance account to the level that would have existed had Remo used 1.5% of credit sales as the basis of calculating the bad debt expense each year.
   i.   What journal entry would be prepared to reduce the balance in the Allowance account to the desired level?
   ii. What would be the effect on net income of making this journal entry?
d. Why are hidden reserves a serious problem that undermines the integrity and usefulness of accounting information?

Using Financial Statements

High Liner Foods Incorporated

High Liner Foods Incorporated (High Liner) is a Canadian publicly traded company in the business of processing and marketing superior quality seafood, frozen pasta, and other food products in North America. The company owns High Liner, the number one seafood brand in Canada; Fisher Boy, its leading frozen seafood brand in the United States and Mexico; and Gina Italian Village, its frozen stuffed pasta brand, which is number one in its core United States markets.[8]

www.highlinerfoods.com

High Liner's consolidated balance sheets and consolidated statements of earnings, along with some extracts from the notes to the financial statements are provided in Exhibit 7-6 (page 430). Use this information to respond to questions FS7-1 to FS7-9.

FS7-1. How much does High Liner report on its balance sheet for accounts receivable on December 30, 2000? What does that amount represent (how would you explain its meaning to a novice user of financial statements)? How much cash does High Liner report on December 30, 2000?

Exhibit 7-6

High Liner Foods Incorporated
Financial Statements

Consolidated Balance Sheets
(In thousands of dollars)

Assets
(Note 8)

	December 30, 2000	January 1, 2000
Current		
Cash	$ 1,106	$ 7,474
Accounts receivable *(note 5)*	30,643	29,955
Inventories *(note 5)*	50,105	54,415
Prepaid expenses	932	1,836
Future income taxes *(notes 2 and 13)*	2,174	2,066
Total current assets	84,960	95,746
Property, plant and equipment *(note 6)*	45,614	46,002
Other		
Goodwill *(note 3)*	54,952	54,515
Deferred charges	2,065	1,053
Future income taxes *(notes 2 and 13)*	13,470	16,505
Other receivables and sundry investments *(note 3)*	6,311	6,080
	76,798	78,153
	$ 207,372	$ 219,901

Liabilities and Shareholders' Equity

	December 30, 2000	January 1, 2000
Current		
Bank loans *(note 7)*	$ 2,337	$ 16,456
Accounts payable and accrued liabilities *(note 7)*	37,163	30,586
Income taxes payable	-	4,594
Current portion of long-term liabilities *(note 8)*	13,227	5,226
Total current liabilities	52,727	56,862
Long-term liabilities *(note 8)*	77,753	92,302
Employee future benefits *(note 2 and 16)*	679	871
Future income taxes *(note 2 and 13)*	762	-
Shareholders' Equity		
Preference shares *(note 9)*	21,442	21,929
Common shares *(note 9)*	28,065	27,966
Retained earnings	25,148	20,448
Foreign currency translation account *(note 10)*	796	(477)
	75,451	69,866
	$ 207,372	$ 219,901

5. Current Assets
A) Accounts Receivable

	Dec. 30, 2000 ($000)	Jan. 1, 2000 ($000)
Canada Trade	$ 14,444	$ 13,793
US Trade (US$9,619; 1999 US$9,949)	14,431	14,360
Other	1,768	1,802
	$ 30,643	$ 29,955

Terms range from 7 to 30 days with most amounts being collected under 35 days. One customer accounts for approximately 11% of outstanding trade amounts. The allowance for trade doubtful accounts amounts to 2.6% of the trade balance outstanding. The Company has experienced a bad debt expense of less than 0.1% of sales over the past five years.

7. Current Liabilities
A) Bank Loans

	Dec. 30, 2000 ($000)	Jan. 1, 2000 ($000)
Bank loans, denominated in Canadian dollars, not exceeding prime plus 0.375%	$ 1,856	$ 6,504
Bank loans, denominated in US dollars, not exceeding prime plus 0.375% (US$321; 1999 US$6,895)	481	9,952
	$ 2,337	$ 16,456

The Company has pledged as collateral for its bank loans a general assignment of accounts receivable and inventory. The Company has the option of borrowing using bankers acceptances, LIBOR or prime loans with the majority of borrowings using LIBOR.

FS7-2. Examine note 5 to High Liner's financial statements and respond to the following questions:
   a. What is the total amount of receivables that High Liner has outstanding on December 30, 2000?
   b. What amount is due from Canadian customers and what amount is due from U.S. customers?
   c. How much do the U.S. customers owe in U.S. dollars?
   d. What is the exchange rate that was applied to the amount of U.S. dollars owed on December 30, 2000 to obtain the balance in Canadian dollars? What was the rate applied to the amount owed on January 1, 2000? Why are the rates different?
   e. Suppose that instead of the rate that you calculated in (d) above, the cost of one U.S. dollar was Cdn$1.40. What amount would be reported for receivables on High Liner's December 30, 2000 balance sheet? Does the rate used affect the number of U.S. dollars owed? Explain.
   f. What are the risks to High Liner associated with doing business with customers that pay in a currency other than Canadian dollars?

FS7-3. High Liner states in Note 5 that approximately 11% of the outstanding trade amounts are due from one customer. Is this information important to users of the financial statements? Explain.

FS7-4. What is the balance in the Allowance for Trade Doubtful Accounts account on December 30, 2000? What is the gross amount of accounts receivable (before deducting the Allowance for Trade Doubtful Accounts) on December 30, 2000? Is it useful to know the gross and net amount of accounts receivables, or is knowing just the net amount enough? Explain.

FS7-5. How much do you think High Liner expensed for bad debts in its fiscal 2000 income statement? Explain. Do you think that an entity's historical rate of bad debts should be the basis for determining the expense in the current year? Explain. What circumstances might justify using a rate different from the actual historical performance?

FS7-6. High Liner has pledged its accounts receivable and inventory as collateral for its bank loans. Which of these current assets do you think is more attractive as collateral to the bank? Explain. Why does the bank want collateral for the loans it makes? What benefits do you think exist to the borrower of providing collateral to a lender?

FS7-7. Calculate High Liner's current and quick ratios, and the amount of working capital on hand on December 30, 2000 and January 1, 2000. Based on the current and quick ratios, and the amount of working capital, how would you evaluate High Liner's liquidity position?

FS7-8. Calculate High Liner's accounts receivable turnover ratio for the years ended December 30, 2000 and January 1, 2000.
   a. Which receivables did you include in the calculation of the accounts receivable turnover ratio? Explain.
   b. What is the average collection period of accounts receivable for the two years?
   c. Do the accounts receivable turnover ratio and the average collection period indicate that High Liner is managing its receivables well? Explain.
   d. Do your calculations correspond with the information that High Liner provides in note 5?

FS7-9. Suppose that instead of showing cash separately on the balance sheet, High Liner combined its cash with its bank borrowings.
   a. How would the balance sheet be affected by this treatment of cash?
   b. How would the current and quick ratios be affected by this treatment?
   c. How would the debt-to-equity ratio be affected by this treatment?
   d. Do you think this approach to reporting cash is confusing or misleading? Explain.
   e. Why do you think some entities combine cash and bank borrowing and others report them separately? Explain.

■ Analyzing Mark's Work Wearhouse

M7-1. What amount of Cash and Cash Equivalents did MWW report on its January 27, 2001 and January 29, 2000 balance sheets?

M7-2. By how much did accounts receivable decrease from the end of fiscal 2000 to the end of fiscal 2001? Is this decrease in accounts receivable surprising? Explain. What are some possible explanations for the decrease?

M7-3. What would be considered *quick assets* on MWW's balance sheet? Explain your answer. What amount of quick assets did MWW report on its January 29, 2000 and January 27, 2001 balance sheets? Calculate MWW's quick and current ratios for fiscal 2000 and 2001.

M7-4. Read Note 4 to MWW's financial statements (page A-52).
   a. How much of MWW's accounts receivable are due to business account sales on January 27, 2001?
   b. How many business customers owe MWW money at the end of fiscal 2001, 2000, and 1999?
   c. How is this information useful to you as a user of financial statements?
   d. Note 4 also explains that "There are no individually significant clients who could create a credit risk to the Company in its operated stores." What does this statement mean and why might it be useful to users of the financial statements?

M7-5. Provide the following information for January 27, 2001 and January 29, 2000:
   a. Amount of accounts receivable reported on the balance sheet.
   b. Allowance for doubtful accounts.
   c. Gross amount of accounts receivable
   d. Amounts owed by Mark's franchise stores.

M7-6. Note 9 to MWW's financial statements (page A-54) shows that MWW has up to $75,000,000 available to it in the form of a "revolving operating facility" (which is a line of credit that can be used as required and paid back when the cash is available). The text under the table provides some of the terms of the $75,000,000 revolving operating facility. What percentage of accounts receivable is used to limit the amount that MWW can borrow against the operating facility? Why do you think that the banks do not use 100% of receivables to define the borrowing limit?

M7-7. Why do you think MWW is not owed money by retail customers? Why do MWW's franchise stores owe it money? What explanation does MWW give for its allowance for doubtful accounts?

Endnotes

1. Extracted from Cadillac Fairview Corporation's 1999 annual report.

2. Extracted from The Boyd Group Inc.'s 2000 annual report.

3. Extracted from Sears Canada Inc.'s 2001 annual report.

4. Clarence Byrd, Ida Chen, and Heather Chapman, *Financial Reporting in Canada*, 26th Edition. The Virtual Professional Library. CD-ROM. 2002.

5. Panel A extracted from Potash Corporation of Saskatchewan Inc.'s 2000 annual report. Panel B extracted from Rogers Communications Inc.'s 2000 annual report. Panel C extracted from Ballard Power Systems Inc.'s 2000 annual report. Panel D extracted from Husky Energy Inc.'s 2000 annual report.

6. Extracted from Nortel Networks Corporation's 2000 annual report.

7. Arthur Levitt, speech to the Financial Executives Institute, New York, New York, November 16, 1998, quoted at the United States Securities and Exchange Commission web site, http://www.sec.gov/news/speech/speecharchive/1998/spch227.htm (accessed April 18, 2002).

8. Extracted from High Liner Foods Incorporated's 2000 annual report.

Chapter 8

Inventory

Chapter Outline

Learning Objectives

After studying the material in this chapter you will be able to:

LO 1. Distinguish between the perpetual and periodic methods of inventory control.

LO 2. Distinguish among the different cost flow assumptions that are used to determine the amount of inventory that is reported on the balance sheet and cost of sales on the income statement, and understand the impact that the different cost flow assumptions have on the amounts reported in the financial statements.

LO 3. Explain the lower of cost and market rule.

LO 4. Characterize the difference between direct and absorption costing.

LO 5. Recognize the issues, choices, and effects on the financial statements of using market values instead of cost for valuing inventory.

LO 6. Discuss the relationship between accounting and income tax.

LO 7. Analyze and interpret inventory information in financial statements.

Introduction

For many entities, inventory is *the* business. Without inventory, many businesses cannot operate. What's a clothing store without clothes? What's a car dealership without cars? What is an appliance manufacturer without the parts to build the appliances? What's a fast food outlet without burgers, fries, or the ingredients to make pizza? In each case, it is the inventory that is directly responsible for the generation of revenue. Even some service businesses rely on inventory to provide their services to customers. Painters require paint. Lawn care companies require fertilizer.

Accounting for inventory can be surprisingly tricky. Our exposure to accounting for inventory so far in the book has simply involved recording inventory in the accounting records at its cost, and then expensing the cost of that particular inventory when it was sold. Pretty straightforward. But imagine an entity with thousands of identical units of inventory that did not all cost the same amount. How do we know the cost of the particular unit that was taken from the warehouse? The fact is, in many cases we don't. However, we still have to determine a cost of the inventory sold so that an income statement and balance sheet can be prepared. This is one of the challenges that faces accounting—determining the value of inventory on hand and the cost of inventory sold when we do not know the cost of the specific inventory sold to customers, used up in the production process, or consumed in providing services to customers.

This chapter examines the issues that affect accounting for inventory and the effect the resolution of those issues has on the numbers reported in the financial statements. The chapter also discusses a number of other issues designed to broaden our perspective of accounting information. Throughout the book the point has been made that historical cost, transactions-based accounting is not the only way to account, although it is the method that dominates financial reporting in Canada. In this chapter we will take a quick look at non-cost-based methods for accounting for inventory to see how financial statements can be affected by using alternatives to cost. We will also discuss the close link that exists between accounting and tax. We have already identified tax minimization as an important objective of financial reporting. In this chapter we will see how the Canadian income tax system has an effect on accounting choices and financial reporting by entities.

What Is Inventory?

Inventory is goods that are available for sale by an entity, or goods that will be used to produce goods that will be sold. Inventory can also include materials used in supplying a service to customers. The type of inventory an entity has depends on what it does: different types of entities have different inventories. For example, Mark's Work Wearhouse's inventory represents the clothing that it has in its warehouses and available for sale in its stores. MWW's January 27, 2001 balance sheet reports $84,483,000 of inventory, representing over 76% of MWW's current assets and almost 54% of its total assets.

That such a large proportion of MWW's assets is inventory is not surprising. MWW's business is selling clothing to customers. MWW does not need heavy investment in capital assets, and the retail nature of the business keeps accounts receivable low (retail customers pay cash or use major credit cards). It is interesting to observe that MWW's financial statements provide no description of the over $84,000,000 of inventory on hand. The reason is that, broadly, MWW has only one type of inventory: clothing available for sale.

Other types of entities have different kinds of inventory. A forestry company like Slocan Forest Products Ltd., a Canadian producer of lumber and other wood products, has inventory that includes logs, lumber, and pulp and paper. A commercial

www.slocan.com

airline such as WestJet Airlines Ltd. has inventory that consists primarily of spare parts, fuel, and supplies. For entities that manufacture or process inputs into finished goods that are sold to customers, inventory is usually broken down into three sub-categories on the balance sheet or in the notes to the financial statements. These sub-categories of inventory are:

1. **Raw materials inventory:** the inputs into the production process of a manufacturer or processor. For example, raw materials inventory for a furniture manufacturer includes the wood that is used to build the furniture.

2. **Work-in-process** inventory or **WIP:** inventory that is partially completed on the financial statement date. For a car manufacturer, a partially completed car would be classified as WIP inventory.

3. **Finished goods inventory:** inventory that has been completed and is ready for sale.

One entity's inventory can be another entity's capital asset. For example, MWW accounts for its display cases as capital assets. But for companies that manufacture display cases, the cases are inventory because they are the goods that these entities sell to customers. For some types of entities it is not obvious whether an item is inventory or something else. A video store will purchase large quantities of the latest videos and rent them to customers. As time passes, the demand for a once-popular video declines and the store will sell "previously viewed" videos to customers. How should the video store classify the videos? As capital assets (because they are rented to customers) or as inventory (because they are sold)? We will discuss this question further in Chapter 9.

What GAAP Say

As we will see, Canadian GAAP provides us with surprisingly little guidance about how to account for inventory. As a result, there are many acceptable ways of accounting for inventory, which allows for many different measurements of the same underlying economic resource. The *CICA Handbook* requires that inventory be accounted for at cost. It uses the term laid-down cost to describe the costs that should be included in inventory.

Laid-down cost can be interpreted to include all costs that are incurred to purchase or make the products and get them ready for sale to customers. For retailers and wholesalers, laid-down cost should include the actual cost of the product purchased, plus shipping and handling, and any taxes. Of course, things are not always straightforward. Consider a company that takes delivery of a variety of goods in a single delivery. It may not be practical to allocate the cost of the shipping to the individual products. Similarly, it may be difficult to allocate the cost of employees who stock the shelves of a store to the individual products. In these cases the costs might not be allocated to inventory.

For manufacturers, laid-down cost would include the cost of the materials that went into the production of the product, direct labour costs that can be traced to the product, and a share of overhead. The *CICA Handbook* is actually quite ambiguous about how much of overhead costs should be included in inventory. As a result, in practice there can be considerable variability in the allocation of overhead to inventory. (We will further discuss the allocation of overhead to inventory later in the chapter.)

Perpetual and Periodic Inventory Systems

There are two ways in which accounting systems are designed to keep track of transactions affecting inventory during a period: perpetual systems and periodic systems.

A **perpetual inventory system** keeps an ongoing tally of purchases and sales of inventory, with the Inventory account adjusted to reflect changes as they occur. When inventory is purchased or sold, the Inventory account is immediately debited or credited to record the change. When inventory is sold, Cost of Sales is debited immediately. With a perpetual system it is possible to determine cost of sales at any time.

The journal entry to record the purchase of inventory using a perpetual inventory system would be:

> Dr. Inventory (asset +)   xxx
>   Cr. Accounts payable (liability +) or Cash (asset −)   xxx
> To record the purchase of inventory using a perpetual
> inventory system.

When inventory is sold, the entity would record the following journal entry:

> Dr. Cash (asset +) or Accounts receivable (asset +)   yyy
>   Cr. Revenue (revenue +, owners' equity +)   yyy
> To record the sale of inventory.

> Dr. Cost of sales (expense +, owners' equity −)   xxx
>   Cr. Inventory (asset −)   xxx
> To record the sale of inventory using a perpetual inventory
> system and the corresponding cost of goods sold.

Because the recording of cost of sales with a perpetual system occurs when the actual exchange with the customer takes place, the entry that records cost of sales is a transactional entry.

With a **periodic inventory system**, the Inventory account is not adjusted whenever a transaction affects inventory. The balance in the Inventory account at the end of a period is determined by actually counting the inventory. Purchases of inventory are not recorded directly to the Inventory account but instead are accumulated in a separate "Purchases" account. With a periodic inventory system, cost of sales is determined indirectly using the following equation:

$$\text{Cost of sales} = \text{Beginning inventory} + \text{Purchases} - \text{Ending inventory}$$

Cost of sales is determined by finding out the beginning and ending Inventory balances (which are known from the inventory counts) and the amount of inventory purchased during the period (from the "Purchases" account). Because it is necessary to count the inventory to calculate cost of sales, cost of sales cannot be determined from the accounting system before the end of a period. If an entity's accountant received an urgent call in the middle of an accounting period from the controller asking for the entity's gross margin to date, the accountant could only shrug. (The accountant might be able to estimate the gross margin indirectly, but the cost of sales information would not be directly available from the accounting system.)

The journal entry to record the purchase of inventory using a periodic inventory system would be:

> Dr. Purchases (asset +)   xxx
>   Cr. Accounts payable (liability +), Cash (asset −)   xxx
> To record the purchase of inventory using a periodic
> inventory system. (Note that the Purchases account is not
> the same as the Inventory account.)

When inventory is sold, the following journal entry is made:

> Dr. Cash (asset +)   yyy
>   Cr. Revenue (revenue +, owners' equity +)   yyy
> To record the sale of inventory. (This entry is the same as
> with the perpetual system. The sale transaction is not
> affected by the inventory control system being used.)

No entry is made to record cost of sales. Cost of sales is recorded at the end of the period after the inventory has been counted. Because the recording of cost of sales occurs separately from the sale of inventory, it is an adjusting entry—it is not triggered by an external transaction.

The journal entries that would be made at the end of the period under a periodic system would be:

Dr. Inventory   zzz
    Cr. Purchases   zzz
To transfer the inventory purchased during the period that
is recorded in the Purchases account to the Inventory account.

Dr. Cost of sales   www
    Cr. Inventory   www
To record cost of sales for the period.

Remember, the debit to Cost of Sales and the credit to Inventory is simply the amount that is necessary to make the ending balance in the Inventory account equal to the amount determined from the actual count of the inventory.

Internal Control

A perpetual inventory system does not eliminate the need for counting the inventory from time to time. The selling of inventory is not the only way inventory is consumed. Inventory can also be stolen, lost, damaged, or destroyed. A perpetual system will only

---

Question for Consideration

Trenche Ltd. provides you with the following information about its inventory:

Inventory on December 31, 2004	$ 175,000
Purchases during 2005	1,245,000
Inventory on December 31, 2005	210,000

Trenche uses a periodic inventory system.

a. Prepare the journal entry to record purchases of inventory during 2005.
b. Prepare the journal entry to transfer the purchases in 2005 to the Inventory account.
c. Calculate Trenche's cost of sales for 2005.
d. Prepare the journal entry to record cost of sales for 2005.

Answer:

a. Journal entry to record purchases of inventory during 2005:

Dr. Purchases   1,245,000
    Cr. Accounts payable/Cash   1,245,000
To record the purchase of inventory.

b. Journal entry to transfer the purchases in 2005 to the Inventory account:

Dr. Inventory   1,245,000
    Cr. Purchases   1,245,000
To transfer inventory purchases to the Inventory account.

c. Trenche's cost of sales for 2005:

Cost of sales = Beginning inventory + Purchases − Ending inventory
Cost of sales = 175,000   + 1,245,000 − 210,000
               = 1,210,000

d. Journal entry to record cost of sales for 2005:

Dr. Cost of sales   1,210,000
    Cr. Inventory   1,210,000
To record cost of sales for 2005.

account for the cost of inventory actually sold. Only a physical count of inventory will identify that inventory has been consumed for reasons other than a sale.

For example, if $5,000 of inventory had been stolen during the year, the perpetual inventory records would show that there was $5,000 more inventory than there was in fact. This is because the theft would not be recorded in the accounting system (thieves usually do not report their activities). If the inventory were not physically counted, the amount of inventory on the balance sheet at the end of the period would be overstated by $5,000 and expenses would be understated by $5,000. (Stolen inventory is an expense in the period the theft occurs or is discovered.) Differences between the accounting records and the count can also occur because of errors in recording transactions. Once the inventory is counted, the accounting records should be adjusted so that they correspond with the actual amount of inventory on hand.

Counting the inventory and discovering differences between the accounting records and the count is valuable for internal control purposes. Differences between the count and the accounting records allow management to identify the "disappearance" of inventory. With this information, management is then able to investigate the cause of the difference and take steps to reduce or eliminate the problem. For example, if management discovered that inventory was being stolen, it could consider steps to better protect the inventory from theft. Information about the amount of inventory being stolen could help stakeholders assess how management is fulfilling its stewardship responsibilities. However, information on the amount of stolen inventory is rarely, if ever, reported in a set of financial statements. The amount of stolen inventory is usually included in cost of sales.

It is important to recognize that with a periodic inventory system, it is not possible to determine whether any theft has taken place because there are no records with which to compare the physical count. Therefore, the cost of stolen items is included, by default, in cost of sales. More important, it is not possible to tell from the accounting records that there is a problem with stolen inventory. This is one of the weaknesses of a periodic inventory system. The periodic system does not allow for as effective control over inventory as a perpetual system does.

Let's consider another situation. It is very common to see scanners in retail and grocery stores. The scanners provide detailed information about what is being sold and quantities on hand. This information is invaluable for management decision-making—including decisions such as when merchandise should be reordered and whether particular products should be stocked. However, the information about physical quantities of inventory may not be integrated with the entity's financial accounting records. The inventory system might keep track of quantities, but may not record the financial effect of a sale by crediting Inventory and debiting Cost of Sales when an item is sold. In other words, even though an entity might be collecting information about physical quantities on a continuous or perpetual basis, it might still be using a periodic system for determining the cost of inventory and cost of sales.

In conclusion, the choice between a periodic and perpetual inventory system is an internal control issue, not an accounting issue. Managers will choose between periodic and perpetual inventory control systems based on the costs and benefits of the two systems. However, as we will see, the choice can have an effect on the amount of inventory reported on the balance sheet and cost of goods sold for the period.

Inventory Valuation Methods

So far, the description of how inventory costs have been accounted for has been quite straightforward. It has been implicitly assumed that when inventory is sold, we know the actual cost of that specific inventory. In fact, the actual cost of the specific inventory sold is often not known. When inventory is purchased or manufactured, the cost

Question for Consideration

Nairn Ltd. (Nairn) uses a perpetual inventory system. The perpetual inventory records show that during the fiscal year ended October 31, 2005 Nairn purchased $475,000 of inventory and sold inventory with a cost of $450,000. The inventory count on October 31, 2005 found inventory on hand of $185,000. The count on October 31, 2004 found inventory of $170,000.

During the fiscal year ended October 31, 2005, determine how much inventory was consumed for reasons other than sales to customers (theft, breakage, etc.). If Nairn was using a periodic inventory system, why would it not be possible to determine the amount of inventory that was consumed for reasons other than sales to customers?

Answer: The amount of inventory consumed by reasons other than sales to customers can be determined by comparing the amount of inventory that should be on hand, as indicated by the perpetual inventory records, with the amount of inventory actually on hand, as determined by the physical count. The perpetual inventory records indicate that there should be $195,000 of inventory on hand on October 31, 2005. This can be calculated using the equation:

$$\begin{aligned}
\text{Ending inventory} &= \text{Beginning inventory} + \text{Purchases} - \text{Cost of sales} \\
&= \$170,000 + \$475,000 - \$450,000 \\
&= \$195,000
\end{aligned}$$

However, the physical count shows that there is only $185,000 of inventory on hand on October 31, 2005. This means that $10,000 ($195,000 − $185,000) of inventory was somehow consumed but not recorded in the perpetual inventory system. The physical count is assumed to provide the actual amount of inventory on hand. The difference between the count and the amount of inventory that the perpetual records indicate there should be is the amount of inventory that has been consumed for reasons other than sales and, therefore, not recorded in the accounting records.

A periodic inventory system does not record inventory as it is sold, so it would not be possible for Nairn to compare the amount of inventory that the accounting records say should be on hand with the actual amount of inventory on hand as determined by the count. Therefore, Nairn can calculate the amount of inventory that was consumed during the period, but it cannot determine the amount of inventory lost because of theft, breakage, and so on.

is recorded in the Inventory account (or in the Purchases account). From then on, the flow of costs from the balance sheet to the income statement (from the Inventory account to Cost of Sales) does not necessarily correspond with the physical flow of the actual goods sold. The cost of Inventory reported on the balance sheet may not be the actual cost of the physical items in inventory. Also, the Cost of Sales that is reported on the income statement may not be the actual cost of the physical units that were received by customers. The reason why the flow of costs through the financial statements does not usually match the physical flow of goods is because in most cases it is not practical, cost effective, or even possible to track the cost of individual units of inventory.

For example, consider an inventory of nails, lumber, flower seeds, or plastic furniture—inventory that is relatively low in cost and homogeneous (that is, the items are virtually identical). To track the cost of individual items would require that the entity be able to identify the cost of each individual nail or seed or piece of lumber. It is difficult to imagine a situation where it would be worthwhile to incur the costs of doing so. Or consider a company that refines crude oil to produce a range of petroleum-based products. The price of crude oil is continually fluctuating. The refiner buys crude oil on the open market and stores it in large storage tanks at the refinery. Batches of oil that cost different amounts will be mixed together in the storage tanks. Once the batches are mixed together, it is impossible to distinguish which batch is being removed from the tank—and therefore it is impossible to know the cost of the oil that is used in the production process.

As a result, in most cases accountants do not keep track of the costs associated with the individual items of inventory. Instead, they have developed methods called *cost flow assumptions* for moving costs through the Inventory account to Cost of Sales without regard for the actual physical movement of the inventory. There are a number of cost flow assumptions that are currently in use. The *CICA Handbook* identifies four:

1. specific identification
2. average cost
3. first in, first out (FIFO)
4. last in, first out (LIFO)

The *CICA Handbook* and GAAP in general do not state a preference for one of these cost flow assumptions over any other. The *CICA Handbook* requires that inventory be valued at cost and that the method an entity uses to value its inventory be the one that results in the "fairest" matching of costs to revenues. In most cases, it is difficult to argue conclusively that one of the cost flow assumptions results in a fairer matching than the others, so the choice is up to the preparer of the financial statements.

The choice of cost flow assumption does not have any effect on the underlying economic activity of the entity (though it may have tax implications, as we will see below), but the numbers reported on the balance sheet and the income statement can be significantly different depending on the cost flow assumption used. The cost flow assumption that an entity uses must be disclosed in the notes to the financial statements.

Cost is not the only basis by which inventory can be valued. There are methods that use measures of current market value to value inventory, such as replacement cost and net realizable value. These methods are not acceptable according to GAAP in most cases because they violate the historical cost measurement convention. (These methods will be examined later in the chapter.)

The remainder of this section will be devoted to discussing four of the common cost flow assumptions. When you study the methods, remember that the purpose of the cost flow assumptions is to have a method of moving costs from the balance sheet to the income statement, and that the method does not necessarily reflect or affect the physical flow of inventory.

Let's begin our look at the four common cost flow assumptions.

First In, First Out (FIFO)

Under **first in, first out** or **FIFO** the cost associated with the inventory that was purchased or produced first is expensed first. For raw materials that are used in a manufacturing process, the cost associated with the raw materials that were purchased first is the cost that is charged to the production process first.

With a FIFO system the cost of inventory reported on the balance sheet represents the cost of inventory that was purchased or produced most recently. The inventory cost that has been on hand for the least amount of time is the inventory cost that will still be on hand at the end of the period. FIFO matches the cost of inventory to revenue in the order the costs arrived at the entity. Oldest costs are matched to revenue first.

We can conceptualize a FIFO system by imagining a warehouse where new purchases of inventory are placed in the warehouse from a loading dock at the back and where customers receive the inventory they buy from the front of the warehouse. This conceptualization is shown in Figure 8-1. When new inventory is purchased and placed in the warehouse, it "pushes" the inventory that was purchased earlier toward the front of the warehouse. The inventory gradually moves from the back of the warehouse to the front. When the inventory reaches the front of the warehouse, it can be sold to customers. The result is that the "oldest" costs (the costs that entered the accounting system the longest time ago) are expensed first, while the "newest" costs (the costs associated with the most recently acquired inventory) remain in inventory at the end of the period. This conceptualization uses the physical flow of goods

Question for Consideration

Thessalon Inc. (Thessalon) manufactures gumballs. Its most popular product is a one-quarter-inch gumball that comes in six colours. This size gumball is commonly found in dispensers in stores, malls, and so on, as well as in candy stores. Thessalon can have as many as 1,000,000 of these gumballs in inventory at a point in time, depending on the time of year. Once they are made, the gumballs are stored in large containers that hold up to 50,000. The gumballs are then packaged into smaller containers for shipment to customers. The cost of gumballs can vary because some of the inputs used in the production of gumballs are commodities whose price can vary from day to day.

Why is it likely that Thessalon would not know the exact cost of a particular order of one-quarter-inch gumballs? Why is it likely that Thessalon would use a cost flow assumption to determine the value of its inventory and its cost of sales?

Answer: With the cost of gumballs varying because of changing input prices and the vast number of gumballs on hand at anytime, it would be impossible to determine the cost of any particular gumball under the current storage arrangement. Once they are produced, gumballs with different costs are presumably mixed together in the large containers, at which time it becomes impossible to distinguish gumballs of different costs (but identical appearance), unless each gumball were given an identifying mark that would allow Thessalon's management to determine its cost.

Giving each gumball an identifying mark seems impractical and costly. It is likely that gumballs of different costs will be drawn from the large storage containers for packaging. Without being able to identify the cost of individual gumballs, it is impossible for Thessalon to determine the cost of a particular gumball order. However, for accounting purposes Thessalon needs to have a cost associated with the gumballs that are sold so that net income and the value of ending inventory can be determined. As a result, it is necessary to use a method of estimating the cost of the gumballs sold.

This is where a cost flow assumption becomes useful. With a large amount of low-cost, identical inventory it would be cost effective and practical for Thessalon to use a cost flow assumption rather than trying to determine the exact cost of the gumballs sold.

through a warehouse as an analogy for how costs move through a FIFO inventory system. However, remember that FIFO and the other cost flow assumptions address the flow of costs, not the physical flow of goods.

Let's consider a simple example to show how a FIFO system works. Figure 8-2 (page 442) provides information about inventory purchases and sales made by Falcon Inc. (Falcon) in January 2004. Falcon had no inventory on hand on January 1, 2004.

Under FIFO the costs associated with the 100 units purchased on January 10 would be expensed first, the costs associated with the 125 units purchased on January 20 would be expensed second, and the costs associated with the 110 units purchased on January 30 would be expensed third.

Figure 8-1

FIFO Inventory Valuation System

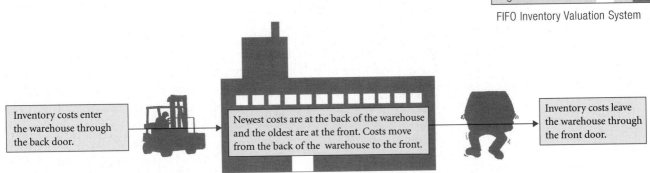

| Inventory costs enter the warehouse through the back door. | Newest costs are at the back of the warehouse and the oldest are at the front. Costs move from the back of the warehouse to the front. | Inventory costs leave the warehouse through the front door. |

In a FIFO valuation system the costs can be conceptualized entering the back door of the warehouse and gradually being "pushed" to the front of the warehouse as new inventory is added. When inventory is sold, the customer "receives" the inventory cost that is closest to the front of the warehouse, which is the oldest cost. The cost of inventory still in the warehouse at the end of the period is reported on the balance sheet. The cost of inventory on hand at the end of the period is the cost of the inventory that was purchased most recently.

Figure 8-2

Inventory Information for
Falcon Inc.

Falcon Inc. Inventory Information For January 2004		
	Number of units purchased	Price paid per unit
Purchased on January 10, 2004	100	$20
Purchased on January 20, 2004	125	$25
Purchased on January 30, 2004	110	$28
Sold on January 31, 2004	195	

On January 31, 2004 Falcon sells 195 units of inventory. Under FIFO the costs that would be expensed if financial statements were being prepared for January 2004 would be the costs associated with the 100 units that were purchased on January 10 and the costs associated with 95 of the units that were purchased on January 20. Again, the reason for this is that under FIFO the oldest costs are expensed first. For Falcon the oldest costs are associated with the inventory purchased on January 10, so those units are expensed first. Once the costs associated with the inventory purchased on January 10 are fully expensed, the costs associated with the next oldest inventory— the inventory purchased on January 20—are expensed.

The Inventory account on the balance sheet would include the costs associated with the most recently acquired inventory units that were still on hand on the balance sheet date. For Falcon the Inventory account would include the cost associated with the 110 units purchased on January 30, plus the costs associated with 30 of the units purchased on January 20 (the costs associated with 95 of the January 20 units would be expensed in January).

The purpose of this example is to show the order in which costs move from the balance sheet to the income statement under a FIFO system. Later in this section we will examine an example that shows the effect of the different cost flow assumptions on the amounts reported for Cost of Sales and Inventory.

Last In, First Out (LIFO)

Under the **last in, first out** or **LIFO** cost flow assumption, the cost associated with the inventory that was purchased or produced most recently is matched to revenue (expensed) first. For raw materials that are used in a manufacturing process, the cost associated with the raw materials that were purchased last or most recently is the cost that is charged to the production process first. With LIFO the cost of inventory reported on the balance sheet represents the cost of old, sometimes very old, inventory. Because under a LIFO system the cost of the newest inventory is expensed first, as long as new inventory keeps being purchased the cost of the older inventory may not be expensed for a long time.

We can also conceptualize a LIFO system using the warehouse analogy. In a LIFO warehouse, new purchases of inventory enter and inventory that is sold leaves the warehouse through the same door. This conceptualization of a LIFO inventory system is shown in Figure 8-3. When new inventory is purchased, it is placed closest to the door so that when a customer comes to purchase inventory it is conveniently available to be sold to the customer. The older inventory that was previously closest to the door is "pushed" towards the back of the warehouse. As older inventory is pushed to the back, the only way it can be sold is if the inventory in front of it is sold first. In Figure 8-3 the only way the inventory costs from two years ago could be expensed is if the costs associated with the inventory from last year, last month, last week, and today were sold first. As an entity expands, the amount of inventory it will have increases, so it is unlikely that costs associated with the older inventory that has been pushed back in the warehouse

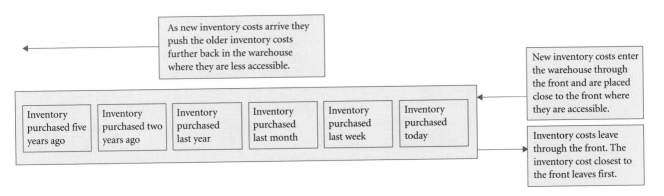

As new inventory costs arrive they push the older inventory costs further back in the warehouse where they are less accessible.

New inventory costs enter the warehouse through the front and are placed close to the front where they are accessible.

| Inventory purchased five years ago | Inventory purchased two years ago | Inventory purchased last year | Inventory purchased last month | Inventory purchased last week | Inventory purchased today |

Inventory costs leave through the front. The inventory cost closest to the front leaves first.

In a LIFO valuation system costs can be thought of as entering and leaving the warehouse through the front door. The inventory cost closest to the front of the warehouse, which is always the inventory cost that was added most recently, is "sold" to customers first. (The customer would be given the inventory costs that are added, the older costs get "pushed" further back in the warehouse where they are less accessible and, therefore, less likely to be "sold." Older inventory costs that are not at the front of the warehouse can only be "sold" if the newer inventory costs ahead of the older costs are "sold" first. The inventory cost still in the warehouse at the end of the period is reported on the balance sheet. The exact composition of the inventory costs on hand at the end of the period will depend on the pattern of the purchase and sale of inventory over time.

Figure 8-3

LIFO Inventory Valuation System

will be expensed. The inventory cost that is expensed first is the cost associated with the newest inventory—the inventory that was placed in the warehouse most recently.

Now let's use the information for Falcon Inc. to show how costs flow under LIFO. With LIFO the costs associated with the inventory acquired most recently are expensed first and the oldest costs are included in inventory at the end of the period. On January 31, 2004 Falcon sells 195 units of inventory. If Falcon used LIFO, at the end of January 2004 it would expense the cost associated with the 110 units purchased on January 30 (since those are the costs associated with the most recent inventory purchase) and the cost associated with 85 of the units purchased on January 20. In inventory on January 31, 2004 will be the costs associated with the 100 units purchased on January 10 and 40 of the units purchased on January 20.

Take a moment to notice how LIFO and FIFO differ in the costs that are matched to revenues during the period and in the costs that remain in inventory at the end of the period. In considering this example, again remember that we are talking about the movement of costs, not the physical movement of the actual units of inventory.

LIFO is not widely used in Canada because it is not acceptable for tax purposes. If an entity chooses to use LIFO for accounting purposes (which it is free to do), it would also have to be able to calculate cost of sales using a method that is acceptable to the Canada Customs and Revenue Agency, a method such as average cost or FIFO.

Average Cost

With the **average cost method,** the average cost of all inventory on hand during the period is calculated and that average is used to calculate cost of sales and the balance in ending inventory. The average cost method does not attempt to distinguish among units of inventory that have different costs and make assumptions about when costs move from Inventory to Cost of Sales (as FIFO and LIFO do). Instead, the average cost method simply assumes that all the inventory units have the same cost. In an average cost system all units of inventory at a point in time are assigned the same cost: the average cost of the inventory on hand. With an average cost system, the cost of individual units of inventory is lost.

We have to conceptualize the average cost inventory cost flow assumption differently than we did LIFO and FIFO. Consider a large storage tank at an oil refinery. The refinery purchases crude oil at market prices and stores the oil in the storage tank. Crude oil prices have fluctuated significantly in recent years, so it will be very common to mix batches of crude oil purchased at different prices in the tank. The differently priced oil mixes and mingles in the tank. When oil is required to produce product, it is impossible to tell what priced oil is coming out of the tank. In fact, the oil drawn will be an average of the various costs of oil put in the storage tank in the first place.

Returning to the Falcon Inc. example, we see that when average cost is used it is necessary to calculate the average cost of the units to determine cost of sales and ending inventory. With average cost, we "create" the cost of the units that are expensed and that are in inventory. The average cost used does not correspond to the cost of a specific unit. Falcon paid a total of $8,205 ($100 \times \$20 + 125 \times \$25 + 110 \times \$28$) for the 335 ($100 + 125 + 110$) units of inventory it had on hand during January 2004. The average cost of each unit of inventory on hand during January is $24.49 ($\$8,205 \div 335$). Each unit of inventory sold during January is assigned the average cost of $24.49 and each unit in inventory at the end of January is also assigned the average cost of $24.49.

Specific Identification

The **specific identification method** assigns the actual cost of a particular unit of inventory to that unit of inventory. Unlike the average cost, FIFO, and LIFO cost flow assumptions, when specific identification is used the physical flow of inventory matches the flow of costs that are recorded in the accounting system. As a result, the inventory cost reported on the balance sheet is the actual cost of the specific items that are in inventory, and cost of sales is the actual cost of the specific items of inventory that were sold during the period. (Strictly speaking, specific identification should not be referred to as a cost flow assumption because it reflects the actual flow of costs and the physical flow of inventory.)

Specific identification has appeal because the physical flow of inventory and the flow of costs correspond. However, aside from the practical problems with using specific identification for homogeneous inventories, specific identification allows for easy manipulation of financial information by managers. If there are a number of identical items in inventory that have different costs, the managers could choose to sell the inventory items that would have a desired effect on the financial statement.

For example, a car dealer might have two of the same model car, each the same colour and with the same features. The two cars may have been purchased from the manufacturer for different amounts. A car buyer is unlikely to be able to differentiate between the vehicles and may not care which vehicle he or she receives. However, if the dealer sells the more expensive car, net income is lower. If the less expensive model is sold, income is increased. Simply by choosing the "appropriate" unit of inventory, the dealer can help achieve an objective of financial reporting.

The other cost flow assumptions are less subject to manipulation than specific identification because these other methods have defined flows of costs that are not subject to arbitrary choices. (Nonetheless, LIFO can be manipulated if managers allow the level of inventory to decrease so that the entity is expensing the costs associated with inventory from much earlier periods.) FIFO and average cost are much more difficult to manipulate.

The specific identification method is suitable for more expensive inventory that is relatively unique (such as works of art or some types of jewellery) or for inventory that is relatively easy to distinguish among individual units (such as cars, major appliances, and home entertainment equipment, which have serial numbers that make it easy to identify the individual items).

Comparison of the Different Cost Flow Assumptions

Now let's examine an example that will allow us to see the effects that the different cost flow assumptions have on the financial statements. Information about the purchases and sales of inventory made by Woolchester Inc. (Woolchester) during October 2005

Question for Consideration

During May 2005 Sanikiluaq Ltd. (Sanikiluaq) made the following purchases of inventory:

Date of purchase	Quantity purchased	Cost per unit
May 6	10,000	$1.00
May 13	12,000	$1.10
May 20	8,000	$1.25
May 27	11,000	$1.50

On May 31, 2005 Sanikiluaq sold 23,000 units of inventory to customers. Sanikiluaq had no inventory on hand on May 1, 2005.

Identify which inventory units would be expensed in May 2005 and which units would be in inventory on May 31, 2005 using the FIFO, LIFO, average cost, and specific identification cost flow assumptions.

Answer:

	Inventory costs that would be expensed during May*	Inventory costs that would be in inventory at the end of May
FIFO	10,000 @ $1.00 (May 6) 12,000 @ $1.10 (May 13) 1,000 @ $1.25 (May 20)	7,000 @ $1.25 (May 20) 11,000 @ $1.50 (May 27)
LIFO	11,000 @ $1.50 (May 27) 8,000 @ $1.25 (May 20) 4,000 @ $1.10 (May 13)	10,000 @ $1.00 (May 6) 8,000 @ $1.10 (May 13)
Average cost	[(10,000 × $1.00 + 12,000 × $1.10 + 8,000 × $1.25 + 11,000 × $1.50) ÷ 41,000**] = $1.212 $1.212 × 23,000** = $27,876	$1.212 × 18,000 = $21,816
Specific identification	It is not possible to determine cost of sales or ending inventory using the specific identification method because we have not been told the cost of the specific units that were sold.	

*Date in brackets is the date the inventory was purchased.

**41,000 is the total number of inventory units available for sale during May 2005 and 23,000 is the number of units sold during May.

is shown in Figure 8-4 (page 446). We will use this information to calculate the ending inventory balance on October 31, 2005, and the cost of sales and the gross margin for October 2005. For each of the cost flow assumptions we will calculate these amounts for both a periodic and a perpetual inventory control system because the outcomes can differ depending on the inventory control system used. We will also see that cash flow is not affected by the choice of inventory cost flow assumption and control method. Regardless of the cost flow assumption used for accounting for inventory, revenue for October is the same: $26,250.

FIFO Perpetual   When a perpetual inventory system is used, additions and reductions to the Inventory account are made when inventory is bought or sold. This means that Cost of Sales is debited and Inventory is credited at the time of the sale. The entries that Woolchester would make for October 2005, along with other information about the Inventory account using FIFO perpetual, are shown in the spreadsheet in Table 8-1 (page 447).

On October 3 Woolchester purchased 100 units of inventory for $5,000. The purchase is recorded by increasing the Inventory account and decreasing the Cash account by $5,000. On October 8 Woolchester sells 80 units for $125 each, so Cash and

Figure 8-4

Purchases and Sales of Inventory
at Woolchester Inc.

Woolchester Inc. Information about the Purchases and Sales of Inventory During October 2005			
	Number of units	Price per unit	Total
Inventory balance on September 30, 2005	0	$ 0	$ 0
Purchases:*			
October 3	100	50	5,000
October 15	125	55	6,875
October 25	75	59	4,425
Sales:**			
October 8	80	125	10,000
October 20	130	125	16,250

*All purchases of inventory are made for cash.
**All sales are for cash.

revenue each increase by $10,000. Since the only inventory costs on hand on October 8 are units that cost $50, we debit Cost of Sales for $4,000 (80 units × $50) and credit Inventory for $4,000. When the accounting for the October 8 transaction is complete, there are 20 units at a cost of $50 each remaining in inventory.

The October 15 purchase of 125 units for $55 each reduces Cash and increases Inventory by $6,875. On October 20 Woolchester sells 130 units, again for $125 each. Before this sale Woolchester has units in inventory that have two different costs associated with them—20 units with a cost of $50 each and 125 units with a cost of $55 each. Since we are using FIFO, the oldest costs are expensed first, which means the cost associated with the 20 remaining $50 units is expensed first, followed by the cost associated with 110 of the $55 units. Therefore, on October 20 Cost of Sales is debited and Inventory is credited for $7,050 (20 units × $50 + 110 units × $55).

On October 25 Woolchester purchases 75 inventory units for $59 each. At the end of October the value of the remaining inventory is $5,250, composed of 15 units with a cost of $55 each and 75 units with a cost of $59 each.

FIFO Periodic   When a periodic inventory control system is used, the entry that records Cost of Sales for the period is an adjusting entry made at the end of the period. The entries of Woolchester for October 2005 using FIFO periodic are shown in Table 8-2. For the remainder of the cost flow assumptions discussed in this section, we will only examine the entries pertaining to the sale of inventory. The entries that record the purchase of inventory and the revenue earned are the same as those described under FIFO perpetual.

On October 31 Woolchester has to make the entry to the spreadsheet to record cost of sales and inventory used during the period. We determine the costs that should be expensed for October by looking at the units and costs available for sale during the month in the order the inventory was purchased.

During October Woolchester had on hand (in order of acquisition) 100 units at $50, 125 units at $55, and 75 units at $59. Under FIFO, to record the cost of selling 210 units during October, Woolchester would expense the cost associated with the 100 units purchased for $50 each on October 3 and the cost associated with 110 of the units purchased for $55 each on October 15. Under FIFO periodic, the total cost of sales for October was $11,050. If Woolchester had a beginning inventory balance at the start of October, the costs associated with that inventory would be expensed first under a FIFO system.

Notice that ending inventory and cost of sales under FIFO periodic are the same as under FIFO perpetual. This is always the case.

Table 8-1   Woolchester Inc.: Spreadsheet 1—FIFO Perpetual

Woolchester Inc.
Spreadsheet for Inventory Transactions for October 2005 Using FIFO Perpetual

		Cash	Inventory	Revenue	Cost of sales
October 3	Purchase 100 units @ $50	$(5,000)	$5,000		
October 8	Sell 80 units @ $125	10,000		$10,000	
Inventory on hand:	Inventory expensed:				
100 units @ $50	80 units @ $50		(4,000)		$ (4,000)
Remaining in inventory:					
20 units @ $50					
October 15	Purchase 125 units @ $55	(6,875)	6,875		
October 20	Sell 130 units @ $125	16,250		16,250	
Inventory on hand:	Inventory expensed:				
20 units @ $50	20 units @ $50				
125 units @ $55	+ 110 units @ $55		(7,050)		(7,050)
Remaining in inventory:					
15 units @ $55					
October 25	Purchase 75 units @ $59	(4,425)	4,425		
October 31 **Ending balances**		$ 9,950	$5,250	$26,250	$(11,050)
Remaining in inventory:					
15 units @ $55 = $ 825 ⎫					
75 units @ $59 = $4,425 ⎭					

Table 8-2   Woolchester Inc.: Spreadsheet 2—FIFO Periodic

Woolchester Inc.
Spreadsheet for Inventory Transactions for October 2005 Using FIFO Periodic

		Cash	Inventory*	Revenue	Cost of sales
October 3	Purchase 100 units @ $50	$(5,000)	$5,000		
October 8	Sell 80 units @ $125	10,000		$10,000	
October 15	Purchase 125 units @ $55	(6,875)	6,875		
October 20	Sell 130 units @ $125	16,250		16,250	
October 25	Purchase 75 units @ $59	(4,425)	4,425		
October 31 Inventory on hand on October 31 (before recording cost of sales): 100 units @ $50 125 units @ $55 75 units @ $59	Inventory expensed for the month of October 2005: 100 units @ $50 + 110 units @ $55		(11,050)		$(11,050)
October 31 **Ending balances**		$ 9,950	$5,250	$26,250	$(11,050)
Remaining in inventory:					
15 units @ $55 = $ 825 ⎫					
75 units @ $59 = $4,425 ⎭					

*In this table purchases are made directly to the Inventory account. These should have been made to the Purchases account. However, for clarity the step of recording purchases to the Purchases account and then moving them to the Inventory account is ignored.

LIFO Perpetual   With LIFO the first inventory costs to be expensed are the costs that were most recently added to inventory. With LIFO perpetual the debit to Cost of Sales and credit to Inventory is based on the inventory costs on hand on the date the transaction is recorded—the date the revenue is recognized and recorded. The spreadsheet entries for Woolchester for October under LIFO perpetual are shown in Table 8-3.

The treatment of the transaction on October 8 is the same as under FIFO because all of the inventory on hand on October 8 had the same cost of $50 per unit. On October 20, just before Woolchester sold 130 inventory units, there were 20 units with a cost of $50 and 125 units with a cost of $55 on hand. Since the $55 cost is associated with inventory units acquired most recently, the cost associated with those units is expensed first. Once the costs associated with the 125 $55 units are expensed, then the costs associated with the older $50 units can be expensed. Therefore, on October 20 Cost of Sales is debited for $7,125, the cost of 125 $55 units and five $50 units.

Notice that the $59 units that were purchased on October 25 do not affect the October 20 transaction because those units had not been purchased as of that date. At the end of October, there are costs associated with 15 $50 units and 75 $59 units in inventory, for an ending inventory balance of $5,175.

LIFO Periodic   When LIFO periodic is used, the costs most recently added to inventory are expensed first. However, the movement of costs from Inventory to Cost of Sales is determined at the end of the reporting period, using all inventory that was on hand during the period.

During October Woolchester had inventory costs of 100 units at $50, 125 units at $55, and 75 units at $59. The most recent costs are the $59 units, so these are expensed first, followed by the $55 units, and then by the $50 units. Since 210 units were sold

Table 8-3   Woolchester Inc.: Spreadsheet 3—LIFO Perpetual

Woolchester Inc.
Spreadsheet for Inventory Transactions for October 2005 Using LIFO Perpetual

		Cash	Inventory	Revenue	Cost of sales
October 3	Purchase 100 units @ $50	$(5,000)	$5,000		
October 8	Sell 80 units @ $125	10,000		$10,000	
Inventory on hand:	Inventory expensed:				
100 units @ $50	80 units @ $50		(4,000)		$(4,000)
Remaining in inventory:					
20 units @ $50					
October 15	Purchase 125 units @ $55	(6,875)	6,875		
October 20	Sell 130 units @ $125	16,250		16,250	
Inventory on hand:	Inventory expensed:				
20 units @ $50	125 units @ $55				
125 units @ $55	+ 5 units @ $50		(7,125)		(7,125)
Remaining in inventory:					
15 units @ $50					
October 25	Purchase 75 units @ $59	(4,425)	4,425		
October 31 **Ending balances**		**$9,950**	**$5,175**	**$26,250**	**$(11,125)**
Remaining in inventory:					
15 units @ $50 = $ 750					
75 units @ $59 = $4,425					

Table 8-4   Woolchester Inc.: Spreadsheet 4—LIFO Periodic

Woolchester Inc.
Spreadsheet for Inventory Transactions for October 2005 Using LIFO Periodic

			Cash	Inventory*	Revenue	Cost of sales
October 3		Purchase 100 units @ $50	$(5,000)	$5,000		
October 8		Sell 80 units @ $125	10,000		$10,000	
October 15		Purchase 125 units @ $55	(6,875)	6,875		
October 20		Sell 130 units @ $125	16,250		16,250	
October 25		Purchase 75 units @ $59	(4,425)	4,425		
October 31	Inventory on hand on October 31 (before recording cost of sales): 100 units @ $50 125 units @ $55 75 units @ $59	Inventory expensed for the month of October 2005: 75 units @ $59 + 125 units @ $55 + 10 units @ $50		(11,800)		$(11,800)
October 31	**Ending balances** Remaining in inventory: } 90 units @ $50 = $4,500 }		**$9,950**	**$4,500**	**$26,250**	**$(11,800)**

*In this table purchases are made directly to the Inventory account. These should have been made to the Purchases account. However, for clarity the step of recording purchases to the Purchases account and then moving them to the Inventory account is ignored.

during October, Cost of Sales must be debited and Inventory credited for the cost of the 75 $59 units, the 125 $55 units, and 10 of the $50 units. At the end of October the costs remaining in inventory are associated with 90 units with a cost of $50 each. The spreadsheet entries for Woolchester for October using LIFO periodic are shown in Table 8-4.

Average Cost Perpetual   When an average cost flow method is used, the average cost of the inventory on hand is determined when the entry that records cost of sales and the reduction to inventory is made. When a perpetual inventory control system is used, the average cost is calculated each time revenue is recognized. The average is based on the inventory costs on hand at the time the entry is made.

For Woolchester it is necessary to calculate an average when the sales are made on October 8 and October 20. The spreadsheet entries for Woolchester for October using average cost perpetual are shown in Table 8-5 (page 450).

On October 8, because there are only inventory units with costs of $50 associated with them, the average cost is $50 per unit and the entry to the spreadsheet is the same as with the other perpetual methods. When inventory is sold on October 20, the average is calculated based on the 20 $50 units and the 125 $55 units on hand on that date. The average cost is approximately $54.31 per unit ([(20 units at $50) + (125 units at $55)] ÷ 145 units) and cost of sales is $7,060.34. The average unit cost is rounded to the nearest cent, which results in the amounts in the spreadsheet being "off" by a little bit. This should not be a problem because the error caused by the rounding is not likely to be material to any user.

The $54.31 now becomes the cost associated with every unit of inventory. Cost of sales is determined simply by multiplying the number of units sold by the average cost. It is important to recognize that this average becomes the cost associated with the units remaining in inventory. We have, in effect, "lost" the actual cost of the remaining units.

Table 8-5   Woolchester Inc.: Spreadsheet 5—Average Cost Perpetual

Woolchester Inc.
Spreadsheet for Inventory Transactions for October 2005 Using Average Cost Perpetual

		Cash	Inventory	Revenue	Cost of sales
October 3	Purchase 100 units @ $50	$(5,000)	$5,000		
October 8					
Average cost per unit $= \dfrac{(100 \text{ units} \times \$50)}{100 \text{ units}}$ $= \$50$ Remaining in inventory: 20 units with an average cost of $50 per unit	Sell 80 units @ $125 Inventory expensed: 80 units @ $50	10,000	(4,000)	$10,000	($4,000)
October 15	Purchase 125 units @ $55	(6,875)	6,875		
October 20					
Average cost per unit $= \dfrac{[(20 \text{ units @ } \$50) + (125 \text{ units @ } \$55)]}{145 \text{ units}}$ $= \$54.31$ Remaining in inventory: 15 units @ $54.31	Sell 130 units @ $125 Inventory expensed: 130 units @ $54.31	16,250	(7,060.34)	16,250	(7,060.34)
October 25	Purchase 75 units @ $59	(4,425)	4,425		
October 31 Ending balances Average cost per unit: $= \dfrac{[(15 \text{ units @ } \$54.31) + (75 \text{ units @ } \$59)]}{90 \text{ units}}$ $= \$58.22$ Ending inventory $= \$58.22 \times 90$		**$9,950**	**$5,239.66***	**$26,250**	**$(11,060.34)**

*The ending inventory balance and the amount that is obtained by multiplying $58.22 × 90 units are not the same because of rounding error.

Note also that with the perpetual system the average cost is recalculated each time revenue is recognized, as well as at the end of the month. At the end of October the average cost per unit is calculated to determine the ending inventory balance and the average cost that will be carried forward to the next period. In this case, the average cost is $58.22 ([(15 units at $54.31) + (75 units at $59)] ÷ 90 units). When a new average has to be calculated in November, the cost associated with the 90 units of inventory left over from October is $58.22 each.

Average Cost Periodic   Average cost periodic works much the same way as average cost perpetual, except that the average cost is only calculated at the end of the period.

The spreadsheet entries for Woolchester for October using average cost periodic are shown in Table 8-6. For Woolchester the average cost per unit of the inventory available for sale during October is $54.33 ([(100 units at $50) + (125 units at $55) + (75 units at $59)]÷ 300 units). Cost of sales for October is simply $11,409.30, the product of the average cost and the number of units sold ($54.33 × 210). The $54.33

Table 8-6   Woolchester Inc.: Spreadsheet 6—Average Cost Periodic

Woolchester Inc.
Spreadsheet for Inventory Transactions for October 2005 Using Average Cost Periodic

		Cash	Inventory	Revenue	Cost of sales
October 3	Purchase 100 units @ $50	$(5,000)	$5,000		
October 8	Inventory expensed: 80 units @ $125	10,000		$10,000	
October 15	Purchase 125 units @ $55	(6,875)	6,875		
October 20	Inventory expensed: 130 units @ $125	16,250		16,250	
October 25	Purchase 75 units @ $59	(4,425)	4,425		
October 31	Sell 210 units @ $54.33		(11,409.30)		$(11,409.30)
Average cost = [(100 units @ $50) + (125 units @ $55) + (75 units @ $59)] ──────────── 300 units = $54.33					
October 31 Ending balances Remaining in inventory: 90 units @ $54.33 = $4,890.70		$9,950	$4,890.70	$26,250	$(11,409.30)

*In this table purchases are made directly to the Inventory account. These should have been made to the Purchases account. However, for clarity the step of recording purchases to the Purchases account and then moving them to the Inventory account is ignored.

becomes the cost associated with the 90 units of inventory on hand at the start of the next period.

Specific Identification   When the specific identification method is used, cost of sales is the actual cost of the particular units of inventory that were sold and the balance in Inventory at the end of the period is the actual cost of the units of inventory that have not yet been sold. As a result, the cost remaining in ending inventory at the end of the period and cost of sales for the period will depend on which physical units are sold.

The spreadsheet entries for Woolchester for October using specific identification are shown in Table 8-7 (page 452). When Woolchester sold 80 units on October 8, the cost of each of the units sold had to be $50. For the sale that occurred on October 20, if we assume that Woolchester sold 12 of the $50 units and 118 of the $55 units, then cost of sales for that transaction would be $7,090. The cost that would be reported in Inventory on October 31 would be $5,210, which would be the cost associated with the eight $50 units, the seven $55 units, and the 75 $59 units that were on hand on October 31.

The specific identification cost flow assumption is shown only with the perpetual method of inventory control because specific identification is typically associated with high-value inventory that requires tight control. Strictly speaking, the specific identification method is not a cost flow assumption because the actual costs of the units being sold and held in inventory are used.

If on October 20, either by design or by chance, Woolchester sold 124 of the $55 units and only six of the $50 units, cost of sales would be $11,120 instead of $11,090. In this case, ending inventory would be $5,180 instead of $5,210. Simply by changing the actual physical units that were given to customers, amounts reported on the income statement and the balance sheet change. One can see that the specific identification method can be easily manipulated by the managers to achieve their reporting objectives.

Table 8-7   Woolchester Inc.: Spreadsheet 7—Specific Identification

Woolchester Inc.
Spreadsheet for Inventory Transactions for October 2005 Using Specific Identification

		Cash	Inventory	Revenue	Cost of sales
October 3	Purchase 100 units @ $50	$(5,000)	$5,000		
October 8	Sell 80 units @ $125	10,000		$10,000	
Inventory on hand:	Inventory expensed:				
100 units @ $50	80 units @ $50		(4,000)		$(4,000)
Remaining in inventory:					
20 units @ $50					
October 15	Purchase 125 units @ $55	(6,875)	6,875		
October 20	Sell 130 units @ $125	16,250		16,250	
Inventory on hand:	Inventory expensed:				
20 units @ $50	12 units @ $50				
125 units @ $55	+ 118 units @ $55		(7,090)		(7,090)
Remaining in inventory:					
8 units @ $50					
7 units @ $55					
October 25	Purchase 75 units @ $59	(4,425)	4,425		
October 31 Ending balances		$9,950	$5,210	$26,250	$(11,090)
Remaining in inventory:					
8 units @ $50 = $ 400					
7 units @ $55 = $ 385					
75 units @ $59 = $4,425					

Summary of the Comparison of Different Cost Flow Assumptions   Figure 8-5 summarizes the data from each of the cost flow assumptions and inventory control methods discussed above. Figure 8-5 highlights a number of important points:

- Cash flow is not directly affected by the cost flow assumption or inventory control method used. In all of the situations described there is a net increase in cash of $9,950 from the purchase and sale of inventory during October. There can be a secondary effect on cash flow because the cost flow assumption and inventory control method that are used for financial reporting purposes are usually also used for tax purposes. Methods that yield higher cost of sales and, therefore, lower income before tax will have a smaller cash outflow because less tax will have to be paid.

- Cost of Sales and Inventory are affected by the choice of cost flow assumption and inventory control method. While there is an effect on the numbers reported in the financial statements, the underlying economic activity of the entity is the same regardless of the methods used.

- Because the amounts reported for Inventory and Cost of Sales differ under the different cost flow assumptions and inventory valuation methods, many other financial accounting measures and ratios are also affected. For example, gross margin and the gross margin percentage will change with the methods, as will net income, return on assets and return on equity, profit margin, current ratio, quick ratio, and debt-to-equity ratio. Again, it is important to emphasize that the underlying economic activity of the entity is not affected by these differences in methods. However, the representations of the underlying economic activity are affected, which may affect the perceptions, interpretations, and inferences of users of the information.

	Revenue	Cost of sales	Gross margin	Gross margin percentage	Cash flow	Ending inventory

Woolchester Inc.
Summary Information on Inventory Transactions for the Month Ended October 31, 2005

	Revenue	Cost of sales	Gross margin	Gross margin percentage	Cash flow	Ending inventory
FIFO perpetual	$26,250	$11,050	$15,200	57.90%	$9,950	$5,250
Average cost perpetual	26,250	11,060.34	15,189.66	57.87%	9,950	5,239.66
LIFO perpetual	26,250	11,125	15,125	57.62%	9,950	5,175
FIFO periodic	26,250	11,050	15,200	57.90%	9,950	5,250
Average cost periodic	26,250	11,409.30	14,840.70	56.54%	9,950	4,890.70
LIFO periodic	26,250	11,800	14,450	55.05%	9,950	4,500
Specific identification	26,250	11,090	15,160	57.75%	9,950	5,210

Figure 8-5

Woolchester Inc.: Summary

- The sum of cost of sales and ending inventory in each case is $16,300. This is not a coincidence. The different cost flow assumptions and inventory control methods affect the allocation of the cost of inventory between the balance sheet and the income statement but they do not affect the total amount. Ultimately, the total cost of the inventory, in this case the full $16,300 that was purchased, will find its way to the income statement. The different cost flow assumptions and inventory control methods affect when the cost of the inventory is expensed.

- When inventory prices are rising for a given inventory control method (periodic or perpetual), FIFO will always give the lowest cost of sales (and the highest gross margin and net income), while LIFO will always give the highest cost of sales (and the lowest gross margin and net income). Average cost will always be between these two. This point will be discussed further.

Which Method Is Best?

That takes care of the mechanics. We now have to figure out what all this means for the numbers that appear in financial statements and for users of financial statements. How and why does an entity choose one cost flow assumption over another? Do GAAP provide any direction for the choice? Is one cost flow assumption better than the others?

According to the *CICA Handbook* and GAAP, none of the cost-based cost flow assumptions described above is recommended or preferred. The *CICA Handbook* merely requires that the method an entity chooses for determining inventory costs should be "one which results in the fairest matching of costs against revenues." The

Question for Consideration

Figure 8-5 shows that cost of sales and gross margin are different with cost flow assumption, while cash flow is the same for each. Explain why this is the case.

Answer: The cost flow assumptions are accounting methods for allocating the cost of inventory between the balance sheet and the income statement. They are accrual accounting concepts that involve economic flows, not necessarily cash flows. The cost flow assumption an entity selects has no effect on the amount of money that is paid in cash to suppliers of inventory or for the inputs used for producing inventory. The actual amount paid in cash is not affected by accrual accounting choices made by the preparers of the financial statements. Therefore, cost of sales and gross margin will change with the cost flow assumption, but cash flows will remain the same.

requirement of fair matching is very ambiguous and pretty much allows the managers to choose the cost flow assumption they prefer, as long as it is a cost-based method. The problem with the matching argument is that it is not clear what it is we are trying to match. All of the cost flow assumptions match a cost to the revenue, although what is being matched depends on the method.

Over the years, accountants have developed many arguments for and against the various cost flow assumptions. None of these arguments has conclusively proved that one cost flow assumption is always better than the others. The implication is that we cannot say that one of the cost flow assumptions is best in all situations. Each cost flow assumption has strengths and weaknesses, and the choice depends on the information the preparers want to convey to the users. In many cases an entity will choose the method that is used by other similar entities for comparison purposes.

The *CICA Handbook* also states that the cost flow assumption that is used does not have to correspond with the physical flow of the inventory. This means that the physical flow of goods is not a criterion that managers have to consider when choosing the cost flow assumption.

We will now discuss implications of each cost flow assumption for the financial statements.

FIFO　When FIFO is used, the costs in inventory at the end of a period are the costs associated with the inventory that was purchased most recently. This means that the amount reported on the balance sheet for Inventory is as close an approximation of the replacement cost of the inventory that is possible while still using a cost-based inventory valuation method. This is a useful feature of FIFO because it provides users more relevant information about the value of an entity's inventory.

Users of financial statements who are interested, for example, in predicting future cash flows might find a FIFO-based inventory value more useful than the alternatives because it gives a more current indication of what it would cost to replace the entity's inventory. When FIFO is used in periods when prices are rising, the reported amount for ending inventory will be higher than with average cost and LIFO because the newest costs are in inventory at the end of a period. Because the more recent, higher costs are reported on the balance sheet, the current ratio will be higher when FIFO is used in a period of rising prices.

On the other hand, the costs associated with the oldest inventory are expensed to cost of sales first under FIFO. The implication of this treatment is that in a period of rising prices, cost of sales is more out of date with FIFO, compared with average cost and LIFO. Being out of date means that the most current cost of inventory is not being matched to the current revenue and, as a result, gross margin and net income are higher when FIFO is used than when LIFO or average cost are used. This effect could be misleading to a user who is attempting to predict future profitability. Future profitability is based on what inventory will cost in the future, not what it cost in the past. If inventory costs are rising and the entity cannot raise prices to offset the increase in costs, the gross margin calculated under FIFO is not as representative of the future as the alternative cost flow assumptions. Consequently, users who base their predictions about future profitability on an income statement that is based on FIFO might overestimate future profitability.

Despite the fact that the flow of inventory costs and the physical flow of inventory do not have to correspond, one of the appeals of FIFO seems to be that in most cases it does follow the physical flow of goods. The use of FIFO provides an approximation of the specific identification method, where there is a matching of the actual cost of the item sold to the revenue recognized. In many situations good inventory management requires that the oldest inventory be sold to customers first. This is, of course, crucial for perishable goods.

LIFO   LIFO matches the most recent inventory costs to revenue first. This means that when the prices of an entity's inputs are rising, cost of sales will be higher and net income will be lower than with the other cost flow assumptions. This result will not be attractive for objectives of financial reporting that are served by higher net income, such as management bonuses.

On the other hand, by matching the newer, more current costs to revenue, the LIFO income statement gives a better approximation of the current cost of operations—a more relevant and current gross margin, profit margin, and net income. This can be useful. One can argue that the wealth of an entity increases only once it is able to replace the resources it has consumed earning the current revenue. In other words, if an entity is going to continue in business, it must replace the inventory that it uses. That inventory must be replaced at the current market price, not some historical cost.

LIFO can create some big problems on the balance sheet. The almost-current cost of sales number on the income statement comes at the expense of the balance sheet. As we discussed earlier in the chapter, the costs in inventory under LIFO can be very, very old. They will certainly not approximate the replacement cost of inventory. If a bank lends money to an entity based on the amount of inventory reported on the balance sheet, LIFO would allow for a smaller amount of borrowing than FIFO would, assuming that prices were rising. This assumes that no consideration was given to the cost flow assumption used by the entity when the terms of the loan were established. The lower inventory value would also result in a lower current ratio. Overall, when prices are rising, LIFO paints a poorer picture of an entity. Also, gross margin and profit margin are lower with LIFO.

There is an additional problem associated with LIFO that can play havoc with the financial statements. The problem arises when an entity reduces the amount of inventory being held. An entity might reduce its inventory levels for efficiency purposes or because it has decided to eliminate some of its products. Whatever the reason, when the amount of inventory is reduced significantly, the entity will expense older costs, which are likely much lower than current costs. The effect will be to match low, old costs with current revenues, which will result in unusually high gross margin and net income. With LIFO managers can intentionally deplete their inventory to boost net income. Therefore, the benefits for income measurement of using LIFO can be lost if inventory levels fluctuate significantly.

Average Cost   Average cost provides results that fall in between FIFO and LIFO. That means the cost of sales is not as current as would be achieved when LIFO is used, but not as old or out of date as is achieved when FIFO is used. Conversely, average cost does not provide balance sheet information that is as current as FIFO, but it is not as out of date as LIFO. As a result of this "in the middle" effect, gross margin, net income, current ratio, and many other financial measurements fall between LIFO and FIFO.

Because average cost yields an income figure that is lower than FIFO, it is attractive for tax purposes in Canada. (Remember that LIFO is not acceptable for tax purposes in Canada.) Entities that have a tax minimization objective would choose average cost over FIFO in periods when prices are rising. One would expect that private companies would tend to prefer average cost because the tax minimization objective is more likely to be dominant. This will not always be the case, since some private firms may be interested in maximizing their net income to satisfy lenders or because of an upcoming sale of shares.

Comment: This section has highlighted the fact that different cost flow assumptions can have a significant effect on the cost of inventory that is reported on the balance sheet and the amount of cost of sales. It is crucial to understand that the different cost flow assumptions provide different results *only* if the cost of inventory is changing. If the cost of inventory remains constant over a period of time, all the methods will yield the same results. That said, it is unusual for the price of anything to remain constant for any length of time. Even in periods of very low inflation, the prices of individual goods and services are rising and falling.

It is important for users of financial statements to be aware of the accounting choices made by the preparers of the statements. As our discussion of cost flow assumptions has shown, the choice of accounting policies can have significant effects on many of the accounting numbers that users will use to analyze an entity. Without knowing the accounting policy choices that an entity has made, it is virtually impossible to make any sense of the information in the financial statements.

Comparisons among entities are very difficult at the best of times. Comparisons are invalid when the entities being compared use different accounting policies. The *CICA Handbook* provides some assistance here because entities are required to disclose the cost flow assumption being used. For comparisons of an entity's accounting information over time, consistency requires that an entity use the same set of accounting policies year after year. While changes in accounting policies are allowable, it is not possible to change accounting policies every period and still adhere to GAAP. In addition, when accounting policies change, it is necessary to restate the financial statements so they present prior years' statements with the new accounting policies.

Retail Method

Note 1E to MWW's financial statements states that "merchandise inventory is accounted for by the retail method…." (page A-49). The **retail method** is a method widely used by retail businesses as a way of estimating the cost of ending inventory and cost of sales that uses the retail price of merchandise and the relationship between the cost and the selling price of the merchandise. The retail method is not a separate cost flow assumption, but a method of estimating inventory and cost of sales under one of the cost flow assumptions. The retail method is useful if an entity values its inventory by assigning retail prices to the inventory rather than the cost. The retail method is also useful if an entity wants to prepare financial statements during a year (perhaps monthly or quarterly) and it is not practical to physically count the inventory each time. This section will briefly explain how the retail method works so that readers will understand how MWW accounts for its inventory.

When the retail method is used, the retail value of inventory on hand is determined rather than its cost. Since inventory must be valued at cost if GAAP are being followed, the retail value of inventory must be adjusted to cost. This adjustment is made by using the relationship between cost and retail price of the inventory that was available for sale during the period. Inventory available for sale during a period is equal to beginning inventory plus inventory purchased during the period. To use the retail method, an entity must know the cost and the retail value of the goods available for sale during the period so that the relationship between cost and retail price can be determined. Ending inventory at retail is determined by a physical count, or by calculating it as the difference between inventory available for sale during the period at retail and sales during the period.

An example will show how the retail method works. As you study the example, remember that the cost of ending inventory is not known and that is why the retail method is used.

Figure 8-6 shows how the cost of ending inventory on July 31, 2006 is estimated for Usk Ltd. (Usk) using the retail method. First, Usk determines the goods that were available for sale during July at cost and at retail. During July 2006 Usk had goods available for sale that had a retail value of $540,000 and cost of $324,000. Then the cost ratio is determined by dividing the cost of the goods available for sale by the retail

Usk Ltd. Estimation of Ending Inventory on July 31, 2006 Using the Retail Method			
	Cost	**Retail**	**Cost ratio** $\left[\dfrac{\text{Cost}}{\text{Retail}}\right]$
Inventory on July 1, 2006 (beginning inventory)	$ 65,000	$120,000	
Purchases during July 2006	259,000	420,000	
Goods available for sale during July	$324,000	$540,000	0.60
Less: Sales during July 2006		390,000	
Inventory on July 31, 2006 (ending inventory), at retail		$150,000	
Inventory on July 31, 2006 (ending inventory), at cost ($150,000 × 0.60)	$ 90,000		

Figure 8-6

Usk Ltd.: Ending Inventory Estimation Using the Retail Method

price of the goods available for sale (note: cost ratio = 1 – gross margin). For July 2006 the cost of Usk's inventory was 60% of its retail value ($324,000 ÷ $540,000).

Next, the ending inventory at retail is calculated by subtracting sales during the period (which of course take place at the retail sales price) from the goods available for sale during the month at retail. The difference gives an estimate of the goods on hand at the end of period at their retail value. During July Usk had goods available for sale at retail of $540,000 and sales of $390,000, which means that the retail value of ending inventory on July 31, 2006 was $150,000 ($540,000 – $390,000). The cost of that inventory is estimated by multiplying the inventory at retail at the end of period by the cost ratio for the period. For Usk, we multiply the ending inventory at retail of $150,000 by the cost ratio of 0.60 to obtain our estimate of the cost of ending inventory of $90,000. Note that if the inventory were counted at the end of the period, the retail price of the inventory determined by the count would be multiplied by the cost ratio to give an estimate of the cost of ending inventory.

In practice, the retail method can involve many more complexities. For example, most retail stores carry goods at a variety of gross margins. Also, during the course of a period the retail price of goods available for sale will decrease and increase.

The Lower of Cost and Market Rule

In the fashion business, what is popular today might be virtually unsaleable in a couple of months. MWW might buy a large supply of fashionable pants and shirts for the 2004 fall season, but when the spring 2005 merchandise arrives it may still have some of the inventory left over from fall that might not be easy to sell at the full retail price. From a business standpoint, it makes sense for MWW to sell those fall fashions for whatever it can get—even if it means selling them for less than their cost.

But how should MWW account for clothes that cannot be sold for more than what they cost? According to GAAP, inventory on hand at the end of a period must be evaluated according to the lower-of-cost-and-market rule. The **lower of cost and market (LCM) rule** requires that when the market value of inventory at the end of a reporting period is lower than its cost, the inventory must be reported on the balance sheet at its market value. If the market value of inventory is less than its cost, the inventory must be written down to its market value. The amount of the write-down is the difference between the inventory's cost and its market value, and it is reported as a loss on the income statement in the period that the market value of the inventory falls, not when the inventory is sold. This treatment is a departure from what is ordinarily done under GAAP, where inventory remains at its cost until it is sold. If the inventory must be written down, the following journal entry is recorded:

> Dr. Cost of sales (expenses +, owner's equity –)   xxx
>   Cr. Inventory (asset –)   xxx
> To record a write-down of inventory.

The effect of this journal entry is to reduce the balance in the Inventory account and increase expenses and thereby decrease net income. This journal entry buries the loss suffered on the decline in the value of inventory in Cost of Sales. The amount of the write-down could also be disclosed separately in the income statement, either on a separate line in the income statement or in the notes.

If the write-down is included in Cost of Sales, a financial statement user will not be able to determine if an inventory write-down has occurred or the amount of the write-down. And when the amount of the write-down is included in Cost of Sales, financial ratios such as gross margin percentage might be distorted. Without adequate disclosure of the existence of the write-down, it is not possible for a user to understand why the gross margin percentage has changed from previous years. Once inventory is written down to its market value, it cannot be written back up in the event that the market price of the inventory increases.

For some entities, writing down inventory is a regular occurrence. For example, most entities that sell fashion goods will have out-of-style merchandise every year that has to be written down to market value. If such write-downs are normal and in the ordinary course of business, then not separately disclosing information about them is probably not a serious problem. However, it would be valuable for users of the financial statements to be aware of unusual write-downs of inventory. Separate disclosure of an unusual inventory write-down would be helpful to users for evaluating the performance of management and for predicting future earnings of the entity.

Let's consider an example. In its fiscal year ended January 29, 2000 Dylex Limited (Dylex), operator of the BiWay, Fairweather, and Tip Top chains, took a $25,000,000 write-down in its BiWay Division, in part to reduce the value of its inventory. If you examine Dylex's annual report, the write-down is discussed in various parts of the report, but it is not mentioned in the financial statements or notes. Exhibit 8-1 provides extracts from Dylex's 1999 annual report.[1] Keep in mind that it is difficult to fully understand the impact of the write-down from the disclosure provided.

As was discussed in Chapter 5, the reason for this departure from the usual transactions-based accounting approach is conservatism. When conservatism is applied to inventory, the historical cost, transactions-based valuation of inventory is replaced with a market value that is not supported by a transaction if the market value of the inventory is less than the cost. If there were no LCM rule and the market value of inventory were below cost, the value of inventory on the balance sheet would be overstated. That is, the actual future benefit associated with the inventory would be less than the amount reported on the balance sheet. From this perspective the LCM rule makes sense. (The LCM rule is also applied to current assets other than inventory, such as temporary investments.)

Probably the major criticism with the use of the LCM rule and conservatism is that decreases in the value of inventory are recognized, whereas increases are not recognized until the inventory is sold. Also, application of the LCM rule sacrifices consistency, because cost is not being applied consistently from period to period.

There are many circumstances in which the market value of inventory can fall, in addition to clothing going out of style. Technological change is another reason. For example, the selling price of last year's leading-edge computer equipment will usually fall dramatically when faster and more powerful computers come on the market. Another example is goods that are damaged. If the market value of damaged goods is less than cost, the inventory should be written down to market. For commodities such as lumber or minerals, market prices rise and fall with market conditions, and in some circumstances the market price may fall below the cost of producing the commodity.

Exhibit 8-1

Dylex Limited: Extract from 1999
Annual Report

consolidated statements of earnings

For the 52 weeks ended	January 29 2000	January 30 1999
(thousands of dollars, except per share data)		
Sales	$1,081,767	$1,077,102
Earnings (loss) from operations before the following	$ (5,101)	$ 47,538
Depreciation	20,119	15,074
Amortization	1,099	89
Interest on long-term debt	29	39
Interest on obligations under capital leases	419	50
Interest income	–	(279)
Interest on operating line	3,016	1,789
	24,682	16,762
Earnings (loss) before the undernoted	(29,783)	30,776
Unusual items (note 8)	(6,000)	(10,200)
Earnings (loss) before income taxes	(35,783)	20,576
Income taxes (note 10)	604	665
Net earnings (loss)	$ (36,387)	$ 19,911
Earnings (loss) per share (note 7g)	$ (0.73)	$ 0.39
Fully diluted earnings per share (note 7g)	$ N.A.	$ 0.38

notes to consolidated financial statements

As at January 29, 2000, and January 30, 1999

1. Summary of Significant Accounting Policies

Inventories

Retail inventories, with the exception of BiWay, are valued at the lower of cost and net realizable value less normal profit margins using the retail inventory method. Inventories of BiWay and manufacturing operations are valued at the lower of average cost and net realizable value.

8. Unusual Items

During the year ended January 29, 2000, the Company recorded unusual items in the amount of $6.0 million. This amount represents costs associated with reorganization of the corporate departments.

During the year ended January 30, 1999, the Company recorded unusual items in the amount of $10.2 million. This amount represents inventory valuation adjustments and other costs related to a strategic repositioning of the Company's Tip Top Tailors division.

management's discussion and analysis

BiWay

BiWay's sales were down 0.8% for the 1999 year to $582.9 million, the division recorded an operating loss of $33.9 million and same-store-sales fell 4.4%. Included in the loss is a $25.0 million one-time write-down taken in the second quarter to reduce the value of BiWay's inventory, address problems relating to the start-up of its distribution facility and correct internal process and control breakdowns. The division continues to improve its merchandise mix and store layout to meet customer needs.

While BiWay encountered significant setbacks in 1999, the issues uncovered throughout the course of the year are being addressed and steps have already been taken to return BiWay to its position as a profitable Canadian discount business. Problems at the BiWay Distribution Centre have been identified and rectified, a full year-end inventory count has indicated that shrink levels are returning to acceptable levels, and recommendations made as part of a business review conducted at Management's request by Ernst & Young Consultants have been, and will continue to be, implemented. As well, BiWay's senior management team has been solidified and is having a positive effect on all levels of the organization.

Application of the LCM rule requires a definition of market. The preparers must choose a definition of market just as they choose the revenue recognition policy or the cost flow assumption that the entity will use. The definition of market is disclosed in the financial statements. Once selected, it should be applied consistently from year to year, barring any change in the constraints, facts, or objectives that would justify a change. It is not necessary to use the same definition of market for all inventory—the preparers can choose different definitions of market for different types of inventory.

The definitions most commonly used for market are replacement cost and net realizable value.

- **Replacement cost** is the amount that an entity would have to pay to replace its existing inventory (or other asset).

- **Net realizable value** (**NRV**) is the amount that the entity would receive from selling the inventory (or other asset) less any additional selling costs that would have to be incurred.

The *CICA Handbook* does not provide much guidance on what definition of market should be used. It merely requires that entities explicitly state their definition of market. *Financial Reporting in Canada*, 26th Edition, reports that of 162 companies in 1999, 75 used only NRV and seven used only replacement cost. Sixty-six other companies used more than one definition, most commonly replacement cost and NRV.[2]

Let's consider an example to show how the LCM rule is applied. Sangree Ltd. (Sangree) values its inventory at the lower of cost and net realizable value (NRV). Sangree carries three inventory items: item 1, item 2, and item 3. The cost and NRV of Sangree's inventory on December 31, 2004, are shown in Figure 8-7. Column 1 in Figure 8-7 shows the cost of each item in inventory, column 2 provides the NRV of each item, and column 3 shows the lower of cost and NRV for each item.

There is actually more than one approach for applying the LCM rule, and the approach used can affect the amount of the write-down and the value of ending inventory. One approach compares the cost and market for the entire inventory. Another approach compares cost and market item by item. Both methods are used in practice.

If cost and market are compared for the entire inventory, the total cost of inventory—the cost of items 1, 2, and 3 in total—is compared with the market value of the entire inventory. For Sangree we compare the total cost in column 1 with the total NRV in column 2 in Figure 8-7. Since the total NRV is lower than total cost, the LCM rule requires that the inventory be written down to its market value or NRV. The amount of the write-down required is $3,950 ($145,500 − $141,550).

Applying LCM on an item-by-item basis is a bit trickier. Instead of looking at the cost and NRV for the entire inventory, we compare cost and NRV for each item in

Figure 8-7

Inventory Information for Sangree Ltd.

	Column 1	Column 2	Column 3
Sangree Ltd. **Inventory Information on December 31, 2004**			
	Cost	**Net realizable value**	**Lower of cost and net realizable value**
Item 1	$ 72,300	$ 69,250	$ 69,250
Item 2	21,200	22,400	21,200
Item 3	52,000	49,900	49,900
Total	$145,500	$141,550	$140,350

inventory. Whichever of cost and market is lower for each item is used as the basis for determining the value of the inventory. For inventory Items 1 and 3, NRV is lower than cost, so NRV is used and included in column 3, while for inventory Item 2, cost is lower than NRV, so cost is used. The total of column 3 is the amount that will appear on the balance sheet for inventory. Since the inventory is recorded at cost, a write-down of $5,150 ($145,500 − $140,350) is required. The item-by-item method provides the lowest possible value for inventory and, therefore, is considered more conservative than looking at the inventory in total.

If Sangree used the total inventory approach to determine the market value of its inventory, the journal entry it would make to record the loss on its inventory would be:

    Dr. Cost of sales (expense +, shareholders' equity −)   3,950
          Cr. Inventory (asset −)   3,950
    To record the write-down of inventory to market.

It is important to remember that the LCM rule is not intended to find the lowest possible value for inventory. The comparison of cost and market is based on whatever definition of cost the entity chooses (cost based on FIFO or LIFO or average cost) and whatever definition of market it chooses. If an entity uses the average cost as its cost flow assumption and NRV as its definition of market, then those two measures are used for comparison. If, for example, replacement cost gave a lower market value than NRV, the entity would not switch its market definition to replacement cost so that it could obtain the lowest possible valuation. In each period the comparison would be based on the definitions that the entity selected. These measures should be applied consistently.

For tax purposes entities are allowed to deduct write-downs of inventory to market.

Question for Consideration

Zoar Inc. values its inventory using the lower of cost and replacement cost. On July 31, 2004 Zoar's records showed the following:

	Cost	Replacement cost
Item 1	$125,000	$115,000
Item 2	220,000	235,000
Total	$345,000	$350,000

Apply the LCM rule and determine the amount that should be reported for inventory on Zoar's July 31, 2004 balance sheet. Determine the amount of the write-down that is required and prepare the journal entry to record the write-down. Answer the question using the total inventory approach and the item-by-item approach.

Answer: Using the total inventory approach, the cost of the inventory ($345,000) is less than its replacement cost. Therefore, the inventory can be reported on the balance sheet at its cost of $345,000. No write-down is required.

If the item-by-item approach is used, the replacement cost of item 1 (replacement cost [$115,000] < cost [$125,000]) and the cost of item 2 (replacement cost [$235,000] > cost [$220,000]) are used to determine the value of ending inventory. Therefore, the value of ending inventory should be $335,000 ($115,000 + $220,000) and a write-down of $10,000 ($345,000 − $335,000) is required. The journal entry to record the write-down is:

    Dr. Cost of sales (expense +, shareholders' equity −)   10,000
         Cr. Inventory (asset −)   10,000
    To record the write-down of inventory.

Direct and Absorption Costing

Determining the cost of inventory of manufacturers and processors has an additional complexity. In a manufacturing or processing company, it is necessary to "build" the cost of inventory from the inputs that go into the production of the finished product. The difficult question that accountants and managers face is, What costs should be included in inventory?

We can classify the costs that go into the production of a product into two broad categories:

1. **Prime costs** are the costs of direct materials and labour used in production. These costs can be easily traced to the product and it is clear that they should be included in inventory. For example, a manufacturer that supplies jeans to MWW will incur costs for the fabric, zippers, buttons, thread, and so on used to make the jeans. In addition, workers will have to cut the fabric and do the stitching and sewing required to make the pants.

2. **Overhead** is the indirect costs of manufacturing a product. Overhead costs are more difficult or even impossible to associate directly with the product being produced. For MWW's jeans, overhead would include supervisors in the factory, the use of sewing machines, utilities, and the factory itself.

The amount of some types of overhead costs vary with the amount of output that is produced. For example, the amount of electricity that is used will increase with the quantity of jeans produced. Overhead that varies with the amount of production is called **variable overhead**.

Other overhead is unaffected by the amount of production. For example, the cost of heating the factory and the utilization of the factory building itself will not be affected by the quantity of jeans produced. Overhead that is unaffected by the amount of production is called **fixed overhead**.

When all costs—prime and overhead—are included in the cost of inventory, the costing method is called **absorption costing**. When prime costs plus variable overhead are included in inventory, the costing method is called **direct costing**. When only prime costs are included, the costing method is called **prime costing**. Costs that are included in inventory are expensed in the period that the inventory is sold. Costs that are not included in the cost of inventory are treated as period costs and are expensed when incurred. With direct costing, fixed overhead is treated as a period cost. With prime costing, all overhead is treated as a period cost. Figure 8-8 shows how costs flow through to the income statement under the three costing methods.

Because the different types of costs are accounted for differently under the three costing methods, the costing method used by an entity can affect the amount of expenses and the net income that are reported in a period. The reason is that the costing method affects the timing of expensing certain costs. Over the life of the business, total production costs will be the same regardless of the costing method used, so cost of sales and net income will be the same.

As with so many accounting problems, the issue is *when* the expense is recognized, not *if* it will be recognized. Ending inventory will always be higher with absorption costing because more costs are included in inventory. Having a larger balance in inventory can be useful if bank lending is tied to the amount of inventory on hand. By including more costs in inventory, a company is able to increase the amount that it can borrow.

There may also be tax implications for the different methods. Direct costing expenses certain costs sooner and, therefore, achieves a deferral of income and income taxes.

GAAP only provide vague guidance about the costs that should be included in

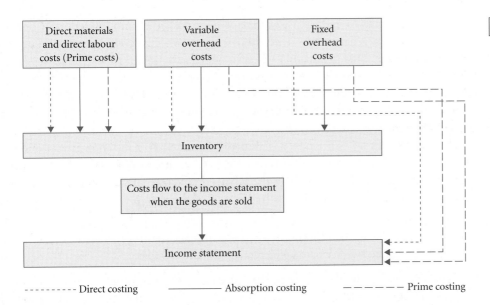

Figure 8-8

Absorption vs. Direct vs. Prime Costing

inventory. The *CICA Handbook* requires that the cost of materials and direct labour be included in inventory, along with "an applicable share of overhead." The *CICA Handbook* clearly requires the inclusion of direct materials and labour, along with some overhead. This means that prime costing will not be seen when an entity is constrained by GAAP.

The problem is that it is up to management to decide what constitutes an applicable share of overhead. The interpretation could range from the inclusion of only variable overhead costs to the full allocation of fixed overhead, or anywhere in between. Some entities may include certain fixed overhead or variable overhead costs in inventory, but not others. Other entities may include different overhead costs in inventory. The result is that the comparability of financial statements—even the financial statements of similar entities—is impaired. Because prime costing is not allowed under GAAP or for tax purposes, its usage in Canada is rare.

Valuing Inventory at Other than Cost

It is easy to forget that it is possible to value inventory and other assets in ways other than cost. Many people who become comfortable with accounting information prepared in accordance with GAAP, or at least in accordance with the cost concept, may forget that there are legitimate, often useful alternatives to cost for valuing assets and liabilities. For many users of financial statements, these alternative valuation methods can provide information that is relevant for their decision making. GAAP's reluctance to embrace market value accounting for inventory is because of the trade-off that exists between relevance and reliability. While many users and uses of accounting information might benefit from the market value of inventory, a market value measure is often less reliable than cost, sometimes much less reliable. Accounting standard setters have concluded that the loss of reliability from having to estimate current values is not worth any benefits that could be derived from having the more relevant information.

The market value measures that are usually given consideration when accountants talk about alternatives to cost are the same ones that were discussed when we examined the lower of cost and market rule—replacement cost and net realizable value. What is different between the LCM rule and using market value for valuing inventory is that the LCM rule only applies when market value is less than cost. When market value accounting is used for inventory, the market value is always used, regardless of the cost of the inventory.

When inventory is valued using replacement cost, the amount reported on the balance sheet is the amount that it would cost to replace the inventory on hand on the balance sheet date. This means that when financial statements are prepared, it is necessary to adjust the balance in the Inventory account for changes in the replacement cost of the inventory since it was purchased. At the time inventory is purchased or manufactured, the cost and the replacement cost are the same. After that, the cost to buy or make the same item can change.

For example, if an entity purchased inventory for $1,000 and then at year end the inventory had a replacement cost of $1,100, the entity would make the following journal entry to record the change in the replacement cost. This example assumes that none of the inventory had been sold by the end of the year.

Dr. Inventory (assets +)   100
    Cr. Holding gain (income statement +, owner's equity +)   100
To record the increase in the replacement cost of inventory.

The amount by which the replacement cost of the inventory changes from the date it was purchased to either the date it was sold or the end of the period is called a **holding gain or loss**. This terminology makes sense. If the value of inventory, or any asset, increases while you own it, you are better off. If the price falls, you are worse off. This change is wealth and the change in value occurred by simply owning or "holding" the inventory—thus the term holding gain or loss.

When replacement cost accounting is used, a holding gain or holding loss is recognized in the financial statements regardless of whether the inventory is sold. This is a major departure from transactions-based, historical cost accounting where gains are recognized only if there is a transaction. If a holding gain or loss occurs on inventory that has not been sold by the end of the period, it is an **unrealized holding gain or loss**. Realization of a gain or loss occurs when there is a transaction or exchange supporting the change in value. If the replacement cost of inventory changes from the date it is purchased (or from the beginning of the period) to the date it sold, there is a holding gain or loss, but it is a **realized holding gain or loss** because the inventory has been sold. Traditional historical cost accounting recognizes realized holding gains when the inventory is sold, but the holding gains are not identified separately in the income statement. GAAP recognize unrealized holding losses because of the LCM rule.

Valuing inventory at its NRV (selling price less additional selling costs) is equivalent to recognizing the revenue from the sale of the inventory as soon as it is received from the supplier. The profit that will be earned from the sale of the inventory is recognized when the inventory is acquired. However, because there is no actual buyer for the inventory, the debit increases the value of Inventory rather than Accounts Receivable. By recording the inventory at NRV users get an idea of the amount of cash that will be realized from the sale of the inventory. This would be useful information for predicting cash flows. Of course, estimating what inventory will be sold for can be difficult in many situations.

One final point about using market value methods for valuing inventory: There is no need for a cost flow assumption. All inventory is valued at the same amount at a point in time, so it is not necessary to make assumptions as to which inventory cost is "sold" first.

Examples of Inventory Disclosures in Financial Statements

When you read the annual report of a company that follows Canadian GAAP, what can you expect to find about inventory? The *CICA Handbook* requires that an entity disclose the method it uses to value its inventory—that is, its cost flow assumption. The *CICA Handbook* goes on to state that if "cost" is not significantly different from the "recent" cost of inventory, then the cost flow assumption used does not have to be stated. This is probably the reason why MWW does not state a cost flow assumption in its annual report. Entities are encouraged (not required) to disclose the amounts of major categories of inventory, such as finished goods, supplies, raw materials, etc.

Exhibit 8-2 provides two examples of the type of information about inventory that appears in entities' financial statements.[3]

- Panel A provides information about Brick Brewing Co. Limited's (Brick) inventory. Brick is a small beer brewer in Ontario. Brick's balance sheet for the year ended January 31, 2000 reports inventory of $2,341,585, representing about 68% of current assets and about 12% of total assets. The balance sheet only reports a single number for the entire inventory held by Brick.

    www.brickbeer.com

    To get more detail about Brick's inventory it is necessary to examine Note 2 to the financial statements. Note 2 shows that Brick's inventory is made up of several components—promotional inventory, returnable containers, raw materials and supplies, and WIP and finished goods. To understand the numbers on the balance sheet and in Note 2, it is necessary to know the accounting policies Brick uses to account for its inventory. Note 1(b) discloses that raw materials, supplies, and promotional materials are valued at the lower of FIFO cost and replacement value. WIP and finished goods are valued at the lower of cost (the cost flow assumption is not stated) determined using absorption costing and net realizable value.

    The Brick example shows that different inventory can be accounted for in different ways. In this case, Brick's definition of market for purposes of the LCM rule depends on the type of inventory. It is also possible for an entity to use different cost flow assumptions for different types of inventory.

- Panel B provides information about TGS Properties Ltd. (TGS). TGS is a rapidly growing and diversified western Canadian commercial real estate company.

    www.tgsproperties.com

    What is interesting about property development companies is that they too have inventory, but it is not usually described as inventory in the financial statements. TGS reports on its balance sheet an account called "Properties under development, construction and held for sale." This is TGS's inventory. The accounting for this asset is described in Note 1. The note explains that properties held under development, construction and held for sale are valued at the lower of cost and net realizable value. The note also describes the costs that are included in the account.

    TGS does not state a cost flow assumption because in this case specific identification is likely used. Each real property project is unique and identifiable so it is possible and appropriate to keep track of each separately.

Consignment Inventory

Sometimes an entity (the owning entity) provides its inventory to another entity (the selling entity) to sell, but the selling entity doesn't buy, own, or assume the rights and risks of ownership of the inventory. Inventory that is held for sale by the selling entity, but not owned by the selling entity, is known as **consignment inventory**. For example, it is very common for art dealers to accept works of art from artists on consignment. The art dealer displays the art and tries to sell it to customers. If a particular piece of art doesn't sell, it is returned to the artist. If a customer purchases a piece of art, the art dealer receives a commission and the artist receives the selling price of the art, less the commission. (A **commission** is a payment made to a seller as compensa-

Exhibit 8-2

Examples of Inventory Disclosures

Panel A: Brick Brewing Co. Ltd.

January 31, 2000 and 1999	2000	1999
Assets		
Current assets:		
Accounts receivable	$ 1,076,364	$ 950,483
Inventories (note 2)	2,341,585	2,546,051
Prepaid expenses	45,944	121,654
Total current assets	3,463,893	3,618,188
Capital assets (note 3)	10,298,446	9,770,452
Trademarks and other deferred costs (note 4)	6,020,287	6,401,183
	$19,782,626	$19,789,823

1. Significant accounting policies:

(b) Inventories:

Raw materials, supplies, and promotional items are valued at the lower of cost (determined on a first-in, first-out basis) and replacement value. Work-in-process and finished goods are valued at the lower of cost (including direct materials, labour and overhead costs) and net realizable value. Returnable containers are recorded at cost.

2. Inventories:

	2000	1999
Promotional inventory	$294,746	$252,487
Returnable containers	802,141	747,903
Raw materials and supplies	713,458	908,711
Work-in-process and finished goods	531,240	636,950
	$2,341,585	$2,546,051

Panel B: TGS Properties Ltd.

CONSOLIDATED BALANCE SHEETS

(In thousands of dollars)

	December 31, 2000	January 31, 2000
Assets		
Revenue producing properties (Note 3)	$ 84,231	$ 62,049
Land held for future development (Note 4)	43,645	—
Properties under development, construction and for sale (Note 5)	6,842	—
Portfolio investment (Note 6)	—	2,757
Cash and term deposits	4,106	3,153
Accounts receivable	5,660	228
Other assets (Note 7)	9,706	4,051
	$154,190	$ 72,238

1. SIGNIFICANT ACCOUNTING POLICIES

Properties Under Development, Construction and For Sale

Properties under development, construction and for sale are recorded at the lower of cost and net realizable value and is property on which significant development activity is taking place. This encompasses costs related to the specific projects, including an allocation of land and capitalized interest, administrative and development costs.

5. PROPERTIES UNDER DEVELOPMENT, CONSTRUCTION AND FOR SALE

	As at December 31, 2000	As at January 31, 2000
Residential land, under development	$1,140	$—
Residential land, serviced	2,891	—
	4,031	—
Interval ownership projects, completed	2,811	—
	$6,842	$—

tion for making a sale. A commission can be based on the selling price of the item, on the gross margin, or be a fixed fee.)

Consignment selling is attractive to the selling entity because it does not have to invest in inventory, so cash is conserved. The risk to the seller is lower because he or she can't get "stuck" with the inventory since it can always be returned to the owner. On the other hand, the inventory's owner has a continuing investment in the inventory and greater risk than with a traditional sale because the owner retains ownership of the inventory.

From an accounting standpoint, consignment inventory is included in the inventory account of the owning entity (not in the inventory account of the selling entity). Revenue on the sale of consignment inventory is only recognized when the inventory is sold by the selling entity to a customer. It is important for the owning entity to remember to include the consignment inventory in its year-end financial statements, even though it does not have physical custody of the inventory.

Inventory Accounting and Income Taxes

The accounting choices that the preparers of financial statements make frequently have tax implications. Often, as we have discussed, preparers must choose among accounting alternatives that can lower the entity's tax burden or achieve some other objective of financial reporting. In situations where the *Income Tax Act* (*ITA*) does not specify a treatment, the method used for financial reporting purposes will often be selected for tax purposes. Inventory accounting is one such situation. The *ITA* is not very specific about how to account for inventory for tax purposes. Therefore, entities will usually use the inventory accounting methods selected for the general purpose financial statements for tax purposes, which means that these accounting choices can have a bearing on the amount of tax an entity pays.

The Canada Customs and Revenue Agency (CCRA), the Canadian government agency responsible for the administration and enforcement of the Canadian federal tax laws, suggests that the same cost flow assumption that is used for financial reporting purposes should also be used for tax purposes. While in principle using different methods for financial reporting and tax is allowable, using different methods may raise a red flag that may encourage the CCRA to investigate. That said, the CCRA does not automatically accept the method used for financial reporting purposes. The CCRA has stated that "the method used for income tax purposes should be the one that gives the truer picture of the taxpayer's income."[4] Even if the method used for financial reporting purposes is acceptable according to GAAP, the CCRA can challenge the choice if it believes that the method is not the one that "gives the truer picture of taxpayer income."

www.ccra-adrc.gc.ca

The LIFO cost flow assumption cannot be used for tax purposes. LIFO is not allowed because it tends to lower taxable income unreasonably, at least in the eyes of the CCRA and the courts. If an entity chooses LIFO for financial reporting purposes, it must switch to an alternative method such as FIFO, average cost, or specific identification, to determine cost of sales for tax purposes. As a result, LIFO is rarely used in Canada. *Financial Reporting in Canada*, 26th Edition, reports that in 1999 only six of 163 firms used LIFO.[5]

In contrast, in the United States LIFO is allowable for tax purposes provided that the entity also uses LIFO for financial reporting purposes. As a result, the use of LIFO is much more widespread in the U.S. because LIFO can defer taxes for a long time. However, preparers in the U.S. are faced with the conflict of lower tax payments by using LIFO versus lower accounting income, which may be inconsistent with other objectives. The fact that so many entities in the U.S. use LIFO suggest how important the tax minimization objective is to many preparers.

The definition of cost for tax purposes is similar to that used for accounting purposes. The CCRA explains that for inventories of merchandise purchased for resale or raw materials acquired for a manufacturing process, cost means laid-down cost. Laid-down cost includes invoice cost, customs and excise duties, transportation and other acquisition costs and, where they are significant, storage costs.[6] For tax purposes, entities can use either direct or absorption costing, but not prime costing—some overhead must be allocated to inventory. If an entity has an objective of minimizing taxes, direct costing is the better choice because all fixed overhead costs are treated as period costs and expensed when they are incurred. If absorption costing is used, some of the overhead costs will be included in inventory at the end of the year instead of being expensed.

Entities are also allowed to use the lower of cost and market rule for inventory valuation purposes. If the fair market value of inventory at the end of a year is less than its cost, then the taxpayer can use fair market value. This treatment allows the taxpayer to reduce income by writing down the value of inventory to fair market value. Taxpayers are expected to use the same definition of market for tax purposes as they do for financial reporting purposes.

The CCRA requires that methods used to account for inventory for tax purposes be applied consistently from period to period. Once a method is used for tax purposes, it can only be changed with the permission of the Minister of National Revenue. The Minister will usually approve a change if the new method proposed by the taxpayer:

a.   is a more appropriate way of determining income,

b.   will be used for financial reporting purposes, and

c.   will be used consistently in future years.[7]

This constraint on the ability of taxpayers to change methods of accounting for inventory is intended to limit an entity's ability to make changes simply to avoid tax.

Interpreting and Analyzing Inventory Information in the Financial Statements

For many businesses, management of inventory is a crucial management responsibility. Management's effectiveness and efficiency in managing inventory can have a significant impact on the performance of the entity. Managing inventory requires careful balance. Carrying too much or too little inventory can be costly. Remember from Chapter 6 that usually at least some of an entity's inventory has been fully paid for. That means that an entity's cash must be invested in inventory and is not available for other purposes. The more inventory that an entity has, the more cash that is tied up. Also, costs incurred for storage, insurance, and taxes will increase with larger amounts of inventory, and higher levels of inventory may mean that the entity may be unable to sell some of the inventory, or may have to sell it at a discount.

On the other hand, too little inventory may mean that an entity runs out of the inventory that it requires to meet customers' needs on a timely basis. When an entity is out of stock, customers may take their business elsewhere, which means a loss of revenue for that particular transaction. The impact may be more serious than the loss of a single sale. The customer may be lost permanently, which means that the stream of revenue that the customer would have generated is lost. Thus the impact of not carrying enough inventory is that revenues will decline. If a manufacturing company runs out of inventory that is required in its production process, the entire production process may be forced to stop, which would be very costly.

A ratio that is often used to evaluate how well inventory is being managed is the inventory turnover ratio. The **inventory turnover ratio** provides information on how efficiently inventory is being managed by measuring how quickly the entity is able to sell its inventory. The inventory turnover ratio is defined as:

$$\text{Inventory turnover ratio} = \frac{\text{Cost of sales}}{\text{Average inventory}}$$

Average inventory can be calculated by summing the amount in the Inventory account at the beginning and the end of the period and dividing by two. A better measure of average inventory can be obtained by using quarterly or monthly data if they are available. This is especially important for entities that are seasonal. For example, MWW has its lowest amount of inventory at its year end and the highest amount just before the winter and Christmas seasons.[8]

Note that if cost of sales for a period other than a year is used to calculate the inventory turnover ratio, it is necessary to annualize the ratio. For example, if the ratio is calculated for an entity's first quarter, the resulting ratio must be multiplied by four. If the calculation is being done for three-quarters of a year then the ratio must be multiplied by 4/3 or 1.333 to give an annualized inventory turnover ratio.

The inventory turnover ratio indicates the number of times during a period the entity is able to purchase and sell its stock of inventory. Usually, the higher the inventory turnover ratio, the better, because a higher ratio indicates that the entity can sell or "turn over" the inventory more quickly. A high turnover ratio indicates that the inventory is more liquid because the inventory is sold more quickly and therefore cash will be realized sooner than with slower-moving inventory. A lower inventory turnover ratio may indicate that inventory is not selling or is slow moving, that there is obsolete inventory, or that there is low demand for the inventory. However, a decreasing inventory turnover ratio could indicate that inventory is being built up in anticipation of increasing sales or because of an expansion of the business.

As with other financial ratios, it is not possible to make sense of the inventory turnover ratio in absolute terms. The ratio must be considered in comparison with other, similar entities, or for a particular entity over time. Inventory turnover ratios can vary significantly among industries.

Another measure used to evaluate the efficiency of inventory management is the average number of days inventory on hand. The **average number of days inventory on hand** indicates the number of days it takes an entity to sell its inventory. The average number of days inventory on hand is defined as:

$$\text{Average number of days inventory on hand} = \frac{365}{\text{Inventory turnover ratio}}$$

An average number of days inventory on hand of 105 means that the entity holds its inventory for an average of 105 days before it is sold. This measure is another way of presenting the inventory turnover ratio and is interpreted in the same way as the inventory turnover ratio, except that a lower average number of days inventory on hand measure indicates better and more efficient inventory management.

Inventory turnover receives a lot of attention in MWW's annual report. MWW sets inventory turnover targets for its senior executives (see the Senior Management Performance section of MWW's annual report on page A-10) and forecasts of inventory turnover are provided (see the Operational Goals section of MWW's annual report on page A-12). MWW's Mark's division achieved an inventory turnover ratio of 2.1 in fiscal 2001 and sets a target for 2002 of 2.3. The emphasis MWW gives to inventory turnover in its annual report suggests that MWW's management believes that the ratio is important for evaluating the performance of the company and its managers. It's interesting to note that in MWW's 2000 annual report the company set an inventory turnover ratio goal of 2.4 for fiscal 2001, but only delivered a ratio of 2.1.

The inventory turnover ratio can be difficult to interpret if an entity has many different types of inventory. Different types of inventory may turn over at different rates. The figure obtained using the aggregate total reported on the balance sheet will just be an average of the turnover ratios of all the different types of inventory. A manufacturer will likely have finished goods, work-in-process, and raw materials. If the total amount of inventory on the balance sheet is used to calculate the inventory turnover ratio, the ratio will reflect the turnover rate of the entire inventory. If a manufacturer breaks down the components of inventory in the notes to the financial statements, for example as Brick Brewing Co. Limited does (see Exhibit 8-1, Panel A, page 459), it is possible to calculate an inventory turnover ratio for finished goods. Note that for Brick Brewing, the breakdown is not ideal because the amount of finished goods alone is not disclosed. Brick Brewing combines finished goods and work-in-process. This is another example of how the information provided in financial statements is not necessarily the best information for user needs.

There are also entities that sell inventory of very different types. For example, a department store will carry a vast range of different products from furniture to art to clothing to jewellery. Each of these product categories is very different and can be expected to have different inventory turnover ratios. Yet despite the different types of inventory, a department store like Sears Canada Inc. provides a single amount in its financial statements for inventory. If the composition of the inventory changes (for example, if the quantity of one product type increased and another was reduced), the inventory turnover ratio can change without there being a change in how inventory is being managed. MWW's inventory is relatively homogeneous—mainly clothing of different types—which makes the inventory turnover ratio more interpretable.

Like other information in the financial statements, information about inventory and cost of sales raises questions and does not necessarily provide answers. For example, the existence of inventory doesn't mean that the inventory can be sold. Suppose that at the end of a year you notice that the amount of inventory reported on the balance sheet had increased significantly from previous years. How can that change be interpreted? If sales had increased along with inventory, we might conclude that inventory has increased to support the increased level of sales. If there was no increase in the amount of sales, then we could conclude that management was building up inventory in anticipation of an expansion or to reflect anticipated sales growth. On the other hand, the increase might reflect over-purchasing of inventory by management or obsolete inventory that had not yet been written off.

It should be clear from the discussion of the different inventory cost flow assumptions that financial analysis and financial ratios will be affected by the cost flow assumption used by an entity. This means that comparisons among firms in an industry may be difficult if the amount of inventory reported differs because the entities are using different cost flow assumptions or inventory control methods, or are applying direct and absorption costing differently. The effect of different treatments can have an impact on the inventory turnover ratio, current ratio, quick ratio, gross margin, and profit margin, to name a few. However, analyzing an entity over time is not affected by differences in accounting treatments for inventory, provided that the entity has applied its inventory accounting policies consistently over the period being examined.

It is important to recognize that while the different accounting methods affect our measures of liquidity, they do not, for the most part, affect liquidity itself. Whether a company uses LIFO, FIFO, or average cost does not affect the actual liquidity of the entity.

A Banker's View of Inventory

When entities borrow money it is common for the lender to request that collateral be provided in the event that the borrower cannot repay the loan. Inventory would seem like a sensible asset to use as collateral, but in general banks do not welcome inventory for this purpose. The reason is that inventory can be difficult to dispose of if the borrower is unable to meet its obligations. After all, if the borrower can't sell the inventory, how will a bank? What will a bank do with large quantities of toasters, shirts, or machine-tooled dies? Generally, banks recover as little as five or ten cents for each dollar of inventory that is reported on the balance sheet.

That said, many businesses require financing for their inventory. This is especially true for seasonal businesses. For example, consider a business that produces Christmas decorations. The decoration maker would build up its inventory during the year until it began shipping its products as the holiday season approached. Most seasonal businesses will not have a stockpile of cash available to self-finance the inventory build-up. Instead, many businesses in this situation will use bank credit to finance the inventory build-up, and despite their concerns banks will lend against inventory. However, when a bank lends against inventory, it will generally expect the loan to be repaid in full at the end of the entity's operating cycle. That is, inventory loans are not permanent. They must be fully repaid each year. In contrast, when accounts receivable is the collateral, the amount borrowed can remain outstanding permanently, based on the amount of receivables the entity has.

■ Solved Problem

In November 2005 Chedder Inc. (Chedder) set up operations as the exclusive western Canada distributor of Pligs, the newest children's toy sensation. Pligs first became popular in Europe and then the fad came to North America. Chedder's lone shareholder contributed $37,000 of her own money to purchase shares in Chedder and borrowed $50,000 from the bank. The terms of the loan required that Chedder have a current ratio of greater than 1.4 on December 31, 2006 or the loan is fully repayable immediately. Chedder began selling Pligs in early 2006. For its December 31, 2005 year end Chedder did not select an inventory cost flow assumption because it had not yet sold anything.

Chedder's December 31, 2005 balance sheet is shown in Table 8-8 and information on sales and purchases of Pligs in fiscal 2006 is shown in Table 8-9 (page 472). During 2006, Chedder's other expenses (all expenses other than the cost of sales) were $150,000. The balances in Chedder's current asset and liability accounts (except for inventory) on December 31, 2006 are shown in Table 8-10 (page 472).

Required:

a. What might be Chedder's objectives of financial reporting? Briefly explain your reasoning.

b. Calculate ending inventory, cost of sales, gross margin, and net income for Chedder under FIFO, average cost, and LIFO for perpetual and periodic inventory control systems. Calculate the gross margin percentage, inventory turnover, and current ratio under each cost flow assumption.

c. Comment on the financial statement amounts and the ratios calculated in (b) above. What are the implications of the amounts calculated under each of the methods?

d. Which inventory cost flow assumption do you recommend for Chedder?

e. Suppose that on December 31, 2006 the replacement cost of the Pligs was $1.86.

Assuming that Chedder decided to use replacement cost as its definition of market for purposes of the lower of cost and market rule, what would be the financial statement implications under each inventory cost flow and inventory control system?

Table 8-8   Balance Sheet for Chedder Inc

Chedder Inc.
Balance Sheet
For the Year Ended December 31, 2005

Assets		Liabilities and shareholders' equity	
Current assets		*Current liabilities*	
Cash	$44,000	Bank loan	$50,000
Accounts receivable	0	Accounts payable	10,000
Inventory	24,000	Total current liabilities	60,000
Other current assets	9,000		
Total current assets	77,000		
Capital assets (net)	20,000	Capital stock	37,000
		Retained earnings	0
Total assets	$97,000	Total liabilities and shareholders' equity	$97,000

Table 8-9   Purchasing Information for Chedder Inc.

Chedder Inc.
Purchasing Information
For the Year Ended December 31, 2006
(including inventory purchased in December 2005)

Date	Quantity purchased	Purchase price per unit
December 28, 2005	15,000	$1.60
April 1, 2006	25,000	$1.75
July 1, 2006	20,000	$1.90
October 1, 2006	40,000	$2.00

Chedder Inc.
Sales Information
For the Year Ended December 31, 2006

Period	Quantity sold	Selling price per unit
January 1 – March 31, 2006	8,000	$3.75
April 1 – June 30, 2006	20,000	$3.75
July 1 – September 30, 2006	17,000	$4.00
October 1 – December 31, 2006	45,000	$4.00

Table 8-10   Current Asset and Liability Account Balances for Chedder Inc.

Chedder Inc.
Current Asset and Liability Account Balances (Excluding Inventory)
As of December 31, 2006

Cash	$13,000
Accounts receivable	88,250
Other current assets	2,000
Bank loan	50,000
Accounts payable	38,000

Solution:

a. Because Chedder is a small, privately owned corporation with a single share-holder who operates the business, the owner would likely want to minimize tax payments. This would mean choosing accounting treatments that lower income for tax purposes. However, Chedder's bank loan has a restrictive covenant that requires that it have a current ratio that is greater than 1.4. Therefore, Chedder would want to ensure that it does not violate the covenant because doing so would likely create financial problems for the company and its owner.

b. Calculation results:

	FIFO Perpetual and Periodic	LIFO Perpetual	LIFO Periodic	Average Cost Perpetual	Average Cost Periodic
Revenue	$353,000	$353,000	$353,000	$353,000	$353,000
Cost of sales	165,750[1]	169,300[3]	169,750[5]	166,210[7]	167,175[9]
Gross margin	187,250	183,700	183,250	186,790	185,825
All other expenses	150,000	150,000	150,000	150,000	150,000
Net income	$ 37,250	$ 33,700	$ 33,250	$ 36,790	$ 35,825
Gross margin percentage	0.530	0.520	0.519	0.529	0.526
Ending inventory	$ 20,000[2]	$ 16,450[4]	$ 16,000[6]	$ 19,540[8]	$ 18,575[10]
Current assets except for inventory (from Table 8-8)	$103,250	$103,250	$103,250	$103,250	$103,250
Total current assets	$123,250	$119,700	$119,250	$122,790	$121,825
Total current liabilities (from Table 8-8)	$ 88,000	$ 88,000	$ 88,000	$ 88,000	$ 88,000
Current ratio $\left(\dfrac{\text{Current assets}}{\text{Current liabilities}}\right)$	1.401	1.360	1.355	1.395	1.384
Inventory turnover $\left(\dfrac{\text{Cost of sales}}{\text{Average inventory}}\right)$	7.534	8.371	8.488	7.635	7.853

[1] Expense:
15,000 @ $1.60 +
25,000 @ $1.75 +
20,000 @ $1.90 +
30,000 @ $2.00

[2] Ending inventory: 10,000 @ $2.00

[3] Expense:
8,000 @ $1.60 +
20,000 @ $1.75 +
17,000 @ $1.90 +
40,000 @ $2.00 +
3,000 @ $1.90 +
2,000 @ $1.75

[4] Ending inventory:
7,000 @ $1.60 +
3,000 @ $1.75

[5] Expense:
40,000 @ $2.00 +
20,000 @ $1.90 +
25,000 @ $1.75 +
5,000 @ $1.60

[6] Ending inventory: 10,000 @ $1.60

[7] Expense:
8,000 @ $1.60 +
20,000 @ $1.717 +
17,000 @ $1.831 +
45,000 @ $1.954 +

[8] Ending inventory: 10,000 @ $1.954

[9] Expense: $185,750 ÷ 100,000 × 90,000 [total cost of inventory purchased ÷ no. of units purchased × no. of units sold]

[10] Ending inventory: $185,750 ÷ 100,000 × 10,000 [total cost of inventory purchased ÷ no. of units purchased × no. of units in ending inventory]

c. While each of the methods produces different numbers, each is actually measuring the same underlying economic phenomenon. For many users and uses of financial information this can be an inconvenience because it impairs the ability to compare the financial information of different entities. In some situations these differences can have serious consequences.

For example, if Chedder uses an inventory cost flow assumption other than FIFO, it is in violation of its current ratio covenant, which would mean that it would have to repay its bank loan immediately. The economic consequence of this violation could be significant. If Chedder uses FIFO, there is no problem with the loan. Either way, it is the same company, yet with FIFO it has no (immediate) problems with the bank, whereas with any of the others it has potentially large problems. The gross margin is slightly different under each of the methods. This can lead to different conclusions about the profitability of Chedder. A 1% difference in margins may not seem significant, but in some industries a 1% difference can have a dramatic effect on the profitability of the entity.

d. Chedder should use FIFO. All the other cost flow assumptions result in the current ratio falling below 1.4, which would require that it repay its bank loan. This could be an especially serious problem because Chedder only had $13,000 cash on hand on December 31, 2006. To meet the repayment requirement Chedder would have to obtain cash from the shareholder or from another investor, or obtain a new loan from a bank or another lender. Clearly, in this situation ensuring that the current ratio covenant is met is more important than minimizing taxes.

e. If the replacement cost of a single unit of inventory is $1.86, then the replacement cost of the 10,000 units on hand on December 31, 2006 is $18,600. The replacement cost of the inventory is less than the cost when FIFO and average cost perpetual are used. If Chedder were using either of these methods, it would be appropriate to write down the inventory on the balance sheet to the market value. In the case of FIFO the write-down would be $1,400 and for average cost perpetual the write-down would be $940. If the write-down were required, Chedder would be in violation of its current ratio covenant and it would be required to pay back the bank loan immediately.

Summary of Key Points

LO 1. There are two types of accounting systems for keeping track of inventory transactions: perpetual systems and periodic systems. A perpetual inventory system keeps an ongoing tally of purchases and sales of inventory, and the inventory account is adjusted to reflect changes as they occur. With a periodic inventory system the balance in the Inventory account at the end of period is determined by actually counting the inventory on hand at the end of a period, and Cost of Sales is determined indirectly using the equation Cost of Sales = Beginning Inventory + Purchases − Ending Inventory. The choice between a periodic and perpetual inventory system is an internal control issue, not an accounting issue. However, the choice can have an effect on the amount of inventory reported on the balance sheet and cost of goods sold for the period.

LO 2. Usually accountants do not keep track of the costs associated with individual items of inventory. Instead, they have developed methods called cost flow assumptions for moving costs through the Inventory account to Cost of Sales without regard for the actual physical flow of the inventory. There are a number of cost flow assumptions that are currently in use, including FIFO, LIFO, average cost, and specific identification, all of which are acceptable under GAAP. The choice of cost flow assumption does not directly affect the cash flow of the entity, but the information reported on the balance sheet and the income statement can be significantly different depending on the cost flow assumption used. When inventory prices are rising, FIFO will always give the lowest cost of sales and the highest inventory value, while LIFO will always give the highest cost of sales and the lowest inventory value. Average cost will always be between these two.

LO 3. According to GAAP, inventory on hand at the end of a period must be reported at the lower of cost and market. If the market value of inventory at the end of a reporting period is lower than its cost, the inventory must be written down to its market value. The amount of the write-down is expensed in the period of the write-down. The LCM rule is an application of conservatism. Once inventory is written down to its market value, it is not written back up in the event that the market price of the inventory increases. Net realizable value and replacement cost are the most commonly used definitions of market.

LO 4. Costs that go into the production of a product can be classified into two broad categories: prime costs and overhead. Prime costs are the costs of direct materials and labour used in production. Overhead is the indirect costs of manufacturing a product. When all costs—prime and overhead—are included in the cost of inventory, the costing method is referred to as absorption costing. When only prime costs plus variable overhead are included in inventory, the costing method is called direct costing. The *CICA Handbook* requires that the cost of materials and direct labour be included in inventory along with "an applicable share of overhead." However, management decides what constitutes an applicable share of overhead.

LO 5. Historical cost, transactions-based accounting is not the only accounting model available. For many users of financial statements alternative valuation methods, such as replacement cost accounting, can provide useful information for decision making. These alternative methods are not in use in Canada because accounting standard setters have concluded that the loss of reliability from having to estimate current values is not worth any benefits. When inventory is valued using replacement cost, the amount reported on the balance sheet is the amount that it would cost to replace the inventory on hand on the balance sheet date.

LO 6. The accounting choices that the preparers of financial statements make often have tax implications. In situations where the *Income Tax Act* does not specify a treatment, the method used for financial reporting purposes will often be used for tax purposes. The Canada Customs and Revenue Agency suggests that the same cost flow assumption that is used for financial reporting purposes should also be used for tax purposes. However, LIFO is not allowed for tax purposes. For tax purposes entities can use either direct or absorption costing and can apply the lower of cost and market rule. The CCRA requires that methods used to account for inventory for tax purposes be applied consistently.

LO 7. Management's effectiveness and efficiency in managing inventory can have a significant impact on the performance of the entity. Managing inventory requires careful balance. Carrying too much or too little inventory can be costly. The inventory turnover ratio and the number of days inventory on hand ratio provide information on how efficiently and effectively inventory is being managed. A low or decreasing inventory turnover ratio can indicate that inventory is not selling or is slow moving or obsolete, or that there is low demand for the inventory. Generally, a higher inventory turnover ratio indicates better management of inventory.

Key Terms

absorption costing, p. 462

average cost method of inventory valuation, p. 443

average number of days inventory on hand, p. 469

commission, p. 465

consignment inventory, p. 465

direct costing, p. 462

finished goods inventory, p. 435

first-in, first-out (FIFO), p. 440

fixed overhead, p. 462

holding gain or loss, p. 464

inventory, p. 434

inventory turnover ratio, p. 469

laid-down cost, p. 435

last-in, first-out (LIFO), p. 442

lower of cost and market (LCM) rule, p. 457

net realizable value (NRV), p. 460

overhead, p. 462

periodic inventory system, p. 436

perpetual inventory system, p. 436

prime costing, p. 462

prime costs, p. 462

raw materials inventory, p. 435

realized holding gain or loss, p. 464

replacement cost, p. 460

retail method, p. 456

specific identification method, p. 444

unrealized holding gain or loss, p. 464

variable overhead, p. 462

work-in-process inventory (WIP), p. 435

Similar Terms

The left column gives alternative terms that are sometimes used for the accounting terms introduced in this chapter, which are listed in the right column.

variable costing   **direct costing, p. 462**

Assignment Materials

Questions

Q8-1. For each of the following entities, describe the type of inventory you would expect the entity to have:
   a. Future Shop (an electronics retailer)
   b. Loblaw Companies Limited (a grocery chain)
   c. Barrick Gold Corporation (a gold mining company)
   d. Torstar Corporation (a newspaper publisher)
   e. Magna International Inc. (an auto parts manufacturer)
   f. Andrés Wines Ltd. (a vintner)
   g. Burger King Corporation (a fast-food chain)

Q8-2. For each of the following entities, describe what would be included in raw materials inventory, work-in-process inventory, and finished goods inventory:
   a. an auto manufacturer
   b. a producer of concentrated orange juice
   c. a tailor shop
   d. a grower of trees (trees often take many years to mature before they are available for sale)
   e. a miner and refiner of gold

Q8-3. Explain why it is not possible to calculate cost of goods sold when a periodic inventory system is used if the inventory is not counted.

Q8-4. Explain and give examples of the following types of inventory:
   a. raw materials
   b. work-in-process
   c. finished goods
   d. supplies

Q8-5. Explain the costs that would be included in inventory under each of the following:
   a. prime costing
   b. direct costing
   c. absorption costing

Q8-6. Why is it not possible to determine the amount of inventory that was stolen during a period when a periodic inventory system is used?

Q8-7. Explain the difference between periodic and perpetual inventory control systems. Which do you think is the better system to use? Why?

Q8-8. Explain why perpetual and periodic inventory control systems can give different ending inventory balances and different cost of sales when average cost and LIFO cost flow assumptions are used.

Q8-9. Why is it necessary to use a cost flow assumption in many situations for valuing inventory and determining cost of sales? Why can't the actual cost of the goods sold be used to calculate cost of sales in these situations?

Q8-10. Regardless of the cost flow assumption being used (FIFO, average cost, LIFO, specific identification), the sum of cost of sales plus ending inventory will be the same. Explain why.

Q8-11. Explain why a FIFO inventory system gives higher inventory valuation and lower cost of sales than LIFO when prices are rising.

Q8-12. Explain the difference between absorption and direct costing. Why is ending inventory always higher when absorption costing is used?

Q8-13. Explain how costs flow through the following cost flow systems: a LIFO versus a FIFO versus an average cost versus a specific identification cost flow system.

Q8-14. What is the lower of cost and market rule? Why is it used? What is meant by the term "market" in lower of cost and market?

Q8-15. Why might it be difficult to actually determine the market value of inventory when applying the lower of cost and market rule? Provide some examples of when determining market might be difficult.

Q8-16. What is a holding gain? How are holding gains accounted for when traditional historical cost, transactions-based accounting is used?

Q8-17. Under the traditional historical cost, transactions-based accounting model, are holding gains and losses always treated the same way? Describe the difference in the accounting treatment used for each and explain the reason for the difference.

Q8-18. The *CICA Handbook* is quite unclear with respect to exactly how preparers of financial statements should account for their inventory. Explain the areas where the *CICA Handbook* is unclear and explain what the implications of this lack of clarity are for users of financial statements.

Q8-19. Why is it necessary to count inventory when a perpetual inventory system is used? Explain. Why is it necessary to count inventory when a periodic inventory system is used? Explain.

Q8-20. Explain how the specific identification method of valuing inventory works. Why do many entities not use this method? Under what circumstances is the method useful? Why is it sometimes easy to manipulate the financial statements when the specific identification method is used?

Q8-21. Why is the choice of the inventory cost flow assumption important for tax purposes? Explain.

Q8-22. Why is it not possible to satisfy a tax minimization objective and an income maximization objective when selecting the inventory cost flow assumption that the entity should use?

Q8-23. Onslow Ltd. (Onslow) is a small public company trading on a Canadian stock exchange. Onslow's managers have a bonus plan that is based on net income and the managers believe that the amount of reported earnings is important for maintaining the company's stock price. Assume that whether Onslow uses FIFO or average cost will have a significant effect on reported earnings (FIFO earnings being higher) and the amount of assets it reports on its balance sheet. Discuss the issues that Onslow's management must consider when choosing between FIFO and average cost.

Q8-24. Why is LIFO so commonly used in the United States but rarely used in Canada?

Q8-25. Does it matter which cost flow assumption an entity uses if the price an entity pays for its inventory is stable? Explain.

Q8-26. How does the choice of cost flow assumption affect financial ratios such as the inventory turnover ratio and the current ratio? Does the choice have any effect on the actual rate at which an entity turns over its inventory or the actual liquidity of the entity? Explain.

Q8-27. Explain why ending inventory and cost of sales are the same under either a perpetual or periodic inventory system when FIFO is used.

Q8-28. What is inventory turnover? What does it tell a user of financial statements about how the entity is managing its inventory? What could be some reasons for a decreasing inventory turnover ratio? What could be some reasons for an increasing inventory turnover ratio?

Q8-29. Which cost flow assumption for valuing inventory is best? Explain.

Q8-30. What is inventory that is on consignment? Which entity should report consignment inventory on its balance sheet: the entity that has the inventory and is selling it or the entity that owns the inventory? Explain.

Q8-31. Ayr Inc. (Ayr) uses a periodic inventory system. During Ayr's inventory count on December 31, 2004, $100,000 of the inventory was counted twice in error. What effect would the double counting of the inventory have on net income for the year ended December 31, 2004 and on the amount of inventory reported on the balance sheet on December 31, 2004?

Q8-32. Explain what the retail method of estimating inventory and cost of sales is. What are the advantages of using the retail method?

Q8-33. Explain why the cash spent on inventory is not affected by the cost flow assumption used for valuing ending inventory and determining cost of sales.

Exercises

E8-1.   **(Determine cost of units sold and cost of units remaining in inventory using average cost, FIFO, and LIFO cost flow assumptions, LO 1, 2)** The following information is provided for Badger Inc. (Badger):

Badger Inc. Inventory Information For October 2004		
	Number of units purchased	Price paid per unit
Purchased on October 8, 2004	1,100	$ 8
Purchased on October 17, 2004	1,325	$ 9
Purchased on October 25, 2004	900	$10

On October 30, 2004, Badger sold 2,400 units of inventory to customers.

Required:

Identify which inventory units would be expensed in October 2004 and which units would be in inventory on October 31, 2004 using the average cost, FIFO, LIFO, and specific identification cost flow assumptions.

E8-2.   **(Calculating cost of sales and ending inventory using average cost, FIFO, and LIFO cost flow assumptions, LO 1, 2)** Information is provided for Olds Ltd. on page 479.

Date	Purchases	Sales	Balance
December 31, 2003			110 units @ $5
January 5, 2004	80 units @ $6		
January 8, 2004		60 units @ $8	
January 15, 2004	120 units @ $7		
January 20, 2004		120 units @ $10	
January 22, 2004	100 units @ $8		
January 29, 2004		80 units @ $11	
January 31, 2004			150 units @ $

Required:

Calculate cost of goods sold and ending inventory for Olds Ltd. using the average cost, FIFO, and LIFO cost flow assumptions under both the perpetual and periodic inventory systems.

E8-3.   **(Using the retail method, LO 2)** Neighbour Inc. (Neighbour) is a small local boutique. Neighbour uses the retail method for determining its ending inventory. The store has an April 30 year end. On May 1, 2003 Neighbour had opening inventory with a cost of $200,000 and retail value of $280,000. During the year Neighbour purchased inventory for $1,000,000. The inventory purchased during the year had a retail value of $1,640,000. When the inventory was counted on April 30, 2004, there was $220,000 of inventory on hand valued at its retail price. Sales during the year ended April 30, 2004 were $1,700,000.

Required:

Estimate the cost of inventory on April 30, 2004 using the retail method.

E8-4.   **(Using the retail method, LO 2)** The CFO of Hilbre Stores Ltd. (Hilbre Stores) rushes into the accounting office, saying that he needs to know the chain's gross margin for the year to date immediately. You tell the CFO that you will be able to give him an estimate of the gross margin by the end of the day. You begin to gather the information you require to answer the CFO's question. You observe that it is a good thing that Hilbre Stores uses the retail method for accounting for inventory. From the inventory count records from the end of last year you find that ending inventory was $925,000 at cost and $1,500,000 at retail. You also determine from the purchase records that so far during the year Hilbre Stores purchased inventory costing $1,750,000. You estimate that the retail price of that inventory would be about $2,712,500. Finally, you check the sales records that are transmitted weekly from each of the stores and find that sales to date are $3,400,000.

Required:

Prepare a report to the CFO showing your calculation of the gross margin for the year to date. Indicate in your report any uncertainties and limitations associated with your calculation.

E8-5.   **(Classifying different costs as prime, variable overhead, or fixed overhead, LO 4)** Whonock Ltd. (Whonock) is a manufacturer of fine wood furniture. For each of the following items, indicate whether Whonock would classify the costs associated with each of the following as a prime cost, variable overhead cost, or fixed overhead cost. Provide a brief explanation for each classification.

a. work done by the furniture makers
b. wood
c. electricity to operate tools
d. heat for the workshop
e. amortization of the tools and equipment used by the furniture makers
f. people who clean the workshop
g. glue, nails, and other supplies
h. shipping crates for the finished furniture

E8-6.   **(Classifying different types of inventory, LO 1)** Whonock Ltd. (Whonock) is a manufacturer of fine wood furniture. For each of the following items, indicate whether Whonock would classify the costs associated with each of the following as inventory and, if it should be classified as inventory, whether it would be considered raw materials, work-in-process, finished goods, or supplies. Provide a brief explanation for each classification.

a. lumber
b. unpainted furniture
c. furniture makers' tools
d. fabric
e. sandpaper

f. furniture awaiting shipment on the loading dock
g. crates used for packing furniture for shipment

E8-7.   **(Calculating cost of sales and ending inventory using average cost, FIFO, and LIFO cost flow assumptions when prices are stable, LO 1, 2)** The following information is provided for Exlou Ltd. (Exlou):

	Number of units	Purchase price per unit	Selling price per unit
Inventory on hand on January 1, 2004	10,000	$10	
Inventory purchases during 2004	40,000	$10	
Inventory purchases during 2005	50,000	$10	
Sales during 2004	38,000		$22
Sales during 2005	54,000		$22

Required:

a. Calculate ending inventory on December 31, 2004 and 2005 and cost of sales and gross margin for the years ended December 31, 2004 and 2005 for Exlou using FIFO, LIFO, and average cost. Assume that Exlou uses a periodic inventory system.
b. Explain the results you obtained in (a). Do you find anything unusual about the amounts you calculated for ending inventory, cost of sales, and gross margin under each of the cost flow assumptions?
c. Would your results be any different if Exlou used a perpetual inventory control system? Explain.

E8-8.   **(Calculating inventory turnover ratio and the average number of days inventory on hand, LO 7)** You are provided with the following information about Kepenkeck Inc. (Kepenkeck):

Cost of sales for the year ended November 30, 2005	$13,525,000
Inventory balance on November 30, 2004	$ 3,450,000
Inventory balance on November 30, 2005	$ 3,900,000

Required:

a. Calculate Kepenkeck's inventory turnover ratio for the year ended November 30, 2005.
b. What is the average length of time that it took Kepenkeck to sell its inventory in 2005?
c. Is Kepenkeck's inventory turnover ratio satisfactory? What would you need to know to fully answer this question?

E8-9.   **(Lower of cost and market, LO 3)** Massawippi Inc. (Massawippi) uses the lower of cost and market rule to value its inventory. Massawippi defines market as net realizable value. Massawippi's inventory on February 28, 2003 had a cost of $375,000 and a NRV of $345,000.

Required:

a. By how much should Massawippi's inventory be written down?
b. Prepare the journal entry that Massawippi should prepare to record the write-down.
c. What amount should be reported for inventory on Massawippi's February 28, 2003 balance sheet?

E8-10. **(Lower of cost and market, LO 3, 7)** Wolf Ltd. (Wolf) reports its inventory at the lower of cost and market. You obtain the following information about Wolf for its year ended August 31, 2004:

Inventory, at cost on August 31, 2003	$ 501,000
Inventory, at cost, on August 31, 2004	525,000
Inventory, at NRV, on August 31, 2004	995,000
Inventory, at replacement cost, on August 31, 2004	497,000
Sales during the year ended August 31, 2004	2,340,000
Cost of sales for the year ended August 31, 2004	1,090,000

Required:

a. If Wolf defines market as replacement cost, by how much should Wolf's inventory be written down?

b. If Wolf defines market as NRV, by how much should Wolf's inventory be written down?

c. If Wolf knew the replacement cost and NRV of its inventory on August 31, 2004, which should it use to determine the lower of cost and market?

d. What would be the effect of applying the lower of cost and market rule on Wolf's gross margin and inventory turnover ratio?

E8-11. **(Working with the inventory turnover ratio and the average number of days inventory on hand, LO 7)** Use the information provided in each row to calculate the missing values (shaded boxes). Each row is an independent situation.

Cost of sales	Average inventory	Inventory turnover ratio	Average number of days inventory on hand
$1,345,000	$ 562,000		
	495,000		65
	2,399,000	2.68	
827,000			82

E8-12. **(Identifying and calculating holding gains and losses, LO 5)** For each of the following situations indicate whether the event is a gain or a loss and whether the gain or loss is realized or unrealized.

a. In 1989, a land development company purchased raw land for later development for $5,000,000. In 2002 development of the land had not yet begun. The company had recently received an offer for the land of $14,000,000.

b. In November 2003 a jeweller purchased $10,000 of gold for making jewellery. In May 2004, when the jeweller sold the jewellery made from the gold, the same amount of gold would have cost $9,000.

c. In March 2004 a company purchased a large supply of lumber for $200,000. By the end of the year the market price of the lumber had doubled because of high demand in the United States.

E8-13. **(Compute missing information, LO 1)** Complete the following table by calculating the missing values (shaded boxes).

	Dec. 31, 2002	Dec. 31, 2003	Dec. 31, 2004	Dec. 31, 2005
Beginning inventory	$100,000	$	$	$
Purchases	950,000		1,200,000	
Ending inventory		125,000	200,000	190,000
Cost of sales	900,000	800,000		1,310,000

E8-14. **(The effect of different cash flow assumptions on liquidity, LO 2, 7)** The balances in the current asset and liability accounts for Feeder Ltd. (Feeder) are provided on page 482. The balances in the inventory account are provided under the FIFO, average cost, and LIFO cost flow assumptions.

Cost flow assumption	Inventory balance on December 31, 2005
FIFO	$89,000
Average cost	68,000
LIFO	47,000

Account	Account balance on December 31, 2005
Cash	$12,000
Accounts receivable	25,000
Prepaid assets	7,000
Bank loan	35,000
Accounts payable and accrued liabilities	60,000

Required:

a. Calculate Feeder's current ratio on December 31, 2005 using the three cost flow assumptions.

b. How do you explain the results you obtained in (a)?

c. What are the implications for analyzing Feeder Ltd.'s financial statements of the different results you obtained in (a)?

d. Which current ratio provides the best measure of Feeder's liquidity? Explain.

E8-15. (**Effect of transactions and economic events on ratios, LO 3, 7**) Complete the following table by indicating whether the following transactions or economic events would increase, decrease, or have no effect on the financial ratios listed. Assume that the current ratio is greater than 1.0 and the quick ratio less than 1.0 before considering the effect of each transaction or economic event.

	Current ratio	Quick ratio	Gross margin percentage	Inventory turnover ratio	Profit margin percentage	Debt-to-equity ratio
a. Inventory is written down						
b. Inventory is sold at its cost						
c. Inventory is stolen						
d. The amount of inventory carried by the entity is increased						
e. Inventory is purchased on credit						

E8-16. (**Recording inventory transactions, LO 1, 2, 3**) For each of the following transactions and economic events, prepare the necessary journal entries. Provide a brief explanation for each journal entry and state any assumptions that you make.

a. Inventory costing $20,000 is purchased on credit.

b. Inventory costing $15,000 is written off because it has become unsaleable.

c. Inventory costing $10,000 is sold to a customer for cash. The entity uses a periodic inventory control system.

d. Inventory costing $8,000 is sold to a customer on credit, with the amount due in 30 days. The entity uses a perpetual inventory control system.

e. Management discovers that the NRV of its inventory is $200,000 and its cost is $215,000.

f. A supplier is paid $5,000 for inventory purchased on credit.

E8-17. (**Inventory cost flow assumptions when prices are falling, LO 2, 3**) Azilda Inc. (Azilda) operates in a part of the computer industry where the cost of inventory has been falling recently. The cost of inventory purchased by Azilda over the last year is summarized on page 483. Azilda values its inventory at the lower of cost and market and defines market as net realizable value. Assume that purchases are made at the start of a month before any sales occur during that month.

Date	Quantity	Cost per unit	Selling price per unit
Purchases			
Opening inventory	35	$950	
October 1, 2003	72	900	
January 2, 2004	54	860	
April 1, 2004	42	810	
July 2, 2004	85	775	
Sales			
October-December, 2003	81		$1,710
January-March, 2004	58		1,620
April-June, 2004	43		1,550
July-September, 2004	79		1,390

Required:

a. Calculate cost of sales for the year ended September 30, 2004 and ending inventory on September 30, 2004 for Azilda using the FIFO, average cost, and LIFO cost flow assumptions.

b. Which cost flow assumption is most attractive for an accounting objective of income maximization?

c. Which cost flow assumption is most attractive for an accounting objective of tax minimization?

d. Compare the relative values under the three cost flow assumptions of ending inventory and cost of sales in this situation versus a situation where prices are rising. What is different between the two situations?

e. Apply the lower of cost and market rule to the year-end inventory. Assume that Azilda's selling costs for inventory are $300 per unit.

E8-18. **(Inventory cost flow assumptions and taxes, LO 2, 6)** Sayabec Ltd.'s (Sayabec) purchases for 2003 were:

Date	Quantity purchased	Cost per unit
March 1	8,000	$2.75
June 4	10,000	3.00
September 9	15,000	3.15
December 4	7,000	3.30

The beginning balance in inventory on January 1, 2003 was 12,000 units with a cost of $2.50 per unit. The inventory count on December 31, 2003 found that there were 11,000 units on hand at the end of the year. Sayabec uses a periodic inventory control system. During 2003 Sayabec had revenues of $246,000 and expenses other than the cost of sales and taxes of $100,000. Saybec pays taxes equal to 20% of its income before taxes.

Required:

a. Prepare income statements for 2003 for Sayabec using FIFO and average cost. Your income statements should show the amount of taxes that the company has to pay for the income it earned in 2003. Taxes are calculated by multiplying income before taxes (revenue – all expenses except taxes) by the tax rate.

b. Which method would you recommend that Sayabec use if its primary objective of financial accounting is to minimize taxes? Explain your answer.

c. What are possible explanations as to why Sayabec would choose not to use the method you recommended in (b)?

Problems

P8-1. **(Calculating cost of sales and ending inventory using average cost, FIFO, and LIFO cost flow assumptions, LO 1, 2)** Adamo Limited (AL) is a wholesaler of machine parts. Jacob Avery recently purchased AL. Previously Mr. Avery was an employee of AL. Mr. Avery purchased AL from the original owner, Mr. Adam, who is retiring. Mr. Avery has come to you for advice on how to calculate ending inventory and cost of goods sold. He asked you to explain your reasoning for any choices you make. Mr. Avery provided you with the following example of his inventory costs using Part 17592a.

Inventory Information for Part 17592a

	Number of units	Date of purchase/sale	Cost per unit	Selling price per unit
Opening inventory	125 units	various	$26.00	
Purchase	100 units	Nov. 10	$27.00	
Sale	80 units	Nov. 12		$60.00
Purchase	75 units	Nov. 20	$27.50	
Sale	160 units	Nov. 22		$60.00
Purchase	90 units	Nov. 25	$27.75	

Required

Calculate ending inventory as at November 30 and cost of goods sold for Part 17592a for November. Provide the explanations requested by Mr. Avery.

P8-2. **(The impact of cost flow assumptions on ratios, LO 1, 2, 7)** Cardigan Corp. (Cardigan), Huskisson Ltd. (Huskisson), and Mallet Inc. (Mallet) are small distribution companies. They are identical in every respect—same amount of sales, same quantity of inventory sold, same number of employees. Everything is the same except that Cardigan uses FIFO as its cost flow assumption, Huskisson uses average cost, and Mallet uses LIFO.

Balance Sheets As of December 31, 2004	Cardigan (FIFO)	Huskisson (Average cost)	Mallet (LIFO)
Assets			
Cash	$ 94,800	$ 94,800	$ 94,800
Accounts receivable	252,000	252,000	252,000
Inventory	1,055,000	784,500	549,500
Other current assets	42,000	42,000	42,000
Total current assets	1,443,800	1,173,300	938,300
Capital assets (net)	1,507,000	1,507,000	1,507,000
Total assets	$2,950,800	$2,680,300	$2,445,300
Liabilities and Owners' Equity			
Bank loan	$ 150,000	$ 150,000	$ 150,000
Accounts payable	755,000	755,000	755,000
Other current liabilities	65,000	65,000	65,000
Total current liabilities	970,000	970,000	970,000
Long-term debt	262,000	262,000	262,000
Other non-current liabilities	50,000	50,000	50,000
Total liabilities	1,282,000	1,282,000	1,282,000
Capital stock	200,000	200,000	200,000
Retained earnings	1,468,800	1,198,300	963,300
Total liabilities and owners' equity	$2,950,800	$2,680,300	$2,445,300

Income Statements For the Year Ended December 31, 2004			
	Cardigan (FIFO)	Huskisson (Average cost)	Mallet (LIFO)
Revenue	$3,540,000	$3,540,000	$3,540,000
Cost of sales	1,699,200	1,911,600	2,053,200
Gross margin	1,840,800	1,628,400	1,486,800
Other expenses	1,450,000	1,450,000	1,450,000
Net income	$ 390,800	$ 178,400	$ 36,800

You also learn that on December 31, 2003 the balances in Inventory for the three companies were:

Ending Inventory Balances on December 31, 2003			
	Cardigan (FIFO)	Huskisson (Average cost)	Mallet (LIFO)
Inventory	$955,100	$714,200	$505,200

Required:

    a. Calculate the following ratios for each of the three companies:

        i.   current ratio

        ii. quick ratio

        iii. inventory turnover ratio

        iv. average number of days inventory on hand

        v. gross margin percentage

        vi. profit margin percentage

    b. Which of the three companies has the strongest liquidity position?

    c. Which of the three companies is the most profitable?

    d. Which of the three companies manages its inventory most effectively?

    e. The three companies' bankers lend money based on the amount of accounts receivable and inventory on hand. Which company will be able to obtain the largest loan? From the banks' point of view, is the company that receives the largest loan the best credit risk? Explain.

P8-3.   (**The impact of cost flow assumptions on ratios, LO 1, 2, 7**) Weybridge Corp. (Weybridge), Kennetcook Ltd. (Kennetcook), and Aaskana Inc. (Aaskana) are small retail stores. They are identical in every respect—same amount of sales, same quantity of inventory sold, same number of employees. Everything is the same except that Weybridge uses FIFO as its cost flow assumption, Kennetcook uses average cost, and Aaskana uses LIFO.

Income Statements For the Year Ended December 31, 2005			
	Weybridge (FIFO)	Kennetcook (Average cost)	Aaskana (LIFO)
Revenue	$442,500	$442,500	$442,500
Cost of sales	276,120	310,635	333,645
Gross margin	166,380	131,865	108,855
Other expenses	121,000	121,000	121,000
Net income (loss)	$ 45,380	$ 10,865	($ 12,145)

Income Statements For the Year Ended December 31, 2005			
	Weybridge (FIFO)	Kennetcook (Average cost)	Aaskana (LIFO)
Assets			
Cash	$ 11,850	$ 11,850	$ 11,850
Accounts receivable	31,500	31,500	31,500
Inventory	131,875	98,063	68,688
Other current assets	5,250	5,250	5,250
Total current assets	180,475	146,663	117,288
Capital assets (net)	188,375	188,375	188,375
Total assets	$368,850	$335,038	$305,663
Liabilities and Owners' Equity			
Bank loan	$ 18,750	$18,750	$ 18,750
Accounts payable	94,375	94,375	94,375
Other current liabilities	8,125	8,125	8,125
Total current liabilities	121,250	121,250	121,250
Long-term debt	32,750	32,750	32,750
Other non-current liabilities	6,250	6,250	6,250
Total liabilities	160,250	160,250	160,250
Capital stock	25,000	25,000	25,000
Retained earnings	183,600	149,788	120,413
Total liabilities and owners' equity	$368,850	$335,038	$305,663

You also learn that on December 31, 2004 the balances in Inventory for the three companies were:

Ending Inventory Balances on December 31, 2004			
	Weybridge (FIFO)	Kennetcook (Average cost)	Aaskana (LIFO)
Inventory	$955,100	$714,200	$505,200

Required:

a. Calculate the following ratios for each of the three companies:
   i.   current ratio
   ii. quick ratio
   iii. inventory turnover ratio
   iv. average number of days inventory on hand
   v.   gross margin percentage
   vi. profit margin percentage
b. Which of the three companies has the strongest liquidity position?
c. Which of the three companies is most profitable?
d. Which of the three companies manages its inventory most effectively?
e. The three companies' bankers lend money based on the amount of accounts receivable and inventory on hand. Which company will be able to obtain the largest loan? From the banks' point of view, is the company that receives the largest loan the best credit risk? Explain.

P8-4.   **(Recommending inventory accounting policies, LO 1, 2, 3, 4, 6)** Tesseralik Inc. (Tesseralik) is a small private manufacturing company that makes inexpensive laptop computers. Tesseralik is owned by three brothers who converted their interest in computers into a business. All three brothers are involved in the management of the company. The company is relatively free of debt, with only a small bank loan outstanding, which is personally guaranteed by the brothers. Tesseralik purchases all component parts from independent manufacturers and assembles them into the laptops.

The company has been successful because it has been able to provide a good-quality product at a low price. Management searches extensively to find the lowest-cost components that meet its quality standards. Tesseralik employs 14 people, mainly assemblers who put together the computers. The major costs that Tesseralik incurs are the cost of labour and parts for the computers. There is as well a significant amount of both fixed and variable overhead that is incurred by the business. While the company has been successful, it is often short of cash.

Required:

Prepare a report to Tesseralik's management recommending accounting policies for inventory. Your report should fully explain your recommendations.

P8-5. **(Recommending inventory accounting policies, LO 1, 2, 3, 4)** Howser Ltd. (Howser) is a Canadian manufacturer of wooden shingles. Howser purchases lumber from saw mills and manufactures the shingles in one of its two factories. The shingles are used in house construction, mainly in the southern and western United States. Howser is owned by 20 investors, all of whom are not involved in the day-to-day management of the company. The professional management team that manages the company receives salary, plus bonuses based on company performance as compensation. Howser has a large loan outstanding from the bank. The amount of the loan is based on accounts receivable and inventory outstanding on the last day of each calendar month. Howser usually has borrowed the maximum amount allowable under the borrowing agreement with the bank. Howser pays surplus cash (cash that is not required for operations and that is available after paying of debts) out to its shareholders.

Required:

Prepare a report to Howser's management recommending accounting policies for inventory. Your report should fully explain your recommendations.

P8-6. **(Considering the effect of inventory errors, LO 1, 4, 7)** Abney Ltd. (Abney) is a small manufacturing company. In the fiscal year just ended a number of errors were made in accounting for inventory. For each of the following errors, indicate the effect on the financial statement elements and ratios shown in the table below. Indicate whether the financial statement element or ratio would be overstated (higher than it would have been had the error not occurred), understated (lower than it would have been had the error not occurred), or not affected by the error. Abney uses a periodic inventory system and direct costing. Abney applies the lower of cost and market rule on an item-by-item basis.

a. Some of the inventory in Abney's warehouse was not counted during the year-end inventory count.
b. Certain fixed costs were included in inventory.
c. The purchase of some inventory on credit was not recorded (both the inventory and the payable) but the inventory was included in the year-end inventory count.
d. Certain direct labour costs were expensed as incurred.

	Net income	Cost of sales	Total assets	Owners' equity	Current ratio	Inventory turnover ratio	Debt-to-equity ratio
a.							
b.							
c.							
d.							

P8-7. **(Considering the effect of inventory errors, LO 1, 3, 4, 7)** Cariboo Ltd. (Cariboo) is a small manufacturing company. In the fiscal year just ended a number of errors were made in accounting for inventory. For each of the following errors, indicate the effect on the financial statement elements and ratios shown in the table on page 488. Indicate whether the financial statement element or ratio would be overstated (higher than it would have been had the error not occurred), understated (lower than it would have been had the error not occurred), or not affected by the error.

Cariboo uses a periodic inventory system and direct costing. Cariboo applies the lower of cost and market rule on an item-by-item basis.

a. Inventory that was on consignment with one of Cariboo's customers was not included in inventory.

b. Certain variable manufacturing overhead costs were expensed as incurred.

c. Several inventory items whose market value was less than cost were not written down to market.

d. Some of the inventory in Cariboo's warehouse was counted twice during the year-end inventory count.

	Net income	Cost of sales	Total assets	Owners' equity	Current ratio	Inventory turnover ratio	Debt-to-equity ratio
a.							
b.							
c.							
d.							

P8-8.   **(Determining the amount of inventory on hand when a periodic inventory system is used, LO 1, 7)** On March 24, 2001 Enterprise Inc. (Enterprise) suffered a serious fire that destroyed its entire inventory of fine paper products. Enterprise uses a periodic inventory system and as a result does not keep track of the amount of inventory that has been removed from inventory. Enterprise last counted its inventory on December 31, 2000, its year end. At that time there was $450,000 of inventory on hand. Enterprise's records indicate that sales from January 1 to March 24, 2001 were $370,000 and that during that time additional inventory was purchased for $325,000. Enterprise's usual gross margin on its sales of fine paper is 45%.

Required:

Enterprise has insurance that covers it fully for losses suffered by fire, except for a $50,000 deductible. Prepare a report to Enterprise's management that computes the amount of the loss that should be claimed from the insurance company as a result of the fire. Explain any factors that management should be aware of that would change the amount of the claim.

P8-9.   **(Determining the amount of inventory on hand when a periodic inventory system is used, LO 1, 7)** On February 19, 2004 Exploits Inc.'s (Exploits) entire inventory was stolen in a daring daylight robbery. The thieves held warehouse personnel at gunpoint while they methodically loaded trucks with the contents of the warehouse. There were no injuries.

Exploits is fully insured against theft and so must file a claim with its insurance company for the loss suffered. Because Exploits uses a periodic inventory system, it does not know for certain the amount of inventory that was stolen. However, from your discussions with company personnel you have learned that Exploits has two categories of inventory. Category one inventory usually generates a gross margin of 60%, while the category two usually generates a gross margin of 35%. Sales of category one since the company's year end on October 31, 2003 were about $850,000. Sales of category two over the same time period were about $1,755,000. During the period since the year end, Exploits purchased $325,000 of category one inventory and $800,000 of category two inventory. The financial records show that on October 31, 2003 there was $450,000 of category one inventory and $1,000,000 of category two inventory on hand.

Required:

Prepare a report to Exploits' management that computes the amount of the loss that should be claimed from the insurance company as a result of the robbery. Explain any factors that management should be aware of that would change the amount of the claim.

P8-10.   **(Lower of cost and market, LO 3, 7)** Tumbell Corp. (Tumbell) reports its inventory at the lower of cost and market, where market is defined as net realizable value. Tumbell has five inventory categories. You are provided with the following cost and NRV information about each category:

Inventory category	Cost	NRV
Category 1	$112,000	$100,000
Category 2	231,000	310,000
Category 3	74,500	105,000
Category 4	98,100	147,500
Category 5	147,000	140,000

Required:

a. What amount should Tumbell report on its balance sheet for inventory if it determines the lower of cost and market for the inventory as a whole? What is the amount of write-down that is required?

b. What amount should Tumbell report on its balance sheet for inventory if it determines the lower of cost and market item by item? What is the amount of write-down that is required?

c. What is the effect on Tumbell's cash flow of determining the lower of cost and market for the inventory as a whole versus on an item-by-item basis?

d. What are the implications of the two methods on the inventory turnover ratio and the gross margin percentage? Explain.

e. Should Tumbell use the inventory-as-a-whole approach or the item-by-item approach to determine the lower of cost and market of its inventory? Explain your answer.

P8-11. **(Lower of cost and market, LO 3, 7)** Wolverine Corp. (Wolverine) reports its inventory at the lower of cost and market, where market is defined as replacement cost. Wolverine has five inventory categories. You are provided with the following cost and replacement cost information about each category:

Inventory category	Cost	Replacement cost
Category 1	$112,000	$125,000
Category 2	231,000	215,000
Category 3	74,500	75,200
Category 4	98,100	78,500
Category 5	147,000	152,000

Required:

a. What amount should Wolverine report on its balance sheet for inventory if it determines the lower of cost and market for the inventory as a whole? What is the amount of write-down that is required?

b. What amount should Wolverine report on its balance sheet for inventory if it determines the lower of cost and market item by item? What is the amount of write-down that is required?

c. What is the effect on Wolverine's cash flow of determining the lower of cost and market for the inventory as a whole versus on an item-by-item basis?

d. What are the implications of the two methods on the inventory turnover ratio and the gross margin percentage? Explain.

e. Should Wolverine use the inventory-as-a-whole approach or the item-by-item approach to determine the lower of cost and market of its inventory? Explain your answer.

P8-12. **(Determine the amount of inventory lost due to theft, LO 1)** Wekusko Ltd. (Wekusko) is a wholesaler of electronic equipment that it imports from Asia. Recently the manager of Wekusko's warehouse in Winnipeg became concerned that a significant amount of goods was being stolen from the warehouse and he wanted to know the extent of the problem so he could take steps to remedy the problem, if necessary. He spoke with the company accountant, who told the warehouse manager that if he would count the inventory on hand, the accountant could give him an idea of how much inventory was being stolen.

The manager closed the warehouse and had the inventory counted. The warehouse manager advised the accountant that there was $2,453,517 of inventory on hand on the date of the count. The manager also told the accountant that since the last year end, goods costing $12,550 had been damaged and had to be thrown away. The accountant examined the financial records pertaining to the Winnipeg warehouse and found that since the last year end, goods costing $995,640 had been purchased and stored in the warehouse, and that goods costing $1,055,456 had been shipped to customers over the same period. The inventory count at the end of the previous reporting period reported inventory of $2,623,765.

Required:

a. Estimate the amount of electronic equipment that might have been stolen from the Winnipeg warehouse.
b. Is it possible to conclude with certainty the amount you calculated in (a) was due to theft? Explain.
c. Why was it necessary to count the inventory to estimate the amount of inventory that was stolen?

P8-13. (**Determine the amount of inventory shrinkage, LO 1**) Magyar Ltd. (Magyar) is a large retail clothing store located in a suburban mall. Recently, the store manager became concerned that a significant amount of goods was being stolen from the store and she wanted an idea of how much was being stolen so that she could decide whether it was worthwhile to install theft-prevention equipment. The accountant told the store manager that if she would count the inventory on hand, the accountant could give her an idea of the amount of inventory being stolen.

The manager had the inventory counted after store closing one Sunday. According to the count there was $480,000 of inventory on hand. The manager also told the accountant that since the year end $42,000 of merchandise had been returned to suppliers. At the last year end Magyar had $420,000 of inventory. Since the year end the store had purchased $405,000 of inventory and had sales of $610,000. The gross margin that Magyar usually earns is 52%.

Required:

a. Determine the amount of electronic equipment that might have been stolen from the store.
b. Is it possible to conclude with certainty the amount you calculated in (a) was due to theft?
c. Why was it necessary to count the inventory to estimate the amount of inventory that was stolen?
d. If Magyar had used a perpetual inventory system, would a count of the inventory have been required to provide the manager with the information she required?

P8-14. (**Consider the effect of different inventories on the inventory turnover ratio, LO 7**) Xena Inc. (Xena) is an importer of gift items from Europe and Asia. Xena classifies its inventory into three categories: porcelain figurines, toys, and linens. Over the years Xena's management has found that the success of the three categories has tended to vary, sometimes quite significantly, although fortunately for the company, poor performance of one category seems to be offset by success in another. On its balance sheet and income statement, Xena does not break down its Inventory, Sales, and Cost of Sales into three categories.

For its years ended October 31, 2004 and 2005, Xena reported inventory of $1,670,000 and $1,733,000 respectively. For the fiscal year ended October 31, 2005, Xena reported sales of $7,844,000 and cost of sales of $3,854,500. However, the following breakdown of Inventory, Sales, and Cost of Sales has been made available to you:

Category	Inventory balance on October 31, 2004	Inventory balance on October 31, 2005	Sales for the year ended October 31, 2005	Cost of Sales for the year ended October 31, 2005
Porcelain figurines	$585,000	$638,000	$3,450,000	$1,380,000
Toys	675,000	505,000	2,771,000	1,663,000
Linens	410,000	590,000	1,623,000	811,500

Required:

    a. Calculate the gross margin percentage, inventory turnover ratio, and the average number of days inventory on hand for the year ended October 31, 2005, using the aggregated amounts reported for inventory, sales, and cost of sales on Xena's balance sheet and income statement.

    b. Calculate the gross margin, inventory turnover ratio, and the average number of days inventory on hand for the year ended October 31, 2005 for each category of inventory that Xena carries.

    c. What are the implications of the results you obtained in parts (a) and (b) of the question?

    d. How is your ability to analyze Xena affected by the aggregated information presented in the company's balance sheet and income statement versus the information that was made available to you? Explain fully.

P8-15. **(Consider the effect of different inventories on the inventory turnover ratio, LO 7)** Herschel Inc. (Herschel) is a small chain of convenience stores. Herschel classifies its inventory into three categories: perishable items, packaged goods, and household items. On its balance sheet and income statement, Herschel does not break down its Inventory, Sales, and Cost of Sales into three categories.

For its years ended December 31, 2005 and 2006, Herschel reported inventory of $268,400 and $349,400 respectively. For the fiscal year ended December 31, 2006, Herschel reported sales of $2,805,200 and cost of sales of $2,230,000. However, the following breakdown of Inventory, Sales, and Cost of Sales has been made available to you:

Category	Inventory balance on December 31, 2005	Inventory balance on December 31, 2006	Sales for the year ended December 31, 2006	Cost of Sales for the year ended December 31, 2006
Perishable items	$ 20,000	$ 17,000	$ 950,000	$800,000
Packaged goods	73,400	122,400	805,200	660,000
Household items	175,000	210,000	1,050,000	770,000

Required:

    a. Calculate the gross margin percentage, inventory turnover ratio, and the average number of days inventory on hand for the year ended December 31, 2006 using the aggregated amounts reported for Inventory, Sales, and Cost of Sales on Herschel's balance sheet and income statement.

    b. Calculate the gross margin percentage, inventory turnover ratio, and the average number of days inventory on hand for the year ended December 31, 2006 for each category of inventory that Herschel carries.

    c. What are the implications of the results you obtained in parts (a) and (b)? How is your ability to analyze Herschel affected by the aggregated information presented in the company's balance sheet and income statement versus the information that was made available to you? Explain fully.

P8-16. **(Cost flow assumptions, LO 1, 2, 3, 6)** The purchase and sale of inventory by Yearly Inc. (Yearly) during the year ended November 30, 2005 is summarized on page 492. Assume that purchases are made on the first day of each quarter and sales on the last day of each quarter. Yearly pays for all its inventory in cash when it is delivered.

Economic event	Quantity	Purchase price per unit	Selling price per unit
Opening inventory	10,000	$12.00	
Purchases—first quarter	8,000	$12.30	
Purchases—second quarter	11,000	$12.90	
Purchases—third quarter	19,000	$13.20	
Purchases—fourth quarter	7,000	$13.55	
Sales—first quarter	13,000		$22.00
Sales—second quarter	10,000		$22.00
Sales—third quarter	22,000		$23.00
Sales—fourth quarter	5,000		$23.00

Required:

a. Determine cost of sales for the year ended November 30, 2005 and ending inventory on November 30, 2005 using FIFO, LIFO, and average cost, assuming that Yearly uses a periodic inventory control system.

b. Determine cost of sales for the year ended November 30, 2005 and ending inventory on November 30, 2005 using FIFO, LIFO, and average cost, assuming that Yearly uses a perpetual inventory control system.

c. How much cash was spent on inventory during 2005 under each cost flow assumption? Is the amount of cash spent on inventory under each cost flow assumption the same or different? Explain.

d. Which cost flow assumption would you recommend if the objective of the entity were to minimize taxes? Explain.

e. Which cost flow assumption would you use if you were Yearly's CEO and your bonus were based on net income? Explain.

f. Which cost flow assumption would you recommend if the amount of Yearly's bank loan were a percentage of inventory? Explain.

g. Yearly uses the lower of cost and market to value its inventory and defines market as net realizable value. Suppose that on November 30, 2005 the NRV of Yearly's inventory plummeted to $12.50 per unit. What would you do under each cost flow assumption and inventory control system?

h. Does it matter which cost flow assumption Yearly uses? Explain fully.

P8-17. **(Cost flow assumptions, LO 1, 2, 3, 6)** The purchase and sale of inventory by Ripple Inc. (Ripple) during the year ended April 30, 2006 is summarized below. Assume that sales are made on the first day of each quarter and purchases are made on the last day of each quarter. Ripple pays for all its inventory in cash when it is delivered.

Economic event	Quantity	Purchase price per unit	Selling price per unit
Opening inventory	75,000	$2.75	
Purchases—first quarter	90,000	$3.50	
Purchases—second quarter	51,000	$4.00	
Purchases—third quarter	70,000	$4.25	
Purchases—fourth quarter	80,000	$3.70	
Sales—first quarter	68,000		$8.00
Sales—second quarter	88,000		$8.00
Sales—third quarter	55,000		$8.00
Sales—fourth quarter	67,000		$8.00

Required:

a. Determine cost of sales for the year ended April 30, 2006 and ending inventory on April 30, 2006 using FIFO, LIFO, and average cost, assuming that Ripple uses a periodic inventory control system.

b. Determine cost of sales for the year ended April 30, 2006 and ending inventory on April 30, 2006 using FIFO, LIFO, and average cost, assuming that Ripple uses a perpetual inventory control system.

c. How much cash was spent on inventory during 2006 under each cost flow assumption? Is the amount of cash spent on inventory under each cost flow assumption the same or different? Explain.

d. Which cost flow assumption would you recommend if the objective of the entity were to minimize taxes? Explain.

e. Which cost flow assumption would you use if you were Ripple's CEO and your bonus was based on net income? Explain.

f. Which cost flow assumption would you recommend if the amount of Ripple's bank loan were a percentage of inventory? Explain.

g. Ripple uses the lower of cost and market to value its inventory and defines market as replacement cost. Is it necessary to make any adjustments to inventory on April 30, 2006 to ensure compliance with the lower of cost and market rule? Explain.

h. Does it matter which cost flow assumption Ripple uses? Explain fully.

P8-18. **(Problems with LIFO, LO 2)** Iffly Ltd. (Iffly) uses LIFO to account for its inventory. Beginning in April 2003, the start of its fiscal year, Iffly's management began to reduce the amount of inventory it carried. Management felt that with the new inventory control techniques that it recently implemented, it would be able to safely operate with 40% less inventory. Iffly uses a periodic inventory control system. The listing of the costs associated with the inventory on hand on March 31, 2003 is provided below:

Iffly Ltd. LIFO Inventory Listing—Costs Remaining in Inventory March 31, 2003		
Year acquired	**Number of units**	**Cost per unit**
2003	5,000	$2.40
1998	5,000	1.95
1995	23,000	1.55
1992	85,000	1.25
1988	91,000	1.10
1987	80,000	1.05
1986	42,000	1.00
Total	331,000	

During fiscal 2004 Iffly purchased an additional 430,000 units of inventory for $2.40 per unit and sold 560,000 units for $5.00 per unit. During fiscal 2003 Iffly sold 550,000 units for $5.00 per unit and purchased 550,000 units for $2.40 per unit. In each of 2003 and 2004, Iffly incurred $1,000,000 in other expenses.

Required:

a. What amount did Iffly report for inventory on its March 31, 2003 balance sheet?

b. Prepare income statements for 2003 and 2004.

c. What was Iffly's gross margin percentage in 2003 and 2004?

d. Assess Iffly's performance in 2004 versus 2003. How do you explain the improvement in the company's performance? Do you think the company is more attractive to investors in 2004 than it was in 2003? Explain.

e. What would Iffly's net income and gross margin percentage have been if Iffly's cost per unit for all units sold in 2004 had been $2.40? Explain why net income in this part is different from what you calculated in (b) for net income in 2004.

P8-19. **(Problems with LIFO, LO 2)** Joyvista Ltd. (Joyvista) uses LIFO to account for its inventory. In early 2005 Joyvista's management realized that it would be difficult to meet earnings targets set by its parent company in the United States that were key for evaluating the performance of the managers and determining their annual bonuses. As a result, Joyvista's management decided to reduce the amount of inventory it was carrying so that it would be able to expense "less expensive" inventory. Joyvista uses a periodic inventory control system. The listing of the costs associated with the inventory on hand on December 31, 2004 is provided below:

Joyvista Ltd.		
LIFO Inventory Listing—Costs Remaining in Inventory December 31, 2004		
Year acquired	Number of units	Cost per unit
2004	400	$23.00
2003	600	22.50
2002	2,000	20.00
2001	4,000	13.75
2000	20,000	13.00
1999	20,000	13.50
1998	15,000	13.50

During fiscal 2005 Joyvista purchased an additional 20,000 units of inventory for $23.00 per unit and sold 35,000 units for $50.00 per unit. During fiscal 2004 Joyvista sold 30,000 units for $48.00 per unit and purchased 30,000 units for $23.00 per unit. In each of 2003 and 2004 Joyvista incurred $500,000 in other expenses.

Required:

a. What amount did Joyvista report for inventory on its December 31, 2005 balance sheet?

b. Prepare income statements for 2004 and 2005.

c. What was Joyvista's gross margin percentage in 2004 and 2005?

d. Assess Joyvista's performance in 2005 versus 2004. How do you explain the improvement in the company's performance? Do you think the company is more attractive to investors in 2005 than it was in 2004? Explain.

e. What would Joyvista's net income and gross margin percentage have been if Joyvista's cost per unit for all units sold in 2005 had been $23.00? Explain why net income in this part is different from what you calculated in (b) for net income in 2005.

■ Using Financial Statements

ATI Technologies Inc.

www.ati.com

Founded in 1985, ATI Technologies Inc. (ATI) has become the world's largest supplier of 3D graphics and multimedia solutions. ATI's cutting-edge technology is bringing cinema-quality images to creative professionals, business users, and consumers. ATI designs, manufactures and markets innovative and award-winning products for the personal computer, set-top box, and game console markets. ATI enjoys strong working relationships with original equipment manufacturers (OEMs), strategic technology partners, system builders, distributors, and retailers worldwide. The Company employs more than 1,900 people with locations around the world.[9]

ATI's consolidated balance sheets and statements of earnings, along with some extracts from the notes to the financial statements and the annual report, are provided in Exhibit 8-3. Use this information to respond to questions FS8-1 to FS8-6.

FS8-1. What amount of inventory did ATI report on its August 31, 2000 balance sheet? What proportion of current assets and what proportion of total assets did inventory

Exhibit 8-3

ATI Technologies Inc. Financial Statements

CONSOLIDATED STATEMENTS OF OPERATIONS AND RETAINED EARNINGS

THOUSANDS OF U.S. DOLLARS, EXCEPT PER SHARE AMOUNTS

	YEARS ENDED AUGUST 31		
	2000	1999	1998
SALES	$ 1,372,043	$ 1,231,261	$ 737,268
Cost of goods sold	1,045,508	780,572	464,524
Gross margin	326,535	450,689	272,744
EXPENSES			
Selling and marketing	174,568	108,284	64,626
Research and development	134,355	102,156	42,425
Administrative	29,072	30,394	19,276
Amortization of intangible assets (note 8)	56,709	52,061	–
	394,704	292,895	126,327
Income (loss) from operations	(68,169)	157,794	146,417
Interest and other income (note 9)	15,225	4,070	3,765
Interest expense	(104)	(379)	(99)
Income (loss) before income taxes	(53,048)	161,485	150,083
Income taxes (note 12)	16,286	54,282	42,752
NET INCOME (LOSS) (note 13)	$ (69,334)	$ 107,203	$ 107,331
RETAINED EARNINGS, beginning of year	275,870	168,667	61,336
Repurchase of common shares (note 11)	(6,580)	–	–
RETAINED EARNINGS, end of year	$ 199,956	$ 275,870	$ 168,667
NET INCOME (LOSS) PER SHARE (note 13)			
Basic	$ (0.32)	$ 0.53	$ 0.55
Fully diluted	$ (0.32)	$ 0.49	$ 0.50

CONSOLIDATED BALANCE SHEETS

THOUSANDS OF U.S. DOLLARS

	AUGUST 31	
	2000	1999
ASSETS		
Current assets		
Cash and cash equivalents	$ 74,835	$ 85,467
Short-term investments	4,403	10,000
Accounts receivable	180,395	178,545
Inventories (note 5)	239,170	190,905
Prepayments and sundry receivables	32,920	15,652
Total current assets	531,723	480,569
Capital assets (note 6)	61,320	55,584
Intangible assets (note 8)	409,412	18,808
Long-term investments (note 9)	12,556	12,500
Total Assets	$ 1,015,011	$ 567,461
LIABILITIES AND SHAREHOLDERS' EQUITY		
Current liabilities		
Accounts payable	$ 183,908	$ 103,097
Accrued liabilities	48,634	52,837
Deferred revenue	3,658	–
Income taxes payable	4,437	30,278
Total current liabilities	240,637	186,212
Deferred income taxes	9,100	4,400
Shareholders' equity		
Share capital (note 11)		
Common shares:		
Authorized – unlimited number of common shares		
Issued and outstanding – 229,436,267 (1999 – 204,963,711)	557,044	92,705
Preferred shares:		
Authorized – unlimited number of preferred shares		
Issued and outstanding – Nil (1999 – Nil)	–	–
Retained earnings	199,956	275,870
Currency translation adjustment (note 2)	8,274	8,274
Total shareholders' equity	765,274	376,849
Total Liabilities and Shareholders' Equity	$ 1,015,011	$ 567,461

3. SIGNIFICANT ACCOUNTING POLICIES

(d) Inventories

Raw materials are stated at the lower of cost and replacement cost. Finished goods and work-in-process are stated at the lower of cost and net realizable value. Cost is determined on a first-in, first-out basis.

Exhibit 8-3 (continued)

ATI Technologies Inc. Financial
Statements and Other Information

5. INVENTORIES

	2000	1999
Raw materials	$ 108,012	$ 90,063
Work-in-process	71,436	60,535
Finished goods	59,722	40,307
	$ 239,170	$ 190,905

13. ADJUSTED NET INCOME AND ADJUSTED NET INCOME PER SHARE

The table below presents adjusted net income and adjusted net income per share, which excludes the
after-tax effect of gain on sale of long-term investments, amortization of intangible assets related to
the Company's acquisitions and special charges. The special charges include a $64 million charge
in cost of goods sold for excess inventory and lower of cost and market adjustments against certain
products and a $24.3 million charge included in selling and marketing expenses that includes the
cost for special programs and incentives provided to customers in order to stimulate demand for the
Company's older and slow-moving product lines.

	2000	1999	1998
Net income (loss)	$ (69,334)	$ 107,203	$ 107,331
Gain on sale of long-term investments	(10,666)	–	–
Amortization of intangible assets	56,709	52,061	–
Inventory special charge	63,997	–	–
Selling and marketing expense special charge	24,303	–	–
Net tax effect	(365)	–	–
Adjusted net income	$ 64,644	$ 159,264	$ 107,331
Adjusted net income per share			
Basic	$ 0.30	$ 0.79	$ 0.55
Fully diluted	$ 0.29	$ 0.73	$ 0.50

Extract from the CEO and Chairman's message to shareholders
Our highly competitive industry saw considerable consolidation in 2000, with some
firms joining forces and others dropping out of the market altogether. Some of our
competitors and those companies exiting the graphics business reverted to excep-
tionally aggressive pricing tactics in an attempt to clear out graphics board inventories. This, combined with stiff competition from both the enthusiast and integrated
segments, created severe pressures in the markets we serve. The result was continuing pricing pressures and much lower profit for everyone.

comprise? What is the breakdown of ATI's inventory? As a user of the financial statements, do you find knowing the breakdown useful? Explain.

FS8-2. Describe the accounting policies that ATI uses to account for its inventory. Why do
you think that raw materials and finished goods are not accounted for in exactly the
same way?

FS8-3. Calculate ATI's inventory turnover ratio for 2000. If ATI's ending inventory on
August 31, 1998 was $110,340,000, what would be the inventory turnover ratio for
1999? How would you interpret the change in the inventory turnover ratio from
1999 to 2000? What might explain the change from 1999 and 2000?

FS8-4. (This is a difficult question.) Examine ATI's statement of earnings, note 13 to the
financial statements, and the extract from the CEO and chairman's message to shareholders. Note 13 introduces a measure of performance that ATI calls adjusted net
income. Adjusted net income removes from the traditional net income unusual
transactions and economic events that were included in the calculation of net

income, as well as the amortization of certain intangible assets. (We will have more to say about the intangibles in Chapter 9.)

    a. How much was the special charge that ATI made for inventory in fiscal 2000? Where did you find the amount?

    b. What journal entry would ATI have prepared to record the special charge?

    c. What would the balance in the Inventory account on the balance sheet have been had the special charge not been made?

    d. What is the reason provided for the special charge for inventory? Interpret the meaning of the words in the note.

    e. Examine ATI's consolidated statement of earnings. Can you find the special charge for inventory in the statement of earnings? Where in the statement of earnings do you think the special charge is included? Why do you think the special charge is not disclosed separately in the statement of earnings? What are the implications to users of the financial statements of not disclosing the special charge separately in the statement of earnings?

    f. Suppose that the special charge was included in cost of sales. How would gross margin and the gross margin percentage be affected? Recalculate gross margin and the gross margin percentage in 2000 with the special charge excluded from cost of sales. How would the inclusion of the special charge in cost of sales affect the comparability of the 2000 statement of earnings with those of previous years?

    g. Why do you think ATI introduces "adjusted net income", instead of simply using the more traditional measure of net income?

FS8-5. Calculate the amount of inventory that ATI purchased during fiscal 2000, assuming that the inventory special charge is included in cost of sales. Is it possible to determine the amount of raw materials that were purchased during 2000? Explain.

FS8-6. Why is careful management of inventory so important for a company like ATI?

■ Analyzing Mark's Work Wearhouse

M8-1. Suppose MWW decided to write off some of its inventory because it could not be sold (perhaps it was damaged or destroyed).

    a. What journal entry (or worksheet entry) would MWW make to record the write-off?

    b. Suppose the amount of the write-off was sizable. How/where would you report the write-off in the income statement? Explain why.

    c. Are there any alternatives to how the amount of the write-off could be reported?

    d. How would different ways of reporting the write-off affect stakeholders' interpretations of the statements?

M8-2. Given the type of business it is in, do you think that MWW is likely to have to address lower of cost and market (LCM) problems on a regular basis? Explain.

M8-3. Calculate the amount of inventory that MWW purchased during its year ended January 27, 2001. Assume that the inventory was purchased in a single transaction. Ignore the implications of the purchase of franchised stores during the year. Prepare the journal entry that MWW would have made to record the purchase.

M8-4. Use the information from MWW's annual financial statements to calculate the inventory turnover ratio for MWW for the years ended January 27, 2001 and January 29, 2000. Use the quarterly information below to calculate the inventory turnover ratios for 2001 and 2000. Why are the ratios different when the quarterly data are used? Which calculation gives a better indication of the inventory turnover? Explain. Remember that the cost of sales is only for the quarter in question, not for the year to date.

	Fiscal 2001		Fiscal 2000	
	Inventory at the end of	Cost of sales during	Inventory at the end of	Cost of sales during
1st Quarter	$ 94,772	$36,730	$ 89,357	$33,386
2nd Quarter	89,915	45,081	83,300	37,578
3rd Quarter	113,720	51,567	106,994	45,388
4th Quarter	84,483	80,983	81,468	70,371

M8-5. Examine the quarterly information shown in question M8-4 above. Why do you think the amount of inventory is so much higher at the end of the third quarter than the other quarters? Why are cost of sales so much higher in the fourth quarter? Why is the amount of inventory lowest at the end of the fourth quarter?

M8-6. MWW does not break down its inventory into sub-categories. Why do you think this is the case? As a user of MWW's financial statements, do you think that it would be useful to have the inventory broken down into sub-categories? Explain. Suggest some possible sub-categories that would be useful for you.

M8-7. Examine the last paragraph in Note 11 to MWW's financial statements (page A-56). Describe the agreement Mark's and Work World have with its banker in the event the banks foreclose on any of the franchise stores. What is the maximum amount that MWW would have to pay to banks in the event of foreclosure of all franchise stores? How many stores have this type of buy-back arrangement?

Endnotes

1. Extracted from Dylex Limited's 1999 annual report.

2. Clarence Byrd, Ida Chen, and Heather Chapman, *Financial Reporting in Canada*, 26th Edition. The Virtual Professional Libarary. CD-ROM 2002.

3. Panel A extracted from Brick Brewing Co. Limited's 2000 annual report. Panel B extracted from TGS Properties Ltd.'s 2000 annual report.

4. Interpretation Bulletin IT473R "Inventory Valuation." Published by the Canadian Customs and Revenue Agency, December 21, 1998; http://www.ccra-adrc.gc.ca/E/pub/tp/it473rem/it473re.html (accessed April 30, 2002).

5. Clarence Byrd, Ida Chen, and Heather Chapman, *Financial Reporting in Canada*, 26th Edition. The Virtual Professional Libarary. CD-ROM 2002.

6. Interpretation Bulletin IT473R "Inventory Valuation." Published by the Canadian Customs and Revenue Agency, December 21, 1998; http://www.ccra-adrc.gc.ca/E/pub/tp/it473rem/it473re.html (accessed April 30, 2002).

7. Interpretation Bulletin IT473R "Inventory Valuation." Published by the Canadian Customs and Revenue Agency, December 21, 1998; http://www.ccra-adrc.gc.ca/E/pub/tp/it473rem/it473re.html (accessed April 30, 2002).

8. Information about MWW's inventory at times other than its year end can be obtained from its quarterly financial statements, which can be viewed at the SEDAR database at http://www.sedar.com.

9. Extracted from ATI Technologies Inc.'s 2000 annual report.

Chapter 9

Capital Assets

Chapter Outline

Learning Objectives

After studying the material in this chapter you will be able to:

LO 1. Explain the strengths and limitations of the different bases for valuing capital assets on the balance sheet.

LO 2. Recognize how to account for the purchase of capital assets.

LO 3. Describe the different methods of amortizing capital assets and understand the implications of the different methods for financial statements and for the users of the statements.

LO 4. Discuss the problems with accounting for intangible assets.

LO 5. Differentiate between capital cost allowance for tax purposes and amortization for financial reporting purposes.

LO 6. Explain how to account for disposals of amortizable capital assets and for write-downs of capital assets.

LO 7. Recognize the implications of changing accounting policies and accounting estimates.

LO 8. Explain how the cash flow statement is affected by whether expenditures on capital assets are expensed or capitalized.

LO 9. Analyze and interpret information about capital assets in financial statements.

Introduction

Capital assets are resources that contribute to the earning of revenue over more than one period by helping an entity to produce, supply, support, or make available the goods or services it offers to its customers. Capital assets contribute indirectly to the earning of revenue—indirectly because selling capital assets is not part of the ordinary activities of the entity (although capital assets are sometimes sold).

For example, Mark's Work Wearhouse's business is selling clothes—but it takes a lot more than a shipment of jeans to make a successful chain of clothing stores. The stores that MWW rents have to be renovated so they are appropriately set up for a MWW store. The costs of these renovations are capital assets. MWW must install display cases, shelving, sales desks, cash registers, lighting, and so on. Furniture and mannequins must be purchased. These too are capital assets. And capital assets are also required to operate the company as a whole. MWW's head office must have the necessary furniture, fixtures, computers, and office equipment to manage the company. These assets are all necessary for MWW to do its business.

Via Rail's capital assets include its trains. TimberWest Forest Corp.'s capital assets include the rights to harvest timber from government land, privately owned timberland, saw and pulp mills, and logging roads. The capital assets of Open Text Corporation (a software company) include computer equipment and software. In each case the capital assets are essential if these companies are going to be able to carry on business. What would Via Rail do if it had no trains or TimberWest Forest if it had no land to harvest trees from?

Capital assets take many forms. They can be tangible—have physical existence—like land, buildings, equipment, and furniture. They can be intangible, like patents, copyrights, brands, and trademarks. Capital assets can be oil in the ground or trees in a forest. Capital assets can have very long lives—like land, which lasts forever, or buildings, which can last for decades. Or they can have relatively short lives.

Not all of an entity's capital assets appear on its balance sheet. The traditional accounting model sometimes has difficulty with certain types of capital assets. As a result assets that most people, including accountants, agree would have future benefit to an entity do not appear on the balance sheet. For example, many software and biotechnology companies do not report the software and pharmaceuticals that they develop as capital assets. Some of the aircraft flown by airlines do not appear as assets because they are leased. Many companies' brand names are not recorded. The investments that entities make in their employees rarely appear as assets.

In this chapter we will take a close look at the accounting for capital assets. We will investigate what amounts are recorded on the balance sheet as capital assets and how these amounts are expensed. We will look at the challenges that contemporary accounting faces with accounting for intangible or "knowledge" assets. And we will evaluate the usefulness of information about capital assets when it is presented on a historical cost basis.

www.viarail.ca
www.timberwest.com
www.opentext.com

Measuring Capital Assets and Limitations to Historical Cost Accounting

GAAP require that entities report their capital assets at historical cost. This means that the purchase price of a capital asset, plus any costs incurred to get the asset ready for use, should be **capitalized**—recorded on the balance sheet as an asset. From the date a capital asset is recorded on the balance sheet, the cost is the basis of valuation. A piece of land purchased in 1953 for $25,000 would be reported on the 2004 balance sheet at $25,000. It makes no difference that the market value of the land may have increased to $1,000,000 in the years after the purchase—the land would be reported at its cost. As we will see in this chapter, only when a capital asset is impaired is its basis of valuation something other than cost.

One has to wonder about the usefulness of historical cost information about capital assets. How useful is it today to know that land cost $25,000 when it was purchased in 1953? Historical cost accounting serves the purpose of matching the cost of capital assets to revenue earned over the life of the asset. But for the purpose of making projections or other future-oriented decisions, it is difficult to understand how the historical cost of capital assets—costs that are sometimes very old—can be useful for most uses and to most users of financial statements. While inventory is also reported at cost, in most cases inventory is bought and sold in a relatively short period of time, so historical information and trends can be used as a basis for making projections and future-oriented decisions. In contrast, capital assets can remain in an organization for a long time, which limits the usefulness of the cost of those assets for making projections and future-oriented decisions. (However, the historical cost of capital assets is relevant for tax purposes because the tax treatment of capital assets is based on their cost.)

There are three alternatives to historical cost accounting for capital assets: net realizable value (NRV), replacement cost, and value-in-use. It is important to recognize that each of these alternatives has shortcomings of its own, and none is ideal for all uses. The usefulness of any method of accounting for capital assets, of course, depends on the decisions a particular user has to make. It should also be remembered that historical cost is the "law of the land," so despite its limitations it is necessary to understand and be able to work with the information presented in traditional financial statements.

NRV and replacement cost were discussed in Chapter 8. Here we will look at them from the perspective of capital assets.

NRV is the amount that would be received from the sale of an asset after the selling costs are deducted. For example, it is common for a bank to have a property appraised when a person is buying a home so that the bank can have an idea of what the property is worth when it makes its lending decision. NRV is more useful than historical cost in this situation because it gives the lender a current estimate of what would be received if the property had to be sold. Historical cost will likely provide no information about a capital asset's NRV. NRV is less objective and less reliable than historical cost because the amount is an estimate—it is not supported by a transaction. It may be difficult to come up with a reasonable estimate of the NRV of capital assets because many used and even new capital assets are not bought and sold very often. Also, NRV does not tell the lender what the asset could be sold for in the future. It is only an estimate of the current NRV.

Replacement cost is the amount that would have to be spent to replace a capital asset. Replacement cost can take a number of forms. It can be the cost of replacing an existing asset with a new identical one. It can be the cost of replacing an existing asset with an equivalent one—for example, if the existing asset were no longer available, it would be necessary to consider an asset with similar capabilities and features. The replacement cost of an asset can be useful for predicting future cash flows associated with replacing an existing asset. Most capital assets have to be replaced from time to time and the timing and amounts involved in replacing assets can have significant consequences for the cash flow of the entity, as well as implications for a user's evaluation of the performance of the entity and its management. Replacement cost has some of the same problems that were noted with NRV. Replacement cost is less objective than historical cost since there is no transaction supporting the amount. Replacement cost today also doesn't say anything about what the asset will cost to replace in the future, when actual replacement is required.

Another method of valuing capital assets is the value-in-use—the value the asset has for doing what it was purchased to do. **Value-in-use** is the net present value of the cash flow that the asset will generate over its life, or the net present value of the cash flow that the asset would allow the entity to avoid paying. Value-in-use would be useful to investors who are trying to figure out the value of an entity. Value-in-use is conceptually an attractive method, but practically it has severe limitations. First, individual assets are rarely responsible for generating cash on their own. They interact with other assets to generate cash flows. For example, what is the value-in-use of a computer that contributes to the development of some software? Second, estimating the future cash flows that an asset will generate can be difficult, requiring many assumptions and estimates that can make the value-in-use estimate very unreliable.

Historical cost also has its uses, although not for future-oriented decisions. For users interested in evaluating historical performance, such as calculating return on investment, historical cost measures can be used. Historical cost information is also of use for the stewardship objective of accounting. As mentioned earlier, historical cost is also appropriate for tax purposes.

Question for Consideration

For each of the following, specify which measurement basis—historical cost, NRV, replacement cost, or value-in-use—is most appropriate for the purpose described. Provide a brief explanation why you chose the measurement basis in each case.

a. Determine the amount of fire insurance needed for a building.

b. Prepare a balance sheet according to GAAP.

c. Determine the value of the assets of an entity going out of business.

d. Evaluate whether the entity should purchase a particular capital asset.

Answer:

Situation	Measurement basis	Explanation
a. Determine the amount of fire insurance needed for a building.	Replacement cost	Fire insurance is intended to allow the insured to replace a building destroyed by fire. Therefore, the replacement cost of a building is the appropriate measurement basis.
b. Prepare a balance sheet according to GAAP.	Historical cost	GAAP require the use of historical cost, transactions-based accounting.
c. Determine the value of the assets of an entity going out of business.	NRV	An entity that is going out of business will likely be looking to sell its assets so that it can satisfy its creditors and/or allow the owners to receive cash from the liquidation of the business. NRV gives the current selling price of assets.
d. Evaluate whether the entity should purchase a particular capital asset.	Value-in-use	The managers should evaluate the present value of the cash flows the asset will generate to assess whether the purchase is desirable. By evaluating the present value of the cash flows, management is measuring the value in use of the asset.

What Is Cost?

For better or for worse, historical cost is the measurement basis that is used for capital assets in almost all financial statements in Canada. It is therefore necessary to have a good understanding of the workings of historical cost accounting for capital assets and the issues and problems surrounding its use.

The cost of an asset that is reported on an entity's balance sheet should include all the costs associated with purchasing the asset and getting it ready for use. This definition casts a fairly broad net around the costs that should be capitalized and includes more than just the purchase price of the asset. Amounts that can be included in this definition of cost are the purchase price of the asset; architectural, design and engineering fees; taxes; delivery costs; transportation insurance costs; duties, testing and preparation charges; installation costs; and legal costs—any and all costs incurred to get the asset up and running. Costs incurred by employees of the purchasing entity to get the asset ready for use, including their wages, should also be capitalized. Only necessary costs should be capitalized. Costs that are not related to the acquisition—such as repairs or unnecessary work caused by poor planning, etc.—should not be capitalized.

Interest can be capitalized up until the time an asset is ready for use. Once an asset is ready for use, interest incurred is expensed. Capitalizing interest is most common when an entity is constructing an asset itself. For example, if an entity is using its own personnel to build an extension to its warehouse, the interest incurred to finance the extension can be capitalized up until the time the extension is complete and ready for use.

Sometimes it is difficult to determine whether certain costs should be capitalized and judgment must be exercised in deciding how to treat those costs. This need for judgment introduces the possibility that different preparers will account for similar costs differently. For example, it may be difficult to determine the amount of employees' wages that should be capitalized as part of the cost of preparing an asset for use. Of course, any time ambiguity exists, the choices made by managers may be influenced by their self-interests. For example, if an entity has tax minimization as it main objective, it may expense as much and as many of the expenses incurred to acquire the asset as it reasonably can. On the other hand, if the entity prefers to maximize current income, then it will capitalize as much as it can to defer expensing the costs.

Let's look at an example. Aillik Corp. (Aillik) purchases a new machine for $700,000 plus $45,000 in taxes. Aillik pays $5,000 to have the machine delivered and $50,000 to have it installed and tested. Legal fees associated with the contract with the seller of the machine were $10,000. According to GAAP, all of these costs should be capitalized as part of the cost of the machine. The journal entry to record the purchase of the machine would be:

Dr. Machine (asset +)	810,000	
Cr. Accounts payable—machine manufacturer (liability +)		700,000
Cr. Taxes payable (liability +)		45,000
Cr. Accounts payable—delivery (liability +)		5,000
Cr. Accounts payable—installation (liability +)		50,000
Cr. Accounts payable—legal fees (liability +)		10,000
To record the purchase of a machine.		

The $810,000 cost of the machine would be recorded as a capital asset on the balance sheet and the cost would be amortized over its expected useful life.

However, suppose that instead of using outsiders to deliver and install the new machine, Aillik used its own personnel and equipment. If the wages Aillik paid to deliver and install the machine were $25,000, it could make the following journal entry:

Dr. Machine (asset +)	780,000	
Cr. Accounts payable—machine manufacturer (liability +)		700,000
Cr. Taxes payable (liability +)		45,000
Cr. Wages payable (liability +)		25,000
Cr. Accounts payable—legal fees (liability +)		10,000

To record the purchase of a machine.

Or if it was too difficult or troublesome to identify the costs of these internally provided services, and if Aillik had tax minimization as it main objective, it might make this journal entry:

Dr. Machine (asset +)	755,000	
Dr. Wage expense (expense +, shareholders' equity –)	25,000	
Cr. Accounts payable—machine manufacturer (liability +)		700,000
Cr. Taxes payable (liability +)		45,000
Cr. Wages payable (liability +)		25,000
Cr. Accounts payable—legal fees (liability +)		10,000

To record the purchase of a machine.

In this case, only $755,000 is capitalized, and the $25,000 that is paid to Aillik's employees is expensed. There is nothing inherently inappropriate about this accounting treatment. Aillik may not have been able to determine the cost of the employees' work on delivering and installing the machine. Or the company may have felt that because the employees would have been paid regardless of whether the machine was acquired, it was not appropriate to capitalize the cost.

This example again highlights the fact that different possible accounting treatments exist for similar transactions. The motivation for different treatments may be the result of several factors:

a. The cost of gathering the information may not be worth the benefit,

b. There may be different, legitimate interpretations of GAAP,

c. There may be different objectives of accounting at play, or

d. A combination of all three factors.

So what theoretically should be capitalized under GAAP, and what is capitalized in fact, may depend on a number of factors, including the reporting objectives of the entity. That is why it is important not to take for granted how an entity has accounted for a transaction. It is important to find out the accounting choices an entity has made if the information is relevant to a decision.

Sometimes expenditures are made that improve an existing capital asset. These types of investments are called betterments. A **betterment** makes a capital asset more valuable to the entity, perhaps by increasing the asset's useful life, or by improving its efficiency or effectiveness. In other words, the betterment stands to make the entity more profitable. Because betterments provide future benefits, the cost is capitalized and amortized over the remaining life of the asset.

In contrast, expenditures that allow an asset to operate as intended—to do what it is designed to do—are considered **repairs** or **maintenance** and should be expensed when incurred. Changing a car's oil regularly does not make the car better—it allows it to operate as intended by the manufacturer. The same goes for brakes. Car brakes wear out from time to time and have to be replaced. Replacing worn brakes does not improve the car; it simply makes the car drivable. On the other hand, the cost of rebuilding an engine so that it is more powerful and efficient should be capitalized. A more powerful, efficient engine might allow the vehicle to do more work (carry heavier loads) and use less fuel, both of which are beneficial to the entity.

While some expenditures can easily be classified as betterments or maintenance, the treatment is not always obvious. As a result, managers' choices may be motivated by their reporting objectives. When tax minimization is the primary objective, managers would expense as much of the expenditures as they could reasonably justify because the accounting treatment might make expensing those outlays for tax purposes more justifiable. If management is more concerned with the bottom line, it would be inclined to capitalize as much of the outlays as possible. The financial statement effect of treating an expenditure as a betterment is that the cost of the betterment is capitalized and amortized over the remaining life of the asset. Treating an expenditure as repairs or maintenance increases expenses and reduces income for the full amount of the expenditure in the period in which it is incurred. In general, it can be assumed that expenditures made on existing capital assets are much more likely to be repairs or maintenance than betterments.

Question for Consideration

Meadow Inc. (Meadow) recently acquired a new computer server for its head office network. The server had a list price of $50,000, but the head of the computing department was able to negotiate a price of $46,900. Taxes added $7,035 to the price and delivery cost $2,000. Replacement of the cables in the offices to meet the needs of the new server cost $8,000. However, a planning error by Meadow's management made it necessary for most of the cabling work to be redone, which cost an additional $2,100. Installation of the server cost $3,000, but once it was installed, management realized that the site for the server was inappropriate because the ventilation was not adequate. Moving and reinstalling the server cost an additional $2,600. Meadow purchased a three-year insurance policy for the server for $3,600.

Calculate the amount that should be capitalized for the purchase of the new server. Also, indicate which cost items should not be included in the capitalized amount. Explain your reasoning.

Solution:

Cost	Amount Capitalized	Explanation
Purchase price	$46,900	The only price that is relevant is the amount actually paid. The list price does not matter.
Taxes	7,035	Taxes are a part of the cost of the server.
Delivery	2,000	Delivery costs are necessary to get the server ready for use. The server must be delivered to be useful.
Cabling	8,000	Cabling costs are necessary to get the server ready for use. The server cannot do its job without adequate cabling.
Cabling required due to error	Not capitalized	The additional costs were incurred due to a mistake. These costs were not required to get the server ready for use and do not add anything to the value of the server. These costs should be expensed when incurred.
Installation	3,000	Installation costs are necessary to get the server ready for use. It cannot serve its purpose if it is not installed.
Reinstallation	Not capitalized	Reinstallation was required because of poor planning. The cost incurred was not necessary and does not make the server more valuable to the entity.
Insurance	Not capitalized	Insurance is not a cost required to get the server ready for use. It is a cost incurred to provide insurance protection for the server when it is operating. The insurance should be recorded as a prepaid asset and expensed as it is used.
Total amount to be capitalized for acquisition of the server	$66,935	

Basket Purchases

Sometimes an entity will purchase a "basket" or bundle of assets at a single price. The price of individual assets will not be stated anywhere. Basket purchases raise the problem of how to allocate the cost of the whole basket to each of the assets in the bundle. Good accounting requires that the purchase price be allocated in proportion to the market values of the assets in the bundle. The allocation is important because the different assets in the bundle may be accounted for differently, and different allocations will result in different financial statement effects (as we will see below).

For example, suppose that Pockwock Ltd. (Pockwock) purchases land and a building for $25,000,000. If the land were worth 40% of the total cost and the building 60%, the journal entry would be

Dr. Land (asset +)	10,000,000	
Dr. Building (asset +)	15,000,000	
Cr. Cash (asset –)		25,000,000

To record the basket purchase of land and building.

The problem in practice is knowing exactly what the market values of the land and building are as separate assets. Consequently, as long as the amount assigned to each asset is reasonable, preparers have the flexibility to make the allocation in a way that suits their reporting objectives. If the preparer's main concern were minimizing taxes, it would be preferable to allocate more of the cost to the building because buildings can be deducted for tax purposes whereas land cannot. By allocating more of the cost to the building, the company will have more to deduct to reduce taxes. If management were more concerned about increasing net income, it could allocate more of the cost of the basket to land, which is not amortized.

If Pockwock obtained independent appraisals that estimated the value of the land at between $9,000,000 and $12,000,000, it could justifiably assign any amount between those two values to the land. If Pockwock's reporting objective were tax minimization, it would allocate $9,000,000 of the purchase price to land and $16,000,000 to the building. This treatment would maximize the amount of expenses available for tax purposes, thereby permanently reducing the amount of tax Pockwock would have to pay. The downside of this choice would be that it would result in lower net income as well as lower taxes. If instead management wanted to minimize the effect of the purchase on income, it would allocate $12,000,000 to the cost of the land and $13,000,000 to building. This treatment would minimize the amount that would have to be amortized.

Remember, the choice being made here is not strictly arbitrary—it is not pure self-interest by the preparers. The amounts in both cases can be justified because they fall within the ranges of the independent appraisals. A reader might be suspicious of any choice management makes in circumstances such as these, but it is important to remember that it is usually not possible to know exactly what is the "truth." The actual market value of the land and building individually are just not known and cannot be known unless they are sold separately. The portion of cost that is assigned to each asset is an informed estimate.

Amortization

Most capital assets get used up. A truck, a machine, a building, a mine, and even an idea don't last forever. The truck eventually breaks down and can deliver no more merchandise. The machine is no longer able to produce goods effectively and has to be replaced by technologically up-to-date equipment. The building no longer meets the needs of the entity. The resource in the mine is exhausted and the patent for the idea expires. Because capital assets get used up while helping to earn revenue, it makes sense that under historical cost accrual accounting the cost of the capital assets should somehow be matched to the revenues they help earn. Expensing the cost of a capital asset is no different conceptually from expensing the cost of inventory when it is sold or salaries when the work is done. It is an application of the matching concept. The hard part about expensing the cost of a capital asset is figuring out a way of doing it. Because capital assets contribute to the earning of revenue indirectly and over more than one period, it is necessary to have a way of allocating the cost to each of the periods that the asset contributes to earning revenue.

The process of allocating the cost of a capital asset to expense over time to reflect the consumption of the asset while it helps to earn revenue is known as **amortization**. There are also specific terms used for the amortization of different types of capital assets. **Depreciation** is usually used to describe the amortization of the cost of tangible assets. **Tangible assets** are capital assets that have physical substance, such as buildings, equipment, vehicles, and furniture. The term amortization is also used specifically to refer to the amortization of intangible assets. **Intangible assets** are capital assets that do not have physical substance, such as patents, copyrights, trademarks, and brand names. A third term—**depletion**—is used to describe the amortization of the cost of natural resources. Note that amortization is the more general term, encompassing depreciation and depletion. The types of capital assets and the associated terms used to describe the amortization of those capital assets are summarized in Figure 9-1.

As mentioned earlier, the hard part about expensing the cost of a capital asset is figuring out a way of doing it. Authoritative sources provide very little specific guidance about how to amortize capital assets. According to the *CICA Handbook*, the cost of an asset less its **residual value** (the amount the asset can be sold for at the end of its useful life) should be amortized over its useful life in a "systematic and rational" manner. There are several difficulties: What is a systematic and rational way of amortizing the cost? What is the useful life? What is the residual value?

These difficulties do not have definitive solutions. Preparers must use their knowledge and judgment in resolving these difficulties, and users must recognize that there is considerable scope for different reasonable decisions. For example, could anyone strongly argue with the assumption that the useful life of a car is three years or five years or seven years? An asset does not come with a tag advising owners how long the asset will last and how much it will be worth when it is sold. The useful life, residual value, and the contribution an asset makes to revenue depend on how the asset is used, what it is used for, and how it is cared for. As long as the estimates are reasonable, any choice is likely acceptable.

We will now look at different methods for amortizing capital assets. First, let's consider the conceptual reasoning behind amortization.

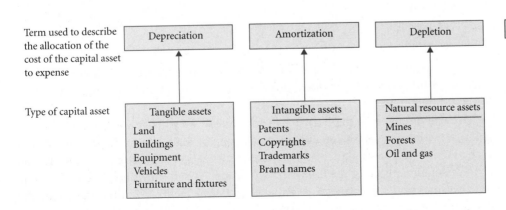

Figure 9-1

Summary of the Types of Capital Assets and Terms Used to Describe the Allocation of the Cost of the Capital Asset

There are two main reasons that explain why capital assets are amortized: physical use and obsolescence. Physical use refers to the effects that the passage of time, wear and tear, and exposure to the elements have on the ability of a capital asset to make a contribution to earning income. The effectiveness and efficiency of a machine decreases with use. As the machine gets older and is used a lot, it may break down more often, use more energy to operate, and produce less and lower quality output. Eventually the machine is not worth operating and must be replaced.

Assets become obsolete because of changes in technology as well as shifts in the business environment. Computers are an excellent example. Most computers purchased three or more years ago can probably still do now what they did when they were purchased. However, in many situations advances in technology have rendered those computers obsolete. These computers may be inadequate because they are too slow, do not have enough memory or multi-media capabilities, or are unable to handle some software applications. These computers have less to contribute to money-making activities of the business than state-of-the-art equipment.

Consider your wardrobe as an analogy. Clothes wear out because they are used: they fade, they tear, they pill. However, you may own an article of clothing that is in excellent condition but that you never wear because the style, colour, or pattern is no longer considered fashionable. That article of clothing has become obsolete.

Land is not amortized because it does not wear out and does not become obsolete. The buildings that are constructed on a piece of land may come and go, but the land on which the buildings were constructed will always be there to receive the next construction project. An exception to this rule is land that is used for extracting natural resources. In that case the cost of the land is expensed as the resource is taken from the land. In the case of a mine, the land is "used up" as the resource is removed.

Amortization and Market Values

According to GAAP, the purpose of amortization is to allocate the cost of an asset to expense in a "rational and systematic manner." Amortization is not intended to reflect the change in a capital asset's market value. The net book value (NBV) of the asset (cost less amortization to date) is not intended to be an estimate of its market value. New accounting students are tempted to think that the NBV of a capital asset is an estimate of market value. Resist the temptation.

Amortization Methods

Now let's look at how capital assets are amortized. There are several methods that are generally accepted in Canada as systematic and rational. These methods can be grouped into four major categories:

1. straight-line
2. accelerated
3. usage-based
4. decelerated

Each method allocates the cost of a capital asset to expense in a different pattern and, as a result, each will provide a different net income in each year over the asset's life and different NBVs.

We will discuss each method. For the discussion we will use an example of a capital asset with a cost of $1,200,000, residual value of $200,000, and useful life of ten years. Figure 9-2 shows plots of the annual amortization expense over the useful life of the asset under each of the four methods (Panel A) and shows how the NBV of the asset declines under each method (Panel B). Refer to Figure 9-2 when you study the discussion of each amortization method.

Panel A: Plots of the Annual Amortization Expense over the Useful Life of the Example Under Each of the Four Amortization Methods

Panel B: How NBV of the Asset Declines Under Each of the Four Amortization Methods

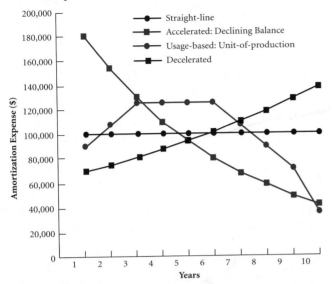

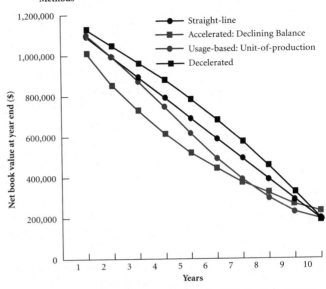

Amortization expenses of an asset costing $1,200,000 with residual value of $200,000 and estimated useful life of ten years. The amount that is amortized in any year differs widely, depending on the method. The straight line method has equal amortization in each year, declining balance has decreasing amounts over time, decelerated methods have an increasing amortization pattern, and the unit-of-production method depends on the amount of production in each year.

The effect of different amortization methods on the NBV of capital assets over time. All methods approach the residual value of the asset at the end of the asset's life, but the NBV of the asset at any time during its life will differ.

Figure 9-2

Annual Amortization Expense Example

When you study the different amortization methods, remember that they all result in the same amount of amortization over the life of the asset. Only the timing of the expense is affected. Also, while these choices do not affect cash flow, they can affect outcomes that are based on financial statement numbers, such as management bonuses and debt covenants.

Now let's look at the example. When the asset is purchased the following journal entry is made:

Dr. Capital Assets—equipment (assets +)   1,200,000
    Cr. Cash (assets –) or Liability (liability +)   1,200,000
To record the purchase of a capital asset.

Under any amortization method, the form of the journal entry that will be made each period to record the amortization expense is:

Dr. Amortization expense (expenses +, owners' equity –)   xxx
    Cr. Accumulated amortization (contra-asset +)   xxx
To record the amortization expense and the increase in
the accumulated amortization account for the year.

The amortization expense is the portion of the cost of the capital asset that is being matched to revenues earned during the period. The credit entry represents the portion of the capital asset that was consumed during the period, so the credit acts to reduce assets on the balance sheet. Notice that the credit is made to a contra-asset account, not to the capital asset account itself. Recall from Chapter 3 that a contra-asset account is used to accumulate reductions in the related asset account. That means that the capital asset itself remains in the capital asset account at full cost while amortization accumulates in the contra-asset account. To obtain the NBV of a capital asset, the cost recorded in the capital asset account must be considered together with the credit balance in the contra-asset account.

Finally, before we examine the different methods, Figure 9-3 (page 510) shows the relative use of each of the amortization methods in Canada, as reported in *Financial Reporting in Canada 2000*, 26th Edition.[1] Figure 9-3 shows that straight-line amorti-

Figure 9-3

Relative Use in Canada of Each of
the Four Amortization Methods

	Number of Firms	**Percentage***
Straight-line	171	87%
Accelerated: Declining Balance	50	25%
Usage-Based: Unit-of-production	48	24%
Decelerated	10	5%
Other	6	3%

*Results are from 2000 annual reports. Percentages are greater than 100% because some firms use more than
one amortization method.

zation is by far the most commonly used method by public companies in Canada.
Most of the public companies surveyed use it for at least some of their assets.

Straight-Line Amortization   With **straight-line amortization** the amortization
expense is the same in each period. This method is straightforward and simple to use,
which makes it appealing. The method implies that the contribution that the capital
asset makes to revenue generation is the same each period. This assumption is probably not entirely valid because the capability of most assets declines with time, repairs
and maintenance increase with time, and sales tend to vary over time. However, since
it can be so difficult to reasonably estimate the contribution an asset makes in each
period, this approach is reasonable (or as reasonable as any other). The equation for
calculating amortization using the straight-line method is:

$$\text{Amortization Expense} = \frac{\text{Cost} - \text{Estimated residual value}}{\text{Estimated useful life}}$$

For our asset costing $1,200,000, with an estimated residual value of $200,000
and estimated useful life of 10 years, the annual amortization expense is $100,000.

$$\text{Amortization Expense} = \frac{\$1,200,000 - \$200,000}{10 \text{ years}}$$

$$= \$100,000 \text{ per year}$$

Figure 9-4 shows the amortization schedule for the life of the asset.

The annual amortization expense will change if different estimates of the asset's
useful life and residual value are made. If we estimated the useful life to be 12 years
and the residual value to be $300,000, the annual amortization expense becomes
$75,000. If everything else stays the same, these changes will result in net income
being $25,000 higher in each of the first ten years than with our original estimates.
These changes have no direct economic impact on the entity, but they may affect the
outcome of contracts that are based on net income and other financial statement
measures. From a user's standpoint, this example shows that the estimates made by
management can affect numbers that may influence perceptions of the entity and
possibly decisions that a user makes. As we will discuss below, the choice of amortization method has no tax implications.

Accelerated Amortization   **Accelerated amortization** methods allocate more of
the cost of a capital asset to expense in the early years of its life and less in the later
years. When an asset's contribution to the revenue-generating ability of the entity is
greater in the early part of its life, an accelerated method of amortization makes sense.
Accelerated amortization would be appropriate for assets that are sensitive to obsolescence, such as computers, and assets that clearly lose efficiency and/or effectiveness

		Balance Sheet		Income statement	
Year	Cost	Accumulated amortization on December 31	NBV on December 31 (cost – accumulated amortization)	Amortization expense for the year ended December 31	
1	$1,200,000	$100,000	$1,100,000	$100,000	
2	1,200,000	200,000	1,000,000	100,000	
3	1,200,000	300,000	900,000	100,000	
4	1,200,000	400,000	800,000	100,000	
5	1,200,000	500,000	700,000	100,000	
6	1,200,000	600,000	600,000	100,000	
7	1,200,000	700,000	500,000	100,000	
8	1,200,000	800,000	400,000	100,000	
9	1,200,000	900,000	300,000	100,000	
10	1,200,000	1,000,000	200,000	100,000	
Total				$1,000,000	

Figure 9-4

Amortization Schedule Using Straight-Line Amortization

with the passage of time, producing less or lower quality output. Look at Figure 9-2 (page 509) to see the pattern of accelerated amortization in graphic form.

The most common accelerated amortization method used in Canada is the **declining balance** method. This method applies an amortization rate to the NBV of the asset at the beginning of the year to calculate the amortization expense. That is,

$$\text{Amortization Expense} = (\text{Cost} - \text{Accumulated amortization}) \times \text{Rate}$$

$$= \text{NBV} \times \text{Rate}$$

Because a fixed rate is being applied to a declining balance, an asset is never amortized to zero. This is one of the reasons why the residual value is usually ignored with this method.

The amortization schedule for our $1,200,000 asset is shown in Figure 9-5 (page 512). The rate that is being applied to this asset is 15%. The amortization expense in the first year is $180,000 ($1,200,000 × 0.15). In the second year the amortization expense is $153,000 ([$1,200,000 – $180,000] × 0.15). You can see how the amortization expense is lower than the year before. You can also see that at the end of Year 10 only $963,751 of the cost has been amortized. If the residual value is estimated to be $200,000 in Year 10, the remaining $36,249 would be expensed then, assuming that the estimate of a ten-year useful life still applies.

For managers who are concerned about the level of income of their company, accelerated amortization is less attractive than straight-line because the amortization expense is larger in the first years of an asset's life, which makes net income lower. Of course, straight-line eventually catches up, so in later years, when the accelerated amortization expense is lower than straight-line amortization, net income will be higher with accelerated amortization. The effect where the accelerated amortization expense eventually becomes less than the straight-line expense can be seen in the plots in Figure 9-2, Panel A (page 509). While this pattern applies to single assets, if an entity is growing and continually purchasing and replacing capital assets, the amortization expense using straight-line will almost always be lower than with declining balance. If an entity is not growing, declining balance eventually produces lower amortization expenses.

There are other accelerated amortization methods, but these methods are rarely used in Canada and will not be discussed further.

Figure 9-5

Amortization Schedule Using
Accelerated Amortization

| Year | Cost | Balance Sheet | | Amortization rate | Income statement |
		Accumulated amortization December 31	NBV on December 31		Amortization expense for the year ended December 31
1	$1,200,000	$180,000	$1,020,000	15%	$180,000
2	1,200,000	333,000	867,000	15%	153,000
3	1,200,000	463,050	736,950	15%	130,050
4	1,200,000	573,593	626,408	15%	110,543
5	1,200,000	667,554	532,446	15%	93,961
6	1,200,000	747,421	452,579	15%	79,867
7	1,200,000	815,307	384,693	15%	67,887
8	1,200,000	873,011	326,989	15%	57,704
9	1,200,000	922,060	277,940	15%	49,048
10	1,200,000	963,751	236,249	15%	41,691
Total					$963,751

Usage-Based Amortization: Unit-of-Production　　If the consumption of an asset can be readily associated with its use and not to the passage of time or obsolescence, then an amortization method based on the actual use of the asset can be employed. One of the more common usage-based methods is unit-of-production. To use unit-of-production the preparer must be able to estimate the number of units that the asset will produce over its life. The amortization expense in a year is the proportion of units produced in the year to total estimated number of units to be produced over the asset's life. In our example, if the estimated production of the asset over its useful life is 280,000 units and 25,000 are produced in the first year, the amortization expense in the first year would be:

$$\text{Amortization Expense} = \frac{\text{Number of units produced in the period}}{\text{Estimated number of units produced over the asset's life}} \times (\text{Cost} - \text{Estimated residual value})$$

$$= \frac{25,000 \text{ units}}{280,000 \text{ units}} \times (\$1,200,000 - \$200,000)$$

$$= \$89,286$$

The amortization schedule using this method is shown in Figure 9-6. Note that it is assumed that the actual production over the asset's life equals the estimated production.

Other measures of assets' use are also available. For example, the number of kilometres a delivery truck travels and the number of hours equipment is used are possible measures of use.

There are a number of difficulties with applying an amortization method that is based on actual use:

- First, it can be difficult to make a reasonable estimate of the production or usage of an asset. Is it possible to make a reasonable, justifiable estimate of the number of kilometres a vehicle will travel, the number of units a machine will produce, or the number of hours equipment will function? For most assets, the answer is probably no. But the estimate is crucial for determining the amount of amortization that will be expensed in a period. For example, estimating that a truck will

Year	Balance Sheet			Percentage of total production in year	Production	Income Statement Amortization expense
	Cost	Accumulated amortization	NBV			
1	$1,200,000	$ 89,286	$1,110,714	0.089	25,000	$ 89,286
2	1,200,000	196,429	1,003,571	0.107	30,000	107,143
3	1,200,000	321,429	878,571	0.125	35,000	125,000
4	1,200,000	446,429	753,571	0.125	35,000	125,000
5	1,200,000	571,429	628,571	0.125	35,000	125,000
6	1,200,000	696,429	503,571	0.125	35,000	125,000
7	1,200,000	803,572	396,428	0.107	30,000	107,143
8	1,200,000	892,858	307,142	0.089	25,000	89,286
9	1,200,000	964,287	235,713	0.071	20,000	71,429
10	1,200,000	1,000,000	200,000	0.036	10,000	35,713
Total				1.000	280,000	$1,000,000

Figure 9-6

Amortization Schedule Using Unit-of-Production Amortization

travel 200,000 kilometres rather than 150,000 will have a significant effect on the amortization expense.

- Second, the usage-based amortization method is not appropriate for many types of assets. For example, buildings or office equipment do not lend themselves well to this method as there is no obvious unit of measurement that could be applied. Could we measure the use of a chair by the number times it is sat on?

- Third, unit-of-production allocates an equal amount of amortization per unit, but the revenue per unit may vary over time. In that case the amortization expense is not a constant proportion of revenue, which will affect ratios such as operating margin and return on investment.

An attractive aspect of usage-based amortization methods, if reasonable measures of usage can be made, is that they result in good matching. With usage-based methods there is a direct association between the amount of amortization and the consumption of the asset. Unfortunately, the difficulties described above limit the usefulness of the methods.

That said, Figure 9-3 (page 510) shows that the unit-of-production method is used quite widely in Canada, by 24% of the firms in the survey. One of the main reasons for its fairly high use is that it is popular in natural resources industries such as mining and forestry. In these industries it is possible to estimate the amount of the resource that is available. The estimated amount of the resource is used as the basis for amortizing the costs of discovering and developing the mine or forest (costs such as the purchase of the land or rights to the land, the cost of finding the resource, and the cost of developing it.)

Exhibit 9-1 (page 514) provides a note to the financial statements of North American Palladium Ltd., a company that uses the unit-of-production amortization method.[2] The note explains that the company uses unit-of-production amortization for some of its plant and equipment, certain exploration and development costs, as well as estimated mine closure costs. When a mine shuts down, companies are required by law to repair environmental damage caused by the mining activities. North American Palladium Ltd. accrues those costs, which will be incurred when the mine actually shuts down, on a unit-of-production basis over the life of the mine.

www.napalladium.com

2.   **Summary of Significant Accounting Policies**

Mining Interests

Plant and equipment are recorded at cost with amortization generally provided either on the unit-of-production method over the estimated economic life of the mine to which they relate or on the straight-line method over their estimated useful lives, which generally range from two to five years.

Mining leases and claims and royalty interests are recorded at cost and are amortized on the unit-of-production method over the estimated economic life of the mine to which they relate.

Exploration and development costs relating to properties that are reasonably certain of a productive result are capitalized and are being amortized on a unit-of-production method, based upon the proven and probable ore reserves of the mine. Development costs incurred to maintain current production are included in operating expenses.

Provision for Mine Closure Costs

Estimated mine closure costs are based primarily on environmental and regulatory requirements and are accrued as a cost of production, when reasonably determined, on a unit-of-production method over the remaining life of the mine.

www.brookfieldproperties.com

Decelerated Amortization   **Decelerated amortization** methods have lower amortization charges in the early years and higher charges in the later ones. A decelerated method called the sinking fund method is used in the property development industry. Exhibit 9-2 shows the note to the financial statements of Brookfield Properties Corporation that explains its use of the sinking fund method.[3] The attraction of this method for real estate companies is that it provides a lower amortization expense in the early years of an asset's life when the interest charges often associated with the financing of real estate projects are highest. The effect of the sinking fund method is to smooth the total of amortization and interest expense over an asset's life.

The calculations for the method are quite complicated and will not be discussed here. The pattern of decelerated amortization can be seen in Figure 9-2 (page 509).

Comparing Methods

Let's now look at an example of how different amortization methods affect a company's financial statements.

In 2005 Vermilion Corp. (Vermilion) began operations and purchased capital assets for $1,000,000. Vermilion estimated that the assets would have no residual value and that their useful lives would be four years, after which Vermilion would terminate operations. Table 9-1 shows summarized income statements, year-end capital assets, and total assets for years 2005 through 2008 using three different amortization methods: straight-line, declining balance (40% per year), and unit-of-production.

Vermilion's revenues and expenses, other than the amortization expense, are identical regardless of the method of amortization. The tax expense is based on the actual rules stated in the *Income Tax Act (ITA)* and is the same under all three

Note 1: Significant accounting policies

(c)   **Properties**

(i)   Commercial properties

Depreciation on buildings is provided on the sinking-fund basis over the useful lives of the properties to a maximum of 60 years. The sinking-fund method provides for a depreciation charge of an annual amount increasing on a compounded basis of 5% per annum. Depreciation is determined with reference to each rental property's carried value, remaining estimated useful life and residual value. Tenant improvements and re-leasing costs are deferred and amortized over the lives of the leases to which they relate.

Table 9-1   Vermilion Corp.: Summarized Financial Statement Information Using Three Different Amortization Methods

Panel A	Vermilion Corp. 2005			Panel D	Vermilion Corp. 2008		
	Straight-Line	40% Declining Balance	Unit-of-production		Straight-Line	40% Declining Balance	Unit-of-production
Revenue	$ 800,000	$ 800,000	$ 800,000	Revenue	$ 700,000	$ 700,000	$ 700,000
Expenses	425,000	425,000	425,000	Expenses	371,875	371,875	371,875
Amort. Exp.	250,000	400,000	176,471	Amort. Exp.	250,000	216,000	205,882
Operating Inc.	125,000	(25,000	198,529	Operating Inc.	78,125	112,125	122,243
Taxes	38,500	38,500	38,500	Taxes	8,828	8,828	8,828
Net Income	$ 86,500	$ (63,500)	$ 160,029	Net Income	$ 69,297	$ 103,297	$ 113,415
Capital assets (at cost)	$1,000,000	$1,000,000	$1,000,000	Capital Assets (at cost)	$1,000,000	$1,000,000	$1,000,000
Accum. amort.	(250,000)	(400,000)	(176,471)	Accum. amort.	(1,000,000)	(1,000,000)	(1,000,000)
Capital Assets (net)	$ 750,000	$ 600,000	$ 823,529	Capital Assets (net)	$ 0	$ 0	$ 0
Total Assets	$1,586,500	$1,436,500	$1,660,029	Total Assets	$1,838,107	$1,838,107	$1,838,107

Panel B	Vermilion Corp. 2006			Panel E	Vermilion Corp. 2005–2008		
	Straight-Line	40% Declining Balance	Unit-of-production		Straight-Line	40% Declining Balance	Unit-of-production
Revenue	$ 900,000	$ 900,000	$ 900,000	Revenue	$3,400,000	$3,400,000	$3,400,000
Expenses	478,125	478,125	478,125	Expenses	1,806,250	1,806,250	1,806,250
Amort. Exp.	250,000	240,000	264,706	Amort. Exp.	1,000,000	1,000,000	1,000,000
Operating Inc.	171,875	181,875	157,169	Operating Inc.	593,750	593,750	593,750
Taxes	105,222	105,222	105,222	Taxes	255,643	255,643	255,643
Net Income	$ 66,653	$ 76,653	$ 51,947	Net Income	$ 338,107	$ 338,107	$ 338,107
Capital assets (at cost)	$1,000,000	$1,000,000	$1,000,000	Capital Assets (at cost)	$1,000,000	$1,000,000	$1,000,000
Accum. amort.	(500,000)	(640,000)	(441,177)	Accum. amort.	(1,000,000)	(1,000,000)	(1,000,000)
Capital Assets (net)	$ 500,000	$ 360,000	$ 558,823	Capital Assets (net)	$ 0	$ 0	$ 0
Total Assets	$1,653,153	$1,513,153	$1,711,976	Total Assets	$1,838,107	$1,838,107	$1,838,107

Panel C	Vermilion Corp. 2007		
	Straight-Line	40% Declining Balance	Unit-of-production
Revenue	$1,000,000	$1,000,000	$1,000,000
Expenses	531,250	531,250	531,250
Amort. Exp.	250,000	144,000	352,941
Operating Inc.	218,750	324,750	115,809
Taxes	103,093	103,093	103,093
Net Income	$ 115,657	$ 221,657	$ 12,716
Capital assets (at cost)	$1,000,000	$1,000,000	$1,000,000
Accum. amort.	(750,000)	(784,000)	(794,118)
Capital Assets (net)	$ 250,000	$ 216,000	$ 205,882
Total Assets	$1,768,810	$1,734,810	$1,724,692

methods. In the fourth year, the unamortized portion of the capital assets under the declining balance method is fully expensed so that the NBV of the capital assets is zero at the end of the fourth year, the assumed residual value. That is why the amortization expense in the fourth year is larger than in the third year with the declining balance method. For the unit-of-production method, it is assumed the number of units produced equals the number of units sold in each year. In the example, there were 30,000 units produced and sold in 2005, 45,000 in 2006, 60,000 in 2007, and 35,000 in 2008.

Notice the significant effect that the amortization method has on Vermilion's net income, net capital assets, and total assets. In 2005, for example, net income ranges from a loss of $63,500 to a profit of $160,029. What does this tell a user? Is Vermilion profitable or is it losing money? Is Vermilion doing well, as might be suggested by the $160,029 profit, or poorly, as indicated by the loss? These questions are not easy to answer because while the numbers are quite different in each of the income statements, the underlying economic position of Vermilion is the same. Accounting choices affect the appearance of the statements, but not the economic reality. And even if we had more information about Vermilion's assets, it would not be possible to definitively conclude that a particular amortization method was superior to the others. The fact is, there is no way of knowing which amortization method is "right" and which measure of net income is "best."

Does this mean that accounting choice doesn't matter? No. It can matter very much. Whether it matters depends on who is using the financial statements, how the statements are being used, and for what reason they are being used. It is unlikely that any but the most unsophisticated users of financial statements would be misled by a company's amortization policy. Research shows that reporting a higher income by changing amortization methods does not result in a higher stock price. However, if a contract depended on the numbers in the financial statements, then the amortization method could make a difference.

While income in individual years differs under the three amortization methods, notice that total net income for the four years is the same for all the methods (see Panel E of Table 9-1, page 515). The cumulative income statements highlight the fact that the different accounting choices affect the timing of revenues and expenses, but not the totals.

So how does a preparer decide which method to use? Practically, no amortization method can be justified over all others because in almost all cases it is impossible to know how a capital asset contributes to earning revenue. Indeed, some people have argued that the choice of amortization method is arbitrary—one method of amortization cannot be proven to be superior to any other. It can also be difficult to estimate the useful life of an asset or its residual value with any precision. As long as an estimate is reasonable under the circumstances, it is acceptable. As a result, preparers have considerable leeway in choosing the amortization methods, useful lives, and residual values for their entity's capital assets. The managers' decision can be influenced by their knowledge of how the assets in question are actually used, by what is used by other firms in the industry, by the information needs of users, and by the interests of the preparers themselves.

In the case of Vermilion Corp., if the preparers had a bonus plan based on net income, they might prefer unit-of-production because their bonus would be higher in the first year. For appearances, perhaps if loans were required, preparers might be reluctant to use the declining balance method because of the loss it produces in the first year. The preparers may believe that lenders may be less willing to invest in an unprofitable entity. For tax purposes, none of these methods is appropriate because the rules in the *ITA* are not followed (as will be discussed below).

Question for Consideration

Dragon Ltd. (Dragon) is a small, privately owned company. A professional manager manages the company, and the shareholders are not involved in day-to-day management. Recently Dragon began to manufacture products that it had previously purchased and sold to its customers. Dragon paid $750,000 for the equipment (the equipment only).

a. What decisions must Dragon's manager make regarding the accounting for the new equipment before she can calculate the amortization expense for the current year?

b. Using the following assumptions, calculate the amortization expense for each year and the ending balance in the accumulated amortization expense using the straight-line, declining balance, and unit-of-production amortization methods. For declining balance, use a rate of 50%.

   i. The cost of buying and getting the equipment operating was $800,000 ($750,000 cost + $50,000 in delivery, set-up, and ancillary costs).

   ii. The residual value of the equipment is estimated to be $80,000.

   ii. The useful life of the equipment is three years.

   iv. The equipment will produce 20,000 units in the first year, 32,000 in the second year, and 28,000 units in the third year.

c. Prepare the journal entries that would be required for each of the three years for the straight-line method.

Answer:

a. Before calculating the amortization expense, the manager must determine the cost of the equipment, select an amortization method, and estimate its useful life and residual value.

b. Calculation results:

	Straight-line		Declining balance		Unit-of-production	
	Amortization expense*	Year end accumulated amortization	Amortization expense**	Year end accumulated amortization	Amortization expense***	Year end accumulated amortization
Year 1	$240,000	$240,000	$400,000	$400,000	$180,000	$180,000
Year 2	240,000	480,000	200,000	600,000	288,000	468,000
Year 3	240,000	720,000	120,000	720,000	252,000	720,000

* Amortization expense each year is $240,000 [($800,000 − 80,000) ÷ 3].

** The calculation of the amortization expense for declining balance ignores the residual value. For Year 1 the calculation is $800,000 × 0.5, for Year 2 ($800,000 − $400,000) × 0.5, and for Year 3 ($800,000 − $600,000) × 0.5). However, at the end of Year 3 the NBV of the equipment has to be $80,000, so an additional $20,000 is expensed in Year 3.

*** Amortization expense in Year 1 is (20,000 units ÷ 80,000 units) × ($800,000 − $80,000), for Year 2 (32,000 units ÷ 80,000 units) × ($800,000 − $80,000), and for Year 3 (28,000 units ÷ 80,000 units) × ($800,000 − $80,000).

c. Journal entries:

Year 1:	Dr. Amortization expense	240,000	
	Cr. Accumulated amortization		240,000

To record the amortization expense for Year 1. The same entry is made for Years 2 and 3.

Summary

In summary, there are a number of amortization issues to be aware of:

1. There are a number of different, acceptable methods of amortizing capital assets, with little restriction on which can be used, and none of the methods stand out as clearly the best.

2. It is difficult to estimate the useful life or the residual value of an asset so one can expect variation in the choices that preparers make. The appropriate estimates depend on how the asset is used and how it is cared for, and these can be difficult to figure out from financial statements.

3. Preparers can use the first and second issues to make choices that serve their reporting objectives.

4. Amortization has no effect on cash flow.

5. The choices that preparers make can impact the outcome of contracts such as management bonuses and debt covenants that are dependent on accounting measurements.

Because of these issues, it is common for similar entities to use different amortization methods and make different assumptions regarding useful life and residual value. As a result, comparability of financial statements can be impaired. Users must pay careful attention to the accounting choices made by entities so that they can understand whether differences between entities reflect actual differences in economic activity or simply differences in how the accounting is done. The same holds true for interpreting the performance of or evaluating an entity. The amortization choices can have a significant effect on the reported numbers such as net income and the NBV of assets.

Entities that require large investments in capital assets to operate their businesses are sometimes referred to as capital intensive. Figure 9-7 shows the percentage that capital assets are of total assets for a number of entities in different capital-intensive industries. Large amounts of capital assets mean that the amortization expense might also be large, meaning that the accounting choices made by the preparers can have a significant impact on income. In comparison, MWW's ratio of capital assets to total assets is only 17% and its ratio of amortization expense to revenue is 3.0%.

Financial Statement Disclosure

Companies that adhere to GAAP and the *CICA Handbook* are required to disclose the following information about their capital assets:

* cost of capital assets
* amortization method and amortization period or rate
* accumulated amortization
* amortization expense

Exhibit 9-3 provides an example of capital asset disclosure.[4] ClubLink Corporation (ClubLink) is Canada's largest owner, operator, and developer of high-quality member golf clubs, daily fee golf clubs, and resorts. ClubLink's balance sheets show the total amount of capital assets, net of accumulated amortization. There is no detail provided, only a single number.

Figure 9-7			
Ratios of Capital Assets to Total Assets in Capital-Intensive Industries			

Company	Industry	Ratio of capital assets to total assets	Ratio of amortization expense to net income	Ratio of amortization expense to revenue
Oxford Properties Group Inc.	Real Estate	94%	51%	10.9%
Dofasco Inc.	Steel	57%	135%	7.9%
Domtar Inc.	Forest Products	70%	87%	6.6%
ClubLink Corporation	Hospitality	79%	115%	7.7%
Newfoundland Power Inc.	Utility	82%	110%	8.5%

To get more details about ClubLink's capital assets, it is necessary to look at note 6 to the financial statements. Note 6 breaks down capital assets into eight operating and three development categories. For 2000 the cost, accumulated amortization, and the NBV are shown in the note. For 1999 only the NBVs are shown. To get the cost and accumulated amortization on December 31, 1999, it would be necessary to examine the 1999 annual report. Note 6 also points out that some capital assets are used as collateral for bank loans and long-term debt.

ClubLink's statements of income report the amortization expense for capital assets as $8,190,000 for 2000 and $6,661,000 for 1999. Although the note is not referenced in the financial statements, there is important information in note 2, the

www.clublink.ca

Exhibit 9-3
ClubLink Corporation Financial Statements

consolidated balance sheets

AS AT DECEMBER 31

(thousands of dollars – except per share amounts)	Reference	2000	1999
ASSETS			
Current assets			
Cash		$ 5,465	$ 15,081
Accounts receivable		2,342	5,351
Inventories and prepaid expenses		2,905	2,450
Membership fees receivable	3	8,178	7,403
Loans receivable	4	1,527	39,110
Capital assets held for sale	6	33,066	–
		53,483	69,395
Membership fees receivable	3	16,642	12,754
Loans receivable	4	15,540	16,934
Long-term portfolio investments	5	11,231	9,275
Capital assets	6	388,686	370,201
Deferred charges	7	4,050	8,143
		$ 489,632	$ 486,702

consolidated statements of income and retained earnings

FOR THE YEARS ENDED DECEMBER 31

(thousands of dollars – except per share amounts)	Reference	2000	1999
REVENUE			
Operating		$ 92,814	$ 80,683
Membership fees	3	12,900	11,642
		105,714	92,325
EXPENSES			
Cost of goods sold		13,506	11,773
Operating		50,502	43,785
Marketing and membership sales		6,298	6,101
General and administrative		8,947	8,031
Provincial capital taxes		1,087	922
		80,340	70,612
INCOME BEFORE AMORTIZATION, INTEREST, OTHER AND TAXES		25,374	21,713
AMORTIZATION OF CAPITAL ASSETS		8,190	6,661
AMORTIZATION OF DEFERRED CHARGES		970	935
INTEREST EXPENSE		7,873	3,212
INTEREST INCOME	13	(2,985)	(5,672)
OTHER EXPENSE	14	3,359	4,286
		17,407	9,422
INCOME BEFORE INCOME TAXES		7,967	12,291
INCOME TAX PROVISION	1, 15		
Current		1,025	3,200
Future		(202)	1,700
		823	4,900
NET INCOME		7,144	7,391

Exhibit 9-3 (continued)

ClubLink Corporation Financial
Statements

2. SUMMARY OF SIGNIFICANT ACCOUNTING POLICIES

Capital assets Direct costs incurred in respect of completed acquisitions are allocated to the asset acquired. Direct costs related to acquisitions not completed are charged to income as general and administrative expenses. Capital assets are recorded at cost. Operating capital assets include Member Golf Clubs, Daily Fee Golf Clubs and Resorts, including land and improvements thereto, buildings and related equipment. Operating capital assets are amortized on a straight-line basis over their estimated useful lives as follows:

Buildings, fixtures and related improvements	40 years
Roads, cart paths and irrigation	20 years
Maintenance equipment	10 years
Furnishings	10 years
Golf carts	10 years
Office and data processing equipment	5 years

Leased golf course land is amortized on a straight-line basis over the term of the lease.

Properties under construction, development and held for future development are recorded at the lower of cost and net realizable value. ClubLink capitalizes all direct costs relating to the acquisition, development and construction of these properties. ClubLink also capitalizes interest and direct general and administrative expenses to properties under construction.

6. CAPITAL ASSETS

(thousands of dollars)	Cost	Accumulated Amortization	2000 Net	1999 Net
Operating capital assets				
Land and improvements	$ 198,308	$ —	$ 198,308	$ 174,798
Leased golf course land	5,301	156	5,145	1,277
Buildings, fixtures and related improvements	88,647	6,899	81,748	70,363
Roads, cart paths and irrigation	26,907	3,450	23,457	18,438
Maintenance equipment	14,984	4,881	10,103	9,426
Furnishings	12,737	4,029	8,708	7,236
Golf carts	6,617	1,757	4,860	3,787
Office and data processing equipment	11,080	4,140	6,940	5,687
	364,581	25,312	339,269	291,012
Development assets				
Properties under construction			35,554	29,296
Properties under development			33,266	26,638
Properties held for future development			21,616	23,255
			90,436	79,189
			429,705	370,201
Less: Capital assets held for sale			33,066	—
Less: Estimated vendor take-back loans on capital assets held for sale (note 4)			7,953	—
			$ 388,686	$ 370,201

Maintenance equipment, golf carts, and office and data processing equipment include assets under capital leases in the amount of $26,875,000 (1999 – $16,715,000) with related accumulated amortization of $8,895,000 (1999 – $5,069,000). Amortization in the amount of $3,867,000 (1999 – $2,291,000) of assets recorded as capital leases is included in amortization expense.

Interest in the amount of $3,755,000 (1999 – $5,494,000), and project development and management costs in the amount of $1,793,000 (1999 – $2,211,000) have been capitalized to capital assets under construction.

Certain capital assets are being held as security for bank indebtedness (note 8) and long-term debt (note 9).

summary of significant accounting policies. The note describes the costs that are cap-italized for capital assets that are purchased and for ones that are constructed. The note also explains that ClubLink uses straight-line amortization for all capital assets (except for land, which is not amortized), and states the amortization period for each category of capital asset.

The information in ClubLink's financial statements provides some context for understanding the accounting it uses for capital assets. The information does not give an idea about whether the accounting methods used are reasonable or appropriate. That insight comes from familiarity with the business. It should also be noted that ClubLink provides fairly detailed information about its capital assets. Not all entities are so generous. For example, Dofasco Inc. (Dofasco) breaks its capital assets into only two categories and provides ranges for the amortization rates used. (Dofasco uses per-centages rather than number of years for the straight-line method. The percentages can be converted to years by dividing the percentage into 1.0. A percentage of 5% means a useful life of 20 years [1.0 ÷ 0.05].) The less extensive detail makes it a bit more difficult to understand the impact of Dofasco's accounting choices on the finan-cial statements. The note describing Dofasco's accounting policies for capital assets is shown in Exhibit 9-4.[5]

www.dofasco.ca

Question for Consideration

Some people argue that the amortization of the cost of capital assets is arbitrary. Explain.

Answer: The purpose of amortization is to match the cost of capital assets to the rev-enues they help generate. But what is the relationship between a delivery vehicle and revenue, a lawn mower and revenue, a computer and revenue, or a machine and revenue? Clearly, these capital assets make contributions to earning revenue, but it is impossible to know exactly what that contribution is. Nevertheless, accrual accounting requires that capital assets have to be amortized, so it is necessary to develop methods to amortize them. As a result, any amortization method can be justified in terms of the facts, as long as it is reasonable. It is impossible to argue that the method selected allocates the cost of capital assets to expense better than any other method. In other words, the choice is arbitrary.

Amortization and Taxes

The *Income Tax Act* (*ITA*) is very specific about how capital assets can be amortized for tax purposes. The *ITA* uses the term **capital cost allowance** (CCA) to describe amortization for tax purposes. The mechanics of CCA are the same for tax as they are for financial accounting—the cost of capital assets is somehow expensed over time—

---

1. Accounting policies

Fixed assets – Fixed assets are recorded at their historical cost.

Depreciation is computed generally by the straight-line method applied to the cost of assets in service at annual rates based on their estimated useful lives, as follows:

Buildings	2.5 to 5%
Equipment and machinery	5 to 25%

but the *ITA* is very detailed about the method and rate that must be used for each type of asset. For most assets the *ITA* requires the declining balance method, though straight-line is required for some assets. For example, buildings are amortized at a rate of 4%, equipment 20%, and cars 30%, all using the declining balance method. There is no choice or discretion available to the preparers—the rules in the *ITA* must be followed exactly. Preparers can do whatever they please for financial reporting purposes, but when the entity's income tax return is prepared, the amortization expense in the general purpose financial statements is replaced with CCA.

While for many assets the CCA rules would be acceptable for accounting purposes, in some cases they might not satisfy the *CICA Handbook*'s requirement that amortization of capital assets must be done in a systematic and rational manner because the government can use the *ITA* to achieve policy objectives. For example, the government might try to encourage investment by allowing entities to expense certain assets quickly. This treatment is fine for tax purposes, but may not achieve the matching objective under GAAP.

Another example is the half-year rule. The **half-year rule** allows an entity to deduct for tax purposes, in the year an asset is purchased, only one-half the amount of CCA that would otherwise be allowable. If an entity purchases a vehicle for $20,000, it should be allowed to deduct 30% of the cost of the vehicle for tax purposes or $6,000 ($20,000 × 0.3) in the first year. The half-year rule allows the entity to deduct only one-half of that amount in the year the vehicle is purchased, or in this case only $3,000 ($20,000 × 0.3 × 0.5). The half-year rule prevents entities from getting the full tax benefit from a new capital asset if the asset is purchased late in the year. On the other hand, an entity that purchases and uses an asset starting in the early part of the year would only be able to deduct 50% of the allowable amount of CCA in the year the asset is purchased. While this treatment may satisfy the policy objectives of the government, it does not really satisfy some of the basic concepts of GAAP, such as matching.

It is easy to make the mistake of thinking that by choosing an amortization policy that minimizes income for financial reporting purposes, taxes are minimized. However, amortization for financial reporting purposes is irrelevant for tax. If an entity uses different methods and rates for financial reporting than what is specified in the *ITA*, an adjustment is required when preparing the entity's tax return. Some companies will use the CCA methods for financial reporting, especially private companies that use their financial statements mainly for tax purposes, to reduce their bookkeeping costs. The irrelevance of amortization for tax purposes contrasts with the ITA treatment of inventory. Because the *ITA* does not specify how to account for inventory for tax purposes, the accounting method selected for the general purpose financial statements is usually used for tax purposes.

This discussion highlights the relationship between the *ITA* and financial reporting. Sometimes the *ITA* is very specific about how accounting must be done for tax purposes. In these situations accounting and tax are completely separate. A company can pursue an objective other than tax minimization and still pay as little tax as possible. In other situations, such as inventory valuation, the *ITA* requires companies to use the same policies for tax purposes as they use in their general purpose financial statements. In that case, a company must choose whether it wants to follow tax minimization or some other objective of accounting.

Intangible Assets

Intangible assets—also known as knowledge assets or intellectual capital—are capital assets that have no physical qualities. Intangible assets cannot be seen, touched, or felt like a machine, a building, or a table, but they are often crucial to the success of an entity. Examples of intangible assets include patents, copyrights, trademarks, franchise rights, brand names, customer lists, software, licenses, human resources, and goodwill.

One of the great challenges currently facing accounting is intangible assets. In the "new economy" of the 21st century, more and more of the investments made by entities are for knowledge assets. Yet investments that build brand names, investments in research that result in new, competitive products, and investments in human resources that allow people do their jobs more efficiently, more effectively, and more profitably, are all but ignored in traditional accounting.

Money spent on knowledge assets is normally expensed when incurred. These investments are never reported as assets on an entity's balance sheet. However, it is difficult to argue that these investments are not assets, at least conceptually. There is no doubt that investments in knowledge assets provide an expectation of future benefits. The future success of technology companies depends on the research that they do to develop their products of the future. Without ongoing research, technology companies would quickly become worthless as their products became obsolete. Successful brand names, customer lists, and skilful personnel clearly provide future benefits to an entity. Yet the current accounting model fails to effectively account for these important assets. The *CICA Handbook* explicitly requires that research costs be expensed when incurred—these costs cannot be capitalized. The *CICA Handbook* does allow for capitalization of development costs if certain strict criteria are met. In the United States research and development must be expensed when incurred.

There are a number of reasons why contemporary accounting fails to recognize knowledge assets. One reason is conservatism. Because the future benefits associated with investments in knowledge assets can be very difficult to measure, conservatism prevails and the expenditures are expensed. Part of the problem is that many knowledge assets are developed internally by entities over time, and in many or most cases it is not at all clear that a valuable resource will ultimately emerge. In contrast, most tangible capital assets are purchased in a completed form—ready or almost ready for use.

Expensing investments in knowledge assets when they are incurred has significant implications for the financial statements. The first is that the matching principle is violated. A major cost associated with earning revenues—the cost of knowledge assets—is not matched to the revenue it helps generate. For example, a pharmaceuticals company will expense all expenditures that it makes in developing a new drug. By the time the new drug has been developed, tested, and approved by Health Canada and other regulators around the world, many years will have passed. When the drug finally makes it to market, most of the costs incurred to develop it would have been expensed. What does profit mean if the costs incurred to earn the revenues are not reported in the period the revenues are recognized? Clearly, net income does not represent the change in wealth that we traditionally think of. This would be similar to expensing the cost of a retailer's inventory when it is purchased rather than when it is sold.

Also, many financial ratios are adversely affected by the accounting treatment used for knowledge assets. Gross margin, profit margin, return on assets (net income ÷ total assets), return on equity (net income ÷ shareholders' equity), and many others tend to be distorted as a result of the accounting used for intangibles. Research has shown that return on assets and return on equity both tend to be higher than they would be if knowledge assets were capitalized.

Let's look at Mosaid Technologies Incorporated's (Mosaid) income statement to get an idea of the magnitude of the issue. Mosaid is an independent Canadian semiconductor company. Mosaid's income statement is shown in Exhibit 9-5.[6] In the year ended April 27, 2001 Mosaid spent $31,428,000 on research and development, representing almost 38% of revenues in the year and over 43% of total operating expenses. In fiscal 2000 Mosaid spent $18,450,000. These are large sums of money and they will not be expensed when the projects they represent start generating revenue for Mosaid.

www.mosaid.com

Instead they are treated as period costs and expensed when incurred. There is a clear and significant mismatching of revenues and expenses as a result of this treatment. In addition, Mosaid's assets are understated. If we assume that the $31,428,000 has future benefit, then assets on the April 27, 2001 balance sheet are understated by that amount, which represents over 35% of total assets.

Another example: Coca-Cola is one of the best-known brand names in the world. If the Coca-Cola company were to be purchased, the buyer would pay a lot of money for the rights to the Coca-Cola name. Yet if you examine Coca-Cola's balance sheet there is no mention of this valuable asset. On December 31, 2000 Coca-Cola's shareholders' equity, as reported on the company's balance sheet, was US$9.316 billion. In contrast, the value of Coca-Cola's shares on the New York Stock Exchange (which is a market measure of the value of the company's shareholders' equity) was in excess of $150 billion. Why this vast difference in these measures of the owners' interest in the company? The missing value of the Coca-Cola brand name certainly plays a significant role.

An introductory financial accounting textbook is not the place to go into detail about this problem. However, students of accounting, even at the introductory level, must be aware of this shortcoming in the current reporting model, especially given the importance of knowledge assets in the contemporary economy. The problem is under investigation by academic researchers and regulators, but it is not clear what the resolution will be.

It is interesting to note that when most knowledge assets are purchased they are accounted for in the traditional way. For example, if an entity purchases the rights to a patent, the cost is capitalized and amortized over its useful life, just as is done with tangible capital assets.

Let's look at an example. Zangwill Ltd. purchased a patent from Roach Research Corp. for $6,000,000. The patent has a remaining life of 12 years and Zangwill's

---

Exhibit 9-5	
Mosaid Technologies Incorporated Income Statement—Research and Development Costs	

MOSAID TECHNOLOGIES INCORPORATED

CONSOLIDATED STATEMENTS OF EARNINGS AND RETAINED EARNINGS

(in thousands, except per share amounts)

Year ended	April 27, 2001	April 28, 2000
REVENUES		
Operations	$ 81,640	$ 47,044
Interest	1,286	1,065
	82,926	48,109
EXPENSES		
Labour and materials	13,367	8,181
Research and development (NOTE 7)	31,428	18,450
Selling and marketing	18,250	11,839
General and administration	8,338	7,015
Bad debt	139	–
Unusual item (NOTE 8)	694	(206)
	72,216	45,279
Earnings from operations	10,710	2,830
Income tax expense (NOTE 9)	3,708	926
NET EARNINGS	7,002	1,904

RESEARCH AND DEVELOPMENT

Research costs are expensed as incurred. Development costs are deferred once technical feasibility has been established and all criteria for deferral under generally accepted accounting principles are met. Such costs are amortized commencing when the product is released, over the expected life of the product. To date, no development costs have met the criteria for deferral.

management believes that it will be able to sell products that rely on the patent for that long. When it purchases the patent Zangwill would record the following journal entry:

> Dr. Patent (asset +)   6,000,000
>   Cr. Cash (asset −) or Liability (liability +)   6,000,000
> To record the purchase of a patent.

Each year Zangwill would amortize a portion of the cost of the patent:

> Dr. Amortization expense (expense +, shareholders' equity −)   500,000
>   Cr. Accumulated amortization—patent (contra-asset +)   500,000
> To record amortization of the patent ($600,000,000 ÷ 12 years).

If Zangwill had developed the patent internally, there would be no recognition of it on the balance sheet. The costs of developing the patent would have been expensed as they were incurred.

We will complete this section on knowledge assets with a brief discussion of goodwill. Most intangible or knowledge assets, regardless of how they are accounted for, can be identified. An entity will own a patent, a copyright, a franchise, a license, and so on. Goodwill, probably the most commonly seen intangible asset on balance sheets, is different. Goodwill does not really represent anything in particular. To understand why goodwill does not represent anything in particular, we need to understand how goodwill arises.

Goodwill arises only when one entity purchases all or part of another entity. When an entity is purchased, the purchaser must allocate the purchase price to the specific assets and liabilities that were purchased. In effect, the purchaser must determine the market value of each asset and liability on the date of the purchase. (**Goodwill** is the amount that the purchaser pays for another entity over and above the fair value of the purchased entity's identifiable assets and liabilities on the date the entity is purchased. Goodwill will be discussed further in Chapter 12 when we examine investments in other corporations.)

A Contrast with Oil and Gas Accounting

An interesting contrast with accounting for knowledge assets is the accounting that is used by companies that explore for oil and gas. Oil and gas exploration companies

---

Question for Consideration

The *CICA Handbook* requires that expenditures on research must be expensed when incurred. Under no circumstances can research costs be capitalized. Why do you think the *Handbook* requires the expensing of research costs when they are incurred? Do you agree with this requirement?

    Answer: Research costs represent important and valuable assets to an entity. Without them many entities would quickly fail because they would be unable to compete. The problem is that it is not clear what the payoff is for investing in research. Investments in research might pay off handsomely or they might not pay off at all. Given the uncertainty, accountants are reluctant to call expenditures made on research assets because they may prove to have no future benefit. This is an application of conservatism.

    If one accepts the importance of conservatism as an accounting concept then the existing treatment for research makes sense. However, it is clear that investments in research pay off on average (although not for any particular investment or for any particular entity). In that case, expensing a research when it is incurred results in a mismatching of expenses and revenues and an understatement of assets on the balance sheet.

must spend large amounts of money to find new sources of fossil fuels in the same way that technology companies must invest heavily in research and development to develop new products. In both of these industries a significant amount of money is spent before anything is sold. Unlike investments on research and development and other knowledge assets, expenditures on oil and gas exploration and development can be capitalized and amortized over the period that the oil or gas is extracted.

There are two methods that oil and gas companies can use to account for their exploration costs: **successful efforts** and **full costing**. Under full costing, a company capitalizes all costs incurred to find new sources of oil and gas, even if some of those costs do not result in successful projects. In contrast, under successful efforts accounting only the costs associated with successful projects are capitalized. The costs associated with failed projects are expensed when they are incurred.

For example, Divide Corp. (Divide) invests $14,000,000 exploring for oil over 50,000 square kilometres in northern Alberta. The exploration efforts result in the drilling of seven test wells, of which two have oil. The cost of each well is $2,000,000. Under full costing, the $14,000,000 would be capitalized, even though $10,000,000 was spent on five wells that do not have any oil. The $14,000,000 would be amortized over the production of the two productive wells. If Divide used the successful efforts method, it would capitalize only the $4,000,000 cost associated with the two wells that have oil. The $10,000,000 associated with the dry wells would be expensed once it was clear they had no oil. With successful efforts the $4,000,000 would be amortized over the production of the two successful wells.

Exhibit 9-6 shows the notes to the financial statements of two companies, Suncor Energy Inc., which uses successful efforts, and Bow Valley Energy Ltd., which uses full cost accounting.[7]

The difference between the accounting rules that oil and gas exploration companies can use versus what companies that invest in research and development must do is striking. The differences in the accounting for these conceptually similar expenditures can result in significantly different financial statements. Oil and gas companies will have lower expenses and more assets than companies investing in research and development. Lenders who rely on financial ratios to assess loan applications may have difficulty with the financial statements of research and development companies because of their low incomes and low asset balances.

Disposal of Capital Assets

In Chapter 4 we discussed gains and losses that arise on the sale of capital assets. When an entity sells an asset that is not usually sold in the ordinary course of its business for an amount that is different from the asset's NBV, a gain or a loss arises. In Chapter 4 the examples were limited to situations where land—an asset that is not amortized—was sold. In this section the discussion is expanded to include amortizable assets.

When an amortizable asset is sold, the cost of the asset and the accumulated amortization associated with the asset must both be removed from the books. A gain or loss on the sale of a capital asset arises when the asset is sold for an amount that is different from the asset's NBV. If the amount received is greater than the NBV, a gain is recorded. If the amount received is less than the NBV, there is a loss.

Before recording the disposal of the asset, it is necessary to record the amortization expense related to the part of the year the asset was sold. The entries to record the amortization expense and accumulated amortization usually take place at the end of a period, whereas sales of capital assets can take place any time, so in most cases part of a year's amortization will not have been recorded. If the amortization expense is

Exhibit 9-6

Suncor Energy Inc. and Bow Valley Energy Ltd.: Successful Efforts and Full Cost Accounting for Oil and Gas Exploration Costs—Notes to the Financial Statements

Panel A—Suncor Energy Inc. Extract from 2000 Annual Report

Summary of Significant Accounting Policies

(d) Capital assets

Cost

Capital assets are recorded at cost.

The company follows the successful efforts method of accounting for its crude oil and natural gas operations. Under the successful efforts method, acquisition costs of proved and unproved properties are capitalized. Costs of unproved properties are transferred to proved properties when proved reserves are confirmed. Exploration costs, including geological and geophysical costs, are expensed as incurred. Exploratory drilling costs are capitalized initially. If it is determined that the well does not contain proved reserves, the capitalized exploratory drilling costs are charged to expense, as dry hole costs, at that time. The related land costs are expensed through the amortization of unproved properties as covered under the Natural Gas section of the following policy.

Development costs, which include the costs of wellhead equipment, development drilling costs, gas plants and handling facilities, applicable geological and geophysical costs and the costs of acquiring or constructing support facilities and equipment are capitalized. Costs incurred to operate and maintain wells and equipment and to lift oil and gas to the surface are expensed as operating costs.

Panel B—Bow Valley Energy Ltd.: Extract from Annual Report

2. Significant Accounting Policies

Oil and Gas

The Corporation follows the full cost method of accounting, whereby all costs associated with the exploration for and development of oil and gas reserves are capitalized. Such amounts include land acquisition costs, geological and geophysical costs, carrying costs of non-producing properties, costs of drilling productive and non-productive wells, administration costs related to exploration and development activities and related plant and equipment costs. These amounts are accumulated in separate cost centres for each country.

not recorded, amortization expense will be understated and the gain or loss on sale will be misstated. Net income will not be affected.

Let's look at an example. At the beginning of 1998, Ycliff Inc. (Ycliff) purchased equipment for $1,200,000. Management estimated that the equipment would have a residual value of $200,000 and useful life of 10 years. Ycliff amortized the equipment on a straight-line basis. In 2005, one-quarter of the way through the year, Ycliff sold the equipment for $400,000 in cash. At the end of 2004, the NBV of the assets was $500,000:

Cost	$1,200,000
Accumulated amortization	700,000
NBV	$ 500,000

Since the equipment was sold one-quarter of the way into 2005, an amortization expense of $25,000 is necessary for 2005. The journal entry is:

Dr. Amortization expense (expense +, shareholders' equity −) 25,000
    Cr. Accumulated amortization (contra-assets +)   25,000
To record the part-year amortization expense for equipment
 sold during 2005.

On the date of the sale, accumulated amortization on the equipment was $725,000 ($700,000 + $25,000) and the NBV was $475,000 ($1,200,000 − $725,000). The journal entry to record the sale is:

Dr. Cash (asset +)	400,000
Dr. Accumulated amortization (contra-asset −)	725,000
Dr. Loss on sale of equipment	75,000
(income statement −, shareholders' equity −)	
Cr. Equipment (asset −)	1,200,000
To record the sale of equipment at a loss.	

The journal entry removes the cost of $1,200,000 and the accumulated amortization of $725,000 from the books. The gain or loss is equal to the proceeds from the sale of the asset less its NBV. In the example,

Proceeds from sale	$400,000
NBV	475,000
Loss	($75,000)

In this scenario there is a loss because the proceeds from sale are less than the NBV. It is interesting to observe that the amount of the gain or loss on the sale of a capital asset is simply a function of how the asset is accounted for. We should assume that the selling price of a capital asset is fixed—that is, the amount a buyer would pay for the asset is not affected by its NBV. Then, the amount of the gain or loss is determined only by the asset's NBV, which in turn is determined by the amount that was capitalized in the first place for the asset and the amount of amortization that has accumulated over its life.

If, for example, Ycliff amortized the equipment over 12 years instead of ten, the NBV when the equipment was sold would have been $595,833 ($1,200,000 − [$1,000,000 ÷ 12] × 7.25) and the loss would have been $195,833 ($400,000 − $595,833). Any changes that affect the NBV of an asset will change the amount of the gain or loss reported (assuming that the selling price is a constant). In some cases, the managers' decision to sell an asset may be affected by the amount of any gain or loss. For example, if an entity requires higher net income to meet the requirements of a loan covenant, the managers may be unwilling to sell a capital asset at a loss, preferring instead to hold on to the asset.

Write-Downs

Sometimes situations arise that impair the value of capital assets. A capital asset is impaired when its **net recoverable amount**—the net cash flow the asset is expected to generate from use over its remaining life, plus its residual value—is less than its NBV. Examples of impaired capital assets include a building destroyed by fire, a plant that is no longer productive, and reductions in the earnings from a mine.

According to GAAP, when capital assets become impaired they should be written down to their net recoverable amount. A write-down reduces the NBV of the capital asset and reduces income. It is important to recognize that capital assets are not assessed in the same way as inventory in the application of the lower of cost and market rule. With the lower of cost and market rule, the cost of inventory must be compared to its market value at the end of each period, and if the market value is less than cost, the inventory must be written down. The assessment of capital assets takes a

Question for Consideration

Suppose that in the Ycliff example (pages 527–528) the company had sold the equipment for $750,000 instead of $400,000. What would be the gain or loss that Ycliff would report for the sale of the equipment in 2005? Prepare the journal entry required to record the sale.

Answer:
First, it would be necessary to record the partial-year amortization expense of $25,000 as was done above. If the equipment was sold for $750,000, the gain would be:

Proceeds from sale	$750,000
NBV	475,000
Gain	$275,000

The journal entry to record the sale would be:

Dr. Cash (asset +)	750,000	
Dr. Accumulated amortization (contra-asset –)	725,000	
Cr. Gain on sale of equipment		275,000
(income statement +, shareholders' equity +)		
Cr. Equipment (asset –)		1,200,000
To record the sale of equipment.		

longer-term perspective—cash flows over the entire life of an asset are considered, not a short-term measure of market value. A short-term decline in net realizable value or replacement cost, or a short-term reduction in net cash flows, is not enough to trigger the write-down of a capital asset. The net recoverable amount must be less than NBV. Once a write-down is made, it is not reversed if the net recoverable amount increases.

For example, Overflow Ltd. (Overflow) owns a small office building. The building is recorded in the accounting records at its cost of $12,000,000, less accumulated amortization of $5,000,000. In recent years the building has become less attractive to potential tenants because the building has become rundown and its neighbourhood has deteriorated. As a result, the rents that Overflow can obtain have declined. Management now estimates that the building will generate $4,000,000 in net cash flows over its remaining life and will be sold at the end of its life for $1,000,000. Therefore, according to GAAP Overflow must write down the building by $2,000,000 to $5,000,000. The net recoverable amount of the building is $5,000,000, which is the sum of the net cash flows to be generated by the building ($4,000,000) and its residual value ($1,000,000), so that is the amount to which the building is written down. The journal entry to record the write-down would be:

Dr. Loss due to impairment of building	2,000,000	
(income statement –, shareholders' equity –)		
Cr. Accumulated amortization (contra-asset +)		2,000,000
To write down the building to its net recoverable amount.		

The write-down is credited to Accumulated Amortization, which serves to decrease the NBV of the asset.

Management has considerable discretion in deciding the timing and amount of a write-down because determining the impairment of a capital asset is very subjective. There is ample evidence that managers will time write-downs of capital assets to accomplish reporting objectives. For example, managers might write down capital assets as part of a big bath. (Big baths were introduced in Chapter 4.)

Exhibit 9-7 (page 530) gives an example of an asset write-down.[8] GenSci Regeneration Sciences Inc. (GenSci) is a company that uses biotechnology to treat

GenSci Regeneration Sciences Inc.:
Write-Down Example

CONSOLIDATED STATEMENTS OF LOSS AND DEFICIT
[in Canadian dollars]

	December 31,		
	2000 $	1999 $	1998 $
REVENUES	**45,827,426**	30,571,305	16,304,139
OPERATING EXPENSES			
Cost of sales	**14,144,268**	10,412,007	6,393,815
Marketing, general and administrative	**30,174,661**	21,141,322	13,533,706
Research and development	**3,876,506**	3,830,869	3,392,759
Amortization	**1,878,793**	3,160,749	3,345,744
Write-down of technology and patents *[note 6]*	**3,300,000**	10,000,000	—
	53,374,228	48,544,947	26,666,024
Loss before the following	**(7,546,802)**	(17,973,642)	(10,361,885)
Interest income	**538,065**	439,530	35,818
Interest expense			
Short-term	**—**	(35,420)	(85,789)
Long-term	**—**	(95,014)	(360,000)
Net loss for the year	**(7,008,737)**	(17,664,546)	(10,771,856)

6. OTHER ASSETS

Other assets consist of the following:

	2000 $	1999 $
Patent costs, net of accumulated amortization of $1,316,942 [1999 - $1,139,885] and write-down of $504,906 [1999 - nil]	**1,355,197**	1,816,904
Technology costs, net of accumulated amortization of $8,083,385 [1999 - $7,546,812] and accumulated write-down of $12,795,094 [1999 - $10,000,000]	**1,841,171**	4,791,314
Deferred development costs, net of accumulated amortization of $1,670,683 [1999 - $1,250,364]	**213,271**	568,285
Goodwill, net of accumulated amortization of $1,862,535 [1999 - $1,753,741]	**550,910**	672,328
	3,960,549	7,848,831

[a] The Company assesses the carrying value of its technology on an ongoing basis *[note 2]*. As a result of the Company's decision to seek alternate funding for certain of its peptide technologies and negotiations to date, management has determined that the current carrying value of these technologies should be adjusted to reflect estimated market values. During 1999, the Company reduced the value of technology by $10,000,000 to reflect the value based on negotiations at that time. Subsequent negotiations during 2000 required that the Company further reduce the carrying value of the technology and patents, related to the peptide technology by $2,795,094 and $504,906 respectively.

www.gensci.bc.ca

musculoskeletal disease and injury. GenSci purchased the rights to a technology for $16,252,000 and was amortizing the cost over the life of the license to use the technology. In 1999 GenSci's management decided that the book value of the technology was much higher than its net recoverable amount and wrote down the rights to the technology by $10,000,000. In 2000, a further assessment resulted in an additional write-down of $2,795,094. Exhibit 9-7 shows the presentation of the write-down on the income statement and the note explaining what happened.

The journal entry that would be recorded in GenSci's accounting system in 2000 to record the write-down would be:

Dr. Write-down of technology	2,795,094	
(income statement –, shareholders' equity –)		
Dr. Write-down of patents	504,906	
(income statement –, shareholders' equity –)		
Cr. Other assets—technology (assets –)		2,795,094
Cr. Other assets—patents (assets –)		504,906

To record the write-down of patents and the rights to a technology.

Accounting Changes—Policies and Estimates

Consistency in the application of accounting choices is an important principle. If an entity could change its accounting on a whim, the integrity and usefulness of the financial statements would be undermined and it would be much more difficult for users to understand and interpret the statements. However, consistency does not mean that an entity can never change how it does its accounting. Sometimes a change makes sense. An accounting change is necessary if GAAP change and the entity is required to use a different accounting policy. Or an entity may decide that a different way of accounting is appropriate because the facts underlying certain transactions have changed or the reporting objectives of the entity have changed.

There are two types of accounting changes—changes in policies and changes in estimates. **Accounting policies** are the methods that an entity selects for financial reporting. Accounting policies include the revenue recognition method, inventory cost flow assumption, and amortization method. **Accounting estimates** are the judgments about uncertain future events that preparers must make to complete accrual accounting financial statements. Accounting estimates include the useful lives and residual values of capital assets, bad debt expenses, warranty expenses, and many more.

What happens if an entity decides to change an accounting policy or estimate? The two types of changes are dealt with quite differently. If a company decides to change an accounting policy—for example, switching from an accelerated method of amortization to the straight-line method—the change is applied retroactively. That is, previous years' financial statements are restated as if the new accounting method had always been used. This treatment also means that retained earnings would have to be restated to adjust for the difference in retained earnings between the old and new methods.

Consider the following example. In 2001 Justice Inc. (Justice) purchased a specialized piece of equipment for its manufacturing facility. The equipment cost $750,000. Management decided to use declining-balance amortization at 40% per year. In 2004 management decided to change from declining-balance to straight-line amortization because most firms in Justice's industry used straight-line. Management estimated that the equipment would continue to be useful until 2006 and would have no residual value at the end of its useful life.

Because this is a change in accounting policy, it must be applied retroactively. (The amortization schedules for the two methods are shown in Figure 9-8.) When Justice prepares its annual report for 2004, the amortization expense reported for 2004 and for all comparative years would be the straight-line amount. That is, if Justice presented in its 2004 financial statements comparative information for 2003 and 2002, the amortization expense in all three years would be $125,000, even though for 2003 and 2002, $108,000 and $180,000 respectively had been originally reported in the previous years' financial statements.

It is also necessary to adjust retained earnings at the start of 2004 to reflect the use of the straight-line method from the time the equipment was purchased. Between 2001 and 2003, Justice would have expensed $588,000 ($300,000 + $180,000 +

	2001	2002	2003	2004	2005	2006
40% Declining balance	$300,000	$180,000	$108,000	$ 64,800	$ 38,880	$ 58,320
Straight line, useful life six years	$125,000	$125,000	$125,000	$125,000	$125,000	$125,000

Current year

Figure 9-8

Justice Inc.: Change in Accounting Policy from Declining Balance to Straight-Line

$108,000) for amortization of the equipment using the declining balance method. Had straight-line amortization been used from the date the equipment was purchased, $375,000 in amortization would have been expensed ($125,000 + $125,000 + $125,000). Since the declining balance method resulted in $213,000 ($588,000 – $375,000) "too much" amortization expense between 2001 and 2003, the following journal entry would be required to adjust retained earnings. The journal entry also reduces the amount of accumulated amortization, which increases the NBV of the equipment.

Dr. Accumulated amortization (contra-asset –)	213,000	
Cr. Retained earnings (shareholders' equity +)		213,000
To record the effect of the change in the accounting policy for the equipment.		

A change in accounting estimate is treated differently. If an entity discovers that an accounting estimate made previously has to be revised—for example, if the initial estimate of an asset's useful life was too long—the error is corrected from the time management decides a revision is necessary. Prior years are not revised.

Let's look at an example. In 2001 Aubigny Ltd. (Aubigny) purchased an asset for $48,000. Management decided to use straight-line amortization and assumed a zero residual value and a useful life of eight years. In each of years 2001, 2002, and 2003, Aubigny expensed $6,000 for amortization of the asset ($48,000 ÷ 8 years). In 2004 it became clear to Aubigny's management that the asset would only last for six years. Because the estimated life of the asset had decreased to six years, it was necessary to expense the unamortized portion of the cost of the asset over three years rather than five. At the end of 2003 Aubigny had amortized $18,000 of the cost of the asset (see Figure 9-9). The unamortized $30,000 ($48,000 – $18,000) would be amortized over the remaining three years on a straight-line basis, so the amortization expense in 2004, 2005, and 2006 would be $10,000 ($30,000 ÷ 3). No adjustment of retained earnings is necessary because the amortization expense in previous years is not restated—unlike changes in accounting policy, previous years' expenses are not changed. The year-by-year amortization expense and accumulated amortization for each year is shown in Figure 9-9.

According to GAAP, accounting policy changes must be disclosed. In contrast, GAAP and the *CICA Handbook* do not require disclosure of changes in estimates. As a result, managers can manage their earnings by adjusting accounting estimates and it would be very difficult for a user to detect the existence and the extent of the change. The ability to manage earnings by adjusting estimates was also explored in Chapter 7 when we looked at hidden reserves.

Exhibit 9-8 gives an example of changes in accounting policy and estimates.[9] Fortis Inc. (Fortis) operates in the electric utility business, commercial real estate, hotels, and financial services. In 1999 Fortis reported a change in accounting policy and a change in accounting estimate in its annual report. The changes are both quite

Figure 9-9

Aubigny Ltd.: Change in Accounting Estimate

	2001	2002	2003	2004	2005	2006
Amortization expense	$6,000	$ 6,000	$ 6,000	$10,000	$10,000	$10,000
Accumulated amortization	$6,000	$12,000	$18,000	$28,000	$38,000	$48,000

Current year

complex, but the reader should focus on how these changes are reported in the financial statements and not on the accounting issue itself. In 1999 Fortis adopted a new accounting recommendation in the *CICA Handbook*. Because the new accounting recommendation represents a change in accounting policy, it was applied retroactively. Panel A of Exhibit 9-8 provides Fortis' note explaining the accounting change and the consolidated statement of retained earnings, where the adjustment for the change is shown. As a result of the change in accounting policy, retained earnings at the beginning of 1999 was decreased by $3,266,000.

Panel B of Exhibit 9-8 shows the note to Fortis' financial statements that explains that the company has increased the estimated useful lives of its income-producing properties to 60 years from between 25 to 40 years. The note explains that the change in estimate will be applied prospectively, which means the change will only affect future periods—no retroactive adjustment is made. The note also provides a reasonable justification for the change in estimate. This note is useful for users of financial statements because the change would likely have a significant effect on net income, but the *CICA Handbook* does not require it.

www.fortisinc.com

Exhibit 9-8

Fortis Inc.: Change in Accounting Policies and Accounting Estimates

---

Panel A—Changes in Accounting Policy

10. Employee Future Benefits

On January 1, 1999 the Corporation, except with respect to Newfoundland Power, adopted the recommendations of Section 3461 of the CICA Handbook, Employee Future Benefits. These recommendations have been applied retroactively. As the effect of this change in accounting policy is not reasonably determinable for individual prior periods, the adjustments were recorded in 1999. The opening balance of retained earnings decreased by $3,266,000 and the associated tax effect reduced deferred income taxes by $2,649,000.

CONSOLIDATED STATEMENT OF RETAINED EARNINGS
For the Year Ended December 31

	1999	(in thousands)	1998
Balance at Beginning of Year	$ 189,585	$	185,480
Change in accounting policy (Note 10)	(3,266)		–
As Restated	186,319		185,480
Earnings applicable to common shares	29,183		27,414
Dividends on common shares	(23,788)		(23,309)
Balance at End of Year	$ 191,714	$	189,585

Panel B—Changes in Accounting Estimates

Amortization

Fortis Properties depreciates income producing buildings on the sinking fund method using an imputed interest rate of 6% over the estimated useful lives of sixty years from date of acquisition. Prior to 1999, estimated useful lives ranged from twenty-five to forty years. Management's decision to change the estimated useful lives was based on architectural assessments of the Corporation's income producing properties in 1999. This change in accounting estimate will be applied prospectively. Fortis Properties amortizes tenant inducements over the initial terms of the leases to which they relate, except where a write-down is required to reflect permanent impairment. The lease terms range from three to twenty years.

Capital Assets and the Cash Flow Statement

When capital assets are bought or sold for cash, the amount is reported as an investing activity in the cash flow statement. Purchases appear as negative amounts because they use cash and disposals are positive because they generate cash. One complexity with the sale of capital assets is the treatment of gains and losses on the cash flow statement. Gains and losses are included in the calculation of net income but they do not affect cash flow, so gains must be subtracted from net income and losses added back when reconciling from net income to cash from operations (CFO) using the indirect method. The only cash flow effect of the sale of a capital asset is the cash received, and the cash received is treated as an investing activity. Write-downs of capital assets do not affect cash flows, so they are added back when calculating CFO using the indirect method.

Does the Way Capital Assets Are Accounted for Affect the Cash Flow Statement?

It may come as a surprise, but how expenditures for capital assets are accounted for can affect the cash flows reported in the cash flow statement. Accounting choices do not affect the actual amount of cash that enters and leaves an entity, but the choices can affect the classification of cash flows. If an expenditure is capitalized, the outlay appears in the cash flow statement as an investing activity. If that same expenditure is expensed when incurred, the expenditure is included in CFO. The amount of cash spent during the year is not affected by the accounting choice. How it is reported is.

Suppose that in 2003 Balaclava Ltd. (Balaclava) spends $1,000,000 in cash on the development of a new product. If the expenditure meets the requirements for capitalization under GAAP, Balaclava could make the following journal entry:

Dr. New product development (asset +)   1,000,000
  Cr. Cash (asset –)   1,000,000
To capitalize development costs associated with a new product.

If Balaclava decides to amortize the development costs over four years, there will be an annual amortization expense of $250,000 in each year from 2003 through 2006:

Dr. Amortization expense (expense +, shareholders' equity –) 250,000
  Cr. Accumulated amortization (contra-asset +)   250,000
To record amortization of new product development costs.

If instead Balaclava decides to expense the new product costs when they are incurred, the journal entry would be:

Dr. New product development expense   1,000,000
  (expense +, shareholders' equity –)
  Cr. Cash (asset –)   1,000,000
To expense expenditures associated with a new product.

Table 9-2 provides summarized income statements for Balaclava Ltd. for 2003 and 2004, for both capitalizing and expensing the new product development costs. It is assumed in the income statements that revenues and expenses other than the amortization expense are in cash, and that the revenues and expenses are the same in both 2003 and 2004. In 2003, if the expenditure is capitalized, net income is reduced by $250,000, the amount of the amortization expense. Net income is also reduced in 2004 (as well as 2005 and 2006) by $250,000 because the $1,000,000 is being amortized over four years. If the product development costs are expensed in full in 2003,

Balaclava Ltd.
Income Statement
For the Years Ended December 31, 2003 and 2004

	December 31, 2003		December 31, 2004	
	Capitalize	**Expense**	**Capitalize**	**Expense**
Revenues	$25,000,000	$25,000,000	$25,000,000	$25,000,000
Expenses	15,000,000	15,000,000	15,000,000	15,000,000
Amortization of product development costs	250,000		250,000	
Product development expense		1,000,000		0
Net Income	$ 9,750,000	$ 9,000,000	$ 9,750,000	$10,000,000

income is reduced by $1,000,000 in 2003. In 2004 (as well as 2005 and 2006) the new product costs have no effect on income.

But what is the effect on the cash flow statement? Table 9-3 provides summarized cash flow statements for Balaclava Ltd. for 2003 and 2004 for both capitalizing and expensing the new product development costs. If the $1,000,000 is capitalized, the outlay is classified as an investing activity and the $250,000 amortization expense is added back to net income in the calculation of CFO using the indirect method. If the cost is expensed in full in 2003, it is classified as CFO. (The product development costs do not appear explicitly in the cash flow statement under the expensing alternative because the costs have already been deducted in the calculation of net income.)

Notice the effect of the accounting choice on the cash flow statement. In 2003 the overall increase in cash is $9,000,000 under both methods, but CFO is $10,000,000 when the product development costs are capitalized and $9,000,000 when the costs are expensed when incurred. If the costs are capitalized, investing activities reflect a $1,000,000 cash outlay, whereas if the costs are expensed, cash expended for investing activities is zero. In 2004 CFO and investing activities are the same under both alternatives because the only financial statement impact of the new product development costs is amortization, which has no effect on cash.

Even the cash flow statement, a statement designed to neutralize the effects of accounting choices by preparers, is affected by accounting choices. In evaluating CFO

Balaclava Ltd.
Cash Flow Statement
For the Year Ended December 31, 2003 and 2004

	December 31, 2003		December 31, 2004	
	Capitalize	**Expense**	**Capitalize**	**Expense**
Cash from Operations:				
Net Income	$ 9,750,000	$9,000,000	$ 9,750,000	$10,000,000
Add back:				
Amortization of product development costs	250,000	0	250,000	0
Cash from Operations	10,000,000	9,000,000	10,000,000	10,000,000
Investing Activities:				
Cost of product development	1,000,000	0	0	0
Increase in Cash	$ 9,000,000	$9,000,000	$10,000,000	$10,000,000

you as a user of the information have to consider the accounting policies used, because if some companies capitalize certain outlays as capital assets while similar entities expense them, your ability to compare the companies' CFO is impaired.

Why Accounting Choice?

Let's take a moment to re-emphasize a central theme of this book. One of the most difficult issues for students of accounting to understand is the reason why there is so much choice available to preparers. Accounting choice is a double-edged sword. Choice provides preparers the opportunity to present information in ways that are useful to the users of the information. Choice also provides an effective means for preparers to achieve their own reporting objectives. There is nothing inherently sinister in allowing preparers the ability to tailor information to suit their own needs and the needs of users. However, the other edge of the sword is that preparers can use the flexibility inherent in accounting to mislead and manipulate the users of the information. It is not always possible for users to tell how the preparers are using accounting choice and this is one of the dangers that users face.

Some might ask why a single set of accounting rules couldn't be applied to every situation. This issue has been argued throughout the book, but it bears repeating through an example. Consider a small business wholly owned and operated by a husband-and-wife team. The financial statements have been used exclusively for management decision making and tax purposes. As such, the owners have always prepared its financial statements with the purpose of minimizing taxes. All accounting choices have been made with the purpose of paying as little tax as possible. This approach makes perfect sense. Why pay more taxes than necessary? Why make the bookkeeping more complicated than necessary?

Then the husband and wife decide to sell the business. A prospective purchaser would want to see financial statements to assess the attractiveness of the business. Are the statements that the couple has been preparing for tax purposes appropriate for the prospective purchaser? Probably not! The financial statements prepared for tax purposes are inappropriate for the purpose of valuing a business because they will tend to understate the performance of the entity. Financial statements for a prospective buyer should reflect the economic activity of the business for the purpose of predicting future performance. In other words, a purchaser wants information to help evaluate how much money he or she will make. Tax-based financial statements don't do that.

The issue of how to deal with accounting policy choice has no easy answer. A system that allows choice opens itself up for abuse by preparers. A system with no choice reduces the likelihood for abuse but may render financial statements useless. For now Canada allows a lot of choice and emphasizes the exercise of judgment. Users should recognize the opportunity for abuse and use accounting information cautiously. Thus far, we have seen the effect that the choice of revenue recognition method, inventory cost flow assumption, and amortization method, along with a number of other estimates that the preparers make, have on the financial statements. With these accounting issues alone a wide range of numbers could appear in the financial statements of an entity, depending on the choices by the preparers, each of which represents the identical underlying economic activity.

Accounting plays a very important role in communicating information about an entity. Ethical behaviour by the preparers of the information, the managers, and any external accountants (including auditors) is essential for the efficient and effective operation of the economy. Users must be able to use accounting information with confidence. If they are unable to do so, the costs of doing business will increase and economic performance will decline.

Users must recognize that it is not always possible to "see through" the financial statements numbers to the "truth". Financial statements should rarely be the finishing point of an investigation. Users should ask detailed questions if they have the opportunity. (For example, if someone is planning to buy a business, they should ask the seller detailed questions about the business and the financial statements.) Other sources of information should also be consulted.

Financial Statement Analysis Issues

Despite the importance of capital assets to many entities, there are limits to the insights about an entity that can be gained from analyzing the historical cost information about them in the financial statements. First, as we discussed earlier in the chapter, the usefulness of historical cost information about capital assets for many decisions is questionable. Second, even under GAAP there is extensive choice for how to account for capital assets. How capital assets are accounted for can have significant effects on the numbers in the financial statements. The list below summarizes the areas of choice that were discussed in the chapter:

- what costs get capitalized
- how capital assets are amortized
- estimates of useful life and residual value
- the existence of unrecorded assets (especially intangible assets)
- write-downs and write-offs of capital assets

These policy and estimate choices will affect expenses, net income, assets and retained earnings, and any ratios that depend on these measures. That said, a ratio often used to measure the performance and operating efficiency of an entity is **return on assets (ROA)**. ROA is defined as:

$$\text{Return on assets} = \frac{\text{Net income} + \text{After-tax interest expense}}{\text{Total assets}}$$

The numerator of the ratio is a measure of how the entity has performed—in this case, net income with the after-tax interest expense added back. The after-tax interest expense is the cost of interest after taking into consideration that the government picks up part of the cost of interest because interest is deductible for tax purposes. That is, if an entity incurs $10,000 in interest and the entity's tax rate is 25%, the actual cost of interest to the entity is $7,500 ($10,000 × [1 − tax rate] = $10,000 × [1 − 0.25]). The reason after-tax interest expense is added back is so that the ratio is a measure of return on assets independent of how the assets are financed. If the interest expense were included in the numerator, the return on assets would be affected by the amount of debt the entity had.

The denominator is the investment—in this case the entity's investment in assets. The denominator can be expressed as average assets for the year or year-end assets. Both the numerator and denominator introduce some problems. In addition to the effect of the accounting choices made by management, the ratio will also be affected by when the assets were purchased. Assets purchased at different times will have different costs. As a result, comparing the ROA of different entities must be done with a great deal of caution.

This ratio can be thought of in the context of a bank account. The denominator—the investment or the assets invested—is the amount of money that you put in your bank account. The numerator—the return—is the interest that the bank pays you over the year. The return on assets is the rate the bank account earned. If you

Figure 9-10

Vermilion Inc.: Effect of Using Straight-Line and Declining Balance Amortization Methods on Profit Margin and ROA

		2005	2006	2007	2008
Profit Margin	Straight-line	10.8%	7.4%	11.6%	9.9%
	Declining balance	−7.9%	8.5%	22.2%	14.8%
Return on Assets	Straight-line	5.5%	4.0%	6.5%	3.8%
	Declining balance	−4.4%	5.1%	12.8%	5.6%

invested $1,000 in a bank account and over the following year the bank paid you $50 in interest, your return would be 5% ($50 ÷ $1,000). Mark's Work Wearhouse's return on assets for the year ended January 27, 2001 is:

$$\text{Return on assets} = \frac{\text{Net income + After-tax interest expense}}{\text{Total assets}}$$

$$= \frac{\$8,180 + (\$2,498 + \$1,480) \times (1 - 0.489)}{(\$157,060 + \$143,084) \div 2}$$

$$= \frac{\$10,213}{\$150,072}$$

$$= \quad 6.8\%$$

The tax rate of 48.9% for fiscal 2001 can be found in Note 17 to MWW's financial statements (see page A-62). MWW's ROA for the year ended January 29, 2000 was 6.2%, so the company showed a slight improvement in 2001 over 2000.

To illustrate the effect of policy choices on financial statement analysis, we will examine the effect of using different amortization methods on two financial ratios for Vermilion Corp. Vermilion Corp.'s financial statements are provided in Table 9-1 of this chapter (see page 515). The two ratios we will examine are profit margin and ROA. For simplicity, we assume that Vermilion incurred no interest expense and we use year-end total assets (instead of the year average) as the denominator in the calculation of ROA. The two ratios are calculated using straight-line and declining-balance amortization.

The results are shown in Figure 9-10. Observe how different the ratios are in each year. In 2005 the profit margin is over 10% when straight-line amortization is used and it is −7.9% when declining balance is used. Comparing 2005 to 2006, the profit margin ratio fell when straight-line is used but increased when declining balance is selected. ROA shows a similar pattern.

Similar results can be expected with other ratios and other accounting choices regarding capital assets. While the economic condition of an entity is unaffected by these accounting choices, the pictures that those ratios paint can be very different. Without care and awareness of the impact of accounting choices, the conclusions one might draw about the entity may be very different simply because of its accounting choices. Any type of financial analysis must be based on an understanding of the accounting choices that went into the financial statements. If comparisons are being made between entities or for a particular entity over time, it is important to ensure that like things are being compared.

■ Solved Problem

This chapter's solved problem is a case analysis in an unusual setting. The case will give readers an opportunity to apply the material that has been covered thus far in the book. The case is challenging and readers should not be discouraged if they struggle in places. Readers are encouraged to take the time to do a complete and thorough analysis before reading the solution.

High-Tech Industries Inc.

High-Tech Industries Inc. (Hi-Tech) develops and manufactures highly sophisticated technical equipment for mining companies. Over the years High-Tech has developed a worldwide reputation for the quality and reliability of its products. High-Tech is one of only a few companies in the world that produces this type of equipment. For many years High-Tech was the only company in this market, but in recent years a number of competitors have entered the industry. All these competitors have been supported by their national governments. In the last three years High-Tech has seen its profits and its margins decline drastically in the face of the new competition. In its most recent fiscal year High-Tech claims it suffered a loss of $42,000,000.

The management of High-Tech has approached government officials for support so that the company can compete on a "level playing field" with its competitors. High-Tech has suggested that it may be forced to move some or all of its operations to another country if it does not obtain adequate support. High-Tech has asked for immediate subsidies of between $50–$75 million.

The government has formed a committee to examine whether High-Tech should receive government funding. While the government itself and many members of the committee seem supportive of High-Tech, there is at least one member of the com-

---

Figure 9-11

Additional Information about High-Tech Industries Inc.

1. High-Tech is a private company. Normally its financial statements are not publicly available, but in an effort to support its position, High-Tech has provided a summarized income statement for its 2004 fiscal year to the government committee.

    High-Tech Industries Inc.
    Summarized Income Statement for the Year Ended October 31, 2004

Revenue		$225,000,000
Cost of sales		106,000,000
Gross margin		119,000,000
Expenses:		
Salaries and benefits	$59,000,000	
Selling, general, marketing and administration	25,000,000	
Loss on sale of technology	22,000,000	
Research and development	40,000,000	
Amortization	15,000,000	161,000,000
Net loss		($ 42,000,000)

2. High-Tech normally uses the percentage-of-completion method for recognizing revenue on its long-term contracts.

3. In 2004 the company entered into a large contract with an Asian company to develop a unique type of mining equipment. Work has begun on the project and it is expected to be completed in 2006. Because of the economic problems in the Asian country, High-Tech has decided to recognize revenue on a completed-contract basis for this contract. Management believes that there is a higher than normal probability that the customer will be unable to pay in full for the technology.

    High-Tech expensed the costs of obtaining the contract in its 2004 income statement. Some other costs pertaining to the contract have also been expensed in the current year. The contract will generate $33,000,000 in revenue and incur estimated costs of $17,000,000. The Asian company has already made $7,000,000 in payments to High-Tech.

4. The majority shareholder of High-Tech owns a company that provides testing and other consulting advice to High-Tech. During 2004 High-Tech paid $18,000,000 to the company owned by the majority shareholder.

5. In 2002 High-Tech purchased the rights to a technology developed by a British company. The technology has proven not to be useful to High-Tech and in 2004 it sold the rights to the technology to another company at a loss of $22,000,000.

6. High-Tech invests heavily in research and development. Research and development expenditures have been increasing significantly in each recent year and this trend is expected to continue. Research and development costs are expensed when they are incurred.

mittee who strongly believes that governments should not be subsidizing private businesses. The dissenting member of the committee has asked you to prepare a report evaluating whether High-Tech's financial information provides a true picture of its financial position. Your report will be used to present the dissenting member's side of the story to the committee, so it is important that your report clearly detail any problems that you identify with the accounting information. Your report should also discuss alternative treatments for the problems you identify and consider the quantitative impact.

The committee member has supplied you with the information in Figure 9-11.

Required:

Prepare the report requested by the dissenting committee member.

Comment: This is a user-oriented case. This means that you are to approach the analysis from the perspective of a specific user of the financial statements—in this situation as an advisor to a member of a government committee who strongly opposes government subsidies to businesses.

High-Tech Industries Inc. (High-Tech) has approached the government for a large subsidy and the committee member wants to make an argument against granting a subsidy. Your task is to assist the committee member by providing an analysis of the income statement that serves the interests of the committee member. Remember that interpreting financial statements requires judgment. Simply because an entity reports a loss does not mean it is in financial distress. The role requires that you look at the financial statements to identify areas where the accounting used by High-Tech does not give a reasonable indication of its need for government support. In other words, you must assess whether High-Tech's income statement is appropriate for the stated purpose.

The report should make clear that High-Tech has incentives to understate its performance, and it should identify situations where High-Tech has taken advantage of accounting to make its situation look bad. The report must establish some criteria for assessing the performance of High-Tech. It could be cash flow (low income does not necessarily mean poor liquidity or financial problems), it could be accrual income adjusted for unusual items or some other measure of performance. Some criteria are necessary so that there is a context for interpreting financial statements.

An important aspect of this case is that GAAP have no bearing for this role. It might be necessary for High-Tech to prepare GAAP financial statements, but GAAP statements may not provide the information needed for the intended purpose. Because of GAAP's rules it is possible that High-Tech's income statement does not reasonably reflect its need for a subsidy. Remember that preparers of financial statements are often constrained by GAAP, but users are not. Users may adjust and modify financial statements to whatever form they please. If GAAP's rules do not provide information that provides that support, then those rules should not be followed. This does not imply a free-for-all. Any basis of accounting must be supported and supportable. So whatever accounting choices are selected, each choice must be well explained and justified so that it will be convincing to other committee members and to High-Tech's representatives.

Solution:

Report to Committee Member on High-Tech Industries Inc.

I have examined the income statement and explanatory information provided by High-Tech Industries. In my opinion, that statement is not appropriate for evaluating the economic condition of High-Tech for purposes of determining whether High-Tech should be provided with a government subsidy. The statement tends to understate the actual economic performance of the company because of the measurement conventions used. The statement takes a conservative approach to reporting and includes at least one item that is not representative of ongoing performance. In addition, the statement is not a good indication of whether High-Tech actually needs cash. Rather, the statement is prepared on what is known as an accrual basis, which measures wealth or economic flows rather than cash flows.

The usual basis for preparing financial statements in Canada is generally accepted accounting principles or GAAP and it appears that High-Tech followed GAAP. While GAAP are a useful set of rules and guidelines for preparing financial statements, they are not useful for all decisions in all situations. In the case of High-Tech, application of GAAP served to understate its income in the current period. The reason is that GAAP are inherently conservative. In my analysis below, I suggest treatments that may deviate from GAAP. In my opinion, this is acceptable because GAAP treatments do not give a reasonable view of the economic situation of the company. Overall, I will use accrual accounting as the basis for evaluating High-Tech's performance, although not necessarily GAAP-based accrual accounting. I think it is also important to assess High-Tech's liquidity.

My review of the statements assesses the information provided. However, there is considerable additional information that would be very useful in assessing High-Tech. Thus my conclusions can only be considered preliminary. Additional information that should be requested includes: comparative financial statements, cash flow statements, balance sheets, details on specific transactions such as related-party transactions, and notes to the financial statements. I have provided my analysis in the absence of a more complete set of information so that you can participate in the upcoming committee meeting in an informed way.

Use of completed contract method

The impact of the completed contract method is to reduce revenue and income by deferring revenue recognition to 2006 when the contract is completed. There is no theoretical problem with using different revenue recognition methods for different contracts, provided that the facts justify the different treatments. That is, the circumstances surrounding the contract with the Asian country must be such that the revenue or costs are difficult to reasonably estimate or collection of cash is questionable.

In this situation it does not appear that the completed-contract method is justified. High-Tech contends that the completed-contract method is justified because cash collection is quite uncertain. The facts do not appear to support this claim. High-Tech has already collected $7,000,000 from the country, which suggests a willingness and an ability to pay. Therefore, there does not seem to be good reason to deviate from the percentage-of-completion method. Since the contract spans three years, I suggest recognizing one-third of the revenue and the expenses related to the contract in 2004. This treatment will add over $5,000,000 to income during the year. (The exact amount may change pending additional information on the work done through the end of 2004.)

Non-arm's length transactions

The non-arm's length transactions raise serious concerns but not answers. If the services provided by the related company have an actual market value of $18,000,000 and were required by High-Tech, then recording them at their transaction value is acceptable. However, it is impossible to determine whether the services provided had a market value of $18,000,000, $8,000,000, $1,800,000, or something else.

Non-arm's length transactions introduce the opportunity for the major shareholder to overstate the value of the services provided to High-Tech with the purpose of understating High-Tech's income to make its financial situation look poorer. There are no negative economic consequences to High-Tech's major shareholder because she has an economic interest in both transacting entities. Additional information is required to evaluate these transactions. It is necessary to know extensive details on the services provided to High-Tech and an indication of their market value. Indeed, it is necessary to confirm the actual existence of these transactions. For the time being, I recommend that these costs be completely removed from the income statement until additional information is provided. This treatment will reduce the reported loss by $18,000,000.

Loss on sale of purchased technology

During 2004 High-Tech sold technology at a significant loss. That loss represents more than half of the reported net loss. A number of issues arise from this loss. First, the loss is likely not recurring. That means that future periods will not reflect this loss. Therefore, if everything else stayed exactly the same as this year, the loss in 2005 would be $20,000,000 instead of $42,000,000. Also, the loss is an accounting loss, not a cash loss. High-Tech paid for this technology a few years ago. Sale of the technology does not leave the company out of pocket in the current period. In fact, by selling the technology it is actually $22,000,000 better off in a cash sense. I recommend that this loss be disregarded when evaluating the company's income statement. Instead the analysis should focus on earnings before non-recurring items. This treatment would reduce High-Tech's loss by $22,000,000.

The question can also be raised as to when the loss in value actually occurred. While the loss was realized in 2004, the actual economic loss may have been suffered in a previous period. This means that the loss should have been recognized earlier. There are a number of possible reasons why the loss might have occurred in previous periods but not recorded. If this is the case, income for 2004 is understated. Finally, there is the question of whether taxpayers should be subsidizing a company for its poor decisions.

Research and development costs

Research and development (R&D) is an investment by an entity in future revenue-generating resources. Standard accounting practice (GAAP) expenses R&D when it is incurred because of conservatism. The future benefits of R&D expenditures are considered too difficult to measure, which is why they are expensed. Conceptually, no one would dispute that R&D is an asset. By expensing R&D currently, High-Tech understates its income because expenses are not being matched to the revenues they generate. Those revenues will presumably be earned sometime in the future.

It makes better sense to capitalize the R&D costs and amortize them over some (probably short) period of time (say four years). That means that only $10,000,000 of the year's expenditures should be expensed this year. This adjustment will increase income by $30,000,000. However, for consistency, R&D expensed in previous years should be capitalized and amortized. Given that R&D spending is increasing, the net effect of these adjustments will be to increase income in the current period. However, it is not possible to state an amount that should be amortized in the current period.

Summary

Net income as reported		($42,000,000)
Add:	Adjustment to percentage-of-completion method	5,000,000
	Loss on sale of technology	22,000,000
	Non-arms length transactions	18,000,000
	Research and development costs	30,000,000
	Change in revenue recognition method	5,000,000
Deduct:	Amortization of previous years' R&D	?
Revised net income		$38,000,000

Revised net income shows that High-Tech was profitable in 2004. Even with additional adjustments for R&D amortization and for the non-arm's length transactions, income will likely continue to be positive. This approach is also more representative of its ongoing economic performance.

Please contact me if you have any questions about my report and if you require assistance at the upcoming hearing.

Comment: A good analysis should have included:

- effective role playing
- an indication of a basis for evaluating whether High-Tech should receive a subsidy
- a solid discussion of the accounting issues and recommendations on appropriate treatments
- an attempt to quantify the impact of the proposed accounting changes

Remember that this analysis represents one approach. Different ones are possible. The preceding is intended to give an idea how this case could be approached, not to serve as the definitive answer.

Summary of Key Points

LO 1. GAAP require that entities report their capital assets at historical cost. While historical cost accounting serves the purpose of matching, for the purpose of making projections or other future-oriented decisions it is difficult to understand how the historical cost of capital assets can be useful for most uses and to most users of financial statements. There are three alternatives to historical cost accounting for capital assets: net realizable value, replacement cost, and value-in-use. The main objection to these alternatives is that the measures are not as reliable as historical cost. None of these measurement bases is ideal for all purposes.

LO 2. The cost of an asset that is reported on an entity's balance sheet should include all the costs associated with purchasing the asset and getting it ready for use. Costs incurred by employees of the entity purchasing the asset, including their wages, should also be capitalized. Costs incurred to improve an existing asset should be capitalized and amortized, whereas costs incurred to maintain an asset should be expensed when incurred.

LO 3. The process of allocating the cost of a capital asset to expense over time to reflect the consumption of the asset is known as amortization. According to the *CICA Handbook*, the cost of an asset less its residual value should be amortized over its useful life in a "systematic and rational" manner. There are four major methods of amortization: straight-line, accelerated, usage-based, and decelerated. All of the amortization methods result in the same amount of amortization over the life of the asset. Only the timing of the expense is affected. Different amortization methods do not affect an entity's cash flow, but the method used can affect the outcomes that are based on financial statement numbers.

LO 4. Intangible assets—also known as knowledge assets or intellectual capital—are capital assets that have no physical qualities. Investments in knowledge assets are all but ignored in traditional accounting, mainly because of conservatism. Money spent on knowledge assets is normally expensed when incurred. However, it is difficult to argue that these investments are not assets, at least conceptually. Expensing investments in knowledge assets when they are incurred has significant implications for the financial statements, including violation of the matching principle, which impairs the meaningfulness of net income.

LO 5. The *Income Tax Act* (*ITA*) uses the term capital cost allowance (CCA) to describe amortization for tax purposes. The mechanics of CCA are the same as they are for financial accounting—the cost of capital assets is somehow expensed over time—but the *ITA* is very detailed about the method and rate that must be used for each type of asset. For most assets the *ITA* requires the declining balance method, though straight line is required for some assets. There is no choice or discretion available to the preparers—the rules in the *ITA* must be followed exactly.

LO 6. When an amortizable asset is sold, the cost of the asset and the accumulated amortization associated with it must be removed from the accounting records. If the proceeds received on disposal of a capital asset are different from the NBV of the asset, a gain or loss is reported on the income statement. The amount of the gain or loss on the sale of a capital asset is simply a function of how the capital asset is accounted for.

Sometimes situations arise that impair the value of capital assets. A capital asset is impaired when its net recoverable amount is less than its NBV. According to GAAP, when capital assets become impaired they should be written down to their net recoverable amount. Management has considerable discretion in deciding the timing and amount of a write-down because determining the impairment of a capital asset is very subjective.

LO 7. There are two categories of accounting changes—changes in policies and changes in estimates. If a company decides to change an accounting policy, the change is applied retroactively. A change in accounting estimate is corrected in future periods, from the period of the change in estimate onward. Under GAAP accounting, policy changes must be disclosed. GAAP and the *CICA Handbook* do not require disclosure of changes in estimates.

LO 8. How expenditures for capital assets are accounted for affects the cash flows reported in the cash flow statement. Accounting choices do not affect the actual amount of cash that enters and leaves an entity, but the choices can affect the amount reported as CFO. If an expenditure is capitalized, the outlay will appear in the cash flow statement as an investing activity. If that same expenditure is expensed when incurred, the expenditure is included in CFO.

LO 9. Despite the importance of capital assets to many entities, there are limits to the insights about an entity that can be gained from analyzing the historical cost information about capital assets in the financial statements. Despite the limitations, a ratio often used to measure the performance and operating efficiency of an entity is return on assets.

Key Terms

accelerated amortization, p. 510

accounting estimate, p. 531

accounting policy, p. 531

amortization, p. 507

betterment, p. 504

capital asset, p. 500

capital cost allowance, p. 521

capitalize, p. 500

decelerated amortization, p. 514

declining balance, p. 511

depletion, p. 507

depreciation, p. 507

full costing, p. 526

goodwill, p. 525

half-year rule, p. 522

intangible asset, p. 507

maintenance, p. 504

net recoverable amount, p. 528

repair, p. 504

residual value, p. 507

return on assets (ROA), p. 537

straight-line amortization, p. 510

successful efforts, p. 526

tangible asset, p. 507

value-in-use, p. 502

Similar Terms

The left column gives alternative terms that are sometimes used for the accounting terms introduced in this chapter, which are listed in the right column.

fixed asset, long-lived asset	**capital asset, p. 500**
depreciation	**amortization, p. 507**
knowledge asset, intellectual capital	**intangible asset, p. 507**
diminishing balance	**declining balance, p. 511**

Assignment Materials

Questions

Q9-1. For each of the following entities, describe the types of capital assets you would expect the entity to have:
a. gas station
b. university
c. convenience store
d. hotel
e. dairy farm
f. electric utility
g. golf course

Q9-2. What is an intangible asset? How do intangible assets differ from tangible ones? Give examples of each.

Q9-3. Why do intangible assets not usually appear on a balance sheet? Under what circumstances will intangible assets be reported on the balance sheet?

Q9-4. What is goodwill? How does it arise?

Q9-5. Why are capital assets amortized?

Q9-6. What costs should be included in the amount capitalized for the purchase of a new delivery vehicle?

Q9-7. What characteristics distinguish capital assets from inventory?

Q9-8. What effect does amortization have on an entity's cash flow? Why is amortization added back to net income when the indirect method of calculating cash from operations is used?

Q9-9. Academic research has shown that the stock price of a public company is not affected by the amortization method an entity uses. Does the amortization method an entity uses matter? Explain.

Q9-10. Why is the amortization of the cost of an asset considered arbitrary?

Q9-11. Identify and explain the two main reasons why capital assets have to be amortized.

Q9-12. Why is the selection of an amortization method never an issue if tax minimization is the main objective of financial reporting?

Q9-13. Why is accounting for knowledge assets such a difficult problem under existing GAAP?

Q9-14. To make room for new equipment that it was installing, Sandwich Inc. had to knock down a wall. The cost of knocking down the wall was $32,000. While the installation was in progress another wall was accidentally knocked down. The cost of replacing that wall was $44,000. Which, if any, of these costs should be capitalized? Explain.

Q9-15. An accounting firm purchases used office furniture for its support staff. For each of the following, would the expenditure be capitalized or expensed? Explain.
a. The office furniture cost $18,000.
b. Some of the furniture required repairs before it could be used. The repairs cost $4,000.
c. Soon after the furniture was delivered, some was damaged because of mishandling by the accounting firm's staff. Additional repairs costing $1,300 were required.
d. The accounting firm had to hire people to help rearrange the furniture to accommodate the new furniture. The work cost $1,500.

Q9-16. Explain why repairs are expensed whereas betterments are capitalized.

Q9-17. An uncle of yours explains that amortization is important because it ensures that money is set aside for replacing the capital assets that are being used up. What would be your response to your uncle?

Q9-18. What effect does a write-down of capital assets have on cash flow? Explain.

Q9-19. What criteria are applied when deciding whether a capital asset should be written down? How does the approach to writing down capital assets differ from the approach used for writing down inventory?

Q9-20. Explain the difference between full cost and successful efforts accounting used by oil and gas exploration companies.

Q9-21. Why do you think GAAP allow the capitalization of oil and gas exploration costs but not research costs?

Q9-22. For each business identified below, explain how the capital asset contributes to generating revenue by the business:

	Business	Asset
a.	Lawn care	Lawn mower
b.	Bank	Banking machine
c.	Arena	Zamboni machine
d.	Jewellery store	Display cases
e.	Doctor's office	Waiting room furniture
f.	Auto parts manufacturer	Warehouse

Q9-23. Explain the difference between a change in accounting policy and a change in accounting estimate. How is each accounted for in the financial statements?

Q9-24. Why does judgment by the preparers of financial statements play such an important role in determining the amortization expense that an entity incurs? Be specific.

Q9-25. You are the accountant for a restaurant. The restaurant has recently started a home delivery service and purchased a car to make deliveries. You have to prepare the year-end financial statements for the restaurant and have to decide how to amortize the car. What useful life and residual value would you assign to the car? Explain your decision fully and discuss the factors you considered. Assume the restaurant prepares its financial statements in accordance with GAAP.

Q9-26. Explain how accounting policies can affect the cash from operations an entity reports when we know that different accounting policies have no effect on cash flow.

Q9-27. Explain the following bases for valuing capital assets. Provide examples of how each might provide useful information to a user:
a. historical cost
b. replacement cost
c. net realizable value
d. value-in-use

Q9-28. Company A owns a world-renowned trademark, but it does not appear on its balance sheet. Company B owns a world-renowned trademark, which is valued on the company's balance sheet at $125,000,000. Explain why this difference might arise.

Q9-29. Wisdom Inc. tries to use very conservative accounting methods. For example, it tends to make conservative estimates of the useful lives of capital assets (shorter lives rather than longer ones) and residual value (lower estimates of residual value).
a. What is the impact of these conservative accounting policies on income? Explain.
b. How could these conservative policies have unconservative effects when Wisdom Inc. disposes of capital assets? Explain.

Q9-30. What is capital cost allowance? How does capital cost allowance differ from amortization?

Q9-31. Define and explain the use of the following terms. Provide examples of when each would be used:
a. amortization
b. depreciation
c. depletion

Q9-32. Is it possible for an entity to use a capital asset that is completely amortized? Explain. What would be the net book value of such an asset?

Q9-33. Esk Ltd. (Esk) recently purchased a fully equipped restaurant at an auction for $500,000. The restaurant included all the equipment, furniture, and fixtures. The building itself is rented. Esk now must allocate the purchase price to the items purchased. Explain how Esk should allocate the purchase price to the specific items. Why is it necessary for the purchase price to be allocated to the specific items? What motivations might influence the allocations that Esk makes?

Exercises

E9-1. **(Straight-line amortization, LO 2, 3, 6)** Roxana Inc. (Roxana) recently purchased new furniture for the reception area of the company's head office. The furniture itself cost $30,000, taxes were $4,500, delivery cost $1,000, and set-up cost $700. Roxanna's management expects to use the furniture for six years, at which time it will be replaced. Management expects that the new furniture will have a residual value after six years of $5,500.

Required:

a. Prepare the journal entry to record the purchase of the new furniture.
b. Prepare an amortization schedule showing the amortization expense for each of the six years Roxana expects to keep the furniture and the NBV of the furniture at the end of each year. Assume that the furniture was purchased midway through the fiscal year and only a half-year's amortization is to be expensed in the first year.
c. Suppose the furniture was sold at the end of the fourth year for $12,000. Prepare the journal entry to record the sale and any other journal entries required with respect to the furniture in the fourth year.

E9-2. **(Accelerated amortization, LO 2, 3, 6)** In early 2003 Jupitagon Ltd. (Jupitagon) purchased new computer equipment. Jupitagon does cutting-edge graphic design work and requires highly sophisticated computer hardware and software. The new equipment cost $125,000 plus $18,750 in taxes, $10,000 for installation, $20,000 for training, and $30,000 for a three-year insurance policy on the equipment.

Jupitagon's management expects to be able to use the computer equipment for about four years, although with the passage of time the equipment will likely be less useful for more sophisticated work because better equipment becomes available very quickly. Accordingly, management has decided to amortize the equipment using the declining-balance method at a rate of 50% per year. Management has indicated that it hopes to be able to sell the equipment at the end of four years for $10,000.

Required:

a. Prepare the journal entry to record the purchase of the new equipment.
b. Prepare an amortization schedule showing the amortization expense for each of the four years Jupitagon expects to use the computer equipment, and the NBV of the equipment at the end of each year.
c. Suppose the computer equipment was sold at the end of 2005 for $22,000. Prepare the journal entry to record the sale and any other journal entries required with respect to the computer equipment in 2005.

E9-3. **(Unit-of-production amortization, LO 2, 3, 6)** Grindstone Corp. (Grindstone) produces fad toys for children. In 2004 Grindstone purchased a new stamping machine to produce the latest fad toy. The machine cost $30,000 plus taxes of $2,100, and delivery and installation of $1,000. Grindstone's management estimates that the market for the toy is about 250,000 units and demand for the toy will last no more than four years. Management expects that it will be able to produce and sell 30,000 units in 2004, 150,000 units in 2005, 65,000 units in 2006, and 5,000 units in 2007. Once the fad dies, the machine will not be useful for any purpose and will have to be sold for scrap, about $2,000. Grindstone will use unit-of-production amortization for the machine.

Required:

    a. Prepare the journal entry to record the purchase of the new machine.

    b. Prepare an amortization schedule showing the amortization expense for each year and the NBV of the machine at the end of each year.

    c. Suppose that at the end 2005 Grindstone's management realized that the fad died more quickly than expected and that there was no more demand for the toy. Prepare the journal entry to record the sale and any other journal entries required with respect to the machine in 2005. Assume that Grindstone produced and sold 150,000 units in 2005 and received $5,000 from a scrap dealer for the machine.

E9-4. **(Change in accounting estimate, LO 7)** Refer to the original information about Grindstone Corp. in Exercise 9-3 above. Suppose that early in 2006 Grindstone's management realized that the fad would last longer than expected and that it would be able to sell 100,000 units in 2006, 50,000 in 2007, and 10,000 in 2008, at which time the machine would be scrapped and Grindstone would receive $1,000.

Required:

Prepare an amortization schedule showing the amortization expense for 2006, 2007, and 2008, and the NBV of the machine at the end of each year.

E9-5. **(Accounting for a basket purchase, LO 2)** In January 2005 Bath Inc. (Bath) purchased a small office building on a half-hectare piece of land in downtown Saskatoon for $9,000,000. An appraiser valued the land at $3,500,000. The building is eight years old and Bath's management expects the building to last for another 16 years, after which time it will have to be demolished. Management has decided to use straight-line amortization.

Required:

Prepare the journal entries that Bath would make to record the purchase of the land and building. What entry would be made to record the amortization expense for the year ended December 31, 2005?

E9-6. **(Determining the gain or loss on the sale of land, LO 6)** In 1995 Chin Corp. purchased a piece of land for $5,000,000. In 2005 the land was sold for $7,000,000.

Required:

Prepare the journal entry to record the sale of Chin Corp's land.

E9-7. **(Classifying capital assets, LO 3)** Indicate whether the following assets would be considered tangible or intangible. Explain your reason for the classification:

    a. licence to sell lottery tickets in an area

    b. machine that dispenses lottery tickets

    c. unique design for beer bottles

    d. beer bottles

    e. right to access another entity's property to enter and leave a lake

    f. land

E9-8. **(Determining cost, LO 2)** Mr. Bogan operates a dairy farm in Québec. Recently one of his cows gave birth to a female calf. The calf will eventually join the dairy herd that produces the milk that Mr. Bogan sells to dairies. When the calf was born, Mr. Bogan had the veterinarian check the calf. For the first while after its birth, the calf drinks its mother's milk. As the calf gets older, it will graze in the pasture, eating the grass that grows there. During the winter the calf will eat hay that Mr. Bogan grows on another part of his farm. Eventually the calf will mature and join the herd as a milk-producing cow.

Required:

    a. How would you report the dairy herd on Mr. Bogan's farm's balance sheet? Explain.

    b. What cost will appear on the farm's balance sheet for the new calf when she is old enough to produce milk? Explain.

c. Explain any limitations you see with the reporting you described above for the new calf.

E9-9. **(Calculation of gains and losses on sale of capital assets, LO 3, 6)** On July 4, 2003 Vroomanton Inc. (Vroomanton) purchased new equipment for its print shop. Vroomanton's accountant determined that the capital cost of the equipment was $34,000. The accountant also estimated that the useful life of equipment would be five years and the residual value $4,000. Assume that Vroomanton took a full year of amortization for the equipment in the year ended June 30, 2004.

Required:

a. Prepare an amortization schedule for the new equipment, assuming the use of straight-line amortization. Set up your amortization schedule like Figure 9-4 in the chapter (page 511).

b. Prepare an amortization schedule for the new equipment assuming the use of declining-balance amortization using an amortization rate of 40%. Set up your amortization schedule like Figure 9-5 in the chapter (page 512).

c. Assume that on June 30 2007, after the amortization expense had been recorded for the year, Vroomanton sold the equipment for $11,000. Prepare the journal entry that is required to record the sale assuming that:
   i.   the amortization schedule in (a) was used, and
   ii. the amortization schedule in (b) was used.

d. Explain the reason for the different income statement effects for the journal entries you recorded in (c).

E9-10. **(Preparing amortization schedules, LO 3)** In July 2004 Savory Inc. (Savory) purchased new equipment for $100,000. Savory's management estimates that the equipment's useful life will be eight years and that its residual value will be $5,000.

Required:

a. Prepare an amortization schedule for each year of the new piece of equipment's life using:
   i.   straight-line amortization
   ii. declining balance amortization (25%)
   iii. unit-of-production method
   Your amortization schedule should show the amortization expense for each year and the net book value of the equipment and accumulated amortization at the end of each year. For the unit-of-production method, assume that 10% of the production was produced in each of 2004, 2005, 2010, and 2011, and 15% in each of the remaining years.

b. Which method do you think Savory's managers would prefer if they have a bonus based on the company's net income? Explain.

E9-11. **(Repairs and maintenance, or betterments, LO 2)** For each of the following independent items, indicate whether the expenditure should be capitalized or expensed. Provide your reasoning.

a. A courier company changes the oil, oil filters, spark plugs, and air filters of the trucks in its delivery fleet.

b. An airline paints its aircraft with its new colours.

c. An office building replaces broken windows with new, energy-efficient windows.

d. An office suite is rewired to allow for more phone lines to be installed so customer service can be improved.

e. The CPUs of 12 computers are replaced because of a defect.

f. The carpets in a law office are cleaned.

E9-12. **(Choosing an amortization period, LO 3)** Wandby Inc. (Wandby) recently replaced the roof on its 32-year-old building. The roofing company guarantees the roof for 15 years and advised Wandby's management that the roof should last 25 years with no problems. Wandby is amortizing the building on a straight-line basis over 40 years and it is expected that the building will have to be demolished and replaced before it is 45 years old.

Required:

How should Wandby amortize the new roof (method, useful life, and residual value)? Explain your answer fully.

E9-13.   (**Determine the cost of a capital asset, LO 2**) The Nameless Cove Hotel (Nameless Cove) is a luxury resort in Atlantic Canada. Recently Nameless Cove built a new, Olympic-size swimming pool on its grounds. The pool was constructed by Deep and Sure Pool Company (Deep and Sure). The following costs were incurred to build the pool:

i.	Building permits	$ 1,000
ii.	Design costs	8,000
iii.	Redesign costs required to make changes that Nameless Cove wanted after construction began	5,000
iv.	Cost of clearing the land of trees and bushes	12,000
v.	Amount paid to Deep and Sure for construction of the pool	150,000
vi.	Damage and repairs to an adjacent property caused when heavy equipment was brought onto the site to do the excavation	22,000
vii.	Cost of meals served to workers	2,000
viii.	Penalties paid to Deep and Sure because Nameless Cove did not want construction to be done on certain regular working days	9,000
ix.	Damage and repair of underground telephone lines that Nameless Cove neglected to advise Deep and Sure about	5,500
x.	Construction of a patio	45,000
xi.	Electrical wiring installed for pool equipment and lighting around the patio	15,000
xii.	Cost of new plants for the patio	9,200

Required:

Determine the amount that should be capitalized as part of the cost of the pool. Explain your reasoning for including or excluding each item in the capitalized cost.

E9-14.   (**Effect of transactions and economic events on ratios, LO 4, 6, 7, 9**) Complete the following table by indicating whether the following transactions or economic events would increase, decrease, or have no effect on the financial ratios listed. Assume the current ratio is greater than 1.0 before considering each of the situations.

	Return on assets	Profit margin percentage	Current ratio	Debt-to-equity ratio	Gross margin percentage
Write-off of a capital asset					
Change of estimate of useful life from ten to eight years					
Change in the estimate of the residual value of an asset from $10,000 to $15,000					
Expense R&D costs					
Capitalize R&D costs					
Change from amortizing a capital asset using declining balance at 20% per year to straight-line over 10 years, in the second year of the asset's life					

E9-15.   (**Effect of transactions and economic events on accounting measures, LO 4, 6, 7, 8, 9**) Complete the following table by indicating whether the following transactions or economic events would increase, decrease, or have no effect on the accounting measurements listed.

	Net income	Gross margin	Total assets	Owners' equity	Cash from operations	Cash from/used in investing activities	Total cash flow
Write-off of a capital asset							
Change of estimate of useful life from ten to eight years							
Change in the estimate of the residual value of an asset from $10,000 to $15,000							
Expense R&D costs							
Capitalize R&D costs							
Change from amortizing a capital asset declining balance at 20% per year to straight-line over 10 years in the second year of the asset's life							

E9-16. **(Evaluating the effect of the sale of a capital asset, LO 6, 8)** In 2001 Triangle Corporation purchased a piece of heavy equipment for $300,000. The equipment was estimated to have a ten-year life and it was amortized on a straight-line basis. In 2005 (after four years of amortization was recorded) the equipment was sold for $140,000 in cash. What journal entry would be made to record the sale of the equipment? How would the sale be reflected in the cash flow statement? Would there be any effect of this transaction on the calculation of cash generated from operations?

E9-17. **(Change in accounting estimate, LO 2, 3, 6, 7)** On November 12, 2001 Griffon Inc. (Griffon) purchased a new front-end loader for $275,000. Management estimated that the loader would have a useful life of eight years and a residual value of $25,000. Near the end of fiscal 2006 management reassessed the useful life of the loader and decided that because the workload of the loader was much lower than was originally expected, its useful life would probably be about 12 years and the residual value of the loader would be about $10,000. Griffon's year end is October 31 and the company uses straight-line amortization for this type of asset.

Required:
   a. Prepare the journal entry to record the purchase of the loader in 2001.
   b. What would be the amortization expense for the loader in 2002? Prepare the journal entry to record the amortization expense in 2002.
   c. What would be the amortization expense for the loader in 2009? Prepare the journal entry to record the amortization expense in 2009.
   d. Suppose the loader was sold in 2010 for $22,000. Prepare the journal entry to record the sale.

E9-18. **(Change in accounting policy, LO 2, 3, 6, 7)** On April 21, 2000 Rustico Inc. (Rustico) purchased a new fishing trawler for $945,000. Rustico initially amortized the trawler on a straight-line basis over 20 years, assuming a residual value of $125,000. Near the end of fiscal 2007 management decided to switch to declining balance amortization using a 10% rate. Rustico's year end is March 31.

Required:
   a. Prepare the journal entry to record the purchase of the trawler in 2000.
   b. What would be the original amortization expense for the trawler in fiscal 2001, 2002, and 2003? Prepare the journal entry to record the amortization expense in each of these years.
   c. What would be the amortization expense for the trawler in 2001, 2002, and 2003 after Rustico changed to the declining-balance method?
   d. Suppose the trawler was sold in 2015 for $195,000. Prepare the journal entry to record the sale.

E9-19. **(Impact of capital asset transactions on the cash flow statement, LO 8)** For each of the following items, indicate whether it would appear on the cash flow statement as cash from operations, an investing cash flow, or a financing cash flow, or that it would not have an effect on cash flows:

a. proceeds from the sale of land

b. amortization expense

c. purchase of a patent for cash

d. gain on the sale of equipment

e. loss on the sale of furniture and fixtures

f. research costs

E9-20. **(CCA versus amortization, LO 3, 5)** On January 3, 2004 Goglin Inc. (Goglin) purchased new equipment to process fresh fruit into jams and jellies for retail sale. The equipment cost $25,000, fully installed, and the amount was capitalized for accounting and tax purposes. Goglin's equipment is classified as class 43, which has a CCA rate of 30% declining balance. Goglin's year end is December 31.

Required:

a. What is the maximum amount of CCA that could be claimed for tax purposes in 2004? Explain.

b. What is the maximum amount of CCA that could be claimed for tax purposes in 2005? Explain.

c. What is the maximum amount of amortization for financial reporting purposes that could be expensed in 2004?

d. If Goglin decides to amortize the equipment on a straight-line basis over 15 years, what would be the maximum amount of amortization that could be expensed in 2004?

e. How does the useful life estimated by Goglin's management affect the amount of CCA that can be claimed? Explain.

f. Why are the amounts calculated in (a) and (c) likely different? Explain.

Problems

P9-1. **(Interpreting a write-down, LO 4, 6, 7, 9)** Fiscal 2005 was an outstanding year for Schmevan Inc. (Schmevan). For a variety of reasons, the company's sales surged and net income was going to exceed financial analysts' expectations by more than 20% or $13,000,000. Schmevan's management recognized that the high earnings during the year were due to some unusual business circumstances and were not likely to be repeated in the foreseeable future.

Before finalizing its financial statements, Schmevan's management evaluated the company's assets and determined that several were overvalued. As a result, Schmevan's assets were written down by a total of $12,000,000 so that the assets would not be reported on its books at more than their market value. All of the assets written down were being amortized, and their remaining useful lives ranged between five and eight years. Schmevan is a public company that is traded on a Canadian stock exchange.

Required:

a. Explain the effect on the current year's financial statements, as well as the implications for future years' financial statements, of the write-down.

b. Explain how users of the financial statements would be affected by the write-down and how the financial statements should be interpreted as a result of recording the write-down.

c. Why do you think Schmevan chose to write down the assets?

d. Does it matter that Schmevan wrote down these assets? Explain.

P9-2. **(Interpreting a write-down, LO 4, 6, 7, 9)** In fiscal 2004 Redlax Technologies Inc. (Redlax) purchased a company that owned a technology that Redlax believed was extremely valuable for its future success. Redlax paid $900,000,000 for the company. Among the assets that Redlax obtained by purchasing the company were "technologies under development" that Redlax estimated to have a fair value of $350,000,000. This means that Redlax estimated that the technologies under development would generate revenues of at least $350,000,000.

Redlax decided to expense the technologies under development in full in fiscal 2004. As an alternative, Redlax could have treated the technologies under development as an asset and amortized them over a period as long as 40 years. Redlax is a public company that is traded on a Canadian stock exchange.

Required:

Explain the effect on the current year's financial statements, as well as the implications for future years' financial statements, of the write-down. Also, explain how users of the financial statements would be affected by how Redlax accounted for the acquired technologies and how the financial statements should be interpreted as a result of how the acquired technologies were accounted for. Why do you think Redlax chose to account for the technologies in the way it did?

P9-3. **(Calculate missing information, LO 2, 3, 6)** Use the following information and determine the NBV of the capital assets of June Inc. (June) on September 30, 2005, the end of its 2005 fiscal year. An accounting equation spreadsheet may help you do this question.

i. On October 1, 2004 the cost of June's capital assets was $750,000 and the accumulated amortization was $225,000.

ii. During fiscal 2005 June sold capital assets with a cost of $110,000 at a loss of $20,000. June received $30,000 for the assets.

iii. During fiscal 2005 June sold land, which is included in the capital asset account, for $145,000 cash, which generated a gain for accounting purposes of $40,000.

iv. During fiscal 2005 capital assets were purchased for $190,000 cash, plus long-term debt of $225,000.

v. During fiscal 2005 June wrote down capital assets by $32,000.

vi. June recorded an amortization expense of $85,000 for fiscal 2005.

P9-4. **(Calculate missing information, LO 2, 3, 6)** Use the following information and determine the NBV of the capital assets of Ziska Ltd. (Ziska) on July 1, 2003, the first day of its 2004 fiscal year. An accounting equation spreadsheet may help you do this question.

i. On June 30, 2004 the cost of Ziska's capital assets was $2,250,000 and the accumulated amortization was $1,025,000.

ii. During fiscal 2004 Ziska purchased capital assets for $475,000 in cash plus $200,000 in notes payable.

iii. During fiscal 2004 Ziska sold capital assets with a cost of $270,000 at a gain of $60,000. Ziska received $100,000 cash for the assets.

iv. During fiscal 2004 Ziska sold land, which is included in the capital asset account, for $215,000, which produced a loss for accounting purposes of $80,000.

v. During fiscal 2004 Ziska wrote down capital assets by $83,000.

vi. Ziska recorded an amortization expense of $230,000.

P9-5. **(Effect of capitalizing versus expensing R&D costs, LO 3, 4, 8, 9)** Utopia Inc. (Utopia) is a biotechnology company located in Montréal. Utopia has successfully marketed a number of products since it went public three years ago. Biotechnology is a highly competitive industry and a company's decline in the marketplace is no further away than a competitor's dramatic scientific breakthrough. To remain competitive, companies must invest heavily in research and development to ensure that they have a pipeline of new medicines to bring to market.

Utopia prepares its financial statements in accordance with GAAP, so it expenses all research costs and any development costs that do not meet the criteria for capitalization. To date, none of Utopia's development costs have met the criteria for capitalization. The following information has been summarized from Utopia's financial statements:

Utopia Inc.					
Extracts from Financial Statements					
	2006	**2005**	**2004**	**2003**	**2002**
Summarized from the					
income statement					
Revenue	$ 7,245,000	$ 4,525,000	$ 3,050,000	$ 850,000	$ 25,000
Expenses*	3,260,000	2,172,000	1,555,000	1,005,000	750,000
Research and develop.					
expenditures	4,500,000	3,500,000	2,000,000	750,000	500,000
Net loss	$ (515,000)	$(1,147,000)	$ (505,000)	$ (905,000)	$(1,225,000)
Summarized from the					
balance sheet					
Total assets	$12,625,000	$11,235,000	$10,550,000	$3,250,000	$1,400,000
Total liabilities	4,923,750	4,044,600	3,692,500	1,365,000	630,000
Total shareholders'					
equity	7,701,250	7,190,400	6,857,500	1,885,000	770,000
Summarized from the					
cash flow statement					
Cash from operations	$ 625,000	$ (900,000)	$ (410,000)	$ (700,000)	$(1,500,000)
Cash expended on					
investing activities	(1,000,500)	(1,235,000)	(5,350,000)	(1,750,000)	(950,000)

*Includes all expenses incurred by Utopia except for research and development.

Required:

a. Recalculate net income for 2004 through 2006, assuming that research and development costs were capitalized and expensed over three years.

b. What would total assets be at the end of 2004 through 2006 if research and development costs were capitalized and expensed over three years?

c. What would shareholders' equity be at the end of 2004 through 2006 if research and development costs were capitalized and expensed over three years?

d. What would cash from operations and cash expended on investing activities be if research and development costs were capitalized and expensed over three years?

e. What would the following ratios be, assuming that (1) research and development costs were expensed as incurred and (2) research and development costs were capitalized and expensed over three years?
   i.   return on assets
   ii.   debt-to-equity ratio
   iii. profit margin percentage

f. How would your interpretation of Utopia differ depending on how research and development costs are accounted for? Which accounting approach do you think is more appropriate? Explain. Your answer should consider the objectives of the users and preparers of accounting information, as well as the accounting concepts discussed in Chapter 5.

P9-6. **(Effect of capitalizing versus expensing R&D costs, LO 3, 4, 8, 9)** Florze Software Inc. (Florze) is a software development company located in Kanata, Ontario. Software is a highly competitive industry and the life of a software product is usually quite short. To remain competitive, companies must invest heavily in research and development to keep their existing products up to date and to develop new ones. Florze expenses all research costs and any development costs that do not meet the criteria for capitalization. Florze has never capitalized any development costs. The following information has been summarized from Florze's financial statements:

Florze Software Inc. Extracts from Financial Statements					
	2006	**2005**	**2004**	**2003**	**2002**
Summarized from the *income statement*					
Revenue	$2,898,000	$1,810,000	$1,220,000	$ 340,000	$ 290,000
Expenses*	1,324,500	1,052,500	905,000	685,000	672,500
Research and development expenditures	1,125,000	875,000	500,000	187,500	125,000
Net loss	$ 448,500	$ (117,500)	$ (185,000)	$(532,500)	$(507,500)
Summarized from the *balance sheet*					
Total assets	$3,156,250	$2,808,750	$2,637,500	$ 812,500	$ 350,000
Total liabilities	1,294,063	983,063	791,250	235,625	87,500
Total shareholders' equity	1,862,187	1,825,687	1,846,250	576,875	262,500
Summarized from the *cash flow statement*					
Cash from operations	$ 150,000	$ (250,000)	$ (75,000)	$(350,000)	$(750,000)
Cash expended on investing activities	(450,000)	(350,000)	(1,750,000)	(500,000)	(285,000)

*Includes all expenses incurred by Florze except for research and development.

Required:

a. Recalculate net income for 2004 through 2006, assuming that research and development costs were capitalized and expensed over three years.

b. What would total assets be at the end of 2004 through 2006 if research and development costs were capitalized and expensed over three years?

c. What would shareholders' equity be at the end of 2004 through 2006 if research and development costs were capitalized and expensed over three years?

d. What would cash from operations and cash expended on investing activities be for 2004 through 2006 if research and development costs were capitalized and expensed over three years?

e. What would the following ratios be, assuming that (1) research and development costs were expensed as incurred and (2) research and development costs were capitalized and expensed over three years?

    i.   return on assets

    ii.   debt-to-equity ratio

    iii. profit margin percentage

f. How would your interpretation of Florze differ depending on how research and development costs are accounted for? Which accounting approach do you think is more appropriate? Explain. Your answer should consider the objectives of the users and preparers of accounting information, as well as the accounting concepts discussed in Chapter 5.

P9-7. **(Effect of a recording error on the financial statements, LO 2, 3, 8, 9)** In 2001 Zumbro Ltd. (Zumbro) purchased a large delivery truck for $72,000. In error, Zumbro's bookkeeper recorded the purchase as an expense rather than capitalizing the cost and recording it on the balance sheet as an asset. The error went unnoticed until late in 2004, when the truck was sold for $12,000 and no record could be found of it in the accounts.

Required:

a. Show the entry that Zumbro's bookkeeper made to record the purchase of the truck. Show the entry that the bookkeeper should have made.

b. Zumbro uses the straight-line method for amortizing its vehicles and the useful life assigned to similar vehicles in the past has been five years. What would be the effect of the error on net income and total assets (amount and direction of the error) in 2001, 2002, and 2003?

c. What would be the effect of the error on net income and total assets (amount and direction of the error) in 2004, the year the truck was sold?

d. What would be the effect of the error on the cash flow statement in each of years 2001 through 2004?

e. Assuming the error is material, what would the implications of this error be for users of the financial statements? Explain.

P9-8. **(Effect of a recording error on the financial statements, LO 2, 3, 8, 9)** In 2004 We-Non-Cha Forest Products Ltd. (We-Non-Cha) purchased and installed a new state-of-the-art lathe line in its lumber manufacturing facility in British Columbia. The new lathe line cost $7,000,000 to purchase and install, all of which was capitalized. The line is being amortized on a declining balance basis at 20% per year. We-Non-Cha used its own employees to install the line. Because of errors made by We-Non-Cha's employees, it was necessary to remove parts of the lathe line after they were already installed to reinforce the building to meet safety standards. The extra work added $800,000 to the cost of the lathe line and is included in the $7,000,000 cost.

Required:

a. How should the cost of the extra work have been accounted for? Explain.

b. What would be the effect of the error on net income and total assets (amount and direction of the error) in 2004, 2005, and 2006? Explain your reasoning.

c. What would be the effect of the error on the cash flow statement in each of years 2004 through 2006?

d. Assuming the error is material, what would the implications of this error be for users of the financial statements? Explain.

P9-9. **(Accounting for a change in accounting estimate, LO 3, 7)** On October 1, 2001 Independent Manufacturing Inc. (Independent) purchased a state-of-the-art mould-casting machine for its manufacturing facility for $8,200,000. Independent's management estimated that the machine would be useful for eight years, at which time the machine could be sold for $500,000. Independent uses straight-line amortization on all its capital assets. In September 2005 management realized that because of rapid technological changes, the machine would not likely be useful beyond fiscal 2007. Therefore, Independent decided to shorten its estimate of the machine's useful life to six years and the estimate of the residual value to zero. Independent's year end is September 30.

Required:

a. Is the change being made by Independent considered a change in accounting policy or a change in accounting estimate? Explain. How would the change be accounted for?

b. What amortization expense would Independent have originally reported in fiscal 2002, 2003, and 2004 for the mould-casting machine?

c. What amortization expense would Independent have reported in fiscal 2002, 2003, and 2004 for the mould-casting machine after the accounting change had been made?

d. What amortization expense will Independent report for the year ended September 30, 2005?

e. What are the implications of this change to users of the financial statements? Explain.

f. Do you think that this type of change can be objectively made? Explain. What possible motivations could Independent's managers have for making the change? Explain.

P9-10. **(Accounting for a change in accounting policy, LO 3, 7)** On October 1, 2001, Eureka Corp. (Eureka) purchased state-of-the-art equipment for $10,200,000. Eureka's management estimated that the machine would be useful for six years, at which time the equipment could be sold for $500,000. Eureka's management decided that it would use declining-balance amortization at 25% for the equipment. In fiscal 2005 management decided that it would switch from declining-balance amortization to straight-line amortization. Management estimated that the equipment had a remaining useful life of four years from September 2005 (eight years from its initial purchase in 2001). Eureka's year end is September 30.

Required:

    a. Is the change being made by Eureka considered a change in accounting policy or a change in accounting estimate? Explain. How should the change be accounted for?

    b. What amortization expense would Eureka have originally reported in 2002, 2003, and 2004 for the equipment?

    c. What amortization expense would Eureka have reported in fiscal 2002, 2003, and 2004 for the equipment after the accounting change had been made?

    d. What amortization expense will Eureka report for the year ended September 30, 2005?

    e. What are the implications of this change to users of the financial statements? Explain.

    f. How do you think Eureka's management could justify the change in accounting? Is it possible that the change could satisfy the self-interests of Eureka's management? Explain.

P9-11. **(Effect of accounting on business decisions, LO 6, 9)** Judge Ltd. (Judge) operates a small chain of auto supply shops. The company has been in business for many years and for most of that time it was owned and operated by the Judge family. In recent years Judge has been in financial difficulty and management has been turned over to a team of professional managers. The managers own 10% of the shares of Judge. The Judge family owns the remainder of the shares. As result of the financial difficulties, Judge agreed to a number of strict accounting-based covenants with its creditors, including a requirement that Judge's debt-to-equity ratio not go above 1.5:1 at the end of any quarter over the term of either its bank loan or its long-term debt. If the covenant is violated, all loans become payable in full in 30 days.

Judge owns a piece of land and a building that it has not used for four years. The building housed the first of Judge's shops, but it is no longer appropriate for use. The building is in very poor condition and is not in a very good part of town. Judge has not been able to find a tenant or a buyer, even though it has been looking for both for over two years. The land and building have a NBV of $1,685,000. Judge Ltd. has received an offer of $1,000,000 for the land and building. The offer is attractive, especially because it would provide some urgently needed cash. The offer expires on June 30, 2005, the last day of Judge's fiscal year, and it appears unlikely that it will be renewed.

It is now June 27, 2005. Judge's management estimates that net income for the year will be about $225,000. Management also projects that on June 30, 2005 current liabilities will be $575,000 and long-term debt will be $1,675,000. Capital stock on June 30, 2005 will be $800,000 and retained earnings on June 30, 2004 were $725,000.

You have been asked by Judge's president to prepare a report discussing all the business and accounting issues relevant to the land and building.

Required:

Prepare the report requested by Judge's president.

P9-12. **(Effect of accounting on business decisions, LO 2, 3, 6)** Togo Ltd. (Togo) and Fairfax Inc. (Fairfax) are small property development companies. Ms. Bessnerdium owns 60% of the shares of each of the companies and the rest of the shares are owned by separate consortiums of investors in the cities where the companies own properties. Togo owns several small apartment buildings in Ottawa and Fairfax owns a number of apartments in Windsor. Recently Togo and Fairfax traded buildings. Fairfax received from Togo a building that had a cost of $3,765,000 and accumulated amortization of $1,950,000, and Togo received from Fairfax a building that had a cost of $4,720,000 and accumulated amortization $1,425,000. Both buildings were appraised by independent appraisers, who estimated that the market value of each building was between $9,300,000 and $10,500,000.

Required:

    a. Prepare the journal entries that Fairfax and Togo would have to make to record the exchange of the buildings.

    b. What would be the effect of the exchange on each company's financial statements in the year of the exchange? Explain.

    c. What would be the effect of the exchange on each company's financial statements in the year following the transactions? Explain.

    d. Why do you think Fairfax and Togo entered into the exchange?

    e. Do you think the accounting treatments you prescribed in (a) make sense? Use the accounting concepts from Chapter 5 to support and oppose the accounting treatment you prescribed.

    f. If you were responsible for setting accounting standards, how would you require companies in the situation of Fairfax and Togo to account for these transactions? Explain your reasoning.

P9-13. (**Basket purchase, LO 2, 3, 5**) Quabbin Corp. (Quabbin) is a small manufacturing company in Regina. It is owned by five shareholders, two of whom manage the company. The other three are silent investors who invested when the company was struggling financially. The three silent investors live in British Columbia. Quabbin also has significant borrowings from the bank and it anticipates that it will have to request a significant increase in its line of credit in the next few months.

Recently Quabbin purchased some land, a building, and a number of pieces of used equipment from a bankrupt company. The total cost of the bundle of goods was $4,500,000. For accounting purposes Quabbin estimates that the building will last about 12 years and the equipment should last about five years. It is expected that neither the building nor the equipment will have any residual value. For tax purposes CCA on the building can be charged at 4% per year on a declining balance basis. CCA on the equipment is 30% per year declining balance. CCA cannot be claimed on the land.

The land, building, and equipment were appraised by Quabbin to ensure it was getting a good deal before they were purchased. The land was appraised at between $950,000 and $1,300,000, the building at between $2,100,000 and $2,800,000, and the equipment at between $1,500,000 and $2,000,000.

You have been asked for advice by Quabbin's controller about how to account for the purchase of the land, building, and equipment. The controller has requested that you explain your recommendation fully so that he can in turn explain the situation to the managers. Your report should also provide the journal entry that Quabbin would make to record its purchase of the land, building, and equipment.

Required:

Prepare the report.

P9-14. (**Preparing amortization schedules, LO 2, 3, 4, 6**) In July 2002 Yreka Palladium Mines Inc. (Yreka), a public company, began operation of its new palladium mine. Geologists estimate that the mine contains about 235,000 ounces of palladium. Yreka incurred the following capital costs in starting up the mine:

Exploration and development	$18,000,000
Mine extraction equipment	22,000,000
Buildings	3,000,000

The exploration and development costs were incurred to find the mine and prepare it for operations. The mine extraction equipment should be useful for the entire life of the mine and Yreka should be able to sell the equipment for $1,500,000 when the mine is exhausted in ten years. The buildings are expected to last much longer than the ten-year life of the mine, but they will not be useful once the mine is shut down.

The production engineers estimate that all the palladium can be removed from the mine over ten years. They estimate the following year-by-year production for the mine:

2002	5,000 ounces
2003	20,000 ounces
2004–2009	30,000 ounces
2010	20,000 ounces
2011	10,000 ounces

Required:

a. Show the journal entries necessary to record the purchase of the extraction equipment and the construction of the buildings.

b. Prepare amortization schedules using the straight-line, declining balance (20% per year), and unit-of-production methods for the three types of capital costs.

c. Which method would you recommend that Yreka use to amortize its capital assets? Explain.

d. The mine is viable as long as the cash cost of extracting the palladium remains below the price Yrkea can obtain for its palladium. If the price falls below the cash cost of extraction, it may be necessary to close the mine temporarily until prices rise. What would be the effect on amortization if the mine were temporarily shut down?

e. Under some circumstances it may become necessary to shut the mine permanently. How would you account for the capital assets if the mine had to be shut down permanently? Show the journal entries that you would make in regard to the capital assets in the event the mine had to close permanently. State any assumptions you make.

P9-15. (**Full costing versus successful efforts, LO 3, 4, 9**) Forillon Exploration Ltd. (Forillon) and Gullbridge Gas Inc. (Gullbridge) are natural gas exploration and development companies. In 2005 both companies did extensive exploration in northern Alberta. Each company drilled seven wells and each found gas in three of the wells. The cost of exploring for the gas and drilling the wells was $2,000,000 per well. During 2005 each successful well produced $945,000 in gas revenue.

Both companies paid royalties to the Alberta government equal to 25% of the revenues from gas sales. In addition, for both companies the cost of producing the natural gas was $56,000 per well, general and administrative costs totalled $220,000, and interest costs were $105,000. Income taxes were $72,000. Geologists estimate that in 2005, 10% of the gas reserves in the wells was extracted and sold. The only difference between the two companies is that Forillon uses the successful efforts method for accounting for gas exploration costs and Gullbridge uses full costing.

Required:

a. Prepare income statements for 2005 for Forillon and Gullbridge. Assume that both companies use the unit-of-production method to amortize exploration costs.

b. Prepare the journal entry required by each company to record the cost of exploring for natural gas. Assume that all expenditures were paid in cash.

c. Suppose that total assets before accounting for gas exploration costs was $27,000,000 for both companies. How would the balance sheets of the two companies differ?

d. Calculate the return on assets and profit margin for the two companies. Explain the difference between the two companies.

e. Which company is more successful? Explain. Which company would you invest in if you could only invest in one of them? Explain.

P9-16. (**Full costing versus successful efforts, LO 3, 4, 9**) Droxford Exploration Ltd. (Droxford) and Bartibog Inc. (Bartibog) are oil exploration and development companies. In 2003 both companies did extensive exploration in Alberta. Each company drilled 12 wells and each found gas in four of the wells. The cost of exploring for the oil and drilling the wells was $1,500,000 per well. During 2005 each successful well produced $1,500,000 in revenue.

Both companies paid royalties to the Alberta government equal to 25% of the revenues from oil sales. In addition, for both companies the cost of producing the oil was $226,000 per well, general and administrative costs totalled $420,000, and interest costs were $305,000. Income taxes were $72,000. Geologists estimate that in 2003, 15% of the oil reserves in the wells was extracted and sold. The only difference between the two companies is that Droxford uses the successful efforts method for accounting for oil exploration costs and Bartibog uses full costing.

Required:

a. Prepare income statements for 2003 for Droxford and Bartibog. Assume that both companies use the unit-of-production method to amortize exploration costs.

b. Prepare the journal entry required by each company to record the cost of exploring for oil. Assume that all expenditures were paid in cash.

c. Suppose that total assets before accounting for oil exploration costs was $42,000,000 for both companies. How would the balance sheets of the two companies differ?

d. Calculate the return on assets and profit margin for the two companies. Explain the differences between the two companies.

e. What difference does it make which method of accounting for exploration a company uses? Why do you think Droxford and Bartibog would choose one over the other? Explain fully. Remember that both methods are allowed by GAAP.

P9-17. **(Observing the effects of accounting choices on the cash flow statement, LO 4, 8)**
Barkway Inc. (Barkway) is in the process of finalizing its cash flow statement for 2006. The statement has been completely prepared except for the new product development costs that the controller has not decided how to account for. Preliminary net income, *before* accounting for the development costs, is $97,000. The product development costs for the year are $82,000. Based on the controller's interpretation of the *CICA Handbook*, an argument could be made for either capitalizing the costs or expensing them. Barkway's preliminary cash flow statement is shown below:

Barkway Inc. Cash Flow Statement For the Year Ended August 31, 2006	
Cash from operations	
Net income	$ ▮▮▮▮
Add: Amortization	37,000
Less: Gain on sale of capital assets	21,000
Less: Net increase in non-cash working capital	35,000
Cash from operations	▮▮▮▮
Investing activities	
Proceeds from the sale of capital assets	49,000
Purchase of capital assets	(98,000)
Cash from (used for) investing activities	▮▮▮▮
Financing activities	
Increase in long-term debt	75,000
Repayment of mortgage loan	(25,000)
Dividends	(10,000)
Cash from (used for) financing activities	▮▮▮▮
Change in cash during 2006	▮▮▮▮
Cash and equivalents, beginning of the year	22,000
Cash and equivalents, end of the year	$ ▮▮▮▮

Required:

   a. Complete the cash flow statement (shaded boxes) assuming that:

     i. the new product development costs are capitalized and amortized, and

     ii. the new product development costs are expensed when incurred.

      Assume that if the product development costs are capitalized, it is not necessary to amortize any of the costs in 2006.

   b. Compare the two cash flow statements. How is your evaluation of Barkway influenced by the two statements?

   c. How are the balance sheet and the income statement affected by the accounting treatment for the new product development costs?

   d. If Barkway's management received their bonuses based on net income, which treatment for the product development costs do you think they would prefer? Explain.

P9-18. **(Observing the effects of accounting choices on the cash flow statement, LO 4, 8)** Juskatla Ltd. (Juskatla) is in the process of finalizing its cash flow statement for 2004. The statement has been completely prepared except for some costs that the controller is not sure whether to classify as repairs or betterments. Normally these types of costs are relatively minor, but this year they were significant and so the classification will have an impact on the financial statements. The preliminary net loss, *before* accounting for the repairs/betterments, is $425,000. The repair/betterment costs for the year are $210,000. The nature of the costs is ambiguous so the controller will likely be able to classify them as either repairs or betterments.

Juskatla Ltd.
Cash Flow Statement
For the Year Ended April 30, 2004

Cash from operations	
Net loss	$
Add: Amortization	275,000
Add: Loss on sale of capital assets	95,000
Add: Net decrease in non-cash working capital	112,000
Cash from operations	
Investing activities	
Proceeds from the sale of capital assets	310,000
Purchase of capital assets	(1,325,000)
Cash from (used for) investing activities	
Financing activities	
Increase in long-term debt	1,000,000
Repayment of long-term loan	(750,000)
Sale of common stock	1,050,000
Cash from (used for) financing activities	
Change in cash during 2004	
Cash and equivalents, beginning of the year	98,000
Cash and equivalents, end of the year	$

Required:

   a. Complete the cash flow statement (shaded boxes) assuming that:

     i. the costs are treated as betterments, and

     ii. the costs are treated as repairs.

      Assume that if the costs are treated as betterments, it will be necessary to amortize $40,000 in 2004.

   b. Compare the two cash flow statements. How is your evaluation of Juskatla influenced by the two statements?

   c. How are the balance sheet and the income statement affected by the accounting treatment for the repairs/betterments?

d. Assuming that the controller is correct in her belief that the costs can be reasonably classified as either repairs or betterments, what factors would you advise the controller to consider in making her decision? Explain.

P9-19. **(Evaluating and interpreting the effects of a write-down, LO 4, 6)** Meridian Ltd. (ML) is a public company that manufactures machine parts. In its most recent financial statements ML wrote down $175,000,000 of its assets. The assets will continue to be used by ML. The new president and CEO of ML announced that the write-downs were the result of competitive pressures and poor performance of the company in the last year. The write-downs were reported separately in ML's income statement as a "non-recurring" item. A non-recurring item is "an item that results from transactions or events that are not expected to occur frequently over several years, or do not typify normal business activities of the entity." The write-off is not included in the calculation of operating income.

ML's summarized income statement for the year ended December 31, 2004 is (amounts in millions of dollars):

Revenue		$625
Operating expenses		
Cost of goods sold	$470	
Amortization	87	
Selling, general, and administrative costs	82	639
Operating income		(14)
Other expenses		
Non-recurring item	175	
Interest expense	33	
Income tax expense	(53)	155
Net income		($169)

The write-downs will reduce the amortization expense by $22,000,000 per year for each of the next eight years. After the announcement and release of the income statement, analysts revised their forecasts of earnings for the next three years to:

Year ended December 31, 2005	$15,000,000
Year ended December 31, 2006	$47,000,000
Year ended December 31, 2007	$95,000,000

Required:

a. What would net income be in each of 2004 through 2007 had ML not written off the assets and continued to amortize them? Assume that the operations of ML do not change regardless of the accounting method used.

b. Why do you think management might have undertaken the decision to write off the assets?

c. As an investor trying to evaluate the performance and predict future profitability, what problems do asset write-downs of this type create for you? Consider how the write-off is reflected in the income statement and use the ML case as a basis for your discussion.

■ Using Financial Statements

Rogers Wireless Communications Inc.

Rogers Wireless Communications Inc. (Rogers) is Canada's largest national wireless communications service provider, offering subscribers a broad spectrum of wireless communications products and services. With 2.9 million wireless customers, its seamless cellular network covers 93% of the Canadian population with analog coverage and over 83% of the population with digital coverage. Rogers Wireless Communications Inc., which operates under the co-brand Rogers AT&T Wireless, is 51% owned by Rogers Communications and 33.3% owned equally by AT&T Corp. and British Telecommunications plc.[10]

www.rogers.com

Rogers's consolidated statements of income, extracts from its consolidated balance sheets and consolidated statements of cash flows, along with some extracts from the notes to the financial statements, are provided in Exhibit 9-9.[11] Use this information to respond to questions FS9-1 to FS9-9.

Exhibit 9-9

Rogers AT&T Wireless Financial Statements

consolidated statements of income

(In thousands of dollars and number of shares, except per share amounts)
Years ended December 31

	2000	1999
Revenue (note 10)	$ 1,532,063	$ 1,351,723
Operating, general and administrative expenses	1,121,139	929,395
Management fees (note 12B)	10,374	9,851
Operating income before depreciation and amortization	400,550	412,477
Depreciation and amortization	334,619	285,458
Operating income	65,931	127,019
Interest expense (income):		
Long-term debt	128,472	153,772
Notes payable to Rogers Communications Inc.	4,107	11,347
Other	—	(1,803)
Loss on early repayment of long-term debt (note 7G)	—	69,331
Other expense	577	142
	133,156	232,789
Loss before income taxes	(67,225)	(105,770)
Income taxes (recovery) (note 11)	4,524	(69,941)
Loss for the year	$ (71,749)	$ (35,829)

consolidated statements of cash flows

(In thousands of dollars)
Years ended December 31

	2000	1999
Cash provided by (used in):		
Operating activities:		
Loss for the year	$ (71,749)	$ (35,829)
Adjustments to reconcile net income to cash flow:		
Depreciation and amortization	334,619	285,458
Loss on early repayment of long-term debt	—	69,331
	262,870	318,960
Changes in:		
Accounts receivable	(36,651)	(23,400)
Other assets	(7,742)	(6,312)
Accounts payable and accrued liabilities and unearned revenue	4,201	(12,698)
Amounts due to/from parent and affiliated companies, net	2,239	(10,668)
Investing activities:		
Additions to fixed assets	(525,993)	(400,959)
Acquisition of business (note 3)	—	(19,750)
	(525,993)	(420,709)

consolidated balance sheets

(In thousands of dollars)
As at December 31

	2000	1999
Assets		
Fixed assets (note 4)	$ 1,972,110	$ 1,778,545
Goodwill	9,549	12,040
Accounts receivable, net of allowance for doubtful accounts of $52,453 (1999 — $39,013)	215,696	179,045
Due from parent and affiliated companies (note 12A)	—	514
Deferred charges (note 5)	90,417	75,124
Other assets (note 6)	76,571	71,349
	$ 2,364,343	$ 2,116,617

Exhibit 9-9 (continued)

Rogers AT&T Wireless Financial
Statements

2. Significant accounting policies

B. Capitalization policy

Fixed assets are recorded at purchase cost. During construction of the wireless communications network, direct costs plus a portion of overhead costs are capitalized. Repairs and maintenance expenditures are charged to operating expense as incurred.

C. Depreciation

Fixed assets are depreciated over their estimated useful lives at the following annual rates:

Asset	Basis	Rate
Buildings	Diminishing balance	5%
Network equipment	Straight line	$6\frac{2}{3}$% to 25%
Network radio base station equipment	Straight line	$12\frac{1}{2}$%
Computer software and hardware	Straight line	$14\frac{1}{3}$% to $33\frac{1}{3}$%
Furniture, fixtures and office equipment	Diminishing balance	20%
Leasehold improvements	Straight line	Over term of lease
Other equipment	Mainly diminishing balance	30% to $33\frac{1}{3}$%

As a result of the introduction of new network technology planned for 2001, the Company undertook a review of the remaining useful life of certain of its network equipment. Effective January 1, 2001, the Company changed the estimated useful lives of certain network equipment, which will result in an increase in depreciation expense in 2001 of approximately $25,000,000.

D. Goodwill

The Company amortizes goodwill related to acquired messaging operations on a straight-line basis over a period of five years. Amortization of goodwill for 2000 amounted to $2,491,000 (1999 — $415,000). Accumulated amortization of goodwill at December 31, 2000 amounted to $2,906,000 (1999 — $415,000).

    The carrying value of goodwill is periodically reviewed to determine if an impairment in value has occurred. The Company measures the potential impairment in value by comparing the carrying value to the undiscounted value of expected future operating income before depreciation and amortization, interest and income taxes. Based on its review, the Company does not believe that an impairment of the carrying value of goodwill has occurred to date.

3. Acquisition

Effective November 8, 1999, the Company acquired the net assets of a messaging business for cash consideration of $19,750,000, including costs of acquisition of $150,000. The acquisition was accounted for using the purchase method and the operating results of the acquired business have been included in the consolidated statements of income from the date of acquisition.

    Net assets acquired, at fair values, were as follows:

(In thousands of dollars)

Goodwill	$ 12,455
Fixed assets	7,524
Other assets	1,792
	21,771
Liabilities	2,021
	$ 19,750

4. Fixed assets

(In thousands of dollars)

	2000	1999
Land and buildings	$ 116,920	$ 116,970
Network equipment	1,800,994	1,579,063
Network radio base station equipment	1,091,739	1,085,389
Computer software and hardware	467,852	393,486
Furniture, fixtures and office equipment	51,950	42,883
Leasehold improvements	34,120	16,725
Other equipment	12,939	10,597
	3,576,514	3,245,113
Less accumulated depreciation	1,604,404	1,466,568
	$ 1,972,110	$ 1,778,545

The Company has a significant ongoing capital expenditure program for the expansion and improvement of its network. The Company estimates that its capital expenditures for 2001 will range between $650,000,000 and $690,000,000.

Exhibit 9-9 (continued)

Rogers AT&T Wireless Financial
Statements

6. Other assets

(In thousands of dollars)

	2000	1999
Brand licence costs, less accumulated amortization of $10,290 (1999 — $7,770)	$ 27,510	$ 30,030
Prepaid expenses	27,691	14,690
Inventories	14,064	21,336
Miscellaneous notes and loans receivable from employees	6,333	4,648
Amounts receivable from employees under RCI share purchase plans	442	509
Other	531	136
	$ 76,571	$ 71,349

In 1996, the Company entered into a brand licence agreement with AT&T Canada Enterprises Inc. ("AT&T") providing the Company with, among other things, the right to use the AT&T brand names. The costs of entering into the brand licence agreement amounted to $37,800,000. These costs are being deferred and amortized on a straight-line basis to expense over the 15-year term of the brand licence agreement. Amortization of the brand licence cost for 2000 was $2,520,000 (1999 — $2,520,000).

FS9-1. The following questions pertain to Rogers' fixed assets:

a. What amount of fixed assets did Rogers report on its December 31, 2000 balance sheet?

b. What does the amount on the balance sheet represent (how would you explain what the amount means to a novice user of financial statements)?

c. What proportion of Rogers' assets are capital assets? Why do you think the proportion is so large? (When you answer, consider the nature of the business.)

d. What is the cost of the capital assets Rogers reported on April 30, 2000?

e. What amortization methods does Rogers use? Do you think that it is reasonable that Rogers uses more than one amortization method?

f. How much amortization has been accumulated against the fixed assets?

g. What was Rogers' amortization expense for the year ended December 31, 2000?

h. What is Rogers' capitalization policy? What does Rogers' capitalize as the cost of the wireless communication network? What do you think that these costs include?

i. How are repairs and maintenance accounted for? Is this a reasonable treatment for these costs? Explain.

j. Can you determine the NBV of Rogers' network equipment? Explain.

k. Over how many years is Rogers amortizing its network radio base station equipment?

FS9-2. Describe the change in accounting estimate that Rogers will be implementing in its 2001 fiscal year. What are the implications of the change to the financial statements and the financial statement users? If the change were implemented for the 2000 fiscal year, and the effect of the change was the same as indicated in the note, what would have been Rogers' net income for the year ended December 31, 2000? What would cash from operations have been?

FS9-3. How does Rogers amortize its leasehold improvements? Do you think that this is a reasonable basis for amortizing the leasehold improvements? Explain. Do you think that it would be more appropriate to amortize the leasehold improvement over the life of the asset being leased? Explain.

FS9-4. How much cash did Rogers spend on fixed assets during 2000? How much money does Rogers estimate that it will spend on capital expenditures in 2001? How is this information useful to users of the financial statements?

FS9-5. The asset side of Rogers' consolidated balance sheet does not have a format that is commonly seen. Describe how Rogers' consolidated balance sheet differs from the more common format and provide an explanation for why the unusual format is used.

FS9-6. The following questions have to do with Rogers' goodwill:

a. How much goodwill does Rogers report on its December 31, 2000 balance sheet?

b. What is the cost of the goodwill?

FS9-7. What was Rogers' net income for the year ended December 31, 2000? What was its cash from operations? How do you explain the large difference between net income and CFO? Based on your assessment of net income and CFO, did Rogers have a good year or a bad year in 2000?

FS9-8. What was Rogers' return on assets for the year ended December 31, 2000? What would the return on assets be for the year ended December 31, 1999 if total assets on December 31, 1998 were $2,023,813,000?

FS9-9. The following questions have to do with "other assets":
   a. How much does Rogers report on its December 31, 2000 balance sheet for other assets?
   b. What are these other assets?
   c. Why do you think they are grouped together on a single line on the balance sheet?
   d. Explain what the "brand license costs" is? What type of asset is brand license costs? Why do you think this expenditure is classified as an asset?
   f. How are the brand license costs being amortized (method and useful life)? Do you think that the useful life that Rogers has estimated is reasonable? Explain.
   g. What was the amortization expense for the brand license costs in 2000? How much of the brand license costs have been amortized?
   h. What will the amortization expense for brand license costs be in the year the license agreement expires?

■ Analyzing Mark's Work Wearhouse

M9-1. Explain what the balance reported on MWW's balance sheet for capital assets represents.

M9-2. What types of capital assets does MWW own? Describe what each category represents.

M9-3. What is the historical cost of MWW's capital assets on January 27, 2001?

M9-4. How much amortization has been accumulated against MWW's capital assets on January 27, 2001?

M9-5. Does MWW own all the capital assets it reports on its balance sheet? Explain.

M9-6. At the end of fiscal 1999 MWW owned a piece of land that had a cost of $45,000 and a NBV of $45,000. Explain why the cost of the land and the NBV of the land were the same.

M9-7. How does MWW amortize its capital assets? Why does MWW amortize its capital assets (aside from the fact it is required by GAAP)?

M9-8. Under what circumstances do you think how MWW amortizes its capital assets would matter to some of its stakeholders?

M9-9. How much cash did MWW spend on capital assets during fiscal 2001? Where did you find the answer?

Endnotes

1. Clarence Byrd, Ida Chen, and Heather Chapman, *Financial Reporting in Canada*, 26th Edition, section 3060. The Virtual Professional Library. CD-ROM. 2002.
2. Extracted from North American Palladium Ltd.'s 2000 annual report.
3. Extracted from Brookfield Properties Corporation's 2000 annual report.
4. Extracted from ClubLink Corporation's 2000 annual report.
5. Extracted from Dofasco Inc.'s 2000 annual report.
6. Extracted from Mosaid Technologies Incorporated's 2001 annual report.
7. Panel A extracted from Suncor Energy Inc.'s 2000 annual report. Panel B extracted from Bow Valley Energy Ltd.'s 2000 annual report.
8. Extracted from GenSci Regeneration Sciences Inc.'s 2000 annual report.
9. Extracted from Fortis Inc.'s 1999 annual report.
10. Extracted from Rogers Wireless Communications Inc.'s web site at http://www.rogers.com.
11. Extracted from Rogers Wireless Communications Inc.'s 2000 annual report.

Chapter 10

Liabilities

Chapter Outline

Learning Objectives

Introduction

What Are Liabilities?

Current Liabilities

Bonds and Other Forms of Long-Term Debt

Leases

Pensions and Other Post-Retirement Benefits

Future Income Taxes

Debt and Taxes

Contingencies

Commitments

Subsequent Events

Financial Statement Analysis Issues

Solved Problem

Summary of Key Points

Key Terms and Similar Terms

Questions, Exercises, and Problems

Using Financial Statements

Analyzing Mark's Work Wearhouse

Learning Objectives

After studying the material in this chapter you will be able to:

LO 1.   Explain what liabilities are and how they are valued.

LO 2.   Describe the nature and type of current liabilities and how current liabilities are accounted for.

LO 3.   Recognize the characteristics of bonds and other forms of long-term debt and explain how the values of these liabilities are determined.

LO 4.   Discuss how to account for bonds and other forms of long-term debt.

LO 5.   Explain the fundamentals of leasing and how leases are accounted for and reported in the financial statements.

LO 6.   Characterize the basics of pensions and pension accounting.

LO 7.   Describe future income taxes and explain how they arise.

LO 8.   Recognize the nature of contingencies, commitments, and subsequent events, and understand the reporting issues surrounding each.

LO 9.   Analyze and interpret information about liabilities in financial statements.

Introduction

We now turn our attention to liabilities. Liabilities are obligations—to provide cash, goods, or services to customers, suppliers, employees, governments, lenders, and anyone else an entity "owes something to." A liability can be very short-term; for example, a loan that a lender can demand repayment of at any time or payments that must be made to suppliers within 10 days. Or a liability can exist for 10, 20, 30, or more years, such as a mortgage from a bank or bonds sold to investors to finance a capital asset, such as a building, that will contribute to earning revenue over a long period of time.

Information about liabilities is very important for assessing the liquidity and solvency of an entity. Liabilities often represent obligations to pay significant amounts of cash at specified times, and the amounts and timing of the payments are usually not negotiable. As a result, knowing the timing and terms of these commitments can be crucial for evaluating the ability of an entity to meet its obligations and achieve its objectives. Of course, like most of the other accounting issues that we have discussed in this book, accounting for liabilities is not always straightforward. For example, some of an entity's "obligations" may not be reported on its balance sheet.

Accounting for liabilities, particularly for public companies, involves the application of complex GAAP rules. Accounting for leases, pensions, and future income taxes are among the most difficult topics of GAAP accounting to understand. These complex rules evolved in response to some difficult economic problems. These complex accounting topics are introduced in this chapter with the objective of providing you with a basic understanding of how the amounts that appear on the balance sheet—amounts that can sometimes be very large—are determined and what they mean. In particular, the three areas of leases, pensions, and future income taxes are examined. Also, these are areas in which a private company might choose not to use GAAP because the rules are complex and the benefit to the users of these companies' financial statements may be limited.

What Are Liabilities?

A liability is an obligation. It can be an obligation to pay money to suppliers, lenders, employees, shareholders, or governments, or to provide goods or services to a customer. A liability can be current: the obligation has to be fulfilled within a year, or one operating cycle. A liability can be non-current: it may not have to be settled for many years. One might think that identifying liabilities is pretty straightforward, but like so many of the topics we have addressed in the book, the matter isn't always clear. To establish a framework for thinking about liabilities, let's look at the criteria GAAP use to determine whether a liability exists.

According to GAAP, liabilities have three characteristics:

1. They require the sacrifice of resources.
2. They are unavoidable.
3. They are the result of past transactions or economic events.

By these criteria, an amount owed to a supplier for inventory purchased—an account payable—is a liability because:

a. The supplier will have to be paid cash to satisfy the obligation. The entity is sacrificing a resource—cash—to meet its obligation.

b. There is a legal obligation to pay. The goods have been delivered and an invoice has been received. The supplier has a right to the money. The entity has to pay or face possible legal action. However, liabilities do not have to be legal obligations to meet this criterion.

c. The amount is owed because the supplier has already delivered the requested goods. This criterion reflects transactions-based historical cost accounting.

Accrued interest payable also meets the GAAP criteria for liabilities. At the end of a reporting period, entities must often make adjusting journal entries to accrue an Interest Expense and Interest Payable so that the cost of borrowing is reflected in the period the money was used, even though the interest does not have to be paid until later. There is a difference between accrued interest and accounts payable though, even though both are considered liabilities by GAAP. For accounts payable, there is a legal obligation to pay the supplier. For accrued interest, there is no legal obligation on the balance sheet date to pay the accrued interest. A legal obligation exists on the payment date, not before. A lender has no legal claim to interest payments before the payment date. The important point here is that a liability does not have to be a legal obligation to be reported under GAAP.

In contrast, agreements that commit an entity to purchase goods or services in the future are not reported as liabilities, according to GAAP. These types of arrangements are called executory contracts. When neither party to a contract has performed its part of the bargain, then neither the liability to pay for nor the asset representing the goods or services to be received is recorded. For example, it is common in professional sports for athletes to sign long-term, high-value, guaranteed contracts. (A very large contract signed in 2001 requires the team to pay the athlete US$250 million over ten years.) Under traditional GAAP, accounting the team's liability to pay the athlete and its right to the athlete's services are not reported on the sport team's balance sheet. This transaction is not reported as a liability because criterion (3) has not, according to GAAP, been met. The signing of the contract does not trigger recognition of the liability. Performance by the athlete triggers recognition. Once the athlete has played (assuming that he or she was not paid in advance), a liability for wages can be set up.

Then there are items that are reported in the liability section of the balance sheet that probably do not meet the GAAP criteria. Two examples of these "non-liability" liabilities are the deferred gains that Mark's Work Wearhouse (MWW) reports on the liability side of its balance sheet, and future income taxes, which are reported as liabilities on many entities' balance sheets. We will leave the discussion of these examples for later in the chapter. For now it can simply be explained that the deferred gains do not require future sacrifices, but are simply gains on the sale of assets that GAAP says cannot be recognized until later periods. Future income taxes may never have to be paid, so they may not meet the first criterion either.

Valuation of Liabilities

In principle, liabilities should be valued at their present value. For many liabilities the timing and amount of the cash flows are known, and in most other cases it is possible to make a reasonable estimate of the cash flows. In contrast, it is usually very difficult to estimate the timing and amount of cash flows that assets, especially capital assets, will produce. It is also possible to identify an appropriate rate for discounting the cash flows associated with liabilities. Long-term liabilities such as bonds and other long-term debt are valued at the present value of the cash flows that will be paid to the creditors. However, not all liabilities are discounted to their present value. Current liabilities, for example, are not discounted.

Let's look at an example that examines how liabilities are valued. On December 31, 2003 Rowena Inc. (Rowena) purchased heavy equipment from a dealer. The dealer, through the manufacturer, financed the purchase by giving Rowena a three-year, $300,000 interest-free loan. Under the terms of the loan Rowena is required to pay $100,000 on December 31 of each of the next three years. How much should Rowena report as a liability for the loan on its balance sheet on December 31, 2003 through 2006?

One possibility is for Rowena to report a liability equal to the actual number of dollars that it owes the dealer on each December 31. The amount that would be reported on each balance sheet can be seen in Column 1 of Table 10-1. With this

Table 10-1	Valuation of Rowena Inc.'s Loan from the Equipment Dealer	
	Column 1	**Column 2**
	Amount of liability using the nominal value of the liability	**Amount of liability using the discounted value of the liability**
December 31, 2003	$300,000	$244,371
December 31, 2004	200,000	171,252
December 31, 2005	100,000	90,090
December 31, 2006	0	0

approach, Rowena would not report an interest expense on its income statement (since the loan is interest free) and the liability would decrease each year by $100,000.

This approach is useful because it informs users of the exact number of dollars that are owed. It is also simple to use and understand. The problem is that it ignores the time value of money. (See Chapter 7 to refresh your understanding of the time value of money.) Even though the loan agreement states that the loan is interest-free, the economic reality is that there is a cost to borrowing; people don't lend money interest-free. When the time value of money is ignored, assets and liabilities are overstated.

Rowena's assets are overstated because the heavy equipment would be valued at $300,000 instead of the present value of the payments. (Remember, in the last chapter we said that interest should not be included in the cost of a capital asset once the asset starts operating.) By using the full amount owed to the dealer, Rowena is capitalizing interest as part of the cost of the heavy equipment. Liabilities are overstated because the amount of the loan implicitly includes the cost of borrowing. Net income is also overstated because the cost of borrowing is not expensed.

When the time value of money is considered, the amount that is reported on the December 31, 2003 balance sheet is equal to the present value of the payments that must be made to the dealer of the equipment. Assuming a discount rate of 11%, the amount that should be reported on December 31, 2003 is equal to the present value of three $100,000 payments made at the end of each of the next three years. The appropriate discount factor can be found in Appendix B, Table B-3 (page B-6), Present Value of a $1 Annuity, because the payments represent an annuity of $100,000 per year for three years. The appropriate discount factor for December 31, 2003 is found at the intersection of the 11% column and the 3-period row. The amount that should be recorded as the liability on December 31, 2003, using the discounting approach, is $244,371. The calculation is shown below:

$$\text{Present value of payments} = \text{Annual payment} \times \text{Discount factor}$$
$$= \$100,000 \times 2.44371$$
$$= \$244,371$$

The amounts that would be reported on the balance sheets over the life of the loan are shown in Column 2 of Table 10-1. The calculations for the other years are left to the reader in the Question for Consideration on page 571.

Current Liabilities

Current liabilities are obligations that will be satisfied in one year or one operating cycle. Information about current obligations is important because it is relevant for assessing the short-term liquidity of an entity. Current liabilities are usually not discounted to their present value because the amount of time until they are settled is

Question for Consideration

Required

a. Use the information from the Rowena Inc. example (pages 569–570) to calculate the amount that would be reported on Rowena's balance sheet on December 31, 2004 and 2005 using the present value approach to valuing the liability.

b. Our discussion has explained that if Rowena's liability were not discounted, the amount of the liability and the amount of the asset would be overstated. Explain why the asset would be overstated if the liability were overstated.

Answer:

a. On December 31, 2004 Rowena still has two payments of $100,000 to make. The payments must be made on December 31, 2005 and December 31, 2006. The present value of these payments using a discount rate of 11% can be determined using the present value of an annuity table in Appendix B, Table 3 (page B-6). The appropriate present value factor of 1.71252 is found at the intersection of the 2-period row and the 11% column. The liability reported on December 31, 2005 would be:

$$\text{Present value of payments} = \text{Annual payment} \times \text{Discount factor}$$
$$= \$100,000 \times 1.71252$$
$$= \$171,252$$

For December 31, 2006 there is an obligation to make a single $100,000 payment in one year. The present value of the payment uses a discount factor of 0.90090. (This discount factor is found at the intersection of the 1-period row and 11% column of either Appendix B, Table B-1 (page B-2 or Table B-2 (page B-4). Either of these tables from Appendix B can be used because the amount is a single payment to be received one period from now, and under those conditions, both tables give the same answer.) The liability reported on December 31, 2006 would be:

$$\text{Present value of payments} = \text{Annual payment} \times \text{Discount factor}$$
$$= \$100,000 \times 0.90090$$
$$= \$90,090$$

b. With historical cost accounting the amount recorded as the cost of an asset is the amount paid when the asset is purchased. When an asset is purchased on credit with an interest-free loan, the question is, What is the actual cost? Using the $300,000 paid over the three years as the cost ignores the economic fact that borrowing money is not free, despite the terms of the loan. If the $300,000 amount is used, the amount capitalized includes the interest. Therefore, using the $300,000 overstates the cost of the asset by the amount of interest implicit in the loan— in this case, $55,629 ($300,000 − $244,371). An interesting question is, If Rowena purchased the heavy equipment for cash, how much would it have paid? A lot of factors come into play in determining the selling price, but it is likely that the amount would have been less than $300,000. How much less? It is hard to answer without actually making the purchase.

relatively short, and as a result the difference between the present value and the stated value will be small. In this section we will look at a number of different types of current liabilities and discuss the issues that affect accounting for them.

Bank and Other Current Loans

Loans are reported as current liabilities in some circumstances. If all or part of a long-term liability must be repaid within the next year or operating cycle, the amount that is to be repaid is classified as current. For example, MWW classifies $10,905,000 of its long-term debt as a current liability because it is to be repaid within one year. This amount can be found in MWW's balance sheet and in Note 10 to the financial statements (see pages A-45 and A-55).

Demand loans are classified as current liabilities. A **demand loan** is a loan that must be repaid whenever the lender requests or demands repayment. Lenders often never demand repayment and the loans remain on the books for a long time, but because demand loans are payable at any time, they are classified as current. Loans from banks are often demand loans.

Revolving loans are also classified as current. A **revolving loan** is a loan that is expected to be renewed when it matures. If the revolving loan matures within the next year or operating cycle, it will be classified as current even though it is likely that the loan will be renewed at maturity. Note 9 to MWW's financial statements (see page A-54) describes a $75,000,000 revolving operating line of credit with a syndicate of Canadian banks. A **line of credit** is an arrangement with a lender that allows an entity to borrow up to a specified maximum amount when and if the entity requires the money. The line of credit is revolving because it matures every 364 days and must be extended at the request of MWW and with the agreement of the lenders.

Accounts Payable

Accounts Payable represents amounts that an entity owes to suppliers for goods and services. These goods and services include anything that the entity uses in the course of its business operations, including inventory, supplies, utilities, cleaning services, and so on. We have seen numerous examples of the recording and settlement of accounts payable throughout the book. Measuring the amount of accounts payable is usually not difficult because the recording is triggered by receipt of an invoice from the supplier. The amount of the invoice is recorded as an account payable, and when the amount owing is paid the balance in Accounts Payable is reduced.

Collections on Behalf of Third Parties

Most entities act as tax collectors for various government taxation authorities. For example, when we purchase merchandise in a store, in addition to the selling price of the merchandise we also pay the GST (goods and services tax) or the HST (harmonized sales tax) and in some provinces provincial sales tax. Employers withhold amounts from their employees' pay for items such as income taxes, employment insurance, and Canada or Québec Pension Plans. Employers also withhold amounts on behalf of employees for items such as employee shares of benefits, union dues, and so on.

GST/HST and provincial sales taxes collected from buyers and money withheld from an employee's pay do not belong to the entity. The entity has an obligation to send these amounts to the appropriate government agency, union, pension plan, and so on, and a liability is set up to reflect the obligation. For example, suppose MWW makes a $100 sale to a customer at one of its stores in Alberta. In addition to collecting $100 for the merchandise, the store will also collect $7 of GST. The entry that would be made to record the sale is:

Dr. Cash (assets +)	107	
Cr. Revenue (revenue +, shareholders' equity +)		100
Cr. GST payable (liabilities +)		7
To record the sale of merchandise and collection of GST.		

The $7 is a liability because the money does not belong to MWW. It belongs to the government. MWW is acting as a collector for the government. When MWW remits the money to the government, it would make the following entry:

Dr. GST payable (liabilities −)	7	
Cr. Cash (assets −)		7
To record remittance of GST to the government.		

An entity also must record liabilities when it withholds money from an employee's pay, again because the money withheld does not belong to the employer. The money has been collected from the employee on behalf third parties. For example, Mr. Barrows is a crane operator for Eyremore Inc. (Eyremore). Mr. Barrows earned $7,000 in May. From his May paycheque Eyremore withheld $2,000 for income taxes, $313 for Canada Pension Plan (CPP), $169 for Employment Insurance (EI), $90 in union dues, $450 for his employee contribution to the company pension plan, $100 for long-term disability insurance, and a $10 contribution to the United Way in Mr. Barrows' community. The journal entry that Eyremore would make to record Mr. Barrows' wages and the withholdings is:

Dr. Wages expense (expenses +, shareholders' equity −)	7,000	
Cr. Income taxes payable—employee (liabilities +)		2,000
Cr. CPP payable (liabilities +)		313
Cr. EI payable (liabilities +)		169
Cr. Union dues payable (liabilities +)		90
Cr. Pension plan contribution payable (liabilities +)		450
Cr. Disability insurance payable (liabilities +)		100
Cr. Charitable donation payable (liabilities +)		10
Cr. Cash (assets −)		3,868

To record wages and employee withholdings.

Of his $7,000 wages Mr. Barrows receives $3,868. The rest is collected and distributed on his behalf. The amount for income taxes payable is not for income taxes owed by Eyremore. These taxes are the income taxes of Mr. Barrows that Eyremore must collect by law on behalf of governments. Also, an entity would not make this entry for each employee. The entry would reflect wages and withholdings for the entire payroll of the company. When Eyremore sends the money owed to the appropriate parties, it would make the following entry:

Dr. Income taxes payable—employee (liabilities −)	2,000	
Dr. CPP payable (liabilities −)	313	
Dr. EI payable (liabilities −)	169	
Dr. Union dues payable (liabilities −)	90	
Dr. Pension plan contribution payable (liabilities −)	450	
Dr. Disability insurance payable (liabilities −)	100	
Dr. Charitable donation payable (liabilities −)	10	
Cr. Cash (assets −)		3,132

To record remittance of payroll withholdings.

Income Taxes Payable

Canadian businesses are required to pay tax on their income to both the federal and provincial governments. Most businesses are required to pay instalments throughout the year, based on their estimate of the amount of tax that will have to be paid for the year. A corporation does not have to file its tax return until six months after its fiscal year end, and an unincorporated business' taxes are included in the tax return of the proprietor or partner. In an entity's financial statements the amount of income taxes that are owed should be accrued. The amount accrued should be the difference between the estimated amount of income tax the entity must pay and the amount already paid for the year. The accrued amount is classified as a current liability.

Dividends Payable

Dividends payable is an obligation to pay the corporation's shareholders a dividend that has been declared. Once the board of directors has declared a dividend, the amount of the dividend is classified as a liability until it is paid. If Usona Ltd.'s

(Usona) board of directors declared a $100,000 dividend on December 15, 2006, but the cheques are not to be mailed to the shareholders until January 10, 2007, Usona would make the following journal entries to record the dividend declaration and subsequent payment of the dividend:

December 15, 2006
Dr. Retained earnings—dividends (shareholders' equity –)   100,000
    Cr. Dividends payable (liabilities +)   100,000
To record the declaration of a dividend on December 15, 2006.

January 10, 2007
Dr. Dividends payable (liabilities –)   100,000
    Cr. Cash (assets –)   100,000
To record the payment of a dividend on January 10, 2007.

If Usona's year end were December 31, the dividend payable would be reported as a current liability on its December 31, 2006 balance sheet.

Accrued Liabilities

An accrued liability is a liability that is recognized and recorded in the financial statements, but for which the recording is not triggered by an external event such as receipt of a bill or invoice. Accrued liabilities must be recorded with adjusting journal entries. Adjusting entries are necessary so that expenses associated with revenues earned in the period are properly matched to the period. Examples of accrued liabilities include:

- wages and salaries for employees that are unpaid at the end of a period
- interest costs incurred but not payable until a later period
- goods and services that have been acquired but not invoiced (and have not been recorded)
- warranty liabilities
- liabilities for affinity programs (for example, airline frequent flyer programs)
- liabilities to redeem coupons (for example, discount coupons for grocery products, Canadian Tire money)

All of these accrued liabilities require that the preparers of the financial statements determine the amount of the expense and associated liability, and record them with an adjusting journal entry. Some accrued liabilities can be estimated quite accurately. Accrued wages and salaries can be determined by referring to the number of hours worked or the proportion of salary earned from the end of the last pay period to the end of the reporting period.

Accrued interest payable can be calculated using the following formula:

$$\text{Accrued interest payable} = \frac{\text{Amount of}}{\text{loan}} \times \frac{\text{Interest}}{\text{rate}} \times \frac{\text{Proportion of the year}}{\text{since the last payment date}}$$

For example, Fordyce Ltd. (Fordyce) has a $250,000 revolving bank loan that carries an interest rate of 8% per year. Interest payments must be made quarterly on the first business day of January, April, July, and October. Fordyce has a December 31 year end. On December 31, 2006 Fordyce must accrue a $5,041($250,000 × 0.08 × 92 ÷ 365) accrued interest payable liability so that the cost of borrowing money is matched to the proper period. The adjusting journal entry that Fordyce would make on December 31, 2006 to accrue the interest expense and interest payable is:

Dr. Interest expense (expenses +, shareholders' equity –)   5,041
    Cr. Accrued interest payable (liabilities +)   5,041
To accrue interest expense and accrued interest payable on the bank loan.

On January 3, 2006 (the first working day in January 2007) Fordyce would record the following entry to record the payment of interest (the entry assumes that the interest expense incurred on January 1 and 2 will be paid in April):

Dr. Accrued interest payable (liabilities –)   5,041
    Cr. Cash (assets –)   5,041
To record the payment of interest on the bank loan.

Some accrued liabilities are more difficult to estimate. To accrue a warranty liability managers must estimate the average cost of providing warranty service to customers. If the entity has experience with a good or service, it can use historical information as a basis for making the estimate. It is more difficult to estimate the cost of providing warranty service to new products. It can also be difficult to make accurate estimates about frequent flyer programs, other affinity programs, and coupon programs. With these types of liabilities the redemption rate and cost must be estimated and there is the potential for significant errors. For example, a pizza chain might distribute $200,000 in discount coupons, but how many of those coupons will be redeemed by customers? It is the value of the redeemed coupons that should be accrued as a liability.

Estimation is integral to accounting. Simply because certain amounts are difficult to estimate does not mean that the estimates should not be made, or that they do not provide useful information to users of the financial statements. It is, however, important to be aware that these measurements are imprecise and that financial statement numbers vary with the estimates that the preparers make. In addition, because it is difficult to know exactly what the actual costs will be, these difficult-to-estimate accruals are attractive for earnings management. Remember in Chapter 7 we discussed how managers can use hidden reserves to manage earnings. Managers can use these more difficult-to-estimate accruals as the basis for creating hidden reserves.

Accrued liabilities for warranties and affinity programs can have non-current as well as current components. Carmakers, for instance, offer warranties of three or more years on their vehicles. The warranty cost must be estimated for each year that the warranty is offered.

Let's look at an example. Irricana Inc. (Irricana) offers a three-year warranty on its high-definition televisions. The television is a new product and a new technology for Irricana, so it does not have much experience in making an estimate of the cost of the warranty service. Based on an analysis by the company's engineers and data from the first sets sold, management has estimated that the average cost per television of warranty service will be $175. During 2004 Irricana sold 22,000 of its high-definition televisions. The estimated warranty expense and liability for televisions sold during 2004 is $3,850,000 (22,000 × $175). The engineers further estimate that 40% of warranty costs will be incurred in the next 12 months. The entry that Irricana would make to accrue the warranty expense and liability for 2004 would be:

Dr. Warranty expense (expenses +, shareholders' equity –)   3,850,000
    Cr. Warranty liability—current (liabilities +)   1,540,000
    Cr. Warranty liability—non-current (liabilities +)   2,310,000
To accrue warranty expense and liability for television sets sold during 2004.

During 2005 Irricana incurred actual warranty costs of $1,625,000, so the journal entry to record all warranty costs would be:

Dr. Warranty liability-current (liabilities –)   1,625,000
    Cr. Cash (assets –)   1,625,000
To record the payment for repairs of high-definition televisions under warranty.

That the actual cost of warranty repairs was not exactly the same as the amount accrued is not surprising or a problem. Estimates by their nature are imprecise, and over time annual deviations will either average out or will be corrected with adjusting entries in later periods. At the end of 2005, in addition to accruing an expense and liability for warranty costs for televisions sold in 2005, Irricana will also need to reclassify part of the warranty liability accrued in 2004 from non-current to current.

Unearned Revenue

When an entity receives cash in advance of providing goods or services, it has an obligation to provide those goods or services. Since cash is in hand but revenue has not been recognized, a liability equal to the amount of cash received is required. Examples of unearned revenue include:

- rent payments received in advance
- deposits for goods and services to be provided in the future
- tickets purchased in advance to sporting events, concerts, and the theatre
- gift certificates

For example, on December 4, 2006, Mr. Wayne purchased a $100 gift certificate at Dromore Books Ltd. (Dromore) as a gift for his daughter. The gift certificate entitles the holder to purchase books in the store worth up to $100. The gift certificate cannot be exchanged for cash. Dromore would make the following entry to record the purchase of the gift certificate:

Dr. Cash (assets +)	100	
Cr. Unearned revenue—gift certificate (liabilities +)		100
To record the sale of a gift certificate on December 4, 2006.		

When Mr. Wayne's daughter purchases books using the gift certificate, Dromore would make the following entry:

Dr. Unearned revenue—gift certificate (liabilities –)	100	
Cr. Revenue (revenue +, shareholders' equity +)		100
To record the use of a $100 gift certificate.		

Since the gift certificate can be used at any time, the liability is classified as current even though it might not be used over the course of the next year. In general, the timing of converting unearned revenue into revenue is determined by when the entity recognizes its revenue. (Revenue recognition would not be an issue for the gift certificate example since it is difficult to identify a reasonable time for recognizing revenue other than at the time the gift certificate is used.)

Disclosure

Disclosure requirements for liabilities by entities that follow GAAP are quite general, and the financial statements of public companies show a wide variation in the classification and the amount of detail that is provided. The *CICA Handbook* requires that current liabilities be segregated by main class (bank loans, accounts payable and accrued liabilities, taxes payable, unearned revenue, current portion of long-term debt, and so on). Interestingly, there is no requirement that current liabilities be shown separately.

MWW does not provide very much detail about its current liabilities. Current liabilities are shown separately, but only three categories are provided. Accounts Payable and Accrued Liabilities, shown as a single account representing about 73% of current liabilities, probably represent a wide variety of different obligations, but it is not possible to tell. The amount of detail that MWW provides about its current liabilities is not unusual—many firms provide the same basic information.

Panel A—Canadian National Railway Company

Consolidated Balance Sheet

In millions December 31,	2000	1999
Accounts payable and accrued charges *(Note 9)*	$ 1,393	$ 1,390
Current portion of long-term debt *(Note 11)*	434	272
Other	76	115

9 Accounts payable and accrued charges

In millions December 31,	2000	1999
Trade payables	$ 407	$ 503
Accrued taxes	244	88
Payroll-related accruals	194	185
Accrued charges	187	195
Current portion of workforce reduction provisions	137	182
Accrued interest on long-term debt	126	119
Accrued operating leases	31	29
Other	67	89
	$1,393	$1,390

Panel B—Salter Street Films Limited

as at October 31	2000	1999
LIABILITIES		
Accounts payable and accrued liabilities	$ 9,293,187	$ 8,238,491
Deferred revenue and government assistance	1,804,234	1,439,238
Income taxes payable	6,007,867	3,738,784
Interim production financing *(note 8)*	24,055,254	23,552,530
Long-term debt *(note 9)*	1,993,917	2,286,969
Non-controlling interest in subsidiary companies	226,677	238,054
	43,381,136	39,494,066

An example of somewhat more detailed disclosure of current liabilities can be seen in the Canadian National Railway Company's (CN Rail) annual report. CN Rail provides a detailed breakdown of its accounts payable and accrued liabilities in the notes to the financial statements. CN Rail's disclosure on current liabilities can be seen in Panel A of Exhibit 10-1. An example of an entity that does not segregate current and non-current liabilities is Salter Street Films Limited (Salter Street), an integrated entertainment company that develops, produces, and distributes original film and television programming. The liability section of Salter Street's balance sheet is shown in Panel B of Exhibit 10-1. This format is common in certain industries, such as the entertainment industry. The problem with not segregating current liabilities is that it is more difficult to assess the liquidity of an entity since it is not clear what is current and what isn't.[1]

www.cn.ca
www.salter.com

Bonds and Other Forms of Long-Term Debt

Debt is amounts borrowed and owed by an entity. Debt can be long-term (non-current) or current. In this chapter we will examine a number of aspects of long-term debt, including how to account for it.

Note 10 to MWW's financial statements (page A-55) provides information on its debt. On January 27, 2001 MWW reported long-term debt of $37,921,000, of which $10,905,000 was classified as current because it was due to be repaid within the next year. A significant amount of MWW's long-term debt is in the form of leases, a topic we will discuss later in this chapter. Many entities use long-term debt as a source of financing their businesses. For example, on December 31, 2000, TransCanada PipeLines Limited reported long-term debt of $10,540,000,000, of which $612,000,000 was classified as current. Dofasco Inc., a major Canadian steel producer, reported $706,200,000 of long-term debt on its December 31, 2000 balance sheet, of which $108,300,000 was classified as current.

www.transcanada.com
www.dofasco.ca

Debt comes in all different shapes and sizes. Money can be borrowed from banks. Money can be raised by selling bonds to investors. Debt can be issued to the public at large or to private organizations such as insurance companies or pension funds. Borrowers can provide receivables, inventory, equipment, buildings, or land to lenders as collateral for the loan. The collateral provides the lenders with some protection should the borrower be unable to pay back the loan. If the borrowers cannot pay, the lenders get the collateral or the proceeds from its sale. The interest rate can be fixed or it can vary with changes in interest rates in the economy. A loan whose interest rate varies with market conditions is called a **variable-rate loan**. If the interest rate does not change, the loan is called a **fixed-rate loan**. The period the debt is outstanding can be long or short. In sum, a debt arrangement can include whatever terms the borrowers and lenders can agree on.

Examples of debt instruments include:

- **bond:** A formal borrowing arrangement in which a borrower agrees to make periodic interest payments to lenders as well as repay the principal at a specified time in the future.

- **debenture:** A bond with no collateral provided to the lenders.

- **mortgage:** A loan that provides the borrower's property as collateral.

- **note payable:** A formal obligation signed by the borrower, promising to repay a debt.

In this section we will focus our attention on bonds, although there are many similarities between bonds and other forms of debt. Mortgages will also be briefly discussed.

There are two ways to finance an entity—debt and equity. Equity represents ownership in the entity and debt is borrowings that have to be repaid. A question that might come to mind is, Why would an entity choose to finance with debt rather than equity, or vice versa?

There are a number of advantages and disadvantages to each. Interest on debt is tax deductible, which means that the actual cost of borrowing is lower than the interest rate stated in the loan. (The tax deductibility of interest will be explained later in the chapter.) Also, debt is less costly to an entity—the cost of debt is lower than the cost of equity. However, debtholders do not have a say in the management of the entity; only equity investors, the owners of the entity, do. Debt is more risky for the issuing entity because the interest and principal payments have to be made when required by the loan agreement. That means that interest and principal payments on debt must be made, regardless of how well the entity is doing. Defaulting on interest or principal payments (failing to make interest or principal payments when they are due) can have significant and costly economic and legal consequences for an entity. But debt is less risky for investors because debt investors must be satisfied before equity investors. If an entity goes out of business, the creditors must be fully repaid before the equity investors receive anything.

An attractive (and risky) feature of debt to an entity is leverage. **Leverage** is the use of debt to increase the return earned on equity. Debt can increase the return on equity because the cost of debt (interest) is fixed, so if an investment earns a return that is greater than the cost of debt, the return above the interest rate belongs to the equity investors. Of course, if the investment earns less than the cost of debt, the lenders still have to be paid the agreed amount. (We will look at an example of the effect of leverage in Chapter 11.)

Characteristics of Bonds

A bond is a formal borrowing arrangement in which a borrower agrees to make periodic interest payments to the lenders and to repay the principal at a specified time in the future. When a bond is issued there is an agreement that lays out the terms and conditions of the bond. When an entity issues a bond it sells individual bond certificates to investors. Each bond certificate will have a face value of an amount such as $1,000 or $5,000. The **face value of a bond** is the amount that is written on the individual bond certificate and represents the amount that the holder of the bond, the investor, will receive when the bond matures. The **maturity date of a bond** is the date on which the borrower has agreed to pay back the principal (the face value of the bond) to the bondholders. A bond will specify an interest rate or **coupon rate**, which is the percentage of the face value that the issuer pays to investors each year. These are the essentials of a bond. A bond with a face value of $1,000, coupon rate of 10%, and maturity of September 15, 2020 pays the holder of the bond $100 per year in interest and will repay the principal of $1,000 on September 15, 2020.

The face value of a bond is not necessarily the amount of money that the issuer receives from the sale of the bond to an investor. The amount of money that an issuer receives, or the **proceeds** from the sale of bonds, is determined by the market interest rate or effective interest rate that is appropriate for the bond being issued. The **effective interest rate** is the real or market rate of interest that is required by investors. If the coupon rate is different from the effective interest rate, the bond must be sold at a price that allows investors to earn the effective interest rate. If the coupon rate on a bond is lower than the effective interest rate, then the proceeds will be less than the face value. If the coupon rate is greater than the effective interest rate, then the proceeds from the issue will be greater than the face value. Only if the effective interest rate is the same as the coupon rate will the proceeds be the same as the face value. How the price of a bond is determined will be discussed in the next section.

There are many other features that a bond can have in addition to the basic ones described above. Any other characteristics are bells and whistles that are added on to meet the needs of the lenders and the borrowers. The additional features come at a price—the price being a change in the interest rate. If a feature is beneficial to the investors who buy the bonds, the entity issuing the bonds should be able to offer a lower interest rate. If a feature is beneficial to the issuing entity, then investors will require a higher interest rate.

For example, some bonds are callable. A **callable bond** gives the bond issuer the option to repurchase the bond from investors at a time other than the maturity date under conditions that are specified in the bond agreement. This feature is attractive to an issuer because if interest rates fall, the issuer can call the bond and then make another issue at a lower interest rate. This feature is not attractive to investors because they lose an investment that was paying a higher-than-market rate of interest. A callable bond will have a higher market rate of interest associated with it than an equivalent bond without the call feature. A **convertible bond** may be exchanged by the investor for other securities of the issuing entity, such as common stock. The investor may be given the option to cash in the bond before the maturity date under certain conditions. This type of bond is called a **retractable bond**.

A bond agreement can also impose restrictions on the activities of the issuer. These restrictions are intended to reduce the risk of the investors and thereby reduce the cost of borrowing. Many restrictions are stated in accounting terms. For example, a borrowing agreement may set a maximum debt-to-equity ratio or a minimum current ratio. Restrictions may prohibit the payment of dividends if retained earnings falls below a certain amount. Violation of restrictive covenants can have significant economic consequences for the entity. These consequences can include an increase in the interest rate on the debt, an increase in the collateral required, additional covenants, or immediate repayment of the loan. Because violation of restrictive covenants is costly, managers will take steps to avoid violating them. These steps can involve operating decisions—for example, reducing spending—or accounting choices.

When bonds are sold to the public, they can be readily traded among investors. It is important to understand that when bonds (and shares as well) are sold and traded by the public, transactions occur in two markets. The primary market involves only transactions between an entity issuing stocks or bonds and the investors buying these securities directly from the issuing entity. The secondary market involves transactions among individual investors. Most trading activity takes place in the secondary market. Transactions in the secondary market do not involve the entities that actually issued the securities. (For example, the Toronto Stock Exchange is a secondary market.) While transactions in the secondary market do not involve the issuing entities directly, managers of the issuing entities are still concerned about what is happening on those markets because the entities and managers are affected by the price of their traded securities, especially their common shares.

Pricing of Bonds

Determining the price of a bond or other long-term debt uses the present value tools discussed in Chapter 7. The price of a bond is equal to the present value of the cash flows that will be paid to the investor, discounted at the effective interest rate. The effective interest rate is not the same for all bonds. The effective interest rate is determined by market forces, and depends on the risk of the bond. The riskier the bond, the higher the effective interest rate. The risk for bond investors is whether they will receive their interest and principal. The higher the risk that the investors will not get paid, the higher the effective interest rate the market will apply to the bonds.

Let's consider an example to examine the pricing of long-term debt. Bardal Ltd. (Bardal) plans to make a bond issue to raise about $5,000,000 to finance a major expansion. The bonds have a face value of $5,000,000 and will be issued on October 1, 2005. The bonds will carry a coupon rate of 9%, with interest paid semi-annually on March 31 and September 30 of each year, and will mature in five years, on September 30, 2010. Each semi-annual interest payment will be $225,000 ($5,000,000 $\times$ 0.09 $\times$ 1/2). For a bond of this type (risk, features, maturity), the effective interest rate is 10%. Therefore, the discount rate that should be used to value the cash flows from this bond is 10%. Bardal's year end is September 30. The cash flows that will be generated by the bond are shown in Figure 10-1.

The proceeds from this bond issue is the present value of a series of 10 payments of $225,000 paid semi-annually, plus a payment of $5,000,000 to be paid at maturity, on September 30, 2010, discounted at the effective interest rate of 10%. Because the interest payments are made semi-annually, there is a little twist from our discussion in Chapter 7. Instead of discounting the interest payments at 10% over five years, we use a 5% discount rate over 10 six-month periods. The interest payments are an annuity, so from the intersection of the 10-period row and the 5% column in Appendix B, Table B-3 (the present value of an annuity of $1 paid at the end of each

Sept. 30/05 Mar. 31/06 Sept. 30/06 Mar. 31/07 Sept. 30/07 Mar. 31/08 Sept. 30/08 Mar. 31/09 Sept. 30/09 Mar. 31/10 Sept. 30/10
($225,000) ($225,000) ($225,000) ($225,000) ($225,000) ($225,000) ($225,000) ($225,000) ($225,000) ($225,000)
($5,000,000)

Figure 10-1

Interest and Principal Payments
for Bardal Ltd.'s $5,000,000
Bond Issue

period; page B-6), we find the appropriate factor of 7.72173. The present value of the interest payments is:

$$\text{PV of interest payments} = \text{Interest payment} \times \text{Discount factor (10 periods, 5\%)}$$
$$= \$225,000 \times 7.72173$$
$$= \$1,737,389$$

(Note that discounting at 5% over 10 periods is not exactly the same as discounting at 10% over five periods. For the purpose of this example the assumption is acceptable. An important point to recognize is that if the interest payments are being discounted at 5% over 10 periods, then the principal repayment should be discounted at 5% over 10 periods as well. Further explanation of this aspect of finding present value will be left for other courses.)

In looking at the Bardal example we also have to consider the present value of the principal that will be repaid on September 15, 2010. The $5,000,000 that will be received is a single payment, so we use Appendix B, Table B-2 (the present value of a payment of $1 to be received at the end of the nth period; page B-4). The $5,000,000 will be paid in five years, so the appropriate discount factor to use is found at the intersection of the 10-period row and the 5% column. The present value of the principal repayment on September 15, 2010 is:

$$\text{PV of the principal repayment} = \text{Principal repayment} \times \text{Discount factor (10 periods, 5\%)}$$
$$= \$5,000,000 \times 0.61391$$
$$= \$3,069,550$$

The proceeds from the bond is the sum of these two present value calculations:

Proceeds from bond issue	=	Present value of interest payments	+	Present value of principal repayment
	=	$1,737,389	+	$3,069,550
	=	$4,806,939		

Once the terms of the bond have been set (interest rate, maturity, other features), the proceeds that Bardal receives are a function of the discount rate that is used. The discount rate is the effective interest rate, which is set by the market. If we assume that the effective interest rate appropriate for Bardal's bond is 8% instead of 10%, the proceeds from the bond would be:

$$\text{PV of interest payments} = \text{Interest payment} \times \text{Discount factor (10 periods, 4\%)}$$
$$= \$225,000 \times 8.11090$$
$$= \$1,824,953$$

$$\text{PV of the principal repayment} = \text{Principal repayment} \times \text{Discount factor (10 periods, 4\%)}$$
$$= \$5,000,000 \times 0.67556$$
$$= \$3,377,800$$

$$\text{Proceeds from the bond issue} = \text{PV of interest payments} + \text{PV of the principal repayment}$$
$$= \$1,824,953 + \$3,377,800$$
$$= \$5,202,753$$

We can do one more calculation. If the effective interest rate were 9%, the same rate as the coupon rate on the bond, the proceeds would be:

$$\text{PV of interest payments} = \text{Interest payment} \times \text{Discount factor (10 periods, 4.5\%)}$$
$$= \$225,000 \times 7.91272$$
$$= \$1,780,362$$

$$\text{PV of the principal repayment} = \text{Principal repayment} \times \text{Discount factor (10 periods, 4.5\%)}$$
$$= \$5,000,000 \times 0.64393$$
$$= \$3,219,650$$

$$\text{Proceeds of the bond offering} = \text{PV of interest payments} + \text{PV of the principal repayment}$$
$$= \$1,780,362 + \$3,219,650$$
$$= \$5,000,000$$

It is not a coincidence in this scenario that the proceeds of the bond (the present value of the cash flows) are the same as its face value. When the effective interest rate and the coupon rate of a bond are the same, the proceeds and the face value of the bond will be the same.

Accounting for Bonds

Now that we've seen how bonds are priced in the marketplace, let's look at how to account for them. We will continue with the example of Bardal Ltd.'s $5,000,000 bond offer that we began in the previous section. We will examine the three scenarios we used for pricing the bonds. The first scenario will be when the effective interest rate is the same as the coupon rate on the bond, the second will be when the effective interest rate is greater than the coupon rate, and the third will be when the effective interest rate is less than the coupon rate.

Scenario 1: Selling Bonds at Face Value   When the market rate of interest is the same as the coupon rate, the bonds sell at their face value, so Bardal will receive $5,000,000 from the offering. The journal entry that Bardal would make on October 1, 2005 to record the issue of the bonds is:

Dr. Cash (asset +)	5,000,000	
Cr. Long-term debt—bonds (liability +)		5,000,000
To record the issue of bonds on October 1, 2005.		

On March 31 and September 30 of each year, Bardal would make the following journal entry to record the payment of interest and the interest expense:

Dr. Interest expense (expense +, shareholders equity −)	225,000	
Cr. Cash (asset −)		225,000
To record the interest expense on the $5,000,000 bond offering.		
(This entry is made on March 31 and September 30 of each year from 2006 through 2010.)		

On September 30, 2010, when the bond matures, Bardal would make the following journal entry to record the retirement of the bond. Retirement of a bond occurs when the liability is settled by paying the principal to the investors:

Dr. Long-term debt—bonds (liability −)	5,000,000	
Cr. Cash (asset −)		5,000,000
To record the retirement of the bonds on September 30, 2010.		

The accounting in this scenario is straightforward. The bonds would be reported as a $5,000,000 non-current liability on Bardal's balance sheet. The bonds would be reclassified as a current liability on the September 30, 2009 balance sheet because the bond would be payable in the next fiscal year. The income statement would show an interest expense of $450,000 (2 × $225,000) each year over the life of the bond.

Scenario 2: Selling Bonds at a Discount

In this scenario the effective interest rate for Bardal's bonds is greater than the coupon rate. Similar bonds provide investors with a return of 10% per year, while the coupon rate on Bardal's bond is only 9%. As a result, Bardal has to sell its bonds for less than their face value so that investors can earn the 10% effective interest rate they require. Recall from the previous section that the price for Bardal's bond when the effective interest rate is 10% is $4,806,939. What this amount means is that investors earn a 10% return by investing $4,806,939 now in exchange for a series of ten $225,000 semi-annual payments, plus a $5,000,000 payment at the end of five years.

When a bond is sold to investors for less than its face value, the bond is said to have been sold at a **discount**. The discount is equal to the difference between the face value of the bonds and the proceeds from their sale. The accounting issue is, How do we account for the discount? How do we account for the fact that Bardal receives $4,806,939 when it issues the bonds, but has to pay investors $5,000,000 when the bond matures? When the bond is issued, the discount is recorded in a contra-liability account. The entry that Bardal would make to record the issue of its bonds is:

Dr. Cash (asset +)	4,806,939	
Dr. Bond discount (contra-liability +)	193,061	
Cr. Long-term debt—bonds (liability +)		5,000,000

To record the issue of bonds on October 1, 2005 at a discount.

The net book value of the bonds—the face value of the bonds less the bond discount—is the net present value of bonds discounted using the effective interest rate when the bonds were sold. By paying less than the face value for the bonds, investors are compensated for the low coupon rate. In effect, the interest that investors must receive to earn the effective interest rate is paid in advance through the discount from the face value of the bond. The discount of $193,061 is accounted for as part of the interest cost of the bonds and is amortized over the life of the bonds. The portion of the discount amortized each period is reported on the income statement as part of the interest expense.

The bonds might be reported on Bardal's balance sheet, if it prepared one on October 1, 2005, as shown in Panel A of Table 10-2 (page 584). Panel A and the journal entry above treat the discount as a contra-liability account, which would be netted against the face value of the bonds to give the net book value of the bonds on the liability side of the balance.

An alternative approach is to include the discount on the asset side of the balance sheet, reported as a deferred charge or other assets. The deferred charge represents interest paid in advance. In this approach the bonds would be shown at their face value on the liability side of the balance sheet and the discount would appear separately on the asset side. This approach is shown in Panel B of Table 10-2. Both methods are seen in practice.

There are two methods for amortizing the discount: the straight-line method and the effective-interest method.

The straight-line method allocates an equal amount of the discount to interest expense each period. The method is straightforward to use and easy to understand. For Bardal's bonds, one-tenth of the discount, or $19,306 ($193,061 ÷ 10), is amortized at the time of each interest payment (remember that there are 10 semi-annual interest payments made over the life of the bond). Application of the straight-line method can be seen in Panel A of Table 10-3 (page 584). With the straight-line method, the interest expense is the same each period ($244,306) and the discount decreases and the net book value (NBV) of the bond increases by the same amount each period ($19,306). Sample journal entries for the interest expense and amortiza-

Table 10-2　Methods of Reporting Bond Discount

Panel A: Discount Reported as a Contra-Liability Account

Bardal Ltd.
Extracts from the October 1, 2005 Balance Sheet

Long-term debt—Bonds payable	$5,000,000
Unamortized discount on October 1, 2005	193,061
Net book value of Long-term debt—Bonds payable	$4,806,939

Panel B: Discount Reported as "Other Assets"

Bardal Ltd.
Extracts from the October 1, 2005 Balance Sheet

Non-current assets:		Non-current liabilities:	
Other assets	$193,061	Long-term debt—Bonds payable	$5,000,000

tion of the discount are shown in Table 10-4 for three dates over the life of the bond. Notice in Table 10-4 that the interest expense has two components: the part paid in cash to investors ($225,000 at each semi-annual payment) and the portion of the bond discount that is amortized. Even though the interest expense recorded at the time of each semi-annual payment is $244,306, the cash payment each time is only $225,000.

The effective interest method is more complicated than the straight-line method. Instead of amortizing the same amount of discount each period, the effective interest method provides a constant rate of borrowing over the life of the bond. That is, the interest expense for a period divided by the NBV of the bonds during the same period is constant and equal to the effective interest rate when the bond was issued. The interest expense for each period can be calculated by multiplying the effective interest

Table 10-3　Bond Discount Amortization Schedule for Bardal Ltd.

Date	Panel A Straight-line method					Panel B Effective interest method			
	Interest payment	Interest expense	Amount of discount amortized	Unamortized discount	NBV of bond	Interest expense	Amount of discount amortized	Unamortized discount	NBV of bond
Oct. 1, 2005				$193,061	$4,806,939			$193,061	$4,806,939
Mar. 31, 2006	$225,000	$244,306	$19,306	173,755	4,826,245	$240,347	$15,347	177,714	4,822,286
Sept. 30, 2006	225,000	244,306	19,306	154,449	4,845,551	241,114	16,114	161,600	4,838,400
Mar. 31, 2007	225,000	244,306	19,306	135,143	4,864,857	241,920	16,920	144,680	4,855,320
Sept. 30, 2007	225,000	244,306	19,306	115,837	4,884,163	242,766	17,766	126,914	4,873,086
Mar. 31, 2008	225,000	244,306	19,306	96,531	4,903,470	243,654	18,654	108,259	4,891,741
Sept. 30, 2008	225,000	244,306	19,306	77,224	4,922,776	244,587	19,587	88,672	4,911,328
Mar. 31, 2009	225,000	244,306	19,306	57,918	4,942,082	245,566	20,566	68,106	4,931,894
Sept. 30, 2009	225,000	244,306	19,306	38,612	4,961,388	246,595	21,595	46,511	4,953,489
Mar. 31, 2010	225,000	244,306	19,306	19,306	4,980,694	247,674	22,674	23,837	4,976,163
Sept. 30, 2010	225,000	244,306	19,306	0	5,000,000	248,837	23,837	0	5,000,000

Table 10-4 Sample Journal Entries for Recording Interest Expense and Amortization of the Bond Discount for Bardal Ltd.

	Straight-line method		Effective interest method	
March 31, 2006				
Dr. Interest expense (expense +, shareholders' equity –)	244,306		240,347	
Cr. Bond discount (contra-liability –)		19,306		15,347
Cr. Cash (asset –)		225,000		225,000
To record the interest expense and the amortization of the bond discount on March 31, 2006.				
September 30, 2007				
Dr. Interest expense (expense +, shareholders' equity –)	244,306		242,766	
Cr. Bond discount (contra-liability –)		19,306		17,766
Cr. Cash (asset –)		225,000		225,000
To record the interest expense and the amortization of the bond discount on September 30, 2007.				
March 31, 2008				
Dr. Interest expense (expense +, shareholders' equity –)	244,306		243,654	
Cr. Bond discount (contra-liability –)		19,306		18,654
Cr. Cash (asset –)		225,000		225,000
To record the interest expense and the amortization of the bond discount on March 31, 2008.				

rate by the NBV of the bond for the period. For example, for the six-month period from October 1, 2005 through March 31, 2006, the interest expense is calculated as follows:

$$\text{Interest expense} = \begin{array}{c}\text{NBV of the bond} \\ \text{during the period}\end{array} \times \begin{array}{c}\text{Effective interest rate when} \\ \text{the bond was issued}\end{array}$$

$$= \quad \$4,806,939 \quad \times \quad 0.05$$

$$= \quad \$240,347$$

The difference between the interest expense as calculated above and the cash interest payment to investors is the amount by which the discount is amortized. For the October 1, 2005 through March 31, 2006 period, $15,347 ($240,347 – $225,000) of the discount is amortized. Application of the effective interest method can be seen for Bardal in Panel B of Table 10-3. For Bardal the interest rate reflected in the interest expense each six-month period is 5%, which was the effective rate of interest (on a semi-annual basis) when Bardal issued its bonds. The 5% rate is constant over the life of the bond. The straight-line method gives a constant interest expense, not a constant interest rate. Sample journal entries for the interest expense and amortization of the discount are shown in Table 10-4 for three periods.

Notice that for both amortization methods the interest expense is not the same as the amount of cash paid to investors as interest. The reason is that the bond discount is considered part of the cost of borrowing and the amortization of the discount is included in the interest expense. Note too that the straight-line and effective-interest methods each provide a different interest expense and a different amount of discount amortization each period. While the amount of discount amortized and the amount of interest expense in each period is different, over the life of the bonds the amount of interest expensed is the same and the discount is fully amortized (compare Panels A and B of Table 10-3). Finally, notice how the bond discount decreases toward zero and how the NBV of the bond increases toward $5,000,000 over the life of the bond (see Table 10-3).

On September 30, 2010, when the bonds mature, Bardal would make the following journal entries to record the final interest payment and final amortization of the bond discount, and the retirement of the bonds. Retirement of bonds occurs when the liability is settled by repaying the principal to the investors.

	Straight-line method		Effective interest method	
September 30, 2010				
Dr. Interest expense (expense +, shareholders' equity –)	244,306		248,837	
Cr. Bond discount (contra-liability –)		19,306		23,837
Cr. Cash (asset –)		225,000		225,000
To record the interest expense and the amortization of the bond discount on September 30, 2010.				
Dr. Long-term debt-bonds (liability –)	5,000,000		5,000,000	
Cr. Cash (asset –)		5,000,000		5,000,000
To record the retirement of bonds on September 30, 2010.				

These two entries could be combined into a single entry as follows:

	Straight-line method		Effective interest method	
September 30, 2010				
Dr. Long-term debt—bonds (liability –)	5,000,000		5,000,000	
Dr. Interest expense (expense +, shareholders' equity –)	244,306		248,837	
Cr. Bond discount (contra-liability –)		19,306		23,837
Cr. Cash (asset –)		5,225,000		5,225,000
To record the interest expense, amortization of the bond discount, and retirement of bonds on September 30, 2010.				

Scenario 3: Selling Bonds at a Premium In this scenario the bonds are sold to investors for more than their face value; that is, the bonds are sold at a **premium**. A bond is sold at a premium when the coupon rate is greater than the effective rate of interest for a bond of this type. Recall from the section on pricing bonds that Bardal's bond had a coupon rate of 9%, while the effective interest rate was 8% (4% semi-annually). The amount of the premium is the difference between the cash received from investors and the face value of the bonds. The price for the bonds in this scenario was $5,202,753 and the premium $202,753 ($5,202,753 – $5,000,000). The entry that Bardal would make to record the issue of the bonds at a premium is:

Dr. Cash (asset +)	5,202,753	
Cr. Bond premium (contra-liability +)		202,753
Cr. Long-term debt—bonds (liability +)		5,000,000
To record the issue of bonds on October 1, 2005 at a premium.		

Accounting for a premium is essentially the same as for a discount, except that the bond premium account carries a credit balance (instead of a debit balance as with a discount) and the amortization of the premium decreases the interest expense (instead of increasing the expense as with a discount). A premium lowers the interest rate that the investors earn from the coupon rate to the effective rate. In effect, by paying a premium investors are repaying in advance the interest they will collect over the life of the bonds that is over and above the effective interest rate.

As with a discount, a premium is amortized over the life of the bonds using the straight-line method or effective interest method. The application of the two methods for Bardal's bond premium is shown in Table 10-5 (page 588). Sample journal

Question for Consideration

On January 1, 2007 Krydor Inc. (Krydor) issued a two-year, $1,000,000 bond with a 10% coupon, interest paid annually on December 31. The bond matures on December 31, 2008. The effective interest rate for this bond is 11%.

a.   What price will Krydor sell the bond for?

b.   What journal entry will Krydor make to record the issue of the bond?

c.   Prepare a table similar to the one in Table 10-3 (page 584) showing the interest payment and interest expense, the amount of discount amortized, the unamortized discount, and the NBV of the bond over the life of the bond using both the (i) straight-line method and (ii) effective-interest method.

d.   What journal entry will Krydor make when the bond is retired and the investors are repaid the principal? Do not include the interest portion of the entry.

Answer:

a.   The price of the bond is equal to the present value of the cash flows received by the investor over the life of the bond, discounted using the effective-interest rate. The present value of the $100,000 interest payments to be received on December 31, 2007 and 2008, plus the $1,000,000 principal repayment to be received on December 31, 2008, is:

$100,000 × 1.71252   = $171,252
$1,000,000 × 0.81162 = $811,620
Price of the bond   = $982,872

b.   Krydor's journal entry to record issue of the bond:

Dr. Cash (asset +)	982,872	
Dr. Bond discount (contra-liability +)	17,128	
Cr. Long-term debt—bonds (liability +)		1,000,000

To record the issue of a $1,000,000 bond on January 1, 2007 at a discount.

c.   (i) Straight-line method:

Date	Interest payment	Interest expense	Amount of discount amortized	Unamortized discount	NBV of bond
Jan. 1, 2007				$17,128	$ 982,872
Dec. 31, 2007	$100,000	$108,564	$8,564	8,564	991,436
Dec. 31, 2008	100,000	108,564	8,564	0	1,000,000

(ii) Effective interest method:

Date	Interest payment	Interest expense	Amount of discount amortized	Unamortized discount	NBV of bond
Jan. 1, 2007				$17,128	$ 982,872
Dec. 31, 2007	$100,000	$108,116	$8,116	9,012	990,988
Dec. 31, 2008	100,000	109,012	9,012*	0	1,000,000

*The exact amount for this calculation is $9,008 ($1,000,000 − $990,988 × 0.11). The amount shown is adjusted by $4 to correct the rounding error caused by the use of the tables.

d.   Krydor's journal entry when bond is retired and investors are repaid the principal:

Dr. Long-term debt—bonds (liability −)	1,000,000	
Cr. Cash (asset −)		1,000,000

To record the repayment of principal on December 31, 2008.

entries are shown in Table 10-6 (page 589). When the straight-line method is used, the interest expense is $204,725 and $20,275 ($202,753 ÷ 10) of the bond premium is amortized in each period. As was explained in Scenario 2, the effective interest method results in a constant interest rate over the life of the bond. That is, the interest

Table 10-5 — Bond Premium Amortization Schedule for Bardal Ltd.

Date	Interest payment	Panel A Straight-line method				Panel B Effective interest method			
		Interest expense	Amount of premium amortized	Unamortized premium	NBV of bond	Interest expense	Amount of premium amortized	Unamortized premium	NBV of bond
Oct. 1, 2005				$202,753	$5,202,753			$202,753	$5,202,753
Mar. 31, 2006	$225,000	$204,725	$20,275	182,478	5,182,478	$208,110	$16,890	185,863	5,185,863
Sept. 30, 2006	225,000	204,725	20,275	162,202	5,162,202	207,435	17,565	168,298	5,168,298
Mar. 31, 2007	225,000	204,725	20,275	141,927	5,141,927	206,732	18,268	150,030	5,150,030
Sept. 30, 2007	225,000	204,725	20,275	121,652	5,121,652	206,001	18,999	131,031	5,131,031
Mar. 31, 2008	225,000	204,725	20,275	101,377	5,101,377	205,241	19,759	111,272	5,111,272
Sept. 30, 2008	225,000	204,725	20,275	81,101	5,081,101	204,451	20,549	90,723	5,090,723
Mar. 31, 2009	225,000	204,725	20,275	60,826	5,060,826	203,629	21,371	69,352	5,069,352
Sept. 30, 2009	225,000	204,725	20,275	40,551	5,040,551	202,774	22,226	47,126	5,047,126
Mar. 31, 2010	225,000	204,725	20,275	20,275	5,020,275	201,885	23,115	24,011	5,024,011
Sept. 30, 2010	225,000	204,725	20,275	0	5,000,000	200,989	24,011	0	5,000,000

expense for a period divided by the NBV of the bonds during the same period is constant and equal to the effective interest rate when the bond was issued. In this scenario, the interest rate reflected in the interest expense for each six-month period is 4%, which was the effective rate of interest (on a semi-annual basis) when Bardal issued its bonds. For example, the interest expense for the six-month period between October 1, 2005 and March 31, 2006 is:

$$\text{Interest expense} = \text{NBV of the bond during the period} \times \text{Effective interest rate when the bond was issued}$$

$$= \$5,202,753 \times 0.04$$

$$= \$208,110$$

The 4% effective interest rate will be constant over the life of the bond.

On September 30, 2010, when the bond matures, Bardal would make the following journal entries to record the final interest payment and final amortization of the bond discount, and the retirement of the bond:

	Straight-line method		Effective interest method	
September 30, 2010				
Dr. Interest expense (expense +, shareholders' equity −)	204,725		200,989	
Dr. Bond premium (contra-liability −)	20,275		24,011	
Cr. Cash (asset −)		225,000		225,000
To record the interest expense and the amortization of the bond premium on September 30, 2010.				
Dr. Long-term debt-bonds (liability −)	5,000,000		5,000,000	
Cr. Cash (asset −)		5,000,000		5,000,000
To record the retirement of the bond on September 30, 2010.				

These two entries could be combined into a single entry as follows:

	Straight-line method	Effective interest method
September 30, 2010		
Dr. Long-term debt—bonds (liability –)	5,000,000	5,000,000
Dr. Interest expense (expense +, shareholders' equity –)	204,725	200,989
Dr. Bond premium (contra-liability –)	20,275	24,011
Cr. Cash (asset –)	5,225,000	5,225,000

To record the interest expense, amortization of the bond discount, and retirement of the bond on September 30, 2010.

The straight-line and effective interest methods give different measurements for the interest expense, NBV of bonds, and unamortized amounts of discounts and premiums. As a result, the two methods will give different net incomes, total assets and liabilities, and other fundamental accounting measures. Usually the differences between the methods are relatively small. Entities generally do not choose a coupon rate that is different from the effective interest rate so that they have premiums or discounts. However, market interest rates do change over time, so sometimes the effective interest rate changes between the time the coupon rate is set and when the bond is sold to investors. As a result a discount or premium will arise. Because the premiums and discounts tend to be small, there is usually no material difference between the straight-line and effective interest methods and so in practice the straight-line method is commonly used.

One final remark about the effective-interest method is necessary. According to GAAP, bonds and other forms of long-term debt should be valued at the present value of the cash payments to investors, discounted using the effective interest rate on the date the bond is issued. However, interest rates can and do change over the life of a bond, but the financial statements do not reflect the effect of a change in the effective

Table 10-6 Sample Journal Entries for Recording Interest Expense and Amortization of the Bond Premium for Bardal Ltd.

	Straight-line method		Effective interest method	
March 31, 2006				
Dr. Interest expense (expense +, shareholders' equity –)	204,725		208,110	
Dr. Bond premium (contra-liability –)	20,275		16,890	
Cr. Cash (asset –)		225,000		225,000
To record the interest expense and the amortization of the bond premium on March 31, 2006.				
September 30, 2007				
Dr. Interest expense (expense +, shareholders' equity –)	204,725		206,001	
Dr. Bond premium (contra-liability –)	20,275		18,999	
Cr. Cash (asset –)		225,000		225,000
To record the interest expense and the amortization of the bond premium on September 30, 2007.				
March 31, 2008				
Dr. Interest expense (expense +, shareholders' equity –)	204,725		205,241	
Dr. Bond premium (contra-liability –)	20,275		19,759	
Cr. Cash (asset –)		225,000		225,000
To record the interest expense and the amortization of the bond premium on March 31, 2008.				

interest rate. By ignoring changes in effective interest rates, financial statements do not reflect real economic gains and losses on long-term debt.

For example, if interest rates increase after a bond is issued, the issuer benefits because its interest cost is now lower than the new effective interest rate. The benefit of having to pay less than the going market interest rate is reflected in a decrease in the market value of the liability. (Remember, when the discount rate increases, the present value of a given series of cash flows decreases. As a result, an increase in the effective-interest rate decreases the value of the bond.) The decrease in the market value of the debt can be thought of as an economic gain because the entity now has less debt and is therefore better off (less debt is better than more debt). The journal entry to record a decrease in the market value of debt would be:

> Dr. Long-term debt (liability –)   xxx
>   Cr. Gain on decrease in market value of long-term
>   debt (income statement +, shareholders' equity +)   xxx
> To record a decrease in the market value of long-term debt.

The opposite logic applies if interest rates decrease. In that case an entity would be paying a higher-than-market interest rate. As a result, the present value of the debt would increase and the entity would suffer an economic loss.

These gains and losses are not recognized under GAAP because of GAAP's transactional nature and because it is difficult to objectively determine the appropriate effective interest rate in the absence of a transaction. However, GAAP now require disclosure of the market value of debt in the notes to the financial statements.

Accruing Interest on Long-Term Debt

What happens if an entity's year end is not the same as the date that interest is paid? If we are using accrual accounting, it is necessary to accrue the interest expense at the end of the period so that the cost of borrowing is recognized in the appropriate period, even though the interest is not paid until later.

In the Bardal example it was assumed that Bardal's year end was September 30. If we assume instead that Bardal's year end is December 31, then an adjusting entry is necessary on December 31 of each year of the bond's life to accrue the interest expense and interest payable for October 1 to December 31. We will use the facts from Scenario 2 (page 583) to show the adjusting entry that has to be made. We will assume as well that Bardal uses the effective interest method for accounting for the bond discount and we will use the December 31, 2007 year end as the basis for the example.

Between October 1 and December 31, 2007, Bardal incurs three months of interest costs that should be matched to the 2007 fiscal year. From Table 10-3 (page 584) we find that the interest expense for March 31, 2008 is $243,654 and that $18,654 of the bond discount was amortized on that date. (We use the information from March 31, 2008 because the interest expense and amortization recorded on that date is for the period from October 1, 2007 to March 31, 2008). On December 31, 2007 half the interest expense for the period has to be accrued and half the bond discount has to be amortized. The adjusting entry that Bardal would make on December 31, 2007 to accrue the interest expense and interest payable and amortize the bond discount is:

> Dr. Interest expense (expense +, shareholders' equity –)   121,827
>   Cr. Bond discount (contra-liability –)   9,327
>   Cr. Interest payable (liability +)   112,500
> To accrue the interest expense and the record amortization
> of the bond discount on December 31, 2007.

On March 31, 2008, when Bardal actually pays interest to the investors, it would record the following entry:

Dr. Interest expense (expense +, shareholders' equity −)	121,827	
Dr. Interest payable (liability −)	112,500	
Cr. Bond discount (contra-liability −)		9,327
Cr. Cash (asset −)		225,000

To record the interest expense, amortization of the bond discount, and payment of interest on March 31, 2007.

This entry records the following information:

1. The interest expense for the first three months of fiscal 2008.

2. The reduction in the interest payable liability that was accrued on December 31, 2007.

3. The amortization of the discount that pertains to the first three months of fiscal 2008.

4. The payment of interest earned by investors from October 1, 2007 through March 31, 2008 (part of the payment is for interest that was expensed in fiscal 2007 and part is being expensed in fiscal 2008).

The approach is the same for situations when bonds are sold at a premium or at their face value.

Early Retirement of Debt

Entities sometimes retire their long-term debt before it matures. For example, lower market interest rates can make it worthwhile to retire existing high-interest-rate debt and then reissue at a lower rate. An entity can do this relatively easily if the debt has a provision that gives the issuer the option to redeem the debt. Alternatively, an entity could repurchase its debt on the open market if it is publicly traded.

Question for Consideration

Use the facts from Scenario 3 above for Bardal (bond sold at a premium; see page 586) and assume that Bardal has a December 31 year end. Also assume that Bardal uses the effective interest method to amortize the premium.

a. Prepare the adjusting journal entry that Bardal should make on December 31, 2008 to accrue the interest expense and amortization of the bond premium.

b. Prepare the entry that Bardal would make on March 31, 2009.

Answer:

a. Bardal's journal entry on December 31, 2008:

Dr. Interest expense (expense +, shareholders' equity −)	101,814.50	
Dr. Bond premium (contra-liability −)	10,685.50	
Cr. Interest payable (liability +)		112,500.00

To accrue the interest expense and the record amortization of the bond discount on December 31, 2008.

b. Bardal's journal entry on March 31, 2009, when it pays the interest to the investors:

Dr. Interest expense (expense +, shareholders' equity −)	101,814.50	
Dr. Interest payable (liability −)	112,500.00	
Dr. Bond premium (contra-liability −)	10,685.50	
Cr. Cash (asset −)		225,000.00

To record the interest expense, amortization of the bond discount, and payment of interest on March 31, 2009.

Accounting for the early retirement of debt requires that any unamortized discount or premium be removed from the books when the debt is retired. The impact is that the unamortized premium or discount is included on the income statement in full when the debt is retired, instead of being amortized. A gain or loss will arise on the early retirement of long-term debt if the NBV of the debt is different from the amount that has to be paid to retire it. A gain arises if the cost of retiring the debt is less than its NBV and a loss occurs if the cost of retiring the debt is greater than its NBV. We will continue with the Bardal Ltd. example to show how the early retirement of debt is recorded.

Scenario 4 (Based on Scenario 2, Selling Bonds at a Discount)
As part of the agreement signed with the bondholders, Bardal is entitled to redeem its $5,000,000 in bonds by paying investors $5,100,000. On October 1, 2008 Bardal's management decided to take advantage of market conditions and exercise its option to redeem the bonds. Note that on October 1, 2008, the unamortized discount (using the effective interest method) was $88,672 (see Table 10-3, page 584) and this amount must be removed from the books when the bonds are retired. The loss of $188,672 ([$5,000,000 − $88,672] − $5,100,000) arises because the NBV of the bonds (face value − unamortized discount) is less than the cost of retiring them. Bardal would make the following journal entry to record the early retirement of the bonds.

October 1, 2008

Dr. Long-term debt—bonds (liability −)	5,000,000	
Dr. Loss on redemption of bond		
(income statement +, shareholders' equity −)	188,672	
Cr. Bond discount (contra-liability −)		88,672
Cr. Cash (asset −)		5,100,000
To record the early retirement of bonds on October 1, 2008.		

Scenario 5 (Based on Scenario 3, Selling Bonds at a Premium)
On April 1, 2009 Bardal decided to repurchase all of its bonds on the open market at the market price of $4,850,000. On April 1, 2009 the unamortized bond premium (using the straight-line method) was $60,826 (see Table 10-5, page 588) and this amount must be removed from the books when the bonds are retired. A gain of $210,826 ([$5,000,000 + $60,826] − $4,850,000) arises because the NBV of the bonds is greater than the cost of retiring them. Bardal would make the following journal entry to record the early retirement of the bonds.

April 1, 2009

Dr. Long-term debt—bonds (liability −)	5,000,000	
Dr. Bond premium (contra-liability −)	60,826	
Cr. Gain on redemption of bond (income statement +,		
equity −)		210,826
Cr. Cash (asset −)		4,850,000
To record the interest expense and the amortization of the bond premium on September 30, 2010.		

The amount that Bardal had to pay to retire its bonds in Scenario 5 means that interest rates have increased since the bond was issued. As interest rates increase, the market price of bonds will decrease. If an entity repurchases a bond with a low coupon rate relative to the current effective interest rate, it is quite possible that it would report a gain and be able to pay off the liability at a lower cost than at maturity. The downside of this strategy is that if the entity had to borrow money to pay off its debt early, the new debt (the borrowed money) would be issued at the higher effective interest rate, which means that the actual interest cost would be higher.

Mortgages

In the bond example only interest was paid over the term of the bond. When the bonds matured, the full amount of the principal was repaid. Some loans are structured so that the borrower pays interest and principal throughout the life of the loan. Payments that are a combination of interest and principal are called **blended payments**. Mortgages commonly require blended payments of a fixed amount over the life of the mortgage. In the early years of a mortgage most of the payment is for interest, with only a small proportion for reducing the principal. As the principal balance declines, less of the payment goes to interest and more to principal repayment.

Let's consider an example. On April 1, 2004 Journois Inc. (Journois) purchased a new office building for $11,750,000. Journois paid $1,750,000 in cash and arranged a 25-year, 11% mortgage with a bank for the balance. The mortgage requires equal annual payments on March 31 of each year over the term of the mortgage. Journois' year end is March 31. The first question to address is how much each annual payment should be. The payments should be the amount required to have the mortgage fully paid off at the end of the 25th year. This is another present value calculation, but with a bit of a twist. What we have to figure out is the amount that has to be paid each year for 25 years using a discount rate of 11% to fully pay off the mortgage. The calculation is:

$$\text{Present value of an annuity} = \text{Annual (periodic) payment} \times \text{Present value of annuity factor}$$

$$
\begin{aligned}
\text{Annual (periodic) payment} &= \frac{\text{Present value of an annuity}}{\text{Present value factor}} \\
&= \frac{\$10,000,000}{8.42174} \\
&= \$1,187,403
\end{aligned}
$$

Journois must pay $1,187,403 on March 31 of each of the next 25 years. In the calculation the present value of the mortgage is $10,000,000, assuming that 11% is the effective interest rate. From Appendix B, Table B-3 (page B-6) the appropriate present value of an annuity factor, found at the intersection of the 11% column and 25-year row, is 8.42174. Rearranging the terms in the equation we obtain the annual payment.

Table 10-7 (page 594) provides a table showing the interest and principal component of each annual mortgage payment. The interest expense each year is simply the product of the interest rate and the unpaid balance on the mortgage during the year. For example, in 2015 the mortgage expense is $939,229 (0.11 × $8,538,446). Notice in Table 10-7 the small proportion of the payment that goes toward reducing the principal in the early years of the mortgage and how that proportion increases over the life of the mortgage. Also notice that the mortgage principal decreases each year by the amount in the mortgage principal reduction column.

The journal entry Journois would make to record the mortgage is:

Dr. Cash (asset +)	10,000,000	
Cr. Mortgage payable (liability +)		10,000,000

To record the mortgage payable on the office building purchased on April, 1 2004.

The cash received from the bank would then be paid (or be paid directly) to the seller of the building. Each year Journois makes a journal entry to record the payment to the bank. Of course, the amount of interest and principal paid each year will vary. The entry made on March 31, 2009 would be as follows (the amounts can be found in Table 10-7):

>   Dr. Mortgage payable (liability –)   132,684
>   Dr. Interest expense (expense +, shareholders' equity –)   1,054,719
>   Cr. Cash (asset –)   1,187,403
>   To record the mortgage payment to the bank on March 31, 2009.

If the annual payments were required on a date other than Journois' year end, it would be necessary to accrue the interest expense at each year end.

Disclosure

The balance sheet itself usually only reveals the total amount of long-term debt outstanding and the amount of that long-term debt that is maturing within the next year. Many users of the financial statements want more information than that. The totals might provide a small bit of information about the riskiness of the entity, but much more information is required so that users can estimate future cash flows, funding requirements, and earnings, and evaluate the management and stewardship of the entity. The notes to MWW's financial statements provide additional detail on its long-term debt that may be useful in assessing these areas.

Table 10-7   Mortgage Amortization Schedule for Journois Inc.

Date	Payment	Interest expense	Mortgage principal reduction	Unpaid balance on mortgage
April 1, 2004				$10,000,000
March 31, 2005	$1,187,403	$1,100,000	$ 87,403	9,912,597
March 31, 2006	1,187,403	1,090,386	97,017	9,815,580
March 31, 2007	1,187,403	1,079,714	107,689	9,707,890
March 31, 2008	1,187,403	1,067,868	119,535	9,588,355
March 31, 2009	1,187,403	1,054,719	132,684	9,455,671
March 31, 2010	1,187,403	1,040,124	147,279	9,308,392
March 31, 2011	1,187,403	1,023,923	163,480	9,144,912
March 31, 2012	1,187,403	1,005,940	181,463	8,963,450
March 31, 2013	1,187,403	985,979	201,424	8,762,026
March 31, 2014	1,187,403	963,823	223,580	8,538,446
March 31, 2015	1,187,403	939,229	248,174	8,290,272
March 31, 2016	1,187,403	911,930	275,473	8,014,799
March 31, 2017	1,187,403	881,628	305,775	7,709,024
March 31, 2018	1,187,403	847,993	339,410	7,369,614
March 31, 2019	1,187,403	810,658	376,745	6,992,868
March 31, 2020	1,187,403	769,216	418,187	6,574,681
March 31, 2021	1,187,403	723,215	464,188	6,110,493
March 31, 2022	1,187,403	672,154	515,249	5,595,244
March 31, 2023	1,187,403	615,477	571,926	5,023,318
March 31, 2024	1,187,403	552,565	634,838	4,388,480
March 31, 2025	1,187,403	482,733	704,670	3,683,810
March 31, 2026	1,187,403	405,219	782,184	2,901,626
March 31, 2027	1,187,403	319,179	868,224	2,033,402
March 31, 2028	1,187,403	223,674	963,729	1,069,673
March 31, 2029	1,187,403	117,730	1,069,673	0

The table at the top of Note 10 to MWW's financial statements (page A-55) provides a listing of the different long-term debt obligations that were outstanding on the balance sheet date, along with the amounts outstanding and some information on the terms, such as interest rate. For example, MWW had a bank loan of $1,400,000 outstanding on January 27, 2001. The interest rate on the bank loan is 7.5%. The table shows that a large portion of MWW's debt pertains to leases of fixtures, equipment, computer equipment, and software. (Lease accounting is discussed in the next section.) The text below the table provides additional information about the long-term debt. For example, the text explains that the bank loan was originally a $7,000,000 loan that had to be repaid in 20 equal instalments over five years. The table at the very end of Note 10 discloses the repayments that MWW will have to make in each of the next five years on its long-term debt. This information is important for assessing future cash flows, cash requirements, and financing needs.

Note 9 (page A-54) also provides important information about MWW's liabilities. Note 9 describes amounts available and the terms of certain loan agreements and the security that has been provided. However, the notes do not tell everything a reader might want to know. For example, the interest rates on the syndicated bank term loans depend on "certain interest coverage tests," but what the tests are and how they affect the interest rate are not stated. It is also not entirely clear which debts are classified as current, although it is possible to figure some of that out from the information provided.

Most public companies provide similar disclosure about their long-term liabilities, though the extensiveness of the disclosure will vary from entity to entity. Private companies may provide less information than what appears in MWW's statements because the users of the statements do not require, or the preparers do not wish to provide, the information. However, powerful users of the financial statements may require and therefore request additional detail on liabilities.

Leases

When an entity purchases an asset, it will often finance the purchase by borrowing money. When an asset purchase is financed this way, an asset and a liability are reported on the balance sheet. The asset, of course, is recorded at its cost and is amortized over its useful life. The liability is the amount owed to the lender and the liability decreases as repayments of principal are made.

Financial arrangements can be sophisticated, though. What happens if instead of borrowing money to buy the asset, the entity leases it? (A **lease** is a contractual arrangement where one entity, the lessee, agrees to pay another entity, the lessor, a fee in exchange for the use of an asset. A **lessee** is an entity that leases an asset from the asset's owner and a **lessor** is an entity that leases assets that it owns to other entities.) A lease can be short- or long-term. An asset can be leased for an hour, a day, a week, a year, five years, or more. Many different assets are available through leasing—individuals lease or rent homes, cars, and garden equipment.

The lessor owns the leased asset, but the lessee has certain rights and obligations that are defined in the lease agreement. Leasing has become a very common way for entities to obtain the use of assets without actually buying them. MWW leases furniture and fixtures, computer equipment and software, and its stores. Air Canada, Canada's largest airline and the twelfth-largest airline in the world, has a fleet of 241 aircraft, yet the company owns only 66 of those planes; the rest are leased.

There are a number of reasons why entities prefer to lease assets instead of buying them. With a lease an entity does not have to obtain separate financing for the purchase. This can be important when the entity already has a lot of debt and lenders such as banks are reluctant to lend more. Leasing also allows for financing of 100% of the cost of the asset. A lender will often lend only a portion of the amount required to purchase the asset. Leases can also provide flexibility to lessees. For example, a lease agreement could allow a lessee to exchange leased computer equipment during the term of the lease for more up-to-date equipment. This arrangement provides the lessee some protection from technological obsolescence. Leasing is attractive for entities that do not need certain assets continuously. For example, a company may require heavy equipment only at certain stages of a project. A lease allows the entity to use the equipment when it is needed but not incur the cost of owning assets that are idle for a significant amount of time. The terms of a lease are the outcome of negotiation between the lessee and the lessor—any terms are possible if both parties agree.

Leasing has accounting implications. When leasing began to be popular, entities used it to achieve a "trick" called off-balance-sheet financing. **Off-balance-sheet financing** occurs when an entity incurs an obligation without reporting a liability on its balance sheet. Leasing allowed for off-balance-sheet financing because the lessee would have to record a lease or rent expense only when payment to the lessor was paid or payable. The lessee could have use of the leased asset in much the same way a purchaser would, but neither the leased asset nor the financing associated with the asset would be reported on the balance sheet.

Off-balance-sheet financing allows an entity to have the benefit of incurring a liability without suffering balance sheet consequences, such as a higher debt-to-equity ratio. This can be attractive to entities that are in danger of violating debt-to-equity covenants or for simply limiting the amount of debt the entity appears to have. Also, since the debt-to-equity ratio is a measure of an entity's risk, off-balance-sheet financing makes an entity appear less risky. Of course, an entity's risk is not affected by how liabilities are accounted for, but measures of risk are affected.

Eventually accounting standard-setters recognized that many of these leasing contracts were actually purchases in disguise that allowed entities to avoid recording liabilities on their balance sheets. To attempt to remedy the perceived abuse of the financial statements, rules were established in the *CICA Handbook*. The *CICA Handbook* requires that if a lease results in the transfer of the "benefits and risks of ownership to the lessee," the leased asset and associated liability must be reported on the lessee's balance sheet. Effectively, a lease transaction would be accounted for in the same way as a purchase and sale of assets if the criteria in the *CICA Handbook* are met.

The *CICA Handbook* defines two categories of leases: capital leases and operating leases.

A **capital lease** is a lease that transfers the benefits and risks of ownership to the lessee. Assets associated with a capital lease are capitalized on the balance sheet of the lessee and a liability that is equal to the present value of the lease payments to be made over the life of the lease is recorded. At the beginning of a capital lease the amount recorded for the asset and the related liability are both equal to the present value of the lease payments. (As we will see below, after the initial recording of the lease, the asset and liability will most likely not be equal.) The lessor removes the leased asset from its books and reports a receivable equal to the present value of lease payments to be received from the lessee. Under a capital lease the lessee amortizes the leased asset, not the lessor.

If the rights and risks of ownership are not transferred to the lessee but are retained by the lessor, then the lease is an **operating lease**. When a lease is classified as an operating lease, the lessee does not record the assets or the associated liability on its balance sheet. Under an operating lease, the lessee recognizes an expense when the payment to the lessor is paid or payable and the lessor recognizes revenue from the lease when payments are received or receivable. When a lease is classified as an operating lease, the entity has off-balance-sheet financing.

The key to lease accounting is whether the "benefits and risks of ownership" are transferred to the lessee. The *CICA Handbook* does not precisely define the term, but the idea is that if the lease is, for all intents and purposes, a sale and purchase, it should be accounted for as a sale and purchase. This notion is conceptually reasonable, but under what circumstances are the "benefits and risks of ownership" transferred? The *CICA Handbook* provides some criteria for determining the type of lease.

For a lessee, a lease should be classified as a capital lease if any of the following three criteria are met:

1. It is likely that the lessee will take title of the asset;

2. The lease term is long enough that the lessee receives most of the economic benefits available from the asset (usually defined as 75% or more of the leased asset's life); or

3. The lessor is assured of recovering its investment in the leased asset and earning a return on the investment (usually defined as the present value of the lease payments being greater than or equal to 90% of the asset's fair value).

For a lessor, a lease is considered a capital lease if

1. Any of the three criteria described for the lessee is met;

2. The credit risk of the lessee is normal; and

3. The lessor is able to estimate any unreimbursable costs the lessor must incur as part of the lease agreement.

These criteria are intended to provide guidance for classifying leases, but in Canada the classification of a lease is supposed to be a matter of judgment. In practice, the existence of concrete criteria are often interpreted as hard and fast rules. Indeed, in the United States the same criteria exist, but they are rules—judgment is not required. The criteria provide preparers with the ability to design lease contracts that allow them to achieve their reporting objectives. If preparers want to avoid accounting for a lease as a capital lease, the terms can be negotiated so that the criteria are not met.

Let's look at an example to see how lease accounting works. On March 31, 2004 Outram Inc. (Outram) signed an agreement to lease eight buses from the Cheekye Bus Corp. (Cheekye) for its new inter-city bus service between Calgary and Edmonton. The buses were leased for 12 years and Outram agreed to pay Cheekye $170,000 on March 31 of each year, beginning in 2005. Outram took delivery of the buses immediately upon the signing of the lease. At the end of the lease Outram can purchase the buses for $1 each. Outram is responsible for maintaining, repairing, and insuring the buses. If Outram purchased the buses from Cheekye, they would have cost $150,000 each. Outram's year end is March 31.

Outram should account for this lease as a capital lease because not one, but all three *CICA Handbook* criteria appear to be met.

- First, Outram is likely to gain title of the buses at the end of the lease because it can purchase them for $1 each. At such a low price Outram would certainly purchase the buses if they could still be used or if they could be sold for more than $1.

- We do not know the useful life of these buses, but if it is 16 years or less the lease term represents at least 75% of the life of the buses. Sixteen years seems a reasonable ceiling for the life of a bus, so the second criterion is likely met.

- The third criterion is also met. The present value of a series of 12 payments of $170,000 beginning in one year is $1,158,328 ($170,000 × 6.81369), assuming a discount rate of 10%, so the present value of the lease payments is over 96% ($1,158,328 ÷ [$150,000 × 8 buses]) of the purchase price of the buses. Note, though, that the third criterion is sensitive to the discount rate used. If a discount rate of 12% were used instead, the present value of the lease payments would be only about 88% of the purchase price of the buses, which would mean that the third criterion is not met.

Table 10-8   Income Statement Effect of Capital Versus Operating Leases

	Capital Lease*					Operating Lease
	Column A	Column B	Column C	Column D	Column E	Column F	Column G
	Liability on March 31	NBV of the buses on March 31	Principal repayment	Interest expense	Amortization expense	Total expense	Lease expense
2004	$1,158,328	$1,158,328					
2005	1,104,161	1,085,933	$ 54,167	$115,833	$72,395	$188,228	$170,000
2006	1,044,577	1,013,538	59,584	110,416	72,395	182,811	170,000
2007	979,035	941,143	65,542	104,458	72,395	176,853	170,000
2008	906,939	868,748	72,096	97,904	72,395	170,299	170,000
2009	827,633	796,353	79,306	90,694	72,395	163,089	170,000
2010	740,396	723,958	87,237	82,763	72,395	155,158	170,000
2011	644,436	651,563	95,960	74,040	72,395	146,435	170,000
2012	538,880	579,168	105,556	64,444	72,395	136,839	170,000
2013	422,768	506,773	116,112	53,888	72,395	126,283	170,000
2014	295,045	434,378	127,723	42,277	72,395	114,672	170,000
2015	154,550	361,983	140,495	29,505	72,395	101,900	170,000
2016	0	289,588	154,550	15,450	72,395	87,845	170,000
2017	0	217,193	0	0	72,395	72,395	0
2018	0	144,798	0	0	72,395	72,395	0
2019	0	72,403	0	0	72,395	72,395	0
2020	0	0	0	0	72,403	72,403	0

*Some amounts in this exhibit do not total exactly because of rounding errors due to use of the present value tables. These errors are small and should not be of any concern. Adjustments have been made in the last year to adjust for these errors.

The amount that Outram should capitalize for the buses is the present value of the lease payments that will be made over the life of the lease, which is $1,158,328. The journal entry to record the acquisition of the buses by a capital lease is:

Dr. Assets under capital lease (asset +)   1,158,328
   Cr. Lease liability (liability +)   1,158,328
To record the acquisition of eight buses under a capital lease.

After the initial recording of the leased asset and the related liability, the asset and liability are accounted for separately. (The accounting effects are summarized in the complicated-looking Table 10-8.) Leased capital assets are accounted for in much the same way as any capital asset—they are amortized over their useful lives. Amortization does present some interesting issues, though. If the term of the capital lease is shorter than the useful life of the asset and the lessee is not likely to take title of the leased asset, the asset should be amortized over the term of the lease.

Since Outram will likely own the buses at the end of the lease, amortizing them over an estimated 16-year life is reasonable. If Outram were not likely to take title to the buses at the end of the lease, then a 12-year amortization period, the period of the lease, would be appropriate because that would be the period that Outram would have the buses to earn revenue. Outram can select the amortization method for its leased assets as it would for capital assets it owns, though it should probably use the same method for the leased buses that it uses for any similar buses it owns. If Outram uses straight-line amortization, the annual amortization expense will be $72,395 ($1,158,328 ÷ 16). The amortization expense is shown in Column E of Table 10-8 and the NBV of the buses at the end of each fiscal year is shown in Column B. If Outram chose a different amortization method or made different estimates of the useful life or residual value of the buses, the annual amortization expense would be different. The journal entry to record the amortization expense each year is:

Dr. Amortization expense (expense +, shareholders' equity –)   72,395
    Cr. Accumulated amortization (contra-asset +)   72,395
To record the amortization of leased buses.

The lease liability is treated in much the same way as the mortgage with blended payments that we discussed in the previous section. One difference between a capital lease liability and, for example, a bond, is that the interest rate in a lease is not usually stated explicitly and so a rate must be assumed. The assumption is needed so that the initial amount recorded for the capital lease asset and liability can be determined, and for calculating the annual interest expense. In this example, a rate of 10% has been assumed. Again, remember that the numbers in the financial statements will be affected by the rate chosen and the preparers have some flexibility in choosing the rate.

Throughout fiscal 2005 Outram's liability to Cheekye was $1,158,328, so the interest expense for 2005 is $115,833 ($1,158,328 × 0.10). The remainder of the $170,000 paid to Cheekye (the portion that is not for interest) is repayment of principal and it reduces the amount of the liability. In 2005 the liability is reduced by $54,167 ($170,000 – $115,833), so the liability on March 31, 2005 is $1,104,161 ($1,158,328 – $54,167). For 2006 the interest expense is calculated on the $1,104,161 liability that is outstanding for the entire fiscal year.

Notice that, as was the case with the mortgage discussed in the previous section, as time passes the interest portion of the annual payment decreases and the principal portion increases. The reason for this is that as the liability decreases, less interest must be paid and more of the payment is applied to paying down the liability. This effect can be seen in Columns A, C, and D of Table 10-8.

The journal entry that would be recorded to record the lease payment in 2005 is:

Dr. Interest expense (expenses +, shareholders' equity –)   115,833
Dr. Lease liability (liability–)   54,167
    Cr. Cash (asset –)   170,000
To record the lease payment to Cheekye for 2005.

The journal entry for 2010 would be:

Dr. Interest expense (expenses +, shareholders' equity –)   82,763
Dr. Lease liability (liability–)   87,237
    Cr. Cash (asset –)   170,000
To record the lease payment to Cheekye for 2010.

Notice in Table 10-8 that the NBV of the buses (Column B) and the associated liability (Column A) are different in each of 16 years shown, except when the lease is initially recorded. This is expected because the asset and liability are accounted for separately after the initial recording of the lease.

If Outram were able to treat the lease as an operating lease (which in this example it could not), the only entries required would occur when a payment to Cheekye was made or became payable. The entry that Outram would make on March 31, 2005 (and in 2006 through 2016) if the lease were classified as an operating lease would be:

Dr. Rent expense (expense +, shareholders' equity –)   170,000
    Cr. Cash (asset –)   170,000
To record the annual payment to Cheekye for the buses
leased under an operating lease.

The annual lease expense for Outram under an operating lease is shown in Column G of Table 10-8 and is $170,000 each year. Another point to observe in Table 10-8 is the total amount expensed each year under capital and operating leases. Notice that in the early years of the lease the amount expensed for interest plus amortization under the capital lease (Column F) is greater than the lease expense under the operating lease (Column G). This is another reason why preparers prefer having leases classified as operating leases.

The *CICA Handbook* requires extensive disclosure about an entity's lease transactions. The *CICA Handbook* is our source for what should be disclosed because lease accounting is strictly a *Handbook* requirement. For operating leases, an entity should disclose in the notes to the financial statements the minimum lease payments that must be made under operating leases in each of the next five years. For capital leases, an entity should disclose the amount of assets it has under capital leases, along with accumulated amortization associated with those assets, as well as information about capital lease liabilities.

An example of lease-related disclosures can be found in MWW's annual report. Examine notes 1F, 4, 7, 10, and 11 to MWW's financial statements to see the type of disclosures entities provide about their lease arrangements (pages A-49, 52, 53, 55, and 56).

An additional remark about MWW's leasing arrangements is necessary. MWW reports a deferred gain of $2,101,000 among the liabilities on its January 27, 2001 balance sheet. This amount pertains to a number of leasing-related transactions. (Note 7 to MWW's financial statements describes these transactions.) MWW finances some of its capital expenditures by selling capital assets to a purchaser who immediately leases the property back to MWW. This type of arrangement is called a **sale-leaseback transaction**.

With a sale-leaseback transaction the entity receives cash for the property being sold and then makes regular lease payments to the lessor. Recall from Chapter 9 that when capital assets are sold, gains or losses arise if the assets are sold for amounts that are different from their NBV. When assets are sold in sale-leaseback transactions, GAAP do not allow gains or losses to be fully recognized on the income statement in the year of the sale. Instead, the gains or losses must be deferred and recorded on the balance sheet, and amortized over the term of the lease.

Gains, as is the case with MWW, are reported as deferred gains on the liability side of the balance sheet and losses are reported as deferred losses on the asset side. Because the sale and the lease are closely linked, it is not possible to be sure that the selling price reflects the market value of the asset, which means that the gain or loss may be artificial. If gains and losses could be recognized in full immediately, one could envision entities arranging sale-leaseback transactions to generate gains when management wanted higher net income. While these deferred gains are included among the liabilities on the balance sheet, they do not meet the definition of a liability because there is no future sacrifice required. The deferred gain is being placed on the balance sheet to avoid full recognition on the income statement when the capital asset was sold.

Also included in the deferred gains on MWW's balance sheet are financial inducements received from property owners to sign leases. A property owner might make a cash payment to MWW or waive or reduce rent payments in exchange for signing a lease. In these cases GAAP require that the inducement be spread over the life of the lease and not be recognized in full immediately.

For example, suppose Chokio Inc. (Chokio) received a $50,000 cash payment to sign a five-year lease for space in a downtown office complex. Annual rent required by the lease is $100,000. The journal entry Chokio would make to record the inducement payment is:

Dr. Cash (asset +)	50,000	
Cr. Deferred rent inducement (liability +)		50,000
To record the receipt of a rent inducement payment.		

Chokio would record the following entry when it made its annual rent payment

Dr. Deferred rent inducement (liability −)	10,000	
Dr. Rent expense (expense +, shareholders' equity −)	90,000	
Cr. Cash (asset −)		100,000
To record the payment for use of office space.		

The $50,000 payment has the effect of reducing the actual amount of rent that Chokio has to pay. According to GAAP the benefit is spread over the life of the lease. It is recognized as revenue when it is received. The result is that the rent expense that Chokio incurs each year is $90,000 instead of $100,000, even though Chokio pays the property owner $100,000.

Accounting for leases by lessors follows the same pattern as for lessees, but from the opposite perspective. If a lessor classifies a lease as a capital lease, the leased asset is removed from the lessor's books and a receivable is recorded for the present value of the lease payments to be received.

There are two types of capital leases from the lessor's perspective, as follows:

- A **sales-type lease** is a capital lease used by manufacturers and dealers to sell a product. A sales-type lease is a combination of a sale and a financing arrangement, so the lessor earns income in two ways: profit on the "sale" of the leased asset and interest from financing the sale. With a sales-type lease the lessor records the sale of the leased asset when the lease comes into effect and recognizes interest revenue over the term of the lease.

- A **direct financing lease** is a capital lease that is a straight financing arrangement where the lessor purchases assets on behalf of a lessee and leases them to the lessee. The lessor earns interest revenue over the term of the lease in much the same way a bank earns its revenue from lending money.

With an operating lease the lessor simply recognizes revenue when lease payments are received or are receivable.

This will be the extent of our discussion of accounting for lessors. While lessor accounting could be discussed at length, most entities do not act as lessors so this topic will be left for more advanced accounting courses.

To conclude, lease accounting is an area where a private company might choose not to follow GAAP. For example, if the main or only reason for preparing financial statements is for tax purposes, then not following GAAP for leases makes sense if capital leases for accounting purposes are considered operating leases for tax purposes. It may also be sensible for small businesses to avoid the complexities of lease accounting if the users of the financial statements do not require them. Of course, public companies must follow GAAP for leases, and private companies whose financial statements are audited must follow GAAP or they will receive a qualified audit opinion.

Question for Consideration

Explain why companies might prefer to have their leases classified as operating leases instead of capital leases. Explain why and how companies are able to arrange their leases to satisfy this preference under GAAP.

Answer:

The disadvantage of a capital lease is that a liability equal to the present value of the lease payments must be reported on the balance sheet. This accounting treatment increases the amount of debt an entity reports on its balance sheet, which may affect the perceived risk of the entity and the perceived ability of the entity to carry additional debt. Measurements such as the debt-to-equity ratio increase when leases are capitalized, which may have economic consequences if a covenant exists that sets a limit on the debt-to-equity ratio and similar measures. Operating leases, on the other hand, have no effect on the liabilities of the entity. An operating lease allows the entity to keep its lease liabilities "off the balance sheet."

A lease is classified as a capital lease if the benefits and risks of ownership are transferred to the lessee. The *CICA Handbook* does not clearly define benefits and risks of ownership, but provides criteria for guiding preparers. These criteria are often interpreted as firm rules and preparers will structure leases so that none of the criteria are met, which allows the leases to be classified as operating.

Pensions and Other Post-Retirement Benefits

One of the benefits the employees of some entities receive as part of their compensation packages is a pension. A **pension** is income provided to a person after he or she retires. Pensions are also provided to Canadians by government, through the Canada and Québec Pension Plans. Retired employees can also receive benefits such as extended medical coverage (medical costs not covered by a provincial health plan), as well as dental, vision, and prescription coverage. The pension and other post-retirement benefits that retirees receive are negotiated between the employer and its employees.

Post-retirement benefits are an extremely important issue in Canada, for both economic and accounting reasons. The magnitude of the amounts that are involved in pension plans gives an idea of their economic significance. For example, the fair value of the assets in Air Canada's employee pension plan was in excess of $9,000,000,000 on December 31, 2000, and the Canadian National Railway Company's employee pension plan had assets with a fair value in excess of $14,000,000,000 on December 31, 2000. The economic significance of pensions and other post-retirement benefits will continue to grow as Canada's population ages.

Accounting for pensions and post-retirement benefits can be complex and the reporting of the information in the financial statements can be confusing. Most of the issues in pension accounting are beyond the scope of this book. However, because of the economic significance of pensions and post-retirement benefits and their prominence in many entities' financial statements, a brief introduction to the subject is appropriate.

Employees earn their pensions and other post-retirement benefits while they are working, even though they receive the money after they retire. In effect, instead of receiving their full compensation in cash while they are working, the employer funds a pension plan that provides income to employees after they retire. Since a pension is part of employees' compensation while they are working, for accounting purposes the cost of providing a pension should be expensed over the employee's working career. In other words, it is a question of matching. But how much should be expensed in any given period? How much should an employer expense in 2005 for a pension that will be paid beginning in 2030?

Usually an independent arm's length party called a trustee manages a pension plan, not the employer itself. While it is not required that a pension plan be managed by a trustee, most are because an employer cannot deduct for tax purposes contributions to a plan that is not managed by a trustee. The accounting implication of having a trustee manage a pension plan is that the assets in the plan are not included on the employer's balance sheet because the employer does not control them. The money contributed to a pension plan by the employer and the income earned on the investments in the plan are not accessible to the employer.

There are two types of pension plans: defined-contribution plans and defined-benefit plans. In a **defined-contribution plan** the employer makes cash contributions to the plan as specified in the pension agreement with the employees. For example, the employer's contribution to the plan might be a percentage of each employee's wage or salary. Employees are often able to make their own contributions to the plan to increase the amount invested. The pension benefits that an employee receives upon retirement depend on the amount contributed to the plan on behalf of that employee (by the employer and the employee) and on the performance of the investments made with the funds in the pension plan. The employer's obligation is limited to making the required contribution each year. The employee is entitled only to his or her share of what is in the plan on retirement.

Accounting for a defined-contribution plan is fairly straightforward. The pension expense for a year is the contribution that the employer is required to make to the plan according to the agreement with the employees. A pension liability is reported on an employer's balance sheet if the full contribution to the plan has not been made by the end of the period.

Consider the following example. Under its employee defined-contribution pension plan, Nojack Ltd. (Nojack) is required to contribute $250,000 to the plan in 2005. On December 15, 2005 Nojack's treasurer wrote a cheque for $250,000 to the trustee managing the plan. The entry that Nojack would make to record its contribution in 2005 is:

Dr. Pension expense (expense +, shareholders' equity −)	250,000	
Cr. Cash (asset −)		250,000

To record the contribution to the employee defined-contribution pension plan for 2005.

If Nojack did not make the required contribution by its year end on December 31, 2005, the credit would be to a pension liability account. The liability would be reduced as the employer made payments to the plan.

The second type of pension plan is a defined-benefit plan. In a **defined-benefit plan** the employer promises to provide employees with certain specified benefits in each year they are retired. A defined-benefit plan might specify that employees receive 2.5% of the salary earned in the final year of employment for each year worked for the entity. For example, if an employee worked for 30 years and his/her salary in the last year was $125,000, the employee would receive an annual pension of $93,750 ($125,000 × 0.025 × 30 years).

There is a variety of ways of determining the amount of pension a retired employee receives. The method of determining an employee's benefits is the result of negotiations between the employer and its employees. With a defined-benefit plan the employer is obligated to provide the specified benefits to employees, regardless of how the investments in the pension plan have performed. If there is not enough money in the pension plan to pay employees their pensions, the employer is responsible for making up the difference.

There are two decisions that an entity must make about its defined-benefit pension plan. The first is the accounting question—what should the annual pension expense be? The second is the funding question—how much money should the employer contribute to the plan each year? The pension expense in a year does not have to be the same, and will usually not be the same, as the amount of cash that the employer contributes to the plan.

Determining the amount to expense and the amount to fund are complex present value problems. The objective of a defined-benefit plan is to provide an employee regular payments of a specified amount (an annuity) for the rest of the employee's life after he or she retires. The calculation itself is relatively straightforward, but the assumptions that must be made to do the calculation are difficult.

For example, consider the employee described previously who is to receive an annual pension of $93,750. Conceptually, the pension plan must have enough money on hand when the employee retires to purchase an annuity that will pay the employee $93,750 for the rest of his or her life. If the employee is expected to live for 15 years after retirement and the appropriate discount rate is 8%, the plan would have to have $802,406.25 ($93,750 × 8.559 [from Appendix B, Table B-3, page B-6]) to purchase an annuity that guaranteed an annual payment of $93,750 for 15 years.

Two crucial assumptions have been made to come up with this amount: the number of years that the employee would live after retirement and the appropriate discount rate. If either of these assumptions changes, the amount that must be available in the retirement year to purchase the annuity would change, possibly dramatically.

But hold on. We have addressed only part of the problem. We also have to determine the amount that must be invested in the pension plan each year over the employee's working life so that the $802,406.25 will be in the plan when the employee retires. (Remember that the money invested in the plan earns a return, so that has to be factored into the analysis). As well, we have to figure out how much should be expensed each year for accounting purposes. Then consider that we have to figure this out for an entire workforce.

Things can get very complicated. The whole exercise is dependent on a series of assumptions. These assumptions include:

- the number of years employees will work for the employer
- the number of employees who will qualify for benefits
- the number of employees who will die before they retire
- the age at which employees will retire
- the salary employees will earn in the year or years on which the pension is based
- the number of years employees will live after retirement
- the return the money in the pension fund will earn (the higher the expected return, the less money that needs to be invested in the pension fund by the employer)

Now remember that funding pension plans and calculating pension expenses is based on events that will take place over the many years until an employee retires—20, 25, 30, or even more years into the future! It is these assumptions and the length of time involved that makes pension accounting so complex.

As mentioned above, the pension expense and the amount of funding each year are not usually the same. Among the reasons that these amounts are different is that there is no requirement that the same method and assumptions be used to calculate each. The *CICA Handbook* specifies the method that must be used to calculate the pension expense and provides some direction on the assumptions that must be made. But the *CICA Handbook* has nothing to say about how pension plans are funded. That is the domain of legislation, the pension agreements between the employer and its employees, and actuaries. (An **actuary** is a person who assesses insurance risks and sets insurance premiums. Actuaries help determine the funding requirements of pension plans.)

In contrast to accounting, there are several methods that are acceptable for calculating the funding of a pension plan. Also, the assumptions that actuaries make tend to be more conservative than those made by accountants. As a result, the funding of a pension plan and the pension expense for a year are often different. The difference between the two amounts gives rise to a balancing pension asset or liability. If the amount of funding is greater than the pension expense, a pension asset is reported on the balance sheet. If the expense is greater than the funding, a pension liability is reported.

Pension information is important to many users of financial statements. The condition of a pension plan provides information about cash flow requirements of an entity. A pension plan that has significantly fewer resources than are required to meet its obligations will have to be "topped up" by the employer. (By law, a pension plan must be adequately funded.) This requirement will draw cash away from other possible uses. The funding status of a pension plan is also important to employees, who should be interested in knowing whether the pension fund has the resources to pay the pensions they have been promised.

A crucial point for understanding balance sheet information about pensions is that the pension asset or liability does not provide information about the condition of the pension plan—the ability of a plan to meet the obligations to retirees. It is simply the difference between the accounting measure of the pension expense and the amount funded. The pension asset or liability informs users of the extent to which funding has exceeded recognition in the accounting records (pension asset) or recognition in the accounting records has exceeded funding (pension liability).

To conclude that the difference between the accounting expense and the amount funded is an indication of how well funded the plan is implies that the pension expense is the correct measure of the amount that should be funded. This is not a valid interpretation. The pension expense is just one of many possible measures of the amount that should be expensed—other measures are possible and reasonable. The pension expense is also a function of the assumptions made. Change the assumptions and you change the pension expense. If the funding remains the same in light of changes in the accounting assumptions, the amount of the pension asset or liability will change, but the condition of the pension plan will be the same.

There are two other points about pension accounting that are worth mentioning. First, the rules in the *CICA Handbook* are designed to allow preparers to smooth income. The full economic impact of events that could cause significant fluctuations in the annual pension expense are not reflected when they occur but instead are often amortized, thereby smoothing out their effects. Second, because of the complexity of the assumptions that must be made to calculate the pension expense, preparers must exercise considerable judgment in making those assumptions. These judgments can significantly affect the numbers that are reported in the financial statements, and as a result preparers have some flexibility with which to achieve their reporting objectives.

The disclosure requirements for pensions under GAAP are detailed and extensive. The information in the financial statements themselves is limited to the pension expense and the pension asset or liability. The notes provide information about the amount that has been expensed to date (since the inception of the plan) and the fair value of the assets in the plan. Remember that neither of these amounts appears on the balance sheet of the entity.

Question for Consideration

Gulch Inc. (Gulch) has reported on its latest balance sheet a large pension liability. A friend has asked you to explain whether the liability means that Gulch has not contributed enough money to the pension plan. Respond to your friend's question.

Answer:

A pension liability simply means that the pension expense for accounting purposes is greater than the amount of cash contributed to the pension fund. The liability says nothing about the ability of the pension fund to meet Gulch's obligation to its employees. The pension expense that Gulch reports is determined by accountants and accounting rules, and the amount contributed to the pension plan is determined by legislation, the agreement between the employees and employer, and actuaries. The methods and assumptions used in the determination of each element do not have to be the same.

Future Income Taxes

Perhaps one of the most confusing, misunderstood, and abused topics in accounting is *future income taxes*. The topic is worthy of attention in an introductory financial accounting course because it is very common to see future income taxes (or deferred income taxes, as they used to be called) reported on companies' balance sheets. MWW reports a $2,997,000 future income tax asset on its January 27, 2000 balance sheet. Petro-Canada reported a $1.533 billion future income tax liability on its December 31, 2000 balance sheet, which represents over 27% of its liabilities and over

15% of its liabilities and equities. With numbers that big it is important to understand where they come from, what they represent and, perhaps even more importantly, what they do not represent.

The first point to make about future income taxes is that they have nothing to do with the amount of tax an entity has to pay. **Future income tax assets and liabilities** arise because the accounting methods used to prepare the general purpose financial statements are sometimes different from the methods used to calculate taxable income and the amount of income tax an entity must pay. **Taxable income** is the measure of income, as defined by the *Income Tax Act* (*ITA*), that is used to calculate the amount of tax an entity must pay. In many situations the *ITA* specifies how an entity must account for certain transactions and economic events for tax purposes. When a method is specified in the *ITA*, it must be used for tax purposes regardless of what is done for financial reporting. In other words, an entity can do what it wants for financial reporting purposes, but for calculating its taxes it must use the rules in the *ITA*.

If you examine MWW's statement of earnings (page A-46), you will notice that the *income tax expense* is split into two parts: current expense and future expense. The current expense is the income taxes that MWW must pay currently to the federal and provincial governments—it is the amount that is reported on MWW's tax return. The current expense represents cash that either has already been paid or is currently payable to government. For the year ended January 27, 2001, MWW had to pay income taxes of $8,317,000. We cannot tell from the financial statements how much of that amount has been paid because taxes payable is included in the accounts payable and accrued liabilities account. The future expense (benefit) portion is the result of differences between how the *ITA* and GAAP require or allow income to be calculated.

There are two categories of differences between tax accounting and financial reporting: temporary differences and permanent differences. **Temporary differences** are a matter of timing. Many revenues and expenses are recognized at different times for tax and financial reporting. These revenues and expenses will be fully recognized for both tax and financial reporting purposes, but recognition will happen at different times. For example, a warranty expense is accrued for financial reporting purposes when the revenue from the sale of the product or good under warranty is recognized. For tax purposes warranty costs are deducted when the cost is actually incurred—when the warranty work is actually done. For both financial reporting and tax, the cost of providing warranty services will be expensed, but the expense will be recognized at different times. When temporary differences exist between tax and financial reporting, future income taxes arise.

Permanent differences are revenues and expenses that are recognized for tax purposes but never recognized for financial reporting purposes, or are recognized for financial reporting purposes but never recognized for tax purposes. These differences between tax and financial reporting are permanent—they never reverse. For example, for tax purposes businesses can deduct only 50% of amounts spent on meals and entertainment when calculating taxable income. For financial reporting purposes, 100% of these costs are expensed when calculating net income. The 50% that is not deductible for tax purposes is a permanent difference between tax and financial reporting. Permanent differences do not have an effect on future income taxes. Examples of temporary and permanent differences between tax and financial reporting are listed in Table 10-9.

Let's now look at some specifics. We will start by looking at the journal entry an entity makes to record income taxes. The form of the journal entry is:

Dr. Income tax expense (expenses +, shareholders' equity −)   xxx
     Cr. Future income tax asset or liability   yyy
     Cr. Taxes payable (liabilities +)   zzz

Table 10-9   Temporary and Permanent Differences Between Tax and Financial Reporting

Issue	Type of difference	Tax	GAAP
Amortization of assets	Temporary	CCA (capital cost allowance) at prescribed rates	Amortization in a "rationale" way
Revenue recognition	Temporary	Percentage of completion for contracts lasting more than two years	Completed contract allowable if consistent with the facts
Warranty costs	Temporary	Deduct when the work is done	Accrue the expense when the revenue is recognized
Discounts and premiums on long-term debt	Temporary	Recognized when the principal is repaid	Amortized over the term of the debt
Pension costs	Temporary	Deduct when money contributed to the pension fund	Expense based on accounting estimate of the pension obligation
Capital gains	Permanent	50% of capital gains and losses are taken into income for tax purposes	100% of capital gains and losses are taken into income for financial reporting purposes
Meals and entertainment expenses	Permanent	Only 50% of the amount spent is deductible for tax purposes	100% is expensed for financial reporting purposes
Interest and penalties on late payment of taxes	Permanent	Not deductible for tax purposes	Expensed for financial reporting purposes

or

Dr. Income tax expense (expenses +, shareholders' equity −)	xxx
Dr. Future income tax asset or liability	yyy
Cr. Taxes payable (liabilities +)	zzz

The taxes payable entry is easiest. It is the amount that the entity has to pay in taxes and is obtained from the entity's tax return. Determining the amount of tax an entity must pay can be very complex. We will not deal with those complexities in this book. Our challenge will be determining the debit or credit to future income taxes. The entry to future income taxes increases or decreases the amount in the future income taxes account on the balance sheet. Finally, the income tax expense is the amount that is reported on the entity's income statement. MWW's income tax expense for the year ended January 27, 2001 is $8,346,000, which is made up of a $8,317,000 current expense and a $29,000 future expense. As we will see, the income tax expense is a "plug". It is the amount that balances the journal entry and does not have to be calculated.

The future income tax balance on the balance sheet reflects temporary differences between the accounting value of assets and liabilities and the tax value of assets and liabilities on the balance sheet date, multiplied by the entity's tax rate. The debit or credit to future income taxes in the journal entry is the amount required to adjust the opening balance in the future income tax account to the required closing balance. Don't get alarmed if this sounds very complicated. We will go through a (long) example to show how it's done. As the basis for the example, we will use the largest contributor to most entities' temporary differences—the difference between capital cost allowance (CCA) and amortization.

Askilton Inc. (Askilton) began business in 2005. The company owns a single asset that it purchased for $100,000 in early 2005. For tax purposes the asset is in a CCA class that allows Askilton to deduct 100% of the capital cost of the asset. However, because of the half-year rule Askilton can claim only one-half of the allowable amount in 2005 and the remainder in 2006. For accounting purposes management has decided to amortize the asset on a straight-line basis over four years. Askilton has an income tax rate of 30% and its income before amortization and taxes is $300,000 in each year from 2005 through 2008. Askilton has no temporary differences between tax and financial reporting, except for the difference between amortization and CCA, and there are no permanent differences. Askilton's year end is December 31.

The first step will be to determine how much tax Askilton has to pay. Extracts from Askilton's tax returns are shown in Table 10-10. As stated above, income before CCA and taxes is assumed to be $300,000 each year, and this amount applies to both tax and financial reporting. To calculate taxable income, CCA is deducted each year. CCA in 2005 is $50,000 ($100,000 × 100% × 0.5) and in 2006 $50,000 ([$100,000 − $50,000] × 100%). After 2006 the full capital cost of the asset has been deducted for tax purposes, so no CCA can be deducted in 2007 and 2008. Askilton's tax liability is calculated by multiplying taxable income by the tax rate of 30%. Askilton must pay $75,000 in taxes in 2005 and 2006, and $90,000 in 2007 and 2008. We have now completed the first element of the income tax journal entry, taxes payable.

The way to determine the balance in the future income taxes account at a point in time is to compare the tax basis of an asset or liability with the accounting basis. The accounting basis of an asset (or liability) is its NBV for financial reporting purposes. For a capital asset, NBV equals the cost of the asset less accumulated amortization. The tax basis of an asset (or liability) is a similar concept, except that it is determined using tax rules instead of accounting rules. For a capital asset, the tax basis or **undepreciated capital cost (UCC)** is the part of the cost of the asset that has not been deducted for tax purposes. UCC is the tax equivalent of NBV and equals the cost of the asset less the total amount of CCA that has been deducted.

Table 10-11 provides a comparison of the tax basis and the accounting basis for Askilton's asset in each of the four years.

Table 10-11 shows that at the end of 2005 the tax basis (UCC) of Askilton's asset is $50,000 and its accounting basis (NBV) is $75,000. To the Canada Customs and Revenue Agency (CCRA) the value of the asset at the end of 2005 is $50,000. To Askilton's auditor the value at the end of 2005 is $75,000. All this means is that the income tax people measure Askilton's assets differently than do accountants.

Different ways of measuring the same thing is nothing new to us. The reason for the difference at the end of 2005 is that Askilton could deduct $50,000 of CCA in 2005, while for accounting purposes Askilton amortized $25,000 of the cost of the asset ($100,000 ÷ 4). At the end of 2006 the tax basis is $0 and the accounting basis is $50,000. At the end of 2008 the tax basis and the accounting basis of the asset are the same because it is fully amortized for both accounting and tax purposes. At the end of 2008 UCC = NBV = 0.

Table 10-10 Extracts from Askilton Inc.'s Tax Return

Askilton Inc. Extracts from Tax Returns for the Years Ended December 31, 2005–2008				
	2005	**2006**	**2007**	**2008**
Income before CCA and taxes	$300,000	$300,000	$300,000	$300,000
Less: CCA	50,000	50,000	0	0
Taxable income	250,000	250,000	300,000	300,000
Income taxes (30% of taxable income)	$75,000	$75,000	$90,000	$90,000

Table 10-11 Comparison of Tax Basis and Accounting Basis for
Askilton Inc.'s Asset

	Tax Basis			Accounting Basis		
	UCC at the beginning of the year	CCA claimed for the year	UCC at the end of the year	NBV at the beginning of the year	Amortization expense	NBV at the end of the year
2005	$100,000	$50,000	$50,000	$100,000	$25,000	$75,000
2006	50,000	50,000	0	75,000	25,000	50,000
2007	0	0	0	50,000	25,000	25,000
2008	0	0	0	25,000	25,000	0

With the information from Table 10-11 we can calculate the amount of future income taxes that should be reported on Askilton's balance sheet each year. Askilton's future income tax asset or liability is calculated by multiplying the difference between the asset's tax basis (UCC) and its accounting basis (NBV) by the tax rate. Table 10-12 shows the calculation.

The rightmost column of Table 10-12 shows the balance that will appear on Askilton's balance sheet each year for future income taxes. In this case, the future income tax balance is a liability. On Askilton's December 31, 2005 balance sheet a future income tax liability of $7,500 will be reported. A future income tax liability arises when the tax basis of an asset is less than the accounting basis of the asset or when the tax basis of a liability is greater than the accounting basis of the liability. A future income tax asset arises when the tax basis of an asset is greater than the accounting basis of the asset or when the tax basis of a liability is less than the accounting basis of the liability. These relationships are summarized in Table 10-13 (page 610).

Notice that over the four-year period the temporary differences reverse and in the end the same amount that is deducted for tax purposes is expensed for accounting purposes. In Table 10-12 the tax basis of Askilton's asset at the end of 2005 is $50,000, which is less that the accounting basis of $75,000, and therefore the future income tax balance is a liability.

While the rightmost column in Table 10-12 tells us the balance that is required on the balance sheet at the end of each year, it does not tell us what the debit or credit to future income taxes should be to give us that balance. At the beginning of 2005 the balance in the future income tax account is zero (Askilton began business in 2005). At the end of 2005 we need the future income tax account to be a liability of $7,500 (see Table 10-13). To obtain this balance, a credit to future income taxes of $7,500 is

Table 10-12 Calculating Askilton's Future Income Tax Asset or Liability

	Tax Basis	Accounting Basis			
	UCC at the end of the year	NBV at the end of the year	Difference	Tax rate	Future income tax asset (liability)
2005	$50,000	$75,000	($25,000)	30%	($7,500)
2006	0	50,000	(50,000)	30%	(15,000)
2007	0	25,000	(25,000)	30%	(7,500)
2008	0	0	0	30%	0

Table 10-13   Tax Bases and Accounting Bases and the Balance in the Future Income Taxes Account

			Future income tax balance
Tax basis of an asset	>	Accounting basis of an asset ⟶	Asset
Tax basis of an asset	<	Accounting basis of an asset ⟶	Liability
Tax basis of an liability	>	Accounting basis of an liability ⟶	Liability
Tax basis of an liability	<	Accounting basis of an liability ⟶	Asset

needed. At the end of 2006 a liability of $15,000 is required, so another credit to future income taxes of $7,500 must be made. In 2007 the credit balance in the account decreases from $15,000 to $7,500. To account for this change, a debit to the future income tax account of $7,500 is needed. A summary of the debits and credits needed is shown in Table 10-14.

We now have all the pieces to the puzzle. We know the amount of tax that has to be paid (see Table 10-10, page 608) and the entries required to the future income tax account (Table 10-14). All we need now is the income tax expense that is reported on the income statement. That, as was pointed out earlier, is a plug. With the method described here, it is not actually possible to calculate the income tax expense directly.

The journal entries for each year are shown in Table 10-15. For 2005 we know that Askilton must pay taxes of $75,000 (credit Taxes Payable or Cash) and that to obtain the required balance in the Future Income Tax account on December 31, 2005, a credit of $7,500 to Future Income Taxes is required. Therefore, the Income Tax Expense for 2005 must be $82,500. Examine the entries in Table 10-16 and notice how the tax expense is determined from the other amounts that are known.

The income tax expense in Askilton's income statement would be reported as shown in Table 10-16. The *CICA Handbook* requires the financial statements disclose the portion of the income tax expense that is attributable to future income taxes. The amount can be shown in the income statement as in Table 10-17 (page 612) and MWW (page A-46), or in the notes to the financial statements.

Notice that taxable income (Table 10-10) and income before taxes (Table 10-17, page 612) are different in each year and that the tax expense reported on the income statement and the amount of tax that Askilton must pay (Table 10-10) are different in each year. These differences occur because the *ITA* required Askilton to calculate its CCA deduction one way and GAAP allowed it to calculate amortization on the asset another way.

Things would be simpler if the income tax expense were simply the actual amount of tax an entity actually had to pay—an approach we can call the taxes

Table 10-14   Entries Required to Obtain the Desired Balance in Future Income Tax Account on December 31, 2005–2008

Year	Opening balance in future income tax asset (liability) account	Entry required to the future income tax account	Ending balance in future income tax asset (liability) account
2005	0	$7,500 Cr.	($7,500)
2006	($7,500)	7,500 Cr.	(15,000)
2007	(15,000)	7,500 Dr.	(7,500)
2008	(7,500)	7,500 Dr.	0

Table 10-15 Tax Journal Entries for Askilton Inc.

Dr. Tax expense (expenses +, shareholders' equity–)	82,500	
Cr. Future income tax liability (liabilities +)		7,500
Cr. Taxes payable (liabilities +)		75,000
To record the tax expense and future income tax liability for 2005.		
Dr. Tax expense (expenses +, shareholders' equity–)	82,500	
Cr. Future income tax liability (liabilities +)		7,500
Cr. Taxes payable (liabilities +)		75,000
To record the tax expense and future income tax liability for 2006.		
Dr. Tax expense (expenses +, shareholders' equity–)	82,500	
Dr. Future income tax liability (liabilities +)	7,500	
Cr. Taxes payable (liabilities +)		90,000
To record the tax expense and future income tax liability for 2007.		
Dr. Tax expense (expenses +, shareholders' equity–)	82,500	
Dr. Future income tax liability (liabilities +)	7,500	
Cr. Taxes payable (liabilities +)		90,000
To record the tax expense and future income tax liability for 2008.		

payable method. If the taxes payable method were used, there would be no future income taxes to account for because income tax expense would be equal to income taxes payable. The problem with the taxes payable method for some accountants is that the income tax expense would be measured using a different method than the other numbers on the income statement. The income tax expense would be based on the requirements of the *ITA* and the rest of the numbers would be based on GAAP, accrual accounting, or whatever basis of accounting the entity chose to use. Of course, as we have seen throughout the book, a variety of different ways of measuring things is reflected in contemporary financial statements. The taxes payable method can have some interesting effects on net income.

Net income calculated using the taxes payable method for Askilton is shown in Table 10-17 (page 612).

Notice that in Table 10-17 net income varies over the four years, whereas in Table 10-16 net income is the same each year. In general the taxes payable approach makes earnings more variable, which can make an entity look more risky. Which approach is better? That depends on the users and uses of the information. The taxes payable

Table 10-16 Financial Statement Presentation of Future Income Taxes

Askilton Inc.
Extracts from the Income Statement
December 31, 2005–2008

	2005	2006	2007	2008
Income before amortization				
and income taxes	$300,000	$300,000	$300,000	$300,000
Amortization expense	25,000	25,000	25,000	25,000
Income before taxes	275,000	275,000	275,000	275,000
Income tax expense				
Current expense	75,000	75,000	90,000	90,000
Future expense (benefit)	7,500	7,500	(7,500)	(7,500)
	82,500	82,500	82,500	82,500
Net income	$192,500	$192,500	$192,500	$192,500

| Table 10-17 | Net Income Calculated using the Taxes Payable Method |

Askilton Inc.
Extracts from the Income Statement
December 31, 2005–2008

	2005	2006	2007	2008
Income before amortization and income taxes	$300,000	$300,000	$300,000	$300,000
Amortization expense	25,000	25,000	25,000	25,000
Income before taxes	275,000	275,000	275,000	275,000
Income tax expense	75,000	75,000	90,000	90,000
Net income	$200,000	$200,000	$185,000	$185,000

method is the cash approach. The future income tax method is based on accounting measurement criteria. Remember, however, that regardless of which method is used, the actual cash flow, the amount of tax the entity pays, remains the same.

The Askilton example only gave rise to future income tax liabilities. Future income tax assets are also commonly reported. For example, MWW reports a non-current future income tax asset in its balance sheets (page A-45). As shown in Table 10-13 (page 610), whether a future income tax asset or liability arises is simply a matter of the tax basis of assets and liabilities versus their accounting basis. If at the end of 2005 the NBV of Askilton's asset were $45,000 instead of $75,000, Askilton would have reported a future income tax asset of $1,500 ([(UCC – NBV) × tax rate] = [($50,000 – $45,000) × 30%]). The example also did not deal with current and non-current future income tax assets and liabilities. Current future income tax assets and liabilities are the result of differences between the tax and accounting bases of current assets and liabilities, and non-current future income tax assets and liabilities are the result of differences between the tax and accounting bases of non-current assets and liabilities.

The purpose of this discussion was to show with a "simple" example where a balance in the future income tax account comes from. In reality, a future income tax balance is a complex mix of differences between financial reporting and tax for many different assets and liabilities. But the more important question for introductory students of accounting is, How should a future income tax balance be interpreted when examining an entity's financial statements? Here are some points to consider:

- Future income taxes (and its predecessor, deferred taxes) have long been misinterpreted and abused. Every now and then in the media or among politicians the future income tax liability is pointed to as evidence that corporations are not paying "their fair share" of taxes. This interpretation is false and misleading. Future income taxes also do not represent actual claims of governments against a company's assets or refunds that are forthcoming. As we discussed at length, future income taxes are the result of differences between financial reporting and tax. By using the taxes payable method, future income tax liabilities would disappear, but entities would be paying exactly the same amount of income tax. Perhaps the new name, future income taxes, instead of deferred income taxes, will discourage people from misinterpreting the meaning of this account.

- Only the current portion of the income tax expense on the income statement represents a current cash flow. The future portion represents a non-cash accrual. As a result, future income tax accounting reduces the association between earnings and cash flows.

- Tax and accounting rules are different. Most entities do not prepare their financial statements on a tax basis (although some will, if it serves their objectives of financial reporting). But tax rules do have an important impact on entities. An asset with CCA still available to be claimed is more valuable than an asset with no CCA because the remaining CCA will reduce the amount of tax the entity has to pay.

In principle, future income tax balances give some insight into the remaining tax value of assets and liabilities because it bridges the difference between accounting and tax. For example, at the end of 2006 Askilton's asset had a tax value of zero and an accounting value of $50,000. From the accounting records alone, it is not possible to tell that the asset had no tax value. Information about the tax value of an asset is useful because it helps users assess future cash flows. The future tax liability of $15,000 tells users that the tax value of the asset is $50,000 (future tax liability ÷ tax rate = $15,000 ÷ 0.3) less than the accounting value. On December 31, 2006 the accounting value of the asset is $50,000, so the tax value is zero.

MWW provides a table in Note 17 (page A-62) that allocates future income tax assets and liabilities to specific asset and liability categories. This disclosure helps users figure out the tax value of different groups of assets and liabilities. An alternative to this approach would be to disclose the tax value of assets and liabilities in the notes to the financial statements.

- The temporary differences that give rise to future income taxes are often not very temporary. If an entity is growing, the temporary differences between the amount of CCA deducted and the amount of amortization expensed will usually grow as well, with the result that the future income tax liability will increase year after year. In those circumstances it is questionable whether the credit balance should be considered a liability.

- Future income tax liabilities are not discounted. As a result, amounts reported on the balance sheet are overstated because the time value of money is not taken into consideration. If future income tax balances will not decrease for a long time, some of the very large future income tax liability balances can actually represent some relatively small liabilities in present value terms. For example, if Petro-Canada's $1.533 billion future income tax liability will not decrease for 50 years, the present value of the liability discounted at 8% is only about $32,700,000.

www.petro-canada.ca

- Future income taxes are affected by the accounting policies used. Assuming that the amount of income tax an entity pays is not affected by the accounting choices it makes for financial reporting purposes, accounting choices that increase income will increase the future income tax liability (or decrease the future income tax asset).

- Entities that do not have to follow GAAP might choose not to use future income tax accounting. A small private company whose financial statements are used for tax purposes and by a banker might choose to forego following this GAAP rule. Future income tax accounting is complex and confusing, can be costly to use, and in many situations may provide little useful information to financial statement users.

- The financial statements of public companies provide additional disclosures that can be useful to understanding the tax status of an entity. The first table in Note 17 to MWW's financial statements (page A-62) provides a reconciliation from the tax rate that MWW would be expected to pay (the statutory rate) and the tax rate reflected in the income statement (tax expense ÷ earnings before income taxes and goodwill amortization). Using the income statement numbers gives a tax rate of 48.9% ($8,346,000 ÷ $17,074,000), whereas the statutory rate for MWW in fiscal 2001 is 44%. MWW does not provide any detail about what gives rise to the difference, but the financial statements of other entities often do. The *CICA Handbook* requires disclosure of the information shown in MWW's Note 17.

Debt and Taxes

We briefly discussed earlier the tax implications of debt. Entities are allowed to deduct interest when calculating taxable income. This means the actual cost of borrowing money is less than the amount that is paid to the lender. In effect, the taxpayers pay for part of the cost of borrowing. The **after-tax cost of borrowing** is the interest rate an entity pays after taking into consideration the savings that come from being able to deduct interest in the calculation of taxable income. The after-tax cost of borrowing is calculated using the following formula:

$$\text{After-tax cost of borrowing} = \text{Stated interest rate} \times (1 - \text{tax rate})$$

Estmere Inc. (Estmere) has a $10,000,000 long-term bond outstanding that has an interest rate of 11.5%. Estmere pays the bondholder $1,150,000 in interest on December 31 of each year. Estmere's tax rate is 40%. Estmere's after-tax cost of borrowing is:

After-tax cost of borrowing	=	Stated interest rate	×	(1 − tax rate)
	=	11.5%	×	1 − 0.4
	=	11.5%	×	0.6
	=	6.9%		

Since Estmere is able to reduce its income by $1,150,000 each year because it can deduct the interest cost, it has to pay $460,000 ($1,150,000 × 0.4) less tax than it would if the cost of borrowing were not deductible.

Suppose Estmere's income for tax purposes before deducting interest and taxes were $5,000,000. Estmere would have to pay $2,000,000 ($5,000,000 × 0.4) in taxes if interest were not deductible, whereas it would have to pay $1,540,000 ([$5,000,000 − $1,150,000] × 0.4) if interest were deductible. The deductibility of interest makes debt a desirable way to obtain financing because the entity does not have to pay the full cost of borrowing. Dividends, on the other hand, are not tax deductible.

Contingencies

Suppose an entity realizes that it may incur a gain or a loss as a result of events that have already happened, but the amount of the gain or loss, or even the existence of the gain or loss, is uncertain and will not be known until some future event occurs. What, if anything, should the financial statement impact be?

For example, in 2002 Rosyth Ltd. (Rosyth) was sued for $10,000,000. As of the end of fiscal 2006 no settlement had been reached or judgment made by the courts, so the amount that Rosyth will ultimately have to pay is unknown. What, if anything, should Rosyth report in its 2006 financial statements about the lawsuit? These types of situations are known as contingencies. A **contingency** is a possible liability or asset whose existence and amount depend on some future event. The lawsuit against Rosyth is a contingency because whether Rosyth has to pay out as a result of the law-suit and the amount it will have to pay out depend on a future event—a settlement or a judgment by the courts.

There are three possible ways to account for a contingency: it could be accrued, disclosed in the notes to the financial statements, or ignored for financial reporting purposes. Perhaps it would be best if all contingencies were accrued in the financial statements. That way, the economic impact of contingencies would be reflected in the financial statement numbers.

But does it make sense to accrue contingencies if they have a low probability of being realized—for example, a frivolous lawsuit launched by a disgruntled employee? Such recognition in the accounts would have an impact on the financial statements but would eventually have to be reversed when the lawsuit failed. And what about the case of Rosyth's lawsuit? Just because someone is suing for $10,000,000 does not mean that that will be the amount of the settlement. It can be very difficult to determine the outcome of a case before the courts.

On the other hand, ignoring contingencies would deprive users of important information about risks that the entity faces. Failing to disclose significant contingen-cies could open entities and their auditors to lawsuits for failing to provide important information. Disclosure could provide information about the existence and signifi-cance of contingencies, but disclosure does not have any measurement implications—it does not affect the financial statement numbers—so outcomes such as bonus payments or covenants that depend on financial statement numbers are not affected. Clearly, accounting for contingencies is a tricky business, and there is no easy solution for what to do.

The *CICA Handbook* provides guidance for accounting for contingencies for those entities that follow GAAP. The *Handbook* requires that contingent losses that are likely to occur and can be reasonably measured be accrued in the financial statements. Contingent losses that are likely to occur but cannot be reasonably mea-sured should be disclosed in the notes to the financial statements, but do not have to be accrued. The *CICA Handbook* suggests, but does not require, disclosure of con-tingent losses that are not likely to occur but are significant.

For many contingent losses it is not possible to determine if they are likely or unlikely to occur. In situations where the likelihood of outcome of a contingency is not determinable, the *CICA Handbook* requires that the contingency be disclosed in the notes to the financial statements.

Contingent gains should never be accrued, according to the *CICA Handbook*. This treatment is consistent with the concept of conservatism. The *Handbook* requires dis-closure of a contingent gain if it is likely to occur. Managers often have to exercise con-siderable judgment in applying this *CICA Handbook* section. The terms "likely", "unlikely" and, "reasonably measurable" are subjective, and the judgments made by management can have an impact on the numbers reported in and the information provided by financial statements.

Panel A—Fortis Inc. 2000 Annual Report

22. Contingent Liability

In 2000, the Canada Customs and Revenue Agency (CCRA) issued Notices of Reassessment to Newfoundland Power confirming the deductibility of certain amounts capitalized by Newfoundland Power for regulatory and accounting purposes, and reconfirming a 1995 reassessment, which included in income the value of electricity consumed in December but not billed until January. Newfoundland Power's practice, which has been consistent and is in accordance with regulatory requirements, is to record revenue on a billed basis.

Newfoundland Power believes it has reported its tax position appropriately and has filed a Notice of Objection with the Minister of National Revenue. No provision has been made in the accounts for additional income taxes, if any, which may be determined to be payable. Should Newfoundland Power be unsuccessful in defending its position, a liability of approximately $14 million, including accrued interest, would arise. In this event, Newfoundland Power would apply to the PUB to include the amount in the rate making process. The application may include a request to change the current accounting practice of recognizing revenue when billed. If the PUB approves this change in accounting practice, electricity, valued at approximately $17 million, consumed in December but not billed until January would be included in income.

The provisions of the Income Tax Act require Newfoundland Power to deposit one half of the amount in dispute with CCRA. The amount currently withheld by CCRA arising from the 2000 reassessment is approximately $14 million. This amount exceeds the required deposit by approximately $7 million and, accordingly, Newfoundland Power has requested that this amount be refunded.

Panel B—Four Seasons Hotels and Resorts 2001 Annual Report

Years ended December 31, 2000 and 1999
(In thousands of dollars except per share amounts)

12) Commitments and contingencies:

(c) **Contingencies:**

(i) The Corporation estimates and accrues for the losses, if any, it is likely to incur relating to uninsured contingent liabilities such as guarantees of third party debt, environmental matters, personal injury and property damage at owned or managed hotels, workers' compensation claims, etc. The Corporation's assessment of its potential liability for such matters could change, with the result that the accruals for contingent liabilities recorded in the Corporation's financial statements could increase by a material amount.

(ii) Until 1982, the Corporation held a co-ownership interest in an office building in Toronto. In 1981, the co-owners obtained financing of approximately $22,000 (of which approximately $20,600 plus accrued interest was outstanding as at December 31, 2000) in connection with the property and the Corporation provided a several guarantee with respect to the financing. The Corporation sold its interest in the property to a Canadian insurance company in 1982 for consideration consisting of a cash payment and an assumption by the purchaser of the Corporation's obligations under the mortgage. The Corporation has been advised by the mortgagee that a default has occurred under the mortgage and the mortgagee has commenced a proceeding against the Corporation and another guarantor. The Corporation is vigorously defending the suit and believes that, as a result of, among other things, the sale by the Corporation of its interest in the property and the resulting obligations of the purchaser, obligations of the Corporation, if any, to the mortgagee should be offset by corresponding claims against the purchaser.

(iii) In the ordinary course of its business, the Corporation is named as defendant in legal proceedings resulting from incidents taking place at hotels owned or managed by it. The Corporation maintains comprehensive liability insurance and also requires hotel owners to maintain adequate insurance coverage. The Corporation believes such coverage to be of a nature and amount sufficient to ensure that it is adequately protected from suffering any material financial loss as a result of such claims.

(iv) A number of the Corporation's management contracts are subject to certain performance tests which, if not met, could allow a contract to be terminated prior to its maturity. The Corporation generally has various rights to cure any such defaults to avoid termination. In addition, certain management contracts are terminable by the hotel owner on a defined change of control of FSHI.

(v) The Corporation has guaranteed certain obligations of various directors, officers, and employees in the amount of $941.

According to *Financial Reporting in Canada,* 26th Edition, lawsuits, environmental matters, guarantees of the debts of others, and possible tax reassessments were the most common contingent losses reported by entities in 2000. The *Financial Reporting in Canada* survey finds that the reporting of contingent gains is quite rare. In 2000 none of the 200 firms surveyed reported contingent gains while only one firm in 1999 and two in 1998 disclosed contingent gains.[2]

Examples of contingencies reported in financial statements are provided in Exhibit 10-2. Fortis Inc. reports a contingent liability related to a tax reassessment from the CCRA. The reassessment pertains to the company's 1995 tax return. Four Seasons Hotels Inc. describes five different contingencies in its annual report. Contingency (i) describes its general accounting policy for contingencies and (iii) states that the company gets sued fairly regularly and that it believes it carries adequate liability insurance. The note does not seem to describe the lawsuits that are currently outstanding. Contingencies (ii), (iv), and (v) describe specific contingencies.[3]

Recognizing contingencies in the financial statements, either in the statements

www.fortisinc.com
www.fourseasons.com

themselves or in the notes, is not a violation of historical cost accounting. The trigger for recognizing a contingency is an event that occurs in the past, before the financial statement date. The difficulty with accounting for contingencies is the uncertainty about the outcome—whether there will actually be a loss and a liability or a gain and an asset.

Commitments

A **commitment** is a contractual agreement to enter into a transaction in the future. It was explained earlier in the chapter that when neither party to the commitment has performed its side of the bargain, under GAAP the contract is not recorded in the entity's accounting records. These types of circumstances are called executory contracts.

The GAAP approach is not the only way of accounting for executory contracts. An alternative would be to record the asset and liability associated with the contract (perhaps only when it is not possible for either party to cancel the contract). For example, in December 2004, Chopaka Inc. (Chopaka) signed a contract to purchase $400,000 of lumber that it requires for the construction of homes in a new subdivision. The lumber is to be delivered over the construction period between March and October 2005. The contract is not cancellable by either Chopaka or the supplier. Under GAAP this contract would not appear in the financial statements. However, if executory contracts were recognized, Chopaka would report an asset representing the lumber to be delivered and a liability to pay for the lumber when it is delivered. The asset and liability would each be reported at $400,000.

This non-GAAP approach treats the commitment to purchase the lumber as an obligation for Chopaka to pay the supplier for the lumber (because it is a binding, non-cancellable contract). An asset is recorded because Chopaka has obtained a future benefit—an assured supply of lumber at a fixed price. There are no income statement effects of this treatment, but it increases assets and liabilities. There is no effect on working capital (current assets − current liabilities), but the current ratio (current assets ÷ current liabilities) is affected if the ratio is not equal to 1.0.

Note that the asset is not called inventory. It is really inventory receivable because the actual inventory has not yet been delivered. The liability is not an account payable because money is not owed to the supplier until the lumber is delivered.

While Canadian GAAP generally do not allow for recognition of executory contracts, it is recognized that information about contracts that represent significant commitments by an entity can be important to users of the financial statements. The *CICA Handbook* requires disclosure of information about contracts that are significant to the entity. The *Handbook* mentions that contracts should be disclosed when they (a) involve an unusual degree of risk, (b) commit the entity to significant expenditures, or (c) commit the entity to issue shares.

If Chopaka followed GAAP, it might disclose information about its contract to purchase lumber if the contract were considered significant. No entries would be made to the financial records until lumber was actually delivered. The decision to disclose a contract is a judgment call made by the managers. Managers could avoid disclosing contracts that might be of interest to stakeholders by exercising that judgment. The managers could contend that there was nothing significant about a contract that would merit separate disclosure.

MWW describes commitments that it has with suppliers of merchandise in Note 11 to the financial statements (page A-56). Two additional examples of commitments are shown in Exhibit 10-3 (page 618). Boralex Inc. (Boralex) is a non-government producer of hydroelectric and thermal power in Quebec. Boralex has commitments to sell its electricity production, to allow another entity to manage one of its plants, and to purchase capital assets for construction projects. Air Canada has commitments to purchase a number of aircraft, lease commitments, and commit-

www.boralex.com
www.aircanada.ca

Exhibit 10-3

Examples of Commitments

Panel A—Boralex Inc. 2001 Annual Report

13 Commitments and contingency

a) The Corporation is committed to sell all of its electricity production in Canada under long-term contracts maturing from 2010 to 2022 and renewable, except the one maturing in 2022, for periods of 10 to 25 years. The steam production from its two cogeneration power stations in Canada is sold under long-term contracts maturing in 2006 and 2023, respectively. The Corporation is also committed to sell most of its electricity production in the United States under contracts maturing from September 2001 to December 2001.

b) The Corporation is committed, under the terms of a service agreement ending January 28, 2023, to allow a third party, under its overview, the entire management of the operation and maintenance of one of its stations. The agreement covers the wood-residue supply cost, salaries, supplies and spare parts, minor maintenance work, and operating and administration costs. Major maintenance work and capital expenditures are assumed in addition to the service fees. Fees related to this service agreement amounted to $8,635,000 for the year. They are adjusted annually based on the consumer products index rate and, if applicable, to give effect to changes in the wood-residue supply costs.

c) With respect to construction projects in Senneterre, Québec and Blendecques, France, the Corporation is committed to the acquisition of capital assets amounting to $11,400,000 and $3,800,000 respectively (see also note 16 b).

Panel B—Air Canada 2000 Annual Report

13. Commitments

The Corporation has commitments to purchase, along with spare engines, four Airbus A330-300 and five Airbus A321 in 2001, seven Airbus A321, five Airbus A319 and two Airbus A340-500 in 2002 and three Airbus A340-500 and two Airbus A319 in 2003. Payments under the commitments of US $1,370 are payable as follows:

		US
2001	$	511
2002		552
2003		307

The Corporation has received financing commitments for 100% of two of the Airbus A330 aircraft, and for a number of Airbus A319 and A321 aircraft not to exceed US $384, as well as up to 85% of the other aircraft purchases. The Corporation has entered into certain interest rate swaps in 2000 with a credit worthy counterparty in support of the anticipated financing of four Airbus A330 aircraft in 2001. The fair value of these interest rate swaps at December 31, 2000 was $16 in favour of the counterparty (1999 $0).

The Corporation has also committed to leasing, under operating leases, aircraft on a long term basis to be delivered as follows: four Boeing 767-300 and three Airbus A319 in 2001, three Airbus A319 and three Airbus A320 in 2002. The total lease payments over the full term of the leases will be approximately US $780. The Corporation has entered into certain interest rate swaps in 2000 with a credit worthy counterparty in support of the leasing of two Boeing 767-300 aircraft in 2001. The fair value of these interest rate swaps at December 31, 2000 was $9 in favour of the counterparty (1999 $0).

Other commitments in 2001 and 2002 for property, ground equipment and spare parts, amount to approximately $146.

Future minimum lease payments under existing operating leases of aircraft and other property total $5,761 and are payable as follows:

	Operating Leases of Aircraft		Operating Leases of Other Property	
2001	$	964	$	105
2002		882		93
2003		852		85
2004		750		75
2005		584		66
Remaining years		961		344
	$	4,993	$	768

ments for property, ground equipment, and spare parts. The amounts for Air Canada in Exhibit 10-3 are in millions of dollars. The Air Canada note puts dollar figures on many of its commitments. Boralex does not put a dollar figure or disclose the terms of its long-term contracts to sell its power.[4]

Subsequent Events

What happens if a significant economic event occurs after the end of an entity's fiscal year? Strictly speaking, transactions-based, historical cost accounting should ignore the event until the financial statements are prepared for the fiscal year in which the event took place. On the other hand, any information that is potentially useful to stakeholders should be provided on a timely basis. GAAP and the *CICA Handbook* recognize that it can be important to disclose certain economic events even if they occur after the end of the fiscal year being reported on. A **subsequent event** is an economic event that occurs after an entity's year end, but before the financial statements are released to users.

The *CICA Handbook* identifies two types of subsequent events:

1. Events that provide additional information about circumstances that existed at the year end; and

2. Events that happened after the balance sheet date.

When the first type of subsequent event occurs, the financial statements themselves should be adjusted to reflect the new information. The availability of the new information allows preparers to make better estimates than they could at the financial statement date. For example, if a debtor filed for bankruptcy after the year end, the information could be used to improve the estimate of uncollectables. If new information about a contingent liability such as a lawsuit becomes available after the year end, the entity may be able to accrue the cost of the lawsuit rather than just disclosing it. Additional information about the warranty costs associated with a new product may allow for an improved estimate of the warranty provision.

The second type of subsequent event is unrelated to circumstances that existed at year end and should be disclosed only in the notes to the financial statements. The financial statements are not adjusted in response to this type of subsequent event. Of course, many events occur after the year end and virtually none of them are disclosed as subsequent events. What should be disclosed is not well defined. The *CICA Handbook* states that events that will have a significant effect on the entity in a subsequent period should be disclosed. Ultimately, what constitutes a subsequent event of either type is a matter of judgment and the preparers of the financial statements have flexibility in many cases as to whether and how an event that occurs after the year end will be reported in the financial statements.

For public companies, most events of any consequence would be disclosed to the public by means such as newspaper reports or press releases long before the financial statements were released. Thus, disclosing the second type of subsequent event in the financial statements would for the most part be redundant. For example, stock prices would probably not be affected by a subsequent event disclosed in the notes to the financial statements. The stock price effect would have occurred when the market first became aware of the event. The usefulness of a subsequent event disclosure of the second type for private companies, especially those that get little media scrutiny or public attention, would be much more likely to be "news" to users of the financial statements.

Not all users and uses of financial statements benefit from the disclosure of the second type of subsequent event. The second type of subsequent event is not relevant for tax purposes because it has no bearing on the calculation of the previous year's taxable income. Any use of the financial statements that requires measurement—such

Exhibit 10-4

Examples of Subsequent Evevnts

Panel A—Fortis Inc. 2000 Annual Report

23. Subsequent Event

On January 26, 2001, the Corporation purchased a 95% interest in Belize Electric Company Limited U.S. $62 million representing the fair market value of the assets acquired.

Panel B—Canadian Pacific Enterprises Limited 2000 Annual Report

17.   SUBSEQUENT EVENT

On February 13, 2001, Canadian Pacific Limited (the Company) announced a major reorganization which is intended to divide the Company into five separate public companies - Canadian Pacific Railway, CP Ships, PanCanadian Petroleum Ltd., Fording Inc. and Canadian Pacific Hotels & Resorts Inc.

Under the proposed plan, the Company intends to distribute its approximately 86% investment in PanCanadian Petroleum Ltd. and its wholly owned subsidiaries, Canadian Pacific Railway, CP Ships and Fording Inc. to its common shareholders. All of the distributed companies will be publicly traded. At this stage, it is proposed that Canadian Pacific Hotels & Resorts Inc. would remain with the Company as its principal ongoing business.

The distribution will be implemented by a Plan of Arrangement, contingent upon shareholder and court approval, a favourable Canadian tax ruling and other requisite consents.

Panel C—Boralex Inc. 2001 Annual Report

16 Subsequent events

a) On October 4, 2000, the Corporation completed a private placement of $33,000,000 in consideration of 6,000,000 Special Warrants at a price of $5.50 each. Each Special Warrant entitles its holder to acquire one Class A share of the Corporation at no additional cost. The Corporation has committed to obtain, before March 5, 2001, a receipt from the securities commissions for a final prospectus qualifying for distribution 4,000,000 new Class A shares of the Corporation and 2,000,000 Class A shares of the Corporation held directly or indirectly by Cascades Inc. Otherwise, each holder of Special Warrants will be entitled to receive at its election, either (i) 1.1 Class A shares upon exercise or deemed exercise of each Special Warrant, or (ii) as to one-third of its Special Warrants, the purchase price of such Special Warrants along with any interest earned thereon, and, as to two-thirds of its Special Warrants, 1.1 Class A shares for each Special Warrant surrendered on or prior to March 5, 2001. The net amount of $20,900,000 received by the Corporation will be used to finance its current and future projects.

b) On November 1, 2000, the Corporation finalized a $42,000,000 financing for the construction in Senneterre, Québec of its wood-residue power station with a capacity of 34 MW. The total costs of construction are estimated at $55,000,000, of which $33,000,000 remain to be incurred as at September 30, 2000.

as calculation of an income-based bonus or determination of whether a debt-to-equity or current ratio covenant is violated—would not be affected by disclosure of the second type of subsequent event. Disclosure would be useful to users who are interested in forecasting future earnings or cash flows.

MWW discloses a subsequent event in Note 19 to its financial statements (see page A-64). The note explains that MWW contracted with an independent company to handle its distribution activities for the next five years. The arrangement is disclosed presumably because it commits MWW to the service for a fairly long period of time. Other examples of subsequent events are provided in Exhibit 10-4. These examples include disclosure of the acquisition of a company by Fortis Inc., a major reorganization by Canadian Pacific Enterprises Limited, and the placement of securities and the completion of financing arrangements for a new plant by Boralex Inc.[5]

Financial Statement Analysis Issues

Analyzing an entity's liabilities can provide important information about its financial situation and its prospects. This analysis can also provide insight into the financial management of the entity. For example, creditors can obtain information that allows them to assess the amount that they would be willing to lend the entity and the terms of the loan, including interest rate, amount and type of collateral, and restrictive covenants. Two tools for analyzing liabilities are described below, along with some other important characteristics of debt.

Debt-to-Equity Ratio

The debt-to-equity ratio provides a measure of the amount of debt relative to equity an entity uses for financing. The ratio gives an indication of the riskiness of the entity and its ability to carry more debt. More debt makes an entity more risky. The reason is that more debt means more fixed interest charges must be paid—regardless of whether the entity is performing well or poorly. If interest and principal payments are not paid when required, the entity faces significant economic and legal consequences. As well, as the proportion of debt increases, the cost of debt—interest—will increase because lenders will charge a higher interest rate as the debt becomes more risky. Higher interest rates are how lenders are compensated for higher risk.

The debt-to-equity ratio is defined as:

$$\text{Debt-to-equity ratio} = \frac{\text{Total liabilities}}{\text{Total shareholders' equity}}$$

MWW's debt-to-equity ratio on January 27, 2001, using the numbers directly from the financial statements, was:

$$= \frac{\$92,339,000}{\$64,721,000}$$

$$= 1.427$$

The interpretation of the debt-to-equity ratio must be done carefully. MWW's debt-to-equity ratio of 1.427 means that it has $1.43 of liabilities for every $1 of equity. Is that too much? It is not possible to answer without a context. What is too high a ratio depends on many factors, including industry and circumstances. Entities that have highly reliable cash flows can carry more debt because they can be confident that the cash flows will be available to make interest and principal payments as required. Examples of average debt-to-equity ratios for different industries in 2000 are shown in Table 10-18.[6] Notice the variation in the ratio across the industries.

The use of the debt-to-equity ratio by simply using the numbers on the balance sheet can provide misleading results and interpretations. Leases, pensions, and future income taxes all present problems that can impair the interpretation of the debt-to-equity and other ratios that incorporate liabilities. If an entity makes extensive use of operating leases, liabilities and the debt-to-equity ratio will be understated because

Table 10-18 Seven Year Average Debt-to-Equity Ratios for Several Industries

Industry	Debt-to-equity ratio
Communications and media	1.06
Fabricating and engineering	0.27
Food and beverage	1.35
Paper and forest products	1.21
Telephone and utilities	2.03
Wholesale and retail	0.73

operating leases are a form of off-balance-sheet financing. This situation makes it difficult to compare debt-to-equity ratios of entities that have borrowed money to purchase assets or use capital leases.

Financial statement users can adjust total liabilities by using the disclosures in the notes to the financial statements about future lease payments required under operating leases. For example, Note 11 to MWW's financial statements (page A-56) provides a table of operating lease payments that will be made from 2002 through 2006. These amounts would have to be discounted to estimate the value of the liability, but the information is available to make adjustments.

Pensions pose similar problems. As we discussed, the pension liability on the balance sheet does not necessarily reflect the amount the entity must invest in the pension plan to meet the obligations of the plan. Footnote disclosure may help assess this shortfall. In any case, an adjustment to liabilities may be required so that the condition of the pension plan is reflected in the ratio.

Future income taxes present another problem. First, future income taxes are not liabilities in the sense that there is an obligation to anyone on the balance sheet date. Instead, it is simply the result of how accountants account for income taxes versus how income taxes are accounted for according to the *Income Tax Act*. Second, future income tax liabilities are not discounted. This means that even if the liability represents a cash flow that will actually occur, the amount is overstated because the reported balance ignores the time value of money. Third, future income taxes may not reverse. As long as an entity keeps expanding and the differences between the tax basis and accounting basis of the assets and liability continue to grow, the balance in the future income tax account may never decline (or at least not for a long time). In circumstances where it is unlikely that the future income taxes will decline, excluding them from liabilities and classifying them as equity makes sense. If the future income taxes are likely to decline, then treating them as liabilities makes sense. A combination of both approaches is also possible. The exact treatment in any situation is a matter of judgment.

Interest Coverage Ratio

The **interest coverage ratio** is one of a number of coverage ratios designed to measure the ability of an entity to meet its fixed financing charges. In particular, the interest coverage ratio indicates the ease with which an entity can meet its interest payments. The interest coverage ratio is defined as:

$$\text{Interest coverage ratio} = \frac{\text{Net income} + \text{Interest expense} + \text{Tax expense}}{\text{Interest expense}}$$

The larger the ratio, the better able the entity is to meet its interest payments. The interest coverage ratio is limiting in that it ignores the fact that entities have financial charges other than interest. Other fixed financial charges include debt repayment and payments on operating leases. This ratio can be modified to include these other charges, but for introductory purposes the interest coverage ratio is appropriate. The interest coverage ratio can also be calculated on a cash basis.

The interest coverage ratio for MWW for the year ended January 27, 2001 is calculated as:

$$\text{Interest coverage ratio} = \frac{\text{Net income} + \text{Interest expense} + \text{Tax expense}}{\text{Interest expense}}$$

$$= \frac{\$8,180,000 + (\$1,480,000 + \$2,498,000) + \$8,346,000}{\$1,480,000 + \$2,498,000}$$

$$= 5.154$$

The interest coverage ratio of 5.154 means that MWW's income before taxes and interest expense is enough to cover its interest cost over five times. This suggests reasonable protection for lenders. Of course, earnings and cash flows can be volatile and coverage ratios can change dramatically from period to period. MWW's interest coverage ratio for the year ended January 29, 2000 is 4.064.

Other Issues

Another characteristic of debt worth noting is the currency of the borrowed money. Canadian firms sometimes borrow money in currencies other than Canadian dollars and the interest and repayment of those debts are made in that foreign currency. Debt in foreign currency can add significant risk to an entity because of the fluctuations in currency exchange rates. For example, in the early 1990s it cost between $1.15 and $1.20 Canadian to buy one United States dollar. In the early 2000s one United States dollar cost as much as Cdn$1.60. If a Canadian firm borrowed U.S.$1,000,000 when the exchange rate was $1.20, the firm would receive Cdn$1,200,000. If the firm then had to repay the loan in U.S. dollars when the exchange rate was $1.50, the firm would have to pay Cdn$1,500,000 so that the lender would receive US$1,000,000. The firm incurred an extra $300,000 in borrowing costs, not to mention the higher cost of interest.

Loans that have interest rates that vary also add risk. MWW's syndicated bank loans have interest rates that vary with the prime lending rate. This means that as interest rates in the economy increase, the interest rate on the loan increases. An increase in the interest rate on a loan, of course, increases the entity's cost of borrowing.

■ Solved Problem

On December 1, 2005 Caxton Inc. (Caxton) issued a $10,000,000 bond to a private borrower. The bond will carry a 10% coupon rate and will mature in six years on November 30, 2011. Interest will be paid annually on November 30. Caxton's year end is March 31. The effective interest rate on December 1, 2005 was 9%.

Required:

a. What were the proceeds from the bond issue?

b. Prepare the journal entry to record issue of the bond on December 1, 2005.

c. Prepare an amortization schedule using both the straight-line and effective interest methods for any premium or discount that arose from the issue of the bond.

d. Prepare the journal entry required to accrue the interest expense and accrued interest payable on March 31, 2008. Make the entry for both the straight-line and effective interest amortization methods.

e. Prepare the journal entry required to record the interest expense and the payment to investors on November 30, 2008. Make the entry for both the straight-line and effective interest amortization methods.

f. Prepare the journal entry required to record the retirement of the bond on maturity. Include the interest expense and amortization of any bond premium or discount for 2011 in the entry. Make the entry for both the straight-line and effective interest amortization methods. When responding, remember that interest would have been accrued on March 31, 2011.

g. Assume that Caxton's bond agreement allowed the company to redeem the bond on November 30, 2008 for $11,500,000. Prepare the journal entry required to record early retirement of the bond. When responding, remember that interest would have been accrued on March 31, 2008. Also, remember that the entry to record the regular interest payment for 2008 would be made before making the entry for the early retirement.

h.   It is January 2008. You are a pension fund manager and Caxton has approached you for a $2,000,000 loan. What information would you want to have about the $10,000,000 bond issued in 2005 to help you decide whether to make the loan? Explain your reasoning.

Solution:

a.   The proceeds from the bond issue are the present value of a series of six annual interest payments of $1,000,000 plus the repayment of the $10,000,000 principal at the end of the sixth year, discounted at the effective interest rate of 9%. From the tables:

$$\text{PV of interest payments} = \text{Interest payment} \times \text{Discount factor (6 periods, 9\%)}$$
$$= \$1,000,000 \times 4.48592$$
$$= \$4,485,920$$

$$\text{PV of the principal repayment} = \text{Principal repayment} \times \text{Discount factor (6 periods, 9\%)}$$
$$= \$10,000,000 \times 0.59627$$
$$= \$5,962,700$$

$$\text{Proceeds from the bond issue} = \text{PV of interest payments} + \text{PV of the principal repayment}$$
$$= \$4,485,920 + \$5,962,700$$
$$= \$10,448,620$$

b.   Caxton would make the following journal entry to record the issue of the bond:

Dr. Cash (asset +)   10,448,620
   Cr. Bond premium (contra-liability +)   448,620
   Cr. Long-term debt—bonds (liability +)   10,000,000
To record the issue of bonds on December 1, 2005 at a premium.

c.   Amortization schedule for the bond premium:

| Date | Straight-line method | | | | | Effective interest method* | | | |
	Interest payment	Interest expense	Amount of premium amortized	Unamortized premium	NBV of bond	Interest expense	Amount of premium amortized	Unamortized premium	NBV of bond
Dec 1, 2005				$448,620	$10,448,620			$448,620	$10,448,620
Nov 30, 2006	$1,000,000	$925,230	$74,770	373,850	10,373,850	$940,376	$59,624	388,996	10,388,996
Nov 30, 2007	1,000,000	925,230	74,770	299,080	10,299,080	935,010	64,990	324,006	10,324,006
Nov 30, 2008	1,000,000	925,230	74,770	224,310	10,224,310	929,160	70,840	253,166	10,253,166
Nov 30, 2009	1,000,000	925,230	74,770	149,540	10,149,540	922,785	77,215	175,951	10,175,951
Nov 30, 2010	1,000,000	925,230	74,770	74,770	10,074,770	915,836	84,164	91,787	10,091,787
Nov 30, 2011	1,000,000	925,230	74,770	0	10,000,000	908,213	91,787	0	10,000,000

*Amounts for 2011 were adjusted by $47 because of rounding errors from the present value tables.

d. Journal entry to accrue the interest expense and accrued interest payable on March 31, 2008.

	Straight-line method		Effective interest method	
Dr. Interest expense (expense +, shareholders' equity −)	308,410[1]		309,720[3]	
Dr. Bond premium (contra-liability −)	24,923[2]			23,613[4]
Cr. Interest payable (liability +)		333,333[5]		333,333[5]

To accrue the interest expense and the record amortization of the bond discount on March 31, 2008.

[1] = (interest expense for fiscal 2008) × 4 months (December–March) ÷ 12 months.
= \$925,230 × 4 ÷ 12

[2] = (bond premium amortized in fiscal 2008) × 4 months (December–March) ÷ 12 months
= \$74,770 × 4 ÷ 12

[3] = (interest expense for fiscal 2008) × 4 months (December–March) ÷ 12 months
= \$929,160 × 4 ÷ 12

[4] = (bond premium amortized in fiscal 2008) × 4 months (December–March) ÷ 12 months
= \$70,840 × 4 ÷ 12

[5] = (interest payment for 2008) × 4 months (December–March) ÷ 12 months
= \$1,000,000 × 4 ÷ 12

e. Journal entry required to record the interest expense and the payment to investors on November 30, 2008.

	Straight-line method		Effective interest method	
Dr. Interest expense (expense +, shareholders' equity −)	616,820[1]		619,440[3]	
Dr. Interest payable (liability +)	333,333		333,333	
Dr. Bond premium (contra-liability −)	49,847[2]		47,227[4]	
Cr. Cash		1,000,000		1,000,000

To record payment of interest and interest expense on November 30, 2008.

[1] = (interest expense for fiscal 2008) × 8 months (March–November) ÷ 12 months
= \$925,230 × 8 ÷ 12

[2] = (bond premium amortized in fiscal 2008) × 8 months (March–November) ÷ 12 months
= \$74,770 × 8 ÷ 12

[3] = (interest expense for fiscal 2008) × 8 months (March–November) ÷ 12 months
= \$929,160 × 8 ÷ 12

[4] = (bond premium amortized in fiscal 2008) × 8 months (March–November) ÷ 12 months
= \$70,840 × 4 ÷ 12

f. Journal entry required to record the retirement Caxton's bond on maturity.

	Straight-line method		Effective interest method	
Dr. Long-term debt—bonds (liability −)	10,000,000		10,000,000	
Dr. Interest expense (expense +, shareholders' equity −)	616,820		605,475	
Dr. Interest payable	333,333		333,333	
Dr. Bond premium (contra-liability −)	49,847		61,192	
Cr. Cash (asset −)		11,000,000		11,000,000

To record the interest expense, amortization of the bond discount, and retirement of the bond on November 30, 2011.

g. The entries made in parts (d) and (e) must be considered because the entry to record the interest expense, interest payment, and bond premium amortization would be made before making the entry to record the early retirement of the bond. The amount of bond premium that would have to be written off when the bond was retired would be the amount outstanding after the normal entries for the year had been made. The bondholder would be entitled to the $1,000,000 interest payment for fiscal 2008. The journal entry to record the early retirement of the bond is:

	Straight-line method	Effective interest method
Dr. Long-term debt—bonds (liability –)	10,000,000	10,000,000
Dr. Bond premium (contra-liability –)	224,310	253,166
Dr. Loss on redemption of bond (income statement +, equity –)	1,275,690	1,246,834
Cr. Cash (asset –)	11,500,000	11,500,000

To record the early retirement of bonds on November 30, 2008.

h. As a prospective lender, you will be interested in assessing the likelihood that Caxton will make its interest and principal payments. This will involve estimating future cash flows and evaluating whether these cash flows will be adequate to support the loan. You will also want to know whether there is any collateral available in the event that Caxton does default. Information that might help with the decision includes:

- The timing of the cash payments required by the bond. These payments are the interest payments each year and the principal repayment in November 2011. This information allows you to include information about the bond in your cash flow analysis. The principal repayment in 2011 will require a significant amount of cash or refinancing of the bond. Is this going to be a problem?

- Any collateral that has been provided to secure the bond. This information will let you know which of Caxton's assets are still available as security.

- Any special terms that will affect cash flows. The redemption privilege can change the timing of the cash flows, which may affect your assessment of Caxton's ability to meet its obligations.

- Any restrictive covenants such as maximum debt-to-equity ratio or minimum current ratio. Knowing about these covenants will allow you to assess the likelihood that these covenants will be violated. Violation of the covenants may change the timing of the cash flows and may impose significant costs on Caxton, and these may affect the pension fund's loan.

Summary of Key Points

LO 1. Liabilities are obligations to provide cash, goods, and services to customers, suppliers, employees, governments, lenders, and any other creditors. According to GAAP, liabilities have three characteristics: (i) they require the sacrifice of resources; (ii) they are unavoidable; and (iii) they are the result of past transactions or economic events. In principle, liabilities should be valued at their present value, and in many cases they are. There are some exceptions, though.

LO 2. Current liabilities are obligations that will be satisfied in one year or one operating cycle. Information about current obligations is important because it is relevant for assessing the short-term liquidity of an entity. Current liabilities are usually not discounted to their present value because the amount of time until they are settled is relatively short, and as a result the difference between the present value and the stated value will be small. There are many different types of current liabilities, including loans, accounts payable, collections on behalf of third parties, accrued liabilities, and unearned revenue.

LO 3. A bond is a formal borrowing arrangement in which a borrower agrees to make periodic interest payments to the lenders, as well as to repay the principal at a specified time in the future. The essential characteristics of a bond are its face value, maturity date, and coupon rate. In addition, a bond can have a large array of features and restrictions that are agreed to by the lender and borrowers. These features and restrictions will affect the price of the bond. The price of bonds and other long-term debt is determined by discounting the interest and principal payments to investors using the effective interest rate. The effective interest rate is the market rate of interest appropriate for the long-term debt and is influenced by the risk and other characteristics of the debt.

LO 4. Long-term debt is usually recorded at its present value, discounted using the effective interest rate on the date the debt is issued. If the coupon rate is not the same as the effective interest rate, a premium or discount arises. The premium or discount is amortized over the life of the debt using the straight-line or the effective interest method. The amount amortized each period is included in the interest expense for the period. Once long-term debt is recorded, its value is not adjusted for changes in market interest rates. If the end of the reporting period does not correspond with the date when interest payments are made, it is necessary to accrue the interest expense and accrued interest payable. When debt is retired early, any premium or discount must be removed from the books immediately and a gain or a loss may arise on retirement. Some debt instruments require that blended payments of principal and interest be made over the term of the debt.

LO 5. A lease is a contractual arrangement whereby a lessee agrees to pay a lessor a fee in exchange for the use of an asset. Leases have a number of advantages to lessees, including 100% financing and flexibility. There are two types of leases—capital leases and operating leases. A capital lease is a lease that transfers the benefits and risks of ownership to the lessee. Assets associated with a capital lease are capitalized on the balance sheet of the lessee, along with a liability that is equal to the present value of the lease payments to be made over the life of the lease. An important accounting and reporting benefit of treating a lease as a capital lease is that it overcomes the problem of off-balance-sheet financing. If the rights and risks of ownership are not transferred to the lessee but are retained by the lessor, then the lease is an operating lease. Under an operating lease, the lessee recognizes an expense when the payment to the lessor is paid or payable. The assets and related liabilities do not appear on the lessee's balance sheet.

LO 6. A pension is income provided to a person after he or she retires. Employees earn their pensions and other post-retirement benefits while they are working, even though they receive the money after they retire. There are two types of pension plans: defined-contribution plans and defined-benefit plans. In a defined-contribution plan the employer makes cash contributions to the plan as specified in the pension agreement with the employees. In a defined-benefit plan the employer promises to provide employees with certain specified benefits in each year they are retired. Accounting for defined-contribution plans is relatively straightforward, but accounting for defined-benefit plans is complex because it is necessary to estimate and accrue the cost currently of benefits that will be received many years in the future. The pension asset or liability does not provide information about the condition of the pension plan—the ability of a plan to meet the obligations to retirees. It is simply the difference between the accounting measure of the pension expense and the amount funded.

LO 7. The future income tax method is a method of accounting for an entity's income taxes where the income tax expense is calculated using accounting measurements, not the actual amount of taxes payable. Future income taxes arise because the accounting policies used to prepare general purpose financial statements are sometimes different from the rules entities must follow when calculating the amount of income tax they must pay. The differences that give rise to future income taxes are temporary and they eventually reverse. Future income taxes do not represent money owed to or owed by the government.

LO 8. A contingency is a possible liability or asset whose existence and amount depend on some future event. How contingencies are accounted for according to GAAP depends on the likelihood of them occurring, whether they can be reasonably measured, and whether the contingency will result in a gain or a loss.

A commitment is a contractual agreement to enter into a transaction in the future. Commitments are executory contracts and under GAAP these contracts are not recorded in the accounting records. Significant commitments should be disclosed in the notes to the financial statements.

A subsequent event is an economic event that occurs after an entity's year end, but before the financial statements are released to users. According to GAAP, when a subsequent event occurs that provides additional information about circumstances that existed at the year end, the financial statements should be adjusted to reflect the new information. When a subsequent event occurs that is unrelated to circumstances that existed at year end, the event should be disclosed only in the notes to the financial statements.

LO 9. Analyzing an entity's liabilities can provide important information about its financial situation and prospects. This analysis can also provide insight into the financial management of the entity. Two tools for analyzing liabilities are the debt-to-equity ratio and the interest coverage ratio. Caution must be taken in using ratios that incorporate liabilities because of measurement problems associated with leases, pensions, and future income taxes. Failure to adjust for these problems may result in misinterpretation of the ratios.

Key Terms

actuary, p. 604

after-tax cost of borrowing, p. 614

blended payment, p. 593

bond, p. 578

callable bond, p. 579

capital lease, p. 596

commitment, p. 617

contingency, p. 615

convertible bond, p. 579

coupon rate, p. 579

debenture, p. 578

debt, p. 578

defined-benefit plan, p. 603

defined-contribution plan, p. 602

demand loan, p. 572

direct financing lease, p. 601

discount (on debt), p. 583

effective interest rate, p. 579

face value of a bond, p. 579

fixed-rate loan, p. 578

future income tax assets and liabilities, p. 606

interest coverage ratio, p. 622

lease, p. 595

lessee, p. 595

lessor, p. 595

leverage, p. 579

line of credit, p. 572

maturity date of a bond, p. 579

mortgage, p. 578

note payable, p. 578

off-balance-sheet financing, p. 596

operating lease, p. 596

pension, p. 602

permanent differences, p. 606

premium (on debt), p. 586

proceeds, p. 579

retractable bond, p. 580

revolving loan, p. 572

sale-leaseback transaction, p. 600

sales-type lease, p. 601

subsequent event, p. 619

taxable income, p. 606

temporary differences, p. 606

undepreciated capital cost (UCC), p. 608

variable-rate loan, p. 578

Similar Terms

The left column gives alternative terms that are sometimes used for the accounting terms introduced in this chapter, which are listed in the right column.

long-term debt	**non-current debt, p. 578**
deferred income taxes	**future income taxes, p. 605**
provision for income taxes, income tax provision	**income tax expense, p. 606**
security	**collateral, p. 578; see also p. 270**

Assignment Materials

Questions

Q10-1. What happens to the market value of a bond if the effective interest rate decreases after the bond is issued? Explain. How is the change in the effective interest rate reflected in the financial statements?

Q10-2. Explain the following terms as they relate to bonds:
a. effective rate of interest
b. coupon rate
c. maturity date
d. proceeds
e. face value

Q10-3. What is off-balance-sheet financing? Why is off-balance-sheet financing attractive for some entities? How does off-balance-sheet financing affect financial statement users' ability to interpret financial statements?

Q10-4. Hyannas Inc. has recently arranged financing for its planned expansion. The company arranged a $5,000,000 bank loan that is secured against the inventory, receivables, and certain capital assets. The second loan is for $2,000,000 and is an unsecured loan. Which loan would you expect to have a higher interest rate? Explain.

Q10-5. What is a sale-leaseback transaction? Why do entities enter into sale-leaseback transactions? How are gains and losses on sale-leaseback transactions accounted for? Do you agree with this treatment? Explain.

Q10-6. A labour union leader said at a recent rally that there would be plenty of money for health care, education, and other social programs if governments simply collected the future income taxes that corporations owe and are reported on their balance sheets. A friend of yours asked you, in response to the union leader's comments, how it is that businesses can avoid paying their taxes whereas working people cannot.

Required:

Respond to your friend.

Q10-7. Why does recording an "interest-free" loan at its face value result in the understatement of net income? Explain.

Q10-8. What is an executory contract? How are executory contracts accounted for according to GAAP? What is the reason for this treatment? What are some of the problems with it? Can you think of any executory contracts that are reported on GAAP-based financial statements?

Q10-9. Do you agree with the statement, "All liabilities reported on a GAAP balance sheet are legally enforceable"? Explain.

Q10-10. What are bond discounts and premiums? Why are bonds sometimes sold at a discount or premium?

Q10-11. What are restrictive covenants? Why are restrictive covenants sometimes included as part of debt agreements? How does a borrower benefit from a restrictive covenant? Why would a borrower prefer to avoid having restrictive covenants in loan agreements, assuming nothing changes as a result?

Q10-12. Because of an increase in competition in the industry, a respected bond-rating agency recently downgraded its rating on Quaw Inc.'s (Quaw) corporate bonds. A downgrade means that the bonds are considered more risky. What do you think would be the effect of the downgrade on the market price of Quaw's bonds? Explain. What do you think the impact would be the next time Quaw issued bonds?

Q10-13. Distinguish between primary and secondary capital markets.

Q10-14. What are future income taxes and what circumstances cause them to appear on an entity's balance sheet?

Q10-15. According to the GAAP characteristics for liabilities, is a future income tax liability really a liability? Explain.

Q10-16. How do bond discounts and premiums affect an entity's interest expense? Explain.

Q10-17. Explain the effective interest method of amortizing bond discounts and premiums. How does the effective interest method differ from the straight-line method?

Q10-18. Why do gains and losses arise when an entity redeems its bonds before they mature? How are the gains and losses calculated?

Q10-19. Explain the difference between a capital lease and an operating lease. Explain how each type of lease is accounted for and the effect that each has on the balance sheet and income statement.

Q10-20. What amount is reported on a lessee's balance sheet at the start of a lease for a leased asset and the associated liability? Why do the amounts reported for the asset and liability differ for balance sheets prepared after the start of the lease?

Q10-21. What is a subsequent event? How are subsequent events accounted for?

Q10-22. What is a commitment? How are commitments accounted for?

Q10-23. Distinguish between a defined-benefit pension plan and defined-contribution pension plan. Which plan is more attractive for employees? Explain. Which plan is less risky for employers? Explain.

Q10-24. What is a contingency in accounting? Under what circumstances should a contingency be accrued in the financial statements? Under what circumstances should a contingency be disclosed in the notes to the financial statements? Under what circumstances should a contingency not be reflected in the financial statements or notes? What do you think is the best way to account for a contingency? Explain.

Q10-25. One of the criticisms often made about accounting for future income taxes is that the amounts reported on the financial statements are not discounted. What is the problem with not discounting future income taxes? What problems do not discounting impose on users of the financial statements?

Q10-26. What is an accrued liability? How does an accrued liability differ from an account payable? Under what circumstances are accrued liabilities required?

Q10-27. Because it is so difficult to estimate the cost of providing defined-benefit pensions to employees who will retire many years in the future, it would make more sense, and result in more accurate financial statements, to simply expense the pension when it is paid. Discuss this statement. In your discussion address relevant accounting concepts and the impact of the proposed approach on the financial statements.

Q10-28. What is a current liability? Why is it important to know the amount of current liabilities an entity has?

Q10-29. Why is the current portion of long-term debt classified separately as a current asset? What would be the impact on users of the financial statements if the current portion of long-term debt were not reported separately?

Q10-30. What is the interest coverage ratio? What information does the interest coverage ratio provide?

Q10-31. What is a liability? What are the three characteristics that, according to GAAP, a liability must have? Do you think these characteristics capture every obligation an entity has? Explain.

Q10-32. Rykerts Ltd. reports a pension liability of $3,250,000 on its December 31, 2004 balance sheet. Provide an interpretation of this account and the balance in the account.

Q10-33. Why do managers sometimes have incentives to understate liabilities? What are the implications for the financial statements of understating liabilities? Provide examples of how a manager could understate his or her entity's liabilities.

Q10-34. What are the characteristics of debt that make it risky? Why do these characteristics make debt risky?

Q10-35. Why are long-term liabilities such as bonds valued for financial reporting purposes at their present value, but capital assets are not?

Q10-36. What is the relationship between the coupon rate and effective interest rate when a bond is sold at a discount? What is the relationship when a bond is sold at a premium?

Q10-37. Distinguish the future income tax method of accounting for income taxes from the taxes payable method.

Q10-38. Why is the actual cost of borrowing usually lower than the stated rate of interest that the borrower pays to a lender such as a bank? Can you think of a situation where the actual cost of borrowing will not be lower than the stated rate of interest?

Q10-39. Why are the assets in a pension plan not reported on the balance sheet of the entity sponsoring the pension plan? Does this treatment result in an understatement of the sponsoring entity's assets?

Q10-40. What is unearned revenue? Why is it considered a liability?

Q10-41. Identify and explain the criteria that the *CICA Handbook* provides to assist in the classification of leases. What are the problems and benefits of providing preparers of the financial statements with these criteria?

Q10-42. Entities that use future income tax accounting show two components of the income tax expense: the current expense and the future expense. Define and explain these two components of the income tax expense.

Q10-43. In its most recent balance sheet, Vosburg Inc. reported a debt-to-equity ratio of 1.85 to 1. This ratio has increased slightly from the previous year when the ratio was 1.55 to 1. Assess Vosburg Inc.'s debt-to-equity ratio and the change in the ratio over the last year.

Exercises

E10-1.   **(Determining the proceeds from a bond, LO 3)** On July 15, 2006, Dyce Inc. (Dyce) will be making a $2,000,000 bond issue to public investors. The bond matures in five years on July 14, 2011, has a coupon rate of 8%, and pays interest annually on July 14. Indicate how much Dyce will receive in proceeds from its bond if the effective interest rate when the bond is issued is:

a. 7%

b. 8%

c. 9%

E10-2.   **(Determining the proceeds from a bond, LO 3)** On December 1, 2005 Koidern Inc. (Koidern) will be making a $5,000,000 bond issue to public investors. The bond matures in eight years on November 30, 2013 and pays interest annually on November 30. The effective interest rate on December 1, 2005 is expected to be 9%. Indicate how much Koidern will receive in proceeds from its bond if the coupon rate on the bond is:

a. 10%

b. 9%

c. 8%

E10-3.   **(Accounting for gift certificates, LO 2, 9)** Juno Boutique Inc. (Juno) operates a small chain of fashion boutiques. Juno usually opens its stores in upscale shopping malls in major cities. In 2004 Juno began offering gift certificates for sale to customers. The certificates can be exchanged for any merchandise in Juno's stores. The certificates cannot be redeemed for cash. During 2004 gift certificates worth $31,000 were sold. By the end of the year, $12,000 of the gift certificates had been redeemed by customers to purchase merchandise that cost Juno $7,500.

Required:

a. Prepare the journal entry required to record the sale of the gift certificates.

b. Prepare the journal entry required to record the redemption of the gift certificates.

c. How would the unused gift certificates be reported in Juno's financial statements?

d. What effect does the sale of gift certificates have on Juno's current ratio?

E10-4. **(Classifying liabilities, LO 2, 3)** How would each of the following items be classified on Atluck Grocery Store Corp.'s (Atluck) September 30, 2006 balance sheet? Explain your reasoning.

     a. A $250,000 20-year mortgage on Atluck's land and building. The mortgage requires annual equal payments of $29,365.

     b. $1,200 withheld from employee paycheques for income taxes.

     c. A $2,500 deposit received from a customer for food platters to be served at a local company's annual meeting to be held on October 17, 2006.

     d. $30,000 owed to a supplier for renovations on the store; $15,000 of the amount owed is due on December 15, 2006 and the remainder on November 1, 2007.

     e. A $25,000 demand loan from the bank.

E10-5. **(Valuing liabilities, LO 1)** On March 31, 2005 Etzikom Inc. (Etzikom) purchased a corporate jet from the manufacturer for $7,500,000. Etzikom paid $500,000 in cash to the manufacturer and received a four-year, $7,000,000, interest-free loan for the remainder of the purchase price. The terms of the loan require Etzikom to pay the manufacturer $1,750,000 on March 31 of each of the next four years, beginning on March 31, 2006.

     a. What alternatives exist for reporting the liability to the manufacturer of the jet? What are the problems and benefits of the alternative approaches?

     b. Prepare the journal entry that Etzikom should make to record the purchase of the jet. Explain the amount that you have recorded for the jet on the balance sheet.

     c. Prepare the journal entries that Etzikom should make on March 31 of 2005 through 2009 to record payments on the loan.

     d. How much should Etzikom report as a liability for the loan on its balance sheet on December 31, 2005 through 2009?

E10-6. **(Collections on behalf of third parties, LO 2)** For the following two independent situations, prepare the journal entry that Durrell Ltd. (Durrell) should record. Record the entry for both the amounts collected or withheld and for the remittances.

     a. During November 2006 Durrell sold and delivered $220,000 of services to customers. In addition, customers were charged and paid 7% GST on the services provided. Durrell remits the GST it collects from customers on the tenth day of each month.

     b. During November Durrell's employees earned $42,000. From this amount Durrell withheld $13,000 for income taxes, $4,105 for Canada Pension Plan (CPP), $1,860 for Employment Insurance (EI), $750 in union dues, $1,450 for employee contributions to the company pension plan, $1,000 for long-term disability insurance, and $200 in contributions to local charities. Durrell remits the withholdings on the tenth day of each month.

E10-7. **(Calculating the interest expense, LO 3, 4)** During 2005 Goffs Ltd. (Goffs) had the following amount of debt outstanding in each quarter of the year:

1st Quarter	$ 760,000
2nd Quarter	925,000
3rd Quarter	1,100,000
4th Quarter	535,000

The average interest rate that Goffs paid on its debt was 9.8% in the first and second quarters and 10.1% in the third and fourth quarters.

Required:

Calculate the interest expense that Goffs would report for 2005.

E10-8. **(Understanding bond accounting relationships, LO 3, 4)** Complete the following table by indicating whether the stated components of a bond will increase, decrease, or be unchanged as the bond approaches maturity and when the bond is sold at a premium, a discount, and at its face value. Assume the effective interest method is used.

	Premium	Discount	Face value
a. Interest expense			
b. Interest payment			
c. NBV of the bond			
d. Amortization of the discount or premium			

E10-9. **(Classifying transactions and economic events, LO 8)** Classify the following transactions and economic events that Floral Ltd. (Floral) was involved with as commitments, subsequent events, or contingencies. Some may fit more than one classification. Assume that the year end is December 31, 2007. Indicate how each should be reflected in the financial statements and explain your reasoning. In responding, consider the usefulness of the information to different users of the financial statements.

a. On January 15, 2008 Floral signed a three-year contract with a supplier to provide raw materials. The contract is the largest ever agreed to by Floral.

b. In November 2007 a company that Floral was suing for damages for breaching a contract made an offer of $200,000 to settle the case. As of the year end Floral had not decided whether to accept the offer or go to court. The offer is far below what Floral is suing for.

c. On January 21, 2008 Floral signed a five-year lease for storage space in a building near its main facility. The annual lease payments will be $5,000 per year.

d. On January 18 the company lost a lawsuit launched by a disgruntled former senior executive. Floral is required to pay the former employee $500,000 in damages.

e. In May 2007 Floral guaranteed a $1,000,000 bank loan made to a company Floral owns. Floral is responsible for paying the principal and any outstanding interest in the event that the company is unable to make its payments.

E10-10. **(Future income taxes, LO 7)** Use the following information to calculate the balance in the future income tax account for a machine owned by the entity:

Cost of the machine when it was purchased:	$700,000
Total amount of CCA deducted since the machine was purchased:	410,000
Total amount of amortization expensed since the machine was purchased:	575,000
Tax rate:	25%

E10-11. **(Future income taxes, LO 7)** Use the following information to calculate the balance in the future income tax account for a building owned by the entity:

Cost of the machine when it was purchased:	$10,000,000
Total amount of CCA deducted since the machine was purchased:	4,610,000
Total amount of amortization expensed since the machine was purchased:	3,575,000
Tax rate:	40%

E10-12. **(Future income taxes, LO 7)** For the fiscal year ended November 30, 2004 Vibank Ltd. (Vibank) has income before taxes of $4,500,000. Vibank's tax return shows taxable income of $4,950,000 for that year. The tax basis of Vibank's assets exceeded the accounting basis by $800,000 on November 30, 2004, and the balance in the future income tax account on November 30, 2003 was a credit of $300,000. Vibank has a tax rate of 30%.

Required:

a. Prepare the journal entry that Vibank should make to record its income tax expense for fiscal 2004.

b. What is Vibank's net income for fiscal 2004?

c. What would Vibank's net income be if it used the taxes payable method?

d. Explain the difference between (b) and (c).

E10-13.   **(Accounting for bonds, LO 3, 4)** On November 1, 2005 Nordin Inc. (Nordin) issued a $2,000,000 bond with a 7% coupon rate and a maturity date of October 31, 2010. Interest is paid annually on October 31. The effective interest rate for a bond of this type on November 1, 2005 was 9%. Nordin's year end is October 31.

Required:

a. What will be the proceeds from the bond issue?

b. Prepare the journal entry to record issue of the bond on November 1, 2005.

c. Prepare an amortization schedule using both the straight-line and effective interest methods for any premium or discount that arose on issue of the bond.

d. Prepare the journal entry required to record the interest expense and the interest payment to investors on October 31 of each year over the life of the bond. Make the entries for both the straight-line and effective interest amortization methods.

e. Prepare the journal entry required to record the retirement of the bond on maturity.

E10-14.   **(Accounting for bonds, LO 3, 4)** On September 1, 2004 Yone Ltd. (Yone) issued a $4,000,000 bond with a 10% coupon rate and a maturity date of August 31, 2010. Interest is paid annually on August 31. The effective interest rate for a bond of this type on September 1, 2004 was 8%. Yone's year end is August 31.

Required:

a. What will be the proceeds from the bond issue?

b. Prepare the journal entry to record issue of the bond on September 1, 2004.

c. Prepare an amortization schedule using both the straight-line and effective interest methods for any premium or discount that arose on issue of the bond.

d. Prepare the journal entry required to record the interest expense and the interest payment to investors on August 31 of each year over the life of the bond. Make the entries for both the straight-line and effective interest amortization methods.

e. Prepare the journal entry required to record the retirement of the bond on maturity.

E10-15.   **(Accounting for bonds, LO 3, 4)** On February 1, 2006 Jura Corp. (Jura) issued a $12,000,000 bond with an 8% coupon rate and a maturity date of January 31, 2012. Interest is paid annually on January 31. The effective interest rate for a bond of this type on February 1, 2006 was 8%. Jura's year end is January 31.

Required:

a. What will be the proceeds from the bond issue?

b. Prepare the journal entry to record issue of the bond on February 1, 2006.

c. Prepare an amortization schedule using both the straight-line and effective interest methods for any premium or discount that arose on issue of the bond.

d. Prepare the journal entry required to record the interest expense and the interest payment to investors on June 30 of each year over the life of the bond. Make the entries for both the straight-line and effective interest amortization methods.

e. Prepare the journal entry required to record the retirement of the bond on maturity.

E10-16.   **(Future income taxes and pensions, LO 8)** Orthez Inc. (Orthez) funds a defined-benefit pension plan for its employees. The plan began in 2003. Contributions to the pension plan are made in accordance with actuarial assumptions, while the pension expense that Orthez records each year is determined in accordance with GAAP. In the first three years of the plan Orthez contributed to the plan and expensed for financial reporting purposes the following amounts:

	Contributed to the plan	Pension expense
2003	$2,250,000	$2,000,000
2004	3,000,000	3,125,000
2005	3,250,000	3,000,000

Required:

    a. Prepare the journal entry that Orthez would make each year to record the pension expense and the contribution to the pension plan.

    b. What is the balance in the pension asset or liability account at the end of 2003 through 2005?

E10-17. **(Early retirement of bonds, LO 4)** In fiscal 2008 Ruthilda Inc. (Ruthilda) decided to exercise its option to redeem its outstanding bond issue before the bonds matured in 2015. The bonds had a face value of $3,000,000 and Ruthilda paid $3,200,000 to redeem them. The bonds were originally issued at a premium of $130,000, and at the time the bonds were redeemed $60,000 of the premium had been amortized.

Required:

    a. Prepare the journal entry to record the early retirement of the bonds.

    b. What would be the entry if Ruthilda were able to redeem the bonds on the open market at a cost of $2,800,000?

    c. What is the economic significance of a gain or loss on the redemption of bonds? How do you think the gain or loss should be reported in the financial statements? Explain. In responding, consider the information needs of users of the financial statements.

E10-18. **(Early retirement of bonds, LO 4)** In fiscal 2006 Hurette Inc. (Hurette) decided to exercise its option to redeem its outstanding bond issue before the bonds matured in 2011. The bonds had a face value of $2,000,000 and Hurette paid $2,100,000 to redeem them. The bonds were originally issued at a discount of $100,000, and at the time the bonds were redeemed $40,000 of the discount had been amortized.

Required:

    a. Prepare the journal entry to record the early retirement of the bonds.

    b. What would be the entry if Hurette were able to redeem the bonds on the open market at a cost of $1,900,000?

    c. What is the economic significance of a gain or loss on the redemption of bonds? How do you think the gain or loss should be reported in the financial statements? Explain. In responding, consider the information needs of users of the financial statements.

E10-19. **(The effect of different amortization methods on future income taxes, LO 7)** Caycuse Inc. (Caycuse) has just completed its first year of operations on December 31, 2005. The company owns a single asset that cost $100,000. For tax purposes Caycuse can deduct $15,000 in CCA in calculating its taxable income. Assume that Caycuse's tax rate is 20%.

Required:

    a. Determine the future income tax asset or liability on December 31, 2005 if Caycuse amortizes its asset on a straight-line basis over 10 years.

    b. Determine the future income tax asset or liability on December 31, 2005 if Caycuse amortizes its asset on a straight-line basis over five years.

    c. Determine the future income tax asset or liability on December 31, 2005 if Caycuse amortizes its asset on a declining balance basis at 30% per year.

    d. Determine the future income tax asset or liability on December 31, 2005 if Caycuse amortizes its asset using the same basis used for tax purposes.

    e. According to the three GAAP characteristics for determining whether a liability exists, is a future income tax liability really a liability? Should a future income tax asset be considered an asset? How would you interpret the future income tax assets or liabilities that you calculated in parts (a) through (d) above?

E10-20. **(Cost of borrowing, LO 3)** For each of the following situations, determine the entity's after-tax cost of borrowing:

a. A corporation has a $1,000,000 bond with a coupon rate of 10%. The corporation has a tax rate of 38%.

b. A small business has a three-year, $100,000, 6% note payable with a supplier. The small business has a tax rate of 20%.

c. A not-for-profit organization, which does not have to pay tax, has a $25,000 bank loan at the prime lending rate plus 2%. For the year just ended the prime lending rate was 6.5%.

d. What is the relationship between an entity's tax rate and its after-tax cost of borrowing? Is it more desirable for an entity to have a higher tax rate so that it can lower its after-tax cost of borrowing? Explain.

E10-21. **(Accounting for mortgages, LO 4)** On November 1, 2006 Astwood Inc. (Astwood) purchased a small apartment building for $3,000,000. Astwood paid $500,000 in cash and arranged a 10-year, 8% mortgage with a bank for the balance. The mortgage requires equal annual blended payments on October 31 of each year over the term of the mortgage. Astwood's year end is October 31.

Required:

a. Prepare the journal entry to record the mortgage and the purchase of the apartment building.

b. What will be Astwood's annual mortgage payments?

c. Prepare a schedule similar to the one in Table 10-7 (page 594) showing the interest and principal components of each annual payment.

d. Prepare the journal entries to record the mortgage payment made on October 31, 2009 and on October 31, 2012.

e. If Astwood has a tax rate of 24%, what would be its after-tax cost of the mortgage?

E10-22. **(Accounting for mortgages, LO 4)** On May 1, 2005 Duricle Inc. (Duricle) purchased land for $1,000,000. Duricle plans to build an office building or a condominium on the land some time in the future. Duricle paid $300,000 in cash and arranged a 5-year, 10% mortgage with a bank for the balance. The mortgage requires equal semi-annual blended payments on October 31 and April 30 of each year over the term of the mortgage. Duricle's year end is December 31.

Required:

a. Prepare the journal entry to record the mortgage and the purchase of the land.

b. What will be Duricle's annual mortgage payments?

c. Prepare a schedule similar to the one in Table 10-7 (page 594) showing the interest and principal components of each semi-annual payment.

d. Prepare the journal entry to accrue the interest expense on December 31, 2007 and on December 31, 2008.

e. Prepare the journal entries to record the mortgage payment made on April 30, 2007 and on October 31, 2009.

f. If Duricle has a tax rate of 40%, what would be its after-tax cost of the mortgage?

E10-23. **(Accounting for leases, LO 5)** On February 1, 2005 Flatwater Ltd. (Flatwater) signed a five-year lease for four delivery trucks. According to the terms of the lease, Flatwater must make annual lease payments of $35,000 on January 31, commencing in 2006. The interest rate that applies to the lease is 9%.

Required:

a. If Flatwater's lease were accounted for as an operating lease, what amount would be recorded as an asset for the leased delivery trucks on February 1, 2005?

b. If the lease were accounted for as an operating lease, prepare the journal entries that would have to be made in fiscal 2006 and fiscal 2008 to account for the lease.

   c. If Flatwater's lease were accounted for as a capital lease, what amount would be recorded as an asset for the leased delivery trucks on February 1, 2005?

   d. If the lease were accounted for as a capital lease, what journal entry would be required on February 1, 2005?

   e. If the lease were accounted for as a capital lease, what journal entries would be required on January 31, 2006 to record the lease payment?

   f. If the lease were accounted for as a capital lease, what journal entry would be required on January 31, 2006 to record the amortization of the delivery vehicles?

   g. What would be the NBV of the leased delivery trucks and the lease liability on Flatwater's January 31, 2006 balance sheet?

E10-24. **(The effect of interest rates on capital leases, LO 5)** On June 1, 2006 Grumbler Corp. (Grumbler) signed a six-year lease for heavy equipment. The lease requires Grumbler to make annual lease payments of $250,000 on May 31 of each year beginning in 2007. The lease is to be treated as a capital lease.

Required:

   a. Indicate the amount that would be recorded for heavy equipment and for the lease liability on June 1, 2006 assuming:

     i.   The appropriate interest rate for the lease was 8%.

     ii. The appropriate interest rate for the lease was 10%.

     iii. The appropriate interest rate for the lease was 12%.

   b. Indicate the annual amortization expense for the heavy equipment, assuming straight-line amortization over six years and assuming:

     i.   The appropriate interest rate for the lease was 8%.

     ii. The appropriate interest rate for the lease was 10%.

     iii. The appropriate interest rate for the lease was 12%.

   c. Indicate the interest expense pertaining to the lease in the fiscal year ended May 31, 2007, assuming:

     i.   The appropriate interest rate for the lease was 8%.

     ii. The appropriate interest rate for the lease was 10%.

     iii. The appropriate interest rate for the lease was 12%.

E10-25. **(The effect of bond transactions on the cash flow statement, LO 3, 4)** Wivenhoe Ltd. (Wivenhoe) includes a cash flow statement in the financial statement package it prepares for the bank. Wivenhoe uses the indirect method for calculating cash from operations. For each of the following items, indicate how it would be reported in Wivenhoe's cash flow statement as operating, financing, or investing. For items classified as operating, indicate how the amount would affect the calculation of cash from operations.

   a. Amortization of a bond premium.

   b. Proceeds from the issue of a bond.

   c. Interest payment to investors.

   d. Repayment of a bond on maturity.

   e. Gain on early retirement of a bond.

   f. Amortization of a bond discount.

E10-26. **(Lease accounting and financial ratios, LO 5, 9)** Zeballos Inc. (Zeballos) is planning to lease new equipment for its distribution centre. The terms that Zeballos has agreed to require that it pay $250,000 per year for the next five years. The interest rate for the lease is 8%. Zeballos has provided you with the following balance sheet information before the new lease has been accounted for:

Current assets	$ 785,000
Non-current assets	3,456,000
Current liabilities	545,000
Non-current liabilities	2,100,000
Shareholders' equity	1,596,000

Required:

    a. Calculate the current ratio and debt-to-equity ratio for Zeballos, assuming the lease is accounted for as an operating lease.

    b. Calculate the current ratio and debt-to-equity ratio for Zeballos, assuming the lease is accounted for as a capital lease.

    c. Which calculations provide a better representation of Zeballos' liquidity and underlying risk? Explain.

    d. Does it matter how Zeballos accounts for its lease (GAAP notwithstanding)? Explain.

E10-27. **(Accounting for bonds, LO 4)** On June 1, 2006 Joffre Inc. (Joffre) issued a $2,000,000, 10-year bond with a 10% coupon rate. Proceeds from the bond issue were $2,200,000. Interest is to be paid annually on May 31. Joffre's year end is December 31. Assume that Joffre uses the straight-line method to amortize any bond premiums or discounts.

Required:

    a. Prepare the journal entry to record the issue of the bond on June 1, 2006.

    b. Prepare the journal entry to accrue the interest expense on December 31, 2006.

    c. Prepare the journal entry to record the payment of interest to bondholders on May 31, 2007.

Problems

P10-1.   **(Determining whether certain economic events are liabilities, LO 1)** Explain whether each of the following would be considered a liability according to GAAP (using the three criteria from the chapter) on December 31, 2005. Intuitively, would you consider each of these items an obligation, regardless of how it is accounted for according to GAAP? Explain.

    a. The cost of providing warranty services to a customer who purchased a product in 2005. The warranty covers parts and labour for three years from the date of purchase.

    b. A company borrows $950,000 on January 8, 2006. The loan is revolving, bears an annual interest rate of 7.5%, and must be renewed each year.

    c. A small business signs a two-year, non-cancellable lease on office space in a downtown building in December 2005. The lease requires the business to pay $10,000 in rent over the two years of the lease.

P10-2.   **(Determining whether certain economic events are liabilities, LO 1)** Explain whether each of the following would be considered a liability according to GAAP (using the three criteria from the chapter) on December 31, 2005. Intuitively, would you consider each of these items an obligation, regardless of how it is accounted for according to GAAP? Explain.

    a. Interest on a bank loan outstanding on December 31, 2005. Interest is not payable until the loan must be repaid on September 30, 2006.

    b. A $1,000,000 loan from a shareholder that bears no interest and has no scheduled repayment date.

    c. The cost of closing a landfill when it is full. Significant costs will have to be incurred to ensure that it meets government standards. The landfill is expected to close in 15 years.

P10-3.   **(Effect of transactions and economic events on ratios, LO 2, 4, 5, 7, 8, 9)** The president of Oskelaneo Ltd. (Oskelaneo) wants to know the effect that a number of transactions and economic events will have on several financial measures for the company's fiscal year ended September 30, 2007. Complete the following table by indicating whether the listed transactions or economic events would increase, decrease, or have no effect on the financial measures listed. Explain your reasoning and state any assumptions that you make. Consider each item independently.

		Debt-to-equity ratio	Current ratio	Interest coverage ratio	Cash from operations	Return on assets
	Ratio/amount before taking the transaction/economic event into effect.	1.2:1	1.87	4.38	$750,000	5.3%
a.	Oskelaneo paid interest on a bank loan.					
b.	Oskelaneo arranged a new capital lease.					
c.	Oskelaneo had a decrease in its future income taxes.					
d.	Oskelaneo repaid a bond that was classified as the current portion of long-term debt.					
e.	Oskelaneo received cash from a customer for services that will be provided in February 2008.					
f.	Oskelaneo retired a bond early and recognized a gain of $55,000 (the bond retired was not classified as a current liability).					
g.	A customer sued Oskelaneo in January 2007 for negligence. A decision by the court is not expected for at least two years. The company's lawyers state that it is unlikely the company will lose the lawsuit.					

P10-4. **(Effect of transactions and economic events on ratios, LO 4, 5, 6, 7, 8, 9)** The president of Ruskin Inc. (Ruskin) wants to know the effect that a number of transactions and economic events will have on several financial measures for the company's fiscal year ended April 30, 2006. Complete the following table by indicating whether the listed transactions or economic events would increase, decrease or have no effect on the financial measures listed. Explain your reasoning and state any assumptions that you make.

		Debt-to-equity ratio	Current ratio	Interest coverage ratio	Cash from operations	Return on assets
	Ratio/amount before taking the transaction/economic event into effect.	0.8:1	0.95	5.21	$2,250,000	7.1%
a.	Ruskin signed a contract to purchase raw materials beginning in 2007 at an agreed-to price.					
b.	Ruskin provided services to a customer that were paid for in the previous fiscal year.					
c.	Ruskin made a contribution to its defined-contribution pension plan.					
d.	A fire destroyed a small building owned by Ruskin on May 4, 2006.					
e.	Ruskin had a decrease in its future income taxes.					
f.	Ruskin arranged a new operating lease.					
g.	Ruskin paid $1,000,000 to settle a lawsuit that was launched three years ago.					

P10-5.　**(Accounting for possible unexpected warranty costs, LO 8)** Nouvelle Ltd. (Nouvelle) is a privately owned industrial-products manufacturer located in Sherbrooke, Québec. The president of Nouvelle owns 25% of the shares of the company and three investors who are not active in managing the company own the remaining 75% of the shares. The company has a large demand loan outstanding at the bank. The terms of the loan require that Nouvelle maintain a current ratio of 1.5 and a debt-to-equity ratio of 1.25 to 1. Nouvelle's senior executives have an employment contract that entitles them to share a bonus pool equal to 10% of the company's net income. The financial statements are also used for tax purposes.

On December 21, 2006 Nouvelle's quality control engineer presented a report to the president where she expressed concern about problems with a new line of the company's products. The engineer believes that these new products were rushed into production and as a result there are some technical flaws that have not been corrected in products that have been sold to customers. The engineer has reported that there has been an increase of about 20% in service calls required on the new products, as compared with other company products, but she believes that repairs will increase dramatically once the products have been used by customers for more than 2,500 hours. The engineer estimates that she expects to see a sharp increase in repairs on these products from 12 to 18 months from the date of purchase and that the cost of repairing these products will be $3,000,000 higher than the amount originally budgeted. To date, repair costs on the new product line are about $250,000 higher than budgeted. The engineer bases her concerns on extensive tests she has carried out in the quality control laboratory.

Nouvelle's product design engineer, who was responsible for development of the products, has stated flatly that there are no technical flaws and that the increase in service calls is reasonable for a new product line.

On December 15, 2006 Nouvelle's vice-president of finance provided the president with the following estimates of the December 31, 2006 financial statements:

Net income	$ 2,540,000
Current assets	22,300,000
Current liabilities	18,200,000
Non-current liabilities	57,500,000
Shareholders' equity	62,800,000

Required:

Prepare a report to Nouvelle's president discussing the accounting and financial reporting issues regarding treatment of the concerns raised by the quality control engineer. Your report should identify alternative ways that the possible future costs could be treated and explain the implications of the alternatives. The president would also like your supported recommendations on what should be done.

P10-6.　**(Accounting for a rebate promotion, LO 1, 2, 8)** Urling Inc. (Urling) is a small public company that produces packaged consumer foods. Urling began operations about 22 years ago and has been a public company for about eight years. The company is managed by professional managers, who own about 10% of Urling's stock. About 30% of the shares are owned by members of the family who originally founded the company and the rest are widely held by private and institutional investors. Urling stock has struggled in recent years. The company has failed to meet earnings targets for the last two fiscal years. For the current fiscal year management has projected earnings of $2,500,000, which is about a 2% increase from the previous year.

Recently Urling introduced a new line of upscale frozen entrées to satisfy the tastes and lifestyles of busy baby boomers. For the first time Urling's management decided to promote the sale of the new entrées by offering rebates to customers. In the past the company had promoted its products through advertising and in-store price reductions. The new promotion entitles customers to a $5.00 rebate if they purchase four entrées and mail in the UPC labels from the packages. Urling used special packaging highlighting the promotion, provided in-store signs, and advertised it in newspaper and magazines. Since the promotion began several months ago, approximately 250,000 entrées have been sold and sales of an additional 70,000 are expected by year end. Approximately 1,500 customers have already mailed in their requests for rebates.

Because Urling has never used this type of promotion before, its marketing manager is not sure how to account for the promotion. The marketing manager has indicated that the number of rebate claims can be very difficult to estimate, especially because it is a new promotion and a new product. The manager has indicated that the number of claims can range between 2% and 25% of the product sold. Urling's controller has projected that net income before accounting for the new promotion will be about $2,555,000. Because projected earnings are so close to the forecast, the president is quite uneasy about the effect the new promotion will have.

Required:

    a. Prepare a report to Urling's president outlining the accounting issues and problems with the new rebate promotion. Provide recommendations on how the promotion should be accounted for and provide support for your recommendations that can be used in any discussions with the company's auditors. Indicate how the rebate promotion will be reported in the financial statements.

    b. Prepare a journal entry that will account for the rebate promotion in the current fiscal year.

P10-7. **(Accounting for a possible loss, LO 8)** Hoselaw Ltd. (Hoselaw) is a privately owned manufacturing company in eastern Ontario. The company is owned by five shareholders, three of whom are not active in management of the business. The company has a large demand loan outstanding at the bank.

The government recently informed Hoselaw's management that seepage from a dumpsite on its property might have polluted the ground water that is used by a local community. The company has denied responsibility, but the local community has launched a $2,000,000 lawsuit against Hoselaw to compensate the community for additional costs of obtaining fresh water and for cleaning up the contaminated water. The lawyers for the community and the company have met to discuss possible settlement terms, but little progress has been reported. Hoselaw's net income over the last five years has averaged $725,000 and its assets, as reported on the most recent balance sheet, have a NBV of $3,750,000.

Required:

Prepare a report to Hoselaw's president discussing the issues surrounding how to account for the environmental incident and the lawsuit. Your report should include a discussion of the alternative accounting treatments available and the implications of each.

P10-8. **(Future income taxes, LO 7)** Noggle Inc. (Noggle) processes fresh apples that it purchases from local farmers into apple juice and applesauce. All of Noggle's processing equipment was purchased in 2003 for $1,000,000. For accounting purposes, Noggle is amortizing the equipment on a straight-line basis over 10 years. For tax purposes, the asset is in a CCA class that allows Noggle to deduct 30% of the capital cost of the asset on a declining-balance basis. Because of the half-year rule Noggle can deduct only one-half of the allowable amount (15%) of the cost. Noggle has an income tax rate of 20% and its income before amortization and taxes is $350,000 in each year from 2003 through 2005. Noggle has no temporary differences between tax and financial reporting, except for the difference between amortization and CCA on the processing equipment, and there are no permanent differences.

Required:

    a. Calculate Noggle's taxable income in 2003 through 2005.

    b. Calculate the amount of income tax that Noggle must pay in 2003 through 2005.

    c. Calculate the accounting and tax bases of the processing equipment in 2003 through 2005.

    d. Calculate the future tax asset or liability that would be reported on Noggle's balance sheet at the end of 2003 through 2005.

    e. Prepare the journal entry that Noggle would make each year to record its income tax expense in 2003 through 2005.

    f. Calculate Noggle's net income in 2003 through 2005.

    g. What would Noggle's net income be in 2003 through 2005 if it used the taxes payable method?

    h. As a banker, which measure of net income is more useful to you? Explain.

P10-9. **(Future income taxes and pensions, LO 7, 8)** Azen Inc. (Azen) funds a defined-benefit pension plan for its employees. The plan began in 2005. Contributions to the pension plan are made in accordance with actuarial assumptions, while the pension expense that Azen records each year is determined in accordance with GAAP. For income tax purposes Azen can deduct only amounts actually contributed to the plan. The difference between the amount contributed to the plan and the amount expensed for financial reporting purposes is a temporary difference between accounting and tax. In the first three years of the plan Azen contributed to the plan and expensed for financial reporting purposes the following amounts:

	Contributed to the plan	**Pension expense**
2005	$1,000,000	$ 925,000
2006	1,000,000	950,000
2007	1,250,000	1,000,000

Azen has an income tax rate of 40% and its income before amortization and taxes is $7,500,000 in each year from 2005 through 2007. Azen has no temporary differences between tax and financial reporting, except for the difference between the tax and accounting bases of the pension asset or liability, and there are no permanent differences.

(Note that the temporary difference is the difference between the pension asset or liability for accounting purposes and the pension asset and liability for tax purposes. For tax purposes, a pension asset or liability always has a value of zero.)

Required:

    a. Prepare the journal entry that Azen would make each year to record the pension expense and the contribution to the pension plan.

    b. What is the balance in the pension asset or liability account at the end of 2005 through 2007?

    c. Calculate Azen's taxable income in 2005 through 2007.

    d. Calculate the amount of income tax that Azen must pay in 2005 through 2007.

    e. Calculate the accounting and tax basis of the pension plan amounts in 2005 through 2007.

    f. Calculate the future tax asset or liability that would be reported on Azen's balance sheet at the end of 2005 through 2007.

    g. Prepare the journal entry that Azen would make each year to record its income tax expense in 2005 through 2007.

    h. Calculate Azen's net income in 2005 through 2007.

    i. What would Azen's net income be in 2005 through 2007 if it used the taxes payable method?

    j. As a prospective investor in Azen's stock, which measure of net income is more useful to you? Explain.

P10-10. **(Accounting for leases, LO 5)** Vista Inc. (Vista) is a new manufacturing company that was formed in January 2007 to supply certain specialized machine parts to a large public company. Vista's managers decided to arrange long-term leases for the company's equipment, rather than to arrange financing and buy the equipment. Had Vista purchased the equipment, it would have cost about $1,000,000. Instead, Vista signed a 10-year lease for the equipment in January 2007 that required it to make annual payments of $150,000 on December 31, the company's year end. At the end of the lease Vista has the option to purchase the equipment at its fair market value at the time. However, Vista's management thinks that it is unlikely that it will exercise the option, since after 10 years the equipment is likely to be technologically out of date. The interest rate appropriate for this lease is 10%.

On December 31, 2007 Vista had total liabilities (before accounting for the lease obligation) of $800,000, capital stock of $500,000, and income before lease-related expenses and taxes of $350,000. Vista's tax expense for 2007 is estimated to be $40,000.

Required:

a. What are some of the reasons that Vista might have leased rather than purchased the equipment?

b. Should the lease be accounted for as a capital lease or an operating lease? Explain.

c. What journal entry would be required when the lease agreement was signed if the lease were considered a capital lease? What entry would be required if it were classified as an operating lease?

d. Prepare a schedule showing the principal and interest components of each annual payment over the life of the lease, assuming the lease is treated as a capital lease. Prepare the journal entries that Vista would make on December 31, 2007 and December 31, 2010 to record the lease payment. What would the entries be if the lease were classified as an operating lease?

e. Compare the effect on the income statement of classifying the lease as a capital lease versus an operating lease. Make the comparison for the years ended December 31, 2007 and 2010.

f. What amount would be reported on Vista's balance sheet for the machinery when the lease was signed in January 2007? What does this amount represent?

g. Over what period of time should the equipment be amortized? Explain. Prepare the journal entry to record the amortization expense for the year ended December 31, 2007. Assume Vista uses straight-line amortization.

h. How would Vista's debt-to-equity ratio be affected by accounting for the lease as a capital lease? Compare the debt-to-equity ratio on December 31, 2007 when the lease is classified as a capital lease versus an operating lease.

i. What steps could Vista take to have the lease classified as an operating lease? Why might Vista prefer that classification?

j. For purposes of determining a bonus for Vista's managers, do you think it is more appropriate to treat the lease as a capital lease or an operating lease? In answering, focus on determining management's bonus, not how GAAP would require the lease to be classified.

P10-11. **(Accounting for leases, LO 5)** In May 2005 Isachsen Inc. (Isachsen) signed a four-year lease with an office supply company to supply Isachsen with all required office equipment over the lease period. Had Isachsen purchased the office equipment, it would have cost about $500,000. The lease requires Isachsen to make annual lease payments of $150,000 on April 30, the company's year end. At the end of the lease Isachsen will own the equipment. Isachsen's management believes that the office equipment will be useful for between six and eight years. The interest rate appropriate for this lease is 12%.

On April 30, 2006 Isachsen had total liabilities (before accounting for the lease obligation) of $2,750,000 and capital stock of $1,500,000. Isachsen's income before lease related-expenses and taxes for the year ended April 30, 2006 is $550,000. Isachsen's tax expense for fiscal 2006 is estimated to be $160,000 and retained earnings on April 30, 2005 was $900,000.

Required:

a. What are some of the reasons that Isachsen might have leased rather than purchased the office equipment?

b. Should the lease be accounted for as a capital lease or an operating lease? Explain.

c. What journal entry would be required when the lease agreement was signed if the lease were considered a capital lease? What entry would be required if it were classified as an operating lease?

d. Prepare a schedule showing the principal and interest components of each annual payment over the life of the lease, assuming the lease is treated as a capital lease. Prepare the journal entries that Isachsen would make on April 30, 2006 and April 30, 2008 to record the lease payment. What would the entries be if the lease were classified as an operating lease?

e. Compare the effect on the income statement of classifying the lease as a capital lease versus an operating lease. Make the comparison for the years ended April 30, 2006 and 2008.

f. What amount would be reported on Isachsen's balance sheet for the equipment when the lease was signed in May 2005? What does this amount represent?

g. Over what period of time should the equipment be amortized? Explain. Prepare the journal entry to record the amortization expense for the year ended April 30, 2006. Assume Isachsen uses straight-line amortization.

h. How would Isachsen's debt-to-equity ratio be affected by accounting for the lease as a capital lease? Compare the debt-to-equity ratio on April 30, 2006 when the lease is classified as a capital lease versus an operating lease.

i. What steps could Isachsen take to have the lease classified as an operating lease? Why might Isachsen prefer that classification?

j. Suppose you were considering buying all the shares of Isachsen. Which balance sheet and income statement would be more useful to you in assessing the company—statements where the lease was classified as a capital lease or as an operating lease?

P10-12. **(The effects of buying versus leasing on the financial statements, LO 5)** Winterton Rail Ltd. (Winterton) is considering obtaining some new locomotives. The purchase price of the locomotives is $59,724,975. Winterton is considering whether it should purchase the locomotives or lease them directly from the manufacturer. If Winterton buys the locomotives, it would borrow the full purchase price from a large institutional lender and repay the loan by making an annual blended payment of $7,500,000 on the last day of each of the next 20 years. If Winterton leases the locomotives, it would make annual lease payments of $7,500,000 to the manufacturer on the last day of each of the next 20 years.

Required:

a. Prepare the journal entries that Winterton would make if it borrowed the money and purchased the locomotives.

b. Prepare the journal entries that Winterton would make when the lease agreement is signed if it leased the locomotives and the lease were considered a capital lease.

c. Prepare the journal entries that Winterton would make when the lease agreement is signed if it leased the locomotives and the lease were considered an operating lease.

d. Compare the three alternatives in (a), (b), and (c). Explain the similarities and differences among them. Under what circumstances might one of the alternatives be preferred over the others? Explain.

P10-13. **(Lease accounting and financial ratios, LO 5, 9)** Uphill Corp. (Uphill) operates four amusement arcades in Calgary. Uphill's summarized balance sheet on March 31, 2004 is shown on page 645.

The non-current liabilities of $115,000 include an $80,000 eight-year term note that matures in 2009. The terms of the note stipulate that Uphill must maintain a current ratio greater than 1.6 and a debt-to-equity ratio of less than 1.0. If either of these covenants is violated, the term note becomes payable immediately.

On April 1, 2004 management decided to upgrade the quality of the games in the arcades, many of which were no longer popular with the young people who are Uphill's primary customers. Uphill arranged a five-year lease for new games. The terms of the lease require annual payments of $22,000. The lease allows Uphill to replace up to 25% of the leased arcade games each year with newer games that are carried by the lessor.

Uphill Corp.
Balance Sheet
As of March 31, 2004

Assets		Liabilities and shareholders' equity	
Current assets	$ 45,000	Current liabilities	$ 30,000
Capital assets and		Non-current liabilities	115,000
other non-current			145,000
assets	295,000	Shareholders' equity	195,000
		Total liabilities and	
Total assets	$340,000	shareholders' equity	$340,000

Required:

a. Calculate the current ratio and debt-to-equity ratio on March 31, 2004.

b. Calculate the current ratio and debt-to-equity ratio on April 1, 2004 if the new lease is accounted for as an operating lease.

c. Calculate the current ratio and debt-to-equity ratio on April 1, 2004 if the new lease is accounted for as a capital lease. Assume that the appropriate interest rate that should be applied to the lease is 10%.

d. You are Uphill's controller. The president of the company has just informed you of his plan to lease the new arcade equipment. Write a memo to the president raising any concerns you have with the plan and providing advice and recommendations on how he should proceed.

P10-14. **(Accounting for bonds, LO 3, 4)** On May 1, 2003 Kuldo Inc. (Kuldo) issued a $20,000,000 bond with a 7% coupon rate and a maturity date of April 30, 2007. Interest will be paid semi-annually on April 30 and October 31. Kuldo's year end is December 31. The effective interest rate for a bond of this type on May 1, 2003 was 9%.

Required:

a. What will be the proceeds from the bond issue?

b. Prepare the journal entry to record issue of the bond on May 1, 2003.

c. Prepare an amortization schedule using both the straight-line and effective interest methods for any premium or discount that arose from the issue of the bond.

d. Prepare the journal entry required to accrue the interest expense and interest payable on December 31, 2005. Make the entry for both the straight-line and effective interest amortization methods.

e. Prepare the journal entry required to record the interest expense and the payment to investors on April 30, 2006. Make the entry for both the straight-line and effective interest amortization methods.

f. Prepare the journal entry required to record the retirement of the bond on maturity. Include the interest expense and amortization of any bond premium or discount in the entry. Make the entry for both the straight-line and effective interest amortization methods.

g. Assume that Kuldo's bond agreement allowed the company to redeem the bond on April 30, 2005 for $22,500,000. Prepare the journal entry required to record early retirement of the bond.

h. Assume the role of a shareholder in Kuldo. How would you interpret the gain or loss that would be reported on Kuldo's income statement as a result of the early retirement of the bond? Explain.

P10-15. **(Accounting for bonds, LO 3, 4)** On August 1, 2004 Quilty Inc. (Quilty) issued an $8,000,000 bond with a 9% coupon rate and a maturity date of July 31, 2010. Interest will be paid semi-annually on July 31 and January 31. Quilty's year end is December 31. The effective interest rate for a bond of this type on August 1, 2004 was 8%.

Required:

a. What will be the proceeds from the bond issue?

b. Prepare the journal entry to record issue of the bond on August 1, 2004.

c. Prepare an amortization schedule using both the straight-line and effective interest methods for any premium or discount that arose from the issue of the bond.

d. Prepare the journal entry required to accrue the interest expense and accrued interest payable on December 31, 2005. Make the entry for both the straight-line and effective interest amortization methods.

e. Prepare the journal entry required to record the interest expense and the payment to investors on January 31, 2006. Make the entry for both the straight-line and effective interest amortization methods.

f. Prepare the journal entry required to record the retirement of the bond on maturity. Include the interest expense and amortization of any bond premium or discount in the entry. Make the entry for both the straight-line and effective interest amortization methods.

g. On July 31, 2007, Quilty was able to buy back all the outstanding bonds on the open market for $7,250,000. Prepare the journal entry required to record early retirement of the bond.

h. Do you think that the decision to buy back the bonds early was a good decision? Explain.

■ Using Financial Statements

Extendicare Inc.

www.extendicare.com

Extendicare Inc. (Extendicare) is one of the largest operators of long-term care facilities in North America. On December 31, 2000 the Company operated 274 facilities, with capacity for more than 27,000 residents, and employed approximately 38,800 people in the United States and Canada. Extendicare provides medical specialty services in the United States, including subacute care and rehabilitative therapy services, as well as home health care and rehabilitative therapy services in Canada.

Extendicare's consolidated balance sheets, statements of earnings and statements of cash flows, along with extracts from the notes to the financial statements from its 2000 annual report, are provided in Exhibit 10-5.[7] Use this information to respond to questions FS10-1 to FS10-6.

FS10-1. Use the information in Exhibit 10-5 to respond to the following questions:

a. What amount of current liabilities did Extendicare have on December 31, 1999 and 2000? What amount of non-current liabilities did it have?

b. What was Extendicare's debt-to-equity ratio on December 31, 1999 and 2000? Interpret the ratios you calculated.

c. Which liabilities on Extendicare's balance sheet are valued at their present value?

d. What was Extendicare's interest coverage ratio in 2000? Does an interest coverage ratio make any sense when an entity is losing money? Explain.

e. Calculate Extendicare's current ratio on December 31, 1999 and 2000. What is your assessment of the company's liquidity?

f. How informative is Extendicare's statement of earnings? What information is missing from the statement that you would find useful in your assessment of its performance? Based on the information provided in the statement of earnings, how has the company performed over the last three years?

g. What is Extendicare's cash from operations for 1999 and 2000? Why is cash from operations so different from net earnings?

consolidated balance sheets

Exhibit 10-5

Extendicare Inc. Financial Statements

(thousands of dollars) December 31	2000	1999
Assets		
Current assets		
Cash and short-term investments	10,181	35,894
Accounts receivable	222,477	236,387
Income taxes recoverable	34,550	67,671
Future income tax assets, net *(notes 1K, 10)*	15,346	35,229
Inventories, supplies and prepaid expenses	15,745	16,438
	298,299	391,619
Property and equipment *(note 3)*	920,231	1,017,382
Goodwill	112,775	114,940
Other assets *(note 4)*	257,040	173,859
	1,588,345	1,697,800
Investment in Crown Life Insurance Company *(note 5)*	147,407	136,323
	1,735,752	1,834,123
Liabilities and Shareholders' Equity		
Current liabilities		
Bank overdraft	1,147	8,664
Accounts payable and accrued liabilities	247,719	253,540
Current maturities of long-term debt *(note 7)*	21,876	33,069
	270,742	295,273
Accrual for self-insured liabilities *(note 6)*	182,026	135,733
Long-term debt *(note 7)*	802,426	891,955
Deposits under divestiture agreement *(note 4)*	44,985	–
Future income tax liabilities, net *(notes 1K, 10)*	53,549	73,782
Minority interests	587	1,447
	1,354,315	1,398,190
Shareholders' equity	381,437	435,933
	1,735,752	1,834,123

FS10-2. The following questions pertain to Extendicare's self-insured liabilities:

   a. What are "self-insured liabilities"? Why does Extendicare have this account on its balance sheet? What do you think Extendicare self-insures?

   b. How much did Extendicare expense during 2000 to increase the balance in the self-insured liability account? Prepare the journal entry that was required in 2000 to record the increase in the amount in the self-insured liabilities account. (This information is not on the income statement. You will have to look at information elsewhere in the statements, such as the statement of cash flows.)

   c. What journal entry would be made if Extendicare had to pay a $1,000,000 claim against the company?

   d. Do you think that Extendicare's self-insured liabilities meets the GAAP characteristics of a liability? Explain.

   e. How much does Extendicare have invested to cover claims against the company? Why is this amount different from the amount of the liability? Does it concern you that the amount invested to cover self-insured liabilities decreased in 2000 while the amount of the liability has increased? Explain.

   f. Do you think Extendicare's management could use this account to manage its earnings? Explain.

FS10-3. The following questions pertain to Extendicare's long-term debt:

   a. How much long-term debt was outstanding on December 31, 2000? How much of that long-term debt was classified as current? What does it mean when long-term debt is classified as a current liability?

   b. How much long-term debt did Extendicare issue in 1999 and 2000? How much long-term debt did it repay?

Exhibit 10-5 (continued)

Extendicare Inc. Financial
Statements

consolidated statements of earnings (loss)

(thousands of dollars except per share amounts) Year ended December 31	2000	1999	1998
Revenue *(note 9)*			
Nursing and assisted living centres			
United States	1,346,033	1,364,084	1,470,539
Canada	266,671	260,723	240,782
United Kingdom	–	35,985	38,412
Medical supplies and outpatient therapy – United States	14,430	63,989	209,308
Home health – Canada	161,323	150,280	134,984
Other	18,949	17,626	18,843
	1,807,406	1,892,687	2,112,868
Operating and administrative costs	1,683,990	1,749,613	1,859,780
Earnings before undernoted	123,416	143,074	253,088
Lease costs	30,947	32,327	27,792
Depreciation and amortization	75,002	86,880	82,685
Interest, net	78,484	91,888	99,240
Loss (gain) from asset impairment, disposals and other items *(note 2)*	42,747	183,889	(131,566)
Earnings (loss) before income taxes	(103,764)	(251,910)	174,937
Income taxes *(notes 1K, 10)*			
Current (recovery)	(20,625)	(58,414)	129,475
Future (reduction)	(16,291)	(10,805)	(17,326)
	(36,916)	(69,219)	112,149
Net earnings (loss) from health care before minority interests	(66,848)	(182,691)	62,788
Minority interests	257	(171)	976
Net earnings (loss) from health care	(67,105)	(182,520)	61,812
Share of earnings of Crown Life *(note 5)*	7,827	22,818	3,520
Net earnings (loss) for the year	(59,278)	(159,702)	65,332
Earnings (loss) per share *(note 11)*	(0.81)	(2.14)	0.85

c. How much of Extendicare's long-term debt is payable in Canadian dollars and how much is payable in U.S. dollars? What are the risks that Extendicare faces because it borrows in U.S. dollars? Do you think those risks are reduced because Extendicare conducts much of its business in the United States?

d. What was Extendicare's interest expense in 1999 and 2000? How much interest did Extendicare pay in those years? Why are the interest expense and the amount of interest paid different?

e. What is the difference between fixed rate and variable (or floating) rate debt? What do you think are the benefits and limitations of each? What proportion of Extendicare's long-term debt is fixed rate?

f. Use library or Internet resources to define the following:
   i. LIBOR
   ii. letter of credit
   iii. senior debt
   iv. subordinated debt

g. Some of Extendicare's debt is secured and some is unsecured. Explain the difference between secured and unsecured debt. Do you think that the interest rate that Extendicare has to pay on its debt is affected by whether it is secured or unsecured? Explain.

h. What is included in Extendicare's "credit facility"? Explain the interest rate terms that apply to the components of the credit facility. Describe the covenants associated with the credit facility. What is the purpose of these covenants? Do you think Extendicare would prefer not to have them? Explain. Why do you think Extendicare agreed to them?

CONSOLIDATED STATEMENTS OF CASH FLOWS

Exhibit 10-5 (continued)

Extendicare Inc. Financial
Statements

(thousands of dollars) Year ended December 31	2000	1999	1998
Cash provided by operations			
Net earnings (loss)	(59,278)	(159,702)	65,332
Items not involving cash			
Depreciation and amortization	75,002	86,880	82,685
Increase in accrual for self-insured liabilities	40,615	65,167	15,185
Provision for punitive damages *(note 17)*	13,249	–	–
Future income taxes *(notes 1K, 10)*	(16,291)	(10,805)	(17,326)
Undistributed share of earnings of Crown Life	(7,827)	(22,818)	(3,520)
Loss (gain) from asset impairment, disposals and other			
items, net of current taxes *(note 2)*	42,747	93,780	(33,911)
Reserve (recovery) for settlements with third parties	(17,794)	39,546	–
Other	2,709	2,090	3,924
	73,132	94,138	112,369
Net change in operating working capital, excluding cash			
Accounts receivable	7,825	14,455	(24,508)
Inventories, supplies and prepaid expenses	2,593	1,068	(6,079)
Accounts payable	(41,967)	(48,092)	(16,027)
Income taxes payable (recoverable)	6,066	(22,284)	5,524
	47,649	39,285	71,279
Cash provided by (used in) investment activities			
Property and equipment	(46,292)	(50,268)	(113,342)
Acquisitions, net of cash acquired	–	–	(28,616)
Net cash proceeds from divestiture agreement *(note 4)*	43,774	–	–
Net cash proceeds from dispositions *(note 2)*	10,677	132,002	365,377
Income taxes recovered (paid) related to dispositions	42,584	(37,790)	(60,767)
Other assets	71	3,586	(2,358)
	50,814	47,530	160,294
Cash provided by (used in) financing activities			
Issue of long-term debt	–	65,886	42,402
Repayment of long-term debt	(115,501)	(128,119)	(301,661)
Decrease (increase) in investments held for			
self-insured liabilities	13,161	(8,865)	13,535
Purchase of shares for cancellation	(4,036)	(5,932)	(1,029)
Issue of Subordinate Voting Shares	–	–	547
Financing costs	(2,894)	(3,102)	(1,254)
Other	(7,327)	(89)	548
	(116,597)	(80,221)	(246,912)
Foreign exchange gain (loss) on cash held in foreign currency	(62)	(283)	813
Increase (decrease) in cash and cash equivalents	(18,196)	6,311	(14,526)
Cash and cash equivalents at beginning of year	27,230	20,919	35,445
Cash and cash equivalents at end of year	9,034	27,230	20,919

i. The note explains that Extendicare has a $40,000,000 operating line of credit in Canada, of which $31,050,000 has been utilized by a standby letter of credit. However, this amount does not appear in the list of borrowing provided in the note. Explain why the $31,050,000 does not appear as an amount borrowed. (Use the results of your research in (f) to answer.)

j. The note provides a list of principal repayments that Extendicare must make over the next five years. How might users of the financial statements use this information?

FS10-4. The following questions pertain to Extendicare's income taxes:

a. What amounts does Extendicare report on its December 31, 1999 and 2000 balance sheet for future income taxes?

b. What was Extendicare's statutory tax rate in 1998, 1999, and 2000? What is the tax rate using the income tax expense in 1998, 1999, and 2000? What is

Exhibit 10-5 (continued)

Extendicare Inc. Financial
Statements

1. Summary of Accounting Policies

(I) Accrual and Investments Held for Self-insured Liabilities

The Company self-insures certain risks related to general and professional liability, auto liability, health benefits, employers' liability and workers' compensation. The accrual for self-insured liabilities includes estimates of the costs of both reported claims and claims incurred but not reported and is based on estimates of loss based on assumptions made by management, including consideration of actuarial projections.

The Company invests funds to support the accrual for self-insured liabilities. These funds are investment grade, are carried at amortized cost approximating market value and are classified in other assets as investments held for self-insured liabilities.

(K) Income Taxes

Effective January 1, 2000, the Company adopted, on a retroactive basis, the new requirements of the Canadian Institute of Chartered Accountants (CICA) with respect to accounting for income taxes. The Company has not restated prior periods and therefore, shareholders' equity includes a cumulative charge to opening retained earnings of $1,250,000. Under the new requirements, the liability method of tax allocation is used, based on differences between financial reporting and tax bases of assets and liabilities. Future income tax liabilities or assets are calculated using tax rates anticipated to apply in the periods that the temporary differences are expected to reverse. The income tax rates used to measure income tax assets and liabilities are those rates enacted or substantially enacted at the balance sheet date. Realization of the deferred tax assets is dependent on the availability of taxable income, of similar character. Previously, the deferral method was used, based on differences in the timing of reporting income and expenses in financial statements and tax returns.

4. Other Assets

(thousands of dollars)	2000	1999
Investments held for self-insured liabilities	68,199	78,433

6. Self-insured Liabilities and Measurement Uncertainty

The accrual for self-insured liabilities is based on management's best estimate of the ultimate cost to settle claims. Management regularly evaluates the appropriateness of the carrying value of this liability. Of the risks for which the Company self-insures, general and professional liability claims are the most volatile and significant.

Management's estimate of the accrual for general and professional liability costs is significantly influenced by assumptions, which are limited by the uncertainty of predictions concerning future events, and assessments regarding expectations of several factors. Such factors include, but are not limited to: the frequency and severity of claims, which can differ materially by jurisdiction in which the Company operates; coverage limits of third-party reinsurance; the effectiveness of the claims management process; and uncertainty regarding the outcome of litigation.

The Company is experiencing adverse claims development resulting in an increase in the accrual for self-insured liabilities. Consequently, effective January 1, 2000 the Company's per claim retained risk increased significantly. Changes in the Company's level of retained risk, and other significant assumptions that underlie management's estimates of self-insured liabilities, could have a material effect on the future carrying value of the self-insured liabilities as well as the Company's operating results and liquidity.

The Company invests funds to support the accrual for self-insured liabilities. General and professional liability and workers' compensation risks are long-term in nature and accordingly, claim payments for any one policy year occur over a period of up to 10 years. The Company believes that it has sufficient cash resources to meet its estimated current claims payment obligations.

Extendicare's tax rate based on the actual amount of tax that it must pay for income earned in 1998, 1999, and 2000?

c. What journal entry did Extendicare make in 1998, 1999, and 2000 to record its income tax expense?

d. Explain why property and equipment gives rise to a future income tax liability of $107,583,000 and why the self-insurance liability (reserve) gives rise to a future income tax asset of $40,850,000.

FS10-5. The following questions pertain to Extendicare's commitments:

a. Suppose the operating lease payments reported in Note 14 were to be reported as capital leases:

Exhibit 10-5 (continued)

Extendicare Inc. Financial
Statements

7. Long-term Debt

(thousands of dollars)	2000	1999
Payable in Canadian Dollars		
Mortgages, 5.81% to 9.81%, maturing through to 2013	161,153	163,738
Payable in United States Dollars		
Bank term loans, at rates varying with prime and/or LIBOR,		
maturing through to 2004	298,050	391,586
Senior Subordinated Notes at 9.35%, due 2007	286,553	288,659
Mortgages and Industrial Development Bonds		
6.25% to 13.61%, maturing through to 2010	12,530	61,635
At varying rates, due 2015	56,374	8,653
Notes payable, 3.00% to 10.00%, maturing through to 2008	9,531	10,556
Obligations under capital leases (note 14)	111	197
	824,302	925,024
Less due within one year and included in current liabilities	21,876	33,069
	802,426	891,955

The weighted average interest rate of all long-term debt at December 31, 2000 was approximately 8.8% (1999 – 8.7%). After taking into account swaps to fix certain floating rate debt, 75.0% of the Company's total long-term debt at December 31, 2000 was subject to fixed rates. Interest paid in 2000, 1999 and 1998 was $78,984,000, $88,950,000 and $97,309,000, respectively.

EHSI entered into a syndicated bank credit agreement (the "Credit Facility") dated November 26, 1997, which provided EHSI with senior secured credit facilities of up to US$600,000,000. The Credit Facility consisted of three term loans, each in the amount of US$200,000,000, as follows: a six-year revolving credit facility (the "Revolving Credit Facility"); a six-year term loan (the "Tranche A Term Loan"); and a seven-year term loan (the "Tranche B Term Loan"). Borrowings under the Credit Facility are secured by the outstanding common shares and various assets of EHSI and each of its existing and future domestic subsidiaries. As a result of the decline in financial results, amendments to EHSI's Credit Facility in the second quarter of 1999 included revisions to the financial covenants, increased interest rates and asset securitization. The Credit Facility was further amended in the first quarter of 2000 for the 1999 general provision for Medicare settlements and non-cash provisions for general and professional liability costs.

On December 2, 1997, EHSI issued US$200,000,000 9.35% Senior Subordinated Notes due 2007 (the "Subordinated Notes"). The Subordinated Notes are unsecured senior subordinated obligations of EHSI subordinated in right of payment to all existing and future senior indebtedness of EHSI, which includes all borrowings under the Credit Facility as well as all indebtedness not refinanced by the Credit Facility. At December 31, 2000, US$8,900,000 of the Senior Subordinated Notes was held by Extendicare Inc. and had been deducted from long-term debt.

The Revolving Credit Facility matures on December 31, 2003, at which time all outstanding borrowings are due. As part of the amendments to the Credit Facility, EHSI waived its right to US$25,000,000 of the Revolving Credit Facility. The unused portion of the Revolving Credit Facility at December 31, 2000, was US$23,500,000 (net of letters of credit of US$36,500,000 and the US$25,000,000 unavailable portion), which is available for working capital and general corporate purposes. The Tranche A Term Loan matures on December 31, 2003 with escalating annual repayments, payable in quarterly instalments. The Tranche B Term Loan matures on December 31, 2004 with annual repayments of US$655,000, payable in quarterly instalments, with the balance of US$61,530,000 due in 2004.

Borrowings under the Credit Facility bear interest at EHSI's option at rates equal to the prime rate or LIBOR, plus applicable margins, depending upon leverage ratios of EHSI. Applicable margins at December 31, 2000, under the Revolving Credit Facility and the Tranche A Term Loan, were 1.75% for prime rate loans and 2.50% for LIBOR-based borrowings. The applicable margin at December 31, 2000, under the Tranche B Term Loan, was 2.50% for prime rate borrowings and 3.00% for LIBOR-based borrowings.

EHSI is party to two interest rate swap agreements to reduce the impact of changes in interest rates on certain of its floating rate long-term debt with two banks. The swaps effectively change the interest rates on US$100,000,000 of LIBOR-based borrowings under the Credit Facility to fixed rates ranging from 5.53% to 5.74% (average of 5.63%), plus the applicable margins, over periods of three to four years. The Company may be exposed to credit loss in the event of non-performance by the banks under the swap agreements but does not anticipate such non-performance.

The Credit Facility contains a number of covenants, such as: restrictions on the payment of dividends by EHSI; redemption of EHSI's common stock and change of control, as defined, of the Company; as well as financial covenants, including fixed charge coverage, debt leverage, and net worth ratios. EHSI is required to make mandatory prepayments of principal upon the occurrence of

Exhibit 10-5 (continued)

Extendicare Inc. Financial
Statements

certain events, such as certain asset sales and certain issuances of securities. EHSI is permitted to make voluntary prepayments at any time. Such prepayments may, under certain conditions, reduce the amounts available to be borrowed under the Credit Facility.

In Canada, the Company has two lines of credit, a $40,000,000 operating line, of which $31,050,000 has been utilized by a standby letter of credit to secure pension obligations. A second line of credit has been secured for $20,000,000 and is available for construction costs on the new nursing facilities.

Principal payments on long-term debt due within the next five fiscal years, exclusive of those obligations under capital leases, after giving effect to renewal privileges, are as follows:

	(thousands of dollars)
2001	21,855
2002	16,261
2003	189,006
2004	97,653
2005	5,745

10. Income Taxes

The provision (recovery) for income taxes is comprised as follows:

(thousands of dollars)	2000	1999	1998
Earnings (loss) from health care before income taxes	(103,764)	(251,910)	174,937
Income taxes at statutory Canadian rate of 43.95% (1999 – 44.62%; 1998 – 44.62%)	(45,609)	(112,402)	78,057
Income tax effect relating to the following items:			
Non-deductible goodwill and accounting provisions	924	14,520	51,354
Tax rate variance of foreign subsidiaries	6,891	49,545	258
Benefit of operating and capital loss utilization	–	(42,200)	(14,920)
Capital losses not benefited	–	14,738	–
Non-taxable income	(531)	(695)	(2,712)
Other items	1,409	7,275	112
	(36,916)	(69,219)	112,149

In the United States, the Company has state net operating loss carryforwards of $111,263,000, which expire in years 2001 through 2020. Because the realizability of these losses is uncertain, they have not been benefited in the accounts.

There are capital losses available for income tax purposes amounting to $64,679,000 (1999 – $63,301,000) that can be carried forward indefinitely to apply against future capital gains. The full benefit of these capital losses is offset by a valuation allowance.

Cash taxes recovered during 2000 were $69,275,000, and cash taxes paid in 1999 and 1998 were $43,517,000 and $74,892,000, respectively.

Future income taxes are provided for temporary differences. The significant components of future income tax assets and liabilities are as follows:

(thousands of dollars)	2000	*(thousands of dollars)*	2000
Future income tax assets		Future income tax liabilities	
Self-insurance reserves	40,850	Property and equipment	107,583
Investment in Crown Life	13,764	Leasehold rights	4,061
Employee benefit accruals	13,086	Other	9,828
Accounts receivable reserves	12,272		
Net capital loss carryforwards	11,590		121,472
Goodwill	3,879	Future income tax liabilities, net	38,203
Operating loss carryforwards	3,176	Less current portion of future	
Operating reserves	3,273	income tax assets, net	15,346
Other	9,066		
		Long-term future	
	110,956	income tax liabilities, net	53,549
Valuation allowance	(27,687)		
	83,269		

Exhibit 10-5 (continued)

Extendicare Inc. Financial
Statements

14. Other Commitments

At December 31, 2000, the Company was committed under non-cancellable leases requiring future minimum rentals as follows:

(thousands of dollars)	Capital Leases	Operating Leases	Total
2001	25	17,733	17,758
2002	27	14,414	14,441
2003	27	12,492	12,519
2004	27	11,494	11,521
2005	16	11,290	11,306
Thereafter	–	58,247	58,247
Total minimum payments	122	125,670	125,792
Less amount representing interest	11		
Obligations under capital leases	111		

At December 31, 2000, EHSI had capital expenditure purchase commitments outstanding of approximately $8,397,000 (US$5,600,000).

The Company has undertaken to construct eight new facilities in Ontario, at an estimated total cost of $125,000,000. At December 31, 2000, property and equipment includes $24,155,000 of construction-in-progress related to these facilities. Construction costs of up to $75,000 per bed will be repaid to the Company by the Government of Ontario over a 20-year period, based on a per bed occupancy formula. In an agreement finalized in February 2001, the Company obtained financing of $125,000,000 to build the new facilities from Borealis Long-Term Care Facilities Inc. (Borealis), a wholly owned subsidiary of the Ontario Municipal Employees Retirement System. Extendicare intends to operate the facilities for Borealis during the 25-year capital lease arrangement at a financing cost of approximately 8.0%.

During 2000, the Company duly exercised its right to purchase seven nursing facilities in the United States that it had operated under a lease agreement. The Company continues to lease and operate the facilities in good faith and has held ongoing negotiations with the landlord to conclude issues involved in completing the transaction. Though negotiations are not finalized, the Company believes it has complied fully with the terms of the option and believes that settlement of outstanding issues can be resolved. Should the matters be resolved, approximately US$6,400,000 of the purchase price would be paid in cash. There are however, no assurances that the transaction will be completed, and as of December 31, 2000, the Company had $6,298,000 in leaseholds and equipment relating to these facilities.

17. Contingent Liabilities

The Company and its consolidated subsidiaries are defendants in actions brought against them from time to time in connection with their operations. It is not possible to predict the ultimate outcome of the various proceedings at this time or to estimate additional costs that may result.

During September 2000, a Florida jury awarded US$3,000,000 in compensatory damages and US$17,000,000 in punitive damages to a plaintiff in a lawsuit filed against the Company. In the third quarter of 2000, EHSI accrued a reserve of $13,249,000 (US$9,000,000) in conjunction with its appeal of the verdict. Subsequent to year-end, the Company settled the lawsuit with the plaintiff within the amount reserved.

    i.   What would be the journal entry that you would record on January 1, 2001 to record these leases as capital leases, assuming the leases went into effect on that date? Assume a discount rate of 12% and assume the payments to be made "thereafter" are evenly distributed over 2006 through 2010.

   ii.   What effect would classifying these leases as capital leases have on Extendicare's debt-to-equity ratio? Explain and show your calculations.

  iii.   Do you think that treating all leases as capital leases gives a better indication of an entity's debt load?

  b. How much money did Extendicare have committed for capital expenditures on December 31, 2000? Why is this disclosure useful if Extendicare has not yet spent the money?

c. How much does Extendicare expect to spend on the eight facilities that will be built in Ontario? Would this information be useful to a prospective lender? Explain. Would it be of interest to the Canada Customs and Revenue Agency? Explain.

FS10-6. The following questions pertain to Extendicare's contingent liabilities:

a. What was the outcome of the lawsuit that was concluded in September 2000? How much did Extendicare accrue in respect of the case? Why was this amount added back to net earnings in the calculation of cash from operations in 2000? What was the ultimate resolution of the lawsuit?

b. The first paragraph of Note 17 explains that Extendicare is sued from time to time and that it is not possible to estimate the outcome of these suits and the costs associated with them. What are the accounting implications of this statement?

■ Analyzing Mark's Work Wearhouse

M10-1. Examine MWW's balance sheet, statement of earnings, and statement of cash flow (including the supplementary schedules):

a. How much does MWW report in current liabilities on January 27, 2001?

b. What was the percentage increase in current liabilities from January 29, 2000 to January 27, 2001? What is the reason for the increase? Do you think the increase is reasonable? Explain.

c. What additional information might you want about MWW's current liabilities? Explain what you would want that information for.

d. How much long-term debt did MWW retire during fiscal 2001? How much new long-term debt did MWW obtain during fiscal 2001?

e. How much interest did MWW expense during fiscal 2001? How much interest was paid to lenders in cash? How do you explain the fact that these amounts are not the same?

M10-2. Examine Note 11 to MWW's financial statements on commitments and contingent liabilities (page A-56).

a. Which users of financial statements would be interested in the information in Note 11? Explain. Answer by making reference to specific information disclosed in the notes.

b. How much is MWW committed to pay in operating lease payments in 2004 and 2005? Could this amount change in future years? How?

c. Suppose the operating lease payments reported in the note were to be reported as capital leases.

i. What would be the journal entry that you would record on January 28, 2001 to record these leases as capital leases, assuming the leases went into effect on that date? Assume a discount rate of 11% and assume the payments to be made "thereafter" are evenly distributed over 2007 through 2010.

ii. What effect would classifying these leases as capital leases have on MWW's debt-to-equity ratio? Explain and show your calculations.

iii. Does it matter how MWW accounts for its leases? Explain.

d. The following questions pertain to the buy-back agreement that Mark's and Work World have with Canadian chartered banks:

i. Describe the buy-back agreement that Mark's and Work World have regarding inventory owned by franchise stores.

ii. As of January 27, 2001, what is the maximum amount for which MWW is responsible?

iii. This amount is disclosed only in the notes to the financial statements. Do you think that it should be accrued in the financial statements? Explain. Do you think that it would have been a problem if the information had not been disclosed at all? Explain.

iv. What would be the effect on the financial statements of accruing the maximum amount for which MWW is responsible?

M10-3. Examine Note 10 to MWW's financial statements (page A-55). During the fiscal year ended January 27, 2001, MWW purchased some of its franchise stores and converted them to corporate stores.

    a. How much long-term debt did MWW record as due to the vendors of the franchise stores?

    b. How much of that debt should be classified as current on the January 27, 2001 balance sheet? Explain.

    c. What interest rate is being paid on this debt?

    d. What are the repayment terms of this debt?

    e. Why is it useful to know when the debt is to be repaid? What users and uses of accounting does this information serve?

    f. It does not appear that this debt has been recorded at its present value. If the effective interest rate on the non-interest-bearing portion of the debt were 7%, what amount would have been reported on the January 27, 2001 balance sheet had it been recorded at its present value? What journal entry would have been made to record the debt? What journal entry would be required to record the payment on April 1, 2001?

M10-4. Examine Note 9 to MWW's financial statements (page A-54) and consider the $75,000,000 credit facility available from a syndication of Canadian chartered banks.

    a. What is the interest rate that applies to this credit facility? Can the rate change? Explain.

    b. Would amounts borrowed from this credit facility be classified as a current or non-current liability? Explain.

    c. On January 27, 2001, what is the maximum amount of the $75,000,000 credit facility that MWW could have borrowed? Explain your answer.

    d. Under what circumstances can borrowings against this credit facility be extended? What happens if the credit is not extended?

    e. What amount of the credit facility is outstanding on January 27, 2001? (See Note 10, page A-55, to respond.)

M10-5. Examine Note 10 to MWW's financial statements (page A-55).

    a. How much long-term debt did MWW have on January 27, 2001? How much of that debt was interest-bearing?

    b. What amount of principal repayments is MWW required to make in 2001, 2003, and 2005? Why and to whom might this information be useful?

    c. What was the market value of MWW's debt on January 27, 2001? Explain why the market value is different from the amount included in the balance sheet.

M10-6. Examine Note 10 to MWW's financial statements (page A-55).

    a. What amount of MWW's long-term debt pertains to leased assets under capital leases?

    b. What is the average interest rate on the fixture and equipment capital leases? What is the relevance of the interest rate on capital leases?

    c. Why do you think that MWW makes such extensive use of leases?

    d. What are the cost and the NBV of MWW's assets under capital lease (see Note 7, page A-53)? Why does this amount differ from capital lease liabilities listed in Note 10 (page A-55)?

    e. What assets has MWW given the lessor as security for the leases?

M10-7. Note 10 to MWW's financial statements includes among the company's long-term debt an "estimated future earnout payable—on Paul John Enterprises acquisition" of $2,000,000. Explain what this long-term debt represents. Why is the amount owed estimated instead of being the exact amount owed? You will have to read the third to last paragraph in Note 10 and Note 2 to answer this question (pages A-55, A-51).

M10-8. Examine the financial statements and Note 17 to the financial statements.

    a. What is the combined federal and provincial tax rate that applies to MWW's taxable income?

b. How much is MWW liable for in income taxes for the fiscal year ended January 27, 2001? How much was MWW liable for the fiscal year ended January 29, 2000?

c. Use the combined federal and provincial tax rate that applies to MWW's taxable income to estimate its taxable income for the fiscal year ended January 27, 2001.

d. Prepare the journal entry that MWW would make to record its income tax expense for the year ended January 27, 2001.

e. What was the balance in the future income tax account on January 27, 2001 and on January 29, 2000?

f. Explain the difference between the income tax expense, or as MWW calls it, the provision for income taxes, and taxes payable.

g. Note 17 (page A-62) discloses the major components of MWW's future tax assets and liabilities. What contribution do capital assets make to the future income tax balance on January 27, 2001? Explain what this amount means. What contribution do other assets make to the future income tax balance on January 27, 2001? Explain what this amount means.

h. On MWW's statement of cash flows, future income taxes (benefits) are added back in the calculation of funds from operations. Explain why.

i. Prepare a schedule reconciling the balance in the income taxes payable account on January 29, 2000 to the balance in that account on January 27, 2001. To answer this question you will have to use information from the balance sheet, statement of earnings, and the supplementary schedules to the consolidated statement of cash flows.

j. Examine the first table in Note 17 (page A-62). What is the tax rate that MWW would have been expected to pay in fiscal 1999 and 2000 according to the *Income Tax Act* and provincial tax laws? What is the tax rate reflected in the accounting numbers in the income statement in fiscal 1999 and 2000? What is MWW's tax rate based on the actual amount of tax that it must pay for income earned in fiscal 1999 and 2000? Explain why these three rates are different and what each means. Is information about these different tax rates important to users of the financial statements? Explain.

Endnotes

1. Panel A extracted from Canadian National Railway Company's 2000 annual report. Panel B extracted from Salter Street Films Limited's 2000 annual report.

2. Clarence Byrd, Ida Chen, and Heather Chapman, *Financial Reporting in Canada*, 26th Edition. The Virtual Professional Library. CD-ROM. 2002.

3. Panel A extracted from Fortis Inc.'s 2000 annual report. Panel B extracted from Four Seasons Hotels Inc.'s 2001 annual report.

4. Panel A extracted from Boralex Inc.'s 2001 annual report. Panel B extracted from Air Canada's 2000 annual report.

5. Panel A extracted from Fortis Inc.'s 2000 annual report. Panel B extracted from Canadian Pacific Enterprises Limited's 2000 annual report. Panel C extracted from Boralex Inc.'s 2001 annual report.

6. Data obtained from *Financial Post Industry Report* at the *Financial Post* web site, http://www.fpdata.finpost.com/suite/autologreports.asp (accessed May 14, 2002).

7. Extracted from Extendicare Inc.'s 2000 annual report.

Chapter 11

Owners' Equity

Learning Objectives

After studying the material in this chapter you will be able to:

LO 1. Recognize the differences among proprietorships, partnerships, corporations, and not-for-profit organizations, and be familiar with accounting and reporting differences among these different types of entities.

LO 2. Characterize equity and the different types of equity securities, and explain the accounting for the issuance and repurchase of shares.

LO 3. Describe the transactions and economic events that affect retained earnings, and explain the nature of cash, property, stock dividends, and stock splits, and the accounting for them.

LO 4. Define leverage and explain the effects it has on the return earned by equity investors and on the profitability of an entity.

LO 5. Discuss the nature and purpose of employee stock options, and the accounting issues and controversy surrounding them.

LO 6. Analyze and interpret information about equity that is provided in financial statements.

Introduction

Entities finance their assets from two sources: debt and equity. These two sources of financing are seen in the structure of the accounting equation:

$$\text{Assets} = \text{Liabilities} + \text{Owners' (Shareholders') Equity}$$

Liabilities represent assets financed by debt, and equity represents assets financed by the owners. Owners can invest in an entity in two ways. An investor can invest directly by purchasing an ownership interest from an entity in exchange for cash or other assets. Indirect investments are made when an entity reinvests the profits it earns into its own activities, instead of distributing those profits to owners as dividends or distributions.

The accounting equation provides another view of equity: equity as the residual interest of owners. When the accounting equation is rearranged as follows—

$$\text{Assets} - \text{Liabilities} = \text{Owners' (Shareholders') Equity}$$

—equity can now be viewed as what is left over after the entity's assets have been used to satisfy the creditors. As we will see, the equity section of the balance sheet represents the owners' interest as measured by accountants; it does not represent the market value of the entity.

Many of the accounting issues we will look at in this chapter are straightforward and have been touched on earlier in the book (for example, accounting for the sale of shares to investors and payment of cash dividends). Other issues can be a bit trickier, such as accounting for when an entity buys its own shares back from investors. The chapter also uses a current accounting controversy to highlight the important concept of economic consequences: the notion that how an entity reports its transactions and economic events has an economic impact on the entity and its stakeholders.

Corporations, Partnerships, and Proprietorships

The different types of accounting entities were introduced and discussed in Chapter 1. These accounting entities include proprietorships, partnerships, corporations, and not-for-profit organizations such as charities, social clubs, governments, professional organizations, and so on. Readers might find it useful to return to Chapter 1 at this time to review the section on the different types of accounting entities (pages 10–13).

Our focus throughout most of the book has been on corporations, so let's begin there. A corporation is a separate legal and taxable entity. The owners of a corporation are its shareholders. One of the main attractions of a corporation is the limited liability that is provided by its corporate status. Shareholders of a corporation are not liable for the obligations of and losses suffered by the corporation, beyond what they have invested in the corporation.

This limited liability is especially important for public companies, where most shareholders have little involvement in the management and operation of the entity. If the owner of 1,000 shares of a large public corporation were liable for fulfilling obligations that the corporation was not able to meet—for example, paying off a bank loan that corporation was unable to pay—that shareholder would probably be much more reluctant to invest. If shareholders are responsible for a corporation's liabilities, they bear higher risks and investment in equity is less attractive. After all, how many people would want to hold stock in public companies if there were a chance that they could lose their savings, cars, or houses?

In some circumstances shareholders might agree to waive the limited liability protection of a corporation. For example, lenders often demand that the shareholders of smaller, private corporations personally guarantee to repay amounts borrowed by the corporation in the event it is not able to repay.

Corporations divide the shareholders' equity section of their balance sheets into two broad classifications: capital stock and retained earnings. Capital stock represents direct investments by shareholders—the purchase of shares by shareholders directly from the corporation. Retained earnings represents indirect investment by shareholders—earnings that are not distributed to the shareholders. The separation of direct and indirect investment on the balance sheet is important because the shareholders need to know whether dividends represent a distribution of earnings or a distribution of the money directly invested by shareholders.

Partnerships and proprietorships are not incorporated. Partnerships and proprietorships do not pay income taxes and do not file income tax returns. Instead, earnings are taxed in the hands of the proprietor or partners. At the end of each year a proprietor determines the income of the proprietorship and includes the amount in his or her personal tax return. The income of a partnership is divided among the partners at the end of each year in a way agreed to by the partners, and each partner includes that amount in his or her tax return. Because proprietorships and partnerships do not pay income taxes, their income statements do not report an income tax expense.

Partnerships and proprietorships do not have legal liability, which means that partners and proprietors are personally liable for any obligations that the partnership or proprietorship is unable to meet. However, there are exceptions to this unlimited liability rule. In partnerships known as **limited liability partnerships** or **LLPs** some of the partners have limited liability protection.

There are two types of partners in an LLP: limited partners and general partners.

- **Limited partners** have the same limited liability protection as they would if the entity were a corporation—they are not personally liable for the debts and obligations of the partnership.

- **General partners** do not have limited liability and are liable for all debts and obligations of the partnership. An LLP must have at least one general partner.

LLPs are useful when a partnership is the preferred form of organizing a business, but some of the investors are not actively involved and would not be prepared to accept the risk associated with unlimited liability.

Most accounting done by partnerships and proprietorships is not very different from that done by corporations. There are no legal requirements that partnerships or proprietorships use GAAP, although GAAP would be used if, for example, a lender demanded it. However, the equity section of financial statements for partnerships and proprietorships is structured differently than that of corporations. See, for example, Table 11-1 (page 660), which shows the balance sheet of a partnership that operates a nursing home. (This is the balance sheet of an actual partnership. The name has been removed because the partnership is private and, therefore, the financial statements are not publicly available.)

In the equity section of the balance sheet in Table 11-1 there is a single line called Partners' Deficiency. (Had the partnership been profitable, the account title would have been Partners' Equity.) The Statement of Partners' Deficiency provides additional detail about the partners' capital. Notice that the direct investment by the partners is not separated from the earnings of the partnership, as it is in a corporation. In a partnership an account is kept for each partner. The partners' accounts keep track of the capital contributed by each, the portion of the partnership's earnings that is attributable to each partner, and the drawings made by each partner. (Drawings are amounts taken by the partners from the partnership.) This format can be seen in

Table 11-1   Partnership Balance Sheet

Nursing Home Partnership
Balance Sheet
As of December 31, 2002 and 2003

	2003	2002
Assets		
Current		
Cash	$ 947,512	$ 171,894
Accounts receivable	1,171,838	1,299,429
Prepaid expenses	829,394	978,148
	2,948,744	2,449,471
Capital assets (Note 3)	30,091,895	31,464,292
Deferred financing charges (Note 4)	—	687,782
Goodwill (Note 5)	12,797,549	13,291,350
	$45,838,188	$47,892,895
Liabilities		
Current		
Payables and accruals	$ 5,047,227	$ 4,662,064
Payable to Ministry of Health	661,536	1,183,373
Due to management company	1,560,269	962,753
Current portion of long term debt	734,185	667,046
	8,003,217	7,475,236
Long term debt (Note 7)	73,361,917	74,096,106
Cash flow deficiency loan (Note 8)	2,807,355	2,807,355
Deferred management fees (Note 9)	5,135,348	6,346,406
	89,307,837	90,725,103
Partners' Deficiency	(43,469,649)	(42,832,208)
	$45,838,188	$47,892,895

Statement of Partners' Deficiency
For the Year Ended December 31, 2002 and 2003

	General Partner	Limited Partners	2003 Total	2002 Total
Deficiency, beginning of year	$(46,588)	$(44,570,296)	$(44,616,884)	$(43,641,368)
Net income (loss)	372	371,920	372,292	(21,724)
Drawings	—	(1,036,292)	(1,036,292)	(953,792)
Deficiency, end of year	$(46,216)	$(45,234,668)	$(45,280,884)	$(44,616,884)

Table 11-1, where the deficiency attributable to the general partner is shown separately from that of the limited partners.

In a non-LLP partnership, the equity section of the balance sheet would have a single line for partners' capital and the statement of partners' equity would have a column for each partner. In a three-partner partnership, the statement of partners' equity might appear as shown in Table 11-2.

Not-for-profit organizations (NFPOs) are economic entities whose objective is to provide services and not to make a profit. NFPOs do not have owners or ownership shares that can be traded or sold. Any "net income" earned by the NFPO is reinvested in the organization. Because NFPOs are not organized to earn a profit, it is not appropriate to use the term net income when discussing an NFPO. Usually the "bottom line" on an NFPO's statement of operations (the term sometimes used for an NFPO's "income statement") is called the excess of revenues over expenses. The idea of this terminology is to convey whether the NFPO produced revenues that were greater than expenses or vice versa.

Table 11-2 Statement of Partners' Equity for a Partnership with Three Partners

Statement of Partners' Equity
For the Year Ended December 31, 2005

	Partner 1	Partner 2	Partner 3	Total
Capital on January 1, 2005	$85,000	$117,000	$49,000	$251,000
Share of net income	22,000	31,000	15,000	68,000
Withdrawals	(15,000)	(8,000)	(6,000)	(29,000)
Capital on December 31, 2005	$92,000	$140,000	$58,000	$290,000

Revenues for an NFPO should not be thought of in the same way as revenues earned by a business. While some of the revenue of some NFPO's may be paid directly by those consuming the services, many of an NFPOs revenues come from donations, contributions, and grants. For example, the Canadian Cancer Society provides support to cancer patients across Canada. The cancer patients do not pay for these support services. The services are paid for by contributors to the cancer society. Thus the relationship that exists between expenses and revenues in a for-profit organization may not exist in an NFPO.

www.cancer.ca
www.heartandstroke.ca

Because an NFPO does not have owners, it will not have an owners' or shareholders' equity section in its financial statements. However, if a balance sheet is to be prepared, the difference between assets and liabilities must be referred to somehow. Different NFPOs use different terms; for example, the Heart and Stroke Foundation of Ontario refers to its "equity" as *net assets*, while the Canadian Cancer Society uses the term *resources.*

The Canadian Cancer Society's statement of resources (that's what it calls its balance sheet) is presented in Exhibit 11-1 (page 662).[1] Accounting for NFPOs is somewhat specialized and we will not be able to go into detail here. However, notice in the Resources section of Exhibit 11-1 that the Canadian Cancer Society allocates its net resources—its assets less its liabilities—to a number of categories. These resources categories are *invested in capital assets, externally restricted, internally restricted,* and *unrestricted.*

- Resources invested in capital assets represents the amount the Canadian Cancer Society has invested in capital assets.

- Externally restricted resources are available to the Canadian Cancer Society, but some external stakeholders have imposed limits how those resources can be used. For example, a contributor might require that funds he or she contributes be used for a specific purpose, such as research.

- The use of internally restricted resources is limited by the Canadian Cancer Society.

- Unrestricted resources can be used however the Canadian Cancer Society chooses.

Characteristics of Equity

Unlike debt, equity offers no promises. When a corporation borrows money, the rate of interest, the timing of payments, and other terms of the loan are usually laid out in a contract. If the corporation is unable to meet the terms of the contract, it faces potentially significant economic and legal consequences. In contrast, a shareholder is not entitled to dividends or any other type of payments from the corporation, and no return of principal is guaranteed. The rights of shareholders come after those of

Consolidated Statement of Resources

(In thousands of dollars)

September 30, 2000, with comparative figures for 1999

	2000	1999
Assets		
Current assets:		
Cash	$ 8,851	$ 5,820
Accounts receivable	1,647	2,122
Prepaid expenses	1,454	1,734
Investments	34,278	30,354
	46,230	40,030
Deferred pension costs	1,894	2,456
Capital assets	11,664	11,335
	$ 59,788	$ 53,821
Liabilities and Resources		
Current liabilities:		
Accounts payable	$ 3,485	$ 3,081
Research contribution payable to National Cancer Institute of Canada	3,441	1,723
Deferred revenue	2,760	2,982
	9,686	7,786
Obligation for post-retirement benefits other than pensions	4,915	4,356
Resources:		
Externally restricted	2,758	3,160
Invested in capital assets	11,664	11,335
Internally restricted	18,435	13,705
Unrestricted	12,330	13,479
	45,187	41,679
	$ 59,788	$ 53,821

The data on these pages are extracted from audited financial statements. For a complete set of consolidated financial statements including the notes that accompany these statements, please visit our website at www.cancer.ca or call the national office at (416) 961-7223.

debtholders. That means that if the corporation goes bankrupt, the debtholders must be paid what they are owed before shareholders receive anything.

From the corporation's standpoint, issuing equity is more attractive than debt because equity does not commit the corporation to make any payments at any time. The corporation has more flexibility to manage, particularly through difficult times.

However, there are drawbacks to issuing equity for the corporation and its existing shareholders. New shareholders have a voice in the corporation—not necessarily a say in its day-to-day affairs, but certainly the right to be heard on certain issues. In many situations the shareholders of a corporation vote on important issues. The voice provided to new shareholders dilutes the voice of the existing ones. Consider a small business operated by a single entrepreneur. The entrepreneur needs money for expansion and finds an investor who is willing to invest in exchange for a 50% interest in the corporation. The new shareholder will own 50% of the corporation and will be able to participate in the key decision making of the company. The entrepreneur will no longer be able to act alone.

Unlike debt, the cost of equity is not deductible for tax purposes. This treatment raises the cost of equity relative to debt. Also, dividends are not expensed for accounting purposes. This treatment is consistent with the view that net income reflect changes in the wealth of the shareholders. In this view, dividends are not a cost of doing business but a distribution to the shareholders. Interest payments, in contrast, are expensed on the income statement because interest is a cost that the shareholders must incur to borrow money.

When a corporation is formed it must file articles of incorporation with the appropriate government agency. The articles of incorporation define the terms of reference of the new corporation. Any changes to these terms of reference must be approved by the shareholders. The articles of incorporation define the types and characteristics of the shares the corporation can issue. The maximum number of each type of share that can be issued is the **authorized capital stock** of the corporation.

MWW's authorized capital stock is 100,000,000 first preferred shares and an unlimited number of common shares. This means that MWW can issue up to 100,000,000 first preferred shares and as many common shares as is deemed appropriate, without having to consult the shareholders.

The number of shares that have been distributed to shareholders is the **issued shares** of the corporation. The **outstanding shares** of a corporation are the number of shares currently in the hands of shareholders. The number of shares outstanding may differ from the number of shares issued because shares are sometimes repurchased by a corporation and retired. On January 27, 2001, MWW had 26,527,159 common shares and no preferred shares outstanding.

Corporations or companies acts are laws of the federal and provincial governments that govern companies incorporated in a particular jurisdiction. For example, the **Canada Business Corporations Act** is the federal legislation that governs federally incorporated companies. These laws give shareholders certain rights and privileges, regardless of whether their investments are large or small. For example, shareholders of a corporation are entitled to attend its annual general meeting, where they can ask questions of management. Shareholders can usually vote on the composition of the board of directors, the appointment of auditors, amendments to the corporation's articles of incorporation, and other matters. For smaller shareholders the annual general meeting of a public company may be the only place that their voices can be heard.

Even though every shareholder has the right to attend the annual meeting, the ability of smaller shareholders to influence management is limited. For example, a shareholder who owns 1,000 shares of Nortel Networks Corporation owns about 0.00003% of the votes. Nortel had over 3.2 billion shares outstanding on December 31, 2001.

Common and Preferred Shares

Broadly speaking, there are two types of shares that a corporation can issue: common shares and preferred shares. Because these shares can have various features added to them, many different varieties of shares are possible.

Common Shares   **Common shares** represent the residual ownership in an entity. Common shareholders are entitled to whatever earnings and assets are left after obligations to debtholders and preferred shareholders have been satisfied.

For example, consider a one-year venture into which common shareholders invest $50,000 and creditors lend $50,000 at 10% interest for the year. If the venture earned $150,000, the creditors would receive $55,000—their $50,000 of principal plus $5,000 in interest. The common shareholders would get the rest—$95,000 ($150,000 − $55,000). The creditors are entitled only to the loan principal plus interest. They do not share in the profits of the venture. On the other hand, common shareholders are the last ones to be satisfied. If the venture earned $60,000, the common shareholders would receive only $5,000 because $55,000 would have to be used to satisfy the lenders.

Common shares do not have a specified dividend associated with them. Dividend declarations are made at the discretion of the board of directors. A corporation is under no obligation to pay a dividend at any time, and the board can eliminate or reduce dividends if it so chooses. Public companies do not like to cut their dividends because it suggests the company is in serious trouble. Usually when a public company cuts its dividend its share price falls dramatically. In small private companies dividends are used to compensate the owner-manager and are an important part of the tax planning program for the corporation and its shareholders.

www.bombardier.com

> **12. SHARE CAPITAL**
>
> **Common shares**
>
> 1,792,000,000 Class A (Multiple Voting) Shares, without nominal or par value, ten votes each, convertible at the option of the holder into one Class B (Subordinate Voting) Share; and
>
> 1,792,000,000 Class B (Subordinate Voting) Shares, without nominal or par value, one vote each, with an annual non-cumulative preferential dividend of $0.001563 per share, and convertible, at the option of the holder, into one Class A (Multiple Voting) Share, after the occurrence of one of the following events: (i) an offer made to Class A (Multiple Voting) shareholders is accepted by the present controlling shareholder (the Bombardier family); (ii) such controlling shareholder ceases to hold more than 50% of all outstanding Class A (Multiple Voting) Shares of the Corporation.

There can be more than one class of common shares (and more than one class of preferred shares as well). Each class of shares that a corporation is authorized to issue must be described in the articles of incorporation. Some corporations issue common shares that have different voting rights and different dividends. For example, Bombardier Inc. has two classes of common shares outstanding. The Class A common shares are multiple voting shares that have ten votes per share. The Class B common shares have only one vote per share. This difference in voting power allows the Bombardier family to control the company without owning more than 50% of the company' common shares. (Descriptions of Bombardier's two classes of common shares are provided in Exhibit 11-2.[2]). In contrast, MWW has only a single class of common shares.

Some shares have a par value. **Par value** is a value assigned to each share of common stock in the articles of incorporation. At one time the par value of a share had legal significance, but that is no longer the case. The *Canada Business Corporations Act* and the corporations acts of a number of provinces do not permit par value shares. As a result, shares of most Canadian corporations are no par value shares. **No par value shares** are shares that do not have a par value assigned to them. Par value shares are now uncommon, although they do appear. The par value of a share has no economic significance and bears no relationship to its market value.

The accounting implication of par value versus no par value shares is quite minor, but there is an impact. When no par value shares are issued, the full amount of the proceeds is credited to the Common Stock account. When par value shares are issued, the par value of the shares is credited to the Common Stock account, and the difference between the proceeds from the sale of the shares and the par value is credited to an account called contributed surplus. **Contributed surplus** is a shareholders' equity account that shows amounts an entity received from the sale of its shares in excess of the par value.

For example, on January 19, 2007, Knutsford Ltd. (Knutsford) issued 100,000 shares of no par value common stock for $11 per share. Knutsford would make the following entry to record the sale of the shares:

Dr. Cash (assets +)	1,100,000	
Cr. Common stock (shareholders' equity +)		1,100,000
To record the issue and sale of 100,000 no par value common shares for $11 per share.		

This entry is the same one we have seen throughout the book when an entity sold its stock. If Knutsford's shares had a par value of $0.01 per share, the entry would be:

Dr. Cash (assets +)	1,100,000	
Cr. Common stock (shareholders' equity +)		1,000
Cr. Contributed surplus (shareholders' equity +)		1,099,000
To record the issue and sale of 100,000 common shares with par value of $0.01 per share for $11 per share.		

The Common Stock account is credited for the par value of the shares (100,000

× $0.01) and the amount in excess of par is credited to Contributed Surplus (100,000 × [$11.00 − $0.01]). The Common Stock and Contributed Surplus accounts together equal the amount received from the sale of par value common shares.

While equity is usually sold for cash, it does not have to be. An investor can exchange property or expertise for an equity interest. For example, a company might issue shares in exchange for a patent or land. In this situation the challenge is to determine the amount that should be recorded for the property received and the shares issued. If a market value is readily available for either the shares or the property received, then that amount can be used. For publicly traded companies, a share price is readily available and should be used to record the transaction. However, since most corporations' shares are not publicly traded, determining a value for them is more difficult. It may also be difficult to estimate the value of the property being exchanged for the shares, especially property that is not bought and sold very often, such as land, or property that is unique, such as a patent.

If the value of either the shares issued or the property received is not readily known, it is necessary to estimate an amount. The estimate must be reasonable and the preparers have to exercise judgment when making the choice. In these situations there could be a wide possible range of reasonable amounts.

For example, on October 11, 2007, Juniata Corp. (Juniata), a private company, issued 50,000 common shares to Professor Evan Alexander in exchange for his patent for a specific type of gene therapy. The board of directors decided, based on independent appraisals and reports, that the patent and the shares should be valued at $1,240,000. The journal entry required to record the exchange is:

Dr. Patent (assets +)	1,240,000	
Cr. Common stock (shareholders' equity +)		1,240,000
To record the exchange of 50,000 common shares for a patent.		

Because Juniata is a private company and the market value of a patent can be very difficult to estimate, the amount that should be used to record this transaction is subjective. There are methods for estimating the value of shares, but these cannot be exact. The amount that is selected can have an effect on financial measures such as the debt-to-equity ratio, return on equity, return on assets, and net income (because the patent has to be amortized). The patent would be amortized over its estimated useful life, as would any patent.

When equity is exchanged for non-cash assets or for a reduction in liabilities, the transaction is not included in the cash flow statement. As we discussed in Chapter 6, the cash flow statement only reports financing and investing activities that involve cash. According to GAAP, non-cash exchanges must be disclosed somewhere in the financial statements or notes. Sales of shares for cash are shown as financing activities in the cash flow statement.

Preferred Shares   **Preferred shares** are shares of a corporation that have rights that must be satisfied before common shareholders' rights. These preferred rights pertain to the payment of dividends and/or to the distribution of assets in the event of liquidation. Dividends on preferred shares must be paid before dividends can be paid to common shareholders. If the corporation is liquidated, preferred shareholders' claims to assets must be satisfied before the common shareholders' claims.

Preferred shares often have characteristics of debt. Some preferred shares specify a dividend payment that must be paid before the common shareholders can receive their dividends. A preferred share might specify the dollar amount of the dividend (for example, a $7 dividend per preferred share) or the percentage of the face value of the shares (for example, 7% per $100 face value preferred share). This is similar to the interest required on a bond. However, a crucial difference between debt and preferred shares is that preferred shareholders cannot take any action against the corporation if the dividend is not paid. Dividends on any shares are not guaranteed, and if the management of a corporation decides that it will not pay a dividend, then the shareholders are out of luck.

Preferred shares are often **cumulative**, which means that any dividends on the preferred shares that have not been paid in the current year or in previous years must be paid before the common shareholders can receive any dividends.

There are various other features that preferred shares can have. Some of the more common features of preferred shares include:

- **convertible:** Shareholders can choose to exchange their preferred shares for a specified number of common shares for each preferred share that they convert.

- **redeemable:** The issuer can repurchase the preferred shares from the shareholders if it chooses, according to specified terms.

- **retractable:** Shareholders can require the issuer to purchase the preferred shares from them, if they choose, according to specified terms.

- **participating:** The amount of the preferred share dividend increases above the stated amount if certain conditions are met. The amount of the preferred dividend is often tied to the dividend paid on the common shares.

One of the attractions of preferred shares for investors is that they can expect to receive periodic payments (as they would with debt), but the preferred dividends are taxed at a lower rate than interest. On the other hand, corporations that pay investors preferred dividends cannot deduct them for income tax purposes. Private companies sometimes use preferred shares for tax and estate-planning purposes.

www.bmo.com

Exhibit 11-3 provides a description of the preferred shares that Bank of Montreal (BMO) has sold to investors[3]. BMO's articles of incorporation authorize it to issue an unlimited number of Class A or Class B preferred shares. The Class B shares can be issued in a foreign currency. The preferred shares are issued in series. Each series of preferred shares can have different features. The Class B—Series 1 preferred shares have the following features:

- redeemable starting on February 25, 2001 for $25 cash or an equivalent value in BMO common shares.

- convertible into BMO common shares starting on August 25, 2001 (but BMO has the option of paying $25 for each share instead of allowing conversion).

- non-cumulative with a quarterly dividend of $0.5625 per share.

The other series of Class B shares has similar features with some variations. The Series 2 preferred shares pay their dividend in U.S. dollars, the Series 5 shares are not convertible, and the Series 6 shares pay a premium if they are redeemed before November 25, 2007. The Class A—Series 4 and 5 preferred shares were redeemed by BMO in 1998. The Class A Series 4 preferred shares were participating, with a quarterly dividend of the greater of $0.5625 per share or 113.2% of cash dividend paid on BMO's common stock.

Preferred shares are among a category of securities known as hybrid securities. **Hybrid securities** have characteristics of both debt and equity. (Convertible debt is another example of a hybrid security.) Because preferred shares have the characteristics of both debt and equity, they introduce some interpretation and classification problems when financial statements are analyzed. Dividends on preferred shares represent a committed cash flow that is likely to be paid in most circumstances. This is a characteristic that is common, in some ways, with interest payments. However, the amount the preferred shareholders paid the corporation for their shares does not have to be repaid, a characteristic of equity. Of course, as we saw in the Bank of Montreal example, preferred shares sometimes have features that make repayment possible—

Exhibit 11-3

The Bank of Montreal's Preferred Shares

Note 13   Share Capital

Outstanding
(Canadian $ in millions, except per share information)

Preferred Shares	2000 Number of shares	2000 Amount	2000 Dividends declared per share	1999 Number of shares	1999 Amount	1999 Dividends declared per share	1998 Number of shares	1998 Amount	1998 Dividends declared per share
Class A – Series 4	–	$ –	$ –	–	$ –	$ 1.87	8,000,000	$ 200	$ 2.25
Class A – Series 5	–	–	–	–	–	522.26	288	72	19,062.50
Class B – Series 1	10,000,000	250	2.25	10,000,000	250	2.25	10,000,000	250	2.25
Class B – Series 2	10,000,000	381	US$1.69	10,000,000	368	US$1.69	10,000,000	386	US$1.69
Class B – Series 3	16,000,000	400	1.39	16,000,000	400	1.39	16,000,000	400	1.39
Class B – Series 4	8,000,000	200	1.20	8,000,000	200	1.20	8,000,000	200	0.90
Class B – Series 5	8,000,000	200	1.33	8,000,000	200	1.33	8,000,000	200	0.99
Class B – Series 6	10,000,000	250	1.19	10,000,000	250	1.19	10,000,000	250	0.63
		1,681			1,668			1,958	
Common Shares	261,291,947	3,173	2.00	267,032,100	3,190	1.88	264,433,198	3,095	1.76
Total Outstanding Share Capital		$ 4,854			$ 4,858			$ 5,053	

Preferred Shares

We are authorized by our shareholders to issue an unlimited number of Class A Preferred Shares and Class B Preferred Shares without par value, in series, for unlimited consideration. Class B Preferred Shares may be issued in a foreign currency.

Class B – Series 1 shares are redeemable at our option starting February 25, 2001 for $25.00 cash per share or an equivalent value of our common shares, and are convertible at the shareholder's option starting August 25, 2001 into our common shares; however, we have the right to pay $25.00 cash per share instead. The shares carry a non-cumulative quarterly dividend of $0.5625 per share.

Class B – Series 2 shares are redeemable at our option starting August 25, 2001 for US$25.00 cash per share or an equivalent value of our common shares, and are convertible at the shareholder's option starting February 25, 2002 into our common shares; however, we have the right to pay US$25.00 cash per share instead. The shares carry a non-cumulative quarterly dividend of US$0.4219 per share.

Class B – Series 3 shares are redeemable at our option starting August 25, 2004 for $25.00 cash per share, plus a premium if we redeem the shares before August 25, 2006, or an equivalent value of our common shares, and are convertible at the shareholder's option starting May 25, 2007 into our common shares; however, we have the right to pay $25.00 cash per share instead. The shares carry a non-cumulative quarterly dividend of $0.346875 per share.

Class B – Series 4 shares are redeemable at our option starting August 25, 2005 for $25.00 cash per share, plus a premium if we redeem the shares before August 25, 2007, or an equivalent value of our common shares, and are convertible at the shareholder's option starting May 25, 2008 into our common shares; however, we have the right to pay $25.00 cash per share instead. The shares carry a non-cumulative quarterly dividend of $0.30 per share.

Class B – Series 5 shares are redeemable at our option starting February 25, 2013 for $25.00 cash per share, and are not convertible. The shares carry a non-cumulative quarterly dividend of $0.33125 per share.

Class B – Series 6 shares are redeemable at our option starting November 25, 2005 for $25.00 cash per share, plus a premium if we redeem the shares before November 25, 2007, or an equivalent value of our common shares, and are convertible at the shareholder's option starting November 25, 2008 into our common shares; however, we have the right to pay $25.00 cash per share instead. The shares carry a non-cumulative quarterly dividend of $0.296875 per share.

the redeemable and retractable features. By issuing preferred shares an entity is able to issue a security that has many of the characteristics of debt, but without increasing its debt-to-equity ratio and without diluting the existing common shares.

Accounting for hybrid securities can be quite complex. According to GAAP and the *CICA Handbook*, entities are required to classify hybrid securities according to their economic nature, not simply by what they are called. The application of this accounting standard is complicated and beyond the scope of this book. However, as a result of the standard, some preferred shares would be classified as debt if they are to be repaid. Some convertible debt would be classified as equity if the bonds are convertible at the issuer's option. Other convertible debt would be partially classified as debt and partially as equity because these securities have attributes of both debt and equity.

Hybrid securities are not necessarily classified the same way for tax purposes as they are for accounting. The tax system applies different principles for the classification of hybrid securities, so it is quite possible that an entity could issue a hybrid security that would be classified as debt for tax purposes and as equity for accounting purposes. This arrangement would be very attractive to an entity because it would be able to deduct the payments to the holders of the security for tax purposes without increasing the debt-to-equity ratio.

The journal entry to record the issuance of preferred shares is similar to the one made to record the issuance of common shares. The difference is that the credit is made to a Preferred Stock account, instead of the Common Stock account.

For example, on June 7, 2006 Nunalla Inc. issued 50,000 no par, cumulative preferred shares for $25 per share. The entry Nunalla Inc. would make to record the issuance is:

Dr. Cash (assets +)	1,250,000	
Cr. Preferred stock (shareholders' equity +)		1,250,000

To record the issue and sale of 50,000 no par, cumulative preferred shares for $25 per share.

Share Repurchases

Sometimes a corporation will buy its own common stock from the shareholders. For example, during fiscal 2001 MWW purchased 1,379,348 of its common shares from shareholders for $3,102,000. Why an entity will repurchase its shares is not entirely clear, but some explanations have been suggested and investigated:

- If an entity has excess cash, repurchasing shares is a way of distributing the cash to investors without establishing a precedent for paying regular or higher dividends.

- Repurchasing shares increases the earnings per share (net income ÷ common shares outstanding) and should increase share price because there are fewer shares to participate in the company's earnings, assuming that the operating activity of the entity is not affected by the repurchase.

- Repurchasing shares is a way for management to communicate to the market that it thinks the market is understating the value of its shares.

When an entity repurchases its shares there is no effect on the income statement. Any transaction involving an entity's own equity is accounted for on the balance sheet only. The accounting for share repurchases depends on whether the shares were purchased for more or less than the average amount paid for the common shares outstanding.

For example, on May 17, 2006 Granum Ltd. (Granum) repurchased 200,000 of its common shares on the open market for $10 per share. The average price paid by Granum's investors for its common shares was $8 per share. (For no par value shares the average amount paid for the common shares is the amount in the Common Stock account divided by the number of shares outstanding on the date of the repurchase.) Granum would make the following journal entry to record the repurchase of the common shares:

Dr. Common stock (shareholders' equity –)	1,600,000	
Dr. Retained earnings (shareholders' equity –)	400,000	
Cr. Cash (assets –)		2,000,000

To record the repurchase of 200,000 shares for $10 per share.

The debit to Common Stock is the average price paid by shareholders for the shares outstanding on the date of the repurchase, multiplied by the number of shares repurchased. Retained earnings is debited for the amount paid in excess of the average price invested per share. Since shareholders are receiving more than they paid for their shares, the amount in excess of the average price paid can be considered a distribution of Granum's profit and, therefore, a reduction in retained earnings. Cash is credited for the amount paid out.

If Granum paid $7 per share to repurchase its shares, the journal entry that would be recorded is:

Dr. Common stock (shareholders' equity –)	1,600,000	
Cr. Contributed surplus (shareholders' equity +)		200,000
Cr. Cash (assets –)		1,400,000

To record the repurchase of 200,000 shares for $7 per share.

When an entity repurchases its shares for less than the average price paid by investors, Common Stock is again debited for the average price paid by shareholders for the shares outstanding on the date of the repurchase, multiplied by the number of shares repurchased. The difference between the average amount paid by investors and the amount of cash paid for the shares is credited to Contributed Surplus. The credit to contributed surplus is the way the "gain" on the repurchase of the shares is accounted for (investors paid $8 per share while Granum only had to pay $7 to repurchase them) without involving the income statement. In other words, because the investors sold their shares back to Granum for less that what they paid for them, they have left some of their original investment in the company and the company gets to keep that surplus.

In most jurisdictions in Canada shares that are repurchased must be retired immediately. That means the shares no longer exist. In some jurisdictions in Canada, and in the United States, entities are allowed to own their own shares. Shares that were previously sold to investors and that the issuing corporation has repurchased but not retired are called **treasury stock**. Treasury stock may not vote and cannot receive dividends, but it is available for resale by the entity. We will not discuss accounting for treasury stock any further, but you should be familiar with the term because it may show up from time to time in the financial statements of some companies and in the press.

Remember that an entry is made in the accounting records only when an entity issues shares to or repurchases shares from shareholders. For public companies in particular, the vast majority of purchase and sale transactions of shares takes place between individual investors in the secondary market. For example, most trades that take place on the Toronto Stock Exchange (TSX) occur between individual investors. The entity whose shares are being exchanged is not a party to these transactions and the transactions have no financial statement effect.

www.tsx.ca

That is not to say that the managers of an entity are not keenly interested in its share price. The entity's share price can have an effect on the managers' wealth (because managers' compensation is sometimes related to share price and because managers are often shareholders), on their job prospects (managers of entities whose share price is not doing well will sometimes lose their jobs or may have fewer opportunities in the job market), and because market price provides information about the market's perceptions of the entity.

Retained Earnings, Dividends, and Stock Splits

Retained Earnings

Retained earnings represents the accumulated earnings of an entity over its entire life, less all dividends paid to shareholders over its life. Retained earnings can be thought of as profits that have been reinvested in the entity by the shareholders. It represents an indirect investment by shareholders—indirect because investors do not decide for themselves to make the investment. Instead, the board of directors decides if dividends should be paid and, if so, the amount of the dividends. Any amount not paid to the shareholders is "reinvested" in the company and is included in retained earnings. While net income or loss and dividends are the most common economic events that affect retained earnings, there are others. A list of the transactions and economic events that affect retained earnings is provided in Figure 11-1 (page 670). (There are actually a couple of other events that affect retained earnings, but they are beyond the scope of this book.)

Correction of errors affects retained earnings when an error made in a previous period is discovered. The prior years' financial statements are restated so that they appear in their corrected form. For example, in 2003 Auld Ltd. (Auld) purchased land for $700,000. The cost of the land was incorrectly expensed instead of capitalized. The

Economic event	Description
Net income or net loss	A measure of how the owners' wealth has changed over a period.
Dividends	Distributions of earnings to shareholders.
Correction of errors	When an accounting error is discovered that was made in a previous period, the error should be corrected retro-actively.
Retroactive application of a change in accounting policy	When an entity is changing an accounting policy, the financial statements are restated as if the new accounting policy had always been used.
Share retirement	When an entity repurchases its shares from shareholders and pays more than the average price paid when the shareholders purchased them.

Figure 11-1

Transactions and Economic Events that Affect Retained Earnings

error was not discovered until 2005. To correct the error, Auld would make the following journal entry in 2005:

Dr. Land (assets +)   700,000
    Cr. Retained earnings (shareholders' equity +)   700,000
To correct an error in accounting for the purchase of land in 2003.

The credit to retained earnings is required because when the land was incorrectly expensed in 2003, net income was reduced by $700,000 (tax effects are ignored). At the end of 2003 retained earnings was then $700,000 lower than it should have been because the land should have been capitalized, not expensed. The entry shown above restates retained earnings so that the balance is what it would have been had the error not occurred.

Changes in accounting policy were discussed in Chapter 9. When an entity changes an accounting policy, either because it is required to by GAAP or because management decides to change a policy, the financial statements must be restated so that it appears as if the entity had always been using the new accounting policy. This means that current amounts in balance sheet accounts, including retained earnings, must be restated to reflect the new accounting policy.

It is worth mentioning that retained earnings receives the impact of all the accounting choices that the preparers of the financial statements make. Throughout the book it has been emphasized that preparers of financial statements have considerable latitude, even under GAAP, in deciding how to account for many transactions and economic events. The effects of these differences accumulate in retained earnings. Over the life of an entity, retained earnings will not be affected by different accounting choices. However, at any point in time during the life of an entity retained earnings can vary significantly, depending on the accounting choices used in the preparation of the financial statements.

The statement of retained earnings is probably the most overlooked of the financial statements. The purpose of the statement of retained earnings is to show the changes in the Retained Earnings account over the period. MWW incorporates its statement of retained earnings into its statement of earnings (see page A-46). MWW's statement includes two items: net earnings and the purchase of stock for cancellation (MWW bought back some of its own stock).

The statements of retained earnings and the related notes to the financial statements of Quebecor Inc. (Quebecor), the Québec-based media and publishing company, are shown in Exhibit 11-4 (page 672).[4] Unlike MWW, Quebecor provides a

www.quebecor.com

separate statement of retained earnings in its financial statement package. The statement shows the impact of the following events:

- net income
- dividends, which reduced retained earnings by $33,000,000
- a redemption of shares, which reduced retained earnings by $400,000

These events are shown in Panel A of Exhibit 11-4 (page 672).

A fourth event is the restatement of retained earnings, which occurred because Quebecor adopted two new *CICA Handbook* sections. The adoption of these new sections result in changes in accounting policy. The changes are not explicitly shown in the statement, but are the cause of the restatement of retained earnings in 1999 and 1998 (note that the columns for both years include "Restated" in their headings). A description of these accounting changes and their impact on retained earnings is shown in Panel B of Exhibit 11-4.

Dividends

Dividends are distributions of a corporation's earnings to its shareholders. There are three types of dividends:

- cash
- property
- stock

As explained earlier, dividends are discretionary and must be declared by the board of directors. Dividends are declared on a per share basis and every share of a specific class must receive the same dividend. If, for example, an entity has a single class of common shares, it is not possible to pay some of the shareholders a dividend and not others. Once a dividend is declared, it is classified as a liability on the balance sheet.

Corporations do not have an unlimited ability to pay dividends. There are legal restrictions and there can be contractual restrictions against paying dividends. These restrictions are not the result of accounting rules, although the accounting methods used by an entity can have an impact if accounting numbers are used to determine whether dividends can be paid.

Generally a corporation is not allowed to pay dividends if it does not have any retained earnings. The *Canada Business Corporations Act* prohibits the payment of dividends if it is reasonable to believe that the corporation would be unable to pay its liabilities if the dividends were paid. Finally, some debt agreements have covenants that restrict the payment of dividends. For example, Call-Net Enterprises Inc. (Call-Net), as part of its loan agreements, is restricted from borrowing more money, paying dividends, and repurchasing its capital stock. Exhibit 11-5 (page 673) shows extracts from Call-Net's financial statements that disclose the restrictions.[5]

www.callnet.ca

For accounting purposes, there are two important dates pertaining to dividends: the **date of declaration**—the date when the board of directors of a corporation declares a dividend, and the **date of payment**—the date when the dividends are actually paid to shareholders.

Cash Dividends   Cash dividends are the most common form of dividend. A **cash dividend** is a cash payment from the corporation to its shareholders. It is sometimes said that dividends are "paid out of retained earnings." This expression means that retained earnings decrease when dividends are paid. However, to pay a cash dividend the cash must be available. For example, on January 27, 2001 MWW had retained earnings of $33,493,000 but only $6,993,000 of cash and cash equivalents. The maximum amount of cash dividend that MWW could have paid on January 27, 2001 is $6,993,000 (ignoring the possibility of borrowing to pay a larger dividend).

Exhibit 11-4

Quebecor Inc.'s Statements of Retained Earnings and Related Notes to the Financial Statements

Panel A

Consolidated Statements of Retained Earnings

Years ended December 31, 2000, 1999 and 1998
(in millions of Canadian dollars)

	2000	1999 (Restated)	1998 (Restated)
Balance at beginning of year	$ 1,376.9	$ 937.3	$ 821.7
Net income	1,084.4	477.3	172.3
	2,461.3	1,414.6	994.0
Premium paid on redemption of shares	(0.4)	(6.6)	(28.0)
Dividends	(33.0)	(31.1)	(28.7)
Balance at end of year	$ 2,427.9	$ 1,376.9	$ 937.3

Panel B

SUMMARY OF SIGNIFICANT ACCOUNTING POLICIES

The consolidated financial statements are prepared in conformity with Canadian generally accepted accounting principles. The material differences between generally accepted accounting principles in Canada and in the United States are described in note 21.

Accounting changes

Effective January 1, 2000, the Canadian Institute of Chartered Accountants ("CICA") changed the accounting standards relating to the accounting for income taxes and the accounting for employee future benefits, including pension and non-pension postretirement benefits.

(a) Income taxes

In December 1997, the Accounting Standards Board issued Section 3465 of the CICA Handbook, Income Taxes. Under the asset and liability method of Section 3465, future income tax assets and liabilities are recognized for the estimated future tax consequences attributable to differences between the financial statements carrying amounts of existing assets and liabilities and their respective tax bases. Future income tax assets and liabilities are measured using enacted or substantively enacted tax rates in effect for the year in which those temporary differences are expected to be recovered or settled. Future income tax assets and liabilities of a change in tax rates is recognized in income in the period that includes the enactment date. Future income tax assets are recognized and if realization is not considered "more likely than not" a valuation allowance is provided.

The Company has adopted the new recommendations of the CICA in 2000 and has applied the provisions of Section 3465 retroactively. The cumulative effect of this accounting change for income taxes is reported as a restatement which increased the opening balance of retained earnings for the year ended December 31, 1998 by $3.5 million.

Accordingly, the financial statements for the years ended December 31, 1999 and 1998 have been restated to comply with the provisions of Section 3465. In addition to restating the future income tax accounts, an allocation between short- and long-term portions is now presented in the consolidated balance sheets.

(b) Employee future benefits

In March 1999, the Accounting Standards Board issued Section 3461 of the CICA Handbook, Employee Future Benefits. Under the Section 3461, the Company is required to accrue, during employees' active service period, the estimated cost of pension, retiree benefit payments other than pensions, and workers' compensation. The Company previously expensed the cost of postretirement benefits other than pension, which are principally health care, as claims were incurred by the employees and paid by the Company. In addition, the Company will now use the corridor method to amortize actuarial gains or losses (such as changes in actuarial assumptions and experience gains or losses). Under the corridor method, amortization is recorded only if the accumulated net actuarial gains or losses exceed 10% of the greater of accrued pension benefit obligation and the value of the plan assets. Previously, actuarial gains and losses were amortized on a straight-line basis over the average remaining service life of the employees.

The Company has elected to recognize this change in accounting on the immediate recognition basis retroactively. The cumulative effect of this accounting change for pension and postretirement benefits other than pension is reported as a restatement which decreased the opening balance of retained earnings for the year ended December 31, 1998 by $10.2 million.

Accordingly, the financial statements for the years ended December 31, 1999 and 1998 were restated to comply with the provisions of Section 3461.

(c) Summary effect

The following summarizes the impact of applying Sections 3465 and 3461 on income before income taxes, net income, earnings per share, and retained earnings for the years ended December 31, 1999 and 1998 and retained earnings as at December 31, 1997. The presentation of property, plant and equipment, goodwill, future income taxes, other liabilities and non-controlling interest are also affected by these changes.

	Income before income taxes	Net income	Earnings per share	Retained earnings 1999
As previously reported	$ 693.0	$ 481.0	$ 7.43	$ 1,387.7
Effect of Section 3465	—	(2.1)	(0.03)	2.6
Effect of Section 3461	(2.3)	(1.6)	(0.03)	(13.4)
As restated	$ 690.7	$ 477.3	$ 7.37	$ 1,376.9

	Income before income taxes	Net income	Earnings per share	Retained earnings 1998
As previously reported	$ 414.9	$ 172.7	$ 2.64	$ 944.4
Effect of Section 3465	—	1.2	0.02	4.7
Effect of Section 3461	(2.3)	(1.6)	(0.02)	(11.8)
As restated	$ 412.6	$ 172.3	$ 2.64	$ 937.3

	Retained earnings 1997
As previously reported	$ 828.4
Effect of Section 3465	3.5
Effect of Section 3461	(10.2)
As restated	$ 821.7

Exhibit 11-5

Call-Net Enterprises Inc.: Dividend Restrictions

---

7. LONG-TERM DEBT

Each of the Company's Senior Notes and Senior Discount Notes are unsecured obligations and rank *pari passu* in right of payment with all unsubordinated, unsecured indebtedness of the Company. The Senior Discount Notes and the Senior Notes are governed by trust indentures which contain certain covenants which, among other things, restrict the ability of the Company to incur additional indebtedness, incur liens, pay dividends or repurchase the Company's capital stock.

8. CAPITAL STOCK

Certain restrictions on the payment of dividends exist as a result of the long-term debt issued in 1997, 1998 and 1999.

Let's look at an example of accounting for cash dividends. On December 15, 2004 Bankeir Inc. (Bankeir) declared a $0.10 quarterly dividend on its common shares and a $0.25 quarterly dividend on its preferred shares. On the date of declaration Bankeir had 500,000 common shares and 250,000 preferred shares outstanding. Bankeir paid the dividend on January 12, 2005. The company's year end is December 31. The journal entries required to record the declaration and payment of the dividends are:

Dr. Retained earnings (shareholders' equity –)	112,500	
Cr. Dividend payable on common shares (liability +)		50,000
Cr. Dividend payable on preferred shares (liability +)		62,500

To record the declaration of a $0.25 per preferred share and $0.10 per common share dividend on December 15, 2004.

Dr. Dividend payable on common shares (liability –)	50,000	
Dr. Dividend payable on preferred shares (liability –)	62,500	
Cr. Cash (asset –)		112,500

To record payment of the preferred and common share dividends on January 12, 2005.

The first entry records the reduction of retained earnings and the liability to pay the preferred and common share dividends. The second entry records the cash payment to the shareholders and removes the liabilities to pay the dividends from the balance sheet. Bankeir's December 31, 2004 balance sheet would report the dividends payable on the preferred and common stock as current liabilities.

Property Dividends   **Property dividends** are dividends paid with property instead of cash. In theory, a property dividend could be paid using any property the entity has: inventory, capital assets, investments, etc. In practice, for public companies or for private companies with many shareholders, there are practical limitations to declaring property dividends. Since every share of the same class must receive the same dividend, the entity must have property that can be divided to allow equal distribution. One type of property that can be readily used for a property dividend is shares of a corporation owned by the issuing entity (not its own shares).

If an entity pays a property dividend, the dividend is recorded at the market value of the property distributed on the date the dividend is declared. If the market value of the property is not equal to its book value on the date the dividend is declared, a gain or loss is reported on the income statement.

For example, Drook Corp. (Drook) decided to distribute the shares it owned of Rylstone Inc. (Rylstone) as a dividend. The book value of the shares was $5,000,000 and their market value on the date the dividend was declared was $7,200,000. The journal entries that Drook would make to record the property dividend are:

Dr. Investment in Rylstone (assets +)	2,200,000	
Cr. Gain on disposal of investments		2,200,000
(income statement +, shareholders' equity +)		

To record the gain on the shares of Rylstone being distributed to shareholders as a property dividend.

Dr. Retained earnings (shareholders' equity –)	7,200,000	
Cr. Property dividend payable (liability +)		7,200,000
To record the declaration of a property dividend.		

Dr. Property dividend payable (liability –)	7,200,000	
Cr. Investment in Rylstone (assets –)		7,200,000
To record payment of the property dividend.		

The first entry adjusts the value of the property to its market value on the date the dividend was declared. Because the market value of the dividend was greater than its book value, a gain is recognized on the income statement. The second entry records the declaration of the dividend. The amount of the property dividend is the market value of the property on the date the dividend is declared. The third entry records the actual payment of the dividend—the distribution of the Rylstone shares to Drook's shareholders.

Stock Dividends   A **stock dividend** is the distribution of a corporation's own shares to its existing shareholders. The number of shares a shareholder receives depends on the number of shares owned on the date of declaration.

For example, if Hylo Ltd. (Hylo) declared a 5% stock dividend, a shareholder that owned 100 shares would receive five shares of Hylo stock as a dividend. After the stock dividend the investor would have 105 shares of Hylo stock. If Hylo had 100,000 shares outstanding before the distribution of the stock dividend, there would be 105,000 after the distribution. Each shareholder would own exactly the same proportion of Hylo before and after the dividend. The shareholder that owned 100 shares before the dividend and 105 shares after always owned 0.1% (100 ÷ 100,000 = 105 ÷ 105,000) of the outstanding shares. The market price of Hylo's share price should fall by 5% as a result of the stock dividend because nothing about the entity has changed except for the number of shares outstanding. Thus the value of Hylo is spread over a larger number of shares (and therefore the value of each share is less after the stock dividend), but the total value of Hylo's shares should be the same before and after the stock dividend.

A stock dividend results in a decrease in Retained Earnings and an increase in the Capital Stock account (assuming the shares are no par value), but there is more than one method of assigning an amount to the shares distributed. In the first method, the market value of the shares just before they are issued is used. In the second method, the board of directors can assign a value to the shares—for example, the average amount paid by shareholders for the shares already outstanding.

Returning to the Hylo Ltd. example, suppose that Hylo declared and distributed its stock dividend on June 23, 2004, when the market price of its common shares was $10 and the average amount paid for common shares issued before June 23, 2004 was $3.25 per share. If Hylo used the market value method of accounting for stock dividends, it would make the following entry:

Dr. Retained earnings (shareholders' equity –)	50,000	
Cr. Common stock (shareholders' equity +)		50,000
To record the declaration and distribution of a 5% stock dividend using the market value method.		

This entry results in an increase in common stock and a decrease in retained earnings of $50,000, the market value of the stock dividend (5,000 shares × $10 per share). If the average amount paid for the common shares were used, the entry Hylo would make is:

Dr. Retained earnings (shareholders' equity –)	16,250	
Cr. Common stock (shareholders' equity +)		16,250
To record the declaration and distribution of a 5% stock dividend using the average amount paid for the common shares method.		

Both approaches affect only the shareholders' equity section of the balance sheet. There is no effect on assets, liabilities, or the income statement.

Stock Splits

A **stock split** is the division of an entity's shares into a larger number of units, each with a smaller value. A stock split is really nothing more than a big stock dividend. A stock split might split an entity's existing shares two-for-one, which means that a shareholder that previously had 1,000 shares would have 2,000 after the split. A three-for-two split means that a shareholder that initially had 1,000 shares would have 1,500 after the split.

The accounting for stock splits is different from accounting for stock dividends. There is no accounting effect of a stock split—the amounts in the retained earnings and common stock accounts are unchanged. No journal entries are required to record a stock split. What changes as a result of a stock split is the number of shares outstanding, so any measurements that are based on the number of shares will change. For example, if an entity's shares split three-for-one, retained earnings will be unchanged, but earnings per share will be one-third of what it was before the split.

Exhibit 11-6 (page 676) shows an example of the financial statement effects of a stock split.[6] On July 7, 2000 the voting common shares of Bombardier Inc. split two for one. Exhibit 11-6 compares selected information about Bombardier's 2000 fiscal year as reported in its 2000 annual report (before the stock split) and in its 2001 annual report (after the stock split). After a stock split an entity restates previous years' financial statements so that the comparable financial statements are prepared on the same basis. Notice that the number of shares doubled from the 2000 annual report to the 2001 annual report, but the dollar amounts in the Common Stock account assigned to those shares is the same. The amount of Retained Earnings is the same, but earnings per share has been cut in half—Bombardier's earnings have been divided among twice as many shares.

Various explanations have been offered for stock dividends and stock splits. One explanation for a stock dividend is that it allows shareholders to receive "something"

Question for Consideration

Several years ago a friend of yours received 1,000 shares of a public company as a gift from her uncle. Recently the company shares split four-for-one and now she has 4,000 shares. Your friend is not sure what this means, but she is concerned that the shares that were trading for $104 per share before the split are now trading for around $26 per share.

Explain to your friend the meaning of a stock split and its economic significance. Should she be concerned about the decrease in the share price?

Answer: A stock split is the division of an entity's shares into a larger number of units, each with a smaller value. A stock split does not really have any economic significance. A stock split is like cutting a pie into six pieces and then, when you realize that you will be having more than six guests, cutting the pie into 12 pieces. You have the same amount of pie, just more pieces. There is no difference between getting one slice of a pie cut into six pieces or two pieces of a pie cut into 12 pieces.

The same is true for a stock split. You have 4,000 shares instead of 1,000, but there are also four times as many shares outstanding. You own exactly the same percentage of the outstanding shares. The decrease in the share price makes perfect sense because after the split each share represents 25% of what it did before the split. Therefore, it is reasonable to expect that each share would be worth 25% of what it was before the split. The market value of your shares is the same before and after the split. Before the split the shares were worth $104,000 (1,000 × $104) and after the split they were worth $104,000 (4,000 × $26).

when the entity is unable or unwilling to pay a cash dividend. A reason given for a stock split is that it lowers the price of a stock into a range that makes it accessible to more investors.

The reality is that both stock splits and stock dividends are a bit of sleight of hand. Neither has any real economic significance—they merely divide the entity into a different number of pieces. In other words, there are more pieces of pie, not more pie. Stock dividends and stock splits have no effect on the assets, liabilities, or net income of an entity, and do not change the underlying value of a shareholder's interest in an entity. There is no evidence from research that suggests that shareholders are better off after a stock dividend or split than they were before.

Exhibit 11-6

Bombardier Inc.: The Effect of a Stock Split

12. SHARE CAPITAL

Share split

On June 20, 2000, the shareholders of the Corportion approved a Class A (Multiple Voting) and Class B (Subordinate Voting) common share split on a two-for-one basis, effective as of the close of business on July 7, 2000. The number of shares and per share amounts included in these consolidated financial statements have been adjusted to give retroactive effect to the share split.

	2000 common share information As reported in the 2001 Annual Report		2000 common share information As reported in the 2000 Annual report	
	Number of shares	Amount (in millions)	Number of shares	Amount (in millions)
Common shares				
Class A Shares (multiple voting)				
Balance at beginning of year	353,415,352	$49.1	176,707,676	$49.1
Converted from Class A to Class B	(1,821,224)	(0.5)	(910,612)	(0.5)
Balance at end of year	351,594,128	48.6	175,797,064	48.6
Class B Subordinate Voting Shares				
Balance at beginning of year	1,012,930,638	796.4	506,465,319	796.4
Issued under the share option plans	11,270,840	16.8	5,635,420	16.8
Issued to employees for cash	1,186	—	593	—
Converted from Class A to Class B	1,821,224	0.5	910,612	0.5
Balance at end of year	501,652,790	813.7	250,826,395	813.7
Balance at end of year—common shares	678,918,448	862.3	339,459,224	862.3
Common stock		1,162.3		1,162.3
Retained earnings		2,392.5		2,392.5
Earnings per share		1.02		0.51

Leverage

Leverage is the use of debt to attempt to increase the return earned on the equity investment of the owners. (The concept of leverage was introduced in Chapter 10.) Leverage is attractive because any profits earned from investing borrowed money, above the cost of borrowing, go to the owners. But leverage is risky because the cost of borrowing must be paid, regardless of how well or poorly the entity is performing.

Let's look at an example to demonstrate. Four Friends Partnership (FFP) was recently formed by four friends to operate a one-year business venture. The friends have decided that $100,000 of invested capital is required to safely launch the venture, but they are not sure how much debt and how much equity should be used. They have three possible financing arrangements in mind:

1. 100% equity financing: the friends invest $100,000 of their own money and do not borrow any from the bank.

2. 50% debt and 50% equity: the friends invest $50,000 of their own money and borrow $50,000 from the bank.

3. 90% debt and 10% equity: the friends invest $10,000 of their own money and borrow $90,000 from the bank.

The friends have predicted two possible outcomes for their venture: a good news outcome where revenues will be $80,000 and expenses $60,000 (excluding interest), and a bad news outcome where revenues will be $50,000 and expenses will be $48,000 (excluding interest). If the friends decide to borrow, the bank will charge them an interest rate of 10%. At the completion of the venture the friends will have to repay any money borrowed from the bank.

We will examine the effect of leverage by using return on equity (ROE). ROE was introduced in Chapter 3 and is defined thus:

$$\text{Return on equity} = \frac{\text{Net income} - \text{Preferred dividends}}{\text{Average common shareholders' equity}}$$

ROE is a measure of the profitability of an entity and its effectiveness in using the assets provided by the owners of the entity to generate net income. The effects of leverage for FFP's venture are shown in Table 11-3 (page 678). When 100% equity is used, the friends simply earn what the venture earns. If the good news outcome occurs, the friends earn $20,000, which is a 20% return on their $100,000 equity investment ($20,000 ÷ $100,000). If the bad news outcome occurs, the friends earn $2,000, a 2% ROE ($2,000 ÷ $100,000). With both outcomes the friends also get their original investment back.

If the friends borrow some of the money to finance their venture, they must pay interest. The effect of leverage is that they have to pay a fixed amount of interest to use the borrowed money, but anything the venture makes in excess of the interest cost belongs to them. When 50% debt and 50% equity is used, FFP must pay $5,000 ($50,000 × 10%) in interest, so net income is $15,000 in the good news outcome (see Table 11-3). While net income is lower than in the 100% equity alternative, the ROE earned by FFP increases from 20% to 30%. The reason is that the friends invested half as much money as before ($50,000) and earned 20% or $10,000 on their own investment. They also earned an additional $5,000 on the borrowed money. The bank supplied $50,000, that $50,000 earned 20% or $10,000, and FFP had to pay the bank $5,000 for the use of its money, so there is $5,000 left that goes to the four friends after the bank is paid. The friends' return is 30% because they earned $15,000 ($10,000 from their own investment and $5,000 from the bank's investment) on an investment of $50,000.

This is the effect of leverage: using "someone else's" money can increase equity

Table 11-3   Scenarios Showing the Effect of Leverage on Performance

Four Friends Partnership
Information Regarding New Venture

| | Financing Alternatives | | |
	100% equity	50% debt and 50% equity	90% debt and 10% equity
Debt	$ 0	$50,000	$90,000
Equity	100,000	50,000	10,000

	Projected performance outcomes		
	Good news outcome		
Revenue	$80,000	$80,000	$80,000
Expenses	60,000	60,000	60,000
Operating income	20,000	20,000	20,000
Interest expense	0	5,000	9,000
Net income	$20,000	$15,000	$11,000
Return on equity	20%	30%	110%
	Bad news outcome		
Revenue	$50,000	$50,000	$50,000
Expenses	48,000	48,000	48,000
Operating income	2,000	2,000	2,000
Interest expense	0	5,000	9,000
Net income	$ 2,000	$(3,000)	$(7,000)
Return on equity	2%	–6%	–70%

investors' returns. Notice that the borrowed money does not increase the size of the venture. In all the alternatives the amount of capital invested is $100,000. What is different are the sources of the capital.

But there is a dark side to leverage. While leverage makes the good news better, it also makes the bad news worse. If the bad news outcome occurs, the four friends earn a small return of 2% on their $100,000 investment with the 100% equity investment. The friends get to take home $2,000 in profits and their initial investment is intact. With the 50% debt and 50% equity alternative, the cost of borrowing is more than what the borrowed money earned. The equity investors, the four friends, must pay this shortfall. The friends earn $1,000 ($50,000 × 2%) on their investment. The money from the bank also earns $1,000, but the bank still has to be paid $5,000 in interest for the use of its money. To satisfy the bank, the $1,000 earned by the friends' investment and the $1,000 earned by the bank's investment goes to pay the bank. In addition, $3,000 of the friends' initial investment must be used to pay the bank. The $3,000 loss on the venture means that the friends lose some of their initial investment. In this scenario, the ROE is –6% (–$3000 ÷ $50,000). In sum, leverage makes a good situation better and a bad situation worse.

The effect of leverage in the 90% debt and 10% equity alternative is even more dramatic. In the good news outcome the four friends earn 110% on their $10,000 investment because the bank's money earns $18,000 ($90,000 × 20%), but the bank has to be paid only $9,000 ($90,000 × 10%). The friends earn $11,0000 ($2,000 on the equity investment and $9,000 on the borrowed money) on a $10,000 investment. On the other hand, the friends have a return of –70% in the bad news outcome, because while the venture itself earned $2,000, the bank has to be paid $9,000. The loss on the venture is $7,000 and 70% of the friends' original investment is lost.

How, you might ask, can the friends' return be increasing when the net income of the venture is decreasing? The answer is that the amount of income being earned as a proportion of the equity investment is increasing, even though the actual dollar amount of net income is decreasing. The friends will have more profit from the venture if only equity is used, but if the bank finances part of the venture the friends will have a higher return and be able to keep some of their money for other purposes.

This example raises another interesting point. In all three financing alternatives the amount invested was the same and the performance of the business activity itself—the operating income—was the same. (The operating income was $20,000 in the good news outcome and $20,000 in the bad news outcome.) What differed in the income statements under the three alternatives was the cost of financing. By separating operating income and the cost of financing, we can evaluate the performance of the entity separately from the cost of financing it.

It is also important to remember that there are limits to the amount of money that an entity can borrow. It is possible that if FFP wanted to borrow $90,000 when the owners were investing only $10,000, the bank might charge a higher interest rate or not lend at all.

Note that the FFP example ignores income taxes. This approach makes sense because FFP is a partnership and partnerships do not pay taxes. The individual partners take care of the taxes. Taxes are important, though. Taxes reduce the cash that the partners are left with (in the case of FPP) and reduce the cash a corporation has available to distribute. (The tax implications of debt were discussed in Chapter 10.)

Question for Consideration

What are the advantages and disadvantages of using leverage when financing a business?

Answer: Leverage is the use of borrowed money to finance a business. Leverage magnifies the results earned by the owners of an entity. The more debt or leverage that an entity uses, the greater the return the owners can earn. However, leverage will lower the return if the entity performs poorly. Leverage reduces the amount that the owners have to invest, which may be valuable if the owners have limited resources. Leverage also puts less of the owners' money at risk (because less of their own money is invested). One of the biggest risks with leverage is that interest must be paid, regardless of the success of the business.

Employee Stock Options

One of the interesting challenges that accountants have had to address in recent years is accounting for stock options offered to employees as part of their compensation packages. Stock options have become an increasingly important way of compensating employees. In the high technology field in particular, stock options have become an extremely effective way of attracting and keeping talented people.

Stock options have been very controversial because they can result in employees, particularly senior executives, receiving extremely large pay packages. The controversy extends to the accounting realm because, while stock options are used to compensate employees, their cost is not usually reflected in the financial statements. Stock options are also attractive to the issuing entity because they do not cost the entity any cash, which can be important for a new or growing entity. Whether stock options are an effective or appropriate way of compensating employees will not be discussed here. The focus will be on the nature of employee stock options and the accounting issues surrounding them. First, some stock option basics:

- An **employee stock option** gives an employee the right to purchase a specified number of shares of the employer's stock at a specified price over a specified period of time. Employee stock options represent the right to purchase shares, not shares themselves.

- The price at which a stock option allows the employee to purchase shares is called the **exercise price**. For tax reasons, the exercise price of a stock option is usually the same as or greater than the market price of the shares on the date it is granted.

- The terms of a stock option also state an expiry date. The **expiry date** is the final date that the option can be exercised. If the employee has not exercised or used the option by its expiry date, the option is worthless—it cannot be used to purchase shares. An employee will exercise an option only if the exercise price is less than the market price. If an employee has stock options to purchase shares at $10 per share, the employee will exercise the options only if the market price of the shares on the date the options are exercised is greater than $10. The reason is obvious: Why would someone pay $10 for an asset that has a market value of less than $10?

- When the exercise price is less than the market price, the stock option is said to be "**in-the-money**."

- When the exercise price is greater than the market price, the stock option is said to be "**out-of-the-money**."

Note 12 to MWW's financial statements (page A-57) describes its incentive stock option plan. Under the terms of the plan the board of directors can grant stock options to directors, officers, employees, and consultants of the company. As of January 27, 2001, there were 2,016,100 options outstanding, which represent 7.6% (2,016,100 ÷ 26,527,159) of the number of shares outstanding on January 27, 2001. If all of the options were exercised, an additional 2,016,100 shares in MWW would be sold, most being sold at prices below the market value of the shares.

A table in Note 12 (page A-58) describes the options that were outstanding on January 27, 2001, and provides the exercise price, number outstanding at that price, and the expiry date. For example, on January 27, 2001 there were 200,000 options with an exercise price of $1.65 and expiry date of January 25, 2002, and 598,000 options with an exercise price of $2.38 and expiry date of March 26, 2004. If sometime before March 27, 2004 the 598,000 options were exercised, MWW would receive $1,423,240 ($2.38 × 598,000) and the employees would receive 598,000 shares of MWW stock. If the market price of the shares on the date they were exercised was $3.50, the employees would be receiving, and MWW would be giving up, shares worth $2,093,000 ($3.50 × 598,000) in exchange for $1,423,240.

Figure 11-2 shows the compensation earned by the CEOs of ten well-known Canadian companies. Figure 11-2 breaks down the CEOs' compensation into cash, which includes salary and bonus, and long-term incentives, which are mainly stock options. Aside from the fact that these CEOs earn a lot of money, it is interesting to note that, for eight of the ten, more than 50% of their compensation is in the form of stock options. Long-term incentives such as stock options are usually provided to other employees in the organization, so the economic impact on the entity will be much greater than what is indicated in Figure 11-2.

The accounting problem with employee stock options is that according to GAAP, they do not have to be reported as an expense in the income statement. The impact of this treatment is that a significant economic cost incurred by an entity is not reflected in the income statement. As a result, expenses are understated and net income is overstated.

The treatment also impairs the comparability of financial statements because the form of employees' compensation affects an entity's salary expense. For example, the CEOs of Canadian Tire and Petro-Canada each received total compensation of about

$3,000,000 in 2000. However, Canadian Tire's CEO received more of his compensation in stock options and less in cash than his Petro-Canada counterpart. As a result, Canadian Tire would expense $750,000 in CEO compensation, whereas Petro-Canada would expense $1,312,000. A research study of ten Canadian technology firms whose shares are listed on U.S. as well as Canadian stock exchanges showed that had the economic cost of stock options been expensed, earnings in fiscal 2000 would have been 48.7% lower than originally reported.[7]

Some people argue that since stock options are usually out-of-the-money when they are granted, they have no value. This is clearly false. As long as there is time before the stock option expires, the option has an economic value, even if it is out-of-the-money. There is always some chance that the price of the underlying stock will rise above the exercise price and the option will be in-the-money. For example, would you pay for the right to be able to purchase MWW shares at $4.20 each sometime over the next three years if the current market price of the shares was $3.00? Many people would pay something for that right (they might not pay very much, but they would pay something). By buying this right, the purchaser is betting that the stock price will increase.

Moreover, if stock options have no value, why would employees negotiate for and accept them as compensation? Clearly the options are worth something. This is a very important point. Even though a stock option is not in-the-money, it has economic value. The entity granting the option is giving something that is valuable: the opportunity to purchase stock at below-market prices. Methods have been developed that estimate the economic value of stock options. An introductory textbook in financial accounting is not the place to discuss these methods. What is important is that GAAP accounting ignores what is clearly an economic cost to the entity.

For many years the GAAP treatment for stock options was to record a compensation expense for the difference between the market value of the shares on the date the options were awarded and the exercise price of the options. Since most stock options are not in-the-money when they are granted, the difference between the market value of the shares and the exercise price is usually zero or less. As a result, the compensation expense associated with stock options was usually zero.

Accounting standard setters in the United States studied this issue for a long time and eventually attempted to implement a standard that required entities to expense the economic value of stock options granted to employees on the date the options were issued. There were very strong objections from the business community, especially in the high technology sector, to the proposed standard. In the end the U.S. stan-

Company	Cash compensation	Long-term incentives	Total compensation	Long-term incentives ÷ Total compensation
Air Canada	$1,600,000	$3,489,000	$5,089,000	68.56%
Canadian Tire	750,000	2,412,000	3,162,000	76.28%
Celestica	2,748,000	5,881,000	8,629,000	68.15%
CN Rail	2,100,000	2,573,000	4,673,000	55.06%
Loblaw	1,675,000	0	1,675,000	0.00%
Magna International	7,866,000	145,000	8,011,000	1.81%
Nortel Networks	10,227,000	60,527,000	70,754,000	85.55%
Petro-Canada	1,312,000	1,646,000	2,958,000	55.65%
Rogers Communications	2,850,000	6,014,000	8,864,000	67.85%
Royal Bank	4,082,000	4,664,000	8,746,000	53.33%

Figure 11-2

Compensation of CEOs of Major Canadian Companies, 2001[8]

dard setters backed off. Now only disclosure of the economic value of employee stock options is required.

One of the main reasons for the objections was that the accounting standard would significantly lower net income. To be fair, the issue is much more complex than simply the effect on accounting numbers. Accounting standard setting can be very political, which many readers may find surprising. However, accounting standards often affect the wealth of various stakeholders, and when people see themselves being adversely affect by a change, they react against it. Nobody wants "their ox gored."

The *CICA Handbook* has a new section that addresses accounting for employee stock options. The new *Handbook* section must be applied commencing in fiscal years that begin on or after January 1, 2002. The new Canadian standard is very similar to the U.S. standard. Canadian companies are encouraged to expense the economic value of stock options awarded to employees in the year they are awarded, but they are not required to do so. If the U.S. experience is any indication, very few firms will choose to accrue the value of the options and, as a result, income for firms granting stock options to employees will be overstated. However, in May 2002 the TD Bank Financial Group became the first Canadian company to announce that it would expense the cost of executive stock options.

www.td.com

However, while Canadian GAAP does not require expensing of the economic value of the stock options, it does require disclosure of the information. Under the new *CICA Handbook* section companies will have to report in the notes to the financial statements what their net income would have been had they expensed the economic value of the stock options. Previously it was not possible to determine the value of the options granted employees. Now financial statement users will know the full economic cost of employee stock options, although the amount will not be reported in the income statement.

United States GAAP already require companies to disclose information about stock options. Some Canadian companies whose shares are traded on U.S. as well as Canadian stock exchanges prepare their financial statements in accordance with U.S. GAAP. One example is Nortel Networks Corporation (Nortel). Exhibit 11-7 shows an extract from Note 17 to Nortel's financial statements, in which the company discloses the economic impact of its employee stock options as required under U.S. GAAP.[9] The note shows Nortel's net loss and earnings per share as reported in its income statement and the *pro forma* net loss and earnings per share. (**Pro forma** means that the net income or loss and earnings per share are restated using accounting policies that are different from those used in the actual financial statements.) The *pro forma* net loss and earnings per share are the amounts that would have been reported had Nortel expensed the economic cost of its stock options.

An important implication of the heavy use of stock options to compensate employees is that it can result in a significant dilution of the shareholders' ownership interest. When employees purchase shares using stock options, the future earnings of the entity have to be divided among more shares, but those future earnings are being purchased for less than what they are worth. The existing shareholders lose out.

Financial statement users need to be aware that different forms of compensation are not treated the same way in financial statements. A company that grants stock options to its employees and does not accrue their cost in the financial statements will report a higher net income than a company that pays equivalent compensation in cash.

Let's look at an example to show the effects of the different accounting treatments on the financial statements. Ottertail Inc. (Ottertail) recently introduced an employee stock option plan whereby certain employees receive options to purchase shares of company stock. For the year ended December 31, 2005, Ottertail's board of directors granted employees 200,000 stock options to purchase Ottertail stock at $18.00 per

17.   Stock-based compensation plans

Stock options

The Company has adopted the disclosure requirements of SFAS No. 123, "Accounting for Stock-based Compensation" ("SFAS 123"), and, as permitted under SFAS 123, applies Accounting Principles Board Opinion No. 25 and related interpretations in accounting for its plans. SFAS 123 requires disclosure of pro forma amounts to reflect the impact if the Company had elected to adopt the optional recognition provisions of SFAS 123 for its stock option plans and employee stock purchase plans. Accordingly, the Company's net loss applicable to common shares and loss per common share would have been increased to the *pro forma* amounts as indicated below:

	2000	1999	1998
Net loss applicable to common shares:			
– reported	$ (3,470)	$ (351)	$ (1,282)
– *pro forma*	$ (4,874)	$ (839)	$ (1,399)
Basic and diluted loss per common share:			
– reported	$ (1.17)	$ (0.13)	$ (0.56)
– *pro forma*	$ (1.65)	$ (0.31)	$ (0.61)

The fair value of stock options used to compute pro forma net loss applicable to common shares and loss per common share disclosures is the estimated fair value at grant date using the Black-Scholes option-pricing model with the following assumptions as at December 31:

Weighted-average assumptions	2000	1999	1998
Dividend yield	0.13%	0.22%	0.28%
Expected volatility	54.01%	56.44%	42.34%
Risk-free interest rate	4.94%	6.21%	4.81%
Expected option life	4 yrs	4 yrs	4 yrs

share. The market price of the shares on the date the options were granted was $18.25. The market value of the options on the date of issue, calculated using an appropriate method for determining the economic value of stock options, was $2,925,000. In addition, these employees received $2,200,000 in salary and bonus. According to Canadian accounting standards, Ottertail does not have to expense the economic value of the stock options. As a result, Ottertail would make the following journal entry to record the compensation expense for the year:

Dr. Compensation expense (expense +,		
shareholders' equity –)	2,200,000	
Cr. Cash (assets –)		2,200,000
To record the compensation expense for 2005.		

Note that there is no recognition of the stock options in the entry. Only the cash compensation is recorded. The notes to the financial statements would disclose the market value of the options. If the options are exercised in 2008, when Ottertail's shares are trading at $31 per share, the entry the Ottertail would make is:

Dr. Cash (assets +)	3,600,000	
Cr. Common stock (shareholders' equity +)		3,600,000
To record the exercise of 200,000 stock options at $18.		

The exercise of the stock options is treated as would be any sale of equity. There is no recognition that the shares are being sold for less than their market value at the time.

Now let's consider what happens if the stock options are treated as part of the compensation expense. In that case, the expense would include the salary and bonus, and the value of the stock options:

Dr. Compensation expense (expense +,		
shareholders' equity –)	5,125,000	
Cr. Contributed surplus (shareholders' equity +)		2,925,000
Cr. Cash (assets –)		2,200,000
To record the compensation expense for 2005.		

Now the full economic cost of the compensation being provided to the employees is being recognized when it is granted to the employees. The value of the stock options is credited to Contributed Surplus because the granting of the options does not mean that new shares were issued. Only when the shares are issued would the amount be credited to the Common Stock account. When the stock options are exercised in 2008, when Ottertail's shares are trading at $31, the following entry would be made:

Dr. Cash (assets +)	3,600,000	
Dr. Contributed surplus (shareholders' equity −)	2,925,000	
Cr. Common stock (shareholders' equity +)		6,525,000
To record the exercise of 200,000 stock options at $18.		

When the stock options are exercised, the amount that was credited to contributed surplus when the stock options were granted is moved to the common stock account. In 2005 Ottertail's net income would be $2,925,000 lower when the value of the stock options is accrued than when the options' value is not accrued.

Question for Consideration

Some people argue that employee stock options do not represent an economic cost to an entity and that is why it is reasonable not to record them as an expense.

Do you agree that employee stock options do not represent an economic cost to the entity that issues them? Explain.

Answer: Employee stock options do not require that an entity pay cash or any other assets to the employees. That does not mean there is no economic cost. The common shares of an entity represent valuable economic assets (although they are not accounted for as assets by the entity itself) and if they are "given away" or are sold for less than market value, the economic value of the shares held by existing shareholders decreases. The value of existing shares decreases because the ownership interest of the existing shares is being diluted. Since net income is intended to reflect the change in wealth of the shareholders, a real cost to the shareholders is ignored when the cost of employee stock options is not accounted for.

Economic Consequences

Accounting matters. The discussion in the previous section about employee stock options and the controversy surrounding the attempt by United States standard setters to require that employee stock options be accrued provides an opportunity to emphasize that accounting does matter. If accounting didn't matter, why would people get so excited about a new accounting standard? Clearly, stopping the new accounting standard mattered to the people who objected to it.

But why does accounting matter? Accounting matters because it has economic consequences for an entity and its stakeholders. Economic consequences mean that the wealth of the stakeholders of an entity is affected by how the entity accounts for various transactions and economic events. There are many decisions and outcomes that can be affected simply by how an entity decides to represent its economic circumstances in its financial statements. Some of the decisions and outcomes affected by accounting include:

- management compensation
- compliance with debt covenants that are based on accounting measurements
- the selling price of an entity when the price is based on net income or other accounting measurements
- the amount of tax an entity pays
- rate changes for regulated companies when the rate is based on accounting measurements

- the ability of an entity to receive subsidies from government
- the ability of an entity to raise capital (some entities have argued that their ability to raise capital has been adversely affected by certain accounting standards)

This list does not include the effect that accounting choices might have on the decisions of individual stakeholders—decisions such as whether to buy shares of a particular entity, to sell shares already owned, or to lend money. While economic consequences mean that how an entity accounts affects the wealth of an entity and its stakeholders, the underlying economic activity is not affected by how the entity accounts. Whether employee stock options are accrued, disclosed, or ignored does not change the economic cost of those options. What is affected are the financial statements and the economic consequences of using those statements.

Financial Statement Analysis Issues

The equity section of an entity's balance sheet represents the book value of its equity. **Book value** is the amount recorded in the accounting records for the assets, liabilities, and equities—it is the accounting value of these items. The **book value of equity** is the balance sheet or accounting value of an entity's equity and is equal to assets minus liabilities as reported on the balance sheet. Book value of equity is also referred to as the net assets or net worth of the entity.

Importantly, the book value of equity is not a measure of the market value of equity. As we have discussed throughout the text, there are many reasons why book values and market values do not correspond. Mainly, historical cost, GAAP-based accounting is not designed or intended to measure the market value of all assets and liabilities. For example, assets are recorded at their cost and are not adjusted for changes in market value, and not all assets are even recorded on the balance sheet. (Remember that research and development, advertising, and human resources usually do not appear on a GAAP balance sheet.)

The **market value of equity** is the market price of an entity's shares multiplied by the number of shares outstanding. For public companies, determining the market value of equity is straightforward because the shares trade publicly and so a market price is readily available. For example, the market value of MWW's equity on January 27, 2001 was $63,665,181.60 ($2.40 per share × 26,527,159 shares). The book value of MWW's equity on January 27, 2001 was $64,721,000 or $2.44 per share ($64,721,000 ÷ 26,527,159 shares).

While the market and book values of equity are quite close in value for MWW, one should not infer that book value is a consistently good measure of the market value. It isn't. Table 11-4 provides the market and book values of MWW's shares on its fiscal year ends between 1998 and 2001. The table shows that the relationship between the market and book values of MWW's shares has varied quite significantly from year to year.

Table 11-4   Market Values and Book Values of Mark's Work Wearhouse's Shares

Year	Market value per share	Book value per share	Market-to-book ratio
2001	2.40	2.44	0.98
2000	1.80	2.14	0.84
1999	3.25	1.91	1.70
1998	3.70	1.71	2.16

Earnings Per Share

One of the most often quoted financial ratios is **earnings per share** or **EPS**. EPS is the amount of net income that is attributable to each individual share of common stock. The investing public pays close attention to EPS and anxiously awaits the announcement of companies' quarterly and annual earnings and earnings per share. Analysts project earnings per share, and whether an entity has had a successful quarter or year is often measured by whether it met the analysts' forecasts.

EPS comes in a number of variations. We will look at two of them. The first and most straightforward is **basic earnings per share**. Basic EPS is calculated using the following formula:

$$\text{Basic EPS} = \frac{\text{Net income} - \text{Preferred dividends}}{\text{Weighted-average number of common shares outstanding during the period}}$$

Preferred dividends are deducted from net income in the numerator of the formula because preferred dividends have preference over the rights of common shareholders. Therefore, the amount of preferred dividends is not available to common shareholders, but is not deducted in the calculation of net income. The denominator is the weighted-average number of shares that were outstanding during the year. The weighted-average number of common shares outstanding is the average number of shares outstanding during the period, taking into consideration when during the period changes in the number of shares outstanding occurred. An example of how to calculate the weighted-average number of shares outstanding is shown in Figure 11-3.

For MWW, basic EPS is:

$$\text{Basic earnings per share} = \frac{\$8,180,000 - \$0}{27,596,847} = \$0.296$$

EPS is reported at the bottom of MWW's income statement. In Note 12 (page A-57), MWW provides the weighted-average number of shares outstanding during the year. However, not all entities provide the weighted-average number of shares outstanding. EPS will be disclosed in virtually all financial statements that you are likely to examine.

The second EPS measure we will look at is called fully diluted EPS. In this chapter and in Chapter 10, we discussed securities such as convertible bonds, convertible preferred shares, and stock options that can be converted into or exchanged for common shares. Some of these securities, if they are converted or exercised, will dilute an entity's earnings. They will increase the number of common shares that will share the entity's earnings and thereby lower EPS. **Fully diluted earnings per share** is designed to show the effect that these dilutive securities would have on EPS if the securities were converted or exchanged for common stock.

The actual calculations can get complicated and will not be shown here, but fully diluted EPS can be thought of as a worst-case scenario of EPS. Fully diluted EPS is provided because one of the uses of financial statements is to help investors predict future earnings. Fully diluted EPS is intended to help users understand how EPS in future periods would be affected if the securities that can increase the number of common shares outstanding were converted or exercised.

MWW reports a third EPS measure called EPS before goodwill amortization. This measure is reported because of the change in Canadian accounting standards that states that goodwill does not have to be amortized. However, the new accounting standard can be used only for fiscal years beginning after December 31, 2001, which means that MWW could not use it in its January 27, 2001 financial statements. Presumably, MWW wanted to show the effect of the new standard on EPS in advance, possibly because it results in a slightly higher EPS amount.

The weighted average number of shares outstanding reflects the average number of shares that were outstanding throughout a period, taking into consideration that new shares can be issued and existing shares repurchased at any time during the period.

For example, on January 1, 2005, the start of its fiscal year, Chisasibi Inc. (Chisasibi) had 500,000 common shares outstanding. On March 31, 2005, Chisasibi repurchased 90,000 common shares from investors. On September 30, 2005, Chisasibi issued 40,000 shares to employees who exercised their stock options. The calculation of weighted-average number of shares outstanding is based on the percentage of the year that a certain number of shares are outstanding.

Column 1 Months outstanding	Column 2 Percentage of year	Column 3 Number of shares	Column 4 Weighted-average
January–March	25%	500,000	125,000
April–September	50%	410,000	205,000
October–December	25%	450,000	112,500
			442,500

For the first quarter of the year, January through March, Chisasibi had 500,000 common shares outstanding. For the next six months, April through September, representing half of the year, there were 410,000 (500,000 – 90,000) common shares outstanding. For the last quarter of the year, October through December, there were 450,000 (500,000 – 90,000 + 40,000) common shares outstanding.

The weighted-average is calculated by determining how many shares were outstanding for each part of the year and multiplying that amount by the proportion of the year (the weight) that the amount was outstanding. In the table above, these amounts are obtained by multiplying Column 2 by Column 3. The amount from each of these calculations is added to give the weighted-average for the year. For Chisasibi, the weighted-average number of shares outstanding in 2005 is 442,500.

Figure 11-3

Calculating the Weighted-Average Number of Shares Outstanding

Despite all the attention it receives in the media, EPS has significant limitations:

- First, like any ratio, EPS has no absolute meaning. It must be considered in relation to some benchmark. For example, current EPS could be compared with previous years' EPS to observe trends, or with forecasts of EPS that analysts who follow public companies often make.

- Second, EPS depends on the accounting policies and estimates reflected in the financial statements.

- Third, EPS may be affected by changes in the number of shares outstanding during a period. For example, if an entity repurchases some of its shares, EPS will increase. Another point worth noting is that EPS does not give an indication of the ability or willingness of an entity to pay dividends. It is simply the amount of earnings attributable to each common share.

- Fourth, it can also be very difficult to compare the EPS figures of different entities. Aside from the effect of different accounting choices, EPS is also affected by the way the entity is financed. Entities with identical assets and operating performance will have different EPS if they are financed differently—that is, if they have different amounts of debt and equity.

There is a link between the market price of a public company's shares and the accounting earnings it reports. However, the relationship is not simple. An entity that makes accounting choices that are simply designed to increase its net income will not be rewarded with an increase in stock price. The market is looking for information that gives insights into an entity's future cash flows. The market actually responds to whether an entity's earnings meet expectations, not to the actual amount of earnings. So if an entity reported an increase in EPS of $0.25 per share when the market was expecting an increase of $0.30 per share, the price of the entity's shares would likely fall because earnings did not meet expectations. If the entity reported a decrease in EPS of $0.05 per share when the market was expecting a decrease of $0.10 per share, the price of the entity's shares would be expected to rise because earnings exceeded expectations.

It is important to understand that an entity's share price is a reflection of what the market expects the entity to earn in the future, not a reward for what it earned in the past. In theory, the market value of an entity's stock is the present value of the future cash flows that the shareholders expect to receive.

In Canada our perceptions tend to be overwhelmed by the activities and performance of public companies. For a lot of reasons, this is understandable. Many members of the public have an interest in these companies, either directly or indirectly through pension plans and mutual funds. These companies tend to be large and in the public eye. There is a lot of information available about public companies.

However, most corporations and businesses in Canada are private. That means that there is no market price to obtain a reasonable estimate of the market value of these entities. This is one of the reasons that accounting information is so important for evaluating an entity. For example, how much would you pay to buy a small business in your community? How much would you pay to join a partnership of accountants? Without a market-determined measure of value, it is difficult to know. It is also why accounting information is relied on for determining the value of a private company for purposes of a purchase and sale, or in a divorce.

Return on Shareholders' Equity

In Chapter 9 return on assets (ROA) was introduced as a measure of the performance and operating efficiency of an entity. ROA provides a measure of the return the entity earns regardless of how the entity is financed. **Return on equity (ROE)** provides a measure of return earned by resources invested only by the common shareholders. ROE is defined as:

$$\text{Return on equity} = \frac{\text{Net income} - \text{preferred dividends}}{\text{Average common shareholders' equity}}$$

Because ROE is a measure of return to the common shareholders, preferred dividends are deducted from net income. Preferred dividends are not available to the common shareholders, but the amount is not deducted in the calculation of net income. The denominator, average common shareholders' equity, excludes equity contributed by the preferred shareholders. The denominator includes retained earnings since that amount belongs to the common shareholders. As was discussed in the section in this chapter on leverage, ROE will be affected by how the entity is financed. The more leverage or debt that an entity uses, the more volatile ROE will be.

For MWW, ROE for fiscal 2001 was:

$$\text{Return on equity} = \frac{\$8,180,000 - \$0}{(\$64,721,000 + \$59,571,000) \div 2}$$

$$= \frac{\$8,180,000}{\$62,146,000}$$

$$= 13.2\%$$

MWW's common shareholders earned 13.2% on their investment in MWW. ROE gives common shareholders an indication of the return they are earning on their

Question for Consideration

You are provided the following information about Euston Inc.:

	2007	2006
Common shares outstanding on January 1	125,000	125,000
Common shares issued—on April 30, 2007	20,000	
Common shares issued—on June 30, 2007	10,000	
Common shares outstanding on December 31	155,000	125,000
Net income	$750,000	$695,000
Preferred dividends declared and paid	$100,000	$100,000

Calculate basic EPS for Euston Inc. for the years ended December 31, 2006 and 2007. Interpret the change in EPS over the two years.

Answer:

For the year ended December 31, 2006, the weighted-average number of shares outstanding was 125,000, since that was the number outstanding for the entire year. EPS for 2006 is:

$$\text{Basic EPS} = \frac{\text{Net income} - \text{Preferred dividends}}{\text{Weighted-average number of common shares outstanding during the period}}$$

$$= \frac{\$695,000 - \$100,000}{125,000}$$

$$= \$4.76$$

For the year ended December 31, 2007, the weighted-average number of shares outstanding for the year was:

Months outstanding	Percentage of year	Number of shares	Weighted-average
January–April	33%	125,000	41,667
May–June	17%	145,000	24,167
July–December	50%	155,000	77,500
			143,334

$$\text{Basic EPS} = \frac{\$750,000 - \$100,000}{143,334}$$

$$= \$4.53$$

Basic EPS decreased by $0.23 a share from 2006 to 2007, even though net income increased by $55,000. The reason for the decrease in EPS despite the rise in net income is that additional shares were issued during 2007, but the earnings generated by the additional money contributed by investors was not enough to compensate for the dilution of earnings caused by the new shares issued. This decrease may not be permanent if the additional money invested during 2007 will generate increased earnings in future years.

investment in the company. Investors can compare the ROEs of different entities as part of their evaluation of investment alternatives.

Higher ROEs mean an investment is more attractive, but risk must be considered as well when evaluating investments. Generally, the higher the risk of an investment, the higher the return expected by investors. Thus, when comparing investments, a higher return may indicate more risk. At that point the investor must decide whether he or she is willing to accept the additional risk in exchange for the higher return. This risk-return relationship—the trade-off that exists between risk and return—explains why interest rates that banks pay tend to be low, whereas expected returns on speculative investments tend to be high.

■ Solved Problem

You have been provided with the following information about Wrixon Ltd. (Wrixon):

- Wrixon's year end is December 31.
- Net income for the year ended December 31, 2005 was $3,250,000.
- Wrixon had an unlimited number of common shares authorized and 100,000 outstanding on December 31, 2005.
- There were 500,000 preferred shares with a dividend rate of $5 per share authorized and 400,000 outstanding on December 31, 2005.
- Retained earnings on December 31, 2005 was $4,750,000.
- Balance in the Common Stock account on December 31, 2005 was $1,000,000.
- Balance in the Preferred Stock account on December 31, 2005 was $2,400,000.

During the year ended December 31, 2006 the following events occurred:

i. On March 15 Wrixon issued 50,000 preferred shares at $62 per share.

ii. On August 31 Wrixon declared a dividend of 0.25 shares of Battersea Corp. (Battersea), a public company, for each share of Wrixon stock an investor owned. On the date the dividend was declared, Battersea's shares were trading at $3.90. The dividend was distributed to investors on September 15, 2006. Wrixon originally paid $4.80 per share for the Battersea stock that it distributed to its investors.

iii. On October 1, 2006 Wrixon purchased 10,000 common shares from investors for $11 per share.

iv. On November 1, 2006 Wrixon declared and distributed a 10% stock dividend, with each shareholder receiving an additional share of Wrixon common stock for every 10 shares owned. The market value of Wrixon's shares on November 1, 2006 was $10.75.

v. On December 8, 2006 Wrixon announced a two-for-one stock split.

vi. On December 31, 2006 Wrixon exchanged 30,000 of its common shares for marketing rights for certain products produced by a European company. The price of Wrixon's shares on December 14 was $5.65.

vii. On December 31, 2006 Wrixon's board of directors declared a dividend of $5 per share on each outstanding preferred share. The dividend is to be paid on January 10, 2007.

Required:

a. Prepare the journal entries for each of the items described in the information about Wrixon Ltd.

b. How many common shares were outstanding on December 31, 2006?

c. Calculate the balances in the Preferred Stock and Common Stock accounts on December 31, 2006.

d. Calculate Retained Earnings on December 31, 2006.

e. Calculate basic earnings per share for the year ended December 31, 2006. Assume that the weighted-average number of common shares outstanding during 2006 was 198,000 shares, after taking into consideration the stock split on December 8.

f. Calculate return on equity for the year ended December 31, 2006.

Solution

a. Journal entries for Wrixon Ltd.:

i. The following journal entry is made:

Dr. Cash (assets +)	3,100,000	
Cr. Preferred stock (shareholders' equity +)		3,100,000

To record the issuance and sale of 50,000 shares of preferred stock.

ii. The following journal entries are made:

Dr. Investment in Battersea stock (assets +)	22,500	
Cr. Loss on disposal of investments		
(income statement –, shareholders' equity –)		22,500

To record the loss on the shares of Battersea being distributed to shareholders as a property dividend.

Dr. Retained earnings (shareholders' equity –)	97,500	
Cr. Property dividend payable (liability +)		97,500

To record the declaration of a property dividend on August 31, 2006.

Dr. Property dividend payable (liability –)	97,500	
Cr. Investment in Battersea (assets –)		97,500

To record payment of the property dividend on September 15, 2006.

iii. The average price paid by investors for Wrixon's shares was $10 per share ($1,000,000 ÷ 100,000). Since the price paid to purchase the shares is greater than the average price investors paid for the shares, Wrixon would make the following journal entry to record the transaction:

Dr. Common stock (shareholders' equity –)	100,000	
Dr. Retained earnings (shareholders' equity –)	10,000	
Cr. Cash (assets –)		110,000

To record the repurchase of 10,000 shares for $11 per share.

iv. Assume that Wrixon uses the market value method for accounting for stock dividends.

Dr. Retained earnings (shareholders' equity –)	96,750	
Cr. Common stock (shareholders' equity +)		96,750

To record the 10% stock dividend declared and paid on the 90,000 oustanding common shares.

v. According to GAAP, no entry is made when there is a stock split.

vi. The following journal entry is made:

Dr. Marketing rights (assets +)	169,500	
Cr. Common stock (shareholders' equity +)		169,500

To record the exchange of 30,000 Wrixon common shares for marketing rights for certain products.

vii. The following journal entry is made:

Dr. Retained earnings (shareholders' equity –)	2,250,000	
Cr. Preferred dividend payable (liabilities +)		2,250,000

To record payment of a $5 dividend per share on the 450,000 outstanding preferred shares.

b.

Common shares outstanding on December 31, 2005	100,000
Repurchase of shares	(10,000)
Stock dividend	9,000
Common shares outstanding on December 1, 2006 (before the stock split):	99,000

	Common shares outstanding on December 8, 2006 (after the stock split)	198,000
	Shares issued in exchange for marketing rights	30,000
	Common shares outstanding on December 31, 2006:	228,000

c.
Balance in Preferred Stock account on December 31, 2005	$2,400,000
Preferred shares (50,000 @ $62 per share)	3,100,000
Balance in Preferred Stock account on December 31, 2006	$5,500,000
Balance in Common Stock account on December 31, 2005	$1,000,000
Repurchase of common shares	(100,000)
Stock dividend	96,750
Exchange of common shares for marketing rights	169,500
Balance in Common Stock account on December 31, 2006:	$1,166,250

d.
Retained earnings on December 31, 2005	$4,750,000
+ Net income	3,250,000
– Property dividend on common shares	(97,500)
– Premium paid on repurchase of shares	(10,000)
– Stock dividend	(96,750)
– Preferred share dividend	(2,250,000)
Retained earnings on December 31, 2006:	$5,545,750

e. Calculation of results:

$$\text{Basic EPS} = \frac{\text{Net income} - \text{Preferred dividends}}{\text{Weighted-average number of common shares outstanding during the period}}$$

$$= \frac{\$3,250,000 - \$2,250,000}{198,000}$$

$$= \$5.05$$

f. Calculation of results:

$$\text{Return on equity} = \frac{\text{Net income} - \text{Preferred dividends}}{\text{Average common shareholders' equity}}$$

$$= \frac{\$3,250,000 - \$2,250,000}{\$6,231,000}$$

$$= 16.0\%$$

Summary of Key Points

LO 1. A corporation is a separate legal and taxable entity. The shareholders of a corporation are not liable for the obligations of and losses suffered by the corporation beyond what they have invested in the corporation. Corporations divide the shareholders' equity section of their balance sheets into two broad classifications: capital stock and retained earnings.

Partnerships and proprietorships are not incorporated. Partnerships and proprietorships do not pay tax and do not file tax returns—earnings are taxed in the hands of the proprietor or partners. Partners and proprietors are personally liable for any obligations that the partnership or proprietorship is unable to fulfil, except in the case of limited liability partnerships. The equity section of a partnership has a separate account for each partner to keep track of the capital contributed by, the share of the partnership's earnings of, and the drawings made by each partner.

Not-for-profit organizations (NFPOs) are economic entities whose objective is to provide services and not to make a profit. NFPOs do not have owners or ownership shares that can be traded or sold. Any "income" earned by the NFPO is reinvested in the organization.

LO 2. Common shares represent the residual ownership in an entity. Common share-holders are entitled to whatever earnings and assets are left after obligations to debtholders and preferred shareholders have been satisfied. Preferred shares have rights that must be satisfied before common shareholders' rights. These preferred rights per-tain to the payment of dividends and/or to the distribution of assets in the event of liq-uidation. Unlike debt, the cost of equity is not deductible for tax purposes. Dividends are also not expensed for accounting purposes. Dividends are declared at the discretion of the board of directors. Shareholders are not entitled to dividends or any other type of payments from the corporation, and no return of principal is guaranteed.

Sometimes a corporation will buy its own common stock from the shareholders. When an entity repurchases its shares there is no effect on the income statement. In most juris-dictions in Canada shares that are repurchased must be retired immediately.

LO 3. Retained earnings represents the accumulated earnings of an entity over its entire life, less all dividends paid to shareholders over the entity's life. Retained earnings rep-resents an indirect investment by shareholders. Dividends are distributions of a corpo-ration's earnings to its shareholders. There are three types of dividends: cash, property, and stock. Dividends are discretionary and must be declared by the board of directors. Dividends are declared on a per share basis and every share of a specific class must receive the same dividend. Once a dividend is declared, it is classified as a liability on the balance sheet. A stock split is the division of an entity's shares into a larger number of units, each with a smaller value.

LO 4. Leverage is the use of debt to attempt to increase the return earned on the equity investment of the owners. Leverage is attractive because any profits earned from invest-ing borrowed money, above the cost of borrowing, go to the owners. Leverage is risky because the cost of borrowing must be paid, regardless of how well or poorly the entity is performing.

LO 5. Employee stock options give employees the right to purchase a specified number of shares of the employer's stock at a specified price over a specified period of time. Stock options have become an increasingly important way of compensating employees. Stock options have been very controversial in accounting because, while stock options are used to compensate employees, their economic value is not usually expensed. As a result, expenses are understated and net income is overstated.

LO 6. The equity section of an entity's balance sheet represents the book value of its equity. The book value of equity is the balance sheet or accounting value of an entity and is equal to assets minus liabilities as reported on the balance sheet. The book value of equity is not a measure of the market value of the equity.

Earnings per share (EPS) is the amount of net income that is attributable to each indi-vidual share of common stock. Basic earnings per share equals net income less preferred dividends divided by the weighted-average number of common shares outstanding during the period. Fully diluted EPS is designed to show the effect that these dilutive securities would have on EPS if the securities were converted or exchanged for common stock. Return on equity provides a measure of return earned by resources invested only by the common shareholders.

Key Terms

authorized capital stock, p. 663

basic earnings per share (basic EPS), p. 686

book value, p. 685

book value of equity, p. 685

Canada Business Corporations Act, p. 603

cash dividend, p. 671

common share, p. 663

contributed surplus, p. 664

convertible preferred share, p. 666

cumulative preferred share, p. 666

date of declaration of a dividend, p. 671

date of payment of a dividend, p. 671

earnings per share (EPS), p. 686

employee stock option, p. 679

exercise price, p. 680

expiry date, p. 680

fully diluted earnings per share, p. 686	par value, p. 664
general partner, p. 659	participating preferred share, p. 666
hybrid security, p. 666	preferred share, p. 665
in-the-money, p. 680	*pro forma*, p. 682
issued share, p. 663	property dividend, p. 673
leverage, p. 677	redeemable preferred share, p. 666
limited liability partnership (LLP), p. 659	retractable preferred share, p. 666
limited partner, p. 659	return on equity (ROE), p. 688
market value of equity, p. 685	stock dividend, p. 674
no par value share, p. 664	stock split, p. 675
out-of-the-money, p. 680	treasury stock, p. 669
outstanding share, p. 663	

Similar Terms

The left column gives alternative terms that are sometimes used for the accounting terms introduced in this chapter, which are listed in the right column.

additional paid-in capital	**contributed surplus, p. 664**
authorized share capital, authorized share	**authorized capital stock, p. 663**
dividend in kind	**property dividend, p. 673**
issued share capital	**issued share, p. 663**
net assets, net worth	**book value of equity, p. 685**

Assignment Materials

Questions

Q11-1. Explain the difference between common and preferred shares.

Q11-2. Explain the following features that are sometimes associated with preferred shares:
a. cumulative
b. retractable
c. redeemable
d. participating
e. convertible

Q11-3. What does it mean when an entity uses leverage to finance itself? What are the advantages and disadvantages of using leverage?

Q11-4. Describe and explain the characteristics that distinguish corporations from partnerships and proprietorships.

Q11-5. Why are common shares said to represent the residual interest in an entity?

Q11-6. Why is it important in a corporation's financial statements that contributed capital be separated from retained earnings?

Q11-7. Explain the differences between debt and equity. What are the advantages and disadvantages of each? Which do you think is preferable for an entity to use? Explain.

Q11-8. What is a not-for-profit organization? If the objective of not-for-profit organizations is not to make a profit, then what is their objective? Why is a traditional income statement not appropriate for a not-for-profit organization?

Q11-9. Explain why not-for-profit organizations do not have an owners' equity section on their balance sheets. What do they have instead of an owners' equity section? What does that section of the balance sheet represent? How should it be interpreted?

Q11-10. What is a limited liability partnership? What is the difference between limited partners and general partners? Why must a limited liability partnership have at least one general partner?

Q11-11. What are dividends? Why are dividends not expensed when calculating net income, whereas interest is expensed?

Q11-12. What does par value mean? How does the entry to record the issuance of common stock differ depending on whether the shares have a par value? Provide an example.

Q11-13. Grosvenor Ltd. has the following securities outstanding:
   i. $1,000,000 bond with 10% coupon rate.
   ii. $1,000,000 of cumulative preferred shares with a 6.5% dividend rate.

   What effect would payments to investors for each security have on the income statement? What would be the net cash cost of each security? Assume that Grosvenor Ltd. has a tax rate of 30%.

Q11-14. Over the last six months the price on the stock exchange of Ixworth Inc.'s (Ixworth) shares has fallen from a high of $32 per share to the current price of $18 per share. Ixworth does not plan to issue common shares in the foreseeable future, yet management has expressed concern about the falling share price. Explain why Ixworth's management might be concerned about its share price.

Q11-15. Distinguish between stock splits and stock dividends. How is each accounted for? What is the economic significance of stock splits and stock dividends?

Q11-16. What is retained earnings? What transactions and economic events have an effect on retained earnings? Why is retained earnings considered an indirect investment in an entity?

Q11-17. What are property dividends? How are they accounted for?

Q11-18. What are employee stock options? How are they accounted for? What are the advantages to an entity of issuing stock options to its employees?

Q11-19. You are a shareholder in a public company. The company is proposing to introduce an employee stock option program for its senior executives. Do you think that this proposal is a good idea? In your response, focus on the incentives that the stock option plan would create for the senior executives.

Q11-20. Why do employee stock options impose a cost on shareholders? Explain.

Q11-21. Car prices tend to increase over time. One car manufacturer has offered students the opportunity to lock in the price of a new car for when they graduate. By paying $500 today, a student can purchase any car made by the manufacturer at today's price at any time over the next three years. The $500 fee is not refundable once it is paid.

Required:

Do you think it is worthwhile to spend $500 to lock in the price of a car for three years? Explain. What are the risks associated with purchasing this price guarantee? Suppose you could sell the price guarantee to somebody else. What do you think would happen to the amount for which you could sell the price guarantee if the price of cars increased? What would happen to the amount you could receive if the price of cars decreased? Explain.

Q11-22. What is meant by the term "economic consequences"? Why does accounting have economic consequences?

Q11-23. Since the underlying economic activity of an entity is not affected by accounting choices such as when revenue is recognized or how capital assets are amortized, why does anyone care what accounting choices an entity makes?

Q11-24. Distinguish between the book value and market value of equity. Why are the two amounts usually different? How is book value per share calculated?

Q11-25. Corporations disclose the number of shares authorized and the number of shares outstanding. Explain what these terms mean.

Q11-26. Why are preferred shares "preferred"? Are dividends on preferred shares guaranteed? If the preferred shares have a cumulative feature, are the dividends guaranteed? Explain.

Q11-27. Would you rather receive a cash dividend or a stock dividend from a corporation? Explain.

Q11-28. Why do most companies not pay out 100% of their earnings each year in dividends? Explain.

Q11-29. Why are preferred dividends deducted from net income when calculating earnings per share? Explain. Does earnings per share give an indication of the amount of dividends shareholders can expect to receive? Explain.

Q11-30. Explain why changes in accounting policies and corrections of errors have an effect on retained earnings.

Q11-31. Why might a loan agreement limit or prevent the payment of dividends by the borrower?

Q11-32. Why do you think that property dividends are accounted for at their market value instead of their book value? Why are property dividends relatively uncommon?

Q11-33. What are hybrid securities? Why do they sometimes pose a difficult accounting problem?

Q11-34. Explain why it would be attractive for an entity to be able to classify a hybrid security as debt for tax purposes and as equity for accounting purposes.

Exercises

E11-1.   **(Preparing journal entries, LO 2, 3, 4, 5)** For each of the following transactions or economic events, prepare the journal entry that would be required:

a. On April 2, 2010 Barthel Inc. issued 100,000 common shares for $1,500,000.

b. On May 17, 2010 Cayley Corp. announced a two-for-one stock split.

c. On October 11, 2010 Duro Ltd. declared a $0.15 per share cash dividend. The dividend was paid on February 11, 2010.

d. On August 17, 2010 Gullies Inc. issued 300,000 common shares with a par value of $0.01 for $6,000,000.

e. On December 9, 2010 Ireton Ltd. repurchased 100,000 shares of its common stock on the open market at an average price of $11.25 per share. On December 9, 2010 the balance in Ireton Ltd.'s Common Stock account was $35,000,000 and there were 6,000,000 common shares outstanding.

f. On June 7, 2010 Nilrem Ltd. repurchased 50,000 shares of its common stock on the open market at an average price of $3.75 per share. On June 7, 2010 the balance in Nilrem Ltd.'s Common Stock account was $5,000,000 and there were 1,000,000 common shares outstanding.

g. On April 21, 2010 Quimper Corp. declared and distributed a 5% common stock dividend. On April 21, 2010 Quimper had 25,000,000 common shares outstanding and the market price per share was $2.75. The balance in the Common Stock account on April 21, 2010 was $20,000,000.

h. On February 19, 2010 Vidora Inc. granted 100,000 stock options with an exercise price of $12.00. The market price of the Vidora Inc.'s shares on February 19, 2011 was $11.75. The options were exercised on February 19, 2009, when the market price was $14.20.

i. On December 4, 2010 Yarrow Ltd. declared a property dividend of some of the company's products. Each shareholder received an identical case of products that was taken directly from inventory. The book value of the inventory on December 4, 2010 was $1,200,000 and its market value, based on the most recent selling price to customers, was $2,100,000. The dividend was distributed to the shareholders on December 21, 2010.

j. On March 5, 2010 Zoria Corp. exchanged 50,000 shares of its common stock for equipment it needed for its research lab. Zoria Corp. is a privately owned corporation, so its share price is not readily available, but a recent valuation of the company estimated the value of its shares at between $2.50 and $3.10. The list price of the equipment received is $172,000.

E11-2.   **(Accounting for equity transactions and preparing the shareholders' equity section of the balance sheet, LO 2, 3)** You are provided with the following information from the equity section of Aurora Ltd.'s balance sheet on December 31, 2005:

Preferred stock—Authorized, 100,000 shares, outstanding 30,000	$ 750,000
Common stock—Authorized, unlimited, outstanding 200,000	600,000
Retained earnings	4,555,000

During the year ended December 31, 2006, the following occurred (events are recorded in the order they occurred during the year):

i. Semi-annual dividend on common stock of $100,000 was declared and paid.

ii. 100,000 shares of common stock were issued for $1,500,000.

iii. 20,000 shares of preferred stock were issued for $500,000.

iv. 10,000 shares of common stock were issued in exchange for capital assets. The capital assets received had a list price on the vendor's price list of $190,000.

v. Preferred dividends were declared and paid, $100,000.

vi. 10% stock dividend was declared on the outstanding common shares.

vii. Net income was $1,250,000.

viii. Semi-annual dividend on common stock of $100,000 was declared. The dividend will be paid in January 2008.

Required:

a. Prepare the journal entries required to record the above events.

b. Prepare the shareholders' equity section of Aurora Ltd.'s balance sheet on December 31, 2007.

E11-3. **(Correction of an accounting error, LO 3)** In fiscal 2004 Upshall Ltd. (Upshall) purchased land for $500,000. For some reason, the land was amortized over 10 years on a straight-line basis. A new employee in the accounting department who was asked to review the company's capital assets discovered the error in 2006. Retained earnings on December 31, 2005, Upshall's last year end, was $4,100,000.

Required:

Prepare the journal entry that must be made in Upshall's books to correct the error. What would retained earnings be on December 31, 2005 after the error had been corrected? Explain why the error is corrected in this way.

E11-4. **(Correction of an accounting error, LO 3)** In fiscal 2002, Ioco Inc. (Ioco) purchased capital assets for $1,000,000. The capital assets were supposed to be amortized over five years on a straight-line basis. However, for some reason, these assets were not amortized. Ioco's new controller discovered the error while she was reviewing the accounting records in late 2008. Retained earnings on December 31, 2007, Ioco's last year end, was $12,340,000.

Required:

Prepare the journal entry that must be made in Ioco's books to correct the error. What would retained earnings be on December 31, 2007 after the error had been corrected? Explain why the error is corrected in this way.

E11-5. **(Equity transactions, LO 2, 3, 6)** The shareholders' equity section of Fogo Ltd.'s balance sheet is shown below:

Fogo Ltd.
Extracts from the November 30, 2004 Balance Sheet

Shareholders' equity

Preferred stock (Authorized 100,000, Outstanding, 25,000)	$ 625,000
Common stock (Authorized 1,000,000, Outstanding 500,000)	900,000
Retained earnings	3,440,000
Total shareholders' equity	$4,965,000

During fiscal 2005, the following occurred:

i. On January 31, 50,000 common shares were issued for $100,000.

ii. On July 31, 75,000 common shares were issued for $175,000.

    iii. Dividends on preferred stock of $50,000 were declared and paid.

    iv. Dividends on common stock of $200,000 were declared and paid.

    v. Net income for fiscal 2005 was $975,000.

Required:

a. Calculate the weighted-average number of common shares outstanding during the year.

b. Calculate basic earnings per share for the year ended November 30, 2005.

c. Calculate return on shareholders' equity for the year ended November 30, 2005.

d. Prepare the shareholders' equity section for Fogo Ltd.'s November 30, 2005 balance sheet.

E11-6. **(Repurchase of shares, LO 2)** For the following two transactions, prepare the required journal entries:

a. On July 4, 2006 Nourse Inc. (Nourse) announced that it would be repurchasing up to 100,000 of its common shares on the open market. On July 12, 2006 Nourse repurchased 80,000 shares for $1,000,000. On the date of the repurchase Nourse had 2,000,000 shares outstanding and the amount in the Common Stock account was $4,000,000.

b. On August 15, 2006 Ryley Ltd. (Ryley) announced that it would be repurchasing up to 50,000 of its common shares on the open market. On August 25, 2006 Ryley repurchased 45,000 shares for $300,000. On the date of the repurchase Ryley had 500,000 shares outstanding and the amount in the Common Stock account was $2,500,000.

E11-7. **(Accounting for equity transactions, LO 2, 3)** During the year ended December 31, 2006 Oyama Corp. (Oyama) had the following equity related transactions and economic events. On December 31, 2005 the balance in Oyama's Common Stock account was $8,000,000 with 1,000,000 shares outstanding, the balance in its Preferred Stock account was $0 with no shares outstanding, and Retained Earnings was $4,750,000.

    i. On January 2 Oyama issued 200,000 common shares for $2,000,000.

    ii. On February 28 Oyama issued 50,000 preferred shares for $2,500,000.

    iii. On June 30 Oyama paid a dividend of $0.10 per common share.

    iv. On September 30 Oyama declared a reverse stock split whereby the number of shares outstanding was reduced by half. A shareholder that had 1,000 shares before the reverse stock split would have 500 after the split.

    v. On December 31 Oyama paid dividends to preferred shareholders of $2 per share.

    vi. On December 31 Oyama paid a dividend of $0.10 per common share.

    vii. Net income for 2006 was $2,300,000.

Required:

a. Prepare the journal entries required to record items (i) through (vi).

b. Prepare the equity section of Oyama's balance sheet on December 31, 2006 and provide comparative information for December 31, 2005.

c. Show the equity section of Oyama's balance sheet as it would have been reported in the December 31, 2005 financial statements. Explain the difference between the equity section for 2005 as reported in the 2006 annual report versus the 2005 annual report.

d. Calculate earnings per share and return on shareholders' equity for the year ended December 31, 2006. If earnings per share for 2005 had been reported as $1.75 per share, what amount would be reported for the year ended December 31, 2005 in the 2006 annual report?

e. How did the reverse stock split affect the performance of Oyama?

E11-8. **(Accounting for equity transactions, LO 2, 3)** During the year ended June 30, 2007, Utusivik Inc. (Utusivik) had the following equity-related transactions and economic events. On June 30, 2006 the balance in Utusivik's Common Stock account was $5,000,000 with 2,000,000 shares outstanding, the balance in its

Preferred Stock account was $1,000,000 with 50,000 shares outstanding, and Retained Earnings was $8,200,000.

i. On August 1, 2006 Utusivik issued 400,000 common shares for $3,200,000.

ii. On November 30, 2006 Utusivik issued 100,000 preferred shares for $2,000,000.

iii. On December 31, 2006 Utusivik paid a dividend of $0.25 per common share.

iv. On April 30, 2007 Utusivik declared a two-for-one stock split.

v. On June 30, 2007 Utusivik paid dividends to preferred shareholders of $1.50 per share.

vi. On June 30, 2007 Utusivik paid a dividend of $0.25 per common share.

vii. On June 30, 2007 Utusivik obtained the rights to a patent in exchange for 100,000 shares of Utusivik common stock. The market value of Utusivik stock on June 30, 2007 was $12 per share.

viii. Net income for 2007 was $2,300,000.

Required:

a. Prepare the journal entries required to record items (i) through (vii).

b. Prepare the equity section of Utusivik's balance sheet on June 30, 2007 and provide comparative information for June 30, 2006.

c. Show the equity section of Utusivik's balance sheet as it would have been reported in the June 30, 2006 annual report. Explain the difference between the equity section for 2006 as reported in the 2007 annual report versus the 2006 annual report.

d. Calculate earnings per share and return on shareholders' equity for the year ended June 30, 2007. If earnings per share for 2006 had been reported as $1.75 per share, what amount would be reported for 2006 in the 2007 annual report?

e. How did the stock split affect the performance of Utusivik?

E11-9. **(Calculating earnings per share, LO 2, 3, 6)** For the year ended September 30, 2004 Queylus Inc. (Queylus) reported net income of $250,000. On September 30, 2003, Queylus had the following capital stock outstanding:

Preferred stock, no par, $5 annual dividend, cumulative, authorized 25,000 shares outstanding	$ 250,000
Common stock, no par, authorized 200,000 issued and outstanding	1,000,000

On January 31, 2004 Queylus issued 20,000 common shares for $160,000 and on April 30, 2004 it issued 25,000 common shares for $250,000.

Required:

a. Calculate Queylus's basic earnings per share for the year ended September 30, 2004.

b. How much of a dividend should Queylus's shareholders expect to receive in 2004?

E11-10. **(Impact of equity transactions on the statement of cash flows, LO 2, 3, 6)** For each of the following transactions and economic events, indicate whether it would appear in the cash flow statement. If the transaction or economic event does appear in the cash flow statements would it be reported as cash from operations, an investing cash flow, or a financing cash flow? Explain your reasoning.

a. Issuance of common shares for cash.

b. Declaration of a stock split.

c. Payment of cash dividends on preferred shares.

d. Issuance of preferred shares for cash.

e. Declaration of cash dividends on common shares.

f. Issuance of common shares for capital assets.

g. Distribution of a stock dividend.

h. Repurchase of common shares for cash.

i. Payment of cash dividends on common shares.

j. Granting of stock options to employees.

k. Exercise of stock options by employees.

E11-11. **(The difference between par and no par value shares, LO 2)** For each of the following transactions, record the required journal entry:
   a. 25,000 shares of no par value shares are issued for $30 per share.
   b. 25,000 shares of $0.10 par value shares are issued for $30 per share.
   c. 25,000 shares of $1.00 par value shares are issued for $30 per share.
   d. What effect does par value have on the financial statements? Does par value affect any ratios or the interpretation of the financial statements? Explain.

E11-12. **(Accounting for dividends, LO 3, 6)** Gogama Ltd. (Gogama) is planning on declaring a dividend for its common shareholders and is considering three alternatives:
   i.   Declare a cash dividend of $5.00 per share.
   ii. Declare a property dividend. Shareholders would receive two shares of Judson Inc. (Judson) common stock for each share of Gogama stock owned. Judson's common stock has a market value of $2.50 per share and was originally purchased by Gogama for $1.00 per share.
   iii. Declare a 5% stock dividend. Shareholders would receive one share of Gogama common stock for each 20 shares of Gogama stock owned. The current market value of Gogama's stock is $100.

   Gogama's year end is December 31. The balances in the Common Stock and Retained Earnings accounts on December 31, 2007 are $15,000,000 and $25,000,000 respectively, after accounting for net income for the year but before accounting for the dividend. Gogama currently has 500,000 shares of common stock outstanding and net income for 2007 is $3,500,000.

   Required:
   a. Prepare the journal entries required to record each of the dividends. State any assumptions you make.
   b. How would the equity section of Gogama's December 31, 2007 balance sheet be affected by the three dividends? Show the effect of each dividend separately.
   c. What would basic earnings per share be under each dividend alternative?
   d. What difference does it make which dividend alternative Gogama chooses? Is there an economic difference among the three? Explain. Under what circumstances might one dividend alternative be preferred over the others?
   e. Suppose that instead of paying a property dividend, Gogama sold its shares in Judson and used the proceeds of the sale to pay a cash dividend. Prepare the journal entries required to record the sale of the Judson shares and the declaration and payment of the dividend. What is the difference between paying a property dividend and selling the shares and using the proceeds to pay a dividend?

E11-13. **(Accounting for a partnership, LO 1)** In July 2006 Mr. Irving and Ms. Ruth formed a partnership to offer consulting services. Mr. Irving contributed $20,000 in cash to the partnership and Ms. Ruth contributed non-cash assets to the partnership with a market value of $50,000. During its first year of operations the partnership earned revenues of $92,000 and incurred expenses of $50,000. Mr. Irving and Ms. Ruth agreed to divide the profits of the partnership in proportion to the value of their initial contributions. During the year Mr. Irving withdrew $5,000 in cash from the partnership and Ms. Ruth withdrew $7,000 in cash. The partnership's first year end is December 31, 2006.

   Required:
   a. Record the journal entries required to record formation of the partnership.
   b. Prepare the statement of partners' capital on December 31, 2006.

Problems

P11-1. **(Explaining the differences between preferred shares, LO 2)** Exhibit 11-3 (page 667) provides a description of Bank of Montreal's preferred shares. Class B—Series 4 and 5 were both issued in 1998 and have very similar features, yet the Series 5 shares pay a dividend that is about $0.13 more per year than the Series 4 shares.

Examine the features of the Class B—Series 4 and Series 5 preferred shares and provide some possible explanations for why the dividends on the shares are different but they were sold for the same price.

P11-2. **(Effect of transactions and economic events on ratios, LO 2, 3, 4, 5, 6)** Complete the following table by indicating whether the listed transactions or economic events would increase, decrease, or have no effect on the financial ratios listed. Explain your reasoning and state any assumptions that you make.

	Debt-to-equity ratio	Current ratio	Return on equity	Basic earnings per share	Return on assets
Ratio/amount before taking the transaction/economic event into effect	0.9:1	1.3	11.5%	$3.42	7.1%
1. Issuance of common shares for cash.					
2. Granting of stock options to employees.					
3. Stock dividend.					
4. Issuance of common shares in exchange for capital assets.					
5. Declaration of a preferred stock dividend.					
6. Declaration of a cash dividend.					

P11-3. **(Effect of transactions and economic events on ratios, LO 2, 3, 4, 5, 6)** Complete the following table by indicating whether the listed transactions or economic events would increase, decrease, or have no effect on the financial ratios listed. Explain your reasoning and state any assumptions that you make.

	Debt-to-equity ratio	Current ratio	Return on equity	Basic earnings per share	Return on assets
Ratio/amount before taking the transaction/economic event into effect	1.8:1	1.6	9.8%	$1.82	6.5%
1. Three-for-one stock split.					
2. Payment of a cash dividend that was declared in the previous month.					
3. Repurchase of common shares.					
4. Issuance of preferred shares for cash.					
5. Declaration of a property dividend. The property being distributed has a book value that is greater than its market value.					

P11-4.   **(The effects of leverage, LO 4)** Chitek Inc. (Chitek) is an oil and gas exploration company operating in northern Canada. Chitek has not yet begun extracting oil or gas from the ground, but it is close to the stage when extraction will occur. When Chitek was formed about 18 months ago, shareholders contributed $12,000,000 in exchange for 6,000,000 common shares in the company. Chitek now requires $8,000,000 of additional capital to exploit the resources that it believes it has discovered.

Chitek's CEO is considering two options: selling additional shares in the company or borrowing the required funds. If the company borrows, it will have to pay 12% interest per year. If it uses equity, it will have to sell 2,000,000 shares to raise the required amount of money.

Oil and gas exploration is a risky business. The performance of an oil and gas exploration company is subject to many factors, including the quantity of oil and gas that can be economically extracted from a particular location, the market price of the resource, and the ability of the entity to control its costs. Chitek's CEO has projected two possible outcomes: a good outcome and a poor outcome. Under the good outcome, the CEO estimates that income from operations (income before considering financing costs) will be $2,000,000 in the first year. Under the poor outcome, the CEO estimates that income from operations will be $500,000 in the first year.

Required:

   a. Prepare partial income statements for Chitek assuming:
      i.   Equity financing of the additional $8,000,000 and the good outcome.
      ii.   Equity financing of the additional $8,000,000 and the poor outcome.
      iii.   Debt financing of the additional $8,000,000 and the good outcome.
      iv.   Debt financing of the additional $8,000,000 and the poor outcome.
   b. Calculate basic earnings per share and return on shareholders' equity for the four scenarios described in (a).
   c. Explain the advantages and disadvantages of Chitek using debt, and the advantages and disadvantages of it using equity.
   d. If you were a prospective lender, would you lend $8,000,000 to Chitek? Explain.
   e. Would you advise Chitek to use debt or equity to obtain the additional $8,000,000? Explain.

P11-5.   **(The effects of leverage, LO 4)** Greenway Television (Greenway) owns licenses to operate eight new digital specialty television channels. Greenway was recently granted the licenses by the CRTC and plans to begin broadcasting within six to eight months. Greenway already has agreements in principle with cable and satellite operators to include Greenway's channels on their systems (although these agreements are not binding).

When Greenway was organized two years ago with the purpose of developing specialty channels, the company raised $5,000,000 by selling 2,000,000 common shares to investors. Now that Greenway has received its licenses from the CRTC, it is in need of an additional $5,000,000 to prepare the channels for going on air. Greenway's CEO is considering two options: selling additional shares in the company or borrowing the required funds. If the company borrows, it will have to pay 10% interest per year. If it uses equity, it will have to sell 1,000,000 shares to raise the required amount of money.

The success of Greenway has two main elements—subscribers and advertising revenues. The more subscribers it has and the more money advertisers are prepared to spend to buy advertising time on a channel, the more financially successful Greenway will be. Once the channels are operating, Greenway will receive a fixed fee for each person who subscribes to a channel. Cable and satellite operators sometimes bundle channels, so if a channel is bundled with other channels that are very attractive to viewers, the channel in question will generate revenues regardless of whether many people watch it.

Greenway's CEO has projected two possible outcomes: a good outcome and a poor outcome. Under the good outcome, the CEO estimates that income from operations (income before considering financing costs) will be $1,500,000 in the first year. Under the poor outcome, the CEO estimates that income from operations will be $300,000 in the first year.

Required:

a. Prepare partial income statements for Greenway assuming:
    i.   Equity financing of the additional $5,000,000 and the good outcome.
    ii. Equity financing of the additional $5,000,000 and the poor outcome.
    iii. Debt financing of the additional $5,000,000 and the good outcome.
    iv. Debt financing of the additional $5,000,000 and the poor outcome.

b. Calculate basic earnings per share and return on shareholders' equity for the four scenarios described in (a).

c. Explain the advantages and disadvantages of Greenway using debt, and the advantages and disadvantages of it using equity.

d. If you were a prospective lender, would you lend $5,000,000 to Greenway? Explain.

e. Would you advise Greenway to use debt or equity to obtain the additional $5,000,000? Explain.

P11-6. **(Effect of employee stock options, LO 5, 6)** At its annual meeting in March 2006 the shareholders of Jasper Inc. (Jasper) approved an employee stock option plan that allows the company's board of directors to grant stock options to certain employees as part of their compensation packages. During the year ended December 31, 2006 the board granted 200,000 options to its senior executives. The stock options were issued when Jasper's shares had a market price of $22 per share. The exercise price of the options is $24 per share.

During fiscal 2006, Jasper earned revenues of $37,345,000, and had cost of sales of $18,525,000; selling, general, and administrative expenses of $4,560,000; interest expense of $3,535,000; other expenses of $5,700,000; and an income tax expense of $1,340,000. The economic value of the stock options when they were issued was $1,200,000.

On December 31, 2005, the equity section showed the following:

Capital stock (unlimited number of common shares authorized, 7,000,000 outstanding)	$21,500,000
Retained earnings	18,950,000

During fiscal 2006 Jasper did not issue or repurchase any common shares. Dividends of $0.10 were declared and paid during the year.

Required:

a. Prepare Jasper's income statement for the year ended December 31, 2006.

b. Calculate basic earnings per share and return on shareholders' equity under the two accounting treatments for employee stock options.

c. What effect on cash flow do the two accounting treatments for employee stock options have?

d. Which accounting approach do you think Jasper's managers would prefer? Explain.

e. Which accounting approach do you think gives a better representation of Jasper's economic performance?

f. If Jasper did not accrue the cost of the options in its financial statements, what information would you want disclosed about them? Explain.

P11-7. **(Effect of employee stock options, LO 5, 6)** At its annual meeting in June 2005 the shareholders of Rusylvia Ltd. (Rusylvia) approved an employee stock option plan that allows the company's board of directors to grant stock options to certain employees as part of their compensation packages. During the year ended March 31, 2006 the board granted 100,000 options to its senior executives. The stock options were issued when Rusylvia's shares had a market price of $10 per share. The exercise price of the options is $10.25 per share.

During fiscal 2006, Rusylvia earned revenues of $17,250,000, and had cost of sales of $7,600,000; selling, general, and administrative expenses of $2,400,000; interest expense of $1,750,000; other expenses of $2,950,000; and an income tax expense of $610,000. The economic value of the stock options when they were issued was $900,000.

On March 31, 2005, the equity section showed the following:

Capital stock:

Preferred shares (unlimited number authorized, 200,000 outstanding, $3 annual dividend, cumulative)	$8,000,000
Common shares (unlimited number authorized, 4,000,000 outstanding)	4,500,000
Retained earnings	7,425,000

On February 1, 2006 Rusylvia issued 300,000 shares of common stock for $10 per share. In March 2006 Rusylvia declared and paid the dividend on the preferred shares and declared and paid a cash dividend of $0.25 per share on the common shares.

Required:

a. Prepare Rusylvia's income statement for the year ended March 31, 2006.

b. Calculate basic earnings per share and return on shareholders' equity under the two accounting treatments for employee stock options.

c. What effect on cash flow do the two accounting treatments for employee stock options have?

d. Which accounting approach do you think Rusylvia's managers would prefer? Explain.

e. Which accounting approach do you think gives a better representation of Rusylvia's economic performance?

f. If Rusylvia did not accrue the cost of the options in its financial statements, what information would you want disclosed about them? Explain.

P11-8.   **(Hybrid securities, LO 2)** In May 2005 Kugluktuk Ltd. (Kugluktuk) sold $200,000 in convertible bonds to investors. The bonds have a coupon rate of 9% and mature in May 2015. The bonds are convertible into common shares at the option of the company. The terms of the bond agreement make it highly likely that the bonds will be converted before they mature. Kugluktuk's summarized balance sheet just before the convertible bonds were sold was:

Kugluktuk Ltd.
Summarized Balance Sheet
(Just before the sale of convertible bonds)

Assets	$2,400,000	Liabilities	$1,000,000
		Shareholders' equity	1,400,000
		Total liabilities and shareholders'	
Total assets	$2,400,000	equity	$2,400,000

Required:

a. Do you think that the convertible bonds are really debt or equity? Explain. (Consider the characteristics of debt and equity in your response.)

b. Prepare the journal entry to record the issuance of the convertible bond and calculate the resulting debt-to-equity ratio, assuming that the bonds are classified as debt.

c. Prepare the journal entry to record the issuance of the convertible bond and calculate the resulting debt-to-equity ratio, assuming that the bonds are classified as equity.

d. How do you think Kugluktuk's management would want to classify the convertible bonds for accounting purposes? Explain.

e. How do you think Kugluktuk's management would want to classify the convertible bonds for tax purposes? Explain.

f. How do you think Kugluktuk's management would account for the convertible bonds if the classification for tax purposes had to be the same as the classification for accounting purposes?

g. Does it matter how the convertible bonds are classified? Explain.

P11-9. **(Hybrid securities, LO 2)** In August, 2006 Ethelbert Ltd. (Ethelbert) issued 10,000 shares of cumulative, redeemable preferred stock to investors for $500,000. The preferred shares pay an annual dividend of $4 per share and are redeemable beginning in 2011. Ethelbert must redeem the preferred shares before September 1, 2020. Ethelbert's summarized balance sheet just before the preferred shares were sold was:

Ethelbert Ltd.
Summarized Balance Sheet
(Just before the sale of preferred shares)

Assets	$4,400,000	Liabilities	$2,000,000
		Shareholders' equity	2,400,000
		Total liabilities and shareholders'	
Total assets	$4,400,000	equity	$4,400,000

Required:

a. Do you think that the preferred shares are really debt or equity? Explain. (Consider the characteristics of debt and equity in your response.)

b. Prepare the journal entry to record the issuance of the preferred shares and calculate the resulting debt-to-equity ratio, assuming that the shares are classified as debt.

c. Prepare the journal entry to record the issuance of the preferred shares and calculate the resulting debt-to-equity ratio, assuming that the shares are classified as equity.

d. How do you think Ethelbert's management would want to classify the preferred shares for accounting purposes? Explain.

e. How do you think Ethelbert's management would want to classify the preferred shares for tax purposes? Explain.

f. How do you think Ethelbert's management would account for the preferred shares if the classification for tax purposes had to be the same as the classification for accounting purposes?

g. Does it matter how the preferred shares are classified? Explain.

P11-10. **(Analyzing the effects of different financing alternatives, LO 2, 6)** Owakonze Inc. (Owakonze) is in need of $1,000,000 to finance an expansion of its operations. Management is considering three financing alternatives:

i. Issue 100,000 common shares to a group of private investors for $10 per share. In recent years dividends of $0.40 per share have been paid on the common shares.

ii. Issue 40,000 cumulative preferred shares with an annual dividend of $2 per share. The preferred shares are redeemable after 10 years for $27 per share.

iii. Issue a $1,000,000 bond with a coupon rate of 11% per year and maturity in 15 years.

It is now late July 2006. Owakonze's year end is July 31. Owakonze plans to raise the needed money at the beginning of its 2007 fiscal year, but management wants to know the financial statement effects and implications of each of the alternatives. Owakonze's accounting department has provided a projection of the right-hand side of the balance sheet as of July 31, 2007 and a summarized projected income statement for the year ended July 31, 2007. The projected statements do not reflect any of the proposed financing alternatives. If the current expansion plan is successful, Owakonze anticipates the need to raise additional money in the near future. One of Owakonze's loans has a covenant that requires the debt-to-equity ratio be below 1.1. Owakonze has a tax rate of 30%.

Owakonze Ltd.
Summarized Projected Income Statement as of July 31, 2007

Revenue	$1,900,000
Expenses	1,400,000
Income tax expense	150,000
Net income	$ 350,000

Owakonze Ltd.
Summarized Projected Liabilities and Shareholders' Equity as of July 31, 2007

Liabilities	$ 750,000
Shareholders' equity:	
Preferred stock (200,000 shares authorized, 0 issued)	0
Common stock (unlimited number of shares authorized,	
200,000 outstanding)	950,000
Retained earnings	800,000
Total liabilities and shareholders' equity	$2,500,000

Required:

    a. Calculate net income for Owakonze under the three financing alternatives.

    b. Calculate basic earnings per share and return on shareholders' equity.

    c. Prepare a report to Owakonze's management explaining the effect of each of the financing alternatives on the financial statements. Include in your report a discussion of the pros and cons of each financing alternative. Also, make a recommendation as to which alternative it should choose. Support your recommendation.

P11-11. **(Different ways of looking at income, LO 2, 6)** In the traditional income statement prepared in accordance with GAAP, net income is thought of as the increase of wealth that belongs to the owners of the entity. In this view, interest is an expense, whereas dividends are a reduction of retained earnings. However, this is only one way to view an entity and its financial statements. Net income could also be calculated by expensing both interest and dividends. Another alternative would not treat interest, dividends, or income taxes as expenses.

During the year ended December 31, 2006 Atnarko Ltd. (Atnarko) had revenues of $2,450,000, expenses of $1,500,000, and income taxes of $237,000. In addition, Atnarko incurred interest costs of $150,000, and declared preferred share dividends of $70,000 and common share dividends of $110,000.

Required:

    a. Prepare an income statement for Atnarko using the traditional GAAP approach. Explain why the measure of income is useful from the perspective of shareholders.

    b. Devise three alternative measures of net income and prepare income statements on these bases. Explain which users of the income statement would find your alternative measures useful.

P11-12. **(Assessing the payment of dividends, LO 6)** Dunsinane Ltd. (Dunsinane) is a publicly traded manufacturing company that makes computer components for resale to end-product manufacturers. Extracts from the last five years financial statements are shown on page 707.

Dunsinane completed an expansion in 2004 that was financed by a share issuance made in late 2003. Management believes that cash from operations should now be fairly stable and the net cash outflows on investing activities should range between $900,000 and $1,500,000 per year. To date, Dunsinane has not faced the effects of any economic slowdowns. There is concern of the effects of a prolonged slowdown on Dunsinane's revenues, income, and cash flow. Dunsinane has access to a $1,000,000 line of credit secured against accounts receivable that it has not used to date. After two years of satisfactory and steady performance since the expansion was completed, the board of directors is considering a proposal to implement an annual common share dividend. Dunsinane has never paid dividends before.

	2006	2005	2004	2003	2002
Assets					
Cash	$ 512,000	$ 375,000	$ 430,000	$1,900,000	$ 175,000
All other assets	8,908,000	7,710,000	6,775,000	4,500,000	3,050,000
Total assets	$9,420,000	$8,085,000	$7,205,000	$6,400,000	$3,225,000
Liabilities	$2,900,000	$2,600,000	$2,400,000	$2,200,000	$1,400,000
Shareholders' equity					
Capital stock (unlimited number of common shares authorized, 1,000,000 outstanding)	3,765,000	3,625,000	3,560,000	3,425,000	1,200,000
Retained earnings	2,755,000	1,860,000	1,245,000	775,000	625,000
Total shareholders' equity	6,520,000	5,485,000	4,805,000	4,200,000	1,825,000
Total liabilities and shareholders' equity	$9,420,000	$8,085,000	$7,205,000	$6,400,000	$3,225,000
Extracts from the cash flow statement					
Cash from operations	$1,130,000	$975,000	($250,000)	($75,000)	$225,000
Cash spent on investing activities	(765,000)	(600,000)	(1,550,000)	(1,200,000)	(900,000)

Required:

Prepare a report to Dunsinane's board of directors, assessing the pros and cons of implementing an annual common share dividend. Identify additional information that you would want to have to make a definitive decision. If you recommend that a dividend should be paid, what amount per share should be paid? Provide support for your positions.

P11-13. (**Examining financial statements, LO 1, 6**) The Convenience Store (or The Store) is a family-run, unincorporated business owned and operated by the Shar family. The Store offers food staples, basic household goods, newspapers and magazines, and candy, drinks, and snacks. The Store is operated 80% of the time by family members. Family members are not paid regular salaries. Instead, cash is distributed to family members as they require it. Income is allocated to family members with the purpose of minimizing taxes. Local people are hired to work in the store at other times, and they are paid the minimum wage.

The store is operated out of a building owned by the Shar family. The family lives in a large apartment above the store. The building has a 6%, $235,000 mortgage. The Shar family obtains most of its food and household needs from the shelves of The Convenience Store. The Shar family will also often purchase goods and services through The Store for their own use. The Store has a fairly simple accounting system. Inventory is kept track of manually. Sales are recorded when a transaction is "rung up" on the cash register. Not all transactions are rung up.

The Shar family has earned a satisfactory living from The Convenience Store, but running a store of this type is difficult because it is necessary to be open for business 18 hours a day, seven days a week. A representative of a small chain of convenience stores has recently approached the Shar family with a proposal to buy The Convenience Store. The chain's executives feel the area where The Convenience Store operates has reached the necessary density to justify one of the chain's stores. The chain could open its store elsewhere in the area, but the executives feel that if it could buy The Convenience Store at a reasonable price it would obtain the best location in the area for the store and remove a source of competition.

As part of the negotiations, The Convenience Store has provided its income statements for the last two years to the chain. This is the first time that the chain has attempted to purchase an unincorporated, family-run store, and the controller is not sure what to make of the income statements. The controller has asked you to examine The Convenience Store's income statements and to prepare a report identifying and explaining concerns you have with them. The controller would also like you to indicate any other information that should be obtained and explain the purpose of the information.

The Convenience Store
Income Statements
For the Years Ended December 31, 2006 and 2007

	2006	2007
Revenue	$285,000	$275,025
Cost of merchandise sold	151,050	152,364
Wages	11,900	11,662
Utilities	13,200	13,464
Supplies	11,300	11,074
Amortization of capital assets*	15,900	15,900
Advertising and promotion	7,500	7,000
Interest on bank loans and mortgage	18,100	17,738
Other expenses	20,200	21,000
Net income	$ 35,850	$ 24,823

*Amortization is based on rates specified in the *Income Tax Act.*

Required:

Prepare the report requested by the controller.

■ Using Financial Statements

CanWest Global Communications Corp.

www.canwestglobal.com

CanWest Global Communications Corp. (CanWest) is Canada's leading international, diversified media company. CanWest's strength as a content provider has been built through its coast-to-coast Canadian broadcasting network, Global Television, which reaches over 94% of English-speaking Canada; its leading film and TV production and distribution operation, CanWest Entertainment; a growing new media business, CanWest Interactive; and the Company's significant international broadcasting presence in New Zealand, Australia, and Ireland. Most recently, CanWest was transformed into Canada's largest daily newspaper publisher with the acquisition from Hollinger Inc. of 14 major metropolitan newspapers, 126 community newspapers, and the *National Post.*[10]

CanWest's consolidated balance sheets, statements of retained earnings, extracts from its statements of earnings, and extracts from the notes to the financial statements and the annual report are provided in Exhibit 11-8.[11] Use this information to respond to questions FS11-1 to FS11-8.

FS11-1.   Examine the information provided in Exhibit 11-8 and find the following information:
    a. Retained earnings on August 31, 1999 and 2000.
    b. Dividends paid on common and preferred shares in 1999 and 2000.
    c. Total shareholders' equity on August 31, 1999 and 2000.
    d. Balance in the capital stock account on August 31, 1999 and 2000.
    e. Net income for the years ended August 31, 1999 and 2000.
    f. Net assets on August 31, 1999 and 2000.

FS11-2.   Use the information provided in Exhibit 11-8 and calculate the following ratios for the years ended August 31, 1999 and 2000:
    a. Earnings per share.
    b. Return on shareholders' equity.
    c. Debt-to-equity ratio.
    Interpret and explain your findings.

FS11-3.   Examine Note 9 to CanWest's financial statements and the information on CanWest's shares and stock exchange listings, and respond to the following questions:
    a. Describe the different types of shares that CanWest is authorized to issue. How do the classes differ and how are they the same?
    b. How many shares of each class of share were outstanding on August 31, 2000?

Exhibit 11-8

CanWest Global Communications
Corp. Financial Statements

C O N S O L I D A T E D
B A L A N C E   S H E E T S

As at August 31

	2000	1999
	$000	$000
ASSETS		
Current Assets		
Cash and short term investments	76,298	34,148
Accounts receivable	237,845	126,534
Investment in film and television program rights	57,390	76,791
Other	4,508	8,318
	376,041	245,791
Other receivables	10,310	—
Investment in Network TEN	141,897	159,996
Other investments	360,755	667,028
Investment in film and television programs rights	251,114	45,503
Property and equipment	185,224	110,011
Broadcast licences and goodwill	1,095,066	287,452
Other assets	92,674	52,672
	2,513,081	1,568,453
LIABILITIES		
Current Liabilities		
Bank loans and advances	16,255	13,820
Accounts payable and accrued liabilities	195,302	98,097
Income taxes payable	42,759	18,609
Film and program accounts payable	18,030	27,328
Deferred revenue	41,022	4,144
	313,368	161,998
Long term debt	1,172,532	548,925
Film and program accounts payable	22,260	4,028
Deferred income taxes	43,672	30,336
Other accrued liabilities	74,236	7,552
Minority interests	21,722	19,399
	1,647,790	772,238
SHAREHOLDERS' EQUITY		
Capital stock	420,260	416,083
Contributed surplus	3,647	3,647
Retained earnings	529,112	412,833
Cumulative foreign currency translation adjustments	(87,728)	(36,348)
	865,291	796,215
	2,513,081	1,568,453

c. How many shares of each class of share were issued during fiscal 2000?

d. How much capital (cash and property) was contributed by each class of shares?

e. Why do you think CanWest has these different classes of common shares?

FS11-4. CanWest's multiple voting shares are not traded publicly. They are closely held by members of the CanWest's founder's family and organizations associated with the founder of the company. Why do you think the multiple voting shares are closely held?

CanWest Global Communications
Corp. Financial Statements

CONSOLIDATED STATEMENTS OF RETAINED EARNINGS

For the years ended August 31

	2000	1999
	$000	$000
Retained earnings – beginning of year	412,833	311,544
Net earnings for the year	162,680	146,103
Dividends	(44,933)	(44,814)
Excess of redemption amount over stated amount of shares redeemed	(1,468)	—
Retained earnings – end of year	529,112	412,833

The notes constitute an integral part of the consolidated financial statements.

	2000	1999
Weighted average number of shares outstanding	149,786,882	149,502,365

9. CAPITAL STOCK

AUTHORIZED

Authorized capital consists of an unlimited number of preference shares issuable in series, an unlimited number of multiple voting shares, an unlimited number of subordinate voting shares and an unlimited number of non-voting shares.

The multiple voting shares, the subordinate voting shares and the non-voting shares rank equally on a per share basis in respect of dividends and distributions of capital and are subordinate to the preference shares. Subordinate voting shares carry one vote per share and multiple voting shares carry ten votes per share. Non-voting shares do not vote, except at meetings where the holders of such shares would be entitled by law to vote separately as a class.

Multiple voting shares are convertible into subordinate voting shares and non-voting shares on a one-for-one basis at any time at the option of the holder. Subordinate voting shares are convertible into non-voting shares on a one-for-one basis at any time at the option of the holder. Non-voting shares are convertible into subordinate voting shares on a one-for-one basis provided the holder is Canadian.

ISSUED

	2000	1999
	$000	$000
78,040,908 (1999 – 78,040,908) multiple voting shares	3,252	3,252
69,395,035 (1999 – 67,706,697) subordinate voting shares	394,050	378,385
2,607,837 (1999 – 3,847,291) non-voting shares	22,958	34,446
	420,260	416,083

Changes in outstanding share capital during the two years ended August 31, 2000 were as follows:

	# of Shares	$000
MULTIPLE VOTING SHARE CAPITAL:		
Balance – August 31, 1999 & 2000	78,040,908	3,252
SUBORDINATE VOTING SHARE CAPITAL:		
Balance – August 31, 1998	62,777,825	332,103
Changes pursuant to:		
Share purchase plans	42,476	804
Exercise of stock options	46,483	122
Dividend reinvestment plan	157,168	2,693
Conversion from non-voting shares – net	4,682,745	42,663
Balance – August 31, 1999	67,706,697	378,385
Changes pursuant to:		
Share purchase plans	44,030	713
Exercise of stock options	340,039	900
Dividend reinvestment plan	201,705	3,304
Share repurchase program	(139,600)	(785)
Conversion from non-voting shares – net	1,242,164	11,533
Balance – August 31, 2000	69,395,035	394,050

NON-VOTING SHARE CAPITAL:

Balance – August 31, 1998	8,528,337	77,079
Changes pursuant to:		
Dividend reinvestment plan	1,699	30
Conversion to subordinate voting shares – net	(4,682,745)	(42,663)
Balance – August 31, 1999	3,847,291	34,446
Changes pursuant to:		
Dividend reinvestment plan	2,710	45
Conversion to subordinate voting shares – net	(1,242,164)	(11,533)
Balance – August 31, 2000	2,607,837	22,958

SHARE COMPENSATION PLANS

The Company's board of directors has approved share compensation plans, the purpose of which is to provide employees and certain directors of the Company and its subsidiaries with the opportunity to participate in the growth and development of the Company through the granting of options and share purchase loans. At any time, the number of subordinate voting and non-voting shares reserved and set aside for purposes of the plans may not exceed 10% of the issued shares of the Company.

Options vest over a five or six year period and are exercisable on a cumulative basis over a ten year period, except that under certain specified conditions the options become exercisable immediately. The exercise price represents the market trading price at the date on which the option was granted.

Under management and employee share purchase plans, employees may purchase subordinate voting shares or non-voting shares from treasury at the market trading price using non-interest bearing short-term loans provided by the Company. The shares are held as collateral by a trustee until the loans are repaid.

Changes in outstanding options to purchase subordinate voting shares or non-voting shares for the two years ended August 31 were as follows:

	2000		1999	
	Options	Average Price	Options	Average Price
Options outstanding – beginning of year	1,493,946	11.27	1,470,697	10.53
Changes pursuant to:				
Options granted	478,250	16.86	76,009	21.13
Options exercised	(340,039)	2.65	(46,483)	2.62
Options expired	(596)	15.84	(6,277)	20.27
Options outstanding – end of year	1,631,561	14.70	1,493,946	11.27

The following options to purchase subordinate voting shares or non-voting shares were outstanding as at August 31, 2000:

Year Granted	Exercise Price		Expiry Date	Number Outstanding
1992	$1.63 –	$1.93	2002	122,257
1993	$2.15 –	$2.86	2003	10,750
1994	$3.58		2004	10,753
1995	$4.60		2005	13,279
1996	$7.13 –	$12.92	2006	624,275
1997	$14.24 –	$22.50	2007	151,684
1998	$22.95 –	$25.99	2008	150,563
1999	$18.93 –	$21.40	2009	69,750
2000	$16.20 –	$17.00	2010	478,250
				1,631,561

16. SUBSEQUENT EVENTS

(a) On November 16, 2000, the Company acquired substantially all of the Canadian newspaper and other media assets of Hollinger International Inc. and certain of its affiliates (the "Southam Publications") for an aggregate consideration of approximately $3,000,000,000. The consideration paid was as follows:

	$000
Cash	1,859,000
24.3 million non-voting shares and 2.7 million Series I preference shares	376,000
Note payable to Vendor	751,000
	2,986,000

FS11-5. Use the information provided to calculate the dividend per share paid by CanWest to its shareholders during fiscal 2000.

FS11-6. Use the information in Exhibit 11-8 to respond to the following questions:

    a. How many of its shares were repurchased by CanWest during fiscal 2000? What type of shares were repurchased?

**CANWEST SHARES AND
STOCK EXCHANGE LISTINGS**

The Subordinate Voting Shares and Non-Voting Shares of the Company are listed on the Toronto Stock Exchange under the symbols CGS.S and CGS.A respectively. The Non-Voting Shares of the Company are also listed on the New York Stock Exchange under the symbol CWG.

Issued and outstanding shares as at August 31, 2000 were comprised of:

- Multiple Voting Shares   78,040,908
- Subordinate Voting Shares   69,395,035
- Non-Voting Shares   2,607,837

Each of the share classes has a different number of votes per share. There are 10 votes per Multiple Voting Share and one vote per Subordinate Voting Share. Non-Voting Shares do not vote, except at meetings where the holders of such shares would be entitled by law to vote separately as a class.

CanWest Global Communications Corp. is a constrained-share company, of which at least 66.7% of the voting shares must be beneficially owned by persons who are Canadian citizens or corporations controlled in Canada. There is no limit on the number of non-voting shares that a non-Canadian can hold.

Any Canadian citizen purchasing Non-Voting Shares can present them for registration as either Subordinate Voting Shares or Non-Voting Shares. Non-Voting Shares can be purchased by anyone, Canadian or otherwise. Subordinate Voting Shares purchased by a non-Canadian will, upon registration of transfer, be converted into Non-Voting Shares.

b. What was the total amount paid by CanWest to repurchase its shares? What was the average price paid for each share repurchased?

c. What is the journal entry that CanWest would have made to record the repurchase of shares in fiscal 2000?

d. How would you expect the repurchase of shares to appear in the cash flow statement? Explain.

FS11-7. Examine the information in Note 9 to CanWest's financial statements pertaining to the company's share compensation plan (stock option plan) and respond to the following questions:

a. Describe the terms and limitations to the share compensation plan.

b. How many employee stock options were outstanding on August 31, 2000?

c. How many options were issued during fiscal 2000? What was the average exercise price of the options? Prepare the journal entry that CanWest would have made to record the issuance of the options.

d. How many options were exercised during fiscal 2000? What was the price paid for the shares purchased by the employees? Prepare the journal entry that CanWest would have made to record the exercise of the options in fiscal 2000.

e. How many options expired during fiscal 2000? Why would an employee allow an option to expire without exercising it?

f. Suppose that the options granted in 2000 had an economic value of $3,116,000 on the date they were granted. What would be the effect on net income, earnings per share, and return on shareholders' equity if the options were accrued in the financial statements in the year they were granted? Which measure of net income, the one presented by CanWest or the one that takes into consideration the value of the options, gives a better indication of CanWest's economic performance? Explain.

g. What do you think is the purpose of CanWest's share compensation plan?

FS11-8. Examine Note 16 to CanWest's financial statements and respond to the following questions:

a. Describe the event disclosed in the note. Why is this event disclosed in the fiscal 2000 financial statements?

b. What effect would this event have on the August 31, 2000 financial statements? Explain.

c. Assuming that the price of CanWest's non-voting shares on November 16, 2000 was $14.25 per share, prepare the journal entry that CanWest would have made to record the transaction.

■ Analyzing Mark's Work Wearhouse

M11-1. How much did shareholders contribute to MWW in money and property for the purchase of common stock in the company as of January 27, 2001? What is the average amount paid per share by investors?

M11-2. What was MWW's authorized capital stock on January 27, 2001? What is the par value of the authorized capital stock? How many shares were outstanding on January 27, 2001?

M11-3. How many shares of its own stock did MWW purchase in fiscal 2000 and 2001? How much did it pay in each year for the shares? What amount is reported in the statement of cash flows for the repurchase of MWW stock? Where in the statement of cash flows is this amount reported? Explain why it is reported there. Prepare the journal entry that MWW would have made in fiscal 2000 and 2001 to record the repurchase of its shares.

M11-4. Calculate basic earnings per share and return on equity for fiscal 2000 and fiscal 2001.

M11-5. Use the information in Note 12 (page A-57) to reconcile the number of common shares outstanding on January 29, 2000 to the number outstanding on January 27, 2001.

M11-6. How many MWW shares were purchased during fiscal 2001 by employees exercising their stock options? What was the average price paid for each share purchased? How much did MWW receive in total from the employees exercising their stock options? How much is reported in MWW's statement of cash flows for the sale of shares? Where in the statement of cash flows is this amount reported? Explain why it is reported there. What journal entry would MWW make to record the exercise of the stock options?

M11-7. How many stock options did MWW grant its employees in fiscal 2001? What was the weighted-average exercise price of the options awarded in fiscal 2001? What entry did MWW make to record the granting of the stock options? Suppose that the market value of the stock options issued in fiscal 2001 was $512,000. Calculate net income, basic earnings per share, and return on common shareholders' equity for 2001.

Endnotes

1. Extracted from the Canadian Cancer Society's 2000 annual report.

2. Extracted from Bombardier Inc.'s 2000 annual report.

3. Extracted from the Bank of Montreal's 2000 annual report.

4. Extracted from Quebecor Inc.'s 2000 annual report.

5. Extracted from Call-Net Enterprises Inc.'s 2000 annual report.

6. Extracted from Bombardier Inc.'s 2001 and 2000 annual reports.

7. C.I. Wiedman and D. J. Goldberg, "Accounting for stock-based compensation: As easy as SFAS 123," *Ivey Business Journal*, July/August 2001, pp. 6-9.

8. *National Post*, May 22, 2001.

9. Extracted from Nortel Networks Corporation 2000 annual report.

10. Extracted from CanWest Global Communications Corp.'s corporate web site at www.canwest-global.com (accessed May 15, 2002).

11. Extracted from CanWest Global Communications Corp.'s 2000 annual report.

Chapter 12

Investments in Other Companies

Chapter Outline

Learning Objectives

After studying the material in this chapter you will be able to:

LO 1.　Describe how corporations account for their subsidiaries.

LO 2.　Discuss the accounting for investments where there is significant influence.

LO 3.　Explain the accounting for passive investments.

Introduction

One of the first things pointed out when we looked at Mark's Work Wearhouse's (MWW's) financial statements for the first time in Chapter 2 was that the statements were consolidated. MWW's financial statements combine the activities of its Mark's Work Wearhouse, Work World, and DOCKERS® stores into a single set of financial statements.

MWW is not unusual. The financial statements of most public companies are consolidated. Consolidated financial statements are required under GAAP when one company, the parent, controls another company, the subsidiary.

Consolidated financial statements combine the financial statements of a parent and all its subsidiaries into a single set of financial statements. The idea behind consolidated financial statements is to provide financial information about an entire economic entity, not just about the parent corporation alone.

Gaining control of another company is only one outcome of investment by one corporation in another. Some investments allow the investing corporation to influence the decisions of those companies, but not control them. Other investments, usually small ones, give the investing corporation no more influence than any small investor would have. These investments, with their different degrees of influence, are each accounted for differently.

While the concept of consolidated financial statements may seem straightforward—combining the financial statements of several entities into a single set of statements—in fact, consolidation accounting and accounting for investments in other corporations in general are among the more complicated topics in accounting. People who study to become accountants can spend an entire course on the subject. In many ways, this topic is beyond the scope of an introductory accounting course. However, because consolidated financial statements are encountered so frequently, and because accounts like Goodwill and Non-controlling Interest are so commonly seen in financial statements, it is important, even for the accounting novice, to be familiar with the subject.

To that end, this chapter will provide a discussion of how corporations account for investments in other corporations and how those investments affect the financial statements. The intent is to provide enough of the mechanics to give you insight into the effect on financial statements without being overwhelming.

Why Do Companies Invest in Other Companies?

There are many reasons why one company will invest in another. The reason can be as simple as the need to find a place to invest a temporary surplus of cash. For example, companies in seasonal businesses may have excess cash on hand at certain points during a year. Or companies may accumulate cash over a period of time in anticipation of expansion or acquisitions. Prudent management requires that the cash not be idle—that it be invested to earn a reasonable return. This can be achieved by purchasing the debt or equity of other companies. Securities of other companies might be purchased because they represent good investment opportunities that will generate dividend, interest, and capital gains income for the investing company.

Some companies invest in other companies for strategic reasons—so that they can influence or control the decisions made by those companies. For example, in 2000 CanWest Global Communications Corp. (CanWest) purchased the Canadian newspaper and Internet assets of Hollinger Inc. and a 50% partnership interest in the

National Post newspaper for over $3 billion in cash, CanWest shares, and debt. (Soon afterwards, CanWest purchased the remaining 50% of the *National Post*.) CanWest made the investment to take advantage of media convergence by adding print and Internet businesses to its existing broadcasting and entertainment businesses.

Companies might purchase all or part of other companies in the same business as a way of expanding their existing operations. For example, in 1998 Loblaw Companies Limited (Loblaw), a large grocery store chain, purchased 100% of the shares of Provigo Inc., a Québec-based grocery chain, for $1.7 billion in cash and Loblaw shares. By making the purchase, Loblaw was able to expand into Québec, a market where it previously had no stores. Alternatively, a company might purchase competitors in a market where it already does business to reduce competition and expand its presence in that market.

Companies may also invest in their customers to ensure markets for their products and in their suppliers to ensure the availability of needed inputs. For example, Imperial Oil Limited is a large producer, refiner, and marketer of petroleum products in Canada. By operating at all these levels, Imperial Oil ensures its refineries serve as guaranteed customers for the oil and gas it extracts from the ground, and its gas stations are customers for its gasoline and lubricants.

Companies may also purchase all or part of other companies to diversify. Some businesses are cyclical—their performance depends on where in the business cycle the economy is. Cyclical businesses will be profitable in some years and unprofitable in others. By diversifying their investments in different business and geographic areas, companies try to mitigate the effect of the business cycle. For example, Brascan Corporation has major investments in natural resources, energy, property, and financial management companies that are active in many parts of the world.

www.imperialoil.ca
www.brascancorp.com

Accounting for Investments in Other Corporations: Introduction

How an entity accounts for its investments in other corporations depends on the influence that it has over those corporations. For accounting purposes, there are three levels of influence that an **investor corporation** (a corporation that has an investment in another corporation) can have over an **investee corporation** (a corporation in which an investor corporation has invested). (Throughout this chapter, the investor and investee corporations will be referred to as the investor and the investee.) These levels of influence are:

1. Control. If an investor controls an investee, it can make all the important decisions of the investee. An investee that is controlled is called a subsidiary of the investor, and the financial statements of the investor and investee are aggregated into a single set of consolidated financial statements.

2. Significant influence. If the investor does not control an investee, but can affect its important decisions, the investor corporation is said to have significant influence and, according to GAAP, should use the equity method of accounting.

3. Passive investment. If the investor has no influence over the decision making of the investee (or at least no more influence than any other small investor), the investment is called a passive investment and it is accounted for using the cost method of accounting.

The different types of investments in other corporations are summarized in Figure 12-1. We will discuss each of the methods of accounting for investments in other corporations in detail in the following sections.

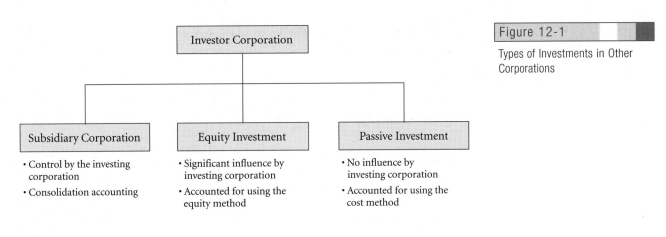

Figure 12-1

Types of Investments in Other
Corporations

Control: Accounting for Subsidiaries

The first level of influence we will examine is control. When an investor has **control** of an investee, the investor is able to make the important decisions of the investee and determine its strategic operating, financing, and investing policies on an ongoing basis, without the support of other shareholders. In other words, the managers of the investor can set the key policies of the investee.

Control usually means that the investor owns more than 50% of the votes of the investee, although there are rare situations where the investor has fewer than 50% of the votes. Note that 50% of the votes is not necessarily the same as 50% of the common shares. For example, Onex Corporation (Onex) controls a number of companies, despite owning less than 50% of the common shares. Onex owns 20% of the outstanding common shares of Celestica Inc., but has 86% of the votes. This is because each of the common shares that Onex owns has 25 votes, whereas the common shares held by other shareholders have only one vote each. Exhibit 12-1 (page 718) lists the companies that Onex controls, the percentage of the common shares that it owns, and the percentage of the votes that it owns.[1]

When an investor has control it is often referred to as the **parent corporation** (or parent) and the investee is called a **subsidiary corporation** (or subsidiary). When an investor controls an investee, the investor prepares consolidated financial statements.

Consolidated financial statements aggregate the accounting information of a parent corporation and all of its subsidiaries into single set of financial statements. This means that each line in a set of consolidated financial statements reflects the assets, liabilities, revenues, expenses, and cash flows of the parent and all its subsidiaries. A parent corporation may have many subsidiaries, each of which is reflected in the single set of consolidated financial statements. Onex Corporation, for example, consolidates 14 subsidiaries into its consolidated financial statements (see Exhibit 12-1 for a list of Onex's subsidiaries). These subsidiaries are in a variety of different industries—electronics manufacturing, airline catering, automotive products, and building products. But the financial information about all these diverse companies is reported in the single set of consolidated financial statements.

Consolidated financial statements are an application of the entity assumption. The entity represented by the financial statements is a group of corporations that are under the control of a parent. The purpose of consolidated statements is to provide users who are interested in the parent—for example, shareholders of the parent—with statements that reflect the assets, liabilities, equities, revenues, and expenses of all the corporations controlled by the parent in a single set of financial statements.

It is important to recognize that a consolidated group of companies is an accounting creation. The individual subsidiaries and the parent are each separate legal entities and each one must file its own tax return. Each corporation has its own

www.onexcorp.com
www.celestica.com

The principal operating companies and the Company's ownership and voting interests for consolidated entities are as follows:

	December 31, 2000		December 31, 1999	
	Ownership	Voting	Ownership	Voting
Celestica	20%	86%	22%	87%
Sky Chefs				
(including Caterair)	47%	54%	47%	54%
ClientLogic	70%	87%	81%	100%
Dura Automotive	8%	70%	8%	70%
J.L. French				
Automotive Castings	37%	81%	45%	88%
Performance				
Logistics Group	49%	100%	62%	100%
Commercial				
Vehicle Systems	45%	100%	–	–
Performance				
Marketing Global	62%	100%	–	–
Bostrom	52%	100%	–	–
MAGNATRAX	53%	80%	55%	75%
Lantic Sugar	61%	75%	61%	75%
InsLogic	49%	63%	–	–
ONCAP	25%	100%	–	–
Vencap	99%	100%	99%	100%

limited legal liability. The consolidated group is not a legal entity and it does not file a tax return.

Conceptually, consolidated financial statements may sound simple—just a matter of adding together the individual financial statements of the parent and subsidiaries. In fact, however, they are very complicated. The complications arise because consolidated statements are not just the sum of the statements of the entities in the economic group. There are many adjustments that must be made to arrive at the consolidated statements.

From an accounting perspective, the first event of consequence occurs when the investor purchases control of the investee. When the purchase is made, the investor records the investment at cost in its financial records. The investment is recorded in a single account that appears on the parent's balance sheet. (As we will see, the parent's financial statements are *not* the same as the consolidated financial statements.) In the consolidated balance sheet the assets and liabilities of a subsidiary are recorded at the amount the parent paid for them. That is, the consolidated balance sheet reports the subsidiary's assets and liabilities at their cost to the parent on the date the subsidiary was purchased. However, on the subsidiary's own balance sheet, the assets and liabilities are reported at their cost to the subsidiary when the subsidiary purchased them.

Thus, there are two valuations for the subsidiary's assets and liabilities: the valuation used on the subsidiary's balance sheet, which is the cost to the subsidiary itself, and the valuation on the consolidated balance sheet, which is the cost to the parent. Both valuations are valid applications of GAAP. The two valuations represent the cost of the assets and liabilities at different times. Because the amounts that appear on the subsidiary's balance sheet are different from what is reported on the consolidated balance sheet, the balance sheets of the parent and the subsidiary cannot be simply added together to get the consolidated statement. Adjustments are required.

We will examine the accounting for the purchase of a subsidiary with an example. (Throughout this chapter the examples assume that the investor used cash to make the investment. Note that investments can also involve shares of the parent, debt, and non-cash assets.)

On June 30, 2005 Pentz Ltd. (Pentz) bought 100% of the shares of Sahtlam Corp. (Sahtlam) from its shareholders for $20,000,000. Pentz would make the following journal entry in its accounting records to record the investment in Sahtlam:

Dr. Investment in Sahtlam (asset +)	$20,000,000	
Cr. Cash (asset −)		$20,000,000

To record the purchase of 100% of the shares of
Sahtlam Corp on June 30, 2005.

The investment has no effect at all on Sahtlam's accounting records or its financial statements. Pentz purchased the shares from Sahtlam's shareholders, not from the corporation itself. Only the ownership of Sahtlam's shares has changed.

Pentz has purchased 100% of Sahtlam for $20,000,000. But what exactly did Pentz buy and how much did it pay for the specific assets and liabilities? For Pentz to be able to prepare consolidated financial statements, it must identify the assets and liabilities that it purchased and determine their cost—the amount Pentz paid for them.

This process can be difficult because Pentz purchased an entire entity, not individual assets and liabilities. As a result, the purchase price must be allocated to the individual assets and liabilities that were purchased. To accomplish this, the market or fair values of all of Sahtlam's assets and liabilities must be determined as of the date of the purchase, and these are the amounts that are reported in the consolidated financial statements. (Remember, the cost of an asset or liability is its market value on the date the asset or liability was acquired.)

This is a straightforward application of GAAP's historical cost measurement convention. Since Pentz has purchased Sahtlam, the assets and liabilities that were purchased should be treated the same way as any purchase, at cost. This process of determining the fair value of the assets and liabilities of a subsidiary occurs only once, when the subsidiary is purchased. After that, the consolidated financial statements are based on the amounts determined as of the date of the purchase.

(Throughout this chapter the term **fair value** is used when referring to the estimated market value of the subsidiary's assets and liabilities on the date the subsidiary was purchased. This is the term commonly used in accounting for subsidiaries.)

Table 12-1 summarizes the book and fair values of Sahtlam's assets and liabilities on June 30, 2005.

There are a couple of things to notice in Table 12-1:

- First, there are two measurements of Sahtlam's assets and liabilities. One measurement is the amount that actually appears in Sahtlam's own financial statements. The second measurement is the fair values on the date Sahtlam was purchased by Pentz, which are the amounts Pentz paid for Sahtlam's assets and

Table 12-1   Fair Values and Book Values of Sahtlam Corp.'s Net Assets on June 30, 2005

	Fair Value on June 30, 2005	Book Value of Sahtlam's Financial Statements on June 30, 2005	Difference
Current assets	$ 5,500,000	$ 5,000,000	$ 500,000
Capital assets	21,500,000	14,000,000	7,500,000
Liabilities	(9,000,000)	(8,000,000)	(1,000,000)
	$18,000,000	$11,000,000	$7,000,000

liabilities. The fair values are the amounts that appear on Pentz's consolidated balance sheet.

- Second, only $18,000,000 of the purchase price has been attributed to specific assets and liabilities. The remaining $2,000,000 is called goodwill.

Goodwill

Goodwill is the amount that a parent pays for a subsidiary over and above the fair value of the subsidiary's identifiable assets and liabilities on the date the subsidiary is purchased. That is,

$$\text{Goodwill} = \frac{\text{Purchase}}{\text{price}} - \frac{\text{Fair value of identifiable assets}}{\text{and liabilities purchased}}$$

Identifiable assets and liabilities are tangible and intangible assets and liabilities that can be specifically identified and measured with some objectivity. Identifiable assets include cash, inventory, land, buildings, patents, copyrights, and research and development.

The goodwill that arose as a result of the purchase of 100% of Sahtlam's shares by Pentz is calculated as:

$$
\begin{aligned}
\text{Goodwill} &= \frac{\text{Purchase}}{\text{price}} - \frac{\text{Fair value of identifiable assets}}{\text{and liabilities purchased}} \\
&= \$20,000,000 - \$18,000,000 \\
&= \$2,000,000
\end{aligned}
$$

Why would Pentz pay $2,000,000 more than the fair value of the identifiable assets and liabilities for Sahtlam? What does the goodwill actually represent? Well, it is hard to be sure because goodwill is a residual—it is the amount that is left over after the identifiable assets and liabilities have been valued. It is assumed that if an investor paid more than the fair value of the identifiable assets and liabilities for a subsidiary, the extra amount paid is for something of value, even if it is not clear exactly what. Goodwill is often attributed to things such as management ability, location, synergies created by the acquisition, customer loyalty, reputation, and benefits associated with the elimination of a competitor—all things that are of value but that are very difficult to specifically identify and measure.

Of course, another possible explanation for paying more than the fair value of the identifiable assets and liabilities is that the investor paid too much. However, it would probably be imprudent for a manager to admit that too soon after the purchase of a subsidiary!

It is interesting to observe that assets such as management skill, location, reputation, and so on that are considered goodwill all exist before a subsidiary is purchased. However, according to GAAP, internally generated goodwill cannot appear on the balance sheet. This is the nature of historical cost, transactions-based accounting: Goodwill can be recognized only when one entity purchases another—it is determined only on the date a subsidiary is purchased. Because of conservatism and reliability, costs incurred to generate goodwill internally are expensed when incurred because it is difficult to measure the future benefits associated with the money spent. This treatment is also consistent with the accounting used for other intangible assets such as research and development, and copyrights.

It is important to emphasize that, conceptually, goodwill is an asset. The existence of higher management ability, reputation, customer loyalty, and so on should lead to higher profits than would be earned in their absence. The challenge with the accounting is determining the existence and the value of the future benefit.

According to GAAP, goodwill is not amortized. Instead, management must estimate the fair value of the goodwill each year. If the fair value is less than the book value, the goodwill must be written down to its fair value. The amount of any write-down of goodwill is expensed in the income statement in the year.

The *CICA Handbook* provides guidelines for estimating the fair value of goodwill. However, because of its nature, estimating the fair value of goodwill is very subjective and requires judgment. Because so much judgment is required to determine if goodwill's value is impaired, management has considerable leeway in deciding the timing and amount of any write-down.

It is important to note that the accounting treatment for goodwill just described is new. Before 2003 goodwill had to be amortized over a period not longer than 40 years. When you examine MWW's financial statements in Appendix A, you will notice that the goodwill is being amortized.

Goodwill can represent a significant proportion of a company's assets. For example, on December 31, 2000 goodwill represented almost 24% of Onex Corporation's assets. From an analytical standpoint, goodwill does not tell the reader of consolidated financial statements very much. It provides information about the amount that was spent for an investment, but nothing about what the goodwill represents, if it represents anything at all. Financial statement readers can only speculate whether it represents a wise expenditure of company resources.

Question for Consideration

Why is it difficult to say for sure what goodwill is in any given situation? Do you think goodwill meets the definition of an asset under GAAP? (See Chapter 2 for the criteria for an asset.)

Answer: It is difficult to say for sure what goodwill is in any given situation because goodwill is not specifically identified as an asset. Instead, goodwill is a residual—it is what is left over after assets and liabilities that can be specifically identified have been identified and fair values assigned to them. Therefore, it is not necessary to identify what is represented by the goodwill that an entity reports on its balance sheet. This situation also makes it difficult to assess whether an entity's goodwill really has any future benefit because it is hard to assess future benefit if you do not know what it is you are assessing.

The three GAAP criteria for an asset that were identified in Chapter 2 are:

1. An asset must be the result of a transaction with another entity;

2. The cost of an asset can be determined; and

3. An asset must provide a future benefit to the entity and the benefit must be reasonably measurable. (If you are not sure what the benefit is or that there will be a benefit, you cannot call an item an asset.)

The first criterion is met because goodwill is recorded only when another company is purchased. Whether the second criterion is met can be questioned. Since the cost of goodwill itself is not determined—rather, it is the portion of the purchase price that is not assigned to specific assets and liabilities—one can question whether the cost of goodwill is actually determinable. Goodwill's cost depends on how well the cost of the identifiable assets and liabilities can be determined. The third criterion is the most debatable. If we do not really know what goodwill is, how can we be reasonably sure that there is a future benefit and reasonably measure what that future benefit is?

The rationale for classifying goodwill as an asset is that since goodwill is purchased when an entity is acquired, it should be accounted for as an asset.

The Consolidated Balance Sheet on the Date the Subsidiary Is Purchased

We now have the information to prepare Pentz's consolidated balance sheet on June 30, 2005, the date that Pentz purchased all of the shares of Sahtlam. Pentz's consolidated balance sheet will be the sum of the balance sheets of Pentz and Sahtlam, adjusted so that:

a. The market values of Sahtlam's net assets are reflected in the consolidated balance sheet;

b. The goodwill purchased is reported in the consolidated financial statements;

c. The Investment in Sahtlam that is reported in Pentz's (not consolidated Pentz's) balance sheet is eliminated to avoid double counting; and

d. Sahtlam's shareholders' equity is eliminated to avoid double counting.

Adjustments (c) and (d) require some additional explanation. Regarding adjustment (c), the Investment in Sahtlam account must be eliminated because the specific assets and liabilities that were purchased replace the Investment account. The Investment account on Pentz's balance sheet and Sahtlam's assets and liabilities that are reported in the consolidated balance sheet represent the same thing—the investment in Sahtlam. If the Investment account is not eliminated, the net assets of the subsidiary are reported twice in the consolidated financial statements.

Let's now look at adjustment (d). Sahtlam's shareholders' equity is also not reported in the consolidated balance sheet because Pentz's ownership of Sahtlam is reflected in Pentz's shareholders' equity. Pentz's shareholders' equity represents Pentz's shareholders' interest in Pentz's assets, which includes Sahtlam. Since Pentz's interest in Sahtlam is already reflected in Pentz's shareholders' equity, the inclusion of Sahtlam's equity in the consolidated balance sheet would result in double counting—Sahtlam's equity would be counted twice.

In general, when consolidated financial statements are prepared as of the date the subsidiary is purchased, the Investment in Subsidiary account on the parent's balance sheet must not be reflected in the consolidated balance and neither must the shareholders' equity of the subsidiary.

It is important to understand that a parent's financial statements are not the same as its consolidated financial statements. The parent itself prepares unconsolidated financial statements that report on the parent alone. All that is reported about a parent's subsidiaries in the unconsolidated financial statements is a single line reporting the investment in the subsidiaries. The unconsolidated statements are required for tax purposes and may be provided to other users, such as bankers. A parent's unconsolidated financial statements are not usually widely distributed.

The construction of Pentz's consolidated balance sheet on June 30, 2005, the date Pentz purchased the shares of Sahtlam, is shown in Table 12-2. Specifically,

• Column 1 of Table 12-2 shows the balance sheets of the individual corporations. (The information from Pentz's balance sheet has not been shown before.)

• Column 2 shows the adjustments that must be made to the accounts on Pentz's and Sahtlam's balance sheets to obtain the consolidated balance sheet. The increases to Current Assets, Capital Assets, and Liabilities adjust the amounts on Sahtlam's balance sheet so that their fair values on June 30, 2005 are reflected in the consolidated balance sheet. (These are the same amounts shown in the difference column in Table 12-1, page 719.) The decrease of $20,000,000 in the Investment in Sahtlam account eliminates the investment reported on Pentz's balance sheet from the consolidated balance sheet. The reductions in the Capital Stock and Retained Earnings accounts eliminate Sahtlam's shareholders' equity

Table 12-2	Pentz Ltd.'s Consolidated Balance Sheet on June 30, 2005			
	Column 1		**Column 2**	**Column 3**
			Adjustments to Prepare Consolidated Balance Sheet	Consolidated Balance Sheet As of June 30, 2005
	Balance Sheets As of June 30, 2005			
	Pentz Ltd.[1]	**Sahtlam Corp.[1]**		
Current assets	$ 29,000,000	$ 5,000,000	+500,000[2]	$ 34,500,000
Capital assets	52,000,000	14,000,000	+7,500,000[2]	73,500,000
Investment in Sahtlam	20,000,000		−20,000,000[3]	0
Goodwill			+2,000,000[4]	2,000,000
	$101,000,000	$19,000,000		$110,000,000
Liabilities	$ 38,000,000	$ 8,000,000	+1,000,000[2]	$ 47,000,000
Capital stock	22,000,000	3,500,000	−3,500,000[5]	22,000,000
Retained earnings	41,000,000	7,500,000	−7,500,000[5]	41,000,000
	$101,000,000	$19,000,000		$110,000,000

[1] These are the balance sheets of Pentz (not consolidated Pentz) and Sahtlam on June 30, 2005, immediately after the purchase of Sahtlam occurred.

[2] Adjustments to the book values of Sahtlam's assets and liabilities so that they will be included in Pentz's consolidated balance sheet at their fair values on June 30, 2005. The adjustments are the differences between Sahtlam's book and fair values on June 30, 2005, as shown in Table 12-1 (page 719).

[3] The investment in Sahtlam must be eliminated to avoid double counting of Sahtlam's net assets.

[4] Goodwill as calculated by the formula

$$\text{Goodwill} = \frac{\text{Purchase}}{\text{price}} - \frac{\text{Fair value of identifiable assets}}{\text{and liabilities purchased}}$$

$$\$2,000,000 = \$20,000,000 - \$18,000,000$$

[5] Sahtlam's owners' equity accounts are eliminated to avoid double counting.

from the consolidated balance sheet. The increase to the Goodwill account results in goodwill appearing on the consolidated balance sheet. (Notice that there is no goodwill reported on the balance sheets of Pentz or Sahtlam. The Goodwill appears only on the consolidated balance sheet.)

- Column 3 is the consolidated balance sheet.

The purchase of Sahtlam does not affect its income statement in the year ended June 30, 2005. The purchase took place on the last day of Sahtlam's fiscal year, and the revenues and expenses of a subsidiary are incorporated into the consolidated income statement only after the date of the purchase. The income statement effects of consolidation are discussed in the next section.

The Consolidated Balance Sheet in Periods After a Subsidiary Is Purchased

The previous discussion addressed the accounting for a subsidiary on the date the subsidiary was purchased. Adjustments to the financial statements of the parent and its subsidiaries are required whenever consolidated financial statements are prepared. The assets and liabilities that were reported on a subsidiary's balance sheet when it was purchased by the parent continue to be reported at their fair value on the date of the purchase, less any amortization. As long as a subsidiary has assets and liabilities that were on hand when the subsidiary was purchased, the adjustments for differences between the date of purchase book values and fair values of those assets are required. Also, the Investment in Subsidiary account on the parent's balance sheet and the Shareholders' Equity accounts on the subsidiary's balance sheet must be eliminated whenever consolidated financial statements are prepared. In effect, the adjustments

Question for Consideration

When an entity purchases a subsidiary, the fair value of the subsidiary's assets and liabilities on the date the subsidiary is purchased are included in the consolidated balance sheet, not the amounts reported in the subsidiary's own balance sheet. Explain why this treatment is not a violation of the historical cost measurement convention.

Answer: Recording a subsidiary's assets and liabilities at their fair values in the consolidated balance sheet on the date the subsidiary was purchased is not a violation of the historical cost measurement convention because the subsidiary's assets and liabilities were purchased when the parent purchased the subsidiary. The purchase does not affect the subsidiary's balance sheet because the purchase transaction occurs between the parent and the previous owners of the subsidiary. That is why the amounts reported on the subsidiary's balance sheet are usually different from the amounts that are included in the consolidated balance sheet.

It is important to remember that assigning fair values to the assets and liabilities of a subsidiary occurs only once—when the subsidiary is actually purchased. The fair values assigned on the date the subsidiary is purchased form the basis of valuing those assets and liabilities in the consolidated financial statements from then on. If the fair values were determined each time consolidated financial statements were prepared, the historical cost measurement convention would be violated.

that were made on the date the subsidiary was purchased are repeated whenever consolidated financial statements are prepared, with some modifications.

But there's more. There are three other types of adjustments that have to be made:

- amortization of fair value adjustments
- possible write-down of goodwill
- elimination of the effects of intercompany transactions

These items will affect the consolidated income statement as well as the consolidated balance sheet. The consolidated income statement combines the revenues and expenses of the parent and its subsidiaries. That is, the revenues and expenses reported on the income statements of the parent and the subsidiaries are added together in the consolidated income statement, but with the three types of adjustments made. Each of the adjustments is discussed next.

It is important to recognize that the fair values of a subsidiary's assets and liabilities are not determined each time consolidated financial statements are prepared. Consolidated financial statements reflect the cost of a subsidiary's assets and liabilities on the date they are purchased. This treatment is no different than when an entity purchases an asset. The asset is recorded at its cost, which is also its market value on the date it is purchased, and the cost is the basis of valuation from then on. Assets and liabilities of the subsidiary that were incurred *after* the parent purchased the subsidiary do not require adjustment because the cost to the subsidiary and the cost to the parent are the same.

Amortization of Fair Value Adjustments   A subsidiary amortizes the cost of its capital assets over their useful lives. If Sahtlam were amortizing its $14,000,000 (see Table 12-2, page 723) of capital assets over ten years, it would report an amortization expense of $1,400,000 on its fiscal 2006 income statement. The problem is that Sahtlam's capital assets are reported in the consolidated financial statements at $21,500,000 ($14,000,000 + $7,500,000). The full cost of Sahtlam's capital assets as reported on the consolidated financial statements must be amortized, not just the portion that is reported in Sahtlam's financial statements. As a result, an additional

$750,000 ($7,500,000 ÷ 10 years) of amortization expense is required in the fiscal 2006 consolidated financial statements to amortize the $7,500,000 fair value adjustment.

Similarly, if the fair value of inventory on hand when the subsidiary was purchased is different from the cost of the inventory reported on the subsidiary's balance sheet, that difference must be expensed when the inventory is sold. That is, cost of sales on the subsidiary's income statement must be adjusted when preparing the consolidated income statement, so that the cost of inventory when the subsidiary was purchased is expensed. (That is, the cost of inventory to the parent as opposed to the subsidiary.) If the full amount of the difference between the book value and fair value of Sahtlam's current assets on June 30, 2005 were due to inventory, then when that inventory was sold consolidated cost of sales would have to be increased by the $500,000 difference.

Decline in the Value of Goodwill

As mentioned earlier, according to the *CICA Handbook*, goodwill does not have to be amortized. Management must regularly evaluate the company's goodwill and write it down if its value is somehow impaired. Writing down goodwill means that if it is determined that the goodwill is impaired, the amount of goodwill on the consolidated balance sheet must be reduced and the amount of the reduction expensed on the consolidated income statement.

Intercompany Transactions

An important and useful feature of how subsidiaries are accounted for is that **intercompany transactions**—transactions among the corporations in a consolidated group—are eliminated when consolidated financial statements are prepared. This means that sales and expenses, and changes in the value of assets and liabilities that occur as a result of transactions among subsidiaries and with the parent, are not reflected in the consolidated statements. Transactions that take place among the entities in a consolidated group are recorded in the accounting systems of the individual corporations, but from the perspective of the consolidated entity, these transactions have no economic significance. Only transactions with entities external to the consolidated group have economic significance. After all, has there been a change in wealth of the consolidated entity if a subsidiary sells merchandise to its parent at a profit? If sales among entities in a corporate group are not eliminated, sales and expenses in the consolidated income statement will be overstated, and receivables, inventory, and payables on the balance sheet may be overstated.

Let's use an example to examine the effect on the consolidated financial statements of sales by a subsidiary to its parent. Seech Inc. (Seech) is a 100%-owned subsidiary of Pitaga Ltd. (Pitaga). During the year ended December 31, 2005, Seech sold merchandise costing $2,000,000 to Pitaga for $4,500,000. These were the only transactions that Pitaga and Seech entered into during 2005. Seech recorded the sale with the following journal entries:

Dr. Accounts receivable (asset +)	4,500,000	
Cr. Revenue (revenue +, shareholders' equity +)		4,500,000
To record the sale of merchandise to Pitaga.		
Dr. Cost of sales (expense +, shareholders' equity –)	2,000,000	
Cr. Inventory (asset –)		2,000,000
To record the cost of the merchandise sold to Pitaga.		

Pitaga recorded its purchase of the merchandise from Seech with the following journal entry:

Dr. Inventory (asset +)	4,500,000	
Cr. Accounts payable (liability +)		4,500,000
To record the purchase of merchandise from Seech.		

Notice the effect of this transaction. Seech has earned a profit of $2,500,000 ($4,500,000 − $2,000,000) and the inventory it sold to Pitaga is now valued at $4,500,000 on Pitaga's balance sheet. There are receivables and payables of $4,500,000. In the context of historical cost, transactions-based accounting and from the view of the consolidated group, nothing has happened to justify reporting the profit and the increase in the value of inventory. From the perspective of the consolidated entity, this is no different from recognizing a profit, increasing the value of inventory, and reporting payables and receivables when moving goods from one warehouse to another.

Table 12-3 sets out the effect of intercompany transactions between Pitago and Seech:

- Column 1 shows the summarized income statements and extracts from the balance sheets of the two companies.

- Column 2 shows Pitaga's consolidated financial statements if the intercompany transactions are not eliminated. From the information in Column 2, consolidated Pitaga appears to be an active, perhaps successful enterprise with sales of $4,500,000 and net income of $2,500,000. It is not possible to tell from these statements that no real economic activity has occurred.

- Column 3 shows the consolidated statements if the intercompany transactions are eliminated. These statements show no activity: no revenues, no expenses, inventory reported at its cost to Seech, and no receivables or payables.

Because the transactions between Pitaga and Seech do not have economic significance to the consolidated entity, intercompany transactions are eliminated when the consolidated financial statements are prepared. Imagine the effect if Pitaga and Seech sold the same items back and forth many times. Sales and inventory would be huge, but would the transactions have any economic significance?

Now let's suppose that Pitaga sold the inventory it purchased from Seech to third parties for $6,200,000 during 2005, instead of having it on hand at the end of the year. Pitaga would make the following journal entries to record the sale:

Dr. Accounts receivable (asset +)	6,200,000	
Cr. Revenue (revenue +, shareholders' equity +)		6,200,000
To record the sale of merchandise to customers.		
Dr. Cost of sales (expense +, shareholders' equity −)	4,500,000	
Cr. Inventory (asset −)		4,500,000
To record the cost of the merchandise sold to customers.		

Once the inventory has been sold to a third party, problems with intercompany transactions still exist. The consolidated financial statements should reflect only the effect of transactions with entities external to the consolidated entity. This means that only sales of merchandise to third parties by Pitaga and the cost of the merchandise to the consolidated entity, which is the cost that Seech originally incurred, should be recorded. This means that the effects of the sale by Seech to Pitaga still have to be eliminated.

The summarized income statements and extracts from the balance sheets of Pitaga and Seech and the consolidated information under this scenario are provided in Table 12-4. The inventory is no longer an issue because it has been sold. The accounts receivable and payable that were recorded when Seech sold the merchandise to Pitaga still have to be eliminated until they are actually settled by the two companies; otherwise, receivables and payables will be overstated. The only receivable that should appear on the consolidated statements is the amount owed by the third party customers ($6,200,000). The revenue recorded by Seech from the sale to Pitaga still must be eliminated. Otherwise, the sale of the inventory appears twice—once when it was sold to Pitaga and once when Pitaga sold it to the third parties.

Table 12-3 The Effect of Intercompany Transactions: Scenario 1 (Seech Sells Merchandise to Pitaga—Merchandise Held by Pitaga at the End of the Year)

	Column 1		Column 2	Column 3
	Accounting Information for the Year Ended and As of December 31, 2005		Consolidated Statements (intercompany transactions not eliminated)	Consolidated Statements (intercompany transactions eliminated)
	Pitaga Ltd.	Seech Inc.		
Revenue	$ 0	$4,500,000	$4,500,000	$ 0
Cost of Sales	0	2,000,000	2,000,000	0
Net Income	$ 0	$2,500,000	$2,500,000	$ 0
Accounts Receivable	0	$4,500,000	$4,500,000	$0
Inventory	$4,500,000	0	$2,500,000	$2,000,000
Accounts Payable	$4,500,000	0	$4,500,000	$0

Columns 2 and 3 of Table 12-4 provide a comparison of the financial statement impact of not eliminating (Column 2) and eliminating (Column 3) the effects of the intercompany transactions. Column 3 shows only the effect of transactions with outside entities. Revenue is only revenue earned from third parties. Cost of sales reflects only the cost of the merchandise to the consolidated entity ($2,000,000). If intercompany transactions are not eliminated, Column 2 in Table 12-4 is the result. Revenues, cost of sales, accounts receivable, and accounts payable are all overstated because of the effects of intercompany transactions. The entity looks much more active than it really is when intercompany transactions are not eliminated. Clearly, from the perspective of the consolidated entity, Column 3 is a better representation of its economic activity than is Column 2.

These examples highlight the effect that intercompany transactions can have on the numbers that appear in financial statements, and the difficulties that can be created for users who want to interpret and analyze the information in the financial statements if intercompany transactions are not eliminated. Fortunately, under GAAP intercompany transactions must be eliminated. When the financial statements of a subsidiary are being examined (that is, not the consolidated financial statements), it is important to be aware that intercompany transactions can have a significant effect on those financial statements.

Table 12-4 The Effect of Intercompany Transactions: Scenario 2 (Pitaga Sells Inventory Purchased from Seech to Third Parties)

	Column 1		Column 2	Column 3
	Accounting Information for the Year Ended and As of December 31, 2005		Consolidated Statements (intercompany transactions not eliminated)	Consolidated Statements (intercompany transactions eliminated)
	Pitaga Ltd.	Seech Inc.		
Revenue	$6,200,000	$4,500,000	$10,700,000	$6,200,000
Cost of Sales	4,500,000	2,000,000	6,500,000	2,000,000
Net Income	$1,700,000	$2,500,000	4,200,000	$4,200,000
Accounts Receivable	$6,200,000	$4,500,000	$10,700,000	$6,200,000
Accounts Payable	$4,500,000		$ 4,500,000	$ 0

Question for Consideration

Explain why including intercompany transactions in consolidated financial statements can make those statements misleading to users of the statements.

Answer: If intercompany transactions are not eliminated from consolidated financial statements, a number of problems exist that can mislead users.

1. Revenue from sales by one member of the consolidated entity to another will be included in the consolidated revenue reported on the income statement. This will overstate the economic activity of the entity, making it appear that the entity is generating more revenue than it really is.

2. If an entity that purchased inventory from another entity in the consolidated group still owns the inventory at the end of the period, that inventory will be valued at the price in the internal transaction. If the inventory was sold internally at a profit, the effect is to increase the value of the inventory on the balance sheet, which violates the historical cost measurement convention of GAAP. While there may be merit to changing the value of inventory, this is not usually done when statements are prepared in accordance with GAAP. As a result, a user who is assuming that GAAP's concepts are being followed could be misled.

3. If the transactions between the corporations in the consolidated entity are not settled in cash, receivables and payables will be increased by the amounts owing between the entities, thereby overstating current assets and liabilities.

4. As a result of the effects in (1) to (3), financial ratios will be distorted from the amounts that would be reported if intercompany transactions were eliminated.

Non-Controlling Interest

When a parent owns less than 100% of the shares of a subsidiary, but still controls it, accounts called "Non-controlling Interest" (or Minority Interest) are reported in the consolidated financial statements. Non-controlling Interest accounts appear because of how the *CICA Handbook* requires parent corporations to account for subsidiaries that are less than 100% owned. The *CICA Handbook* requires that the consolidated balance sheet include 100% of the book values of the subsidiary's assets and liabilities, even if the parent owns less than 100% of those assets and liabilities. The *CICA Handbook* also requires that the consolidated income statement report 100% of the revenues and expenses of a subsidiary.

The rationale for this approach is that since the parent controls 100% of the subsidiary's net assets, even if it doesn't own 100% of them, the consolidated statements should report what is under the parent's control. The problem with this approach is that the consolidated statements contain assets, liabilities, revenues, and expenses that do not belong to the parent's shareholders. If these amounts are going to be included in the consolidated financial statements, then what is to be done with the portions that are not owned by the parent's shareholders?

The answer is non-controlling interest. **Non-controlling interest** on the balance sheet represents the net assets of a subsidiary that are owned by the shareholders of the subsidiary other than the parent. Non-controlling interest on the income statement represents the portion of net income of the consolidated entity that belongs to the shareholders of subsidiaries other than the parent.

For example, on January 31, 2004, Padlei Ltd. (Padlei) purchased 80% of the common shares of Schyan Inc. (Schyan) for $800,000 cash. On January 31, 2004, Schyan's balance sheet reported net assets of $1,000,000 and on that date the book value of the net assets equalled their fair value. Table 12-5 (page 730) shows how this transaction affects the consolidated balance sheet.

Notice that net assets on the consolidated balance sheet are $6,500,000, which

Question for Consideration

The summarized income statements for Pentz Ltd. and Sahtlam Corp. for the fiscal year ended June 30, 2006 are shown below. (This question builds on the example of Pentz and Sahtlam used on pages 719–723.)

Summarized Income Statements
For the Year Ended June 30, 2006

	Pentz Ltd.	Sahtlam Corp.
Revenue	$21,000,000	$ 5,000,000
Expenses	12,000,000	14,000,000
Net income	$ 9,000,000	$ 2,000,000

Required: Consider the following information and prepare the summarized consolidated income statement for fiscal 2006.

i. During fiscal 2006, Sahtlam sold merchandise to Pentz for $250,000. Sahtlam had paid $110,000 for the merchandise. At the end of 2006, Pentz had sold none of the merchandise.

ii. Sahtlam reports capital assets of $14,000,000 on its balance sheet. This amount is being amortized on a straight-line basis over the next 10 years. These assets are reported on the consolidated balance sheet at $21,500,000. The fair value adjustment is also being amortized on a straight-line basis over the next ten years.

iii. At the end of fiscal 2006, management determined that the goodwill that was recorded when Pentz purchased Sahtlam was impaired and had to be written down by $400,000.

iv. During fiscal 2006, Sahtlam sold all of the inventory that was on hand when it was purchased on June 30, 2005. The difference between the cost of the inventory to Sahtlam and its fair value on June 30, 2005 was $500,000 (which was the full difference between the fair value and book value of Sahtlam's current assets on June 30, 2005).

Answer: This is a difficult question. It shows how the adjustments described above affect the consolidated income statement.

Summarized Income Statements
For the Year Ended June 30, 2006

	Pentz Ltd.	Sahtlam Corp.	Adjustments	Consolidated Income Statement
Revenue	$21,000,000	$5,000,000	−$250,000[1]	$25,750,000
Expenses	12,000,000	3,000,000	−110,000[2]	16,540,000
			+750,000[3]	
			+400,000[4]	
			+500,000[5]	
Net income	$ 9,000,000	$2,000,000		$ 9,210,000

[1] Eliminates revenue recognized by Sahtlam on intercompany sale of merchandise to Pentz.

[2] Eliminates cost of intercompany sale of merchandise by Sahtlam to Pentz.

[3] Records additional amortization expense for amortization of fair value adjustment to capital assets ([$21,500,000 − $14,000,000] ÷ 10 years).

[4] Records the write-down of goodwill.

[5] Records the additional expense for cost of inventory sold that is required because the fair value of inventory on the date Sahtlam was purchased was greater than the cost reported on Sahtlam's balance sheet.

includes the $1,000,000 of Schyan's net assets, even though Padlei's interest in those net assets is only $800,000 ($1,000,000 × 80%). The other $200,000 is the net assets that belong to the non-controlling shareholders of Schyan ($1,000,000 × 20%). The consolidated balance sheet is reporting 100% of the net assets that the parent controls, not just the 80% that the parent owns. The non-controlling interest represents the

Table 12-5   The Effect of Non-Controlling Interest: Scenario 1 (Book Value of Subsidiary's Net Assets Equals Their Cost on the Date the Subsidiary Is Purchased)

	Summarized Balance Sheets As of January 31, 2004		Adjustments	Summarized Consolidated Balance Sheet As of January 31, 2004
	Padlei Ltd	Schyan Inc.		
Net assets	$5,500,000	$1,000,000		$6,500,000
Investment in Schyan (at cost)	800,000		−800,000	0
Non-controlling shareholders' interest in consolidated Padlei's net assets			+200,000	200,000
Shareholders' equity	6,300,000	1,000,000	−1,000,000	6,300,000

equity that Schyan's shareholders have in Padlei's consolidated net assets. The Non-controlling Interest account appears on the liabilities and shareholders' equity side of the balance sheet.

Perhaps surprisingly, the amount reported for non-controlling interest on the balance sheet is not affected if the market value of the subsidiary's net assets is not the same as their book value on the date a subsidiary is purchased. The reason is that GAAP allows only the parent's share of the fair value adjustments and goodwill to appear on the consolidated balance sheet. The non-controlling interest on the balance sheet is simply the book value of the non-controlling shareholders' interest in the net assets of the subsidiary.

The result is that a consolidated balance sheet includes a potentially confusing mix of measurements—100% of the book value of a subsidiary's net assets (the parent's and the non-controlling interest's share), plus the parent's share of the difference between fair value and book value. The rationale for this treatment is an application of the historical cost measurement convention. Since only the parent's share of the subsidiary has been purchased, only the parent's share of the fair value is recorded.

Returning to the Padlei–Schyan example, suppose that the market value of Schyan's net assets were $1,125,000 and Padlei paid $900,000 for its 80% interest ($1,125,000 × 80%) in Schyan (assume no goodwill). The consolidated balance sheet would include 100% of the book value of Schyan's net assets ($1,000,000—the

Table 12-6   The Effect of Non-Controlling Interest: Scenario 2 (Fair Value of Subsidiary's Net Assets Greater than Their Cost on the Date the Subsidiary is Purchased))

	Summarized Balance Sheets As of January 31, 2004		Adjustments	Summarized Consolidated Balance Sheet As of January 31, 2004
	Padlei Ltd	Schyan Inc.		
Net assets	$5,400,000	$1,000,000	+$100,000	$6,500,000
Investment in Schyan (at cost)	900,000		−900,000	
Non-controlling shareholders' interest in consolidated Padlei's net assets			+200,000	200,000
Shareholders' equity	6,300,000	1,000,000	−1,000,000	6,300,000

amount on Schyan's balance sheet) plus 80% of the difference between the fair value and book value of Schyan's net assets on the date the subsidiary was purchased— $100,000 ([$1,125,000 – $1,000,000] × 80%). The non-controlling interest would still be $200,000 ($1,000,000 × 20%) because only the parent's share of the difference between the fair value and book value of the net assets is included in the consolidated balance sheet. Therefore, the non-controlling shareholders' equity in Padlei's net assets is $200,000.

The effects of this situation are shown in Table 12-6. As we will discuss next, non-controlling interest does change over time, reflecting the non-controlling shareholders' share of consolidated net income.

Now let's look at the income statement. The summarized income statements of Padlei and Schyan and the summarized consolidated income statement for fiscal 2005 are shown in Table 12-7. Notice that 100% of Schyan's revenues and expenses are included in the consolidated income statement, even though 20% of those revenues and expenses belong to the non-controlling interest. Remember that net income is a measure of the change in wealth of the owners of an entity—in this case the owners of Padlei. The $50,000 ($250,000 × 20%) of Schyan's net income that belongs to Schyan's non-controlling interest should not be included in Padlei's consolidated net income because it doesn't belong to the owners of Padlei. If it were included, Padlei's consolidated net income would be overstated. There would be $50,000 in net income that belonged to others. Therefore, $50,000 is deducted in the calculation of consolidated net income.

The amount deducted not only reduces consolidated net income, it also increases the balance in the non-controlling interest account on the balance sheet. The reason is that the non-controlling interest's equity in the consolidated entity's net assets has increased by $50,000. The non-controlling interest account on the consolidated balance sheet can be thought of as the non-controlling interest's equity in the consolidated entity's net assets.

The non-controlling interest appears on the consolidated balance sheet between liabilities and shareholders' equity. Non-controlling interest is equity, but it is the equity of the non-controlling shareholders of the subsidiaries, not the equity of the parent's shareholders. It is not a liability because there is no obligation to anyone.

On the consolidated income statement, non-controlling interest appears as a deduction in the calculation of consolidated net income.

On the consolidated cash flow statement, the non-controlling interest reported on the consolidated income statement is added back to net income when calculating

Table 12-7   Non-Controlling Interest and the Income Statement

	Summarized Income Statement For the Year Ended January 31, 2005		Consolidated Income Statement For the Year Ended January 31, 2005
	Padlei Ltd.	**Schyan Inc.**	
Revenues	$1,000,000	$750,000	$1,750,000
Expenses	700,000	500,000	1,200,000
Income before non-controlling interest			550,000
Non-controlling interest			(50,000)*
Net Income	$ 300,000	$250,000	$ 500,000

* The non-controlling interest's share of Padlei's net income is equal to 20% of Schyan Inc.'s net income ($250,000 × 20%).

cash from operations using the indirect method. The non-controlling interest is added back because it does not represent cash distributed to the non-controlling shareholders—it is the allocation of income to the non-controlling shareholders.

The amount of cash within the consolidated entity is not affected by the deduction of non-controlling interest on the income statement. Cash is affected only when a dividend is paid to the shareholders.

Let's look at an example. As we discussed earlier, Onex Corporation (Onex) does not own 100% of any of its subsidiaries. Onex's consolidated balance sheets, consolidated income statements, and the operating activities section from its consolidated statement of cash flows are shown in Exhibit 12-2.[2] Notice how non-controlling interest is reported on each of these statements. (In contrast, MWW does not report non-controlling interest on its balance sheet or income statement because it owns 100% of all its subsidiaries.)

One final remark: Non-controlling interest appears in consolidated financial statements only because GAAP require that 100% of a subsidiary's net assets, revenues, and expenses be reported even if the parent owns less than 100% of the subsidiary. If GAAP required that only the parent's share of the subsidiary's net assets, revenues, and expenses be included, there would be no non-controlling interest.

Exhibit 12-2
Onex Corporation: Non-Controlling Interest

Consolidated Balance Sheets

As at December 31 *(in millions of dollars)*	2000	1999
Assets		
Current assets		
Cash and short-term investments	$ 2,229	$ 1,023
Accounts receivable	4,071	2,319
Inventories (note 4)	3,036	1,409
Other current assets	718	489
	10,054	5,240
Capital assets (note 5)	3,267	2,159
Investments and other assets (note 6)	1,221	861
Goodwill and intangible assets (note 7)	5,177	4,153
	$ 19,719	$ 12,413
Liabilities and Shareholders' Equity		
Current liabilities		
Bank indebtedness. Without recourse to Onex	$ 48	$ 34
Accounts payable and accrued liabilities	5,395	3,109
Current portion of long-term debt and obligations under capital leases of subsidiaries. Without recourse to Onex	400	173
	5,843	3,316
Long-term debt of subsidiaries. Without recourse to Onex (note 8)	4,864	4,111
Obligations under capital leases. Without recourse to Onex (note 9)	98	82
Exchangeable debentures (note 10)	746	–
Future income taxes (note 16)	481	411
Other liabilities	583	405
	12,615	8,325
Non-controlling interests	5,673	2,810
Shareholders' equity	1,431	1,278
	$ 19,719	$ 12,413

Exhibit 12-2 (continued)

Onex Corporation: Non-Controlling Interest

Consolidated Statements of Earnings

Year ended December 31 (in millions of dollars)	2000	1999
Revenues	$ 24,531	$ 14,869
Earnings Before the Undernoted Items	$ 1,612	$ 1,025
Amortization of capital assets	(458)	(266)
Amortization of goodwill, intangible assets and deferred charges	(322)	(206)
Interest expense of operating companies (note 12)	(506)	(320)
Interest and other income	134	62
Gains on shares of operating companies, net (note 3)	252	514
	712	809
Acquisition, integration and other expenses (note 13)	(43)	(60)
Debt prepayment costs (note 14)	(3)	(19)
Writedown of goodwill and intangible assets by operating companies (note 15)	(22)	(33)
Earnings before income taxes and non-controlling interests	644	697
Provision for income taxes (note 16)	(197)	(272)
Earnings before non-controlling interests	447	425
Non-controlling interests in results of operating companies	(259)	(131)
Net Earnings for the Year	$ 188	$ 294

Earnings per Subordinate Voting Share are reported in note 17.

Consolidated Statements of Cash Flows

Year ended December 31 (in millions of dollars)	2000	1999
Operating Activities		
Net earnings	$ 188	$ 294
Items not affecting cash:		
Amortization of capital assets	458	266
Amortization of goodwill and intangible assets	314	195
Amortization of deferred charges	8	11
Writedown of goodwill and intangible assets by operating companies	22	33
Non-controlling interests in results of operating companies	259	131
Future income taxes	(22)	116
Gains on shares of operating companies, net (note 3)	(252)	(514)
Other	(44)	7
	931	539
Decrease in other liabilities	(30)	(80)
Increase in non-cash net working capital related to operations	(898)	(422)
	3	37

Question for Consideration

Paisly Inc. (Paisly) recently purchased 65% of the shares of Sackville Ltd. (Sackville). Paisly will be accounting for Sackville as a subsidiary. Among the assets that Sackville reported on its balance sheet on the date of its purchase by Paisly was land valued at $2,400,000. Management determined that the fair value of the land on the date Paisly purchased Sackville was $4,000,000.

According to GAAP, what amount would be reported on Paisly's consolidated balance sheet for the land? Explain the rationale an accountant would give for this treatment.

Answer: Paisly would report $3,440,000 for the land on its consolidated balance sheet. According to GAAP, 100% of the book value of a subsidiary's assets and liabilities, plus the parent's share of the fair value adjustment, appears on the consolidated balance sheet. As a result, Paisly's consolidated balance sheet would include 100% of the book value of the land

(continued)

Are Consolidated Financial Statements Useful?

Now that we have looked at the basics of accounting for subsidiaries (which aren't all that basic!), we can consider the usefulness of consolidated financial statements. Consolidated statements provide, in a single set of financial statements, financial information about a group of corporations that are under the control of a parent—a single economic entity. This information might be useful to users who want stewardship information about the entire economic entity, or to evaluate the performance of the corporate group as a whole. Consolidated financial statements may be an effective way for a corporate group to communicate the "big picture" to various stakeholders. Since the parent company controls its subsidiaries, the parent is able to move assets from corporation to corporation and control the operations of the subsidiaries. For example, a parent company that is short of cash could have a subsidiary declare a dividend, make a loan, or pay management fees to the parent to help it meet its cash needs. Consolidated statements allow users to see the resources that are under the management of the entire corporate group.

Consolidated financial statements eliminate intercompany transactions and profits. Intercompany transactions and profits can be misleading because they misstate the real economic activity and performance of the consolidated group. Transactions within a consolidated group do not have any economic significance from the perspective of the parent—such transactions are equivalent to moving money from one pocket to another. A parent could improve its reported economic performance or financial position, or that of a subsidiary, by ordering transactions between companies in the consolidated group (perhaps transactions that are not required), or by dictating the terms of these transactions. The financial statements of the individual corporations in a consolidated group do not eliminate intercompany transactions, whereas consolidated statements do not report them.

For many users, however, consolidated financial statements are an obstacle to effective decision making because they aggregate information about the individual corporations in the consolidated group. The details about the different businesses that a parent and its subsidiaries are engaged in are lost in consolidated financial statements. It is virtually impossible to determine, by examining consolidated financial statements, which companies, lines of business, and geographical areas in a consolidated group are doing well and which are doing poorly.

Consolidated statements alone do not serve the interests of users such as financial analysts and other sophisticated users who want to use historical accounting information as a starting point for predicting future earnings or cash flows. For example, consolidated financial statements can significantly limit the usefulness of ratio analysis. By combining the accounting information of several companies, often companies in different industries, ratios will not be representative of any industry. For example, what sense can be made of Onex Corporation's inventory turnover ratio, when inventory and cost of sales relate to companies in industries as different as electronics manufacturing, catering, automotive products, and building products?

The aggregation problem can be mitigated if the financial statements of the individual companies in a consolidated group are available in addition to the consolidated statements. The financial statements of corporations in a consolidated group are available under some circumstances. A subsidiary's annual report would be available if its shares that are not controlled by the parent are publicly traded. Also, a powerful user could request and obtain the financial statements of a subsidiary from the subsidiary itself. A shareholder of a subsidiary, whether public or private, is entitled to receive the subsidiary's financial statements, regardless of whether it is controlled by a parent. Outside these situations, a user will not have access to the financial statements of the subsidiaries in the consolidated group.

GAAP attempt to assist users by requiring public companies to provide information about the different business activities and the different economic environments in which they operate. The disaggregation of information by types of products and services, geographic location, and major customers is called **segment disclosure**.

MWW provides segment disclosure in Note 18 to its financial statements (see page A-63). MWW operates in the retail clothing and footwear business, and segments its information by division (Mark's, Work World, and DOCKERS). The sales information is for all stores—corporate and franchise—whereas the remaining information is for only MWW itself. Notice that complete financial statements are not provided for each segment. MWW probably could have avoided providing segment information by defining itself simply as a clothing and footwear retailer. Managers do have some flexibility in defining the segments they report, and as a result can influence what information is provided to users and its level of detail.

The segment information of BCE Inc. (BCE) for 2000 is shown in Exhibit 12-3.[3] BCE reports four operating segments, plus a segment for non-core businesses. Again, complete financial statements are not provided for each segment. Indeed, no balance sheet or cash flow information is provided at all by BCE. The sum of the revenue of the individual segments ($18,747,000,000) is actually greater than the total revenue reported on the income statement ($18,094,000,000). The reason is that there are sales among entities in the different segments—that is, there were intercompany transactions. These revenues are eliminated in the reconciliation that is shown at the bottom of Exhibit 12-3. Similarly, the total earnings from continuing operations of the individual segments ($679,000,000) is significantly different from the earnings from continuing operations reported on the consolidated income statement ($886,000,000). This difference is also reconciled at the bottom of Exhibit 12-3.

www.bce.ca

For some users, consolidated financial statements, even with segment information, are not adequate for their needs. For lenders, consolidated financial statements and segment disclosure are not useful because loans are made to legal entities, not to consolidated ones. A lender will be concerned about the ability of the legal entity that borrowed the money to repay a loan. Consolidated financial statements do not provide information about individual subsidiaries, and segment disclosure provides information about business segments, not necessarily about separate corporations. Only if a loan is being made to the parent, or if the parent is guaranteeing a loan to a subsidiary, would the lender be interested in the consolidated statements. Otherwise, a lender needs the financial statements of the corporation actually borrowing the money.

Consolidated financial statements are of little interest to the non-controlling shareholders and other stakeholders of a subsidiary. The consolidated statements are intended for stakeholders of the consolidated entity. The non-controlling interest on the consolidated statements provides little useful information to users who are inter-

2. SEGMENTED INFORMATION

Effective December 1, 2000, BCE centres its activities around four operating businesses: a) **Bell Canada**: This segment provides an integrated platform of substantially domestic telecommunications services including voice, data, wireline, wireless and directory communications and satellite entertainment to Canadian customers; b) **Bell Globemedia**: This segment provides integrated information, communications and entertainment services to Canadian customers and access to distinctive Canadian content that allows the creation of unique destinations for Internet users through the various portal properties; c) **Teleglobe**: This segment provides, on a world-wide basis, a broad portfolio of voice, data and Internet services, including connectivity services, to Internet service providers, Internet content providers, application service providers, carriers and global enterprises; d) **BCE Emergis**: This segment provides business to business (B2B) e-commerce infrastructures, strategically focusing on market leadership in the transaction-intensive eHealth and financial services sectors, through its three strategic business units (eHealth, Canadian and U.S.), e) All other non-core businesses are combined in a new group called **BCE Ventures**.

BCE Ventures – reflects BCE's interests in Bell Canada International Inc. (BCI), Telesat Canada (Telesat), CGI Group Inc. (CGI), Excel Communications Inc., acquired as part of the Teleglobe Inc. acquisition (Note 3) and other BCE investments.

The Corporation evaluates each segment's performance based on its contribution to consolidated net earnings. The accounting policies of the segments are the same as those described in Note 1, Significant Accounting Policies. Inter-segment sales are negotiated on arm's length terms. The following tables present summarized financial information for the years ended December 31, 2000 and 1999:

GEOGRAPHIC INFORMATION [i]

	2000		1999	
	Revenues from external customers	Capital assets & goodwill	Revenues from external customers	Capital assets & goodwill
Canada	16,124	25,372	13,129	16,774
United States	1,646	12,541	139	157
Other foreign countries	324	692	946	2,412
Total	18,094	38,605	14,214	19,343

[i] The point of origin (the location of the selling organization) of revenues and the location of capital assets and goodwill determine the geographic areas.

BUSINESS SEGMENTS

	Bell Canada	Bell Globemedia [iii]	Teleglobe [iv]	BCE Emergis	BCE Ventures
2000					
Total revenues	15,791	98	326	468	2,064
Interest income	14	1	4	6	23
Interest expense	1,028	4	39	36	442
Depreciation and amortization	2,829	7	84	346	385
Equity in net earnings (losses) of significantly influenced companies	3	15	(122)	–	(9)
Income tax expense	1,241	7	(57)	6	104
Earnings (losses) from continuing operations [i]	994	(78)	(237)	(209)	209
1999					
Total revenues	12,716	3	–	188	1,810
Interest income	18	–	–	4	59
Interest expense	793	–	–	1	510
Depreciation and amortization	2,810	–	–	86	303
Equity in net earnings (losses) of significantly influenced companies	52	–	–	–	(11)
Income tax expense	880	116	–	–	–
Earnings (losses) from continuing operations [i]	1,024	–	–	(69)	(306)
Other significant non-cash items:					
– Gain on reduction of ownership in a significantly influenced company	–	–	–	–	69
– Restructuring and other charges	345	–	–	–	113

RECONCILIATIONS

Revenues	2000	1999
Total revenues for reportable segments	18,747	14,717
Corporate and other (including elimination of inter-segment revenues) [ii]	(653)	(503)
Total consolidated revenues	18,094	14,214
Net earnings		
Total earnings from continuing operations for reportable segments	679	649
Corporate and other (including elimination of inter-segment earnings)	207	4,420
Earnings from continuing operations	886	5,069
Discontinued operations (Note 8)	3,975	390
Net earnings	4,861	5,459
Other significant non-cash items in corporate and other (including elimination of inter-segment earnings)		
– Gain on reduction of ownership in a subsidiary company	–	4,242

[i] Represents each segment's contribution to BCE's net earnings.
[ii] The majority of inter-segment revenues were between Bell Canada and Nortel Networks in 1999 and up to May 2000.
[iii] CTV is consolidated effective December 1, 2000.
[iv] Includes unallocated corporate expenses. Teleglobe is consolidated effective November 1, 2000.

Exhibit 12-3

BCE Inc.: Segmented Reporting

ested in subsidiaries. The non-controlling shareholders and other stakeholders in the subsidiary would want to see the financial statements of the subsidiary itself. The shareholders in the subsidiaries are entitled to receive financial statements of the subsidiaries in which they own shares.

Consolidated financial statements are not relevant for tax purposes. Each individual corporation is required to file tax returns with the Canada Customs and Revenue Agency and provincial taxation authorities. This means that each corporation must prepare financial statements for tax purposes regardless of who owns it.

Accounting for subsidiaries provides managers with significant opportunities to make choices that will influence the consolidated financial statements for many years. When a new subsidiary is acquired, the fair values of the assets and liabilities must be determined. A subsidiary is a bundle of assets and liabilities purchased for a single price, so the exact price paid for individual assets and liabilities is not known. Management must allocate the purchase price of the subsidiary to individual assets and liabilities and to goodwill. Because the process of assigning market values is imprecise, management can make choices that help it satisfy its reporting objectives. Different preparers could come up with very different reasonable amounts of goodwill for the same acquisition and different reasonable valuations for the identifiable assets and liabilities. Because goodwill does not have to be amortized, managers who are concerned about net income might allocate less of the purchase price to amortizable assets and inventory so that more would be included in goodwill.

Purchasing Assets Instead of Shares

In this chapter, the focus has been on situations where one corporation buys the shares of another corporation. However, purchasing shares is not the only way that a corporation can buy another business. An investor corporation can also buy another business's assets. These could be the assets of a corporation, partnership, or proprietorship.

The purchase of the assets of an entire business is accounted for in the same way as any purchase of assets—the assets are recorded at their cost. The accounting is a bit more complicated because instead of a single asset being purchased, all the assets that comprise the business are acquired. As was discussed in Chapter 9, when a basket of assets is purchased, the purchase price must be allocated to the individual assets in the basket. If the amount paid for the assets was greater than the fair value of the identifiable assets on the date of the purchase, goodwill would be recorded. However, goodwill arises only if the assets of an entire business are purchased.

The purchase of the assets of a business does not require the preparation of consolidated financial statements. If the assets being purchased are included among the assets of the investor corporation, consolidated financial statements are not required because there is no subsidiary corporation to consolidate.

Whether to buy the assets or shares of another corporation is a complex decision. One of the main factors that must be considered is tax. Tax issues affect the buyer and the seller, and the ultimate terms of the purchase are the result of negotiations. One advantage of purchasing the assets is that the investor corporation does not acquire any unknown liabilities, such as lawsuits that have not yet been launched. Finally, when assets are purchased there are no issues regarding the influence the purchaser has. The purchaser has 100% control of the purchased assets.

Significant Influence

When a corporation has significant influence on the decision making of another corporation as a result of its investment in that corporation, the *CICA Handbook* requires that the equity method of accounting be used. **Significant influence** means that the investor corporation can affect the strategic operating, investing, and financing decisions of the investee corporation, even though it does not have control.

The *CICA Handbook* suggests that owning between 20% and 50% of the votes of an investee company is an indication of significant influence. However, judgment must be used to determine whether significant influence exists in a particular situation. An investor corporation could own 30% of the voting shares of another company, but another investor could own more than 50% of the voting shares of that company and have control. In that case significant influence does not exist. On the other hand, even with an investment of less than 20%, an investor corporation may be able to exert significant influence if, for example, the investor corporation has representation on the investee corporation's board of directors.

The **equity method of accounting** is essentially the same as accounting for subsidiaries using the consolidation method. However, the information appears in the financial statements in a very different way. Unlike accounting for subsidiaries, where the financial statements of the parent and subsidiary are combined line by line, information about investments accounted for using the equity method is presented on a single line on the balance sheet and a single line on the income statement.

An investment accounted for using the equity method is initially recorded on the investor's balance sheet at cost. The balance sheet amount is then adjusted each period by the investor's share of the investee's net income, less dividends declared by the investee. The income statement reports the investor's share of the investee's net income. The investor's share is determined by multiplying the investee's net income by the percentage of the investee that the investor owns, and adjusting the investee's net income for amortization of differences between the fair value and book value of the investee's net assets (fair value adjustments), intercompany transactions, and write-downs of goodwill.

The rationale for the equity method is that if an investor corporation has significant influence, it can affect the important policies of the investee, such as the timing and amount of dividends. By being able to influence the timing and amount of the investee's dividends, an investor can manage its own earnings by having the investee declare dividends when the investor wants them. Since dividends from an investment in an investee corporation accounted for using the equity method are not considered income, this type of income manipulation is not available.

Let's examine an example to see how the equity method of accounting works. On September 30, 2005, Ozerna Inc. (Ozerna) purchased 30% of the voting shares of Hyndford Ltd. (Hyndford) for $5,000,000 cash. Ozerna is assumed to have significant influence over Hyndford. Ozerna and Hyndford both have September 30 year ends. Ozerna makes the following entry to record its investment in Hyndford:

Dr. Investment in Hyndford (assets +)	5,000,000	
Cr. Cash (assets –)		5,000,000
To record the investment in Hyndford Ltd.		

At the time of its investment in Hyndford, Ozerna determines the fair values of Hyndford's identifiable assets and liabilities and the amount of goodwill purchased. The fair values of the identifiable assets and liabilities and goodwill do not appear explicitly on Ozerna's financial statements, but they are needed to calculate the amount of income that Ozerna will recognize from its investment in Hyndford each year. Also, Ozerna does not consolidate Hyndford because it does not have control. Based on its analysis, Ozerna determines that the fair value of its 30% share of Hyndford's net assets is $4,200,000, which is $2,000,000 greater than their book value of $2,200,000, and that it purchased goodwill of $800,000.

On Ozerna's September 30, 2005 balance sheet, the date Ozerna purchased Hyndford, the investment in Hyndford would be reported on a single line at $5,000,000.

For its year ended September 30, 2006, Hyndford reported a net income of $3,000,000. Since Ozerna owns 30% of Hyndford, its share of Hyndford's reported net income is $900,000. However, this amount must be adjusted for the amortization of the fair value adjustment to the net assets, the elimination of intercompany transactions, and any write-down of goodwill. At the end of fiscal 2006, Ozerna's share of profits on intercompany transactions between Hyndford and Ozerna was $100,000. Also, Ozerna is amortizing the fair value adjustments over 10 years and goodwill must be written down by $150,000.

Therefore, the amount of income from its investment in Hyndford that Ozerna will report in its September 30, 2006 financial statements is:

Share of income as reported by Hyndford ($3,000,000 × 30%)		$900,000
Less: Amortization of fair value adjustments ($2,000,000 ÷ 10)		200,000
Profit on intercompany transactions		100,000
Write-down of goodwill		150,000
Adjusted income from Hyndford		$450,000

To reflect its share of Hyndford's earnings in its financial statements, Ozerna makes the following journal entry:

Dr. Investment in Hyndford (assets +)	450,000	
Cr. Investment income from Hyndford		450,000
(investment income +, shareholders' equity +)		
To record the income from Ozerna's		
equity investment in Hyndford.		

The book value of the Investment in Hyndford account on Ozerna's balance sheet increases by the amount of investment income recognized from Hyndford. If Hyndford suffered a loss during a year, Ozerna would recognize a loss on its income statement, and the balance sheet amount would be reduced by the amount of its share of the loss.

On September 30, 2006, Hyndford declared and paid a $1,000,000 dividend. Ozerna's share of the dividend is $300,000 ($1,000,000 × 30%). The journal entry that Ozerna makes to record the dividend from Hyndford is:

Dr. Cash (assets +)	300,000	
Cr. Investment in Hyndford (assets −)		300,000
To record the dividend received from Hyndford Ltd.		

The dividend reduces the Investment in Hyndford account on the balance sheet by $300,000. Typically, one would expect that receiving a dividend would be treated as income. However, under the equity method of accounting the amount of income recognized is based on the investee's net income. A dividend is a distribution of the wealth or equity of an entity. Since the Investment in Hyndford account represents Ozerna's equity in Hyndford, a dividend is a reduction in its equity and a conversion of Ozerna's equity in Hyndford into another asset, Cash.

On Ozerna's September 30, 2006 balance sheet, the Investment in Hyndford account would have a balance of $5,150,000 ($5,000,000 + $450,000 − $300,000).

A few points about the equity method of accounting are worth noting:

1. The adjustments made using the equity method are the same as those made when consolidated financial statements are prepared, except that the effect is summarized in a single line instead of on a line-by-line basis.

2. While an equity investment account changes to reflect the earnings of an investee and the dividends it declares, the amount reported on the balance sheet does not reflect the market value of the investment. The changes to the balance sheet amount are based on historical cost, transactions-based accounting, not on changes in the investee's market value. Just as the shareholders' equity section of an entity's balance sheet does not provide the market value of its shares, the amount reported on the balance sheet for an investment accounted for using the equity method does not represent the market value of the investment.

3. The income reported from an investment accounted for using the equity method is not an indication of the amount of dividends or cash that will be forthcoming from the investee. The amount of income recorded is simply an allocation of the investor's share of the investee's income. An equity investment may not be very liquid and the investor may be limited in its ability to obtain cash from the investee. A user who is interested in predicting cash flows would probably be

better served by looking at the dividends received from the investee corporation, rather than the amount of income accrued from it.

4. The equity investment account on the investor's balance sheet provides virtually no information about the investee corporation. Information about investments over which the investor has significant influence is not included in the segment disclosures described earlier in the chapter. If the investee corporation is public, the financial statements of the investee can be examined. If the investee is private, then little will be known about it.

Exhibit 12-4 shows how Trimac Corporation (Trimac) reports its investments accounted for using the equity method.[4] Trimac reports income from equity-accounted investments of $7,655,000. Trimac's balance sheet reports almost $180,000,000 of investments. Note 7 to Trimac's financial statements shows that about $46,000,000 of this amount is investments accounted for using the equity method while $134,000,000 is accounted for using the cost method. The top panel of Note 7 lists Trimac's equity accounted investments.

www.trimac.com

Exhibit 12-4

Trimac Corporation: Equity Accounting

Consolidated Balance Sheet

	December 31	
(thousands of dollars)	1998	1997
Assets		
Current Assets		
Cash and term deposits	$ 7,256	$ 4,912
Accounts receivable	69,021	67,052
Income taxes recoverable	—	1,626
Materials and supplies	7,519	6,993
Prepaid expenses	18,658	18,142
	102,454	98,725
Investments (Note 7)	179,965	255,639
Fixed Assets, Net (Note 9)	447,125	425,549
Goodwill (Note 10)	6,494	7,038
Other	309	1,199
	$ 736,347	$ 788,150

Consolidated Statement of Earnings

	Year ended December 31 (Note 1)	
(thousands of dollars except per share amounts)	1998	1997
Revenues	$ 607,658	$ 597,669
Operating Costs and Expenses		
Direct	404,780	401,956
Selling and administrative	86,898	82,685
Depreciation and amortization	86,137	79,825
Gain on sale of assets (net)	(8,767)	(5,365)
	569,048	559,101
Operating Earnings	38,610	38,568
Interest – long term debt	22,015	16,465
– other interest (net)	36	1,091
	22,051	17,556
Earnings Before Unusual Items	16,559	21,012
Unusual items - (loss) gain recognized on disposal or write down of investments (Note 6)	(36,067)	77,430
Earnings Before Taxes	(19,508)	98,442
Income tax (recovery) expense (Note 5)	(20,332)	47,688
Earnings Before Equity Accounted Investments	824	50,754
Equity accounted investments (Note 7)	7,655	9,393
Net Earnings	$ 8,479	$ 60,147

Exhibit 12-4 (continued)

Overview of an Accounting System

Consolidated Financial Statements   (tabular amounts in thousands of Canadian dollars)

Note 7 – Investments

The Corporation's share of net earnings from investments and the related carrying and market values at December 31 were as follows:

| | Year ended December 31 | | | | | |
| | 1998 | | | 1997 | | |
Equity accounted investments	Net earnings (loss)	Carrying value	Market value	Net earnings (loss)	Carrying value	Market value
BFC Construction Corporation	$ 3,334	$ 29,509	$ 17,904	$ 226	$ 26,175	$ 20,795
Bantrel Inc. (a)	2,018	2,682	2,682	1,025	2,264	2,264
BOVAR Inc. (b)	2,142	6,731	9,780	2,150	24,148	29,339
Chauvco Resources Ltd. (c)	—	—	—	5,133	—	—
CleanCare Corporation (d)	—	—	—	81	—	—
IITC Holdings Ltd. (e)	579	509	509	374	1,939	2,243
Taro Industries Limited (f)	—	—	—	404	7,409	7,409
Transportation Implementing Services Limited Partnership (g)	—	4,192	4,192	—	—	—
Other (h)	(418)	2,290	2,290	—	2,345	2,345
	$ 7,655	$ 45,913	$ 37,357	$ 9,393	$ 64,280	$ 64,395
Cost accounted investments						
Chauvco Resources International Ltd. (c)	$ —	$ —	$ —	$ —	$ 3,004	$ 8,248
Fort Chicago Energy Partners L.P. (c)	—	39,522	42,613	—	39,522	41,582
Intermap Technologies Ltd. (e)	—	—	—	—	2,276	2,914
Newalta Corporation	—	12,775	7,500	—	12,775	22,125
Pioneer Natural Resources Company (c)	—	76,865	66,470	—	133,782	140,710
Other (i)	—	4,890	4,890	—	—	—
	$ —	$ 134,052	$ 121,473	$ —	$ 191,359	$ 215,579
Total Investments	$ 7,655	$ 179,965	$ 158,830	$ 9,393	$ 255,639	$ 279,974

(Note: This example is a bit old, but it is used because it shows clearly how the equity accounting method works in an actual company's financial statement. Most other companies' disclosures of their equity investments are much less clear. Trimac become a private company in 2000.)

You can see the application of the equity method by examining how the book value of some of Trimac's investments changed from 1997 to 1998. For example, Bantrel Inc. had a book value of $2,264,000 at the end of 1997. (The term *carrying value* used in Trimac's financial statements has the same meaning as book value). In 1998 Trimac's share of Bantrel's net income was $2,018,000 and Trimac received $1,600,000 in dividends from Bantrel (the dividend information is available elsewhere in Trimac's financial statements). Therefore, the amount that Trimac reports on its balance sheet for its investment in Bantrel (or the investment's book value) on its December 31, 1998 balance sheet is calculated as follows:

Book value of Bantrel at December 31, 1998	=	Book value of Bantrel at December 31, 1997	+	Trimac's share of Banter's net income	–	Dividends received by Trimac
$2,682,000	=	$2,264,000	+	$2,018,000	–	$1,600,000

Question for Consideration

On June 30, 2004 Kreepeeshaw Ltd. (Kreepeeshaw) purchased 45% of the common shares of Vinsulla Corp. (Vinsulla) for $12,000,000. The book value of Kreepeeshaw's 45% interest in Vinsulla was $8,550,000, the fair value adjustments of net assets equalled $2,500,000, and goodwill was $950,000. Kreepeeshaw has significant influence but not control over Vinsulla. Kreepeeshaw and Vinsulla both have June 30 year ends. Kreepeeshaw will amortize the fair value adjustments over five years. For the year ended June 30, 2005 Vinsulla reported net

(continued)

income of $4,200,000, and declared and paid dividends to its shareholders of $500,000. On June 30, 2005 Kreepeeshaw's share of profits on intercompany transactions reported in Vinsulla's income statement was $230,000. On June 30, 2005 management estimated that its share of goodwill had to be written down by $125,000.

a. Prepare the journal entry that Kreepeeshaw would make to record its purchase of 45% of Vinsulla's common shares.

b. Calculate the amount of income that Kreepeeshaw would report on its income statement from its investment in Vinsulla for the year ended June 30, 2005. Record the journal entry that Kreepeeshaw would make to record its income from Vinsulla.

c. Prepare the journal entry Kreepeeshaw would make to record the dividend received from Vinsulla.

d. What amount would be reported on Kreepeeshaw's June 30, 2005 balance sheet for its investment in Vinsulla?

Answer:

a. Dr. Investment in Vinsulla Corp. (assets +)   12,000,000
        Cr. Cash (assets –)   12,000,000
    To record the investment in Vinsulla Corp.

b.   Share of income as reported by Vinsulla ($4,200,000 × 45%) $1,890,000
    Less: Amortization of fair value adjustments ($2,500,000 ÷ 5)   500,000
            Unrealized profit on intercompany transactions   230,000
            Write-down of goodwill   125,000
            Adjusted income from Vinsulla $1,035,000

    Dr. Investment in Vinsulla Corp. (assets +)   1,035,000
        Cr. Investment income from Hyndford   1,035,000
            (investment income +, shareholders' equity +)
    To record the income from Kreepeeshaw's
    equity investment in Vinsulla Corp.

c. Dr. Cash (assets +)   225,000
        Cr. Investment in Vinsulla Corp. (assets –)   225,000
    To record dividends received from Vinsulla Corp.

d. On June 30, 2005 Kreepeeshaw would report $12,810,000 ($12,000,000 + $1,035,000 – 225,000) in the investment in Vinsulla Corp. account.

Passive Investments

Passive investments are investments for which the investor corporation cannot influence the strategic decision making of the investee corporation. All investments in non-voting securities—securities such as debt, preferred shares, or non-voting common shares—are accounted for as passive investments because without voting power it is not possible to have influence. Voting shares are accounted for as passive investments when the investing company holds a relatively small proportion of the investee's voting shares.

The *CICA Handbook* suggests that if an investor corporation owns less than 20% of the voting shares of an investee, it should be treated as a passive investment. However, 20% is only a guideline. A 10% investment could give the investor corporation significant influence if, for example, the investment allows it to have representation on the board of directors.

Passive investments can be classified as temporary or portfolio investments. A

temporary investment is one that can be converted to cash reasonably easily and that management intends to sell within a year. If a company holds bonds that will mature within three months, the bonds would be classified as temporary investments. If the company owns shares in a public corporation that were purchased as a short-term investment of surplus cash—for example, the shares will be sold when the company needs cash to purchase equipment in the next few months—the investment would be classified as temporary because management intends to sell the shares within a year. Temporary investments are classified as current assets on the balance sheet.

Passive investments that cannot be readily converted to cash within a year, or that management does not intend to convert to cash within a year, are classified as **portfolio investments**. They are reported on the balance sheet as non-current assets. Passive investments in the securities of private companies, which tend to be more difficult to liquidate because there is no ready market for them, would be classified as portfolio investments.

All passive investments are accounted for using the cost method. Under the **cost method**, a passive investment is initially recorded at its cost. Income from passive investments is recognized when a dividend is declared or interest is earned. The lower of cost and market rule is applied to temporary investments (but not to portfolio investments). If the market value of a temporary investment is below its cost at year end, the investment is written down to market and the loss is reported on the income statement. Portfolio investments are not subject to the lower of cost and market rule. Instead, portfolio investments are written down only if the decline in value is not temporary. Increases in the market value of passive investments are not recorded unless the gain is realized—that is, when the investment is sold.

For example, Cayamant Corporation (Cayamant) invested surplus cash by purchasing 100,000 shares of Petro-Canada at $40 per share. This investment represents less than 0.04% of the outstanding voting shares held by investors. Clearly, Cayamant would have little influence on Petro-Canada's decision making, so the investment would be treated as a passive investment. Representatives of Cayamant could attend the annual meeting of Petro-Canada and vote on questions put before the shareholders, but that would be the extent of its influence. Cayamant would make the following journal entry to record the purchase:

Dr. Investment in shares (assets +)	4,000,000	
Cr. Cash (assets –)		4,000,000
To record the purchase of 100,000 Petro Canada shares at $40 per share.		

When Petro-Canada declares and pays a dividend, Cayamant would recognize income. If Petro-Canada paid a quarterly dividend of $0.10 per share, Cayamant would make the following entry:

Dr. Cash (assets +)	10,000	
Cr. Dividend income		10,000
(revenue +, shareholders' equity +)		
To record dividend income from the investment in Petro-Canada shares.		

If at year end Petro-Canada's share price were $39, the following journal entry would be required *if* the investment were accounted for as temporary:

Dr. Write-down of investment in Petro-Canada shares	100,000	
(expenses +, shareholders' equity–)		
Cr. Investment in shares (assets –)		100,000
To record the write-down of the investment in Petro-Canada shares.		

If the investment were accounted for as a portfolio investment, it would be written down only if the decline in value were considered permanent. Absent any specific evidence that Petro-Canada's economic value was permanently impaired, the decline of $1 per share would be ignored. The usual fluctuations in the prices of public companies' shares would not be considered permanent.

Notice that whether a portfolio investment is permanently impaired is a judgment made by management. This can be a subjective decision and it provides management with flexibility in deciding when a permanent decline in value has occurred and the amount of the decline.

Selling the securities would generate a gain or loss if their book value were different from the amount they were sold for. If Cayamant sold 40,000 of its Petro-Canada shares for $42 per share (assuming no previous write-down had occurred), the journal entry to record the sale would be:

Dr. Cash (asset +)	1,680,000	
Cr. Investment in shares (asset −)		1,600,000
Cr. Gain on sale of shares (income statement +)		80,000
To record the sale of 40,000 Petro-Canada shares		
at $42 per share.		

The credit to the investment in shares account of $1,600,000 is the cost of the shares times the number sold ($40 × 40,000 shares). The gain on the sale of shares is the difference between the selling price and the cost times the number of shares sold ([$42 −$40] × 40,000 shares). If the shares were sold for less than their book value, a loss on the sale of shares would be reported.

The accounting treatment for passive investments is another demonstration of conservatism in GAAP accounting. Gains are recognized only when the investments are sold, but losses are often accrued before they are realized (that is, before the investments are sold). Yet for investments in marketable securities (securities that are publicly traded), there are reliable and objective measures of the market prices available each day from the stock exchange listings.

From a user's standpoint, it is difficult to imagine many situations where the historical cost of the shares would be more useful than the current market value.

A lender, for example, would want to know market values in deciding the amount to lend against the shares as collateral. Shareholders might want to know both the cost and the market value so that they could evaluate management's investment decisions. An exception would be tax purposes, where only realized gains and losses have tax implications. GAAP recognize the relevance of market values because disclosure of market values of passive securities is required. However, the disclosure does not affect the income statement.

For securities that are not publicly traded, valuation is problematic because determining the value of such a security can be difficult.

In the United States a debate has been going on about the use of historical cost accounting versus market value accounting. Changes have been made to U.S. GAAP, which now require that temporary investments in debt and equity securities be reported at market value, with the gains and losses included in the income statement. Portfolio investments are also reported at market value, but the gains and losses are reported in shareholders' equity, not on the income statement.

The classification of passive investments depends in part on management intentions and, therefore, management's choices can affect the financial statements. If a security is classified as a temporary investment, the amount of working capital will be increased, the current ratio will increase, and cash from operations may be affected. Managers can also influence income if the specific identification method of accounting for the investments is used to account for the securities. As was the case with inventory, when specific identification is used, the cost of the actual security sold is used to calculate the gain or loss. If a company has identical securities that it purchased at different prices, the managers can determine the gain or loss by choosing which securities are sold.

■ Solved Problem

On December 31, 2006 Penryn Ltd. (Penryn) purchased 100% of the common shares of Seahorse Inc. (Seahorse) from its shareholders for $10,000,000. The summarized balance sheets of Penryn and Seahorse on December 31, 2006 immediately before the purchase are shown below:

Balance Sheets
As of December 31, 2006

	Penryn Ltd.	Seahorse Inc.
Current assets	$19,000,000	$2,000,000
Capital assets	31,000,000	6,000,000
	$50,000,000	$8,000,000
Liabilities	$12,000,000	$3,000,000
Capital stock	15,000,000	2,000,000
Retained earnings	23,000,000	3,000,000
	$50,000,000	$8,000,000

On December 31, 2006 the fair value of Seahorse's current assets was $2,700,000, the fair value of its capital assets was $7,200,000, and the fair value of its liabilities was $3,200,000.

Required:

a. What journal entry would Penryn make in its accounting system to record its purchase of Seahorse?

b. What journal entry would Seahorse make in its accounting system to record its purchase by Penryn?

c. How much goodwill would be reported on Penryn's consolidated balance sheet on December 31, 2006, immediately following the purchase of Seahorse?

d. Prepare the consolidated balance sheet for Penryn and its subsidiary on December 31, 2006.

e. Why is it necessary to make adjustments to the book values of the assets and liabilities reported on Seahorse's balance sheet when preparing consolidated financial statements?

Solution:

a. Dr. Investment in Seahorse (asset +)   10,000,000
        Cr. Cash (asset −)   10,000,000
    To record the purchase of 100% of the shares of
    Seahorse Corp on December 31, 2006.

b. Seahorse would not make any journal entry to record the purchase. The shares were purchased from Searhorse's shareholders, so there is no direct impact on its financial statements.

c. Goodwill = Purchase −   Fair value of identifiable assets
                    price   and liabilities purchased

          = $10,000,000 − ($2,700,000 + $7,200,000 − $3,200,000)

          = $3,300,000

d. Consolidated Balance Sheet for Penryn and Subsidiary:

	Balance Sheets As of December 31, 2006		Adjustments to Prepare Consolidated Balance Sheet	Consolidated Balance Sheet As of Dec. 31, 2006
	Penryn Ltd.[1]	Seahorse Corp.[1]		
Current assets	$ 9,000,000	$2,000,000	+700,000[2]	$11,700,000
Capital assets	31,000,000	6,000,000	+1,200,000[2]	38,200,000
Investment in Seahorse	10,000,000		−10,000,000[3]	
Goodwill			+3,300,000[4]	3,300,000
	$50,000,000	$8,000,000		$53,200,000
Liabilities	$12,000,000	$3,000,000	+200,000	$15,200,000
Capital stock	15,000,000	2,000,000	−2,000,000	15,000,000
Retained earnings	23,000,000	3,000,000	−3,000,000	23,000,000
	$50,000,000	$8,000,000		$53,200,000

[1] These are the balance sheets of Penryn (not consolidated Penryn) and Seahorse on December 31, 2006 after accounting for the purchase of Seahorse.

[2] Adjustments to the book values of Seahorse's assets and liabilities so that they will be included in Penryn's consolidated balance sheet at their fair values on December 31, 2006. The adjustments are the differences between Seahorse's book and fair values on December 31, 2006 as follows:

Account	Fair Value on December 31, 2006	Book Value on December 31, 2006	Adjustment
Current assets	$2,700,000	$2,000,000	$ 700,000
Capital assets	7,200,000	6,000,000	1,200,000
Liabilities	3,200,000	3,000,000	200,000

[3]The investment in Seahorse must be eliminated to avoid double counting of Seahorse's net assets.

[4]Goodwill as calculated by the formula:

$$\text{Goodwill} = \text{Purchase price} - \text{Fair value of identifiable assets and liabilities purchased}$$

$$\$3,300,000 = \$10,000,000 - \$6,700,000$$

[5] Seahorse's owners' equity accounts are eliminated to avoid double counting.

e. Adjustments to the book values of Seahorse's assets and liabilities are necessary because the consolidated statements are supposed to reflect the fair value of the subsidiary's assets and liabilities on the date the subsidiary was purchased by the parent. This is an application of the historical cost measurement convention. However, the amounts on Seahorse's balance sheet are recorded at the cost to Seahorse, not the cost to Penryn. Therefore, it is necessary to make adjustments so that the consolidated balance sheet will reflect the fair value (Penryn's cost) on the date of the purchase.

Summary of Key Points

LO 1. When an investor has control of an investee, the investor prepares consolidated financial statements. Consolidated financial statements aggregate the accounting information of a parent corporation and all of its subsidiaries into a single set of financial statements. On the consolidated balance sheet, the assets and liabilities of a subsidiary are reported at their fair value on the date the subsidiary was purchased. The consolidated income statement combines the revenues and expenses of the parent and its subsidiaries, but with three types of adjustments: amortization of fair value adjustments, possible write-down of goodwill, and elimination of the effects of intercompany transactions.

If a parent pays more than the fair value of the subsidiary's identifiable assets and liabilities on the date the subsidiary is purchased, goodwill arises. Goodwill can be recognized only when one entity purchases another and, according to GAAP, goodwill is not amortized. Instead, management must estimate the fair value of the goodwill each year, and if the fair value is less than the book value, the goodwill must be written down to its fair value.

When a parent company owns less than 100% of the shares of a subsidiary, but still controls it, accounts called non-controlling interest are reported on the consolidated balance sheet and income statement. GAAP require that the consolidated balance sheet include 100% of the book values of a subsidiary's assets and liabilities, even though the parent owns less than 100% of those assets and liabilities. GAAP also require that the consolidated income statement report 100% of the revenues and expenses of a subsidiary. Non-controlling interest on the balance sheet represents the net assets of a subsidiary that are owned by the shareholders of the subsidiary corporation other than the parent. Non-controlling interest on the income statement represents the portion of net income of the consolidated entity that belongs to the shareholders of subsidiaries other than the parent.

LO 2. When a corporation has significant influence on the decision making of another corporation, the equity method of accounting is used. The equity method of accounting is essentially the same as accounting for subsidiaries using the consolidation method, except that the information about equity-accounted-for investments is presented on a single line on the balance sheet and a single line on the income statement. An investment accounted for using the equity method is initially recorded on the investor's balance sheet at cost. The balance sheet amount is then adjusted each period by the investor's share of the investee's net income, less dividends declared by the investee. The investor's share is determined by multiplying the investee's net income by the percentage of the investee that the investor owns, and adjusting the investee's net income for amortization of differences between the fair value and book value of the investee's net assets (fair value adjustments), intercompany transactions, and write-downs of goodwill.

The rationale for the equity method is that if an investor corporation has significant influence, it can affect the important policies of an investee corporation, such as the timing and amount of the dividends the latter pays.

LO 3. Passive investments are investments for which the investor corporation cannot influence the strategic decision making of the investee corporation. All investments in non-voting securities are accounted for as passive investments. Voting shares are accounted for as passive investments when the investing company holds a relatively small proportion of the investee corporation's voting shares.

Passive investments can be classified as temporary or portfolio investments. A temporary investment is one that can be converted to cash reasonably easily and management intends sell the investment within a year. Temporary investments are classified as current assets. Passive investments that cannot be readily converted to cash within a year, or that management does not intend to convert to cash within a year, are classified as portfolio investments and are reported as non-current assets. All passive investments are accounted for using the cost method. Income from passive investments is recognized when a dividend is declared or interest is earned. The lower of cost and market rule is applied to temporary investments. Portfolio investments are written down only if the decline in value is not temporary.

The classification of passive investments depends in part on management intentions and, therefore, management's choices can affect the financial statements.

Key Terms

consolidated financial statement, p. 717

control, p. 717

cost method (of accounting for investments in other companies), p. 743

equity method of accounting, p. 738

fair value, p. 719

goodwill, p. 720

identifiable assets, p. 720

identifiable liabilities, p. 720

intercompany transaction, p. 725

investee corporation, p. 716

investor corporation, p. 716

Similar Terms

The left column gives alternative terms that are sometimes used for the accounting terms introduced in this chapter, which are listed in the right column.

minority interest	**non-controlling interest, p. 728**
market value	**fair value, p. 719**
carrying value	**book value, p. 741; see also p. 685**

Assignment Materials

Questions

Q12-1. What is goodwill? Under what circumstances is it recorded on financial statements?

Q12-2. Why is understanding the extent to which one corporation influences another important for accounting purposes? What impact does the degree of influence an entity has over another have on accounting?

Q12-3. Explain the following degrees of influence that one corporation can have over another and the implications of each for financial reporting:
a. control
b. significant influence
c. no influence

Q12-4. What are consolidated financial statements? What are some of the benefits and limitations of them?

Q12-5. Why do companies invest in other companies? Explain.

Q12-6. What are intercompany transactions? Why are the effects of intercompany transactions eliminated when consolidated financial statements are prepared?

Q12-7. What is a subsidiary? How are subsidiaries accounted for? Explain.

Q12-8. What is meant by the term "non-controlling interest"? What does the non-controlling interest on a company's balance sheet represent? What does non-controlling interest on the income statement represent?

Q12-9. Why is non-controlling interest added back to net income when calculating cash from operations using the indirect method?

Q12-10. Explain how a non-controlling shareholder in a subsidiary would use the non-controlling interest accounts on the parent's consolidated balance sheet and income statement.

Q12-11. When a subsidiary is acquired, the managers of the parent must allocate the purchase price to the specific identifiable assets and liabilities. Because the subsidiary's assets and liabilities are bought as a bundle, management has some flexibility in how it allocates the purchase price. Given this flexibility, how do you think the objectives of financial reporting would affect how management allocates the purchase price? Explain.

Q12-12. What is segment disclosure? Why is segment information required in the financial statements of public companies?

Q12-13. Describe the similarities and differences between consolidation and equity accounting.

Q12-14. Explain the usefulness of the consolidated financial statements of a parent corporation for the following stakeholders:

a. shareholder of the parent corporation
b. major supplier of one of the subsidiaries
c. Canada Customs and Revenue Agency (for income tax determination)

Q12-15. What are passive investments? Why do companies make passive portfolio invest-ments? What are the differences between portfolio investments and temporary investments? What are the differences in how each type of passive investment is accounted for?

Q12-16. Explain why consolidated financial statements are not just the sum of the amounts reported on the parent's and subsidiaries' financial statements.

Q12-17. Explain the following terms:
a. investor corporation
b. investee corporation
c. parent corporation
d. subsidiary corporation

Q12-18. Explain why the following adjustments must be made each time consolidated financial statements are prepared:
a. amortization of fair value adjustments
b. elimination of intercompany transactions
c. possible write-down of goodwill
d. elimination of the equity accounts of the subsidiary
e. elimination of the investment account reported on the parent's balance sheet

Q12-19. Explain why the following adjustments must be made when preparing the consol-idated balance sheet on the date a subsidiary is purchased:
a. elimination of the equity accounts of the subsidiary
b. elimination of the investment account reported on the parent's balance sheet
c. adjustment of the book values of the subsidiary's assets and liabilities to their fair values

Q12-20. When the equity method of accounting for investments is used, dividends received from the investee corporation reduce the balance in the investment account on the investor's balance sheet. The dividends are not treated as investment income on the income statement. Explain.

Q12-21. Explain the difference between the parent's consolidated financial statements and the financial statements of the parent alone.

Q12-22. Usually, passive investments are reported at cost on the investor corporation's bal-ance sheet. However, for passive investments in public corporations, market values are readily available. Why do you think managers of investor corporations would prefer not to have their passive investments in public corporations reported at mar-ket value? (In your answer consider the effect that using market values would have year to year on the income statement.)

Q12-23. How should an investor corporation account for the following investments?
a. Ownership of 51% of the shares of a company.
b. Ownership of 20% of the outstanding common shares of a company. These common shares represent 60% of the votes.
c. Ownership of 25% of the shares of a company.
d. Ownership of 0.05% of the shares of a company.

Exercises

E12-1. **(Accounting for different types of investments in securities, LO 1, 2, 3)** State how the investor corporation would account for the following investments. Explain your choice.
a. Purchase of $1,000,000 of bonds that management intends to hold until they mature in three years.
b. Investment in non-voting shares of a private corporation. Management hopes to sell the shares within six months.

c. Investment in voting shares of a private corporation. The investment represents 15% of the voting shares of the corporation. One person owns the remaining shares.

d. Investment in 52% of the voting shares of a private corporation. One person owns the remaining shares.

e. Investment in 30% of the voting shares of a public corporation. The investor corporation is the largest single investor in the public corporation and it has five representatives on its board of directors.

f. Investment in 60% of the voting shares of a public corporation. The investor corporation intends to sell its investment within six months.

E12-2.   **(Calculation of goodwill, LO 1)** On December 31, 2005 Resolute Inc. (Resolute) purchased 100% of the common shares of Uno Ltd. (Uno) for $22,000,000. At the time of the purchase, Resolute's management made the following estimates of the fair values of Uno's assets and liabilities:

Assets	$25,000,000
Liabilities	6,000,000

Required:

Calculate the amount of goodwill that Resolute would report on its December 31, 2005 consolidated balance sheet as a result of its purchase of Uno. How much goodwill would Resolute report on its unconsolidated balance sheet on December 31, 2005 as a result of the purchase? Explain.

E12-3.   **(Calculate the amount of goodwill, LO 1)** On April 15, 2003 Cashtown Inc. (Cashtown) purchased 100% of the common shares of Shakespeare Ltd. (Shakespeare) for $16,000,000. At the time of the purchase, Cashtown's management made the following estimates of the fair values of Shakespeare's assets and liabilities:

Current assets	$ 7,000,000
Tangible capital assets	17,000,000
Patents	3,500,000
Current liabilities	4,750,000
Long-term debt	10,250,000

Required:

a. Calculate the amount of goodwill that Cashtown recorded when it purchased Shakespeare on April 15, 2003.

b. In fiscal 2007, management determined that the goodwill associated with the purchase of Shakespeare was impaired and that it should be written down to $2,500,000. Prepare the journal entry that Cashtown would make to the consolidated financial statements to record the impairment of the goodwill. What amount would be reported on the fiscal 2007 balance sheet for goodwill and what expense would be reported in the income statement?

E12-4.   **(Calculation of goodwill when the parent purchases less than 100% of a subsidiary, LO 1)** On July 31, 2005 Janow Inc. (Janow) purchased 80% of the common shares of Worby Ltd. (Worby) for $5,200,000. The book and market values of Worby's assets and liabilities on July 31, 2005 were:

	Book Value on Worby's July 31, 2005 Balance Sheet	Fair Value of Worby's Assets and Liabilities on July 15, 2005
Assets	$8,000,000	$11,500,000
Liabilities	5,000,000	6,000,000

Required:

Calculate the amount of goodwill that Janow would report on its July 31, 2005 consolidated balance sheet as a result of its purchase of Worby.

E12-5.   **(Non-controlling interest, LO 1)** On December 31, 2005, Kootuk Inc. (Kootuk) purchased 80% of the common shares of Grimmer Ltd. (Grimmer) for $3,500,000. At the time of the purchase, Kootuk's management made the following estimates of the fair values of Grimmer's assets and liabilities:

	Book Value of Grimmer's Assets and Liabilities on December 31, 2005	Fair Value of Grimmer's Assets and Liabilities on December 31, 2005
Assets	$5,000,000	$6,000,000
Liabilities	2,000,000	2,400,000

Required:

    a. Calculate the amount of non-controlling interest that Kootuk would report on its December 31, 2005 consolidated balance sheet as a result of its purchase of Grimmer.

    b. What amount would be included in the assets and liabilities on the Kootuk's December 31, 2005 consolidated balance sheet as a result of the purchase of Grimmer?

E12-6.   **(Calculate the amount of goodwill, LO 1)** On August 31, 2006 Hoselaw Inc. (Hoselaw) purchased 100% of the common shares of Upsalquitch Ltd. (Upsalquitch) for $16,000,000. At the time of the purchase, Upsalquitch's management made the following estimates of the fair values of Upsalquitch's assets and liabilities:

	Book Value of Upsalquitch's Assets and Liabilities on August 31, 2006	Fair Value of Upsalquitch's Assets and Liabilities on August 31, 2006
Current assets	$2,000,000	$2,500,000
Tangible capital assets	6,000,000	7,200,000
Patents	200,000	2,000,000
Current liabilities	1,750,000	1,800,000
Long-term debt	4,250,000	4,000,000

Required:

    a. Calculate the amount of non-controlling interest that Hoselaw would report on its August 31, 2006 consolidated balance sheet as a result of its purchase of Upsalquitch.

    b. What amount would be included in each asset and liability account on the August 31, 2006 consolidated balance sheet as a result of the purchase of Upsalquitch?

    c. What does non-controlling interest on the balance sheet represent? Explain why it appears. How should users of financial statements interpret non-controlling interest?

E12-7.   **(Accounting for passive investments, LO 3)** Chockpish Inc. (Chockpish) has provided you with the following list of transactions and economic events that involved its investment portfolio in 2005. For each of the items on the list, prepare any necessary journal entries required. Explain your entries fully. Chockpish's year end is December 31.

    a. On January 15, 2,000 shares of Inwood Corp. were purchased at $37 per share.

    b. On February 12, a cheque for $10,000 was received from Guthrie Inc. for dividends.

    c. On March 6, 2,500 shares of Antigonish Inc. were sold for $9 per share. The shares were originally purchased in 2001 for $3 per share.

    d. On April 2, 4,200 shares of Hydraulic Corp. were sold for $12 per share. The shares were originally purchased in 1999 for $20 per share.

    e. At the close of trading on December 31, shares of Kynoch Ltd. were priced at

$12 per share. Chockpish's 5,000 shares of Kynoch Ltd. have a book value of $15 per share. Chockpish plans to continue holding these shares for the foreseeable future.

f. At the close of trading on December 31, shares of Jobrin Inc. were priced at $19 per share. Chockpish's 3,000 shares of Jobrin Ltd. have a book value of $22 per share. Chockpish plans to sell the shares by March 31, 2006.

E12-8. **(Accounting for portfolio investments, LO 3)** Yellek Inc. (Yellek) is a private corporation owned by the Yellek family. Yellek maintains a significant investment portfolio of publicly traded shares as a method of maximizing the return on surplus cash that the family keeps in the company. In March 2006 Yellek purchased 50,000 shares of Viking Corp. (Viking), a public company that trades on the Toronto Stock Exchange, for $20 per share. Then in May 2006 Yellek purchased an additional 20,000 shares of Viking for $23 per share. During 2006 Viking declared and paid a dividend of $0.12 a share on April 30 and a dividend of $0.12 a share on September 30. On November 12, 2006 Yellek sold 30,000 of its Viking shares for $25 per share because it needed cash to pay dividends to members of the family.

On December 12, 2006 Viking made an announcement that stunned the investment community. Viking was being forced to close one of its operating facilities permanently because of environmental concerns. The facility was responsible for about 20% of its annual production and the company said that it did not think it would be able to make up the lost production in the short term. Immediately after the announcement Viking's share price fell to $13 per share. On December 31, 2006 Viking's shares closed at $13.25.

Required:

a. Prepare the journal entries to record the purchase of Viking shares during 2006.

b. Prepare the journal entries to account for the dividends declared and paid by Viking during 2006.

c. Prepare the journal entry to record the sale of Viking shares on November 12, 2006. Assume that Viking uses the specific identification method of accounting for its securities. Explain your entry.

d. How would you account for the effects of the announcement made by Viking on December 12, 2006? Explain. Prepare any journal entry required. Indicate the amount that would be reported on Yellek's balance sheet for its investment in Viking.

E12-9. **(Comparison of equity and cost methods of accounting, LO 2, 3)** On January 1, 2005 Fletwode Corp. (Fletwode) purchased 2,250,000 common shares of Irvine Ltd. (Irvine) for $10,000,000. The investment represents a 30% interest in Irvine and gives Fletwode significant influence over Irvine. During 2005 Irvine reported net income of $1,300,000 and paid dividends of $0.10 per share. No adjustments to Irvine's net income for fair value adjustments, intercompany transactions, or goodwill are required. Both companies have December 31 year ends.

Required:

a. Prepare the journal entry that Fletwode would make to record its investment in Irvine.

b. What amount would be reported on Fletwode's December 31, 2005 balance sheet for its investment in Irvine? How much would Fletwode report on its December 31, 2005 income statement from its investment in Irvine?

c. Suppose Fletwode used the cost method to account for its investment in Fletwode. What amounts would be reported on its December 31, 2005 balance sheet and income statement?

E12-10. **(The equity method of accounting, LO 2)** On June 1, 2006 Wostok Corp. (Wostok) purchased 1,000,000 common shares of Griffin Ltd. (Griffin) for $2,000,000. The investment represents a 40% interest in Griffin and gives Wostok significant influence over Griffin. During fiscal 2007 Griffin reported net income of $1,100,000 and paid dividends of $0.50 per share. No adjustments to Griffin's net income for fair value adjustments, intercompany transactions, or goodwill are required. Both companies have May 31 year ends.

Required:

a. Prepare the journal entry that Wostok would make to record its investment in Griffin.

b. How much would Wostok report on its May 31, 2007 income statement from its investment in Griffin?

c. What amount would be reported on Wostok's May 31, 2007 balance sheet for its investment in Griffin?

E12-11. **(Investments with significant influence, LO 2)** On May 1, 2006 Owlseye Inc. (Owlseye) purchased 25% of the voting shares of Wyse Ltd. (Wyse) for $2,000,000 cash. As a result of the purchase, Owlseye has significant influence over Wyse because it can appoint two members to Wyse's board of directors. For the year ended April 30, 2007, Wyse reported net income of $800,000. On the date that Owlseye purchased Wyse, the fair value of Wyse's net assets exceeded the book value by $200,000. The difference is being amortized over four years. In addition, Owlseye's share of profit on intercompany transactions included in Wyse's net income was $25,000. During fiscal 2007 Owlseye received $30,000 in dividends from Wyse. Owlseye also has an April 30 year end.

Required:

a. Prepare the journal entry that would be made to record Owlseye's investment in Wyse.

b. What amount would be reported on Owlseye's April 30, 2007 income statement as income from its equity investment in Wyse?

c. What amount would be reported on Owlseye's April 30, 2007 balance sheet for its investment in Wyse?

d. Why is the amount reported on Owlseye's income statement as income from its equity investment in Wyse not simply Wyse's reported net income multiplied by Owlseye's ownership interest?

E12-12. **(Investments with significant influence, LO 2)** On October 1, 2005 Rowanton Inc. (Rowanton) purchased 40% of the voting shares of Durward Ltd. (Durward) for $1,000,000 cash. As a result of the purchase, Rowanton has significant influence over Durward because it can appoint four members to Durward's board of directors. For the year ended September 30, 2006, Durward reported net income of $650,000. On the date that Rowanton purchased Durward, the fair value of Durward's net assets exceeded the book value by $400,000. The difference is being amortized over four years. In addition, Rowanton's share of profit on intercompany transactions included in Durward's net income was $50,000 and the goodwill that was identified on acquisition had to be written down by $15,000. During fiscal 2006 Rowanton received $100,000 in dividends from Durward. Rowanton also has a September 30 year end.

Required:

a. Prepare the journal entry that would be made to record Rowanton's investment in Durward.

b. What amount would be reported on Rowanton's September 30, 2006 income statement as income from its equity investment in Durward?

c. What amount would be reported on Rowanton's September 30, 2006 balance sheet for its investment in Durward?

d. Explain why the amount reported on Rowanton's balance sheet for its equity investment in Durward changes from year to year.

E12-13. **(Consolidated income statement, LO 1)** Explain how the following items would affect consolidated net income in the year the subsidiary is purchased and the year after it is purchased:

a. Impairment of the value of goodwill.

b. Land with a book value of $2,000,000 on the subsidiary's balance sheet on the date the subsidiary was purchased has a fair value of $5,000,000 on that date.

c. Equipment with a book value of $1,000,000 on the subsidiary's balance sheet on the date the subsidiary was purchased has a fair value of $1,500,000 on that date. The equipment has a remaining useful life of five years.

d. Inventory with a book value of $200,000 on the subsidiary's balance sheet on the date the subsidiary was purchased has a fair value of $230,000 on that date.

e. Dividends paid by the subsidiary to the parent.

f. Services sold at a profit by the subsidiary to the parent.

g. The subsidiary is 80% owned by the parent.

Problems

P12-1. **(Problems with cost, LO 3)** In June 2004 Jolicure Inc. (Jolicure) and Horsefly Inc. (Horsefly) each began operations. Each company was formed with an initial capital contribution of $100,000. During the year ended May 31, 2005, each company had revenue of $225,000 and total expenses of $175,000. In addition, during the first year of operations each company purchased 1,000 shares of Nictaux Ltd. (Nictaux), a public company, for $12 per share. In May 2005 Horsefly sold its shares in Nictaux for $20 per share and immediately repurchased them at the same price. Jolicure did not sell its shares during fiscal 2005. On May 31, 2005 each company had total assets (excluding the shares in Nictaux) of $168,000 and total liabilities of $30,000.

Required:

a. Prepare summarized balance sheets for Jolicure and Horsefly as of May 31, 2005.

b. Prepare summarized income statements for Jolicure and Horsefly for the year ended May 31, 2005.

c. Which company performed better in fiscal 2005?

d. Which company was in a better financial position on May 31, 2005?

e. Why do you think Horsefly sold and repurchased the shares in Nictaux? Do you think that this was a wise transaction to enter into? Explain.

P12-2. **(Preparation of a consolidated balance sheet on the date a subsidiary is purchased, LO 1)** On August 31, 2007 Pacquet Inc. (Pacquet) purchased 100% of the common shares of Schwitzer Ltd. (Schwitzer) for $4,000,000 cash. Pacquet's and Schwitzer's balance sheets on August 31, 2007 just before the purchase were:

Balance Sheets As of August 31, 2007		
	Pacquet Inc.	**Schwitzer Ltd.**
Current assets	$ 7,000,000	$1,250,000
Capital assets	6,500,000	2,500,000
Total assets	$13,500,000	$3,750,000
Current liabilities	$ 2,700,000	$ 750,000
Non-current liabilities	2,500,000	1,000,000
Capital stock	4,000,000	500,000
Retained earnings	4,300,000	1,500,000
Total liabilities and shareholders' equity	$13,500,000	$3,750,000

Management determined that the fair values of Schwitzer's assets and liabilities were as follows:

	Fair Value of Schwitzer's Assets and Liabilities on August 31, 2007
Current assets	$1,750,000
Capital assets	3,900,000
Current liabilities	750,000
Non-current liabilities	1,100,000

Required

    a. Prepare the journal entry that Pacquet would prepare to record its purchase of Schwitzer's shares.

    b. Prepare the journal entry that Schwitzer would prepare to record its purchase by Pacquet.

    c. Prepare Pacquet's balance sheet immediately following the purchase.

    d. Calculate the amount of goodwill that would be reported on Pacquet's consolidated balance sheet on August 31, 2007.

    e. Prepare Pacquet's consolidated balance sheet on August 31, 2007.

    f. Calculate the current ratios and debt-to-equity ratios for Pacquet, Schwitzer, and for the consolidated balance sheet. Interpret the differences between the ratios. When calculating the ratios, use Pacquet and Schwitzer's balance sheets after the purchase had been made and recorded.

    g. You are a lender who has been asked to make a sizeable loan to Schwitzer. Which balance sheets would you be interested in viewing? Explain. How would you use Pacquet's consolidated financial statements in making your lending decision?

P12-3. **(Preparation of a consolidated balance sheet on the date a subsidiary is purchased, LO 1)** On January 31, 2006, Paju Inc. (Paju) purchased 100% of the common shares of Shellmouth Ltd. (Shellmouth) for $5,000,000 in cash. Paju's and Shellmouth's balance sheets on January 31, 2006 just before the purchase were:

Balance Sheets
As of January 31, 2006

	Paju Inc.	Shellmouth Ltd.
Current assets	$ 6,000,000	$4,500,000
Capital assets	11,750,000	1,500,000
Total assets	$17,750,000	$6,000,000
Current liabilities	$ 1,200,000	$1,500,000
Non-current liabilities	6,000,000	500,000
Capital stock	7,500,000	3,000,000
Retained earnings	3,050,000	1,000,000
Total liabilities and shareholders' equity	$17,750,000	$6,000,000

Management determined that the fair values of Shellmouth's assets and liabilities were as follows:

Fair Value of Shellmouth's Assets **and Liabilities on January 31, 2006**	
Current assets	$3,900,000
Capital assets	1,900,000
Current liabilities	1,600,000
Non-current liabilities	750,000

Required

    a. Prepare the journal entry that Paju would prepare to record its purchase of Shellmouth's shares.

    b. Prepare the journal entry that Shellmouth would prepare to record its purchase by Paju.

    c. Prepare Paju's balance sheet immediately following the purchase.

    d. Calculate the amount of goodwill that would be reported on Paju's consolidated balance sheet on January 31, 2006.

    e. Prepare Paju's consolidated balance sheet on January 31, 2006.

    f. Calculate the current ratios and debt-to-equity ratios for Paju, Shellmouth, and for the consolidated balance sheet. Interpret the differences between the ratios. When calculating the ratios, use Paju's and Shellmouth's balance sheets after the purchase had been made and recorded.

g. You are a potential investor who has been asked to purchase a 25% equity interest in Shellmouth (you would purchase the shares from Shellmouth, not from Paju). Which balance sheets would you be interested in viewing? Explain. How would you use Paju's consolidated financial statements in making your lending decision? What concerns would you have about making an equity investment in Shellmouth?

P12-4.   **(Preparation of a consolidated balance sheet on the date a subsidiary is purchased when less than 100% of the subsidiary is purchased, LO 1)** On March 31, 2005 Popkum Inc. (Popkum) purchased 60% of the common shares of Saguay Ltd. (Saguay) for $1,500,000. Popkum's and Saguay's balance sheets on March 31, 2005 just before the purchase were:

Balance Sheets As of March 31, 2005		
	Popkum Inc.	**Saguay Ltd.**
Current assets	$3,500,000	$ 625,000
Capital assets	3,250,000	1,250,000
Total assets	$6,750,000	$1,875,000
Current liabilities	$1,350,000	$ 375,000
Non-current liabilities	1,250,000	500,000
Capital stock	2,000,000	250,000
Retained earnings	2,150,000	750,000
Total liabilities and shareholders' equity	$6,750,000	$1,875,000

Management determined that the fair values of Saguay's assets and liabilities were as follows:

	Fair Value of Saguay's Assets and Liabilities on March 31, 2005
Current assets	$ 875,000
Capital assets	1,950,000
Current liabilities	375,000
Non-current liabilities	550,000

Required

a. Prepare the journal entry that Popkum would prepare to record its purchase of Saguay's shares.

b. Prepare the journal entry that Saguay would prepare to record its purchase by Popkum.

c. Calculate the amount of goodwill that would be reported on Popkum's consolidated balance sheet on March 31, 2005.

d. Calculate the amount of non-controlling interest that would be reported on the consolidated balance sheet on March 31, 2005.

e. Prepare Popkum's consolidated balance sheet on March 31, 2005.

f. Calculate the current ratios and debt-to-equity ratios for Popkum, Saguay, and for the consolidated balance sheet. Interpret the differences between the ratios.

g. Explain what the non-controlling interest on the balance sheet represents. How would you interpret it from the perspective of a shareholder of Popkum? How would you interpret it from the perspective of a shareholder in Saguay? How would you interpret it from the perspective of a lender?

P12-5.   **(Preparation of a consolidated balance sheet on the date a subsidiary is purchased when less than 100% of the subsidiary is purchased, LO 1)** On October 31, 2006, Pahonan Inc. (Pahonan) purchased 75% of the common shares of Seebe Ltd. (Seebe) for $1,500,000. Pahonan's and Seebe's balance sheets on October 31, 2006 just before the purchase were:

Balance Sheets As of October 31, 2006		
	Pahonan Inc.	**Seebe Ltd.**
Current assets	$2,000,000	$2,250,000
Capital assets	6,875,000	750,000
Total assets	$8,875,000	$3,000,000
Current liabilities	$ 600,000	$ 750,000
Non-current liabilities	3,000,000	250,000
Capital stock	3,750,000	1,500,000
Retained earnings	1,525,000	500,000
Total liabilities and shareholders' equity	$5,875,000	$3,000,000

Management determined that the fair values of Seebe's assets and liabilities were as follows:

Fair Value of Seebe's Assets and Liabilities on October 31, 2006	
Current assets	$1,950,000
Capital assets	950,000
Current liabilities	800,000
Non-current liabilities	375,000

Required

    a. Prepare the journal entry that Pahonan would prepare to record its purchase of Seebe's shares.

    b. Prepare the journal entry that Seebe would prepare to record its purchase by Pahonan.

    c. Calculate the amount of goodwill that would be reported on Pahonan's consolidated balance sheet on October 31, 2006.

    d. Calculate the amount of non-controlling interest that would be reported on the consolidated balance sheet on October 31, 2006.

    e. Prepare Pahonan's consolidated balance sheet on October 31, 2006.

    f. Calculate the current ratios and debt-to-equity ratios for Pahonan and Seebe, and for the consolidated balance sheet. Interpret the differences between the ratios.

    g. Explain what the non-controlling interest on the balance sheet represents. How would you interpret it from the perspective of a shareholder of Pahonan? How would you interpret it from the perspective of a shareholder in Seebe? How would you interpret it from the perspective of a lender?

P12-6.   **(Intercompany transactions, LO 1)** Vonda Inc. (Vonda) is a 100%-owned subsidiary of Atik Ltd. (Atik). During the year ended March 31, 2006, Vonda sold, on credit, merchandise costing $1,000,000 to Atik for $2,000,000. These were the only transactions that Atik and Vonda entered into during 2005 (with each other or with third parties) and there were no other costs incurred.

Required:

    a. Prepare an income statement for Vonda for the year ended March 31, 2006.

    b. What amount of accounts receivable would Vonda report on its March 31, 2006 balance sheet?

    c. What amount of inventory and accounts payable would Atik report on its March 31, 2006 balance sheet?

    d. Prepare Atik's March 31, 2006 consolidated income statement assuming that intercompany transactions are not eliminated. How much would be reported for accounts receivable, inventory, and accounts payable on the March 31, 2006 consolidated balance sheet?

e. Prepare Atik's March 31, 2006 consolidated income statement assuming that intercompany transactions are eliminated. How much would be reported for accounts receivable, inventory, and accounts payable on the March 31, 2006 consolidated balance sheet?

f. Discuss the differences in the information you prepared in parts (d) and (e). Which information is more useful to stakeholders? Explain.

P12-7.   **(Intercompany transactions, LO 1)** Batteau Inc. (Batteau) is a 100%-owned subsidiary of Castaway Ltd. (Castaway). During the year ended May 31, 2006, Batteau sold, on credit, merchandise costing $700,000 to Castaway for $1,200,000. During fiscal 2006 Castaway sold, on credit, the merchandise it had purchased from Batteau to third parties for $2,000,000. These were the only transactions that Castaway and Batteau entered into during 2006 (with each other or with third parties) and there were no other costs incurred.

Required:

a. Prepare an income statement for Batteau for the year ended May 31, 2006.

b. What amount of accounts receivable would Batteau report on its May 31, 2006 balance sheet?

c. What amount of inventory and accounts payable would Castaway report on its May 31, 2006 balance sheet?

d. Prepare Castaway's May 31, 2006 consolidated income statement assuming that intercompany transactions are not eliminated. How much would be reported for accounts receivable, inventory, and accounts payable on the May 31, 2006 consolidated balance sheet?

e. Prepare Castaway's May 31, 2006 consolidated income statement assuming that intercompany transactions are eliminated. How much would be reported for accounts receivable, inventory, and accounts payable on the May 31, 2006 consolidated balance sheet?

f. Discuss the differences in the information you prepared in parts (d) and (e). Which information is more useful to stakeholders? Explain.

P12-8.   **(Intercompany transactions, LO 1)** Guilds Inc. (Guilds) is a 100%-owned subsidiary of Nutak Ltd. (Nutak). During the year ended August 31, 2006, Guilds sold merchandise costing $200,000 to Nutak for $500,000. These were the only transactions that Nutak and Guilds entered into during 2005 (with each other or with third parties) and there were no other costs incurred. The sale was on credit.

Required:

a. Prepare an income statement for Guilds for the year ended August 31, 2006.

b. What amount of accounts receivable would Guilds report on its August 31, 2006 balance sheet?

c. What amount of inventory and accounts payable would Nutak report on its August 31, 2006 balance sheet?

d. Prepare Nutak's August 31, 2006 consolidated income statement assuming that intercompany transactions are not eliminated. How much would be reported for accounts receivable, inventory, and accounts payable on the August 31, 2006 consolidated balance sheet?

e. Prepare Nutak's August 31, 2006 consolidated income statement assuming that intercompany transactions are eliminated. How much would be reported for accounts receivable, inventory, and accounts payable on the August 31, 2006 consolidated balance sheet?

f. Discuss the differences in the information you prepared in parts (d) and (e). Which information is more useful to stakeholders? Explain.

P12-9.   **(Intercompany transactions, LO 1)** Dozois Inc. (Dozois) is a 100%-owned subsidiary of Yarbo Ltd. (Yarbo). During the year ended July 31, 2006, Dozois sold merchandise costing $2,200,000 to Yarbo for $3,000,000. During fiscal 2006 Yarbo sold, on credit, the merchandise it had purchased from Dozois to third parties for $3,800,000. These were the only transactions that Yarbo and Dozois entered into during 2006 (with each other or with third parties) and there were no other costs incurred.

Required:

    a. Prepare an income statement for Dozois for the year ended July 31, 2006.

    b. What amount of accounts receivable would Dozois report on its July 31, 2006 balance sheet?

    c. What amount of inventory and accounts payable would Yarbo report on its July 31, 2006 balance sheet?

    d. Suppose that during fiscal 2006, Yarbo sold the merchandise it had purchased from Dozois for $3,200,000. Prepare Yarbo's July 31, 2006 consolidated income statement assuming that intercompany transactions are not eliminated. How much would be reported for accounts receivable, inventory, and accounts payable on the July 31, 2006 consolidated balance sheet?

    e. Suppose that during fiscal 2006, Yarbo sold the merchandise it had purchased from Dozois for $3,200,000. Prepare Yarbo's July 31, 2006 consolidated income statement assuming that intercompany transactions are eliminated. How much would be reported for accounts receivable, inventory, and accounts payable on the July 31, 2006 consolidated balance sheet?

    f. Discuss the differences in the information you prepared in parts (d) and (e). Which information is more useful to stakeholders? Explain.

P12-10. **(Investments in public companies, LO 3)** In July 2005 Roddickton Ltd. (Roddickton) purchased 100,000 shares of Kola Inc. (Kola), a publicly traded company, for $37 per share. From the time of purchase to its year end on December 31, 2005, Roddickton received dividends of $0.70 per share from its investment in Kola. On December 31, 2005 the closing price for Kola's shares was $34. There were 100,000,000 shares of Kola's common stock outstanding during 2005.

Required:

    a. Prepare the journal entry that would be made to record the purchase of the shares.

    b. Prepare the journal entry to record the dividends received by Kola during 2005.

    c. How might you determine whether this investment should be treated as a temporary investment or a portfolio investment?

    d. If the investment in Kola were considered a portfolio investment, what amount would be reported on Roddickton's December 31, 2005 balance sheet? Explain.

    e. If the investment in Kola were considered a temporary investment, what amount would be reported on Roddickton's December 31, 2005 balance sheet? Explain.

    f. Do you think a management cares whether its passive investments are classified as portfolio or temporary? Explain.

P12-11. **(Consolidated income statement, LO 1)** The summarized income statements for Pakan Ltd. (Pakan) and Shemogue (Shemogue) Corp. for the fiscal year ended September 30, 2005 are shown below:

	Summarized Income Statements For the Year Ended September 30, 2005	
	Pakan Ltd.	Shemogue Corp.
Revenue	$3,500,000	$1,250,000
Expenses	2,000,000	825,000
Net income	$1,500,000	$ 425,000

The following information is provided:

    i. During fiscal 2005, Shemogue sold, on credit, merchandise to Pakan for $200,000. Shemogue paid $125,000 for the merchandise. At the end of fiscal 2005, Pakan had sold none of the merchandise.

    ii. On the date it was purchased by Pakan, Shemogue reported capital assets of $1,400,000 on its balance sheet. This amount is being amortized on a straight-line basis over seven years from the date of the purchase. These assets had fair values of $2,100,000 on the date Shemogue was purchased. The fair value adjustment is also being amortized on a straight-line basis over seven years.

iii. At the end of fiscal 2005 management determined that the goodwill that was recorded when Pakan purchased Shemogue was impaired and had to be written down by $50,000.

iv. During fiscal 2005 Shemogue sold all of the inventory that was on hand when it was purchased on September 30, 2004. The difference between the cost of the inventory to Shemogue and its fair value on September 30, 2004 was $75,000 (which was the full difference between the fair value and book value of Shemogue's current assets on September 30, 2004).

Required:

a. Prepare the summarized consolidated income statement for fiscal 2005.

b. Which do you think is a better measure of Shemogue's economic performance: its net income reported on its own income statement, or its net income as incorporated in Pakan's consolidated balance sheet?

P12-12. **(Consolidated income statement, LO 1)** The summarized income statements for Pirogue Ltd. (Pirogue) and Seaview (Seaview) Corp. for the fiscal year ended April 30, 2005 are shown below:

	Summarized Income Statements For the Year Ended September 30, 2005	
	Pirogue Ltd.	**Seaview Corp.**
Revenue	$6,400,000	$4,750,000
Expenses	3,500,000	4,100,000
Net income	$2,900,000	$ 650,000

The following information is provided:

i. During fiscal 2005, Seaview sold, on credit, merchandise to Pirogue for $500,000. Seaview paid $275,000 for the merchandise. At the end of fiscal 2005, Pirogue had sold none of the merchandise.

ii. On the date it was purchased by Pirogue, Seaview reported capital assets of $3,100,000 on its balance sheet. This amount is being amortized on a straight-line basis over ten years from the date of the purchase. These assets had fair values of $4,100,000 on the date Seaview was purchased. The fair value adjustment is also being amortized on a straight-line basis over ten years.

iii. At the end of fiscal 2005 management determined that the goodwill that was recorded when Pirogue purchased Seaview was impaired and had to be written down by $250,000.

iv. During fiscal 2005 Seaview sold all of the inventory that was on hand when it was purchased on April 30, 2004. The difference between the cost of the inventory to Seaview and its fair value on April 30, 2004 was $175,000 (which was the full difference between the fair value and book value of Seaview's current assets on April 30, 2004).

Required:

a. Prepare the summarized consolidated income statement for fiscal 2005.

b. Explain why Seaview's net income has to be adjusted when preparing the consolidated income statement.

■ Using Financial Statements

Brascan Corporation

Brascan Corporation (Brascan) owns and operates real estate, power generating, natural resource, and financial businesses, located principally in North and South America. Together with its affiliates, Brascan has a combined asset base of $35 billion and employs over 50,000 people.[5]

Brascan's consolidated balance sheet, statements of income, statement of cash flows, and extracts from the notes to the financial statements are provided in Exhibit 12-5 (pages 762–765).[6] Use this information to respond to questions FS12-1 to FS12-7.

FS12-1. What are the companies that Brascan consolidates into its financial statements? What is Brascan's ownership interest in each of these companies? Why are these companies consolidated?

FS12-2. What are the companies that Brascan accounts for using the equity method of accounting? What is Brascan's ownership interest in each of these companies? Why are these companies accounted for using the equity method? What is the book value of each of the equity-accounted-for investments?

FS12-3. On Brascan's consolidated statement of income, why are group revenues of $13,524,000,000 reported, but only $1,194,000,000 included in the calculation of consolidated net income?

FS12-4. How much did Brascan receive in dividends from companies that it accounts for using the equity method? (This question is tricky and requires that you use information from the consolidated statement of income and consolidated statement of cash flows.)

FS12-5. The following questions pertain to Brascan's non-controlling (minority) interest:
   a. What amount of minority interest is reported on Brascan's December 31, 2000 balance sheet? What does this amount represent?
   b. Where on the balance sheet is the minority interest reported? Explain why it is reported there.
   c. What amount of minority interest is reported on Brascan's statement of income for the year ended December 31, 2000? What does this amount represent?
   d. Why is the minority interest added back to income from continuing operations when calculating cash from operations?
   e. If you were an investor in Trilon Financial Corporation, how would you use the minority interest information included in Brascan's financial statements?

FS12-6. Examine Note 19 to Brascan's financial statements and answer the following questions on segment disclosure:
   a. Identify the business segments in which Brascan operates. Which segment has the most revenues? Which has the most assets? Which has the most income?
   b. Identify the geographic segments that Brascan reports in Note 19. Which segment has the most revenues? Which has the most assets? Why do you think segment income information isn't provided for the geographic segments?
   c. Is the segmented information provided only for the entities that are consolidated into Brascan's consolidated financial statements? Explain.
   d. Why is segment disclosure required under GAAP? As a user of Brascan's annual report, how would your ability to use the financial statements be impaired by not having the segmented information?
   e. What are the limitations of the segment disclosure provided by Brascan?

FS12-7. What are the problems and limitations of analyzing financial ratios based on Brascan's consolidated financial statements?

■ Analyzing Mark's Work Wearhouse

M12-1. The following questions pertain to MWW's goodwill.
   a. How much goodwill did MWW report on its January 27, 2001 balance sheet?
   b. How much new goodwill did MWW acquire in fiscal 2000 from the purchase of franchise stores?
   c. Do you think MWW's consolidated balance sheet fully reflects MWW's goodwill? (In other words, if MWW were purchased, would there be additional goodwill not currently reported on the balance sheet?) Why is this goodwill not currently reported on the consolidated balance sheet? What might be the sources of this unrecorded goodwill?

Consolidated Balance Sheet

YEARS ENDED DECEMBER 31
MILLIONS

	Note	2000	1999
Assets			
Cash and cash equivalents		$ 347	$ 100
Securities	2	2,371	2,509
Loans and other receivables	3	2,833	2,691
Corporate investments	4	3,654	3,614
Property and equipment	5	2,018	1,832
Other assets		378	314
		$ 11,601	$ 11,060
Liabilities			
Accounts payable and other		$ 812	$ 639
Corporate borrowings	6	1,360	1,718
Subsidiary company borrowings	7	2,420	2,161
		4,592	4,518
Deferred credits	8	395	332
Capital base			
Minority interests	9	1,701	1,596
Shareholders' equity	10	4,913	4,614
		6,614	6,210
		$ 11,601	$ 11,060

Consolidated Statement of Income

YEARS ENDED DECEMBER 31
MILLIONS, EXCEPT PER SHARE AMOUNTS

	Note	2000	1999
Group revenues	1	$ 13,524	$ 12,729
Revenue of equity accounted affiliates		12,330	11,652
Consolidated revenues		1,194	1,077
Equity in pre-tax earnings of affiliates		376	290
Income before the undernoted items		1,570	1,367
Operating expenses		608	561
Interest expense		276	262
Minority interests		147	130
Taxes and other provisions	12	151	128
Income from continuing operations		388	286
Income from discontinued operations		10	27
Gain on sale of discontinued operations	13	250	110
Net income		$ 648	$ 423
Per Class A and Class B common share	14		
Income from continuing operations		$ 1.96	$ 1.38
Net income		$ 3.41	$ 2.15

Exhibit 12-5 (continued)

Brascan Corporation Financial Statements

Consolidated Statement of **Cash Flows**

YEARS ENDED DECEMBER 31
MILLIONS

	Note	2000	1999
Group operating cash flows		$ 1,708	$ 1,546
Operating cash flows of equity accounted affiliates		1,265	1,147
Consolidated cash flow from operations	14	443	399
Financing and shareholder distributions			
Corporate borrowings:			
Issuances		–	145
Repayments		(382)	(60)
Subsidiary company borrowings:			
Issuances		417	290
Repayments		(219)	(260)
Minority interests		48	(109)
Convertible notes repurchased		(40)	–
Shares:	10		
Issued		–	1
Repurchased		(92)	–
Convertible note interest paid		(6)	(9)
Dividends paid		(213)	(208)
		(487)	(210)
Investing			
Securities:			
Purchases		(256)	(197)
Sales		395	151
Loans and other receivables:			
Advanced		(707)	(330)
Collected		477	351
Investment in property and equipment		(201)	(115)
Corporate investments sold		619	–
Other		(36)	(99)
		291	(239)
Cash and cash equivalents			
Increase (Decrease)		247	(50)
Balance, beginning of year		100	150
Balance, end of year		$ 347	$ 100

Cash flow from operations

MILLIONS	2000	1999
Income from continuing operations	$ 388	$ 286
Add (deduct) non-cash items:		
Depreciation and amortization	46	42
Minority interests	147	130
Equity income in excess of dividends received	(144)	(103)
Other	6	44
Cash flow from operations	$ 443	$ 399

1. SUMMARY OF ACCOUNTING POLICIES

These consolidated financial statements have been prepared in accordance with accounting principles generally accepted in Canada.

Basis of presentation

The consolidated financial statements include the accounts of Brascan Corporation (the "company") and the companies over which it has and intends to maintain control.

The company's principal affiliates and ownership interests are as follows:

FULLY DILUTED OWNERSHIP	2000	1999
Companies consolidated:		
Great Lakes Power Inc. [1]	100%	93%
Trilon Financial Corporation [1]	71%	65%
Brascan Brazil Ltd.	100%	100%
Companies equity accounted:		
Noranda Inc.	40%	40%
Nexfor Inc.	33%	31%
Brookfield Properties Corporation	48%	49%
Canadian Hunter Exploration Ltd.	–	40%

1 *These ownership figures are pro-forma to reflect transactions that occurred in January and February 2001. As at December 31, 2000, these ownership percentages were unchanged from 1999.*

The cost of acquiring each affiliate is allocated to its identifiable net assets on the basis of the estimated fair values at the date of purchase. The excess of acquisition costs over the underlying net book values of the affiliates is amortized over the estimated useful lives of the assets acquired. The company evaluates the carrying value of this excess for potential impairment on a regular basis. Management assesses the recoverability of this excess based on a review of estimated future operating income and cash flows of the affiliates on an undiscounted basis.

The company accounts for its long-term corporate investments over which significant influence exists on the equity basis. Interests in jointly controlled partnerships and corporate joint ventures are proportionately consolidated. The accounting policies of the long-term corporate investments are, in all material respects, in accordance with those of the company.

2. SECURITIES

MILLIONS	2000	1999
Common shares	$ 938	$ 767
Preference shares	1,433	1,742
Total securities	$2,371	$2,509

The fair value of the company's securities at December 31, 2000 was $2,355 million (1999 – $2,438 million). In determining fair values, quoted market prices are used where available and, where not available, management's estimates of the amounts which could be recovered over time or through a transaction between knowledgeable and willing third parties under no compulsion to act.

4. CORPORATE INVESTMENTS

MILLIONS	2000	1999
Noranda Inc.	$1,809	$1,787
Brookfield Properties Corporation	1,332	1,226
Nexfor Inc.	400	377
Canadian Hunter Exploration Ltd.	–	207
Other investments	113	17
Total corporate investments	$3,654	$3,614

Included in the carrying value of the company's long-term corporate investments is $390 million (1999 – $456 million), representing the unamortized excess of acquisition costs over the company's share of the net book value of these investments which are being amortized over periods of up to 40 years.

In addition to the company's common shareholdings, the company and its consolidated subsidiaries own $1,391 million (1999 – $1,563 million) of securities and loans receivable of the company's corporate investments, and $388 million (1999 – $235 million) of property mortgages of affiliates held for syndication. Revenues received from these assets in 2000 totalled approximately $165 million (1999 – $133 million).

Exhibit 12-5 (continued)

Brascan Corporation Financial
Statements

9. MINORITY INTERESTS

Minority interests include Class A, Series 1 and Series 5 retractable preference shares issued by the company and common and preference shares owned by minority shareholders in the company's consolidated subsidiaries, as follows:

MILLIONS	2000	1999
Preference shares issued by the company with retractable features	$ 65	$ 65
Preference shares issued by consolidated subsidiaries	574	550
Common shares issued by consolidated subsidiaries	1,062	981
Total minority interests	$ 1,701	$ 1,596

19. SEGMENTED INFORMATION

The company's business segments are based on the way management organizes the business in making operating decisions and assessing performance. These business segments are as follows:

(a) property operations, which represent the company's investment in Brookfield, a North American office property company;

(b) natural resource operations, which represent the company's investments in Noranda, an international mining and metals company, and Nexfor, a diversified forest products company;

(c) energy operations, which include Great Lakes' electric energy generation, transmission and distribution operations; and

(d) financial and other operations, which include Trilon's financial and related advisory services, and Brascan's Brazilian property, financial services and other operations.

Group revenues, segmented income and assets by business segment are as follows:

	2000			1999		
MILLIONS	Group Revenues	Segmented Income	Assets	Group Revenues	Segmented Income	Assets
Property operations	$ 3,129	$ 111	$ 6,168	$ 2,721	$ 100	$ 5,850
Natural resource operations	9,091	148	5,616	8,824	106	5,344
Energy operations	333	68	2,303	286	66	2,237
Financial and other operations	858	154	3,995	807	132	3,480
Corporate	113	113	1,137	91	91	1,481
	13,524	594	19,219	12,729	495	18,392
Equity accounted affiliates	12,330	–	7,618	11,652	–	7,332
Consolidated revenues/assets	$ 1,194	–	$ 11,601	$ 1,077	–	$ 11,060
Interest and other unallocated expenses		206			209	
Earnings from continuing operations		$ 388			$ 286	

Group revenues and assets by geographic segment are as follows:

	2000		1999	
MILLIONS	Group Revenues	Assets	Group Revenues	Assets
Canada	$ 5,948	$ 9,607	$ 6,037	$ 9,829
United States	5,363	5,819	4,883	5,253
South America	1,362	2,845	1,238	2,506
Europe and other	851	948	571	804
	13,524	19,219	12,729	18,392
Equity accounted affiliates	12,330	7,618	11,652	7,332
Consolidated revenues / assets	$ 1,194	$ 11,601	$ 1,077	$ 11,060

Exhibit 12-5 (continued)

Brascan Corporation Financial Statements

M12-2. You are considering purchasing a Work World franchise from Mark's Work Wearhouse. Are MWW's consolidated financial statements useful to you in making your decision? Explain. What financial information would you want that is not included in the consolidated financial statements? Explain.

M12-3. What would MWW's net income for fiscal 2001 and 2002 be if the new accounting standard that does not require that goodwill be amortized were in effect? How is cash from operations affected by this accounting change? What difference might this accounting change mean for users of MWW's financial statements?

M12-4. Examine Notes 2 and 8 to MWW's financial statements (pages A-51 and A-54). The following questions pertain to MWW's purchase of Paul John Enterprises Ltd. (Paul John) in fiscal 1999.
   a. Describe what MWW acquired with its purchase of Paul John.
   b. How much did MWW pay for Paul John on the date of the purchase? Is this the final price that MWW will have to pay? Explain. How much has MWW paid to date?
   c. Why was the amount of goodwill associated with the purchase of Paul John increased during fiscal 2000? What was the amount of the increase?
   d. On the date Paul John was purchased, what amounts of cash, other current assets, capital assets, and liabilities were obtained? Do you think that these amounts are the same as the amounts that were reported on Paul John's balance sheet? Explain.
   e. The table in Note 2 identifies assumed goodwill and acquisition goodwill. What do you think is the difference between these two types of goodwill?

M12-5. Examine Note 3 to MWW's financial statements (page A-52). The following questions pertain to MWW's purchase of franchise stores in fiscal 2001.
   a. How many franchise stores did MWW buy in fiscal 2001?
   b. What was the purchase price for these stores? How much of the purchase price was paid in cash? (You should be able to determine the amount from two places in the financial statements and notes.)
   c. On the date the franchise stores were purchased, what amounts of cash, other current assets, capital assets, and liabilities were obtained? Do you think that these amounts are the same as the amounts that were reported on the individual stores' balance sheets? Explain.
   d. How much of the cost of the franchise store purchases was attributed to goodwill? What do you think the goodwill was for? (Tie your explanation to the specifics of the entities purchased. Do not give a general answer.)

M12-6. Examine Note 18 to MWW's financial statements (see page A-63). These questions pertain to MWW's segment disclosures.
   a. Identify the different segments that MWW reports. What were the sales and earnings before interest, taxes, depreciation, and amortization for each segment in fiscal 2001?
   b. Are the segment disclosures useful? Explain. Tie your answer to specific users of the financial statements.
   c. In fiscal 1999 and 2000, small amounts of inter-group sales are reported. Explain what these amounts might represent and why they are deducted when coming to total sales.

Endnotes

1. Extracted from Onex Corporation's 2000 annual report.

2. Extracted from Onex Corporation's 2000 annual report.

3. Extracted from BCE Inc.'s 2000 annual report.

4. Extracted from Trimac Corporation's 1998 annual report.

5. Extracted from Brascan Corporation's web site at www.brascancorp.com (accessed April 3, 2002).

6. Extracted from Brascan Corporation's 2001 annual report.

Chapter 13

Analyzing and Interpreting Financial Statements

Chapter Outline

Learning Objectives

After studying the material in this chapter you will be able to:

LO 1. Distinguish between permanent and transitory earnings, and discuss the concept of earning quality.

LO 2. Analyze and evaluate entities through the use of financial ratios.

LO 3. Recognize the limitations of using financial statements and ratio analysis for evaluating an entity.

Introduction

Chapter 1 of this book began with the following statement:

> Accounting is full of mystery and intrigue. The reader of an accounting report, like the reader of a good mystery, must sort through clues, interpret and analyze information, exercise judgment, decide which information is relevant and which should be ignored, and use the information to come to a conclusion. …Solving an accounting mystery requires detective work. The numbers tell a story, but it is usually necessary to read between the lines.

The first 12 chapters of this book explained why accounting information is full of mystery and intrigue. It should be clear to readers that there is nothing straightforward about the information that is reported in financial statements. Despite the complexity, ambiguity, and limitations of the information, financial statements are crucial for decision making. It would be extremely difficult for people to make their decisions without the information that is in the financial statements.

Without financial statements it would be difficult to determine whether to purchase a business and how much to pay. It would be difficult to decide whether to lend money to an entity and how much to lend. It would be difficult for regulators to set rates for regulated companies. Indeed, Mark's Work Wearhouse's (MWW's) financial statements, along with other accounting-based information that was probably provided by the company, likely played an important role in the decision of Canadian Tire Corporation, Limited to purchase MWW in late 2001.

But using the information in financial statements for making decisions usually isn't easy. The answers to most questions are not laid out in the statements. Users must analyze and interpret the financial statements to help them get the answers they need. Even then, the financial statements do not usually provide the answers. They provide clues and insights, but rarely definitive answers.

This chapter begins by providing some perspective on how different users approach the task of analyzing financial statements. It discusses the importance of having a good understanding of an entity before beginning the analysis. The chapter also explains the concepts of permanent and transitory earnings, which are valuable for understanding how current earnings are useful for predicting future earnings.

Throughout the book tools for analyzing and interpreting financial statements have been discussed. The chapter reviews those analytical tools and provides additional methods for interpreting financial statements. Two techniques that eliminate the impact of size from the financial statement numbers and restate them as proportions are introduced: common size financial statements and trend statements. The ratios and analytical tools are grouped into four analytical themes:

1. evaluating performance
2. liquidity
3. solvency and leverage
4. other common ratios

Why Analyze and Interpret Financial Statements?

Analysis and interpretation of financial information is not an end in itself. People analyze financial statements to help them make better decisions. The type of analysis that one does depends on the decision one has to make. Different stakeholders will have different questions that they need resolved. As a result, each stakeholder group will approach their analysis differently.

Let's look at some stakeholders and discuss reasons why they would want to analyze financial statements.

Creditors   Creditors come in many shapes and sizes. They may be suppliers of goods and services that accept payment sometime (usually in a short time) after supplying the goods or services. Creditors may be banks that provide short-term or permanent working capital loans, or long-term financing through term loans. They may be suppliers of long-term financing through notes payable, bonds, debentures, or mortgages. Creditors may be public or private investors.

Creditors have two broad concerns:

- First, they are concerned about the ability of the borrower to make payments. To assess this concern, creditors consider the resources the entity has and the reliability, timing, and stability of its future cash flows. Creditors will be particularly concerned about an entity's ability to make payments as economic conditions change—for example, if the economy enters a recession. A creditor will want to be confident that the borrower can weather poorer economic conditions and meet its obligations.

- Second, creditors are concerned about security. Security can be assets that a creditor can sell or arrange to sell if the borrower does not meet its obligations. For this purpose a creditor will want to know the fair market value of the assets that have been given as security. Security can also be provided through specified restrictions on the behaviour of the borrower. These restrictions can be in the form of actual limitations on the borrower's activities—for example, restrictions on the payment of dividends, additional borrowing, or the sale of certain assets. Restrictions can also require that borrowers comply with specified accounting measures, such as the current ratio or the debt-to-equity ratio, where the borrower agrees not to exceed specified levels of these measures.

    Restrictions that impose limits on the actions of borrowers are known as **covenants**. Violation of covenants can have significant economic consequences on the borrower, such as requiring immediate repayment of the loan or an increase in the interest rate charged on the loan.

The type of analysis required by a creditor depends on the nature of the credit being provided. Short-term creditors will be concerned about an entity's financial situation at the time the credit is offered, the liquidity of current assets, and how quickly the current assets turn over. Long-term creditors will want to forecast future cash flows and evaluate the borrower's ability to generate earnings. The ability of an entity to generate earnings is important because it serves as an indicator of the borrower's ability to generate cash flows to meet its obligations.

Equity Investors   In many ways equity investors need to know everything. That's because most decisions and factors that affect an entity affect the equity investors. Remember that equity investors have a residual interest in the entity. A residual interest means that equity investors are entitled to what is left over after all other interests, in particular creditors, have been satisfied. Because of their residual interest in an entity, equity investors' analyses are much more complex than those of creditors. Whereas a creditor has to assess the ability of an entity to make specified payments at specified times, payments to equity investors are not specified or required.

There are many questions that equity investors (or prospective equity investors) can ask. A fundamental question is the value of the entity or its shares. This is an extremely important question for people considering investing in or purchasing a privately owned entity. Privately owned companies do not have prices set by trading on a stock market to serve as a benchmark for evaluation, so financial statement analysis is crucial for determining a reasonable price for a prospective investment. Public companies are also thoroughly analyzed by individual investors, analysts for investment bankers, and mutual and pension fund managers to determine whether the market has "properly" priced the shares. Equity investors could analyze an entity to determine strengths and weaknesses in its performance, perhaps relative to competitors. Equity investors could also analyze an entity to assess its risk.

As well as creditors and equity investors, we should keep in mind the many stakeholders that were identified in Chapter 1 and that have been referred to throughout the book, including:

- Employees and their representatives, who could analyze the financial statements of the employer to determine the employer's ability to pay increased wages.

- The Canada Customs and Revenue Agency (CCRA), which might analyze financial statements to assess the reasonableness of amounts reported in tax returns.

- Regulators, which could use financial information to evaluate requests by regulated companies for permission to increase their prices.

We could continue. The point is that while stakeholders use financial accounting information in their decision making, in most cases the financial statements do not present the answers to stakeholders' questions "on a silver platter." Usually, the information in the financial statements must be analyzed, massaged, evaluated, and interpreted before it can provide insights about the entity.

Know the Entity

Financial statements are only one source of information about an entity, albeit an important one. The successful analysis of an entity cannot be achieved only by examining its financial statements. In fact, the analysis of an entity shouldn't even begin with the financial statements.

Financial statements are nothing more than numbers on pages. To understand what those numbers are saying requires an understanding of the entity's business, its industry, and its environment. Much of that information will come from sources other than the financial statements. Chapter 2 of this book is titled *Financial Statements: A Window on an Entity*. Why is this title significant? Because it emphasizes that financial statements provide important information about an entity and are essential for investigating various aspects of the entity, but that while financial statements are *a* window on an entity, they are not the *only* window. Just as looking in only one window of a house cannot give the observer a complete view of all its rooms, examining only the financial statements cannot provide a complete view of the entity.

Information about entities can be obtained from many sources. The media often provide news items about entities. Brokerage firms provide research that analyzes the investment prospects of publicly traded companies. There are also many online services that provide information, such as Globeinvestor.com and Hoovers.com.

Information about a particular entity is not the only relevant information that someone might consider. Information about competitors can also be important, as it provides another benchmark against which to evaluate the entity of interest.

Information about the entity's industry can also be relevant. Industry information can be obtained from industry and trade associations that represent the interests of all members of a particular industry. Statistics Canada, a department of the Government of Canada, provides extensive industry information. Statistics Canada also provides detailed economic and demographic data.

There are many more possible sources and types of information that people can

www.statcan.ca

consider and access in their investigation of an entity. Keep in mind, though, that not all of these sources provide information for free.

What does one need to know about an entity, its industry, and environment? A list could be endless and much depends on the entity being investigated and its environment. Some questions to consider include:

- What does the entity do—what business or businesses is it in?
- What strategies does the entity use to make money?
- What is the entity's competitive environment? (Are there many competitors? Is it easy for new competitors to enter the market?)
- What are the entity's competitive advantages?
- Who are the managers of the entity? What experience do the managers' have? What has their performance been?
- What are the risks faced by the entity?
- Is the entity regulated? How does regulation affect the way it can conduct business?
- How do economic conditions and changes in economic conditions affect the entity?
- What are the conditions in the entity's businesses?
- How does the entity produce, market, and distribute its products?
- What are the key inputs for the entity and how does it obtain them? What are the conditions in the supplier market?
- What are the entity's key success factors?

While one should examine sources other than the annual report to learn about an entity, its industry, and its environment, the annual reports of public companies can provide considerable useful information beyond what is reported in the financial statements and notes. One very valuable section of an annual report is the **management discussion and analysis (MD&A)**. The MD&A must be prepared by publicly traded companies (but not by private companies). The MD&A is prepared by an entity's managers and provides them the opportunity to discuss its financial results, position, and future prospects. The MD&A is intended to provide readers with a view of the entity through the eyes of management.

MWW's MD&A can be found between pages A-23 and A-43 in Appendix A of this book. MWW's MD&A provides extensive interpretation, discussion, and analysis that compliments and supplements the information in the financial statements. Some examples of the information in MWW's MD&A are:

- Analysis of MWW's performance against the industry.
- Breakdown of the financial statements by operating component (Mark's, Work World, DOCKERS®).
- Additional details about numbers reported in the financial statements (for example, Table 7 on page A-29 provides additional detail on MWW's front-line expenses).
- Explanation of significant changes from previous years.
- Highlights of the risks and uncertainties affecting MWW.

A user of MWW's financial statements would be in a much better position to understand the statements after having carefully read the MD&A. However, it should be noted that the quality of MD&As varies widely from entity to entity and depends on what management puts into it. Some entities provide very informative MD&As, whereas others do little more than state the obvious. MWW's MD&A is excellent.

While the MD&A can be a very valuable source of information about an entity, it is important to remember that management prepares it. This raises an interesting paradox. An entity's management is, for the most part, the best source of information and insight about the entity. But management will not likely be unbiased in its presentation of information about the entity. That is not to say that the information provided by management will be false. Rather, management is likely to focus on positive aspects of the entity, its performance, and its prospects, and provided favourable and optimistic interpretations of events.

Private companies are not required to provide a MD&A. In general, one can expect to find far less information about private companies than public ones, both from the private companies themselves and from non-company sources. To begin with, private companies are not required to disclose their financial statements to the public. Private companies can limit the disclosure of their statements to whichever entities they chose—for instance, the CCRA, the company's bankers, and possibly suppliers who want to do a credit analysis. Also, there will usually be little interest in private companies by the investment community. People in the investment community will gather information about public companies in an effort to gain insight into the desirability of investing in their equity and debt. The same incentives for gathering information about private companies do not exist.

There are other parts of annual reports that can provide useful information. Annual reports usually have a message from the CEO and/or the chair of the board of directors. They also typically include information about the entity's senior executives and the members of the board of directors. All this information can be useful, depending on the user and use.

Companies often issue press releases about their activities. While press releases and other disclosures by an entity are prepared by management and can therefore be biased, they can still be a useful source of information.

Of course, as a user of financial information you should evaluate all information you receive for its usefulness and credibility. You should recognize that just because information is provided by a source other than the entity itself, it does not mean that the information is unbiased. For example, information from industry associations would take views favourable to the interests of that industry. Also, research by brokerages and investment bankers has been assailed in recent years because it has been suggested that these organizations have incentives not to offend entities that might use their services in the future. As a result, these organizations are unlikely to make negative statements about potential future clients.

Permanent Earnings and the Quality of Earnings

Permanent Earnings

One of the themes that has been emphasized throughout this book is that net income is not an absolute or true number. Net income reflects the economic gain or loss of the owners of the entity; it is a representation of the underlying economic performance of an entity, albeit not a complete or comprehensive representation. We have seen that measuring economic gains or losses is extremely complex. As a result, it is not possible to determine an entity's "true" net income. The amount of income an entity reports is a function of the accounting policies it chooses and the estimates it makes. Despite all the difficulties that exist in measuring income, the measurement of income is important.

For many stakeholders or prospective stakeholders, an important use for current earnings is for forecasting future earnings. The *CICA Handbook* states that an objective of financial statements is for investors and creditors to predict earnings and cash flow. Even absent this specific statement in the *CICA Handbook*, it is clear that for many users and uses, knowing future net incomes would be quite valuable. Any information that would help these users make better forecasts of future earnings would also be helpful.

That said, Canadian GAAP, as well as financial reporting regulations in most jurisdictions around the world, do not require or support providing forecasted financial statements. As a result, stakeholders are left to their own devices in trying to make these forecasts. Of course, stakeholders are not completely abandoned in Canada. Disclosure requirements and information from other sources can improve stakeholders' ability to make forecasts.

For the purpose of forecasting future earnings, historical earnings can be used as a starting point. Historical earnings can be adjusted to reflect changes that are expected to affect the entity. An important aspect of interpreting historical earnings is being able to determine the components of earnings that can be expected to recur in future periods. These **permanent earnings**—earnings that are expected to be repeated in the future—are a good indicator of future earnings. In contrast, **transitory earnings** are earnings that are not expected to be repeated in future periods. The net income of an entity can have both permanent and transitory components.

The distinction between permanent and transitory earnings and their impact on forecasting future earnings can be shown with the following example.

In mid-2006 Rusagonis Ltd. (Rusagonis) signed a $100,000 contract with a customer. After considering all costs, Rusagonis' management expects to earn $31,000 as a result of the contract. If the revenue and earnings associated with this contract are repeated year after year, the contract will increase permanent earnings. This is an appropriate interpretation if Rusagonis' management expects that the customer is going to become permanent or if the contract will be indicative of Rusagonis' growth. If we measure the value of a company as the present value of its future earnings, we would expect the value of Rusagonis to increase by the present value of a series of $31,000 payments to be received for the foreseeable future. (It is assumed here that the annual earnings increase translates into annual cash flows of $31,000, which in fact may not be the case. However, the principle should be clear.) To a lender, the new contract would mean that Rusagonis could support more debt. Because of the new contract, shareholders might anticipate increased dividends. The new contact might enable unions and employees to argue for increased wages and salaries.

But now let's suppose that the $100,000 contract was a just a one-time event. In this situation Rusagonis is clearly better off, but only by $31,000 (the amount of profit earned on the contract). This contract and contracts like it are not expected to occur in the future, so the contract has no implications for future earnings. There is no permanent effect on the performance of Rusagonis. If a stakeholder were estimating future earnings, the contract would be ignored because it has no effect on permanent or future earnings—it was simply a one-time event. In other words, the effect of this contract on earnings is transitory. There would be a one-year increase in earnings of $31,000, but everything else being equal, earnings would be expected to decrease in the next year by $31,000 and return to the pre-2006 level.

This discussion should highlight the importance to users of understanding the sources of an entity's earnings and the reason for changes in its earnings. Permanent and transitory earnings should be interpreted differently. As a result, it is desirable for financial statements to provide information the helps users distinguish permanent and transitory earnings.

GAAP and the *CICA Handbook* provide some help in this regard. The *CICA Handbook* requires or allows disclosure of information that is helpful for understanding the components of earnings. We will look at three areas:

1. extraordinary items

2. unusual items

3. discontinued operations

Extraordinary Items   An **extraordinary item** (EOI) is defined in the *CICA Handbook* as an event or transaction that is:

- not expected to occur frequently,

- not typical of the entity's business, and

- not primarily the result of decisions or determinations by the managers or owners of the entity.

The *CICA Handbook* requires that EOIs be disclosed separately in the income statement. The designation as extraordinary clearly indicates that an event is transitory. Because of the stringent criteria for determining whether a transaction or event should be treated as extraordinary (particularly the third one), EOIs are rarely reported in Canadian financial statements. *Financial Reporting in Canada,* 26th Edition reports that in its sample of 200 public companies, there was only one EOI reported in 2000, one in 1999, four in 1998, and six in 1997.[1] Examples of events and transactions that could be considered extraordinary include losses caused by natural disasters (earthquakes, tornadoes) and expropriations.

Interestingly, the *CICA Handbook* distinguishes between natural disasters that are part of the normal risks faced by an entity and those that are out of the ordinary. For example, crop losses by a farmer because of a drought would not be considered extraordinary if drought conditions are normally experienced every few years. On the other hand, destruction of a crop because of a tornado might fit the definition of an extraordinary item. The classification of a transaction or event as extraordinary is often a matter of judgment.

Exhibit 13-1 provides an example of an EOI.[2] It shows TransAlta Corporation's (TransAlta) statements of income, Note 4 to the financial statements, and an extract from the management discussion and analysis. For its year ended December 31, 2000, TransAlta reported an extraordinary loss of $209,700,000 as a result of a change from regulatory accounting to GAAP for non-regulated businesses. This extraordinary item is unusual in that it is an accounting change and, therefore, has no real economic impact. This accounting change is treated as extraordinary because it is the result of a change in the environment caused by the Alberta government's decision to deregulate the electricity industry. Normally, an accounting change would not be considered extraordinary because accounting changes are not infrequent or atypical. However, changes in the regulatory environment *are* infrequent and atypical.

www.transalta.com

Unusual Items   At one time the criteria for classifying a transaction or event as extraordinary were much looser than they are today. Many events that were actually quite ordinary—for example, losses on the sale of capital assets—were classified as extraordinary. When the criteria for extraordinary items were tightened, standard setters recognized that it was necessary to allow preparers to distinguish permanent and transitory events. As a result, Section 1520 of the *CICA Handbook*, the section on the income statement, was modified to require separate disclosure of "unusual" revenue, expenses, gains, and losses.

Unusual items are revenue, expenses, gains, and losses that do not meet the definition of an extraordinary item, but that are not expected to occur frequently, or that are not considered part of the normal business activities of the entity. While unusual items are included among the ordinary operating activities of the entity, identifying them separately is helpful because it allows users to distinguish events that are

TRANSALTA CORPORATION

CONSOLIDATED STATEMENTS OF EARNINGS & RETAINED EARNINGS

Years ended December 31 (in millions except earnings per common share)	2000	1999
Revenues	$ 1,587.0	$ 1,029.4
Operating expenses		
Fuel and purchased power	479.1	205.4
Operations, maintenance and administration	359.6	262.7
Depreciation and amortization	252.0	210.3
Taxes, other than income taxes	36.9	35.7
	1,127.6	714.1
Operating income	459.4	315.3
Other income (expense)	(1.0)	2.4
Net interest charges (Note 11)	(100.8)	(79.1)
Earnings from continuing operations before regulatory decisions, income taxes and non-controlling interests	357.6	238.6
Prior period regulatory decisions (Note 17)	44.1	–
Earnings from continuing operations before income taxes and non-controlling interests	401.7	238.6
Income taxes (Note 18)	169.4	105.5
Non-controlling interests (Note 13)	41.6	30.9
Earnings from continuing operations	190.7	102.2
Earnings from discontinued operations (Notes 3 and 17)	44.8	53.4
Net gain on disposal of discontinued operations (Note 3)	266.8	19.7
Net earnings before extraordinary item	502.3	175.3
Extraordinary item (Note 4)	(209.7)	–
Net earnings	292.6	175.3
Preferred securities distributions, net of tax (Note 14)	12.8	5.2
Net earnings applicable to common shareholders	$ 279.8	$ 170.1
Common share dividends	(168.7)	(169.5)
Adjustment arising from normal course issuer bid (Note 15)	(7.5)	–
Retained earnings		
Opening balance (Note 1)	723.3	722.7
Closing balance	$ 826.9	$ 723.3
Weighted average common shares outstanding in the period	168.8	169.5
Basic earnings per share		
Continuing operations	$ 1.05	$ 0.57
Earnings from discontinued operations (Note 3)	0.27	0.32
Net earnings from operations	1.32	0.89
Net gain on disposal of discontinued operations (Note 3)	1.58	0.11
Extraordinary item (Note 4)	(1.24)	–
Net earnings	$ 1.66	$ 1.00
Fully diluted earnings per share (Note 14)		
Continuing operations	$ 1.03	$ 0.55
Net earnings from operations	$ 1.29	$ 0.87
Net earnings	$ 1.62	$ 0.97

See accompanying notes.

4: EXTRAORDINARY ITEM

In December 2000, the corporation discontinued regulatory accounting and commenced the application of generally accepted accounting principles for non-regulated businesses for its Alberta generation operations, consistent with the deregulation of the electricity generation industry in Alberta beginning on Jan. 1, 2001.

As a result of the discontinuance of regulatory accounting, the corporation recorded an extraordinary non-cash after-tax charge of $209.7 million ($1.24 per share) comprised of the following:

Write-off of regulatory accounts	$	2.5
Write-down of net carrying values of capital assets		17.3
Recognition of previously unrecognized future income tax liabilities		189.9
	$	209.7

(continued)

Exhibit 13-1

TransAlta Corporation: Extraordinary Item

permanent, transitory, or a little of each. This classification allows users to forecast earnings and cash flows better.

How particular transactions and events are classified in the income statement is often a matter of judgment. Managers may have incentives to classify bad news as unusual and to not classify good news as unusual. The reason is that unusual items are

Exhibit 13-1 (continued)

TransAlta Corporation:
Extraordinary Item

B: Extraordinary Item

On Dec. 31, 2000, TransAlta discontinued regulatory accounting and commenced the application of generally accepted accounting principles for non-regulated businesses for its Alberta generation operations, following final confirmation of deregulation of the electricity generation industry in Alberta beginning on Jan. 1, 2001. As a result of the discontinuance of regulatory accounting, the corporation recorded an extraordinary non-cash after-tax charge of $209.7 million ($1.24 EPS). Of this amount, $189.9 million ($1.13 EPS) results from the recognition of future income tax liabilities that the corporation was previously exempted from recording due to the regulatory environment.

In 1993, the Government of Alberta began a process to deregulate aspects of the Alberta electricity industry. Under this process, long-term power purchase arrangements (PPAs) were developed for existing regulated electricity generation. These PPAs were then auctioned to the public in 2000. Under the PPAs, which commenced Jan. 1, 2001, owners of the generating plants receive capacity payments and compensation for variable costs of producing electricity. The PPAs also provide incentives for exceeding specific plant availability targets. Owners are penalized, however, if the specific plant availability targets are not met and therefore full recovery of their costs is not assured in the future. In December 1999, the EUB approved the PPAs. Uncertainty as to the commencement of deregulation continued as a result of the requirement of Government of Alberta acceptance of the results of the PPA auctions. In August and December 2000, the results of the auctions of PPAs were accepted by the Government of Alberta, thereby removing this uncertainty.

more likely to be interpreted as transitory. For public companies, a transitory event should have less of an effect on an entity's stock price, so classifying bad news as unusual may lessen the stock price impact of the event. The logic is opposite for good news. If a good news event is not treated as unusual, the stock market may include the impact of the event in permanent earnings. Similarly, if managers' bonuses are based on earnings before unusual items, there would be incentives for them to classify bad news as unusual and good news as part of "ordinary" operations.

Financial Reporting in Canada, 26th Edition, reports that the classification of transactions and events as unusual is not uncommon. In 2000, 116 of the 200 companies surveyed (58% of the firms in the survey) reported unusual items. The percentage of firms reporting unusual items in other years was also high—64% in 1996 and 1997, 72% in 1998, and 71% in 1999.[3]

The *CICA Handbook* does not require that a transaction or event be designated as unusual, just that it be separately disclosed. As a result, users of the financial statements must carefully evaluate and consider the items reported in the income statement and disclosed in the notes to assess the implications an event may have for future periods. Users should also consider the implications of information from other sources and from financial statement analysis in evaluating earnings.

Exhibits 13-2 and 13-3 provide examples of unusual items. Exhibit 13-2 provides the statement of earnings, Note 6 to the financial statements, and an extract from the management discussion and analysis from the December 31, 2000 annual report of Alliance Forest Products Inc. (Alliance).[4] For its year ended December 31, 2000, Alliance reports two unusual items: a gain on disposal of certain fixed assets and the write-down of assets associated with closure of some of the facilities at one of Alliance's plants. Notice that the unusual items are not included in operating income. This treatment makes sense if these items are genuinely transitory. However, disposals and write-downs of assets can be fairly regular occurrences for some entities, so the classification as unusual can be confusing or even misleading. Alliance does not report any unusual items in 1999 or 1998, which provides some comfort that these two items are at least somewhat unusual. (Update note: Alliance was acquired by Bowater Incorporated in 2001.)

Exhibit 13-3 (page 778) provides the statement of income and Notes 2, 5, and 8 to Rogers Communications Inc. (Rogers).[5] In 2000 and 1999 Rogers reports a number of items below its operating income line that could be considered unusual. Rogers does not label these items as unusual, but it does disclose them separately. Because they are disclosed separately, users might evaluate them differently from ordinary operations.

www.rogers.com

Exhibit 13-2

Alliance Forest Products Inc.:
Unusual Items

Consolidated statements of earnings
Years ended December 31,

(In millions of Canadian dollars, except net earnings per share)

	2000	1999	1998
Sales	$1,085.1	$1,052.7	$1,085.1
Operating costs and expenses			
Cost of goods sold	910.6	914.0	864.2
Selling, general and administrative expenses	31.7	37.8	37.9
Depreciation, amortization and depletion	78.7	89.4	87.3
Amortization of the deferred gain (Note 4)	(34.4)	—	—
	986.6	1,041.2	989.4
Operating income	98.5	11.5	95.7
Net financing expenses	11.4	35.7	60.2
Earnings (loss) before unusual items and income taxes	87.1	(24.2)	35.5
Unusual items (Note 6)			
Gain on disposal of assets	11.0	—	—
Write-down of assets	(62.8)	—	—
	(51.8)	—	—
Earnings (loss) before income taxes	35.3	(24.2)	35.5
Income taxes (Note 7)			
Current (recovery)	53.1	(0.5)	(2.6)
Future	(39.1)	(7.5)	12.2
	14.0	(8.0)	9.6
Net earnings (loss)	21.3	(16.2)	25.9
Net earnings (loss) per common share	$0.68	$(0.44)	$0.68
Net earnings (loss) per common share before unusual items	$1.70	$(0.44)	$0.68

6. Unusual items

Gain on disposal of assets

On June 30, 2000, the Company disposed of the fixed assets relating to the manufacture of I-joists for a cash consideration of $15.8.

Write down of assets

During the second quarter, the Company recorded a $62.8 charge relating to the permanent closure at the end of 2001 of the deinking, mechanical pulp, thermo-mechanical pulp and hardwood pulp installations at Coosa Pines.

Extract from Alliance Forest Products Inc.'s Management Discussion and Analysis

Owing to the permanent closure in late 2001 of the current de-inking, mechanical pulp, thermomechanical pulp, and SBHK kraft pulp facilities, the Company recorded an unusual before-tax charge of $62.8 million in the second quarter. The start-up of the new recylced pulp plant and shutdown of the hardwood kraft pulping facilities will lead to the elimination of about 200 positions at the Coosa Pines complex. Once the project is complete, 338 positions will have been eliminated at Coosa Pines since the acquisition.

These items do have a significant effect on Rogers' bottom line. While Rogers' operating income minus interest on long-term debt is negative in 2000 and 1999, the company reports a profit in both years after these unusual items are considered. The proceeds received on termination of the merger agreement and the loss on early repayment of long-term debt would seem to be relatively uncommon events and could be reasonably considered unusual. The gain on the sale of assets and investments does not seem to be all that unusual, especially given that gains are reported in both 2000 and 1999.

It is important to recognize that there is wide variation in how unusual items are classified and disclosed in the financial statements. Users must stay on their toes to make sure they understand the actual nature of transactions and events being reported. Users should not accept the presentation in the financial statements at face value.

Discontinued Operations   Another helpful income statement classification that is required by the *CICA Handbook* is discontinued operations. A **discontinued operation** is a business segment that an entity has stopped operating or plans to stop operating. When management decides to discontinue operating a particular business segment, the *CICA Handbook* requires that the results from the discontinued opera-

Exhibit 13-3

Rogers Communications Inc.:
Unusual Items

consolidated statements of income

(In thousands of dollars, except per share amounts)
Years ended December 31

	2000	(As restated — note 1D) 1999
Revenue	$ 3,504,247	$ 3,107,846
Operating, general and administrative expenses	2,586,522	2,214,018
Operating income before the following	917,725	893,828
Integration costs on cablesystems exchange (note 2B)	10,612	—
Depreciation and amortization	730,779	619,113
Operating income	176,334	274,715
Interest on long-term debt	359,612	440,816
	(183,278)	(166,101)
Gain on sale and issuance of subsidiary shares (note 2C)	—	1,084,701
Gain on sale of assets and investments (note 5)	112,472	159,679
Proceeds received on termination of merger agreement, net (note 2D)	222,456	—
Loss on early repayment of long-term debt (note 8F)	—	(210,587)
Investment and other income	2,408	42,560
Income before income taxes and non-controlling interest	154,058	910,252
Income taxes (note 10):		
Current	14,935	10,524
Future	32,527	69,705
	47,462	80,229
Income before non-controlling interest	106,596	830,023
Non-controlling interest	34,846	34,698
Net income	$ 141,442	$ 864,721
Earnings per share (note 11):		
Basic	$ 0.44	$ 4.41
Adjusted basic	0.44	4.25
Fully diluted	0.44	3.79
Weighted-average number of Class A Voting and Class B Non-Voting shares outstanding (in thousands):		
Basic	203,761	189,805
Adjusted basic	203,761	200,857
Fully diluted	204,092	231,379

See accompanying Notes to Consolidated Financial Statements.

2. Acquisitions and divestitures

C. 1999 Divestitures

On August 16, 1999, the Company sold 12,313,435 Class A Multiple Voting shares of its subsidiary, Rogers Wireless Communications Inc. ("Wireless"), formerly Rogers Cantel Mobile Communications Inc., to AT&T Corp. ("AT&T") and British Telecommunications plc ("BT"). Contemporaneously, Wireless issued Preferred shares convertible into 15,334,453 Class A Multiple Voting shares and 12,443,324 Class B Restricted Voting shares of Wireless to AT&T and BT. These transactions, which reduced the Company's ownership in Wireless from 79.92% to 51.58%, yielded net proceeds of $1,382,165,000 and generated a combined gain on sale and dilution gain of $1,084,701,000 before income taxes.

D. Proceeds received on termination of merger agreement

On February 7, 2000, the Company announced that it had agreed to merge with Le Groupe Vidéotron ltée ("Vidéotron"). This agreement was subsequently terminated and, as a result, the Company received $241,000,000, which has been recorded as income net of expenses incurred.

tion be disclosed separately in the income statement. This means that the revenue and expenses associated with the discontinued operation are not included in normal operating revenue and expenses. Instead, these amounts are shown separately, usually toward the bottom of the income statement. Information about the current and comparative years for the discontinued operation is shown separately. Information about the assets and liabilities associated with the discontinued operation is also disclosed.

Exhibit 13-3 (continued)

Rogers Communications Inc.:
Unusual Items

5.   Investments

B.   Dispositions in 2000

i.   In 1999, the Company acquired 833,333 common shares of Liberate for $11,680,000 and received 216,666 warrants to purchase Liberate common shares at an exercise price of US$13.80 per warrant. Of these warrants, 116,666 vested immediately, however, any shares obtained on the exercise of these warrants may only be sold after December 30, 2000. The remaining 100,000 warrants vest over time based on certain conditions relating to subscriber set-top box deployment, with 70,000 warrants vesting automatically by March 2003. In 1999, the Company also acquired and subsequently sold 10,000 common shares of Liberate for proceeds of $1,696,000, recording a gain on sale of $1,555,000 before income taxes.

On January 18, 2000, Liberate completed a two-for-one share split. In 2000, the Company converted 116,666 pre split warrants which had vested upon signing of the agreement into 220,282 common shares post split, through a cashless exercise. In 2000, the Company also sold 350,000 shares of Liberate for proceeds of $11,227,000 resulting in a gain on sale of $8,753,000 before income taxes.

ii.   During 1999, the Company purchased for nominal consideration 2,000,000 warrants to acquire common shares of Terayon for an aggregate exercise price of US$38,000,000. The warrants were converted into 1,843,809 common shares through a cashless exercise in March 2000, and underwent a two-for-one share split on May 8, 2000. In 2000, the Company sold 450,000 common shares of Terayon for proceeds and a gain on sale of $30,891,000 before income taxes.

iii.   In 1998, the Company acquired 1,500,000 common shares and 100,000 warrants to acquire common shares of Bid.com for $1,900,000. These warrants have an exercise price of $1.40 per share. In 1998, the Company sold 200,000 common shares of Bid.com for proceeds of $656,000 and recorded a gain on sale of $403,000 before income taxes. In 1999, the Company sold 1,016,400 common shares of Bid.com for proceeds of $18,791,000 and recorded a gain on sale of $17,489,000 before income taxes. The Company also exercised warrants to acquire an additional 100,000 common shares of Bid.com at an exercise price of $1.40 per share. In 2000, the Company sold 181,300 common shares of Bid.com for proceeds of $1,527,000 and recorded a gain on sale of $1,292,000 before income taxes.

iv.   During 2000, the Company sold 2,035,211 common shares of CanCom to Shaw Communications Inc. for proceeds of $95,655,000 and recorded a gain on sale of $74,508,000 before income taxes.

8.   Long-term debt

F.   Debt repayment

In 1999, the Company repurchased US$860,624,000 of U.S. dollar denominated long-term debt with partial repurchases of: Corporate's Senior Notes due 2006 and 2007; Wireless, Senior Secured Notes due 2007 and Senior Secured Debentures due 2008 and 2016; and Cable's Senior Secured Second Priority Notes due 2002, 2005 and 2007 and Senior Secured Second Priority Debentures due 2012. As a result, the Company paid a prepayment premium of $106,376,000, incurred a loss from redesignating certain cross-currency interest rate exchange agreements of $4,324,000, and wrote off deferred financing costs of $17,147,000 and deferred foreign exchange of $82,740,000, resulting in a net loss on repayment of $210,587,000 (note 6).

Once the decision is made to stop operating a business segment, information about the segment gets disclosed separately. It doesn't matter if the segment being discontinued continues operating after the decision is made. Also, the costs associated with ceasing to operate a business segment are also included in the income statement. These costs can include termination pay for employees, costs of shutting or selling facilities, gains and losses on the disposition of assets, and so on. Discontinuing a business segment has implications for future revenues, expenses, and income of the entity, and prediction of future earnings and cash flows must take into account the changes caused by the discontinued operation.

Exhibit 13-4 (page 780) provides an example of discontinued operations.[6] In 2000 Cambior Inc. (Cambior), a major Canadian gold producer, decided that it would no longer operate in the base metal sector. Exhibit 13-4 provides Cambior's statement of operations and Note 4 to its financial statements. As a result of the decision, Cambior reported the revenues and expenses pertaining to the base metal sector as discontinued operations. What is reported in revenues and expenses in Cambior's statement of operations are the revenues and expenses of the business segments that Cambior is continuing to operate. The revenues and expenses pertaining to the base

www.cambior.com

CONSOLIDATED OPERATIONS

Years ended December 31	2000	1999	1998
(in thousands of United States dollars, except for amounts per share)	$	$	$
REVENUES			
Mining operations	209,921	227,186	252,136
Investments	720	1,776	1,998
	210,641	228,962	254,134
EXPENSES			
Mining operations	152,420	152,231	159,411
Depreciation, depletion and amortization	53,984	56,581	50,700
Exploration	2,441	8,033	7,948
General and administrative	4,458	6,427	6,070
Financial expenses	18,204	7,546	5,744
Loss (Gain) on foreign exchange	64	(86)	495
Gain on disposal of exploration properties and other	—	(1,156)	(4,232)
Writedown of investments	393	2,411	6,110
Writedown of mining assets *(Note 7)*	93,589	102,134	18,020
Unrealized loss (gain) on derivative instruments *(Note 2(a))*	(41,761)	18,600	3,400
Restructuring charge *(Note 15)*	518	49,261	—
	284,310	401,982	253,666
Earnings (Loss) before the undernoted items	(73,669)	(173,020)	468
Income and mining taxes *(Note 16)*	148	(7,729)	(6,572)
	(73,521)	(180,749)	(6,104)
Minority interest *(Note 11)*	—	(694)	(1,801)
Loss from continuing operations	(73,521)	(181,443)	(7,905)
Results of discontinued operations *(Note 4)*	(8,089)	(192,174)	(5,851)
Net loss	(81,610)	(373,617)	(13,756)
Loss per share			
Continuing operations	(1.01)	(2.57)	(0.12)
Discontinued operations	(0.11)	(2.72)	(0.08)
	(1.12)	(5.29)	(0.20)
Weighted average number of common shares outstanding (in thousands)	73,104	70,563	69,627

4 – DISCONTINUED OPERATIONS

Subsequent to the March 2000 agreement for the sale of the Bouchard-Hébert and Langlois mines, the Company decided to actively pursue the process of reducing its level of indebtedness by concentrating on the disposal of its other base metal assets. Consequently and in accordance with generally accepted accounting principles in Canada, the Company now presents its results from its base metal sector as discontinued operations.

During the year, the Bouchard-Hébert and Langlois mines and the Company's 100% interest in the La Granja property were sold for total net cash proceeds of $75,750,000, including working capital items of $5,868,000. Since the net book value of these assets totaled $79,277,000, a loss of $9,395,000 was charged to operations in 2000 as results of discontinued operations.

The elements of the consolidated statement of operations relating to discontinued operations are detailed as follows:

	2000	1999	1998
	$	$	$
Revenues from mining operations	32,392	102,842	89,327
Depreciation, depletion and amortization	1,576	16,274	12,491
Writedown of mining assets	—	188,704	365
Income and mining taxes	59	(12,128)	(2,689)
Earnings (Loss) from operations	1,306	(192,174)	(5,851)
Loss from disposal of assets	(9,395)	—	—
Results of discontinued operations	(8,089)	(192,174)	(5,851)

Exhibit 13-4 (continued)

Cambior Inc.: Discontinued Operations

As at December 31, 1999, the Company had commitments through forward sales and option contracts for its zinc and copper production. The mark-to-market loss of the hedge totaled $7,153,000 at December 31, 1999 of which, a mark-to-market loss of $6,162,000 was accounted for in the calculation of the writedown of the Bouchard-Hébert and Langlois mines in 1999. The balance was accounted for in the results of the discontinued operations in 2000.

Assets and liabilities relating to the discontinued operations are detailed as follows:

	2000	1999
	$	$
Current assets	57	16,151
Property, plant and equipment[1]	27,132	107,435
Current liabilities	364	6,215
Non-current liabilities	—	3,257

[1] These amounts are included in the tables presented in Note 7. They include provisions for the estimated care and maintenance expenses of the remaining assets held for sale.

As at December 31, 2000, assets from discontinued operations include the Carlota and Pachón copper projects.

metal sector are not included. As a result, operating income represents only income from ongoing business segments. This separation of operating activities and discontinued operations is helpful for predicting future earnings and cash flows.

Cambior reports only a single line on its statement of operations for discontinued operations. Additional information is provided in Note 4. Note 4 provides descriptions of the circumstances giving rise to the discontinued operations, details from the statement of operations and balance sheet related to the discontinued operations, and some additional information. Notice that Cambior's statement of operations classifies base metal sector operations for 1999 and 1998 as well for 2000 as discontinued, even though the decision to discontinue the base metal sector did not occur until 2000. This treatment is important because it makes the revenues and expenses related to ongoing operating activities comparable for the three reported years.

MWW also provides us with an example of transitory earnings. In fiscal 1999 MWW recorded a $2,961,000 provision for closure of its U.S. stores. This means that MWW expensed $2,961,000 as the estimated cost of ending its retailing experiment in the U.S. This is an example of transitory earnings because MWW would not be expected to incur these costs every year, so if a user were trying to predict earnings it would make sense to ignore this provision.

This is not to say that the store closing costs have no relevance. The cost of closing the stores is a real economic cost to MWW and the decision to end the U.S. venture can give some insights for management evaluation and stewardship purposes. However, for prediction purposes the provision is not relevant (assuming the costs are genuinely transitory).

Note 16 to MWW's financial statements provides additional information about the closure, including sales, expenses, and assets. (See page A-61.) The note also explains how much of the provision had actually been spent by the end of fiscal 2001. Notice that while the cost of closing the stores was accrued in fiscal 1999, the actual money was spent in subsequent fiscal years.

There is some evidence that managers sometimes use unusual items as a way of managing earnings. For example, if MWW overestimated the cost of closing its U.S.

stores, the amount of the overstatement would eventually have to be included in income. The amount might be included as part of permanent earnings rather than being disclosed as transitory. As a result, the entity would be able to categorize part of a loss as transitory, which would be ignored for purposes of making predictions, and the reversal would be included as permanent earnings, which would result in flawed predictions of future earnings.

Our discussion in this section has focussed on the reporting requirements of the *CICA Handbook*. It must be recognized that the interpretation of transactions and other economic events as permanent or transitory have significance beyond GAAP and the *CICA Handbook*. Regardless of the accounting basis being used, users should distinguish between events that have permanent and transitory implications for the financial statements.

Quality of Earnings

The discussion of permanent and transitory earnings leads us to another concept for evaluating the usefulness of the income statement and net income—earnings quality. **Earnings quality** refers to the usefulness of current earnings for predicting future earnings.

Earnings quality is high if there is a close relationship between current earnings and future earnings. Earnings quality is low if the relationship between current and future earnings is not close. Another way of thinking about earnings quality is as the extent to which reported earnings are permanent. If an entity's earnings contain a lot of transitory elements, those earnings would be considered to be of low quality.

Low earnings quality is not simply a matter of identifying and removing the transitory components of earnings that were discussed earlier. The lowering of earnings quality can be much more insidious than these obvious items. Managers can also lower earnings quality when they manage earnings through their accounting policies, estimates, and accruals. The crucial aspect of earnings management is that it allows managers to move earnings among periods to achieve their reporting objectives, but in doing so the managers lower earnings quality and distort the relationship between current and future earnings.

The concept of moving earnings among periods requires some explanation. First, let's review why it is possible for managers to manage earnings. As has been explained earlier in the book, there are two main culprits. The first is accrual accounting. Accrual accounting creates the need for judgment in determining when economic events occur and how they should be accounted for. The second is periodic reporting. Periodic reporting makes it necessary to provide financial information for periods of time that are shorter than the life of the entity. These two factors provide managers with the flexibility for deciding when and how revenues and expenses will be reported.

As we know, accounting does not affect an entity's cash flows (at least not directly, although there can be secondary cash flow effects caused by taxes, bonus plans, and so on). Earnings during a period can be thought of as being comprised of two elements: cash flow and accruals. These components can be expressed in equation form as:

$$\text{Earnings} = \text{Cash from operations} + \text{Accruals}$$

Cash from operations is real. An entity collects and spends a specific number of dollars during the period and accounting can do nothing to change that. Accruals represent the non-cash part of earnings. Accruals include things like amortization, bad debt expense, accrued liabilities, provisions for losses, write-downs of assets, and allowances for returns, to name a few. Accruals require judgment. The managers must estimate the amounts of the accruals because the actual amounts are not known.

Ultimately, the actual amounts of these estimates become known and are reflected in earnings. Accrual of a little too much bad debt expense this year means that at some time in the future, a little bit less of an expense will be required. In other words, if managers make accruals that lower earnings in one period, earnings will have to be higher in another period to offset this.

Let's consider the case of the bad debt expense referred to earlier. At the end of the life of an entity, the amount of receivables that will be collected will be known. The problem is that at the time a bad debt estimate is made, the amount that will be collected is not known. Over the life of an entity the "right" amount of bad debts will have to be expensed. The right amount is the amount of credit sales that were not collected. While over the life of an entity earnings cannot be managed, in the short term managers can use the uncertainty surrounding estimates and accruals to shift earnings among periods.

When managers use accruals to influence earnings in a given period, earnings quality can be impaired because by shifting earnings to satisfy short-term reporting objectives, the relationship between current and future earnings may be impaired. And remember, adherence to GAAP doesn't solve the problem. In most cases, earnings management is done in accordance with GAAP.

We have only covered part of the story. Quality of earnings can also be affected by an entity's operating decisions—the timing of its actual transactions. For example, if an entity wants to increase its income in a period, it can defer discretionary expenditures to a later period. Expenditures for research and development, advertising, and repairs and maintenance are possible candidates for this type of treatment. It is an important responsibility of management to determine how to spend the entity's money. Cutting back spending on advertising or research that management does not believe is productive makes sense. However, cutting these expenditures just to boost the bottom line can be counter-productive. Current expenditures on research can have a significant effect on an entity's future earnings. By reducing spending on research, current earnings might rise, but at the cost of future earnings. The same is true for advertising expenditures. Cutting advertising may provide a short-term boost to the bottom line, but at the expense of future earnings.

One of the problems with research and advertising is that they are usually expensed when incurred. (Under GAAP research expenditures must be expensed when incurred.) As a result, reducing spending for research and advertising will have an immediate effect on income, making it an attractive way for managers to manage earnings. Deferring repairs and maintenance will also have a positive effect on current earnings, but delaying the work may result in additional or more costly repairs and maintenance, or result in the need to replace the assets sooner.

In each case the decision to defer the expenditure can lower earnings quality. By reducing expenditures in the current period. earnings are higher, but future earnings will likely be lower. As a result, the relationship between current and future earnings is weakened and earnings quality is reduced. Remember that operational choices affect accounting but they do not represent accounting choice. Delaying or forgoing discretionary spending is properly not recorded under GAAP. Thus following GAAP does not ensure the absence of earnings management in these types of situations either.

There are a number of ways that discretionary spending can be evaluated. One way is to look at the expenditure in question in relation to the sales of the entity. For example, for research and development costs the following ratio could be calculated:

$$\text{Ratio of research and development expense to sales} = \frac{\text{Research and development expense}}{\text{Sales}}$$

Similar ratios can be calculated for other discretionary expenses. A significant decrease in the ratio in a period could indicate an attempt by management to bolster earnings by cutting discretionary spending. Of course there could be legitimate business reasons for a reduction in spending, relative to sales, on research, repairs and maintenance, or advertising. This conclusion reconfirms that financial statement analysis provides clues to potential problems. These analyses do not usually provide definitive answers.

Management can also affect the quality of earnings by recognizing sales in one period rather than another. For example, if management wanted to increase income, it could ship goods to customers early, or create incentives for customers to make purchases sooner than they otherwise would have. Such "channel stuffing" has the effect of increasing sales and income legitimately in a strict accounting sense, but this action makes current sales and earnings a poorer indicator of future earnings. The impact of channel stuffing is that customers will not have to buy as much in future periods, or they will return merchandise in larger-than-expected amounts. This type of behaviour is difficult to identify from financial statements.

Managers can also affect earnings by managing the accruals and estimates related to sales. These accruals and estimates include the allowance for bad debts, warranty provision, allowance for returns, and unearned revenue. What is ultimately important about sales is the cash that is realized from them. It is possible to gain some insight in management of these estimates by looking at the relationship between these estimates and sales. For example, the relationship between warranty liabilities and sales could be analyzed by examining the ratio of sales to warranty liabilities. If the ratio showed a significant change during a period, a user could consider the possibility of earnings management and question the quality of the entity's earnings. Similar ratios and analyses could be conducted for the other accruals and estimates that are related to sales.

An in-depth examination of earnings management and financial statement analysis is beyond the scope of this book. Indeed, it could be the subject of a book itself. However, below are some additional points to consider:

- Disclosure is one of the most effective ways of overcoming difficulties in understanding the effects of an entity's accounting choices on its financial statements. If users were informed about the impact of accounting choices and estimates, they would be better able to assess the quality of an entity's earnings and then be able to make better forecasts and to better assess the quality of information management is providing. The *CICA Handbook* has disclosure requirements, as do securities regulations, and as we discussed in Chapter 5, the measurement convention of full disclosure requires that an entity provide all relevant information about the economic activities of the entity. For example, entities could be required to disclose all the estimates that they make and the amounts that actually occur. However, it is important to remember that too much information can be a problem. There are limits to the amount of information that human beings can process. Also, the cost of going through large quantities of information could exceed any benefit derived from doing so.

- When analyzing financial statements for purposes of predicting future earnings and cash flows, one's starting point should be a measure of earnings that excludes transitory items such as unusual items, extraordinary items, and discontinued operations. Clearly, net income is not the appropriate measure because it includes transitory items. In many cases, the appropriate definition of earnings may not be reported as a separate line on the income statement. It may be necessary for a user to make his or her own adjustments to the income statement to determine an appropriate measure of income. The challenge then is rooting out the elements that lower the earnings quality of this preliminary measure of earnings.

- Accounting choices in one period often have implications that go beyond that period. For example, when an entity takes a big bath by writing off or writing down some of its assets, earnings in periods after the big bath will be higher than they would have been had the big bath not occurred because there are less costs to expense. If, as part of a big bath, an entity wrote down equipment initially with a book value of $10,000,000 to $4,000,000, income in the year of the bath would be reduced by $6,000,000, but in subsequent years there would be $6,000,000 less equipment to amortize. If the equipment had a remaining useful life of ten years, amortization each year would be $600,000 lower than it would have been had the big bath not occurred. The big bath would likely have been interpreted as a transitory item, but the effect in subsequent years could easily be included in permanent earnings.

Question for Consideration

Explain the concept of earnings quality. Give two examples of accounting treatments that could lower an entity's earnings quality and explain why each lowers earnings quality.

Answer: Earnings quality refers to the usefulness of current earnings for predicting future earnings. Earnings quality is high if there is a close relationship between current earnings and future earnings. Earnings quality is low if the relationship between current and future earnings is not close. Another way of thinking about earnings quality is as the extent to which reported earnings are permanent. If an entity's earnings contain a lot of transitory elements, those earnings would be considered to be of low quality.

Biased estimates, such as underestimating the bad debt expense, lower earnings quality because by overstating current earnings, an entity is trying to make itself look more profitable than it really is. If the current earnings are used as a basis for forecasting future earnings, the forecast will be overstated because current earnings are overstated.

Reducing discretionary expenditures, such as for advertising, research, or repairs and maintenance, will lower earnings quality if the reduction is temporary. Reduction of these expenditures makes the entity appear more profitable than it actually is, which lowers earnings quality.

Using Ratios to Analyze Accounting Information

Throughout this book we have discussed using financial statement information for analyzing entities. In most chapters ratios and other analytical tools were introduced. In this chapter, some of the same ratios and analytical tools are discussed, but here they are grouped into four analytical themes:

1. evaluating performance

2. liquidity

3. solvency and leverage

4. other common ratios

However, before that discussion begins, two new analytical tools, common size financial statements and trend analysis, are introduced.

If you have been working carefully with the financial statement analysis material in each chapter, you probably already have some good skills for analyzing and interpreting financial statements. Because the material from earlier chapters is not repeated in its entirety here, you may find it helpful to review the earlier parts of the book in which the ratio or tool was initially introduced. Figure 13-1 summarizes the financial statement analysis material covered in each chapter.

Before we begin our discussion, here are a few points to keep in mind:

- There are no GAAP for ratio analysis or financial statement analysis. A person can modify or create any ratios that he or she feels is appropriate for the intended purpose. What is important is making sure that the right tool is used for the task at hand.

- While many of the topics, ratios, and tools are presented separately in this section, they cannot be considered independently. The information obtained from different analyses often has to be integrated to obtain the most informed insights.

- As was discussed earlier in this chapter, financial information has to be integrated with information from other sources to get a more complete picture of the entity and its circumstances.

- Materiality is important. Small changes in some accounts (such as gross margin) can be very significant and important, whereas large changes in other accounts may be unimportant.

- Financial statement information cannot be interpreted in a vacuum. The information must be compared to previous years' information from the same entity, the performance of other entities, industry standards, forecasts, and other benchmarks.

Common Size Financial Statements and Trend Analysis

Interpreting the raw numbers—the numbers actually presented in a set of financial statements—can be a challenge. It is certainly necessary to examine the actual numbers that an entity reports, but it can be difficult to make sense of trends in and relationships between the numbers in the statements by examining only the raw numbers. It can also be difficult to compare the raw numbers of different entities.

In this section we will discuss two tools that make this type of analysis easier:

- common size financial statements or vertical analysis

- trend or horizontal analysis

Figure 13-1

Summary of Financial Statement Analysis Coverage in Chapters 1 Through 12

Chapter	Coverage
Chapter 2	• Current ratio, pp. 46–47 • Debt-to-equity ratio, p. 49
Chapter 3	• Profit margin ratio, p. 113 • Return on equity, p. 113
Chapter 4	• The effect of accounting choices on financial statement numbers, pp. 190–203
Chapter 6	• Interpreting the cash flow statement, pp. 340–345 • The effect of accrual accounting choices on the cash flow statement, pp. 345–348
Chapter 7	• Hidden reserves, pp. 404–406 • Quick ratios and limitations of the current ratio for measuring liquidity, pp. 406–408 • Accounts receivable turnover ratio and average collection period of accounts receivable—limitations of these measures, pp. 408-410
Chapter 8	• Inventory turnover ratio and average number of days inventory on hand—evaluation of inventory management, pp. 468–470 • A banker's view of inventory, p. 471
Chapter 9	• Return on assets—measurement of performance and operating efficiency of an entity, pp. 537–538 • Limitations to using historical information about capital assets for decision making, pp. 500–502 • The effect of accounting policy choices on the cash flow statement, pp. 531–537 • The effect of accounting policy choice on ratios, pp. 537–538
Chapter 10	• Debt-to-equity ratio—measure of risk and debt carrying ability, pp. 621–622 • Interest coverage ratio—ability to cover fixed financing charges, pp. 622–623
Chapter 11	• Leverage, pp. 677–679 • Book value versus market value of equity—why the accounting value of equity can differ from the market value, p. 685 • Earnings per share (basic and fully diluted)—summary measure of performance, pp. 685–688 • Return on shareholders' equity—measure of return earned by common shareholders, pp. 688–689
Chapter 12	• Limitations of consolidated financial statements for ratio analysis, pp. 734–737

These tools eliminate the impact of size from the financial statement numbers by restating them as proportions.

Common Size Financial Statements or Vertical Analysis **Common size financial statements** or **vertical analysis** is an analytical tool in which the amounts in the balance sheet and income statement are expressed as percentages of other elements in the same year's statements. On the balance sheet, assets and liabilities and equities can be expressed as a percentage of total assets. On the income statement, amounts can be stated as a percentage of revenue. If amounts on the balance sheet are presented as percentages of total assets, the common size balance sheet will show the percentages that cash, inventory, capital assets, long-term debt, and so on are of total assets.

This presentation gives a person a good view of the asset and liability composition of the entity. Similarly, if income statement elements are stated as a percentage of revenues, the user can see the proportion of sales that each expense represents. This type of analysis can provide some useful insights into the relative importance of different expenses and allow comparisons over time and with other entities. For example, comparing common size income statements would allow users to see the percentage of each sales dollar that is expended for advertising, research and development, or wages. By examining the common size financial statements of an entity over a number of years, it may be possible to explain developments such as changes in profitability.

Figure 13-2 shows common size financial statements for MWW. On MWW's statements of earnings, each line is presented as a percentage of sales for the year. As a result, the sales line in each is 100% (for fiscal 2001, sales $_{\text{fiscal 2001}}$ ÷ sales $_{\text{fiscal 2001}}$ × 100% = $363,870,000 ÷ $363,870,000 × 100%). Similarly, gross margin for fiscal 2001 is 41.1% of sales (gross margin $_{\text{fiscal 2001}}$ ÷ sales $_{\text{fiscal 2001}}$ × 100% = $149,509,000 ÷ $363,870,000 × 100%).

The common size statement of earnings makes year-to-year comparisons very convenient. By comparing each row we see how each amount as a proportion of sales has changed over time. For example, MWW's gross margin as a percentage of sales increased from 40.3% in fiscal 1999 to 40.6% in fiscal 2000 to 41.1% in fiscal 2001. By looking at MWW's actual statement of earnings it is not possible to tell at a glance that the gross margin percentage has increased. It is easy enough to see that the gross margin has increased, because the dollar amount in fiscal 2001 is greater than the amounts in 1999 or 2000. However, the dollar increase in gross margin could have been due to the increase in sales, to an increase in the gross margin percentage, or to both. The common size statements of earnings shows clearly that the gross margin percentage has increased.

Figure 13-2

Common Size Financial Statements for Mark's Work Wearhouse Ltd.

Mark's Work Wearhouse Ltd.
Common Size Consolidated Balance Sheets

	As at January 30, 1999	As at January 29, 2000	As at January 27, 2001
ASSETS			
Current assets			
Cash and cash equivalents	2.0%	1.2%	4.5%
Accounts receivable	10.0%	10.5%	8.9%
Merchandise inventories	57.9%	56.9%	53.8%
Other current assets	2.5%	2.3%	3.1%
	72.5%	70.9%	70.3%
Other assets	0.7%	1.1%	0.7%
Capital assets	17.7%	18.1%	17.9%
Future income taxes	2.6%	2.1%	1.9%
Goodwill	6.6%	7.7%	9.2%
	100.0%	100.0%	100.0%
LIABILITIES			
Current liabilities			
Accounts payable and accrued liabilities	32.8%	32.0%	29.4%
Income taxes payable	3.7%	1.6%	3.9%
Current portion of long-term debt	6.0%	6.5%	6.9%
	42.5%	40.0%	40.3%
Long-term debt	16.6%	16.7%	17.2%
Deferred gains	0.8%	1.6%	1.3%
	59.9%	58.4%	58.8%
SHAREHOLDERS' EQUITY			
Capital stock	24.6%	22.9%	19.9%
Retained earnings	15.5%	18.8%	21.3%
	40.1%	41.6%	41.2%
	100.0%	100.0%	100.0%

Figure 13-2 (continued)

Common Size Financial Statements for Mark's Work Wearhouse Ltd.

Mark's Work Wearhouse Ltd.
Common Size Consolidated Statements of Earnings and Retained Earnings

	52 weeks ended January 30, 1999	52 weeks ended January 29, 2000	52 weeks ended January 27, 2001
Corporate and franchise sales	147.3%	139.1%	134.1%
Corporate operations			
Front-line operations			
Sales	100.0%	100.0%	100.0%
Cost of sales	59.7%	59.4%	58.9%
Gross margin	**40.3%**	**40.6%**	**41.1%**
Front-line expenses			
Personnel, advertising, and other	18.3%	18.2%	18.5%
Occupancy	9.1%	9.9%	9.8%
Depreciation and amortization	1.9%	2.0%	1.8%
Interest—short term	0.7%	0.5%	0.4%
	30.0%	30.6%	30.6%
Front-line contribution	**10.3%**	**10.1%**	**10.5%**
Franchise royalties and other	2.5%	2.1%	1.8%
Net front-line contribution before back-line expenses	**12.8%**	**12.2%**	**12.3%**
Back-line operations			
Back-line expenses			
Personnel, administration, and other	5.3%	5.3%	5.2%
Occupancy	0.4%	0.3%	0.3%
Depreciation and amortization	1.0%	1.1%	1.0%
Software development and maintenance costs	0.3%	0.4%	0.3%
Computer services	0.2%	0.2%	0.2%
Interest—long term	0.5%	0.8%	0.7%
Franchise bad debt provisions (recoveries)	0.1%	0.1%	(0.1%)
	7.7%	8.1%	7.6%
Earnings before provision for closure of U.S. pilot stores, income taxes and goodwill amortization	**5.0%**	**4.0%**	**4.7%**
Provision for closure of U.S. pilot stores	1.0%	–	–
Earnings before income taxes and goodwill amortization	**4.0%**	**4.0%**	**4.7%**
Income taxes			
Current expense	2.3%	1.8%	2.3%
Future expense (benefit)	(0.5%)	0.1%	0.0%
	1.9%	1.9%	2.3%
Net earnings before goodwill amortization	**2.1%**	**2.1%**	**2.4%**
Goodwill amortization	0.1%	0.1%	0.2%
Net earnings	**2.0%**	**2.0%**	**2.2%**

Similar analyses can be carried out for any line on the statement of earnings. Examination of MWW's common size statements of earnings shows that relative to sales, performance has been very stable over the last three years. Some items that stand out on the statement of earnings include:

- Front-line occupancy costs have increase from 9.1% of sales in fiscal 1999 to 9.8% in fiscal 2001.

- Franchise royalties and other have decreased from 2.5% of sales in fiscal 1999 to 1.8% in fiscal 2001. This decline is due, at least in part, to the decrease in the number of franchise stores over the period.

- Net earnings as a percentage of sales is 0.2% higher in fiscal 2001 than in fiscal 1999 or 2000. However, ignoring the effect in fiscal 1999 of the provision for the closure of U.S. pilot stores, net earnings as a percentage of sales was actually higher in 1999.

Though this point has been made many times in the book, it bears repeating again: *Financial statement analysis may help identify problems, but it will not usually explain them.* For example, it is not evident from MWW's statement of earnings that the reason for the decline in franchise royalties and other is due to the decrease in the number of franchise stores. This conclusion can only be drawn from further investigation or knowledge of the entity. In this case an explanation can be found elsewhere in the annual report. Another example: It is not clear why MWW's gross margin percentage has increased over the last three years. Some answers may be found in the MD&A, but that may not always be the case. In many cases explanations may not be found in the annual report at all. Users would have to look elsewhere for help to answer the question at hand.

We can do similar analyses on the balance sheet. In the common size balance sheets in Figure 13-2, each amount is stated as a percentage of total assets. For example, inventory on January 27, 2001 is stated as 53.8% of total assets (inventory $_{\text{January 27, 2001}}$ ÷ total assets $_{\text{January 27, 2001}}$ × 100% = $84,483,000 ÷ $157,060,000 × 100%). Similarly, accounts payable and accrued liabilities on January 27, 2001 represent 29.4% of total assets, or total liabilities plus equities since the two are equal (accounts payable $_{\text{January 27, 2001}}$ ÷ total assets $_{\text{January 27, 2001}}$ × 100% = $46,131,000 ÷ $157,060,000 × 100%). Comparing the percentages year to year allows the user to see any changes in the relative proportion of assets and liabilities.

Some of the items that stand out when examining MWW's common size balance sheets include:

- The relative amount of inventory has decreased by 4.1% from the end of fiscal 1999 to the end of fiscal 2001, despite an increase in sales over the same period.

- The proportion goodwill is of total assets has increased from 6.6% at the end of fiscal 1999 to 9.2% at the end of fiscal 2001. This increase is due to the purchase of franchise stores and the acquisition of Paul John Enterprises Inc.

- The proportion of accounts payable and accrued liabilities has decreased from 32.8% of total assets at the end of fiscal 1999 to 29.4% at the end of fiscal 2001.

- Overall, the elements of the balance sheet have remained relatively stable over the three reported years.

As with any type of analysis, there is a lot of flexibility in common size financial statement analysis. For example, a user might be interested in analyzing inventory as a proportion of current assets, rather than as a proportion of total assets. This type of analysis would give insights into the entity's liquidity. By comparing the percentage of total current assets represented by inventory with percentages from previous years, users can gain insight into whether the liquidity of the current assets is changing.

Common size financial statements are also very useful for comparing the financial statements of different entities. It can be very difficult to compare raw financial statement numbers of different entities because the entities may differ in size. Common size financial statements eliminate the effects of size and allow users to see the financial statement components of different entities on a common basis. Of course, differences between entities have to be interpreted carefully because they can be due to different accounting choices, as well as to differences in the economic performance and nature of the entities.

Horizontal Analysis or Trend Statements

Another type of analysis that eliminates the effects of size from financial statements is called horizontal analysis or trend statements. **Horizontal analysis** or **trend statements** is an analytical tool in which the amounts in the balance sheet and income statement are expressed as percentages of a base year set of financial statements.

Trend statements provide information that shows the change in each account in the financial statements relative to that account's base year. To construct trend statements, it is first necessary to specify a base year. The base year serves as the basis for determining the trend in each account in the financial statements. For each year reported in the financial statements, each account is stated as a proportion of that particular account's base year.

MWW's trend statements are presented in Figure 13-3 (page 792–793). For the statements in Figure 13-3, 1999 was selected as the base year. Notice that each row on MWW's 1999 balance sheet and statement of earnings is 100%. The amounts for 2000 and 2001 are stated as percentages of the 1999 amounts. The calculation of the trend statement amount for sales are shown below:

$$\text{Trend statement amount} = \frac{\text{Current year amount}}{\text{Base year amount}} \times 100\%$$

$$\text{Trend statement amount for sales for 1999} = \frac{\$283,401,000}{\$283,401,000} \times 100\% = 100.0\%$$

$$\text{Trend statement amount for sales for 2000} = \frac{\$314,547,000}{\$283,401,000} \times 100\% = 111.0\%$$

$$\text{Trend statement amount for sales for 2001} = \frac{\$363,870,000}{\$283,401,000} \times 100\% = 128.4\%$$

For each year the denominator is sales for 1999 and the numerator is sales for the year for which the trend statement is being calculated. Thus for 2001, sales in 2001 is the numerator and sales in 1999 is the denominator. When the trend statement amount is calculated for another line on the financial statements, the amounts from that line are used. For cash, the balance in the cash account in 1999 is the base year amount and the cash balances in 1999, 2000, and 2001 are the numerators.

The trend statements give a different view of the entity. These statements allow the user to view the change in each account over time relative to the base year. Thus, from fiscal 1999 to fiscal 2000 sales increased by 11%. From fiscal 1999 to fiscal 2001 sales increased by 28.4%. If you want to know the growth in sales from fiscal 2000 to fiscal 2001 additional calculations are required.

Some issues that arise from an examination of MWW's trend financial statements include:

- MWW has significantly more cash at the end of fiscal 2001 than it did at the end of fiscal 1999, and the amount of cash seems to be quite variable.

- Growth in receivables (4.7%) and inventories (9.7%) has been quite small between 1999 and 2001. This is surprising, given that sales increased over that period by 28.4%.

- Noticeable changes in some expense categories include:
  a. An increase of 38.2% in front-line occupancy costs.
  b. A decrease in short-term interest costs of 26.6%, and an increase in long-term interest costs of 85%.

Mark's Work Wearhouse Ltd. Trend Consolidated Balance Sheets			
	As at January 30, 1999	As at January 29, 2000	As at January 27, 2001
ASSETS			
Current assets			
Cash and cash equivalents	100.0%	65.5%	258.0%
Accounts receivable	100.0%	112.3%	104.7%
Merchandise inventories	100.0%	105.8%	109.7%
Other current assets	100.0%	97.5%	148.7%
	100.0%	105.3%	114.6%
Other assets	100.0%	165.5%	108.3%
Capital assets	100.0%	110.0%	119.6%
Future income taxes	100.0%	88.7%	87.8%
Goodwill	100.0%	127.1%	166.1%
	100.0%	107.6%	118.1%
LIABILITIES			
Current liabilities			
Accounts payable and accrued liabilities	100.0%	105.0%	105.9%
Income taxes payable	100.0%	45.0%	124.3%
Current portion of long-term debt	100.0%	116.7%	136.4%
	100.0%	101.4%	111.8%
Long-term debt	100.0%	108.6%	122.5%
Deferred gains	100.0%	204.2%	189.4%
	100.0%	104.8%	115.9%
SHAREHOLDERS' EQUITY			
Capital stock	100.0%	100.1%	95.5%
Retained earnings	100.0%	130.3%	162.5%
	100.0%	111.8%	121.4%
	100.0%	**107.6%**	**118.1%**

Some interpretational issues with using trend statements should be noted. When the balance in an account changes from positive to negative, or from negative to positive—for example, MWW's franchise bad debt provision and future income taxes on the statement of earnings—the change cannot be interpreted simply by looking at the percentage change relative to the base year. Also, if the balance in an account in the base year is zero, it is not possible to calculate a trend number for subsequent years because division by zero infinite. In addition, very small balances in the base year can result in huge percentage changes that may not be meaningful.

Trend statements give a better indication of growth and decline than do common size financial statements because the proportion in the trend data is relative to another year. Trend statements remove the effects of size from the numbers, which facilitates comparisons among periods and entities. However, the actual numbers in a set of financial statements cannot be ignored. Only by examining the actual numbers can one get a sense of the importance of a particular account.

For example, from 1999 to 2001 MWW's Other Current Assets account increased by almost 49%. This is a large increase compared with the increase in total assets and most of the other asset accounts over the same period. But on January 27, 2001 Other Current Assets was only $4,913,000 or just 3.1% of total assets, so spending much time investigating this relatively minor account would probably not be very produc-

Mark's Work Wearhouse Ltd. Trend Consolidated Statements of Earnings and Retained Earnings	52 weeks ended January 30, 1999	52 weeks ended January 29, 2000	52 weeks ended January 27, 2001
Corporate and franchise sales	100.0%	104.8%	116.9%
Corporate operations			
Front-line operations			
Sales	100.0%	111.0%	128.4%
Cost of sales	100.0%	110.4%	126.7%
Gross margin	**100.0%**	**111.9%**	**130.9%**
Front-line expenses			
Personnel, advertising, and other	100.0%	110.4%	129.9%
Occupancy	100.0%	120.2%	138.2%
Depreciation and amortization	100.0%	116.5%	124.6%
Interest—short term	100.0%	79.9%	73.4%
	100.0%	113.0%	130.7%
Front-line contribution	**100.0%**	**108.5%**	**131.3%**
Franchise royalties and other	100.0%	94.6%	93.5%
Net front-line contribution before back-line expenses	**100.0%**	**105.8%**	**124.0%**
Back-line operations			
Back-line expenses			
Personnel, administration, and other	100.0%	109.7%	123.9%
Occupancy	100.0%	101.7%	104.0%
Depreciation and amortization	100.0%	124.4%	133.7%
Software development and maintenance costs	100.0%	132.6%	136.6%
Computer services	100.0%	120.3%	149.6%
Interest—long term	100.0%	178.3%	185.0%
Franchise bad debt provisions (recoveries)	100.0%	137.0%	(114.6%)
	100.0%	116.9%	126.8%
Earnings before provision for closure of U.S. pilot stores, income taxes and goodwill amortization	**100.0%**	**88.9%**	**119.6%**
Provision for closure of U.S. pilot stores	100.0%	–	–
Earnings before income taxes and goodwill amortization	**100.0%**	**112.1%**	**150.9%**
Income taxes	100.0%	84.3%	126.7%
Current expense			
Future expense (benefit)	100.0%	(29.3%)	(2.2%)
	100.0%	112.9%	159.2%
Net earnings before goodwill amortization	**100.0%**	**111.4%**	**143.8%**
Goodwill amortization	100.0%	118.7%	173.4%
Net earnings	**100.0%**	**111.0%**	**142.2%**

Figure 13-3 (continued)

Trend Financial Statements for Mark's Work Wearhouse Ltd.

tive. That said, it is not always the case that a small balance in an account makes the account unimportant. The absence of certain amounts may be very important in some situations.

Question for Consideration

Calculate (a) the common size financial statement and (b) trend statement amounts for MWW for 1999 through 2001 for the "personnel, advertising and other" expense account on MWW's statement of earnings. For the trend statements use 1999 as the base year.

Answer:

a. Common size statements of earnings base the restatement on sales in each year. The denominator in each year is revenue in the year in question and the numerator is the "personnel, advertising and other" expense for that year.

1999: $\dfrac{\text{Personnel, advertising and other expense}_{\text{fiscal 1999}}}{\text{Sales}_{\text{fiscal 1999}}} = \dfrac{\$51,869,000}{\$283,401,000} \times 100\% = 18.3\%$

2000: $\dfrac{\text{Personnel, advertising and other expense}_{\text{fiscal 2000}}}{\text{Sales}_{\text{fiscal 2000}}} = \dfrac{\$57,272,000}{\$314,547,000} \times 100\% = 18.2\%$

2001: $\dfrac{\text{Personnel, advertising and other expense}_{\text{fiscal 2001}}}{\text{Sales}_{\text{fiscal 2001}}} = \dfrac{\$67,366,000}{\$363,870,000} \times 100\% = 18.5\%$

b. Trend statements are prepared by restating each line on the statement as a percentage of the balance in the account of the same line in the base year. Since 1999 is the base year for this question, the denominator in each case is the balance in the "personnel, advertising and other" expense account in 1999. The numerator for each year is the balance in the "personnel, advertising and other" expense account for that year.

1999: $\dfrac{\text{Personnel, advertising and other expense}_{\text{fiscal 1999}}}{\text{Personnel, advertising and other expense}_{\text{fiscal 1999}}} = \dfrac{\$51,869,000}{\$51,869,000} \times 100\% = 100.0\%$

2000: $\dfrac{\text{Personnel, advertising and other expense}_{\text{fiscal 2000}}}{\text{Personnel, advertising and other expense}_{\text{fiscal 1999}}} = \dfrac{\$57,272,000}{\$51,869,000} \times 100\% = 110.4\%$

2001: $\dfrac{\text{Personnel, advertising and other expense}_{\text{fiscal 2001}}}{\text{Personnel, advertising and other expense}_{\text{fiscal 1999}}} = \dfrac{\$67,366,000}{\$51,869,000} \times 100\% = 129.9\%$

Evaluating Performance

Many users of financial statements want to evaluate the performance of entities. They want to know how a particular entity "did." This is often easier said than done, because measuring performance can be very difficult. Performance is a multi-faceted concept that can be measured in different ways. Different performance indicators can often tell conflicting stories about how an entity is doing.

In this section we discuss different ways of evaluating the performance of an entity. Before we do, it is important to keep in mind some of the measurement difficulties that exist with determining income. These points have been raised before, but they bear repeating:

- There are many different choices available to managers in accounting for an entity's transactions and economic events. In many cases, it is not possible to point to one of the alternatives as being the best way of measuring income. As a result, there can be many reasonable measures of income that can be obtained, depending on the accounting policies used.

- Another measurement problem relates to the use of estimates. While traditional GAAP reporting is historical and transactions-based, there is usually uncertainty reflected in the amounts reported in the financial statements. The amount of accounts receivable that will not be collected cannot be known with certainty on the financial statement date. The cost of fulfilling an entity's warranty obligations must be estimated when financial statements are prepared. The pattern by which capital assets are consumed must be estimated so that amortization can be calculated. The list goes on and on. The actual amount of cash that will be collected, costs incurred, and so on, depends on future, uncertain events. Management can make their best efforts to estimate these unknown amounts, but in the end they are estimates.

- As a result, we cannot contend that the current GAAP accounting system can provide an entity's true income. Thus, while there might be a "true" income or economic reality out there, it is not possible to know what it is. And while accountants, managers, and users do their best to find that "right" number, it is not possible to know whether it has been found. Only when an entity winds up, and all its liabilities are settled and its assets converted to cash, is it possible to know and understand the performance of the entity over its life.

But we evade the issue. While there are many problems associated with measuring performance, those problems don't take away the need to measure it. Despite all its limitations, measuring performance is essential to users so that they can make decisions about how to invest their resources, so that they can evaluate how well managers have done their jobs, and so they can address many other performance-related questions. So how does one approach this task?

A logical place to start is with the income statement. The income statement was described in Chapter 2 as a statement of performance. In accrual accounting the income statement provides an indication of an entity's economic gains (revenues) and the economic costs (expenses) that were incurred to generate those gains. Net income is a representation of the net economic gain or loss to the owners of the entity over a period.

We can also look at subtotals within the income statement to get different indicators of performance. Gross margin (sales – cost of sales), operating income, income before taxes, and others are examples of different, potentially informative measures that are reported on an income statement.

One of the most commonly used tools for analyzing financial statements is ratios. Ratios allow people to examine relationships between numbers in the financial statements to gain insights about the entity. Also, like common size financial statements and trend statements, ratios eliminate the effect of size from the data.

Let's examine some of the common income statement performance measures.

Gross Margin   Gross margin is the difference between sales and cost of sales. (Cost of sales is the cost of the goods or services actually provided to customers.) Gross margin is an important measure of performance. From gross margin an entity must be able to cover all its other costs of operations and provide profit. Gross margin is often stated as a percentage of sales and called the gross margin percentage. The gross margin percentage indicates the percentage of each dollar of sales that is available to cover other costs and return a profit to the entity's owners.

The gross margin percentage is defined as:

$$\text{Gross margin percentage} = \frac{\text{Sales} - \text{Cost of sales}}{\text{Sales}} \times 100\% = \frac{\text{Gross margin}}{\text{Sales}} \times 100\%$$

MWW's gross margin in fiscal 2001 is \$149,509,000 (sales – cost of sales = \$363,870,000 – \$214,361,000). This means that MWW sold its clothes for \$149,509,000 more than what they cost. MWW's gross margin percentage in fiscal 2001 was 41.1% (\$149,509,000 ÷ \$363,870,000), which means that for every dollar of sales, MWW had \$0.41 to apply to costs other than clothing and for profit.

This percentage has been fairly stable over the last three years at around 40% (see Figure 13-2, page 789). However, the 0.5% increase in gross margin that MWW reported between fiscal 2000 and 2001 should not be dismissed as trivial. If all of MWW's costs for fiscal 2001 remained the same, but the gross margin percentage was 40.6% (the amount reported in fiscal 2000), gross margin in fiscal 2001 would have been over \$1,641,000 lower than actually reported. In addition, net earnings before income taxes and goodwill amortization would have been \$15,433,000 (instead of \$17,074,000) and net earnings would have been \$7,886,000 (assuming the same tax rate of 48.9%; see Note 17), a decrease of almost 5%. Clearly, for MWW a small increase in the gross margin percentage can have very positive effects on the bottom line.

The reason for the increase in MWW's gross margin percentage is not obvious and would require further analysis. The increase could be due to slightly higher selling prices, lower costs of inventory, or a slight change in the mix of products that MWW sold during the year (a shift from lower-margin products to higher-margin ones). A change in the gross margin and gross margin percentage could also be due to accounting choices made the MWW's management. For example, an inventory write-down could affect the gross margin percentage.

An entity's gross margin percentage can be influenced in two ways:

1. The entity can increase its gross margin percentage by being able to charge a premium for its goods or services. Charging a premium is not a matter of simply increasing the price of the entity's products. For an entity to be able to charge a premium, its customers must believe they are getting something in return. In other words, an entity must be able to somehow distinguish its products. For example, an entity might offer higher quality or better service. If an entity cannot somehow distinguish its products, it will not be able to charge a premium.

2. An entity can influence its gross margin percentage through cost control and efficiency. If an entity can obtain the inputs it requires to provide its goods or services at a lower cost, or use those inputs more efficiently, the entity will have a higher gross margin percentage.

Gross margin percentages can vary dramatically from entity to entity and industry to industry. For example, computer software companies often have very high gross margin percentages because a major cost of developing software—research and development—is expensed when incurred. Research and development is accounted for as a period cost and is therefore not included in cost of sales.

Gross margin percentages for a number of entities in different industries are shown in Figure 13-4.

A financial statement user cannot always determine an entity's gross margin because some entities do not provide the information in their income statements. Also, some entities do not specifically show the gross margin on their income statements, but do provide cost of sales, making it possible to calculate the amount.

Exhibit 13-5 provides the statement of earnings for Falconbridge Limited (Falconbridge), a mining company, and Sobeys Inc., an operator and franchiser of grocery stores.[7] Notice that Falconbridge includes cost of metal and other product

Figure 13-4

Gross Margin Percentages for Selected Companies in Different Industries

Entity	Industry	Gross Margin in Most Recent Fiscal Period
Angoss Software Corporation	Software	97.8% (year ended November 30, 2000)
Domtar Inc.	Forest and paper products	24.9% (year ended December 31, 2000)
Falconbridge Limited	Mining	38.6% (year ended December 31, 2000)
Leon's Furniture Limited	Furniture retailing	41.6% (year ended December 31, 2000)
Mitec Telecom Inc.	Computer hardware	23.6% (year ended April 30, 2001)
Premdor Inc.		
(now Masonite International Incorporated)	Door manufacturing	16.7% (year ended December 31, 2000)
TransCanada Pipelines Limited	Pipeline	18.5% (year ended December 31, 2000)

Exhibit 13-5

Income Statement Presentation of Gross Margin

Panel A: Falconbridge Limited

CONSOLIDATED STATEMENTS OF EARNINGS

IN THOUSANDS OF CANADIAN DOLLARS	YEAR ENDED DECEMBER 31, 2000	YEAR ENDED DECEMBER 31, 1999
REVENUES	$ 2,614,596	$ 2,173,479
OPERATING EXPENSES		
Costs of metal and other product sales	1,604,588	1,469,524
Selling, general and administrative	122,072	104,573
Amortization of development and preproduction expenditures	71,562	81,493
Depreciation and depletion	219,200	211,599
Exploration	45,815	34,654
Research and process development	27,971	14,435
	2,091,208	1,916,278
OPERATING INCOME	523,388	257,201

Panel B: Sobeys Inc.

CONSOLIDATED STATEMENT OF EARNINGS

(in millions) Year Ended May 5, 2001	2001 (52 weeks)	2000 (53 weeks)
Sales	$ 11,370.5	$ 11,006.1
Cost of sales, selling and administrative expenses	11,006.4	10,642.5
Depreciation	99.5	98.0
Operating Income	264.6	265.6
Interest expense		
Long term debt	63.5	79.8
Short term debt	10.3	9.2
	73.8	89.0
	190.8	176.6
Restructuring (Note 9)	(89.1)	-
Earnings before the following items	101.7	176.6
Income taxes (Note 10)		
Restructuring (Note 9)		
Future income tax benefit	(39.9)	-
Other operations		
Current income tax expense	32.4	46.0
Future income tax expense	48.1	31.5
	40.6	77.5
	61.1	99.1
Earnings before goodwill charges	19.1	18.9
Goodwill charges (Note 1)	$ 42.0	$ 80.2
Net earnings		
Earnings per share, basic and fully diluted (Note 11)		
Earnings before goodwill charges	$ 1.00	$ 1.77
Net earnings	$ 0.69	$ 1.43

sales (its cost of sales) among its other operating expenses (Panel A). With this information a user can calculate Falconbridge's gross margin and gross margin percentage. Sobeys Inc. reports virtually all its expenses on a single line on its statement of earnings, making calculation of gross margin impossible (Panel B). Some entities are reluctant to provide information about measures such as gross margin and gross margin percentage because they fear it will disclose valuable information to competitors.

www.falconbridge.com

Profit Margin Ratio The profit margin ratio is a bottom line measure of performance. The ratio indicates the percentage of each sales dollar that the entity earns in profit. The ratio is defined as:

$$\text{Profit margin ratio} = \frac{\text{Net income}}{\text{Sales}} \times 100\%$$

A higher profit margin ratio indicates greater profitability because the entity earns a larger proportion of each dollar of sales in profit. MWW's profit margin for the fiscal year ended January 27, 2001 is calculated as:

$$\text{Profit margin ratio} = \frac{\text{Net income}}{\text{Sales}} \times 100\%$$

$$= \frac{\$8,180,000}{\$363,870,000} \times 100\%$$

$$= 2.2\%$$

The profit margin ratio of 2.2% means that MWW earned $0.022 for every dollar of sales that it made. MWW's profit margin in fiscal 2000 and fiscal 1999 was 2.0%.

There are some different variations of the profit margin ratio. The numerator can be defined as operating income or income before discontinued operations and non-controlling interest. These provide measures of profitability that reflect ongoing operations rather than overall profitability.

Figure 13-5 shows the profit margin ratios for a number of industries. The profit margins shown are seven-year averages (1994–2000) for firms in each industry. Figure 13-5 shows that there is a wide variation of profit margin among industries. Considerable variation can also be seen within each industry across the reported years.

Return on Investment   Our discussion of performance to this point has focussed on the income statement. We have looked at three measures of performance, each calculated as a percentage of sales. These measures provide some insight into the operating profitability of an entity. However, these income statement measures ignore what it cost to generate those sales and earn those profits. An entity could have a high gross margin and profit margin, but the amount of investment required to earn those margins—the amount of assets required—might indicate that the performance of the entity was unsatisfactory. In other words, a profit of $1,000,000 will be evaluated differently if the investment required to earn that profit was $5,000,000 or $50,000,000.

This is where our measures of return on investment come in. Earlier in the book two measures of return on investment were discussed: return on assets (ROA) and return on equity (ROE). These two return measures allow us to assess the performance of an entity in relation to the investment made in the entity. They differ in the investment base that each uses. ROA uses all investment, debt and equity, to determine the return. ROA is a measure of the performance of the entity that is independent of how the entity's assets were financed. In contrast, ROE determines the return on the investment made by the common equity investors. Both are legitimate, valid, and widely used measures. The two measures are also closely related, as we will see.

Here are the definitions of ROA and ROE in equation form:

$$\text{Return on assets} = \frac{\text{Net Income} + \text{After-tax interest expense}}{\text{Average total assets}} \times 100\% = \frac{\text{Net income} + \text{interest expense} (1 - \text{tax rate})}{\text{Average total assets}} \times 100\%$$

$$\text{Return on equity} = \frac{\text{Net income} - \text{preferred dividends}}{\text{Average common shareholders' equity}} \times 100\%$$

The numerator in ROA has after-tax interest expense added back because the ratio is a measure of return that is supposed to be independent of how the assets are

Figure 13-5		
Profit Margins in Selected Canadian Industries	**Industry**	**Seven-Year Average Profit Margin (1994–2001)*** Profit margin equals net income before discontinued operations and non-controlling interest
	Auto parts and transportation equipment	4.86%
	Banks and trusts	18.25%
	Communications and media	−3.40%
	Consumer products	1.19%
	Metals and minerals	0.75%
	Paper and forest products	3.22%
	Steel	3.44%
	Wholesale and retail	2.79%

*Data from the *Financial Post Industry Reports*, http://www.fpdata.finpost.com/suite/autologreports.asp (accessed May 31, 2002).

	Fiscal 2001	Fiscal 2000	Fiscal 1999
Return on assets—MWW	6.80%	6.20%	6.30%
Return on equity—MWW	13.20%	11.30%	11.50%
Return on assets—wholesale and retail industry*	5.97%	5.79%	4.90%
Return on equity—wholesale and retail industry*	10.98%	11.61%	8.73%

*Data from the *Financial Post Industry Reports*, http://www.fpdata.finpost.com/suite/autologreports.asp (accessed May 31, 2002).

Figure 13-6

Return on Assets and Return on Equity for MWW and the Wholesale and Retail Industry

financed. If the interest expense were included in the numerator, ROA would be affected by the amount of debt because the interest expense would increase with the amount of debt.

Preferred dividends are deducted from net income when calculating ROE because ROE is a measure of return to the common shareholders. Preferred dividends are paid to the preferred shareholders, so the amount paid is not available to the common shareholders. Remember that preferred share dividends are not expensed in the calculation of net income.

ROA and ROE for MWW and the wholesale and retail industry are shown in Figure 13-6.

MWW's ROE shows that equity investors are earning a better return than they would if they had their money in bank accounts or in guaranteed investment certificates (GICs). The higher return is expected because investing in a retail business is much more risky than keeping money in the bank.

Are these returns high enough? It is difficult to say simply by looking at MWW's returns. It is positive that both ROA and ROE were higher in fiscal 2001 than in fiscal 2000. We can also compare MWW's returns with firms in the same industry. Figure 13-6 shows that MWW's ROA was higher than the industry average for fiscal years 1999 through 2001. MWW's ROE was greater than the industry average in fiscal 2001 and fiscal 1999, but not in fiscal 2000.

It is important to keep in mind, of course, that these measures of return on investment are affected by the accounting choices the managers make. Different accounting choices mean different measures of return on investment. That means that comparisons among firms may not be valid, though it might be possible to interpret trends among different firms. Also, remember that the returns earned by an entity are related to risk. The higher the risk, the higher the return should be. Therefore, differences in returns may be reflecting differences in risk as well as different performance levels.

It is common to break down ROA into components to provide insight into how an entity is generating its return and help identify how its performance can be improved. ROA can be broken down into two components: profit margin and asset turnover. Generally then, ROA can be stated as follows:

$$\text{Return on assets} = \text{Asset turnover ratio} \times \text{Profit margin percentage} \times 100\%$$
$$= \frac{\text{Sales}}{\text{Average total assets}} \times \frac{\text{Net income}}{\text{Sales}} \times 100\%$$
$$= \frac{\text{Income}}{\text{Average total assets}} \times 100\%$$

(Note: The ROA equation is shown in very general terms. This is because there are a number of variations in determining the component parts. For purposes of the discussion in this book, the analysis will keep to the basic concepts.)

We discussed profit margin earlier in this section. Profit margin indicates the amount of each sales dollar the entity earns as profit. **Asset turnover** is a measure of

Figure 13-7

How Different Combinations of
Profit Margin and Asset Turnover
Can Generate a Specific ROA

	Company A	Company B	Company C
Sales	$8,000,000	$1,000,000	$4,000,000
Net income	640,000	20,000	40,000
Average assets	8,000,000	250,000	500,000
Profit margin ratio	8%	2%	1%
Asset turnover ratio	1	4	8
Return on assets	8%	8%	8%

how effectively an entity can generate sales from its asset base. The more sales an entity can generate from its asset base, the higher its asset turnover ratio and the higher its ROA. If an entity can produce the same amount of sales by carrying less inventory than its competitors, everything else being equal, that entity will have a higher asset turnover ratio and a higher ROA.

An entity can generate a given ROA through different combinations of profit margin and asset turnover. The objective for any entity will be to maximize the ROA. It is up to an entity's managers to design strategies to achieve this objective. Some businesses or industries might pursue a strategy of accepting a low profit margin but compensate by having a high asset turnover ratio. In other words— make a small amount of money on each sale, but make a lot of sales. Business and industries that have a relatively low asset turnover ratio would try to compensate with a higher profit margin.

In Figure 13-7 three combinations for earning an 8% ROA are shown. Company A generates its 8% ROA with a relatively high profit margin (8%) but a relatively low asset turnover ratio (1%). Company C does the opposite. Company C has a very small profit margin ratio but its assets turnover quickly. Company B is in between.

By breaking down ROA into its components, it is possible to identify sources of problems with an entity's performance. An entity with a low profit margin would require different corrective steps than an entity with a low asset turnover ratio. An entity with a low profit margin might focus on product pricing (for example, it might try to increase its prices) or find ways of controlling or reducing costs, identifying inefficiencies in the production and delivery of the entity's product, and so on. A company with a low asset turnover ratio might examine whether there are unproductive or idle assets, ones perhaps that could be sold, or whether some assets could be managed more efficiently and effectively (for example, inventory or receivables levels that are unreasonably high).

Of course, there are limits to the improvements management can make. If an entity is already performing well in either profit margin or asset turnover, there is only so much the managers could do to make improvements. Also, the nature of different industries imposes limits on the magnitude of these ratios. For example, industries that require very large capital investments will tend to have lower asset turnover ratios.

Seven-year average asset turnover ratios for a number of industries are shown in Figure 13-8.

Now let's examine the components of MWW's ROA. The information needed from MWW's annual report to do the analysis is shown in Figure 13-9.

For the purpose of this analysis the profit margin ratio will be defined as net income divided by sales. This definition will produce a ROA that is different from what was calculated earlier. The difference is that in the earlier calculation the numerator was defined as net income plus after tax interest expense. The definition used here will make the discussion easier. For fiscal 2001 the breakdown of ROA is calculated as follows:

$$
\begin{array}{rlcl}
\text{Return on assets} \\
\text{for 2001} & = & \text{Asset turnover ratio} & \times & \text{Profit margin percentage} & \times & 100\% \\[2ex]
& = & \dfrac{\text{Sales}}{\text{Average total assets}} & \times & \dfrac{\text{Net income}}{\text{Sales}} & \times & 100\% \\[3ex]
& = & \dfrac{\$363,870}{(\$157,060 + \$143,084) \div 2} & \times & \dfrac{\$8,180}{\$363,870} & \times & 100\% \\[3ex]
& = & 2.425 & \times & 2.248\% \\[2ex]
& = & 5.45\%
\end{array}
$$

We can use the information in Figure 13-9 to calculate return on assets and its components for the fiscal years 1999 through 2001. The results are shown in Figure 13-10.

Over the last three fiscal years MWW has managed to increase its ROA significantly. ROA declined in 2000 compared with 1999, but 2001 represents an improvement compared with both years. Over the three years MWW's profit margin percentage increased. The increase in profit margin in 2001 seems to be due in large measure to the improvement in gross margin (see Figure 13-2, page 789). The decrease in ROA in 2000 versus 1999 was due to a decrease in the asset turnover ratio. This decline was recovered and then some in fiscal 2001. We could further break down the asset turnover ratio into additional component parts such as receivables turnover

Industry	Seven-Year Average Asset Turnover Ratios (1994–2000)*
Auto parts and transportation equipment	1.53
Communications and media	0.66
Consumer products	1.48
Food and beverage	1.69
Insurance	0.33
Metals and minerals	0.46
Paper and forest products	0.84
Real estate	0.26
Steel	1.08
Telephone and utilities	0.43
Wholesale and retail	2.07

Figure 13-8

Seven-Year Average Asset Turnover Ratios for Selected Industries

*Data from the *Financial Post Industry Reports*, http://www.fpdata.finpost.com/suite/autologreports.asp (accessed May 31, 2002).

	Fiscal 2001	Fiscal 2000	Fiscal 1999	Fiscal 1998
Sales	$363,870	$314,547	$283,401	$ –
Net income	8,180	6,387	5,752	–
Total assets	157,060	143,084	132,992	105,617
Shareholders' equity	64,721	59,571	53,306	46,746

Figure 13-9

Information From MWW's Annual Report to Calculate Return on Investment

	Return on Assets	=	Asset Turnover Ratio	×	Profit Margin Percentage*
Fiscal 2001	5.45%	=	2.425	×	2.248%
Fiscal 2000	4.63%	=	2.279	×	2.031%
Fiscal 1999	4.82%	=	2.375	×	2.030%

Figure 13-10

Return on Assets for MWW, 1999–2001

*Profit margin = Net income ÷ Sales

	Return on Equity	=	Return on Assets	×	Financial Leverage
Fiscal 2001	13.13%	=	5.45%	×	2.41
Fiscal 2000	11.34%	=	4.63%	×	2.45
Fiscal 1999	11.47%	=	4.82%	×	2.38

(see Chapter 7) and inventory turnover (see Chapter 8) to gain further insight into changes in the asset turnover ratio. We can obtain further information about the profit margin percentage by examining the common size financial statements (see Figure 13-2, pages 788–789) to see changes in the income statement components.

We can now turn our attention to ROE. ROE can be disaggregated into the entity's ROA, how effectively it uses its assets, and financial leverage (the proportion of the entity's assets that are financed by the shareholders). The disaggregation of ROE is:

$$\text{Return on equity} = \text{Return on assets} \times \text{Financial leverage}$$

$$= \frac{\text{Net income}}{\text{Average total assets}} \times \frac{\text{Average total assets}}{\text{Average shareholders' equity}}$$

$$= \frac{\text{Net income}}{\text{Average shareholders' equity}}$$

Financial leverage is a measure of the proportion of assets financed by common shareholders. An entity that has few liabilities will have low financial leverage and the financial leverage ratio will be close to one. As the amount of liabilities increases, the financial leverage ratio will get larger. Remember from the discussion of leverage in Chapter 11 that the owners of an entity can increase their return by borrowing. Financing by debt, however, introduces risk because the interest must be paid regardless of the performance of the entity.

Using the information in Figure 13-9 (page 801) and the calculation of ROA in Figure 13-6 (page 799) we can calculate MWW's ROE for 2001.

$$\text{ROE for 2001} = \text{Return on assets} \times \text{Financial leverage}$$

$$= \text{Return on assets} \times \frac{\text{Average total assets}}{\text{Average shareholders' equity}}$$

$$= 6.81\% \times \frac{(\$157{,}060 + \$143{,}084) \div 2}{(64{,}721 + 59{,}571) \div 2}$$

$$= 6.81\% \times 2.41$$

$$= 16.41\%$$

We can use the information in Figures 13-9 and 13-10 (page 801) to calculate return on equity and its components for the fiscal years 1999 through 2001. The results are shown in Figure 13-11.

Figure 13-9 shows that MWW's ROE was significantly higher in 2001 than in the other two years. Because financial leverage remained stable over the three-year period, the increase is due to the increase in ROA.

Earnings per Share   Earnings per share or EPS is the amount of net income that is attributable to each individual share of common stock. EPS was discussed in depth in Chapter 11. This section will serve as a brief summary of that discussion.

EPS comes in a number of variations. The first and most straightforward is basic EPS. Basic EPS is calculated using the following formula:

$$\text{Basic EPS} = \frac{\text{Net income} - \text{Preferred dividends}}{\text{Weighted-average number of common shares outstanding during the period}}$$

Preferred dividends are deducted from net income in the numerator because the amount of preferred dividends is not available to common shareholders, but is not deducted in the calculation of net income. The denominator is the weighted-average number of shares that were outstanding during the year—the average number of shares outstanding during the period, taking into consideration when during the period changes occurred in the number of shares outstanding.

Another EPS measure is fully diluted EPS. Fully diluted EPS is designed to show the effect that dilutive securities (securities such as convertible bonds, convertible preferred shares, and stock options that can be converted into common stock) would have on EPS if they were converted or exchanged for common stock. Fully diluted EPS can be thought of as a worst-case scenario of EPS. It is provided because one of the uses of financial statements is to help investors predict future earnings.

Liquidity

Liquidity is an entity's ability to make payments as they come due. This means an entity must have adequate cash resources and/or the ability to generate cash to make payments to suppliers, creditors, lenders, employees, and so on. Lenders and creditors want to assess the liquidity of an entity to ensure that it will be able to pay amounts owed. If there is concern that the entity will not be able to meet its obligations, lenders and creditors may not want to provide credit. At the very least they will attach terms to any credit offered that will reflect the level of risk associated with the entity.

In Chapter 7 two commonly used measures of liquidity were introduced:

- the current ratio
- the quick or acid test ratio

The current ratio provides a measure of the resources an entity has to meet its short-term obligations. The higher the current ratio, the more likely it is that an entity will be able to meet its existing current obligations. A larger current ratio also indicates greater protection in the event the entity's cash flow somehow becomes impaired. The ratio assumes that inventory, receivables, and other current assets can be converted to cash on a timely basis.

The current ratio is defined as:

$$\text{Current ratio} = \frac{\text{Current assets}}{\text{Current liabilities}}$$

The quick or acid test ratio is a stricter test of an entity's ability to meet its obligations because it excludes less liquid assets such as inventory, prepaids, and the current portion of store opening costs. The concept behind the quick ratio is that it can take a fairly long time to convert inventory into cash. Remember, in the normal course of events inventory must be sold and the purchase price collected from the customer before cash is realized. For businesses in which inventory turns over relatively slowly, considerable time can pass before the inventory is realized in cash. In these cases inventory cannot be considered very liquid. Other current assets (for example, prepaids and store opening costs) are not liquid at all. They will never be realized in cash, so it makes sense to exclude them from an assessment of liquidity.

The quick or acid test ratio is defined as:

$$\text{Quick ratio or acid test ratio} = \frac{\text{Quick assets}^*}{\text{Current liabilities}}$$

*Quick assets include cash, temporary investments, accounts receivable, and any other current assets that can be quickly converted to cash.

A major problem with both the current and quick ratios is that they are static measures. These ratios reflect the existing current resources an entity has available to meet its existing obligations. But the ratios say nothing about an entity's ability to generate cash flow to meet existing and future obligations. Ultimately, an entity's liquidity depends on its ability to generate cash flows in the future to pay its liabilities. As long as an entity has a steady and reliable flow of cash coming in, a low current ratio is not going to be a concern. However, if cash flow is unpredictable—for example, if an entity is sensitive to changes in the economy or competitive changes in the industry—then the current ratio gives an indication of the entity's ability to weather any cash flow disturbances in the short term. A higher current (or quick) ratio means that an entity has some insurance in the event that cash flow becomes impaired.

It is important to understand that many of the liquidity problems that entities come to face arise because of changes in the environment. If an entity's environment remains stable and predictable, it is unlikely to face liquidity problems (assuming that it does not already have liquidity problems). Why? If an entity is operating successfully in a given environment, as long as that environment remains constant there is no reason for the entity's cash flows to change.

However, change is another matter. A changing environment can create significant liquidity pressures. Change can take many forms. It can be economy-wide (an economic slowdown) or specific to the entity (growth). Change in the environment can affect the timing and amount of cash flows. An economic slowdown might reduce an entity's sales, force a reduction in the prices it charges its customers, increase the amount of uncollectable accounts receivable, increase the time it takes to collect receivables, and make inventory less saleable. For example, suppose MWW purchased inventory in anticipation of a certain level of sales. If the sales targets are not met, MWW would be left with surplus inventory that it might not be able to sell, or that it would have to sell at discounted prices. Regardless of these problems, MWW's suppliers would still have to be paid the full agreed-upon amount.

Additional insights into the liquidity of an entity can be obtained by examining the turnover of receivables and inventory. Receivables and inventory usually represent the major part of current assets, so understanding how long it takes to realize them in cash can help a user predict cash flows and identify liquidity problems. (For MWW, receivables and inventory represent over 89% of current assets.) In Chapter 7 the accounts receivable turnover ratio and the average collection period of accounts receivable were introduced. In Chapter 8 the inventory turnover ratio and the average number of days inventory on hand were explained. For in-depth discussions of these ratios you should review those chapters.

The accounts receivable turnover ratio indicates how quickly an entity is collecting its receivables. The larger the ratio, the more quickly receivables are being collected. The average collection period of receivables conveys the same idea as the receivables turnover ratio, except it is stated as the number of days, on average, it takes to collect receivables. A decrease in the receivables turnover ratio (or an increase in the average collection period) relative to previous years, or a deterioration in these measures relative to similar firms or industry benchmarks, may suggest a liquidity problem. A decrease in the receivables turnover ratio may suggest that receivables have become less collectable (the amount of receivables that will not be collected has increased) and/or the period of time it takes to collect receivables has increased. A decrease in the receivables turnover ratio means that it takes more time for the entity to receive cash and, as a result, it has less cash to meet its obligations.

The formulas for the accounts receivable turnover ratio and the average collection period for accounts receivable are:

$$\text{Accounts receivable turnover ratio} = \frac{\text{Credit sales}}{\text{Average accounts receivable}}$$

$$\text{Average collection period of accounts receivable} = \frac{365}{\text{Accounts receivable turnover ratio}}$$

The inventory turnover ratio indicates the number of times during a period the entity is able to purchase and sell (or use) its stock of inventory. The average number of days inventory on hand conveys the same idea as the inventory turnover ratio, except it is stated as the number of days, on average, it takes to sell or use inventory. A high turnover rate (or low average number of days inventory on hand) indicates that the inventory is more liquid because it is sold quickly and, therefore, cash is realized sooner than with slower-moving inventory. An inventory turnover ratio that is decreasing (or average number of days inventory on hand that is increasing) relative to previous years, or that is deteriorating relative to similar firms or industry benchmarks, may suggest a liquidity problem. Inventory may not be selling. It could be slow-moving or obsolete, or there could be low demand for the inventory. A decreasing inventory turnover ratio indicates that it is taking more time to sell inventory, which implies that it will take more time to realize the inventory in cash. In the meantime, suppliers of inventory and other goods and services still have to be paid.

The formulas for the inventory turnover ratio and the average number of days inventory on hand are:

$$\text{Inventory turnover ratio} = \frac{\text{Cost of sales}}{\text{Average inventory}}$$

$$\text{Average number of days inventory on hand} = \frac{365}{\text{Inventory turnover ratio}}$$

A third turnover ratio can be added to the previous two, one we haven't examined before. The **accounts payable turnover ratio** provides information about how quickly an entity pays its accounts payable. The accounts payable turnover ratio is calculated using the following formula:

$$\text{Accounts payable turnover ratio} = \frac{\text{Credit purchases}}{\text{Average accounts payable}}$$

There are some practical difficulties with applying this ratio. First, credit purchases or purchases, for that matter, are not usually disclosed in the financial statements. It is possible to estimate purchases during a period using the equation:

$$\text{Purchases} = \text{Cost of sales} - \text{Beginning inventory} + \text{Ending inventory}$$

This equation will provide a reasonable estimate of purchases for a retail business because cost of sales includes mainly the cost of inventory, which, we can reasonably assume, is purchased mainly on credit. For manufacturing companies this estimate is less reliable because cost of sales will include much more than the cost of goods purchased on credit. It includes costs such as wages and possibly amortization.

MWW's accounts payable turnover ratio is calculated below. The first step is to calculate purchases; then that amount is used to calculate the turnover ratio.

Purchases	=	Cost of sales	−	Beginning inventory	+	Ending inventory
	=	214,361,000	−	81,468,000	+	84,483,000
	=	217,376,000				

$$\text{Accounts payable turnover ratio} = \frac{\text{Purchases}}{\text{Average accounts payable}}$$

$$= \frac{217,376,000}{(45,730,000 + 46,131,000) \div 2}$$

$$= 4.73$$

A problem with this calculation for MWW is that average accounts payable includes much more than just amounts owed to suppliers of inventory. MWW's accounts payable account includes all amounts owing, including accrued liabilities, except for income taxes and the current portion of long-term debt. Purchases likely includes only purchases of inventory. As a result, our calculation of 4.73 for MWW's accounts payable turnover ratio is likely lower than it actually would be because accounts payable pertains to more than just purchases of inventory.

The accounts payable turnover ratio can also be stated as the number of days that the entity takes to pay its accounts payable. This ratio, the **average payment period for accounts payable**, is calculated as follows:

$$\text{Average payment period for accounts payable} = \frac{365}{\text{Accounts payable turnover ratio}}$$

MWW's average payment period for accounts payable is:

$$\text{Average payment period for accounts payable} = \frac{365}{\text{Accounts payable turnover ratio}}$$

$$= \frac{365}{4.73}$$

$$= 77.2 \text{ days}$$

This amount means that, on average, MWW takes just over 77 days to pay it suppliers. The actual period is probably lower than this because, as explained above, the accounts payable turnover ratio is probably greater than what was calculated. This means that comparing either MWW's turnover ratio or average payment period with those of other entities can be dangerous because the inputs to the calculations may be quite different.

Examining these amounts for an entity over time may provide some reasonable insights. A decreasing accounts payable turnover ratio or increasing average payment period may indicate that the entity is having cash flow problems and is extending the time it takes to pay its accounts payable.

Taken together, these three turnover ratios, when expressed in number of days, give an idea of how well operating cash inflows and outflows are matched. Recall that in Chapter 6 we discussed the lag that exists between the expenditure of cash and the receipt of cash. The three turnover ratios allow us to estimate that lag. The lag can be estimated using the following equation:

$$\text{Cash lag} = \frac{\text{Average collection period}}{\text{of accounts receivable}} + \frac{\text{Average number of days}}{\text{inventory on hand}} - \frac{\text{Average payment period}}{\text{for accounts payable}}$$

The larger the cash lag, the longer the period of time the entity must finance its inventory and accounts receivable. In times of financial distress the length of the lag will likely increase. This information can important to users such as lenders, who want to predict cash flows and assess the risk associated with a loan.

The above ratios provide only part of the information required to analyze an entity's liquidity. Other tools, which we will not investigate here, are available. However, analyzing liquidity is not only a matter of using ratios. The notes to the financial statements often provide information that is useful for evaluating an entity's liquidity, even though the information is not reflected in the financial statements themselves. For example, many entities have access to lines of credit from which they can borrow money as it is needed. That is, a lender will make a specified amount of money available to an entity. and it can borrow up to the amount specified if and when it is needed. If an entity has lines of credit available that have not yet been fully used, the amount not yet borrowed is not reported on the balance sheet. However, that available credit can be an important source of liquidity for the entity that should be taken into consideration when its liquidity position is analyzed.

Exhibit 13-6 provides two examples of notes to financial statements that describe the availability of credit.[8] The examples in Exhibit 13-6 are from the financial statements of AlarmForce Industries Inc., a home security company (Panel A), and Causeway Energy Corporation, an oil and gas exploration, development, and production company (Panel B).

Entities sometimes make commitments that require them to make cash payments in the future. These were described earlier in the book as executory contracts—arrangements in which neither party to a contract has performed its side of the arrangement, so there are no financial statement effects. These commitments, such as payments required under operating leases, have implications for an entity's liquidity because they commit an entity to expend cash. MWW discloses its commitments in Note 10 to its financial statements (see page A-55).

www.alarmforce.com
www.causewayenergy.com

Solvency and Leverage

We discussed solvency and leverage in several places in the book. In Chapter 2 the debt-to-equity ratio was introduced. In Chapter 10 the debt-to-equity ratio and another tool for analyzing liabilities and credit worthiness, the interest coverage ratio, were discussed in detail. In Chapter 11 the nature and implications of leverage were

---

Exhibit 13-6

Disclosures About Available Credit

Panel A: AlarmForce Industries Inc.

5. Bank Loans

	2000 $	1999 $
Revolving term loans *(i)*	2,776,561	1,147,319
Other	-	38,847
	2,776,561	1,186,166
Less current portion	975,813	566,416
	1,800,748	**619,750**

(i) The company has revolving lines of credit in the aggregate amount of $5,500,000. Loans made under the respective facilities are repayable over a term of either forty-eight or sixty months, in monthly instalments of principal plus interest at prime rate plus 0.75% per annum, corresponding to individual contract periods.

A general assignment of book debts, a general security agreement and an assignment of the proceeds of a $300,000 life insurance policy have been pledged as collateral.

Panel B: Causeway Energy Corporation

3. Long-Term Debt

	2000	1999
Revolving demand loan	$ –	$ 2,300,000
Term loan	1,052,907	–
Current portion	(205,869)	–
	$ 847,038	$ 2,300,000

The Company has a revolving demand multi-currency facility with a credit limit of $6,000,000 CDN or $3,500,000 US, subject to a monthly reduction commencing March 1, 2001 of $216,000 CDN. The outstanding loan bears interest at a floating rate equal to prime plus 0.5% per annum on the outstanding Canadian dollar balance and US prime on any US balance outstanding. This credit facility is to be reviewed annually by the Bank, and subject to their satisfactory review no principal repayments will be required in the next twelve months. The facility currently comes due for review on May 1, 2001. Collateral for this credit facility is provided by fixed and floating debentures in the amount of $12,500,000 on the Canadian assets and a first mortgage on

the U.S. assets. The Company is currently negotiating a further increase to the facility.

In addition, the Company's wholly owned pipeline subsidiary, Chinook Pipeline Company had a $1 million US line of credit with a local Montana bank for construction of the Chinook Pipeline. Upon drawing down the $1 million and commencement of gas flow on the Chinook Pipeline, the line of credit converted on January 31, 2001 to a 5 year term loan. The loan bears interest at US prime and is secured by the pipeline assets. Monthly payments of principal and interest are $21,156 US.

Interest accrued was paid out in the current years.

explained. This section reviews the earlier coverage and adds some additional insights to the topic.

In the last section liquidity was defined as an entity's short-term ability to make payments as they come due. In contrast, **solvency** refers to the financial viability of an entity—its ability to meet its long-term obligations.

One of the important sources of insight into an entity's solvency is its capital structure. **Capital structure** refers to an entity's sources of financing—its relative proportions of debt and equity. Capital structure is important in the assessment of solvency because the more debt that an entity has in its capital structure, the more risk there is to its long-term solvency. A common tool for evaluating capital structure is the debt-to-equity ratio.

The debt-to-equity ratio provides a measure of the relative amount of debt to equity an entity is using. The ratio gives an indication of the riskiness of the entity and its ability to carry more debt. More debt makes an entity more risky. Why? More debt means there are more fixed interest charges that must be paid—paid regardless of whether the entity is performing well or poorly. If interest and principal payments are not paid when required, the entity faces significant economic and legal consequences. Also, as the proportion of debt increases, the cost of debt—interest—will also increase, because lenders will charge higher interest rates. Higher interest rates are how lenders are compensated for higher risk.

There are many variations of the debt-to-equity ratio. The debt-to-equity ratio we have discussed so far in the book is defined as:

$$\text{Debt-to-equity ratio} = \frac{\text{Total liabilities}}{\text{Total shareholders' equity}}$$

This ratio includes all liabilities and all equity. Other variations on the debt-to-equity ratio include:

$$\text{Long-term debt-to-equity ratio} = \frac{\text{Long-term debt}}{\text{Total shareholders' equity}}$$

$$\text{Debt-to-total-assets ratio} = \frac{\text{Total liabilities}}{\text{Total liabilities} + \text{Total shareholders' equity}} = \frac{\text{Total liabilities}}{\text{Total assets}}$$

We will not discuss these alternatives further, but it is important to recognize that there are different ways of measuring the same concept. The alternatives are not necessarily identical, however. For example, the long-term debt-to-equity ratio does not include current liabilities in the numerator.

The use of the debt-to-equity ratio by simply using the numbers on the balance sheet can provide misleading results and interpretations. Leases, pensions, and future income taxes all present problems that can impair the interpretation of the debt-to-equity and other ratios that incorporate liabilities. If an entity makes extensive use of operating leases, liabilities and the debt-to-equity ratio will be understated because operating leases are a form of off-balance-sheet financing. If this is the case, users might want to incorporate the operating lease "liability" into their assessment of the entity's capital structure. (The impact of leases, pensions, and future income taxes on the debt-to-equity ratio is discussed in Chapter 10.)

Because interest has to be paid regardless of whether an entity is performing well or poorly, debt makes an entity more risky. That does not mean, however, that entities should carry no debt. While debt does add risk, it offers some benefits as well:

- Debt is usually less costly than equity because the payments to debt-holders are specified and debt-holders are entitled to be paid before equity investors.

- Interest on debt is tax deductible, whereas dividends to shareholders are not.

An entity needs a balance between debt and equity financing. Too much debt may result in the entity being unable to pay its obligations. Also, at some point debt will become too expensive because of the increasing interest rates that are charged as the proportion of debt in the capital structure increases. The optimal amount of debt an entity should have depends on the entity. An entity with reliable cash flows can afford to carry more debt than an entity with cash flows that are less predictable. Factors that affect the reliability of cash flows include competition, threat of technological change, sensitivity to economic cycles, and predictability of capital expenditures.

Another important aspect for assessing the solvency of an entity is its ability to generate cash from operations. An entity that can reliably generate cash is best equipped to meet its obligations. Earnings are often used in place of cash flow to assess cash flow generating ability. While earnings are not cash flow, and while, in the short term, earnings and cash flow can differ significantly, earnings do tend to be a good indicator of long-term cash flow. A reliable flow of earnings or cash flow provides creditors with assurance that the entity will be able to meet its obligations.

The **interest coverage ratio (accrual basis)** is one of a number of coverage ratios designed to measure the ability of an entity to meet its fixed financing charges. In particular, the interest coverage ratio indicates the ease with which an entity can meet its interest payments. The interest coverage ratio is defined as:

$$\text{Interest coverage ratio} = \frac{\text{Net income} + \text{Interest expense} + \text{Tax expense}}{\text{Interest expense}}$$

The larger the ratio, the better able the entity is to meet its interest payments. However, the interest coverage ratio is limiting in that it ignores the fact that entities have financial charges other than interest. Other fixed financial charges can include debt repayment and lease payments on operating leases. This ratio can be modified to include these other charges.

The interest coverage ratio can also be calculated on a cash basis. The **interest coverage ratio (cash basis)** is calculated as follows:

$$\text{Interest coverage ratio (cash-based)} = \frac{\text{Cash from operations excluding interest}}{\text{Interest paid}}$$

Some users prefer the cash-based interest coverage ratio because debt-holders have to be paid in cash, not in earnings. The cash-based measure shows the number of dollars of cash generated by operations for each dollar of interest that had to be paid.

The cash-based interest coverage ratio for MWW for the year ended January 27, 2001 is:

$$\text{Interest coverage ratio (cash-based)} = \frac{\text{Cash from operations excluding interest}}{\text{Interest paid}}$$

$$= \frac{\$21,140,000 + \$3,982,000}{\$3,982,000}$$

$$= \$6.31$$

This may be compared with the earnings-based interest coverage ratio of $5.29 that was calculated in Chapter 10 (see page 622). The cash-based interest coverage ratio shows that MWW generated $6.31 of cash from operations for each dollar of interest that had to be paid. Note that the amount of interest that MWW paid can be found in the Supplementary Schedules to Consolidated Statements of Cash Flows (see page A-48). MWW's cash-based interest coverage ratio for the year ended January 29, 2000 was 3.52 and the earnings-based interest coverage ratio was 4.06.

The interest coverage ratio and other measures of an entity's ability to meet its fixed charges are very important indicators for creditors. A higher coverage ratio gives more assurance that the creditors will be paid. The acceptable level of a coverage ratio will depend on the entity. A creditor can accept a lower coverage ratio for an entity with highly reliable earnings and cash flows. A creditor would want a higher coverage ratio for an entity in a cyclical industry or with highly variable earnings and cash flows.

It is important to remember that the interest coverage and similar ratios are historical measures. They show what happened, not necessarily what will happen. Examining historical trends can help give users of financial information insight into the ability of an entity to generate adequate earnings to cover current and future obligations, but it is also important to consider any changes that may affect that ability. For example, increased competition or changing economic conditions could impair an entity's ability to generate earnings and cash flow in future, despite its historical success in doing so.

Other Common Ratios

Price-to-Earnings Ratio

The **price-to-earnings** or **P/E ratio** is commonly mentioned and discussed. The stock market listings that are published daily in most major newspapers usually provide each entity's P/E ratio. The P/E ratio is defined as:

$$P/E \text{ ratio} = \frac{\text{Market price per share}}{\text{Earnings per share}}$$

Conceptually, the P/E ratio gives an indication of how the market values an entity's earnings. The P/E ratio is seen as indicator of the growth prospects of an entity. The higher the P/E ratio, the more the market expects earnings to grow in the future. Another way of thinking about this is that the higher an entity's P/E ratio, the more sensitive is the entity's share price to changes in earnings. For example, a P/E ratio of 10 means that a $1 increase in earnings per share will result in a $10 increase in share price. A P/E ratio of 25 means that a $1 decrease in earnings will result in a $25 decrease in share price.

The P/E ratio is also an indicator of the risk associated with future earnings. The higher the risk of an entity, the lower will be its P/E ratio for a given level of earnings. (The reason for this is that when risk is higher, future cash flows are discounted at a higher rate to reflect the risk. See Chapter 7 for further discussion of the present value technique.)

For a number of reasons the P/E ratio must be interpreted carefully. Remember from our discussion of earnings quality that earnings in any given period will contain permanent and transitory components. Permanent and transitory earnings will have different effects on the market price of shares, which in turn will have implications for the P/E ratio.

Also, conceptually the market price of a share represents the present value of the cash flows that will be received by the shareholder. This is a future-oriented perspective. Earnings, on the other hand, is largely a historically focused measure. As a result, the link between GAAP earnings and share price is not perfect. Current information will be reflected in the price of an entity's shares immediately, whereas the information might not affect earnings until a later time. If an entity has very low but positive earnings in a period, the P/E ratio will be very large. In that case the P/E ratio may not say anything about the prospective growth of an entity. It will simply be the mathematical result of division by a small number.

In addition, a P/E ratio is not meaningful if an entity has a loss. Finally, earnings are affected by the accounting choices an entity makes, so the P/E ratio will vary with different ways of accounting for the same underlying economic activity.

(Note that it is not possible to determine the P/E ratios of private companies because they do not have readily available market prices for their shares.)

Since share prices of companies change from day to day, while annual earnings for a given year are constant for that year, the P/E ratio will vary with share price. In its Eleven-Year Financial Review (page A-70), MWW reports its P/E ratio based on its year-end share price. The calculation of the P/E ratio on January 27, 2001 is:

$$\text{P/E ratio} = \frac{\text{Market price per share}}{\text{Earnings per share}} = \frac{\$2.40}{\$0.30} = 8.00$$

MWW reports P/E ratios of 7.83 on January 29, 2000 and 15.48 on January 30, 1999.

In general, it can be hard to make sense of the changes in P/E ratios because of the many factors that can influence their value.

Dividend Payout Ratio   The **dividend payout ratio** indicates the proportion of earnings that is being paid to common shareholders as dividends. The dividend payout ratio is defined as:

$$\text{Dividend payout ratio} = \frac{\text{Common dividends paid}}{\text{Net income}}$$

A dividend payout ratio of 0.25 means that 25% of earnings are paid in dividends. The portion of earnings that is not paid out as a dividend is retained in the entity. In any given year, an entity does not have to report a profit to pay a dividend. In other words, an entity with a net loss can pay a dividend. If the losses continue, it is likely that the entity's cash flow will be affected, and eventually it will not have the resources to sustain the dividend. A dividend payout ratio greater than 1.0 is also possible. What is necessary for dividends is the cash to pay them. If net income is negative, the dividend payout ratio is not meaningful.

Since MWW has never paid out dividends, its dividend payout ratio is 0%.

An entity's dividend payout ratio can vary quite a bit from period to period if its strategy is to pay a fixed dividend, regardless of the level of earnings. That is, an entity may decide to pay a certain dividend per share and it will attempt to maintain that dividend, regardless of any variation in year-to-year earnings. This approach is common with public companies. For public companies, dividends tend to be constant over time, increasing when the managers feel there will be adequate future cash flow

---

Question for Consideration

Zehner Ltd. (Zehner) is a publicly traded Canadian company. On December 28, 2006, the last day of the company's fiscal year, Zehner's management announced the signing of a new, long-term contract with a customer. The contract will increase Zehner's revenue significantly, and management and financial analysts agree that the contract will be very profitable. The contract begins in the middle of 2007.

Required: How do you think Zehner's share price will be affected by the announcement of the new contract? How will Zehner's December 31, 2006 earnings be affected by the new contract? Explain.

Answer: Zehner's share price should increase because of the new contract. The new contract is expected to be very profitable, which means that the company is now more valuable. Larger earnings mean investors can ultimately expect more cash in the future. In contrast, the announcement of the contract will have no effect on Zehner's December 31, 2006 earnings. Earnings reflects mainly transactions that have occurred. As of December 31, 2006 Zehner has earned no revenue and would report no profits as a result of the new contract (under GAAP at least). Earnings will only be affected when the contract comes into effect, in the middle of 2007. Since the contract commences part way through 2007, the full effect will not be reflected in earnings until 2008.

to permanently support that level of dividends. Managers of public companies are very reluctant to decrease dividends because a decrease suggests to investors that current and future cash flows are declining and that the decline is expected to be permanent. The stock prices of public companies usually fall significantly when a decrease in dividend is announced.

Private companies will be much less concerned about maintaining a given level of dividends because they will not be concerned about the impact of dividend changes on the market value of the shares. The shareholders of private companies will likely consider tax issues, their personal cash needs, and the cash requirements of the entity in any dividend decisions.

Some Limitations and Caveats About Financial Statements and Financial Statement Analysis

Financial ratios are a powerful and informative tool for analyzing and evaluating entities. Financial ratios provide valuable insights into the performance and prospects of an entity. However, ratio analysis has limitations, some of them quite severe. The limitations with doing analysis on GAAP-based information are largely due to the limitations of the GAAP information itself.

It is important to remember that the existence of these limitations and caveats does not mean that financial statement and ratio analysis is not useful or should not be done. Nothing could be further from the truth. But to get the most out of financial statement and ratio analysis, it is important for users to understand the strengths and limitations of the tools being used. Let's examine some of the limitations and caveats associated with financial statement and ratio analysis.

- *GAAP financial statements are historical.* For many users and uses of financial statements, it is the future that matters. However, GAAP-based financial statements report on transactions and economic events that have already happened. They are not forecasts or reports on what will happen. Therefore, the results of analyzing GAAP financial statements may not be useful for assessing what will happen in the future. In most cases, GAAP financial statements can be used as a starting point of an analysis, but the user has to incorporate his or her own future-oriented information to project the future.

  The reason for limitations to using GAAP financial statements is change. Economic conditions change. Technology changes. An entity's marketplace changes. Entities themselves change. As a result, the future may be different from the past and the usefulness of the results of analyzing historical financial statements may be limited. Historical financial statements will be most useful for entities that are stable and where the effects of change are predictable. They will be least informative about entities that are subject to rapid and unpredictable change. For example, entities in the high technology industries are subject to a rapidly changing environment and are often growing. These circumstances make the past a poor indicator of the future.

- *Managers prepare financial statements.* This is good news and bad news. The managers are the people best equipped to prepare financial statements because they are the ones who know and understand the entity best. The managers can incorporate their insights and understanding of the entity into the financial statements. However, managers' self-interests can influence the accounting choices they make. Also, because an entity can only prepare one set of general purpose financial statements, managers often have to choose among the information needs of the different stakeholders and users when deciding how to orient the financial statements.

- *Financial statements are not comprehensive.* Financial statements do not reflect all of an entity's assets and liabilities, or all of its economic activity. Many valuable resources and important obligations are not reported. As a result, financial statements do not give a complete picture of an entity.

  There are many examples. Human resources—for many entities the most valuable asset—are not reported as assets. Research, the lifeblood of many entities in the knowledge-based economy, are expensed as incurred, not classified as assets. Also, the obligations associated with commitments the entity makes are not recorded as liabilities, even though the entity may have made significant and binding obligations to third parties. In addition, traditional financial statements ignore significant amounts of economic activity. For example, financial statements provide little in the way of information about market values or changes in market values. For the most part, assets are recorded at their cost and are left at cost, even though the market values of those assets may change, often significantly. As a result, potentially useful information is omitted from the financial statements.

- *Accounting policy choices and estimates affect ratios.* Under GAAP there are often alternative acceptable accounting policies available. The implication of using these different policies is that similar underlying economic activity can appear very differently in financial statements, depending on the accounting policies chosen. GAAP require that an entity disclose its accounting policies in the notes to the financial statements. It is, therefore, important for users to carefully read the note that describes the entity's significant accounting policies. Even if the accounting policy choices of an entity are known, it can be very difficult to restate financial statements so that they conform to the accounting policies preferred by the user.

  Also, the nature of accrual accounting requires that managers make estimates of future, uncertain events that are reflected in the financial statements. Estimates require judgment by the preparers. Because estimates are predictions, the actual amounts cannot be known at the time they are made. As a result, the assumptions, information, biases, and self-interests of the managers will affect the estimates reflected in the financial statements and, therefore, the numbers reported in the financial statements. Even if self-interest does not play a role in the making of estimates, it is reasonable to expect that there will be a range of acceptable estimates that could be made for most circumstances. Many of the accounting estimates an entity makes are not explicitly stated in the financial statements, which can give rise to unknown differences among different entities' financial statements.

- *Comparing financial statements can be difficult to do.* One of the desirable uses of accounting is to compare entities. Tools such as common size financial statements, return on investment, and other financial ratios are often used to compare entities. However, comparison of entities should always be approached with a great deal of caution. Certainly, the numbers in different entities' financial statements should not be directly compared. Adjustments for different accounting policies and estimates are needed so the basis of comparison is valid.

- *Financial statements are not the only source of information.* It is not possible to analyze an entity by only relying on financial statements. A comprehensive analysis of an entity will integrate information from financial statements as well as from other sources. As explained above in this section, financial statements are not comprehensive. They generally do not include future-oriented information, market values, and information about some important assets and liabilities.

- *Financial analysis is a diagnostic tool. It does not necessarily provide explanations for problems that are identified.* The accounting information on which financial analysis is performed reflects the economic activity of an entity—the entity's strategies, management, operations, and environment. Problem areas identified using financial analysis reflect these factors, but to get to the root of the problem a user must understand the entity's strategies, operations, and environment.

You've now completed your long and challenging journey through this book. Think back to what you knew about accounting when you first started. Now pick up the annual report of an entity and notice how you are able to make sense of the information in the financial statements. You should be able to interpret the numbers and recognize and understand the impact of the accounting choices. You should now be able to unravel some of the mysteries and intrigues of accounting.

■ Solved Problem

Esperanza Stores Corp. (Esperanza) operates two small retail stores in malls in Charlottetown. The two stores were opened in late 2000 and, according to Minh Tran, the president and majority shareholder, they have grown spectacularly over the last few years. In order to provide customers with the merchandise they want, Esperanza has once moved into larger stores and subsequently increased the size of its stores by taking over adjacent retail space as it became available. These expansions have significantly increased the amount of floor space in the stores and allowed Esperanza to expand the range and variety of products sold. Ms. Tran is currently thinking about opening additional stores.

Ms. Tran has approached the bank for an expanded line of credit. Esperanza's current line of credit is $30,000 and as of December 31, 2006 the line of credit has almost been fully used. Ms. Tran has provided the bank with Esperanza's financial statements for 2003 through 2006. The statements are available in Table 13-1. Additional information provided by Ms. Tran accompanies the financial statements.

Required:

Review the information provided by Ms. Tran and prepare a report for the small business lender that provides an assessment of Esperanza and a recommendation on whether additional money should be made available to the company.

Additional information:

- All sales of merchandise to customers are for cash or major credit card. No credit terms are offered to customers. Esperanza recognizes revenue at the time of sale.
- All purchases of inventory from suppliers are purchased on credit.
- The long-term loan is from a private lender. The loan must be repaid in full by 2009. Esperanza has been making payments on the loan since cash has been available to do so.
- Esperanza has never paid dividends.

Table 13-1   Esperanza Stores Corp.: Financial Statements

Esperanza Stores Corp.
Balance Sheets
As of December 31, 2003–2006

	2006	2005	2004	2003
ASSETS				
Cash	$ 10,000	$ 25,000	$ 50,000	$ 75,000
Inventory	200,000	160,000	125,000	78,000
Other current assets	16,298	17,322	8,440	6,000
Total current assets	226,298	202,322	183,440	159,000
Capital assets	182,000	151,000	110,000	75,000
Accumulated amortization	(75,530)	(60,400)	(41,800)	(22,500)
	$332,768	$292,922	$251,640	$211,500
LIABILITIES AND SHAREHOLDERS' EQUITY				
Bank loan	$ 29,371	$ 23,821	$ 11,966	$ 0
Accounts payable	101,000	81,500	65,000	45,000
Other payables	3,000	13,000	19,000	24,000
Current portion of long-term debt	20,000	5,000	5,000	5,000
Total current liabilities	153,371	123,321	100,966	74,000
Long-term debt	20,000	40,000	45,000	50,000
Capital stock	50,000	50,000	50,000	50,000
Retained earnings	109,397	79,601	55,674	37,500
	$332,768	$292,922	$251,640	$211,500

Esperanza Stores Corp.
Income Statements
For the Years Ended December 31, 2003–2006

	2006	2005	2004	2003
Revenue	$535,000	$485,000	$450,000	$350,000
Cost of sales	299,600	264,325	238,500	182,000
Gross margin	235,400	220,675	211,500	168,000
Selling, general, and administrative costs	180,000	170,000	165,000	140,000
Interest expense	6,200	6,000	5,200	5,000
Other expenses	11,000	14,000	18,000	20,000
Income before taxes	38,200	30,675	23,300	3,000
Income tax\se	8,404	6,749	5,126	660
Net income	$ 29,796	$ 23,927	$ 18,174	$ 2,340

Solution:

REPORT ON ESPERANZA STORES CORP.

I have completed my examination of Esperanza Stores Corp. (Esperanza) and while on the surface the stores appear to be performing well, there are some serious concerns. In essence, it appears that Esperanza is facing a serious liquidity problem and may have difficulty generating the cash flows necessary to support a significant loan. It is possible that improvements could be made that make Esperanza a more viable candidate for a loan. This is not to say that Esperanza is a lost cause. It isn't. As my report details, there are many positive accomplishments. The data I refer to in my report are presented in Tables 1, 2, 3, 4, and 5 [pages 818–820].

Performance

Esperanza has performed well over the last four years. Net income has increased each year, from $2,340 in 2003 to $29,796 in 2004, a very significant improvement. In addition, Esperanza's profit margin (Table 1 or 3), return on assets (Table 3), and return on equity (Table 3) have all increased in each reported year. Sales have been growing over the four years as well, with sales in 2006 almost 53% greater than they were in 2003. In absolute numbers, sales have grown from $350,000 in 2003 to $535,000 in 2006. Clearly, the company has done a good job building the business.

On the other hand, gross margin percentage (Table 3) has decreased steadily over the last four years from 48% in 2003 to 44% in 2006. This is a significant and alarming drop. Had Esperanza been able to maintain its 48% gross margin in 2006, net income would have been more than $21,000 higher and there would have been significantly more cash coming in.

Further information is needed to explain the reason for the decline. Is it due to increased competition or a pricing strategy that tried to increase sales by lowering prices? Additional information is also required about what the gross margin percentage is likely to be in future, as this will have significant implications for cash flows.

Despite the decline in the gross margin percentage, the gross margin has increased each year because of the increase in sales. Also, despite the decline in the gross margin percentage, the profit margin percentage has increased each year. Esperanza has achieved a rising profit margin percentage, while its gross margin percentage has been decreasing, through cost control. Selling, general, and administrative costs have increased at a much slower rate than sales, and the proportion of these costs as a percentage of revenue has fallen over the four-year period.

An important question is whether spending has been permanently reduced, or whether expenditures have been deferred. Also, there is a question about whether the reduction in spending will have implications for Esperanza's ability to maintain and increase sales in the future.

Overall, Esperanza has performed well. The company has grown its business with sales, profits, and profitability improving. The company's liquidity is another matter.

Liquidity

While the performance of Esperanza has been fine, I have serious concerns about its liquidity. All liquidity indicators have been deteriorating over the past four years and the company is in danger of running out of cash. The current ratio has decreased from 2.149 in 2003 to 1.475 in 2006. While a current ratio of 1.475 in and of itself is not a problem, the significant decline is.

The current ratio also masks the fact that an increasing proportion of Esperanza's assets is inventory. Since 2003 the proportion of total assets represented by inventory has increased from 36.9% to 60.1%. In addition, the amount of inventory on hand has increased much more rapidly than revenues. In most situations, one would expect inventory to grow at a rate similar to that of sales. Over the period 2003 to 2006, the amount of inventory on hand has increased 256%, while revenues have grown by only about 53%.

This difference in growth suggests that Esperanza may be carrying significant amounts of unsaleable inventory. If the inventory cannot be sold or can only be sold at a discount, the implication is that the current ratio overstates the liquidity of the company. There are other possible explanations for the large increase in inventory, such as failure to meet expected sales forecasts or because a wider range of merchandise is being carried in the stores. The increase could also be the result of poor inventory management.

The quick ratio, which focuses on the availability of very liquid current assets to cover current liabilities, supports a liquidity problem. Esperanza's only quick assets are cash, and over the last four years the amount of cash that the company is holding has declined significantly. As of December 31, 2006 the company had only $10,000 in cash with which to meet its obligations. If, for example, the current portion of long-term debt had to be paid immediately, Esperanza would not have the resources to do so.

The inventory turnover and accounts payable turnover ratios raise similar concerns. Since 2003 Esperanza is taking much longer to sell its inventory and to pay suppliers. The average number of days inventory is held before being sold has increased from 155 days in 2004 to 219 days in 2006, an increase of over 40%. The average number of days the company takes to pay its suppliers has increased from 70 days in 2004 to 98 days in 2006. The increased number of days to pay suppliers suggests that Esperanza is responding to its liquidity problems by delaying payments to suppliers for as long as possible. Taking the average number of days inventory and the average payment period for accounts payable together, the period over which Esperanza is self-financing its inventory has increased from 85 days in 2004 (155 – 70) to 121 days in 2006 (219 – 98).

From the information provided I constructed cash flow statements for 2004 through 2006. These statements are rough because of missing information, particularly about the amortization expense. It seems likely that, given the small change in accumulated amortization year to year, some capital assets were sold during some of the years. As a result, using the change in the accumulated amortization expense as an estimate of the amortization expense may be in error. If my assumption regarding the sale of assets is correct, cash from operations in my cash flow statements is likely lower than it actually is.

Cash from operations in each of the three years has been positive, growing, but is still quite small. Depending on sales in 2007, the company might not have enough cash to make its planned payment on the long-term debt. The company's operating cash flow is crucial for assessing a loan. While the current and quick ratios suggest liquidity problems, the problems could be mitigated if the business were generating enough cash flow. At this point, the cash flow statement and my interpretation of the turnover ratios do not relieve my uneasiness. That said, despite the liquidity problems Esperanza has been able to reduce its long-term debt over the last three years. However, it has done so by increasing its bank loan each year.

There is also potential for trouble if suppliers become more aggressive trying to collect amounts owing to them or if they stop providing credit. If this were the case, any loan that our bank makes could be in jeopardy. In the event a loan is made, Esperanza has little in the way of security to offer. There are no receivables, and it is possible that capital assets and inventory will be unlikely to produce much cash if they had to be sold.

Over the last three years Esperanza has made significant investments in capital assets. An important question is whether additional expenditures for capital assets will continue to be required. Esperanza has been expanding and, as a result, additional capital assets are required. However, the depletion of the company's cash can be largely attributed to the purchases of capital assets each year.

Overall, Esperanza seems to be an attractive and successful business. Its challenge is to survive its liquidity problems. At this point I do not recommend extending additional credit to the company. I think that Esperanza should take immediate steps to reduce its inventory levels to free up cash and reduce its investment in working capital. Also, the company should limit its spending on capital assets until its liquidity position becomes more solid.

Table 1   Common Size Financial Statements

Esperanza Stores Corp.
Common Size Balance Sheets
As of December 31, 2003–2006

	2006	2005	2004	2003
Cash	0.030	0.085	0.199	0.355
Inventory	0.601	0.546	0.497	0.369
Other current assets	0.049	0.059	0.034	0.028
Total current assets	0.680	0.691	0.729	0.752
Capital assets	0.547	0.515	0.437	0.355
Accumulated amortization	−0.227	−0.206	−0.166	−0.106
	1.000	1.000	1.000	1.000
Bank loan	0.088	0.081	0.048	0.000
Accounts payable	0.304	0.278	0.258	0.213
Other payables	0.009	0.044	0.076	0.113
Current portion of long-term debt	0.060	0.017	0.020	0.024
Total current liabilities	0.461	0.421	0.401	0.350
Long-term debt	0.060	0.137	0.179	0.236
Capital stock	0.150	0.171	0.199	0.236
Retained earnings	0.329	0.272	0.221	0.177
	1.000	1.000	1.000	1.000

Esperanza Stores Corp.
Common Size Income Statements
For the Years Ended December 31, 2003–2006

	2006	2005	2004	2003
Revenue	1.000	1.000	1.000	1.000
Cost of sales	0.560	0.545	0.530	0.520
Gross margin	0.440	0.455	0.470	0.480
Selling, general, and administrative costs	0.336	0.351	0.367	0.400
Interest expense	0.012	0.012	0.012	0.014
Other expenses	0.021	0.029	0.040	0.057
	0.071	0.063	0.052	0.009
Income tax expense	0.016	0.014	0.011	0.002
Net income	0.056	0.049	0.040	0.007

Table 2   Trend Financial Statements

Esperanza Stores Corp.
Trend Balance Sheets
As of December 31, 2003–2006

	2006	2005	2004	2003
Cash	0.133	0.333	0.667	1.000
Inventory	2.564	2.051	1.603	1.000
Other current assets	2.716	2.887	1.407	1.000
Total current assets	1.423	1.272	1.154	1.000
Capital assets	2.427	2.013	1.467	1.000
Accumulated amortization	3.357	2.684	1.858	1.000
	1.573	1.385	1.190	1.000
Bank loan	–	–	–	–
Accounts payable	2.244	1.811	1.444	1.000
Other payables	0.125	0.542	0.792	1.000
Current portion of long-term debt	4.000	1.000	1.000	1.000
Total current liabilities	2.073	1.667	1.364	1.000
Long-term debt	0.400	0.800	0.900	1.000
Capital stock	1.000	1.000	1.000	1.000
Retained earnings	2.917	2.123	1.485	1.000
	1.573	1.385	1.190	1.000

Esperanza Stores Corp.
Trend Income Statements
For the Years Ended December 31, 2003–2006

	2006	2005	2004	2003
Revenue	1.529	1.386	1.286	1.000
Cost of sales	1.646	1.452	1.310	1.000
Gross margin	1.401	1.314	1.259	1.000
Selling, general, and administrative costs	1.286	1.214	1.179	1.000
Interest expense	1.240	1.200	1.040	1.000
Other expenses	0.550	0.700	0.900	1.000
	12.733	0.225	7.767	1.000
Income tax expense	12.733	0.225	7.767	1.000
Net income	12.733	0.225	7.767	1.000

Table 3   Table of Financial Ratios

Esperanza Stores Corp.
Selected Financial Ratios, 2003–2006

	2006	2005	2004	2003
Current ratio	1.475	1.641	1.817	2.149
Quick ratio	0.065	0.203	0.495	1.014
Inventory turnover ratio	1.664	1.855	2.350	
Average number of days inventory on hand	219.292	196.775	155.335	
Accounts payable turnover ratio	3.722	4.086	5.191	
Average payment period for accounts payable	98.075	89.322	70.315	
Purchases (= cost of sales – beginning inventory + ending inventory)	$339,600	$299,325	$285,500	$260,000
Gross margin percentage	0.440	0.455	0.470	0.480
Profit margin percentage	0.056	0.049	0.040	0.007
Asset turnover	1.710	1.781	1.943	
Return on assets	0.111	0.106	0.096	
Return on equity	0.206	0.203	0.188	
Debt-to-equity ratio (liabilities ÷ shareholders' equity)	1.088	1.260	1.381	1.417

Table 4   Cash Flow Statements

Esperanza Stores Corp.
Cash Flow Statements
For the Years Ended December 31, 2004–2006

	2006	2005	2004
Net income	$29,796	$23,927	$18,174
Add: Amortization expense	15,130	18,600	19,300
	44,926	42,527	37,474
Adjustments for changes in current operating accounts			
Increase in inventory	(40,000)	(35,000)	(47,000)
Decrease/(increase) in other current assets	1,024	(8,882)	(2,440)
Increase in accounts payable	19,500	16,500	20,000
(Decrease) in other payables	(10,000)	(6,000)	(5,000)
Increase in current portion of long-term debt	15,000	0	0
Cash from operations	30,450	9,145	3,034
Investing activities—purchase of capital assets	(31,000)	(41,000)	(35,000)
Financing activities			
Repayment of long-term debt	(20,000)	(5,000)	(5,000)
Bank loan	5,550	11,855	11,966
	(14,450)	6,855	6,966
Decrease in cash during year	(15,000)	(25,000)	(25,000)
Cash balance at beginning of year	25,000	50,000	75,000
Cash balance at end of year	$10,000	$25,000	$50,000

Summary of Key Points

LO 1. An important use for current income is for forecasting future income. For the purpose of forecasting future earnings, historical earnings can be used as a starting point. Permanent earnings are earnings that are expected to be repeated in the future. As a result, permanent earnings are a useful indicator of future earnings. Earnings that are not considered permanent are called transitory. An entity's net income can have both permanent and transitory components. GAAP and the *CICA Handbook* require disclosure of information that is helpful for understanding the components of earnings. These disclosures include extraordinary items, unusual items, and discontinued operations.

Earnings quality refers to the usefulness of current earnings for predicting future earnings. Earnings quality is high if there is a close relationship between current earnings and future earnings. Earnings quality is low if the relationship between current and future earnings is not close. Another way of thinking about earnings quality is the extent to which reported earnings are permanent. Managers lower earnings quality when they manage earnings through their accounting policies, estimates, and accruals, and through the timing of actual transactions, such as discretionary expenditures and sales.

LO 2. To gain insight into the numbers and other information provided in a set of financial statements, it is usually necessary to analyze them. Financial ratios are a common tool used for examining, evaluating, and assessing an entity. There is a vast number of different ratios that have been developed for various purposes. In this chapter, ratios and analytical tools are grouped into four analytical themes: (1) evaluating performance, (2) liquidity, (3) solvency and leverage, and (4) other common ratios. Two tools that make this type of analysis easier are common size financial statements and trend analysis. These tools eliminate the impact of size from the financial statement numbers and restate them as proportions. While the ratios and other analytical tools introduced in this chapter are valuable for identifying problems, they do not usually provide answers.

LO 3. Financial ratios are a powerful and informative tool for analyzing and evaluating entities. Financial ratios provide valuable insights into the performance and prospects of an entity. However, ratio analysis has limitations, some of them quite severe. To get the most out of financial statement analysis it is important to understand the strength and limitations of the tools being used. The limitations include:

- GAAP financial statements are historical.

- Managers prepare financial statements.

- Financial statements are not comprehensive.

- Accounting policy choices and estimates affect ratios.

- Comparing financial statements can be difficult to do.

- Financial statements are not the only source of information.

- Financial analysis is a diagnostic tool. It does not necessarily provide explanations for problems that are identified.

Key Terms

accounts payable turnover ratio, p. 805

asset turnover, p. 799

average payment period for accounts payable, p. 806

capital structure, p. 808

common size financial statement (vertical analysis), p. 787

covenant, p. 769

discontinued operation, p. 777

dividend payout ratio, p. 811

earnings quality, p. 782

extraordinary item, p. 774

horizontal analysis (trend statement), p. 791

interest coverage ratio (accrual basis), p. 809

interest coverage ratio (cash basis), p. 809

management discussion and analysis (MD&A), p. 771

permanent earnings, p. 773

price-to-earnings (P/E) ratio, p. 810

solvency, p. 808

transitory earnings, p. 773

trend statements (horizontal analysis), p. 791

unusual item, p. 774

vertical analysis (common size financial statement), p. 787

Similar Terms

The left column gives alternative terms that are sometimes used for the accounting terms introduced in this chapter, which are listed in the right column.

horizontal analysis

trend analysis, p. 791

sustainable earnings, recurring earnings,
   core earnings, persistent earnings

permanent earnings, p. 773

vertical analysis

common size financial statements, p. 787

Assignment Materials

Questions

Q13-1.   What is a contribution margin? Why can it be important to determine an entity's contribution margin? Why is it often difficult to determine an entity's contribution margin from its financial statements?

Q13-2.   What is the difference between permanent and transitory earnings? Why can it be important to distinguish between these different types of earnings?

Q13-3.   Suppose you were considering making an investment in one of Canada's major department store chains. You narrowed your choice to Hudson's Bay Company (The Bay) and Sears Canada Inc. (Sears) and obtained each company's annual report. What concerns would you have in comparing the information presented in each company's financial statements when making your decision? What steps could you take to overcome these concerns?

Q13-4.   Why is it important to learn as much as you possibly can about an entity when doing an analysis of it? Explain.

Q13-5.   Would it be possible to gain useful insights into making a loan to an entity by looking *only* at the entity's financial statements? Explain. Assume that, except for what you could obtain from the financial statements, you had no access to other information about the entity and did not otherwise know anything about the entity.

Q13-6.   For each of the following situations, explain why GAAP-transactions-based financial statements would be of limited use for predicting the entity's future performance:
    a. The entity purchases a major new operating division in a new line of business for the entity.
    b. A large and successful U.S. firm in the same line of business as the entity enters the Canadian market.
    c. The entity just began operations and is growing rapidly.
    d. The entity is in a declining industry and has just closed down a number of its plants.
    e. The entity is a producer of software.

Q13-7.   Identify and explain the limitations and caveats associated with using financial ratio analysis on GAAP-based financial statements.

Q13-8.   What are the implications for financial statement analysis of the fact that preparers of financial statements can often choose among different, acceptable accounting methods? Provide examples of some of the accounting choices that preparers have to make.

Q13-9.   How do different objectives of financial reporting affect financial statement analysis?

Q13-10. Explain how the follow events would affect the usefulness of current earnings as a basis for predicting future earnings:
   a. An entity has a two-month strike during the year.
   b. An entity writes off a significant amount of capital assets.
   c. An entity receives a large payment from a competitor as part of the settlement of a lawsuit. The entity sued the competitor for infringement of a patent.
   d. An entity records a gain on the disposal of one of its vehicles.

Q13-11. Is it possible for an entity to be too liquid? Explain.

Q13-12. Explain why the quick ratio might be a better indicator of an entity's liquidity than the current ratio.

Q13-13. Explain the following and explain why it might be useful for a user of financial statements to have information about these items separately disclosed in the financial statements:
   a. extraordinary items
   b. unusual items
   c. discontinued operations

Q13-14. Describe a situation where the user of a private corporation's financial statements would be interested in segregating permanent and transitory earnings. Explain why the separation of the two types of earnings would be important in the situation.

Q13-15. Explain the concept of quality of earnings. What distinguishes high quality earnings from low quality earnings?

Q13-16. Explain how each of the following would affect the quality of an entity's earnings:
   a. Management decides to increase advertising in the current period as part of a special event. Management expects that the increase will occur only in the current year and spending levels will return to historical levels in the future.
   b. Management increases the estimated useful life of some of the entity's capital assets.
   c. Management decides to write down certain capital assets to reflect changes in market conditions.

Q13-17. Explain the significance of the fact that over the life of an entity, the accruals that are made must add up to zero.

Q13-18. What are common size financial statements? Explain why they can be useful for analyzing an entity over and above the actual financial statements of the entity.

Q13-19. What are trend financial statements? Explain why they can be useful for analyzing an entity over and above the actual financial statements of the entity.

Q13-20. What is liquidity? Why are suppliers concerned about the liquidity of an entity?

Q13-21. Why is it not adequate for stakeholders to focus their analyses of entities only on the financial statements? What type information about an entity that is not included in financial statements might be desirable for a stakeholder? What other sources of information might a stakeholder turn to?

Q13-22. What are covenants? Why are covenants often included in lending agreements? What purpose do they serve? Why are covenants often stated in accounting terms?

Q13-23. Explain the two broad concerns that creditors have about the credit they provide to entities. Describe the different types and sources of information that creditors would require to evaluate these concerns.

Q13-24. What is the difference between short-term and long-term creditors? Why would each approach financial statement analysis differently? What type of information would each require for making a decision to supply credit to a prospective customer? Explain.

Q13-25. The text states, "In many ways equity investors need to know everything." Explain why this is the case.

Q13-26. Would information about each of the following be useful to a prospective

long-term creditor in an entity? Explain. Would information about each item be available from the financial statements? Explain.
a. competitive advantages and disadvantages
b. risks faced by the entity
c. source of supplies and conditions in the supplier market
d. regulatory environment

Q13-27. Would information about each of the following be useful to a prospective equity investor in an entity? Explain. Would information about each item be available from the financial statements? Explain.
a. quality, experience, and performance of the managers
b. strategies for making money
c. competitive environment
d. lines of business

Q13-28. What is the management discussion and analysis (MD&A)? Why do you think public companies are required to provide an MD&A, whereas private companies are not?

Q13-29. Contrast the benefits and limitations of information provided to stakeholders by management versus information from a financial analyst who is independent of the entity.

Q13-30. Explain the implications of using only the financial statements when analyzing an entity.

Q13-31. What are factors that allow managers to manage earnings? What is it about these factors that allows for the management of earnings?

Q13-32. Explain the difference between return on assets and return on equity. Which measure is a more useful measure of the performance of an entity? Explain.

Q13-33. Why is necessary to evaluate financial ratios on a comparative basis rather than in absolute terms? What bases of comparison can be used?

Q13-34. Why is it not possible to carry out an effective financial analysis without knowing the decision that the decision-maker is making?

Exercises

E13-1. **(Classifying transactions and economic events as permanent or transitory, LO 1)** Would you classify each of the following as transitory or permanent in the entity's financial statements? Explain your reasoning.
a. severance pay to a number of executives who were fired during a reorganization
b. increase in wages paid to employees as a result of a union contract settlement
c. costs associated with closing a manufacturing facility
d. gains on the sale of equipment

E13-2. **(Classifying transactions and economic events as permanent or transitory, LO 1)** Would you classify each of the following as transitory or permanent in the entity's financial statements? Explain your reasoning.
a. increase in raw materials costs
b. payment associated with the settlement of a lawsuit
c. revenues associated with a discontinued operation
d. bonuses paid to senior executives

E13-3. **(Preparing common size financial statements, LO 2)** Examine the balance sheets and income statements for Fairplay Inc. (Fairplay).

Fairplay Inc.
Balance Sheets
As of December 31

	2005	2004	2003
Cash	$ 9,000	$ 12,000	$ 10,000
Accounts receivable	52,600	46,400	35,000
Inventory	59,250	46,000	45,000
Other current assets	12,000	11,000	8,000
Total current assets	132,850	115,400	98,000
Capital assets (net of amortization)	255,000	210,000	185,000
Total assets	$387,850	$325,400	$283,000
Bank loans	$ 48,310	$ 27,400	$ 23,000
Accounts payable and accrued liabilities	45,900	41,000	38,000
Total current liabilities	94,210	68,400	61,000
Long-term liabilities	70,000	62,000	50,000
Capital stock	125,000	125,000	125,000
Retained earnings	98,640	70,000	47,000
Total liabilities and shareholders' equity	$387,850	$325,400	$283,000

Fairplay Inc.
Income Statements
For the Years Ended December 31

	2005	2004	2003
Revenue	$520,128	$481,600	$430,000
Cost of sales	246,067	228,900	210,000
Gross margin	274,061	252,700	220,000
Selling, general, and administrative expenses	125,895	115,500	110,000
Amortization	30,000	28,000	23,000
Other expenses	63,245	58,560	48,000
Interest expense	15,000	12,000	8,000
Income before taxes	39,921	38,640	31,000
Income tax expenses	8,783	10,000	8,000
Net income	$ 31,138	$ 28,640	$ 23,000

Additional information:
- All sales are on credit.
- All purchases of inventory are on credit.
- Fairplay must begin repaying its long-term debt in 2007.

Required:
   a. Prepare common size balance sheets and income statements for 2003, 2004, and 2005.
   b. Analyze and interpret the common size financial statements you prepared.
   c. How are these common size statements more useful than the statements originally prepared by Fairplay?
   d. Why would it be unwise to examine the common size financial statements without considering the financial statements originally prepared by Fairplay?

E13-4. **(Preparing trend financial statements, LO 2)** Use the financial statements for Fairplay Inc. provided in Exercise E13-3 to respond to the following:
   a. Prepare trend balance sheets and income statements for 2003, 2004, and 2005.
   b. Analyze and interpret the trend financial statements your prepared.
   c. How are these trend statements more useful than the statements originally prepared by Fairplay?

    d. Why would it be unwise to examine the trend financial statements without considering the financial statements originally prepared by Fairplay?

E13-5. **(Calculating liquidity ratios, LO 2)** Use the information provided about Fairplay Inc. in Exercise E13-3 to respond to the following:

    a. Calculate the following for 2004 and 2005:

        i.   current ratio

        ii.   quick ratio

        iii. accounts receivable turnover ratio

        iv. average collection period of accounts receivable

        v.   inventory turnover ratio

        vi. average number of days inventory on hand

        vii. accounts payable turnover ratio

        viii. average payment period for accounts payable

        ix. cash lag

    b. Assume the role of an important new supplier to Fairplay. Use the amounts calculated in part (a) and prepare a report assessing whether Fairplay should be granted credit terms for purchases from your company. Explain the conclusions you make.

E13-6. **(Using common size and trend statements to evaluate performance, LO 2)** The income statements of Kronau Corp. (Kronau) for the years ended March 31, 2003 through 2005 are shown below:

Kronau Corp.
Income Statements
For the Years Ended March 31

	2005	2004	2003
Sales	$5,750,000	$5,225,000	$4,850,000
Cost of sales	3,150,000	2,750,000	2,561,000
Gross margin	2,600,000	2,475,000	2,289,000
Selling, general, and administrative expenses	1,350,000	1,150,000	1,111,000
Amortization expense	258,000	210,000	190,000
Interest expense	300,000	275,000	260,000
Unusual income	500,000	–	–
Income before income taxes	1,192,000	840,000	728,000
Income tax expense	200,000	160,000	150,000
Net income	$ 992,000	$ 680,000	$ 578,000

Required:

    a. Prepare common size and trend financial statements for Kronau.

    b. Use the information from part (a) to evaluate the performance of Kronau. Explain fully. Your evaluation should include a comparison of Kronau's performance from year to year.

    c. How does the unusual income affect your ability to evaluate the performance of Kronau and to interpret your common size and trend financial statements?

E13-7. **(Calculating accounts payable turnover, LO 2)** You have been provided with the following information from the balance sheets and income statements of Batchawana Inc. (Batchawana). Accounts Payable and Inventory are from the balance sheet as of December 31 of the stated year, and Cost of Sales is for the stated year ended December 31. Assume that all purchases of inventory are made on credit, and cost of sales includes only the cost of inventory sold:

	2005	2004	2003	2002
Accounts payable	$1,254,600	$1,066,410	$ 959,769	$ 767,815
Inventory	1,630,980	1,578,287	1,449,251	1,136,366
Cost of sales	5,056,038	5,208,346	4,811,514	3,613,645

Required:

   a. Calculate the accounts payable turnover ratio for 2003, 2004, and 2005.

   b. Calculate the average payment period for accounts payable for 2003, 2004, and 2005.

   c. What circumstances could explain a declining accounts payable turnover ratio (or increasing average payment period for accounts payable)?

E13-8.   **(Determining the effects of transactions on ratios, LO 2)** Complete the following table by indicating whether the following transactions or economic events would increase, decrease, or have no effect on the financial ratios listed. Consider each item independently. State any assumptions you make. Explain your reasoning.

	Current ratio	Inventory turnover ratio	Return on assets	Gross margin percentage	Debt-to-equity ratio
Ratio before the transactions/ economic events	1.47	3.5	12%	48%	1.8:1
a. Payment of a $1,000,000 dividend.					
b. Accrual of an extraordinary loss on expropriation of land.					
c. Early retirement of a long-term liability.					
d. Payment of an obligation by supplying inventory instead of paying cash.					
e. Write-down of a capital asset to net realizable value.					
f. Purchase of inventory on credit.					

E13-9.   **(Determining the effects of transactions on ratios, LO 2)** Complete the following table by indicating whether the following transactions or economic events would increase, decrease, or have no effect on the financial ratios listed. Consider each item independently. State any assumptions you make. Explain your reasoning.

	Interest coverage ratio	Accounts receivable turnover	Price-to-earnings ratio	Return on assets	Gross margin ratio
Ratio before the transactions/ economic events	5.35	5.5	18.5	10%	52.5%
a. Declaration and payment of preferred shares.					
b. Write-off of an accounts receivable.					
c. Sale of goods costing $5,500 for $12,000. Payment is to be made within 45 days.					
d. Disposal of an asset that was not being used. The asset had a book value of $195,000 when it was disposed of.					
e. Announcement of a new long-term contract with a new customer. The announcement was unexpected by the capital markets.					
f. Write-off of obsolete inventory. The company does this each year.					

E13-10. **(Determining the effects of transactions on ratios, LO 2)** Complete the following table by indicating whether the following transactions or economic events would increase, decrease or have no effect on the financial ratios listed. Consider each item independently. State any assumptions you make. Explain your reasoning.

	Quick ratio	Average payment period for accounts payable	Return on equity	Profit margin percentage	Earnings per share
Ratio before the transactions/economic events	0.82	45	16.5%	4%	$1.10
a. Repayment of a bond on the first day of the fiscal year.					
b. Conversion of a bond with a 10% coupon rate into common stock.					
c. Purchase of equipment for cash.					
d. Sale of 100,000 common shares for cash.					
e. Sale of inventory on credit.					
f. Payment of accounts payable.					

E13-11. **(Evaluating accounts receivable, LO 2)** Oungre Inc. (Oungre) is a small printing business that provides a wide range of printing services to retail and commercial clients. Retail customers pay cash, while Oungre offers its commercial customers 30 days from the delivery date to pay amounts owing. You have been provided with the following information from Oungre's accounting records:

	2002	2003	2004	2005
Accounts receivable (on December 31)	$54,000	$ 60,000	$ 68,000	$ 75,000
Sales (for the year ended)		760,000	805,000	875,000
Proportion of sales to commercial customers		63%	69%	78%

Required:

a. Calculate Oungre's accounts receivable turnover ratio for 2003, 2004, and 2005.

b. Calculate Oungre's average collection period of accounts receivable for 2003, 2004, and 2005.

c. Assess how well Oungre is managing its accounts receivable over the three-year period.

d. What are some possible explanations for why Oungre's collection is not less than 30 days? What steps might Oungre's management take to reduce the collection period further?

e. Suppose you did not know what the proportion of Oungre's sales to commercial customers was. How would your calculation of the accounts receivable turnover ratio and the average collection period of accounts receivable be affected? How would your interpretation of the performance of Oungre's management be affected?

E13-12. **(Evaluating inventory management, LO 2)** Zawale Ltd. (Zawale) is a wholesaler of fresh fruits and vegetables. Zawale purchases fruits and vegetables from growers and supplies them to small grocery stores. You have been provided with the following information from Zawale's accounting records:

	2003	2004	2005	2006
Inventory (on December 31)	$65,000	$ 73,000	$ 81,000	$ 130,000
Cost of sales (for the year ended)		4,200,000	4,830,000	4,588,500

Required:

    a. Calculate Zawale's inventory turnover ratio for 2004, 2005, and 2006.

    b. Calculate Zawale's average number of days inventory on hand for 2004, 2005, and 2006.

    c. Evaluate how well Zawale's management is managing the inventory. Explain.

    d. What are some possible explanations for the amounts you calculated in parts (a) and (b)?

    e. What are the implications for Zawale's performance of the results you found in parts (a) and (b)? Explain.

E13-13. **(Evaluating accounts payable management, LO 2)** Guisachan Books Inc. (Guisachan) is a small book retailer. Guisachan has approached your company, a large publishing house, requesting credit terms on purchases. Guisachan has never purchased from your company. If credit is approved, Guisachan would be given 60 days to pay outstanding amounts. You have been provided with the following information from Guisachan's accounting records:

	2004	2005	2006	2007
Accounts payable (on December 31)	$48,000	$ 52,000	$ 61,000	$ 72,000
Credit purchases (for the year ended)		320,000	330,000	325,000

Required:

    a. Calculate Guisachan's accounts payable turnover ratio for 2005, 2006, and 2007.

    b. Calculate Guisachan's average payment period for accounts payable for 2005, 2006, and 2007.

    c. Assume you are the credit manager of the large publishing house. How would you interpret the information you received about Guisachan's accounts payable? How would this information influence your decision about whether to offer credit to Guisachan? Explain. What additional information would you request before making a final decision? Explain.

    d. What effect will the results you calculated in parts (a) and (b) have on Guisachan's cash from operations? Explain. Is this a good situation? Explain. How might Guisachan's suppliers respond? Explain.

E13-14. **(Calculating EPS, price-to-earnings ratio, and dividend ratios, LO 2)** Junor Inc. (Junor) is a publicly traded company. During its year ended July 31, 2004 Junor reported net income of $3,759,000. During fiscal 2004 Junor declared and paid quarterly dividends of $0.10 per share on its 5,000,000 outstanding common shares. During the year no shares were issued and none were repurchased from investors. In addition, Junor paid $1,000,000 in preferred dividends. On July 31, 2004 Junor's share price was $11.50.

Required:

    a. Calculate the following ratios for 2004. Explain and interpret the meaning of each ratio:

       i. basic earnings per share for fiscal 2004

       ii. price-to-earnings ratio on July 31, 2004

       iii. dividend payout ratio for fiscal 2004

E13-15. **(Calculating EPS, price-to-earnings ratio, and dividend ratios, LO 2)** Kovach Ltd. (Kovach) is a publicly traded company. During its year ended March 31, 2006 Kovach reported a net loss of $18,750,000. During fiscal 2006 Kovach declared and paid quarterly dividends of $0.05 per share on its 12,000,000 outstanding common shares. During the year no shares were issued and none were repurchased from investors. In addition, Kovach paid $2,500,000 in preferred dividends. On March 31, 2006 Kovach's share price was $6.75.

Required:

    a. Calculate the following ratios for 2006. Explain and interpret the meaning of each ratio:

     i.   basic earnings per share for fiscal 2006

     ii. price-to-earnings ratio on March 31, 2006

     iii. dividend payout ratio for fiscal 2006

b.   Explain how it is possible for Kovach to pay a dividend when it reported a loss during fiscal 2006.

c.   Explain why Kovach would have a share price that is greater than zero when the company is losing money.

E13-16. **(Examining the effect of debt covenants on debt and dividends)** During fiscal 2005, Husavick Inc. (Husavick) borrowed $500,000 from a private lender. The loan agreement requires that Husavick's debt-to-equity ratio not exceed 2:1 at any time. You have been provided with the following information from Husavick's accounting records:

Husavick Inc.
Summarized Balance Sheet
For the Year Ended July 31, 2005

Assets:	
Current assets	$ 300,000
Non-current assets	1,230,000
Total assets	$1,530,000
Liabilities and shareholders' equity:	
Current liabilities	$ 230,000
Non-current liabilities	750,000
Shareholders' equity	550,000
Total liabilities and shareholders' equity	$1,530,000

Required:

a. Calculate Husavick's debt-to-equity ratio on July 31, 2005.

b. How much additional debt could Husavick have borrowed without violating the debt covenant?

c. How much could Husavick have paid in dividends during fiscal 2005 without violating the debt covenant?

d. Suppose that on December 15, 2005 Husavick's board of directors declared a dividend of $125,000. The dividend is to be paid on January 15, 2006. What would the impact of this event be on the financial statements and on the debt covenant on December 31, 2005?

E13-17. **(Computing ratios, LO 2)** Hurstwood Wineries Ltd. (Hurstwood) produces and markets wines from a number of wineries across Canada. You have been provided with the following income statements and balance sheets for Hurstwood:

Hurstwood Wineries Ltd.
Income Statements
For the Years Ended March 31, 2004 and 2005
(in thousands of dollars except per share amounts)

	2005	2004
Sales	$87,333	$86,865
Cost of goods sold	55,463	54,816
Gross profit	31,870	32,049
Selling and administration	22,561	21,294
Earnings before interest and amortization	9,309	10,755
Interest	1,435	1,563
Amortization	2,700	2,481
Earnings before unusual items	5,174	6,711
Unusual items	(667)	4,739
Earnings before income taxes	4,507	11,450
Provision for (recovery of) income taxes:		
Current	2,168	3,634
Future	(295)	463
	1,873	4,097
Net earnings for the year	2,634	7,353
Retained earnings—beginning of year	39,395	33,970
Dividends on common shares	1,928	1,928
Retained earnings—end of year	$40,101	$39,395

Hurstwood Wineries Ltd.
Balance Sheets
As of March 31, 2004 and 2005
(in thousands of dollars)

	2005	2004
Assets		
Current assets:		
Accounts receivable	$ 7,542	$ 7,844
Inventories	30,736	31,241
Prepaid expenses	702	557
	38,980	39,642
Capital assets and goodwill	43,884	38,844
Investment	3,565	3,565
	$86,429	$82,051
Liabilities		
Current liabilities:		
Bank indebtedness	$17,883	$13,665
Accounts payable and accrued liabilities	8,548	6,862
Dividends payable	482	482
Income and other taxes payable	928	2,009
Current portion of long-term debt	1,552	1,370
	29,393	24,388
Long-term debt	11,346	12,384
Future income taxes	2,716	3,011
	43,455	39,783
Shareholders' equity		
Capital stock (weighted average number of shares outstanding during 2005 was 3,953,050 and during 2004 was 3,875,200)	2,873	2,873
Retained earnings	40,101	39,395
	42,974	42,268
	$86,429	$82,051

Required:

    a. Compute the following ratios and amounts for Hurstwood for 2005 and 2004:
      i.   gross margin
      ii. gross margin percentage
      iii. profit margin
      iv. profit margin percentage
      v.   earnings per share
      vi. working capital
      vii. current ratio
      viii. quick ratio
      ix. debt-to-equity ratio
      x.   interest coverage ratio
      xi. dividend payout ratio

    b. Compute the following ratios and amounts for Hurstwood for 2005:
      i.   asset turnover
      ii. financial leverage
      iii. return on equity
      iv. return on assets
      v.   inventory turnover ratio
      vi. average number of days inventory on hand
      vii. accounts receivable turnover ratio
      viii. average collection period of accounts receivable
      ix. accounts payable turnover ratio
      x.   average payment period for accounts payable
      xi. cash lag

    c. How do the unusual items reported on the 2004 and 2005 income statements affect your ability to predict Hurstwood's future performance?

    d. Comment on Hurstwood's liquidity, based on amounts you calculated in parts (a) and (b). Be sure to consider the nature of Hurstwood's business in your response.

E13-18. **(Understanding return on assets, LO 2)** You are provided with the following information about Unwin Corp. (Unwin), a small manufacturing company.

	2006	2005	2004	2003	2002
Sales	$654,720	$611,888	$582,750	$525,000	
Net income	28,153	25,699	22,145	18,375	
Total liabilities					
(at year end)	173,137	163,337	147,150	136,250	125,000
Shareholders' equity					
(at year end)	190,840	162,688	136,988	114,844	96,469

Required:

    a. Calculate Unwin's return on assets by determining its profit margin and asset turnover ratio. Assume that profit margin equals net income divided by sales.

    b. Calculate Unwin's return on equity by using its return on assets and its financial leverage.

    c. Explain why is it not possible for an entity's return on assets to be greater than its return on equity.

    d. Assess the profitability of Unwin. In your response, explain the reasons for any changes in Unwin's profitability.

E13-19. **(Understanding return on assets, LO 2)** You are provided with the following information about Wha Ti Inc. (Wha Ti), a vehicle repair company.

	2005	2004	2003	2002	2001
Sales	$3,829,056	$3,418,800	$3,052,500	$2,750,000	
Net income	134,017	129,914	122,100	115,500	
Total liabilities (at year end)	638,141	607,753	578,813	551,250	525,000
Shareholders' equity (at year end)	1,274,493	1,140,476	1,010,562	888,462	772,962

Required:

a. Calculate Wha Ti's return on assets by determining its profit margin and asset turnover ratio. Assume that profit margin equals net income divided by sales.

b. Calculate Wha Ti's return on equity by using its return on assets and its financial leverage.

c. Explain why is it not possible for an entity's return on assets to be greater than its return on equity.

d. Assess the profitability of Wha Ti. In your response, explain the reasons for any changes in Wha Ti's profitability.

E13-20. **(Classifying transactions and economic events, LO 1)** Explain whether you would classify each of the following transactions and economic events as extraordinary, unusual, or ordinary.

a. An entity's property is destroyed in a terrorist attack.

b. A manufacturer sells its old equipment so that it can purchase new equipment.

c. A business settles a large lawsuit by paying $1,000,000.

d. A chain of restaurants closes five of its poorly performing locations.

e. An earthquake destroys a factory of a large company.

Problems

P13-1. **(Find the missing information, LO 2)** Use the information provided about Kynocks Inc. (Kynocks) to determine the missing information from its December 31, 2005 balance sheet and for the income statement for the year ended December 31, 2005. For all final amounts determined for the balance sheet and income statement, round to the thousands of dollars.

Kynocks Inc.
Balance Sheets
As of the Years Ended December 31, 2004 and 2005

	2005	2004
Cash	$	$110,000
Accounts receivable		105,000
Inventory		248,000
Capital assets (net)		146,000
Total assets:	$	$609,000
Accounts payable	$	$184,000
Long-term debt		100,000
Capital stock on January 1, 2005		75,000
Retained earnings on January 1, 2005		250,000
Total liabilities and shareholders' equity:	$	$609,000

Kynocks Inc.
Income Statement
For the Year Ended December 31, 2005

Revenue	$
Cost of sales	1,500,000
Gross margin	
Selling, general, and administrative expenses	
Interest expense	
Income before taxes	
Income tax expense	
Net income	
Number of common shares outstanding during 2005	$

Additional information:

- No dividends were paid during the year.
- There are no preferred shares outstanding.
- All sales and purchases of inventory are on credit.
- No new common shares were issued during the year and no common shares were repurchased during the year.
- Tax rate = 20.63%.
- Gross margin percentage = 40%.
- Profit margin percentage = 2%.
- Interest coverage ratio = 6.2085.
- EPS = $0.40.
- ROA = 9.85.
- Inventory turnover ratio = 5.474.
- Accounts receivable turnover ratio = 21.739.
- Accounts payable turnover ratio = 7.589.
- Debt-to-equity ratio = 0.733.
- Current ratio = 2.222.

P13-2. **(Find the missing information, LO 2)** Use the information provided about Voligny Inc. (Voligny) to determine the missing information from its December 31, 2005 balance sheet and for the income statement for the year ended December 31, 2007. For all final amounts determined for the balance sheet and income statement, round to thousands of dollars.

Voligny Inc.
Balance Sheets
As of the Years Ended December 31, 2006 and 2007

	2007	2006
Cash	$	$ 1,250,000
Accounts receivable		2,000,000
Inventory		1,500,000
Capital assets (net)		12,250,000
Total assets:	$	$17,000,000
Accounts payable	$	$ 1,000,000
Long-term debt		6,000,000
Capital stock on January 1, 2005		2,500,000
Retained earnings on January 1, 2005		7,500,000
Total liabilities and shareholders' equity:	$	$17,000,000

Voligny Inc.
Income Statement
For the Year Ended December 31, 2007

Revenue	$
Cost of sales	
Gross margin	
Selling, general, and administrative expenses	
Interest expense	
Income before taxes	
Income tax expense	
Net income	$1,000,000

Additional information:

- No dividends were paid during the year.
- There are no preferred shares outstanding.
- All sales and purchases of inventory are on credit.
- No new common shares were issued during the year and no common shares were repurchased during the year.
- Tax rate = 25.9%.
- Gross margin percentage = 60%.
- Profit margin percentage = 12.5%.
- Interest coverage ratio = 2.588.
- EPS = $0.75.
- Inventory turnover ratio = 1.828.
- Accounts receivable turnover ratio = 3.333.
- Accounts payable turnover ratio = 2.467.
- Debt-to-equity ratio = 0.826.
- Current ratio = 3.25.

P13-3. **(Determining the effect of a big bath on future earnings and financial ratios, LO 1, 2)** Vogar Ltd. (Vogar) is a public company that manufactures machine parts. In its most recent financial statements Vogar wrote down $20,000,000 of its capital assets. The assets will continue to be used by Vogar. The new president and CEO of Vogar announced that the write-downs were the result of competitive pressures and poor performance of the company in the last year. The write-downs were reported separately in Vogar's income statement as a "non-recurring" item. The write-off is not included in the calculation of operating income. In addition, Vogar wrote down its inventory in fiscal 2004 by $2,000,000. The amount is included in cost of sales.

Vogar's summarized income statement for the year ended December 31, 2004 is (amounts in millions of dollars):

Revenue		$95
Operating expenses:		
Cost of sales	$52	
Amortization	14	
Selling general and administrative costs	18	84
Operating income		11
Other expenses:		
Non-recurring item	20	
Interest expense	5	
Income tax expense	2	27
Net income		($16)

The write-downs will reduce the amortization expense by $2,500,000 per year for each of the next eight years. After the announcement and release of the income statement, analysts revised their forecasts of earnings for the next three years to:

Year ended December 31, 2005	$ 4,000,000
Year ended December 31, 2006	$ 9,000,000
Year ended December 31, 2007	$12,000,000

You also obtained the following information from Vogar's December 31 2003 and 2004 balance sheets:

Vogar Ltd.
Summarized Balance Sheet Information
For the Years Ended December 31, 2003 and 2004
(in millions of dollars)

	2004	2003
Current assets	$ 32,975	$ 37,500
Total assets	142,767	151,597
Current liabilities	24,220	22,150
Non-current liabilities	38,250	33,150
Shareholders' equity	80,297	96,297

Required:

a. What would net income be in each of 2004 through 2007 had Vogar not written off the assets and continued to amortize them? Assume that the operations of Vogar do not change regardless of the accounting method used. Interpret the differences in net income under the two scenarios.

b. What would Vogar's gross margin, profit margin, debt-to-equity ratio, return on assets, and return on equity be in 2004 assuming (i) that the assets had been written off and (ii) assuming that the assets had not been written off and they were continuing to be amortized? Interpret the results under each assumption.

c. How would the write-downs in 2004 affect Vogar's gross margin, profit margin, debt-to-equity ratio, return on assets, and return on equity in 2005 through 2007? How is your ability to analyze and interpret the financial statements affected?

P13-4. **(Evaluating the effect of R&D accounting on financial statement analysis, LO 1, 2, 3)** One controversial accounting issue is accounting for research costs. In Canada research costs must be expensed as incurred. This treatment is an application of the conservatism measurement convention. Some people argue that research is a legitimate asset and requiring that it be expensed results in an understatement of assets and income, violates matching, and makes companies that invest heavily in research appear less successful than they actually are.

Chortitz Ltd. (Chortitz) is a large and successful software development company. You have been provided with Chortitz's balance sheets and income statements for 2004 through 2006. In addition, Chortitz expensed (and expended) $7,906,000 for research in 2003 and $6,612,000 in 2002.

Chortitz Ltd.
Summarized Balance Sheet Information
As of June 30, 2003–2006
(000s)

Extracts from the balance sheet	2006	2005	2004	2003
Current assets	$47,953	$51,563	$41,102	$34,815
Total assets	90,923	92,441	76,024	70,589
Current liabilities	32,154	33,220	22,233	18,569
Non-current liabilities	11,550	9,240	6,188	4,331
Shareholders' equity	47,219	49,981	47,603	47,689

Chortitz Ltd.
Income Statements
For the Years Ended June 30, 2004–2006
(000s)

	2006	2005	2004
Revenues	$121,852	$93,180	$76,343
Cost of revenues:			
License & networking	4,849	2,215	1,501
Customer support	6,296	4,728	2,600
Service	20,596	18,975	12,255
Total cost of revenues	31,741	25,918	16,356
	90,111	67,262	59,987
Operating expenses:			
Research and development	20,057	14,638	9,383
Sales and marketing	42,337	35,416	30,064
General and administrative	10,883	16,361	4,885
Depreciation	5,178	4,586	4,225
Total operating expenses	78,455	71,001	48,557
Income (loss) from operations	11,656	(3,739)	11,430
Interest expense	1,005	765	498
Income before income taxes	10,651	(4,504)	10,932
Provision for (recovery of) income taxes	2,115	(854)	1,995
Net income for the year	$ 8,536	$ (3,650)	$ 8,937
Weighted average number of common shares	20,032,092	22,349,268	20,914,365

Required:

a. Recalculate Chortitz's net income in 2004, 2005, and 2006, assuming that research is capitalized and amortized over three years. Also calculate total assets and shareholders' equity, assuming research is capitalized and amortized. What amount would be reported on the balance sheet for research if research were capitalized instead of expensed? (Assume that one-third of the of the amount expended on research is expensed each year, including the year of the expenditure.)

b. Calculate Chortitz's profit margin, interest coverage ratio, earnings per share, debt-to-equity ratio, ROA, and ROE for 2004, 2005, and 2006 using the information as presented in the company's financial statements. Calculate the same ratios, assuming that Chortitz capitalizes and amortizes its research costs over three years.

c. Evaluate the performance and solvency of Chortitz under the "expense" and "capitalize" scenarios. What are the implications of the differences between the two scenarios? Do you think there is merit in the criticisms some people have expressed about the current GAAP treatment of research costs? Explain fully.

P13-5. **(Evaluating performance, LO2)** Nywening Ltd. (Nywening) operates in a highly competitive industry. Price is very important to most customers and it is very difficult for small operators such as Nywening to differentiate themselves on product quality. It is possible to differentiate based on service, but most competitors offer reasonably comparable service packages.

The president of Nywening is reviewing the company's performance in 2005. During 2005 sales increased by 12% to $3,500,000. Average total assets for the year were $1,950,000, net income was $200,000, and interest expense was $60,000. Nywening's tax rate is 20%.

The president believes that Nywening can improve its performance in 2006. She would like to see a 15% growth in sales in 2006 and a return on assets of 20%. The president estimates that it will be necessary to increase assets by 10% in 2006. The president does not think that any additional borrowing will be required and, as a result, the interest expense for 2006 will be the same as for 2005.

Required:

a. Calculate Nywening's profit margin, asset turnover, and return on assets for 2005.
b. What asset turnover ratio is required in 2006 to achieve the president's objectives? What net income is needed to achieve her objectives? What would the profit margin be if the objectives are achieved? For purposes of this question use net income plus the after tax cost of interest.
c. Do you think the president's objectives are reasonable?

P13-6.   (**Determining the effects of transactions on ratios, LO 2**) You have been provided with the following information about Everell Inc. (Everell).

	2003	2004	2005	2006
Accounts receivable	$ 150,000	$ 157,500	$ 165,375	$ 173,644
Inventory	100,000	105,000	110,250	115,763
Accounts payable	75,000	78,750	82,688	86,822
Revenue	1,000,000	1,050,000	1,155,000	1,270,500
Cost of sales	550,000	577,500	641,025	711,538

Required:

a. Calculate the accounts receivable, inventory, and accounts payable turnover ratios for 2004 through 2006.
b. Calculate the average collection period of accounts receivable, average number of days inventory on hand, and average payment period for accounts payable for 2004 through 2006.
c. Determine Everell's cash lag for 2004 through 2006.
d. Interpret the results you obtained in parts (a) through (c). What do these results tell you about Everell's liquidity over the last three years?
e. What are some possible explanations for the results?
f. Suppose you are a banker who Everell's management approached about an expanded line of credit. How would the results you obtained in parts (a) through (c) affect your decision? Explain.

P13-7.   (**Determining the effects of transactions on ratios, LO 2**) You have been provided with the following information about Yarker Ltd. (Yarker).

	2004	2005	2006	2007
Accounts receivable	$ 1,125,000	$ 1,215,000	$ 1,275,750	$1,339,538
Inventory	2,500,000	2,600,000	2,730,000	2,593,500
Accounts payable	100,000	101,920	104,876	97,639
Revenue	10,000,000	10,500,000	10,290,000	9,775,500
Cost of sales	4,000,000	4,179,000	4,074,943	3,851,840

Required:

a. Calculate the accounts receivable, inventory, and accounts payable turnover ratios for 2005 through 2007.
b. Calculate the average collection period of accounts receivable, average number of days inventory on hand, and average payment period for accounts payable for 2005 through 2007.
c. Determine Yarker's cash lag for 2005 through 2007.
d. Interpret the results you obtained in parts (a) through (c). What do these results tell you about Yarker's liquidity over the last three years?
e. What are some possible explanations for the results?
f. Suppose you are a banker whom Yarker's management approached about an expanded line of credit. How would the results you obtained in parts (a) through (c) affect your decision? Explain.

P13-8. **(The effect of leverage on ROA and ROE, LO 2)** Three companies, Company A, Company B, and Company C, are identical in every respect except for how they are financed. You are provided with the following information about each company.

	Company A			Company B			Company C		
	Jan. 1, 2005	Dec. 31, 2005	Dec. 31, 2006	Jan. 1, 2005	Dec. 31, 2005	Dec. 31, 2006	Jan. 1, 2005	Dec. 31, 2005	Dec. 31, 2006
Income before interest and taxes		$ 28,000	$ 3,000		$ 28,000	$ 3,000		$ 28,000	$ 3,000
Interest expense		0	0		3,000	3,000		7,000	7,000
Income tax expense		6,160	660		5,500	0		4,620	(880)
Net income		21,840	2,340		19,500	0		16,380	(3,120)
Dividends paid		10,000	5,460		7,660	3,120		4,540	0
Total assets	$100,000	111,840	108,720	$100,000	111,840	108,720	$100,000	111,840	108,720
Shareholders' equity	100,000	111,840	108,720	70,000	81,840	78,720	30,000	41,840	38,720
Tax rate		0.22	0.22		0.22	0.22		0.22	0.22

Required:

a. Calculate ROA and ROE for each company for the years ended December 31, 2005 and 2006.
b. Explain the differences in performance among the three companies.
c. Explain the effect of leverage on the performance measures.

P13-9. **(The effect of leasing on ratios, LO 2)** Fodhia Inc. (Fodhia) is a small manufacturing company operating in eastern Canada. Fodhia is a public company. In 2004 Fodhia's management decided to acquire additional manufacturing equipment so that it would be able to meet the increasing demand for its products. However, instead of purchasing the equipment, Fodhia arranged to lease the equipment. The lease came into effect on December 1, 2003. In its 2004 financial statements Fodhia accounted for the leases as operating leases. You have obtained Fodhia's summarized balance sheets and income statements for 2003 and 2004.

Fodhia Inc.
Summarized Balance Sheets
As of November 30, 2003 and 2004
(000s)

	2004	2003
Cash	$ 212	$ 276
Accounts receivable	695	608
Inventory	1,825	1,547
Capital assets (net)	2,895	2,652
Other non-current assets	375	442
Total assets	$6,002	$5,525
Current liabilities	$1,728	$1,823
Long term debt	990	950
Capital stock (1,000,000 shares outstanding)	1,200	1,200
Retained earnings	2,084	1,552
	$6,002	$5,525

Fodhia Inc.
Income Statements
For the Years Ended November 30, 2003 and 2004
(000s)

	2004	2003
Revenue	$17,250	$14,500
Cost of sales	9,401	7,996
Selling, general, and administrative expenses	6,512	5,550
Amortization expense	310	275
Lease expense for equipment	225	
Interest expense	92	86
Income tax expense	177	148
Net income	$ 533	$ 445

Had Fodhia accounted for the equipment leases as capital leases, the following differences would have occurred in the 2004 financial statements:

- No lease expense would have been recorded.
- The leased equipment would have been recorded on the balance sheet as capital assets for $460,000. The equipment will be amortized straight-line over 12 years.
- A liability of $460,000 would have been recorded at the inception of the lease. On November 30, 2004 the current portion of the liability would have been $75,000. The interest expense arising from the lease would have been $46,000. On November 30, 2004 the remaining liability, including the current portion, would have been $431,000.
- There would be no effect on the tax expense for the year.

Required:

a. Prepare revised financial statements, assuming that Fodhia treated the leases as capital leases instead of as operating leases.

b. Calculate the following ratios, first using the financial statements as initially prepared by Fodhia and then using the revised statements you prepared in part (a):
   i. debt-to-equity ratio
   ii. return on assets
   iii. return on equity
   iv. profit margin ratio
   v. current ratio
   vi. asset turnover
   vii. earnings per share
   viii. interest coverage ratio

c. Discuss the differences between the two sets of ratios you calculated in part (b). Why are the ratios different? How might users of the financial statements be affected by these differences? Which set of ratios gives a better perspective on the performance, liquidity, and leverage of Fodhia? Explain.

P13-10. **(Determining the effect of a big bath on future earnings, LO 1, 2)** Quirpon Inc. (Quirpon) is a large mining company. In 2001 Quirpon wrote down $10,000,000 in costs that it incurred finding and developing certain mining properties. If Quirpon had not written down the $10,000,000 in costs, $2,000,000 in amortization would have been expensed in each year from 2001 through 2005. The summarized financial statement information for the years 2001 through 2004 is:

Quirpon Inc.
Summarized Financial Statement Information
(in thousands of dollars)

	2000	2001	2002	2003	2004
Revenue		$30,500	$28,000	$31,000	$33,000
Operating expenses		12,000	11,000	13,000	14,500
Amortization expense		7,000	7,200	7,400	7,800
Interest expense		1,200	1,200	1,200	1,200
Income tax expense		$2,575	$2,150	$2,350	$2,375
Net income		($7,725)	$6,450	$7,050	$7,125
Total assets	$37,000	$34,725	$41,175	$48,225	$55,350
Total shareholders' equity	$25,000	$22,725	$29,175	$36,225	$43,350

Additional information:
- Quirpon has no preferred shares outstanding.
- The amortization expense does not include the amortization of the written-down assets and the write-down is not reflected in the presented information.
- Quirpon's tax rate is 25%.
- Assume that the write-down and any additional amortization expense do not affect Quirpon's tax expense.

Required:

a. Determine Quirpon's net income for 2001 through 2004, assuming that the $10,000,000 write-down (i) occurred and (ii) did not occur. For (ii) amortization of the assets must be expensed each year.

b. Calculate Quirpon's profit margin, return on assets, and return on equity, assuming that the write-down (i) occurred and (ii) did not occur.

c. Should the write-down be considered permanent or transitory earnings? Explain.

d. As an equity investor in Quirpon, how would your evaluation of the company be affected by whether the write-down occurred versus if the assets were amortized over their remaining life? In responding you should consider permanent versus transitory earnings.

P13-11. **(Forecasting future earnings, LO 1)** You have been presented with Peverel Ltd.'s (Peverel) income statement for the year ended September 30, 2005.

Peverel Ltd.
Income Statement
For the Year Ended September 30, 2005

Sales	$12,750,000
Cost of sales	5,737,500
Gross margin	7,012,500
Expenses:	
Salaries and wages	2,754,000
Amortization	987,000
Selling and administrative	1,450,000
Interest	500,000
Other	325,000
Unusual items—lawsuit revenue	1,000,000
Income before income taxes	1,996,500
Income tax expense	598,950
Net income	$ 1,397,550

In addition, you have learned the following:

- Cost of sales in 2005 includes a write-down of inventory of $295,000. The amount of the write-down is about three times larger than the amount usually written down each year to account for non-saleable inventory or inventory that will have to be sold at a deep discount.
- Sales includes $1,250,000 for a one-time-only sale to the government of a foreign country. The profit margin percentage on this sale was 60%, which is significantly higher than what Peverel normally experiences.
- Selling and administrative costs includes a $200,000 retirement bonus paid to the former CEO.
- Peverel signed a contract with its employees that goes into effect on October 1, 2005. The contract increases union employees' wages and benefits by 5%. Wages to employees covered by the contract represent 70% of salaries and wages expense in 2005. Wages to other employees are not expected to change during 2006.
- During 2005 Peverel won a lawsuit against a former employee for divulging confidential information to her new employer. The employee and her new employer are required to pay damages to Peverel of $1,000,000.
- Sales (excluding the one-time sale note above) are expected to grow by 8% during 2006. Inventory costs are expected to increase by 9%, selling and administrative expenses are expected to decrease by 2%, interest expense is not expected to change, amortization expense is expected to increase by 2%, and other expenses are expected to increase by 4%.

Required:

a. Use Peverel's 2005 income statement and the additional information to forecast an income statement for 2006.

b. Explain and interpret Peverel's actual performance in 2005 and the performance that you forecast for 2006.

c. Discuss the difficulties that can occur with forecasting the future performance of an entity and the problems with using GAAP financial statements for forecasting.

P13-12. **(Evaluating liquidity and solvency, LO 2)** Yekooche Inc. (Yekooche) is a small manufacturer of home environmental products such as humidifiers, air cleaners, and ionizers. Yekooche's products are sold across Canada and about 20% of its sales are outside of Canada, mainly in the United States. The president of Yekooche feels that the company has a good product and established markets, and has performed well over the last few years. However, the president is concerned that Yekooche is chronically tight on cash. She has approached your organization for a significant loan to provide the company with additional working capital, as well as to purchase capital assets that need to be replaced. The president of Yekooche has provided income statements and balance sheets for recent years.

Yekooche Inc.
Income Statements
For the Years Ended July 31, 2003–2005

	2005	2004	2003
Sales	$1,852,000	$1,981,640	$1,961,824
Cost of sales	1,038,972	1,099,810	1,075,079
Selling, general, and administrative expenses	652,053	670,758	656,211
Amortization	110,000	102,000	98,000
Research and development	45,000	88,000	125,000
Gain on sale of investment	63,000		
Income tax expense	13,000	3,000	1,000
Net Income	$ 55,975	$ 18,072	$ 6,534

Yekooche Inc.
Balance Sheets
For the Years Ended July 21, 2002–2005

	2005	2004	2003	2002
Cash	$ 5,580	$ 26,606	$ 5,533	$ 40,000
Receivables	275,000	215,000	180,000	145,000
Inventory	315,000	210,000	182,000	165,000
Prepaid expenses	51,000	28,000	81,000	15,000
Current assets	646,580	479,606	448,533	365,000
Capital assets (net of amortization)	649,000	610,000	540,000	410,000
Investment, at cost	0	75,000	75,000	0
	$1,295,580	$1,164,606	$1,063,533	$775,000
Bank loans	$125,000	$92,000	$47,000	$0
Accounts payable and accrued liabilities	350,000	308,000	270,000	210,000
Current liabilities	475,000	400,000	317,000	210,000
Long-term debt	175,000	175,000	175,000	0
Capital stock	500,000	500,000	500,000	500,000
Retained earnings	145,580	89,606	71,533	65,000
	$1,295,580	$1,164,606	$1,063,533	$775,000

Additional information:

- The long-term debt is due to be repaid in early 2007. The amount is owed to a large bank and is secured against certain capital assets.
- Yekooche has a $130,000 line of credit available from its bank. Bank loans represent the amount borrowed against the line of credit.
- All sales to customers and purchases of inventory are made on credit.
- Interest expense is included in selling, general, and administrative expenses. Interest expense was $31,000 in 2005, $25,500 in 2004, and $12,000 in 2003.

Required:

Prepare a report to the corporate lending department evaluating the liquidity and solvency of Yekooche. Provide a preliminary recommendation on whether the loan should be made. Provide support for your recommendation. What additional information would you want before reaching a final decision on the loan application? In your analysis consider Yekooche's cash flow.

P13-13. **(Evaluating an equity investment, LO 2)** Refer to the information about Yekooche Inc. provided in Problem P13-12.

You are an investment analyst for Qualicum Investment Group, Inc. (Qualicum). Qualicum raises capital from individual investors and invests in promising small businesses, with the expectation that the businesses will grow and that it will ultimately be able to sell the investments at a profit. The president of Yekooche has approached your organization to make a significant equity investment in the company.

Required:

Prepare a report to Qualicum's executive board analyzing Yekooche's performance over the last few years and assessing its attractiveness as an investment. What additional information would you want before reaching a final decision on whether to invest? In your analysis consider Yekooche's cash flow.

■ Using Financial Statements

The Forzani Group Ltd.

www.forzanigroup.com

Founded in 1974, The Forzani Group Ltd. (Forzani) is Canada's largest sporting goods retailer. Forzani currently operates 135 corporate stores under five banners: Sport Chek, Forzani's, Sports Experts, Coast Mountain Sports, and Save on Sports. Additionally, the Company is the franchisor of 166 stores under the banners: Sports Experts, Intersport, R'n'R, and Econosports. All outlets offer both brand name sporting goods, as well as a number of private-label lines. Several private-label products are Forzani's best sellers in their categories. The Company employs more than 6,900 people in communities across Canada. The Forzani Group Ltd. trades on the Toronto Stock Exchange.[9]

Forzani's consolidated balance sheets, statements of operations and retained earnings, statements of cash flows, and extracts from the notes to the financial statements are provided in Exhibit 13-7.[10] Use this information to respond to questions FS13-1 to FS13-9.

Exhibit 13-7

The Forzani Group Ltd.: Financial Statements

THE FORZANI GROUP LTD.
Consolidated Balance Sheets
(thousands of dollars)
(audited)

As at		January 28, 2001		January 30, 2000 (restated) (Note 1)
ASSETS				
Current				
Cash	$	13,030	$	355
Accounts receivable		31,600		22,120
Inventory		157,923		113,827
Prepaid expenses		4,528		3,559
		207,081		139,861
Capital assets (Note 2)		92,618		65,890
Other assets (Note 3)		10,354		2,565
Future income tax asset (Note 8)		6,833		15,145
	$	316,886	$	223,461
LIABILITIES				
Current				
Indebtedness under revolving credit facility (Note 4)	$	-	$	14,552
Accounts payable and accrued liabilities		136,864		79,913
Current portion of long-term debt		435		280
		137,299		94,745
Long-term debt (Note 5)		30,243		4,447
Deferred lease inducements		39,239		26,435
		206,781		125,627
SHAREHOLDERS' EQUITY				
Share capital (Note 7)		82,408		82,681
Retained earnings		27,697		15,153
	$	316,886	$	223,461

FS13-1. Prepare common size and trend statements from Forzani's balance sheets and statements of operations. Analyze the statements you prepared to identify any issues that you think might require additional explanation. Explain why you identified the issues you did.

FS13-2. Compute and interpret the following ratios for Forzani for fiscal years 2000 and 2001. Use these ratios to assess Forzani's liquidity. Be sure to use the information provided from Forzani's January 31, 1999 balance sheet.
   a. current ratio

THE FORZANI GROUP LTD.
Consolidated Statements of Operations and Retained Earnings
(thousands of dollars, except per share data)
(audited, except where otherwise noted)

Exhibit 13-7 (continued)

The Forzani Group Ltd.: Financial Statements

		For the years ended	
		January 28, 2001	January 30, 2000 (restated) (Note 1)
Corporate and Franchise Retail Sales (unaudited - Note 10)	$	681,306	$ 563,115
Revenue			
Corporate	$	409,510	\ $ 325,041
Franchise		159,103	129,060
		568,613	454,101
Cost of sales		385,807	310,816
Gross margin		182,806	143,285
Operating and administrative expenses			
Store operating		104,617	84,828
General and administrative		40,031	33,008
		144,648	117,836
Operating income before undernoted items		38,158	25,449
Amortization		13,528	8,564
Interest		3,774	2,542
		17,302	11,106
Income before future income taxes		20,856	14,343
Future income tax expense (Note 8)		8,312	6,193
Net income for the year	$	12,544	$ 8,150
Retained earnings (deficit), beginning of year		15,153	(14,335)
Adjustment of retained earnings as a result of the adoption of the liability method of accounting for future income taxes (Note 1)		-	21,338
Retained earnings, end of year	$	27,697	$ 15,153
Basic earnings per share, before income tax expense (Note 7)	$	0.77	$ 0.53
Basic earnings per share, after income tax expense	$	0.47	$ 0.30
Total number of common shares outstanding		26,918,448	26,970,481
Weighted average number of common shares outstanding		26,971,509	26,947,618

    b. quick ratio
    c. accounts receivable turnover ratio
    d. average collection period of accounts receivable
    e. inventory turnover ratio
    f. average number of days inventory on hand
    g. accounts payable turnover ratio
    h. average payment period for accounts payable

FS13-3. Compute and interpret the following ratios for Forzani for fiscal year 2001. Use these ratios to assess Forzani's performance in fiscal 2001:
    a. gross margin
    b. profit margin
    c. return on assets
    d. return on equity

FS13-4. Compute and interpret the following ratios for Forzani for fiscal year 2001. Use these ratios to assess Forzani's solvency and liquidity. Do not restrict your evaluation to the ratios that you are required to calculate.
    a. debt-to-equity ratio

Exhibit 13-7 (continued)

The Forzani Group Ltd.: Financial
Statements

THE FORZANI GROUP LTD.
Consolidated Statements of Cash Flows
(thousands of dollars, except per share data)
(audited)

	For the years ended	
	January 28, 2001	January 30, 2000 (restated) (Note 1)
Cash provided by (used in) operating activities		
Net income for the year	$ 12,544	$ 8,150
Items not involving cash		
Amortization	13,528	8,564
Amortization of finance charges	525	236
Amortization of deferred lease inducements	(4,886)	(2,925)
Write off of tenant inducement	(320)	-
Future income tax expense	8,312	6,193
Cash flow from operations	29,703	20,218
Changes in non-cash operating elements of working capital (Note 6)	2,406	2,739
	32,109	22,957
Cash provided by (used in) financing activities		
Proceeds from issuance of share capital	52	149
Repurchase of share capital pursuant to normal course issuer bid	(325)	(356)
Proceeds from issuance of long-term debt	26,417	540
Principal repayment of long-term debt	(466)	(1,043)
Repayment of revolving credit facility	(14,552)	(3,554)
Proceeds from deferred lease inducements	18,010	16,539
	29,136	12,275
Cash provided by (used in) investing activities		
Addition of capital assets	(40,434)	(33,980)
Addition of other assets	(8,811)	(3,565)
Disposal of capital assets	567	236
Disposal of other assets	108	2,208
	(48,570)	(35,101)
Increase in cash	12,675	131
Net cash position , beginning of year	355	224
Net cash position , end of year	$ 13,030	$ 355
Cash flow from operations, per share (basic)	$ 1.10	$ 0.75

6. Supplementary Cash Flow Information

Changes in Non-Cash Working Capital

	2001	2000
Accounts receivable	$ (9,480)	$ 2,063
Inventory	(44,096)	(20,734)
Prepaid expenses	(969)	(658)
Accounts payable	56,951	22,068
	$ 2,406	$ 2,739
Interest paid	$ 3,249	$ 2,306

b. interest coverage ratio (earnings based)

c. interest coverage ratio (cash based)

FS13-5. Forzani does not pay dividends. Why do you think that is the case? Do you think that Forzani could pay a regular dividend to its shareholders? What would be the implications to Forzani of paying a regular dividend?

FS13-6. You are the credit analyst for a company that Forzani has approached to become a major supplier of hockey equipment. Prepare a report to the manager of the credit department assessing the credit-worthiness of Forzani and recommending whether the company should extend credit.

FS13-7. You are considering purchasing an equity interest in Forzani. Use the information provided in Exhibit 13-7 to assess the attractiveness of such an investment. What additional information would you want to make a decision?

FS13-8. Examine the accounting policies described in Exhibit 13-7. Compare these policies

Exhibit 13-7 (continued)

The Forzani Group Ltd.: Financial Statements

1.   Significant Accounting Policies

The consolidated financial statements have been prepared by management in accordance with Canadian generally accepted accounting principles. The financial statements have, in management's opinion, been properly prepared within reasonable limits of materiality and within the framework of the accounting policies summarized below:

(b)   Inventory

Inventory is valued at the lower of laid-down cost and net realizable value. Laid-down cost is determined using the weighted average cost method and includes invoice cost, duties, freight, and distribution costs.

Volume rebates and other supplier discounts are included in income when earned.

(c)   Capital assets

Capital assets are recorded at cost and are amortized using the following methods and rates:

Building	- 4% declining balance basis
Building on leased land	- 20 years straight line basis
Furniture, fixtures, equipment and automotive	- straight line over 3-5 years
Leasehold improvements	- straight line over the lesser of the length of the lease and estimated useful life of the improvements, not exceeding 10 years
Trademarks	- 10 years straight line basis

(f)   Store opening expenses

Operating costs incurred prior to the opening of new stores are expensed as incurred.

10.   Corporate and Franchise Retail Sales

Total corporate and franchise retail sales have been shown on the Consolidated Statements of Operations and Retained Earnings to indicate the size of the Company's total retail sales level (on an unaudited basis). Only revenue from corporately owned stores, wholesale sales to, and fees from, franchisees are included in the Consolidated Statements of Operations and Retained Earnings.

with the ones used by MWW. What difficulties does the fact MWW and Forzani use different accounting policies have on your ability to analyze the financial statements? Suppose you wanted to adjust Forzani's financial statements so that the store opening expenses were accounted for the same way as in MWW's financial statements. Could you do so? Explain. Note that all the information in Forzani's annual report about store opening costs is included in Exhibit 13-7.

FS13-9. Forzani and MWW are both classified as specialty merchandisers, meaning they are considered to be in the same industry. Compare the performance, liquidity, and solvency and leverage of the two companies. Which company is a better credit risk? Explain. In your response use all the information that is provided. Do not only use financial ratios.

■ Analyzing Mark's Work Wearhouse

M13-1. Examine the management discussion and analysis section of MWW's annual report and respond to the following questions:
   a. Why is it important to distinguish between growth in sales that result from adding stores from growth in sales that results from growth that occurs in existing stores?
   b. By what amount did the following sectors grow?
      i.   total retail sales from 1999 to 2000
      ii.   total retail sales from 1995 to 2000
      iii. men's wear sales from 1999 to 2000
      iv.   women's clothing store sales from 1997 to 2000
      v.   shoe store sales from 1998 to 2000

Why is this information provided in MWW's MD&A? How would you use it in a financial analysis?

c. Examine Table 5 in MWW's MD&A (page A-27). What are the different product categories that MWW identifies? Is it useful to the analysis of the statements to have information about these different product categories? Explain. Use the information in Table 5 to analyze and interpret the sales performance of MWW. Your analysis should consider the relative contribution of each category and the performance of each category.

d. Summarize the explanation MWW's management provides in its MD&A for the increase in gross margin that the company enjoyed in fiscal 2001. What would MWW's gross margin and earnings before provision for closure of U.S. pilot stores, income taxes, and goodwill amortization have been in fiscal 2000 and 1999 had the gross margin percentage been the same in those years as it was in fiscal 2001?

M13-2. It is February 1, 2001. You have been approached by MWW to replace a line of credit that had been previously supplied by another lender.

a. What information would you want that is not provided in MWW's annual report in Appendix A?

b. What sources might you approach to find the additional information?

c. Would MWW itself be a good source of additional information? Would it be prepared to supply the additional information to you? Explain. If you were a small investor interested in buying 100 shares in MWW (when it was a public company), would the company be prepared to supply information to you over and above what was included in the annual report? Explain.

M13-3. Calculate the following ratios for MWW for fiscal 2000 and 2001. Explain what these ratios tell you individually and collectively:

a. gross margin
b. profit margin
c. return on assets
d. return on equity

M13-4. Calculate the following ratios for MWW for fiscal 2000 and 2001. Explain what these ratios tell you individually and collectively:

a. current ratio
b. quick ratio
c. accounts receivable turnover ratio
d. average collection period of accounts receivable
e. inventory turnover ratio
f. average number of days inventory on hand
g. accounts payable turnover ratio
h. average payment period for accounts payable

M13-5. You are the credit analyst for a company that MWW has approached to become a major supplier of work wear. Prepare a report to the manager of the credit department assessing the credit-worthiness of MWW and recommending whether the company should extend credit.

M13-6. MWW has never paid a dividend. Why do you think that is the case? Do you think that MWW could pay a regular dividend to its shareholders (assuming that it had not been purchased by Canadian Tire Corporation, Limited)? What would be the implications to MWW of paying a regular dividend?

M13-7. In the Forecast Range section of its annual report MWW provides forecasted statements of earnings and forecasted balance sheets under conservative and optimistic scenarios (see page A-000). Use the information in the forecasted statements to prepare common size and trend statements for 2002. Analyze and interpret the statements you prepared to explain how MWW's management expects to achieve the forecasted performance in 2002. (To answer, use the common size and trend financial statements to understand the changes management is predicting. You can also use other financial ratios to analyze the expected performance.)

M13-8. You are considering purchasing an equity interest in MWW (assuming that it had not been purchased by Canadian Tire Corporation, Limited). Use the information provided from MWW's annual report to assess the attractiveness of such an investment. You should analyze and investigate all aspects of MWW's business when responding to this question.

M13-9. MWW provides a "post mortem" on the financial forecast that was provided in the fiscal 2000 annual report (see page A-20). In the post mortem MWW's management explains differences between the company's actual performance in 2000 with the forecast it made a year earlier. Explain the usefulness of the post mortem to users of the financial statements. What are the reasons that MWW gives for differences between the actual performance for fiscal 2001 and the forecasted performance? Use the financial analysis tools in the chapter to compare the actual performance, liquidity, and solvency and leverage with the forecasts.

Endnotes

1. Clarence Byrd, Ida Chen, and Heather Chapman, *Financial Reporting in Canada*, 26th Edition. The Virtual Professional Library. CD-ROM. 2002.

2. Extracted from TransAlta Corporation's 2000 annual report.

3. Clarence Byrd, Ida Chen, and Heather Chapman, *Financial Reporting in Canada*, 26th Edition. The Virtual Professional Library. CD-ROM. 2002.

4. Extracted from Alliance Forest Product Inc.'s 2000 annual report.

5. Extracted from Rogers Communications Inc.'s 2000 annual report.

6. Extracted from Cambior Inc.'s 2000 annual report.

7. Panel A extracted from Falconbridge Limited's 2000 annual report. Panel B extracted from Sobeys Inc.'s 2001 annual report.

8. Panel A extracted from AlarmForce Industries Inc.'s 2000 annual report. Panel B extracted from Causeway Energy Corporation's 2000 annual report.

9. Extracted from The Forzani Group Ltd.'s fiscal 2001 annual report.

10. Extracted from The Forzani Group Ltd.'s fiscal 2001 annual report.

Appendix A

MARK'S WORK WEARHOUSE LTD.

delivering value...

ANNUAL REPORT FOR THE YEAR ENDED JANUARY 27, 2001

Delivering Value

The staff of the Newmarket Mark's Work Wearhouse store delivered over $5.0 million in sales, the first store in our history to reach that milestone.

Our theme for this year's annual report is "Delivering Value", and we have chosen it as a theme for two reasons. First of all, it captures the essence of our daily activities. Our products, stores and people have a requirement to deliver value each and every day to our customers in order for us to be successful in the very competitive arena of apparel and footwear retailing. Secondly, we know that by delivering value to our customers they will reward us, and we will continue to produce the results that create value for all of our stakeholders.

In this report, the output of our efforts to deliver value to our customers is discussed in terms of the Company's financial and operational performance. We will describe our market position within Canada's apparel and footwear sectors, and the factors that we believe are influencing the future of our industry. We will also speak to our Strategic Plan, and provide a forecast of earnings for the current year. In other words, we will share with you how we expect to continue to deliver value to our customers and stakeholders into the future.

With three divisions and over 300 stores from coast to coast, Mark's Work Wearhouse Ltd. has significant market share in each of our major categories of business, and we are one of the largest specialty retailers in the country. Our stores offer men's and ladies' clothing, footwear and accessories for industrial work use, for business casual use, and for after work and recreational use. We also have a strong and growing Business-to-Business operation, and sell our products on line at www.marks.com.

Mark's shares are traded on the Toronto Stock Exchange ("MWW" or "Mark Wrk").

CONTENTS

CONSOLIDATED FINANCIAL HIGHLIGHTS

Consolidated Financial Highlights

Based on the growth initiatives we have identified and the skills of our employees we are forecasting a 20% increase in earnings per share in fiscal 2002 on top of the 30% increase we just delivered.

(all dollar amounts in thousands, except per share)	52 weeks ended January 25, 1997	53 weeks ended January 31, 1998	52 weeks ended January 30, 1999	52 weeks ended January 29, 2000	52 weeks ended January 27, 2001	Forecast Range* 52 weeks ended January 26, 2002 Conservative	Optimistic
Sales							
Corporate	$ 220,902	$ 252,016	$ 283,401***	$ 314,547***	$ 363,870	$ 413,188	$ 427,525
Franchise	$ 82,854**	$ 150,191	$ 134,067***	$ 123,123***	$ 124,109	$ 123,668	$ 127,349
Total system	$ 303,756	$ 402,207	$ 417,468	$ 437,670	$ 487,979	$ 536,856	$ 554,874
Number of retail stores							
Corporate	108	118	165***	177	194	209	209
Franchise	183**	170	134***	131	115	114	114
Total system	291	288	299	308	309	323	323
EBITDA	$ 14,582	$ 21,831	$ 22,738	$ 26,305	$ 31,340	$ 33,656	$ 36,231
Pre-tax earnings after goodwill amortization	$ 8,310	$ 12,404	$ 10,996****	$ 12,310	$ 16,526	$ 15,766	$ 18,237
Net earnings	$ 3,923	$ 6,551	$ 5,752	$ 6,387	$ 8,180	$ 8,183	$ 9,465
Net earnings per Common Share – basic	16¢	24¢	21¢	23¢	30¢	31¢	36¢
Weighted average number of Common Shares outstanding (000s)	24,976	27,058	27,475	27,847	27,597	26,012	26,012
Shareholders' equity at end of period	$ 36,884	$ 46,746	$ 53,306	$ 59,571	$ 64,721	$ 69,478	$ 70,760
Funds flow from operations	$ 7,315	$ 13,609	$ 15,815	$ 16,876	$ 18,881	$ 21,029	$ 22,312
Funds flow from operations per Common Share (CFPS)	29¢	50¢	58¢	61¢	68¢	81¢	86¢
Current ratio	1.55/1	1.71/1	1.70/1	1.77/1	1.75/1	1.87/1	1.85/1
Total liabilities-to-equity ratio	1.57/1	1.26/1	1.49/1	1.40/1	1.43/1	1.26/1	1.28/1
Average funded debt-to-equity ratio	0.51/1	0.71/1	0.92/1	0.94/1	0.84/1	1.11/1	1.03/1
Rent, other operating leases, computer services, distribution activities and interest on long-term debt (including capital leases) coverage	1.45	1.58	1.47	1.42	1.50	1.39*****	1.45*****
Return on average capital employed	23%	26%	19%	19%	21%	20%	23%
Return on average equity	11%	16%	12%	11%	13%	12%	14%
Total system same-store sales increase	4%	8%	4%	0%	10%	5%	8%

* The forecast range set by the conservative and optimistic forecasts is based upon management's judgment and on assumptions outlined on page 18, some or all of which may prove incorrect. Accordingly, actual results achieved during the forecast period will inevitably vary from those forecast, and variations may be material.

** Includes two months' sales from Work World franchise stores from the December 1, 1996 acquisition date forward in fiscal 1997.

*** Two Mark's and 31 Work World franchise stores were converted to corporate stores in the latter part of fiscal 1999.

**** Includes $2,961,000 provision for closure of US pilot stores in fiscal 1999.

***** Effective February 2001, the Company outsourced its distribution activities. See Goal 6 under Financial Goals and Note 19 to the Consolidated Financial Statements.

Summary

By creating value for our customers, we create value for our investors. The defining measurement of a retailer's relationship with its customers is its sales growth compared to the rest of the industry, and during the year ended January 27, 2001, we continued our long term trend of outperforming the market. Our sales growth was much better than both the industry in general and our sector in particular, and our book value increased from $2.14 to $2.44 per share. You will find a comprehensive review of operations and complete financial information in the balance of this annual report.

FISCAL 2001 HIGHLIGHTS*

- The Company's pre-tax earnings increased by 34.2% to $16.5 million from $12.3 million.
- The Company's EPS increased by 30.4% to 30 cents from 23 cents.
- The Company's EBITDA increased by 19.1% to $31.3 million from $26.3 million.
- The Company's CFPS increased by 11.5% to 68 cents from 61 cents.
- The Company delivered 99.9% of its optimistic pre-tax earnings forecast, 99.0% of its optimistic sales forecast and 96.8% of its optimistic EPS forecast.
- With approximately the same number of stores, the Company grew its total system sales by 11.5% to $488.0 million from $437.7 million, which is over four times the total apparel sales growth in Canada in calendar 2000 over calendar 1999 as reported by Trendex.
- The Company improved its consolidated corporate store gross margin rate by 50 basis points to 41.1% from 40.6%.
- The Company recorded exceptional corporate store sales growth in ladies' wear (64.1%) and Business-to-Business (27.7%).
- The Mark's Division produced its first store with sales over the $5.0 million sales barrier and has another half dozen approaching that point.
- The Work World Division improved its EBITDA by $1.0 million.
- The Company's share price outperformed the merchandising, specialty store and department store indexes in fiscal 2001.
- In calendar 2000, the Company was awarded the National Post Gold Medal for best annual report in the merchandising category and the Investor Relations Magazine Grand Prix Trophy for best overall investor relations for small-cap companies.
- The Company's President and Chief Executive Officer was selected as Chairman of the Retail Council of Canada.

* Percent calculated on unrounded numbers.

SUMMARY

1

2

MARK'S WORK WEARHOUSE LTD.
Quarterly Financial Information

(dollar amounts in thousands, except per share)	1st Quarter	2nd Quarter	3rd Quarter	4th Quarter	Total
Fiscal 2001					
Corporate and franchise sales	$ 87,848	$ 100,978	$ 117,449	$ 181,704	$ 487,979
Corporate sales	$ 64,568	$ 74,651	$ 88,077	$ 136,574	$ 363,870
Earnings (loss) before income taxes and goodwill amortization	$ (1,045)	$ (809)	$ 2,370	$ 16,558	$ 17,074
Net earnings (loss)	$ (737)	$ (589)	$ 1,426	$ 8,080	$ 8,180
Earnings (loss) per Common Share before goodwill amortization	(2)¢	(2)¢	6¢	30¢	32¢
Earnings (loss) per Common Share – basic	(3)¢	(2)¢	5¢	30¢	30¢
Fiscal 2000					
Corporate and franchise sales	$ 79,407	$ 87,931	$ 107,175	$ 163,157	$ 437,670
Corporate sales	$ 57,235	$ 62,736	$ 77,146	$ 117,430	$ 314,547
Earnings (loss) before income taxes and goodwill amortization	$ (1,853)	$ (554)	$ 1,884	$ 13,208	$ 12,685
Net earnings (loss)	$ (1,193)	$ (461)	$ 874	$ 7,167	$ 6,387
Earnings (loss) per Common Share before goodwill amortization	(4)¢	(1)¢	3¢	26¢	24¢
Earnings (loss) per Common Share – basic	(4)¢	(2)¢	3¢	26¢	23¢
Fiscal 1999					
Corporate and franchise sales	$ 73,292	$ 79,419	$ 101,697	$ 163,060	$ 417,468
Corporate sales	$ 48,419	$ 51,686	$ 67,336	$ 115,960	$ 283,401
Earnings (loss) before income taxes and goodwill amortization	$ (1,599)	$ (1,936)	$ 2,105	$ 12,742*	$ 11,312*
Net earnings (loss)	$ (1,131)	$ (1,122)	$ 1,025	$ 6,980	$ 5,752
Earnings (loss) per Common Share before goodwill amortization	(4)¢	(4)¢	4¢	26¢	22¢
Earnings (loss) per Common Share – basic	(4)¢	(4)¢	4¢	25¢	21¢

* Includes a $2,961,000 provision for closure of the US pilot stores in fiscal 1999.

5-YEAR MARKET VALUE BY QUARTER
(dollars)

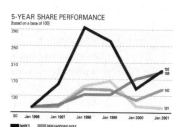

5-YEAR SHARE PERFORMANCE
(based on a base of 100)

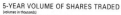

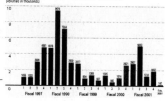

5-YEAR VOLUME OF SHARES TRADED
(volumes in thousands)

Mission Statement

Our mission is to grow consistently as a mature and stable enterprise known for:

- Being the most customer-sensitive and responsive specialty retail organization in the markets within which we operate;
- Having a people-oriented work environment where our people are allowed the greatest possible freedom to carry out their responsibilities, take ownership of what they do, have fun, learn and earn fair financial rewards; and
- Providing a superior financial return to investors as a result of being customer-driven and people-oriented.

Core Values

The Company's divisions are committed to building their respective customer bases and creating shareholder value over time through increasing revenues and earnings, while honoring the Company's three Core Values:

- Product integrity;
- Respect for people; and
- Continuous improvement.

MARK'S DIVISION (L'ÉQUIPEUR)

Mark's Work Wearhouse Division (Mark's Division) comprises 157 stores, including 22 L'Équipeur stores in Quebec. Mark's provides work apparel for both business casual and industrial consumers in 10,000 square foot destination stores. In addition, the division is a market leader in merchandise designed for casual and outdoor pursuits — market share exceeds most national brands across all age, gender and income levels.

Mark's is focused on creating value for its Canadian consumers by broadening its base of "On Concept" stores through new store openings and relocations of existing stores and by enhancing the merchandise assortments in existing stores.

The division is increasing its square footage and expanding its assortments dedicated to women's wear, while maintaining its market leadership position in men's business casual wardrobes, industrial apparel and casual and industrial footwear through continuous product development and innovation.

Mark's is also focused on communicating that value to its customers through the creation of ever-better and more frequent marketing campaigns. Further, Mark's is creating incremental value for its customers with its Business-to-Business initiatives and the continued development of its e-commerce capabilities.

Mark's Division's Top Team (L to R)
Wendy Bennison, Jim Killin, Paul Wilson, Dale Trybuch, Rick Harrison

The following chart shows how the division breaks down into districts:

	Regions	Districts	Corporate Stores	Franchise Stores	Total
Mark's Work	Western Canada/NWT	8	52	8	60
Wearhouse	Ontario	9	51	9	60
(L'Équipeur)	Quebec/Atlantic*	5	29	8	37
	Total	22	132	25	157

* Mark's 19 corporate and three franchise stores in Quebec operate under the name L'Équipeur.

Business-to-Business Division's Top Team *(L to R)*
Harry Bekkema, Marcel Desrochers, Jim Haigh,
Ron McVeetors, Dave Reagan

MARK'S (L'ÉQUIPEUR) BUSINESS-TO-BUSINESS

Mark's Division, Business-to-Business employs a national sales force of over 40 professional sales account managers serving major corporations, the public sector and small businesses — and more account managers will be added as the operation grows.

Sales in this operating unit have risen over 50% in the past two years. This operating unit creates value by developing uniform programs and creating customized fulfillment solutions for its customers. In addition to continuing to add corporate accounts this operating unit is also starting to pursue with more vigor, the promotional corporate wear part of this industry. These Business-to-Business activities also deliver value in the form of incremental sales to the Mark's stores by introducing the Business-to-Business consumer to the stores and the stores' entire assortment.

WORK WORLD DIVISION

There are 144 Work World stores coast to coast across Canada. The stores are typically 3,000 square feet in size located in the best retail location in the market place. That could mean a mall, a strip centre or on a main street depending on the market. The stores are bright, well stocked and easy to shop. Work World generally focuses on the smaller towns and cities across Canada. There is a real need in these markets for a retailer that offers good quality clothing and footwear at a fair price. The target customer is 25 to 60 years old and it does not matter if they work at a construction site, a golf course, a lab, a casual business environment, indoor or outdoor, Work World can accommodate their seasonal clothing and footwear requirements.

In fiscal 2001, the Work World division dramatically strengthened both the buying and store operations teams. The division doubled the number of buyers and added a vice president of store operations. In addition, the district manager team went through some changes so that over half of the group is now new to the organization. The experience of the new buyers and district managers added to the strength of the existing team has already shown positive results and means Work World is now better poised to take on the future.

The following chart shows how the division breaks down into districts.

	Regions	Districts	Corporate Stores	Franchise Stores	Total
Work World Division	British Columbia/Yukon	4	24	29	53
	Prairies/NW Territories	3	13	36	49
	Subtotal	7	37	65	102
	Ontario	3	13	20	33
	Atlantic	1	4	5	9
	Total	11	54	90	144

Work World Division's Top Team *(L to R)*
Mike Strachan and Roy Jopling

The merchandise assortments have continued to evolve and this was reflected in the 5.9% same store sales increase achieved in fiscal 2001, the largest since the division was purchased four years ago. In fiscal 2002, there are a number of specific sales initiatives aimed at continuing to drive the sales growth. In fiscal 2001, the gross margin improved and is on track to achieve the 40% target called for in the Strategic Plan. An increased blend of private label products and a focus on direct sourcing will continue to drive the improvements.

Currently, 70.8 % of the division's stores are in western Canada. Work World continues to see an opportunity to expand mainly into Ontario. Any new stores opened will be corporate as part of the continuing "Corporate Store Strategy". In fiscal 2001, the corporate store results improved considerably. This strengthens the division's belief that this strategy will deliver stronger financial results in the future. The franchise performance and participation also continues to improve. Over time, the number of corporate stores will be increased through the opening of new stores and the buying back of successful franchise stores when they are offered for sale.

DOCKERS® STORES DIVISION

The first five test stores opened in fiscal 2000 — three more test stores were opened in fiscal 2001. Test stores are 3,000 to 4,000 retail square feet in major malls in large and mid-size markets.

Our objective is to expand upon the existing positioning of the DOCKERS® brand for classically and fashionably styled khaki pants, while enhancing the tops and related wardrobe items all targeted to urban customers. Specifically, the target customers are men and women whose personal taste level is classic in nature and who value quality and fit in their clothing. The three core businesses that the DOCKERS® stores focus on are weekend casual, business casual and golf-inspired apparel and we believe that our uniqueness lies in the fact that no specialty retailer currently targets this consumer for these apparel needs.

While we have the opportunity to expand to as many as 120 stores, after completion of the test phase, the operative word today is "test" and the Company is not contemplating any store roll outs in fiscal 2002.

DOCKERS® Stores Division's Top Team *(L to R)*
Peter Roxborough, Cathy Prosser,
Timothea Wiwcharyk

OUR DIVISIONS

(Back, L to R) **Randy Wiebe, John Murphy, Mike Lambert, Robin Lynas,** (Centre, L to R) **Michael Strachan, Garth Mitchell, Cathy Prosser, Linda Mathiesen,** (Front L to R) **Paul Wilson, Michel St. Jean**

President's Message to Shareholders

It is a pleasure to report on the best year in our history. Our total system sales were 12% over the previous year and 99% of our plan. Our pre-tax earnings of $16.5 million were exactly on plan and 33% higher than our previous best year. Our share price at year-end this year was 33% higher than at year-end last year.

It is very tempting to end my conversation with shareholders right now, and not say another word for fear of somehow taking the glow off the first paragraph. However, with three divisions, 309 stores, an Internet business and a Business-to-Business operation, there are obviously many highlights as well as a few lowlights to talk about.

Highlights for the year are dominated by the terrific sales and profit performance of our largest division, the Mark's Division. Same store sales growth for the year was over five times industry averages and in short summary, this occurred because we planned aggressively in some specific areas of the business where we believed we had opportunities and we executed those plans well. For example, we planned to increase our women's business sales by over 50%, and we achieved 58%. We planned a 30% sales increase in our Business-to-Business operation, and we achieved 28%. During the year, our Newmarket store blasted through the milestone of $5 million in sales, and several other stores are knocking on that door. Another significant highlight was the $1 million improvement in EBITDA in the Work World Division, a credit to the new management team and to improved merchandise assortments.

Two lowlights were the fourth quarter sales performance of our DOCKERS® Stores, and our share price performance. In the case of DOCKERS®, we did not meet our customers' expectations for both merchandise content and in-stock position of basics. After substantial effort, we are happy to see improvements in both of these areas so far this year. With regards to share price performance, it is true that on a relative basis our year-over-year performance was better than the Department Store Index and the Specialty Store Index. However, trading at a single digit multiple of earnings is very disappointing to us, given our performance relative to the rest of the industry, especially since we make such an effort to communicate our forecasts and results to the market.

Reflecting on this issue helped us determine the theme of this year's report, which is "Delivering Value". We continue to believe that a well-defined business with solid fundamentals, strength in management and a logical and achievable strategic plan for growth will be recognized and rewarded by investors over time. The care, attention to detail, and disclosure that we inject into the creation of this report is intended to demonstrate to both current and potential shareholders that there is value in owning our shares. In addition, as you will discover when you read the report, the value

of our Company to investors is not based on wishful thinking or unproven plans. Our value has substance because our customers value us, and choose to do business with us more than eight million times a year, based on their appreciation for our merchandise and our people. We believe this report will demonstrate the details of this value to you.

The happy faces that you see throughout the report are employees, and on behalf of all members of our Board of Directors, I would like to thank them for their dedication and efforts. It is on the basis of their skills that we are forecasting a 20% increase in earnings per share in fiscal 2002, on top of the 30% increase we just delivered.

The MVP award for the year goes to our Newmarket Store. Led by Kim McLean and Keith Lim, their store was the first in the Company's history to crack the $5 million sales barrier. That was an outstanding achievement in a record year for the Company.

(signed)

Garth Mitchell
President and Chief Executive Officer

Our technology helps us deliver value

(L to R) **Robin Lynas and Ken Bieber – Technology Group**

How is technology helping us "Deliver Value" at Mark's Work Wearhouse? A challenging question because so much is happening.

Looking back into our history, in the early '90s Mark's Work Wearhouse decided to standardize on the world's leading business-processing system, the IBM AS/400. This decision has served us well and we have continued to build our infrastructure around this platform (now the IBM iSeries Server), which now runs the majority of our front-line, back-line, web and client-server systems. Using a single platform has allowed us to standardize on one database system, which means whatever application tool set we use to develop our products the data is always fully integrated into any business system we build.

Take for example our Multi-Channel Retailing e-Business plan. Whether you order your product over the Internet from www.marks.com, purchase the product from one of our conveniently located stores, or decide to use one of our, soon to be installed, in-store kiosks, you always get the product through the same supply-side model. This is mainly due to the fact that all these channels access the same data interactively as you make your purchasing decision. No matter what channel you choose to shop we use the same inventory and pricing data ensuring a consistent brand message. We then process your sale through the same Point-of-Sale application and either let you walk out of the store with your product or ship it directly to you in a timely fashion.

On the Business-to-Business side we have always supported our corporate business customers with an exceptional corporate business sales staff, that used internal business systems to manage corporate uniform programs and multi-tiered account billing. We are now porting this all to our e-Business infrastructure that will allow corporate accounts to manage their own personalized uniform programs on-line, match purchases to their employees, and will eventually lead to on-line billing. Add to this the fact we have already launched our web based healthwear site, which caters to the needs of all those in the medical profession, and you can see, that by spending the time to build and standardize our systems infrastructure, it has allowed us to continue to leverage existing business processes.

As always our future plans are ambitious but realistic. We are currently switching over our telecommunications network from the older frame relay technology to managed high-speed Internet access wherever the service is affordable and available. This allows us to move that consistent data we have been talking about, up to ten times faster. And you should keep your eyes on our stores where portable cash registers and wireless technology will likely be the norm in the next two to three years.

All in all a challenging situation. But remember, it is all driven by our customers' needs and is meant to support the people who really make it happen, our store staff.

Human Resources focused on value

Superior business results depend on quality products, excellent customer service and strong and efficient front-line and back-line operations, which, in turn, depend on a well-trained staff who feel connected to and proud of the company.

At Mark's Work Wearhouse, we create this sense of connection and pride not by focusing solely on the bottom line, but on the people who create it.

Today, we operate in a world where we often don't see beyond financial measurements to the other important organizational factors, when we describe our worth.

Our core values noted under "Mission Statement" make up those other important organizational factors that guide us and our people in meeting the demands of an ever-challenging environment.

In addition to our core values and internal Code of Conduct, our organization values:

- Inspiration – having a sense of vision and purpose and knowing that each person's role provides a chance to do important things really well;
- Tasks – providing organizational as well as technical knowledge;
- Position – acknowledging effort, accomplishment and ability, and linking them to opportunities that create a sense of belonging; and
- Relationship – giving personal and emotional backing to our people and letting others have ownership and influence within the organization.

At Mark's Work Wearhouse, we firmly believe that these core values, internal Code of Conduct and other values practiced by our employees help make our people and the Company a value-driven organization that is able to continuously redefine itself both in the marketplace and within our corporation in order to maintain our leadership position.

Human Resources Group *(Front)* **Linda Mathiesen** *(Back, L to R)* **Sherri Wright Schweitz, Deb Hunter, Catherine McDade,**

Senior Management Performance

Senior Officer	Business Objective **Fiscal 2001**	Business Objective Result **Fiscal 2001**
Garth Mitchell President and Chief Executive Officer	Consolidated pre-tax profit of $16.5 million	Consolidated pre-tax profit of $16.5 million
Mike Lambert Chief Financial Officer	Major transaction or series of transactions that cause the Company's share price to increase by 30% for a defined period	Business Objective was not achieved.
Paul Wilson President and Chief Operating Officer, Mark's Division	Divisional pre-tax profit growth 15%	Divisional pre-tax profit growth 15%
Rick Harrison Senior Vice President, Merchandising, Mark's Division	Divisional gross margin dollars of $129.1 million and inventory turnover 2.2	Divisional gross margin dollars of $133.1 million and inventory turnover 2.1
Michael Strachan Chief Operating Officer, Work World Division	Divisional pre-tax up $1.5 million	Divisional pre-tax up $0.4 million
Roy Jopling Vice President, Operations Work World Division (Roy joined the Work World Division in June 2000)	Not applicable	Not applicable
Cathy Prosser General Manager, DOCKERS® Stores Division	Divisional pre-tax up $0.7 million	Divisional pre-tax decreased
John Murphy Senior Vice President, Treasurer and Secretary	Consolidated 12-month rolling funded debt-to-equity ratio 1.08-to-1 with $4.1 million store construction capital lease financing	Consolidated 12-month rolling funded debt-to-equity ratio 0.84-to-1 with $5.8 million store construction capital lease financing
Robin Lynas Chief Information Officer	Systems Steering Committee projects and department operations and capex on budget	Most of the Systems Steering Committee projects and department operations and capex on budget
Linda Mathiesen Vice President, Human Resources and Customer Service	Mark's Division total sales dollars per front-line and back-line staff full-time equivalent (including corporate) $243,000	Mark's Division total sales dollars per front-line and back-line staff full-time equivalent (including corporate) $238,000
Michel St. Jean Vice President, Store Design	Planned, new, relocated and refurbished stores at a gross square foot cost of $37, $40 (increased to $50) and $100 in the Mark's, Work World and DOCKERS® Stores Divisions respectively	New relocated and refurbished stores at an average gross square foot cost of $30, $48 and $94 in the Mark's, Work World and DOCKERS® Stores Divisions respectively
Randy Wiebe Vice President, Controller	Timely and accurate internal and external financial reporting and manage the Company's tax affairs on budget	Timely and accurate internal and external financial reporting and manage the Company's tax affairs on budget

Business Objective **Fiscal 2002**	**Fiscal 2002** Key Results and **Fiscal 2001** Key Results Achieved
Consolidated pre-tax profit of $18.2 million	▪ Total system sales growth rate double the Canadian sales growth rate for apparel and footwear ▪ Company's share price to outperform the Toronto Stock Exchange Specialty Stores Index by 5.0% ▪ Both fiscal 2001 Key Results achieved
Major transaction or series of transactions that cause the Company's share price to increase by 30% for a defined period	▪ Have signed letters of intent in place for the acquisition of two Mark's Division franchise stores ▪ Deliver the $500,000 back-line process review cost savings ▪ Both fiscal 2001 Key Results achieved.
Divisional pre-tax profit growth 15%	▪ Twelve new stores and six relocated stores by October 15, 2001 ▪ Fiscal 2001 Key Result achieved
Divisional gross margin dollars of $156.0 million at a 41.8% gross margin rate	▪ Divisional inventory turns 2.3 ▪ Divisional corporate store casual outerwear sales growth 20% ▪ Fiscal 2001 Key Result not achieved
Divisional pre-tax up $1.3 million	▪ Divisional same store corporate sales increase 12.0% ▪ Fiscal 2001 Key Result not achieved
Divisional net front-line contribution up $1.7 million	▪ Fall sales growth in ten focus stores 20% ▪ Divisional Business-to-Business sales to 3.0% of corporate store sales
Divisional pre-tax up $0.9 million	▪ Divisional net front-line contribution up $1.0 million ▪ Fiscal 2001 Key Result not achieved
Consolidated 12-month rolling funded debt-to-equity ratio 1.03-to-1 with $5.0 million store construction capital lease financing	▪ Renew bank operating credits by May 31, 2001 ▪ Back-line expense savings of $0.5 million to plan ▪ One of the two fiscal 2001 Key Results achieved
Systems Steering Committee projects and department operations and capex on budget while keeping the Company technologically current and senior management informed about future retail technology	▪ $0.5 million in revenue or costs savings to plan from continued implementation of e-business strategies ▪ Develop a specific template for arrangements with outside software providers ▪ One of the two fiscal 2001 Key Results achieved
Mark's Division total sales dollars per front-line and back-line staff full-time equivalent (including corporate) $243,000	▪ Sales training services to increase units per transaction in the western region of the Mark's Division to 2.33 ▪ Meet new Privacy Act requirements and standards, including hiring a Privacy Officer ▪ Both of the fiscal 2001 Key Results achieved
Planned new, relocated and refurbished stores at a gross square foot cost of $37 and $45 in the Mark's and Work World Division respectively	▪ Deliver a new store design concept for the Mark's Division store of the future ▪ Deliver the new, relocated and renovated store projects that meet divisional substantial completion guidelines on time ▪ One of the two fiscal 2001 Key Results achieved
Timely and accurate internal and external financial reporting and manage the Company's tax affairs on budget	▪ Deliver $0.25 million in savings in GST, sales, income and capital taxes ▪ Deliver enhanced financial reporting for Mark's Division Business-to-Business activity by September 1, 2001 ▪ One of the two fiscal 2001 Key Results achieved

Operational Goals

Operational goals are key items that the Company monitors to gauge its progress towards the achievement of its Strategic Plan and Mission. Operational goals and other indicators also provide data that can be bench marked against our competitors in the industry.

	Fiscal 1999	Fiscal 2000	Fiscal 2001	Fiscal 2002 Optimistic Forecast*	Fiscal 2006 Master Targets**
Goal 1: Sales per average retail sq. ft.					
Mark's Division corporate stores					
Goal	$ 270	$ 257	$ 258	$ 281	$ 325
Actual and forecast	$ 252	$ 239	$ 259	$ 281	N/A
Total retail sq. ft. of stores with sales greater than $300 per sq. ft.	269,926	289,452	440,005	506,504	N/A
Number of stores with sales greater than $300 per sq. ft.	33	33	47	53	N/A
Work World Division corporate stores					
Goal	N/A	$ 262	$ 235	$ 244	$ 302
Actual and forecast	N/A	$ 217	$ 221	$ 244	N/A
Total retail sq. ft. of stores with sales greater than $300 per sq. ft.	N/A	22,169	24,906	52,400	N/A
Number of stores with sales greater than $300 per sq. ft.	N/A	9	10	17	N/A
DOCKERS® Stores Division corporate stores					
Goal	N/A	N/A	$ 446	$ 387	—****
Actual and forecast	N/A	N/A	$ 333	$ 387	N/A
Total retail sq. ft. of stores with sales greater than $500 per sq. ft.	N/A	2,930	0	2,930	N/A
Number of stores with sales greater than $500 per sq. ft.	N/A	1	0	1	N/A
Goal 2: Gross margin return on investment (times)					
Mark's Division corporate stores					
Goal	1.9	1.5	1.7	1.9	2.6
Actual and forecast	1.5	1.6	1.8	1.9	N/A
Work World Division corporate stores					
Goal	N/A	0.8	0.9	1.0	1.3
Actual and forecast	1.1	0.9	0.9	1.0	N/A
DOCKERS® Stores Division corporate stores					
Goal	N/A	N/A	1.9	1.8	—****
Actual and forecast	N/A	0.3	1.5	1.8	N/A
Goal 3: Front-line contribution as a percentage of corporate store sales					
Goal (consolidated) – corporate stores	11.2%	10.8%	10.9%	10.9%	12.1%***
Actual and forecast					
Mark's Division corporate stores	10.9%	12.2%	12.8%	12.3%	13.2%
Work World Division corporate stores	4.0%	(5.1%)	(1.3%)	4.7%	6.2%
DOCKERS® Stores Division corporate stores	N/A	(52.7%)	(28.2%)	(12.1%)	—****
Consolidated corporate stores***	10.3%	10.1%	10.5%	10.9%	12.1%***
Goal 4: Franchise royalties and other less franchise bad debts as a percent of franchise sales					
Mark's Division franchise stores					
Goal	6.3%	6.3%	6.2%	6.1%	6.0%
Actual and forecast	6.4%	6.2%	6.6%	6.1%	N/A
Work World Division franchise stores					
Goal	3.9%	3.9%	4.0%	4.1%	4.1%
Actual and forecast	3.9%	4.0%	4.2%	4.1%	N/A
Goal 5: Inventory turnover (times)					
Mark's Division corporate stores					
Goal	2.4	2.2	2.4	2.3	3.1
Actual and forecast	1.9	2.0	2.1	2.3	N/A
Work World Division corporate stores					
Goal	N/A	1.2	1.3	1.2	1.6
Actual and forecast	1.1	1.0	1.2	1.2	N/A
DOCKERS® Stores Division corporate stores					
Goal	N/A	N/A	2.9	2.2	—****
Actual and forecast	N/A	0.7	1.8	2.2	N/A

N/A   Not available or not applicable.
*   The reader is cautioned that all forecast data is based upon management's judgment and on assumptions outlined on page 18, some or all of which may prove incorrect. Accordingly, actual results achieved during the forecast period will inevitably vary from those forecast, and variations may be material.
**   The master targets are based on management's judgment and on assumptions some or all of which may prove incorrect. Accordingly, actual results achieved in future years will inevitably vary from those forecasts and variations may be material.
***   The consolidated percentages in fiscal 2000, fiscal 2001, fiscal 2002 include DOCKERS® Stores and in fiscal 2006 exclude DOCKERS® Stores.
****   DOCKERS® Stores Division's Master Targets have not been shown as this venture is still a test.

Other Indicators

Mark's Division Corporate Stores and Mark's Division and Corporate Services Back-Line Operations

	Fiscal 1999	Fiscal 2000	Fiscal 2001	Fiscal 2002 Optimistic Forecast*
Customer service				
Total front-line staff performance rating**	91.2%	92.6%	91.1%	94.0%
All stores performance rating**	84.4%	88.9%	85.3%	91.0%
Payroll management (number of staff at fiscal year end)				
Front-line staff – full time	417	410	446	570
Front-line staff – part time	1,612	1,305	1,767	1,814
Back-line staff – full time	154	178	179	203
Back-line staff – part time	23	24	28	30
	2,206*****	1,917	2,420	2,617
Number of full-time equivalents	1,176*****	1,229	1,344	1,532
Sales dollars per full-time equivalent	$ 229,000*****	$ 230,000	$ 238,000	$ 243,000
Average sales per hour paid	$ 144.27	$ 148.81	$ 152.43	$ 156.85
Sales per dollar of salary (excluding benefits)				
Selling	$ 17.73	$ 17.56	$ 17.34	$ 17.38
Total	$ 9.30	$ 8.77***	$ 8.34***	$ 8.72****
Percentage of front-line staff that is part time	79.4%	76.1%	79.8%	76.1%
Percentage of total staff that is back-line	8.0%	10.5%	8.6%	8.9%
Management payroll				
Front-line management salaries	$ 6,098,944	$ 6,747,178	$ 7,669,686	$ 9,144,965
Back-line management salaries	$ 4,548,103	$ 5,314,328***	$ 5,907,181***	$ 6,350,878
Total management salaries (including benefits)	$ 10,647,047	$ 12,061,506	$ 13,576,867	$ 15,495,843
Total management bonus	$ 606,041	$ 1,178,818	$ 2,486,827	$ 2,050,000
Total management payroll	$ 11,253,088	$ 13,240,324	$ 16,063,694	$ 17,545,843
Total management payroll as a percentage of corporate sales	4.2%	4.7%***	5.0%***	4.7%
Percentage of total management salaries – front-line	57.3%	55.9%	56.5%	59.0%
Percentage of total compensation – bonus-based	5.4%	8.9%	15.5%	11.7%
Percentage of change of total management compensation				
excluding bonus compensation***	11.8%	13.3%	12.6%	14.1%
Percentage of change of total management compensation***	(2.6%)	17.7%	21.3%	9.2%
Advertising as a percentage of corporate store sales	5.3%	4.7%	4.8%	4.8%
Front-line occupancy costs as a percentage of corporate store sales	9.1%	9.5%	9.0%	8.8%
Front-line occupancy costs per average retail sq. ft.	$ 22.78	$ 23.22	$ 23.54	$ 25.01
Total retail sq. ft. at fiscal year end	1,111,985	1,195,053	1,252,213	1,366,824
Corporate stores "On Concept"　Number	103	112	116	129
Percentage	84.4%	88.2%	87.9%	90.2%
Average dollar per transaction (corporate stores)	$ 66.89	$ 68.31	$ 69.28	$ 71.00
Corporate stores' market share of men's clothing stores market	12.1%	12.7%	13.6%	N/A

N/A　Not available or not applicable.
*　The reader is cautioned that all forecast data is based upon management's judgment and on assumptions, outlined on page 18, some or all of which may prove incorrect. Accordingly, actual results achieved during the forecast period will inevitably vary from those forecast and variations may be material.
**　The Mark's Division engages an external organization to shop its stores on a regular basis and evaluate and report on the performance of its staff and stores.
***　Starting in fiscal 2000, includes some additional back-line staff in the Corporate Services operation to support the corporate store initiative in Work World and the DOCKERS* Stores start up and increased back-line staff in the Mark's Division to support increasing Business-to-Business, Internet and marketing activities.
****　Excludes outsourced distribution activities in fiscal 2002 forward. See Note 19 to the Consolidated Financial Statements.
*****　Includes sales and staff from the two US pilot stores in fiscal 1999.

OPERATIONAL GOALS AND OTHER INDICATORS

Financial Goals

Financial goals are set and monitored to ensure that while the Company is aggressively pursing its Strategic Plan and its Mission, it is still being financed conservatively and is providing a superior return to its investors.

Goal 1: To earn a 2% after-tax profit on total corporate and franchise store sales

(thousands of dollars, except percentage items)	Fiscal 1999	Fiscal 2000	Fiscal 2001	Fiscal 2002 (Forecast Range)* Conservative	Optimistic
Corporate and franchise store sales	417,468	437,670	487,979	536,856	554,874
Net earnings	5,752	6,387	8,180	8,183	9,465
After-tax profit return on total systems sales	1.4%	1.5%	1.7%	1.5%	1.7%

Goal 2: To provide a return on capital employed in excess of 25% and a return on average equity in excess of 15%

(thousands of dollars, except per share and percentage items)	Fiscal 1999	Fiscal 2000	Fiscal 2001	Fiscal 2002 (Forecast Range)* Conservative	Optimistic
Average capital employed	73,972	88,101	97,747	104,484	105,125
EBIT	14,361	16,327	20,504	21,209	23,784
Return on average capital employed	19.4%	18.5%	21.0%	20.3%	22.6%
Average equity	50,026	56,439	62,146	67,100	67,741
Return on average shareholders' equity	11.5%	11.3%	13.2%	12.2%	14.0%
Book value per share	1.91	2.14	2.44	2.75	2.81

Goal 3: To maintain a total liabilities-to-equity ratio of no greater than 1.75-to-1 at the Company's fiscal year end, and to have a 12-month rolling average total funded debt-to-equity ratio no greater than 1-to-1 (0.90-to-1 in fiscal 1999)

(thousands of dollars, except ratios)	Fiscal 1999	Fiscal 2000	Fiscal 2001	Fiscal 2002 (Forecast Range)* Conservative	Optimistic
Total liabilities	79,686	83,513	92,339	87,459	90,519
Equity	53,306	59,571	64,721	69,478	70,760
Total liabilities-to-equity ratio	1.49/1	1.40/1	1.43/1	1.26/1	1.28/1
Average funded debt-to-equity ratio	0.92/1	0.94/1	0.84/1	1.11/1	1.03/1

Goal 4: To maintain a current ratio of not less than 1.50-to-1 at the Company's fiscal year end

(thousands of dollars, except ratios)	Fiscal 1999	Fiscal 2000	Fiscal 2001	Fiscal 2002 (Forecast Range)* Conservative	Optimistic
Current assets	96,360	101,475	110,387	112,974	117,316
Current liabilities	56,525	57,296	63,222	60,506	63,566
Working capital	39,835	44,179	47,165	52,468	53,750
Current ratio	1.70/1	1.77/1	1.75/1	1.87/1	1.85/1

* The forecast range set by the conservative and optimistic forecasts is based upon management's judgment and on assumptions outlined on page 18, some or all of which may prove incorrect. Accordingly, actual results achieved during the forecast period will inevitably vary from those forecast and variations may be material.

Goal 5: To restrict unfinanced capital expenditures to no more than the amount that results in at least a 1.3 times coverage of (EBITDA +(-) other non-cash items added or deducted in determining funds flow from operations + rents + CAM + other operating leases - unfinanced capital expenditures) divided by (interest + rents + CAM + other operating leases + scheduled annual principal repayments of long-term debt)

(thousands of dollars, except times coverage)	Fiscal 1999	Fiscal 2000	Fiscal 2001	Fiscal 2002 (Forecast Range)* Conservative	Optimistic
EBITDA	22,738	26,305	31,340	33,656	36,231
Non-cash items	1,686	511	(135)	400	400
Rents + CAM + other operating leases	22,506	27,523	31,705	35,126	35,126
	46,930	54,339	62,910	69,182	71,757
Capital expenditures including capital leases	10,152	11,154	11,150	10,283	10,283
Financing of capital expenditures including lease financing	(7,228)	(10,239)	(8,665)	(9,301)	(9,301)
Unfinanced capital expenditures	2,924	915	2,485	982	982
Numerator	44,006	53,424	60,425	68,200	70,775
Interest, rents, CAM, other operating leases and scheduled annual principal repayments	33,863	40,868	46,588	52,565	52,669
Times coverage	1.30	1.31	1.30	1.30	1.34

Goal 6: To maintain rent, other operating leases, computer services, distribution activities and interest on long-term debt (including capital leases) coverage in the range of 1.50-to-1.75 times. In fiscal 2002, the Company outsourced its distribution activities and those costs have been added to this coverage test in fiscal 2002. As a result, the goal in fiscal 2002 and forward has been reduced to a range of 1.25 to 1.50 times. See Note 19 to the Consolidated Financial Statements.

(thousands of dollars, except times coverage)	Fiscal 1999	Fiscal 2000	Fiscal 2001	Fiscal 2002 (Forecast Range)* Conservative	Optimistic
Earnings from operations before income taxes, rent, other operating leases, computer services, distribution activities and interest on long-term debt (including capital leases)	34,388	41,347	49,428	56,403	58,952
Rent, other operating leases, computer services, distribution activities and interest on long-term debt (including capital leases)	23,392	29,037	32,902	40,637	40,715
Times coverage	1.47	1.42	1.50	1.39	1.45

Goal 7: To achieve back-line costs excluding interest but including goodwill amortization of less than 5% of total system sales (corporate store and franchise store sales combined)

(thousands of dollars, except percentage items)	Fiscal 1999	Fiscal 2000	Fiscal 2001	Fiscal 2002 (Forecast Range)* Conservative	Optimistic
Total system sales	417,468	437,670	487,979	536,856	554,874
Back-line costs, excluding interest but including goodwill amortization**	20,845	23,540	25,795	29,469	30,878
Back-line costs excluding interest but including goodwill amortization as a percentage of total retail sales	5.0%	5.4%	5.3%	5.5%	5.6%

** Back-line costs include back-line depreciation and amortization. See the Consolidated Statement of Earnings and Retained Earnings.

As of January 27, 2001, the Company is meeting one of its five operational goals and four of its seven financial goals.

* The forecast range set by the conservative and optimistic forecasts is based upon management's judgment and on assumptions outlined on page 18, some or all of which may prove incorrect. Accordingly, actual results achieved during the forecast period will inevitably vary from those forecast and variations may be material.

Top Performers *(L to R)* **John Blumenthal, Gail Stone, Pradeep Shakespeare, Ron Iwamoto**

The Value of Strategic Planning

Our Strategic Plan focuses on the requirement to balance resources among reinvesting and improving upon the Mark's Division proven format, executing the growth strategies in less-developed formats — the "Corporate Store" and merchandise development strategies in the Work World Division — testing and proving new formats such as the DOCKERS® test stores and growing new business vehicles such as Business-to-Business and e-Commerce while continuing to grow the company's bottom line.

A review of the Post Mortem On The Prior Year's Forecast Range, the Management's Discussion and Analysis and the Consolidated Financial Statements, shows that the Company achieved its bottom line growth targets in fiscal 2001 because of its strong consolidated sales and gross margin performance.

Mark's (L'Équipeur) Division: The Company continues to invest in and improve its Mark's (L'Équipeur) Division. In fiscal 2002, this will be accomplished by adding 10 new "On Concept" corporate stores, two new corporate clearance centres, relocating six corporate stores, refurbishing two corporate stores and continuing the strong sales growth experienced in the last couple of years in ladies' wear sales and Business-to-Business sales. The division will focus on these value creating growth engines while also continuing to be at or above industry sales growth rates in men's casual wear sales, work wear sales, and casual and work footwear sales.

In addition, in fiscal 2002 and beyond, this division will continue to expand its web capabilities for consumer and Business-to-Business sales as well as for marketing and information exchange activities.

Work World: The Work World Division's strategy in fiscal 2002 will be to improve the merchandise programs, replenishment processes and store formats so that the sales dollars per square foot and store and division front-line contribution rates rise to the required levels, while moderately increasing the number of corporate stores. Further into the future, the number of corporate stores will be increased at a more rapid rate.

DOCKERS® Stores: The division continues to work tirelessly on its merchandise assortments and replenishment processes in its eight pilot stores in order to reach the sales dollars per square foot, gross margin rate, sales mix between men's and ladies' product and sales blend among tops, bottoms and other products that it needs to achieve for success. If these hurdles are met, the Company will then have a third vehicle for future expansion and value creation. Since the DOCKERS® Stores are still very much a test and since early results have not yet met our expectations, master target excerpts from the Strategic Plan have not been shown.

While focusing on its current value creating strategies, the Company is also always on the look-out for new formats, acquisitions or significant transactions that could add shareholder value to Mark's Work Wearhouse Ltd.

Master Targets Excerpts from the Strategic Plan

(dollar amounts in thousands except share price and per retail square foot)	Owner	Actual Fiscal 1999	Actual Fiscal 2000	Actual Fiscal 2001	Master Targets Fiscal 2002*	Master Targets Fiscal 2003*	Master Targets Fiscal 2004*
Mark's Division corporate and franchise sales**	Paul Wilson	$ 328,937	$ 345,803	$ 385,677	$ 440,908	$ 499,248	$ 525,686
Work World Division corporate and franchise sales	Michael Strachan	$ 86,866	$ 89,201	$ 94,532	$ 103,398	$ 114,038	$ 127,677
Mark's Division corporate stores sales per average retail square foot	Paul Wilson	$ 252	$ 239	$ 259	$ 281	$ 303	$ 309
Work World Division corporate stores sales per average retail square foot	Michael Strachan	N/A	$ 217	$ 221	$ 244	$ 271	$ 284
Number of Mark's Division corporate stores	Paul Wilson	122	127	132	143	151	157
Number of Mark's Division franchise stores	Paul Wilson	29	29	25	25	23	21
Number of Work World Division corporate stores	Michael Strachan	41	45	54	58	71	86
Number of Work World Division franchise stores	Michael Strachan	105	102	90	89	83	77
Mark's Division corporate stores gross margin rate	Rick Harrison	40.6%	41.3%	41.6%	41.3%	41.4%	41.4%
Work World Division corporate stores gross margin rate	Michael Strachan	35.6%	36.7%	37.9%	39.7%	40.0%	40.3%
Mark's Division franchise royalties and other	Paul Wilson	$ 3,985	$ 4,075	$ 4,129	$ 4,261	$ 4,066	$ 3,788
Work World Division franchise royalties and other	Michael Strachan	$ 3,031	$ 2,565	$ 2,429	$ 2,513	$ 2,549	$ 2,547
Mark's Division front-line expenses as a percentage of corporate sales	Paul Wilson	29.7%	29.1%	28.8%	28.9%	28.4%	28.5%
Work World Division front-line expenses as a percentage of corporate sales	Michael Strachan	31.6%	41.7%	39.1%	35.0%	36.0%	35.3%
Consolidated back-line expenses, including goodwill amortization, as a percentage of total system sales	John Murphy	5.3%	5.9%	5.8%	6.4%	6.8%	6.3%
Share price at fiscal year end	Garth Mitchell	$ 3.25	$ 1.80	$ 2.40	$ 2.85	$ 3.50	$ 4.25
Consolidated average funded debt-to-equity	Mike Lambert & John Murphy	0.92/1	0.94/1	0.84/1	1.03/1	1.00/1	1.00/1
Mark's Division year-end inventory at retail	Rick Harrison	$ 117,419	$ 123,251	$ 124,564	$ 144,420	$ 152,528	$ 159,360
Consolidated capital expenditures including capital leases	Michel St. Jean & Robin Lynas	$ 10,152	$ 11,154	$ 11,150	$ 10,283	$ 14,286	$ 15,864
Mark's Division corporate stores year-end average store size (retail square feet)	Paul Wilson	9,115	9,410	9,486	9,558	9,617	9,655
Work World Division corporate stores year-end average store size (retail square feet)	Michael Strachan	3,200	3,177	3,144	3,192	3,152	3,142

N/A Not applicable or not available.
*   The master targets are based upon management's judgment and on assumptions some or all of which may prove incorrect. Accordingly, actual results achieved in future years will inevitably vary from those forecast and variations may be material.
**   Includes Business-to-Business and e-Commerce sales.

STRATEGIC PLAN

Forecast Range

Earnings per Common Share, for the 52 weeks ending January 26, 2002 are forecast to be in the range of 31 to 36 cents. This forecast range represents, in management's judgment, the most likely set of conditions and the Company's most likely course of action. The reader is cautioned that some assumptions used while preparing our forecast range, although considered reasonable at the time of preparation, may prove to be incorrect. The actual results achieved during the forecast period will inevitably vary from the forecast range and variations may be material.

KEY ASSUMPTIONS

(dollars and weighted average shares in thousands, except sales per retail sq. ft.)	Actual 52 weeks ended January 27, 2001	Forecast Range (unaudited) 52 weeks ended January 26, 2002	
		Conservative	Optimistic
Growth in GDP	4.7%	2.0%	3.0%
Growth in total retail sales excluding auto, food and drug	5.8% *	2.6%	4.5%
Total sales increase – Mark's Division corporate stores	13.3%	13.3%	16.6%
Total sales increase (decrease) – Mark's Division franchise stores	3.8%	(0.3%)	3.2%
Total sales increase – Work World Division corporate stores	23.0%	13.5%	21.4%
Total sales increase (decrease) – Work World Division franchise stores	(2.4%)	(0.4%)	1.9%
Total sales – DOCKERS® Stores Division corporate stores	$ 7,770	$ 9,685	$ 10,569
Number of DOCKERS® Stores Division store openings***	3	—	—
Same-store sales increase – Mark's Division corporate stores	10.3%	4.6%	8.0%
Same-store sales increase – Mark's Division franchise stores	12.5%	5.0%	8.7%
Same-store sales increase – Work World Division corporate stores	4.7%	4.7%	11.1%
Same-store sales increase – Work World Division franchise stores	7.8%	5.0%	7.5%
Number of new Mark's Division corporate store openings	2	12	12
Sales from new Mark's Division corporate store openings during year	$ 1,330	$ 16,487	$ 16,487
Number of new Work World Division corporate store openings	4	4	4
Sales from new Work World Division corporate store openings during year	$ 1,487	$ 913	$ 1,774
Number of Mark's Division corporate store expansions, relocations,	8	8	8
refurbishments and sales therefrom	$ 24,980	$ 22,732	$ 22,732
Number of Work World Division corporate store expansions, relocations,	2	3	3
refurbishments and sales therefrom	$ 2,089	$ 2,410	$ 2,410
Number of Mark's Division corporate store closings	1	1	1
and sales therefrom	$ 60	$ 593	$ 593
Number of Work World Division corporate store closings	1	—	—
and sales therefrom	$ 227	—	—
Sales per average retail sq. ft. Mark's Division corporate stores**	$ 259	$ 273	$ 281
Sales per average retail sq. ft. Work World Division corporate stores**	$ 221	$ 228	$ 244
Sales per average retail sq. ft. DOCKERS® Stores Division corporate stores**	$ 333	$ 354	$ 387
Number of Mark's Division franchise stores at year end	25	25	25
Number of Work World Division franchise stores at year end	90	89	89
Mark's Division gross margin rate	41.6%	41.4%	41.3%
Work World Division gross margin rate	37.9%	39.3%	39.7%
Consolidated gross margin rate	41.1%	39.3%	39.7%
Consolidated capital expenditures including capital purchases made by capital leases	$ 11,150	$ 10,283	$ 10,283
Operating line – interest rates	7.2%	7.2%	7.2%
Long-term debt financing including capital lease financing and vendor debt on purchase of franchise stores	$ 14,425	$ 9,901	$ 9,901
Consolidated front-line expenses as a percentage of corporate store sales	30.6%	30.7%	30.1%
Consolidated back-line expenses including goodwill amortization as a percentage of total system sales	5.8%	6.3%	6.4%
Weighted average shares outstanding	27,597	26,012	26,012

*   Source: Statistics Canada
**   Calculated on stores open and at the same size for an entire season. The Company divides the year into two seasons.
     Spring – February through July; Fall – August through January.
*** The Company's first five DOCKERS® Stores were opened in fiscal 2000 and three more DOCKERS® Stores were opened in fiscal 2001.

The Company completed this forecast range on March 22, 2001. The quarterly financial reports issued by the Company to its shareholders during the forecast year will contain either a statement that there are no significant changes to be made to the forecast range or an updated earnings per Common Share forecast or forecast range accompanied by explanations of significant changes. The reader is further cautioned that the fourth quarter of the year continues to produce between 37% and 39% of the Company's total system annual sales and most of its annual profits.

CONSOLIDATED STATEMENTS OF EARNINGS

(in thousands, except per Common Share)	Actual 52 weeks ended January 27, 2001	Forecast Range (unaudited) 52 weeks ended January 26, 2002	
		Conservative	Optimistic
Corporate and franchise sales	$ 487,979	$ 536,856	$ 554,874
Franchise sales	124,109	123,668	127,349
Corporate sales	363,870	413,188	427,525
Cost of sales	214,361	243,257	251,916
Gross margin	149,509	169,931	175,609
Front-line expenses	111,248	126,881	128,795
Front-line contribution	38,261	43,050	46,814
Franchise royalties and other	6,558	6,579	6,774
Net front-line contribution	44,819	49,629	53,588
Back-line expenses including goodwill amortization	28,293	33,863	35,351
Earnings before income taxes	16,526	15,766	18,237
Income taxes	8,346	7,583	8,772
Net earnings	$ 8,180	$ 8,183	$ 9,465
Earnings per Common Share – basic	30¢	31¢	36¢
Weighted average number of Common Shares outstanding	27,597	26,012	26,012

CONSOLIDATED BALANCE SHEETS

(in thousands)	Actual as at January 27, 2001	Forecast Range (unaudited) as at January 26, 2002	
		Conservative	Optimistic
Assets			
Cash and cash equivalents	$ 6,993	$ 1,482	$ 7,093
Merchandise inventories	84,483	94,248	92,543
Other current assets	18,911	17,244	17,680
	110,387	112,974	117,316
Other assets	1,056	909	909
Capital assets	28,148	26,590	26,590
Future income taxes	2,997	2,597	2,597
Goodwill	14,472	13,867	13,867
	$ 157,060	$ 156,937	$ 161,279
Liabilities			
Accounts payable, accrued liabilities and income taxes payable	$ 52,317	$ 48,510	$ 51,570
Current portion of long-term debt	10,905	11,996	11,996
	63,222	60,506	63,566
Long-term debt	27,016	24,852	24,852
Deferred gains	2,101	2,101	2,101
	92,339	87,459	90,519
Shareholders' equity			
Capital stock	31,228	29,790	29,790
Retained earnings	33,493	39,688	40,970
	64,721	69,478	70,760
	$ 157,060	$ 156,937	$ 161,279

Forecast Range and Post Mortem on the Prior Year's Forecast Range

CONSOLIDATED STATEMENTS OF CASH FLOWS

(in thousands)	Actual 52 weeks ended January 27, 2001	Forecast Range (unaudited) 52 weeks ended January 26, 2002	
		Conservative	Optimistic
Cash and cash equivalents generated (deployed)			
Operations	$ 18,881	$ 21,029	$ 22,312
Working capital	2,259	(11,907)	(7,579)
Investing*	(5,807)	(835)	(835)
Financing*	(10,114)	(13,798)	(13,798)
Net cash and cash equivalents generated (deployed)	$ 5,219	$ (5,511)	$ 100

* Excludes capital lease investing and financing of $8,665,000 and $3,060,000 of non-cash investing and financing on the acquisition of individual franchise stores during the fiscal year ended January 27, 2001; excludes capital lease investing and financing of $9,301,000 in the conservative and optimistic forecasts for the fiscal year ended January 26, 2002.

Post Mortem on the Prior Year's Forecast Range

CONSOLIDATED STATEMENTS OF EARNINGS

(in thousands, except per Common Share)	Actual 52 weeks ended January 27, 2001	Forecast Range (unaudited) 52 weeks ended January 27, 2001	
		Conservative	Optimistic
Corporate and franchise store sales	$ 487,979	$ 478,937	$ 492,838
Deduct: Franchise store sales – Mark's	65,754	67,016	70,373
Franchise store sales – Work World	58,355	60,260	61,349
Corporate store sales	363,870	351,661	361,116
Gross margin	149,509	144,418	148,804
Add: Franchise royalties and other	6,558	6,873	7,136
Deduct: Expenses including goodwill amortization	139,541	138,166	139,391
Earnings before income taxes	16,526	13,125	16,549
Income taxes	8,346	6,312	7,818
Net earnings	$ 8,180	$ 6,813	$ 8,731
Earnings per Common Share	30¢	25¢	31¢
Weighted average number of Common Shares outstanding	27,597	27,807	27,807

CONSOLIDATED STATEMENTS OF EARNINGS

In its January 29, 2000 annual report, the Company forecast earnings per Common Share in the range of 25 cents to 31 cents for its fiscal year ended January 27, 2001.

In its three quarterly reports issued during fiscal 2001, the Company reported that it was a little ahead or at the upper end of its forecast range and in all cases, advised shareholders that it was staying with its forecast range.

In the final analysis, during the fiscal year ended January 27, 2001, the Company delivered $488.0 million in total system sales — 99.0% of its optimistic forecast. Due to the unplanned purchase of four Mark's Division franchise stores and the purchase of six Work World Division franchise stores, compared to a plan for the purchase of one store during fiscal 2001, corporate store sales came in $2.8 million above the optimistic forecast and franchise store sales came in $3.2 million below the conservative forecast. The higher than optimistic forecast corporate store sales also caused the Company to deliver $0.7 million more in gross margin dollars than the optimistic forecast at a gross margin rate two basis points above the conservative forecast level and 12 basis points below the optimistic forecast level. Franchise royalties and other came in as a percentage of total franchise sales 14 basis points below the rate projected at the optimistic forecast level. The dollar shortfall of $0.6 million in franchise royalties and other from the optimistic forecast level was due to the unplanned conversion of franchise stores to corporate stores as noted above and also due to the fact that franchise store sales, excluding store conversions to corporate, came in closer to the conservative forecast level than optimistic forecast level. The Company's total expenses came in $0.2 million higher than the optimistic forecast dollars but at 25 basis points lower (better) as a percentage of corporate store sales.

The net result of all of the above was that the Company delivered $16.5 million in pre-tax income within

$23,000 of its optimistic forecast. Income taxes came in at a higher rate than planned, as the Company had not anticipated the immediate adverse impact the substantially enacted decline in future income tax rates would have on its future income tax provision. Lower than planned weighted shares outstanding also helped the earnings per share calculation by 22 basis points.

CONSOLIDATED BALANCE SHEETS

The Company's current assets at January 27, 2001 of $110.4 million essentially came in as expected, ending the 2001 fiscal year within the forecast range. Year-end capital assets came in $4.8 million above the forecast, as the Company spent $1.4 million more than forecast on store capital expenditures, $0.7 million more on system capital expenditures (over half of this overage was on Web system capital expenditures), added $0.6 million of capital assets from unplanned purchases of franchise stores and depreciation was $2.1 million below forecast, due to the timing of capital expenditures and capital lease financing during fiscal 2001.

Goodwill came in $3.7 million higher than planned as a result of the $3.9 million of acquisition goodwill less

amortization thereon on the unplanned purchases of franchise stores as summarized in Notes 3 and 8 to the Consolidated Financial Statements.

Total liabilities came in $9.9 million higher than the conservative forecast, primarily as a result of the $5.8 million of long-term debt related to the unplanned purchase of the franchise stores and the funding of $2.7 million more in capital lease financing than forecast.

Year-end shareholders' equity came in $3.4 million below the optimistic forecast as $2.9 million more was spent on shares purchased for cancellation under the Company's Normal Course Issuer Bid than had been planned and net earnings came in $0.5 million below forecast, due to a higher than planned tax provision as noted above.

CONSOLIDATED BALANCE SHEETS

(in thousands)	Actual as at January 27, 2001	Forecast Range (unaudited) as at January 27, 2001	
		Conservative	Optimistic
Assets			
Current assets	$ 110,387	$ 109,908	$ 111,176
Other assets	1,056	1,420	1,420
Capital assets	28,148	23,308	23,308
Future income taxes	2,997	3,301	3,301
Goodwill	14,472	10,729	10,729
	$ 157,060	$ 148,666	$ 149,934
Liabilities			
Current liabilities	$ 63,222	$ 61,327	$ 60,677
Long-term debt	27,016	18,935	18,935
Deferred gains	2,101	2,161	2,161
	92,339	82,423	81,773
Shareholders' equity			
Capital stock	31,228	32,677	32,677
Retained earnings	33,493	33,566	35,484
	64,721	66,243	68,161
	$ 157,060	$ 148,666	$ 149,934

POST MORTEM ON THE PRIOR YEAR'S FORECAST RANGE

Post Mortem on the Prior Year's Forecast Range

CONSOLIDATED STATEMENTS OF CASH FLOWS

The actual net cash generated of $5.2 million in fiscal 2001 came in $5.1 million better than the optimistic forecast of $0.1 million of cash generation. This occurred primarily because of improved inventory and accounts receivable management and higher than planned income taxes payable due to the timing of earnings which caused non-cash working-capital to generate $2.3 million of funds rather than deploying $6.9 million of funds as was forecast resulting in a $9.2 million favorable swing in cash generation.

The $9.2 million favorable swing in non-cash working capital from the optimistic forecast plus the $0.4 million over optimistic forecast in financing activities was partially offset by $2.9 million of investing activities over plan (primarily $3.1 million for the cash component of the unplanned purchases of franchise stores) and $1.6 million of cash flow from operations shortfall from the optimistic forecast ($0.5 million in net earnings shortfall and $1.1 million less in fiscal 2001 depreciation and amortization and other).

CONSOLIDATED STATEMENTS OF CASH FLOWS

(in thousands)	52 weeks ended January 27, 2001 Actual	Forecast (unaudited) 52 weeks ended January 27, 2001		Variance of Actual to Forecast	
		Conservative	Optimistic	Conservative	Optimistic
Cash and cash equivalents generated (deployed)					
Operations	$ 18,881	$ 18,518	$ 20,435	$ 363	$ (1,554)
Non-cash working capital	2,259	(9,468)	(6,909)	11,727	9,168
Investing, excluding capital leases	(5,807)	(2,876)	(2,876)	(2,931)	(2,931)
Financing, excluding capital lease and franchise vendor long-term debt funding	(10,114)	(10,547)	(10,547)	433	433
Net cash and cash equivalents generated (deployed)	$ 5,219	$ (4,373)	$ 103	$ 9,592	$ 5,116

SUPPLEMENTARY SCHEDULES TO CONSOLIDATED STATEMENTS OF CASH FLOWS

(in thousands)	52 weeks ended January 27, 2001 Actual	Forecast (unaudited) 52 weeks ended January 27, 2001		Variance of Actual to Forecast	
		Conservative	Optimistic	Conservative	Optimistic
Capital assets acquired by means of capital leases	$ (8,665)	$ (5,978)	$ (5,978)	$ (2,687)	$ (2,687)
Capital lease funding to acquire capital assets	$ 8,665	$ 5,978	$ 5,978	$ 2,687	$ 2,687
Purchases of individual franchise stores by means of long-term debt	$ (3,060)	$ —	$ —	$ (3,060)	$ (3,060)
Long-term debt from vendors on purchase of individual franchise stores	$ 3,060	$ —	$ —	$ 3,060	$ 3,060

Management's Discussion and Analysis

CONSOLIDATED STATEMENTS OF EARNINGS

SALES

In fiscal 2001, the Company posted strong total system sales growth of 11.5% over the prior year as shown in Table 1.

This strong sales growth story in fiscal 2001 over fiscal 2000 was also true on a same store total system sales basis as shown in Table 2.

A comparison of Tables 1 and 2 shows that 78.4% of the Company's dollar sales growth in fiscal 2001 over fiscal 2000 resulted from initiatives implemented within existing stores and 21.6% of the Company's dollar sales growth resulted from square footage additions.

Performance Against the Industry

The Company's percentage sales increase in fiscal 2001 over fiscal 2000 compares to the retail sales increase in Canada in calendar 2000 over calendar 1999 as shown in Graph 2 and the first row of Table 18.

Tables 1, 2 and 18 and Graph 2 show that in 2000 (fiscal January 2001) the Company's consolidated total system sales growth of 11.5% over 1999 (fiscal January 2000) outperformed the retail sector sales growth in total, and continues to strongly outperform the sales growth in the market segments the Company competes in within the retail sector, namely men's clothing stores (0.1% increase),

CONSOLIDATED TOTAL SYSTEM SALES Table 1

Number of stores as at January 27, 2001		52 weeks ended January 30, 1999 ($000s)	52 weeks ended January 29, 2000 ($000s)	52 weeks ended January 27, 2001 ($000s)	Fiscal 2001 Increase/(Decrease) Over Fiscal 2000 ($000s)	(%)
	Mark's Division					
132	Corporate stores	267,136 **	282,463 **	319,923	37,460	13.3
25	Franchise stores	61,801	63,340	65,754	2,414	3.8
157	Total	328,937	345,803	385,677	39,874	11.5
	Work World Division					
54	Corporate stores	14,600 *	29,418 *	36,177	6,759	23.0
90	Franchise stores	72,266 *	59,783 *	58,355	(1,428)	(2.4)
144	Total	86,866	89,201	94,532	5,331	6.0
	DOCKERS® Stores Division					
8	Corporate stores	—	2,666	7,770	5,104	100.0+
	Mark's U.S. Division					
Nil	Corporate stores	1,665 **	—	—	—	—
309	**Consolidated Total System Sales**	417,468	437,670	487,979	50,309	11.5

* Thirty-one Work World Division franchise stores (19 through the purchase of Paul John Enterprises Ltd.) were acquired during the fiscal year ended January 30, 1999 and those stores became full year corporate stores for the fiscal year ended January 29, 2000.
** Excludes inter-group sales.

CONSOLIDATED SAME STORE TOTAL SYSTEM SALES Table 2

Number of same stores through fiscal 2001 and 2000		52 weeks ended January 29, 2000 ($000s)	52 weeks ended January 27, 2001 ($000s)	Fiscal 2001 Increase Over Fiscal 2000 ($000s)	(%)
	Mark's Division				
148	Corporate and Franchise stores	331,592	366,156	34,564	10.4
	Work World Division				
134	Corporate and Franchise stores	83,217	88,115	4,898	5.9
282	**Consolidated Same Store Total System Sales**	414,809	454,271	39,462	9.5

Management's Discussion and Analysis

total men's wear (3.8% increase), shoe stores (0.4% decline), women's clothing stores (2.7% increase) and total ladies' wear (1.2% increase).

Table 3 shows how the Company's sales percentage increase in fiscal 2001 over fiscal 2000 was strong all year with good healthy total system sales percentage increases in each and every quarter.

The Company's total system sales percentage increase in fiscal 2001 over fiscal 2000 was also strong in most regions of the country as shown in Table 4.

Further, even though on a macro trend apparel as a segment within the retail sector has been losing some of its share of the consumer's wallet to other retail segments such as electronics, furniture, appliances and automobiles over the last five years (see Table 18 under "Risk Factors"), the Company's sales growth has outperformed the total industry and all sectors in the industry. See Graph 3.

Market Share Growth Not surprisingly, an outgrowth of the data above is that the Company continues to increase its share of the men's clothing store market, and in fiscal 2000 (calendar 1999) and fiscal 2001 (calendar 2000) increased its share of the total men's wear market, which includes men's wear sales in department stores and discount stores. See Graph 4.

In addition, now the Company is starting to appear on the radar screen in the ladies' wear market with a 1.3% market share of the women's clothing stores market and a 0.6% market share of the total ladies' wear market (includes ladies' wear sales in department stores and discount stores) in fiscal 2001. While these market share percentages in themselves are not significant today, they are very significant going forward as they mean that the Company is now starting to find sales in the $9.6 billion total ladies' wear market while continuing to maintain or grow its market share in the $6.1 billion men's wear market and continuing to be a dominant player in the $1.0 billion men's footwear market. In other words, as Graph 5 shows, the Company is now playing on a $16.7 billion playing field rather than on a $7.1 billion dollar playing field in terms of future growth potential.

Graph and Table Legend
Source =
- The industry data in Tables 3 and 4 comes from Statistics Canada.
- The industry data in Graphs 2, 3, part of 4 and part of 6 comes from Statistics Canada.
- The industry data in Graph 5, part of 4 and part of 6 comes from Trendex North America.
- All of the industry data in Graphs 7 and 8 comes from Trendex North America.
- The industry data in Table 18 comes partly from Statistics Canada and partly from Trendex North America.
- The share and index data for Graph 18 and the market value by quarter and volumes of shares traded under Summary and Quarterly Financial Information comes from the Toronto Stock Exchange.
- All Mark's, Work World and DOCKERS® Stores data comes from the Company's accounting records.

5-YEAR CONSOLIDATED CORPORATE AND FRANCHISE SALES TO JANUARY 27, 2001 (GRAPH 1)
(rolling 12-month dollars millions)

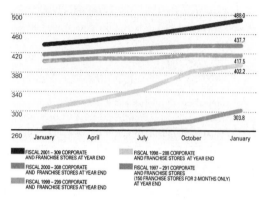

FISCAL 2001 – 309 CORPORATE AND FRANCHISE STORES AT YEAR END
FISCAL 2000 – 308 CORPORATE AND FRANCHISE STORES AT YEAR END
FISCAL 1999 – 299 CORPORATE AND FRANCHISE STORES AT YEAR END
FISCAL 1998 – 288 CORPORATE AND FRANCHISE STORES AT YEAR END
FISCAL 1997 – 291 CORPORATE AND FRANCHISE STORES (150 FRANCHISE STORES FOR 2-MONTHS ONLY) AT YEAR END

2000 RETAIL SALES GROWTH OVER 1999 (GRAPH 2)
(percent change)

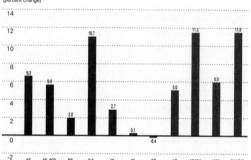

RETAIL TRADE GROWTH IN CANADA (GRAPH 3)
(percent change over 5 years)

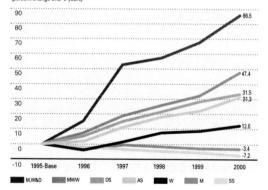

M,W&D   MWW   DS   AS   W   M   SS

AS =	All Stores
SS =	Shoe Stores
AS-AFD =	All Stores less auto, food and drug
AO =	All Others
DS =	Department Stores (includes discount department stores)
MWW =	Mark's Division corporate and franchise stores
F/A =	Furniture and Appliances
WW =	Work World Division corporate and franchise stores
W =	Women's Clothing Stores
M,W&D =	Mark's, Work World and DOCKERS® Stores Divisions total system sales
M =	Men's Clothing Stores

5-YEAR MEN'S APPAREL RETAIL MARKET SHARE (GRAPH 4)

Percentage of Retail Dollar Sales Men's Apparel by Mark's (corporate and franchise stores) plus
Work World (corporate and franchise stores) since 1997 plus DOCKERS® Corporate Stores since 1999
(market share percent)

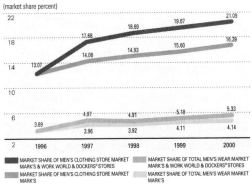

MARKET SHARE OF MEN'S CLOTHING STORE MARKET
MARK'S & WORK WORLD & DOCKERS® STORES

MARKET SHARE OF MEN'S CLOTHING STORE MARKET
MARK'S

MARKET SHARE OF TOTAL MEN'S WEAR MARKET
MARK'S & WORK WORLD & DOCKERS® STORES

MARKET SHARE OF TOTAL MEN'S WEAR MARKET
MARK'S

CANADIAN APPAREL & FOOTWEAR MARKET SIZE (GRAPH 5)

(retail dollar sales – billions)

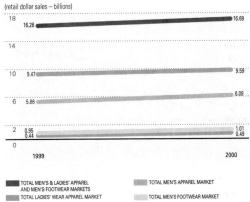

TOTAL MEN'S & LADIES' APPAREL
AND MEN'S FOOTWEAR MARKETS

TOTAL LADIES' WEAR APPAREL MARKET

TOTAL MEN'S APPAREL MARKET

TOTAL MEN'S FOOTWEAR MARKET

M,W&D

That the Company continues to be a dominant player in the footwear business when it does not operate in the dress up or athletic footwear businesses is also quite an accomplishment. The Company's market share of the Canadian men's footwear market and the shoe store market is shown in Graph 6.

Sales Analysis The sales growth engineered by the Company in fiscal 2001 over fiscal 2000 did not simply occur by accident or because the economy was strong. The Company employs very specific strategies to grow its sales. In its Mark's Division, those strategies are "On Concept"

real estate activity, category exploitation of the hot categories through merchandise assortment development, targeted marketing events, the rapid development of ladies' wear sales and Business-to-Business sales and the development of electronic or Internet sales to customers. In the Work World Division, those strategies are the "Corporate Store Strategy," gradual geographic expansion into central and eastern Canada with corporate stores, targeted marketing events and merchandise assortment development to enhance both corporate and franchise store sales. In the DOCKERS® Stores Division, the operative word is "test" as the Company continues to

CONSOLIDATED TOTAL SYSTEM SALES GROWTH BY QUARTER COMPARED TO INDUSTRY SEGMENTS Table 3

	Fiscal 2001 Sales Percentage Increase/(Decrease) over Fiscal 2000				
	M, W & D	M	SS	W	AS
First Quarter	10.6	3.9	2.6	4.2	7.9
Second Quarter	14.8	3.8	(4.2)	1.0	6.4
Third Quarter	9.6	3.2	2.4	4.8	6.7
Fourth Quarter	11.4	(6.1)	(1.0)	1.4	4.7
Total Year	11.5	0.1	(0.4)	2.7	6.3

CONSOLIDATED TOTAL SYSTEM SALES GROWTH BY REGION COMPARED TO RETAIL SALES GROWTH BY REGION Table 4

	Fiscal 2001 Sales Percentage Increase over Fiscal 2000	
	M, W & D	AS
British Columbia	2.1	6.2
Prairies	14.9	7.3
Ontario	13.8	7.2
Quebec	13.5	4.6
Atlantic Canada	8.2	5.0
Total Canada	11.5	6.3

Management's Discussion and Analysis

5-YEAR FOOTWEAR RETAIL MARKET SHARE
(GRAPH 6)

Percentage of Retail Dollar Sales of the Men's Footwear Market and Percentage of Retail Dollar Sales of the Shoe Store Market by Mark's (corporate and franchise stores) plus Work World (corporate and franchise stores) since 1997 plus DOCKERS® Corporate Stores since 1999
(market share percent)

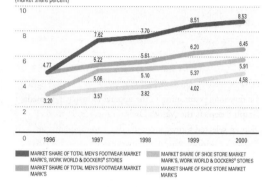

MARKET SHARE OF TOTAL MEN'S FOOTWEAR MARKET MARK'S, WORK WORLD & DOCKERS® STORES
MARKET SHARE OF SHOE STORE MARKET MARK'S, WORK WORLD & DOCKERS® STORES
MARKET SHARE OF TOTAL MEN'S FOOTWEAR MARKET MARK'S
MARKET SHARE OF SHOE STORE MARKET MARK'S

test to find the right merchandise assortment and price points for the division's target customer in the existing eight pilot stores.

In fiscal 2001, the Company's Mark's Division converted four franchise stores to corporate stores, opened two new corporate stores and relocated, expanded or refurbished eight corporate stores. In addition, the six new stores opened in fiscal 2000 went from part-year stores to full-year stores. All this "On Concept" store activity accounted for $17.0 million or 45.3% of the $37.5 million corporate store sales increase delivered in fiscal 2001 over fiscal 2000 as summarized in Table 1. In fiscal 2000, Mark's Division "On Concept" store activity accounted for all of the $15.3 million corporate store sales increase over fiscal 1999. This "On Concept" store strategy has been and continues to be successful for the Mark's Division as the division continues, in a very disciplined fashion, to carry out in-depth "Pre-audit" and "Post-audit" processes on each store project to ensure that the rate of return on real estate related capital expenditures is meeting pre-set internal Company hurdle rates.

In fiscal 2001, the Company's Work World Division converted six franchise stores to corporate stores, opened four new corporate stores and relocated, expanded or refurbished two corporate stores. In addition, the five new stores opened in fiscal 2000 went from part-year stores to full-year stores. All this "Corporate Store" activity accounted for $5.6 million or 82.4% of the $6.8 corporate store sales increase delivered in fiscal 2001 over fiscal 2000 as summarized in Table 1. In fiscal 2000, "Corporate Store" activity accounted for all of the $14.8 million corporate stores sales increase over fiscal 1999.

In fiscal 2001, the Company's DOCKERS® Stores Division opened up three more test stores to bring its total number of test stores to eight. Now that this division has the test store base it needs, it will concentrate all its energy and activities on improving its merchandise assortments in order to increase its sales per square foot in fiscal 2002.

Table 5 summarizes the Company's total sales by major product category. In fiscal 2001, the Company grew its ladies' wear category of corporate store sales (primarily casual pants and casual tops excluding casual outerwear, accessories and footwear grouped in other categories) by $15.4 million (64.1%) on top of corporate store sales growth of $8.0 million (49.9%) in fiscal 2000 over fiscal 1999. In fact, just five years ago in fiscal 1996, the ladies' wear category (primarily casual pants and casual tops excluding casual outerwear, accessories and footwear grouped in other categories) at the Company was only a $5.1 million dollar annual business or a 2.6% blend of total corporate store sales. Clearly the Company's category exploitation initiatives in this category are working.

In fiscal 2001, the Company added new ladies' accessory products, as well as novelty and gift-giving commodities to its accessories category. These additions, combined with an assist from some normal winter weather in the months of November and December 2000 compared to the lack of winter in those months over the last few years, caused the Company to register a strong $7.7 million (18.7%) sales increase in accessories in fiscal 2001 over fiscal 2000.

In fiscal 2001, the Company posted a healthy $5.8 million (16.9%) sales growth in work apparel and industrial outerwear primarily due to the introduction of new work apparel products, the upgrading of the styling on established products and the exploiting of the Company's position as the primary seller of Carhartt product in Canada.

In fiscal 2001, the Company also delivered a strong $10.0 million (16.6%) sales growth in footwear. This growth came mostly in industrial footwear where the Company introduced some new products that were very successful.

In fiscal 2001, in the Company's men's casual wear category, the Company continued to generate strong sales growth (22.6%) in men's casual bottoms (primarily in private label khakis and shorts) and satisfactory sales growth (8.0%) in men's casual tops, but experienced a sales decline (-8.0%) in men's casual outerwear. As well, as noted in the last two years' annual reports, while the Company intends to maintain its position as a dominant cold weather clothing and footwear store in Canada, it has reduced its fourth-quarter sales dependency on winter goods.

More specifically, in the Company's Mark's Division, fourth quarter sales of winter goods have been reduced from 35% of the Mark's Division's fourth quarter corporate store sales in fiscal 1997 to 25% of the Mark's Division's fourth quarter corporate store sales in fiscal 2001. This reduction in dependency on cold weather products has been achieved by growing other businesses that are less weather dependent, thereby reducing the Company's weather dependency risk in the fourth quarter.

The Company's strong sales growth in Business-to-Business sales is included in the sales by category numbers summarized in Table 5. Business-to-Business sales are apparel and footwear sales to corporate and public sector customers ranging from embroidered golf shirts for a corporation's or public sector customer's

annual golf day to full uniforms (industrial or casual) for a customer's entire work force.

In fiscal 2001, the Company's Mark's Division grew the revenue derived from Business-to-Business sales by 27.7% on top of a fiscal 2000 sales increase of 19.0% over fiscal 1999. This activity now contributes 9.2% of the Mark's Division corporate stores sales (fiscal 2000 8.1%; fiscal 1999 7.2%).

Graph 7 shows Mark's Division's fiscal 2001 market share in selected apparel commodities to further highlight the division's positioning in the apparel industry in Canada. Graph 8 depicts the Mark's Division fiscal 2001 market share in selected footwear commodities to highlight the division's positioning in the footwear industry in Canada.

MARK'S DIVISION MARKET SHARE IN FISCAL 2001
(CALENDAR 2000) OF SELECTED APPAREL COMMODITIES
(GRAPH 7)
(market share percent)

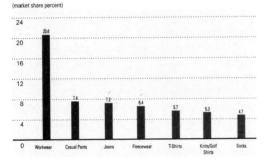

MARK'S DIVISION MARKET SHARE IN FISCAL 2001
(CALENDAR 2000) OF SELECTED FOOTWEAR CATEGORIES
(GRAPH 8)
(market share percent)

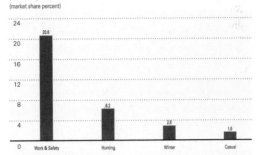

CONSOLIDATED CORPORATE STORE SALES BY CATEGORY Table 5

	52 weeks ended January 30, 1999		52 weeks ended January 29, 2000		52 weeks ended January 27, 2001		Fiscal 2001 Increase/ (Decrease) Over Fiscal 2000
	($000s)	Blend (%)	($000s)	Blend (%)	($000s)	Blend (%)	(%)
Work apparel including industrial outerwear	30,352	10.7	34,107	10.8	39,875	11.0	16.9
Men's casual wear including casual outerwear*	101,985	36.0	114,055	36.3	123,378	33.9	8.2
Men's jeans wear	38,944	13.7	40,170	12.8	41,445	11.4	3.2
Casual and industrial footwear*	55,664	19.6	60,461	19.2	70,505	19.4	16.6
Accessories*	38,567	13.6	41,450	13.2	49,190	13.5	18.7
Ladies' wear*	16,044	5.7	24,051	7.6	39,456	10.8	64.1
Other	1,845	0.7	253	0.1	21	0.0	(91.7)
	283,401	100.0	314,547	100.0	363,870	100.0	15.7

* Depending on the year, approximately 3.5% to 4.5% of the sales in men's casual wear and 5.5% to 7.0% of the sales in accessories are in ladies' items. In addition, approximately 9% to 11% of footwear sales are in ladies' items.

MANAGEMENT'S DISCUSSION AND ANALYSIS

Management's Discussion and Analysis

GROSS MARGIN ANALYSIS

In fiscal 2001, as shown in Table 6, the Company continued its trend of improving its consolidated gross margin rate. The consolidated gross margin rate improved a full 50 basis points to 41.1% from 40.6% a year ago as the 150 basis point improvement in purchase markup was only partially offset by the basis point increases in the cost of freight, markdowns and customer adjustments and shrink.

Within the Company's divisions, the Mark's Division gross margin rate improved by 30 basis points, the Work World Division gross margin rate improved by 120 basis points and the DOCKERS® Stores Division gross margin rate, while still below expectations, significantly improved from the prior year, which had been adversely impacted by start-up issues.

The improvement of the gross margin rate in the Mark's Division can be largely attributed to an improved purchase markup achieved through the continuation of the conversion of the purchase of import merchandise from "indirect import purchases" (purchases through importers) to "direct import purchases" (direct purchases from offshore factories). This activity results in lower landed costs for merchandise. In addition, the Mark's Division has had to move some of its historical domestic product sourcing in the footwear sector offshore as a result of Canadian plant closures and this has also contributed to improved purchase markup.

The improvement in the Work World Division is primarily attributed to improved markdown management, as this division's corporate store operation is now doing a much better job of product quantification and selection than it was during its corporate store start-up phase.

Consolidated markdowns and customer adjustments increased to 7.9% of sales in fiscal 2001, an increase of 70 basis points over the prior year. Most of the increase is attributed to higher than planned markdown activity in the Mark's Division. Although small in dollars from a consolidated perspective in fiscal 2001, markdown activity was also higher than planned in the DOCKERS® Stores Division.

Table 6 also shows that the Company, through its computer processing and store security systems, continues to maintain consolidated shrink levels below one percent of corporate store sales which is better than industry averages.

Of the $21.7 million (17.0%) increase in gross margin dollars in fiscal 2001 over fiscal 2000, $20.0 million or 92.2% is attributable to sales increases and $1.7 million or 7.8% is attributable to the gross margin rate improvement.

The performance of the Mark's Division ladies' wear, accessories and industrial footwear accounted for $13.2 million (80.0%) of the $16.5 million increase in the Mark's Division's gross margin dollars delivered in fiscal 2001 over those delivered in fiscal 2000.

The addition of four new corporate stores, the conversion of six franchise stores to corporate stores and five part-year new stores in fiscal 2000 becoming full-year stores in fiscal 2001 accounted for $2.0 million (69.0%) of the $2.9 million increase in the Work World Division gross margin dollars delivered in fiscal 2001 over fiscal 2000. The strong gross margin dollars growth categories for this division were industrial footwear, men's casual outerwear (even though this category decreased on a consolidated Company basis), men's casual wear and accessories.

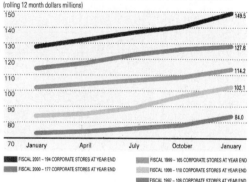

5-YEAR CONSOLIDATED CORPORATE STORE GROSS MARGIN DOLLARS TO JANUARY 27, 2001 (GRAPH 9)
(rolling 12 month dollars millions)

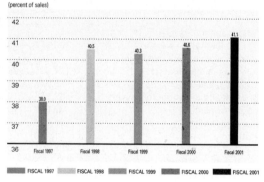

5-YEAR CONSOLIDATED GROSS MARGIN RATE OF CORPORATE STORES SALES TO JANUARY 27, 2001 (GRAPH 10)
(percent of sales)

The more than doubling of the gross margin rate in fiscal 2001 over fiscal 2000 in the DOCKERS® Stores Division was attributable to leaving some of the start-up issues behind and the fact that the division grew from five part-year stores in fiscal 2000 to five full-year stores and three part-year stores in fiscal 2001.

The purchase markup of 50.3% in consolidated corporate store end-of-year inventories is up from 49.5% at January 29, 2000 and 48.8% at January 30, 1999.

FRONT-LINE EXPENSES

During fiscal 2001, consolidated front-line expenses as summarized in Table 7 increased by $15.0 million (15.6%) over fiscal 2000. This increase is less than the $21.7 million (17.0%) increase in consolidated gross margin dollars that was described above under Gross Margin Analysis.

As a percentage of corporate store sales, the front-line expense rate remained unchanged at 30.6% of corporate store sales in fiscal 2001 compared to fiscal 2000. Although front-line expenses per corporate store average retail square foot increased to $79.04 in fiscal 2001 from $74.19 in fiscal 2000, this 6.5% increase is less than the 7.6% increase in

consolidated sales per square foot (see Table 11) and the corporate store same store sales increase of 9.8%.

Fiscal 2001 was a year of investment in front-line expenses. The Mark's Division invested in sales and support staff to support its rapidly growing Business-to-Business sales and in advertising for the addition of three more advertising events and the introduction of "Air Miles" to its Ontario and Quebec regions. Occupancy costs in the Mark's Division also grew in dollars, but remained relatively flat on a cost per retail square foot basis as corporate store retail square footage increased by 57,160 retail square feet in fiscal 2001 over fiscal 2000. See Table 11.

The Mark's Division accounted for $10.1 million ($8.8 million in staff, advertising and occupancy) or 67.3% of the increase in front-line expenses and generated the sales and gross margin dollar increases to justify the investment.

The DOCKERS® Stores Division accounted for $3.0 million of the increase in front-line expenses in fiscal 2001 over fiscal 2000 ($2.2 million in occupancy and depreciation and amortization) as it grew from five part-year stores in fiscal 2000 to five full-year stores and three part-year stores in fiscal 2001.

GROSS MARGIN RATE Table 6

	52 weeks ended January 30, 1999	52 weeks ended January 29, 2000	52 weeks ended January 27, 2001	Fiscal 2001 Improvement/ (Deterioration) Over Fiscal 2000
Purchase markup	49.9%	51.2%	52.7%	1.5%
Freight	(2.0%)	(2.3%)	(2.4%)	(0.1%)
	47.9%	48.9%	50.3%	1.4%
Markdowns and customer adjustments	(6.3%)	(7.2%)	(7.9%)	(0.7%)
Shrink	(0.9%)	(0.6%)	(0.8%)	(0.2%)
Other	(0.4%)	(0.5%)	(0.5%)	0.0%
	40.3%	40.6%	41.1%	0.5%

CONSOLIDATED FRONT-LINE EXPENSES Table 7

	52 weeks Ended January 30,1999 ($000s)	52 weeks ended January 29, 2000 ($000s)	(%) of Corporate Store Sales	Per Corporate Store Avg. Retail sq.ft. ($)	52 weeks ended January 27, 2001 ($000s)	(%) of Corporate Store Sales	Per Corporate Store Avg. Retail sq.ft. ($)	Fiscal 2001 Increase/(Decrease) Over Fiscal 2000 ($000s)	(%)
Staff	25,430	29,602	9.4	22.83	35,398	9.8	25.15	5,796	19.6
Advertising	14,502	14,619	4.6	11.27	16,612	4.6	11.80	1,993	13.6
Occupancy	25,868	31,094	9.9	23.98	35,738	9.8	25.39	4,644	14.9
Other	11,937	13,051	4.2	10.06	15,356	4.2	10.91	2,305	17.7
Depreciation and amortization	5,350	6,231	2.0	4.81	6,664	1.8	4.74	433	6.9
Interest short-term	2,015	1,610	0.5	1.24	1,480	0.4	1.05	(130)	(8.1)
	85,102	96,207	30.6	74.19	111,248	30.6	79.04	15,041	15.6

Management's Discussion and Analysis

The Work World Division accounted for $1.9 million of the increase in front-line expenses in fiscal 2001 over fiscal 2000 ($1.6 million in occupancy and staff) as it grew from 45 corporate stores at the end of fiscal 2000 to 54 corporate stores by the end of fiscal 2001.

FRANCHISE OPERATIONS

Table 8 summarizes the Company's assessment of the contribution it receives from its franchise activities.

During fiscal 2001, the Mark's franchise operations posted a sales increase of $2.4 million or 3.8% over fiscal 2000. Same store sales increased by $6.6 million or 12.5%. The same store sales increase number is larger because during fiscal 2001 four Mark's Division franchise stores were converted to corporate stores. Table 8 shows a franchise contribution after cost allocations of $1.1 million by the Mark's franchisees, a $473,000 or 75% improvement over fiscal 2000. This large improvement was attributable mainly to the recovery of bad debt provisions in fiscal 2001. The Mark's Division franchise operations sales continued to decrease as a percentage of total system sales in the Mark's

Division. They represented 17.0% of the division's corporate and franchise store sales combined in fiscal 2001 (fiscal 2000 18.3%; fiscal 1999 18.8%). The Mark's Division franchise operation is very stable and is expected to shrink a little over time with the occasional franchisee selling his or her store back to the Company. The number of Mark's Division franchise stores repurchased was larger than normal in fiscal 2001, as three franchisees decided to retire.

During fiscal 2001, the Work World Division franchise operations posted a sales decrease of $1.4 million or 2.4%. Same store sales increased by $4.0 million or 7.8%. On a same store basis, there was an increase rather than a decrease primarily because during the course of fiscal 2001 six Work World Division franchise stores were converted to corporate stores and six Work World franchise stores were closed. Table 8 shows a franchise contribution after cost allocations but before acquisition financing costs and goodwill amortization of $358,000 in fiscal 2001, down $74,000 or 17.1% from the $432,000 contribution in fiscal 2000. This decrease was attributable to larger reductions in revenues than in allocated expenses.

FRANCHISE CONTRIBUTION Table 8

(thousands, except for number of stores)	52 weeks ended January 30, 1999		52 weeks ended January 29, 2000		52 weeks ended January 27, 2001		Fiscal 2001 Increase/(Decrease) Over Fiscal 2000	
Mark's franchise operations								
Number of stores at end of year		29		29		25	$ (4)	(13.8%)
Franchise sales	$	61,801	$	63,340	$	65,754	$ 2,414	3.8%
Franchise royalties and other income	$	3,985	$	4,075	$	4,129	$ 54	1.3%
Expenses allocated to franchise operations*	$	3,176	$	3,444	$	3,025	$ (419)	(12.2%)
Contribution by Mark's franchise operations	$	809	$	631	$	1,104	$ 473	75.0%
Work World franchise operations								
Number of stores at end of year		105		102		90	(12)	(11.8%)
Franchise sales	$	72,266***	$	59,783***	$	58,355	$ (1,428)	(2.4%)
Franchise royalties and other income	$	3,031***	$	2,565***	$	2,429	$ (136)	(5.3%)
Expenses allocated to franchise operations**	$	3,244***	$	2,133***	$	2,071	$ (62)	(2.9%)
Contribution by Work World franchise operations before other expenses	$	(213)	$	432	$	358	$ (74)	(17.1%)
Other expenses:								
Acquisition financing costs	$	365	$	260	$	171	$ (89)	(34.2%)
Goodwill amortization	$	211	$	211	$	211	—	—
	$	576	$	471	$	382	$ (89)	(18.9%)
Contribution by Work World franchise operations	$	(789)	$	(39)	$	(24)	$ 15	38.5%
Total franchise operations	$	20	$	592	$	1,080	$ 488	82.4%

*   Mark's Division and Corporate services back-line costs are allocated to Mark's Division franchise operations based on Mark's Division franchise sales as a percentage of Mark's Division total system sales applied to Mark's Division and Corporate Services back-line costs net of cost recoveries and excluding those costs deemed not applicable to the Mark's Division franchise operations. All franchise bad debt provisions (recoveries) applicable to the Mark's Division franchises are also included. The cost of two district managers is assumed for front-line costs related to the operation of the Mark's Division franchise stores. Prior years' Mark's Division and Corporate Services back-line costs charged to franchises were restated to conform to fiscal 2001 calculations.

**   Work World Division back-line costs excluding those costs deemed not applicable to Work World franchise operations are allocated to Work World Division franchise operations based on Work World franchise sales as a percentage of total system sales for the Work World Division. All franchise bad debt provisions (recoveries) applicable to the Work World Division franchises are also included. Prior years' Work World back-line costs charged to franchises were restated to conform to fiscal 2001 calculations.

*** Thirty-one Work World franchise stores were converted to corporate stores in the latter part of fiscal 1999.

BACK-LINE EXPENSES

Table 9 shows that in fiscal 2001 back-line expenses in total increased by $2.2 million or 8.5% from fiscal 2000 amounts.

The Mark's Division and Corporate Services operations account for most of the increase as their combined back-line staff increased by $2.0 million of which $1.1 million related to formula bonus amounts, $0.4 million to increases in benefit costs and the remainder for normal annual staff adjustments and additional technical staff to support the Company's Web activities, additional marketing staff to support increased marketing activities and additional accounting, systems and human resources staff to provide the required level of back-line services to the Work World and DOCKERS® Stores Divisions as they increase in size.

Depreciation and amortization expenses on computer capital leases increased by $0.3 million over a year ago ($0.2 million in the Work World Division, $0.1 million in the Mark's Division and Corporate Services operations) as a result of the $1.9 million of additions at cost of computer

equipment and operating software under capital leases in fiscal 2001 over fiscal 2000.

Interest long-term increased by $0.2 million over the prior year as a result of the $2.5 million net increase in interest-bearing long-term debt in fiscal 2001 over fiscal 2000. See Note 10 to the Consolidated Financial Statements and Table 16 "Long-Term Debt".

In fiscal 2001, due to the good franchise receivable collection results produced by the Company's franchise department and the decrease in the number of franchise stores, franchise bad debt provisions were reduced by $0.6 million (Mark's Division $0.4 million, Work World Division $0.2 million).

In fiscal 2001, consolidated back-line expenses excluding interest long-term and depreciation and amortization were $21.6 million, $1.8 million (9.1%) over last year's $19.8 million and have remained as a similar percentage of total system sales over the last three years: January 27, 2001 at 4.4% (January 29, 2000 4.5%; January 30, 1999 4.3%).

CONSOLIDATED BACK-LINE EXPENSES Table 9

	52 weeks ended January 30, 1999 ($000s)	52 weeks ended January 29, 2000 ($000s)	52 weeks ended January 29, 2000 (%) of Corporate & Franchise Sales	52 weeks ended January 27, 2001 ($000s)	52 weeks ended January 27, 2001 (%) of Corporate & Franchise Sales	Fiscal 2001 Increase/(Decrease) Over Fiscal 2000 ($000s)	Fiscal 2001 Increase/(Decrease) Over Fiscal 2000 (%)
Staff	10,394	12,458	2.8	14,763	3.0	2,305	18.5
Occupancy	998	1,015	0.2	1,038	0.2	23	2.3
Other	4,730	4,132	0.9	3,981	0.8	(151)	(3.7)
Computer services							
Services	571	687	0.2	854	0.2	167	24.3
Depreciation and amortization	2,050	2,751	0.6	3,061	0.6	310	11.3
Interest – long-term	659	668	0.2	609	0.1	(59)	(8.8)
Software development and maintenance costs	906	1,201	0.3	1,238	0.3	37	3.1
Depreciation and amortization	661	621	0.1	563	0.1	(58)	(9.3)
Interest – long-term	691	1,739	0.4	1,889	0.4	150	8.6
Franchise bad debt provisions	219	300	0.1	(251)	(0.0)	(551)	(100.0+)
Total back-line expenses	21,879	25,572	5.8	27,745	5.7	2,173	8.5

MANAGEMENT'S DISCUSSION AND ANALYSIS

Management's Discussion and Analysis

CONSOLIDATED EBITDA

Table 10 shows the pre-tax earnings before interest, depreciation and amortization (EBITDA) increased from $26.3 million a year ago to $31.3 million in fiscal 2001, an increase of 19.1%.

The Mark's Division posted a year-over-year growth in EBITDA of $4.1 million or 11.5% based on strong increases in sales and gross margin dollars in fiscal 2001 over fiscal 2000. The Work World Division posted a year-over-year improvement in EBITDA of $1.0 million as the front-line contribution from the division's corporate stores improved by $1.0 million. Corporate Services EBITDA also improved by $0.4 million.

The DOCKERS® Stores Division posted a decrease in year-over-year EBITDA of $0.6 million or 26.0% as it operated five full-year test stores and three part-year test stores in fiscal 2001 compared to five part-year test stores in fiscal 2000. As noted in the "Sales Analysis" section above, no additional stores are planned to be added in fiscal 2002 as this division will use fiscal 2002 to work

on improving merchandise assortments, delivering sharper price points to its customers on the commodities that require it and improving supplier replenishment.

CONSOLIDATED PRE-TAX EARNINGS BEFORE GOODWILL AMORTIZATION

The combination of the $21.7 million increase in gross margin dollars, $15.0 million increase in front-line expenses, $0.1 million decrease in franchise royalties and other and $2.2 million increase in back-line expenses produced pre-tax earnings before goodwill amortization in fiscal 2001 of $17.1 million, which is $4.4 million or 34.6% higher than the prior year. The Company's pre-tax earnings before goodwill amortization margin on corporate store sales improved from 4.0% in fiscal 1999 and 2000 to 4.7% in fiscal 2001.

Table 11, a three-year operations table, and Table 12, a three-year front-line operations table by division, allow readers to review the Company's performance by season and by division.

Graph 12 allows readers to view how the Company's sales are distributed by region of Canada.

5-YEAR PRE-TAX INCOME AFTER GOODWILL AMORTIZATION (GRAPH 11)

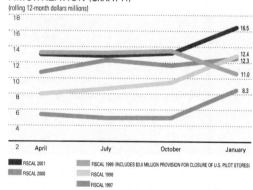

4-YEAR TOTAL SYSTEM SALES PER REGION (GRAPH 12)

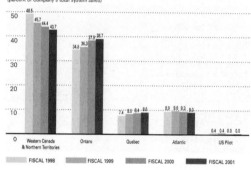

CONSOLIDATED EARNINGS BEFORE INTEREST, INCOME TAXES, DEPRECIATION AND AMORTIZATION (EBITDA) Table 10

	52 weeks ended January 30, 1999	52 weeks ended January 29, 2000	52 weeks ended January 27, 2001	Fiscal 2001 Increase/(Decrease) Over Fiscal 2000	
	($000s)	($000s)	($000s)	($000s)	(%)
Mark's Division	34,026	35,796	39,912	4,116	11.5
Work World Division	510	43	1,088	1,045	100.0+
DOCKERS® Stores Division	—	(2,116)	(2,666)	(550)	(26.0)
Corporate Services	(7,922)	(7,418)	(6,994)	424	5.7
Mark's U.S. Division	(3,876)*	—	—	—	—
	22,738	26,305	31,340	5,035	19.1
EBITDA as percentage of consolidated total systems sales	5.4%	6.0%	6.4%		
EBITDA as percentage of consolidated corporate store sales	8.0%	8.4%	8.6%		

* Mark's U.S. Division includes $2,961,000 of closure costs in fiscal 1999

THREE-YEAR OPERATIONS Table 11

(dollar amounts in thousands, except sales per retail square foot and gross margin return on space)

	52 Weeks Ended January 30, 1999			52 Weeks Ended January 29, 2000			52 Weeks Ended January 27, 2001		
	Spring	Fall	Total	Spring	Fall	Total	Spring	Fall	Total
Consolidated Statement of Earnings									
Corporate and franchise sales	$ 152,711	$ 264,757	$ 417,468	$ 167,338	$ 270,332	$ 437,670	$ 188,826	$ 299,153	$ 487,979
Corporate sales	$ 100,105	$ 183,296	$ 283,401	$ 119,971	$ 194,576	$ 314,547	$ 139,219	$ 224,651	$ 363,870
Gross margin (%)	40.4	40.3	40.3	40.8	40.5	40.6	41.2	41.0	41.1
Front-line expenses	$ 35,975	$ 49,127	$ 85,102	$ 43,269	$ 52,938	$ 96,207	$ 49,664	$ 61,584	$ 111,248
Front-line contribution	$ 4,463	$ 24,673	$ 29,136	$ 5,738	$ 25,879	$ 31,617	$ 7,744	$ 30,517	$ 38,261
Front-line contribution (%)	4.5	13.5	10.3	4.8	13.3	10.1	5.6	13.6	10.5
Franchise royalties and other	$ 2,717	$ 4,299	$ 7,016	$ 2,535	$ 4,105	$ 6,640	$ 2,626	$ 3,932	$ 6,558
Back-line expenses including goodwill amortization	$ 10,863	$ 11,332	$ 22,195	$ 10,853	$ 15,094	$ 25,947	$ 12,441	$ 15,852	$ 28,293
Provision for closure of Mark's U.S. pilot stores	—	$ 2,961	$ 2,961	—	—	—			
Pre-tax earnings (loss)	$ (3,683)	$ 14,679	$ 10,996	$ (2,580)	$ 14,890	$ 12,310	$ (2,071)	$ 18,597	$ 16,526
Mark's corporate stores									
Open at start of period	114	115	114	122	125	122	127	128	127
Opened	1	6	7	3	3	6	—	2	2
Franchise purchases	1	1	2	—	—	—	2	2	4
Closed	(1)	—	(1)	—	(1)	(1)	(1)	—	(1)
Open at end of period	115	122	122	125	127	127	128	132	132
Mark's U.S. corporate stores									
Open at end of period	1	2	2	1	—	—	—	—	—
Work World corporate stores									
Open at end of period	10	41	41	41	45	45	52	54	54
DOCKERS® corporate stores									
Open at end of period	—	—	—	—	5	5	7	8	8
Franchise stores									
Open at end of period									
Mark's	30	29	29	29	29	29	27	25	25
Work World	129	105	105	105	102	102	95	90	90
Corporate stores sales per sales area (sq. ft.)*									
Consolidated*****	$ 95	$ 156	$ 251	$ 94	$ 143	$ 237	$ 101	$ 154	$ 255
Mark's Division	$ 95	$ 157	$ 252	$ 95	$ 144	$ 239	$ 102	$ 157	$ 259
Work World***	—	—	—	$ 86	$ 131	$ 217	$ 87	$ 134	$ 221
DOCKERS® Stores Division****	—	—	—	—	—	—	$ 157	$ 176	$ 333
Corporate operations inventory turns (times)									
Consolidated*****	0.7	1.1	1.8	0.8	1.0	1.8	0.8	1.2	2.0
Mark's Division	0.8	1.1	1.9	0.8	1.2	2.0	0.9	1.2	2.1
Work World Division	0.4	0.7	1.1	0.4	0.6	1.0	0.5	0.7	1.2
DOCKERS® Stores Division	—	—	—	—	0.7	0.7	0.9	0.9	1.8
Mark's U.S. Division	0.4	0.6	1.0						
Operating line**									
highest usage	$ 30,491	$ 44,277	$ 44,277	$ 25,260	$ 32,921	$ 32,921	$ 25,011	$ 35,768	$ 35,768
lowest usage	$ 842	$ 0	$ 0	$ 0	$ 0	$ 0	$ 0	$ 0	$ 0
Mark's corporate stores total sales area (sq. ft.)									
Stores open at beginning of year			1,019,244			1,111,985			1,195,053
Opened/expanded/purchased			98,806			85,984			64,460
from franchisees			(6,065)			(2,916)			(7,300)
Closed/downsized									
Stores open at end of year			1,111,985			1,195,053			1,252,213
Mark's U.S. corporate stores									
total sales area (sq. ft) at end of year			13,282			—			—
Work World corporate stores									
total sales area (sq. ft.)									
Stores open at beginning of year			5,929			131,210			142,979
Opened/expanded/purchased			125,281			20,705			29,646
from franchisees			—			(8,936)			(2,850)
Closed/downsized									
Stores open at end of year			131,210			142,979			169,775
DOCKERS® corporate stores									
total sales area (sq. ft.) end of year			—			16,529			27,337
Gross margin return on investment (times)									
Mark's Division			1.5			1.6			1.8
Work World Division			1.1			0.9			0.9
DOCKERS® Stores Division****			—			0.3			1.5
Gross margin return on space ($ per sq.ft.)									
Mark's Division		$ 101.8			$ 101.1			$ 108.8	
Work World Division		$ 75.8			$ 78.7			$ 87.6	
DOCKERS® Stores Division****		—			—			$ 122.7	

*   Calculated on stores open and at the same store size for an entire season. The Company breaks the year down into two seasons: Spring – February through July; Fall – August through January.

**   Excludes outstanding letters of credit, which had a highest outstanding amount in fiscal 2001 of $11,049,000 in July 2000 (in fiscal 2000 $8,978,000 in January 2000; in fiscal 1999 $8,787,000 in June 1998).

***   All Work World corporate stores are part-year stores in fiscal 1999 and thus no sales per square foot have been calculated.

****   All DOCKERS® Stores were part-year stores in fiscal 2000 and thus no sales per square foot have been calculated. As well, no gross margin return on space for DOCKERS® Stores Division was calculated in fiscal 2000, as the division only opened its initial stores in the fall of fiscal 2000.

***** Includes U.S. pilot stores in fiscal 1999.

Management's Discussion and Analysis

THREE-YEAR FRONT-LINE OPERATIONS BY DIVISION Table 12

(dollar amounts in thousands, except sales per resident and sales per retail sq. ft.)	Mark's	Mark's U.S. Pilot	Work World*	DOCKERS® Stores	Total
Sales – total system**					
Fiscal 2001	$ 385,677	N/A	$ 94,532	$ 7,770	$ 487,979
Fiscal 2000	$ 345,803	N/A	$ 89,201	$ 2,666	$ 437,670
Fiscal 1999	$ 328,937	$ 1,665	$ 86,866	N/A	$ 417,468
Total systems sales per resident***					
Fiscal 2001	$ 12.54	N/A	$ 3.08	$ 0.25	$ 15.87
Fiscal 2000	$ 11.34	N/A	$ 2.92	0.09	$ 14.35
Fiscal 1999	$ 10.88	N/A	$ 2.87	N/A	$ 13.75
Sales – corporate stores**					
Fiscal 2001	$ 319,923	N/A	$ 36,177	$ 7,770	$ 363,870
Fiscal 2000	$ 282,463	N/A	$ 29,418	$ 2,666	$ 314,547
Fiscal 1999	$ 267,136	$ 1,665	$ 14,600	N/A	$ 283,401
Corporate store sales per retail sq. ft.*					
Fiscal 2001	$ 259	N/A	$ 221	$ 333	$ 255
Fiscal 2000	$ 239	N/A	$ 217	N/A	$ 237
Fiscal 1999	$ 252	$ 108	N/A	N/A	$ 251
Sales – franchise stores					
Fiscal 2001	$ 65,754	N/A	$ 58,355	N/A	$ 124,109
Fiscal 2000	$ 63,340	N/A	$ 59,783	N/A	$ 123,123
Fiscal 1999	$ 61,801	N/A	$ 72,266	N/A	$ 134,067
Front-line contribution					
Fiscal 2001	12.8%	N/A	(1.3%)	(28.2%)	10.5%
Fiscal 2000	12.2%	N/A	(5.1%)	(52.7%)	10.1%
Fiscal 1999	10.9%	(40.0%)	4.0%	N/A	10.3%
Franchise royalties and other					
Fiscal 2001	$ 4,129	N/A	$ 2,429	N/A	$ 6,558
Fiscal 2000	$ 4,075	N/A	$ 2,565	N/A	$ 6,640
Fiscal 1999	$ 3,985	N/A	$ 3,031	N/A	$ 7,016
Net front-line contribution from operations					
Fiscal 2001	$ 45,035	N/A	$ 1,976	$ (2,192)	$ 44,819
Fiscal 2000	$ 38,585	N/A	$ 1,076	$ (1,404)	$ 38,257
Fiscal 1999	$ 33,208	$ (668)	$ 3,612	N/A	$ 36,152
Inventory turnover (times)***					
Fiscal 2001	2.1	N/A	1.2	1.8	2.0
Fiscal 2000	2.0	N/A	1.0	0.7	1.8
Fiscal 1999	1.9	1.0	1.1	N/A	1.8
Number of stores at end of year Corporate/Franchise					
Fiscal 2001	132/25	0/0	54/90	8/0	194/115
Fiscal 2000	127/29	0/0	45/102	5/0	177/131
Fiscal 1999	122/29	2/0	41/105	N/A	165/134

N/A   Not applicable.
*   In fiscal 1999, the 31 franchise stores acquired including the 19 from Paul John Enterprises Ltd. appear as franchise stores until their respective purchase dates and as corporate stores thereafter.
**   Excludes inter-group sales.
***   Calculated on stores open and at the same store size for an entire season. The Company breaks the year down into two seasons: Spring – February through July; Fall – August through January.
**** Calculation based on the compilation of regional data plus inventory in the Company's corporate distribution centre. Distribution centre inventories held by Mark's and Work World Divisions contain some amounts intended for their respective franchise stores.
***** Population data obtained from Statistics Canada.

CONSOLIDATED BALANCE SHEETS

The Company's consolidated balance sheets show that the Company's total assets as at January 27, 2001 are up $14.0 million or 9.8% over January 29, 2000. The main increases in asset accounts as at January 27, 2001 over January 29, 2000 are in cash, merchandise inventories, prepaid expenses and supplies (in other current assets) capital assets and goodwill. The increase in cash from a year ago, which is primarily due to reduced investment in non-cash working capital and improved funds provided by operations, is discussed in more detail later on under the heading "Consolidated Statements of Cash Flows".

Most of the $3.0 million or 3.7% increase in merchandise inventories as reflected in Table 13 is the result of $2.6 million of additional inventory for the nine incremental corporate stores in the Work World Division and $1.1 million of additional inventory for the three incremental corporate stores and some increased assortments in the DOCKERS® Stores Division both offset slightly by the $0.7 million decrease in inventory in the Mark's Division.

CONSOLIDATED 5-YEAR INVENTORY TURNS (GRAPH 13)
(dollars millions & retail square feet in thousands)

	FISCAL 1997	FISCAL 1998	FISCAL 1999	FISCAL 2000	FISCAL 2001
	2.3 TURNS	2.2 TURNS	1.8 TURNS	1.8 TURNS	2.0 TURNS

■ RETAIL SQ. FT. AT YEAR END   ■ CORPORATE STORE SALES   ■ AVG. INV. @ RETAIL

CONSOLIDATED MERCHANDISE INVENTORIES Table 13

	As at January 30, 1999	As at January 29, 2000	As at January 27, 2001	Fiscal 2001 Increase/(Decrease) Over Fiscal 2000	
	($000s)	($000s)	($000s)	($000s)	(%)
Mark's Division	62,773	66,499	65,773	(726)	(1.1%)
Work World Division	13,455	13,847	16,510	2,663	19.2%
DOCKERS® Stores Division	—	1,122	2,200	1,078	96.1%
Mark's U.S. Division	754	—	—	—	—
	76,982	81,468	84,483	3,015	3.7%

Management's Discussion and Analysis

Table 14 highlights that, on a consolidated basis in fiscal 2001, year-end inventory per retail square foot and average inventory per average retail square foot were reduced or improved by 3.1% and 1.6% respectively, and consolidated inventory turnover was also improved by 8.2% while average retail square feet and year-end retail square feet grew by 8.6% and 7.0% respectively from fiscal 2000 levels.

As the Company has stated in previous annual reports, while it will continue to monitor inventory turnover and exert effort to improve in this area, it will do so carefully because today's consumers, subject to increasing time pressures, expect that stores, particularly destination stores (Mark's Division concept) will always be "in stock" for them whenever they find the time to shop.

Other current assets detailed in Note 5 to the Consolidated Financial Statements show that the $1.7 million increase in other current assets in fiscal 2001 over fiscal 2000 is a result of the increase in prepaid expenses and supplies. The increased prepaid expenses and supplies consist of increased prepaid advertising and pre-made fixtures for some of the Company's spring 2001 advertising and store construction activities.

Table 15 illustrates that the $2.3 million or 8.7% increase in the Company's capital assets at January 27, 2001 compared to January 29, 2000 is the result of the Company's continuing "On Concept" store program in its Mark's Division, the continuation of the "Corporate Store Strategy" in the Work World Division, the opening of

MERCHANDISE INVENTORIES PER RETAIL SQUARE FOOT Table 14

	Fiscal 1999	Fiscal 2000	Fiscal 2001	Fiscal 2001 Increase/(Decrease) Over Fiscal 2000
				%
Consolidated*				
Inventory at cost per retail sq. ft. at year end (includes warehouse inventory)**	$ 61.27	$ 60.14	$ 58.29	(3.1)
Average inventory at cost per avg. retail sq. ft. throughout the year (includes warehouse inventory)**	$ 72.90	$ 68.43	$ 67.35	(1.6)
Inventory turnover (times)	1.82	1.83	1.98	8.2
Weighted average retail sq. ft. throughout the year	1,116,934	1,296,643	1,407,461	8.6
Year-end retail sq. ft.	1,256,477	1,354,561	1,449,325	7.0

* Includes Mark's U.S. pilot stores in fiscal 1999.
** Warehouse inventories held by the Mark's and Work World Divisions contain some amounts intended for their respective franchise stores.

CAPITAL ASSETS Table 15

	Fiscal 1999 ($000s)	Fiscal 2000 ($000s)	Fiscal 2001 ($000s)
Opening capital assets	20,072	23,531	25,893
Mark's Division store "On Concept" and other additions			
Cash	2,371	127	1,383
Capital leases	3,790	4,464	4,759
Work World Division "Corporate Store Strategy" and other additions			
Cash	812	277	383
Capital leases	429	645	862
DOCKERS® Stores Division "Corporate Stores"			
Cash	—	1,511	719
Capital Leases	—	707	465
Computer system capital lease additions	2,750	3,423	2,579
Paul John acquisition – 19 Work World stores	781	—	—
Franchise purchases – Mark's and Work World Divisions	510	3	565
	31,515	34,688	37,608
Provision for closure of Mark's U.S. pilot stores	(797)	—	—
Disposition of capital assets	160	73	(36)
	30,878	34,761	37,572
Depreciation net of sale leaseback transactions	(7,347)	(8,868)	(9,424)
Closing capital assets	23,531	25,893	28,148

three more stores for the DOCKERS® Stores Division test and the required continuing investment in systems for all divisions and for Corporate Services. Details can also be found in Note 7 to the Consolidated Financial Statements.

The 3.4 million or 30.7% increase in the net book value of goodwill at January 27, 2001 compared to January 29, 2000 is the result of the addition of $3.6 million of goodwill on the purchase of four Mark's Division franchise stores and the addition of $0.3 million of goodwill on the purchase of four of the six Work World Division franchises purchased in fiscal 2001 less $0.5 million of goodwill amortization during fiscal 2001. See Notes 3 and 8 to the Consolidated Financial Statements.

The $1.0 million (6.7%) decline in accounts receivable in fiscal 2001 from fiscal 2000 is due primarily to the $2.4 million decrease in accounts receivable from franchise stores offset by the $1.3 million increase in receivables from the Mark's Division's growing business accounts sales as summarized in Note 4 to the Consolidated Financial Statements.

On the liability side of the balance sheet, most of the $8.8 million or 10.6% increase in total liabilities is a result of the $4.6 million 13.9% increase in long-term debt (current and long-term portion combined) and the $3.9 million increase in income taxes payable. The increase in

income taxes payable is the result of increased third and fourth quarter earnings in fiscal 2001 over fiscal 2000 as summarized in Note 20 to the Consolidated Financial Statements. The increase in long-term debt (current and long-term portion combined) is summarized in Table 16 and Note 10 to the Consolidated Financial Statements.

Table 16 shows that in fiscal 2001, the Company obtained $8.7 million of new capital lease financing to finance 77.7% of its store construction, computer system additions and miscellaneous capital expenditures, made $9.8 million of capital lease and long-term debt repayments and financed 94.2% of its purchase cost of franchise stores (net of liabilities assumed) by drawing down $2.7 million of its syndicated term debt facility and setting up $3.0 million of term debt due to the vendors of the franchise stores over time.

Capital stock decreased by $1.5 million in fiscal 2001 from fiscal 2000 because during fiscal 2001, pursuant to its Normal Course Issuer Bid, the Company purchased for cancellation 1,379,348 Common Shares of the Company for a total consideration of $3,102,000 of which $1,559,000 was charged to capital stock and $1,543,000 was charged to retained earnings. See Note 12 to the Consolidated Financial Statements.

LONG-TERM DEBT (CURRENT AND LONG-TERM) Table 16

	Fiscal 1999 ($000s)	Fiscal 2000 ($000s)	Fiscal 2001 ($000s)
Opening long-term debt (current and long-term)	17,848	30,044	33,280
Store financing (mostly capital leases)			
Mark's Division	3,790	4,464	4,759
Work World Division	429	645	862
DOCKERS® Stores Division	—	707	465
Computer system capital lease financing	2,750	3,423	2,579
Landlord leasehold loans	259	—	—
Leaseholds, fixtures and equipment loan for DOCKERS® test	—	1,000	—
Syndicated bank term loan	5,000	—	—
Syndicated bank term loan for acquisitions and franchise store purchases			
Paul John acquisition purchase price portion	2,250	737	—
Paul John acquisition working capital portion	2,750	(737)	—
Purchases of franchise stores	—	—	2,700
Paul John acquisition – estimated future earnout	—	2,000	—
Long-term debt due to vendors on purchase of individual franchise stores	—	—	3,060
	35,076	42,283	47,705
Principal repayments and capital lease payments	(5,032)	(9,003)	(9,784)
Closing long-term debt (current and long-term)	30,044	33,280	37,921
Current portion	7,992	9,328	10,905
Long-term portion	22,052	23,952	27,016
	30,044	33,280	37,921

Management's Discussion and Analysis

During fiscal 2001, the Company's **$8.2 million** in net earnings (an increase of **$1.8 million** or 28.1% over fiscal 2000 net earnings), less the **$3.1 million** spent on purchasing Company shares for cancellation plus the **$0.1 million** of new share issuance resulted in a **$5.2 million** or 8.6% increase in total equity over fiscal 2000 levels. However, this increase in total equity in fiscal 2001 was **$3.6 million** less than the **$8.8 million** increase in total debt over fiscal 2000 levels. Thus the Company's total liabilities-to-equity ratio at January 27, 2001 is 1.43-to-1 compared to 1.40-to-1 at January 29, 2000 but still better than the 1.49-to-1 at January 30, 1999. Also, this total liabilities-to-equity ratio is still well below the Company's goal of not exceeding 1.75-to-1 at the Company's fiscal year end. In fact, due to improved earnings in fiscal 2001 over fiscal 2000 during the course of the year and reduced average bank indebtedness outstanding during fiscal 2001 compared to fiscal 2000, the Company's 12-month moving average funded debt-to-equity ratio improved to 0.84-to-1 at January 27, 2001 (0.94-to-1 at January 29, 2000; 0.92-to-1 at January 30, 1999) and meets the Company's goal of not exceeding 1.0-to-1.0. See Graph 15 and Financial Goals.

Should the Company achieve its optimistic forecast in fiscal 2002, its 12-month moving average funded debt-to-equity should come in at 1-to-1 and continue to meet the Company's goal. See Financial Goals.

The Company's working capital position also remains healthy with a current ratio at January 27, 2001 of 1.75-to-1 compared to 1.77-to-1 at January 29, 2000 and 1.70-to-1 at January 30, 1999 and meets the Company's goal of not being less than 1.50-to-1 at the Company's fiscal year end. See Financial Goals.

CONSOLIDATED STATEMENTS OF CASH FLOWS

During the year ended January 27, 2001 the Company generated **$18.9 million** in funds flow from operations compared to **$16.9 million** in the prior year, representing an increase of **$2.0 million** or 11.8% over the prior year. The improvement in funds from operations is primarily attributable to improved net earnings and increased depreciation and amortization in fiscal 2001 over fiscal 2000. The changes in non-cash working capital (net of the effect of the purchase of franchise stores and the acquisition of subsidiaries in the prior year) improved significantly from a **$6.6 million** deployment of funds in fiscal 2000 to a **$2.3 million** generation of funds in fiscal 2001, an improvement of **$8.9 million**. This improvement was the result of reduced accounts receivable that generated funds, virtually no ($0.1 million) investment in merchandise inventories in fiscal 2001 compared to **$4.4 million** in fiscal 2000 and increased income taxes payable in fiscal 2001 which provided a **$3.9 million** generation of funds compared to a **$2.7 million** deployment of funds in fiscal 2000. These improvements were partially offset by the **$1.4 million** year-over-year increase in investment in other current assets and the **$1.2 million** pay down of accounts payable and accrued liabilities in fiscal 2001 compared to the **$2.2 million** increase in fiscal 2000.

The above resulted in a net inflow of funds from operations of **$21.1 million**, an increase of **$10.8 million** or 104.9% over the prior year's net inflow of **$10.3 million**. The Company then sourced **$14.5 million** of funds through **$5.8 million** of long-term debt ($3.1 million non-cash) and **$8.7 million** of capital lease financing (all non-cash for statement of cash flow

5-YEAR CAPITAL STRUCTURE (GRAPH 14)
(dollars millions)

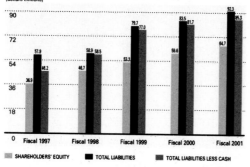

SHAREHOLDERS' EQUITY   TOTAL LIABILITIES   TOTAL LIABILITIES LESS CASH

5-YEAR FUNDED DEBT TO EQUITY TO JANUARY 27, 2001 (GRAPH 15)
(12 month moving average, dollars in millions)

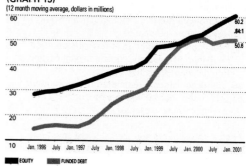

EQUITY   FUNDED DEBT

purposes) to fund the $11.2 million of expenditures on capital assets ($8.7 million non-cash capital leases) and the $6.1 million ($3.1 million non-cash) net of liabilities assumed for the purchase of 10 franchise stores in fiscal 2001. The non-financed $2.8 million of capital investments ($11.2 million plus $6.1 million less $14.5 million) was funded from funds flow from operations. The residual $18.3 million ($21.1 million less $2.8 million used above) net inflow of funds from operations and the $0.1 million generated from the issuance of share capital were used to make $9.8 million of capital lease and long-term debt repayments, to invest $0.3 million in other assets, and to buy back $3.1 million of share capital for cancellation. The net result is an increase in cash and cash equivalents of $5.2 million in fiscal 2001.

The above compares to a decrease in cash and cash equivalents of $0.9 million in fiscal 2000 when the Company obtained $13.3 million in cash and non-cash long-term debt financing, capital lease financing and deferred landlord inducements to cover the $2.7 million ($0.7 million purchase price adjustment and $2.0 million non-cash estimated future earnout) on the Paul John acquisition, $11.1 million in capital expenditures (including capital leases) and $0.1 million on the purchase of one franchise store. The resulting $0.6 million shortfall was funded from funds flow from operations. The residual $9.7 million ($10.3 million less $0.6 million) net inflow of funds from operations and the $0.1 million generated from the issuance of share capital were used to make $9.0 million of capital leases and long-term debt repayments, to invest $1.4 million in other assets, to buy back $0.2 million of share capital for cancellation and to cover the $0.1 million disposition of capital assets.

5-YEAR CASH FLOW TO JANUARY 27, 2001*
(GRAPH 16)
(dollars millions)

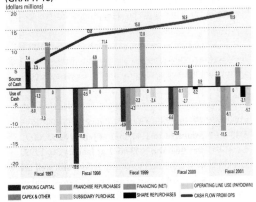

*Includes non-cash investing and financing activities

5-YEAR CASH FLOW FROM OPERATIONS AND CAPITAL EXPENDITURES INCLUDING CAPITAL LEASES*
(GRAPH 17)
(dollars millions)

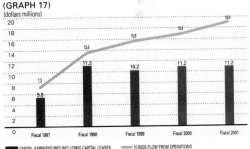

* Includes assumption of $5.3 million of computer capital lease debt in fiscal 1998 on termination of computer services outsourcing arrangements

MANAGEMENT'S DISCUSSION AND ANALYSIS

Management's Discussion and Analysis

RISK AND UNCERTAINTIES

Table 17 shows the external and internal risk factors that affect the Company's business, and ultimately its profitability.

Management's responsibility is to mitigate **external risk factors** to the extent possible, and to achieve an appropriate balance among the **internal risk factors**, in order to optimize profits.

The **consumer environment** in Canada as reflected by the growth in total retail sales and in specific segments within the total retail sector has been as outlined in Table 18 over the last five years.

As can be seen from Table 18, total men's wear sales have grown at a slower rate than the growth in total retail sales and sales in men's clothing stores have declined over the last five years. As well, total sales in women's clothing stores have grown at a slower rate than the growth in total retail sales and sales in shoe stores have declined.

Thus, recent economic slow-down concerns notwithstanding, Table 18 does not provide comfort that consumers will continue to purchase apparel at the rates they have historically. In fact, in recent years consumers have shown a marked preference for bigger-ticket items such as furniture, appliances, autos and electronics. The Company is confident that it has mitigated this risk in its Mark's Division by having developed a stable yet evolving product offering, "On Concept" stores, sound marketing programs and is currently growing its ladies' wear and Business-to-Business sales rapidly, and is developing its e-Commerce sales in order to continue growth in its Mark's Division by increasing its market share in the men's wear, ladies' wear and footwear markets in Canada. In addition, the Company introduced its "Corporate Store Strategy" in its Work World Division three years ago and with eight pilot stores is testing the DOCKERS® Stores concept. The addition of the Work World Division is also

RISK FACTORS Table 17

External	Internal
Consumer environment	Customer service
Competition	Sales blend
Seasonality	Marketing strategies
Weather	Store openings and closings
Merchandise sourcing	Expense rates in payroll, advertising, occupancy and systems
Foreign exchange rates	
Interest rates	Inventory levels
Unsolicited offer to purchase the Company's outstanding Common Shares	Capital expenditure investments in stores and systems
	Number and strength of franchise stores
Small cap company in current Canadian capital markets	"Corporate Store Strategy" in the Work World Division
	Liabilities-to-equity levels
Share trading information	The introduction of new divisions under new store banners, i.e., DOCKERS® Stores Division
	Foreign exchange exposure
	Interest rate exposure

RETAIL SALES GROWTH Table 18

	Percentage Increase/(Decrease) over Prior Period				
	Total Retail*	Men's Clothing Stores*	Total Men's wear**	Women's Clothing Stores*	Shoe Stores*
Year 2000 over Year 1999	6.3	0.1	3.8	2.7***	(0.4)
Year 1999 over Year 1998	5.8	(2.3)	2.9	1.9	(2.6)
Year 1998 over Year 1997	4.3	(0.2)	5.4	2.8	1.4
Year 1997 over Year 1996	7.3	3.0	3.3	3.6	(1.6)
Year 1996 over Year 1995	2.4	(6.1)	3.9	(1.8)	0.4
Year 2000 over Year 1995	31.3	(3.4)	15.4	12.6	(7.2)

*   Statistics Canada
**   Trendex North America (includes men's wear sales in department stores, men's clothing stores and discount stores)
*** Total sales growth in total ladies' wear which includes ladies' wear sales in department stores, women's clothing stores and discount stores was 1.2% in 2000 over 1999 according to Trendex North America.

contributing to the Company's growing market share in the segments of the retail trade in which it operates in Canada and should a DOCKERS® Stores roll out ever become a reality, that would provide a further vehicle to increase the Company's market share in Canada.

Competition in the men's wear apparel sector remains fierce as department stores, discount department stores, other discount stores, unisex stores, sporting goods stores and men's specialty stores battle for market share within this market sector. Many of these stores are large U.S.-based retailers. Some mergers and subsequent store consolidations are also occurring within the sector. Management feels that it has mitigated this risk by keeping the Company well-positioned in this market sector by continually developing and introducing new products to enhance product selection for its customers, by offering products across all price points and by offering its customers different geographic shopping locations through its three divisions (e.g., power centres, strip malls, regional malls, etc.). Clearly, the Company does not believe that it is isolated from the effects of this competition and it intends to continue to be rigorous in maintaining good relationships with its customers, protecting its businesses, generating new customers and continuing to test the introduction of new divisions with new store banners.

The Company's business remains very **seasonal** with the fourth quarter of the last three fiscal years continuing to produce between 37% and 39% of total system annual sales and most of the annual profits, resulting from the general increase in consumer spending in that period. The sales reporting and merchandise planning modules of the Company's information system assist the Company in mitigating the risk and uncertainties associated with seasonal programs, but cannot remove them completely, as inventory orders, especially for a significant portion of offshore commodities, must be placed well ahead of the season.

Five years ago, approximately 33% of the Company's Mark's Division (the Company's largest division) annual business was in seasonal commodities specifically related to winter weather. Today, the Company's Mark's Division does 20% of its annual business in seasonal commodities specifically related to winter weather and does 20% of its annual business in seasonal commodities specifically related to summer weather. While **weather dependency** cannot be totally disassociated from the Company's business, the Company's Mark's Division has clearly spread its winter risk between winter and summer over

the last five years. As the Work World Division matures, it will also follow this pattern. The DOCKERS® Stores Division is not a material part of the Company's sales at this time and because of the nature of its assortments it is less weather dependent.

In the area of **merchandise sourcing**, the Company has several sources of supply for most of its key commodities in order to be able to provide a continuous supply of quality products to its customers. While short-term interruptions could occur, the Company continues to work with both its domestic and foreign sources, to ensure that they have the ability and commitment to supply the Company so that customers' needs are met.

As part of its offshore sourcing practice, the Company advises its importers not to provide it with any goods produced in factories that use child labour or unacceptably paid or treated labour. For direct imports, the Company visits and inspects each factory it deals with to determine if the factory employs child or unacceptably paid or treated labour. The Company uses a comprehensive checklist during each inspection to ensure compliance with its ethical sourcing policies. Nevertheless, the Company cannot guarantee that such activities will not occur in the factories of the offshore suppliers with which it deals.

The Company is also a member of the Retail Council of Canada and the Retail Council's Executive Trade Committee and has adopted the voluntary code of ethical sourcing developed by the Retail Council. In addition, the Company's Corporate Code of Conduct prohibits any employee from accepting gifts, favours or trips other than a nominal amount from anyone with whom they deal on Company business.

The Company's **foreign currency** risk is generally limited to currency fluctuations between the Canadian and U.S. dollars, as most of the Company's offshore suppliers conduct business in U.S. dollars. The Company has no U.S. dollar revenues to use for the purchase of offshore commodities in U.S. dollars. The Company's practice is to enter into forward contracts for over 50% of its anticipated U.S. offshore purchases to help manage this risk. At January 27, 2001, the Company had foreign exchange collar arrangements in place for committed and anticipated foreign purchases during the Company's next fiscal year totaling $6,680,000 U.S. Under the terms of the collars, the Company bears the exchange risk on foreign purchases when the Canadian dollar trades against the U.S. dollar within the ranges and for the time periods listed in Note 13 to the Consolidated Financial

Management's Discussion and Analysis

Statements. At January 27, 2001, there were $102,204 of unrealized gains on the foreign exchange collars based on the January 27, 2001 exchange rate of $1.5063. See Notes lM and 13 to the Consolidated Financial Statements.

In addition, at January 27, 2001, the Company had foreign exchange fixed contract arrangements in place for committed and anticipated foreign merchandise purchases during the Company's next fiscal year totaling $14,064,500 U.S. Under the terms of the fixed contract arrangements, the Company has fixed its exchange risk on foreign purchases at an average Canadian dollar to the U.S. dollar rate of $1.4738 ($20,728,260 Cdn.). At January 27, 2001, the unrealized gains on these contracts were $456,866 based on a January 27, 2001 exchange rate of $1.5063. See Notes lM and 13 to the Consolidated Financial Statements.

In fiscal 2001, the Company purchased approximately 58% of its merchandise from Canadian manufacturers in Canadian dollars (Mark's Division 57%, Work World Division 65% and DOCKERS® Stores Division 60%).

The Company's **interest rate** risk is a result of its short-term floating rate debt requirements during part of every fiscal year. Interest rate swap contracts are used to hedge this interest rate risk on over 50% of the anticipated short-term floating rate debt requirements for the coming year. At January 27, 2001, the Company had fixed its borrowing rate on $20.0 million of its anticipated short-term borrowing requirements at a 7.295% all-in rate and on $14.5 million of its anticipated short-term borrowing requirements at an all-in rate of 6.965%. The mark-to-market value of the interest rate swap contracts is a $7,069 unrecorded gain at January 27, 2001 based on the Company's floating rate interest cost of 7.25% at January 27, 2001. See Notes 1M and 13 to the Consolidated Financial Statements.

Since the Company is a public company without a management control-share block, **unsolicited offers to purchase the Company's outstanding Common Shares** could appear from time to time, as happened during fiscal 1998. This possibility may have a higher probability currently, given that institutional investors seem to be **totally disinterested in investing in small cap stocks**, and given the earnings multiple at which the Company's shares are currently trading. See trading multiples at the end of this section. While management has processes in place to have the Company's Board of Directors and non-operations management deal with such matters should they arise, there is a risk that such activities could distract operations management to the point of affecting

performance and create expenses which, in combination, could cause the Company to fall short of its forecast range. See Forecast.

The **internal risk factors** are often tied together, and thus action taken to stimulate one factor often results in a negative effect on other factors:

- New store openings may increase sales, but, in the first year or two of operations of a new store, the increase in payroll costs, advertising costs, occupancy costs and interest costs may cause that store to contribute an operating loss, until it becomes a mature store from a sales per square foot perspective.
- Additional advertising campaigns may increase sales, but not sufficiently in the short term to cover the cost of the additional advertising.
- Staff reductions can lower payroll costs, but may cause a loss of sales due to lower sales per customer and customer dissatisfaction with the level of sales service and stock outages in the stores.

Management believes that it is achieving an appropriate balance among the internal risk factors in order to optimize profits.

The Mark's Division franchise operations consisted of 25 franchise stores at January 27, 2001, 88% of which meet Company-set capitalization standards. During fiscal 2001, the Mark's Division purchased four of its franchise stores and converted them to corporate stores. This franchise store purchase activity was higher than normal in fiscal 2001 as three franchisees decided to retire during that fiscal year and offered to sell their stores to the Mark's Division. The Mark's Division franchise operation is very stable and is expected to shrink a little over time with the occasional franchisee selling his or her store to the Corporation.

With a "**Corporate Store Strategy**" for new store openings (four in fiscal 2001, five in fiscal 2000 and nine in fiscal 1999) and the purchase of franchise stores as they become available (six purchased franchise stores in fiscal 2001, one in fiscal 2000 and 31 in fiscal 1999) and the closure of non-performing franchise stores, the **Work World franchise operation** has reduced to 90 franchise stores at January 27, 2001 from 150 at January 25, 1997. At January 27, 2001, 51% of the remaining Work World franchises meet Company-set capitalization standards that were developed after the December 1, 1996 acquisition date of Work World, as there were no capitalization standards under the previous administration. Every year, the Work World Division introduces at least half a dozen or so new merchandise programs and continually seeks to improve upon existing assortments in order to positively impact a significant part of the merchandise offering and, it is hoped, store sales in both the Work World Division's franchise and corporate stores.

In addition, over the last several years, the Company has put the necessary credit controls in place to control the level of merchandise shipments and other cost risk services provided to the Work World franchisees. Nevertheless, given the capitalization level of many of these stores, there is a risk that more of the stores could close, causing a loss of royalty and other revenues and bad debt write-offs for the Company.

In its purchased franchise stores and in its new corporate stores, the Work World Division expects to generate the appropriate sales per square foot, gross margin rate, and expense rate to produce a front-line contribution higher than the royalty rates earned from franchisees on franchise sales, although this has not yet occurred and remains a risk factor at this time.

During the second half of 1999 (fiscal 2000), the Company launched its **DOCKERS® Stores Division** with the opening of five test stores. Three more test stores were added during 2000 (fiscal 2001). The business formula for the DOCKERS® Stores Division requires that over time, sales per square foot track to mall averages, a 40% gross margin rate be achieved and that sales be made up of an equal blend of men's and women's products and an equal blend of tops and bottoms. As Table 10 (EBITDA) showed, the near-term adverse impact to earnings to launch this new division have been high. As well, there is still a risk that this or any other new division will not blossom. The Company believes that it has mitigated the risk for the DOCKERS® test by basing

the store banner on an established, internationally recognized brand, by offering customers additional DOCKERS® assortments not carried in other stores, by selecting quality store locations and by providing excellent customer service. No additional stores are planned to be added to this test in 2001 (fiscal 2002) as the division will concentrate on improving merchandise assortments as it must get its sales per square foot to track higher in order to succeed.

During the year ended January 27, 2001, the Company's **shares traded at multiples** ranging from 4.5 to 8.3 times earnings per share. This compares to a range of uncalculated negative price-earnings ratios to 99+ times price-earnings ratios for the TSE Merchandising Index and price-earnings ratios ranging from 12.1 to 19.8 times for the TSE Specialty Stores Index during the Company's fiscal 2001 year. Also during fiscal 2001, the Company's share price ranged from 55.7% to 102.5% of the Company's January 27, 2001 book value per share.

Graph 18 compares the yearly percentage changes over the last five years in the cumulative shareholder return on the Common Shares of the Company (assuming a $100 investment was made on January 28, 1996) with the cumulative total return of the TSE 300 Stock Index, the TSE Merchandising Index and the TSE Specialty Stores Index. No dividends have been paid by the Company; therefore it was not necessary to build a dividend reinvestment feature into the graph. The graph spikes upward in fiscal 1998 because, as noted earlier, the Company was subject to an unsolicited offer to purchase the Company's outstanding Common Shares in the fall of 1997.

5-YEAR SHARE PERFORMANCE (GRAPH 18)
(based on a base of 100)

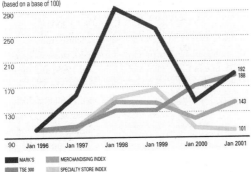

| | MARK'S | | MERCHANDISING INDEX |
| | TSE 300 | | SPECIALTY STORE INDEX |

Management's Responsibility for Financial Statements

The accompanying Consolidated Financial Statements of the Company and all information in the annual report are the responsibility of management. Financial information contained elsewhere in the annual report is consistent with that shown in the financial statements. The Consolidated Financial Statements were prepared by management in accordance with accounting principles generally accepted in Canada, applied on a consistent basis. The significant accounting policies, which management believes are appropriate for the Company, are described in Note 1 to the Consolidated Financial Statements.

Management is responsible for the integrity and objectivity of the Consolidated Financial Statements. Estimates are necessary in the preparation of these statements and, based on careful judgments, have been properly reflected. Management has established systems of internal control which are designed to provide reasonable assurance that assets are safeguarded from loss or unauthorized use, and to produce reliable accounting records for the preparation of financial information.

The Board of Directors is responsible for ensuring that management fulfills its responsibilities for financial reporting and internal control. The Audit Committee of the Board, composed solely of Directors who are not employees of the Company, is appointed annually by the Board of Directors.

The Audit Committee of the Board meets regularly with financial management of the Company and with the shareholders' independent auditors to discuss internal controls, audit matters, including audit scope and auditor remuneration, and financial reporting issues and reports to the Board thereon. The independent shareholders' auditors have unrestricted access to the Audit Committee. The Audit Committee also reviews the annual Consolidated Financial Statements and the Management's Discussion and Analysis, reports to the Board thereon and makes recommendations with respect to acceptance for inclusion thereof in the annual report. The Audit Committee also makes recommendations to the Board with respect to the appointment and remuneration of the Company's auditors.

Management recognizes its responsibility for conducting the Company's affairs in compliance with established financial standards and applicable laws and maintains proper standards of conduct for its activities.

(signed)

Michael Lambert, Chief Financial Officer
Calgary, Alberta, March 9, 2001

Auditors' Report

**TO THE SHAREHOLDERS OF
MARK'S WORK WEARHOUSE LTD.**

We have audited the Consolidated Balance Sheets of Mark's Work Wearhouse Ltd. as at January 30, 1999, January 29, 2000 and January 27, 2001, and the Consolidated Statements of Earnings and Retained Earnings and Cash Flows for each of the years then ended. These financial statements are the responsibility of the Company's management. Our responsibility is to express an opinion on these financial statements based on our audits.

We conducted our audits in accordance with Canadian generally accepted auditing standards. Those standards require that we plan and perform an audit to obtain reasonable assurance whether the financial statements are free of material misstatement. An audit includes examining, on a test basis, evidence supporting the amounts and disclosures in the financial statements. An audit also

includes assessing the accounting principles used and significant estimates made by management, as well as evaluating the overall financial statement presentation.

In our opinion, these Consolidated Financial Statements present fairly, in all material respects, the financial position of the Company as at January 30, 1999, January 29, 2000 and January 27, 2001 and the results of its operations and its cash flows for each of the years then ended, in accordance with Canadian generally accepted accounting principles.

(signed)

PricewaterhouseCoopers LLP, Chartered Accountants
Calgary, Alberta March 9, 2001

Consolidated Balance Sheets

(thousands)	As at January 30, 1999	As at January 29, 2000	As at January 27, 2001
ASSETS			
Current assets			
Cash and cash equivalents (Note 1D)	$ 2,710	$ 1,774	$ 6,993
Accounts receivable (Note 4)	13,364	15,010	13,998
Merchandise inventories	76,982	81,468	84,483
Other current assets (Note 5)	3,304	3,223	4,913
	96,360	101,475	110,387
Other assets (Note 6)	975	1,614	1,056
Capital assets (Note 7)	23,531	25,893	28,148
Future income taxes (Notes 1N & 17)	3,413	3,026	2,997
Goodwill (Note 8)	8,713	11,076	14,472
	$ 132,992	$ 143,084	$ 157,060
LIABILITIES			
Current liabilities			
Accounts payable and accrued liabilities	$ 43,557	$ 45,730	$ 46,131
Income taxes payable	4,976	2,238	6,186
Current portion of long-term debt (Note 10)	7,992	9,328	10,905
	56,525	57,296	63,222
Long-term debt (Note 10)	22,052	23,952	27,016
Deferred gains (Note 7)	1,109	2,265	2,101
	79,686	83,513	92,339
SHAREHOLDERS' EQUITY			
Capital stock (Note 12)	32,696	32,715	31,228
Retained earnings	20,610	26,856	33,493
	53,306	59,571	64,721
	$ 132,992	$ 143,084	$ 157,060

Approved by the Board

(signed)

Michael Fox, Director

(signed)

Garth Mitchell, Director

Consolidated Statements of Earnings and Retained Earnings

(thousands except per Common Share amounts)	52 weeks ended January 30, 1999	52 weeks ended January 29, 2000	52 weeks ended January 27, 2001
Corporate and franchise sales (Note 14)	$ 417,468	$ 437,670	$ 487,979
Corporate operations			
Front-line operations (Note 1B)			
Sales	$ 283,401	$ 314,547	$ 363,870
Cost of sales	169,163	186,723	214,361
Gross margin	114,238	127,824	149,509
Front-line expenses			
Personnel, advertising and other	51,869	57,272	67,366
Occupancy	25,868	31,094	35,738
Depreciation and amortization	5,350	6,231	6,664
Interest – short term	2,015	1,610	1,480
	85,102	96,207	111,248
Front-line contribution	29,136	31,617	38,261
Franchise royalties and other (Note 15)	7,016	6,640	6,558
Net front-line contribution before back-line expenses	36,152	38,257	44,819
Back-line operations (Note 1B)			
Back-line expenses			
Personnel, administration and other	15,124	16,590	18,744
Occupancy	998	1,015	1,038
Depreciation and amortization	2,711	3,372	3,624
Software development and maintenance costs	906	1,201	1,238
Computer services	571	687	854
Interest – long term	1,350	2,407	2,498
Franchise bad debt provisions (recoveries)	219	300	(251)
	21,879	25,572	27,745
Earnings before provision for closure of U.S. pilot stores, income taxes and goodwill amortization	14,273	12,685	17,074
Provision for closure of U.S. pilot stores (Note 16)	2,961	—	—
Earnings before income taxes and goodwill amortization	11,312	12,685	17,074
Income Taxes (Notes 1N and 17)			
Current expense	6,566	5,536	8,317
Future expense (benefit)	(1,322)	387	29
	5,244	5,923	8,346
Net earnings before goodwill amortization	6,068	6,762	8,728
Goodwill amortization	316	375	548
Net earnings	5,752	6,387	8,180
Retained earnings at beginning of year	14,858	20,610	26,856
Purchase of capital stock for cancellation (Note 12)	—	(141)	(1,543)
Retained earnings at end of year	$ 20,610	$ 26,856	$ 33,493
Earnings per Common Share			
Before goodwill amortization	22¢	24¢	32¢
Basic	21¢	23¢	30¢
Fully diluted – restated (Note 1K)	20¢	23¢	29¢

Consolidated Statements of Cash Flows

(thousands)	52 weeks ended January 30 1999	52 weeks ended January 29, 2000	52 weeks ended January 27, 2001
Cash and cash equivalents generated (deployed)			
Operations			
Net earnings	$ 5,752	$ 6,387	$ 8,180
Non-cash items			
Provision for closure of U.S. pilot stores (Note 16)	2,961	—	—
Depreciation and amortization	8,377	9,978	10,836
Loss (gain) on disposition of capital assets	47	124	(164)
Future income taxes (benefits) (Note 1N)	(1,322)	387	29
Funds provided by operations	15,815	16,876	18,881
Changes in non-cash working capital			
(net of effect of acquisition of subsidiaries and purchase of franchise stores)			
Accounts receivable	(605)	(1,646)	1,012
Merchandise inventories	(6,755)	(4,439)	(144)
Other current assets	(614)	73	(1,330)
Accounts payable and accrued liabilities	771	2,173	(1,227)
Income taxes payable	(1,707)	(2,738)	3,948
	(8,910)	(6,577)	2,259
	6,905	10,299	21,140
Investing			
Acquisitions of subsidiaries net of cash acquired (Note 2)	(2,196)	(737)	—
Purchases of franchise stores (Note 3)	(4,320)	(50)	(3,054)
Purchases of capital assets	(3,183)	(1,915)	(2,485)
Other assets	(720)	(1,367)	(304)
Disposition of capital assets	(160)	(73)	36
	(10,579)	(4,142)	(5,807)
Financing			
Proceeds of long-term debt	10,259	1,000	2,700
Retirement of long-term debt	(1,417)	(3,424)	(3,278)
Repayment of capital lease liabilities	(3,615)	(5,579)	(6,506)
Deferred landlord inducements	—	1,032	—
Share capital purchased for cancellation (Note 12)	—	(233)	(3,102)
Issuance of share capital for cash (Note 12)	808	111	72
	6,035	(7,093)	(10,114)
Net cash and cash equivalents generated (deployed)	2,361	(936)	5,219
Cash and cash equivalents at beginning of year (Note 1D)	349	2,710	1,774
Cash and cash equivalents at end of year (Note 1D)	$ 2,710	$ 1,774	$ 6,993

Supplementary Schedules
to Consolidated Statements of Cash Flows

(thousands)	52 weeks ended January 30 1999	52 weeks ended January 29, 2000	52 weeks ended January 27, 2001
Schedule of non-cash investing and financing activities			
Capital assets acquired by means of capital leases	$ (6,969)	$ (9,239)	$ (8,665)
Capital lease funding to acquire capital assets	$ 6,969	$ 9,239	$ 8,665
Acquisition of Paul John Enterprises (Note 2)	$ —	$ (2,000)	$ —
Estimated long-term debt on future earnout of Paul John Enterprises acquisition (Notes 2 and 10)	$ —	$ 2,000	$ —
Purchases of individual franchise stores by means of interest-bearing long-term debt (Notes 3 and 10)	$ —	$ —	$ (900)
Interest-bearing long-term debt on purchases of individual franchise stores (Notes 3 and 10)	$ —	$ —	$ 900
Purchases of individual franchise stores by means of non-interest bearing long-term debt (Notes 3 and 10)	$ —	$ —	$ (2,160)
Non-interest bearing long-term debt on purchases of individual franchise stores (Notes 3 and 10)	$ —	$ —	$ 2,160
Supplemental disclosures of cash flow information			
Cash paid for			
Short-term interest	$ 1,982	$ 1,645	$ 1,448
Long-term interest	$ 1,251	$ 2,435	$ 2,534
Income taxes	$ 8,273	$ 8,274	$ 4,369

Notes to Consolidated Financial Statements

January 27, 2001

(dollar amounts in tables in thousands except operating credit facilities table, financial instrument tables on foreign currencies, earnings per Common Share and exercise price of options to purchase Common Shares)

1. SIGNIFICANT ACCOUNTING POLICIES

The Company operates Mark's Work Wearhouse, (Mark's, called L'Équipeur in Quebec), Work World and DOCKERS® corporate stores and is involved in the operations of franchise-owned Mark's and Work World stores, all operating in the retail clothing and footwear industry within Canada. Through a branch operation in fiscal January 1999, the Company also operated two Mark's pilot stores in the United States. The Mark's U.S. pilot stores were closed in fiscal January 2000. See Note 16. These financial statements are prepared by management in accordance with accounting principles generally accepted in Canada.

A. Fiscal Year

The fiscal year of the Company consists of a 52-week period ending on the last Saturday in January each year. The fiscal year for the Consolidated Financial Statements presented is the 52-week period ended January 27, 2001 and comparably the 52-week periods ended January 29, 2000 and January 30, 1999.

B. Basis of Presentation

The Consolidated Financial Statements include the accounts of the Company and its subsidiaries, all of which are wholly owned.

Front-line operations represent those activities where the Company's people come face-to-face with the customers and back-line operations represent those activities that support the effective performance of front-line activities.

C. Franchise Operations

Initial franchise fees are recorded as income when the store has been opened whether the balance has been received or is receivable. Deposits received on initial franchise fees for stores not yet opened are included in current liabilities on the balance sheet. Royalties, based on sales by the franchisees, are recorded as income as they are earned. Costs are expensed as incurred as part of either front-line or back-line expenses.

D. Cash and Cash Equivalents

Cash and cash equivalents consist of cash on hand and balances with banks and investments in money market instruments.

E. Merchandise Inventories

Merchandise inventories are accounted for by the retail method and are carried at the lower of estimated cost and anticipated selling price, less an expected average gross margin.

F. Capital Assets

Depreciation is designed to amortize the cost of capital assets over their estimated useful lives. Capital assets are amortized at the following annual rates:

- Building — On a straight-line basis at 7% per year
- Leasehold improvements — On a straight-line basis over the term of the lease
- Furniture, fixtures and equipment — On a straight-line basis at 20% per year
- Fixtures, equipment and computer equipment and operating software capital leases — On a straight-line basis over the term of the lease

G. Goodwill

Goodwill is the excess of the cost of investments in subsidiaries or purchased franchise stores over the fair value of the net tangible assets acquired. Goodwill is being amortized on a straight-line basis over the estimated life of the benefit as determined for each acquisition or purchased franchise store. The Company uses the cost recovery method to assess the value of goodwill. The value of goodwill is regularly evaluated by reviewing the financial returns of the related business or purchased franchise stores, taking into account the risk associated with the investment. Any permanent impairment in the value of goodwill is written off against earnings. The weighted average remaining amortization period is 25.7 years (January 29, 2000: 28.7 years; January 30, 1999: 30.2 years). No goodwill is set up on the reacquisition of troubled franchises. See Notes 2, 3 and 8.

H. Translation of Foreign Currencies

Inventory purchases in foreign currencies are translated at the rate of exchange in effect on the dates the purchases occur and payable balances at the balance sheet date, in both cases after taking into account the effect of any related foreign exchange hedging contracts.

Notes to Consolidated Financial Statements

In fiscal 1999, the Mark's U.S. pilot stores were considered integrated and thus were translated using the temporal method, whereby monetary items were translated at the rate of exchange in effect at the balance sheet dates, non-monetary items were translated at historical exchange rates, and revenue and expense items except for depreciation and amortization were translated at the rate of exchange in effect on the dates they occurred.

I. Store Opening Expenses

Store opening expenses are capitalized and amortized over a three-year period commencing in the quarter following the store opening. See Notes 5 and 6.

J. Software Development and Maintenance Costs

Costs incurred, which are primarily programmers' salaries and contracted amounts to develop or maintain software for the Company's proprietary management information systems, including year 2000 modifications made during fiscal 1999 and fiscal 2000, are expensed as incurred.

K. Earnings Per Common Share

Earnings per Common Share before goodwill amortization and basic earnings per Common Share are calculated using the weighted average number of Common Shares outstanding during the year. See Note 12. The Company adopted the treasury stock method of accounting for fully diluted earnings per Common Share in fiscal 2001. Formerly, generally accepted accounting principles required that the imputed earnings method be used for determining the dilutive effect of options. Excluded from the computation of fully diluted earnings per share were options outstanding of 1,201,300 exercisable at prices ranging from $1.95 to $4.25 (2000 – 497,700 at prices ranging from $3.85 to $4.25; 1999 – 260,300 at prices ranging from $4.20 to $4.25) as the options' exercise prices were greater than the average market price of the Company's common stock. The treasury stock method computes the number of incremental shares by assuming the outstanding stock options exercisable at exercise prices below the average market price for the applicable fiscal year are exercised and then that number of incremental shares is reduced by the number of shares that could have been repurchased from the issuance proceeds, using the average market price of the Company's shares for the applicable fiscal year. Fiscal 1999 and fiscal 2000 fully diluted earnings per share have been restated to reflect the treasury stock method. The effect of the restatement of fully diluted earnings per share was nil in fiscal 1999 and an increase of one cent per share in fiscal 2000.

L. Stock-based Compensation Plan

The Company's stock-based compensation plans are described in Note 12. No compensation expenses are recognized for this plan when stock options are issued to employees or directors. Any consideration paid by employees and directors on exercise of stock options is credited to share capital.

M. Financial Instruments

Interest rate swap contracts are used to hedge interest rate risk on over 50% of the Company's anticipated short-term floating rate debt requirements during its next fiscal year. The interest rate differentials to be paid or received under such contracts are recognized as adjustments to interest expenses in that fiscal year.

Foreign currency risks related to the purchase of merchandise for resale are hedged for over 50% of the Company's anticipated purchases. Any costs associated with these purchases are included in the Canadian dollar cost of these products.

The estimated fair values of accounts receivable and accounts payable approximate book value. See Note 10 for the estimated fair value of fixed rate and non-interest bearing debt and Note 13 for the estimated fair value of financial instruments.

N. Future Income Taxes

The Company adopted the asset/liability method of accounting for future income taxes in fiscal 1999. Formerly, generally accepted accounting principles required that the deferred income tax method be used. The future income tax asset results from differences between the tax base and carrying values of capital and other assets and differences in the accounting and tax treatment of certain cost.

O. Future Benefits

The Company has a retirement plan in which all permanent employees may participate after a one-year service period, if they desire. The retirement plan is a combined group registered retirement savings plan and deferred profit-sharing plan, whereby the Company (providing it was profitable in the previous year) matches employees' contributions up to 4% of the employee's salary. Contributions made by the Company to the retirement plan are expensed when they are made.

In addition, for any other future benefit plans, the Company accrues the liability over the estimated remaining service life of the employee. The Company does not provide its employees with post-retirement health, insurance and other benefits at this time.

P. Prior Year Amounts

Certain prior years' amounts are reclassified to conform to the current year's presentation. None of these reclassifications are significant.

2. ACQUISITION

Effective November 1, 1998, the Company acquired all of the outstanding shares of Paul John Enterprises Ltd. (Paul John) for a cash down payment of $2,253,000. During the year ended January 29, 2000, the Company recorded a purchase price adjustment of $737,000. This amount was added to the original purchase price as additional goodwill.

In addition, the agreement stated that there could be a further future earnout amount based on sales and capital expenditures of the operation over the five years subsequent to January 30, 1999, payable no later than April 15, 2004. At January 29, 2000, the Company estimated this earnout to be $2,000,000. This amount was added to the purchase price as additional goodwill in the fiscal year ended January 29, 2000. At January 27, 2001, the Company has estimated that no further earnout amount is required. Paul John owned and operated 19 Work World franchise stores in British Columbia and the Yukon, which are now being operated as corporate stores in the Company's Work World Division.

The acquisition was accounted for by the purchase method, with the results of operations from the acquired business included from the November 1, 1998 acquisition date.

The acquisition resulted in goodwill of $328,000 recorded in the Company's January 30, 1999 fiscal year and goodwill of $2,737,000 recorded in the Company's January 29, 2000 fiscal year. The goodwill is being amortized on a straight-line basis over 25.7 years (January 29, 2000: 26.7 years; January 30, 1999: 27.7 years) which represents the average remaining life of the original franchise agreements plus one extension period.

The net assets acquired were:

Cash	$ 57
Other current assets	7,572
Capital assets	781
Assumed goodwill	537
Acquisition goodwill (see Notes 1G and 8)	328
	9,275
Liabilities assumed	(7,022)
Acquisition cost – during fiscal year ended January 30, 1999	2,253
Acquisition goodwill – purchase price adjustment determined during fiscal year ended January 29, 2000 (see Notes 1G and 8)	737
Acquisition goodwill – future earnout estimated during fiscal year ended January 29, 2000 (see Notes 1G and 8)	2,000
Acquisition cost	$ 4,990

NOTES TO CONSOLIDATED FINANCIAL STATEMENTS

Notes to Consolidated Financial Statements

3. PURCHASES OF FRANCHISE STORES

As opportunities arise, both the Mark's and Work World Divisions purchase their division's respective franchise stores and convert them to corporate stores.

Each purchase is accounted for by the purchase method, with the results of the acquired franchise store included from the date of acquisition.

The purchase sometimes results in goodwill, which is being amortized on a straight-line basis. The weighted average remaining amortization period is 20.6 years (January 29, 2000: 23.0 years; January 30, 1999: 22.6 years). The net assets acquired were:

	1999	2000	2001
Number of stores	14	1	10
Current assets	$ 3,160	$ 47	$ 2,989
Capital assets	510	3	565
Other assets	512	—	244
Acquisition goodwill (see Notes 1G and 8)	969	—	3,944
	5,151	50	7,742
Liabilities assumed	(831)	—	(1,628)
Acquisition cost	$ 4,320	$ 50	$ 6,114

The Company recorded interest-bearing long-term debt due to vendors of $900,000 and non-interest bearing long-term debt due to vendors of $2,160,000 on the fiscal 2001 purchases of franchise stores. See Note 10.

4. ACCOUNTS RECEIVABLE

	1999	2000	2001
Receivables from franchise stores			
Mark's stores	$ 5,597	$ 7,232	$ 5,357
Work World stores	1,744	1,460	969
Receivables from business account sales	3,668	4,568	5,851
Landlord leasehold rebates receivable	1,661	1,653	1,145
Co-op advertising receivable	1,142	654	385
Other accounts receivable	1,162	1,242	1,598
	14,974	16,809	15,305
Allowance for doubtful accounts related primarily to receivables from franchise stores	(1,610)	(1,799)	(1,307)
	$ 13,364	$ 15,010	$ 13,998

The Company operates in the retail industry in Canada. The amounts receivable from business account sales are receivable from 5,800 customers (January 29, 2000: 5,000 customers; January 30, 1999: 4,200 customers). There are no individually significant clients who could create a credit risk to the Company in its operated stores. Accounts receivable from Mark's franchise stores for inventory purchases, royalties, and other services can have large balances at certain times of the year. The Company has security instruments in place over the franchise operations of Mark's franchisees, usually postponed to the franchisees' principal banker plus other personal security, the combined value of which may or may not cover the total receivable position. The Company has receivables from Work World franchise stores for royalties, acquisition fees, merchandise surcharges and for the costs of other services. In addition, during the fiscal year ended January 27, 2001, the Company assumed supplier payment responsibility for approximately 3% of the Work World franchise stores' annual sales (January 29, 2000: 7%; January 30, 1999: 15%) for inventory provided by the Company to Work World franchise stores or for inventory provided directly to Work World franchise stores by the Company's suppliers. Accounts receivable from Work World franchise stores are unsecured.

5. OTHER CURRENT ASSETS

	1999	2000	2001
Prepaid expenses and supplies	$ 2,396	$ 2,102	$ 3,785
Deposits	368	379	313
Current portion of store opening expenses (see Note 1l)	540	742	815
	$ 3,304	$ 3,223	$ 4,913

6. OTHER ASSETS

	1999	2000	2001
Employee relocation loans	$ 26	$ 467	$ 145
Store opening expenses (see Note 1l)	471	823	583
Other	478	324	328
	$ 975	$ 1,614	$ 1,056

7. CAPITAL ASSETS AND DEFERRED GAINS

	1999		2000		2001	
	Cost	Net Book Value	Cost	Net Book Value	Cost	Net Book Value
Land	$ 45	$ 45	$ —	$ —	$ —	$ —
Building	452	312	—	—	—	—
Leasehold improvements	4,494	689	5,693	1,763	3,515	1,945
Furniture, fixtures and equipment	21,720	7,453	22,633	6,051	11,039	6,152
Fixtures & equipment under capital leases	13,319	9,520	18,437	11,792	22,379	14,385
Computer equipment and operating software under capital leases	9,047	5,512	11,768	6,287	8,914	5,666
	$ 49,077	$ 23,531	$ 58,531	$ 25,893	$ 45,847	$ 28,148

See Note 2 for the effect on capital assets of the November 1, 1998 acquisition of Paul John. See Note 3 for the effect on capital assets of franchise store purchases.

The Company finances some of its store capital expenditures by selling and then leasing back these capital assets. The gains realized on the sales have been deferred and are being amortized over the terms of the leases. The deferred gain balance at January 27, 2001 is $1,107,000 (January 29, 2000: $1,083,000; January 30, 1999: $890,000).

The Company receives landlord inducements on some of its store lease agreements. The amounts received from landlords have been deferred and are being amortized over the term of the store leases. The deferred gain balance at January 27, 2001 is $913,000 (January 29, 2000 is $1,032,000; January 30, 1999 is nil).

The Company sold and leased back its corporate office building in fiscal 1992. The gain realized on the sale has been deferred and is being amortized over the original 128-month term of the lease. The deferred gain balance at January 27, 2001 is $81,000 (January 29, 2000: $150,000; January 30, 1999: $219,000).

Notes to Consolidated Financial Statements

8. GOODWILL

| | 1999 | | 2000 | | 2001 | |
	Cost	Net Book Value	Cost	Net Book Value	Cost	Net Book Value
Work World acquisition	$ 7,146	$ 6,690	$ 7,146	$ 6,479	$ 7,146	$ 6,268
Paul John acquisition (Note 2)	865	853	3,602	3,540	3,602	3,405
Purchased Mark's Division franchise stores (Note 3)	473	300	473	223	3,970	3,704
Purchased Work World Division franchise stores (Note 3)	898	870	872	834	1,173	1,095
	$ 9,382	$ 8,713	$ 12,093	$ 11,076	$ 15,891	$ 14,472

(See Note 1G)

9. OPERATING CREDIT FACILITIES

The Company's operating credit facilities are:

Facility	Amount	Interest Rate
Extendible 364-day revolving operating facility from a syndication of Canadian chartered banks.	$ 75 million	Rate options based on prime rate (7.25% at January 27, 2001) and bankers' acceptance rates plus margin, if applicable, based on a certain interest coverage test.
Extendible 364-day revolving term credit facility (each advance becomes a non-revolving reducing 5-year term loan) from a syndicate of Canadian chartered banks.	$ 8 million	Rate based on prime rate (7.25% at January 27, 2001) plus margin, if applicable, based on a certain interest coverage test. See Note 10.
Contingent liability demand line to support contingent exposure under foreign exchange and interest rate swap arrangements from a Canadian chartered bank.	$ 5 million	Quoted rates from time to time. See Notes 1M and 13 on financial instruments.
Contingent liability demand line to support contingent exposure under foreign exchange and interest rate swap arrangements from a Canadian chartered bank.	$ 2.9 million	Quoted rates from time to time. See Notes 1M and 13 on financial instruments.

The $75,000,000 operating line of credit includes limits for letters of credit and is limited to the lesser of $75,000,000 and the sum of 60% of eligible inventories as defined, plus 75% of eligible receivables as defined, plus during June through September and to a maximum of $5,000,000, 40% of eligible franchise receivables as defined. Both the $75,000,000 operating line and the $8,000,000 revolving term credit facility are extendible, at the Company's request and the lenders' discretion, for subsequent 364-day periods. Failing renewal of the $75,000,000 operating line, as long as there has not been an event of default, 50% of the then outstanding amounts under such operating facilities could be converted into non-revolving term loans repayable over 36 months.

Security provided includes a general security agreement, a fixed and floating charge demand debenture registered in various jurisdictions, hypothec on movables registered in Quebec, general assignment of accounts receivable and security under the Bank Act over inventory registered in various jurisdictions. The credit agreements require guarantees and postponements of claim from all material subsidiaries (as defined) secured by general security agreements or fixed and floating charge debentures. There are no such material subsidiaries at January 27, 2001.

10. LONG-TERM DEBT

	1999	2000	2001
Syndicated bank term loan at prime plus margin based on a certain interest coverage test plus one quarter (7.50% at January 27, 2001, 6.75% at January 29, 2000 and 7.0% at January 30, 1999).	$ 5,000	$ 4,000	$ 3,000
Syndicated bank term loan at prime plus margin based on a certain interest coverage test plus one quarter (7.50% at January 27, 2001, 6.75% at January 29, 2000 and 7.0% at January 30, 1999). See Note 9.	5,000	4,000	5,850
Bank term loan, 7.5% interest	4,200	2,800	1,400
Fixture and equipment capital lease obligations – 2001, 9.2% average interest rate over 42 months (2000: 9.0% average interest rate over 46 months; 1999: 9.0% average interest rate over 45 months). See Note 7.	9,907	12,784	15,611
Computer equipment and operating software capital lease obligations – 2001, 8.9% average interest rate over 37 months (2000: 10.5% average interest rate over 36 months; 1999: 10.1% average interest rate over 29 months). See Note 7.	5,937	6,696	6,000
Leaseholds, fixture and equipment loan for DOCKERS® Stores test – non-interest bearing	—	1,000	1,000
Estimated future earnout payable – on Paul John Enterprises acquisition – non-interest bearing. See Note 2.	—	2,000	2,000
Long-term debt payable – on acquisition of individual franchise stores – non-interest bearing. See Note 3.	—	—	2,160
Long-term debt payable – on acquisition of individual franchise stores – interest bearing. See Note 3.	—	—	900
	30,044	33,280	37,921
Less: amount due within one year	(7,992)	(9,328)	(10,905)
Total	$ 22,052	$ 23,952	$ 27,016

If rates currently available to the Company for interest-bearing, long-term debt (including amounts due within one year), with similar terms and maturities are used, the estimated fair values of fixed rate debt as at January 27, 2001 are $31,722,000 (January 29, 2000: $30,251,000 and January 30, 1999: $30,130,000). The estimated fair values of non-interest bearing, long-term debt approximate book value.

On December 4, 1998, the Company obtained a $5,000,000 five-year term facility from a syndication of Canadian chartered banks to refinance a portion of pre-existing bank indebtedness. The loan bears interest at prime plus a margin based on a certain interest coverage test plus one quarter (7.50% at January 27, 2001, 6.75% at January 29, 2000 and 7.0% at January 30, 1999) and is repayable in 20 equal quarterly principal plus interest payments that began January 31, 1999. Security provided is described in Note 9.

On December 4, 1998, the Company obtained an extendible, 364-day revolving term credit facility and took a $5,000,000 advance which became a non-revolving five-year term facility from a syndication of Canadian chartered banks to finance the acquisition and working capital funding requirements of Paul John Enterprises. See Note 2. On July 30, 2000, the Company obtained an increase in this facility limit to a revised limit of $8,000,000. See Note 9. During fiscal 2001, $2,700,000 of the facility was advanced to finance the purchase of franchise stores. See Note 3. The loans bear interest at prime plus a margin based on a certain interest coverage test plus one quarter (7.50% at January 27, 2001, 6.75% at January 29, 2000 and 7.0% at January 30, 1999) and are repayable in 20 equal quarterly principal plus interest payments that begin, for each loan, 90 days after the advance. Security provided is described in Note 9.

On December 9, 1996, the Company obtained a $7,000,000, five-year term facility from a Canadian chartered bank to finance the acquisition of Work World. The loan has a fixed interest rate of 7.5% and is repayable in 20 equal quarterly principal plus interest payments that began on March 31, 1997. Security provided is described in Note 9.

Notes to Consolidated Financial Statements

The fixtures and equipment under capital lease obligations and the computer equipment and operating software under capital lease obligations are the security for those respective obligations.

On September 8, 1998, the Company entered into an exclusive agreement with Levi Strauss & Co. (Canada) Inc. (Levi) to operate DOCKERS® Stores in Canada. As part of this agreement, during fiscal 2000 Levi advanced $1,000,000 to the Company to finance a portion of the working capital investment and capital cost of building the Company's first four test stores. The amount advanced does not bear interest and is repayable to Levi within 60 days of the determination that the initial phase of the test is deemed a success as per specific requirements outlined in the agreement between the Company and Levi. If the initial phase is not deemed a success, then amounts advanced by Levi will not be repayable.

Effective November 1, 1998, the Company acquired all of the outstanding shares of Paul John for a cash down payment of $2,253,000. A further $737,000 purchase price adjustment was paid in the year ended January 29, 2000. In addition, there will be a further earnout amount based on sales and capital expenditures of the operation over the five years subsequent to January 30, 1999. At January 29, 2000, the Company estimated this earnout to be an amount of $2,000,000. The Company estimates that no further earnout is required to be recorded at January 27, 2001. The amount does not bear interest and is payable no later than April 15, 2004. See Note 2.

During the fiscal year ended January 27, 2001, the Company acquired various franchise stores and converted them to corporate stores. In addition to cash down payments, the Company has recorded long-term debt due to the vendors of $3,060,000 on the purchases of these franchise stores. The total amount of debt on these franchise store acquisitions that is interest bearing is $900,000. The interest-bearing debt bears interest at 6.45% and is repayable in three equal annual installments that begin June 30, 2001. The $2,160,000 non-interest-bearing debt is repayable in annual installments beginning April 1, 2001 and ending April 1, 2009.

The aggregate repayments of principal required to meet long-term debt obligations are:

2002	$ 10,905
2003	$ 9,986
2004	$ 8,163
2005	$ 5,821
2006	$ 2,075
Thereafter	$ 971

11. COMMITMENTS AND CONTINGENT LIABILITIES

The Company has entered into operating lease agreements terminating at various dates to 2014. The Company has also entered into various operating lease agreements for store security systems and office equipment.

The minimum annual rentals, excluding tenant operating costs are:

2002	$ 28,119
2003	$ 27,686
2004	$ 26,083
2005	$ 24,676
2006	$ 23,986
Thereafter	$ 59,549

In addition to minimum annual rentals, contingent rentals may be payable under certain store leases on the basis of sales in excess of stipulated amounts.

Subsidiary companies of the Company are on head leases for some of the Work World franchise stores. Should those franchise stores cease operations before the end of their respective lease terms and be unable to meet their remaining lease liabilities, those subsidiary companies would have a commitment for $1,005,000 on 14 store leases prior to any subleasing to new franchisees or corporate stores.

The Company has previously signed leases for its two Mark's U.S. pilot stores in Grand Rapids, Michigan and Portland, Maine, which stores the Company decided to close in the fiscal year ended January 30, 1999. The minimum annual rental commitment under these leases is $12,000 (U.S.) net of existing subleasing agreements for each of the first three years, $nil in year four and $nil in year five. The Company has subleased both of the above locations. Should the current subleasees default on the subleases, the Company would have an annual commitment for $255,000 (U.S.) prior to any further subleasing for each of the first two years, $241,000 (U.S.) in year three, $213,000 (U.S.) in year four and $124,000 (U.S.) in year five.

The Company enters into commitments with its domestic and foreign suppliers in the ordinary course of business to obtain the merchandise required to generate the following year's planned sales. In the opinion of management, commitments made to date after having considered the Company's fiscal 2002 forecasts and inventory levels as at January 27, 2001 are consistent with prior years. At January 27, 2001, the Company had letters of credit outstanding for merchandise purchases from foreign suppliers totaling $7,722,050.

Mark's and Work World have merchandise inventory buy-back agreements in place with Canadian chartered banks under which they have agreed to buy back franchise-owned merchandise inventory should the banks foreclose on any of their respective franchisees. In 62 of the Work World buy-back agreements, there is a ceiling on the amount of inventory that has to be purchased. As at January 27, 2001, if there were foreclosures on all franchise stores, where merchandise inventory buy-back agreements are in place, the Company would be required to buy back inventory at 68% of cost which totals $13,555,000 from 87 stores.

12. CAPITAL STOCK

The authorized capital stock of the Company comprises 100,000,000 First Preferred Shares of no par value and an unlimited number of Common Shares of no par value.

The issued capital stock of the Company is:

	Weighted Average Common Shares	Common Shares	Capital Stock
2001	27,596,847	26,527,159	$ 31,228
2000	27,846,950	27,856,967	$ 32,715
1999	27,475,198	27,866,247	$ 32,696

During the year ended January 27, 2001, 49,540 Common Shares were issued pursuant to the exercise of employee and director stock options for a total consideration of $72,000.

On April 20, 2000, the Company filed a Notice of Intention to make a Normal Course Issuer Bid for the purchase of up to 5% of its outstanding Common Shares during the period April 26, 2000 to April 25, 2001. On December 21, 2000, the Company amended its Normal Course Issuer Bid to increase the number of Common Shares it could repurchase from 1,394,000 to 1,838,000, being 10% of the public float as defined under the rules of The Toronto Stock Exchange, during the April 26, 2000 to April 25, 2001 period. Purchases of Common Shares pursuant to the Normal Course Issuer Bid were affected by a registered investment dealer, on behalf of the Company, through the facilities of The Toronto Stock Exchange. The price paid by the Company for any Common Shares purchased by it was the market price of the shares at the time of the purchase. The Company funded the purchase of Common Shares pursuant to the Normal Course Issuer Bid from its working capital. During the period April 26, 2000 to January 27, 2001, 1,379,348 Common Shares were purchased at an average price of $2.23 per Common Share (excluding commissions) for a total of $3,102,000

(including commissions) of which $1,559,000 was charged to capital stock and $1,543,000 was charged to retained earnings.

During the year ended January 29, 2000, 69,320 Common Shares were issued pursuant to the exercise of employee and director stock options for a total consideration of $111,000.

On March 3, 1999, the Company filed a Notice of Intention to make a Normal Course Issuer Bid for the purchase of up to 5% of its outstanding Common Shares during the period March 5, 1999, to March 4, 2000. Purchases of Common Shares pursuant to the Normal Course Issuer Bid were affected by a registered investment dealer, on behalf of the Company, through the facilities of The Toronto Stock Exchange. The price paid by the Company for any Common Shares purchased by it was the market price of the shares at the time of the purchase. The Company funded the purchase of Common Shares pursuant to the Normal Course Issuer Bid from its working capital. During the period March 5, 1999 to January 29, 2000, 78,600 Common Shares were purchased at an average price of $2.94 per Common Share for a total of $233,000 (including commissions) of which $92,000 was charged to capital stock and $141,000 was charged to retained earnings.

During the year ended January 30, 1999, 579,900 Common Shares were issued pursuant to the exercise of employee stock options for a total consideration of $808,000.

Also during the year ended January 30, 1999, the Preferred Shares held in the Company's U.S. subsidiary by three investors were exchanged for 999,337 Common Shares of the Company pursuant to stock exchange agreements dated January 18, 1995. Since the Company could require that such exchanges take place, these holdings have been treated as equity of the Company and as part of the Common Shares and weighted average Common Shares outstanding since January 18, 1995. Thus, this share issuance did not affect the dollar amount of capital stock or number of Common Shares or weighted average Common Shares outstanding.

The Company has a Stock Option Plan that was approved by shareholders at the June 26, 1996 Annual and Special Meeting of Shareholders. On April 6, 1999, the Board of Directors approved a resolution authorizing that the maximum number of Common Shares reserved for issuance pursuant to options granted under the Stock

Notes to Consolidated Financial Statements

Option Plan be increased to 4,175,000. This amendment to the Stock Option Plan was approved by shareholders at the June 24, 1999 Annual and Special Meeting of Shareholders.

Incentive Stock Option Plan

The Incentive Stock Option Plan provides that the Board of Directors of the Company may, from time to time at its discretion, grant to directors, officers, employees and consultants of the Company, or any affiliates of the Company, the option to purchase Common Shares of the Company provided that the number of Common Shares reserved for issuance under the Stock Option Plan shall not exceed 4,175,000 Common Shares less 98,860 options exercised subsequent to June 24, 1999. The plan also specifies that the maximum number of Common Shares issuable pursuant to options at any time be limited to 10% of the total Common Shares outstanding.

The price per Common Share shall not be less than the closing price of the Company's shares on The Toronto Stock Exchange on the trading day immediately preceding the date of the grant. Generally, options are exercisable for up to seven years from the date of the grant. The Board of Directors has the discretion to grant options that are exercisable for a longer or shorter period than seven years, provided that no option shall be exercisable for longer than 10 years. Unless otherwise determined by the Board at the time of grant, an option may be exercised for 20% of the shares immediately upon grant and thereafter for each completed 12-month period for the next four years, provided that an option may not be exercised as to the initial 20% until the holder has been providing services to the Company for at least one year. The Company does not provide financial assistance under the Stock Option Plan.

This table presents a summary of the status of the Company's Incentive Stock Option Plan at January 27, 2001, January 29, 2000 and January 30, 1999.

	January 30, 1999		January 29, 2000		January 27, 2001	
	Shares	Weighted Average Exercise Price	Shares	Weighted Average Exercise Price	Shares	Weighted Average Exercise Price
Outstanding at beginning of year	2,007,400	$ 1.64	1,662,800	$ 2.08	1,592,000	$ 2.09
Options granted	235,300	4.25	75,000	2.85	550,000	2.15
Options exercised	(579,900)	1.44	(69,320)	1.59	(49,540)	1.45
Options forfeited	—	—	(76,480)	3.03	(76,360)	2.90
Outstanding at end of year	1,662,800	$ 2.08	1,592,000	$ 2.09	2,016,100	$ 2.09
Options exercisable at end of year	855,100		1,120,300		1,388,580	

Performance-Based Stock Option Plan

The Company granted to one of its senior executives a special grant of options (the "Special Option") to purchase 250,000 Common Shares of the Company at the closing price of the Company's shares on The Toronto Stock Exchange on November 11, 1998 which was $3.85. These options were cancelled by the grantee during the fiscal year ended January 27, 2001. These Special Options were to vest based on the common stock of the Company trading on The Toronto Stock Exchange at an average for a 90-day period (using the Closing Price each day), at or above certain levels as follows: one-third or 83,333 options would have vested at $6.00; another third or 83,333 would have vested at $8.35; and the last third, or 83,334 would have vested at $10.65. The options were to expire on November 11, 2005.

The table below presents a summary of incentive-based options to purchase Common Shares granted to directors, retired directors, officers and employees outstanding as at January 27, 2001:

Number of Common Shares	Exercise Price	Expiry Date
200,000	$ 1.65	January 25, 2002
350,920	$ 1.45	March 28, 2003
68,880	$ 1.76	December 9, 2003
25,000	$ 1.95	January 29, 2004
598,500	$ 2.38	March 26, 2004
25,000	$ 4.20	November 6, 2004
192,800	$ 4.25	April 2, 2005
25,000	$ 2.55	April 2, 2006
195,000	$ 1.75	February 3, 2007
335,000	$2.40	October 26, 2007

At January 27, 2001, 1,388,580 of the 2,016,100 Common Share options outstanding are vested and exercisable.

The Company introduced a Shareholders' Rights Plan in 1995. The Rights Plan was subsequently confirmed by the shareholders of the Company at the Annual and Special Shareholders meeting held on June 26, 1996. At the Annual and Special Meeting of the Shareholders held June 24, 1999, the shareholders approved an amended and restated Rights Plan.

Pursuant to the Shareholders' Rights Plan Agreement, each shareholder received one Right for each outstanding Common Share they held. The Rights have no economic value and may not be exercised unless and until (a) an individual acquires the beneficial ownership of 20% or more of the outstanding Common Shares of the Company without Board approval, other than pursuant to a Permitted Bid, (b) the commencement of, or first public announcement of the intent of any person, other than the Company or any subsidiary of the Company, to commence a Take-over Bid, or (c) the date upon which a Permitted Bid ceases to be a Permitted Bid, or in any circumstances, such earlier or later date as may be determined by the Board of Directors, acting in good faith (collectively, the "Separation Time"). Without a postponement of the Separation Time by the Board of Directors, the occurrence of any of the above-mentioned events entitles all other shareholders to exercise their Rights and to purchase additional Common Shares at a 50% discount to market value.

The Rights expire upon the termination of the annual meeting of the Company in the year 2002, unless earlier terminated by the Board.

13. FINANCIAL INSTRUMENTS

Interest Rate

At January 27, 2001, the Company had fixed its borrowing rate on $20,000,000 of its anticipated short-term borrowing requirements at a 7.295% all-in rate and on $14,500,000 of its anticipated short-term borrowing requirements at an all-in-rate of 6.965%.

At January 29, 2000, the Company had fixed its borrowing rate at a 7.135% all-in rate on 88.5% of its actual short-term borrowing requirements during the year ended January 27, 2001. During fiscal 2001, the Company fixed its borrowing rate on the remainder of its short-term borrowing requirements at rates ranging from 6.78% to 7.35% all-in rate. These activities caused the Company to pay $56,677 less in interest during the fiscal year ended January 27, 2001 than if the Company had not fixed its borrowing rate.

At January 30, 1999, the Company had fixed its borrowing rate at a 6.60% all-in rate on 92% of its actual short-term borrowing requirements during the year ended January 29, 2000. During fiscal 2000, the Company fixed its borrowing rate on the remainder of its short-term borrowing requirements at a 6.36% all-in rate. These activities caused the Company to pay $59,000 more in interest during the fiscal year ended January 29, 2000 than if the Company had not fixed its borrowing rate.

The mark-to-market value of the interest rate swap contracts is a $7,069 unrecorded gain at January 27, 2001 (January 29, 2000: $102,992 unrecorded loss and January 30, 1999: $22,779 unrecorded gain) based on the Company's floating rate interest cost at January 27, 2001 of 7.25% (January 29, 2000: 6.50%, January 30, 1999: 6.75%).

Foreign Exchange

At January 27, 2001, the Company had six foreign exchange collar arrangements for committed and anticipated foreign merchandise purchases during the Company's next fiscal year ending January 26, 2002 totaling $6,680,000 (U.S.). Under the terms of the collars, the Company bears the exchange risk or benefit on foreign purchases when the Canadian dollar trades against the U.S. dollar within the ranges and time periods set out in the table below:

Collar Exercise Date	Floor Rate	Ceiling Rate	Contract Amount in U.S. $
February 1, 2001	1.4750	1.4910	$ 1,000,000
March 2, 2001	1.4724	1.4910	$ 800,000
April 4, 2001	1.4699	1.4910	$ 400,000
May 2, 2001	1.4676	1.4910	$ 770,000
June 5, 2001	1.4647	1.4910	$ 1,920,000
July 4, 2001	1.4626	1.4910	$ 1,790,000

Notes to Consolidated Financial Statements

At January 27, 2001, the unrealized gain on foreign exchange collars based on a January 27, 2001 exchange rate of $1.5063 was $102,204.

At January 27, 2001, the Company also had 10 foreign exchange fixed contract arrangements in place for committed and anticipated foreign merchandise purchases

for the period February 1, 2001 to January 31, 2002 totaling $14,064,500 (U.S.). Under the terms of the contract arrangements, the Company has fixed its exchange risk on foreign purchases for Canadian dollar trades against the U.S. dollar at the rate and time periods set forth below:

Time Period/Date for Exercising Contract	Fixed Rate	Contract Amount in U.S. $
February 1, 2001 to February 28, 2001	1.45310	$ 1,885,000
March 1, 2001 to March 30, 2001	1.45210	$ 1,055,000
April 3, 2001 to April 27, 2001	1.45100	$ 1,160,000
July 4, 2001 to July 31, 2001	1.46666	$ 71,000
August 1, 2001 to August 31, 2001	1.46559	$ 2,245,000
September 4, 2001 to September 28, 2001	1.46452	$ 2,096,000
October 1, 2001 to October 31, 2001	1.46378	$ 1,475,000
November 1, 2001 to November 30, 2001	1.50890	$ 1,795,000
December 1, 2001 to December 31, 2001	1.50850	$ 1,177,000
January 3, 2002 to January 31, 2002	1.50810	$ 1,105,500

At January 27, 2001, the unrealized gain on the foreign exchange fixed contract arrangements for U.S. dollars based on a January 27, 2001 exchange rate of $1.5063 was $456,866.

At January 29, 2000, the Company had nine foreign exchange collar arrangements totaling $9,748,000 (U.S.) and 19 fixed contract arrangements totaling $25,021,000 (U.S.) in place for committed and anticipated foreign merchandise purchases for the fiscal year ended January 27, 2001. During the fiscal year ended January 27, 2001, the Company also purchased and exercised $2,135,000 (U.S.) in fixed foreign exchange contracts to settle foreign exchange purchases. Under the terms of the collar arrangements, the Company bore the exchange risk or benefit on foreign merchandise purchases when the Canadian dollar traded against the U.S. dollar within the range of the average floor amount of $1.4560 ($14,193,088 Cdn., the floor) and the average ceiling amount of $1.4714 ($14,343,207 Cdn., the ceiling). Under the terms of the foreign exchange fixed contracts, the Company bore the exchange risk or benefit when the Canadian dollar traded against the U.S. dollar outside of an average rate of $1.4669 ($36,703,304 Cdn.). The fixed U.S. dollar contracts purchased and exercised during the year were at an average rate of $1.4835 ($3,167,273 Cdn.). As at January 29, 2000, based on a closing U.S. dollar exchange rate of $1.4423 (Cdn.) the unrealized net losses from U.S. dollar collars were $133,137 and the unrealized net losses from U.S. dollar fixed contracts were $615,533. During the fiscal year ended January 27, 2001, the various arrangements for foreign merchandise purchases cost the Company $479,414 less than if the arrangements had not been entered into.

At January 30, 1999, the Company had 17 foreign exchange collar arrangements totaling $27,442,002 (U.S.) and three fixed contract arrangements totaling 189,000,000$ (Portuguese Escudos) in place for committed and anticipated foreign merchandise purchases for the fiscal year ended January 29, 2000. During the fiscal year ended January 29, 2000, the Company also purchased and exercised $2,630,000 (U.S.) in fixed foreign exchange contracts to settle foreign exchange purchases. Under the terms of the collar arrangements, the Company bore the exchange risk or benefit on foreign merchandise purchases when the Canadian dollar traded against the U.S. dollar within the range of the average floor amount of $1.5053 ($41,308,446 Cdn., the floor) and the average ceiling amount of $1.5320 ($42,041,147 Cdn., the ceiling). Under the terms of the foreign exchange fixed contracts, the Company bore the exchange risk or benefit when the Canadian dollar traded against the Portuguese Escudo outside of an average rate of 0.008816 ($1,666,224 Cdn.). The fixed U.S. dollar contracts purchased and exercised during the year were at an average rate of 1.4765 ($3,883,195 Cdn.). As at January 30, 1999, based on a closing U.S. dollar exchange rate of $1.5074 (Cdn.) and Portuguese Escudo exchange rate of $.00885 (Cdn.), the unrealized net losses from U.S. dollar collars were $79,825 and the unrealized net gains on Portuguese Escudo fixed contracts were $6,458. During the fiscal year ended January 29, 2000, the various arrangements for foreign merchandise purchases cost the Company $975,455 more than if the arrangements had not been entered into.

14. CORPORATE AND FRANCHISE SALES

	1999	2000	2001
Company-owned store sales	$ 283,401	$ 314,547	$ 363,870
Mark's franchisee-owned store sales	61,801	63,340	65,754
Work World franchisee-owned store sales	72,266	59,783	58,355
	$ 417,468	$ 437,670	$ 487,979

Total corporate and franchise sales have been shown as a separate item at the top of the Consolidated Statements of Earnings and Retained Earnings to illustrate the size of the total business. Only the Company-owned store sales and the franchise royalties earned on franchise-owned store sales, initial franchise fees earned on the sale of franchise stores, other sundry income from franchise operations and Company costs related to franchise operations form part of the Consolidated Statements of Earnings and Retained Earnings.

15. FRANCHISE ROYALTIES AND OTHER

	1999	2000	2001
Royalties from Mark's franchise stores	$ 3,965	$ 4,075	$ 4,129
Sundry income from Mark's franchise operations	20	—	—
Royalties from Work World franchise stores	2,863	2,470	2,404
Fees from the sale of Work World franchises	15	11	(1)
Sundry income from Work World franchise operations	153	84	26
	$ 7,016	$ 6,640	$ 6,558
Number of franchise stores at year end			
Mark's	29	29	25
Work World	105	102	90
	134	131	115

16. U.S. OPERATIONS

The Company decided to end its U.S. test in the fiscal year ended January 30, 1999. The impact of the conclusion of the U.S. test was a $2,961,000 additional charge to pre-tax earnings in fiscal 1999, or 6 cents per share after tax, and the elimination of operating losses from this test and reduced current assets going forward. Expenses incurred in fiscal 2000 relating to the closure of the Company's U.S. test have been charged against this provision. The Company has $306,000 of the provision remaining at January 27, 2001, for additional costs expected to be incurred up to January 28, 2006.

	1999	2000	2001
Sales, excluding inter group	$ 1,665	$ —	$ —
Deduct:			
Cost of sales	1,134	—	—
Front-line expenses	1,198	—	—
Back-line expenses	427	—	—
Operating loss before income taxes	(1,094)	—	—
Provisions for closure costs	2,961	—	—
Loss before income taxes	(4,055)	—	—
Income tax benefit	(1,780)	—	—
Net loss	$ (2,275)	$ —	$ —
Net loss per share	(8) ¢	— ¢	— ¢
Current assets	$ 900	$ —	$ —
Capital and other assets	—	—	—
Total assets	$ 900	$ —	$ —

Notes to Consolidated Financial Statements

17. INCOME TAXES

The provision for income taxes varies from the amount computed by applying the combined federal and provincial income tax rates as follows:

	1999		2000		2001	
Federal and provincial income taxes	43.9%	$ 4,966	44.4%	$ 5,632	44.0%	$ 7,513
Increase resulting from						
Other	2.5%	278	2.3%	291	4.9%	833
Provision for income taxes	46.4%	$ 5,244	46.7%	$ 5,923	48.9%	$ 8,346

Future income taxes result from the effect of transactions that are recognized in different periods for financial and tax-reporting purposes. See Note 1N. The major components of the Company's future tax assets and liabilities are:

	1999	2000	2001
Other assets	$ (851)	$ (448)	$ (480)
Capital assets	3,750	2,631	2,983
Goodwill	27	(85)	(431)
Deferred gains	487	928	925
Future income taxes	$ 3,413	$ 3,026	$ 2,997

Mark's Work Wearhouse Ltd. has an August tax year end. Mark's Work Wearhouse Inc. (the Company's inactive U.S. subsidiary) has a January tax year end. The Company has $12,067,000 of goodwill remaining on its balance sheet that is not deductible for tax purposes. Losses carried forward for tax purposes are:

	1999	2000	2001
Capital losses – Mark's Work Wearhouse Ltd.	$ 611	$ 611	$ 611
Non-capital loss – Mark's Work Wearhouse Inc.	$ 1,439	$ 1,439	$ 1,439

18. SEGMENTED INFORMATION

The Company is a specialty retailer of primarily men's and some ladies' apparel and footwear operating in Canada and operated two Mark's pilot stores in the U.S. until January 30, 1999. See Note 16. Financial information by operating group is:

	1999	2000	2001
Sales, Earnings and Depreciation and Amortization			
Corporate and franchise sales			
Mark's and Corporate Services Canada	$ 329,023	$ 345,810	$ 385,677
Work World Canada	86,866	89,201	94,532
DOCKERS® Stores Canada	—	2,666	7,770
Mark's United States	1,865	—	—
Inter group	(286)	(7)	—
	$ 417,468	$ 437,670	$ 487,979
Earnings (loss) before interest, taxes, depreciation and amortization			
Mark's and Corporate Services Canada	$ 26,104	$ 28,378	$ 32,918
Work World Canada	510	43	1,088
DOCKERS® Stores Canada	—	(2,116)	(2,666)
Mark's United States	(915)	—	—
Mark's United States provision for closure costs	(2,961)	—	—
	$ 22,738	$ 26,305	$ 31,340
Depreciation and amortization excluding goodwill amortization (front-line and back-line)			
Mark's and Corporate Services Canada	$ 7,612	$ 8,562	$ 8,510
Work World Canada	122	858	1,146
DOCKERS® Stores Canada	—	183	632
Mark's United States	327	—	—
	$ 8,061	$ 9,603	$ 10,288
Goodwill amortization			
Mark's and Corporate Services Canada	$ 277	$ 289	$ 372
Work World Canada	39	86	176
	$ 316	$ 375	$ 548
Cash flows related to Capital items			
Capital Expenditures			
Mark's and Corporate Services Canada	$ (1,816)	$ (127)	$ (1,383)
Work World Canada	(812)	(277)	(383)
DOCKERS® Stores Canada	—	(1,511)	(719)
Mark's United States	(555)	—	—
	$ (3,183)	$ (1,915)	$ (2,485)
Acquisitions of subsidiaries			
Work World Canada	$ (2,196)	$ (737)	$ —
Purchases of franchise stores			
Mark's and Corporate Services Canada	$ (1,814)	$ —	$ (1,807)
Work World Canada	(2,506)	(50)	$ (1,247)
	$ (4,320)	$ (50)	$ (3,054)
Financial Position			
Total assets			
Mark's and Corporate Services Canada	$ 119,281	$ 126,441	$ 142,943
Goodwill on acquisition of Work World (net of accumulated amortization)	6,690	6,479	6,268
Work World Canada	19,907	19,530	23,642
Goodwill on acquisition of Paul John (net of accumulated amortization)	853	3,540	3,405
DOCKERS® Stores Canada	—	5,195	6,549
Mark's United States	900	—	—
Inter group	(14,639)	(18,101)	(25,747)
	$ 132,992	$ 143,084	$ 157,060

Notes to Consolidated Financial Statements

19. SUBSEQUENT EVENT

Effective February 19, 2001, the Company outsourced its distribution activities to a third-party logistics-service provider for a term of five years. The annual costs of the service for each year of the contract are determined through an annually approved budget process. Exclusive of the amortization of start-up costs and one-time transition costs, these costs are budgeted at $2,500,000 for the Company's fiscal year ending January 26, 2002.

20. SELECTED QUARTERLY
FINANCIAL INFORMATION (UNAUDITED)

	First	Second	Third	Fourth	Total
52 weeks ended January 27, 2001					
Corporate store sales	$ 64,568	$ 74,651	$ 88,077	$ 136,574	$ 363,870
Gross margin percentage	43.1%	39.6%	41.5%	40.7%	41.1%
Earnings (loss) before income taxes and goodwill amortization	$ (1,045)	$ (809)	$ 2,370	$ 16,558	$ 17,074
Net earnings (loss) per Common Share before goodwill amortization	(2)¢	(2)¢	6¢	30¢	32¢
Net earnings (loss) per Common Share	(3)¢	(2)¢	5¢	30¢	30¢
Corporate stores at end of quarter	182	187	191	194	194
52 weeks ended January 29, 2000					
Corporate store sales	$ 57,235	$ 62,736	$ 77,146	$ 117,430	$ 314,547
Gross margin percentage	41.7%	40.1%	41.2%	40.0%	40.6%
Earnings (loss) before income taxes and goodwill amortization	$ (1,853)	$ (554)	$ 1,884	$ 13,208	$ 12,685
Net earnings (loss) per Common Share before goodwill amortization	(4)¢	(1)¢	3¢	26¢	24¢
Net earnings (loss) per Common Share	(4)¢	(2)¢	3¢	26¢	23¢
Corporate stores at end of quarter	166	167	173	177	177
52 weeks ended January 30, 1999					
Corporate store sales	$ 48,419	$ 51,686	$ 67,336	$ 115,960	$ 283,401
Gross margin percentage	41.4%	39.4%	41.6%	39.5%	40.3%
Earnings (loss) before income taxes and goodwill amortization	$ (1,599)	$ (1,936)	$ 2,105	$ 12,742	$ 11,312
Net earnings (loss) per Common Share before goodwill amortization	(4)¢	(4)¢	4¢	26¢	22¢
Net earnings (loss) per Common Share	(4)¢	(4)¢	4¢	25¢	21¢
Corporate stores at end of quarter	123	126	160	165	165

Glossary of Terms

The following glossary defines terms used throughout this report.

Back-line Expenses: All expenses associated with supporting stores but not directly related to face-to-face customer contact. These expenses include non-store personnel administrative and other expenses, distribution centre costs, computer costs (net of recoveries from the front-line), software development and maintenance costs, interest long-term, franchise bad debts and non-store occupancy, depreciation and amortization.

Base Rent: Rent payable to the landlord prior to paying for Common Area Maintenance (CAM) and property taxes.

Basis Point: A basis point corresponds to 1/100 of a percentage point.

Blend: The percentage that results from dividing the sales of a category by the total Company's corporate store sales.

Business Objective: A measurable target set for each management employee upon which job evaluation and bonuses are based.

Business-to-Business Sales: From the Company's perspective, these sales are apparel and footwear sales, sometimes with embroidery work added, for the account of a corporate customer either directly to the corporate customer or to the corporate customer's employees.

Business-to-Consumer Electronic Sales: See e-Commerce sales.

CAM: The Common Area Maintenance cost component of the total rent payable to a landlord.

Capex: A short form term to describe capital expenditures.

Capital Expenditures: Costs recognized as a portion of long-term assets. These costs relate to the purchase of leasehold improvements, furniture, fixtures, equipment and capital lease purchases.

Captive Label: Labels owned by Mark's or Work World but not associated with the name of the store. These include WindRiver, Denver Hayes, Dakota, Canyon Creek, etc.

Conservative Forecast: The lower end of the Company's published forecast range as depicted on page 19, and based upon the assumptions on page 18.

Corporate Services: The back-line services group that provides the operating divisions with the appropriate level of high-quality, standardized support in the areas of customer service, human resources, warehouse distribution, store design, real estate, systems, finance and accounting and CEO leadership, while ensuring that the divisions are adhering to the Company's corporate value system.

Corporate Store Strategy, Work World Division: A strategy whereby new stores in the Work World Division are opened as corporate stores rather than franchise stores and, as opportunities present themselves, franchise stores are purchased and converted to corporate stores. The Company believes this is the preferred strategy in its Work World Division as the Company believes that, over time, its corporate stores business model will deliver better financial returns than the franchise store model.

CPFS: Cash flow per share calculated by dividing the Company's funds provided by operations by the weighted average shares outstanding during the fiscal year.

Destination Store: A store that is large enough and dominant enough in its retail location to draw its own customer traffic and is not dependent upon its neighbours. A destination store is typically free-standing, but can be located in a strip mall or power centre. The Company's Mark's Division operates destination stores.

Direct Import Purchases: The purchase of merchandise for resale directly from offshore factories without using the services of a Canadian importer.

DOCKERS® or DOCKERS® Stores: The Company's DOCKERS® Stores Division operation excluding Mark's, Work World and Corporate Services.

EBIT: Earnings before interest and income taxes.

EBITDA: Earnings before interest, income taxes and depreciation and amortization: more specifically, sales revenues available after all merchandise costs, front-line and back-line expenses, except for interest, depreciation and amortization, goodwill amortization and income taxes are subtracted, plus franchise royalties.

e-Commerce Sales: From the Company's perspective, these sales are apparel and footwear sales to customers executed electronically through the Internet and fulfilled through the Company's Mark's Division coast-to-coast store network. The Company sometimes also refers to these sales at Business-to-Consumer Electronic Sales.

EPS: Earnings per share. See Note 1K to the Consolidated Financial Statements for the method of calculation.

Franchise Operations: Mark's and Work World franchise operating results consist of franchise royalties, initial franchise fees and other sundry income from franchisees minus bad debt provisions on franchise receivables. Deducted from that amount is an estimate of the franchise operation's share of selected divisional back-line expenses and, in the case of the Mark's Division franchises, selected Corporate Services back-line costs, based on each division's franchise sales as a percentage of each division's total system sales applied to those selected back-line costs. In addition, the Mark's franchise operations are charged with the front-line cost of two district managers and the Work World franchise operations are charged with acquisition financing costs and goodwill amortization.

Front-line Contribution: Sales revenues available after all merchandise costs and front-line expenses are subtracted.

Front-line Expenses: Expenses incurred from having direct contact with customers, including store personnel, advertising, occupancy, store variable and store other expenses. Depreciation and amortization of store assets and short-term interest costs are also included.

Funded Debt: The aggregate of all interest-bearing and non-interest bearing contracted debt on the Company's balance sheet (currently bank indebtedness, bank term debt, capital lease debt, leasehold fixtures and equipment loan for the DOCKERS® Stores test, estimated future earnout payable on the Paul John acquisition and long-term debt payable on acquisitions of individual franchise stores).

Gross Margin: Sales revenues available after all merchandise costs.

Gross Margin Return on Investment (GMROI): A financial ratio comparing a division's or the Company's gross margin dollars to the division's or the Company's average inventory at cost. This ratio provides an indication of the division's or the Company's inventory efficiency.

Gross Margin Return on Space: A financial ratio comparing a division's or the Company's gross margin dollars to a division's or to the Company's average square feet of selling. This ratio provides an indication of the division's or the Company's space efficiency.

Glossary of Terms

Indirect Import Purchases: The purchase of merchandise for resale from Canadian importers who source the merchandise offshore.

Inventory Turnover: A measure of the level of investment in inventory by a division or the Company, calculated by averaging inventory at retail on hand at the start of the period and at each month end during the period for a division or the Company and dividing that amount into the sales for the period of a division or the Company.

Key Results: One to three challenging, measurable business targets set by individuals that cause hearts to race and palms to sweat.

L'Équipeur: Mark's store name in the province of Quebec, Canada.

Macro: A term used to describe "big picture" or "global" factors.

Mark's or Mark's Division: Mark's Work Wearhouse and L'Équipeur divisional operations excluding Work World, DOCKERS® and Corporate Services.

MVP: Most valuable employee or group of employees.

Net Front-line Contribution: Sales revenues available after all merchandise costs and front-line expenses are subtracted and the franchise royalties and other are added.

Net Earnings before Goodwill Amortization: Sales revenues available after all merchandise costs and front-line and back-line expenses and non-recurring items and income taxes are subtracted and franchise royalties and other are added, but before goodwill amortization is subtracted.

Occupancy: Base rent plus Common Area Maintenance (CAM) plus property taxes plus business taxes and licenses.

"On Concept" Store: A Mark's store that is 8,000 to 15,000 sq. ft. in size; is a destination store; occupies a dominant position in its retail location (preferably free-standing but can be in a strip mall or power centre); has good parking, signing and access; has properly implemented all store anchors; and leasehold improvements, fixtures, lighting and cleanliness meet current corporate standards.

Optimistic Forecast: The upper end of the Company's published forecast range as depicted on page 19 and based upon the assumptions on page 18.

Performance Contract: A single page document signed by an employee and management that contains the individual's Business Objective and Key Results.

Post-audit: A detailed review of the return on investment and return on capital employed provided by each new, relocated or refurbished store and by purchased franchise stores against pre-set corporate hurdle rates to determine whether the project was a financial success or not.

Pre-audit: Based on history for similar stores, a projection of the return on investment and return on capital employed expected from each new, relocated or refurbished store or purchased franchise store to determine whether the proposed project is expected to meet pre-set corporate hurdle rates or not.

Private Label: A label that uses the store's name, e.g., Mark's jeans or Work World jeans or DOCKERS® khakis and thus brings an instant association between product and store.

Purchase Markup: The difference between the selling price and landed cost of an item purchased for resale in the Company's stores.

Rent, Other Operating Leases, Computer Services, Distribution Activities and Interest on Long-term (including capital leases) Debt Coverage: A financial ratio comparing the Company's fixed commitments under lease, and long-term agreements and interest-bearing and non interest-bearing contracted debt obligations to the earnings available to meet them. This ratio is intended to provide a better measure of the inherent risk in the business than is provided by the total liabilities-to-equity ratio, due to the large rent component and other outsourced activities in a retail company's risk profile.

Rolling Average Funded Debt-to-Equity Ratio: A financial ratio comparing the Company's average funded debt over the most recent 12 months to the Company's average equity over that same most recent 12 months.

Sales Per Resident: Our measure of market penetration calculated by dividing sales from a division's or the Company's total corporate and franchise stores within a region or the entire country by the population of that region, or the entire country.

Same-store Sales Increase: A calculation of the sales increase on a comparative basis, derived by comparing sales of two consecutive years, exclusive of all stores opened or closed within that two-year period.

Seasons: The Company breaks the year down into two seasons for operating purposes: Spring – February through July; Fall – August through January.

Shrink: The difference between opening inventory and closing year-end inventory after accounting for all purchase, costs of goods sold, markdowns, customer adjustments and other discounts.

Strategic Plan: The Company's most recent five-year Plan covering the fiscal years ending January 2002, 2003, 2004, 2005 and 2006.

Total Liabilities: The aggregate of all liabilities, current and long-term, on the Company's balance sheet, including deferred gains.

Total Liabilities-to-Equity Ratio: A financial ratio comparing the Company's total liabilities to shareholders' equity. This ratio provides creditors with some idea of the Company's ability to withstand losses without impairing the interests of creditors.

Total Sales or Total System Sales: Combined sales from Mark's corporate stores, Mark's franchise stores, Work World's corporate stores, Work World's franchise stores and DOCKERS® corporate stores, and in years prior to fiscal 2000, Mark's U.S. pilot stores.

Trendex North America or Trendex: This organization provides statistical data on the Canadian apparel and footwear markets. The Company subscribes to this service.

Work World: Work World Divisional operations excluding Mark's Work Wearhouse, DOCKERS® Stores and Corporate Services.

Corporate Governance

Mark's Work Wearhouse Ltd. is an Alberta corporation. The Alberta Business Corporations Act makes it clear that it is the responsibility of the Board of Directors to manage the business and affairs of the Company. The Board discharges this responsibility by selecting and holding accountable management to whom the Board delegates operations. Business and affairs, and operations are to be managed in the best interests of the shareholders toward the goal of maximizing the long-term value of the Company to shareholders.

The key governance issues facing the Company's Board relate to seeking the appropriate balance between structures and mechanisms that facilitate management's capacity to manage the business and those that facilitate appropriate stewardship by the Board. The Board recognizes the need for, and encourages management led by the President and Chief Executive Officer, to make clear and appropriate executive decisions and to be strong leaders. The need is not to rein in management but rather to equip the Board with the capacity to exercise its responsibilities, to be good critics as well as supporters and constructive skeptics. A healthy, friendly tension is appropriate.

During fiscal 2001 (January 30, 2000 to January 27, 2001), the Company held five Board meetings in person and one telephone meeting. During fiscal 2001, six directors attended all six meetings and two directors attended five of the six meetings.

During fiscal 2001, two Compensation Committee meetings, three Audit committee meetings and four Governance Committee meetings were held. All respective committee members attended all their respective committee meetings, except for one Audit Committee member who was absent for one Audit Committee meeting.

The following analysis uses definitions contained in the Toronto Stock Exchange Report on Corporate Governance ("Governance Guidelines") and is numbered in response to the specific Governance Guidelines with an indication of the Company's alignment. This analysis was adopted by the Board of Directors of the Company on April 26, 2001.

TSE CORPORATE GOVERNANCE GUIDELINES	DOES MARK'S ALIGN?	COMMENTS
1. Board should explicitly assume responsibility for stewardship of the corporation and specifically for: a) Adoption of a strategic planning process;	Yes	The Board reviews and approves management-developed strategic planning methodology and the Strategic Plan. The Board delegates to management the responsibility for tabling with the Board, a draft Strategic Plan. The Board's input is incorporated by management and, following an iterative process, the Strategic Plan is adopted by the Board at a subsequent meeting. The Board uses the Strategic Plan as a tool to measure the Company's progress.
b) Identification of principal risks and implementation of appropriate risk management systems;	Yes	The principal risks of the Company's business are outlined in the annual report under Management's Discussion and Analysis of Risk and Uncertainties. The Board and particularly its Audit Committee, review these risks, set policy for the management of these risks, and receive reports from the Company's management on how these risks are being assessed and managed.
c) Succession planning, including appointing, training and monitoring senior management;	Yes	The Board takes responsibility for appointing and monitoring senior management. The Board regularly has senior management explain its succession plans for the Company's managers and their own positions. The Board encourages management to participate in professional and personal development activities, courses and programs, and supports management's commitment to the training and development of all permanent employees. An amount is allocated in the Company's budgets each year for this.
d) Communications policy; and	Yes	The Board has instructed senior management to develop a clearly articulated policy for effective two-way communications with shareholders, employees, suppliers, other stakeholders and the public in general, including the media. The Board recognizes this to be, except in rare circumstances, solely the province of management. The Board believes that the quality of the Company's communication with outsiders is an element to be considered in evaluating management.
e) Integrity of internal control and management information systems.	Yes	Directly and through its Audit Committee, the Board assesses the integrity of the Company's internal control and management information systems. The Audit Committee meets with senior management and the independent auditors twice annually to discuss and review these matters, and then reports its findings to the Board.
2. Majority of Directors should be "unrelated" (free from conflicting interest).	Yes	In fiscal 2001, the Board consisted of eight members: six unrelated directors and two members of management. The directors to be proposed by the Board to the shareholders for election at the June 13, 2001 annual meeting are the eight existing directors, of whom two are members of management. The Board intends to maintain a significant proportion of independent unrelated directors. The Company does not have a "significant shareholder" as defined by the Governance Guidelines as a shareholder with the ability to exercise a majority of votes for the election of directors.

Corporate Governance

TSE CORPORATE GOVERNANCE GUIDELINES	DOES MARK'S ALIGN?	COMMENTS
3. Disclose for each Director whether the Director is related and how that conclusion was reached.	Yes	The two management directors are related to the Company. The principal occupation/employment of each of the other directors is set out in the annual report under the heading "Directors". The Board has considered the relationship of each outside director to the Company and has concluded that none are related.
4. a) Appoint a Committee responsible for proposing new nominees for appointment/ assessment of Directors; and	Yes	The Board has constituted a Governance Committee that recommends nominees to the Board, reflecting the Board's expertise and needs and being mindful of potential conflicts of interest.
b) Composed exclusively of outside (non-management) Directors, a majority of whom are unrelated.	Yes	The Governance Committee consists of four unrelated directors.
5. Implement a process for assessing the effectiveness of the Board, its Committees and individual Directors.	Yes	The Governance Committee is responsible for the continuing assessment of the Board as a whole and the Audit, Compensation and Governance Committees. The Governance Committee, in its March 22, 2001 report to the Board, assessed the Board, Audit, Compensation, and Governance Committees as effective in the discharge of their duties, including statutory fiduciary duties. The Governance Committee also assessed that each of the returning nominees for director ably discharges their roles and responsibilities as a director and adds value to the governance of the Company.
6. Provide orientation and education programs for new Directors.	Yes	The Company has an orientation package for new Board members.
7. Consider size of Board with a view to improving effectiveness.	Yes	The Governance Committee reports periodically on the impact of size upon the effectiveness of the Board, ensuring that the Board brings together the right mix of skills, backgrounds, ages and attitudes. In its March 22, 2001 report to the Board, the Governance Committee concluded that the number of directors in the range as presently constituted is appropriate for a company the size and complexity of Mark's Work Wearhouse.
8. Review the adequacy and form of compensation of Directors in light of risks and responsibilities.	Yes	As directed by the Board, the Compensation Committee has used independent compensation studies in assessing the level of senior executive compensation. In the fall of 2000, the Governance and Compensation Committees jointly undertook to review the remuneration of the directors in order to attract and retain talented directors. In this undertaking, the Committees reviewed reports by specialists on director compensation in Canada, including benchmarking materials on public companies of various sectors and sizes. Based on this review, the Committees recommended that stock-based compensation in addition to annual retainers and meeting fees form a portion of the directors' remuneration. The recommendations were adopted by the Board on October 26, 2000.
9. Board Committees should generally be composed of outside Directors, a majority of whom are unrelated.	Yes	The Board has three committees, the Governance Committee, the Compensation Committee and the Audit Committee. All three are made up of four outside, unrelated Directors.
10. Appoint a Committee responsible for approach to corporate governance issues and the guidelines.	Yes	The Governance Committee is responsible for developing and monitoring the Company's approach to governance issues and for responding to The Toronto Stock Exchange governance guidelines.
11. a) Define limits to management's responsibilities by developing mandates for the Board and the Chief Executive Officer; and	Yes	The Governance Committee completed position descriptions for the Board and the President and Chief Executive Officer that have been approved by the Board. These position descriptions are reviewed regularly by the Governance Committee. During the past fiscal year, the Compensation Committee reviewed the compensation and performance of the President and Chief Executive Officer, and Chief Financial Officer. In its February 3, 2000 report to the Board, based on a report received from a national compensation and benefits firm, the Compensation Committee recommended and the Board approved a retirement compensation plan for the current President and Chief Executive Officer of Mark's Work Wearhouse Ltd. In its March 22, 2001 report to the Board, the Compensation Committee addressed and the Board approved senior executive compensation.
b) The Board should approve the Chief Executive Officer's corporate objectives.	Yes	The Board annually approves the Business Objective and Key Results for which the President and Chief Executive Officer is responsible and accountable. The Business Objective and Key Results for fiscal 2002 and a review of the results for fiscal 2001 are published in the annual report under Senior Management Performance.

TSE CORPORATE GOVERNANCE GUIDELINES	DOES MARK'S ALIGN?	COMMENTS
12. Establish procedures to enable the Board to function independently of management.	Yes	In December 1995, the Board decided to appoint an outside independent director as Chairman of the Board based on the position description for a non-management Chairman completed by the Governance Committee. The non-executive Chairman's responsibilities include ensuring that adequate and proper information is made available to the Board and maintaining good lines of communication between the Board and senior management. The Governance Committee also recommended and the Board approved that adequate time be allocated in the Board agenda at each of the March and October Board meetings for the outside directors to meet without management present. These sessions have as agenda items at least the following: (i) evaluation of senior management; (ii) assessment of overall corporate progress and progress against the Strategic Plan; (iii) assessment of overall management capability, strength and depth; (iv) succession planning; (v) Board governance matters; and (vi) issues on the minds of outside directors. The Board has met on several occasions this past fiscal year without management present.
13. a) The Audit Committee should have a specifically-defined mandate; and	Yes	The roles and responsibilities of the Audit Committee have been defined to include responsibility for overseeing management reporting on internal control and management information systems, compliance with the Company's Code of Conduct, and the normal statutory responsibilities. As a result of recent requirements by regulatory authorities, at its March 22, 2001 Board meeting, the Board authorized the Audit Committee to review and approve the Company's quarterly financial statements and quarterly management discussion and analysis beginning with the quarter ending April 28, 2001. The Audit Committee has direct communication channels with the Company's independent auditors and regularly meets with the auditors without management present. The Company has no formal internal audit process at this time, a policy that is reviewed periodically by the Audit Committee and with which the Audit Committee and the independent auditors concur. The Audit Committee meets regularly with management and the external auditors to review the annual audited financial statements of the Company, the auditors' report thereon and Management's Discussion and Analysis included in the Company's annual report. The Audit Committee then recommends to the Board the approval of the annual audited financial statements. Each year the Audit Committee receives regular normal course updates from the external auditors on the Company's internal controls and monitors management's implementation of the recommendations that the Audit Committee, management and the external auditors agree need to be acted upon. The Audit Committee annually reviews the Information Circular and the Annual Information Form and the "Post Audit" analysis of the Company's capital projects. The Audit Committee meets regularly with management to discuss and approve any new accounting or financial policies, including foreign currency and interest rate hedging policies. The Audit Committee annually reviews all material provisions requiring management's judgment and best estimates.
b) All members should be outside Directors.	Yes	The Audit Committee consists of four outside, unrelated directors.
14. Implement a system to enable individual Directors to engage outside advisors, at the Corporation's expense.	Yes	The Governance Committee is responsible for approving the engagement by individual directors of outside advisors at the expense of the Company in appropriate circumstances. Any such engagement is subject to the approval of the Governance Committee and requires senior management to be informed of any such action.

Eleven-Year Financial Review (unaudited)

(amounts in thousands of dollars except where indicated)	Jan. 2001	Jan. 2000	Jan. 1999	Jan. 1998
STATEMENTS OF EARNINGS				
Total sales	487,979	437,670	417,468	402,207
Mark's franchise store retail sales	65,754	63,340	61,801	62,696
Work World franchise store retail sales*	58,355	59,783	72,266	87,495
Mark's corporate store retail sales***	319,923	282,463	267,136	249,339
Work World corporate store retail sales*	36,177	29,418	14,600	1,002
DOCKERS® corporate store retail sales	7,770	2,666	N/A	N/A
Mark's U.S. corporate store retail sales***	N/A	N/A	1,665	1,675
Gross Margin	149,509	127,824	114,238	102,093
Percent	41.09 %	40.64 %	40.31 %	40.51 %
Franchise royalties and other	6,558	6,640	7,016	7,604
Operating expenses	124,727	108,159	95,555	87,866
Interest expense	3,978	4,017	3,365	2,332
Depreciation and amortization including goodwill amortization	10,836	9,978	8,377	7,095
Operating earnings (loss) before U.S. closure provision, discontinued operations and income taxes	16,526	12,310	13,957	12,404
Provision for closure of U.S. pilot stores	N/A	N/A	2,961	N/A
Earnings (loss) from discontinued operations	N/A	N/A	N/A	N/A
Income taxes (recovery)	8,346	5,923	5,244	5,853
Net earnings (loss)	8,180	6,387	5,752	6,551
EBITDA	31,340	26,305	22,738	21,831
EBIT	20,504	16,327	14,361	14,736
STATEMENTS OF CASH FLOWS**				
Funds flow (deficiency) from operations	18,881	16,876	15,815	13,609
Change in non-cash working capital	2,259	(6,577)	(8,910)	(19,610)
Investing	(5,807)	(4,142)	(10,579)	(1,885)
Financing	(10,114)	(7,093)	6,035	(3,514)
Net cash and cash equivalents generated (deployed)	5,219	(936)	2,361	(11,400)
FINANCIAL POSITION				
Current assets	110,387	101,475	96,360	75,810
Current liabilities	63,222	57,296	56,525	44,397
Working capital	47,165	44,179	39,835	31,413
Capital assets (net)	28,148	25,893	23,531	20,072
Goodwill	14,472	11,076	8,713	7,195
Total assets*****	157,060	143,084	132,992	105,617
Long-term debt excluding current portion	27,016	23,952	22,052	13,414
Total debt*****	92,339	83,513	79,686	58,871
Shareholders' equity	64,721	59,571	53,306	46,746
Average capital employed	97,747	88,101	73,972	57,858
SHARE DATA (per Common Share data in dollars)				
Common Shares outstanding at year end (000s)	26,527	27,857	27,866	27,286
Weighted average number of Common Shares outstanding (000s)	27,597	27,847	27,475	27,058
Earnings (loss) per Common Share	0.30	0.23	0.21	0.24
Funds flow (deficiency) from operations per Common Share (CFPS)	0.68	0.61	0.58	0.50
Price/Earnings ratio at year end (times)	8.00	7.83	15.48	15.42
Book value per share (year end)	2.44	2.14	1.91	1.71
Market value per share – high	2.50	3.60	5.00	4.45
– low	1.36	1.50	2.95	1.95
– year end	2.40	1.80	3.25	3.70
Dividends declared	0	0	0	0
FINANCIAL RATIOS				
Return on average shareholders' equity	13.2 %	11.3 %	11.5 %	15.7 %
Return on average capital employed	21.0 %	18.5 %	19.4 %	25.5 %
Current ratio (times)	1.75	1.77	1.70	1.71
Total liabilities to equity ratio (times)	1.43	1.40	1.49	1.26
Rent, other operating leases, computer services, distribution activities and interest on long-term debt (including capital leases) coverage (times)	1.50	1.42	1.47	1.58
STATISTICS				
Consolidated corporate stores same store sales increase (decrease)	9.8 %	(0.6 %)	4.7 %	8.0 %
Consolidated corporate operations inventory turnover (times)	2.0	1.8	1.8	2.2
Consolidated corporate store retail SF (year end)	1,449,325	1,354,561	1,256,477	1,038,523
Consolidated corporate store sales per SF*****	255	237	251	253
No. of Mark's Division corporate stores end of period	132	127	122	114
No. of Work World Division corporate stores end of period	54	45	41	3
No. of DOCKERS® Stores Division corporate stores end of period	8	5	N/A	N/A
No. of Mark's U.S. corporate stores end of period	N/A	N/A	2	1
No. of Mark's Division franchise stores end of period	25	29	29	31
No. of Work World Division franchise stores end of period*	90	102	105	139
Consolidated staff at year end	2,863	2,271	2,512	2,145

*   Mark's acquired Work World effective December 1, 1996 and during fiscal 1999, 31 Work World franchise stores were converted to corporate stores.
** The statements of cash flows exclude non-cash items, primarily non-cash working capital related to the acquisition of subsidiaries and franchise store purchases, capital assets acquired through capital leases and purchases of individual franchise stores by means of long-term debt.

ELEVEN-YEAR FINANCIAL REVIEW (UNAUDITED)

Jan. 1997	Jan. 1996	Jan. 1995	Jan. 1994	Jan. 1993	Jan. 1992	Jan. 1991
303,756	262,575	247,768	220,055	190,082	185,694	234,190
60,682	64,313	66,143	61,989	56,629	52,952	55,872
22,172	N/A	N/A	N/A	N/A	N/A	N/A
219,492	197,416	181,625	158,066	133,453	132,742	178,318
N/A	N/A	N/A	N/A	N/A	N/A	N/A
N/A	N/A	N/A	N/A	N/A	N/A	N/A
1,410	846	N/A	N/A	N/A	N/A	N/A
83,969	73,481	66,853	58,067	48,390	46,783	55,725
38.01 %	37.06 %	36.81 %	36.74 %	36.26 %	35.24 %	31.25 %
4,981	4,266	4,299	4,071	3,473	3,438	3,619
74,368	66,589	61,134	55,126	49,449	50,818	63,663
1,849	1,672	1,139	2,186	2,130	2,354	3,310
4,423	3,112	2,364	3,560	3,030	3,805	3,112
8,310	6,374	6,515	1,266	(2,746)	(6,756)	(10,741)
N/A	N/A	N/A	N/A	N/A	N/A	N/A
N/A	N/A	N/A	N/A	N/A	(2,564)	128
4,387	3,257	200	0	0	(561)	(4,259)
3,923	3,117	6,315	1,266	(2,746)	(8,759)	(6,354)
14,582	11,158	10,018	7,012	2,414	(3,161)	(4,191)
10,159	8,046	7,654	3,452	(616)	(6,966)	(7,303)
7,315	4,860	8,354	6,478	313	(1,157)	(2,894)
7,416	(2,716)	(3,735)	360	(7,537)	(14,758)	14,297
(10,125)	(7,741)	(4,834)	1,418	474	2,361	(4,238)
7,058	274	1,862	(5,435)	10,468	(7,092)	(89)
11,664	(5,323)	1,647	2,821	3,718	(20,646)	7,076
70,377	57,101	56,074	50,173	38,195	44,387	51,268
45,304	34,845	31,217	30,923	23,325	39,991	44,488
25,073	22,256	24,857	19,250	14,870	4,396	6,780
14,608	11,853	7,439	5,590	8,909	8,955	12,306
7,368	140	118	182	N/A	N/A	N/A
94,822	72,187	64,541	56,395	47,635	54,528	72,465
11,952	4,025	3,000	3,000	8,166	3,280	8,465
57,938	40,033	35,619	35,650	31,968	43,775	52,953
36,884	32,154	28,922	20,745	15,667	10,753	19,512
43,775	34,175	27,924	24,845	20,325	22,572	31,516
25,381	24,585	24,400	23,140	18,292	9,842	9,842
24,976	24,515	23,187	22,392	15,794	9,842	9,840
0.16	0.13	0.27	0.06	(0.17)	(0.89)	(0.65)
0.29	0.20	0.36	0.29	0.02	(0.12)	(0.29)
12.31	9.62	6.30	23.33	(4.41)	(1.17)	(1.77)
1.45	1.31	1.19	0.90	0.86	1.09	1.98
2.20	1.85	1.95	1.79	1.40	1.50	2.65
1.10	1.15	1.12	0.74	0.70	0.75	0.90
1.97	1.25	1.70	1.40	0.75	1.04	1.15
0	0	0	0	0	0	0
11.4 %	10.2 %	25.4 %	7.0 %	(20.8 %)	(57.9 %)	(28.0 %)
23.2 %	23.5 %	27.4 %	13.9 %	(3.0 %)	(30.9 %)	(23.2 %)
1.55	1.64	1.80	1.62	1.64	1.11	1.15
1.57	1.25	1.23	1.72	2.04	4.07	2.71
1.45	1.43	1.51	1.11	0.70	0.35	0.18
4.2 %	1.3 %	13.7 %	14.6 %	3.0 %	(18.3 %)	(1.0 %)
2.3	2.1	2.4	2.4	2.3	1.4	2.5
927,972	814,977	657,775	600,028	587,881	547,685	547,983
245	266	289	268	240	242	296
107	102	94	91	91	86	91
N/A	N/A	N/A	N/A	N/A	N/A	N/A
N/A	N/A	N/A	N/A	N/A	N/A	N/A
1	1	N/A	N/A	N/A	N/A	N/A
33	38	42	43	45	57	53
150	N/A	N/A	N/A	N/A	N/A	N/A
1,860	1,657	1,776	1,419	1,199	1,138	1,290

***   Excludes inter-group sales.
****   Calculated on stores open and at the same size for an entire season. The Company breaks the year into two seasons.
***** Within total assets or total debt as the case may be future income taxes reflect the asset/liability method of accounting
        for the January 27, 1996 year forward. The deferred income tax method is used in years prior to January 27, 1996.

N/A   Not applicable

Directors

ART BERLINER (2) (3)

Mr. Berliner is a founding partner of the Walden Group, an experienced international venture capital firm managing funds in excess of $1.0 billion U.S. Mr. Berliner was invited to join the Board when Walden made a $1.6 million investment in Mark's Work Wearhouse Inc., in January of 1995, exchangeable into shares of the Company, to fund the Company's U.S. test at that time. The share exchange was completed on April 3, 1998. Mr. Berliner's experience as a director of private and public companies in the United States, including the U.S. retail sector, provides a valuable resource for the Company.

CLARE COPELAND (2) (3)

Mr. Copeland has been a Director since the fall of 2000 and is currently Chairman and CEO of Ontario Store Fixtures Inc., North America's leading store fixture company. For the past 35 years, Mr. Copeland has held senior executive positions with major corporations such as Peoples Jewellers, Zale Corporation, Granada Canada, and Drake International. Mr. Copeland is also Chairman of Toronto Hydro and holds directorships with Danier Leather, RioCan, White Rose Crafts and Nurseries and several other Canadian companies. Mr. Copeland is also on the Advisory Board for the Richard Ivey School of Business and the Molson Indy Foundation.

MICHAEL FOX (1) (2)

Mr. Fox, a director of the Company since 1981, became the non-management Chairman of the Board in January 1996. Currently owner of a successful business venture and private consulting practice in Whistler, British Columbia, Mr. Fox received his Bachelor of Commerce degree at the University of Manitoba and became a member of the Institute of Chartered Accountants of British Columbia in 1970. He was a partner of a national accounting firm in Vancouver until February 1981.

MICHAEL LAMBERT

Mr. Lambert, Chief Financial Officer and a member of the Board has been with Mark's since 1994, other than for a brief period in 1999, when he was the Chief Financial Officer of Indigo Books, Music and More. Prior to joining Mark's Work Wearhouse, Mr. Lambert spent 15 years in progressive financial positions with major Canadian public companies including Loblaw Companies Ltd., George Weston Limited and the Southam Newspaper Group. In 1981, while at Coopers and Lybrand, Chartered Accountants in Toronto, Mr. Lambert obtained his C.A. designation. In 1978, he earned his Bachelor of Commerce degree from the University of Windsor.

BRUCE R. LIBIN Q.C. (1) (3)

Mr. Libin, a director of the Company since July 1978, is President of B.R. Libin Capital Corp., an investment, merchant banking and investment banking advisory services company since 1995. Mr. Libin is also Chairman and Managing Director of Destiny Resource Services Corp., a resource services company since 1997 and December 2000 respectively. Prior to that, Mr. Libin was a partner with the law firm Bennett Jones. Mr. Libin is also a director of several public and private corporations and community organizations.

GARTH MITCHELL

Mr. Mitchell's retail career spans more than 30 years as a merchant, commencing with senior management positions with the Hudson's Bay Company; seven years as a founding partner and President of a successful women's specialty chain; and seven years as the President of Department Store and Specialty Store Divisions of Comark, the Canadian Division of a large international retailer. Mr. Mitchell joined Mark's Work Wearhouse Ltd. as a Senior Vice President in 1991, became Chief Operating Officer in 1992, President and COO in 1994, and President and CEO in 1995. Mr. Mitchell is currently Chairman of the Retail Council of Canada, an Advisory Council member for Ryerson School of Retail Management, and is a past member of the Advisory Council for the Southern Alberta Institute of Technology.

BRUCE REID (1) (2)

Mr. Reid retired as President and CEO of The Brick Warehouse Corp. in January 1997. Prior to The Brick, he held CEO positions in the retail industry in both Canada and the US and is currently a director of a number of private and public organizations. Since his retirement, Mr. Reid has taught in the MBA programs at The Richard Ivey (Western) and Michel G. DeGroote (McMaster) Business Schools and is currently completing a short-term assignment as President & CEO of RTO Enterprises Inc., where he also serves as a Director. Mr. Reid is a Past Chairman of the Retail Council of Canada.

JAKE SCUDAMORE (1) (3)

Mr. Scudamore is President of Scudamore and Associates Inc., a corporate consulting company specializing in strategic planning, marketing and new media. He sits on an advisory board for George Brown College and was formerly Vice President, Marketing, of The Sports Network (TSN). Under his guidance, TSN won numerous national and international awards in virtually all marketing disciplines. Mr. Scudamore is a recipient of the Commemorative Medal for the 125th Anniversary of Canadian Confederation. Mr. Scudamore has been a director of the Company since January 1994.

Key: (1) Audit Committee Member
(2) Compensation Committee Member
(3) Governance Committee Member

Corporate Information

MARK'S WORK WEARHOUSE LTD.
#30, 1035 – 64th Avenue S.E.
Calgary, Alberta T2H 2J7
Telephone: (403) 255-9220
Fax: (403) 255-6005

INQUIRIES
Customer Service
Linda Mathiesen 1-800-663-6275
Toll Free Customer Service Number
1-800-663-6275; 1-800-663-MARK
Website
www.marks.com
Industrial and Corporate Wear
Jim Haigh (403) 692-7790
Property Management
Doreen Busby (403) 692-7571
Store Design
Michel St. Jean (403) 692-7502

Please call if we can assist you with any of your
clothing or footwear needs.

INVESTOR INFORMATION
Shareholders with inquiries regarding share transfer
requirements, lost certificates, changes of address or the
elimination of duplicate mailings should contact the
Company's transfer agent, Computershare Investor Services
in Calgary, Alberta (403) 267-6800.
Toll free 1-800-267-6555
e-mail caregistry@computershare.com

INVESTOR RELATIONS INQUIRIES
Investors seeking other information about the
Company may contact Karen Bentley at
(403) 692-7572 or karen.bentley@marks.com

INTERNET SITE
To access Mark's corporate and divisional store, product or
financial information, including quarterly reports, quarterly
analyst presentation materials and news releases, visit our
Internet site http://www.marks.com.

NOTICE OF ANNUAL MEETING
The Annual Meeting of Shareholders will be held in the
Wildrose Ballroom of The Sheraton Suites Eau Claire
Calgary on Wednesday, June 13, 2001 at 11:00 a.m.

SENIOR OFFICERS
Corporate Services
Garth Mitchell
President and Chief Executive Officer
Michael Lambert
Chief Financial Officer
John Murphy
Senior Vice President, Treasurer and Secretary
Robin Lynas
Chief Information Officer
Linda Mathiesen
Vice President, Human Resources and Customer Service
Michel St. Jean
Vice President, Store Design
Randy Wiebe
Vice President, Controller

Mark's Division
Paul Wilson
President and Chief Operating Officer
Richard Harrison
Senior Vice President, Merchandising

Work World Division
Michael Strachan
Chief Operating Officer
Roy Jopling
Vice President, Operations

DOCKERS® Stores Division
Cathy Prosser
General Manager

BANKERS
Canadian Imperial Bank of Commerce, Calgary
Bank of Nova Scotia, Calgary
National Bank of Canada, Calgary

LEGAL COUNSEL
Bennett Jones
Barristers and Solicitors, Calgary

AUDITORS
PricewaterhouseCoopers LLP
Chartered Accountants, Calgary

TRANSFER AGENT
Computershare Investor Services of Canada, Calgary

LISTING OF COMMON SHARES
The Toronto Stock Exchange
Trading symbol – MWW or Mark Wrk

Forward-Looking Information – This Annual Report to Shareholders of the Company contains forward-looking information relating to the Company's operations that is based on the Company's current assumptions, expectations, estimates, forecasts and projections. The forward-looking information is not a guarantee of future performance and involves risks, uncertainties, estimates and assumptions that are difficult to predict. Therefore, actual outcomes and results may differ materially from those expressed in the forward-looking information. Readers, therefore, should not place undue reliance on any such forward-looking information. Further, any forward-looking information speaks only as of the date on which such statement is made. A number of important assumptions and factors could cause actual results to differ materially from those indicated by the forward-looking information. Such assumptions and factors include those set forth in the Forecast Range, Key Assumptions and the Risk Factors sections in the Company's Annual Report.

The cover and text stock of this year's annual report is acid free, oxygen bleached and elemental chlorine free. Printed in Canada.

CORPORATE INFORMATION

A Career Choice That Works...

Successful companies are built

one position at a time...

We are always looking

to add talent to our future...

We are an energetic company in an exciting industry. One look inside this report will show you that we are a leader in results and innovative thinking. If your personal ambitions support these attributes, join us for a rewarding career in purchasing, sales management, finance, marketing or systems. E-mail your resume to linda.mathiesen@marks.com to begin your future!

MARK'S WORK WEARHOUSE LTD.

MARK'S WORK WEARHOUSE DIVISION

L'ÉQUIPEUR DIVISION

WORK WORLD DIVISION

DOCKERS® STORES DIVISION

Appendix B

Present and Future Value Tables

Table B-1—Future Value of $1 to Be Received or Paid at the End of Period n

r

n	1.0%	2.0%	2.5%	3.0%	3.5%	4.0%	4.5%	5.0%	5.5%	6.0%	7.0%	8.0%	9.0%	10.0%	11.0%	12.0%
1	1.01000	1.02000	1.02500	1.03000	1.03500	1.04000	1.04500	1.05000	1.05500	1.06000	1.07000	1.08000	1.09000	1.10000	1.11000	1.12000
2	1.02010	1.04040	1.05063	1.06090	1.07123	1.08160	1.09203	1.10250	1.11303	1.12360	1.14490	1.16640	1.18810	1.21000	1.23210	1.25440
3	1.03030	1.06121	1.07689	1.09273	1.10872	1.12486	1.14117	1.15763	1.17424	1.19102	1.22504	1.25971	1.29503	1.33100	1.36763	1.40493
4	1.04060	1.08243	1.10381	1.12551	1.14752	1.16986	1.19252	1.21551	1.23882	1.26248	1.31080	1.36049	1.41158	1.46410	1.51807	1.57352
5	1.05101	1.10408	1.13141	1.15927	1.18769	1.21665	1.24618	1.27628	1.30696	1.33823	1.40255	1.46933	1.53862	1.61051	1.68506	1.76234
6	1.06152	1.12616	1.15969	1.19405	1.22926	1.26532	1.30226	1.34010	1.37884	1.41852	1.50073	1.58687	1.67710	1.77156	1.87041	1.97382
7	1.07214	1.14869	1.18869	1.22987	1.27228	1.31593	1.36086	1.40710	1.45468	1.50363	1.60578	1.71382	1.82804	1.94872	2.07616	2.21068
8	1.08286	1.17166	1.21840	1.26677	1.31681	1.36857	1.42210	1.47746	1.53469	1.59385	1.71819	1.85093	1.99256	2.14359	2.30454	2.47596
9	1.09369	1.19509	1.24886	1.30477	1.36290	1.42331	1.48610	1.55133	1.61909	1.68948	1.83846	1.99900	2.17189	2.35795	2.55804	2.77308
10	1.10462	1.21899	1.28008	1.34392	1.41060	1.48024	1.55297	1.62889	1.70814	1.79085	1.96715	2.15892	2.36736	2.59374	2.83942	3.10585
11	1.11567	1.24337	1.31209	1.38423	1.45997	1.53945	1.62285	1.71034	1.80209	1.89830	2.10485	2.33164	2.58043	2.85312	3.15176	3.47855
12	1.12683	1.26824	1.34489	1.42576	1.51107	1.60103	1.69588	1.79586	1.90121	2.01220	2.25219	2.51817	2.81266	3.13843	3.49845	3.89598
13	1.13809	1.29361	1.37851	1.46853	1.56396	1.66507	1.77220	1.88565	2.00577	2.13293	2.40985	2.71962	3.06580	3.45227	3.88328	4.36349
14	1.14947	1.31948	1.41297	1.51259	1.61869	1.73168	1.85194	1.97993	2.11609	2.26090	2.57853	2.93719	3.34173	3.79750	4.31044	4.88711
15	1.16097	1.34587	1.44830	1.55797	1.67535	1.80094	1.93528	2.07893	2.23248	2.39656	2.75903	3.17217	3.64248	4.17725	4.78459	5.47357
16	1.17258	1.37279	1.48451	1.60471	1.73399	1.87298	2.02237	2.18287	2.35526	2.54035	2.95216	3.42594	3.97031	4.59497	5.31089	6.13039
17	1.18430	1.40024	1.52162	1.65285	1.79468	1.94790	2.11338	2.29202	2.48480	2.69277	3.15882	3.70002	4.32763	5.05447	5.89509	6.86604
18	1.19615	1.42825	1.55966	1.70243	1.85749	2.02582	2.20848	2.40662	2.62147	2.85434	3.37993	3.99602	4.71712	5.55992	6.54355	7.68997
19	1.20811	1.45681	1.59865	1.75351	1.92250	2.10685	2.30786	2.52695	2.76565	3.02560	3.61653	4.31570	5.14166	6.11591	7.26334	8.61276
20	1.22019	1.48595	1.63862	1.80611	1.98979	2.19112	2.41171	2.65330	2.91776	3.20714	3.86968	4.66096	5.60441	6.72750	8.06231	9.64629
21	1.23239	1.51567	1.67958	1.86029	2.05943	2.27877	2.52024	2.78596	3.07823	3.39956	4.14056	5.03383	6.10881	7.40025	8.94917	10.80385
22	1.24472	1.54598	1.72157	1.91610	2.13151	2.36992	2.63365	2.92526	3.24754	3.60354	4.43040	5.43654	6.65860	8.14027	9.93357	12.10031
23	1.25716	1.57690	1.76461	1.97359	2.20611	2.46472	2.75217	3.07152	3.42615	3.81975	4.74053	5.87146	7.25787	8.95430	11.02627	13.55235
24	1.26973	1.60844	1.80873	2.03279	2.28333	2.56330	2.87601	3.22510	3.61459	4.04893	5.07237	6.34118	7.91108	9.84973	12.23916	15.17863
25	1.28243	1.64061	1.85394	2.09378	2.36324	2.66584	3.00543	3.38635	3.81339	4.29187	5.42743	6.84848	8.62308	10.83471	13.58546	17.00006
26	1.29526	1.67342	1.90029	2.15659	2.44596	2.77247	3.14068	3.55567	4.02313	4.54938	5.80735	7.39635	9.39916	11.91818	15.07986	19.04007
27	1.30821	1.70689	1.94780	2.22129	2.53157	2.88337	3.28201	3.73346	4.24440	4.82235	6.21387	7.98806	10.24508	13.10999	16.73865	21.32488
28	1.32129	1.74102	1.99650	2.28793	2.62017	2.99870	3.42970	3.92013	4.47784	5.11169	6.64884	8.62711	11.16714	14.42099	18.57990	23.88387
29	1.33450	1.77584	2.04641	2.35657	2.71188	3.11865	3.58404	4.11614	4.72412	5.41839	7.11426	9.31727	12.17218	15.86309	20.62369	26.74993
30	1.34785	1.81136	2.09757	2.42726	2.80679	3.24340	3.74532	4.32194	4.98395	5.74349	7.61226	10.06266	13.26768	17.44940	22.89230	29.95992
31	1.36133	1.84759	2.15001	2.50008	2.90503	3.37313	3.91386	4.53804	5.25807	6.08810	8.14511	10.86767	14.46177	19.19434	25.41045	33.55511
32	1.37494	1.88454	2.20376	2.57508	3.00671	3.50806	4.08998	4.76494	5.54726	6.45339	8.71527	11.73708	15.76333	21.11378	28.20560	37.58173
33	1.38869	1.92223	2.25885	2.65234	3.11194	3.64838	4.27403	5.00319	5.85236	6.84059	9.32534	12.67605	17.18203	23.22515	31.30821	42.09153
34	1.40258	1.96068	2.31532	2.73191	3.22086	3.79432	4.46636	5.25335	6.17424	7.25103	9.97811	13.69013	18.72841	25.54767	34.75212	47.14252
35	1.41660	1.99989	2.37321	2.81386	3.33359	3.94609	4.66735	5.51602	6.51383	7.68609	10.67658	14.78534	20.41397	28.10244	38.57485	52.79962
36	1.43077	2.03989	2.43254	2.89828	3.45027	4.10393	4.87738	5.79182	6.87209	8.14725	11.42394	15.96817	22.25123	30.91268	42.81808	59.13557
37	1.44508	2.08069	2.49335	2.98523	3.57103	4.26809	5.09686	6.08141	7.25005	8.63609	12.22362	17.24563	24.25384	34.00395	47.52807	66.23184
38	1.45953	2.12230	2.55568	3.07478	3.69601	4.43881	5.32622	6.38548	7.64880	9.15425	13.07927	18.62528	26.43668	37.40434	52.75616	74.17966
39	1.47412	2.16474	2.61957	3.16703	3.82537	4.61637	5.56590	6.70475	8.06949	9.70351	13.99482	20.11530	28.81598	41.14478	58.55934	83.08122
40	1.48886	2.20804	2.68506	3.26204	3.95926	4.80102	5.81636	7.03999	8.51331	10.28572	14.97446	21.72452	31.40942	45.25926	65.00087	93.05097
41	1.50375	2.25220	2.75219	3.35990	4.09783	4.99306	6.07810	7.39199	8.98154	10.90286	16.02267	23.46248	34.23627	49.78518	72.15096	104.21709
42	1.51879	2.29724	2.82100	3.46070	4.24126	5.19278	6.35162	7.76159	9.47553	11.55703	17.14426	25.33948	37.31753	54.76370	80.08757	116.72314
43	1.53398	2.34319	2.89152	3.56452	4.38970	5.40050	6.63744	8.14967	9.99668	12.25045	18.34435	27.36664	40.67611	60.24007	88.89720	130.72991
44	1.54932	2.39005	2.96381	3.67145	4.54334	5.61652	6.93612	8.55715	10.54650	12.98548	19.62846	29.55597	44.33696	66.26408	98.67589	146.41750
45	1.56481	2.43785	3.03790	3.78160	4.70236	5.84118	7.24825	8.98501	11.12655	13.76461	21.00245	31.92045	48.32729	72.89048	109.53024	163.98760
46	1.58046	2.48661	3.11385	3.89504	4.86694	6.07482	7.57442	9.43426	11.73851	14.59049	22.47262	34.47409	52.67674	80.17953	121.57857	183.66612
47	1.59626	2.53634	3.19170	4.01190	5.03728	6.31782	7.91527	9.90597	12.38413	15.46592	24.04571	37.23201	57.41765	88.19749	134.95221	205.70605
48	1.61223	2.58707	3.27149	4.13225	5.21359	6.57053	8.27146	10.40127	13.06526	16.39387	25.72891	40.21057	62.58524	97.01723	149.79695	230.39078
49	1.62835	2.63881	3.35328	4.25622	5.39606	6.83335	8.64367	10.92133	13.78385	17.37750	27.52993	43.42742	68.21791	106.71896	166.27462	258.03767
50	1.64463	2.69159	3.43711	4.38391	5.58493	7.10668	9.03264	11.46740	14.54196	18.42015	29.45703	46.90161	74.35752	117.39085	184.56483	289.00219

r

13.0%	14.0%	15.0%	16.0%	17.0%	18.0%	19.0%	20.0%	21.0%	22.0%	23.0%	24.0%	25.0%
1.13000	1.14000	1.15000	1.16000	1.17000	1.18000	1.19000	1.20000	1.21000	1.22000	1.23000	1.24000	1.25000
1.27690	1.29960	1.32250	1.34560	1.36890	1.39240	1.41610	1.44000	1.46410	1.48840	1.51290	1.53760	1.56250
1.44290	1.48154	1.52088	1.56090	1.60161	1.64303	1.68516	1.72800	1.77156	1.81585	1.86087	1.90662	1.95313
1.63047	1.68896	1.74901	1.81064	1.87389	1.93878	2.00534	2.07360	2.14359	2.21533	2.28887	2.36421	2.44141
1.84244	1.92541	2.01136	2.10034	2.19245	2.28776	2.38635	2.48832	2.59374	2.70271	2.81531	2.93163	3.05176
2.08195	2.19497	2.31306	2.43640	2.56516	2.69955	2.83976	2.98598	3.13843	3.29730	3.46283	3.63522	3.81470
2.35261	2.50227	2.66002	2.82622	3.00124	3.18547	3.37932	3.58318	3.79750	4.02271	4.25928	4.50767	4.76837
2.65844	2.85259	3.05902	3.27841	3.51145	3.75886	4.02139	4.29982	4.59497	4.90771	5.23891	5.58951	5.96046
3.00404	3.25195	3.51788	3.80296	4.10840	4.43545	4.78545	5.15978	5.55992	5.98740	6.44386	6.93099	7.45058
3.39457	3.70722	4.04556	4.41144	4.80683	5.23384	5.69468	6.19174	6.72750	7.30463	7.92595	8.59443	9.31323
3.83586	4.22623	4.65239	5.11726	5.62399	6.17593	6.77667	7.43008	8.14027	8.91165	9.74891	10.65709	11.64153
4.33452	4.81790	5.35025	5.93603	6.58007	7.28759	8.06424	8.91610	9.84973	10.87221	11.99116	13.21479	14.55192
4.89801	5.49241	6.15279	6.88579	7.69868	8.59936	9.59645	10.69932	11.91818	13.26410	14.74913	16.38634	18.18989
5.53475	6.26135	7.07571	7.98752	9.00745	10.14724	11.41977	12.83918	14.42099	16.18220	18.14143	20.31906	22.73737
6.25427	7.13794	8.13706	9.26552	10.53872	11.97375	13.58953	15.40702	17.44940	19.74229	22.31396	25.19563	28.42171
7.06733	8.13725	9.35762	10.74800	12.33030	14.12902	16.17154	18.48843	21.11378	24.08559	27.44617	31.24259	35.52714
7.98608	9.27646	10.76126	12.46768	14.42646	16.67225	19.24413	22.18611	25.54767	29.38442	33.75879	38.74081	44.40892
9.02427	10.57517	12.37545	14.46251	16.87895	19.67325	22.90052	26.62333	30.91268	35.84899	41.52331	48.03860	55.51115
10.19742	12.05569	14.23177	16.77652	19.74838	23.21444	27.25162	31.94800	37.40434	43.73577	51.07368	59.56786	69.38894
11.52309	13.74349	16.36654	19.46076	23.10560	27.39303	32.42942	38.33760	45.25926	53.35764	62.82062	73.86415	86.73617
13.02109	15.66758	18.82152	22.57448	27.03355	32.32378	38.59101	46.00512	54.76370	65.09632	77.26936	91.59155	108.42022
14.71383	17.86104	21.64475	26.18640	31.62925	38.14206	45.92331	55.20614	66.26408	79.41751	95.04132	113.57352	135.52527
16.62663	20.36158	24.89146	30.37622	37.00623	45.00763	54.64873	66.24737	80.17953	96.88936	116.90082	140.83116	169.40659
18.78809	23.21221	28.62518	35.23642	43.29729	53.10901	65.03199	79.49685	97.01723	118.20502	143.78801	174.63064	211.75824
21.23054	26.46192	32.91895	40.87424	50.65783	62.66863	77.38807	95.39622	117.39085	144.21013	176.85925	216.54199	264.69780
23.99051	30.16658	37.85680	47.41412	59.26966	73.94898	92.09181	114.47546	142.04293	175.93636	217.53688	268.51207	330.87225
27.10928	34.38991	43.53531	55.00038	69.34550	87.25980	109.58925	137.37055	171.87195	214.64236	267.57036	332.95497	413.59031
30.63349	39.20449	50.06561	63.80044	81.13423	102.96656	130.41121	164.84466	207.96506	261.86368	329.11155	412.86416	516.98788
34.61584	44.69312	57.57545	74.00851	94.92705	121.50054	155.18934	197.81359	251.63772	319.47368	404.80720	511.95156	646.23485
39.11590	50.95016	66.21177	85.84988	111.06465	143.37064	184.67531	237.37631	304.48164	389.75789	497.91286	634.81993	807.79357
44.20096	58.08318	76.14354	99.58586	129.94564	169.17735	219.76362	284.85158	368.42278	475.50463	612.43282	787.17672	1009.74196
49.94709	66.21483	87.56507	115.51959	152.03640	199.62928	261.51871	341.82189	445.79157	580.11565	753.29237	976.09913	1262.17745
56.44021	75.48490	100.69983	134.00273	177.88259	235.56255	311.20726	410.18627	539.40780	707.74109	926.54961	1210.36292	1577.72181
63.77744	86.05279	115.80480	155.44317	208.12263	277.96381	370.33664	492.22352	652.68344	863.44413	1139.65602	1500.85002	1972.15226
72.06851	98.10018	133.17552	180.31407	243.50347	327.99729	440.70061	590.66823	789.74696	1053.40184	1401.77690	1861.05403	2465.19033
81.43741	111.83420	153.15185	209.16432	284.89906	387.03680	524.43372	708.80187	955.59382	1285.15025	1724.18559	2307.70699	3081.48791
92.02428	127.49099	176.12463	242.63062	333.33191	456.70343	624.07613	850.56225	1156.26852	1567.88330	2120.74828	2861.55667	3851.85989
103.98743	145.33973	202.54332	281.45151	389.99833	538.91004	742.65059	1020.67470	1399.08491	1912.81763	2608.52038	3548.33027	4814.82486
117.50580	165.68729	232.92482	326.48376	456.29805	635.91385	883.75421	1224.80964	1692.89274	2333.63751	3208.48007	4399.92954	6018.53108
132.78155	188.88351	267.86355	378.72116	533.86871	750.37834	1051.66751	1469.77157	2048.40021	2847.03776	3946.43049	5455.91262	7523.16385
150.04315	215.32721	308.04308	439.31654	624.62639	885.44645	1251.48433	1763.72588	2478.56426	3473.38607	4854.10950	6765.33165	9403.95481
169.54876	245.47301	354.24954	509.60719	730.81288	1044.82681	1489.26636	2116.47106	2999.06275	4237.53100	5970.55469	8389.01125	11754.94381
191.59010	279.83924	407.38697	591.14434	855.05107	1232.89563	1772.22696	2539.76527	3628.86593	5169.78782	7343.78226	10402.37395	14693.67939
216.49682	319.01673	468.49502	685.72744	1000.40975	1454.81685	2108.95009	3047.71832	4390.92778	6307.14114	9032.85218	12898.94370	18367.09923
244.64140	363.67907	538.76927	795.44383	1170.47941	1716.68388	2509.65060	3657.26199	5313.02261	7694.71219	11110.40819	15994.69019	22958.87404
276.44478	414.59414	619.58466	922.71484	1369.46091	2025.68698	2986.48422	4388.71439	6428.75736	9387.54887	13665.80207	19833.41583	28698.59255
312.38261	472.63732	712.52236	1070.34921	1602.26927	2390.31063	3553.91622	5266.45726	7778.79641	11452.80963	16808.93654	24593.43563	35873.24069
352.99234	538.80655	819.40071	1241.60509	1874.65504	2820.56655	4229.16030	6319.74872	9412.34365	13972.42774	20674.99195	30495.86018	44841.55086
398.88135	614.23946	942.31082	1440.26190	2193.34640	3328.26853	5032.70076	7583.69846	11388.93582	17046.36185	25430.24010	37814.86662	56051.93857
450.73593	700.23299	1083.65744	1670.70380	2566.21528	3927.35686	5988.91390	9100.43815	13780.61234	20796.56145	31279.19532	46890.43461	70064.92322

Table B-2—Present Value of $1 to Be Received or Paid at the End of Period *n*

r

n	1.0%	2.0%	2.5%	3.0%	3.5%	4.0%	4.5%	5.0%	5.5%	6.0%	7.0%	8.0%	9.0%	10.0%	11.0%	12.0%
1	0.99010	0.98039	0.97561	0.97087	0.96618	0.96154	0.95694	0.95238	0.94787	0.94340	0.93458	0.92593	0.91743	0.90909	0.90090	0.89286
2	0.98030	0.96117	0.95181	0.94260	0.93351	0.92456	0.91573	0.90703	0.89845	0.89000	0.87344	0.85734	0.84168	0.82645	0.81162	0.79719
3	0.97059	0.94232	0.92860	0.91514	0.90194	0.88900	0.87630	0.86384	0.85161	0.83962	0.81630	0.79383	0.77218	0.75131	0.73119	0.71178
4	0.96098	0.92385	0.90595	0.88849	0.87144	0.85480	0.83856	0.82270	0.80722	0.79209	0.76290	0.73503	0.70843	0.68301	0.65873	0.63552
5	0.95147	0.90573	0.88385	0.86261	0.84197	0.82193	0.80245	0.78353	0.76513	0.74726	0.71299	0.68058	0.64993	0.62092	0.59345	0.56743
6	0.94205	0.88797	0.86230	0.83748	0.81350	0.79031	0.76790	0.74622	0.72525	0.70496	0.66634	0.63017	0.59627	0.56447	0.53464	0.50663
7	0.93272	0.87056	0.84127	0.81309	0.78599	0.75992	0.73483	0.71068	0.68744	0.66506	0.62275	0.58349	0.54703	0.51316	0.48166	0.45235
8	0.92348	0.85349	0.82075	0.78941	0.75941	0.73069	0.70319	0.67684	0.65160	0.62741	0.58201	0.54027	0.50187	0.46651	0.43393	0.40388
9	0.91434	0.83676	0.80073	0.76642	0.73373	0.70259	0.67290	0.64461	0.61763	0.59190	0.54393	0.50025	0.46043	0.42410	0.39092	0.36061
10	0.90529	0.82035	0.78120	0.74409	0.70892	0.67556	0.64393	0.61391	0.58543	0.55839	0.50835	0.46319	0.42241	0.38554	0.35218	0.32197
11	0.89632	0.80426	0.76214	0.72242	0.68495	0.64958	0.61620	0.58468	0.55491	0.52679	0.47509	0.42888	0.38753	0.35049	0.31728	0.28748
12	0.88745	0.78849	0.74356	0.70138	0.66178	0.62460	0.58966	0.55684	0.52598	0.49697	0.44401	0.39711	0.35553	0.31863	0.28584	0.25668
13	0.87866	0.77303	0.72542	0.68095	0.63940	0.60057	0.56427	0.53032	0.49856	0.46884	0.41496	0.36770	0.32618	0.28966	0.25751	0.22917
14	0.86996	0.75788	0.70773	0.66112	0.61778	0.57748	0.53997	0.50507	0.47257	0.44230	0.38782	0.34046	0.29925	0.26333	0.23199	0.20462
15	0.86135	0.74301	0.69047	0.64186	0.59689	0.55526	0.51672	0.48102	0.44793	0.41727	0.36245	0.31524	0.27454	0.23939	0.20900	0.18270
16	0.85282	0.72845	0.67362	0.62317	0.57671	0.53391	0.49447	0.45811	0.42458	0.39365	0.33873	0.29189	0.25187	0.21763	0.18829	0.16312
17	0.84438	0.71416	0.65720	0.60502	0.55720	0.51337	0.47318	0.43630	0.40245	0.37136	0.31657	0.27027	0.23107	0.19784	0.16963	0.14564
18	0.83602	0.70016	0.64117	0.58739	0.53836	0.49363	0.45280	0.41552	0.38147	0.35034	0.29586	0.25025	0.21199	0.17986	0.15282	0.13004
19	0.82774	0.68643	0.62553	0.57029	0.52016	0.47464	0.43330	0.39573	0.36158	0.33051	0.27651	0.23171	0.19449	0.16351	0.13768	0.11611
20	0.81954	0.67297	0.61027	0.55368	0.50257	0.45639	0.41464	0.37689	0.34273	0.31180	0.25842	0.21455	0.17843	0.14864	0.12403	0.10367
21	0.81143	0.65978	0.59539	0.53755	0.48557	0.43883	0.39679	0.35894	0.32486	0.29416	0.24151	0.19866	0.16370	0.13513	0.11174	0.09256
22	0.80340	0.64684	0.58086	0.52189	0.46915	0.42196	0.37970	0.34185	0.30793	0.27751	0.22571	0.18394	0.15018	0.12285	0.10067	0.08264
23	0.79544	0.63416	0.56670	0.50669	0.45329	0.40573	0.36335	0.32557	0.29187	0.26180	0.21095	0.17032	0.13778	0.11168	0.09069	0.07379
24	0.78757	0.62172	0.55288	0.49193	0.43796	0.39012	0.34770	0.31007	0.27666	0.24698	0.19715	0.15770	0.12640	0.10153	0.08170	0.06588
25	0.77977	0.60953	0.53939	0.47761	0.42315	0.37512	0.33273	0.29530	0.26223	0.23300	0.18425	0.14602	0.11597	0.09230	0.07361	0.05882
26	0.77205	0.59758	0.52623	0.46369	0.40884	0.36069	0.31840	0.28124	0.24856	0.21981	0.17220	0.13520	0.10639	0.08391	0.06631	0.05252
27	0.76440	0.58586	0.51340	0.45019	0.39501	0.34682	0.30469	0.26785	0.23560	0.20737	0.16093	0.12519	0.09761	0.07628	0.05974	0.04689
28	0.75684	0.57437	0.50088	0.43708	0.38165	0.33348	0.29157	0.25509	0.22332	0.19563	0.15040	0.11591	0.08955	0.06934	0.05382	0.04187
29	0.74934	0.56311	0.48866	0.42435	0.36875	0.32065	0.27902	0.24295	0.21168	0.18456	0.14056	0.10733	0.08215	0.06304	0.04849	0.03738
30	0.74192	0.55207	0.47674	0.41199	0.35628	0.30832	0.26700	0.23138	0.20064	0.17411	0.13137	0.09938	0.07537	0.05731	0.04368	0.03338
31	0.73458	0.54125	0.46511	0.39999	0.34423	0.29646	0.25550	0.22036	0.19018	0.16425	0.12277	0.09202	0.06915	0.05210	0.03935	0.02980
32	0.72730	0.53063	0.45377	0.38834	0.33259	0.28506	0.24450	0.20987	0.18027	0.15496	0.11474	0.08520	0.06344	0.04736	0.03545	0.02661
33	0.72010	0.52023	0.44270	0.37703	0.32134	0.27409	0.23397	0.19987	0.17087	0.14619	0.10723	0.07889	0.05820	0.04306	0.03194	0.02376
34	0.71297	0.51003	0.43191	0.36604	0.31048	0.26355	0.22390	0.19035	0.16196	0.13791	0.10022	0.07305	0.05339	0.03914	0.02878	0.02121
35	0.70591	0.50003	0.42137	0.35538	0.29998	0.25342	0.21425	0.18129	0.15352	0.13011	0.09366	0.06763	0.04899	0.03558	0.02592	0.01894
36	0.69892	0.49022	0.41109	0.34503	0.28983	0.24367	0.20503	0.17266	0.14552	0.12274	0.08754	0.06262	0.04494	0.03235	0.02335	0.01691
37	0.69200	0.48061	0.40107	0.33498	0.28003	0.23430	0.19620	0.16444	0.13793	0.11579	0.08181	0.05799	0.04123	0.02941	0.02104	0.01510
38	0.68515	0.47119	0.39128	0.32523	0.27056	0.22529	0.18775	0.15661	0.13074	0.10924	0.07646	0.05369	0.03783	0.02673	0.01896	0.01348
39	0.67837	0.46195	0.38174	0.31575	0.26141	0.21662	0.17967	0.14915	0.12392	0.10306	0.07146	0.04971	0.03470	0.02430	0.01708	0.01204
40	0.67165	0.45289	0.37243	0.30656	0.25257	0.20829	0.17193	0.14205	0.11746	0.09722	0.06678	0.04603	0.03184	0.02209	0.01538	0.01075
41	0.66500	0.44401	0.36335	0.29763	0.24403	0.20028	0.16453	0.13528	0.11134	0.09172	0.06241	0.04262	0.02921	0.02009	0.01386	0.00960
42	0.65842	0.43530	0.35448	0.28896	0.23578	0.19257	0.15744	0.12884	0.10554	0.08653	0.05833	0.03946	0.02680	0.01826	0.01249	0.00857
43	0.65190	0.42677	0.34584	0.28054	0.22781	0.18517	0.15066	0.12270	0.10003	0.08163	0.05451	0.03654	0.02458	0.01660	0.01125	0.00765
44	0.64545	0.41840	0.33740	0.27237	0.22010	0.17805	0.14417	0.11686	0.09482	0.07701	0.05095	0.03383	0.02255	0.01509	0.01013	0.00683
45	0.63905	0.41020	0.32917	0.26444	0.21266	0.17120	0.13796	0.11130	0.08988	0.07265	0.04761	0.03133	0.02069	0.01372	0.00913	0.00610
46	0.63273	0.40215	0.32115	0.25674	0.20547	0.16461	0.13202	0.10600	0.08519	0.06854	0.04450	0.02901	0.01898	0.01247	0.00823	0.00544
47	0.62646	0.39427	0.31331	0.24926	0.19852	0.15828	0.12634	0.10095	0.08075	0.06466	0.04159	0.02686	0.01742	0.01134	0.00741	0.00486
48	0.62026	0.38654	0.30567	0.24200	0.19181	0.15219	0.12090	0.09614	0.07654	0.06100	0.03887	0.02487	0.01598	0.01031	0.00668	0.00434
49	0.61412	0.37896	0.29822	0.23495	0.18532	0.14634	0.11569	0.09156	0.07255	0.05755	0.03632	0.02303	0.01466	0.00937	0.00601	0.00388
50	0.60804	0.37153	0.29094	0.22811	0.17905	0.14071	0.11071	0.08720	0.06877	0.05429	0.03395	0.02132	0.01345	0.00852	0.00542	0.00346

r

13.0%	14.0%	15.0%	16.0%	17.0%	18.0%	19.0%	20.0%	21.0%	22.0%	23.0%	24.0%	25.0%
0.88496	0.87719	0.86957	0.86207	0.85470	0.84746	0.84034	0.83333	0.82645	0.81967	0.81301	0.80645	0.80000
0.78315	0.76947	0.75614	0.74316	0.73051	0.71818	0.70616	0.69444	0.68301	0.67186	0.66098	0.65036	0.64000
0.69305	0.67497	0.65752	0.64066	0.62437	0.60863	0.59342	0.57870	0.56447	0.55071	0.53738	0.52449	0.51200
0.61332	0.59208	0.57175	0.55229	0.53365	0.51579	0.49867	0.48225	0.46651	0.45140	0.43690	0.42297	0.40960
0.54276	0.51937	0.49718	0.47611	0.45611	0.43711	0.41905	0.40188	0.38554	0.37000	0.35520	0.34111	0.32768
0.48032	0.45559	0.43233	0.41044	0.38984	0.37043	0.35214	0.33490	0.31863	0.30328	0.28878	0.27509	0.26214
0.42506	0.39964	0.37594	0.35383	0.33320	0.31393	0.29592	0.27908	0.26333	0.24859	0.23478	0.22184	0.20972
0.37616	0.35056	0.32690	0.30503	0.28478	0.26604	0.24867	0.23257	0.21763	0.20376	0.19088	0.17891	0.16777
0.33288	0.30751	0.28426	0.26295	0.24340	0.22546	0.20897	0.19381	0.17986	0.16702	0.15519	0.14428	0.13422
0.29459	0.26974	0.24718	0.22668	0.20804	0.19106	0.17560	0.16151	0.14864	0.13690	0.12617	0.11635	0.10737
0.26070	0.23662	0.21494	0.19542	0.17781	0.16192	0.14757	0.13459	0.12285	0.11221	0.10258	0.09383	0.08590
0.23071	0.20756	0.18691	0.16846	0.15197	0.13722	0.12400	0.11216	0.10153	0.09198	0.08339	0.07567	0.06872
0.20416	0.18207	0.16253	0.14523	0.12989	0.11629	0.10421	0.09346	0.08391	0.07539	0.06780	0.06103	0.05498
0.18068	0.15971	0.14133	0.12520	0.11102	0.09855	0.08757	0.07789	0.06934	0.06180	0.05512	0.04921	0.04398
0.15989	0.14010	0.12289	0.10793	0.09489	0.08352	0.07359	0.06491	0.05731	0.05065	0.04481	0.03969	0.03518
0.14150	0.12289	0.10686	0.09304	0.08110	0.07078	0.06184	0.05409	0.04736	0.04152	0.03643	0.03201	0.02815
0.12522	0.10780	0.09293	0.08021	0.06932	0.05998	0.05196	0.04507	0.03914	0.03403	0.02962	0.02581	0.02252
0.11081	0.09456	0.08081	0.06914	0.05925	0.05083	0.04367	0.03756	0.03235	0.02789	0.02408	0.02082	0.01801
0.09806	0.08295	0.07027	0.05961	0.05064	0.04308	0.03670	0.03130	0.02673	0.02286	0.01958	0.01679	0.01441
0.08678	0.07276	0.06110	0.05139	0.04328	0.03651	0.03084	0.02608	0.02209	0.01874	0.01592	0.01354	0.01153
0.07680	0.06383	0.05313	0.04430	0.03699	0.03094	0.02591	0.02174	0.01826	0.01536	0.01294	0.01092	0.00922
0.06796	0.05599	0.04620	0.03819	0.03162	0.02622	0.02178	0.01811	0.01509	0.01259	0.01052	0.00880	0.00738
0.06014	0.04911	0.04017	0.03292	0.02702	0.02222	0.01830	0.01509	0.01247	0.01032	0.00855	0.00710	0.00590
0.05323	0.04308	0.03493	0.02838	0.02310	0.01883	0.01538	0.01258	0.01031	0.00846	0.00695	0.00573	0.00472
0.04710	0.03779	0.03038	0.02447	0.01974	0.01596	0.01292	0.01048	0.00852	0.00693	0.00565	0.00462	0.00378
0.04168	0.03315	0.02642	0.02109	0.01687	0.01352	0.01086	0.00874	0.00704	0.00568	0.00460	0.00372	0.00302
0.03689	0.02908	0.02297	0.01818	0.01442	0.01146	0.00912	0.00728	0.00582	0.00466	0.00374	0.00300	0.00242
0.03264	0.02551	0.01997	0.01567	0.01233	0.00971	0.00767	0.00607	0.00481	0.00382	0.00304	0.00242	0.00193
0.02889	0.02237	0.01737	0.01351	0.01053	0.00823	0.00644	0.00506	0.00397	0.00313	0.00247	0.00195	0.00155
0.02557	0.01963	0.01510	0.01165	0.00900	0.00697	0.00541	0.00421	0.00328	0.00257	0.00201	0.00158	0.00124
0.02262	0.01722	0.01313	0.01004	0.00770	0.00591	0.00455	0.00351	0.00271	0.00210	0.00163	0.00127	0.00099
0.02002	0.01510	0.01142	0.00866	0.00658	0.00501	0.00382	0.00293	0.00224	0.00172	0.00133	0.00102	0.00079
0.01772	0.01325	0.00993	0.00746	0.00562	0.00425	0.00321	0.00244	0.00185	0.00141	0.00108	0.00083	0.00063
0.01568	0.01162	0.00864	0.00643	0.00480	0.00360	0.00270	0.00203	0.00153	0.00116	0.00088	0.00067	0.00051
0.01388	0.01019	0.00751	0.00555	0.00411	0.00305	0.00227	0.00169	0.00127	0.00095	0.00071	0.00054	0.00041
0.01228	0.00894	0.00653	0.00478	0.00351	0.00258	0.00191	0.00141	0.00105	0.00078	0.00058	0.00043	0.00032
0.01087	0.00784	0.00568	0.00412	0.00300	0.00219	0.00160	0.00118	0.00086	0.00064	0.00047	0.00035	0.00026
0.00962	0.00688	0.00494	0.00355	0.00256	0.00186	0.00135	0.00098	0.00071	0.00052	0.00038	0.00028	0.00021
0.00851	0.00604	0.00429	0.00306	0.00219	0.00157	0.00113	0.00082	0.00059	0.00043	0.00031	0.00023	0.00017
0.00753	0.00529	0.00373	0.00264	0.00187	0.00133	0.00095	0.00068	0.00049	0.00035	0.00025	0.00018	0.00013
0.00666	0.00464	0.00325	0.00228	0.00160	0.00113	0.00080	0.00057	0.00040	0.00029	0.00021	0.00015	0.00011
0.00590	0.00407	0.00282	0.00196	0.00137	0.00096	0.00067	0.00047	0.00033	0.00024	0.00017	0.00012	0.00009
0.00522	0.00357	0.00245	0.00169	0.00117	0.00081	0.00056	0.00039	0.00028	0.00019	0.00014	0.00010	0.00007
0.00462	0.00313	0.00213	0.00146	0.00100	0.00069	0.00047	0.00033	0.00023	0.00016	0.00011	0.00008	0.00005
0.00409	0.00275	0.00186	0.00126	0.00085	0.00058	0.00040	0.00027	0.00019	0.00013	0.00009	0.00006	0.00004
0.00362	0.00241	0.00161	0.00108	0.00073	0.00049	0.00033	0.00023	0.00016	0.00011	0.00007	0.00005	0.00003
0.00320	0.00212	0.00140	0.00093	0.00062	0.00042	0.00028	0.00019	0.00013	0.00009	0.00006	0.00004	0.00003
0.00283	0.00186	0.00122	0.00081	0.00053	0.00035	0.00024	0.00016	0.00011	0.00007	0.00005	0.00003	0.00002
0.00251	0.00163	0.00106	0.00069	0.00046	0.00030	0.00020	0.00013	0.00009	0.00006	0.00004	0.00003	0.00002
0.00222	0.00143	0.00092	0.00060	0.00039	0.00025	0.00017	0.00011	0.00007	0.00005	0.00003	0.00002	0.00001

Table B-3—Present Value of a $1 Annuity Paid or Received at the End of Each Period

r

n	1.0%	2.0%	2.5%	3.0%	3.5%	4.0%	4.5%	5.0%	5.5%	6.0%	7.0%	8.0%	9.0%	10.0%	11.0%	12.0%
1	0.99010	0.98039	0.97561	0.97087	0.96618	0.96154	0.95694	0.95238	0.94787	0.94340	0.93458	0.92593	0.91743	0.90909	0.90090	0.89286
2	1.97040	1.94156	1.92742	1.91347	1.89969	1.88609	1.87267	1.85941	1.84632	1.83339	1.80802	1.78326	1.75911	1.73554	1.71252	1.69005
3	2.94099	2.88388	2.85602	2.82861	2.80164	2.77509	2.74896	2.72325	2.69793	2.67301	2.62432	2.57710	2.53129	2.48685	2.44371	2.40183
4	3.90197	3.80773	3.76197	3.71710	3.67308	3.62990	3.58753	3.54595	3.50515	3.46511	3.38721	3.31213	3.23972	3.16987	3.10245	3.03735
5	4.85343	4.71346	4.64583	4.57971	4.51505	4.45182	4.38998	4.32948	4.27028	4.21236	4.10020	3.99271	3.88965	3.79079	3.69590	3.60478
6	5.79548	5.60143	5.50813	5.41719	5.32855	5.24214	5.15787	5.07569	4.99553	4.91732	4.76654	4.62288	4.48592	4.35526	4.23054	4.11141
7	6.72819	6.47199	6.34939	6.23028	6.11454	6.00205	5.89270	5.78637	5.68297	5.58238	5.38929	5.20637	5.03295	4.86842	4.71220	4.56376
8	7.65168	7.32548	7.17014	7.01969	6.87396	6.73274	6.59589	6.46321	6.33457	6.20979	5.97130	5.74664	5.53482	5.33493	5.14612	4.96764
9	8.56602	8.16224	7.97087	7.78611	7.60769	7.43533	7.26879	7.10782	6.95220	6.80169	6.51523	6.24689	5.99525	5.75902	5.53705	5.32825
10	9.47130	8.98259	8.75206	8.53020	8.31661	8.11090	7.91272	7.72173	7.53763	7.36009	7.02358	6.71008	6.41766	6.14457	5.88923	5.65022
11	10.36763	9.78685	9.51421	9.25262	9.00155	8.76048	8.52892	8.30641	8.09254	7.88687	7.49867	7.13896	6.80519	6.49506	6.20652	5.93770
12	11.25508	10.57534	10.25776	9.95400	9.66333	9.38507	9.11858	8.86325	8.61852	8.38384	7.94269	7.53608	7.16073	6.81369	6.49236	6.19437
13	12.13374	11.34837	10.98318	10.63496	10.30274	9.98565	9.68285	9.39357	9.11708	8.85268	8.35765	7.90378	7.48690	7.10336	6.74987	6.42355
14	13.00370	12.10625	11.69091	11.29607	10.92052	10.56312	10.22283	9.89864	9.58965	9.29498	8.74547	8.24424	7.78615	7.36669	6.98187	6.62817
15	13.86505	12.84926	12.38138	11.93794	11.51741	11.11839	10.73955	10.37966	10.03758	9.71225	9.10791	8.55948	8.06069	7.60608	7.19087	6.81086
16	14.71787	13.57771	13.05500	12.56110	12.09412	11.65230	11.23402	10.83777	10.46216	10.10590	9.44665	8.85137	8.31256	7.82371	7.37916	6.97399
17	15.56225	14.29187	13.71220	13.16612	12.65132	12.16567	11.70719	11.27407	10.86461	10.47726	9.76322	9.12164	8.54363	8.02155	7.54879	7.11963
18	16.39827	14.99203	14.35336	13.75351	13.18968	12.65930	12.15999	11.68959	11.24607	10.82760	10.05909	9.37189	8.75563	8.20141	7.70162	7.24967
19	17.22601	15.67846	14.97889	14.32380	13.70984	13.13394	12.59329	12.08532	11.60765	11.15812	10.33560	9.60360	8.95011	8.36492	7.83929	7.36578
20	18.04555	16.35143	15.58916	14.87747	14.21240	13.59033	13.00794	12.46221	11.95038	11.46992	10.59401	9.81815	9.12855	8.51356	7.96333	7.46944
21	18.85698	17.01121	16.18455	15.41502	14.69797	14.02916	13.40472	12.82115	12.27524	11.76408	10.83553	10.01680	9.29224	8.64869	8.07507	7.56200
22	19.66038	17.65805	16.76541	15.93692	15.16712	14.45112	13.78442	13.16300	12.58317	12.04158	11.06124	10.20074	9.44243	8.77154	8.17574	7.64465
23	20.45582	18.29220	17.33211	16.44361	15.62041	14.85684	14.14777	13.48857	12.87504	12.30338	11.27219	10.37106	9.58021	8.88322	8.26643	7.71843
24	21.24339	18.91393	17.88499	16.93554	16.05837	15.24696	14.49548	13.79864	13.15170	12.55036	11.46933	10.52876	9.70661	8.98474	8.34814	7.78432
25	22.02316	19.52346	18.42438	17.41315	16.48151	15.62208	14.82821	14.09394	13.41393	12.78336	11.65358	10.67478	9.82258	9.07704	8.42174	7.84314
26	22.79520	20.12104	18.95061	17.87684	16.89035	15.98277	15.14661	14.37519	13.66250	13.00317	11.82578	10.80998	9.92897	9.16095	8.48806	7.89566
27	23.55961	20.70690	19.46401	18.32703	17.28536	16.32959	15.45130	14.64303	13.89810	13.21053	11.98671	10.93516	10.02658	9.23722	8.54780	7.94255
28	24.31644	21.28127	19.96489	18.76411	17.66702	16.66306	15.74287	14.89813	14.12142	13.40616	12.13711	11.05108	10.11613	9.30657	8.60162	7.98442
29	25.06579	21.84438	20.45355	19.18845	18.03577	16.98371	16.02189	15.14107	14.33310	13.59072	12.27767	11.15841	10.19828	9.36961	8.65011	8.02181
30	25.80771	22.39646	20.93029	19.60044	18.39205	17.29203	16.28889	15.37245	14.53375	13.76483	12.40904	11.25778	10.27365	9.42691	8.69379	8.05518
31	26.54229	22.93770	21.39541	20.00043	18.73628	17.58849	16.54439	15.59281	14.72393	13.92909	12.53181	11.34980	10.34280	9.47901	8.73315	8.08499
32	27.26959	23.46833	21.84918	20.38877	19.06887	17.87355	16.78889	15.80268	14.90420	14.08404	12.64656	11.43500	10.40624	9.52638	8.76860	8.11159
33	27.98969	23.98856	22.29188	20.76579	19.39021	18.14765	17.02286	16.00255	15.07507	14.23023	12.75379	11.51389	10.46444	9.56943	8.80054	8.13535
34	28.70267	24.49859	22.72379	21.13184	19.70068	18.41120	17.24676	16.19290	15.23703	14.36814	12.85401	11.58693	10.51784	9.60857	8.82932	8.15656
35	29.40858	24.99862	23.14516	21.48722	20.00066	18.66461	17.46101	16.37419	15.39055	14.49825	12.94767	11.65457	10.56682	9.64416	8.85524	8.17550
36	30.10751	25.48884	23.55625	21.83225	20.29049	18.90828	17.66604	16.54685	15.53607	14.62099	13.03521	11.71719	10.61176	9.67651	8.87859	8.19241
37	30.79951	25.96945	23.95732	22.16724	20.57053	19.14258	17.86224	16.71129	15.67400	14.73678	13.11702	11.77518	10.65299	9.70592	8.89963	8.20751
38	31.48466	26.44064	24.34860	22.49246	20.84109	19.36786	18.04999	16.86789	15.80474	14.84602	13.19347	11.82887	10.69082	9.73265	8.91859	8.22099
39	32.16303	26.90259	24.73034	22.80822	21.10250	19.58448	18.22966	17.01704	15.92866	14.94907	13.26493	11.87858	10.72552	9.75696	8.93567	8.23303
40	32.83469	27.35548	25.10278	23.11477	21.35507	19.79277	18.40158	17.15909	16.04612	15.04630	13.33171	11.92461	10.75736	9.77905	8.95105	8.24378
41	33.49969	27.79949	25.46612	23.41240	21.59910	19.99305	18.56611	17.29437	16.15746	15.13802	13.39412	11.96723	10.78657	9.79914	8.96491	8.25337
42	34.15811	28.23479	25.82061	23.70136	21.83488	20.18563	18.72355	17.42321	16.26300	15.22454	13.45245	12.00670	10.81337	9.81740	8.97740	8.26194
43	34.81001	28.66156	26.16645	23.98190	22.06269	20.37079	18.87421	17.54591	16.36303	15.30617	13.50696	12.04324	10.83795	9.83400	8.98865	8.26959
44	35.45545	29.07996	26.50385	24.25427	22.28279	20.54884	19.01838	17.66277	16.45785	15.38318	13.55791	12.07707	10.86051	9.84909	8.99878	8.27642
45	36.09451	29.49016	26.83302	24.51871	22.49545	20.72004	19.15635	17.77407	16.54773	15.45583	13.60552	12.10840	10.88120	9.86281	9.00791	8.28252
46	36.72724	29.89231	27.15417	24.77545	22.70092	20.88465	19.28837	17.88007	16.63292	15.52437	13.65002	12.13741	10.90018	9.87528	9.01614	8.28796
47	37.35370	30.28658	27.46748	25.02471	22.89944	21.04294	19.41471	17.98102	16.71366	15.58903	13.69161	12.16427	10.91760	9.88662	9.02355	8.29282
48	37.97396	30.67312	27.77315	25.26671	23.09124	21.19513	19.53561	18.07716	16.79020	15.65003	13.73047	12.18914	10.93358	9.89693	9.03022	8.29716
49	38.58808	31.05208	28.07137	25.50166	23.27656	21.34147	19.65130	18.16872	16.86275	15.70757	13.76680	12.21216	10.94823	9.90630	9.03624	8.30104
50	39.19612	31.42361	28.36231	25.72976	23.45562	21.48218	19.76201	18.25593	16.93152	15.76186	13.80075	12.23348	10.96168	9.91481	9.04165	8.30450

r

13.0%	14.0%	15.0%	16.0%	17.0%	18.0%	19.0%	20.0%	21.0%	22.0%	23.0%	24.0%	25.0%
0.88496	0.87719	0.86957	0.86207	0.85470	0.84746	0.84034	0.83333	0.82645	0.81967	0.81301	0.80645	0.80000
1.66810	1.64666	1.62571	1.60523	1.58521	1.56564	1.54650	1.52778	1.50946	1.49153	1.47399	1.45682	1.44000
2.36115	2.32163	2.28323	2.24589	2.20958	2.17427	2.13992	2.10648	2.07393	2.04224	2.01137	1.98130	1.95200
2.97447	2.91371	2.85498	2.79818	2.74324	2.69006	2.63859	2.58873	2.54044	2.49364	2.44827	2.40428	2.36160
3.51723	3.43308	3.35216	3.27429	3.19935	3.12717	3.05763	2.99061	2.92598	2.86364	2.80347	2.74538	2.68928
3.99755	3.88867	3.78448	3.68474	3.58918	3.49760	3.40978	3.32551	3.24462	3.16692	3.09225	3.02047	2.95142
4.42261	4.28830	4.16042	4.03857	3.92238	3.81153	3.70570	3.60459	3.50795	3.41551	3.32704	3.24232	3.16114
4.79877	4.63886	4.48732	4.34359	4.20716	4.07757	3.95437	3.83716	3.72558	3.61927	3.51792	3.42122	3.32891
5.13166	4.94637	4.77158	4.60654	4.45057	4.30302	4.16333	4.03097	3.90543	3.78628	3.67310	3.56550	3.46313
5.42624	5.21612	5.01877	4.83323	4.65860	4.49409	4.33893	4.19247	4.05408	3.92318	3.79927	3.68186	3.57050
5.68694	5.45273	5.23371	5.02864	4.83641	4.65601	4.48650	4.32706	4.17692	4.03540	3.90185	3.77569	3.65640
5.91765	5.66029	5.42062	5.19711	4.98839	4.79322	4.61050	4.43922	4.27845	4.12737	3.98524	3.85136	3.72512
6.12181	5.84236	5.58315	5.34233	5.11828	4.90951	4.71471	4.53268	4.36235	4.20277	4.05304	3.91239	3.78010
6.30249	6.00207	5.72448	5.46753	5.22930	5.00806	4.80228	4.61057	4.43170	4.26456	4.10816	3.96160	3.82408
6.46238	6.14217	5.84737	5.57546	5.32419	5.09158	4.87586	4.67547	4.48901	4.31522	4.15298	4.00129	3.85926
6.60388	6.26506	5.95423	5.66850	5.40529	5.16235	4.93770	4.72956	4.53637	4.35673	4.18941	4.03330	3.88741
6.72909	6.37286	6.04716	5.74870	5.47461	5.22233	4.98966	4.77463	4.57551	4.39077	4.21904	4.05911	3.90993
6.83991	6.46742	6.12797	5.81785	5.53385	5.27316	5.03333	4.81219	4.60786	4.41866	4.24312	4.07993	3.92794
6.93797	6.55037	6.19823	5.87746	5.58449	5.31624	5.07003	4.84350	4.63460	4.44152	4.26270	4.09672	3.94235
7.02475	6.62313	6.25933	5.92884	5.62777	5.35275	5.10086	4.86958	4.65669	4.46027	4.27862	4.11026	3.95388
7.10155	6.68696	6.31246	5.97314	5.66476	5.38368	5.12677	4.89132	4.67495	4.47563	4.29156	4.12117	3.96311
7.16951	6.74294	6.35866	6.01133	5.69637	5.40990	5.14855	4.90943	4.69004	4.48822	4.30208	4.12998	3.97049
7.22966	6.79206	6.39884	6.04425	5.72340	5.43212	5.16685	4.92453	4.70251	4.49854	4.31063	4.13708	3.97639
7.28288	6.83514	6.43377	6.07263	5.74649	5.45095	5.18223	4.93710	4.71282	4.50700	4.31759	4.14281	3.98111
7.32998	6.87293	6.46415	6.09709	5.76623	5.46691	5.19515	4.94759	4.72134	4.51393	4.32324	4.14742	3.98489
7.37167	6.90608	6.49056	6.11818	5.78311	5.48043	5.20601	4.95632	4.72838	4.51962	4.32784	4.15115	3.98791
7.40856	6.93515	6.51353	6.13636	5.79753	5.49189	5.21513	4.96360	4.73420	4.52428	4.33158	4.15415	3.99033
7.44120	6.96066	6.53351	6.15204	5.80985	5.50160	5.22280	4.96967	4.73901	4.52810	4.33462	4.15657	3.99226
7.47009	6.98304	6.55088	6.16555	5.82039	5.50983	5.22924	4.97472	4.74298	4.53123	4.33709	4.15853	3.99381
7.49565	7.00266	6.56598	6.17720	5.82939	5.51681	5.23466	4.97894	4.74627	4.53379	4.33909	4.16010	3.99505
7.51828	7.01988	6.57911	6.18724	5.83709	5.52272	5.23921	4.98245	4.74898	4.53590	4.34073	4.16137	3.99604
7.53830	7.03498	6.59053	6.19590	5.84366	5.52773	5.24303	4.98537	4.75122	4.53762	4.34205	4.16240	3.99683
7.55602	7.04823	6.60046	6.20336	5.84928	5.53197	5.24625	4.98781	4.75308	4.53903	4.34313	4.16322	3.99746
7.57170	7.05985	6.60910	6.20979	5.85409	5.53557	5.24895	4.98984	4.75461	4.54019	4.34401	4.16389	3.99797
7.58557	7.07005	6.61661	6.21534	5.85820	5.53862	5.25122	4.99154	4.75588	4.54114	4.34472	4.16443	3.99838
7.59785	7.07899	6.62314	6.22012	5.86171	5.54120	5.25312	4.99295	4.75692	4.54192	4.34530	4.16486	3.99870
7.60872	7.08683	6.62881	6.22424	5.86471	5.54339	5.25472	4.99412	4.75779	4.54256	4.34578	4.16521	3.99896
7.61833	7.09371	6.63375	6.22779	5.86727	5.54525	5.25607	4.99510	4.75850	4.54308	4.34616	4.16549	3.99917
7.62684	7.09975	6.63805	6.23086	5.86946	5.54682	5.25720	4.99592	4.75909	4.54351	4.34647	4.16572	3.99934
7.63438	7.10504	6.64178	6.23350	5.87133	5.54815	5.25815	4.99660	4.75958	4.54386	4.34672	4.16590	3.99947
7.64104	7.10969	6.64502	6.23577	5.87294	5.54928	5.25895	4.99717	4.75998	4.54415	4.34693	4.16605	3.99957
7.64694	7.11376	6.64785	6.23774	5.87430	5.55024	5.25962	4.99764	4.76032	4.54438	4.34710	4.16617	3.99966
7.65216	7.11733	6.65030	6.23943	5.87547	5.55105	5.26019	4.99803	4.76059	4.54458	4.34723	4.16627	3.99973
7.65678	7.12047	6.65244	6.24089	5.87647	5.55174	5.26066	4.99836	4.76082	4.54473	4.34734	4.16634	3.99978
7.66086	7.12322	6.65429	6.24214	5.87733	5.55232	5.26106	4.99863	4.76101	4.54486	4.34743	4.16641	3.99983
7.66448	7.12563	6.65591	6.24323	5.87806	5.55281	5.26140	4.99886	4.76116	4.54497	4.34751	4.16646	3.99986
7.66768	7.12774	6.65731	6.24416	5.87868	5.55323	5.26168	4.99905	4.76129	4.54506	4.34757	4.16650	3.99989
7.67052	7.12960	6.65853	6.24497	5.87922	5.55359	5.26191	4.99921	4.76140	4.54513	4.34762	4.16653	3.99991
7.67302	7.13123	6.65959	6.24566	5.87967	5.55389	5.26211	4.99934	4.76149	4.54519	4.34766	4.16656	3.99993
7.67524	7.13266	6.66051	6.24626	5.88006	5.55414	5.26228	4.99945	4.76156	4.54524	4.34769	4.16658	3.99994

Appendix C

Cases

Case 1: Zordef of the Deep

In 2002 Evan Alexander developed a computer game called Zordef of the Deep (Zordef). The game was a big hit among Evan's friends and they suggested that the game might be successful commercially. At first Evan tried to market Zordef on his own by contacting computer stores and clubs, and by placing announcements on computer bulletin boards. However, it quickly became obvious that this approach was not going to be very successful. In the six months that Evan tried to distribute the game on his own, he managed to sell only 154 copies.

In mid-2003 Evan had a chance meeting with a marketing representative from Wonder Software Ltd. (WS), a company that produces computer software. WS is a privately owned corporation, with its head office and production facilities near Ottawa. Evan demonstrated Zordef to the representative, who offered to bring the product to the executives of WS for evaluation. After testing and discussions, WS offered to market Zordef. Evan and WS agreed that Evan would transfer title to the game to WS in exchange for 30% of the net income earned on sales of the game. The contract between the parties stipulated that WS could deduct appropriate, reasonable expenses in determining net income. Zordef of the Deep was released in November 2004.

Games of this type have a life of about three years. Most sales are generated in the first few months and then tail off quickly. Sales of Zordef in the ten months ended August 31, 2005 were $824,000. WS estimates that sales of Zordef for the twelve months ending August 31, 2006 will be about $420,000 and perhaps $100,000 in the twelve months after that. WS recently presented Evan with an income statement for the ten months ended August 31, 2005 and a cheque for $18,000. The income statement and related notes are provided as follows:

Zordef of the Deep Computer Game
Income Statement
For the Ten Months Ended August 31, 2005

Sales (Note 1)		$824,000
Cost of goods sold (Note 2)	$160,000	
Selling and administrative costs (Note 3)	252,000	
Packaging design costs (Note 4)	97,000	
Advertising (Note 5)	85,000	
Customer support (Note 6)	80,000	
Research and development (Note 7)	50,000	
Product development costs (Note 8)	32,000	
Taxes	8,000	764,000
Net income		$ 60,000

Notes:

Note 1. Revenue is recognized when the product is shipped to the customer. The sales figure is net of an allowance for doubtful accounts and an accrual for volume discounts. Volume discounts are offered to customers who purchase more than a specified dollar amount of WS's products, and are allocated to products based on total sales dollars of each product sold.

Note 2. Cost of goods sold includes production costs of the game. Approximately $100,000 represents direct costs of production (labour and materials), and the remainder is an allocation of overhead costs, including amortization of plant and equipment, supervisory staff, quality control staff, and so on.

Note 3. Selling and administrative costs include commissions paid to salespeople, an allocation of salespeople's salaries, and an allocation of general office overhead. A special charge of $50,000 was levied against Zordef of the Deep to account for senior management's time spent on the game.

Note 4. The packaging design charge represents money spent to develop packaging for Zordef of the Deep. The packaging was designed by an outside agency and the charge represents the full amount charged for the design.

Note 5. The company spent $40,000 directly advertising and promoting Zordef of the Deep to consumers and retailers. The remaining amount is an allocation of the overall corporate advertising budget that includes promotion of the WS full product line.

Note 6. WS provides customer support to users of its software. Customers can call a toll-free help line, or visit the WS web site to receive advice and help if they have problems with any of WS's products. The charge to Zordef is an allocation of its share of the cost of the customer support, based on revenues and estimated use of the support by each product's customers.

Note 7. The research and development charge represents Zordef's share of WS's research and development costs incurred for the development of new software products. The amount represents an allocation of the total cost incurred for research and development by WS.

Note 8. Before Zordef of the Deep hit the market, WS made modifications to the program. The cost represents the time of WS's programmer, charged at the prevailing market rate. This is the rate WS charges outsiders who contract with WS to do programming.

Evan Alexander is disturbed that despite the amount of sales of the game, the profit figure is very low. He does not think that he is being dealt with fairly. He has asked you to prepare a report examining the accounting methods used by WS in calculating Zordef's net income. The report will be used in negotiations with WS and may potentially be used in any legal action taken by Evan.

Required:

Prepare the report to Evan Alexander.

Case 2: Patriot Meats Limited (I)[1]

Patriot Meats Limited (Patriot) is incorporated under federal corporate legislation. The company's founder, Patricia Wolford, holds 60% of the shares. Four private individuals, who have very little involvement in operating decisions, each own 10%. All of the company's operations are located in Manitoba. Patriot has produced a variety of packaged meats, which it sells nationally through grocery chains, for ten years. The primary inputs for the company's products are beef, pork, and chicken, which are purchased live at various livestock auctions throughout the western provinces and through contract relationships with farmers.

Labour and management at Patriot have had an acrimonious relationship. Over the past ten years the union representing Patriot's factory employees has made significant wage concessions to avoid job losses. In the last contract negotiations, Patriot and the union agreed that the union could have access to the company's financial statements. The upcoming negotiation will be the first time that the union will see the financial statements. The union negotiators have indicated clearly that they will scrutinize the statements very closely to determine Patriot's ability to pay higher wages to the factory employees without jeopardizing competitiveness.

Patricia Wolford has hired you to provide advice on the appropriate accounting policies for the financial statements for the year ending September 30, 2004. She has asked you to prepare a report on the appropriate treatment of the following items:

1. At the insistence of National Grocers, one of Patriot's major customers, the company has decided to acquire certification for meeting certain quality standards. Patriot has paid $25,000 in advance to a consulting firm for work that will begin in November 2004 and will take about six months to complete, with an expected total cost of $125,000.

2. Since the youth unemployment rate is particularly high in Manitoba, the provincial government subsidizes employers that hire people under the age of 25 who have not previously held full-time employment. The amount is calculated by the employer at the end of December of each year and is paid by the government by mid-February. Patriot estimates that as of September 30, it will be entitled to $300,000 under the plan.

3. Patriot operates several retail stores that offer a variety of additional merchandise, as well as the company's own packaged meats. A line of souvenir-type merchandise was added three years ago but has not been successful. In fact, no additional merchandise has been ordered since the original shipment from Worldwide Imports, the distributor of the merchandise. As of September 13, 2004, Patricia determined the following information related to the remaining inventory:

Total retail price of all remaining stock	$200,000
Original invoice cost of the remaining stock	140,000
Cost based on Worldwide Import's current price list	165,000

    In addition, Patricia asked Manitoba Liquidators, which specializes in purchasing unwanted inventories, for an estimate of what they would pay Patriot for the souvenir merchandise. Their offer, which Patricia is seriously considering, was $45,000.

4. Patriot was invited to join a group of Manitoba companies on a trade mission to China. The trip took place in June 2004 and several large orders were received for shipment in January 2005. However, the negotiators for the Chinese companies were very aggressive and the prices were reduced such that very little profit is expected. The $40,000 cost of the trip included travel costs and product samples. About $5,000 of

that cost was incurred for an extended personal vacation in China that Patricia and her husband took after the conclusion of the trade mission.

5. In June 2004 Patriot signed a three-year contract with Cariboo Foods, a major supplier of in-flight meals to the Canadian airline industry. The additional volume required the construction of a new processing facility. Because Patriot found it difficult to obtain financing for the expansion, Patricia persuaded Cariboo to pay an up-front fee of $300,000 when the contract was signed. In return, Patriot's selling prices under the contract were decreased slightly.

6. In November 2003 the company signed an agreement with Babby Hill (a well-known figure skater) to endorse the Patriot product line. Recently, however, Babby upset many Canadians when she made certain racially offensive comments to a reporter for a foreign newspaper. Patriot has decided not to use Babby's endorsement, although the company's lawyer advises that the contract does not provide any way to avoid paying the agreed fee of $20,000 per month from July 1, 2004 to June 1, 2005.

Required:

Provide the report to Patricia Wolford.

Case 3: Patriot Meats Limited (II)[2]

Use the information provided in Patriot Meats Ltd. I. You have been engaged by the head of the union representing Patriot's employees to prepare a report on how to account for a number of controversial issues that arose when the union reviewed Patriot's financial statements and held its preliminary discussions with Patriot's management. The union will use your report in its assessment of Patriot's financial position, performance, and ability to pay higher wages and benefits to employees. The union head has asked that your report fully explain your recommendations, discuss arguments that Patriot's management might use to counter your recommendations, and identify and discuss alternative treatments that Patriot might present for the outstanding issues.

Required:

Provide the report to the head of the union.

Case 4: The Divorce of Donna and Michael Leaf (I)

In November 2003 Donna and Michael Leaf decided to divorce after 20 years of marriage. Among the assets owned by the couple is a business, Ontario Printing Limited (OPL), which they organized together in 1993. The Leafs are equal shareholders in OPL, but Donna operates it. The Leafs agree that Donna will purchase the shares of OPL from Michael at fair market value. Since the shares are not traded on an exchange and no market price is available, they agree that fair market value will be equal to five times average net income for the past three years, including the fiscal year ending December 31, 2003. Donna and Michael also agree that the accounting policies should be reasonable for determining representative net income for the business. They recognize that adjustments to the final selling price might be necessary to take specific circumstances into consideration.

You obtain the following information about OPL:

1. OPL produces printed materials and makes copies for customers.
2. OPL has used its financial statements primarily for tax purposes. The company writes off any expenditures it makes that can be justified for tax purposes, regardless of whether they have any future benefit.
3. Most transactions are on a cash basis. OPL offers credit terms to its larger customers.
4. OPL has $100,000 in loans from the shareholders. The loans are interest-free.
5. The company owns a small building in the north end of the city. Its offices occupy the ground floor of the building, and the rest of the building is leased to tenants. Since the building was acquired, its market value has increased from $2,500,000 to $3,000,000.

6. The Leafs have charged many personal expenses to the business.
7. In recent months paper prices have risen significantly. Anticipating the increase, OPL stockpiled an additional year's supply of paper. Since OPL purchased the paper, the price has increased by 50%.
8. Donna Leaf took a salary of $200,000 during the year. A manager doing Donna's work at a competitor's company would be paid about $65,000.
9. During the summer of 2003, Michael Leaf, on behalf of OPL, negotiated a long-term contract with a customer to produce instruction manuals for its products. The contract begins in January 2004. In exchange for lower printing rates, the customer has guaranteed a minimum of $200,000 work over two years. The customer will pay as work is done. Any shortfall from the $200,000 will be paid at the end of the contract term.

Required:

Donna and Michael have asked you to prepare a report that they can use to determine the selling price of Michael's shares. The report should state the accounting policies that should be used to prepare the financial statements that will be used to set the selling price of OPL, as well as any adjustments that should be made to the final price because of other information and concerns you have. Since this divorce is less than friendly, you should explain your reasoning fully so that lawyers for the respective parties will have a basis for discussion.

Case 5: The Divorce of Donna and Michael Leaf (II)

Use the information provided in Case 4: The Divorce of Donna and Michael Leaf (I). You have been engaged by Michael Leaf's lawyer to prepare a report that she can use in negotiations with Donna's lawyer. The report should state the accounting policies that should be used to prepare the financial statements that will be used to set the selling price of OPL, as well as any adjustments that should be made to the final price because of other information and concerns you have. The report should explain your reasoning fully so that Michael's lawyer can understand your recommendations and anticipate any alternatives Donna's lawyer might propose.

Required:

Prepare the report for Michael Leaf's lawyer.

Case 6: The Divorce of Donna and Michael Leaf (III)

Use the information provided in Case 4: The Divorce of Donna and Michael Leaf (I). You have been engaged by Donna Leaf's lawyer to prepare a report that he can use in his negotiations with Michael's lawyer. The report should state the accounting policies that should be used for preparing the financial statements that will be used to set the selling price of OPL, as well as any adjustments that should be made to the final price because of other information and concerns you have. The report should explain your reasoning fully so that Donna's lawyer can understand your recommendations and anticipate any alternatives Michael's lawyer might propose.

Required:

Prepare the report for Donna Leaf's lawyer.

Case 7: International Productions Corporation[3]

International Productions Corporation (IPC) is a diversified, privately owned entertainment company with operations throughout Canada. IPC's operations include movie theatres, live theatre productions, and television productions. IPC has been expanding rapidly, financed mainly by large bank loans and by debt and equity investments by private investors. The CEO of IPC owns 30% of the shares of the company and is the largest single investor. The

CEO is also the founder and main creative force behind the company. IPC is in the process of finalizing its fiscal 2004 financial statements (its year end is October 31). The CEO has asked you for advice on a number of outstanding accounting issues that need to be resolved before the financial statements can be issued to the various stakeholders. The CEO has informed you of the following issues:

1. IPC purchases real estate in prime locations where an existing theatre chain does not adequately serve the market. After purchasing the real estate, IPC engages a contractor to build a theatre complex. During fiscal 2004, IPC received a $2,000,000 payment from a contractor who had built a theatre complex in Montréal. The payment represents a penalty for not completing the theatre complex on time. Construction began in February 2003 and was to have been completed by December 2003. Instead, the complex was not completed until the end of May 2004.

2. The company is staging the Canadian production of *Accounting: What Could Be Better?*, which is to open in January 2005. The smash-hit musical has been running in Paris for three years and is still playing to sold-out audiences. IPC started receiving advance bookings in November 2003, and the first 40 weeks of the show's run are completely sold out. Average ticket prices are $65 and the show will play seven nights a week. The theatre used for the production is relatively small, with about 1,200 seats. As of October 31, 2004, IPC had included in revenue $900,000 in interest collected on the funds received from advance ticket sales. IPC has already invested $4,000,000 in advertising for the production. It will have invested $15,000,000 in pre-production costs by January 2005 (pre-production costs are the costs incurred before a show is actually presented to audiences). Once the show opens, IPC will incur weekly production costs of $250,000.

3. IPC started selling some of its movie theatres a couple of years ago. Each theatre's contribution to long-run operating cash flow is assessed and, if the value of the real estate is greater than the present value of future theatre operating profits, the theatre is sold. In the past, revenue from these sales has been relatively minor, but this year 25% of net income (about $6,000,000) came from the sale of theatres. Since these sales are considered an ongoing part of the company's operations, proceeds from the sale of theatres are recorded as revenue in the income statement.

4. During November 2003, IPC purchased a library of "classic" movies and television programs for $5,000,000. Management thought that the library would be a good source of revenue for IPC because of the many new television channels that would be looking to find suitable programming. Management is now concerned that its decision to purchase the library was a poor one because broadcasters have shown little interest in purchasing the rights to show movies and programs from IPC's library. In October 2004, a large broadcaster signed a contract to use certain movies in the library over the next four years. The contract guarantees IPC $1,000,000 over the four years, but payment is only required when the broadcaster actually shows one of the movies. At the end of the four years the broadcaster must make a payment to IPC so that the total payment over the life of the contract is $1,000,000. The broadcaster that signed the contract is the only potential client who has shown interest in the contents of the library.

Required:

Prepare a report for the CEO of IPC, advising him on these accounting issues. Your report should clearly explain the reasoning for your recommendations and should address possible alternatives. The CEO may use your report as the basis for discussions with IPC's auditors.

Case 8: Vulcanzap Inc. [4]

Vulcanzap Inc. (VZAP) is a high-technology company that develops, designs, and manufactures telecommunications equipment. VZAP was founded in 2002 by Dr. Jordan Warman, the former assistant head of research and development at a major telephone company. Dr. Warman and the director of marketing left the company to found VZAP. VZAP has been very successful. Sales reached $5,300,000 in its first year and have grown by 80% annually since then. The key to VZAP's success has been the sophisticated software contained in the equipment it sells.

VZAP's board of directors recently decided to issue shares to raise funds for strategic objectives through an initial public offering of common shares. The shares will be listed on the Toronto Stock Exchange. VZAP's underwriter believes that an offering price of 18 to 20 times the most recent fiscal year's earnings per share can be achieved.

VZAP has announced its intention to go public, and work has begun on the preparation of a preliminary prospectus. The prospectus will be filed with the relevant securities commission in 40 days. The offering is expected to be completed in about 75 days. The company has an October 31 year end. It is now November 9, 2005.

Dr. Warman has provided you with the following information regarding a number of unresolved accounting issues. He has asked you for a report that analyzes the issues and makes recommendations on how they should be treated in the October 31, 2005 financial statements.

1. The job market for top software and hardware engineering talent is very tight. As a result, VZAP has turned to information technology headhunters to attract key personnel from other high-technology companies. During the year VZAP paid $178,000 in placement fees. The search firm offers a one-year, money-back guarantee if any of the people hired leaves the company or proves to be unsatisfactory.

2. On July 29, 2005, the company made a payment of $250,000 to a computer hacker. The hacker had given the company ten days to pay her the funds. Otherwise, she said, she would post information on the Internet about a security flaw she had detected in the VZAP's Firewall Plus software. Disclosure of the security flaw would limit the usefulness of the software. VZAP has been aware of the flaw for some time, but has not been able to figure out a solution for it. The hacker did not provide any information that would be useful for correcting the security flaw. VZAP currently has $500,000 in unamortized development costs pertaining to Firewall Plus that is classified as assets on the balance sheet.

3. Jordan Warman had been working on a photon phaser when he left the telephone company. He has advanced this technology significantly at VZAP and the product is close to being ready to market. To date VZAP has capitalized $1,750,000 in development costs. But in September a competitor introduced a product very similar to the photon phaser and the product has already captured significant attention from customers. Jordan Warman thinks his product will still be successful, but it is not likely that VZAP will be able to command the market share that it originally anticipated.

4. One of VZAP's products, the ATM 4000, has been unsuccessful. High rates of failure and customer dissatisfaction led VZAP to issue an offer, dated July 30, 2005, to buy back all units currently in service for a total of $1,467,500. Southwestern Utah Telephone is suing VZAP for $4,000,000 in damages related to two ATM 4000 devices that it had purchased through a distributor. The devices broke down, affecting telephone traffic for two weeks before they were replaced.

5. During the first two years of operation VZAP expensed all desktop computers (PCs) when purchased, on the grounds that they become obsolete so fast that their value after one year is almost negligible. In the current year, VZAP bought $429,000 worth of PCs and plans to write them off over two years.

Required:

Prepare the report requested by Jordan Warman.

Case 9: Lamberton Lumber Ltd.

Lamberton Lumber Ltd. (LLL) is a retail lumberyard. LLL sells lumber to individuals and small contractors and builders. LLL also sells other building supplies. Until recently LLL was part of a chain of stores, but the chain decided to sell off stores that were not in its core business. Several local investors purchased LLL. The purchasers believe that LLL will be successful, but that it had not been well managed by the chain. None of the new owners will be involved in the day-to-day management of LLL, but some of them will sit on the board of directors.

It is now mid-December 2003. LLL is getting ready to prepare its financial statements for its fiscal year ended November 30, 2003. The chair of LLL's board of directors has asked you to help select appropriate accounting policies and treatments that the company should use, given its new ownership. After your recommendations have been discussed by the board, they will be given to LLL's management team for implementation. In your discussions you have gathered the following information:

1. The new investors paid $5,000,000 in cash for LLL. LLL will also pay the investors 25% of the profits LLL earns in excess of $500,000 for each of the next three years (including fiscal 2003), as reported in LLL's general purpose financial statements.

2. LLL hired a new management team for the store. Members of the team have significant experience in the business. The managers will receive performance-based bonuses, in part based on net income as reported in the general purpose financial statements.

3. The investors agreed that they would receive cash dividends each year. The amount that would be paid in dividends would be equal to 20% of net income each year, as reported in the general purpose financial statements.

4. LLL's business with most customers is transacted in cash or with major credit cards. LLL offers credit terms to builders and contractors, allowing them up to 90 days to pay. LLL has agreed to extend credit terms for one struggling builder of homes. The builder began constructing new homes, but sales have been slower than expected. LLL has agreed to accept payment each time the builder sells one of its homes.

5. During the year LLL sold some vacant land adjacent to its store. A family-owned grocery chain purchased the land to build a large new store. LLL believes that the new store will attract new business to its own store. LLL originally paid $510,000 for the land, and the grocery chain has agreed to pay $2,000,000 for it. The chain paid $550,000 in cash and will pay the remainder on December 31, 2008. The amount owing is secured by the land and personal guarantees of the grocery chain's owners.

6. In mid-1999 LLL obtained an exclusive dealership for a line of high-quality kitchen cabinets. The dealership rights were for an initial five-year period, with five-year renewals possible at the option of the manufacturer. LLL was assured at the time it signed the initial agreement that a renewal was virtually certain. LLL spent $80,000 to set up displays to promote the line. These costs were capitalized and are being amortized over ten years. In November LLL learned that the exclusive dealership arrangement will not be renewed and LLL will not be able to sell the products beyond April 2004.

7. LLL purchased some heavy equipment for use in the lumberyard for $100,000 at an auction. The equipment was fairly old and in poor condition. It required significant repairs and maintenance, which cost $25,000. LLL believes that the equipment is in nearly new condition (new equipment of a similar type would have cost over $200,000) and will likely be usable for at least ten years.

8. In May 2005 a large plumbing department opened in LLL. Because LLL had little expertise in plumbing but wanted to provide for customers' plumbing needs, LLL contracted with J. Alexander & Sons Plumbing Ltd. (J. Alexander) to own and operate the plumbing department. J. Alexander will pay LLL $20,000 per year, plus 5% of gross sales. LLL paid $55,000 to assist J. Alexander in getting the plumbing department ready for business. The contract between J. Alexander and LLL is for seven years.

Required:

Prepare the report requested by the chair of the board of directors.

Case 10: The Cadalex Ruffians

The Cadalex Ruffians (Ruffians) is a major-league Canadian sports franchise. The Cadalex family has owned the Ruffians since the team's inception over 30 years ago. The Ruffians have struggled both financially and on the field for the last few years—attendance at games is among the lowest in the league and the team has not made the playoffs for several years. The Cadalex family has come to realize that the economics of the sport will make it difficult for them to make the team successful. As a result, in July 2003 the Cadalex family sold the team and its brand new sports facility (where the Ruffians play their home games) to a group of 30 businesses and wealthy individuals in the community. The new owners hope that the Ruffians will once again be successful on the field and become a profitable investment. The ownership percentage of each of the investors ranges from 2% to 20% of the Ruffians.

It is now December 2003. The new owners of the Cadalex Ruffians have hired you to make recommendations on a number of unresolved accounting issues facing the team for its December 31, 2003 year end. The owners have asked for a report that identifies and discusses reasonable treatments and alternatives for the unresolved issues, along with your recommendations and the rationale for your choices. From your discussions with the owners and managers, you have learned the following information:

1. The new owners hired a management team to operate the franchise, beginning August 1, 2003. The management team has been instructed to make the Ruffians successful on the field and profitable for the owners. Management's contract specifies that it will receive a bonus based on the profitability of the franchise.

2. The large number of owners makes it impossible for all of them to be involved in ongoing decision making. Most of the owners will receive information about the team from regular briefings from management and from the Ruffians' annual financial statements.

3. The new owners have made a representation to local governments requesting financial assistance. The new owners have stated that since purchasing the team, they have come to realize that it may be difficult for them to keep the team in the community without assistance. The governments have asked for the Ruffians' December 31, 2003 year-end financial statements as soon as they are available.

4. The team sold the rights to name its new facility to a major corporation for an initial payment of $5,000,000, plus $2,000,000 per year in each of the next twenty years. The payments entitle the corporation to attach its corporate name to the new facility. The contract is binding for five years, after which time the corporation can terminate the deal by not making annual payments. The initial payment was made on December 15, 2003. The annual $2,000,000 payments are to be made on March 1 of each year, beginning in 2004.

5. In an effort to generate new excitement and interest in the team, season ticket subscribers are being given coupons to purchase team merchandise at significant discounts. The coupons allow the purchaser 50% off the price of merchandise purchased.

6. The Ruffians recently awarded the rights to broadcast the team's games for the next three seasons to a radio network owned by one of the team's larger investors. The network will pay the Ruffians $2,500,000 per season for the rights. The amount is slightly less than what the previous contract holder paid last season for the rights. The lower price has been justified by the poor performance of the team and the declining number of listeners.

7. The new owners of the team are making an effort to improve the Ruffians for the upcoming season. The team recently signed one of the league's top players to a long-term contract. The Ruffians paid the player $8,000,000 to sign with the team and will pay him $6,000,000 per year in each of the next six years. The $8,000,000 paid to the player for signing with the team is not refundable in the event the player does not make the team or does not play well.

8. One of the team's players has been released from the team effective December 15, 2003. However, the terms of the player's contract require that he receive $500,000 per year in each of the next five years, regardless of whether he plays or not. Payments must be made to the player by July 1 of each year, beginning in 2004.

Required:

Prepare the report for the owners of the Ruffians.

Case 11: Shmevan Stores Ltd.[5]

Shmevan Stores Ltd. (Shmevan) is a national chain of franchised business supplies stores. Currently there are 75 stores in the chain. Each store is owned and operated by people who live in the communities where the stores are located. The stores sell a complete line of business supplies, office furniture, computer hardware and software, and other business-related products. Shmevan supplies all merchandise to the stores. Shmevan is able to obtain lower prices because of its significant buyer power. Shmevan receives a royalty on all sales made by the franchise stores.

In May 2004, in response to the tough and increased competition in the business supplies market, Shmevan's management introduced a contest to motivate franchise store owners and to encourage innovation of new and profitable business practices. The winner of the contest is to receive a cash prize of $150,000. The prize is to be awarded to the store that reports the highest percentage increase in net income before taxes for the year ended October 31, 2005.

In a preliminary review of the financial statements, Shmevan's management determined that the franchise store in Saskatoon was the winner. The Saskatoon store reported a percentage increase in income before taxes of 278%, using the formula specified for the contest. However, the judging panel, which is made up of Shmevan's management along with five people representing the owners of the franchise stores, has concerns about the results reported by the Saskatoon store. Some members of the committee believe that Saskatoon has misrepresented its financial position. As a result of these concerns, a number of stores have protested the awarding of the prize to the Saskatoon store. The second-place finisher in the contest, the store in Fredericton, reported a percentage increase in income before taxes of 201%.

You have been engaged by Shmevan to review the financial information prepared by the Saskatoon store. Shmevan would like a report assessing the appropriateness of the accounting methods Saskatoon used and whether the accounting methods used by the Saskatoon store were "fair in the context of the contest." In preparing to write your report, you have gathered the following information:

1. The formula used to calculate the percentage increase in net income before taxes is:

$$\frac{\text{Income before taxes in 2005} - \text{Income before taxes in 2004}}{\text{Income before taxes in 2004}}$$

   In the event that income before taxes in 2004 is below $100,000, for the purpose of the formula net income before taxes in 2004 is assumed to be $100,000.

2. For the year ended October 31, 2004, the Saskatoon store reported income before taxes of $42,000.

3. The Saskatoon store normally recognizes revenue when goods are delivered to customers.

4. During 2005 the Saskatoon store changed its inventory valuation method from average cost to FIFO. Saskatoon's owner explained that the change was made so the store's accounting records would be consistent with those of other stores in the chain. As of October 31, 2005, 58 of the Shmevan stores use FIFO. The effect of the change was to increase income by $18,000 in 2004 and by $21,000 in 2005, versus the amount that would have been reported using average cost.

5. During the fiscal year ended October 31, 2004, the Saskatoon store wrote off $50,000 of inventory because management deemed that the inventory could not be sold. In February 2005, the inventory was sold to three separate customers for $72,000.

6. In October 2005 the president of the Saskatoon store made three television commercials that are to be broadcast in the Saskatoon area beginning in December. As of October 31, the commercials have not been shown on television, although they have been completed. The commercials cost $15,000 to produce. The amount has been capitalized and is reported on the October 31, 2005 balance sheet.

7. In September and October 2005 the Saskatoon store ran a promotion that offered significant discounts to customers who made large purchases. These customers were

assured that they could return any purchases after 90 days for a full refund for any reason if the customer decided that the merchandise was not required. Sales in September and October 2005 were significantly higher than in the same months of the previous year, and preliminary evidence suggests that sales in November 2005 have declined from 2004.

8. In October 2004 the Saskatoon store paid employees $22,000 in advances against commissions that would be earned in fiscal 2005. The advances were accounted for as wage expenses in 2004. The amount was paid because some employees were facing financial difficulties and the owner of the store wanted to help them out.

9. During fiscal 2005 the Saskatoon store sold a delivery vehicle, some furniture and fixtures, and a number of miscellaneous other assets. Most items were sold for more than their net book values (gains), but some were sold at a loss. Overall, the sales produced a gain of $17,000.

Required:

Prepare the report requested by Shmevan.

Case 12: Good Quality Auto Parts Limited[6]

Good Quality Auto Parts Limited (GQAP) is a medium-sized, privately owned producer of auto parts that are sold to car manufacturers, repair shops, and retail outlets. In March 2004 the union negotiated a new three-year contract with the company for the 200 shop-floor employees. At the time, GQAP was in financial difficulty and management felt unable to meet the contract demands of the union. Management also believed that a strike of any length would force the company into bankruptcy.

The company proposed that, in exchange for wage concessions, the company would implement a profit-sharing plan whereby the shop floor employees would receive 10% of the company's annual after-tax profit as a bonus in each year of the contract. Although the union generally finds this type of contract undesirable, it believed that insisting on the prevailing industry settlement would jeopardize GQAP's survival. As a result, the contract terms were accepted.

The contract specifies that no major changes in accounting policies may be made without the change being approved by GQAP's auditor. Another clause in the contract allows the union to engage an accountant to examine the accounting records of the company and meet with GQAP's management and auditor to discuss any issues. Under the terms of the contract, any controversial accounting issues are to be negotiated by the union and management to arrive at a mutual agreement. If the parties cannot agree, the positions of the parties are to be presented to an independent arbitrator for resolution.

On April 10, 2005 GQAP's management presented to the union its annual financial statements and the unqualified audit report for the year ended February 28, 2005, the first year that the profit-sharing plan was in effect. The union engaged you to examine these financial statements and determine whether there are any controversial accounting issues. As a result of your examination, you identified a number of issues that are of concern to you. You met with the GQAP's controller and obtained the following information:

1. GQAP wrote off $250,000 of inventory manufactured between 1998 and 2001. There have been no sales from this inventory in over two years. The controller explained that up until this year, she had some hope that the inventory could be sold as replacement parts. However, she now believes that the parts cannot be sold.

2. The contracts GQAP has with the large auto manufacturers allow the purchaser to return items for any reason. The company has increased the allowance for returned items by 10% in the year just ended. The controller contends that, because of stiff competition faced by the auto manufacturers with which GQAP does business, there will likely be a significant increase in the number of parts returned.

3. GQAP has a policy of writing off any small tool acquisitions, even though the tools will be used over several periods. For the year just ended, small tools costing $170,000 were acquired.

4. In April 2004 GQAP purchased $500,000 of new manufacturing equipment. To reduce the financial strain of the acquisition, the company negotiated a six-year payment schedule. GQAP decided to use accelerated depreciation at a rate of 40% for the new equipment. The controller argued that because of the rapid technological changes occurring in the industry, equipment purchased now is more likely to become technologically, rather than operationally, obsolete. The straight-line depreciation method applied to the existing equipment has not been changed. Existing equipment similar to that purchased is amortized over ten years.

5. In 1999 GQAP purchased a small auto parts manufacturer and merged it into its own operation. At the time of acquisition, $435,000 of goodwill was recorded. The company has written off the goodwill in the year just ended. The controller explained that GQAP's poor performance has made the goodwill worthless.

6. In February 2005 the president and the chairman of the board, who between them own 75% of the voting shares of the company, received bonuses of $250,000 each. GQAP did not pay any dividends during the current year. In the prior year, dividends amounting to $650,000 were paid. The controller said that the board of directors justified the bonuses as a reward for keeping the company afloat despite extremely difficult economic times.

7. Until this year, GQAP calculated its tax expense based on the actual amount of income tax it had to pay. In all previous years the company received a qualified audit opinion from the auditors due to this deviation from generally accepted accounting principles (GAAP). This year, the company has used future income tax accounting as required by GAAP. The change has been made retroactively. The effect of the change has been to reduce net income for fiscal 2005 by a significant amount. The controller argued that because the company is likely to need significant external financing from new sources in the upcoming year, a clean audit opinion would reduce any fears prospective lenders might have about the company. The controller also believed that in light of the contract with the union, the financial statements should be prepared in accordance with GAAP.

The union has asked you to prepare a report on the position it should take on the issues you identified when it discusses them with management. The union also wants to know what additional information you require in order to support this position.

Required:

Prepare the report for the union.

Case 13: Jeremy Langer

Jeremy Langer is a young entrepreneur who lives in a large Canadian city. In early 2005 he identified a good opportunity to make some money selling souvenirs designed especially for the upcoming International World Festival, a six-week event to be held in June and July 2005. The International World Festival is held every three years in a different city. The Festival has never been held in Canada and it was last held in North America in 1982. The city is expecting a large influx of tourists for the event. You obtain the following information on Jeremy's venture:

1. In January Jeremy opened a bank account in the name of his business venture and deposited $20,000 of his own money into the account. Jeremy also developed a number of designs for the souvenirs that he plans to sell. The designs cost $1,200 and he paid cash from the venture's bank account.

2. In early February Jeremy presented his designs to the Festival organizing committee. Use of the Festival name or logos on souvenirs requires approval by the committee if they are to be legally sold. Jeremy's designs were approved and he paid a licensing fee of $2,000 that allows him to legally sell the souvenirs.

3. In late February Jeremy borrowed $30,000 from the bank. Jeremy agreed to repay the $30,000, plus $1,000 in interest, on August 1, 2005.

4. In May Jeremy signed a contract with a company to produce the souvenirs. Because of the nature of the souvenirs, it was necessary to produce them all before the Festival began. Jeremy had 5,000 souvenirs produced at a cost of $10 each. It was not possible to produce additional souvenirs. Jeremy paid the producer $40,000 in cash, and agreed to pay an additional $5,000 on June 30 and the remainder at the end of the Festival.
5. Jeremy purchased an old van to transport the souvenirs for $5,000 in cash.
6. Jeremy hired a number of vendors who operate street carts to sell merchandise. He agreed to pay the vendors $5 for each souvenir sold. The selling price of Jeremy's souvenirs is $19 each. The vendors will pay Jeremy $14 for each souvenir they sell and will keep $5 from each sale.
7. On June 30 Jeremy made the $5,000 payment to the producer of the souvenirs.
8. On July 3 Jeremy had 3,000 unsold souvenirs.
9. Jeremy has incurred other costs of $1,000 to date, all in cash.

It is July 3, 2005. The Festival has been underway for three and half weeks and Jeremy hasn't had a chance to sit down and take stock of how his venture is doing. He asks you to help him.

Required:

a. Prepare an income statement and balance sheet for Jeremy's venture as of July 3, 2005. Explain the accounting choices you made and why you made them. Be sure to discuss the users and uses of the income statement in your response.

b. Assume the role of Jeremy's banker. Jeremy has provided you with the statements that were prepared in part (a). Are these statements useful to you? Explain. What concerns do you have about the venture at this point? Explain. What suggestions would you give to Jeremy?

c. Use the statements you prepared in part (a) to advise Jeremy about how his venture has performed to date. What suggestions would you give to Jeremy for operating the venture for the remainder of the Festival? Jeremy has asked whether he can withdraw money from the venture for some personal needs. What would you advise Jeremy?

Case 14: Dymo Manufacturing Limited

Dymo Manufacturing Limited (Dymo) is a small manufacturer of appliances. Its products are manufactured under the brand names of the stores that buy from Dymo. (Dymo does not sell any appliances under its own brand name.) The company is wholly owned and managed by Jon and Crystell Karpoff, a married couple. Recently the Karpoffs have been considering retiring and they have been approached by a prospective buyer. The prospective buyer has requested a set of financial statements so that she can analyze the company. The buyer is a sophisticated business person. Until now, the only use of the financial statements has been for calculation of income taxes and internal management purposes.

In your discussion with the Karpoffs, you learn the following:

1. Dymo manufactures several different types of household appliances. It usually carries enough inventory to be able to respond to most orders quickly. When a store places an order with Dymo for these products, the goods are shipped within days.
2. Dymo also carries a significant inventory of parts and supplies used in the production of the appliances. On a recent examination of the inventory Mr. Karpoff observed that there was some stock (both input materials and finished goods) that had been on hand for some time, including stock relating to products that are no longer made.
3. Dymo allows retailers to return, for any reason, up to 20% of the appliances purchased.
4. Dymo offers a two-year warranty on the appliances it makes. Appliances requiring repairs are returned to the retailer, which ships them to Dymo for repair. All costs are paid by Dymo.
5. Dymo uses capital cost allowance (CCA) rates, the rates prescribed in the *Income Tax Act*, to calculate amortization.

6. One of Dymo's major suppliers is a sheet metal manufacturer that is owned by the Karpoffs' son.

7. Recently Dymo agreed to produce a significantly modified version of an existing product for a local chain of appliance stores. The chain promised to purchase a minimum of 7,000 appliances per year for three years. Dymo incurred $75,000 in costs to modify the design of the existing appliance. Production of the new product is scheduled to begin in about a month.

8. The Karpoffs pay themselves enough to cover their living requirements.

Required:

The Karpoffs have come to you requesting advice on the selection of appropriate accounting policies for the financial statements that will be prepared for the prospective buyer. In case the buyer questions the choice, they would like full explanations for the recommendations you make.

Case 15: Discount Stores Limited

Discount Stores Limited (Discount) is a chain of retail stores with locations in several medium-sized Ontario communities. Discount sells a wide range of clothing and household items that it obtains at discounts from wholesalers and jobbers. The company is wholly owned by Ruth and Irving Bogan, who use the cash generated by Discount to live on. Two years ago, the Bogans hired Harry Highpaid as the chief executive officer of the company to help turn the company around after a number of unprofitable years. At the time Harry was hired, the Bogans were worried that Discount would go bankrupt and they would lose their main source of income. Harry was well known as an excellent manager, and the Bogans were prepared to pay for someone who could reverse the fortunes of their business. The Bogans agreed to pay Harry a salary plus 25% of income after taxes in each year of a three-year contract. In his first year with Discount, Harry made significant improvements to the business, but it still suffered a small loss. This year, the company has continued to improve, and the Bogans once again feel confident about the viability of Discount.

Harry has just presented the financial statements for the current year to the Bogans for their approval. The Bogans are pleased about Discount's improvement, but they are concerned about some accounting treatments that appear to have contributed to a significant increase in net income.

1. Harry launched an extensive advertising campaign to improve the image of Discount and to attract new customers. According to Harry, the campaign has been a success, and as a result Discount has been able to increase its profit margins and has increased the flow of customers through all stores. Harry has capitalized 50% of the advertising costs and is amortizing them over five years, arguing that they will benefit the firm over a number of years. In the past, Discount expensed all advertising costs as they were incurred.

2. Discount has had a policy of writing off slow-moving inventory at the end of each fiscal period. Slow-moving inventory is defined as merchandise that has been on hand for six months or more. Harry has suspended the policy and now only writes off inventory that he believes cannot be sold.

3. To attract more customers, Harry has begun offering credit to customers. He has not, however, recorded an allowance for bad debt or a bad debt expense for the period.

Ruth Bogan has come to you for advice on the above accounting issues. Since Ruth and Irving are the only members of Discount's board of directors, they can make any changes they wish to the financial statements. However, they are not very sophisticated with respect to financial issues and are not sure what to do.

Required:

Prepare a report to the Bogans, providing them with the advice they seek.

Case 16: Extreme Sporting Goods Inc.[7]

Paul Pistone was delighted when he was offered a position as president of Extreme Sporting Goods Inc. (Extreme), a small manufacturer of sporting goods. The company had a long history and once dominated its market. Unfortunately, increased competition resulted in declining profitability. Paul believed that with the marketing skills he had gained in product management with a major consumer products company, he could easily turn the company around. He was so confident of his ability that he agreed to sign a rather unusual contract with the company at the request of Gil Gerrard, the president of Acme Industries Corporation (Acme), the company that owned Extreme. The contract specified that Paul would resign after one year if he did not increase the company's return on assets (ROA) to at least 10%.

After one year, Paul has made many changes at Extreme with many positive results. Revenues have increased significantly without the addition of staff, and inventory turnover has increased. However, Paul has just had a meeting with Gil Gerrard, who presented him with the Extreme financial statements for the year ending December 31, 2006. Those statements show a significant loss. Gil has given Paul an ultimatum. Paul must resign from his position or accept a 40% salary cut.

Paul is puzzled by this outcome. He knows that Gil and he have not gotten along very well recently. In fact, a meeting a few months ago ended in a shouting match. However, Paul doesn't understand how the income statement can show a loss, given the increase in revenues. Paul has discussed his situation with his lawyer and believes that legal action against Acme may be appropriate. He has asked you to prepare a briefing memo for the lawyer on the accounting treatment of the transactions described in the additional notes to the financial statements. Paul would also like your memo to include an analysis of the performance of Extreme over the past year.

Extreme Sporting Goods, Inc.
Income Statement
For the Years Ending December 31, 2004–2006

	2006	2005	2004
Revenues	$17,437,400	$13,712,500	$14,535,250
Cost of sales	11,334,310	9,461,625	9,883,970
Gross profit	6,103,090	4,250,875	4,651,280
Selling, general, and administrative expenses	5,754,342	4,662,250	4,651,280
Operating profit	348,748	(411,375)	0
Other income (expense):			
Interest expense	(110,000)	0	0
Other income, net	156,000	197,000	71,000
	46,000	197,000	71,000
Income before income taxes:	394,748	(214,375)	71,000
Income taxes	157,899	(85,750)	28,400
Net income	$ 236,849	$ (128,625)	$ 42,600

Extreme Sporting Goods Inc.
Balance Sheet
As of December 31, 2004–2006

	2006	2005	2004
ASSETS			
Current assets			
Cash and cash equivalents	$ 224,324	$ 495,000	$ 210,000
Accounts receivable	4,625,900	3,892,000	3,954,100
Inventories	6,041,000	5,642,000	5,152,000
Loan due from parent	2,000,000	0	0
Other current assets	275,000	591,000	475,000
Total current assets	13,166,224	10,620,000	9,791,100
Property, plant, and equipment			
Land	900,000	650,000	650,000
Buildings and improvements	5,450,000	3,950,000	3,950,000
Machinery and equipment	6,245,000	5,885,000	5,525,000
	12,595,000	10,485,000	10,125,000
Less accumulated amortization	7,990,000	7,240,000	6,125,000
Total property, plant and equipment, net	4,605,000	3,245,000	4,000,000
Other assets	1,250,000	906,375	785,000
Total assets	$19,021,224	$14,771,375	$14,576,100
LIABILITIES AND SHAREHOLDERS' EQUITY			
Current liabilities			
Bank loan	$ 2,000,000	$ 0	$ 0
Accounts payable	2,875,000	2,050,000	1,802,100
Accrued liabilities	2,163,000	975,000	899,000
Total current liabilities	7,038,000	3,025,000	2,701,100
Shareholders' equity:			
Common stock	3,750,000	3,750,000	3,750,000
Retained earnings	8,233,224	7,996,375	8,125,000
Total shareholders' equity	11,983,224	11,746,375	11,875,000
Total liabilities and shareholders' equity	$19,021,224	$14,771,375	$14,576,100

Notes to the financial statements:

1. The warehouse that Extreme has used for 20 years was originally purchased for $1,000,000 and was reported on the December 31, 2005 balance sheet at $400,000 net of accumulated amortization. In early January, shortly after Paul took over as president, Acme insisted that Extreme sell the warehouse to another Acme subsidiary for $400,000, and purchase an identical warehouse one block away for $2,500,000. The property was purchased on January 11, 2006. All related amortization is recorded (at CCA rates) in selling and administrative expenses. (The CCA rate for buildings is 4% per year declining balance.)

2. Paul replaced several senior managers with some colleagues from his former employer. Generous settlements were arranged with the managers who were replaced. The settlements include two years of salary and benefits for each employee, beginning July 1, 2006. On the December 31, 2006 balance sheet, there is a liability for the remaining 18 months, and the full $900,000 expense for the two years is included in selling and administrative expenses.

3. Acme needed cash for expansion and "arranged" an interest-free loan from Extreme for $2,000,000. Since Extreme needed cash at certain times of the year, an operating loan was required that would not have been otherwise necessary. The interest incurred

was $110,000 and Paul estimates Extreme could have earned an additional $160,000 of interest on the surplus funds if Acme had not "borrowed" the money.

4. One of Paul's first decisions was to drop several poorly performing product lines. The remaining inventory of those products, reported on the December 31, 2005 balance sheet at $1,050,000, was sold on January 20, 2006 for $255,000. The $255,000 is in 2006 revenue and the $1,050,000 is in cost of goods sold.

5. Paul spent $300,000 on a new information system, of which $14,000 of the cost was for computer hardware, while the remainder was for software. It is Acme's policy to use capital cost allowance (CCA) rules for all assets. As a result, 50% of the cost of software is expensed in the year it is purchased (with the remainder expensed in the subsequent year). Acme amortizes all computer hardware on the financial statements at the maximum CCA rates of 30% declining balance.

6. Paul was so excited by the successes of the first year that he took a number of key employees to Aruba for a training session. Any employee who met his or her goals for 2006 was included. The trip occurred on January 20, 2007, but the resort required payment in November 2006. The full amount of $100,000 was included in selling and administrative expenses for 2006.

Required:

Provide the memo to Paul's lawyer.

Endnotes:

1. Case 2, Patriot Meats Limited (I), was written by Daniel Armishaw and is used with permission.

2. Case 3, Patriot Meats Limited (II), was written by Daniel Armishaw and is used with permission.

3. Case 7, International Productions Corporation was adapted from the 1997 Uniform Final Examination, Canadian Institute of Chartered Accountants.

4. Case 8, Vulcanzap Inc., was adapted from the 1998 Uniform Final Examination, Canadian Institute of Chartered Accountants.

5. Case 11, Schmevan Stores Ltd., was adapted from the 2000 Uniform Final Examination, Canadian Institute of Chartered Accountants.

6. Case 12, Good Quality Auto Parts Limited, was adapted from the 1991 Uniform Final Examination, Canadian Institute of Chartered Accountants.

7. Case 16, Extreme Sporting Goods Inc., was written by Daniel Armishaw and is used with permission.

Glossary

At times the definition of a term in the text may differ slightly from the Glossary definition. This is because the chapter definitions are worded to help students understand the concept based on what they have learned to that point. Similar terms are printed in *italics* and cross-referenced to the key term definition.

absorption costing (page 462) A method of costing inventory that includes all prime and overhead costs in the cost of inventory.

accelerated amortization (page 510) Amortization methods that allocate more of the cost of an asset to expense in the early years of its life and less in the later years.

account (page 98) A category of asset, liability, or owners' equity. Each column in an accounting equation spreadsheet represents an account.

accounting (page 5) A system for producing information about an entity and communicating that information to people who want or need the information for making decisions.

accounting cycle (page 95) The process by which data about economic events are entered into an accounting system, processed, organized, and used to produce information such as financial statements.

accounting equation (page 39) The conceptual foundation of accounting that states that assets equal liabilities plus owners' equity.

accounting estimates (pages 223, 531) The judgments about uncertain future events that preparers must make to complete accrual accounting financial statements. Examples of accounting estimates include the amount of accounts receivable that will not be collected, the useful lives of capital assets, and the cost of warranty services that have not yet been provided.

accounting policies (pages 60, 531) The methods, principles, and practices used by an entity to report its financial results. Accounting policies include when revenue is recognized, inventory cost flow assumption, and amortization method.

accounts payable (page 45) Amounts owed to suppliers for goods and services purchased on credit.

accounts payable turnover ratio (page 805) A ratio that provides information about how quickly an entity pays its accounts payable. It is calculated as credit purchases divided by average accounts payable.

accounts receivable (page 43) Money owed by customers who bought on credit.

accounts receivable turnover ratio (page 408) A measure of how well an entity's credit program is being managed by giving an idea of how quickly the entity is collecting its receivables. The accounts receivable turnover ratio is defined as credit sales divided by average accounts receivable.

accrual basis of accounting (page 50) A system of accounting that measures the economic impact of transactions and economic events rather than cash flows.

accrued asset (page 132) An asset that is recorded before cash is received.

accrued liability (page 130) A liability that is recognized and recorded in the financial statements but that is not triggered by an external event such as receipt of a bill or invoice.

accumulated amortization (page 128) A contra-asset account that accumulates subtractions from capital asset and other amortizable asset accounts.

acid test ratio See **quick ratio**.

actuary (page 604) A person who assesses insurance risks and sets insurance premiums. Actuaries help determine the funding requirements of pension plans.

additional paid-in capital See **contributed surplus**.

adjusting entry (page 124) A journal entry recorded at the end of a reporting period that reflects economic changes that may have occurred during the period but have not been recorded in the accounting system. Adjusting entries are not triggered by exchanges with outside entities.

adverse opinion (page 287) The audit opinion given when the financial statements are so materially misstated or misleading that they do not present fairly the financial position, results of operations, and/or cash flows of the entity.

after-tax cost of borrowing (page 614) The interest rate an entity pays after taking into consideration the savings that come from being able to deduct interest in the calculation of taxable income. The after-tax cost of borrowing is calculated as interest rate $\times$ (1 − tax rate).

aging schedule (page 394) A schedule that classifies accounts receivable by the length of time they have been outstanding.

allowance for bad debts See **allowance for uncollectable accounts**.

allowance for doubtful accounts See **allowance for uncollectable accounts**.

allowance for uncollectable accounts (page 392) A contra-asset account to accounts receivable (or another receivables account) that represents the amount of the receivables that management estimates will not be collected.

amortization (pages 53, 507) The process of allocating the cost of a capital asset to expense over time to reflect the consumption of the asset while it helps to earn revenue. Also used specifically for the amortization of intangible assets.

annuity (page 386) A series of equal cash flows (inflows or outflows), usually made at equally spaced time intervals.

arm's length transaction (page 280) A transaction that takes place between unrelated parties, each of whom is acting in his or her own self-interests. Therefore, the exchange amount is considered to be fair market value.

ASB Accounting Standards Board.

asset (page 39) An economic resource that provides future benefits to an entity for carrying out its business activities.

asset turnover (page 799) Asset turnover is a measure of how effectively an entity can generate sales from its asset base. The more sales an entity can generate from its asset base, the higher its asset turnover ratio and the higher its ROA. Asset turnover is defined as sales divided by average total assets.

authorized capital stock (page 663) The maximum number of each type of share that can be issued by a corporation.

authorized share capital See **authorized capital stock**.

authorized shares See **authorized capital stock**.

average collection period of accounts receivable (page 308) A measure of how well an entity's credit program is being managed by giving the number of days receivables are outstanding before they are collected. The average collection period of accounts receivable is calculated by dividing the accounts receivable turnover ratio into 365.

average cost method of inventory valuation (page 443) An inventory cost-flow assumption that determines the average cost of all inventory on hand during the period and uses that average to calculate cost of sales and the balance in ending inventory.

average number of days inventory on hand

(page 469) A measure used to evaluate the efficiency of inventory management. The average number of days inventory on hand indicates the number of days it takes an entity to sell its inventory. It is defined as 365 divided by the inventory turnover ratio.

average payment period for accounts payable (page 806) The average number of days an entity takes to pay its accounts payable. It is calculated as 365 divided by the accounts payable turnover ratio.

balance sheet (page 39) The financial statement that provides information about the financial position of the entity—its assets, liabilities, and owners' equity—at a specific point in time.

bank overdraft (page 325) When an entity removes more money from its bank account than there is in the bank account, effectively creating an amount owing to the bank. The amount of the overdraft is treated as a liability.

bank reconciliation (page 375) An internal control procedure that is used to explain differences between the accounting records and the bank records.

barter transaction See **non-monetary transaction**.

basic earnings per share (basic EPS) (page 686) Net income minus preferred share dividends divided by the weighted-average number of shares outstanding during the period.

basic EPS See **basic earnings per share**.

betterment (page 504) An expenditure made that improves an existing capital asset, thereby making it more valuable to the entity. A betterment might increase a capital asset's useful life or improve its efficiency.

big bath (page 221) The expensing of a significant amount of assets that would normally have been amortized or otherwise expensed in future periods.

blended payments (page 593) Debt payments that are a combination of interest and principal.

bond (page 578) A formal borrowing arrangement in which a borrower agrees to make periodic interest payments to lenders as well as repay the principal at a specified time in the future.

book value (page 685) The amount shown in the accounting records for assets, liabilities, and equities.

book value of equity (page 685) The balance sheet value of the equity section of the balance sheet, equal to assets minus liabilities. Book value of equity is also referred to as the net assets or net worth of the entity.

callable bond (page 579) A bond that gives the bond issuer the option to repurchase

the bond from investors at a time other than the maturity date under conditions that are specified in the bond agreement.

Canada Business Corporations Act (page 663) The federal legislation that governs federally incorporated companies.

Canada Customs and Revenue Agency (CCRA) (page 12) The Canadian government agency responsible for administration and enforcement of the Canadian federal tax laws (www.ccra-adrc.gc.ca).

capital asset (pages 43, 500) A resource that contributes to the earning of revenue over more than one period by helping an entity to produce, supply, support, or make available the goods or services it offers to its customers. Capital assets contribute indirectly to the earning of revenue—indirectly because selling capital assets is not part of the ordinary activities of the entity.

capital cost allowance (CCA) (page 521) Amortization for tax purposes.

capital lease (pages 327, 596) A lease that transfers the benefits and risks of ownership to the lessee. Assets associated with a capital lease are capitalized on the balance sheet of the lessee and a liability that is equal to the present value of the lease payments to be made over the life of the lease is recorded.

capital stock (page 48) A balance sheet account that shows the amount of money (or other assets) that shareholders have contributed to the corporation in exchange for shares in the corporation.

capital structure (page 808) An entity's sources of financing—the relative proportions of debt and equity.

capitalize (page 500) To expend or accrue an amount that is recorded on the balance sheet as an asset.

carrying value See **net book value (NBV)**.

carrying value See **book value**.

cash accounting See **cash basis of accounting**.

cash basis of accounting (page 50) A system of accounting that records the cash flowing into and out of the entity. Under the cash basis of accounting, revenue is recorded when cash is received and expenses are recorded when cash is spent.

cash cycle (page 317) The cycle by which an entity begins with cash, invests in resources, provides goods or services to customers using those resources, and then collects cash from customers.

cash dividend (page 671) A cash payment from a corporation to its shareholders, representing a distribution of the corporation's earnings.

cash flow from operating activities See **cash flow from operations**.

cash flow statement (pages 58, 323) The source of cash flow information in a set of general purpose financial statements. It shows how cash was obtained and used during a period and classifies cash flows as operating, investing or financing.

cash flows from financing activities (pages 59, 323) The cash an entity raises and pays to equity investors and lenders.

cash flows from investing activities (page 323) The cash an entity spends on business capital and other long-term assets and the cash it receives from selling those assets.

cash from financing activities See **cash flows from financing activities**.

cash from investing activities (page 58) The cash an entity spends buying capital and other long-term assets and the cash received from selling those assets.

cash from operating activities See **cash from operations**.

cash from operations (CFO) (pages 58, 323) The cash an entity generates from or uses in its regular business activities.

CCA See **capital cost allowance**.

CCRA See **Canada Customs and Revenue Agency**.

CDNX Canadian Venture Exchange (www.cdnx.ca).

CFO See **cash from operations**.

CGA Certified General Accountants (www.cga-canada.org).

CICA Canadian Institute of Chartered Accountants (www.cica.ca).

clean audit opinion See **unqualified audit opinion**.

closing journal entry (page 134) The journal entry required for resetting temporary account balances to zero and transferring the balances in the temporary accounts to retained earnings or owners' equity.

CMA Certified Management Accountants (www.cma-canada.org).

collateral (page 272) Assets that are pledged by a borrower and that are turned over to the lender in the event the borrower is unable to repay a loan.

commission (page 465) A payment made to a seller as compensation for making a sale. A commission can be based on the selling price of the item, on the gross margin, or be a fixed fee.

commitment (page 617) A contractual agreement to enter into a transaction in the future.

common share (page 663) A share representing the residual ownership in an entity. Common shareholders are entitled to whatever earnings and assets are left after obligations to debtholders and preferred shareholders have been satisfied.

common size financial statements (vertical analysis) (page 787) An analytical tool in which the amounts in the balance sheet and income statement are expressed as percentages of other elements in the statements.

common stock See **capital stock**.

comparability (page 25) The qualitative characteristic of accounting information under Canadian GAAP that states that users should be able to compare the accounting information provided by different entities and the information of a particular entity from period to period.

completed-contract method (page 204) A critical-event approach to revenue recognition that recognizes revenue in full when a contract is completed. The completed-contract method is used for long-term contracts for which it is not appropriate to use the percentage-of-completion method.

compound interest (page 380) Interest that is calculated on the principal amount and on interest accumulated in previous periods.

conservatism (page 110) A fundamental GAAP accounting concept that serves to ensure that assets, revenue, and net income are not overstated and that liabilities and expenses are not understated. The implication is that when preparers are faced with reasonable alternative accounting treatments, they should choose the one that is more conservative.

consignment inventory (page 465) Inventory that is held for sale by an entity, but not owned by the selling entity. Consignment inventory is included in the inventory account of the entity that owns the inventory (not in the inventory account of the entity selling the inventory). Revenue on the sale of consignment inventory is not recognized until is sold to the final customer.

consistency (page 267) The use by an entity of the same accounting policies from period to period.

consolidated financial statement (pages 38, 717) Financial statement that combines the financial information of two or more entities into a single set of statements.

contingency (page 615) A possible liability or asset whose existence and amount depend on some future event.

contingent liability (page 312) A liability that may arise in the future if certain future events occur and a commitment is an executory contract.

contra-asset account (page 128) An account that is used to accumulate subtractions from a related asset account.

contributed surplus (page 664) A shareholders' equity account that shows amounts an entity receives from the sale of its shares in excess of par value of the shares.

control (page 717) When an investor (parent) corporation is able to make the important decisions of the investee (subsidiary) corporation, and determine its strategic operating, financing, and investing policies on an ongoing basis, without the support of other shareholders.

convertible bond (page 579) A bond that may be exchanged by the investor for other securities of the issuing entity, such as common stock.

convertible preferred share (page 666) A preferred share that shareholders can choose to exchange for a specified number of common shares for each preferred share that they convert.

core earnings See **permanent earnings**.

corporation (page 10) A separate legal entity created under the corporation laws of Canada or of a province. A corporation has many of the rights and responsibilities that an individual has.

cost method of accounting for investments in other companies (page 743) The method of accounting for investments in other companies that is used for passive investments. Passive investments are initially recorded at cost. Income is recognized when a dividend is declared or interest is earned.

cost of goods sold See **cost of sales**.

cost of sales (page 54) The cost of the inventory that was sold to customers.

cost/benefit trade-off (page 6) The concept of comparing the benefits of an action with the costs of the action, and taking action only if the benefits are greater than the costs.

coupon rate (page 579) The percentage of the face value that the issuer of a bond pays to investors each year as interest.

covenant (page 769) A restriction that imposes limits and the actions of borrowers.

Cr. See **credit**.

credit (page 116) An entry to an account that has the effect of decreasing assets and expenses, and increasing liabilities, owners' equity, and revenues (abbreviated as Cr.)

creditor (pages 24, 39) An entity to which money is owed. (In other words, another entity has an obligation to provide it with cash or other assets in the future.)

critical-event approach (page 191) A revenue recognition approach where an entity chooses an instant in the earnings process that it considers an appropriate time to recognize revenue. That instance is called the critical event. When the critical event occurs, 100% of the revenue is recognized.

CRTC Canadian Radio-Television and Telecommunications Commission (www.crtc.gc.ca), the government body that regulates telephone, television, and radio companies.

cumulative preferred share (page 666) A preferred share that requires payment of any dividends on the share that have not been paid in respect of the current year or previous years before the common shareholders can receive any dividends.

current asset (page 43) An asset that will be used up, sold, or converted to cash within one year or one operating cycle.

current liability (page 46) A liability that will be paid or satisfied within one year or one operating cycle.

current portion of long-term debt (page 45) Money borrowed for more than one year that is due to be repaid within the next year.

current ratio (working capital ratio) (page 46) A ratio for examining working capital, defined as current assets divided by current liabilities.

date of declaration of a dividend (page 671) The date when the board of directors of a corporation declares a dividend.

date of payment of a dividend (page 671) The date when the dividends are actually paid to shareholders.

debenture (page 578) A bond with no collateral provided to the lenders.

debit (page 116) An entry to an account that has the effect of increasing assets and expenses, and decreasing liabilities, owners' equity, and revenues (abbreviated as Dr.).

debt (page 578) Amounts borrowed and owed by an entity.

debt-to-equity ratio (page 49) A ratio that provides a measure of the amount of debt relative to equity an entity uses for financing. The debt-to-equity ratio (liabilities divided by owners' equity) gives an indication of the riskiness of the entity and its ability to carry more debt.

decelerated amortization (page 514) Amortization methods that have lower amortization charges in the early years and higher charges in the later years.

declining balance method (page 511) The most common accelerated amortization method used in Canada. It applies an amortization to the net realizable value

(NRV) of the asset at the beginning of the year to calculate the amortization expense.

deferred charges See **prepaid expenses**.

deferred costs See **prepaid expenses**.

deferred debits See **prepaid expenses**.

deferred expense (page 126) An asset that is acquired in one period but not expensed, at least in part, until a later period or periods.

deferred income taxes See *future income taxes*, page 605.

deferred revenue See **unearned revenue**.

defined-benefit plan (page 603) A pension plan in which the employer promises to provide employees certain specified benefits in each year they are retired.

defined-contribution plan (page 602) A pension plan in which the employer makes cash contributions to the pension fund as specified in the pension agreement with the employees. The pension benefits that an employee receives upon retirement depend on the amount contributed to the plan on behalf of the employee (by the employer and the employee) and on how well the investments that are made with the funds in the pension fund perform.

deflation (page 377) A period when, on average, prices in the economy are falling.

demand loan (page 572) A loan that must be repaid whenever the lender requests or demands repayment.

denial of opinion (page 287) The audit opinion given when the auditors do not have enough evidence to support an opinion on the financial statements. In that case, the auditors do not give an opinion.

depletion (page 507) The term used to describe the amortization of the cost of natural resources.

depreciation (page 507) Amortization of the cost of tangible capital assets. Also used as a similar term for **amortization**.

diminishing balance See **declining balance method**.

direct costing (page 462) A method of costing inventory that includes all prime costs and variable overhead costs in the cost of inventory.

direct financing lease (page 601) A capital lease that is a straight financing arrangement where the lessor purchases assets on behalf of a lessee and leases them to the lessee. The lessor earns interest revenue over the term of the lease in much the same way a bank earns its revenue from lending money.

direct method (of calculating cash from operations) (page 327) A method of calculating/reporting cash from operations by showing cash collections and cash disbursements related to operations during the period.

direct write-off method (page 392) A method of accounting for uncollectable receivables where the receivable is removed from the list of accounts receivable and an expense is recorded when management decides that a receivable will not be collected.

discontinued operation (pages 345, 777) A business segment that an entity has stopped operating or plans to stop operating.

discount (on debt) (page 583) When a bond is sold to investors for less than its face value. A discount arises when the coupon rate is greater than the effective rate of interest for the bond.

discount rate (page 382) The rate used to calculate the present value of future cash flows.

dividend (page 48) A payment of a corporation's assets, usually cash, to its shareholders. Dividends represent distributions of the corporation's net income to the shareholders.

dividend in kind See **property dividend**.

dividend payout ratio (page 811) A ratio that indicates the proportion of earnings that is being paid to common shareholders as dividends. It is defined as common dividends paid divided by net income.

double-entry bookkeeping (page 95) A record-keeping system in which each transaction or economic event is recorded in two places in the accounts.

Dr. See **debit**.

earnings See **net income**.

earnings per share (EPS) (page 686) The amount of net income that is attributable to each individual share of common stock.

earnings quality (page 782) The usefulness of current earnings for predicting future earnings.

effective interest rate (page 579) The real or market rate of interest that is paid or earned on debt.

Efficient Market Hypothesis (EMH) (page 276) A hypothesis that states that all publicly available information is reflected quickly in the price of publicly traded securities such as stocks and bonds.

EMH See **Efficient Market Hypothesis**.

employee stock option (page 679) A right granted to an employee to purchase a specified number of shares of the employer's stock at a specified price over a specified period of time. Employee stock options represent the right to purchase shares, not shares themselves.

entity (page 5) An economic unit such as an individual, proprietorship, partnership, corporation, government, not-for-profit organization, etc. In an accounting environment, an entity is an economic unit about which a stakeholder wants accounting information.

EOI See **extraordinary item**.

EPS See **earnings per share**.

equity method of accounting (page 738) An investment accounted for using the equity method is initially recorded on the balance sheet at cost. The balance sheet amount is adjusted each period for the investor's share of the investee company's income, less dividends declared. The income statement reports the investor company's share of the investee's net income.

exchange rate (page 379) The price to buy one currency, stated in terms of another currency.

executory contract (page 104) An exchange of promises where one party promises to supply goods or services and the other party promises to pay for them, but neither side has fulfilled its side of the bargain.

exercise price (page 680) The price at which an employee holding a stock option is allowed to purchase the shares.

expenses (page 52) Economic sacrifices or costs made or costs incurred to earn revenue. Sacrifices can be the result of using up an asset or incurring a liability. Expenses result in a decrease in owners' equity.

expiry date (page 680) The final date that a stock option can be exercised. After a stock option expires, it cannot be used to purchase shares.

external audit (page 16) The process of examining, on behalf of an entity's external stakeholders, the entity's financial statements and the data supporting the information in the financial statements, for the purpose of determining whether the statements adhere to principles such as fairness and GAAP.

external auditors (page 16) The people who examine entities' financial information on behalf of the entity's external stakeholders.

extraordinary item (EOI) (page 774) An event or transaction that is not expected to occur frequently, that is not typical of the entity's business, and that is not primarily the result of decisions or determinations by the managers or owners of the entity. According to the *CICA Handbook*, extraordinary items should be disclosed separately in the income statement.

face value of a bond (page 579) The amount that is written on the individual bond certificate. It represents the amount that the holder of the bond, the investor, will receive when the bond matures.

fair value (page 719) In accounting for subsidiaries, the term used when referring to the estimated market value of the subsidiary's assets and liabilities on the date the subsidiary was purchased.

FIFO See **first-in, first-out**.

financial accounting (page 8) The field of accounting that provides information to people who are external to an entity—people who do not have direct access to an entity's information.

finished goods inventory (page 435) Inventory that has been completed and is ready for sale.

first-in, first-out (FIFO) (page 440) An inventory cost-flow assumption in which the cost of inventory that is purchased or produced first is expensed first. For raw materials that are used in a manufacturing process, the cost of the raw materials that were purchased first is the cost that is used in the production process first. With a FIFO system the cost of inventory reported on the balance sheet represents the cost of inventory that was purchased or produced most recently.

fiscal year (page 38) The 12-month period (or 52-week period) for which performance of an entity is measured and at the end of which a balance sheet is prepared.

fixed asset See **capital asset** and **non-current asset**.

fixed overhead (page 462) Overhead that is unaffected by the amount of production.

fixed-rate loan (page 578) A loan whose interest rate does not change.

full costing (page 526) A method used by oil and gas companies to account for the exploration costs, under which a company capitalizes all the costs incurred to find new sources of oil and gas, even if some of those costs do not result in successful prospects.

full disclosure (page 275) The accounting principle that requires that financial statements include all relevant information about the economic activities of the entity.

fully diluted earnings per share (fully diluted EPS) (page 686) An earnings per share measure that reflects the effect that dilutive securities would have on basic EPS if the dilutive securities were converted or exchanged for common shares.

fully diluted EPS See **fully diluted earnings per share**.

future income tax assets and liabilities (page 606) Assets and liabilities that arise when the accounting methods used to prepare general purpose financial statements are different from the methods used to calculate taxable income and the amount of income tax an entity must pay.

future value (of cash flows) (page 380) The amount of money you will receive in the future by investing it today at a given interest rate.

GAAP See **generally accepted accounting principles**.

GAAS See **generally accepted auditing standards**.

general journal (page 146) The chronological record of the journal entries that have been entered into the accounting system.

general ledger (page 146) A record of all the accounts of an entity.

general partner (page 659) A member of a limited liability partnership (LLP) who does not have limited liability and is liable for all debts and obligations of the partnership. An LLP must have at least one general partner.

general purpose financial statements (page 37) Financial statements that are prepared for a wide range of stakeholders and for many different purposes, and are not necessarily tailored to the needs of any or all of them.

generally accepted accounting principles (GAAP) (page 23) The principles, conventions, practices, procedures and rules that define acceptable accounting practices and guide the preparation of financial statements in certain situations. In other words, GAAP represent a structure for preparing financial statements.

generally accepted auditing standards (GAAS) (page 286) A set of general guidelines, stated in the *CICA Handbook*, that provide guidance to auditors in the conduct of their audits.

going concern assumption (page 264) One of the basic assumptions underlying GAAP. The going concern assumption states an entity that will be continuing its operations for the foreseeable future.

goodwill (page 720) The amount that a parent pays for a subsidiary over and above the fair value of the subsidiary's identifiable assets and liabilities on the date the subsidiary is purchased.

gradual approach (page 192) A revenue recognition approach that results in revenue being recognized gradually over a period of time.

gross margin (page 54) Sales minus cost of goods sold. The amount available for covering the other costs of operating the

business and for providing profit to the owners.

gross margin percentage (page 55) The ratio of gross margin to sales (gross margin divided by sales). It indicates the percentage of each dollar of sales that is available to cover other costs and return a profit to the entity's owners.

gross profit See **gross margin**.

half-year rule (page 522) A requirement in the *Income Tax Act* that an entity can deduct for tax purposes in the year an asset is purchased only one-half the amount of capital cost allowance (CCA) that would otherwise be allowable.

hidden reserves (page 404) Undisclosed accounting choices used to manage earnings and other financial information with the intention of satisfying the self-interests of the preparers.

historical cost (page 274) The measurement convention that requires that transactions and economic events be valued in the financial statements at the actual dollar amounts involved when the transaction or economic event took place.

holding gain or loss (page 464) A change in the value of inventory or some other asset while the asset is owned by the entity. A holding gain or loss is realized if the asset is sold before the financial statement date and the holding gain or loss is unrealized if the asset is still owned by the entity on the financial statement date.

horizontal analysis (trend statements) (page 791) An analytical tool in which the amounts in the balance sheet and income statement are expressed as percentages of a base year set of financial statements.

hybrid securities (page 666) Securities that have characteristics of debt and equity.

IAS International Accounting Standards.

identifiable assets (page 720) Tangible or intangible assets that can be specifically identified and measured with some objectivity.

identifiable liabilities (page 720) Tangible or intangible liabilities that can be specifically identified and measured with some objectivity.

income statement (page 49) The financial statement that provides a measure of the economic performance of an entity over a period of time. The income statement summarizes an entity's revenues and expenses for a period.

income tax provision See *income tax expense*, page 606.

indirect method (of calculating cash from operations) (page 327) A method of calculating/reporting cash from operations by reconciling from net income to cash from operations by adjusting net income for non-cash amounts that are included in the calculation of net income and for operating cash flows that are not included in the calculation of net income.

inflation (page 377) A period when, on average, prices in the economy are rising.

instalment method (page 196) A revenue-recognition method that recognizes revenue when each payment in a series of payments is received. The expenses incurred to earn the revenue are matched to the revenue on a proportional basis to the revenue recognized.

intangible asset (page 507) A capital asset that does not have physical substance, such as patents, copyrights, trademarks, brand names and goodwill.

intellectual capital See **intangible asset.**

intercompany transactions (page 725) Transactions among the corporations in a consolidated group. Intercompany transactions are eliminated when preparing consolidated financial statements. This means that sales and expenses, and changes in the value of assets and liabilities that occur as a result of transactions among subsidiaries and with the parent, are not reflected in the consolidated statements.

interest (page 49) The cost of borrowing money, usually calculated as a percentage of the amount borrowed.

interest coverage ratio (accrual basis) (page 622) One of a number of coverage ratios designed to measure the ability of an entity to meet its fixed financing charges. In particular, the interest coverage ratio indicates the ease with which an entity can meet its interest payments. The interest coverage ratio is defined as net income plus interest expense plus tax expense divided by interest expense.

interest coverage ratio (accrual basis) (page 809) A coverage ratio that indicates the ease with which an entity can meet its interest payments. It is defined as net income plus interest expense plus tax expense divided by interest expense.

interest coverage ratio (cash basis) (page 809) One of a number of coverage ratios designed to measure the ability of an entity to meet its fixed financing charges. In particular, the interest coverage ratio indicates the ease with which an entity can meet its interest payments. It is defined as cash from operations excluding interest divided by interest paid.

internal control (page 374) Policies and procedures that management implements to protect the entity's assets and to ensure the integrity of the accounting information system.

in-the-money (page 680) A stock option whose exercise price is less than the market price.

inventory (page 43) Goods available for sale to customers or materials that will be used to produce goods that will be sold.

inventory (page 434) Goods that are available for sale by an entity, or goods that will be used to produce goods that will be sold. Inventory can also include materials used in supplying a service to customers.

inventory turnover ratio (page 469) A ratio used to provide information on how efficiently inventory is being managed by measuring how quickly the entity is able to sell its inventory. The inventory turnover ratio is defined as cost of sales divided by average inventory.

investee corporation (page 716) A corporation in which an investor corporation has invested.

investor corporation (page 716) A corporation that has an investment in another company.

issued share (page 663) An authorized share that has been distributed to shareholders.

issued share capital See **issued share.**

ITA Income Tax Act.

journal entry (page 98) The method used to enter information about economic events into the accounting system.

knowledge-based assets See **intangible assets.**

laid-down cost (page 435) All costs that are incurred to purchase or make the products and get them ready for sale to customers.

last-in, first-out (LIFO) (page 442) An inventory cost flow assumption in which the cost of inventory that was purchased or produced most recently is matched to revenue first. For raw materials that are used in a manufacturing process, the cost of the raw materials that were purchased last or most recently is the cost that is used in the production process first. With LIFO, the cost of inventory reported on the balance sheet represents the cost of old, sometimes very old, inventory.

LCM rule See **lower of cost and market rule.**

lease (pages 327, 595) A contractual arrangement where one entity (the lessee) agrees to pay another entity (the lessor) a fee in exchange for the use of an asset.

lender See **creditor.**

lessee (page 595) An entity that leases an asset from the asset's owner.

lessor (page 595) An entity that leases assets that it owns to other entities.

leverage (page 579) The use of debt to increase the return earned on equity.

leverage (page 677) The use of debt to increase the return earned on the equity investment of the owners.

liability (page 39) An obligation of an entity, such as to pay debts or provide goods or services.

LIFO See **last-in, first-out.**

limited liability (page 10) Restrictions that protect the shareholders of a corporation from being liable for the obligations of and losses suffered by the corporation, beyond the amount of their initial investment.

limited liability partnership (LLP) (page 659) A partnership in which some of the partners have limited liability protection.

limited partner (page 659) A member of a limited liability partnership who has limited liability protection and as a result is not personally liable for the debts and obligations of the partnership.

line of credit (pages 325, 572) An arrangement with a lender that allows an entity to borrow up to a specified maximum amount when and if the entity requires the money.

liquidity (page 46) An entity's ability to pay its obligations as they come due. Liquidity refers to the availability of cash or near-cash resources to meet obligations.

LLP See **limited liability partnership.**

long-lived asset See **capital asset** and **non-current asset.**

long-term asset See **non-current asset.**

long-term debt (page 45) Money borrowed that has to be repaid in more than one year.

lower of cost and market (LCM) rule (page 457) A rule that requires that when the market value of inventory at the end of a reporting period is lower than the cost of the inventory, the inventory must be reported on the balance sheet at its market value. The amount of the write-down (the difference between the cost of the inventory and its market value) is reported as a loss in the income statement. The loss is recorded in the period the inventory decreases in value, not when the inventory is sold.

maintenance (page 504) An expenditure that allows an asset to operate as intended—to do what it is designed to do. Maintenance costs should be expensed when incurred.

management discussion and analysis (MD&A) (page 771) A discussion by an entity's management of the entity's financial results, position and future prospects. The MD&A is intended to provide readers with a view of the entity through the eyes of management. The MD&A is required in the annual reports of public companies.

managerial accounting (page 8) The field of accounting that provides information to the managers of the entity and other decision makers who work for the entity, to assist them in making decisions related to operating the entity.

market value See **fair value**.

market value of equity (page 685) The market price of an entity's shares multiplied by the number of shares outstanding.

matching (matching concept) (page 108) The process of recording and reporting expenses in the same period as when the revenue those expenses help earn is recorded and reported.

materiality (page 284) The significance of financial information to users. Information is material if its omission or misstatement would affect the judgment of a user of the information.

maturity date of a bond (page 579) The date on which the borrower or bond issuer has agreed to pay back the principal (the face value of the bond) to the bondholders.

MD&A See **management discussion and analysis**.

minority interest See **non-controlling interest**.

mortgage (page 578) A loan that provides the borrower's property as collateral.

MWW Mark's Work Wearhouse Ltd. (www.marks.com).

Nasdaq National Association of Securities Dealers Automated Quotations (www.nasdaq.com).

NBV See **net book value**.

NEB National Energy Board (www.neb.gc.ca), the government body that regulates the oil and gas industry.

net assets (page 54) Assets minus liabilities. Also a similar term for **book value of equity**.

net book value (NBV) (page 128) The cost of a capital asset less the accumulated amortization.

net earnings See **net income**.

net income (page 49) A measure of how an entity performed over a period and of how the owners' wealth has changed over a period of time. Net income equals an entity's revenue less all the expenses incurred to earn that revenue.

net profit See **net income**.

net realizable value (NRV) (pages 274, 460)

The amount that the entity would receive from selling inventory (or another asset), less any additional costs that must be incurred before the asset is sold.

net recoverable amount (page 528) The net cash flow a capital asset is expected to generated from use over its remaining life, plus its residual value. A capital asset should be written down to its net recoverable amount when its net recoverable amount is less than its net book value (NBV).

net worth See **book value of equity**.

no par value share (page 664) A share that does not have a par value assigned to it.

nominal accounts See **temporary accounts**.

non-controlling interest (page 728) An account on a consolidated balance sheet that represents the net assets of a subsidiary that are owned by the shareholders of the subsidiary other than the parent. On a consolidated income statement, non-controlling interest represents the portion of net income of the consolidated entity that belongs to shareholders of the subsidiaries other than the parent. Non-controlling interest arises in consolidated financial statements when a parent owns less than 100% of the common shares of a subsidiary because GAAP requires that the consolidated statements include 100% of the subsidiary's assets, liabilities, revenues, and expenses.

non-current asset (page 43) An asset that will not be used up, sold, or converted to cash within one year or one operating cycle.

non-current liability (page 46) A liability that will be paid or satisfied in more than one year or one operating cycle.

non-monetary transaction (page 103) An exchange or trading of goods or services that does not involve cash.

non-profit organization See **not-for-profit organization**.

note payable (page 578) A formal obligation signed by the borrower, promising to repay a debt.

not-for-profit organization (page 11) An entity whose objective is to provide services and not to make a profit. Examples include hospitals, charities, religious organizations, unions, clubs, daycare centres, and universities.

NRV See **net realizable value**.

off-balance-sheet financing (page 596) A financing arrangement that occurs when an entity incurs an obligation (can borrow money) without reporting a liability on its balance sheet.

operating cycle (page 43) The time it takes from the initial investment an entity

makes in goods and services to when cash is received from customers.

operating lease (page 596) A lease that does not transfer the rights and risks of ownership to the lessee. Assets associated with an operating lease remain on the books of the lessor, the lessor recognizes revenue from the lease when payments are received or receivable, and the lessee recognizes an expense when the payment to the lessor is paid or payable.

out-of-the-money (page 680) A stock option whose exercise price is greater than the market price.

outstanding cheque (page 375) A cheque the entity has written and recorded in the accounting system but that has not yet been cashed.

outstanding deposit (page 375) A deposit the entity has made and recorded in the accounting system but that has not been recorded by the bank as of the bank statement date.

outstanding share (page 663) A share of a corporation currently in the hands of shareholders.

overhead (page 462) The indirect costs of manufacturing a product. These costs can be difficult to trace directly to the product being produced.

owners' equity (page 39) The investment the owners of an entity have made in the entity.

P/E ratio See **price-to-earnings ratio**.

par value (page 664) A value assigned to each share of common stock in an entity's articles of incorporation. The *Canada Business Corporations Act* and the corporations acts of a number of provinces do not permit par value shares.

parent corporation (page 717) An investor corporation that controls an investee corporation.

participating preferred share (page 666) A preferred share for which the amount of the dividend increases above the stated amount if certain conditions are met. The amount of the preferred dividend is often tied to the dividend paid on the common shares.

partner (page 11) An entity that is one of two or more owners of a partnership. A partner can be a corporation or an individual.

partners' equity (for a partnership) See **owners' equity**.

partnership (page 11) An unincorporated business owned by two or more entities. Partners can be corporations or individual people. A partnership is not legally separate from the partners who own it.

passive investment (page 742) An investment for which the investor corporation cannot influence the strategic decision making of the investee corporation.

pension (page 602) Income provided to a person after he or she retires.

percentage-of-completion method (page 204) A revenue-recognition method used with the gradual approach to revenue recognition. With the percentage-of-completion method, revenues and expenses associated with a long-term contract are spread over the life of the contract, based on a measure of the effort completed in each period.

percentage-of-credit-sales method (page 397) A method of estimating uncollectable receivables that is based on management's estimate of the percentage of credit sales that will not be collected in a period.

percentage-of-receivables method (page 393) A method of estimating uncollectable receivables that is based on management's estimate of the percentage of receivables at the end of the period that will not be collected.

period costs (page 214) Costs that are expensed in the period in which they are incurred.

periodic inventory system (page 436) An inventory system where the Inventory account is not adjusted whenever a transaction affects inventory. The balance in the Inventory account at the end of the period and cost of goods sold for the period are determined by counting the inventory on hand on the period ending date.

periodic reporting assumption (page 265) One of the basic assumptions underlying GAAP. The periodic reporting assumption states that meaningful financial information about an entity can be provided for periods of time that are shorter than the life of an entity.

permanent differences (page 606) Revenues and expenses that are recognized for tax purposes but never recognized for financial reporting purposes, or are recognized for financial reporting purposes but never recognized for tax purposes.

permanent earnings (page 773) Earnings that are expected to be repeated in the future.

perpetual inventory system (page 436) A system of inventory control that keeps an ongoing record of purchases and sales of inventory. When inventory is purchased or sold, the inventory account is immediately debited or credited to record the change. When inventory is sold, cost of sales is immediately debited.

persistent earnings See **permanent earnings**.

petty cash (page 324) Cash kept on hand to make cash payments that are required on an immediate basis.

portfolio investment (page 743) A passive investment that cannot be readily converted to cash within a year or that management does not intend to convert to cash.

posting (page 146) The process of transferring each line of a journal entry to the corresponding account in the general ledger.

preferred share (page 665) A share of a corporation that has rights that must be satisfied before common shareholders' rights. These preferred rights pertain to the payment of dividends and/or to the distribution of assets in the event of liquidation.

premium (on debt) (page 586) When a bond is sold to investors for more than its face value. A premium arises when the coupon rate is greater than the effective rate of interest for the bond.

prepaid expense (page 126) An asset that is acquired in one period but not expensed, at least in part, until a later period or periods.

preparers (page 15) The people responsible for deciding what, how, and when information is going to be presented in an entity's financial statements and other accounting information. Preparers are the people who make the decisions—senior managers such as controllers, chief financial offers, and even chief executive officers—and not the people who physically prepare the statements.

present value (of cash flows) (page 380) The worth today of money that will be received in the future.

price-to-earnings (P/E) ratio (page 810) An indication of how the market values an entity's earnings. It is defined as market price per share divided by earnings per share.

prime costing (page 462) A method of costing inventory that includes only prime costs in the cost of inventory.

prime costs (page 462) The costs of direct materials and labour used in the production of a product.

principal (page 49) The amount borrowed from a lender.

private corporation (page 11) A corporation whose shares and other securities are not available for purchase without agreement by the private corporation or its shareholders.

pro forma (page 682) When net income or loss and earnings per share are restated using accounting policies that are different from those used in the actual financial statements.

proceeds (page 579) The amount of money a bond issuer receives from selling bonds to investors.

product costs (page 214) Costs that can be matched to specific revenues and that are expensed when the revenue they help generate is recognized.

profit See **net income**.

profit margin ratio (page 113) A measure of how effective the entity is at controlling expenses and reflects the amount of income earned for each dollar of sales. The profit margin ratio is expressed as net income divided by revenue.

property dividend (page 673) A dividend paid with property instead of cash.

proprietor (page 11) A person who owns a proprietorship (an unincorporated business that is not legally separate from the person who owns it).

proprietorship (page 11) An unincorporated business owned by one person. A proprietorship is not legally separate from the person who owns it.

provision for income taxes See *income tax expense*, page 606.

public corporation (page 11) A corporation whose shares or other securities are available for purchase by any entity that has an interest in owning the securities and has the money to buy them. The shares of public corporations are usually traded on a stock exchange.

qualified opinion (page 287) The audit opinion given when, overall, the financial statements present the entity's situation fairly, but the statements do deviate from GAAP (or from whatever set of accounting standards the auditor is auditing to). A qualified audit opinion always contains the term "except for", which prefaces the explanation why the qualified audit report was given.

quick (or acid test) ratio (page 407) A measure of an entity's liquidity. The quick ratio is defined as an entity's most liquid assets (cash, cash equivalents, temporary investments, receivables) divided by current liabilities.

raw materials inventory (page 435) The inputs into the production process of a manufacturer or processor.

realized holding gain or loss (page 464) A holding gain or loss on inventory (or other asset) that was sold during the period.

receivables (page 388) Amounts owed to an entity. The amounts can be due from customers (accounts receivable), taxation authorities (taxes receivable), investments (interest and dividends receivable), shareholders or employees (shareholder/employee loans receivable), etc.

recognition (page 277) The process whereby any financial statement element—asset, liability, equity, expense or revenue—is entered into the accounting system and reported in the financial statements.

recurring earnings See **permanent earnings**.

redeemable preferred share (page 666) A preferred share that the issuer can purchase back from the shareholders if it chooses, according to specified terms.

related parties (page 280) The relationship between entities when one entity has the ability to influence the decision making of another other. Examples of related parties include close family members, corporations owned or controlled by a single shareholder, and senior management.

related party transactions (page 282) Transactions between related parties.

relevance (page 25) The qualitative characteristic of accounting information under Canadian GAAP that states that the information provided to users must be useful for the decisions they have to make.

reliability (page 25) The qualitative characteristic of accounting information under Canadian GAAP that states that the information provided to users must be a reasonable representation of what it is intended to measure.

repair (page 504) An expenditure that allows an asset to operate as intended—to do what it is designed to do. Repair costs should be expensed when incurred.

replacement cost (page 274, 460) The amount that an entity would have to pay to replace the existing inventory (or other asset).

residual value (page 507) The amount a capital asset can be sold for at the end of its useful life.

retail method (page 456) A method widely used by retail businesses as a way of estimating the cost of ending inventory and cost of sales that uses the retail price of merchandise and the relationship between the cost and the selling price of the merchandise.

retained earnings (page 48) A balance sheet account that shows the sum of all the net incomes a corporation has earned since it began operations, less the dividends paid to shareholders.

retractable bond (page 580) A bond that gives the investor the option to cash in the bond before the maturity date under certain conditions.

retractable preferred share (page 666) A preferred share that shareholders can require the issuer to purchase from them, if they choose, according to specified terms.

return on assets (ROA) (page 537) A measure of the performance and operating efficiency of an entity. ROA is defined as net income plus after-tax interest expense divided by total assets.

return on equity (ROE) (page 113) A measure of the profitability of an entity and its effectiveness in using the assets provided by the owners of the entity to generate net income. Return on equity is expressed as net income ÷ owners' equity. Owners' equity can be the period-end amount or the average for the period.

returned cheque (page 375) A cheque that has been cashed by the receiving entity but that has not been honoured by the bank because the entity that wrote the cheque did not have enough money in the bank account to cover the cheque.

revenue (page 51) Economic benefits earned by providing goods or services to customers. Revenue results in an increase in owners' equity or the wealth of the owners of the entity.

revenue recognition (page 122) The point in time when revenue is recorded in the accounting system and is reported in the income statement.

review engagement (page 288) A form of assurance that provides less assurance to users than an audit does about whether an entity's financial statements are in accordance with GAAP. Review engagements are never performed on public companies because securities laws require audits. A review will be done for private companies when external stakeholders require some assurance, but these stakeholders are satisfied with less assurance than is provided by an audit.

revolving loan (page 572) A loan that is expected to be renewed when it matures.

ROA See **return on assets**.

ROE See **return on equity**.

sale-leaseback transaction (page 600) A transaction whereby an entity sells property to a purchaser and the purchaser immediately leases the property back to the seller.

sales See **revenue**.

sales revenue See **revenue**.

sales-type lease (page 601) A capital lease used by manufacturers and dealers to sell a product. A sales-type lease is a combination of a sale and a financing arrangement, so the lessor earns income in two ways: profit on the "sale" of the leased asset and interest from financing the sale.

security See **collateral**.

segment disclosure (page 735) Disaggregation of information about an entity by types of products and services, geographic location, and major customers.

segregation of duties (page 375) An internal control procedure that requires that people who handle an asset should not be responsible for record-keeping for that asset.

share (page 10) A unit of ownership in a corporation.

share capital See **capital stock**.

shareholder (page 10) An entity that owns shares of a corporation and that is, therefore, an owner of the corporation.

shareholders' equity (for a corporation) See **owners' equity**.

significant influence (page 737) An ownership interest in an investee corporation that allows the investor corporation to affect the strategic operating, investing, and financing decisions of the investee corporation, even though it does not have control.

simple interest (page 380) Interest that is paid or earned on the principal amount only.

solvency (page 808) The financial viability of an entity—its ability to meet its long-term obligations.

special purpose report (page 62) An accounting report that is prepared to meet the needs of specific users and/or a specific use (in contrast to a general purpose report).

specific identification method of inventory valuation (page 444) An inventory valuation method that assigns the actual cost of a unit of inventory to that unit of inventory.

stakeholder (page 13) A group or individual that is interested in or has a "stake" in an entity.

statement of cash flows See **cash flow statement**.

statement of changes in financial position See **cash flow statement**.

statement of earnings See **income statement**.

statement of financial position See **balance sheet**.

statement of operations See **income statement**.

statement of profit and loss See **income statement**.

statement of retained earnings (page 57) The financial statement that summarizes the changes to retained earnings during a period.

Statistics Canada (page 12) Canada's national statistical agency. Statistics Canada (www.statcan.ca) has a mandate to collect, compile, analyze, abstract, and publish statistical information on virtually every aspect of the nation's society and economy.

stewardship accounting (page 95) An objective of accounting information that provides the owners of assets with information about how those who have responsibility for looking after the assets have carried out their responsibilities.

stock dividend (page 674) The distribution of a corporation's own shares to its existing shareholders.

stock exchange (page 11) A place (physical or virtual) where entities can buy and sell shares and other securities of publicly traded entities.

stock market See **stock exchange**.

stock split (page 675) The division of an entity's shares into a larger number of units, each with a smaller value.

stockholder See **shareholder**.

stockholders' equity (for a corporation) See **owners' equity**.

straight-line amortization (pages 128, 510) An amortization method where the cost of a capital asset is allocated equally to each year of its life.

subsequent event (page 619) An economic event that occurs after an entity's year end, but before the financial statements are released to users.

subsidiary corporation (page 717) An investee corporation that is controlled by an investor corporation.

successful effort (page 526) A method used by oil and gas companies to account for their exploration costs, under which only the costs associated with successful projects are capitalized. The costs associated with failed projects are expensed when they are incurred.

sustainable earnings See **permanent earnings**.

T-account (page 148) A simplified version of ledger accounts, so-called because it takes the shape of the letter T.

tangible capital asset (pages 109, 507) A capital asset that has physical form or substance, such as buildings, equipment, computers, and vehicles.

taxable income (page 606) The measure of income, as defined by the *Income Tax Act*, that is used to calculate the amount of tax an entity must pay.

temporary account (page 134) An account whose balance is reset to zero at the end of a period by closing it to retained earnings or owners' equity. All income statement accounts are temporary accounts. The balances in temporary accounts are not carried forward from one period to the next.

temporary differences (page 606) Revenues and expenses that are fully recognized for both tax and financial reporting purposes, but the recognition happens at different times.

temporary investment (page 743) A passive investment that can be converted to cash reasonably easily and that management intends sell to within a year.

time value of money (page 379) The concept that people would prefer to receive a given amount of money sooner rather than later.

transactional entry (page 125) An entry that is triggered by an exchange with another entity.

transitory earnings (page 773) Earnings that are not expected to be repeated in future periods.

treasury stock (page 669) Shares that were previously sold to investors and that the issuing corporation has repurchased but not retired.

trend statements (horizontal analysis) (page 791) An analytical tool in which the amounts in the balance sheet and income statement are expressed as percentages of a base year set of financial statements.

trial balance (page 149) A listing of all the accounts in the general ledger by their balances. The main purposes of the trial balance are to ensure that the debits equal the credits and to provide a summary of the balances in each account.

TSX Toronto Stock Exchange (www.tsx.ca), formerly known as the TSE.

UCC See **undepreciated capital cost**.

undepreciated capital cost (UCC) (page 608) The part of the cost of the asset that has not been deducted for tax purposes.

understandability (page 24) The qualitative characteristic of accounting information under Canadian GAAP that states that users must be able to understand information if it is to be useful to them.

unearned revenue (page 129) A liability that is recorded when cash is received before revenue is recognized.

unit-of-measure assumption (page 263) One of the basic assumptions underlying GAAP. The unit-of-measure assumption states that economic activity of an entity can be effectively stated in terms of a single unit of measure. The unit of measure that is almost always used is money, and in Canada the monetary unit used is usually the Canadian dollar.

unqualified opinion (page 285) The audit opinion that is given when the auditors are satisfied that the financial statements present the financial situation of the entity fairly and the statements follow GAAP.

unrealized gain (loss) (page 197) Increases or decreases in the market value of assets that are not supported by a transaction with an outside party.

unrealized holding gain or loss (page 464) A holding gain or loss on inventory (or other asset) that was not sold during the period and was still on hand at the end of the period.

unusual item (page 774) A revenue, expense, gain, or loss that does not meet the definition of an extraordinary item but that is not expected to occur frequently or that is not considered part of the normal business activities of the entity. The *CICA Handbook* requires separate disclosure of these items.

value-in-use (page 502) The net present value of the cash flow an asset will generate over its life, or the net present value of the cash flows the asset will allow the entity to avoid paying.

variable costing See **direct costing**.

variable overhead (page 462) Overhead that varies with the amount of production.

variable-rate loan (page 578) A loan whose interest rate varies with market conditions.

vertical analysis (common size financial statements) (page 787) An analytical tool in which the amounts in the balance sheet and income statement are expressed as percentages of other elements in the statements.

warranty (page 197) A promise by a seller or producer of a product to correct specified problems with the product.

WIP See **work-in-process inventory**.

working capital (page 46) Current assets minus current liabilities.

working capital ratio (current ratio) (page 46) A ratio for examining working capital, defined as current assets divided by current liabilities.

work-in-process inventory (WIP) (page 435) Inventory that is partially completed on the financial statement date.

write-down (page 280) A reduction in the net book value of an asset to some measure of the market value of the asset. A write-down is achieved by debiting an expense and crediting the asset.

write-off (page 280) The write-down of an asset to zero.

Index